TRAVELS IN TARTARY,
THIBET AND CHINA

THE BROADWAY TRAVELLERS

THE BROADWAY TRAVELLERS
In 26 Volumes

I	An Account of Tibet	*Desideri*
II	Akbar and the Jesuits	*du Jarric*
III	Commentaries of Ruy Freyre de Andrada	*de Andrada*
IV	The Diary of Henry Teonge	*Teonge*
V	The Discovery and Conquest of Mexico	*del Castillo*
VI	Don Juan of Persia	*Juan*
VII	Embassy to Tamerlane	*Clavijo*
VIII	The English-American	*Gage*
IX	The First Englishmen in India	*Locke*
X	Five Letters	*Cortés*
XI	Jahangir and the Jesuits	*Guerreiro*
XII	Jewish Travellers	*Adler*
XIII	Memoirs of an Eighteenth Century Footman	*Macdonald*
XIV	Memorable Description of the East Indian Voyage	*Bontekoe*
XV	Nova Francia	*Lescarbot*
XVI	Sir Anthony Sherley and His Persian Adventure	*Sherley*
XVII	Travels and Adventures	*Tafur*
XVIII	Travels in Asia and Africa	*Battúta*
XIX	Travels in India, Ceylon and Borneo	*Hall*
XX	Travels in Persia	*Herbert*
XXI	Travels in Tartary, Thibet and China Vol. I	*Huc and Gabet*
XXII	Travels in Tartary, Thibet and China Vol. II	*Huc and Gabet*
XXIII	Travels into Spain	*D'Aulnoy*
XXIV	The Travels of an Alchemist	*Li*
XXV	The Travels of Marco Polo	*Benedetto*
XXVI	The True History of His Captivity	*Staden*

TRAVELS IN TARTARY, THIBET AND CHINA

1844-1846

Volume One

HUC AND GABET

LONDON AND NEW YORK

First published 1928 by RoutledgeCurzon
Published 2014 by Routledge
2 Park Square, Milton Park, Abingdon, Oxfordshire OX14 4RN
711 Third Avenue, New York, NY 10017

First issued in paperback 2014

*Routledge is an imprint of the Taylor & Francis Group,
an informa business*

All rights reserved. No part of this book may be reprinted or reproduced or utilized in any form or by any electronic, mechanical, or other means, now known or hereafter invented, including photocopying and recording, or in any information storage or retrieval system, without permission in writing from the publishers.

The publishers have made every effort to contact authors/copyright holders of the works reprinted in *The Broadway Travellers*. This has not been possible in every case, however, and we would welcome correspondence from those individuals/companies we have been unable to trace.

These reprints are taken from original copies of each book. In many cases the condition of these originals is not perfect. The publisher has gone to great lengths to ensure the quality of these reprints, but wishes to point out that certain characteristics of the original copies will, of necessity, be apparent in reprints thereof.

British Library Cataloguing in Publication Data
A CIP catalogue record for this book
is available from the British Library

Travels in Tartary, Thibet and China VI

The Broadway Travellers

ISBN 978-0-415-34483-8 (hbk)
ISBN 978-1-138-87812-9 (pbk)

MAP OF TARTARY.

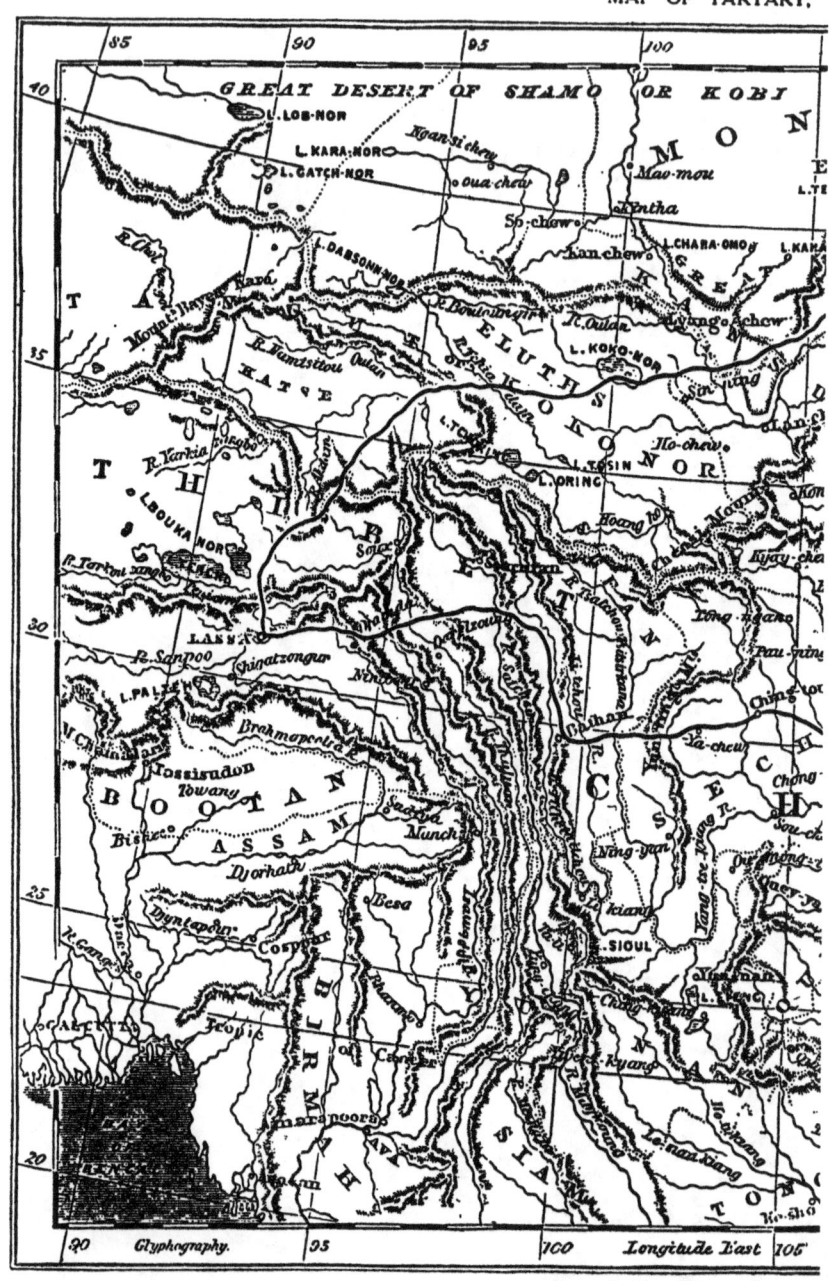

THE DARK LINE INDICATES THE ROUTE

THIBET, AND CHINA

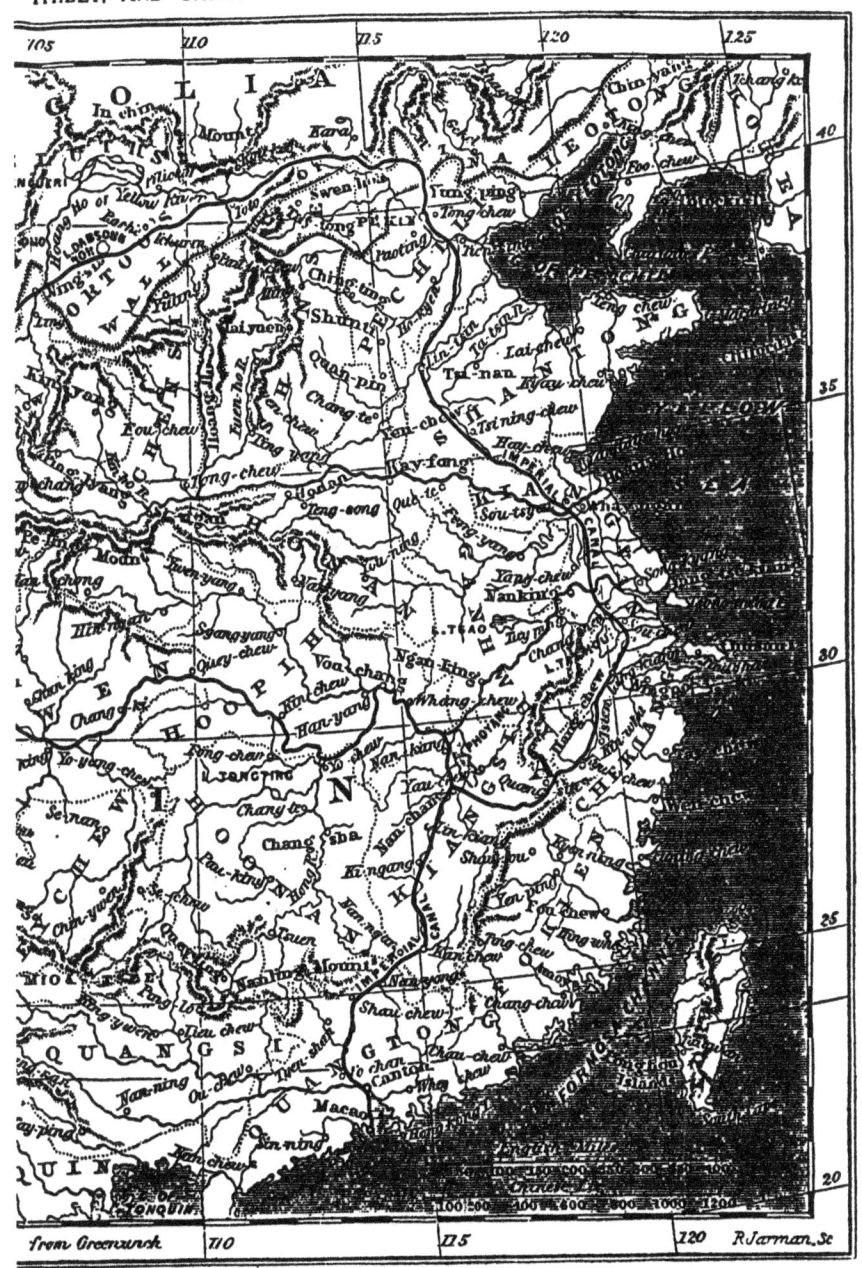

OF THE TRAVELLERS, MM. HUC AND GABET.

THE BROADWAY TRAVELLERS

EDITED BY SIR E. DENISON ROSS
AND EILEEN POWER

HUC AND GABET

TRAVELS IN TARTARY THIBET AND CHINA
1844—1846

*Translated by William Hazlitt
Now edited with an Introduction
by Professor Paul Pelliot*

VOLUME ONE

Published by
GEORGE ROUTLEDGE & SONS, LTD.
BROADWAY HOUSE, CARTER LANE, LONDON

First published in this Series in 1928

PRINTED IN GREAT BRITAIN BY HEADLEY BROTHERS,
18, DEVONSHIRE STREET, E.C.2; AND ASHFORD, KENT.

INTRODUCTION
BY
PAUL PELLIOT

In the literature of travel the *Souvenirs*, in which the Abbé Huc described the journey which led him and his fellow-worker Gabet across Mongolia to Lhasa, won an instant success and continue after the lapse of three quarters of a century to hold a place in the front rank. The attraction of almost unknown lands and the very real dangers run by the two missionaries are not enough to explain this singular good fortune; other explorers have made equally difficult journeys and their accounts have quickly fallen into oblivion. The lasting success of the *Souvenirs* is due above all to the literary gifts of their author. Huc had eyes to see and the power to recall what he had seen to life; but these very gifts have their counterpart in a somewhat ardent imagination, which led him on occasion to invent what he supposed himself to be merely reporting; he had the artist's instinct, which with a few lively touches heightens the colours of reality, at times too drab. Some writers used to make this a pretext for denying the actuality of the journey itself; but there is no question that Huc and Gabet really did spend some time in Lhasa. It must, however, be admitted that Huc went rather far in arranging his facts, and I shall show later that he cannot be trusted in details, even in those which

INTRODUCTION

concern him personally and which he was in a better position to know than anyone else.[1]

Of the two travellers Gabet was the elder. Joseph Gabet, born at Névy-sur-Seille (Jura) on December 4th, 1808, was ordained priest on October 27th, 1833, and entered Saint Lazare on February 22nd, 1834. On March 21st, 1835, he embarked for China on the *Edmond* at Havre and on June 26th he reached Batavia and transhipped to the *Royal George*, which left the roads of Soerabaya on August 7th for Macao, where he landed on the 29th of the same month. There he took the vows of religion on March 6th, 1836, and on August 15th set out for the Mongolian mission, which he reached at the beginning of March, 1837. He passed several years at " Black Waters " (Hei-Shui) and at Jehol he converted two lamas, one of whom, a man of twenty-five, was baptised under the name of Paul, and the other, who was barely twenty, under that of Peter; the latter was sent to Macao and became the Lazarist M. Fong; here too Gabet converted a bonze, John-Baptist, who is the famous " Samdadchiemba " spoken of by Huc. In the summer of 1844 Gabet set out with his colleague, M. Huc, and reached Lhasa. When the travellers arrived at Macao early in October, 1846, M. Guillet, Procurator of the Lazarists, informed Gabet that he had been nominated

---

[1] The details which I am about to sketch are mainly borrowed from an article entitled *Le Voyage de MM. Gabet et Huc* which I published in the *T'oung Pao* for 1925-1926, pp. 133-178; but I have also taken into consideration fresh information hitherto unpublished. Certain details and a number of dates are here corrected from documents contained in the archives of the Lazarist Fathers of the Rue de Sèvres. Data supplied by English writers for the Biographies of Huc and Gabet are far from satisfactory, particularly those of Graham Sandberg in his *The Exploration of Tibet* (Calcutta, 1906); *all* his dates are false.

INTRODUCTION

bishop of Troad *in partibus*, but that his bulls had been sent to Hsi-wan-tzŭ, which was then the seat of the Mongolian mission, ten leagues north of Hsüan-hua-fu in Chih-li. Such, at all events, is the account given in Gindre's *Biographie de Mgr. Gabet* (Poligny, 1867, 8vo), but the publications of the Lazarists are silent on the subject. Undoubtedly Gabet was at one time thought of for the bishopric. At a meeting of the Council of Lazarists at Paris on April 4th, 1844, it was announced that a papal brief to Mgr. Mouly, Vicar Apostolic of Mongolia, had authorized Mgr. Mouly to "nominate a coadjutor with the title of Bishop of Troad"; the Superior General proposed to name M. Gabet and the Council agreed. On the other hand in *La Hiérarchie catholique en Chine, en Corée et au Japon* (Shanghai, 1914, 8vo, p. 118), Father de Moidrey S.J., relying on a *Catalogue* published by the Lazarists of Peking in 1911, says that Florent Daguin was made bishop of Troad and coadjutor to Mgr. Mouly on March 22nd, 1844. and consecrated in 1847; Gabet could not have received the same title about the same time. It is not unlikely that Gindre, who mistakes the name of the See ("Troan" for "Troad") improved upon the talk of Gabet's elder brother, the curé of Besain (Jura), who was wont to say that, thanks to his younger brother, the family had had the honour of entering the ranks of the episcopate. On the other hand the decision taken by the Council on April 4th, 1844, which names Gabet, makes it impossible that Mgr. Mouly should have nominated Daguin on March 2nd, 1844, as Father de Moidrey says. The date, March 2nd, 1844, is perhaps that of the papal authorization in question at the meeting of April 4th,

INTRODUCTION

and Daguin was not then thought of. Moreover, letters written by Daguin on April 22nd, 1845, and May 15th, 1846 (the latter unpublished) show that at these dates he was in charge of the mission of the "Three Towers" and was not residing at Hsi-wan-tzŭ near Mgr. Mouly. Finally, whatever alteration they may have undergone before being reproduced by Gindre, the terms in which M. Guillet, the procurator of the Lazarists, spoke to Gabet in October, 1846, on the subject of his nomination to the bishopric of Troad cannot be explained if Daguin had already received the nomination to this episcopal title in 1844. The truth probably is that in conformity with the Council's resolution, Mgr. Mouly "nominated" Gabet to the bishopric of Troad when he received papal authorization and the Council's resolution, that is to say at the end of 1844, after the departure of Gabet and Huc on their great journey. It is even possible that the new bishop's bulls were afterwards sent to Hsi-wan-tzŭ; but on Gabet's arrival in Europe at the beginning of 1847, there was no longer any idea of consecrating him. The bulls, if any had been sent, were annulled and Daguin replaced Gabet as Bishop of Troad; if Daguin was really consecrated in 1847, even his nomination cannot have been earlier than the beginning of the same year. In any case, instead of resting at Macao on the conclusion of his ordeal and then setting out once more for the Mongolian mission, Gabet in November, 1846, sailed for Europe; he chose the Red Sea route and disembarked at Marseilles in January, 1847. From there he went to Paris, where he remained until April 6th, then to his native province of Jura, and at last arrived in Rome on August 14th,

INTRODUCTION

accompanied by his elder brother, the curé of Besain. His attempts at interference were not regarded with favour there. On his return to Paris he begged his superiors in vain to send him back to Mongolia. Not without hesitation he was appointed in October, 1848, to Brazil, where complaints were made of him. The Council of Lazarists decided on April 26th, 1852, to "notify his dismissal" to him, but matters were still in this position when Gabet died on the Isle of Gésu, half a league from Rio-de-Janeiro, on March 3rd, 1853.

Régis-Evariste Huc was born on June 1st, 1813, at Caylus (Tarn-et-Garonne) of a family originally settled in Martinique. He entered the Lazarist order on October 5th, 1836, took his vows on October 15th, 1838, was ordained priest on January 28th, 1839 (?), left Havre on the *Adhémar* on March 6th, was still in the roads of Batavia on June 24th, disembarked at Macao towards the middle of July, left there again on Saturday, February 20th, 1841, and arrived at Hsi-wan-tzŭ on June 17th. He remained for about two years at Hsi-wan-tzŭ or in that district, to accustom himself to mission life there and to learn Chinese; then, according to M. Planchet, "a little before Ascension Day, 1843" (i.e., before May 26th) he left for the mission of "Black Waters" and Pieh-lieh-kou, where he applied himself to the study of the Manchu and Mongol languages under the direction of the head of his district, M. Gabet. After his return from Lhasa to Macao on October 4th, 1846, Huc remained at Macao until the end of 1848 or the beginning of 1849 and then went again up into Northern China, but his health, enfeebled by the hardships which he had suffered on

INTRODUCTION

his journey to Tibet, obliged him to come down to Ning-po and eventually to return to France. He disembarked at Suez and visited Syria and the Holy Places, finally reaching his native land in June, 1852. The Superior General of the Lazarists, M. Etienne, immediately dispatched him as director of the great seminary of Montpellier. Huc was not at all contented there and on May 31st, 1853, when the session was coming to an end, he requested to be allowed to visit his mother and then to take the waters at Dax. In reality he had already decided to leave the congregation; "community life is incompatible with my temperament" he wrote to M. Etienne on December 25th, 1853. The next day, December 26th, the Council of the Lazarists accepted his resignation. The disagreement was of long standing and Huc had mistaken his vocation. In the very beginning, at the end of his two years' probation in 1838, Huc had been the only seminarist whose profession had been postponed by the Council on the ground that he "left something to be desired in certain directions". His journey, as we shall see, had deviated strangely from the programme drawn up by the Apostolic Vicar of Mongolia and the question had been still further complicated by Gabet's ill-timed proceedings at Rome. On his return to France Huc had not been insensible to the welcome given him by persons of importance. He was received by Drouyn de Lhuys, to whom he later allowed it to be known that he wished to borrow for his own books certain ideas on the invasions and revolutions in Asia, which the minister had explained to him in conversation; and in a letter to a fellow-worker in Paris, Huc, with a touch of vanity, repeated

INTRODUCTION

Drouyn de Lhuys's answer that he would be extremely honoured. These adroit flatteries were no doubt not unconnected with the cross of the Légion d'honneur which Huc received at the end of 1852 or at the very beginning of 1853. M. Etienne was not at all pleased. On January 16th, 1853, Huc wrote to him from Montpellier affecting surprise and, even while protesting that " a son of St Vincent ought not to wear the red ribbon in the button-hole of his soutane " added that " such a nomination is one of those things which it is impossible to refuse " ; in his heart of hearts he was enchanted. The real reason, however, which led him to leave the congregation is of a more delicate nature. Huc, like Gabet, had in the course of his journeys taken certain liberties with his priestly vows, nor had he acted otherwise afterwards. After he had once more become a secular priest the Ministers of Public Worship, Fortoul in 1856 and Rouland in 1857, wanted to propose him for a bishopric, but on both occasions the ecclesiastical authorities opposed this, for reasons of personal conduct, reasons unconnected with dogma. Meanwhile the ex-missionary, whose *Souvenirs* had made him famous, was living by his pen. The two volumes of *L'empire chinois* appeared in 1854, then, in 1857-8, the four of *Christianisme en Chine, en Tartarie et au Thibet*. In 1857 Huc urged Napoleon III to seize the port of Tourane in Annam. He died on March 25th, 1860.

In 1840, Mongolia, where Gabet and afterwards Huc exercised their apostolate, and Tibet, whither circumstances were to lead them, were not *terræ incognitæ*, but there was no longer to be had such direct and

INTRODUCTION

valuable knowledge of these lands as a whole as had been acquired a century earlier. Mongolia and Tibet had been brought under the immediate suzerainty of China by the Manchu emperors of the seventeenth and early eighteenth centuries; Jesuit missionaries had then accompanied K'ang-hi on his campaigns in Mongolia and other Jesuits had assisted him to map the country. The Jesuit accounts, which appeared to the *Lettres édifiantes*, or as independent works, were further supplemented by information derived from Russian travellers or diplomats or from Swedish prisoners banished to Siberia after Charles XII's campaigns. Tibet had remained more mysterious. It is true that in 1661 the Jesuits Grueber and d'Orville had travelled from Peking to India by Lhasa, but they had merely passed through the country, and the Dutchman Van de Putte, who made the same journey in the opposite direction three quarters of a century later, was known only as a name. Moreover, the accounts of the Jesuits and Capuchins who had penetrated into Tibet from India and lived there, were still buried in the archives of their orders and in those of the Propaganda, or remained unknown in public or private libraries. Although the Jesuit cartographers of Peking had not been authorized to map Tibet themselves, maps made by them from the observations of disciples whom they had trained were, and long remained, the best source of information on the physical configuration of the country. As to its political and religious condition, the journals of Bogle's mission to the Teshu Lama in 1774 and that of Manning, who saw the Dalai Lama in 1811-12, were not published till 1879 by Markham. Thus it

INTRODUCTION

was to Samuel Turner, who was sent as envoy to the Teshu Lama in 1783 and whose *Account of an Embassy to the Court of the Teshu Lama* appeared in 1800, that the West owed such detailed ideas on the great theocratic state of Upper Asia as it then possessed.

Although the beginning of the nineteenth century did not bring with it much that was new concerning these distant lands,[1] and even a good deal of what had been known in the eighteenth century had been forgotten, the great impulse towards the " propagation of the faith ", which was then much in evidence in the catholic world and particularly in France, could not pass by lands which offered a field at once so vast and so new for conversion. Some hoped to find there compensation for the wretched condition of the Chinese missions which, hard hit by the suppression of the Jesuits in 1773, were managing to maintain only a precarious existence in the face of a more and more rigorous official proscription. The Lazarists, who had succeeded the Jesuits at Peking, had been obliged practically to abandon the capital, and their headquarters in Chih-li was the mission-station of Hsi-wan-tzŭ, founded in 1834 by a Chinese priest, which we have already met with in our sketch of the biographies of Gabet and Huc. Now the Christian mission of Hsi-wan-tzŭ was at the gates of Mongolia; Mgr. Mouly, who was its superior, at least from 1836, very naturally had been led to send Gabet to the north, to visit the Chinese colonies established at the edge of

---

[1] Timkovskiï's *Voyage en Chine à travers la Mongolie en 1820-1821* appeared in Russian in 1824. Between 1825 and 1827 it was translated into German, Dutch, French, and English. He had acquired much information about Mongolia, but we are unaware of a single copy of the book's reaching the Catholic missions of Northern China before 1844. Neither was their knowledge of Csoma de Körös's work on Tibet any more considerable.

INTRODUCTION

the nomad country, and Gabet, no less naturally, tried to convert the lamas. At the same time the "Missions Etrangères" were entrusted with an apostolic vicariate in Corea (1831); Mgr. Bruguière tried in vain to enter his vicariate by way of Eastern Mongolia and Manchuria; he died in 1835 at Pieh-lieh-kou, that is to say at those "Contiguous Defiles" whence Gabet and Huc set out nine years later for their journey into Upper Asia. Gabet soon found himself in danger of being separated from the mission-stations which he had founded; a decision of the Holy See, dated November 8th, 1838, assigned the whole of Mongolia and Manchuria to the Foreign Missions. However, the titular holder of this new vicariate, Mgr. Verrolles, made his way there at the end of 1840, via Hsi-wan-tzŭ, where he arranged with Mgr. Mouly to leave the whole of Mongolia east of the meridian of Peking to the Lazarists. Indeed, Rome had anticipated the provisional agreement of the two prelates; a papal brief of August 23rd, 1840, which was still unknown at Hsi-wan-tzŭ, had just separated Mongolia from Manchuria and assigned it to the Lazarists. The fate of the mission-stations founded by Gabet in the Jehol region remained, however, uncertain; even when the brief of 1840 had been received in the Far East, the business of fixing the boundaries between the two vicariates gave rise to somewhat lengthy disputes and twice obliged Mgr. Verrolles to undertake the journey to Rome.

Tibet likewise attracted the missionaries and here again we meet the name of Mgr. Verrolles. Before his nomination as Vicar Apostolic in Manchuria, he belonged to the Ssŭ-ch'uan mission, where he had

INTRODUCTION

arrived at the end of 1832 and he had never ceased requesting his superiors, Mgr. Fontana and then Mgr. Pérocheau, for permission to go and evangelize Tibet. Mgr. Fontana had been almost won over; he wrote in 1836 to the directors of the Paris Seminary: " Two months' journey from here, in Tibet, the capital of which is Lhasa, the residence of the Grand Lama, there is an immense region still sunk in idolatry, the inhabitants of which are simple people, very poor, without luxury and without ambition. . . . Oh, my dear brothers, what a fair field for the Gospel! " And Mgr. Verrolles unbosomed himself to one of his sisters in 1838: " Just now there is a question of carrying the gospel to Tibet, the great Tibet. Look at the map; it's 500 leagues long and 400 broad! It is a new country which has never yet received the torch of Faith, and in spite of my sins, I am the happy mortal destined to carry the good news there; pray yourself and get others to pray for this enterprise . . . " Mgr. Pérocheau, who had just succeeded Mgr. Fontana, gave his consent in principle, but not even that before he had received from Rome jurisdiction over Tibet, which till then he still believed to be in dependence on the Bishop of Agra, in India. It was not until August, 1844, that the Bishop of Agra granted Mgr. Pérocheau the right to send priests to Tibet, and two years later, on March 27th, 1846, a papal brief created an apostolic vicariate of Lhasa and gave it into the charge of the Foreign Missions; but by this time Mgr. Verrolles had been nominated to Manchuria these six years past, almost.[1] Gabet and

---

[1] Cf. A. Launay, *Monseigneur Verrolles et la mission de Mandchourie*, Paris, Téqui, 1895, 8vo, pp. 89-94; *Histoire de la Mission du Thibet*, Lille and Paris, no date (1902 ?) I, 65-66.

INTRODUCTION

Huc could as yet have known nothing of these choppings and changings when they set out on their journey in the middle of 1844.

Huc has sometimes been unjuſtly attacked, for Prževal'skiï went as far as to deny the reality of the journey to Lhasa; nor do I share the fiery indignation of one author who, speaking of the " plagiarisms of Father Evariſte Huc", finds fault with all Huc's works and puts them all in the same category. Whatever the inaccuracies of his narrative and its weakness from a scientific point of view, the faƈt remains that he made a very remarkable journey and consequently everything that relates to it direƈtly in Huc's account is important. As for the reſt of his material, especially in the books which appeared in 1854 and in 1857-8, the Abbé was pot-boiling and borrowed at length from other writers and occasionally from himself. On Chinese hiſtory, in particular, no orientaliſt would ever dream of looking to the works of Huc for authoritative information.

The *Souvenirs* were drawn up by Huc at Macao between the end of 1846 and the end of 1848, and appeared in 1850, when he was ſtill on mission work in the Far Eaſt; the firſt edition correƈted by him was consequently the *ne varietur* edition of 1853. The book ſtops at the point where the two travellers have been brought back from Tibet to the frontiers of China, or, more properly speaking, into Ssŭ-Ch'uan. The conclusion of the journey, from Ssŭ-Ch'uan to Canton, forms the frame-work of *L'Empire chinois*, but it appears there in scraps, swamped by interminable digressions. Finally, Huc's journeys in Mongolia and

INTRODUCTION

Tibet are once more described in *Le Chriſtianisme* (IV, 359-420).

These, however, are not our only sources of information. To them muſt be added the letters, both published and unpublished, of the two missionaries and of certain of their co-workers, consular reports and above all, the accounts of Gabet and Huc, which, before the publication of the *Souvenirs*, had already been issued in the *Annales de la Congregation de la Mission* and in the *Annales de la Propagation de la Foi*. A document, mentioned in Hazlitt's preface but hitherto unprinted, is published for the firſt time at the end of this Introduction.[1] Sir E. Denison Ross has kindly had it searched for and copied at the Public Record Office, London. It is a letter written by A. R. Johnſton to Sir John Francis Davis on February 16th, 1847; Johnſton had then juſt been travelling with Gabet from Hong-Kong to Ceylon. Even so other documents are ſtill missing; in particular a long letter concerning the Tibetan mission, which Gabet sent from Paris to the Propaganda in 1847; and, what is ſtill more serious from the point of view of our enquiry, the firſt part also of the *Rapport* presented by Gabet to Pope Pius IX in the second half of 1847 in which he described the journey from the "Contiguous Defiles" to Lhasa.

As to the materials utilized in the drawing-up of the *Souvenirs*, it seems clear that they are of three kinds: notes made on the journey, the traveller's memories, and researches in books made at Macao. In this laſt category muſt obviously be included the long citations from Jacquet, Rémusat, and Klaproth. As for the

---

[1] Below, p. xxxvii.

INTRODUCTION

others, one would much like to know what remains in the *Souvenirs* of the notes made day by day. It is to be feared that Huc's note-books—containing a few notes gathered as he journeyed along, he says in his Preface of 1852—were not very carefully kept. In any case, though, Huc had by him everything he had written. Some papers, chosen, moreover, by the missionaries themselves and contained in a " wooden box ", had been taken from them and confiscated at Lhasa, but were restored to them at Canton.[1] The travellers even appeared to have saved the whole of their meagre effects, since Gabet brought from Lhasa to Europe several stones bearing the formula *Oṃ maṇi padme hūm*, one of which he presented to the Bibliothèque Nationale. Further, he had begun at Lhasa and finished in Hu-Pei a translation of the *Sūtra in Forty-two Articles*, done from the Mongol text; the *Journal Asiatique* published it in its issue for June, 1848 (pp. 535-557).[2] I know nothing further of the papers of Gabet and Huc and am unaware of what has become of them.

The first question which arises in dealing with this famous journey to Lhasa is what induced the two Lazarists to undertake it. It is sometimes said that they were " appointed by their ecclesiastical superiors to make their way to the city of the Dalai Lama " (Markham, *Tibet*, XCIV). Sir Thomas Holdich likewise says that Mgr. Mouly " deputed Huc (with one companion, Gabet) to visit Tibet " (*Tibet the*

---

[1] *L'Empire chinois*, I, 58-59, 65, 84-85; Cordier, *L'Expulsion de MM. Huc et Gabet*, in *Mélanges d'histoire*, I, 291, 292, 294.

[2] To the references which I gave for the study of this topic in my article in the *T'oung Pao* I should like to add L. Feer, *Le Sutra en 42 articles*, Paris, 1878, 12mo, pp. XV-XVI and LV-LVI.

INTRODUCTION

Mysterious, 128). Yule, who has defended Huc against Prževal'skiī, stated definitely nevertheless that Huc, as a traveller, had no " geographical sense ", to which M. Planchet answered, in his recent Peking edition (I, 68 ; 1924), that this was not his business and that the object of his journey was the spreading of the Gospel. In this connection M. Planchet cites Mgr. Mouly's letter of March, 1845, which says : " These expedients in the end allowed us to send two European missionaries, holding the apostolic license, to the northern part of Mongolia last year. They set out from the Mongol-Chinese Mission—that is to say, that usually occupied by the Chinese—on September 10th, 1844. They were MM. Gabet and Huc, both fairly well acquainted with the Manchu and Mongol languages, and knowing enough Tibetan to enable them to carry on their ministry usefully among the nomadic Mongols and to attempt to found a mission in their midst ". M. Planchet further invokes Mgr. Mouly's letter of February 8th, 1846 : " We have had no news of MM. Gabet and Huc, who left almost two years ago to evangelize the nomadic Mongols of the north ".

In spite of Mgr. Mouly's remark it was believed for a while at the Mongol mission that they had almost certain news of the arrival of Gabet and Huc in Northern Mongolia, among the Khalkhas. This is shown by a letter of Daguin's written from the Three Towers Mission, August 22nd, 1845 : " First of all let me mention the arrival of MM. Gabet and Huc in Halha, which contains more than eighty Mongol Kingdoms. I learnt of their arrival without their knowing it, in the way I am about to tell you . . ."

INTRODUCTION

Daguin then narrates the departure of the missionaries, his own movements, then his return to Pieh-Lieh-Kou, where a Mongol back from the Khalkha country " had told the catechists on the spot that Fathers Tseu (Gabet) and Kou (Huc) had become lamas ". In the Khalkha country the Mongol had seen the pagoda out of which " all the objects connected with the superstitious cult of Fo had been ignominiously thrown; three great images had been placed in it. One, according to his tale, represented a woman carrying a child in her arms; the second a man carrying a sheep on his shoulders; I cannot recall the picture he made of the third. This Mongol of Pieh-Lieh-Kou also said that they had had a debate with a grand lama who had come from Tibet, who replied that he was going to Peking and wanted to consult the Emperor about this new doctrine; he also told them that Fathers Tseu and Kou had left and travelled on beyond Halha towards the North-West without his being able to see them. It is certain that this Mongol cannot have been lying in talking so, as he knew nothing of the objects of our cult and had no knowledge either of the departure, or even of the proposed departure, of our two colleagues ".

The following year, in the absence of definite news of the two missionaries, the Mongol's story was still partly believed in at Hsi-wan-tzŭ, and the seminarists of the place in writing to the seminarists of Paris on April 30th, 1846, said, still speaking of Gabet and Huc : " If we are to believe certain rumours, they have converted many lamas and broken their idols, setting up in their place images of Our Lord carrying a lamb on his shoulders and of the Blessed Virgin Mary

INTRODUCTION

bearing the Infant Jesus in her arms. Expounding the Gospel and teaching prayers has doubtless been taking up much of their time."

In July, 1847, an article on *The Mongolian Missions* (*Ann. Prop. Foi*, XIX, 268), after speaking of the Chriſtians of inner Mongolia, adds: " There is not a single Chriſtian to be found among the nomad tribes in the north, which wander about with their movable tents as far even as the frontiers of Asiatic Russia. On this vaſt plateau, which is about 800 leagues in circumference, no Cross of Chriſt had yet been planted to point the way towards the Land of Salvation to these eternal pilgrims of the desert, when, in 1844, two Fathers of the Mission undertook to penetrate into the utmoſt depths of their unknown ſteppes . . ." Following this comes Huc's letter of December 20th, 1846, which is in no way contrary to what preceded; it begins as follows: " Reverend Father, undoubtedly you have long known that Mgr. Mouly, our Apoſtolic Vicar, had charged us, M. Gabet and me, to explore Mongol Tartary, and to ſtudy carefully the cuſtoms and charaćter of these nomad peoples, whom it is our mission to evangelize. As we had been bidden to go as far as possible, we had to make certain preparations and to organize ourselves into a caravan . . ."

The text moſt to the point, however, is a letter written from Macao by Gabet (almoſt certainly, therefore, in Oćtober, 1846) to his successor, M. Daguin. This was, I believe, unpublished till its partial publication by M. Planchet (I, 2), and it is worth reproducing here: " When we left Pieh-Lieh-Kou to make for the Khalkha country, the certainty

INTRODUCTION

of being taken for Russians made us prefer to take the western route; we crossed the Ch'akar, and then the Yellow River, we passed through the Kingdoms of Ordos and Alashan, and eventually arrived at the famous lamasery known as T'a-erh-ssŭ.[1] We hoped to found there the first Christian mission-station in Mongolia. We stayed there eight months, at the end of which, seeing no chance of the hopes we had conceived being realized, and not being able to continue living there, because we should have had to take the lama habit which they wished to force upon us, we were obliged to seek fresh fields. A war which broke out between the Chinese and the Tibetans made our return impossible.[2] As we were obliged to turn our steps westwards, we plunged into the great Kalmuck desert and, after travelling some months, we reached Lhasa, the capital of Tibet. There, from the moment of our very first effort, we were comforted by seeing success surpass all our hopes; we built a small chapel and for the first time the prayers of the true faith were offered in this capital of Buddhism . . ."

In the *Report on the Chinese Missions* made to Pius IX in the second half of the year 1847, Gabet also writes that in August, 1844, he received instructions about his journey from Mgr. Mouly: " He made me head of the future Mission and M. Huc had the title of Procurator ". One passage in the letter ran thus: " You will go on from tent to tent, from tribe to tribe, from lamasery to lamasery, until God makes

---

[1] This is the great lamasery of Kumbum; Gabet gives it its Chinese name, while Huc uses the Tibetan form.

[2] There is no mention of this " war " in the *Souvenirs*.

INTRODUCTION

known to you the spot where he wishes you to stop to make a definite beginning. So these instructions left us, and rightly, with full latitude to decide the direction of our journey ". After saying how reasons of expediency made them prefer the route towards the West, Gabet merely adds that " we had further the benefit of going to the mysterious source whence these people insist so obstinately on drawing all their beliefs ".

All these texts show clearly enough that the Lazarists' instructions sent them to the North-West into Outer Mongolia, to the Khalkha country, towards Urga, and that we must attribute to a combination of fortuitous circumstances the changes in the itinerary which, leading them to the South-West, eventually brought them to Lhasa. Even after his arrival at Macao towards the end of 1846, Gabet speaks of their détour to Lhasa as an accident. At Rome, in 1847, we find for the first time in his writings an allusion to the " mysterious source " which the western route caused them to approach ; he still does not describe it more precisely.

When, however, the missionaries charged with founding a mission in Mongolia appeared suddenly, after lying rumours had aroused belief in the success of their mission in this region, and appeared from Tibet, which was allotted to another order, and when on this account they found that they had made a journey which was fruitless from the point of view of their own mission, it is practically certain that, had any mention been made of either Tibet or Lhasa, in Mgr. Mouly's instructions, Gabet would not have failed to quote the passage at full length. In these

INTRODUCTION

circumstances how, then, is it possible that thoughtful scholars like Markham can have believed that Gabet and Huc had orders to go to the capital of Tibet? It seems to me that the fault lies with Huc himself. In the *Souvenirs* (I, 3) he says that "towards the beginning of 1844 . . ." Mgr. Mouly "sent us instructions for the great journey that we were on the point of undertaking with the purpose of studying the manners and customs of the Tartars and of exploring, if possible, the extent and boundaries of the vicariate". This is vague enough, especially if we recall that Mgr. Mouly, in his letters, speaks of the "North of Mongolia" and of the "nomadic Mongols of the North", and that Gabet says expressly that they had started off intending to go "into the Khalkha country". In his preface of August 7th, 1852, Huc is, to say the least of it, ambiguous. "It was in 1844 that we began to study Buddhist religion in the monasteries of the lamas more particularly, and that the wish to go to the source whence are derived the superstitions which dominate the peoples of Central Asia, caused us to undertake these long journeys that led us to the very capital of Tibet." Every reader, unaware of Mgr. Mouly's instructions but knowing that Huc went to Lhasa, naturally has the impression that it is Lhasa which is meant as "the source of the superstitions which dominate the peoples of Central Asia". And throughout the length of this preface there is never a word either of Mgr. Mouly or of Gabet, though Gabet was the head of Huc's district and all the while his chief on the mission. Lastly, in 1858, in his *Christianisme* (IV, 376-377) Huc relates the conversion of the lamas, Paul, Peter and Samdadchiemba

INTRODUCTION

and then continues thus : " The conversion of these three Buddhi∫t monks was a great encouragement to the missionaries in Mongolia. From all they had learned in the various lamaseries, they became convinced that Lha-Ssa, the capital of Tibet and the seat of the Grand Lama, was in the eyes of all the peoples of Central Asia the very Rome of Buddhism ; that Lha-Ssa exercised a decisive influence over the beliefs of the Tartars and that Chri∫tian propaganda, directed from that city, could not fail to obtain considerable results in the future. Two missionaries then made up their minds to cross Tartary and Tibet and to reach Lhasa, without allowing themselves to be frightened by the pictures of fatigue and danger which had unfailingly been conjured up before their eyes. One of these missionaries was M. Gobet [i.e. Gabet] and the other the writer of these lines."

Here the text is perfectly clear. Huc asserts that from the ∫tart, and in spite of the objections raised by their colleagues, the initial objective of the journey undertaken in 1844 was Lhasa. We know, however, that it was nothing of the sort. If the idea of going there occurred to Huc, or even to Gabet either, it was entertained without the knowledge of Mgr. Mouly and was not considered in his in∫tructions. Besides, Gabet's letter to Daguin, unless we are gratuitously to suspect its sincerity, gives the lie to such an hypothesis. Then what really happened ? What I imagine is this, and it is human enough. On their return to Canton, the welcome given to them made Gabet and Huc realize that they had performed a remarkable journey. The French Consul, M. Lefebvre de Bécour, living at Macao, had learned of the passage

INTRODUCTION

through Ch'eng-tu of the two missionaries and even before their arrival in Canton and Macao he had informed the Minister of Foreign Affairs that "since the mission of the Englishman, Turner (who had not actually got as far as Lhasa), they were the only Europeans, with the possible exception of the Transylvanian scholar (i.e. *Csoma de Körös*), to penetrate into one of the most extraordinary countries of Central Asia." In a new letter from Macao dated October 24th, 1846, Lefebvre de Bécour noted that "MM. Huc and Gabet" had been well treated throughout their journey. He added: "It is to be hoped that after they have rested and regained their self-possession sufficiently to undertake such work and when they have made themselves acquainted with what has already been published on Tibet, they will draw up an account of their journey and of their stay there, which cannot fail to be of great interest to the learned world." Gabet, to judge from his letter to M. Daguin, seems to have retained from the first the self-possession recommended by the consul, but Huc, with the impetuosity and loquacity of a true southerner, allowed his head to be turned a little. He did not wish it thought that he had become a great traveller by accident, as it were, and, after preserving a discreet silence about all the chance happenings which had caused the missionaries to turn aside from their path towards the South-West, he finished in 1858 by affirming that, if he had gone to Lhasa, it was because from the very beginning and as the result of mature deliberation he had had this town as his objective.

Unpublished documents, which were still not known

INTRODUCTION

to me when I composed my article in the *T'oung Pao*, prove moreover that the first reaction of Gabet's and Huc's colleagues, when they heard of the journey to Lhasa, was even more unfavourable than I had thought. The two travellers were making complaints against the Chinese commissioner for Lhasa, and Gabet will insist on this point again when he is travelling with A. R. Johnston from Hong-Kong to Galle Point; but the real reason why Gabet returned to Europe so quickly was that he hoped to get the Tibet mission restored once more to the Lazarists and to become himself the first Apostolic Vicar of Lhasa. He thus put himself into complete opposition to his Bishop, Mgr. Mouly; the latter, in sending one of his priests, J. F. Faivre, to Rome several months later, entrusted him with detailed instructions, dated May 10th, 1847, in which what follows is particularly to the point. " Letters lately brought by courier inform us that M. Gabet left last November for Europe, where he has gone to request for himself the Vicariate of Tibet . . . Seeing . . . that M. Gabet . . . went without orders, on no suggestion, real or inferred, from his superior, the bishop, who is both Apostolic Vicar and visitor [of the Lazarists], and whom he did not deign to consult . . . you alone are our representative, and you alone must be regarded as such . . . We feel that the little Company [of Lazarists] cannot and ought not to assume responsibility for Tibet. This vicariate, far away from our own, has already been given to other missionaries, who are stationed near Tibet; its Vicar Apostolic has probably been consecrated and has probably begun his duties . . . This request [of M. Gabet] is at the present

INTRODUCTION

time and in the circumstances most unseemly." It is evident enough that Mgr. Mouly was not particularly pleased with the journey to Lhasa made by his two subordinates and, with this in mind, it is easier to understand why subsequently the Propaganda showed itself much prepossessed against Gabet.

The chronology of the journey also brings up difficulties; though they are not so vital as those raised by its purport, they are none the less both real and astonishing. In my article in the *T'oung Pao* I have shown that Huc gives false dates in his *Souvenirs* both for the start of the journey and for his stay in the region of Kuku-nor, as well as for his arrival in Lhasa which he fixes as January 29th, 1846, while it really took place at the end of December, 1845. Even the date of his sailing for Europe on the *Cassini* on December 28th, 1851, is wrong. From beginning to end Huc has been unlucky with his dates.[1]

Finally, if Huc " manipulated " the purport of his journey after the event, and if he gives dates that are often suspicious, I am afraid that he was equally easy in his presentation of facts. I should like to illustrate this by a couple of examples.

A. (*Souvenirs*, I, 6).[2] " Hail is of frequent occurrence in these unhappy districts and the dimensions of the hailstones are generally enormous. We have ourselves seen some that weighed twelve pounds. One moment sometimes suffices to exterminate whole flocks. In 1843 during one of these storms there was heard in the air a sound as of a rushing wind and

---

[1] I have not spoken of the dates which Huc gives for historical incidents; they are on occasion no less astonishing.

[2] Below, Vol. I, p. 5.

INTRODUCTION

therewith fell in a field near a house, a mass of ice larger than an ordinary millstone. It was broken to pieces with hatchets, yet, though the sun burned fiercely, three days elapsed before these pieces entirely melted." M. Planchet (I, 73-74) gives an interesting note showing that these enormous hail-stones, however rare they may be, are not without parallel in Mongolia. I readily agree; I do not believe that Huc invented the story, but merely that he has declared himself an eye-witness of what someone else really had told him; for in an unpublished letter which Gabet wrote to his brother Ferdinand on August 20th, 1842, we read as follows: "In the first days of June—the month which has just gone by—such a terrible shower of hail fell that whole flocks of sheep were completely wiped out. Last year near the place where I was on mission work . . . a frightful hail-storm occurred, so bad that some of the hailstones, which were weighed, were as much as ten and twelve pounds each. Two years ago a piece of ice, larger than three mill-stones, fell during a perfect tempest of hail a day's journey away from the place where I was, at a spot inhabited by pagans which I often pass through; it was broken to pieces with picks and clubs and the bits took three or four days to melt, although it was the hottest part of July."

In August, 1842, and therefore still more certainly at an earlier date, Huc was not in the district where Gabet was ordinarily living. We saw above quite definitely that Huc arrived from Macao at Hsi-wan-tsŭ on June 17th, 1841, and stayed there till about May 26th, 1843; it was not till then that he started off for the missions at "Black Waters" and "The

INTRODUCTION

Contiguous Defiles ". Besides, this is confirmed by a passage from Gabet's letter to his brother. " Peter and Paul [the two lamas whom Gabet had converted and baptized] are not with me; the first is teaching Mongol to M. Huc, a colleague who has come to join us[1]; the other is at Macao, where he is studying. I am going to try to get hold of another of them." On the other hand, the likeness between Gabet's letter and Huc's text is so clear, that fresh storms at exactly a year's space, where every incident was repeated so closely, are hardly to be thought of. I am more inclined to think that Huc has narrated as if he had seen it himself what really he had only heard from Gabet.

B. The second example is even more to the point. In his *Souvenirs* (I, 134-137)[2] Huc speaks of the Living Buddha of Urga, or, as he calls him, the Living Buddha of " Great Küren ", which is really the native name. He prefixes these words to his description of the lamasery: " As we had an opportunity of visiting this edifice in one of our journeys into Northern Tartary, we will here give some details respecting it." And, further on, talking of the Chinese merchants' post some half-league away from the lamasery, he says: " A watch and some ingots of silver, stolen during the night from M. Gabet, left us no doubt as to the want of probity in the Holy One's disciples." Every reader of these pages would naturally conclude that Huc had accompanied Gabet at least once on a trip to Urga; and some have, as it happens, not failed to do so—

---

[1] That is to say he had come to join the Mongolian mission, the head-quarter of which were at Hsi-wan-tzŭ.

[2] Below, Vol. I, pp. 108-112.

INTRODUCTION

Markham, for inſtance (*Tibet*, XLIX). Now Gabet actually did go from Hsi-wan-tzŭ, but it was in the summer of 1839 ; and it was then that he was robbed, not near Urga, but when, to the north of Urga, he was trying to push on as far as Kiakhta. We have a detailed account of this journey by Gabet himself in his letter from " Tartary, June, 1842 " (*Ann. Prop. Foi.*, XX, 4-33). Gabet's only companions were the former lamas, Peter and Paul. At this date Huc had not even arrived at Macao.[1] Further ſtill, it is unlikely that Huc ever went to Urga. He arrived at Hsi-wan-tzŭ on June 17th, 1841, and did not leave for the missions opened by Gabet more to the north until the second half of May, 1843. Now it is obvious that on his arrival the chief of his diſtrict gave him mission work to do and did not send a new-comer off alone on an expedition into a diſtant country, which he himself had already explored.

On the other hand, Huc himself tells us (*Souvenirs*, I, 29)[2] that " towards the commencement of the year 1844 " Gabet and he received Mgr. Mouly's inſtructions as to the great journey, and we know from Mgr. Mouly as well as from Gabet that their firſt goal was precisely Outer Mongolia, the Khalkha country where Urga is situated. So Huc assuredly did not go to Urga in this particular year either. Only one solution remains : that Huc owed his information about Urga and the Living Buddha to Gabet. As a skilled writer however, he felt that the public prefers a ſtory told at firſt, rather than at second, hand ; and to please

---

[1] Since my article in the *T'oung Pao* unpublished letters of Gabet have been communicated to me, which confirm the fact that his journey to Urga took place before 1841.

[2] Below, Vol. I, p. 2.

INTRODUCTION

the public he made out that he had undertaken the trip himself.

On the linguistic acquirements of the two missionaries M. Planchet (I, 66-67) has some very judicious remarks. Gabet must have spoken fluently enough both Chinese and Mongol; in addition he set about studying Manchu. His *Rapport* to Pius IX gives information on the various pieces of work he undertook. Immediately after Paul's conversion in 1837 Gabet drew up " A small collection of prayers in the Mongol tongue " and also " a small elementary Catechism of Catholic doctrine ". " Paul, who knows the Manchu language perfectly, is giving me lessons, and these two small books, written in Mongol, were translated into Manchu." After Peter's conversion he says of all three : " We wrote in Mongol a complete statement of Catholic doctrine drawn from the Council of Trent and set out in the form of question and answer; then an historic treatise on the Christian religion with a refutation of the superstitions of Buddhism; and, finally, a tract for teaching purposes on the existence of God. All these works have remained unpublished. The fear, that, in the earlier parts, there might have slipped in some expression that was inexact theologically, has always hindered us from giving them to be printed and from multiplying them."[1] Later, about 1842, Gabet drew up " a Manchu grammar and then a tract on the connections between this language and the Mongol tongue". All this seems to presuppose a fairly wide knowledge of these two languages; we are all the more surprised to find Gabet, in the same

---

[1] Gabet was not aware that old translations of the works of Ricci and Aleni into Mongol and Manchu existed.

INTRODUCTION

Rapport to Pius IX, translating the Mongol name "Dzün-Uliaſti" on two several occasions (pp. 145-146 and 156) as "Eaſtern Reeds", where there seems to be a confusion involved between *qolosun*, a reed, and *uliyasun*, a poplar.

As for Huc, he is considered to have spoken Chinese very well, but he was certainly not in a position to read any but easy texts. Besides that, he had a knowledge of Mongol, sufficient for everyday needs. As regards Tibetan, in spite of some preliminary ſtudies and the seven or eight months spent in the Kumbum diſtrict doing Tibetan with "Sandara the bearded", the ſtage the two missionaries reached is made clear by the fact that, in all their writings, including Gabet's note in the *Journal Asiatique* of May, 1847 (p. 464), they called the Potala "Bouddhala", a name they translated as "mountain of Buddha". Such being the ſtate of affairs we naturally ask ourselves how they were able to carry on at Lhasa the Tibetan conversations, of which Huc has left us such pleasantly highly-flavoured accounts in his *Souvenirs*.

Of the aſtonishing sections in the *Souvenirs* one of the moſt brilliant is the "Invocation to Timur", which Huc says he heard from a wandering singer or "*toolholos*". This is one of the rare passages for which the letter of December 20th, 1846 (*Ann. Prop. Fid.*, XIX, 281-282) already gives us word for word the final version of the *Souvenirs* (I, 90-91).[1] "*Toolholos*, said we, the songs you have sung were all excellent. But you have as yet said nothing about the Immortal Tamerlane: the 'Invocation to Timur', we have

[1] Below, Vol. I, pp. 73-4.

INTRODUCTION

heard, is a famous song, dear to the Mongols.—Yes, yes, exclaimed several voices at once,—sing us the 'Invocation to Timur'." Then follows an epic fragment, in which the Mongols recall the happy times when "the divine Timur dwelt within our tents" and which ends "Return! Return! We await thee, O Timur!" The Mongols, however, particularly those of Inner Mongolia, have no reason to know Tamerlane, who ruled in Russian Turkeſtan and never in Mongolia. I imagine that Huc has here adapted a Mongol folk-song, which, among the Mongols, has as its subjeƈt some great man quite other than Tamerlane.

I will now add that if, in Huc's two accounts, the wording is identical in the whole of both passages, yet the places where the scene is said to occur are not the same. According to the *Souvenirs* the missionaries heard the "Invocation to Timur" at "Chaberté", otherwise called Shabartai, "a hundred leagues" to the eaſt of Kui-hua-ch'eng, at a spot where their route crossed the road from Kiakhta and Urga to Peking. In a letter of December 26th, 1846, however, all this is related of a camping ground in a loop of the Ordos, well to the weſt of Kui-hua-ch'eng, and when the travellers had already crossed the Yellow River ten days before. I see no reason to choose between these two sites, of which one is, in all likelihood, no less arbitrary than the other. Huc in his notes had this scrap of bravura-writing: he localized it at a spot where the surroundings ſtruck him as being beſt suited to show it off.

The conclusion from these remarks is that Huc, in writing up his *Souvenirs*, trimmed them liberally

INTRODUCTION

for public consumption. He "invented" nothing, but he transposed his material in order to please, and he succeeded. The *Souvenirs* are an artistic creation which leaves the reader with the impression of a whole, which is the more true for the very lack of exactitude in the detailed relation of facts.[1] We should very much like to know more of what Gabet thought of all this. Huc's marvellously animated narrative has thrown into the shade his companion who was both his elder and his chief. Huc must have put himself to the forefront straight away. From October, 1846, the very day after the arrival of our travellers, the French consul in Macao is already talking of MM. " Huc and Gabet ". Current usage follows suit. It is our duty to-day to make an effort, having the letters of Mgr. Mouly and Daguin in mind, to reestablish the proper ecclesiastical order—Gabet and Huc.

---

[1] I do not want to discuss in this place the complex question of Moorcroft's fate. Although the positive statements of Huc have either shaken or convinced Waddell G. Sandberg, Landon, Holdich, and Kühner, I think it more probable that Moorcroft really did die in Afghanistan in 1825 and that Huc, by making him come to Lhasa, was guilty of an oversight, from the consequences of which he did not know how to clear himself afterwards.

EDITORIAL NOTE

In the present reprint of Hazlitt's translation the original spellings have been kept throughout except in the rare cases of obvious misprints in the original, such as Isao-ti for Tsao-ti (Vol. I, p. 2), Monhe-Dhot (Vol. I, p. 34), and Monhe Dehot (Vol. II, p. 163) for Monhe Dchot. All the Chinese, Tibetan, and Mongol names and words occurring in the text will be found in the Index with their modern scientific transcription which has been supplied by Professor Pelliot. These transcriptions have throughout the text been inserted in square brackets where these names and words appear for the first time.

APPENDIX

LETTER FROM MR. A. R. JOHNSTON TO SIR JOHN FRANCIS DAVIS, BART.,
HER MAJESTY'S PLENIPOTENTIARY IN PEKING[1]

Victoria [Hong Kong],
16th February, 1847.

I WAS recently a fellow passenger on board the steamer from Hong Kong to Point de Galle with a French lazarist Missionary of the name of Joseph Gabet. He was going to Paris, conceiving that he had been ill-used in L'Hassa by Ke-Shen the Chinese representative there, and if on his arrival in Paris he thought it advisable he intended to bring his case to the notice of the French Government.

Joseph Gabet entered China by the Province of Fokien in 1836, and has since been in the provinces of Se-Shewn, Hoo-Pe, Tche-Lee, Quangtung, Quang-Si, in Thibet, among the Turcomans, and the Mongols. He showed me a Mantchoo Grammar which he had written. He had lived in a large " Bonzarie " on the frontier of Thibet, for ten months, which he describes as a very fine establishment.

The *Church* covering an area of 400 feet square (40 Chang of 10 feet square). He was at L'Hassa for some time, and hoped, and still wishes to establish a mission there, but his funds having run short he wanted to open a communication with Calcutta in order to supply his Mission with resources, for this purpose he obtained the permission of the Regent of Thibet to go to Calcutta through Gorgat [? Gourkak] but Ke-Shen who is at L'Hassa as Chinese Envoy, heard of it, and has sufficient influence to prevent his executing this plan, and by his interference, to get him handed over to him in order that he might be sent to Canton, on the plea that he would shew the English the way to Thibet if he was permitted to go to Calcutta as he wanted.

The Government of Thibet is composed of the Ta-Lee Lama or " Universal Saint " and there is a King under him who is a Lama—

[1] Public Record Office, F.O. 17/123. The document is Letter 22 in the Correspondence of Sir J. Davis, January and February, 1847. It is enclosed in a short explanatory letter from Sir John Davis to Lord Palmerston.

INTRODUCTION

time and in the circumstances most unseemly." It is evident enough that Mgr. Mouly was not particularly pleased with the journey to Lhasa made by his two subordinates and, with this in mind, it is easier to understand why subsequently the Propaganda showed itself much prepossessed against Gabet.

The chronology of the journey also brings up difficulties; though they are not so vital as those raised by its purport, they are none the less both real and astonishing. In my article in the *T'oung Pao* I have shown that Huc gives false dates in his *Souvenirs* both for the start of the journey and for his stay in the region of Kuku-nor, as well as for his arrival in Lhasa which he fixes as January 29th, 1846, while it really took place at the end of December, 1845. Even the date of his sailing for Europe on the *Cassini* on December 28th, 1851, is wrong. From beginning to end Huc has been unlucky with his dates.[1]

Finally, if Huc "manipulated" the purport of his journey after the event, and if he gives dates that are often suspicious, I am afraid that he was equally easy in his presentation of facts. I should like to illustrate this by a couple of examples.

A. (*Souvenirs*, I, 6).[2] "Hail is of frequent occurrence in these unhappy districts and the dimensions of the hailstones are generally enormous. We have ourselves seen some that weighed twelve pounds. One moment sometimes suffices to exterminate whole flocks. In 1843 during one of these storms there was heard in the air a sound as of a rushing wind and

---

[1] I have not spoken of the dates which Huc gives for historical incidents; they are on occasion no less astonishing.

[2] Below, Vol. I, p. 5.

APPENDIX

to have been so complete, Père Gabet believes him already to have commenced amassing wealth. When he left L'Hassa he says he could only procure two bullocks for himself, but Ke-Shen sent with him under his particular care four bullocks laden with baggage, which Ke-Shen instructed him to keep an eye upon, and to see these bullocks loaded and unloaded whenever they stopped as if the baggage was his own, and he was to have it deposited with his own in the room when he slept at night. Père Gabet did as he was told, and finally left the baggage belonging to Ke-Shen at the Treasury in Se-Shewn, and he believed it to have contained diamonds and other valuable gems abounding in Thibet, and which Ke-Shen for some time back had been purchasing up through Agents. The common people even wear diamond rings, and the women gold pins in their hair.

While the war was waging with the English the Emperor of China consulted the Ta-Lee Lama on the subject, and got for reply, that he must use all his exertions and efforts to repel and subdue the English, but if he was not successful, the Ta-Lee Lama would come and with a breath drive them away. When success did not attend the armies of the Chinese, the oracle was again consulted, and this time said, you must accede to all their wishes and the war will be at an end.

Père Gabet was in China during the time of our hostilities and says the events connected with the war were much talked of in the North where he was. The accounts always appear to have been grossly misrepresented, for instance he saw a series of four pictures. The first representing Lin going on board the opium ship disguised as an opium merchant, purchasing all the opium and paying down for it the *Bargain money*. The next picture represented Lin going on board the ship with his satellites and followers all disguised as persons who were to carry away the opium he had purchased, but who, in the next picture no sooner get on board than they throw off their disguise and take the crews of the vessels prisoners. The next and last in the series is Lin sitting in judgement over the prisoners and superintending the destruction of the opium. These pictures were accompanied by descriptions and were sold in numbers about the streets for little or nothing. Opium, Père Gabet says is extensively used by all the Mandarins and he knew one who wanted to leave it off but was not allowed to do so by his mother, because his father in leaving it off died. He thinks the empire of China must soon crumble to pieces. The people have lost their veneration for the Emperors since the War with the English. The Mandarins feel themselves in a false position,

APPENDIX

being all of them addicted to the smoking of Opium while they are ordered to sentence to death those that smoke it.

The Chinese are also at war in three parts of the frontier, at one place with a tribe of Thibetians, at another in trying to subdue some rebellious Mongols, and, at a third in suppressing rebellion.

The Members of the Water Lily Society are becoming more numerous than ever and are much dreaded by the authorities. People are heard not infrequently to talk of the descendants of the last dynasty who live in Se-Shewn.

Not having any maps with me on board the Steamer I was unable to point out his route, but I hope to learn this from a companion of his who resides at Macao and will await his return to China.

These notes were hastily drawn up after conversing with Père Gabet on the subjects they treat of, and in hopes they may be of use to Her Majesty's Government. I now gladly furnish them to Her Majesty's Plenipotentiary in China.

(*Signed*) A. R. JOHNSTON.

True copy.

Signature A. R. JOHNSTON

CONTENTS OF VOLUME I

	PAGE
INTRODUCTION BY PROFESSOR PELLIOT	v
APPENDIX	xxxvii

CHAPTER ONE

French Mission of Peking—Glance at the Kingdom of Ouniot—Preparations for Departure—Tartar-Chinese Inn—Change of Costume—Portrait and Character of Samdadchiemba—Sain-Oula (the Good Mountain)—The Frosts on Sain-Oula, and its Robbers—First Encampment in the Desert—Great Imperial Forest—Buddhist Monuments on the summit of the Mountains—Topography of the Kingdom of Gechekten—Character of its Inhabitants—Tragical Working of a Mine—Two Mongols desire to have their horoscope taken—Adventure of Samdadchiemba—Environs of the town of Tolon-Noor . 1

CHAPTER TWO

Inn at Tolon-Noor—Aspect of the City—Great Foundries of Bells and Idols—Conversation with the Lamas of Tolon-Noor—Encampment—Tea Bricks—Meetings with Queen Mourgue-van—Taste of the Mongols for Pilgrimages—Violent Storm—Account from a Mongol Chief of the War of the English against China—Topography of the Eight Banners of the Tchakar—The Imperial Herds—Form and Interior of the Tents—Tartar Manners and Customs—Encampment at the Three Lakes—Nocturnal Apparitions—Samdadchiemba relates the Adventures of his Youth—Grey Squirrels of Tartary—Arrival at Chaborté 30

CHAPTER THREE

Festival of the Loaves of the Moon—Entertainment in a Mongol Tent—Toolholos, or Rhapsodists of Tartary—Invocation to Timour—Tartar Education—Industry of the Women—Mongols in quest of missing Animals—Remains of an abandoned City—Road from Peking to Kiaktha—Commerce between China and Russia—Russian Convent at Peking—A Tartar solicits us to cure his Mother from a dangerous Illness—Tartar Physicians—The Intermittent Fever Devil—Various forms

CONTENTS

of Sepulture in use among the Mongols—Lamasery of the Five Towers—Obsequies of the Tartar Kings—Origin of the Kingdom of Efe—Gymnastic Exercises of the Tartars—Encounters with three Wolves—Mongol Carts . . . 68

CHAPTER FOUR

Young Lama converted to Christianity—Lamasery of Tchortchi—Alms for the Construction of Religious Houses—Aspect of the Buddhist Temples—Recitation of Lama Prayers—Decorations, Paintings, and Sculptures of the Buddhist Temples—Topography of the Great Kouren in the country of the Khalkhas—Journey of the Guison-Tamba to Peking—The Kouren of the Thousand Lamas—Suit between the Lama-King and his Ministers—Purchase of a Kid—Eagles of Tartary—Western Toumet—Agricultural Tartars—Arrival at the Blue Town—Glance at the Mantchou Nation—Mantchou Literature—State of Christianity in Mantchouria—Topography and Productions of Eastern Tartary—Skill of the Mantchous with the Bow 102

CHAPTER FIVE

The Old Blue Town—Quarter of the Tanners—Knavery of the Chinese Traders—Hotel of the Three Perfections—Spoliation of the Tartars by the Chinese—Money Changer's Office—Tartar Coiner—Purchase of two Sheep-skin Robes—Camel Market—Customs of the Cameleers—Assassination of a Grand Lama of the Blue Town—Insurrection of the Lamaseries—Negociation between the Court of Peking and that of Lha-Ssa—Domestic Lamas—Wandering Lamas—Lamas in Community—Policy of the Mantchou Dynasty with reference to the Lamaseries—Interview with a Thibetian Lama—Departure from the Blue Town 133

CHAPTER SIX

A Tartar-eater—Loss of Arsalan—Great Caravan of Camels—Night Arrival at Tchagan-Kouren—We are refused Admission into the Inns—We take up our abode with a Shepherd—Overflow of the Yellow River—Aspects of Tchagan-Kouren—Departure across the Marshes—Hiring a Bark—Arrival on the

xlii

CONTENTS

Banks of the Yellow River—Encampment under the Portico of a Pagoda—Embarkation of the Camels—Passage of the Yellow River—Laborious Journey across the Inundated Country—Encampment on the Banks of the River . . 159

CHAPTER SEVEN

Mercurial Preparation for the Destruction of Lice—Dirtiness of the Mongols—Lama Notions about the Metempsychosis—Washing—Regulations of Nomadic Life—Aquatic and Passage Birds—The Yuen-Yang—The Dragon's Foot—Fishermen of the Paga-Gol—Fishing Party—Fisherman Bit by a Dog—Kou-Kouo, or St. Ignatius's Bean—Preparation for Departure—Passage of the Paga-Gol—Dangers of the Voyage—Devotion of Samdadchiemba—The Prime Minister of the King of the Ortous—Encampment 184

CHAPTER EIGHT

Glance at the Country of the Ortous—Cultivated Lands—Sterile, sandy steppes of the Ortous—Form of the Tartar-Mongol Government—Nobility—Slavery—A small Lamasery—Election and Enthronization of a Living Buddha—Discipline of the Lamaseries—Lama Studies—Violent Storm—Shelter in some Artificial Grottoes—Tartar concealed in a Cavern—Tartaro-Chinese Anecdote—Ceremonies of Tartar Marriages—Polygamy—Divorce—Character and Costume of the Mongol Women 208

CHAPTER NINE

Departure of the Caravan—Encampment in a fertile Valley—Intensity of the Cold—Meeting with numerous Pilgrims—Barbarous and Diabolical Ceremonies of Lamanism—Project of the Lamasery of Rache-Tchurin—Dispersion and Rallying of the little Caravan—Anger of Samdadchiemba—Aspect of the Lamasery of Rache-Tchurin—Different Kinds of Pilgrimages around the Lamaseries—Turning Prayers—Quarrel between two Lamas—Similarity of the Soil—Description of the Tabsoun-Noor or Salt Sea—Remarks on the Camels of Tartary 240

CONTENTS

CHAPTER TEN

Purchase of a Sheep—A Mongol Butcher—Great Feast à la Tartare—Tartar Veterinary Surgeons—Strange Cure of a Cow—Depth of the Wells of the Ortous—Manner of Watering the Animals—Encampment at the Hundred Wells—Meeting with the King of the Alechan—Annual Embassies of the Tartar Sovereigns to Peking—Grand Ceremony in the Temple of the Ancestors—The Emperor gives Counterfeit Money to the Mongol Kings—Inspection of our Geographical Map—The Devil's Cistern—Purification of the Water—A Lame Dog—Curious Aspect of the Mountains—Passage of the Yellow River 270

CHAPTER ELEVEN

Sketch of the Tartar Nations 307

CHAPTER TWELVE

Hotel of Justice and Mercy—Province of Kan-Sou—Agriculture—Great Works for the Irrigation of the Fields—Manner of Living in Inns—Great Confusion in a Town caused by our Camels—Chinese Lifeguard—Mandarin Inspector of the Public Works—Ning-Hia—Historical and Topographical Details—Inn of the Five Felicities—Contest with a Mandarin, Tchong-Wei—Immense Mountains of Sand—Road to Ili—Unfavourable aspect of Kao-Tan-Dze—Glance at the Great Wall—Inquiry after the Passports—Tartars travelling in China—Dreadful Hurricane—Origin and Manners of the Inhabitants of Kan-Sou—The Dchiahours—Interview with a Living Buddha—Hotel of the Temperate Climates—Family of Samdadchiemba—Mountain of Ping-Keou—Fight between an Innkeeper and his Wife—Water-mills—Knitting—Si-Ning-Fou—House of Rest—Arrival at Tang-Keou-Eul . 342

Travels in Tartary, Thibet, and China

VOLUME I

CHAPTER I

THE French mission of Peking, once so flourishing under the early emperors of the Tartar-Mantchou [Manchu] dynasty, was almost extirpated by the constant persecutions of Kia-King [Chia-ch'ing], the fifth monarch of that dynasty, who ascended the throne in 1799. The missionaries were dispersed or put to death, and at that time Europe was herself too deeply agitated to enable her to send succour to this distant Christendom, which remained for a time abandoned. Accordingly, when the French Lazarists re-appeared at Peking, they found there scarce a vestige of the true faith. A great number of Christians, to avoid the persecutions of the Chinese authorities, had passed the Great Wall, and sought peace and liberty in the deserts of Tartary, where they lived dispersed upon small patches of land which the Mongols permitted them to cultivate. By dint of perseverance the missionaries collected together these dispersed Christians, placed themselves at their head, and hence superintended the mission of Peking, the immediate administration of which was in the hands of a few Chinese Lazarists. The French missionaries could not, with any prudence, have resumed their former position in the capital of the empire. Their presence would have compromised the prospects of the scarcely reviving mission.

In visiting the Chinese Christians of Mongolia, we more than once had occasion to make excursions into the Land of Grass (Tsao-Ti [Ts'ao-ti]), as the uncultivated portions of Tartary are designated, and to take up our temporary abode beneath the tents of the Mongols. We were no sooner acquainted with this nomadic people than we loved them, and our hearts were filled with a passionate desire to announce the gospel to them. Our whole leisure was therefore devoted to acquiring the Tartar dialects, and in 1842, the Holy See at length fulfilled our desires, by erecting Mongolia into an Apostolical Vicariat.

Towards the commencement of the year 1844, couriers arrived at Si-wan [Hsi-wan], a small Christian community, where the vicar apostolic of Mongolia had fixed his episcopal residence. Si-wan itself is a village, north of the Great Wall, one day's journey from Suen-hoa-Fou [Hsüan-hua-fu]. The prelate sent us instructions for an extended voyage we were to undertake for the purpose of studying the character and manners of the Tartars, and of ascertaining as nearly as possible the extent and limits of the Vicariat. This journey, then, which we had so long meditated, was now determined upon; and we sent a young Lama convert in search of some camels which we had put to pasture in the kingdom of Naiman. Pending his absence, we hastened the completion of several Mongol works, the translation of which had occupied us for a considerable time. Our little books of prayer and doctrine were ready, still our young Lama had not returned; but thinking he could not delay much longer, we quitted the Valley of Black Waters (Hé Chuy [Hei-shui]), and proceeded on to await his arrival at the Contiguous Defiles (Pié-lié-Keou [Pieh-lieh-kou]), which seemed more favourable for the completion of our preparations. The days passed away in futile expectation; the coolness of the autumn was becoming somewhat biting, and we feared that we should have to begin our journey across the deserts of Tartary during the frosts of winter. We determined, therefore, to dispatch some one in quest of our camels and our Lama. A friendly catechist, a good walker, and a man of expedition, proceeded on this mission. On the day fixed for that purpose, he returned; his researches had been wholly without result. All he had ascertained at the place which he had visited was that our Lama had started several days before with our camels. The surprise of our courier was extreme when he found that the Lama had not reached us before himself. "What!" exclaimed he, "are my legs quicker than a camel's! They left Naiman before me, and here I am arrived before them! My spiritual fathers, have patience for another day. I'll answer that both Lama and camels will be here in that time." Several days, however, passed away, and we were still in the same position. We once more dispatched the courier in search of the Lama, enjoining him to proceed to the very place where the camels had been put to pasture, to examine things with his own eyes, and not to trust to any statement that other people might make.

During this interval of painful suspense, we continued to inhabit the Contiguous Defiles, a Tartar district dependent on the kingdom of Ouniot [Ougniut].[1] These regions appear to have been affected by great revolutions. The present inhabitants state that, in the olden time, the country was occupied by Corean tribes, who, expelled thence in the course of various wars, took refuge in the peninsula which they still

[1] Notwithstanding the slight importance of the Tartar tribes, we shall give them the name of kingdoms, because the chiefs of these tribes are called *Wang* (King).

possess, between the Yellow Sea and the sea of Japan. You often, in those parts of Tartary, meet with the remains of great towns, and the ruins of fortresses, very nearly resembling those of the middle ages in Europe, and, upon turning up the soil in those places, it is not unusual to find lances, arrows, portions of farming implements, and urns filled with Corean money.

Towards the middle of the seventeenth century, the Chinese began to penetrate into this diſtrict. At that period, the whole landscape was ſtill one of rude grandeur; the mountains were covered with fine foreſts, and the Mongol tents whitened the valleys, amid rich paſturages. For a very moderate sum the Chinese obtained permission to cultivate the desert, and as cultivation advanced, the Mongols were obliged to retreat, conducting their flocks and herds elsewhere.

From that time forth, the aspect of the country became entirely changed. All the trees were grubbed up, the foreſts disappeared from the hills, the prairies were cleared by means of fire, and the new cultivators set busily to work in exhauſting the fecundity of the soil. Almoſt the entire region is now in the hands of the Chinese, and it is probably to their syſtem of devaſtation that we muſt attribute the extreme irregularity of the seasons which now desolate this unhappy land. Droughts are of almoſt annual occurrence; the spring winds setting in, dry up the soil; the heavens assume a siniſter aspect, and the unfortunate population await, in utter terror, the manifeſtation of some terrible calamity; the winds by degrees redouble their violence, and sometimes continue to blow far into the summer months. Then the duſt rises in clouds, the atmosphere becomes thick and dark; and often, at mid-day, you are environed with the terrors of night, or rather, with an intense and almoſt palpable blackness, a thousand times more fearful than the moſt sombre night. Next after these hurricanes comes the rain : but so comes, that inſtead of being an objeƈt of desire, it is an objeƈt of dread, for it pours down in furious raging torrents. Sometimes the heavens, suddenly opening, pour forth in, as it were, an immense cascade, all the water with which they are charged in that quarter; and immediately the fields and their crops disappear under a sea of mud, whose enormous waves follow the course of the valleys, and carry everything before them. The torrent rushes on, and in a few hours the earth reappears; but the crops are gone, and worse even than that, the arable soil also has gone with them. Nothing remains but a ramification of deep ruts, filled with gravel, and thenceforward incapable of being ploughed.

Hail is of frequent occurrence in these unhappy diſtriƈts, and the dimensions of the hailſtones are generally enormous. We have ourselves seen some that weighed twelve pounds. One moment sometimes suffices to exterminate whole flocks. In 1843, during one of these ſtorms, there was heard in the air a sound as of a rushing wind, and therewith fell, in a field near a house, a mass of ice larger than an ordinary mill-ſtone. It was broken to pieces with hatchets, yet, though the sun burned fiercely, three days elapsed before these pieces entirely melted.

The droughts and the inundations together sometimes occasion famines which well nigh exterminate the inhabitants. That of 1832, in the twelfth year of the reign of Tao-Kouang [Tao-kuang],[1] is the moſt terrible of these on record. The Chinese report that it was everywhere announced by a general presentiment, the exaƈt nature of which no one could explain or comprehend. During the winter of 1831,

[1] Sixth Emperor of the Tartar-Mantchou dynaſty. He died in the year 1849.

a dark rumour grew into circulation. *Next year*, it was said, *there will be neither rich nor poor ; blood will cover the mountains ; bones will fill the valleys* (Ou fou, ou kioung ; hue man chan, kou man tchouan [*wu fu, wu ch'iung ; hsüeh man shan, ku man ch'uan*]). These words were in everyone's mouth ; the children repeated them in their sports ; all were under the domination of these sinister apprehensions when the year 1832 commenced. Spring and summer passed away without rain, and the frosts of autumn set in while the crops were yet green ; these crops of course perished, and there was absolutely no harvest. The population was soon reduced to the most entire destitution. Houses, fields, cattle, everything was exchanged for grain, the price of which attained its weight in gold. When the grass on the mountain sides was devoured by the starving creatures, the depths of the earth were dug into for roots. The fearful prognostic, that had been so often repeated, became accomplished. Thousands died upon the hills, whither they had crawled in search of grass ; dead bodies filled the roads and houses ; whole villages were depopulated to the last man. There was, indeed, *neither rich nor poor* ; pitiless famine had levelled all alike.

It was in this dismal region that we waited with impatience the courier, whom, for a second time we had dispatched into the kingdom of Naiman. The day fixed for his return came and passed, and several others followed, but brought no camels, nor Lama, nor courier, which seemed to us most astonishing of all. We became desperate ; we could not longer endure this painful and futile suspense. We devised other means of proceeding, since those we had arranged appeared to be frustrated. The day of our departure was fixed ; it was settled, further, that one of our Christians should convey us in his car to Tolon-Noor

[Dolôn-nôr], distant from the Contiguous Defiles about fifty leagues. At Tolon-Noor we were to dismiss our temporary conveyance, proceed alone into the desert, and thus start on our pilgrimage as well as we could. This project absolutely stupified our Christian friends; they could not comprehend how two Europeans should undertake by themselves a long journey through an unknown and inimical country: but we had reasons for abiding by our resolution. We did not desire that any Chinese should accompany us. It appeared to us absolutely necessary to throw aside the fetters with which the authorities had hitherto contrived to shackle missionaries in China. The excessive caution, or rather the imbecile pusillanimity of a Chinese catechist, was calculated rather to impede than to facilitate our progress in Tartary.

On the Sunday, the day preceding our arranged departure, every thing was ready; our small trunks were packed and padlocked, and the Christians had assembled to bid us adieu. On this very evening, to the infinite surprise of all of us, our courier arrived. As he advanced, his mournful countenance told us before he spoke, that his intelligence was unfavourable. "My spiritual fathers," said he, " all is lost; you have nothing to hope; in the kingdom of Naiman there no longer exist any camels of the Holy Church. The Lama doubtless has been killed; and I have no doubt the devil has had a direct hand in the matter."

Doubts and fears are often harder to bear than the certainty of evil. The intelligence thus received, though lamentable in itself, relieved us from our perplexity as to the past, without in any way altering our plan for the future. After having received the condolences of our Christians, we retired to rest, convinced that this night would certainly be that preceding our nomadic life.

TRAVELS IN TARTARY,

The night was far advanced, when suddenly numerous voices were heard outside our abode, and the door was shaken with loud and repeated knocks. We rose at once; the Lama, the camels, all had arrived; there was quite a little revolution. The order of the day was instantly changed. We resolved to depart, not on the Monday, but on the Tuesday; not in a car, but on camels, in true Tartar fashion. We returned to our beds perfectly delighted; but we could not sleep, each of us occupying the remainder of the night with plans for effecting the equipment of the caravan in the most expeditious manner possible.

Next day, while we were making our preparations for departure, our Lama explained his extraordinary delay. First, he had undergone a long illness; then he had been occupied a considerable time in pursuing a camel which had escaped into the desert; and, finally, he had to go before some tribunal, in order to procure the restitution of a mule which had been stolen from him. A law-suit, an illness, and a camel hunt were amply sufficient reasons for excusing the delay which had occurred. Our courier was the only person who did not participate in the general joy; he saw it must be evident to everyone that he had not fulfilled his mission with any sort of skill.

All Monday was occupied in the equipment of our caravan. Every person gave his assistance to this object. Some repaired our travelling-house, that is to say, mended or patched a great blue linen tent; others cut for us a supply of wooden tent pins; others mended the holes in our copper kettle, and renovated the broken leg of a joint stool; others prepared cords and put together the thousand and one pieces of a camel's pack. Tailors, carpenters, braziers, rope-makers, saddle-makers, people of all trades assembled in active co-operation in the court-yard of our humble abode. For all, great and small, among our Christians, were resolved that their spiritual fathers should proceed on their journey as comfortably as possible.

On Tuesday morning there remained nothing to be done but to perforate the noſtrils of the camels, and to insert in the aperture a wooden peg, to use as a sort of bit. The arrangement of this was left to our Lama. The wild piercing cries of the poor animals pending the painful operation, soon colleƈted together all the Chriſtians of the village. At this moment, our Lama became exclusively the hero of the expedition. The crowd ranged themselves in a circle around him; everyone was curious to see how, by gently pulling the cord attached to the peg in its nose, our Lama could make the animal obey him, and kneel at his pleasure. Then, again, it was an intereſting thing for the Chinese to watch our Lama packing on the camels' backs the baggage of the two missionary travellers. When the arrangements were completed, we drank a cup of tea, and proceeded to the chapel; the Chriſtians recited prayers for our safe journey; we received their farewell, interrupted with tears, and proceeded on our way. Samdadchiemba [Samdachiemba (bSam-gtan-'dzin-pa)], our Lama cameleer, gravely mounted on a black, ſtunted, meagre mule opened the march, leading two camels laden with our baggage; then came the two missionaries, MM. Gabet and Huc, the former mounted on a tall camel, the latter on a white horse.

Upon our departure we were resolved to lay aside our accuſtomed usages, and to become regular Tartars. Yet we did not at the outset, and all at once, become exempt from the Chinese syſtem, Besides that, for the firſt mile or two of our journey, we were escorted by our Chinese Chriſtians, some on foot, and some on horseback; our firſt ſtage was to be an inn kept by the Grand Catechiſt of the Contiguous Defiles.

The progress of our little caravan was not at firſt

wholly successful. We were quite novices in the art of saddling and girthing camels, so that every five minutes we had to halt, either to re-arrange some cord or piece of wood that hurt and irritated the camels, or to consolidate upon their backs, as well as we could, the ill-packed baggage that threatened, ever and anon, to fall to the ground. We advanced, indeed despite all these delays, but still very slowly. After journeying about thirty-five lis,[1] we quitted the cultivated district, and entered upon the Land of Grass. There we got on much better; the camels were more at their ease in the desert, and the pace became more rapid.

We ascended a high mountain, where the camels evinced a decided tendency to compensate themselves for their trouble by browsing, on either side, upon the tender stems of the elder tree or the green leaves of the wild rose. The shouts we were obliged to keep up, in order to urge forward the indolent beasts, alarmed infinite foxes, who issued from their holes, and rushed off in all directions. On attaining the summit of the rugged hill we saw in the hollow beneath the Christian inn of Yan-Pa-Eul [Yang-pa-êrh]. We proceeded towards it, our road constantly crossed by fresh and limpid streams, which, issuing from the sides of the mountain, reunite at its foot and form a rivulet which encircles the inn. We were received by the landlord, or, as the Chinese call him, the Comptroller of the Chest.

Inns of this description occur at intervals in the deserts of Tartary, along the confines of China. They consist almost universally of a large square enclosure, formed by high poles interlaced with brushwood. In the centre of this enclosure is a mudhouse, never more than ten feet high. With the exception of a few

[1] The Chinese *Li* is about equivalent to the quarter of an English mile.

THIBET, AND CHINA

wretched rooms at each extremity, the entire ſtructure consiſts of one large apartment, serving at once for cooking, eating, and sleeping; thoroughly dirty, and full of smoke and intolerable ſtench. Into this pleasant place all travellers, without diſtinƈtion, are ushered, the portion of space applied to their accommodation being a long, wide *Kang* [*k'ang*], as it is called, a sort of furnace, occupying more than three-fourths of the apartment, about four feet high, and the flat, smooth surface of which is covered with a reed mat, which the richer gueſts cover again with a travelling carpet of felt, or with furs. In front of it, three immense coppers set in glazed earth, serve for the preparation of the traveller's milk-broth. The apertures by which these monſter boilers are heated communicate with the interior of the *Kang* so that its temperature is conſtantly maintained at a high elevation even in the terrible cold of winter. Upon the arrival of gueſts, the Comptroller of the Cheſt invites them to ascend the *Kang*, where they seat themselves, their legs crossed tailor-fashion, round a large table, not more than six inches high. The lower part of the room is reserved for the people of the inn, who there busy themselves in keeping up the fire under the cauldrons, boiling tea, and pounding oats and buck-wheat into flour for the repaſt of the travellers. The *Kang* of these Tartar-Chinese inns is, till evening, a ſtage full of animation, where the gueſts eat, drink, smoke, gamble, dispute, and fight: with night-fall, the refeƈtory, tavern, and gambling-house of the day is suddenly converted into a dormitory. The travellers who have any bed-clothes unroll and arrange them; those who have none settle themselves as beſt they may in their personal attire, and lie down, side by side, round the table. When the gueſts are very numerous they arrange themselves in two circles, feet to feet. Thus reclined, those so disposed, sleep; others, awaiting sleep, smoke, drink tea, and gossip. The effect of the scene, dimly exhibited by an imperfect wick floating amid thick, dirty, stinking oil, whose receptacle is ordinarily a broken tea-cup, is fantastic, and to the stranger, fearful.

The Comptroller of the Chest had prepared his own room for our accommodation. We washed, but would not sleep there; being now Tartar travellers, and in possession of a good tent, we determined to try our apprentice hand at setting it up. This resolution offended no one, it was quite understood we adopted this course, not out of contempt towards the inn, but out of love for a patriarchal life. When we had set up our tent, and unrolled on the ground our goat-skin beds, we lighted a pile of brushwood, for the nights were already growing cold. Just as we were closing our eyes, the Inspector of Darkness startled us with beating the official night alarum, upon his brazen tam-tam, the sonorous sound of which, reverberating through the adjacent valleys struck with terror the tigers and wolves frequenting them, and drove them off.

We were on foot before daylight. Previous to our departure we had to perform an operation of considerable importance—no other than an entire change of costume, a complete metamorphosis. The missionaries who reside in China, all, without exception, wear the secular dress of the people, and are in no way distinguishable from them; they bear no outward sign of their religious character. It is a great pity that they should be thus obliged to wear the secular costume, for it is an obstacle in the way of their preaching the gospel. Among the Tartars, a *black man*—so they discriminate the laity, as wearing their hair, from the clergy, who have their heads close shaved—who should talk about religion would be laughed at, as

THIBET, AND CHINA

impertinently meddling with things the special province of the Lamas, and in no way concerning him. The reasons which appear to have introduced and maintained the custom of wearing the secular habit on the part of the missionaries in China, no longer applying to us, we resolved at length to appear in an ecclesiastical exterior becoming our sacred mission. The views of our vicar apostolic on the subject, as explained in his written instructions, being conformable with our wish, we did not hesitate. We resolved to adopt the secular dress of the Thibetian [Tibetan] Lamas ; that is to say, the dress which they wear when not actually performing their idolatrous ministry in the Pagodas. The costume of the Thibetian Lamas suggested itself to our preference as being in unison with that worn by our young neophyte, Samdadchiemba.

We announced to the Christians of the inn that we were resolved no longer to look like Chinese merchants ; that we were about to cut off our long tails and to shave our heads. This intimation created great agitation : some of our disciples even wept ; all sought by their eloquence to divert us from a resolution which seemed to them fraught with danger ; but their pathetic remonstrances were of no avail ; one touch of a razor, in the hands of Samdadchiemba, sufficed to sever the long tail of hair, which, to accommodate Chinese fashions, we had so carefully cultivated ever since our departure from France. We put on a long yellow robe, fastened at the right side with five gilt buttons, and round the waist by a long red sash ; over this was a red jacket, with a collar of purple velvet ; a yellow cap, surmounted by a red tuft, completed our new costume. Breakfast followed this decisive operation, but it was silent and sad. When the Comptroller of the Chest brought in some glasses and an urn, wherein smoked the hot wine drunk by the Chinese, we told him that having changed our habit of dress, we should change also our habit of living. "Take away," said we, "that wine and that chafing dish; henceforth we renounce drink and smoking. You know," added we, laughing, " that good Lamas abstain from wine and tobacco." The Chinese Christians who surrounded us did not join in the laugh; they looked at us without speaking and with deep commiseration, fully persuaded that we should inevitably perish of privation and misery in the deserts of Tartary. Breakfast finished, while the people of the inn were packing up our tent, saddling the camels, and preparing for our departure, we took a couple of rolls, baked in the steam of the furnace, and walked out to complete our meal with some wild currants growing on the banks of the adjacent rivulet. It was soon announced to us that everything was ready—so, mounting our respective animals, we proceeded on the road to Tolon-Noor, accompanied by Samdadchiemba.

We were now launched, alone and without a guide, amid a new world. We had no longer before us paths traced out by the old missionaries, for we were in a country where none before us had preached Gospel truth. We should no longer have by our side those earnest Christian converts, so zealous to serve us; so anxious, by their friendly care, to create around us as it were an atmosphere of home. We were abandoned to ourselves, in a hostile land, without a friend to advise or to aid us, save Him by whose strength we were supported, and whose name we were seeking to make known to all the nations of the earth.

As we have just observed, Samdadchiemba was our only travelling companion. This young man was neither Chinese, nor Tartar, nor Thibetian. Yet, at the first glance, it was easy to recognize in him the features characterizing that which naturalists call the Mongol race. A great flat nose, insolently turned

THIBET, AND CHINA

up; a large mouth, slit in a perfectly straight line, thick, projecting lips, a deep bronze complexion, every feature contributed to give to his physiognomy a wild and scornful aspect. When his little eyes seemed starting out of his head from under their lids, wholly destitute of eyelash, and he looked at you wrinkling his brow, he inspired you at once with feelings of dread, and yet of confidence. The face was without any decisive character: it exhibited neither the mischievous knavery of the Chinese, nor the frank good nature of the Tartar, nor the courageous energy of the Thibetian; but was made up of a mixture of all three. Samdadchiemba was a Dchiahour [rgya-hor]. We shall hereafter have occasion to speak more in detail of the native country of our young cameleer.

At the age of eleven, Samdadchiemba had escaped from his Lamasery, in order to avoid the too frequent and too severe corrections of the master under whom he was more immediately placed. He afterwards passed the greater portion of his vagabond youth, sometimes in the Chinese towns, sometimes in the deserts of Tartary. It is easy to comprehend that this independent course of life had not tended to modify the natural asperity of his character; his intellect was entirely uncultivated; but, on the other hand, his muscular power was enormous, and he was not a little vain of this quality, which he took great pleasure in parading. After having been instructed and baptized by M. Gabet, he had attached himself to the service of the missionaries. The journey we were now undertaking was perfectly in harmony with his erratic and adventurous taste. He was, however, of no mortal service to us as a guide across the desert of Tartary, for he knew no more of the country than we knew ourselves. Our only informants were a compass, and the excellent map of the Chinese empire by Andriveau-Goujon.

TRAVELS IN TARTARY,

The first portion of our journey, after leaving Yan-Pa-Eul, was accomplished without interruption, sundry anathemas excepted, which were hurled against us, as we ascended a mountain, by a party of Chinese merchants, whose mules, upon sight of our camels and our own yellow attire, became frightened, and took to their heels at full speed, dragging after them, and in one or two instances, overturning the waggons to which they were harnessed.

The mountain in question is called Sain-Oula [Sâin-ûla] "Good Mountain," doubtless *ut lucus a non lucendo*, since it is notorious for the dismal accidents and tragical adventures of which it is the theatre. The ascent is by a rough, steep path, half-choked up with fallen rocks. Mid-way up is a small temple, dedicated to the divinity of the mountain, Sain-Nai [Sâin-nai] "the good old Woman" the occupant is a priest, whose business it is from time to time to fill up the cavities in the road, occasioned by the previous rains, in consideration of which service he receives from each passenger a small gratuity, constituting his revenue. After a toilsome journey of nearly three hours we found ourselves at the summit of the mountain, upon an immense plateau, extending from east to west a long day's journey, and from north to south still more widely. From this summit you discern, afar off in the plains of Tartary, the tents of the Mongols, ranged semi-circularly on the slopes of the hills, and looking in the distance like so many bee-hives. Several rivers derive their source from the sides of this mountain. Chief among these is the Chara-Mouren [Shira-müren] (Yellow River—distinct, of course, from the great Yellow River of China, the Hoang-Ho [Huang-ho])—the capricious course of which the eye can follow on through the kingdom of Gechekten [Keshikten], after traversing which, and then the district of Naiman, it passes the stake-boundary into Mantchouria [Manchuria], and flowing from north to south, falls into the sea, approaching which it assumes the name of Léao-Ho [Liao-ho].

The Good Mountain is noted for its intense frosts. There is not a winter passes in which the cold there does not kill many travellers. Frequently whole caravans, not arriving at their destination on the other side of the mountain, are sought and found in its bleak road, man and beast frozen to death. Nor is the danger less from the robbers and the wild beasts with whom the mountain is a favourite haunt, or rather a permanent station. Assailed by the brigands, the unlucky traveller is stripped, not merely of horse and money, and baggage, but absolutely of the clothes he wears, and then left to perish from cold and hunger.

Not but that the brigands of these parts are extremely polite all the while; they do not rudely clap a pistol to your ear, and bawl at you: "Your money or your life!" No! they mildly advance with a courteous salutation: "Venerable elder brother, I am on foot; pray lend me your horse—I've got no money, be good enough to lend me your purse—It's quite cold to-day, oblige me with the loan of your coat." If the venerable elder brother charitably complies, the matter ends with, "Thanks, brother;" but otherwise, the request is forthwith emphasized with the arguments of a cudgel; and if these do not convince, recourse is had to the sabre.

The sun declining ere we had traversed this platform, we resolved to encamp for the night. Our first business was to seek a position combining the three essentials of fuel, water, and pasturage; and, having due regard to the ill reputation of the Good Mountain, privacy from observation as complete as could be effected. Being novices in travelling, the idea of robbers haunted us incessantly, and we took everybody we saw to be a suspicious character, against whom we must be on our guard. A grassy nook, surrounded by tall trees, appertaining to the Imperial Forest, fulfilled our requisites. Unlading our dromedaries, we raised, with no slight labour, our tent beneath the foliage, and at its entrance installed our faithful porter, Arsalan a dog whose size, strength, and courage well entitled him to his appellation, which, in the Tartar-Mongol dialect, means "Lion." Collecting some *argols* [*argol*][1] and dry branches of trees, our kettle was soon in agitation, and we threw into the boiling water some *Koua-mien* [*kua-mien*], prepared paste, something like Vermicelli, which, seasoned with some parings of bacon, given us by our friends at Yan-Pa-Eul, we hoped would furnish satisfaction for the hunger that began to gnaw us. No sooner was the repast ready than each of us, drawing forth from his girdle his wooden cup, filled it with *Kouamien*, and raised it to his lips. The preparation was detestable—uneatable. The manufacturers of *Kouamien* always salt it for its longer preservation; but this paste of ours had been salted beyond all endurance. Even Arsalan would not eat the composition. Soaking it for a while in cold water, we once more boiled it up, but in vain; the dish remained nearly as salt as ever: so, abandoning it to Arsalan and to Samdadchiemba, whose stomach by long use was capable of anything, we were fain to content ourselves with the *dry-cold*, as the Chinese say; and, taking with us a couple of small loaves, walked into the Imperial Forest, in order at least to season our repast with an agreeable walk. Our first nomad supper, however, turned out better than we had expected, Providence placing in our path numerous *Ngao-la-Eul* [*ao-li-êrh*] and *Chan-ly-Houng* [*shan-li-hung*] trees,

[1] Dried dung, which constitutes the chief, and indeed in many places the sole fuel in Tartary.

THIBET, AND CHINA

the former, a shrub about five inches high, which bears a pleasant wild cherry; the other, also a low but very bushy shrub, producing a small scarlet apple, of a sharp agreeable flavour, of which a very succulent jelly is made.

The Imperial Forest extends more than a hundred leagues from north to south, and nearly eighty from east to west. The Emperor Khang-Hi [K'ang-hsi], in one of his expeditions into Mongolia, adopted it as a hunting ground. He repaired thither every year, and his successors regularly followed his example, down to Kia-King, who, upon a hunting excursion, was killed by lightning at Gé-ho-Eul [Jehol]. There has been no imperial hunting there since that time —now twenty-seven years ago. Tao-Kouang, son and successor of Kia-King, being persuaded that a fatality impends over the exercise of the chase, since his accession to the throne has never set foot in Gé-ho-Eul, which may be regarded as the Versailles of the Chinese potentates. The forest, however, and the animals which inhabit it, have been no gainers by the circumstance. Despite the penalty of perpetual exile decreed against all who shall be found, with arms in their hands, in the forest, it is always half-full of poachers and wood-cutters. Gamekeepers, indeed, are stationed at intervals throughout the forest; but they seem there merely for the purpose of enjoying a monopoly of the sale of game and wood. They let anyone steal either, provided they themselves get the larger share of the booty. The poachers are in especial force from the fourth to the seventh moon. At this period the antlers of the stags send forth new shoots, which contain a sort of half-coagulated blood, called *Lou-joung* [*Lu-jung*], which plays a distinguished part in the Chinese *Materia Medica*, for its supposed chemical qualities, and fetches accordingly an exorbitant price. A *Lou-joung* sometimes sells for as much as a hundred and fifty ounces of silver.

TRAVELS IN TARTARY,

Deer of all kinds abound in the forest; and tigers, bears, wild boars, panthers, and wolves are scarcely less numerous. Woe to the hunters and wood-cutters who venture otherwise than in large parties into the recesses of the forest; they disappear, leaving no vestige behind.

The fear of encountering one of these wild beasts kept us from prolonging our walk. Besides, night was setting in, and we hastened back to our tent. Our first slumber in the desert was peaceful, and next morning early, after a breakfast of oatmeal steeped in tea, we resumed our march along the great Plateau. We soon reached the great *Obo* whither the Tartars resort to worship the Spirit of the Mountain. The monument is simply an enormous pile of stones, heaped up without any order, and surmounted with dried branches of trees, from which hang bones and strips of cloth, on which are inscribed verses in the Thibet [Tibet] and Mongol languages. At its base is a large granite urn in which the devotees burn incense. They offer, besides, pieces of money, which the next Chinese passenger, after sundry ceremonious genuflexions before the *Obo*, carefully collects and pockets for his own particular benefit.

These *Obos*, which occur so frequently throughout Tartary, and which are the objects of constant pilgrimages on the part of the Mongols, remind one of the *loca excelsa* denounced by the Jewish prophets.

It was near noon before the ground, beginning to slope, intimated that we approached the termination of the plateau. We then descended rapidly into a deep valley, where we found a small Mongolian encampment, which we passed without pausing, and set up our tent for the night on the margin of a pool further on. We were now in the kingdom of Gechekten, an undulating country, well watered, with abundance of fuel and pasturage, but desolated by

THIBET, AND CHINA

bands of robbers. The Chinese, who have long since taken possession of it, have rendered it a sort of general refuge for malefactors; so that " man of Gechekten " has become a synonyme for a person without fear of God or man, who will commit any murder and shrink from no crime. It would seem as though, in this country, nature resented the encroachments of man upon her rights. Wherever the plough has passed the soil has become poor, arid, and sandy, producing nothing but oats, which constitute the food of the people. In the whole district there is but one trading town, which the Mongols call Altan-Somé [Altansümé], "Temple of Gold." This was at first a great Lamasery, containing nearly 2,000 Lamas. By degrees Chinese have settled there, in order to traffic with the Tartars. In 1843, when we had occasion to visit this place, it had already acquired the importance of a town. A highway, commencing at Altan-Somé, proceeds towards the north, and after traversing the country of the Khalkhas [Khalkha], the river Keroulan [Kerulen], and the Khinggan mountains, reaches Nertechink [Nerchinsk], a town of Siberia.

The sun had just set, and we were occupied inside the tent boiling our tea, when Arsalan warned us, by his barking, of the approach of some stranger. We soon heard the trot of a horse, and presently a mounted Tartar appeared at the door. " *Mendou* " [" *Mendu* "] he exclaimed, by way of respectful salutation to the supposed Lamas, raising his joined hands at the same time to his forehead. When we invited him to drink a cup of tea with us, he fastened his horse to one of the tent-pegs, and seated himself by the hearth. " Sirs Lamas," said he, " under what quarter of the heaven were you born ? " " We are from the western heaven ; and you, whence come you ? " " My poor abode is towards the north, at the end of the valley you see there on the right." "Your country is a fine country." The Mongol shook his head sadly, and made no reply. "Brother," we proceeded, after a moment's silence, "the Land of Grass is still very extensive in the kingdom of Gechekten. Would it not be better to cultivate your plains? What good are these bare lands to you? Would not fine crops of corn be preferable to mere grass?" He replied, with a tone of deep and settled conviction, "We Mongols are formed for living in tents, and pasturing cattle. So long as we kept to that in the kingdom of Gechekten, we were rich and happy. Now, ever since the Mongols have set themselves to cultivating the land, and building houses, they have become poor. The Kitats [Kitat] (Chinese) have taken possession of the country; flocks, herds, lands, houses, all have passed into their hands. There remain to us only a few prairies, on which still live, under their tents, such of the Mongols as have not been forced by utter destitution to emigrate to other lands." "But if the Chinese are so baneful to you why did you let them penetrate into your country?" "Your words are the words of truth, Sirs Lamas; but you are aware that the Mongols are men of simple hearts. We took pity on these wicked Kitats, who came to us weeping, to solicit our charity. We allowed them, through pure compassion, to cultivate a few patches of land. The Mongols insensibly followed their example, and abandoned the nomadic life. They drank the wine of the Kitats, and smoked their tobacco, on credit; they bought their manufactures on credit at double the real value. When the day of payment came, there was no money ready, and the Mongols had to yield, to the violence of their creditors, houses, lands, flocks, everything." "But could you not seek justice from the tribunals?" "Justice from the tribunals! Oh, that is out of the question. The

THIBET, AND CHINA

Kitats are skilful to talk and to lie. It is impossible for a Mongol to gain a suit against a Kitat. Sirs Lamas, the kingdom of Gechekten is undone!" So saying, the poor Mongol rose, bowed, mounted his horse, and rapidly disappeared in the desert.

We travelled two more days through this kingdom, and everywhere witnessed the poverty and wretchedness of its scattered inhabitants. Yet the country is naturally endowed with astonishing wealth, especially in gold and silver mines, which of themselves have occasioned many of its worst calamities. Notwithstanding the rigorous prohibition to work these mines, it sometimes happens that large bands of Chinese outlaws assemble together, and march, sword in hand, to dig into them. These are men professing to be endowed with a peculiar capacity for discovering the precious metals, guided, according to their own account, by the conformation of mountains, and the sorts of plants they produce. One single man, possessed of this fatal gift, will suffice to spread desolation over a whole district. He speedily finds himself at the head of thousands and thousands of outcasts, who overspread the country, and render it the theatre of every crime. While some are occupied in working the mines others pillage the surrounding districts, sparing neither persons nor property, and committing excesses which the imagination could not conceive, and which continue until some mandarin, powerful and courageous enough to suppress them, is brought within their operation, and takes measures against them accordingly.

Calamities of this nature have frequently desolated the kingdom of Gechekten; but none of them are comparable with what happened in the kingdom of Ouniot in 1841. A Chinese *mine discoverer*, having ascertained the presence of gold in a particular mountain, announced the discovery, and robbers and vagabonds at once congregated around him, from far and near, to the number of 12,000. This hideous mob put the whole country under subjection, and exercised for two years its fearful sway. Almost the entire mountain passed through the crucible, and such enormous quantities of metal were produced that the price of gold fell in China fifty per cent. The inhabitants complained incessantly to the Chinese mandarins, but in vain; for these worthies only interfere where they can do so with some benefit to themselves. The King of Ouniot himself feared to measure his strength with such an army of desperadoes.

One day, however, the Queen of Ouniot, repairing on a pilgrimage to the tomb of her ancestors, had to pass the valley in which the army of miners was assembled. Her car was surrounded; she was rudely compelled to alight, and it was only upon the sacrifice of her jewels that she was permitted to proceed. Upon her return home, she reproached the king bitterly for his cowardice. At length, stung by her words, he assembled the troops of his two banners, and marched against the miners. The engagement which ensued was for a while doubtful; but at length the miners were driven in by the Tartar cavalry, who massacred them without mercy. The bulk of the survivors took refuge in the mine. The Mongols blocked up the apertures with huge stones. The cries of the despairing wretches within were heard for a few days, and then ceased for ever. Those of the miners who were taken alive had their eyes put out and were then dismissed.

We had just quitted the kingdom of Gechekten, and entered that of Tchakar [Chakhar], when we came to a military encampment, where were stationed a party of Chinese soldiers charged with the preservation of the public safety. The hour of repose had arrived; but these soldiers, instead of giving us confidence by their presence, increased, on the contrary, our fears; for we knew that they were themselves the most daring robbers in the whole district. We turned aside, therefore, and ensconced ourselves between two rocks, where we found just space enough for our tent. We had scarcely set up our temporary abode, when we observed, in the distance, on the slope of the mountains, a numerous body of horsemen at full gallop. Their rapid but irregular evolutions seemed to indicate that they were pursuing something which constantly evaded them. By-and-by, two of the horsemen, perceiving us, dashed up to our tent, dismounted, and threw themselves on the ground at the door. They were Tartar-Mongols. "Men of prayer," said they, with voices full of emotion, "we come to ask you to draw our horoscope. We have this day had two horses stolen from us. We have fruitlessly sought traces of the robbers, and we therefore come to you, men whose power and learning is beyond all limit, to tell us where we shall find our property." "Brothers," said we; "We are not Lamas of Buddha; we do not believe in horoscopes. For a man to say that he can, by any such means, discover that which is stolen, is for them to put forth the words of falsehood and deception." The poor Tartars redoubled their solicitations; but when they found we were inflexible in our resolution, they remounted their horses, in order to return to the mountains.

Samdadchiemba, meanwhile, had been silent, apparently paying no attention to the incident, but fixed at the fire-place, with his bowl of tea to his lips. All of a sudden he knitted his brows, rose, and came to the door. The horsemen were at some distance; but the Dchiahour, by an exertion of his strong lungs, induced them to turn round in their saddles. He motioned to them, and they, supposing we had relented, and were willing to draw the desired horoscope, galloped once more towards us. When they had come within speaking diſtance :—" My Mongol brothers," cried Samdadchiemba, " in future be more careful ; watch your herds well, and you won't be robbed. Retain these words of mine on your memory : they are worth all the horoscopes in the world." After this friendly address, he gravely re-entered the tent, and seating himself at the hearth, resumed his tea.

We were at firſt somewhat disconcerted by this singular proceeding ; but as the horsemen themselves did not take the matter in ill part, but quietly rode off, we burst into a laugh. " Stupid Mongols ! " grumbled Samdadchiemba ; " they don't give themselves the trouble to watch their animals, and then, when they are ſtolen from them, they run about wanting people to draw horoscopes for them. After all, perhaps it's no wonder, for nobody but ourselves tells them the truth. The Lamas encourage them in their credulity ; for they turn it into a source of income. It is difficult to deal with such people. If you tell them you can't draw a horoscope, they don't believe you, and merely suppose you don't choose to oblige them. To get rid of them, the beſt way is to give them an answer haphazard." And here Samdadchiemba laughed with such expansion, that his little eyes were completely buried. " Did you ever draw a horoscope ? " asked we. " Yes," replied he, ſtill laughing. " I was very young at the time, not more than fifteen. I was travelling through the Red Banner of Tchakar, when I was addressed by some Mongols who led me into their tent. There they entreated me to tell them, by means of divination, where a bull had ſtrayed, which had been missing three days. It was to no purpose that I proteſted to them I could not perform divination, that I could not even read. ' You deceive us,' said they ; ' you are a Dchiahour,

THIBET, AND CHINA

and we know that the Western Lamas can all divine more or less.' As the only way of extricating myself from the dilemma, I resolved to imitate what I had seen the Lamas do in their divinations. I directed one person to collect eleven sheep's droppings, the dryest he could find. They were immediately brought. I then seated myself very gravely; I counted the droppings over and over; I arranged them in rows, and then counted them again; I rolled them up and down in threes; and then appeared to mediate. At last I said to the Mongols, who were impatiently awaiting the result of the horoscope: 'If you would find your bull, go seek him towards the north.' Before the words were well out of my mouth, four men were on horseback, galloping off towards the north. By the most curious chance in the world, they had not proceeded far before the missing animal made its appearance, quietly browsing. I at once got the character of a diviner of the first class, was entertained in the most liberal manner for a week, and when I departed had a stock of butter and tea given me enough for another week. Now that I belong to Holy Church I know that these things are wicked and prohibited; otherwise I would have given these horsemen a word or two of horoscope, which perhaps would have procured for us, in return, a good cup of tea with butter."

The stolen horses confirmed in our minds the ill reputation of the country in which we were now encamped; and we felt ourselves necessitated to take additional precaution. Before night-fall we brought in the horse and the mule, and fastened them by cords to pins at the door of our tent, and made the camels kneel by their side, so as to close up the entrance. By this arrangement no one could get near us without our having full warning given us by the camels, which, at the least noise, always make an outcry loud enough to awaken the deepest sleeper. Finally, having suspended from one of the tent-poles our travelling lantern, which we kept burning all the night, we endeavoured to obtain a little repose, but in vain ; the night passed away without our getting a wink of sleep. As to the Dchiahour, whom nothing ever troubled, we heard him snoring with all the might of his lungs until daybreak.

We made our preparations for departure very early, for we were eager to quit this ill-famed place, and to reach Tolon-Noor, which was now distant only a few leagues.

On our way thither, a horseman stopped his galloping steed, and, after looking at us for a moment, addressed us : " You are the chiefs of the Christians of the Contiguous Defiles ? " Upon our replying in the affirmative, he dashed off again ; but turned his head once or twice to have another look at us. He was a Mongol, who had charge of some herds at the Contiguous Defiles. He had often seen us there ; but the novelty of our present costume at first prevented him recognizing us. We met also the Tartars who, the day before, had asked us to draw a horoscope for them. They had repaired by daybreak to the horse-fair at Tolon-Noor, in the hope of finding their stolen animals : but their search had been unsuccessful.

The increasing number of travellers, Tartars and Chinese, whom we now met, indicated the approach to the great town of Tolon-Noor. We already saw in the distance, glittering under the sun's rays, the gilt roofs of two magnificent Lamaseries that stand in the northern suburbs of the town. We journeyed for some time through a succession of cemeteries ; for here, as elsewhere, the present generation is surrounded by the ornamental sepulchres of past generations. As we observed the numerous population of that large town, environed as it were by a vaſt circle of bones and monumental ſtones, it seemed as though death was continuously engaged in the blockade of life. Here and there, in the vaſt cemetery which completely encircles the city, we remarked little gardens, where, by dint of extreme labour, a few miserable vegetables were extraćted from the earth : leeks, spinach, hard bitter lettuces, and cabbages, which, introduced some years since from Russia, have adapted themselves exceedingly well to the climate of Northern China.

With the exception of these few esculents, the environs of Tolon-Noor produce absolutely nothing whatever. The soil is dry and sandy, and water terribly scarce. It is only here and there that a few limited springs are found, and these are dried up in the hot season.

CHAPTER II

Our entrance into the city of Tolon-Noor was fatiguing and full of perplexity; for we knew not where to take up our abode. We wandered about a long time in a labyrinth of narrow, tortuous streets, encumbered with men and animals and goods. At last we found an inn. We unloaded our dromedaries, deposited the baggage in a small room, foddered the animals, and then, having affixed to the door of our room the padlock which, as is the custom, our landlord gave us for that purpose, we sallied forth in quest of dinner. A triangular flag floating before a house in the next street indicated to our joyful hearts an eating-house. A long passage led us into a spacious apartment, in which were symmetrically set forth a number of little tables. Seating ourselves at one of these, a tea-pot, the inevitable prelude in these countries to every meal, was set before each of us. You must swallow infinite tea, and that boiling hot, before they will consent to bring you anything else. At last, when they see you thus occupied, the Comptroller of the Table pays you his official visit, a personage of immensely elegant manners, and ceaseless volubility of tongue, who, after entertaining you with his views upon the affairs of the world in general, and each country in particular, concludes by announcing what there is to eat, and requesting your judgment thereupon. As you mention the dishes you desire, he repeats their names in a measured chant, for the information of the Governor of the Pot. Your dinner is served up with admirable promptitude; but before you commence the meal, etiquette requires that you rise from your seat, and invite all the other company present to partake. "Come," you say, with an engaging gesture, "come, my friends, come and drink a glass of wine with me; come and eat a plate of rice"; and so on. "No, thank you," replies everybody; "do you rather come and seat yourself at my table. It is I who invite you;" and so the matter ends. By this ceremony you have "manifested your honour," as the phrase runs, and you may now sit down and eat it in comfort, your character as a gentleman perfectly established.

When you rise to depart, the Comptroller of the Table again appears. As you cross the apartment with him, he chants over again the names of the dishes you have had, this time appending the prices, and terminating with the sum total, announced with special emphasis, which, proceeding to the counter, you then deposit in the money-box. In general, the Chinese restaurateurs are quite as skilful as those of France in exciting the vanity of the guests, and promoting the consumption of their commodities.

Two motives had induced us to direct our steps, in the first instance, to Tolon-Noor: we desired to make more purchases there to complete our travelling equipment, and, secondly, it appeared to us necessary to place ourselves in communication with the Lamas of the country, in order to obtain information from them as to the more important localities of Tartary. The purchases we needed to make gave us occasion to visit the different quarters of the town. Tolon-Noor "Seven Lakes" is called by the Chinese Lama-Miao "Convent of Lamas." The Mantchous designate it Nadan-Omo and the Thibetians Tsot-Dun [mts'o-bdun], both translations of Tolon-Noor, and, equally with it, meaning "Seven Lakes." On the

TRAVELS IN TARTARY,

map published by M. Andriveau-Goujon,[1] this town is called Djo-Naiman-Soumé [Jo-naiman-sümé], which in Mongul means, "The Hundred and Eight Convents." The name is perfectly unknown in the country itself.

Tolon-Noor is not a walled city, but a vast agglomeration of hideous houses, which seem to have been thrown together with a pitchfork. The carriage portion of the streets is a marsh of mud and putrid filth, deep enough to stifle and bury the smaller beasts of burden that not infrequently fall within it, and whose carcases remain to aggravate the general stench; while their loads become the prey of the innumerable thieves who are ever on the alert. The foot-path is a narrow, rugged, slippery line on either side, just wide enough to admit the passage of one person.

Yet, despite the nastiness of the town itself, the sterility of the environs, the excessive cold of its winter, and the intolerable heat of its summer, its population is immense, and its commerce enormous. Russian merchandise is brought hither in large quantities by the way of [Kiakhta]. The Tartars bring incessant herds of camels, oxen, and horses, and carry back in exchange tobacco, linen and tea. This constant arrival and departure of strangers communicates to the city an animated and varied aspect. All sorts of hawkers are at every corner offering their petty wares; the regular traders from behind their counters, invite, with honeyed words and tempting offers, the passers-by to come in and buy. The Lamas, in their red and yellow robes, gallop up and down, seeking admiration for their

[1] With the exception of a few inaccuracies, this map of the Chinese empire is a most excellent one. We found it of the most valuable aid throughout our journey.—HUC.

THIBET, AND CHINA

equestrianism, and the skilful management of their fiery steeds.

The trade of Tolon-Noor is mostly in the hands of men from the provinces of Chan-Si [Shansi], who seldom establish themselves permanently in the town; but after a few years, when their money chest is filled, return to their own country. In this vast emporium, the Chinese invariably make fortunes, and the Tartars invariably are ruined. Tolon-Noor, in fact, is a sort of great pneumatic pump, constantly at work in emptying the pockets of the unlucky Mongols.

The magnificent statues, in bronze and brass, which issue from the great foundries of Tolon-Noor are celebrated not only throughout Tartary, but in the remotest districts of Thibet. Its immense workshops supply all the countries subject to the worship of Buddha with idols, bells, and vases employed in that idolatry. While we were in the town, a monster statue of Buddha, a present from a friend of Oudchou-Mourdchin [Ujumchin] to the Talè-Lama [Dalai-lama], was packed for Thibet, on the backs of six camels. The larger statues are cast in detail, the component parts being afterwards soldered together.

We availed ourselves of our stay at Tolon-Noor to have a figure of Christ constructed on the model of a bronze original which we had brought with us from France. The workmen so marvellously excelled, that it was difficult to distinguish the copy from the original. The Chinese work more rapidly and cheaply, and their complaisance contrasts most favourably with the tenacious self-opinion of their brethren in Europe.

During our stay at Tolon-Noor, we had frequent occasion to visit the Lamaseries, or Lama monasteries, and to converse with the idolatrous priests of Buddhism. The Lamas appeared to us persons of very limited information; and as to their symbolism, in general, it is little more refined or purer than the creed of the vulgar. Their doctrine is still undecided, fluctuating amidst a vast fanaticism of which they can give no intelligible account. When we asked them for some distinct, clear, positive idea what they meant, they were always thrown into utter embarrassment, and stared at one another. The disciples told us that their masters knew all about it; the masters referred us to the omniscience of the Grand Lamas; the Grand Lamas confessed themselves ignorant, but talked of some wonderful saint, in some Lamasery, at the other end of the country: *he* could explain the whole affair. However, all of them, disciples and masters, great Lamas and small, agreed in this, that their doctrine came from the West: " The nearer you approach the West," said they unanimously, " the purer and more luminous will the doctrine manifest itself." When we expounded to them the truths of Christianity, they never discussed the matter; they contented themselves with calmly saying, " Well, we don't suppose that our prayers are the only prayers in the world. The Lamas of the West will explain everything to you. We believe in the traditions that have come from the West."

In point of fact there is no Lamasery of any importance in Tartary, the Grand Lama or superior of which is not a man from Thibet. Any Tartar Lama who has visited Lha-Ssa [Lha-sa] "Land of Spirits," or Monhe-Dchot [Möngke-jot] "Eternal Sanctuary," as it is called in the Mongol dialect, is received, on his return, as a man to whom the mysteries of the past and of the future have been unveiled.

After maturely weighing the information we had obtained from the Lamas, it was decided that we should direct our steps towards the West. On October 1st we quitted Tolon-Noor; and it was not without infinite trouble that we managed to traverse the filthy town with our camels. The poor animals could only get through the quagmire ſtreets by fits and ſtarts; it was firſt a ſtumble, then a convulsive jump, then another ſtumble and another jump, and so on. Their loads shook on their backs, and at every ſtep we expeɛted to see the camel and camel-load proſtrate in the mud. We considered ourselves lucky when, at diſtant intervals, we came to a comparatively dry spot, where the camels could travel, and we were thus enabled to re-adjuſt and tighten the baggage. Samdad-chiemba got into a desperate ill-temper; he went on, and slipped, and went on again, without uttering a single word, reſtriɛting the visible manifeſtation of his wrath to a continuous biting of the lips.

Upon attaining at length the weſtern extremity of the town, we got clear of the filth indeed, but found ourselves involved in another evil. Before us there was no road marked out, not the slighteſt trace of even a path. There is nothing but an apparently interminable chain of small hills, composed of fine, moving sand, over which it was impossible to advance at more than a snail's pace, and this only with extreme labour. Among these sand-hills, moreover, we were oppressed with an absolutely ſtifling heat. Our animals were covered with perspiration, ourselves devoured with a burning thirst; but it was in vain that we looked round in all direɛtions, as we proceeded, for water; not a spring, not a pool, not a drop presented itself.

It was already late, and we began to fear we should find no spot favourable for the ereɛtion of our tent. The ground, however, grew by degrees firmer, and we at laſt discerned some sign of vegetation. By and by the sand almoſt disappeared, and our eyes were rejoiced with the sight of continuous verdure. On our left, at no great diſtance, we saw the opening of a defile. M. Gabet urged on his camel, and went to examine the spot. He soon made his appearance at the summit of a hill, and with voice and hand directed us to follow him. We haſtened on, and found that Providence had led us to a favourable position. A small pool, the waters of which were half concealed by thick reeds and other marshy vegetation, some brushwood, a plot of grass : what could we under the circumſtances desire more ? Hungry, thirſty, weary, as we were, the place seemed a perfect Eden.

The camels were no sooner squatted, than we all three, with one accord, and without a word said, seized each man his wooden cup, and rushed to the pond to satisfy his thirſt. The water was fresh enough ; but it affected the nose violently with its ſtrong muriatic odour. I remembered to have drunk water juſt like it in the Pyrenees, at the good town of Ax, and to have seen it for sale in the chemiſts' shops elsewhere in France : and I remembered, further, that by reason of its being particularly ſtinking and particularly naſty, it was sold there at fifteen sous per bottle.

After having quenched our thirſt, our ſtrength by degrees returned, and we were then able to fix our tent, and each man to set about his especial task. M. Gabet proceeded to cut some bundles of horn-beam wood ; Samdadchiemba collected *argols* in the flap of his jacket ; and M. Huc, seated at the entrance of the tent, tried his hand at drawing a fowl, a process which Arsalan, ſtretched at his side, watched with greedy eye, having immediate reference to the entrails in course of removal. We were resolved, for once and away, to have a little feſtival in the desert ; and to take the opportunity to indulge our patriotism by initiating our Dchiahour in the luxury of a dish prepared according to the rules of the *cuisinier Français*. The fowl, artiſtically dismembered, was placed at the bottom of our great pot. A few roots of synapia, prepared in salt water, some onions, a clove of garlic, and some allspice, constituted the seasoning. The preparation was soon boiling, for we were that day rich in fuel. Samdadchiemba, by-and-by, plunged his hand into the pot, drew out a limb of the fowl, and, after carefully inspecting it, pronounced supper to be ready. The pot was taken from the trivet, and placed upon the grass. We all three seated ourselves around it, so that our knees almost touched it, and each, armed with two chopsticks, fished out the pieces he desired from the abundant broth before him.

When the meal was completed, and we had thanked God for the repast he had thus provided us with in the desert, Samdadchiemba went and washed the cauldron in the pond. That done, he brewed us some tea. The tea used by the Tartars is not prepared in the same way as that consumed by the Chinese. The latter, it is known, merely employ the smaller and tenderer leaves of the plant, which they simply infuse in boiling water, so as to give it a golden tint; the coarser leaves, with which are mixed up the smaller tendrils, are pressed together in a mould, in the form and of the size of the ordinary house brick. Thus prepared, it becomes an article of considerable commerce, under the designation of Tartar-tea, the Tartars being its exclusive consumers, with the exception of the Russians, who drink great quantities of it. When required for use, a piece of the brick is broken off, pulverised, and boiled in the kettle, until the water assumes a reddish hue. Some salt is then thrown in, and effervescence commences. When the liquid has become almost black, milk is added, and the beverage, the grand luxury of the Tartars, is then transferred to the tea-pot. Samdadchiemba was a perfect enthusiast of this tea. For our part, we drank it in default of something better.

Next morning, after rolling up our tent, we quitted

this asylum without regret indeed, for we had selected and occupied it altogether without preference. However, before departing, we set up, as an *ex-voto* of our gratitude for its reception of us for a night, a small wooden cross, on the site of our fire-place, and this precedent we afterwards followed, at all our encamping places. Could missionaries leave a more appropriate memorial of their journey through the desert!

We had not advanced an hour's journey on our way, when we heard behind us the tramping of many horses, and the confused sound of many voices. We looked back, and saw hastening in our direction a numerous caravan. Three horsemen soon overtook us, one of whom, whose costume bespoke him a Tartar mandarin, addressed us with a loud voice, " Sirs, where is your country ? " " We come from the west." " Through what districts has your beneficial shadow passed ? " We have last come from Tolon-Noor." " Has peace accompanied your progress ? " " Hitherto we have journeyed in all tranquillity. And you : are you at peace ? And what is your country ? " " We are Khalkhas, of the kingdom of Mourguevan [Murgevan]." " Have the rains been abundant ? Are your flocks and herds flourishing ? " " All goes well in our pasture-grounds." " Whither proceeds your caravan ? " " We go to incline our foreheads before the Five Towers." The rest of the caravan had joined us in the course of this abrupt and hurried conversation. We were on the banks of a small stream, bordered with brushwood. The chief of the caravan ordered a halt, and the camels formed, as each came up, a circle, in the centre of which was drawn up a close carriage upon four wheels. " *Sok! sok!* " cried the camel drivers, and at the word, and as with one motion, the entire circle of intelligent animals knelt. While numerous tents, taken from their backs, were set up, as it were, by enchantment, two mandarins, decorated with the blue button, approached the carriages, opened the door, and handed out a Tartar lady, covered with a long silk robe. She was the Queen of the Khalkhas repairing in pilgrimage to the famous Lamasery of the Five Towers, in the province of Chan-Si. When she saw us, she saluted us with the ordinary form of raising both her hands: " Sirs Lamas," she said, " is this place auspicious for an encampment ? " " Royal Pilgrim of Mourguevan," we replied, " you may light your fires here in all security. For ourselves, we muſt proceed on our way, for the sun was already high when we folded our tent." And so saying, we took our leave of the Tartars of Mourguevan.

Our minds were deeply excited upon beholding this queen and her numerous suite performing their long pilgrimage through the desert; no danger, no diſtance, no expense, no privation deters the Mongols from their prosecution. The Mongols are, indeed, an essentially religious people; with them the future life is everything; the things of this world nothing. They live in the world as though they were not of it; they cultivate no lands, they build no houses; they regard themselves as foreigners travelling through life; and this feeling, deep and universal, developes itself in the practical form of incessant journeys.

The taſte for pilgrimages which, at all periods of the world's hiſtory, has manifeſted itself in religious people, is a thing worthy of earneſt attention. The worship of the true God led the Jews, several times a year, to Jerusalem. In profane antiquity, those who took any heed to religious belief at all repaired to Egypt, in order to be initiated in the myſteries of Osiris, and to seek lessons of wisdom from his prieſts. It was to travellers that the myſterious sphynx of Mount Phicæus proposed the profound enigma of which Œdipus discovered the solution. In the middle ages, the spirit of pilgrimage held predominant sway in Europe, and the Christians of that epoch were full of fervour for this species of devotion. The Turks, while they were yet believers, repaired to Mecca in great caravans; and in our travels in Central Asia, we constantly met numerous pilgrims going to or fro, all of them profoundly filled with and earnestly impelled by a sincere sentiment of religion. It is to be remarked that pilgrimages have diminished in Europe, in proportion as faith has become rationalist, and as people have taken to discuss the truths of religion. Wherever faith remains earnest, simple, unquestioning, in the breasts of men, these pilgrimages are in vigour. The reason is, that the intensity of simple faith creates a peculiarly profound and energetic feeling of the condition of man, as a wayfarer upon the earth; and it is natural that this feeling should manifest itself in pious wayfarings. Indeed, the Catholic Church, which is the depository of all truth, has introduced processions into the liturgy, as a memorial of pilgrimages, and to remind men that this earth is a desert, wherein we commence, with our birth, the awful journey of eternity.

We had left far behind us the pilgrims of Mourguevan, and began to regret that we had not encamped in their company upon the banks of the pleasant stream, and amid the fat pastures which it fed. Sensations of fear grew upon us as we saw great clouds arise in the horizon, spread, and gradually obscure the sky. We looked anxiously around, in all directions, for a place in which we could commodiously halt for the night, but we saw no indication whatever of water. While we were deep in this perplexity, some large drops of rain told us that we had no time to lose. "Let us make haste and set up the tent," cried Samdadchiemba, vehemently. "You need not trouble yourselves any more in looking for water;

you will have enough water presently. Let us get under shelter before the sky falls on our heads." "That is all very well," said we, " but we muſt have some water for the animals and ourselves to drink. You alone require a bucket of water for your tea every evening. Where shall we find some water ? " " My fathers, you will very speedily have more water than you like. Let us encamp, that's the firſt thing to be done. As to thirſt, no one will need to die of that this evening : dig but a few holes about the tent and they'll soon overflow with rain-water. But we need not even dig holes," cried Samdadchiemba, extending his right hand : " do you see that shepherd there and his flock ? You may be sure water is not far off." Following with our eyes the direction of his finger, we perceived in a lateral valley a man driving a large flock of sheep. We immediately turned aside, and haſtened after the man. The rain which now began to fall in torrents redoubled our celerity. To aggravate our diſtress the lading of one of the camels juſt at this moment became loose, and slipped right round towards the ground, and we had to wait while the camel knelt, and Samdadchiemba readjuſted the baggage on its back. We were, consequently, thoroughly wet through before we reached a small lake, now agitated and swollen by the falling torrent. There was no occasion for deliberating that evening as to the particular site on which we could set up our tent ; selection was out of the queſtion, when the ground all about was deeply saturated with the rain.

The violence of the rain itself mitigated ; but the wind absolutely raged. We had infinite trouble to unroll our miserable tent, heavy and impracticable with wet, like a large sheet juſt taken from the washing-tub. The difficulty seemed insuperable when we attempted to ſtretch it upon its poles, and we should never have succeeded at all but for the extraordinary muscular power with which Samdadchiemba was endowed. At length we effected a shelter from the wind, and from a small cold rain with which it was accompanied. When our lodging was established, Samdadchiemba addressed us in these consolatory words :—" My spiritual fathers, I told you we should not die to-day of thirst; but I am not at all sure that we don't run some risk of dying of hunger." In point of fact, there seemed no possibility of making a fire. There was not a tree, not a shrub, not a root to be seen. As to *argols*, they were out of the question; the rain had long since reduced that combustible of the desert to a liquid pulp.

We had formed our resolution, and were on the point of making a supper of meal steeped in a little cold water, when we saw approaching us two Tartars, leading a small camel. After the usual salutations, one of them said: " Sirs Lamas, this day the heavens have fallen ; you, doubtless have been unable to make a fire." " Alas ! how should we make a fire, when we have no *argols* ? " " Men are all brothers and belong to each other. But laymen should honour and serve the holy ones ; therefore it is that we have come to make a fire for you." The worthy Tartars had seen us setting up our tent, and conceiving our embarrassment, had hastened to relieve it by a present of two bundles of *argols*. We thanked Providence for this unexpected succour, and the Dchiahour immediately made a fire, and set about the preparation of an oatmeal supper. The quantity was on this occasion augmented in favour of the two friends who had so opportunely presented themselves.

During our modest repast, we noticed that one of these Tartars was the object of special attention on the part of his comrade. We asked him what military grade he occupied in the Blue Banner. " When the banners of Tchakar marched two years ago against the rebels of the South,[1] I held the rank of *Tchouanda* [*juvani-da*]." "What! were you in the famous war of the South? But how is it that you, shepherds of the plains, have also the courage of soldiers? Accustomed to a life of peace, one would imagine that you would never be reconciled to the terrible trade of a soldier, which consists in killing others or being killed yourselves." "Yes, yes, we are shepherds, it is true; but we never forget that we are soldiers also, and that the Eight Banners compose the army of reserve of the Grand Master (the Emperor). You know the rule of the Empire; when the enemy appears, they send against them, first—the Kitat soldiers; next, the banners of the Solon country are set in motion. If the war is not finished then, all they have to do is to give the signal to the banners of the Tchakar, the mere sound of whose march always suffices to reduce the rebels to subjection."

"Were all the banners of Tchakar called together for this southern war?" "Yes, all; at first it was thought a small matter, and everyone said that it would never affect the Tchakar. The troops of Kitat went first, but they did nothing; the banners of Solon also marched; but they could not bear the heat of the South;—then the Emperor sent us his sacred order. Each man selected his best horse, removed the dust from his bow and quiver, and scraped the rust from his lance. In every tent a sheep was killed for the feast of departure. Women and children wept, but we addressed to them the words of reason. 'Here,' said we, 'for six generations have we received the benefits of the Sacred Master, and he has asked from us nothing in return. Now that he has need of us can we hold back? He has given to us this

[1] The English, then at war with the Chinese, were designated by the Tartars the *Rebels of the South.*

fine region of Tchakar to be a pasture-land for our cattle, and at the same time a barrier for him against the Khalkhas. But now, since it is from the South the rebels came, we must march to the South.' Was not reason in our mouths, Sirs Lamas? Yes, we resolved to march. The Sacred Ordinance reached us at sun-rise, and already by noon the *Bochehons* [*Khoshigun*] at the head of their men, stood by the *Tchouanda*; next to these were the *Nourou-Tchayn* [*niru-i-jangin*], and then the *Ou-gourdha* [*uheri-da*]. The same day we marched to Peking; from Peking they led us to Tien-Tsin-Veï [T'ien-chin-wei (Tientsin)], where we remained for three months." "Did you fight," asked Samdadchiemba; "did you see the enemy?" "No, they did not dare to appear. The Kitat told us everywhere that we were marching upon certain and unavailing death. 'What can you do,' asked they, 'against sea-monsters? They live in the water like fish When you least expect them, they appear on the surface, and hurl their fire-bombs at you; while, the instant your bow is bent to shoot them, down they dive like frogs.' Then they essayed to frighten us; but we soldiers of the Eight Banners knew not fear. Before our departure the great Lamas had opened the Book of Celestial Secrets, and had thence learned that the matter would end well for us. The Emperor had attached to each Tchouanda a Lama, learned in medicine, and skilled in all the sacred auguries, who was to cure all the soldiers under him of the diseases of the climate, and to protect us from the magic of the sea-monsters. What then had we to fear? The rebels, hearing that the invincible troops of Tchakar were approaching, were seized with fear, and sought peace. The Sacred Master, of his immense mercy, granted it, and we returned to the care of our flocks."

The narrative of this Illustrious Sword was to us full of

intense interest. We forgot for a moment the misery of our position amid the desert. We were eager to collect further details of the expedition of the English against China; but night falling, the two Tartars took their way homeward.

Thus left once more alone, our thoughts became exceedingly sad and sombre. We shuddered at the idea so recalled to us of the long night just commencing. How were we to get any sleep? The interior of the tent was little better than a mud-heap; the great fire we had been keeping up had not half dried our clothes; it had merely resolved a portion of the water into a thick vapour that steamed about us. The furs, which we used at night by way of mattress, were in a deplorable condition, not a whit better for the purpose than the skin of a drowned cat. In this doleful condition of things, a reflection, full of gentle melancholy, came into our minds, and consoled us; we remembered that we were the disciples of him who said, " The foxes have holes, and the birds of the air have nests; but the Son of Man hath not where to lay his head."

We became so fatigued after remaining awake the greater part of the night, that sleep conquering us, we fell into a restless doze, seated over the embers of the fire, our arms crossed, and our heads bent forward, in the most uncomfortable position possible.

It was with extreme delight that we hailed the termination of that long and dreary night. At daybreak, the blue, cloudless sky presaged compensation for the wretchedness of the preceding evening. By-and-by, the sun rising clear and brilliant, inspired us with the hope that our still wet clothes would soon get dry as we proceeded on our way. We speedily made all preparations for departure, and the caravan set forth. The weather was magnificent. By degrees, the large grass of the prairie raised its broad head, which had been depressed by the heavy rain; the ground became firmer, and we experienced, with delight, the gentle heat of the sun's ascending rays. At last, to complete our satisfaction, we entered upon the plains of the Red Banner, the most picturesque of the whole Tchakar.

Tchakar signifies, in the Mongol tongue, Border Land. This country is limited, on the east by the kingdom of Gechekten on the west by Western Toumet [Tümet], on the north by the Souniot [Suniut], on the South by the Great Wall. Its extent is 150 leagues long, by 100 broad. The inhabitants of the Tchakar are all paid soldiers of the Emperor. The foot soldiers receive twelve ounces of silver per annum, and the cavalry twenty-four.

The Tchakar is divided into eight banners—in Chinese *Pa-Ki* [*pa-ch'i*]—distinguished by the name of eight colours: white, blue, red, yellow, French white, light blue, pink, and light yellow. Each banner has its separate territory, and a tribunal, named *Nourou-Tchayn*, having jurisdiction over all the matters that may occur in the Banner. Besides this tribunal, there is, in each of the Eight Banners, a chief called *Ou-Gourdha*. Of the eight *Ou-Gourdhas* one is selected to fill at the same time, the post of governor-general of the Eight Banners. All these dignitaries are nominated and paid by the Emperor of China. In fact, the Tchakar is nothing more nor less than a vast camp, occupied by an army of reserve. In order, no doubt, that this army may be at all times ready to march at the first signal, the Tartars are severely prohibited to cultivate the land. They must live upon their pay, and upon the produce of their flocks and herds. The entire soil of the Eight Banners is inalienable. It sometimes happens that an individual sells his portion to some Chinese; but the sale is always declared null and void if it comes in any shape before the tribunals.

THIBET, AND CHINA

It is in these pasturages of the Tchakar that are found the numerous and magnificent herds and flocks of the Emperor, consisting of camels, horses, cattle, and sheep. There are 360 herds of horses alone, each numbering 1,200 horses. It is easy from this one detail to imagine the enormous extent of animals possessed here by the Emperor. A Tartar, decorated with the white button, has charge of each herd. At certain intervals, inspectors-general visit the herds, and if any deficiency in the number is discovered the chief herdsman has to make it good at his own cost. Notwithstanding this impending penalty, the Tartars do not fail to convert to their own use the wealth of the Sacred Master, by means of a fraudulent exchange. Whenever a Chinese has a broken-winded horse, or a lame ox, he takes it to the imperial herdsman, who, for a trifling consideration, allows him to select what animal he pleases in exchange, from among the imperial herds. Being thus always provided with the actual number of animals, they can benefit by their frauds in perfect security.

Never in more splendid weather had we traversed a more splendid country. The desert is at times horrible, hideous; but it has also its charms—charms all the more intensely appreciated, because they are rare in themselves, and because they would in vain be sought in populated countries. Tartary has an aspect altogether peculiar to itself: there is nothing in the world that at all resembles a Tartar landscape. In civilized countries you find, at every step, populous towns, a rich and varied cultivation, the thousand and one productions of arts and industry, the incessant movements of commerce. You are constantly impelled onwards, carried away, as it were, by some vast whirlwind. On the other hand, in countries where civilization has not as yet made its way into the light, you ordinarily find nothing but primeval forests in all the pomp of their exuberant and gigantic vegetation. The soul seems crushed beneath a nature all powerful and majestic. There is nothing of the kind in Tartary. There are no towns, no edifices, no arts, no industry, no cultivation, no forests; everywhere it is prairie, sometimes interrupted by immense lakes, by majestic rivers, by rugged and imposing mountains; sometimes spreading out into vast limitless plains. There, in these verdant solitudes, the bounds of which seem lost in the remote horizon, you might imagine yourself gently rocking on the calm waves of some broad ocean. The aspect of the prairies of Mongolia excites neither joy nor sorrow, but rather a mixture of the two, a sentiment of gentle, religious melancholy, which gradually elevates the soul, without wholly excluding from its contemplation the things of this world; a sentiment which belongs rather to Heaven than to earth, and which seems in admirable conformity with the nature of intellect served by organs.

You sometimes in Tartary come upon plains more animated than those you have just traversed; they are those, whither the greater supply of water and the choicest pastures have attracted for a time a number of nomadic families. There you see rising in all directions tents of various dimensions, looking like balloons newly inflated, and just about to take their flight into the air. Children, with a sort of hod at their backs, run about collecting *argols*, which they pile up in heaps around their respective tents. The matrons look after the calves, make tea in the open air, or prepare milk in various ways; the men, mounted on fiery horses, and armed with a long pole, gallop about, guiding to the best pastures the great herds of cattle which undulate, in the distance all around, like waves of the sea.

All of a sudden, these pictures, so full of animation,

THIBET, AND CHINA

disappear, and you see nothing of that which of late was so full of life. Men, tents, herds, all have vanished in the twinkling of an eye. You merely see in the desert heaps of embers, half-extinguished fires, and a few bones, of which birds of prey are disputing the possession. Such are the sole vestiges which announce that a Mongol tribe has just passed that way. If you ask the reason of these abrupt migrations, it is simply this:—the animals having devoured all the grass that grew in the vicinity, the chief has given the signal for departure; and all the shepherds, folding their tents, had driven their herds before them, and proceeded, no matter whither, in search of fresh fields and pastures new.

After having journeyed the entire day through the delicious prairies of the Red Banner, we halted to encamp for the night in a valley that seemed full of people. We had scarcely alighted when a number of Tartars approached, and offered their services. After having assisted us to unload our camels, and set up our house of blue linen, they invited us to come and take tea in their tents. As it was late, however, we stayed at home, promising to pay them a visit next morning; for the hospitable invitation of our new neighbours determined us to remain for a day amongst them. We were, moreover, very well pleased to profit by the beauty of the weather, and of the locality, to recover from the fatigues we had undergone the day before.

Next morning, the time not appropriated to our little household cares, and the recitation of our Breviary, was devoted to visiting the Mongol tents, Samdadchiemba being left at home in charge of the tent.

We had to take especial care to the safety of our legs, menaced by a whole host of watchdogs. A small stick sufficed for the purpose; but Tartar etiquette required us to leave these weapons at the threshold of our host's abode. To enter a man's tent with a whip or a stick in your hand is as great an insult as you can offer to the family; and quite tantamount to saying, " You are all dogs."

Visiting among the Tartars is a frank, simple affair, altogether exempt from the endless formalities of Chinese gentility. On entering, you give the word of peace *amor* or *mendou*, to the company generally. You then seat yourself on the right of the head of the family, whom you find squatting on the floor, opposite the entrance. Next, everybody takes from a purse suspended at his girdle a little snuff-bottle, and mutual pinches accompany such phrases as these: " Is the pasturage with you rich and abundant?" " Are your herds in fine condition?" " Are your mares productive?" " Did you travel in peace?" " Does tranquillity prevail?" and so on. These questions and their answers being interchanged always with intense gravity on both sides, the mistress of the tent, without saying a word, holds out her hand to the visitor. He as silently takes from his breast-pocket the small wooden bowl, the indispensable vade-mecum of all Tartars, and presents it to his hostess, who fills it with tea and milk, and returns it. In the richer, more easily circumstanced families, visitors have a small table placed before them, on which is butter, oatmeal, grated millet, and bits of cheese, separately contained in little boxes of polished wood. These Tartar delicacies the visitors take mixed with their tea. Such as propose to treat their guests in a style of perfect magnificence make them partakers of a bottle of Mongol wine, warmed in the ashes. This wine is nothing more than skimmed milk, subjected for awhile to vinous fermentation, and distilled through a rude apparatus that does the office of an alembic. One must be a thorough Tartar to relish or even endure this beverage, the flavour and odour of which are alike insipid.

The Mongol tent, for about three feet from the ground, is cylindrical in form. It then becomes conical, like a pointed hat. The woodwork of the tent is composed below of a trellis-work of crossed bars which fold up and expand at pleasure. Above these, a circle of poles, fixed in the trellis-work, meets at the top, like the sticks of an umbrella. Over the woodwork is stretched, once or twice, a thick covering of coarse linen, and thus the tent is composed. The door, which is always a folding door, is low and narrow. A beam crosses it at the bottom by way of threshold, so that on entering you have at once to raise your feet and lower your head. Besides the door there is another opening at the top of the tent to let out the smoke. This opening can at any time be closed with a piece of felt fastened above it in the tent, and which can be pulled over it by means of a string, the end of which hangs by the door.

The interior is divided into two compartments; that on the left, as you enter, is reserved for the men, thither the visitors proceed. Any man who should enter on the right side would be considered excessively rude. The right compartment is occupied by the women, and there you will find the culinary utensils: large earthen vessels of glazed earth, wherein to keep the store of water; trunks of trees of different sizes, hollowed into the shape of pails, and destined to contain the preparations of milk, in the various forms which they make it undergo. In the centre of the tent is a large trivet, planted in the earth, and always ready to receive the large iron bell-shaped cauldron that stands by, ready for use.

Behind the hearth, and facing the door, is a kind of sofa, the most singular piece of furniture that we met with among the Tartars. At the two ends are two pillows, having at their extremity plates of copper, gilt, and skilfully engraved. There is probably not a single tent where you do not find this little couch, which seems to be an essential article of furniture; but, strange to say, during our long journey we never saw one of them which seemed to have been recently made. We had occasion to visit Mongol families where everything bore the mark of easy circumstances even of affluence, but everywhere alike this singular couch was shabby, and of ancient fabric. But yet it seems made to last for ever, and is regularly transmitted from generation to generation.

In the towns where Tartar commerce is carried on, you may hunt through every furniture shop, every broker's, every pawnbroker's, but you meet with not one of these pieces of furniture, new or old.

At the side of the couch, towards the men's quarters, there is ordinarily a small square press, which contains the various odds and ends that serve to set off the costume of this simple people. This chest serves likewise as an altar for a small image of Buddha. The divinity, in wood or copper, is usually in a sitting posture, the legs crossed, and enveloped up to the neck in a scarf of old yellow silk. Nine copper vases, of the size and form of our liqueur glasses, are symmetrically arranged before Buddha. It is in these small chalices that the Tartars daily make to their idol offerings of water, milk, butter and meal. A few Thibetian books, wrapped in yellow silk, perfect the decoration of the little pagoda. Those whose heads are shaved, and who observe celibacy, have alone the privilege of touching these prayer-books. A layman, who should venture to take them into his impure and profane hands, would commit a sacrilege.

A number of goats' horns, fixed in the woodwork of the tent, complete the furniture of the Mongol habitation. On these hang the joints of beef or

THIBET, AND CHINA

mutton deſtined for the family's use; vessels filled with butter; bows, arrows and matchlocks; for there is scarcely a Tartar family which does not possess at leaſt one fire-arm. We were, therefore, surprised to find M. Timkouski, in his *Journey to Peking*,[1] make this ſtrange ſtatement: "The sound of our fire-arms attraćted the attention of the Mongols, who are acquainted only with bows and arrows." The Russian writer should have known that fire-arms are not so foreign to the Tartars as he imagined; since it is proved that already, as early as the commencement of the thirteenth century, Tchinggiskhan [Chingiz-Khan] had artillery in his armies.

The odour pervading the interior of the Mongol tents, is, to those not accuſtomed to it, disguſting and almoſt insupportable. This smell, so potent sometimes that it seems to make one's heart rise to one's throat, is occasioned by the mutton grease and butter with which everything on or about a Tartar is impregnated. It is on account of this habitual filth that they are called *Tsao-ta-Dze* [*Sao-ta-tzŭ*], "Stinking Tartars", by the Chinese, themselves not altogether inodorous, or by any means particular about cleanliness.

Among the Tartars, household and family cares reſt entirely upon the woman; it is she who milks the cows, and prepares the butter, cheese, etc.; who goes, no matter how far, to draw water; who collećts the *argol* fuel, dries it, and piles it around the tent. The making of clothes, the tanning of skins, the fulling of cloth, all appertains to her; the sole assiſtance she obtains, in these various labours, being that of her sons, and then only while they are quite young.

The occupations of the men are of very limited range; they consiſt wholly in condućting the flocks

[1] *Voyage à Peking à travers la Mongolie*, by M. G. Timkouski, chap. II, p. 57.

and herds to pasture. This for men accustomed from their infancy to horseback is rather an amusement than a labour. In point of fact, the nearest approach to fatigue they ever incur is when some of their cattle escape; they then dash off at full gallop, in pursuit, up hill and down dale, until they have found the missing animals, and brought them back to the herd. The Tartars sometimes hunt; but it is rather with a view to what they can catch than from any amusement they derive from the exercise; the only occasions on which they go out with their bows and matchlocks are when they desire to shoot roebucks, deer, or pheasants, as presents for their chiefs. Foxes they always course. To shoot them, or take them in traps, would, they consider, injure their skin, which is held in high estimation among them. They ridicule the Chinese immensely on account of their trapping these animals at night. "We," said a famous hunter of the Red Banner to us, "set about the thing in an honest straightforward way. When we see a fox, we jump on horseback, and gallop after him till we have run him down."

With the exception of their equestrian exercises, the Mongol Tartars pass their time in an absolute *far niente*, sleeping all night, and squatting all day in their tents, dosing, drinking tea, or smoking. At intervals, however, the Tartar conceives a fancy to take a lounge abroad; and his lounge is somewhat different from that of the Parisian idler; he needs neither cane nor quizzing glass; but when the fancy occurs, he takes down his whip from its place above the door, mounts his horse, always ready saddled outside the door, and dashes off into the desert, no matter whither. When he sees another horseman in the distance, he rides up to him; when he sees the smoke of a tent, he rides up to that; the only object in either case being to have a chat with some new person.

THIBET, AND CHINA

The two days we passed in these fine plains of the Tchakar were not without good use. We were able at leisure to dry and repair our clothes and our baggage; but, above all, it gave us an opportunity to study the Tartars close at hand, and to initiate ourselves in the habits of the nomad peoples. As we were making preparations for departure, these temporary neighbours aided us to fold our tent and to load our camels. "Sirs Lamas," said they, "you had better encamp to-night at the Three Lakes; the pasturage there is good and abundant. If you make haste you will reach the place before sunset. On this side, and on the other side of the Three Lakes, there is no water for a considerable distance. Sirs Lamas, a good journey to you!" "Peace be with you, and farewell!" responded we, and with that proceeded once more on our way, Samdadchiemba heading the caravan, mounted on his little black mule. We quitted this encampment without regret, just as we had quitted preceding encampments; except indeed, that here we left, on the spot where our tent had stood, a greater heap of ashes, and that the grass around it was more trodden than was usual with us.

During the morning the weather was magnificent, though somewhat cold. But in the afternoon the north wind rose, and began to blow with extreme violence. It soon became so cutting that we regretted that we had not with us our great fur caps, to operate as a protector for the face. We hurried on, in order the sooner to reach the Three Lakes, and to have the shelter there of our dear tent. In the hope of discovering these lakes, that had been promised us by our late friends, we were constantly looking right and left, but in vain. It grew late, and according to the information of the Tartars, we began to fear we must have passed the only encampment we were likely to find that day. By dint of straining our eyes, we at length got sight of a horseman, slowly riding along the bottom of a lateral valley. He was at some distance from us; but it was essential that we should obtain information from him. M. Gabet accordingly hastened after him, at the utmost speed of his tall camel's long legs. The horseman heard the cries of the animal, looked back, and seeing that someone was approaching him, turned his horse round, and galloped towards M. Gabet. As soon as he got within earshot: "Holy personage," cried he, "has your eye perceived the yellow goats? I have lost all trace of them." "I have not seen the yellow goats; I seek water, and cannot find it. Is it far hence?" "Whence came you? Whither go you?" "I belong to the little caravan you see yonder. We have been told that we should this evening, on our way, find lakes, upon the banks of which we could commodiously encamp; but hitherto we have seen nothing of the kind." "How could that be? 'Tis but a few minutes ago you passed within a few yards of the water. Sir Lama, permit me to attend your shadow; I will guide you to the Three Lakes." And so saying, he gave his horse three swinging lashes with his whip, in order to put it into a pace commensurate with that of the camel. In a minute he had joined us. "Men of prayer," said the hunter, "you have come somewhat too far; you must turn back. Look" (pointing with his bow) "yonder; you see those storks hovering over some reeds: there you will find the Three Lakes." "Thanks, brother," said we; "we regret that we cannot show you your yellow goats as clearly as you have shown us the Three Lakes." The Mongol hunter saluted us, with his clasped hands raised to his forehead, and we proceeded with entire confidence towards the spot he had pointed out. We had advanced but a few paces before we found indications of the near presence of some peculiar waters.

THIBET, AND CHINA

The grass was less continuous and less green, and cracked under our animals' hoofs like dried leaves; the white efflorescence of saltpetre manifested itself more and more thickly. At last we found ourselves on the bank of one lake, near which were two others. We immediately alighted, and set about erecting our tents; but the wind was so violent that it was only after long labour and much patience that we completed the task.

While Samdadchiemba was boiling our tea, we amused ourselves with watching the camels as they luxuriously licked up the saltpetre with which the ground was powdered. Next they bent over the edge of the lake, and inhaled long, insatiable draughts of the brackish water, which we could see ascending their long necks as up some flexible pump.

We had been for some time occupied in this not unpicturesque recreation, when, all of a sudden, we heard behind us a confused, tumultuous noise, resembling the vehement flapping of sails, beaten about by contrary and violent winds. Soon we distinguished, amid the uproar, loud cries proceeding from Samdadchiemba. We hastened towards him, and were just in time to prevent, by our co-operation, the typhoon from uprooting and carrying off our linen *louvre*. Since our arrival, the wind, augmenting in violence, had also changed its direction; so that it now blew exactly from the quarter facing which we had placed the opening of our tent. We had especial occasion to fear that the tent would be set on fire by the lighted *argols* that were driven about by the wind. Our first business, therefore, was to tack about; and after a while we succeeded in making our tent secure, and so got off with our fear and a little fatigue. The misadventure, however, put Samdadchiemba into a desperately bad humour throughout the evening; for the wind, by extinguishing the fire, delayed the preparation of his darling tea.

The wind fell as the night advanced, and by degrees the weather became magnificent; the sky was clear, the moon full and bright, and the stars glittered like diamonds. Alone, in this vast solitude, we distinguished in the distance only the fantastic and indistinct outline of the mountains which loomed in the horizon like gigantic phantoms, while the only sound we heard was the cries of the thousand aquatic birds as, on the surface of the lakes, they contended for the ends of the reeds and the broad leaves of the water-lily. Samdadchiemba was by no means a person to appreciate the charms of this tranquil scene. He had succeeded in again lighting the fire, and was absorbed in the preparation of his tea. We accordingly left him squatted before the kettle, and went to recite the service, walking round the larger lake, which was nearly half a league in circuit. We had proceeded about half round it, praying alternately, when insensibly our voices fell, and our steps were stayed. We both stopped spontaneously, and listened intently, without venturing to interchange a word, and even endeavouring to suppress our respiration. At last we expressed to each other the cause of our mutual terror, but it was in tones low and full of emotion: "Did you not hear, just now, and quite close to us, what seemed the voices of men?" "Yes, a number of voices speaking as though in secret consultation." "Yet we are alone here:—'tis very surprising. Hist! let us listen again." "I hear nothing; doubtless we were under some illusion." We resumed our walk and the recitation of our prayers. But we had not advanced ten steps, before we again stopped; for we heard, and very distinctly, the noise which had before alarmed us, and which seemed the confused vague murmur of several voices discussing some point in undertones. Yet nothing was visible. We got upon a hillock, and thence, by the moon's

THIBET, AND CHINA

light, saw, at a short diſtance, some human forms moving in the long grass. We could hear their voices too, but not diſtinctly enough to know whether they spoke Chinese or Tartar. We retraced our ſteps to our tent, as rapidly as was consistent with the maintenance of silence; for we took these people to be robbers, who, having perceived our tent, were deliberating as to the beſt means of pillaging us.

"We are not in safety here," said we to Samdadchiemba; "we have discovered, quite close to us, a number of men, and we have heard their voices. Go and collect the animals, and bring them to the tent." "But," asked Samdadchiemba, knitting his brows, "if the robbers come what shall we do? May we fight them? May we kill them? Will Holy Church permit that?" "Firſt go and collect the animals; afterwards we will tell you what we muſt do." The animals being brought together, and faſtened outside the tent, we directed our intrepid Samdadchiemba to finish his tea, and we returned on tip-toe to the spot where we had seen and heard our myſterious visitors. We looked around in every direction, with eye and ear intent; but we could neither see nor hear anyone. A well-trodden pathway, however, which we discovered among the reeds of tall grass on the margin of the greater lake, indicated to us that those whom we had taken to be robbers were inoffensive passengers, whose route lay in that direction. We returned joyfully to our tent, where we found our valorous Samdadchiemba actively employed in sharpening, upon the top of his leather boots, a great Russian cutlass, which he had purchased at Tolon-Noor. "Well," exclaimed he, fiercely, trying with his thumb the edge of his sword, "where are the robbers?" "There are no robbers; unroll the goat-skins that we may go to sleep." "'Tis a pity there are no robbers; for here is something that would have cut into them famously!" "Ay, ay, Samdadchiemba, you are wonderfully brave now, because you know there are no robbers." "Oh, my spiritual fathers, it is not so; one should always speak the words of candour. I admit that my memory is very bad, and that I have never been able to learn many prayers; but as to courage, I may boast of having as much of it as another.' We laughed at this singularly expressed sally. "You laugh, my spiritual fathers," said Samdadchiemba. "Oh, you do not know the Dchiahours. In the west, the land of San-Tchouan [San-ch'uan] "Three Valleys" enjoys much renown. My countrymen hold life in little value; they have always a sabre by their side, and a long matchlock on their shoulder. For a word, for a look, they fight and kill one another. A Dchiahour, who has never killed any one, is considered to have no right to hold his head up among his countrymen. He cannot pretend to the character of a brave man." "Very fine! Well, you are a brave man, you say: tell us how many men did you kill when you were in the Three Valleys?" Samdadchiemba seemed somewhat disconcerted by this question; he looked away, and broke out into a forced laugh. At last, by way of diverting the subject, he plunged his cup into the kettle, and drew it out full of tea. "Come," said we, "drink your tea, and then tell us about your exploits."

Samdadchiemba wiped his cup with the skirt of his jacket, and having replaced it in his bosom, addressed us gravely, thus: "My spiritual fathers, since you desire I should speak to you about myself, I will do so; it was a great sin I committed, but I think Jehovah pardoned me when I entered the Holy Church.

"I was quite a child, not more at the utmost than seven years old. I was in the fields about my father's house, tending an old she-donkey, the only animal we possessed. One of my companions, a boy about my own age, came to play with me. We began quarrelling, and from words fell to blows. I struck him on the head with a great root of a tree that I had in my hand, and the blow was so heavy that he fell motionless at my feet. When I saw my companion stretched on the earth, I stood for a moment as it were paralysed, not knowing what to think or to do. Then an awful fear came over me, that I should be seized and killed. I looked all about me in search of a hole wherein I might conceal my companion, but I saw nothing of the kind. I then thought of hiding myself. At a short distance from our house there was a great pile of brushwood, collected for fuel. I directed my steps thither, and with great labour made a hole, into which, after desperately scratching myself, I managed to creep up to my neck, resolved never to come out of it.

"When night fell, I found they were seeking me. My mother was calling me in all directions; but I took good care not to answer. I was even anxious not to move the brushwood, lest the sound should lead to my discovery, and, as I anticipated, to my being killed. I was terribly frightened when I heard a number of people crying out, and disputing, I concluded, about me. The night passed away; in the morning I felt devouringly hungry. I began to cry; but I could not even cry at my ease, for I feared to be discovered by the people whom I heard moving about, and I was resolved never to quit the brushwood."
" But were you not afraid you should die of hunger?"
" The idea never occurred to me; I felt hungry indeed, but that was all. The reason I had for concealing myself was that I might not die; for I thought that if they did not find me, of course they could not kill me." " Well, and how long did you remain in the brushwood?" " Well, I have often heard people say that you can't remain long without eating; but

those who say so never tried the experiment. I can answer for it, that a boy of seven years old can live, at all events, three days and four nights without eating anything whatever.

"After the fourth night, early in the morning, they found me in my hole. When I felt they were taking me out, I struggled as well as I could, and endeavoured to get away. My father took me by the arm. I cried and sobbed, 'Do not kill me, do not kill me,' cried I; 'it was not I who killed Nasamboyan.' They carried me to the house, for I would not walk. While I wept, in utter despair, the people about me laughed. At last they told me not to be afraid, for that Nasamboyan was not dead, and soon afterwards Nasamboyan came into the room as well as ever, only that he had a great bruise on his face. The blow I had struck him had merely knocked him down and stunned him."

When the Dchiahour had finished his narrative, he looked at us in turns, laughing and repeating, again and again, "Who will say people cannot live without eating?" "Well," said we, "this is a very good beginning, Samdadchiemba; but you have not told us yet how many men you have killed." "I never killed anyone; but that was merely because I did not stay long enough in my native Three Valleys; for at the age of ten they put me into a great Lamasery. I had for my especial master a very rough, cross man, who gave me the strap every day, because I could not repeat the prayers he taught me. But it was to no purpose he beat me; I could learn nothing: so he left off teaching me, and sent me out to fetch water and collect fuel. But he continued to thrash me as hard as ever, until the life I led became quite insupportable, and at last I ran off with some provisions, and made my way towards Tartary. After walking several days, haphazard, and perfectly ignorant where I was, I encountered the train of a Grand Lama who was repairing to Peking. I joined the caravan, and was employed to take charge of a flock of sheep that accompanied the party and served for its food. There was no room for me in any of the tents, so I had to sleep in the open air. One evening I took up my quarters behind a rock, which sheltered me from the wind. In the morning, waking somewhat later than usual, I found the encampment ſtruck, and the people all gone. I was left alone in the desert. At this time I knew nothing about eaſt, weſt, north, or south; I had consequently no resources but to wander on at random, until I should find some Tartar ſtation. I lived in this way for three years—now here, now there, exchanging such slight services as I could render for my food and tent room. At laſt I reached Peking, and presented myself at the gate of the Great Lamasery of Hoang-Sse [Huang-Ssŭ], which is entirely composed of Dchiahour and Thibetian Lamas. I was at once admitted, and my countrymen having clubbed together to buy me a red scarf and a yellow cap, I was enabled to join the chorus in the recitation of prayers, and, of consequence, to claim my share in the diſtribution of alms." We interrupted Samdadchiemba at this point, in order to learn from him how he could take part in the recitation of prayers, without having learned either to read or pray. "Oh," said he, "the thing was easy enough. They gave me an old book; I held it on my knees, and mumbling out some gibberish between my lips, endeavoured to catch the tone of my neighbours. When they turned over a leaf, I turned over a leaf; so that, altogether, there was no reason why the leader of the chorus should take any notice of my manœuvre.

"One day, however, a circumſtance occurred that very nearly occasioned my expulsion from the Lamasery. An ill-natured Lama, who had remarked my method

TRAVELS IN TARTARY,

of reciting the prayers, used to amuse himself with mocking me, and creating a laugh at my expense. When the Emperor's mother died, we were all invited to the Yellow Palace to recite prayers. Before the ceremony commenced, I was sitting quietly in my place, with my book on my knees, when this roguish fellow came gently behind me, and looking over my shoulder mumbled out something or other in imitation of my manner. Losing all self-possession, I gave him so hard a blow upon the face, that he fell on his back. The incident excited great confusion in the Yellow Palace. The superiors were informed of the matter, and by the severe rules of Thibetian discipline, I was liable to be flogged for three days with the black whip, and then, my hands and feet in irons, to be imprisoned for a year in the tower of the Lamasery. One of the principals, however, who had taken notice of me before, interposed in my favour. We went to the Lamas who conftituted the council of discipline, and represented to them the fact that the disciple who had been ftruck was a person notorious for annoying his companions, and that I had received extreme provocation from him. He spoke so warmly in my favour that I was pardoned on the mere condition of making an apology. I accordingly placed myself in the way of the Lama whom I had offended : ' Brother,' said I, ' shall we go and drink a cup of tea together ? ' ' Certainly,' replied he ; ' there is no reason why I should not drink a cup of tea with you.' We went out, and entered the first tea-house that presented itself. Seating ourselves at one of the tables in the tea-room, I offered my snuff-bottle to my companion, saying, ' Elder brother, the other day we had a little disagreement ; that was not well. You muft confess that you were not altogether free from blame. I, on my part, admit that I dealt too heavy a blow. But the matter has grown old ; we will think no more about it.' We then drank our tea, interchanged various civilities, and so the thing ended."

These and similar anecdotes of our Dchiahour had carried us far into the night. The camels, indeed, were already up and browsing their breakfaſt on the banks of the lake. We had but brief time before us for repose. "For my part," said Samdadchiemba, "I will not lie down at all, but look after the camels. Day will soon break. Meantime I'll make a good fire, and prepare the *pan-tan*."

It was not long before Samdadchiemba roused us with the intimation that the sun was up, and the *pan-tan* ready. We at once rose, and after eating a cup of *pan-tan*, or, in other words, of oatmeal diluted with boiling water, we planted our little cross upon a hillock, and proceeded upon our pilgrimage.

It was paſt noon when we came to a place where three wells had been dug, at short diſtances, the one from the other. Although it was early in the day, we ſtill thought we had better encamp here. A vaſt plain, on which we could discern no sort of habitation, ſtretched out before us to the diſtant horizon; and we might fairly conclude it deſtitute of water, since the Tartars had taken the trouble to dig these wells. We therefore set up our tent. We soon found, however, that we had selected a deteſtable encampment. With excessive nastiness of very brackish and very fetid water was combined extreme scarcity of fuel. We looked about for *argols*, but in vain. At last Samdadchiemba, whose eyes were better than ours, discerned in the diſtance a sort of enclosure, in which he concluded that cattle had been folded. He took a camel with him to the place in the hope of finding plenty of *argols* there, and he certainly returned with an ample supply of the article; but unfortunately the precious manure-fuel was not quite dry; it absolutely refused to burn. The Dchiahour essayed an experiment. He hollowed out a sort of furnace in the ground, surmounting it with a turf chimney. The structure was extremely picturesque, but it laboured under the enormous disadvantage of being wholly useless. Samdadchiemba arranged and re-arranged his fuel, and puffed, and puffed, with the full force of his potent lungs. It was all lost labour. There was smoke enough, and to spare; we were enveloped in smoke, but not a spark of fire: and the water in the kettle remained relentlessly passive. It was obvious that to boil our tea or heat oatmeal was out of the question. Yet we were anxious, at all events, to take the chill off the water, so as to disguise by the warmth, its brackish flavour and its disagreeable smell. We adopted this expedient:

You meet in the plains of Mongolia a sort of grey squirrel, living in holes like rats. These animals construct over the opening of their little dens, a sort of miniature dome, composed of grass, artistically twisted, and designed as a shelter from wind and rain. These little heaps of dry grass are of the form and size of mole-hills. The place where we had now set up our tent abounded with these grey squirrels. Thirst made us cruel, and we proceeded to level the house-domes of these poor little animals, which retreated into their holes below as we approached them. By means of this vandalism we managed to collect a sackful of efficient fuel, and so warmed the water of the well, which was our only aliment during the day.

Our provisions had materially diminished, notwithstanding the economy to which the want of fire on this and other occasions had reduced us. There remained very little meal or millet in our store bags, when we learned, from a Tartar whom we met on the way, that we were at no great distance from a trading station called Chaborté [Shabartai] "Slough." It lay, indeed, somewhat out of the route we were pursuing; but there was no other place at which we could supply ourselves with provisions, until we came to Blue-Town, from which we were distant a hundred leagues. We turned therefore obliquely to the left, and soon reached Chaborté.

CHAPTER III

WE arrived at Chaborté on the fifteenth day of the eighth moon, the anniversary of great rejoicings among the Chinese. This festival, known as the *Yué-Ping* [*yüeh-ping*] "Loaves of the Moon," dates from the remotest antiquity. Its original purpose was to honour the moon with superstitious rites. On this solemn day all labour is suspended; the workmen receive from their employers a present of money; every person puts on his best clothes; and there is merry-making in every family. Relations and friends interchange cakes of various sizes, on which is stamped the image of the moon; that is to say, a hare crouching amid a small group of trees.

Since the fourteenth century, this festival has borne a political character, little understood, apparently, by the Mongols; but the tradition of which is carefully preserved by the Chinese. About the year 1368, the Chinese were desirous of shaking off the yoke of Tartar dynasty, founded by Tchinggiskhan, and which had then swayed the empire for nearly a hundred years. A vast conspiracy was formed throughout all the provinces, which was simultaneously to develop itself, on the 15th day of the eighth moon, by the massacre of the Mongol soldiers, who were billeted upon each Chinese family, for the double purpose of maintaining themselves and their conquest. The signal was given by a letter concealed in the cakes which, as we have stated, are on that day mutually interchanged throughout the country. The massacre was effected, and the Tartar army dispersed in the

THIBET, AND CHINA
houses of the Chinese, utterly annihilated. This cataſtrophe put an end to the Mongol domination; and ever since, the Chinese, in celebrating the feſtival of *Yué-ping*, have been less intent upon the superſtitious worship of the moon, than upon the tragic event to which they owed the recovery of their national independence.

The Mongols seem to have entirely loſt all memory of the sanguinary revolution; for every year they take their full part in the feſtival of the Loaves of the Moon, and thus celebrate, without apparently knowing it, the triumph which their enemies heretofore gained over their anceſtors.

At a gun-shot from the place where we were encamped, we perceived several Mongol tents, the size and charaćter of which indicated easiness of circumſtances in the proprietors. This indication was confirmed by the large herds of cattle, sheep and horses, which were paſturing around. While we were reciting the Breviary in our tent, Samdadchiemba went to pay a visit to these Mongols. Soon afterwards, we saw approaching an old man with a long white beard, and whose features bespoke him a person of diſtinćtion. He was accompanied by a young Lama, and by a little boy who held his hand. " Sirs Lamas," said the old man, " all men are brothers; but they who dwell in tents are united one with another as flesh with bone. Sirs Lamas, will you come and seat yourselves, for a while, in my poor abode ? The fifteenth of this moon is a solemn epoch; you are ſtrangers and travellers, and therefore cannot this evening occupy your places at the hearth of your own noble family. Come and repose for a few days with us; your presence will bring us peace and happiness." We told the good old man that we could not wholly accept his offer, but that, in the evening, after prayers, we would come and take tea with him, and converse for a while about the Mongol nation. The venerable Tartar hereupon took his leave; but he had not been gone long, before the young Lama who had accompanied him returned, and told us that his people were awaiting our presence. We felt that we could not refuse at once to comply with an invitation so full of frank cordiality, and accordingly, having directed our Dchiahour to take good care of the tent, we followed the young Lama who had come in quest of us.

Upon entering the Mongol tent we were struck and astonished at finding a cleanliness one is little accustomed to see in Tartary. There was not the ordinary coarse fire-place in the centre, and the eye was not offended with the rude dirty kitchen utensils which generally encumber Tartar habitations. It was obvious, besides, that everything had been prepared for a festival. We seated ourselves upon a large red carpet; and there was almost immediately brought to us, from the adjacent tent, which served as a kitchen, some tea with milk, some small loaves fried in butter; cheese, raisins, and jujubs.

After having been introduced to the numerous Mongols by whom we found ourselves surrounded, the conversation insensibly turned upon the festival of the Loaves of the Moon. "In our Western Land," said we, "this festival is unknown; men there adore only Jehovah, the Creator of the heavens, and of the earth, of the sun, of the moon, and of all that exists." "Oh, what a holy doctrine!" exclaimed the old man, raising his clasped hands to his forehead; "the Tartars themselves, for that matter, do not worship the moon; but seeing that the Chinese celebrate this festival, they follow the custom without very well knowing why." "You say truly; you do not, indeed, know why you celebrate this festival. That is what we heard in the land of the Kitat. But do you know why the Kitat celebrate it?" and thereupon we related to these Mongols what we knew of the terrible massacre of their anceftors. Upon the completion of our narrative, we saw the faces of all our audiences full of aftonishment. The young men whispered to one another; the old man preserved a mournful silence his head bent down, and big tears flowing from his eyes. " Brother rich in years," said we, " this ftory does not seem to surprise you as it does your young men, but it fills your heart with emotion." " Holy personages," replied the elder, raising his head, and wiping away the tears with the back of his hand, "the terrible event which occasions such confternation in the minds of my young men was not unknown to me, but I would I had never heard of it, and I always ftruggle againft its recollection, for it brings the hot blood into the forehead of every Tartar, whose heart is not sold to the Kitat. A day known to our great Lamas will come, when the blood of our fathers, so shamefully assassinated, will at length be avenged. When the holy man who is to lead us to vengeance shall appear, every one of us will rise and follow in his train; then we shall march, in the face of day, and require from the Kitat an account of the Tartar blood which they shed in the silence and dark secrecy of their houses. The Mongols celebrate every year this feftival, moft of them seeing in it merely an indifferent ceremony; but the Loaves of the Moon-day ever recalls, in the hearts of a few amongst us, the memory of the treachery to which our fathers fell victims, and the hope of juft vengeance."

After a brief silence, the old man went on: " Holy personages, whatever may be the associations of this day, in other respects it is truly a feftival for us, since you have deigned to enter our poor habitation. Let us not further occupy our breafts with sad thoughts. Child," said he to a young man seated on the threshold of the tent, " if the mutton is boiled enough, clear away these things." This command having been executed, the eldeſt son of the family entered, bearing in both hands a small oblong table, on which was a boiled sheep, cut into four quarters, heaped one on the other. The family being assembled round the table, the chief drew a knife from his girdle, severed the sheep's tail, and divided into it two equal pieces, which he placed before us.

With the Tartars the tail is considered the moſt delicious portion of their sheep, and accordingly the moſt honourable. These tails of the Tartarian sheep are of immense size and weight, the fat upon them alone weighing from six to eight pounds.

The fat and juicy tail having thus been offered a homage to the two ſtranger gueſts, the reſt of the company, knife in hand, attacked the four quarters of the animal, and had speedily, each man, a huge piece before him. Plate or fork there was none, the knees supplied the absence of the one, the hands of the other, the flowing grease being wiped off, from time to time, upon the front of the jacket. Our own embarrassment was extreme. That great white mass of fat had been given to us with the beſt intentions, but, not quite clear of European prejudices, we could not make up our ſtomachs to venture, without bread or salt, upon the lumps of tallow that quivered in our hands. We briefly consulted, in our native tongue, as to what on earth was to be done under these distressing circumſtances. Furtively to replace the horrible masses upon the table would be imprudent; openly to express to our Amphytrion our repugnance to this *par excellence* Tartarian delicacy, was impossible, as wholly opposed to Tartar etiquette. We devised this plan: we cut the villainous tail into numerous pieces, and insisted, in that day of general rejoicing, upon the company's partaking with us of this precious dish. There was infinite reluctance to deprive us of the treat; but we persisted, and by degrees got entirely clear of the abominable mess, ourselves rejoicing, instead, in a cut from the leg, the savour of which was more agreeable to our early training. The Homeric repast completed, a heap of polished bones alone remaining to recall it, a boy, taking from the goat's-horn on which it hung a rude three-stringed violin, presented it to the chief, who, in his turn handed it to the young man of modest mien, whose eyes lighted up as he received the instrument. "Noble and holy travellers," said the chief, "I have invited a *Toolholos* [*toolholos* (= *da'ulgachi, dôlgachi*)] to embellish this entertainment with some recitations." The minstrel was already preluding with his fingers upon the strings of his instrument. Presently he began to sing, in a strong, emphatic voice, at times interweaving with his verses recitations full of fire and animation. It was interesting to see all those Tartar faces bent towards the minstrel, and accompanying the meaning of his words with the movements of their features. The *Toolholos* selected, for his subjects, national traditions, which warmly excited the feelings of his audience. As to ourselves, very slightly acquainted with the history of Tartary, we took small interest in all those illustrious unknown, whom the Mongol rhapsodist marshalled over the scene.

When he had sung for some time, the old man presented to him a large cup of milk-wine. The minstrel placed his instrument upon his knees, and with evident relish proceeded to moisten his throat, parched with the infinitude of marvels he had been relating. While, having finished his draught, he was licking the brim of his cup: "*Toolholos*," said we, "the songs you have sung were all excellent. But you have as yet said nothing about the Immortal Tamerlane: the 'Invocation to Timour [Timur]', we have heard, is a famous song, dear to the Mongols."

"Yes, yes," exclaimed several voices, "sing us the 'Invocation to Timour.'" There was a moment's silence, and then the *Toolholos*, having refreshed his memory, sang, in a vigorous and warlike tone, the following ſtrophes :

"When the divine Timour dwelt within our tents, the Mongol nation was redoubtable and warlike ; its leaſt movements made the earth bend ; its mere look froze with fear the ten thousand peoples upon whom the sun shines.

"O divine Timour, will thy great soul soon revive ?
Return ! return ! we await thee, O Timour !

"We live in our vaſt plains, tranquil and peaceful as sheep ; yet our hearts are fervent and full of life. The memory of the glorious age of Timour is ever present to our minds. Where is the chief who is to place himself at our head, and render us once more great warriors ?

"O divine Timour, will thy great soul soon revive ?
Return ! return ! we await thee, O Timour !

"The young Mongol has arms wherewith to quell the wild horse, eyes wherewith he sees afar off in the desert the traces of the loſt camel. Alas ! his arms can no longer bend the bow of his anceſtors ; his eye cannot see the wiles of the enemy.

"O divine Timour, will thy great soul soon revive ?
Return ! return ! we await thee, O Timour !

"We have burned the sweet smelling wood at the feet of the divine Timour, our foreheads bent to the earth ; we have offered him the green leaf of tea and the milk of our herds. We are ready; the Mongols are on foot, O Timour ! And do thou, O Lama, send down good fortune upon our arrows and our lances.

"O divine Timour, will thy great soul soon revive ?
Return ! return ! we await thee, O Timour !"

When the Tartar troubadour had completed his national song, he rose, made a low bow to the company, and, having suspended his inſtrument upon a wooden pin, took his leave. "Our neighbours," said the old man, "are also keeping the feſtival, and expect the *Toolholos* : but, since you seem to liſten with intereſt to Tartar songs, we will offer some other melodies to your notice. We have in our family a brother who has in his memory a great number of airs, cherished by the Mongols; but, he cannot play; he is not a *Toolholos*. Come, brother Nymbo [Nimbo], sing; you have not got Lamas of the Weſt to liſten to you every day."

A Mongol, whom, seated as he was in a corner, we had not before noticed, at once rose, and took the place of the departed *Toolholos*. The appearance of this personage was truly remarkable; his neck was completely buried in his enormous shoulders; his great dull staring eyes contraſted ſtrangely with his dark face, half-calcined as it were by the sun; his hair, or rather a coarse uncombed mane, ſtraggling down his back, completed the savageness of his aſpect. He began to sing: but his singing was a mere counterfeit, an absurd parody. His grand quality was extreme long-windedness, which enabled him to execute roulades, complicated and continuous enough to throw any rational audience into fits. We soon became desperately tired of his noise, and watched with impatience a moment's cessation, that might give us an opportunity of retiring. But this was no easy matter; the villain divined our thoughts, and was resolved to spite us. No sooner had he finished one air than he dovetailed another into it, and so ſtarted afresh. In this way he went on, until it was really quite late in the night. At length he paused for a moment to drink a cup of tea; he threw the beverage down his throat, and was juſt clearing his throat to commence anew, when we ſtarted up, offered to the head of the family a pinch of snuff, and, having saluted the reſt of the company, withdrew.

You often meet in Tartary these *Toolholos*, or wandering singers, who go about from tent to tent celebrating in their melodies national events and personages. They are generally very poor; a violin and a flute, suspended from the girdle, are their only property; but they are always received by the Mongol families with kindness and honour; they often remain in one tent for several days, and on their departure are supplied with cheese, wine, tea, and so on, to support them on their way. These poet-singers, who remind us of the minstrels and rhapsodists of Greece, are also very numerous in China: but they are probably nowhere so numerous or so popular as in Thibet.

The day after the festival the sun had scarcely risen, when a little boy presented himself at the entrance of our tent, carrying in one hand a wooden vessel full of milk, and in the other hand a rude rush basket, in which were some new cheese and some butter. He was followed soon after by an old Lama, attended by a Tartar who had on his shoulder a large bag of fuel. We invited them all to be seated. "Brothers of the West," said the Lama, "accept these trifling presents from my master." We bowed in token of thanks, and Samdadchiemba hastened to prepare some tea, which we pressed the Lama to stay and partake of. "I will come and see you this evening," said he; "but I cannot remain at present; for I have not set my pupil the prayer he has to learn this morning." The pupil in question was the little boy who had brought the milk. The old man then took his pupil by the hand, and they returned together to their tent.

The old Lama was the preceptor of the family, and his function consisted in directing the little boy in the study of the Thibetian prayers. The education of the Tartars is very limited. They who shave the head, the Lamas, are, as a general rule, the only persons who learn to read and pray. There is no such thing throughout the country as a public school. With the exception of a few rich Mongols, who have their children taught at home, all the young Lamas are obliged to resort to the Lamaseries, wherein is concentrated all that exists in Tartary of arts, of sciences, or intellectual industry. The Lama is not merely a priest; he is the painter, poet, sculptor, architect, physician; the head, heart, and oracle of the laity. The training of the young Mongols, who do not resort to the Lamaseries, is limited, with the men, to perfecting the use of the bow and arrow and matchlock, and to their obtaining a thorough mastery of equestrianism. When a mere infant, the Mongol is weaned, and as soon as he is strong enough he is stuck upon a horse's back behind a man, the animal is put to a gallop, and the juvenile rider, in order not to fall off, has to cling with both hands to his teacher's jacket. The Tartars thus become accustomed, at a very early age, to the movements of the horse, and by degrees and the force of habit, they identify themselves, as it were, with the animal.

There is, perhaps, no spectacle more exciting than that of Mongol riders in chase of a wild horse. They are armed with a long, heavy pole, at the end of which is a running knot. They gallop, they fly after the horse they are pursuing down rugged ravines, and up precipitous hills, in and out twisting and twining in their rapid course, until they come up with their game. They then take the bridle of their own horse in their teeth, seize with both hands their heavy pole, and bending forward throw, by a powerful effort, the running knot round the wild horse's neck. In this exercise the greatest vigour must be combined with the greatest dexterity, in order to enable them to stop short the powerful untamed animals with which they have to deal. It sometimes happens that pole and cord are broken; but as to a horseman being thrown, it is an occurrence we never saw or heard of.

TRAVELS IN TARTARY,

The Mongol is so accuſtomed to horseback that he is altogether like a fish out of water when he sets foot on the ground. His ſtep is heavy and awkward; and his bowed legs, his cheſt bent forward, his conſtant looking around him, all indicate a person who spends the greater portion of is time on the back of a horse or a camel.

When night overtakes the travelling Tartar, it often happens that he will not even take the trouble to alight for the purpose of repose. Ask people whom you meet in the desert where they slept laſt night, and you will as frequently as not have for answer, in a melancholy tone, " *Temên dêro* [*temên dêre*] " " on the camel." It is a singular speƈtacle to see caravans halting at noon, when they come to a rich paſturage. The camels disperse in all direƈtions, browsing upon the high grass of the prairie, while the Tartars, aſtride between the two humps of the animal, sleep as profoundly as though they were sheltered in a good bed.

This incessant activity, this conſtant travelling, contributes to render the Tartars very vigorous, and capable of supporting the moſt terrible cold, without appearing to be in the leaſt affeƈted by it. In the deserts of Tartary, and especially in the country of the Khalkhas, the cold is so intense, that for a considerable portion of the winter the thermometer will not aƈt, on account of the congelation of the mercury. The whole diſtriƈt is often covered with snow; and if at these times the south-weſt wind blows, the plain wears the aspeƈt of a raging sea. The wind raises the snow in immense waves, and impels the gigantic avalanches vehemently before it. Then the Tartars hurry courageously to the aid of their herds and flocks, and you see them dashing in all direƈtions, exciting the animals by their cries, and driving them to the shelter of some rock or mountain. Sometimes these intrepid shepherds ſtop short amid

THIBET, AND CHINA

the tempeſt, and ſtand erect for a time, as if defying the cold and the fury of the elements.

The training of the Tartar women is not more refined than that of the men. They are not, indeed, taught the use of the bow and the matchlock; but in equitation they are as expert and as fearless as the men. Yet it is only on occasions that they mount on horseback; such, for example, as travelling, or when there is no man at home to go in search of a ſtray animal. As a general rule, they have nothing to do with the care of the herds and flocks.

Their chief occupation is to prepare the family meals, and to make the family clothes. They are perfect miſtresses of the needle; it is they who fabricate the hats, boots, coats, and other portions of the Mongol attire. The leather boots, for example, which they make are not indeed very elegant in form, but, on the other hand, their solidity is aſtonishing.

It is quite unintelligible to us how, with implements so rude and coarse as theirs, they could manufacture articles almoſt indeſtructible in their quality. It is true, they take their time about them, and get on very slowly with their work. The Tartar women excel in embroidery, which, for taſte and variety of pattern and for excellence of manipulation, excited our aſtonishment. We think we may venture to say, that nowhere in France would you meet with embroidery more beautiful and more perfect in fabric than that we have seen in Tartary.

The Tartars do not use the needle in the same way as the Chinese. In China they impel the needle perpendicularly down and up; whereas the Tartars impel it perpendicularly up and down. In France the manner is different from both; if we recollect right, the French women impel the needle horizontally from right to left. We will not attempt to pronounce as to the respective merit of the three methods; we will leave the point to the decision of the respectable fraternity of tailors.

On the 17th of the moon, we proceeded very early in the morning to the Chinese station of Chaborté, for the purpose of laying in a store of meal. Chaborté, as its Mongol name intimates, is built upon a slough. The houses are all made of mud, and surrounded each by an enclosure of high walls. The streets are irregular, tortuous and narrow; the aspect of the whole town is sombre and sinister, and the Chinese who inhabit it have, if possible, a more knavish look than their countrymen anywhere else. The trade of the town comprehends all the articles in ordinary use with the Mongols—oatmeal and millet, cotton manufactures, and brick tea, which the Tartars receive in exchange for the products of the desert, salt, mushrooms, and furs. Upon our return, we hastened to prepare for our departure. While we were packing up our baggage in the tent, Samdadchiemba went in search of the animals which had been put to pasture in the vicinity. A moment afterwards he returned with the three camels. "There are the camels," said we, with gloomy anticipation, "but where are the horse and the mule; they were both at hand just now, for we tied their legs to prevent them straying." "They are stolen, in all probability. It never does to encamp too near the Chinese, whom everybody knows to be arrant horse stealers." These words came upon us like a clap of thunder. However, it was not a moment for sterile lamentation; it was necessary to go in search of the thieves. We each mounted a camel and made a circuit in seach of the animals, leaving our tent under the charge of Arsalan. Our search being futile, we resolved to proceed to the Mongol encampment, and inform them that the animals had been lost near their habitation.

By a law among the Tartars, when animals are lost

from a caravan, the persons occupying the nearest encampment are bound either to find them or to replace them. It seems, no doubt, very strange to European views, because, without their consent or even knowledge, without being in the smallest degree known to them, you have chosen to pitch your tent near those of a Mongol party, you and your animals, and your baggage, are to be under their responsibility; but so it is. If a thing disappears, the law supposes that your next neighbour is the thief, or at all events an accomplice. This it is which has contributed to render the Mongols so skilful in tracking animals. A mere glance at the slight traces left by an animal upon the grass, suffices to inform the Mongol pursuer how long since it passed, and whether or not it bore a rider; and the track once found, they follow it throughout all its meanderings, however complicated.

We had no sooner explained our loss to the Mongol chief, than he said to us cheerfully: " Sirs Lamas, do not permit sorrow to invade your hearts. Your animals cannot be lost; in these plains there are neither robbers nor associates of robbers. I will send in quest of your horses. If we do not find them, you may select what others you please in their place, from our herd. We would have you leave this place as happy as you came into it." While he was speaking eight of his people mounted on horseback and dashed off in as many directions, upon the quest, each man trailing after him his lasso, attached to the long, flexible pole we have described. After a while they all collected in one body, and galloped away, as hard as they could, towards the town. " They are on the track now, holy sirs," said the chief, who was watching their movements by our sides " and you will have your horses back very soon. Meanwhile, come within my tent, and drink some tea."

In about two hours a boy appeared at the entrance of the tent, and announced the return of the horsemen. We hastened outside, and in the track which we had pursued saw something amid a cloud of dust which seemed horsemen galloping like the wind. We presently discovered the eight Tartars, dashing along, like so many mad centaurs, our stray animals, each held by a lasso, in the midst of them. On their arrival, they alighted, and with an air of satisfaction said : " We told you nothing was ever lost in our country." We thanked the generous Mongols for the great service they had rendered us; and, bidding adieu to them, saddled our horses, and departed on our way to the Blue City.

On the third day we came, in the solitude, upon an imposing and majestic monument of antiquity—a large city utterly abandoned. Its turreted ramparts, its watch towers, its four great gates, facing the four cardinal points, were all there perfect, in preservation, except that, besides being three-fourths buried in the soil, they were covered with a thick coating of turf. Arrived opposite the southern gate, we directed Samdadchiemba to proceed quietly with the animals, while we paid a visit to the Old Town, as the Tartars designate it. Our impression, as we entered the vast enclosure, was one of mingled awe and sadness. There were no ruins of any sort to be seen, but only the outline of a large and fine town, becoming absorbed below by gradual accumulations of wind-borne soil, and above by a winding sheet of turf. The arrangements of the streets and the position of the principal edifices, were indicated by the inequalities of ground. The only living things we found here were a young Mongol shepherd, silently smoking his pipe, and the flock of goats he tended. We questioned the former as to when the city was built, by whom, when abandoned, and why ? We might as well have interrogated his goats; he knew no more than that the place was called the Old Town.

Such remains of ancient cities are of no unfrequent occurrence in the deserts of Mongolia; but everything connected with their origin and history is buried in darkness. Oh, with what sadness does such a spectacle fill the soul! The ruins of Greece, the superb remains of Egypt,—all these, it is true, tell of death; all belong to the past; yet when you gaze upon them, you know what they are; you can retrace, in memory, the revolutions which have occasioned the ruins and the decay of the country around them. Descend into the tomb, wherein was buried alive the city of Herculaneum,—you find there, it is true, a gigantic skeleton, but you have within you historical associations wherewith to galvanize it. But of these old abandoned cities of Tartary, not a tradition remains; they are tombs without an epitaph, amid solitude and silence, uninterrupted except when the wandering Tartars halt, for a while, within the ruined enclosures, because there the pastures are richer and more abundant.

Although, however, nothing positive can be stated respecting these remains, the probabilities are that they date no earlier back than the thirteenth century, the period when the Mongols rendered themselves masters of the Chinese empire, of which they retained possession for more than one hundred years. During their domination, say the Chinese annals, they erected in Northern Tartary many large and powerful cities. Towards the middle of the fourteenth century the Mongol dynasty was expelled from China; the Emperor Young-Lo [Yung-lo], who desired to exterminate the Tartars, invaded their country, and burned their towns, making no fewer than three expeditions against them into the desert, 200 leagues north of the Great Wall.

TRAVELS IN TARTARY,

After leaving behind us the Old Town, we came to a broad road crossing N.S. that a long which we were travelling E.W. This road, the ordinary route of the Russian embassies to Peking, is called by the Tartars Koutcheou-Dcham [Kinju-jam] "Road of the Emperor's Daughter," because it was constructed for the passage of a princess, whom one of the Celestial Emperors bestowed upon a King of the Khalkhas. After traversing the Tchakar and Western Souniot, it enters the country of the Khalkhas by the kingdom of Mourguevan; thence crossing N.S. the great desert of Gobi, it traverses the river Toula [Tula], near the Great Kouren [Great Kürên], and terminates with the Russian factories at *Kiaktha*.

This town, under a treaty of peace in 1688 between the Emperor Khang-Hi, and the White Khan [Man] of the Oros, i.e. the Czar of Russia, was established as the entrepôt of the trade between the two countries. Its northern portion is occupied by the Russian factories, its southern by the Tartaro-Chinese. The intermediate space is a neutral ground, devoted to the purposes of commerce. The Russians are not permitted to enter the Chinese quarter, nor the Chinese the Russian. The commerce of the town is considerable, and apparently very beneficial to both parties. The Russians bring linen goods, cloths, velvets, soaps and hardware; the Chinese tea in bricks, of which the Russians use large quantities; and these Chinese tea-bricks being taken in payment of the Russian goods at an easy rate, linen goods are sold in China at a lower rate than even in Europe itself. It is owing to their ignorance of this commerce of Russia with China that speculators at Canton so frequently find no market for their commodities.

Under another treaty of peace between the two powers, signed 14th of June, 1728, by Count Vladislavitch, Ambassador Extraordinary of Russia, on the one part, and by the Minister of the Court of Peking on the other, the Russian government maintains, in the capital of the celestial empire, a monastery, to which is attached a school, wherein a certain number of young Russians qualify themselves as Chinese and Tartar-Mantchou interpreters. Every ten years, the pupils, having completed their studies, return with their spiritual pastors of the monastery to St. Petersburg, and are relieved by a new settlement. The little caravan is commanded by a Russian officer, who has it in charge to conduct the new disciples to Peking, and bring back the students and the members who have completed their period. From Kiaktha to Peking the Russians travel at the expense of the Chinese government, and are escorted from station to station by Tartar troops.

M. Timkouski, who in 1820 had charge of the Russian caravan to Peking, tells us, in his account of the journey, that he could never make out why the Chinese guides led him by a different route from that which the preceding ambassadors had pursued. The Tartars explained the matter to us. They said it was a political precaution of the Chinese government, who conceived that, being taken by all sorts of roundabout paths and no-paths, the Russians might be kept from a knowledge of the regular route;—an immensely imbecile precaution, since the Autocrat of all the Russians would not have the slightest difficulty in leading his armies to Peking, should he ever take a fancy to go and beard the Son of Heaven in his celestial seat.

This road to Kiaktha, which we thus came upon unexpectedly amid the deserts of Tartary, created a deep emotion in our hearts: "Here," said we to each other, "here is a road which leads to Europe!" Our native land presented itself before our imagination, and we spontaneously entered upon the road, which connected us with our beloved France. The conversation that rose to our lips from our hearts was so pleasing, that we insensibly advanced. The sight of some Mongol tents, on an adjacent eminence, recalled us to a sense of our position, and at the same moment a loud cry came from a Tartar whom we saw gesticulating in front of the tents. Not understanding the cry to be addressed to us, we turned, and were proceeding on our route, when the Tartar, jumping on his horse, galloped after us; upon reaching us, he alighted and knelt before us: "Holy sirs," said he, raising his hands before Heaven, "have pity upon me, and save my mother from death. I know your power is infinite: come and preserve my mother by your prayers." The parable of the good Samaritan came before us, and we felt that charity forbade us to pass on without doing all we could in the matter. We therefore turned once more, in order to encamp near the Tartars.

While Samdadchiemba arranged our tent, we went, without loss of time, to tend the sick woman, whom we found in a very deplorable state. "Inhabitants of the desert," said we to her friends, "we know not the use of simples, we are unacquainted with the secrets of life, but we will pray to Jehovah for this sick person. You have not heard of this Almighty God—your Lamas know him not: but, be assured, Jehovah is the master of life and of death." Circumstances did not permit us to dwell on the theme to these poor people, who, absorbed in grief and anxiety, could pay little attention to our words. We returned to our tent to pray, the Tartar accompanying us. When he saw our Breviary: "Are these," asked he, "the all-powerful prayers to Jehovah, of which you spoke?" "Yes," said we; "these are the only true prayers; the only prayers that can save." Thereupon he prostrated himself successively before each of us, touching the ground with his forehead; then he took the Breviary, and raised it to his head in token of respect. During our recitation of prayers for the sick, the Tartar remained seated at the entrance of the tent, preserving a profound and religious silence. When he had finished, " Holy men," said he, again prostrating himself, " how can I make acknowledgments for your great benefits? I am poor; I can offer you neither horse nor sheep." " Mongol brother," we replied, " the priests of Jehovah may not offer up prayers for the sake of enriching themselves; since thou art not rich, accept from us this trifling gift;" and we presented to him a fragment of a tea-brick. The Tartar was profoundly moved with this proceeding; he could not say a word, his only answer to us was tears of gratitude.

We heard next morning with pleasure that the Tartar woman was much better. We would fain have remained a few days in the place in order to cultivate the germ of the true faith thus planted in the bosom of this family; but we were compelled to proceed. Some of the Tartars escorted us a short distance on our way.

Medicine in Tartary, as we have already observed, is exclusively practised by the Lamas. When illness attacks anyone, his friends run to the nearest monastery for a Lama, whose first proceeding, upon visiting the patient, is to run his fingers over the pulse of both wrists simultaneously, as the fingers of a musician run over the strings of an instrument. The Chinese physicians feel both pulses also, but in succession. After due deliberation, the Lama pronounces his opinion as to the particular nature of the malady. According to the religious belief of the Tartars, all illness is owing to the visitation of a *Tchutgour* [*jetker*], or demon; but the expulsion of the demon is first a matter of medicine. The Lama physician next proceeds, as Lama apothecary, to give the specific befitting the case; the Tartar pharmacopœia rejecting all mineral chemistry, the Lama remedies consist entirely of vegetables pulverised, and either infused in water, or made up into pills. If the Lama doctor happens not to have any medicine with him, he is by no means disconcerted; he writes the names of the remedies upon little scraps of paper, moistens the papers with his saliva, and rolls them up into pills, which the patient tosses down with the same perfect confidence as though they were genuine medicaments. To swallow the name of a remedy, or the remedy itself, say the Tartars, comes to precisely the same thing.

The medical assault of the usurping demon being applied, the Lama next proceeds to spiritual artillery, in the form of prayers, adapted to the quality of the demon who has to be dislodged. If the patient is poor, the *Tchutgour* visiting him can evidently be only an inferior *Tchutgour*, requiring merely a brief, off-hand prayer, sometimes merely an interjectional exorcism. If the patient is very poor, the Lama troubles himself with neither prayer nor pill, but goes away, recommending the friends to wait with patience until the sick person gets better or dies, according to the decree of Hormoustha [Khormusta]. But where the patient is rich, the possessor of large flocks, the proceedings are altogether different. First, it is obvious that a devil who presumes to visit so eminent a personage must be a potent devil, one of the chiefs of the lower world; and it would not be decent for a great *Tchutgour* to travel like a mere sprite; the family, accordingly, are directed to prepare for him a handsome suit of clothes, a pair of rich boots, a fine horse, ready saddled and bridled, otherwise the devil will never think of going, physic or exorcise him how you may. It is even possible, indeed, that one horse will not suffice, for the demon, in very rich cases, may turn out, upon enquiry, to be so high and mighty a prince, that he has with him a number of courtiers and attendants, all of whom have to be provided with horses.

Everything being arranged, the ceremony commences. The Lama and numerous co-physicians called in from his own and other adjacent monasteries, offer up prayers in the rich man's tents for a week or a fortnight, until they perceive that the devil is gone—that is to say, until they have exhausted all the disposable tea and sheep. If the patient recovers, it is clear proof that the prayers have been efficaciously recited; if he dies, it is still greater proof of the efficaciousness of the prayers, for not only is the devil gone, but the patient has transmigrated to a state far better than that he has quitted.

The prayers recited by the Lamas for the recovery of the sick are sometimes accompanied with very dismal and alarming rites. The aunt of Tokoura [Tokura], chief of an encampment in the Valley of Dark Waters, visited by M. Huc, was seized one evening with an intermittent fever. "I would invite the attendance of the doctor Lama," said Tokoura, "but if he finds that there is a very big *Tchutgour* present, the expenses will ruin me." He waited for some days; but as his aunt grew worse and worse, he at last sent for a Lama; his anticipations were confirmed. The Lama pronounced that a demon of considerable rank was present, and that no time must be lost in expelling him. Eight other Lamas were forthwith called in, who at once set about the construction, in dried herbs, of a great puppet, which they entitled the Demon of Intermittent Fevers, and which, when completed, they placed on its legs by means of a stick, in the patient's tent.

The ceremony began at eleven o'clock at night; the Lamas ranged themselves in a semi-circle round the upper portion of the tent, with cymbals, seashells, bells, tambourines, and other instruments of the noisy Tartar music. The remainder of the circle was completed by members of the family, squatting on the ground close to one another, the patient kneeling, or rather crouched on her heels, opposite the Demon of Intermittent Fevers. The Lama doctor-in-chief had before him a large copper basin filled with millet, and some little images made of paste. The dung-fuel threw, amid much smoke, a fantastic and quivering light over the strange scene.

Upon a given signal, the clerical orchestra executed an overture harsh enough to frighten Satan himself, the lay congregation beating time with their hands to the charivari of clanging instruments and ear-splitting voices. The diabolical concert over, the Grand Lama opened the Book of Exorcisms, which he rested on his knees. As he chanted one of the forms, he took from the basin, from time to time, a handful of millet, which he threw east, west, north and south, according to the rubric. The tones of his voice, as he prayed, were sometimes mournful and suppressed, sometimes vehemently loud and energetic. All of a sudden, he would quit the regular cadence of prayer, and have an outburst of apparently indomitable rage, abusing the herb puppet with fierce invectives and furious gestures. The exorcism terminated, he gave a signal by stretching out his arms, right and left, and the other Lamas struck up a tremendously noisy chorus, in hurried, dashing tones; all the instruments were set to work, and meantime the lay congregation, having started up with one accord, ran out of the tent, one after the other, and tearing round it like mad people, beat it at their hardest with sticks, yelling all the while at the pitch of their voices in a manner to make ordinary hair stand on end. Having thrice performed this demoniac round, they re-entered the tent as precipitately as they had quitted it, and resumed their seats. Then, all the others covering their faces with their hands, the Grand Lama rose and set fire to the herb figure. As soon as the flames rose, he uttered a loud cry, which was repeated with interest by the rest of the company. The laity immediately rose, seized the burning figure, carried it into the plain, away from the tents, and there, as it consumed, anathematized it with all sorts of imprecations; the Lamas meantime squatted in the tent, tranquilly chanting their prayers in a grave, solemn tone.

Upon the return of the family from their valorous expedition, the praying was exchanged for joyous felicitations. By-and-by, each person provided with a lighted torch, the whole party rushed simultaneously from the tent, and formed into a procession, the laymen first, then the patient, supported on either side by a member of the family, and lastly, the nine Lamas, making night hideous with their music. In this style the patient was conducted to another tent, pursuant to the orders of the Lama, who had declared that she must absent herself from her own habitation for an entire month.

After this strange treatment, the malady did not return. The probability is, that the Lamas, having ascertained the precise moment at which the fever-fit would recur, met it at the exact point of time by this tremendous counter-excitement, and overcame it.

Though the majority of the Lamas seek to foster the ignorant credulity of the Tartars, in order to turn it to their own profit, we have met some of them who frankly avowed that duplicity and imposture played a considerable part in all their ceremonies. The superior of a Lamasery said to us one day: " When a person is ill, the recitation of prayers is proper, for Buddha is the master of life and death; it is he who rules the transmigration of beings. To take remedies is also fitting, for the great virtue of medicinal herbs also comes to us from Buddha. That the Evil One may possess a rich person is credible, but that, in order to repel the Evil One, the way is to give him dress, and a horse, and what not, this is a fiction invented by ignorant and deceiving Lamas, who desire to accumulate wealth at the expense of their brothers."

The manner of interring the dead among the Tartars is not uniform. The Lamas are only called in to assist at extremely grand funerals. Towards the Great Wall, where the Mongols are mixed up with the Chinese, the custom of the latter in this particular, as in others, has insensibly prevailed. There the corpse is placed, after the Chinese fashion, in a coffin, and the coffin in a grave. In the desert, among the true nomadic tribes, the entire ceremony consists in conveying the dead to the tops of hills or the bottoms of ravines, there to be devoured by the birds and beasts of prey. It is really horrible to travellers through the deserts of Tartary to see, as they constantly do, human remains, for which the eagles and the wolves are contending.

The richer Tartars sometimes burn their dead with great solemnity. A large furnace of earth is constructed in a pyramidical form. Just before it is completed, the body is placed inside, standing, surrounded with combustibles. The edifice is then completely covered in, with the exception of a small hole at the bottom to admit fire, and another at the top to give egress to the smoke, and keep up a current of air. During the combustion, the Lamas surround the tomb and recite prayers. The corpse being burnt, they demolish the furnace and remove the bones, which they carry to the Grand Lama; he reduces them to a very fine powder, and having added to them an equal quantity of meal, he kneads the whole with care, and constructs, with his own hands, cakes of different sizes, which he places one upon the other, in the form of a pyramid. When the bones have been thus prepared by the Grand Lama, they are transported with great pomp to a little tower built beforehand, in a place indicated by the diviner.

They almost always give to the ashes of the Lamas a sepulture of this description. You meet with a great number of these monumental towers on the summits of the mountains, and in the neighbourhood of the Lamaseries; and you may find them in countries whence the Mongols have been driven by the Chinese. In other respects these countries scarcely retain any trace of the Tartars: the Lamaseries, the pasturages, the shepherds, with their tents and flocks, all have disappeared, to make room for new people, new monuments, new customs. A few small towers raised over graves alone remain there, as if to assert the rights of the ancient possessors of these lands, and to protest against the invasion of the Kitat.

The most celebrated seat of Mongol burials is in the province of Chan-Si, at the famous Lamasery of Five Towers (Ou-Tay) [Wu-t'ai]. According to the Tartars, the Lamasery of the Five Towers is the best place you can be buried in. The ground in it is so holy, that those who are so fortunate as to be interred there are certain of a happy transmigration thence. The marvellous sanctity of this place is attributed to the the presence of Buddha, who for some centuries past has taken up his abode there in the interior of a mountain. In 1842 the noble Tokoura, of whom we have already had occasion to speak, conveying the bones of his father and mother to the Five Towers, had the infinite happiness to behold there the venerable Buddha. " Behind the great monastery," he told us, " there is a very lofty mountain, which you must climb by creeping on your hands and feet. Just towards the summit you come to a portico cut in the rock: you lie down on the earth, and look through a small aperture not larger than the bowl of a pipe. It is some time before you can distinguish anything, but by degrees your eye gets used to the place, and you have the happiness of beholding, at length, in the depths of the mountains, the face of the ancient Buddha. He is seated cross-legged, doing nothing. There are around him Lamas of all countries, who are continually paying homage to him."

Whatever you may think of Tokoura's narrative, it is certain that the Tartars and the Thibetians have given themselves up to an inconceivable degree of fanaticism, in reference to the Lamasery of the Five Towers. You frequently meet, in the deserts of Tartary, Mongols carrying on their shoulders the bones of their parents, to the Five Towers, to purchase, almost at its weight in gold, a few feet of earth, whereon they may raise a small mausoleum. Even the Mongols of Torgot [Turgût] perform journeys occupying a whole year, and attended with immense difficulty, to visit for this purpose the province of Chan-Si.

The Tartar kings sometimes make use of a sepulture which is the height of extravagance and barbarism. The royal corpse is conveyed to a vast edifice, constructed of bricks, and adorned with numerous statues representing men, lions, elephants, tigers, and various subjects of Buddhic mythology. With the illustrious defunct, they bury in a large cavern, constructed in the centre of the building, large sums of gold and silver, royal robes, precious stones, in short, everything which he may need in another life. These monstrous interments sometimes cost the lives of a great number of slaves. They take children of both sexes, remarkable for their beauty, and make them swallow mercury till they are suffocated; in this way they preserve, they say, the freshness and ruddiness of their countenance, so as to make them appear still alive.

THIBET, AND CHINA

These unfortunate victims are placed upright, round the corpse of their master, continuing in this fashion to serve him as during life. They hold in their hands the pipe, fan, the small phial of snuff, and the numerous other nick-nacks of the Tartar kings.

To protect these buried treasures, they place in the cavern a kind of bow, capable of discharging a number of arrows, one after the other. This bow, or rather these several bows joined together, are all bent, and the arrows ready to fly. They place this infernal machine in such a manner that, on opening the door of the cavern, the movement causes the discharge of the first arrow at the man who enters; the discharge of the first arrow causes the discharge of the second, and and so on to the last—so that the unlucky person, whom covetousness or curiosity should induce to open the door, would fall, pierced with many arrows, in the tomb he sought to profane. They sell these murderous machines, ready prepared by the bow-makers. The Chinese sometimes purchase them, to guard their houses in their absence.

After a march of two days we entered the district called the Kingdom of Efe [Efu]; it is a portion of the territory of the Eight Banners, which the Emperor Kien-Loung [Ch'ien-lung] dismembered in favour of a prince of the Khalkhas. Chun-Tche [Shun-chih] founder of the Mantchou dynasty, laid down this maxim: "In the south, establish no kings; in the north, interrupt no alliances." This policy has ever since been exactly pursued by the court of Peking. The Emperor Kien-Loung, in order to attach to his dynasty the prince in question, gave him his daughter in marriage, hoping by this means to fix him at Peking, and thus to weaken the still dreaded power of the Khalkhas sovereigns. He built for him, within the circuit of the Yellow Town itself, a large and magnificent palace, but the Mongol prince could not adapt or reconcile himself to the stiff arbitrary etiquette of a court. Amid the pomp and luxury accumulated for his entertainment, he was incessantly absorbed with the thought of his tents and his herds: even the snows and frosts of his country were matters of regret. The attentions of the court being altogether inadequate to the dissipation of his ennui, he began to talk about returning to his prairies in the Khalkhas. On the other hand, his young wife, accustomed to the refinements of the court at Peking, could not bear the idea of spending the rest of her days in the desert, amongst milkmaids and shepherds. The Emperor resorted to a compromise which sufficiently met the wishes of his son-in-law, without too violently disconcerting the feelings of his daughter. He dismembered a portion of the Tchakar, and assigned it to the Mongol prince; he built for him, amid these solitudes, a small but handsome city, and presented to him a hundred families of slaves skilled in the arts and manufactures of China. In this manner, while the young Mantchou princess was enabled to dwell in a city and to have a court, the Mongol prince, on his part, was in a position to enjoy the tranquility of the Land of Grass, and to resume at will the pleasures of nomadic life, in which he had passed his boyhood.

The King of Efe brought with him into his petty dominions a great number of Mongol Khalkhas, who inhabit, under the tent, the country bestowed upon their prince. These Tartars fully maintain the reputation for strength and active vigour which is generally attributed to the men of their nation. They are considered the most powerful wrestlers in southern Mongolia. From their infancy, they are trained to gymnastic exercises, and at the public wrestling matches, celebrated every year at Peking, a great number of these men attend to compete for the prizes, and to sustain the reputation of their country. Yet,

THIBET, AND CHINA

though far superior in strength to the Chinese, they are sometimes thrown by the latter, generally more active, and especially more tricky.

In the great match of 1843, a wrestler of the kingdom of Efe had overthrown all competitors, Tartars and Chinese. His body, of gigantic proportions, was fixed upon legs which seemed immovable columns; his hands, like great grappling irons, seized his antagonists, raised them, and then hurled them to the ground, almost without effort. No person had been at all able to stand before his prodigious strength, and they were about to assign him the prize, when a Chinese stepped into the ring. He was short, small, meagre, and appeared calculated for no other purpose than to augment the number of the Efeian's victims. He advanced, however, with an air of firm confidence; the Goliath of Efe stretched out his brawny arms to grasp him, when the Chinese, who had his mouth full of water, suddenly discharged the liquid in the giant's face. The Tartar mechanically raised his hands to wipe his eyes, and at the instant, the cunning Chinese rushed in, caught him round the waist, threw him off his balance, and down he went, amid the convulsive laughter of the spectators.

This anecdote was told to us by a Tartar horseman who travelled with us a part of our way through the kingdom of Efe. From time to time he showed us children engaged in wrestling. "This," said he, "is the favourite exercise with all the inhabitants of our kingdom of Efe. We esteem in a man but two things—his being a good horseman and his being a good wrestler." There was one group of youthful wrestlers whom, exercising as they were on the side of our road, we were enabled to watch closely and at leisure; their ardour redoubled when they saw we were looking at them. The tallest of the party, who did not seem more than eight or nine years old, took in his arms one of his companions, nearly his own height, and very fat, and amused himself with tossing him above his head, and catching him again, as you would a ball. He repeated this feat seven or eight times, and at every repetition we trembled for the life of the boy; but the reſt of the children only gambolled about, applauding the success of the performers.

On the 22nd day of the eighth moon, on quitting the petty kingdom of Efe, we ascended a mountain, on the sides of which grew thickets of fir and birch. The sight of these at firſt gave us great pleasure. The deserts of Tartary are in general so monotonously bare, that you cannot fail to experience a pleasurable sensation when you come upon some occasional trees on your way. Our firſt feelings of joy were, however, soon demolished by a sentiment of a very different nature; we were as though frozen with horror, on perceiving at a turn in the mountain, three enormous wolves, that seemed awaiting us with calm intrepidity. At sight of these villainous beaſts we ſtopped suddenly and as it were inſtinctively. After a moment of general ſtupor, Samdadchiemba descended from his mule, and wrung the noses of our camels. The expedient succeeded marvellously; the poor beaſts sent forth such piercing and terrible cries, that the scared wolves dashed off with all speed. Arsalan, who saw them flee, thinking undoubtedly that it was himself they were afraid of, pursued them at the utmoſt speed of his legs; soon the wolves turned round, and our tent-porter would have been infallibly devoured had not M. Gabet rushed to his aid, uttering loud cries, and wringing the nose of his camel; the wolves having taken flight a second time, disappeared without our again thinking of pursuing them.

Although the want of population might seem to abandon the interminable deserts of Tartary to wild beasts, wolves are rarely met with. This arises, no doubt, from the incessant and vindictive warfare which the Mongols wage against them. They pursue them, everywhere, to the death, regarding them as their capital enemy, on account of the great damage they may inflict upon their flocks. The announcement that a wolf has made its appearance in a neighbourhood is for everyone a signal to mount his horse. As there are always near each tent horses ready saddled, in an instant the plain is covered with numerous cavalry, all armed with their long lasso-pole. The wolf in vain flees in every direction: it meets everywhere horsemen who rush upon it. There is no mountain so rugged, or arduous, up which the Tartar horses, agile as goats, cannot pursue it. The horseman who is at length successful in passing round its neck the running knot, gallops off at full speed, dragging the wolf after him to the nearest tent; there they strongly bind its muzzle, so that they may torture it securely; and then, by way of finale, skin it alive, and turn it off. In summer, the wretched brute lives in this condition several days; but in winter, exposed without a skin to the rigours of the season, it dies forthwith, frozen with cold.

Some short time after we had lost sight of our three wolves, we had a singular encounter enough. We saw advancing towards us, on the same road, two chariots each drawn by three oxen. To each chariot were fastened, with great iron chains, twelve dogs of a terrible and ferocious aspect, four on each side, and four behind. These carriages were laden with square boxes, painted red; the drivers sat on the boxes. We could not conjecture what was the nature of the load, on account of which they thought it essential to have this horrible escort of Cerberuses. In accordance with the customs of the country, we could not question them on this point. The slightest indiscretion would have made us pass in their eyes for people actuated by evil intentions. We contented ourselves with asking if we were still very far from the monastery of Tchortchi [Chorchi], where we hoped to arrive that day; but the baying of the dogs, and the clanking of their chains, prevented us from hearing the answer.

As we were going through the hollow of a valley, we remarked on the summit of an elevated mountain before us a long line of objects without motion, and of an indefinite form. By-and-by these objects seemed to resemble a formidable battery of cannons, ranged in line, and the nearer we advanced, the more were we confirmed in this impression. We felt sure that we saw distinctly the wheels of the carriages, the sponge-rods, the mouths of the cannons pointed towards the plain. But how could we bring ourselves to think that an army, with all its train of artillery could be there in the desert, amidst this profound solitude? Giving way to a thousand extravagant conjectures, we hastened our progress, impatient to examine this strange apparition closely. Our illusion was only completely dissipated when we arrived quite at the top of the mountain. What we had taken for a battery of cannons was a long caravan of little Mongol chariots. We laughed at our mistake, but the illusion was not an unnatural one. These small two-wheeled chariots were all standing still on their frames, each laden with a sack of salt, covered with a mat, the ends of which extended beyond the extremities of the sacks so as to resemble exactly the mouths of cannon; the Mongol waggoners were boiling their tea in the open air, whilst their oxen were feeding on the sides of the mountain. The transport of merchandise across the deserts of Tartary, is ordinarily effected, in default of camels, by these small two-wheeled chariots. A few bars of rough wood are the only materials that enter into their construction, and they are so light that a child may lift them with ease. The oxen that draw them, have all a little iron ring passed through their nostrils; to this ring is a cord, which attaches the animal to the preceding chariot; thus, all the carriages from the first to the last are connected together, and form a long uninterrupted line. The Mongol waggoners are generally seated on the oxen, very rarely on the carriage, and scarcely ever on foot. On all the chief roads you meet with these long lines of carriages, and long before you see them, you hear the lugubrious and monotonous sound of the great iron bells, which the oxen carry suspended from their necks.

After drinking a cup of tea with the Mongols whom we had met in the mountain, we proceeded on our way; the sun was on the point of setting, when we set up our tent on the margin of a stream about a hundred yards from the Lamasery of Tchortchi.

CHAPTER IV

ALTHOUGH we had never visited the Lamasery of Tchortchi, we, nevertheless, knew a good deal about it from the information that had been given us. It was here that the young Lama was educated who came to teach M. Gabet the Mongol language, and whose conversion to Christianity gave such great hopes for the propagation of the Gospel among the Tartar tribes. He was twenty-five years of age when he quitted his Lamasery, in 1837; there he had passed fourteen years in the study of Lama books, and had become well acquainted with Mongol and Mantchou literature. He had as yet but a very superficial knowledge of the Thibetian language. His tutor, an old Lama, well educated and much respected, not merely in the Lamasery, but throughout the whole extent of the Yellowish Banner, had cherished great hopes of his disciple; it was, therefore, very reluctantly that he had consented to a temporary separation, which he limited to a month. Before his departure the pupil prostrated himself, according to custom, at the feet of his master, and begged him to consult for him the Book of Oracles. After having turned over some leaves of a Thibetian book, the old Lama addressed to him these words: "For fourteen years thou hast remained by thy master's side like a faithful *Chabi* [*shabi*] "disciple." Now, for the first time, thou art about to go from me. The future fills me with anxiety; be careful then to return at the appointed time. If thy absence is prolonged beyond one moon thy destiny condemns thee never more to set foot in our holy

THIBET, AND CHINA

Lamasery." The youthful pupil departed, resolved to obey to the letter the instructions of his tutor.

When he arrived at our mission of Si-Wan M. Gabet chose, as the subject of his Mongol studies, an historical summary of the Christian religion. The oral and written conferences lasted nearly a month. The young Lama, subdued by the force of truth, publicly abjured Buddhism, received the name of Paul, and was ultimately baptized, after a long course of study. The prediction of the old Lama had its perfect accomplishment; Paul, since his conversion, has never again set foot in the Lamasery which he quitted.

About 2,000 Lamas inhabit the Lamasery of Tchortchi, which, it is said, is the favourite Lamasery of the Emperor, who has loaded it with donations and privileges. The Lamas in charge of it all receive a pension from the court of Peking. Those who absent themselves from it by permission, and for reasons approved by the superiors, continue to share in the distributions of money and the provisions that are made during their absence; on their return they duly receive the full amount of their share. Doubtless that air of ease pervading the Lamasery of Tchortchi is to be attributed to the imperial favours. The houses in it are neat, sometimes even elegant; and you never see there, as in other places, Lamas covered with dirty rags. The study of the Mantchou language is much cultivated there, an incontestable proof of the great devotion of the Lamasery to the reigning dynasty.

With some rare exceptions the imperial benefactions go very little way towards the construction of the Lamaseries. Those grand and sumptuous monuments, so often met with in the desert, are due to the free and spontaneous zeal of the Mongols. So simple and economical in their dress and manner of living, these people are generous, we might say astonishingly prodigal in all that concerns religious worship and expenditure. When it is resolved to construct a Buddhist temple, surrounded by its Lamasery, Lama collectors go on their way forthwith, provided with passports, attesting the authenticity of their mission. They disperse themselves throughout the kingdom of Tartary, beg alms from tent to tent in the name of the Old Buddha. Upon entering a tent and explaining the object of their journey, by showing the sacred basin [*badir*] in which the offerings are placed, they are received with joyful enthusiasm. There is no one but gives something. The rich place in the *badir* ingots of gold and silver; those who do not possess the precious metals, offer oxen, horses, or camels. The poorest contribute according to the extent of their means; they give lumps of butter, furs, ropes made of the hair of camels and horses. Thus, in a short time are collected immense sums. Then, in these deserts, apparently so poor, you see rise up, as if by enchantment, edifices whose grandeur and wealth would defy the resources of the richest potentates. It was, doubtless, in the same manner, by the zealous co-operation of the faithful, that were constructed in Europe those magnificent cathedrals whose stupendous beauty is an abiding reproach to modern selfishness and indifference.

The Lamaseries you see in Tartary are all constructed of brick and stone. Only the poorest Lamas build for themselves habitations of earth, and these are always so well whitewashed that they closely resemble the rest. The temples are generally built with considerable elegance, and with great solidity; but these monuments always seem crushed, being too low in proportion to their dimensions. Around the Lamasery rise, numerous and without order, towers or pyramids, slender and tapering, resting generally on huge bases, little in harmony with the tenuity of the constructions they support. It would be difficult to say to what order of architecture the Buddhic temples of Tartary belong. They are always fantastical constructions of monstrous colonnades, peristyles with twisted columns, and endless ascents. Opposite the great gate is a kind of altar of wood or stone, usually in the form of a cone reversed; on this the idols are placed, mostly seated cross-legged. These idols are of colossal stature, but their faces are fine and regular, except in the preposterous length of the ears; they belong to the Caucasian type, and are wholly distinct from the monstrous, diabolical physiognomies of the Chinese *Pou-Ssa* [*P'u-sa*].

Before the great idol, and on the same level with it, is a gilt seat where the living Fô, the Grand Lama of the Lamasery, is seated. All around the temple are long tables almost level with the ground, a sort of ottomans covered with carpet; and between each row there is a vacant space, so that the Lamas may move about freely.

When the hour for prayer is come, a Lama, whose office it is to summon the guests of the convent, proceeds to the great gate of the temple, and blows, as loud as he can, a sea-conch, successively towards the four cardinal points. Upon hearing this powerful instrument, audible for a league round, the Lamas put on the mantle and cap of ceremony and assemble in the great inner court. When the time is come the sea-conch sounds again, the great gate is opened, and the living Fô enters the temple. As soon as he is seated upon the altar all the Lamas lay their red boots at the vestibule, and advance barefoot and in silence. As they pass him they worship the living Fô by three prostrations, and then place themselves upon the divan, each according to his dignity. They sit cross-legged; always in a circle.

As soon as the master of the ceremonies has given the signal, by tinkling a little bell, each murmurs in a low voice a preliminary prayer, whilst he unrolls, upon his knees, the prayers directed by the rubric. After this short recitation, follows a moment of profound silence; the bell is again rung, and then commences a psalm in double chorus, grave and melodious. The Thibetian prayers, ordinarily in verse, and written in a metrical and well-cadenced style, are marvellously adapted for harmony. At certain pauses, indicated by the rubric, the Lama musicians execute a piece of music, little in concert with the melodious gravity of the psalmody. It is a confused and deafening noise of bells, cymbals, tambourines, sea-conches, trumpets, pipes, etc., each musician playing on his instrument with a kind of ecstatic fury, trying with his brethren who shall make the greatest noise.

The interior of the temple is usually filled with ornaments, statues, and pictures, illustrating the life of Buddha, and the various transmigrations of the more illustrious Lamas. Vases in copper, shining like gold, of the size and form of tea-cups, are placed in great numbers on a succession of steps, in the form of an amphitheatre, before the idols. It is in these vases that the people deposit their offerings of milk, butter, Mongol wine, and meal. The extremities of each step consist of censers, in which are ever burning aromatic plants, gathered on the sacred mountains of Thibet. Rich silk stuffs, covered with tinsel and gold embroidery, form, on the heads of the idols, canopies from which hang pennants and lanterns of painted paper or transparent horn.

The Lamas are the only artists who contribute to the ornament and decoration of the temples. The paintings are quite distinct from the taste and principles of art as understood in Europe. The fantastical and the grotesque predominate inside and out, both in carvings and statuary, and the personages represented, with the exception of Buddha, have generally a monstrous and satanic aspect. The clothes seem never to have been made for the persons upon whom they are placed. The idea given is that of broken limbs concealed beneath awkward garments.

Amongst these Lama paintings, however, you sometimes come across specimens by no means destitute of beauty. One day, during a visit to the kingdom of Gechekten to the great temple called Altan-Somé "Temple of Gold," we saw a picture which struck us with astonishment. It was a large piece representing, in the centre, Buddha seated on a rich carpet. Around this figure, which was of life size, there was a sort of glory, composed of miniatures, allegorically expressing the thousand Virtues of Buddha. We could scarcely withdraw ourselves from this picture, remarkable as it was, not only for the purity and grace of the design, but also for the expression of the faces and the splendour of the colouring. All the personages seemed full of life. We asked an old Lama, who was attending us over the place, what he knew about this admirable work. "Sirs," said he, raising his joined hands to his forehead in token of respect, "this picture is a treasure of the remotest antiquity; it comprehends within its surface the whole doctrine of Buddha. It is not a Mongol painting; it came from Thibet, and was executed by a saint of the Eternal Sanctuary."

The artists here are, in general, more successful in the landscapes than in the epic subjects. Flowers, birds, trees, mythological animals, are represented with great truth and with infinitely pleasing effect. The colouring is wonderfully full of life and freshness. It is only a pity that the painters of these landscapes have so very indifferent a notion as to perspective and chiaro-oscuro.

The Lamas are far better sculptors than painters, and they are accordingly very lavish of carvings in their Buddhist temples. Everywhere in and about these edifices you see works of this class of art, in quantity bespeaking the fecundity of the artist's chisel, but of a quality which says little for his taste. First, outside the temples are an infinite number of tigers, lions and elephants crouching upon blocks of granite; then the stone balustrades of the steps leading to the great gates are covered with fantastic sculptures representing birds, reptiles and beasts, of all kinds, real and imaginary. Inside, the walls are decorated with relievos in wood or stone, executed with great spirit and truth.

Though the Mongol Lamaseries cannot be compared, in point either of extent or wealth, with those of Thibet, there are some of them which are highly celebrated and greatly venerated among the adorers of Buddha.

The most famous of all is that of the Great Kouren "enclosure," in the country of the Khalkhas. As we had an opportunity of visiting this edifice in one of our journeys into Northern Tartary, we will here give some details respecting it. It stands on the bank of the river Toula, at the entrance to an immense forest, which extends thence northwards, six or seven days' journey to the confines of Russia, and eastward, nearly five hundred miles to the land of the Solons, in Mantchouria. On your way to the Great Kouren, over the desert of Gobi, you have to traverse for a whole month, an ocean of sand, the mournful monotony of which is not relieved by a single stream or a single shrub; but on reaching the Kougour [Khougor] mountains, the western boundary of the states of the Guison-Tamba [Jebtsun-Damba] or King-Lama, the scene changes to picturesque and fertile valleys, and verdant pasture-hills crowned

THIBET, AND CHINA

with forests that seem as old as the world itself. Through the largest valley flows the river Toula, which, rising in the Barka [Barka (?=Kentei)] mountains, runs from east to west through the pastures of the Lamasery, and then entering Siberia, falls into Lake Baikal.

The Lamasery stands on the northern bank of the river, on the slope of a mountain. The various temples inhabited by the Guison-Tamba, and other Grand Lamas, are distinguishable from the rest of the structure by their elevation and their gilded roofs. Thirty thousand Lamas dwell in the Lamasery itself, or in smaller Lamaseries erected about it. The plain adjoining is always covered with the tents of the pilgrims who resort hither from all parts to worship Buddha. Here you find the U-Pi-Ta-Dze [Yü-p'i-ta-tzŭ], or "Fish-skin Tartars," encamped beside the Torgot Tartars from the summits of the sacred mountains (Bokte-Oula [Bogda-ula]), the Thibetians and the Péboun [Pebung (?='Bras-spungs)] of the Himalaya, with their long-haired oxen, mingling with the Mantchous from the banks of the Songari and Amour [Amur]. There is an incessant movement of tents set up and taken down, and of pilgrims coming and going on horses, camels, oxen, mules, or waggons, and on foot.

Viewed from the distance, the white cells of the Lamas, built in horizontal lines one above the other on the sides of the mountain, seem the steps of a grand altar, of which the tabernacle is the temple of the Guison-Tamba. In the depths of that sanctuary, all resplendent with gold and bright colouring, the Lama-King, The Holy, as he is called, *par excellence*, receives the homage of the faithful, ever prostrate, in succession, before him. There is not a Khalkha Tartar who does not glory in the title of the Holy One's Disciple. Wherever you meet a man from the district of the

Great Kouren, and ask him who he is, his proud reply is always this: *Koure Bokte-Ain Chabi* [*Kürê bogda-yin-shabi*], "I am a disciple of the Holy Kouren."

Half-a-league from the Lamasery, on the banks of the Toula, is a commercial station of Chinese. Their wooden or mud huts are fortified by a circle of high palisades to keep out the pilgrims, who, despite their devotion, are extremely given to thieving whenever the opportunity occurs. A watch and some ingots of silver, stolen during the night from M. Gabet, left us no doubt as to the want of probity in the Holy One's disciples.

A good deal of trade is carried on here, Chinese and Russian goods changing hands to a very large extent. The payments of the former are invariably made in tea-bricks. Whether the article sold be a house, a horse, a camel, or a bale of goods, the price is settled for in bricks of tea. Five of these represent, in value, an ounce of silver; the monetary system, therefore, which Franklin so much disliked, is not in use by these Northern Tartars.

The Court of Peking entertains several Mandarins at the Great Kouren, ostensibly for the purpose of preserving order among the Chinese traders, but in reality to keep a watch upon the Guison-Tamba, always an object of suspicion to the Chinese Emperors, who bear in mind that the famous Tchinggiskhan was a Khalkha, and that the memory of his conquests has not passed away from the hearts of his warlike people. The slightest movement at the Great Kouren excites alarm at Peking.

In 1839 the Guison-Tamba announced his intention of paying a visit to the Emperor Tao-Kouang. The Court of Peking became horribly alarmed, and negociators were despatched to divert, if possible, the Guison-Tamba from his journey; but all they could effect was, that he should be attended

THIBET, AND CHINA

by only 3,000 Lamas, and that three other Khalkha sovereigns who were to have accompanied him should be left behind.

Immediately upon the Guison-Tamba's departure on his progress, all the tribes of Tartary put themselves in motion, and took up positions on the road he was to travel, in vaſt multitudes, each tribe bringing for his acceptance offerings of horses, oxen, sheep, gold and silver bullion, and precious ſtones. Wells were dug for him at intervals throughout the length of the great desert of Gobi, and at each of these were placed for his use, by the chieftain of the particular locality, a ſtore of provisions of all sorts. The Lama-King was in a yellow palanquin, carried by four horses, each led by a dignitary of the Lamasery. The escort of 3,000 Lamas were before, behind, and on each side of the palanquin, jovially dashing about on horses and camels. The road almoſt throughout was lined with spectators, or rather with worshippers, eagerly awaiting the arrival of the Holy, and upon his approach, falling, firſt on their knees, and then on their faces, before him, their hands crossed over the head. It seemed the progress of a divinity come upon earth to bless its people. On reaching the Great Wall, the Guison-Tamba, ceasing to be a divinity, became only the chief of some nomad tribes, scorned by the people of China, but feared by the Court of China, more alive to political contingencies. Only one half of the 3,000 Lamas were permitted to attend their chief further, the reſt remaining encamped north of the Great Wall.

The Guison-Tamba sojourned at Peking for three months, receiving an occasional visit from the Emperor, and from the Grand Dignitaries. He then relieved the celeſtial city from his troublesome presence, and after paying visits to the Lamaseries of the Five Towers, and of the Blue Town, set out on his return to his own states, where he died, the victim, it was asserted, of a slow poison that had been administered to him by order of the Emperor. The Khalkhas, however, were more irritated than intimidated by his death, for they are persuaded that their Guison-Tamba never actually dies. All he does, when he appears to die, is to transmigrate to some other country, whence he returns to them younger, more vigorous, more active than ever. In 1844, accordingly, they were told that their living Buddha was incarnate in Thibet, and they went thither, in solemn procession, to fetch the child of five years old who was indicated to them, and to place him on his imperishable throne. While we were encamped at Koukou-Noor [Kôkô-nôr], on the banks of the Blue Sea, we saw pass by us the great caravan of the Khalkhas, who were on their way to Lha-Ssa to bring home the Lama-King of the Great Kouren.

The Kouren of the Thousand Lamas—Mingan Lamané Kouré [Mingan-Lama-yin-küren]—is also a celebrated Lamasery, which dates from the invasion of China by the Mantchous. When Chun-Tche,[1] founder of the dynasty now reigning in China, descended from the forests of Mantchouria to march upon Peking, he met on his way a Lama of Thibet, whom he consulted as to the issue of his enterprise. The Lama promised him complete success, whereupon Tchun-Tche ordered him to come and see him when he should be installed at Peking. After the Mantchous had rendered themselves masters of the capital of the empire, the Lama did not fail to keep his appointment. The Emperor at once recognized the person who had favoured him with such an auspicious horoscope; and, in token of his gratitude, allotted to

[1] The ancedote, which we give as we heard it, must have reference to Chun-Tche's father, who died immediately after the conquest. Chun-Tche himself was only four years old at the time.

him a large extent of land whereon to construct a Lamasery, and revenues sufficient for the support of a thousand Lamas. From the time of its erection, however, the Lamasery of the Thousand Lamas has grown and grown, so that at present it contains more than four thousand Lamas, though its original designation still remains. By degrees, traders have established themselves around it, and have built a considerable town, jointly occupied by Chinese and Tartars. The principal commerce of the place is in beasts.

The Grand Lama of the Lamasery is, at the same time, sovereign of the district. It is he who makes laws, who administers justice, and who appoints magistrates. When he dies, his subjects go and seek for him in Thibet, where he is always understood to metempsychosize himself.

At the time of our visit to the Kouren of the Thousand Lamas, everything was in utter confusion, by reason of a suit between the Lama-King and his four ministers, who are called, in the Mongol language, *Dchassak* [*Jassak*]. The latter had taken upon themselves to marry, and to build houses for themselves apart from the Lamasery, things altogether subversive of Lama discipline. The Grand Lama essayed to bring them to order; the four *Dchassak*, instead of submitting, had collected a whole heap of grievances, upon which they framed an accusation against their chief before the *Tou-Toun* [*tu-t'ung*], the high Mantchou Mandarin, who acts as Secretary of State for the Tartar department.

The suit had been under prosecution two months when we visited the Lamasery, and we soon saw how the establishment was suffering from the absence of its principals. Study or prayer there was none; the great outer gate was open, and seemed not to have been closed at all for some time past. We entered the interior; all we found there was silence and solitude.

The grass was growing in the courts and upon the walls. The doors of the temples were padlocked, but through the gratings we could see that the seats, the altars, the paintings, the statues, were all covered with dust; everything manifested that the Lamasery had been for some time in a state of utter neglect. The absence of the superiors, and the uncertainty as to the result of the suit, had unloosened all the bonds of discipline. The Lamas had dispersed, and people began to regard the very existence of the Lamasery as extremely compromised. We have since heard that, thanks to enormous bribery, the suit terminated in favour of the Lama-King, and that the four *Dchassak* were compelled to conform themselves in all respects to the orders of their sovereign.

We may add to the enumeration of the many celebrated Lamaseries, those of Blue Town, of Tolon-Noor, of Gé-Ho-Eul, and within the Great Wall, that of Peking, and that of the Five Towers in Chan-si.

After quitting the Lamasery of Tchortchi, just as we were entering upon the Red Banner we met a Mongol hunter, who was carrying behind him, on his horse, a fine roebuck he had just killed. We had been so long reduced to our insipid oatmeal, seasoned with a few bits of mutton fat, that the sight of the venison inspired us with a somewhat decided desire to vary our entertainment; we felt, moreover, that our stomachs, weakened by our daily privations, imperiously demanded a more substantial alimentation. After saluting the hunter, therefore, we asked him if he was disposed to sell his venison. " Sirs Lamas," replied he, "when I placed myself in ambush to await the deer, I had no thought of trading in my head. The Chinese carmen, stationed up yonder beyond Tchortchi, wanted to buy my game for four hundred sapeks, but I said No! But to you, Sirs Lamas, I speak not as to Kitat; there is my roebuck; give me what you please for it." We told Samdadchiemba to pay the hunter five hundred sapeks; and hanging the venison over the neck of one of the camels, we proceeded on our way.

Five hundred sapeks are equivalent to about 2s. 1d., and this is the ordinary price of a roebuck in Tartary; the price of a sheep is thrice that amount. Venison is little esteemed by the Tartars, and still less by the Chinese; black meat, say they, is never so good as white. Yet in the larger cities of China, and especially at Peking, black meat has honourable place on the tables of the rich and of the mandarins; a circumstance, however, to be attributed to the scarcity of the article, and a desire for variety. The Mantchous, indeed, do not come within the preceding observation; for, great lovers of hunting, they are also great lovers of its produce, and especially of bears, stags, and pheasants.

It was just past noon when we came to a spot marvellously beautiful. After passing through a narrow opening between two rocks, whose summits seemed lost in the clouds, we found ourselves in a large enclosure, surrounded by lofty hills, on which grew a number of scattered pines. An abundant fountain supplied a small stream, whose banks were covered with angelica and wild mint. The rivulet, after making the circuit of the enclosure, amid rich grass, had its issue thence by an opening similar to that by which we had entered the place. No sooner had a glance comprehended the attractions of the spot than Samdadchiemba moved that we should at once set up our tent there. "Let us go no further to-day," said he; "let us encamp here. We have not gone far this morning, it is true, and the sun is still very high; but we have got the venison to prepare, and we should therefore encamp earlier than usual." No one opposing the honourable gentleman's motion, it was put and carried unanimously, and we proceeded to set up our tent by the side of the spring.

Samdadchiemba had often talked of his great dexterity in the dissection of animals, and he was delighted with this opportunity of displaying his excellence in this respect. Having suspended the roebuck from a pine-branch, sharpened his knife upon a tent-pin, and turned up his sleeves to the elbow, he asked whether we would have the animal dismembered *à la Chinoise*, *à la Turque*, or *à la Tartare*. Unprovided with any reason for preferring any one of these modes to the other two, we left it to Samdadchiemba to obey the impulse of his genius in the matter. In a minute he had skinned and gutted the animal, and he then cut away the flesh from the bones, in one piece, without separating the limbs, so as to leave suspended from the tree merely the skeleton of the deer. This, it appeared, was the Turkish fashion, in use upon long journeys, in order to relieve travellers from the useless burden of bones.

This operation completed, Samdadchiemba cut some slices of venison and proceeded to fry them in mutton fat, a manner of preparing venison not perhaps in strict accordance with the rules of the culinary art; but the difficulty of the circumstances did not allow us to do better. Our banquet was soon ready, but, contrary to our expectations, we were not the first to taste it; we had seated ourselves triangularly on the grass, having in the midst the lid of the pot, which served us as a dish, when all of a sudden we heard, as it were, the rushing of a storm over our heads; a great eagle dashed, like a lightning stroke, upon our entertainment, and immediately rose with equal rapidity, bearing off in each claw a large slice of venison. Upon recovering from our fright at this sudden incident, we ourselves were fain to laugh at the ludicrous aspect of the matter, but Samdadchiemba did not laugh by any means; he was in a paroxysm of fury, not indeed at the loss of the venison, but because the eagle, in its flight, had insolently dealt him a sound box on the ears with the extremity of its great wing.

This event served to render us more cautious on the following venison days. During our previous journeyings we had, indeed, on several occasions observed eagles hovering over our heads at meal-times, but no accident of this kind had occurred; probably the royal birds had scorned our mere oatmeal repasts.

You see the eagle almost everywhere throughout the deserts of Tartary; sometimes hovering and making large circles in the air, sometimes perched upon a rising ground, motionless as the hillock itself. No one in these countries hunts the eagle or molests it in any way; it may make its nest where it pleases, and there bring up its eaglets, and itself grow old, without being in the smallest degree interfered with by man. You often see before you an eagle resting on the plain, and looking there larger than a sheep; as you approach, before rising, it leisurely moves along the ground, beating its wings, and then, by degrees ascending, it attains the altitude where it can fly in all its grandeur and power.

After several days journey we quitted the country of the Eight Banners and entered Western Toumet. At the time of the conquest of China by the Mantchous, the king of Toumet, having distinguished himself in the expedition as an auxiliary of the invaders, the conqueror, in order to evince his gratitude for the services which the prince had rendered him, gave him the fine districts situated north of Peking, beyond the Great Wall. From that period they have borne the name of Eastern Toumet, and Old Toumet took that of Western Toumet; the two Toumets are separated from each other by the Tchakar River.

TRAVELS IN TARTARY,

The Mongol Tartars of Western Toumet do not lead the pastoral and nomadic life; they cultivate their lands and apply themselves to the arts of civilized nations. We had been for nearly a month traversing the desert, setting up our tent for the night in the first convenient place we found, and accustomed to see nothing but above us the sky, and below and around us interminable prairies. We had long, as it were, broken with the world, for all we had seen of mankind had been a few Tartar horsemen dashing across the Land of Grass, like so many birds of passage. Without suspecting it, our tastes had insensibly become modified, and the desert of Mongolia had created in us a temperament friendly to the tranquillity of solitude. When, therefore, we found ourselves amid the cultivation, the movement, the bustle, the confusion of civilized existence, we felt, as it were, oppressed, suffocated; we seemed gasping for breath, and as though every moment we were going to be stifled. This impression, however, was evanescent; and we soon got to think that, after all, it was more comfortable and more agreeable, after a day's march, to take up our abode in a warm, well-stored inn, than to have to set up a tent, to collect fuel, and to prepare our own very meagre repast, before we could take our rest.

The inhabitants of Western Toumet, as may well be imagined, have completely lost the stamp of their original Mongol character; they have all become, more or less, Chinese; many of them do not even know a word of the Mongol language. Some, indeed, do not scruple to express contempt for their brothers of the desert, who refuse to subject their prairies to the ploughshare; they say, how ridiculous it is for men to be always vagabondizing about, and to have merely wretched tents wherein to shelter their heads, when they might so easily build houses, and obtain wealth and comforts of all kinds from the land beneath their feet. And, indeed, the Weſtern Toumetians are perfeƈtly right in preferring the occupation of agriculturiſts to that of shepherd, for they have magnificent plains, well watered, fertile, and favourable to the produƈtion of all kinds of grain crops. When we passed through the country, harveſt was over; but the great ſtacks of corn that we saw in all direƈtions told us that the produce had been abundant and fine. Everything throughout Weſtern Toumet bears the impress of affluence; nowhere, go in what direƈtion you may, do you see the wretched tumble-down houses that disfigure the highways and by-ways of China; nowhere do you see the miserable, half-ſtarved, half-clothed creatures that pain the hearts of travellers in every other country; all the peasants here are well fed, well lodged and well clothed. All the villages and roads are beautified with groups and avenues of fine trees, whereas in the other Tartar regions, cultivated by the Chinese, no trees are to be seen; trees are not even planted, for everybody knows they would be pulled up next day by some miserable pauper or other, for fuel.

We had made three days' journey through the cultivated lands of the Toumet, when we entered KouKou-Khoton [Kô Kô-khoto] " Blue Town," called in Chinese Koui-Hoa-Tchen [Kui-Hua-ch'eng]. There are two towns of the same name, five lis diſtant from one another. The people diſtinguish them by calling the one " Old Town," and the other " New Town," or " Commercial Town," and " Military Town." We firſt entered the latter, which was built by the Emperor Khang-Hi, to defend the empire againſt its northern enemies. The town has a beautiful, noble appearance, which might be admired in Europe itself. We refer, however, only to its circuit of embattled walls, made of brick; for inside, the low houses, built in the

Chinese style, are little in unison with the lofty, huge ramparts that surround them. The interior of the town offers nothing remarkable but its regularity, and a large and beautiful street, which runs through it from east to west. A *Kiang-Kian* [*chiang-chün*] or military commandant, resides here with 10,000 soldiers, who are drilled every day; so that the town may be regarded as a garrison town.

The soldiers of the New Town of Koukou Khoton are Mantchou Tartars; but if you did not previously know the fact, you would scarcely suspect it from hearing them speak. Amongst them there is perhaps not a single man who understands the language of his own country. Already two ages have passed away since the Mantchous made themselves masters of the vast empire of China, and you would say that during these two centuries they have been unceasingly working out their own annihilation. Their manners, their language, their very country— all has become Chinese. It may now be affirmed that Mantchou nationality has become irremediably annihilated. In order to account for this strange counter-revolution, and to understand how the Chinese have been able to fuse their conquerors with themselves, and to get possession of Mantchouria, we must look some way back, and enter somewhat into detail.

In the time of the Ming dynasty, which flourished in China from 1368 to 1644, the Mantchous, or Eastern Tartars, after a long series of internal wars, concurred in the selection of a chief, who united all the tribes into one, and established a kingdom. From that time this ferocious and barbarian people insensibly acquired an importance which gave great umbrage to the Court of Peking; and in 1618 its power was so well established that its king did not fear to transmit to the Emperor of China the statement of seven grievances which, he said, he had to avenge. The daring manifesto finished with these words: *"And in order to avenge these seven injuries, I will reduce and subjugate the dynasty of the Ming."* Shortly afterwards the empire was convulsed with revolts in all directions; the rebel chief besieged Peking, and took it. Thereupon the Emperor, despairing of his fortune, hanged himself from a tree in the Imperial garden, leaving near him these words, written in his own blood: *"Since the empire is falling, the Emperor, too, must fall."* Ou-San-Kouei [Wu-San-Kuei], the Imperial general, called in the Mantchous to aid him in reducing the rebels. The latter were put to flight, and while the Chinese general was pursuing them southward, the Tartar chief returned to Peking, and finding the throne vacant, assumed it.

Previous to this event, the Great Wall, carefully maintained by the Ming dynasty, had kept the Mantchous from entering China, while, reciprocally, the Chinese were forbidden to enter Mantchouria. After the Mantchou conquest of the empire, however, there was no longer any frontier separating the two nations. The Great Wall was freely passed, and the communication between the two countries once thrown open, the Chinese populations of Pe-Tche-Li [Pechili] and Chan-Toung [Shan-tung], hitherto confined within their narrow provinces, burst like torrents upon Mantchouria. The Tartar chief had been considered the sole master, the sole possessor of the lands of his kingdom; but, established as Emperor of China, he distributed his vast possessions among the Mantchous, upon the condition that they should pay him heavy rents for them every year. By means of usury and cunning, and persevering machinations, the Chinese have since rendered themselves masters of all the lands of their conquerors, leaving to them merely their empty titles, their onerous statutory labour, and the payment of oppressive rents. The quality of Mantchou has thus by degrees become a very costly affair, and many, of consequence, seek altogether to abnegate it. According to the law, there is, every third year, a census made of the population of each banner, and all persons who do not cause their names to be inscribed on the roll, are deemed no longer to belong to the Mantchou nation; those, therefore, of the Mantchous whose indigence induces them to desire exemption from statute labour and military service, do not present themselves to the census enumerators, and by that omission enter the ranks of the Chinese people. Thus, while on the one hand, constant migration has carried beyond the Great Wall a great number of Chinese, on the other, a great number of Mantchous have voluntarily abdicated their nationality.

The decline, or rather the extinction of the Mantchou nation is now progressing more rapidly than ever. Up to the reign of Tao-Kouang, the regions watered by the Songari were exclusively inhabited by Mantchous: entrance into those vast districts was prohibited to the Chinese, and no man was permitted to cultivate the soil within their range. At the commencement of the present reign, these districts were put up for public sale, in order to supply the deficiency in the Imperial treasury. The Chinese rushed upon them like birds of prey, and a few sufficed to remove everything that could in any way recall the memory of their ancient possessors. It would be vain for anyone now to seek in Mantchouria a single town, a single village, that is not composed entirely of Chinese.

Yet, amid the general transformation, there are still a few tribes, such as the Si-Po [Hsi-po (Sibo)] and the Solon, which faithfully retain the Mantchou type. Up to the present day their territories have been invaded neither by the Chinese nor by cultivation; they continue to dwell in tents and to furnish soldiers to the Imperial armies. It has been remarked, however, that their frequent appearance at Peking, and their long periods of service in the provincial garrisons, are beginning to make terrible inroads upon their habits and taſtes.

When the Mantchous conquered China, they imposed upon the conquered people a portion of their dress and many of their usages. Tobacco smoking, for example, and the manner of dressing the hair, now in use by the Chinese, came to them from the Mantchou Tartars. But the Chinese, in their turn, did far more than this; they managed to make their conquerors adopt their manners and their language. You may now traverse Mantchouria to the river Amour without being at all aware that you are not travelling in a province of China. The local colouring has become totally effaced. With the exception of a few nomadic tribes no one speaks Mantchou: and there would, perhaps, remain no trace of this fine language, had not the Emperors Khang-Hi and Kien-Loung erected, in its honour, monuments imperishable in themselves, and which will ever attract the attention of European orientaliſts.

At one time the Mantchous had no writing of their own; it was not until 1624, that Tai-Tsou-Kao-Hoang-Ti [T'ai-tsu-kao-huang-ti], chief of the Eaſtern Tartars, directed several learned persons of his nation to design a syſtem of letters for the Mantchous, upon the model of those of the Mongols. Subsequently, in 1641, a man of great genius, named Tahai [Ta-hai], perfected the work, and gave to the Mantchou syſtem of letters the elegance, clearness, and refinement which now characterize it.

Chun-Tche had the fineſt productions of Chinese literature translated into Mantchou. Khang-Hi established an academy of learned persons, equally versed in the Chinese and Tartar languages, whom he employed upon the translation of classical and historical works, and in the compilation of several dictionaries. In order to express novel objects and the various conceptions previously unknown to the Mantchous, it was necessary to invent terms, borrowed, for the most part, from the Chinese, and adapted, by slight alterations, as closely as possible, to the Tartar idiom. This process, however, tending to destroy, by imperceptible degrees, the originality of the Mantchou language, the Emperor Kien-Loung, to avert the danger, had a Mantchou dictionary compiled, from which all Chinese words were excluded. The compilers went about questioning old men and other Mantchous deemed most conversant with their mother-tongue, and rewards were given to such as brought forward an obsolescent word or expression which was deemed worthy of revival and perpetuation in the dictionary.

Thanks to the solicitude and enlightened zeal of the first sovereigns of the present dynasty, there is now no good Chinese book which has not been translated into Mantchou; and all these translations are invested with the greatest possible authenticity, as having been executed by learned academies, by order and under the immediate auspices of several emperors: and, as having, moreover, been subsequently revised and corrected by other academies, equally learned, and whose members were versed alike in the Chinese language and in the Mantchou idiom.

The Mantchou language has attained, by means of all these learned labours, a solid basis; it may, indeed, become no longer spoken, but it will ever remain a classic tongue, and ever be of most important aid to philologers applying their studies to the Asiatic tongues. Besides numerous and faithful translations

THIBET, AND CHINA

of the beſt Chinese books, the Mantchou language possesses versions of the principal produćtions in the Lamanesque, Thibetian, and Mongolian literature. A few years labour will thus suffice to place the diligent ſtudent of Mantchou in full possession of all the moſt precious monuments of Eaſtern Asiatic literature.

The Mantchou language is sonorous, harmonious, and, above all, singularly clear. Its ſtudy is now rendered easy and agreeable by H. Conon de la Gabelentz's *Elements de la Grammaire Mantchou*, published at Altemburg, in Saxony, and which develops, with happy lucidity, the mechanism and rules of the language. The excellent work of this learned orientaliſt cannot fail to be of great assiſtance to all who desire to apply themselves to the ſtudy of a language menaced with extinćtion in the very country which gave it birth, but which France, at leaſt, will preserve for the use of the world of letters. M. Conon de la Gabelentz says, in the preface to his grammar: "I have selećted the French language in the preparation of my work, because France is, as yet, the only European country in which Mantchou has been cultivated, so that it seems to me indispensable that all who desire to ſtudy this idiom should firſt know French, as being the tongue in which are composed the only European works which relate to Mantchou literature."

While the French missionaries were enriching their country with the literary treasures which they found in these remote regions, they were, at the same time, ardently engaged in diffusing the light of Chriſtianity amid these idolatrous nations, whose religion is merely a monſtrous medley of doćtrines and praćtices borrowed at once from Lao-Tseu [Lao-tzŭ] Confucius, and Buddha.

It is well known that in the earlier years of the present dynaſty, these missionaries had, by their talents, acquired great influence at court; they always accompanied the Emperors in the long and frequent journeys which at that period they were accustomed to make into the regions of their ancient rule. These zealous preachers of the gospel never failed on all such occasions to avail themselves of the protection and influence they enjoyed, as a means for sowing, wherever they went, the seeds of the true faith. Such was the first origin of the introduction of Christianity into Mantchouria. They reckoned at first but few neophytes; but the number of these was insensibly augmented afterwards by the migrations of the Chinese, in which were always to be found several Christian families. These missions formed part of the diocese of Peking until within a few years past; then the Bishop of Nanking, administrator of the diocese of Peking, finding himself nigh the close of his career, and fearing that the political commotions of which Portugal, his native country, was at that time the theatre, would preclude the Portuguese church from sending an adequate number of labourers to cultivate the vast field which had been confided to him, communicated his apprehensions to the Sacred College *de Propaganda Fide*, and earnestly entreated its members to take under their especial attention a harvest, already ripe, but which was under peril of destruction, for want of husbandmen to gather it in. The sacred congregation, touched with the anxiety of this venerable and zealous old man, among its other arrangements for meeting the requirements of these unfortunate missions, dismembered Mantchouria from the diocese of Peking, and erected it into an Apostolic Vicariat, which was confided to the charge of the Foreign Missionary Society. M. Verolles, Bishop of Colombia, was made the new Vicar Apostolic. Nothing less than the patience, the devotion, the every virtue of an apostle, was essential

THIBET, AND CHINA

for the due administration of this Christendom. The prejudices of the neophytes, not as yet brought within the rules of ecclesiastical discipline, were, for M. Verolles, obstacles more difficult to overcome than even the ruggedness of heart of the pagans; but his experience and his wisdom soon triumphed over all impediments. The mission has assumed a new form; the number of Christians is annually augmenting; and there is now every hope that the Apostolic Vicariat of Mantchouria will become one of the most flourishing missions in Asia.

Mantchouria is bounded on the north by Siberia, on the south by the Gulf Phou-Hai [P'o-hai] and Corea, on the east by the sea of Japan, and on the west by Russian Dauria and Mongolia.

Moukden [Mukden], in Chinese Chen-Yan [Shen-yang], is the chief town of Mantchouria, and may be considered the second capital of the Chinese empire. The Emperor has a palace and courts of justice there on the model of those at Peking. Moukden is a large and fine city, surrounded by thick and lofty ramparts; the streets are broad and regular, and less dirty and tumultuous than those of Peking. One entire quarter is appropriated to the princes of the Yellow Girdle; that is, to the members of the Imperial family. They are all under the direction of a grand mandarin, who is entrusted with the inspection of their conduct, and empowered summarily to punish any offences they may commit.

After Moukden, the most remarkable towns are Ghirin [Girin], surrounded by high wooden palisades, and Ningouta [Ninguta], the native place of the reigning Imperial family. Lao-yan [Lao yang], Kai-Tcheou [Kai-chou], and Kin-Tcheou [Chin-chou] are remarkable for the extensive commerce their maritime position brings them.

Mantchouria, watered by a great number of streams

and rivers, is a country naturally fertile. Since the cultivation has been in the hands of the Chinese, the soil has been enriched by a large number of the products of the interior. In the southern part, they cultivate successfully the dry rice, or that which has no need of watering, and the Imperial rice, discovered by the Emperor Khang-Hi. These two sorts of rice would certainly succeed in France. They have also abundant harvests of millet, of *Kao-Leang* [kao-liang] or Indian corn (*Holcus Sorghum*), from which they distil excellent brandy; sesamum, linseed, hemp, and tobacco the best in the whole Chinese empire.

The Mantchourians pay especial attention to the cultivation of the herbaceous-stemmed cotton plant, which produces cotton in extraordinary abundance. A *Meou* [mou] of these plants, a space of about fifteen square feet, ordinarily produces 2,000 lbs. of cotton. The fruit of the cotton tree grows in the form of a cod or shell, and attains the size of a hazel nut. As it ripens the cod opens, divides into three parts, and develops three or four small tufts of cotton which contain the seeds. In order to separate the seed, they make use of a sort of little bow, firmly strung, the cord of which vibrating over the cotton tufts removes the seeds, of which a portion is retained for next year's sowing, and the rest is made into oil, resembling linseed oil. The upper portion of Mantchouria, too cold to grow cotton, has immense harvests of corn.

Besides these productions, common to China, Mantchouria possesses three treasures[1] peculiar to itself: *jin-seng* [ginseng], sable fur, and the grass *oula* [ula]. The first of these productions has been long known in Europe, though our learned Academy there

---

[1] The Chinese designate them *San Pao* [san pao]; the Mantchous, *Ilan Baobai* [ilan-baobai]; the Mongols, *Korban erdeni* [Gurban-erdeni]; and the Thibetians, *Tchok-Soum* [mch'og-gsum].

ventured some years ago to doubt its exiſtence. *Jin-seng* is perhaps the moſt considerable article of Mantchourian commerce. Throughout China there is no chemiſt's shop unprovided with more or less of it.

The root of *jin-seng* is ſtraight, spindle-shaped, and very knotty; seldom so large as one's little finger, and in length from two to three inches. When it has undergone its fitting preparation, its colour is a transparent white, with sometimes a slight red or yellow tinge. Its appearance, then, is that of a branch of ſtalaċtite.

The Chinese report marvels of the *jin-seng* and no doubt it is, for Chinese organization, a tonic of very great effeċt for old and weak persons; but its nature is too heating, the Chinese physicians admit, for the European temperament, already, in their opinion, too hot. The price is enormous, and doubtless its dearness contributes, with a people like the Chinese, to raise its celebrity so high. The rich and the Mandarins probably use it only because it is above the reach of other people, and out of pure oſtentation.

The *jin-seng*, grown in Corea, and there called *Kao-li-seng* [*kao-li-shên*], is of very inferior quality to that of Mantchouria.

The second special treasure of Eaſtern Tartary is the fur of the sable, which, obtained by the hunters with immense labour and danger, is of such excessive price that only the princes and great dignitaries of the empire can purchase it. The grass called *oula*, the third speciality of Mantchouria, is, on the contrary, of the commoneſt occurrence; its peculiar property is, that if put into your shoes, it communicates to the feet a soothing warmth, even in the depth of winter.

As we have said above, the Mantchou Tartars have almoſt wholly abdicated their own manners, and adopted instead those of the Chinese; yet, amid this transformation of their primitive characters they have still retained their old passion for hunting, for horse exercise, and for archery. At all periods of their history they have attached an astonishing importance to these various exercises; anyone may convince himself of this by merely running his eye over a Mantchou dictionary. Every thing, every incident, every attribute relating to these exercises, has its special expression, so as to need no circumlocution to convey it. There are different names, not only for the different colours of the horse, for example, for its age and qualities, but for all its movements; and it is just the same with reference to hunting and archery.

The Mantchous are excellent archers, and among them the tribe Solon are particularly eminent in this respect. At all the military stations, trials of skill with the bow take place on certain periodical occasions, in presence of the Mandarins and of the assembled people. Three straw men, of the size of life, are placed in a straight line, at from twenty to thirty paces distant from one another; the archer is on a line with them, about fifteen feet off from the first figure, his bow bent, and his finger on the string. The signal being given, he puts his horse to a gallop, and discharges his arrow at the first figure; without checking his horse's speed, he takes a second arrow from his quiver, places it in the bow, and discharges it against the second figure, and so with the third; all this while the horse is dashing at full speed along the line of the figures, so that the rider has to keep himself firm in the stirrups while he manœuvres with the promptitude necessary to avoid the getting beyond his mark. From the first figure to the second, the archer has bare time for drawing his arrow, fixing, and discharging it, so that when he shoots, he has generally

THIBET, AND CHINA

to turn somewhat on his saddle; and as to the third shot, he has to discharge it altogether in the old Parthian fashion. Yet for a competitor to be deemed a good archer, it is essential that he should fire an arrow into every one of the three figures. " To know how to shoot an arrow," writes a Mantchou author, " is the first and most important knowledge for a Tartar to acquire. Though success therein seems an easy matter, success is of rare occurrence. How many are there who practise day and night ? How many are there who sleep with the bow in their arms ? and yet how few are there who have rendered themselves famous! How few are there whose names are proclaimed at the matches ! Keep your frame straight and firm ; avoid vicious postures ; let your shoulders be immovable. Fire every arrow into its mark, and you may be satisfied with your skill."

The day after our arrival at the military town of Koukou-Khoton we repaired on a visit to the mercantile district. Our hearts were painfully affected at finding ourselves in a Mantchou town, and hearing any language spoken there but the Mantchou. We could not reconcile to our minds the idea of a nation renegade of its nationality, of a conquering people, in nothing distinguishable from the conquered, except, perhaps, that they have a little less industry and a little more conceit. When the Thibetian Lama promised to the Tartar chief the conquest of China, and predicted to him that he should soon be seated on the throne at Peking, he would have told him more of truth, had he told him that his whole nation, its manners, its language, its country, was about to be engulphed for ever in the Chinese empire. Let any revolution remove the present dynasty, and the Mantchou will be compelled to complete fusion with the empire. Admission to their own country, occupied entirely by Chinese, will be forbidden to them. In reference to a map of Mantchouria, compiled by the Fathers Jesuits, upon the order of the Emperor Khang-Hi, Father Duhalde says that they abstained from giving the Chinese names of places in the map; and he assigns for this the following reason: "Of what use would it be to a traveller through Mantchouria to be told, for example, that the river Sakhalien-Oula [Sakhalyan-ula] is called by the Chinese He-Loung-Kiang [Hei-lung-chiang], since it is not with Chinese he has there to do; and the Tartars, whose aid he requires, have never heard the Chinese name." This observation might be just enough in the time of Khang-Hi, but now the precise converse would hold good; for in traversing Mantchouria it is always with Chinese you have to deal, and it is always of the He-Loung-Kiang that you hear, and never of the Sakhalien-Oula.

CHAPTER V

FROM the Mantchou town to the Old Blue Town is not more than half an hour's walk, along a broad road, constructed through the large market, which narrowed the town. With the exception of the Lamaseries, which rise above the other buildings, you see before you merely an immense mass of houses and shops huddled confusedly together, without any order or arrangement whatever. The ramparts of the old town still exist in all their integrity; but the increase of the population has compelled the people by degrees to pass this barrier. Houses have risen outside the walls one after another until large suburbs have been formed, and now the extra-mural city is larger than the intra-mural.

We entered the city by a broad street, which exhibited nothing remarkable except the large Lamasery, called, in common with the more celebrated establishment in the province of Chan-Si, the Lamasery of the Five Towers. It derives this appellation from a handsome square tower with five turrets, one, very lofty, in the centre and one at each angle.

Just beyond this the broad street terminated, and there was no exit but a narrow lane running right and left. We turned down what seemed the least dirty of these, but soon found ourselves in a liquid slough of mud and filth, black, and of suffocating stench—we had got into the Street of the Tanners. We advanced slowly and shudderingly, for beneath the mire lay hid now a great stone, over which we stumbled, now a hole, into which we sank. To complete our misfortune, we all at once heard before us deafening cries and shouts, indicating that along the tortuosities of the lane in which we were horsemen and carts were about to meet us. To draw back, or to stand aside, were equally impossible, so that our only resource was to bawl on our own account, and, advancing, take our chance. At the next turning we met the cavalcade, and something extremely disagreeable seemed threatening us, when, upon sight of our camels, the horses of the other party took fright, and, turning right round, galloped off in utter confusion, leaving the way clear before us. Thus, thanks to our beasts of burden, we were enabled to continue our journey without giving the way to anyone, and we at last arrived, without any serious accident, in a spacious street, adorned on each side with fine shops.

We looked about for an inn, but fruitlessly; we saw several inns, indeed, but these were not of the kind we sought. In the great towns of Northern China and Tartary each inn is devoted to a particular class of travellers, and will receive no other. "The Corn-dealers' Arms" inn, for example, will not admit a horse-dealer, and so on. The inns which devote themselves to the entertainment of mere travellers are called the taverns of the Transitory Guests. We were pausing, anxiously looking about for one of these, when a young man, hastening from an adjacent shop, came up to us: "You seek an inn, gentlemen travellers," said he; "suffer me to guide you to one; yet I scarcely know one in the Blue City worthy of you. Men are innumerable here, my Lords Lamas; a few good, but, alas! most bad. I speak it from my heart. In the Blue City you would with difficulty find one man who is guided by his conscience; yet conscience is a treasure! You Tartars, you, indeed, know well what conscience is. Ah! I know the Tartars well! excellent people, right-hearted souls!

THIBET, AND CHINA

We Chinese are altogether different—rascals, rogues. Not one Chinaman in ten thousand heeds conscience. Here, in this Blue City, everybody, with the merest exceptions, makes it his business to cheat the worthy Tartars, and rob them of their goods. Oh! it's shameful!"

And the excellent creature threw up his eyes as he denounced the knavery of his townsmen. We saw very clearly, however, that the direction taken by the eyes thus thrown up was the camel's back, whereon were two large cases, which our disinterested adviser no doubt took to contain precious merchandise. However, we let him lead us on and chatter as he pleased. When we had been wandering about under his escort for a full hour, and yet had reached no inn, we said to him: "We cannot think of troubling you further, since you yourself seem not to know where we may find that which we need." "Be perfectly easy, my lords," replied he; "I am guiding you to an excellent, a super-excellent hotel. Don't mention a word as to troubling me; you pain me by the idea. What! are we not all brothers? Away with the distinction between Tartar and Chinese! True, the language is not the same, nor the dress; but men have but one heart, one conscience, one invariable rule of justice. Just wait one moment for me, my lords; I will be with you again before you can look round," and so saying he dived into a shop on the left. He was soon back with us, making a thousand apologies for having detained us. "You must be very tired, my lords; one cannot be otherwise when one is travelling. 'Tis quite different from being with one's family." As he spoke, we were accosted by another Chinese, a ludicrous contrast with our first friend, whose round shining smiling face was perfectly intense in its aspect of benevolence. The other fellow was meagre and lanky, with thin, pinched lips and little black eyes, half buried in the head, that gave to the whole physiognomy a character of the most thorough knavery. "My Lords Lamas," said he, "I see you have just arrived! Excellent! And you have journeyed safely. Well, well! Your camels are magnificent; 'tis no wonder you travel fast and securely upon such animals. Well, you have arrived: that's a great happiness. Se-Eul [Ssŭ-êrh]," he continued, addressing the Chinese who had first got hold of us, "you are guiding these noble Tartars to an hotel. 'Tis well! Take care that the hotel is a good one, worthy of the distinguished strangers. What think you of the 'Tavern of Eternal Equity?'" "The very hotel whither I was leading the Lords Lamas." "There is none better in the empire. By the way, the host is an acquaintance of mine. I cannot do better than accompany you and recommend these noble Tartars to his best care. In fact, if I were not to go with you, I should have a weight upon my heart. When we are fortunate enough to meet brothers who need our aid, how can we do too much for them, for we are all brothers! My lords, you see this young man and myself; well, we are two clerks in the same establishment, and we make it our pride to serve our brothers the Tartars; for, alas, in this dreadful city there is but too little virtue."

Anyone, hearing their professions of devoted zeal, would have imagined these two personages to have been the friends of our childhood; but we were sufficiently acquainted with Chinese manners to perceive at once that we were the mark of a couple of swindlers. Accordingly, when we saw inscribed on a door, "Hotel of the Three Perfections; transitory guests on horse and camel entertained, and their affairs transacted with infallible success," we at once directed our course up the gateway, despite the vehement remonstrances of our worthy guides, and rode down a long avenue to the great square court of the hotel. The little blue cap worn by the attendants indicated that we were in a Turkish establishment.

This proceeding of ours was not at all what the two Chinese desired; but they still followed us, and, without appearing disconcerted, continued to act their part. "Where are the people of the hotel," cried they, with an immense air; "let them prepare a large apartment, a fine, clean apartment? Their Excellencies have arrived, and must be suitably accommodated." One of the principal waiters presented himself, holding by his teeth a key, in one hand a broom and in the other a watering-pot. Our two protectors immediately took possession of these articles. "Leave everything to us," said they; "it is we who claim the honour of personally waiting upon our illustrious friends; you, attendants of the hotel, you only do things by halves, actuated as you are merely by mercenary considerations." And thereupon they set to work sprinkling, sweeping, and cleaning the room to which the waiter guided us. When this operation was concluded, we seated ourselves on the *kang*, the two Chinese "knew themselves better than to sit by the side of our Eminent Distinctions," and they accordingly squatted on the floor. As tea was being served, a young man, well attired and of exceedingly elegant address, came into the room, carrying by the four corners a silk handkerchief. "Gentlemen Lamas," said the elder of our previous companions, "this young man is the son of our principal, and doubtless has been sent by his father to inquire after your health, and whether you have so far journeyed in peace." The young man placed his handkerchief upon the table that stood before us. "Here are some cakes my father has sent to be eaten with your tea. When you have finished that meal, he entreats you will come and partake of a humble repast in our poor dwelling." "But why wear your hearts out thus for us mere strangers?" "Oh!" exclaimed all three in chorus, "the words you utter cover us with blushes! What! can we do anything in excess for brothers who have thus honoured us with their presence in our poor city!" "Poor Tartars!" said I in French to my colleague, "how thoroughly eaten up they must be when they fall into such hands as these!" These words, in an unknown tongue, excited considerable surprise in our worthy friends. "In which of the illustrious kingdoms of Tartary dwell your Excellencies?" asked one of them. "We are not Tartars at all," was the reply. "Ah! we saw that at once; the Tartars have no such majesty of aspect as yours; their mien has no grandeur about it! May we ask what is the noble country whence you come?" We are from the West; our native land is far hence." "Quite so," replied the eldest of the three knaves. "I knew it, and I said so to these young men, but they are ignorant; they know nothing about physiognomy. Ah! you are from the West. I know your country well; I have been there more than once." "We are delighted to hear this; doubtless, then, you are acquainted with our language?" "Why, I cannot say I know it thoroughly; but there are some few words I understand. I can't speak them, indeed; but that does not matter. You western people are so clever, you know everything, the Chinese language, the Tartarian, the western—you can speak them all. I have always been closely mixed up with your countrymen, and have invariably been selected to manage their affairs for them whenever they come to the Blue Town. It is always I who make their purchases for them."

We had by this time finished our tea; our three friends rose, and with a simultaneous bow, invited us to accompany them. "My lords, the repast is

by this time prepared, and our chief awaits you."
"Liſten," said we, gravely, " while we utter words
full of reason. You have taken the trouble to guide us
to an inn, which shows you to be men of warm hearts;
you have here swept for us and prepared our room,
again in proof of your excellent dispositions; your
maſter has sent us paſtry, which manifeſts in him
a benevolence incapable of exhauſtion towards the
wayfaring ſtranger. You now invite us to go and
dine with you : we cannot possibly trespass so grossly
upon your kindness. No, dear friends, you muſt
excuse us; if we desire to make some purchases in
your eſtablishment, you may rely upon us. For the
present we will not detain you. We are going to dine
at the Turkish Eating House." So saying, we rose
and ushered our excellent friends to the door.

The commercial intercourse between the Tartars
and the Chinese is revoltingly iniquitous on the part
of the latter. So soon as Mongols, simple, ingenuous
men, if such there be at all in the world, arrive in a
trading town, they are snapped up by some Chinese,
who carry them off, as it were, by main force, to their
houses, give them tea for themselves and forage for
their animals, and cajole them in every conceivable
way. The Mongols, themselves without guile and
incapable of conceiving guile in others, take all they
hear to be perfectly genuine, and congratulate themselves, conscious as they are of their inaptitude for
business, upon their good fortune in thus meeting
with brothers, *ahatou* [*aka-de'ü*], as they say, in whom
they can place full confidence, and who will undertake to manage their whole business for them. A
good dinner provided gratis in the back shop, com-
pletes the illusion. " If these people wanted to rob
me," says the Tartar to himself, " they would not go
to all this expense in giving me a dinner for nothing."
When once the Chinese has got hold of the Tartar, he

employs over him all the resources of the skilful and utterly unprincipled knavery of the Chinese character. He keeps him in his house, eating, drinking, and smoking, one day after another, until his subordinates have sold all the poor man's cattle, or whatever else he has to sell, and bought for him, in return, the commodities he requires, at prices double and triple the market value. But so plausible is the Chinese, and so simple is the Tartar, that the latter invariably departs with the most entire conviction of the immense philanthrophy of the former, and with a promise to return, when he has other goods to sell, to the establishment where he has been treated so fraternally.

The next morning we went out to purchase some winter clothing, the want of which began to make itself sensibly felt. But first, in order to facilitate our dealings, we had to sell some ounces of silver. The money of the Chinese consists entirely of small round copper coins, of the size of our halfpenny, with a square hole in the centre, through which the people string them, so that they may be more conveniently carried. These coins the Chinese call, *tsien* [*ch'ien*]; the Tartars, *dchos* [*jôs* (*jo'os*)]; and the Europeans *sapeks* [*sapeca*]. Gold and silver are not coined at all; they are melted into ingots of various sizes, and thus put into circulation. Gold dust and gold leaf are also current in commerce, and they also possess bank notes. The ordinary value of the ounce of silver is 1,700 or 1,800 sapeks, according to the scarcity or abundance of silver in the country.

The money changers have two irregular modes of making a profit by their traffic; if they state the fair price of silver to the customer, they cheat him in the weight; if their scales and their method of weighing are accurate, they diminish the price of the silver accordingly. But when they have to do with Tartars, they employ neither of these methods of fraud; on the contrary, they weigh the silver scrupulously, and sometimes allow a little overweight, and even they pay them above the market price; in fact, they appear to be quite losers by the transaction, and so they would be, if the weight and the price of the silver alone were considered; their advantage is derived, in these cases, from their manner of calculating the amount. When they come to reduce the silver into sapeks, they do indeed reduce it, making the most flagrant miscalculations, which the Tartars, who can count nothing beyond their beads, are quite incapable of detecting, and which they, accordingly, adopt implicitly, and even with satisfaction, always considering they have sold their bullion well, since they know the full weight has been allowed, and that the full market price has been given.

At the money changers in the Blue Town, to which we went to sell some silver, the Chinese dealers essayed, according to custom, to apply this fraud to us but they were disconcerted. The weight shown by their scales was perfectly correct, and the price they offered us was rather above the ordinary course of exchange, and the bargain between us was so far concluded. The chief clerk took the *souan-pan* [*suan-p'an*] the calculation table used by the Chinese, and after calculating with an appearance of intense nicety, announced the result of his operation. "This is an exchange-office," said we; "you are the buyers, we the sellers; you have made your calculations, we will make ours: give us a pencil and a piece of paper."—" Nothing can be more just; you have enunciated a fundamental law of commerce," and so saying, they handed us a writing-case. We took the pencil and a very short calculation exhibited a difference in our favour of a thousand sapeks. "Superintendent of the bank," said we, "your *souan-pan* is in error by a thousand sapeks."—" Impossible! Do you think that all of a sudden I've forgotten my *souan-pan?* Let me go over it again;" and he proceeded with an air of great anxiety to appear correct, to set his calculating machine once more in operation, the other customers by our side looking on with great amazement at all this. When he had done: "Yes," said he, "I knew I was right; see, brother;" and he passed the machine to a colleague behind the counter, who went over his calculation; the result of their operations was exactly the same to a fraction. "You see," said the principal, "there is no error. How is it that our calculation does not agree with that which you have written down there?"—"It is unimportant to inquire why your calculation does not agree with ours: this is certain, that your calculation is wrong and ours right. You see these little characters that we have traced on this paper; they are a very different thing from your *souan-pan;* it is impossible for them to be wrong. Were all the calculators of the world to work the whole of their lives upon this operation, they could arrive at no other result than this; that your statement is wrong by a thousand sapeks."

The money-changers were extremely embarrassed, and began to turn very red, when a bystander, who perceived that the affair was assuming an awkward aspect, presented himself as umpire. "I'll reckon it up for you," said he, and taking the *souan-pan*, his calculation agreed with ours. The superintendent of the bank hereupon made us a profound bow: "Sirs Lamas," said he, "your mathematics are better than mine." "Oh, not at all," replied we, with a bow equally profound; "your *souan-pan* is excellent, but who ever heard of a calculator always exempt from error? People like you may very well be mistaken once and a way, whereas poor simple folks like us make blunders ten thousand times. Now, however, we have fortunately concurred in our reckoning, thanks

THIBET, AND CHINA

to the pains you have taken." These phrases were rigorously required under the circumstances, by Chinese politeness. Whenever any person in China is compromised by an awkward incident, those present always carefully refrain from any observation which may make him blush, or as the Chinese phrase it, take away his face.

After our conciliatory address had restored self-possession to all present, everybody drew round the piece of paper on which we had cast up our sum in Arabic numerals. "That is a fine *souan-pan*," said one to another; "simple, sure, and speedy."—"Sirs Lamas," asked the principal, "what do these characters mean? What *souan-pan* is this?" "This *souan-pan* is infallible," returned we; the "characters are those which the Mandarins of Celestial Literature use in calculating eclipses, and the course of the seasons."[1] After a brief conversation on the merits of the Arabic numerals, the cashier handed us the full amount of sapeks, and we parted good friends.

The Chinese are sometimes victims to their own knavery, and we have known even Tartars catch them in a snare. One day a Mongol presented himself at the counter of a Chinese money-changer, with a *youen-pao* [*yüan-pao*] carefully packed and sealed. A *youen-pao* is an ingot of silver weighing three pounds —in China there are sixteen ounces to the pound; the three pounds are never very rigorously exacted, there being generally four or five ounces over, so that the usual weight of an ingot of silver is fifty-two ounces. The Tartar had no sooner unpacked his *youen-pao* than the Chinese clerk resolved to defraud him of an ounce or two, and weighing it, he pronounced it to be fifty ounces. "My *youen-pao* weighs fifty-two ounces," exclaimed

[1] The Fathers Jesuits introduced the use of Arabic numerals into the Observatory at Peking.

the Tartar. "I weighed it before I left home." "Oh, your Tartar scales are all very well for sheep; but they don't do for weighing bullion." After much haggling, the bargain was concluded, the *youen-pao* was purchased as weighing fifty ounces, and the Tartar, having first required and obtained a certificate of the stated weight and value of the ingot, returned to his tent with a good provision of sapeks and bank notes.

In the evening the principal of the establishment received the usual report from each clerk of the business done in the course of the day. "I," said one of them with a triumphant air, "bought a *youen-pao* of silver and made two ounces by it." He produced the ingot, which the chief received with a smile, soon changing into a frown. "What have you got here?" cried he. "This is not silver!" The ingot was handed round, and all the clerks saw that indeed it was base bullion. "I know the Tartar," said the clerk who had purchased it, "and will have him up before the Mandarin."

The satellites of justice were forthwith dispatched after the roguish Tartar, whose offence, proved against him, was matter of capital punishment. It was obvious that the ingot was base bullion, and on the face of the affair there was clear proof that the Tartar had sold it. The Tartar, however, stoutly repudiated the imputation. "The humblest of the humble," said he, "craves that he may be allowed to put forth a word in his defence." "Speak," said the Mandarin, "but beware how you say aught other than the exact truth." "It is true," proceeded the Tartar, "that I sold a *youen-pao* at this person's shop, but it was all pure silver. I am a Tartar, a poor, simple man, and these people, seeking to take advantage of me, have substituted a false for my genuine ingot. I cannot command many words, but

THIBET, AND CHINA

I pray our father and mother, (*i.e.* the Mandarin), to have this false *youen-pao* weighed." The ingot was weighed, and was found to contain fifty-two ounces. The Tartar now drew from one of his boots a small parcel, containing, wrapped in rags, a piece of paper, which he held up to the Mandarin. " Here is a certificate," cried he, " which I received at the shop, and which attests the value and weight of the *youen-pao* that I sold." The Mandarin looked over the paper with a roguish smile, and then said : " According to the testimony of the clerk himself who wrote this certificate, this Mongol sold to him a *youen-pao* weighing fifty ounces ; this *youen-pao* of base bullion weighs fifty-two ounces ; this, therefore, cannot be the Mongol's *youen-pao* ; but now comes the question, whose is it ? Who are really the persons that have false bullion in their possession ? " Everybody present, the Mandarin included, knew perfectly well how the case stood ; but the Chinese magistrate, tickled with the Tartar's ingenuity, gave him the benefit of the clerk's dull roguery, and dismissed the charge ; but not so the accusers, who were well bastinadoed, and would have been put to death as coiners, had they not found means to appease justice by the present of some ingots of purer metal. It is only, however, upon very rare and extraordinary occasions that the Mongols get the better of the Chinese. In the ordinary course of things, they are everywhere, and always, and in every way, the dupes of their neighbours who by dint of cunning and unprincipled machinations, reduce them to poverty.

Upon receiving our sapeks, we proceeded to buy the winter clothing we needed. Upon a consideration of the meagreness of our exchequer, we came to the resolution that it would be better to purchase what we required at some second-hand shop. In China and Tartary no one has the smallest repugnance to wear other people's clothes; he who has not himself the attire wherein to pay a visit or make a holiday, goes without ceremony to a neighbour and borrows a hat, or a pair of trousers, or boots, or shoes, or whatever else he wants, and nobody is at all surprised at these borrowings, which are quite a custom. The only hesitation anyone has in lending his clothes to a neighbour is lest the borrower should sell them in payment of some debt, or, after using them, pawn them. People who buy clothes buy them indifferently, new or secondhand. The question of price is alone taken into consideration, for there is no more delicacy felt about putting on another man's hat or trousers, than there is about living in a house that some one else has occupied before you.

The custom of wearing other people's things was by no means to our taste, and all the less so, that, ever since our arrival at the mission of Si-Wang [Hsi-wan], we had not been under the necessity of departing from our old habits in this respect. Now, however, the slenderness of our purse compelled us to waive our repugnance. We went out, therefore, in search of a secondhand clothes shop, of which, in every town here, there are a greater or less number, for the most part in connection with pawnshops, called in these countries *Tang-Pou* [*tang-pu*]. Those who borrow upon pledges are seldom able to redeem the articles they have deposited, which they accordingly leave to die, as the Tartars and Chinese express it; or in other words they allow the period of redemption to pass, and the articles pass altogether from them. The old clothes shops of the Blue Town were filled in this way with Tartar spoils, so that we had the opportunity of selecting exactly the sort of things we required, to suit the new costume we had adopted.

At the first shop we visited they showed us a quantity of wretched garments turned up with sheepskin;

but though these rags were exceedingly old, and so covered with grease that it was impossible to guess at their original colour, the price asked for them was exorbitant. After a protracted haggling, we found it impossible to come to terms, and we gave up this first attempt; and we gave it up, be it added, with a certain degree of satisfaction, for our self-respect was somewhat wounded at finding ourselves reduced even to the proposition of wearing such filthy rags. We visited another shop, and another, a third, and a fourth, and still several more. We were shown magnificent garments, handsome garments, fair garments, endurable garments, but the consideration of expense was, in each instance, an impracticable stumbling-block. The journey we had undertaken might endure for several years, and extreme economy, at all events in the outset, was indispensable. After going about the whole day, after making the acquaintance of all the rag-merchants in the Blue Town, after turning over and over all the old clothes, we were fain to return to the secondhand dealer whom we had first visited, and to make the best bargain we could with him. We purchased from him, at last, two ancient robes of sheep-skin, covered with some material, the nature of which it was impossible to identify, and the original colour of which we suspected to have been yellow. We proceeded to try them on, and it was at once evident that the tailor in making them had by no means had us in his eye. M. Gabet's robe was too short, M. Huc's too long; but a friendly exchange was impracticable, the difference in height between the two missionaries being altogether too disproportionate. We at first thought of cutting the excess from the one, in order to make up the deficiency of the other; but then we should have had to call in the aid of a tailor, and this would have involved another drain upon our purse; the pecuniary consideration decided the question, and we determined to wear the clothes as they were, M. Huc adopting the expedient of holding up, by means of a girdle, the surplus of his robe, and M. Gabet resigning himself to the exposure to the public gaze of a portion of his legs; the main inconvenience, after all, being the manifestation to all who saw us that we could not attire ourselves in exact proportion to our size.

Provided with our sheep-skin coats, we next asked the dealer to show us his collection of secondhand winter hats. We examined several of these, and at last selected two caps of fox-skin, the elegant form of which reminded us of the shakos of our sappers. These purchases completed, each of us put under his arm his packet of old clothes, and we returned to the hotel of the " Three Perfections."

We remained two days longer at Koukou-Khoton for, besides that we needed repose, we were glad of the opportunity of seeing this great town and of becoming acquainted with the numerous and celebrated Lamaseries established there.

The Blue Town enjoys considerable commercial importance, which it has acquired chiefly through its Lamaseries, the reputation of which attracts thither Mongols from the most distant parts of the empire. The Mongols bring hither large herds of oxen, camels, horses, sheep and loads of fur, mushrooms, and salt the only produce of the deserts of Tartary. They receive, in return, brick-tea, linen, saddlery, odoriferous sticks to burn before their idols, oatmeal, millet, and kitchen utensils.

The Blue Town is especially noted for its great trade in camels. The camel market is a large square in the centre of the town; the animals are ranged here in long rows, their front feet raised upon a mud elevation constructed for that purpose, the object being to show off the size and height of the creatures. It is impossible to describe the uproar and confusion of this market, what with the incessant bawling of the buyers and sellers as they dispute, their noisy chattering after they have agreed, and the horrible shrieking of the camels at having their noses pulled, for the purpose of making them show their agility in kneeling and rising. In order to teſt the ſtrength of the camel, and the burden it is capable of bearing, they make it kneel, and then pile one thing after another upon its back, causing it to rise under each addition, until it can rise no longer. They sometimes use the following expedient: While the camel is kneeling, a man gets upon its hind heels, and holds on by the long hair of its hump; if the camel can rise then, it is considered an animal of superior power.

The trade in camels is entirely conducted by proxy: the seller and the buyer never settle the matter between themselves. They select indifferent persons to sell their goods, who propose, discuss, and fix the price; the one looking to the intereſts of the seller, the other to those of the purchaser. These "sale-speakers" exercise no other trade; they go from market to market to promote business, as they say. They have generally a great knowledge of cattle, have much fluency of tongue, and are, above all, endowed with a knavery above all shame. They dispute, by turns, furiously and argumentatively, as to the merits and defects of the animal; but as soon as it comes to a queſtion of price, the tongue is laid aside as a medium, and the conversation proceeds altogether in signs. They seize each other by the wrists, and beneath the long wide sleeve of their jackets, indicate with their fingers the progress of the bargain. After the affair is concluded they partake of the dinner which is always given by the purchaser, and then receive a certain number of sapeks, according to the cuſtom of different places.

In the Blue Town there exist five great Lamaseries, each inhabited by more than 2,000 Lamas; besides these, they reckon fifteen less considerable establishments—branches, as it were, of the former. The number of regular Lamas resident in this city may fairly be stated at 20,000. As to those who inhabit the different quarters of the town, engaged in commerce and horse-dealing, they are innumerable. The Lamasery of the Five Towers is the finest and the most famous: here it is that the Hobilgan [hubilgan] lives— that is, a grand Lama—who, after having been identified with the substance of Buddha, has already undergone several times the process of transmigration. He sits here upon the altar once occupied by the Guison-Tamba, having ascended it after a tragical event, which very nearly brought about a revolution in the empire.

The Emperor Khang-Hi, during the great military expedition which he made in the west against the Oelets [Ölet], one day, in traversing the Blue Town, expressed a wish to pay a visit to the Guison-Tamba, at that time the Grand Lama of the Five Towers. The latter received the Emperor without rising from the throne, or manifesting any kind of respect. Just as Khang-Hi drew near to speak to him, a *Kiang-Kian*, or high military Mandarin, indignant at this unceremonious treatment of his master, drew his sabre, fell upon the Guison-Tamba, and laid him dead on the steps of his throne. This terrible event roused the whole Lamasery, and indignation quickly communicated itself to all the Lamas of the Blue Town.

They ran to arms in every quarter, and the life of the Emperor, who had but a small retinue, was exposed to the greatest danger. In order to calm the irritation of the Lamas, he publicly reproached the *Kiang-Kian* with his violence. "If the Guison-Tamba," answered the *Kiang-Kian*, " was not a living Buddha, why did he not rise in the presence of the master of the universe ? If he was a living Buddha, how was it he did not know I was going to kill him ? " Meanwhile the danger to the life of the Emperor became every moment more imminent ; he had no other means of escape than that of taking off his imperial robes, and attiring himself in the dress of a private soldier. Under favour of this disguise, and the general confusion, he was enabled to rejoin his army, which was near at hand. The greater part of the men who had accompanied the Emperor into the Blue Town were massacred, and among the rest, the murderer of the Guison-Tamba.

The Mongols sought to profit by this movement. Shortly afterwards it was announced that the Guison-Tamba had re-appeared, and that he had transmigrated to the country of the Khalkhas, who had taken him under their protection, and had sworn to avenge his murder. The Lamas of the Great Kouren set actively to the work of organization. They stripped off their red and yellow robes, clothed themselves in black, in memory of the disastrous event of the Blue Town, and allowed the hair and beard to grow, in sign of grief. Everything seemed to presage a grand rising of the Tartar tribes. The great energy and rare diplomatic talents of the Emperor Khang-Hi alone sufficed to arrest its progress. He immediately opened negociations with the Talé-Lama, Sovereign of Thibet, who was induced to use all his influence with the Lamas for the re-establishment of order, whilst Khang-Hi was intimidating the Khalkha kings by means of his troops. Gradually peace was restored ; the Lamas resumed their red and yellow robes ; but, as a memorial of their coalition in favour of the Guison-Tamba, they retained a narrow border of black on the collar of their robes. Khalkha Lamas alone bear this badge of distinction.

Ever since that period, a Hobilgan has taken the place in the Blue Town of the Guison-Tamba, who himself is resident at the Great Kouren, in the district of the Khalkhas. Meanwhile, the Emperor Khang-Hi, whose penetrating genius was always occupied with the future, was not entirely satisfied with these arrangements. He did not believe in all these doctrines of transmigration, and clearly saw that the Khalkhas, in pretending that the Guison-Tamba had reappeared among them, had no other end than that of keeping at their disposal a power capable of contending, upon occasion, with that of the Chinese Emperor. To abolish the office of Guison-Tamba would have been a desperate affair; the only course was, whilst tolerating him, to neutralize his influence. It was decreed, with the concurrence of the Court of Lha-Ssa, that the Guison-Tamba should be recognized legitimate sovereign of the Great Kouren but that after his successive deaths, he should always be bound to make his transmigrations to Thibet. Khang-Hi had good reason to believe that a Thibetian by origin would espouse with reluctance the resentments of the Khalkhas against the Court of Peking.

The Guison-Tamba, full of submission and respect for the orders of Khang-Hi and of the Talé-Lama, has never failed since that to go and accomplish his metempsychosis in Thibet. Still, as they fetch him whilst he is yet an infant, he must necessarily be influenced by those about him: and it is said, that as he grows up, he imbibes sentiments little favourable to the reigning dynasty. In 1839, when the Guison-Tamba made that journey to Peking of which we have spoken, the alarm manifested by the Court arose from the recollection of these events. The Lamas who flock from all the districts of Tartary to the Lamaseries of the Blue Town, rarely remain there

THIBET, AND CHINA

permanently. After taking their degrees, as it were, in these quasi universities, they return, one class of them, to their own countries, where they either settle in the small Lamaseries, wherein they can be more independent, or live at home with their families; retaining of their order little more than its red and yellow habit.

Another class consists of those Lamas who live neither in Lamaseries nor at home with their families, but spend their time vagabondizing about like birds of passage, travelling all over their own and the adjacent countries, and subsisting upon the rude hospitality which, in Lamasery and in tent, they are sure to receive, throughout their wandering way. Lamasery or tent they enter without ceremony, seat themselves, and while the tea is preparing for their refreshment, give their hosts an account of the places they have visited in their rambles. If they think fit to sleep where they are, they stretch themselves on the floor and repose until the morning. After breakfast they stand at the entrance of the tent, and watch the clouds for awhile, and see whence the wind blows; then they take their way, no matter whither, by this path or that, east or west, north or south, as their fancy or a smoother turf suggests, and lounge tranquilly on, sure at least, if no other shelter presents itself, by-and-by, of the shelter of the cover, as they express it, of that great tent, the world; and sure, moreover, having no destination before them, never to lose their way.

The wandering Lamas visit all the countries readily accessible to them :—China, Mantchouria, the Khalkhas, the various kingdoms of Southern Mongolia, the Ourianghai [Uriangkhai], the Koukou-Noor the northern and southern slopes of the Celestial Mountains, Thibet, India, and sometimes even Turkestan. There is no stream which they have not crossed, no mountains they have not climbed, no Grand Lama before whom they have not proſtrated themselves, no people with whom they have not associated, and whose cuſtoms and language are unknown to them. Travelling without any end in view, the places they reach are always those they sought. The ſtory of the Wandering Jew, who is for ever a wanderer, is exactly realized in these Lamas. They seem influenced by some secret power, which makes them wander unceasingly from place to place. God seems to have infused into the blood which flows in their veins something of that motive power which propels them on their way, without allowing them to stop.

The Lamas living in community are those who compose the third class. A Lamasery is a collection of small houses built around one or more Buddhic temples. These dwellings are more or less large and beautiful, according to the means of the proprietor. The Lamas who live thus in community are generally more regular than the others; they pay more attention to prayer and ſtudy. They are allowed to keep a few animals; some cows to afford them milk and butter, the principal materials of their daily food; horses; and some sheep to be killed on festivals.

Generally speaking, the Lamaseries have endowments, either royal or imperial. At certain periods of the year, the revenues are diſtributed to the Lamas according to the ſtation which they have obtained in the hierarchy. Those who have the reputation of being learned physicians, or able fortune-tellers, have often the opportunity of acquiring possession of the property of ſtrangers; yet they seldom seem to become rich. A childish and heedless race, they cannot make a moderate use of the riches they acquire; their money goes as quickly as it comes. The same Lama whom you saw yesterday in dirty, torn rags,

THIBET, AND CHINA

to-day rivals in the magnificence of his attire the grandeur of the higheſt dignitaries of the Lamasery. So soon as animals or money are placed within his disposition, he ſtarts off to the next trading town, sells what he has to sell, and clothes himself in the richeſt attire he can purchase. For a month or two he plays the elegant idler, and then, his money all gone, he repairs once more to the Chinese town, this time to pawn his fine clothes for what he can get, and with the certainty that once in the *Tang-Pou*, he will never, except by some chance, redeem them. All the pawnbrokers' shops in the Tartar Chinese towns are full of these Lama relics. The Lamas are very numerous in Tartary; we think we may affirm, without exaggeration, that they compose at leaſt a third of the population. In almoſt all families, with the exception of the eldeſt son, who remains a layman, the male children become Lamas.

The Tartars embrace this profession compulsorily, not of their own free will; they are Lamas or laymen from their birth, according to the will of the parents. But as they grow up, they grow accuſtomed to this life; and, in the end, religious exaltation attaches them ſtrongly to it.

It is said that the policy of the Mantchou dynaſty is to increase the number of Lamas in Tartary; the Chinese Mandarins so assured us, and the thing seems probable enough. It is certain that the Government of Peking, whilſt it leaves to poverty and want the Chinese bonzes, honours and favours Lamanism in a special degree. The secret intention of the Government, in augmenting the number of the Lamas, who are bound to celibacy, is to arreſt, by this means, the progress of the population in Tartary. The recollection of the former power of the Mongols ever fills its mind; it knows that they were formerly maſters of the empire,—and in the fear of a new invasion, it seeks to enfeeble them by all means in its power. Yet, although Mongolia is scantily peopled, in comparison with its immense extent, it could, at a day's notice, send forth a formidable army. A high Lama, the Guison-Tamba, for instance, would have but to raise his finger, and all the Mongols, from the frontiers of Siberia to the extremities of Thibet, rising as one man, would precipitate themselves like a torrent wherever their sainted leader might direct them. The profound peace which they have enjoyed for more than two centuries, might seem to have necessarily enervated their warlike character; nevertheless, you may still observe that they have not altogether lost their taste for warlike adventures. The great campaigns of Tching giskhan, who led them to the conquest of the world, have not escaped their memory during the long period of leisure of their nomadic life; they love to talk of them, and to feed their imagination with vague projects of invasion.

During our short stay at the Blue Town we had constant conversations with the Lamas of the most celebrated Lamaseries, endeavouring to obtain fresh information on the state of Buddhism in Tartary and Thibet. All they told us only served to confirm us more and more in what we had before learnt on this subject. In the Blue Town, as at Tolon-Noor, everyone told us that the doctrine would appear more sublime and more luminous as we advanced towards the west. From what the Lamas said, who had visited Thibet, Lha-Ssa was, as it were, a great focus of light, the rays of which grew more and more feeble in proportion as they became removed from their centre.

One day we had an opportunity of talking with a Thibetian Lama for some time, and the things he told us about religion astounded us greatly. A brief explanation of the Christian doctrine, which we gave to him, seemed scarcely to surprise him; he even

maintained that our views differed little from those
of the Grand Lamas of Thibet. "You muſt not
confound," said he, "religious truths with the super-
ſtitions of the vulgar. The Tartars, poor, simple
people, proſtrate themselves before whatever they
see; everything with them is *Borhan* [*Burkhan*].
Lamas, prayer books, temples, Lamaseries, ſtones,
heaps of bones,—'tis all the same to them: down they
go on their knees, crying, *Borhan! Borhan!*"
"But the Lamas themselves admit innumerable
Borhans?" "Let me explain," said our friend,
smilingly; "there is but one Sovereign of the
universe, the Creator of all things, alike without
beginning and without end. In Dchagar [rGya-gar]
(India) he bears the name of Buddha, in Thibet, that
of Samtche Mitcheba [Sangs-rgyas-mi-skye-va] All
Powerful Eternal; the Dcha-Mi [rGya-mi], (Chinese)
call him Fo, and the Sok-Po-Mi [Sog-po-mi]
(Tartars), Borhan." "You say that Buddha is sole;
in that case, who are the Talé-Lama of Lha-
Ssa, the Bandchan [Pan-ch'en] of Djachi-Loumbo
[Jashilumbo (bkra-shis Lhun-po)], the Tsong-Kaba
[Tsong-kha-pa], of the Sifan [Hsi-fan], the Kaldan
[Galdan (dGa'-ldan)] of Tolon-Noor, the Guison-
Tamba of the Great Kouren, the Hobilgan of Blue
Town, the Houtouktou [Hutuktu] of Peking, the
Chaberon [*shabron*] of the Tartar and Thibetian
Lamaseries generally?" "They are all equally
Buddha." "Is Buddha visible?" "No, he is
without a body; he is a spiritual subſtance." "So
Buddha is sole, and yet there exiſts innumerable
Buddhas: the Talé-Lama, and so on. Buddha is
incorporeal; he cannot be seen, and yet the Talé-
Lama, the Guison-Tamba, and the reſt are visible, and
have bodies like our own. How do you explain all
this?" "The doctrine, I tell you, is true," said the
Lama, raising his arm, and assuming a remarkable

accent of authority, "it is the doctrine of the West, but it is of unfathomable profundity. It cannot be sounded to the bottom."

These words of the Thibetian Lama astonished us strangely; the Unity of God, the mystery of the Incarnation, the dogma of the Real Presence seemed to us enveloped in his creed; yet with ideas so sound in appearance, he admitted the metempsychosis, and a sort of pantheism of which he could give no account.

These new indications respecting the religion of Buddha gave us hopes that we should really find among the Lamas of Thibet a symbolism more refined and superior to the common belief, and confirmed us in the resolution we had adopted, of keeping on our course westward.

Previous to quitting the inn we called in the landlord, to settle our bill. We had calculated that the entertainment, during four days, of three men and our animals, would cost us at least two ounces of silver; we were therefore agreeably surprised to hear the landlord say, " Sirs Lamas, there is no occasion for going into any accounts; put 300 sapeks into the till, and that will do very well. My house," he added, "is recently established, and I want to give it a good character. You are come from a distant land, and I would enable you to say to your countrymen that my establishment is worthy of their confidence." We replied that we would everywhere mention his disinterestedness; and that our countrymen, whenever they had occasion to visit the Blue Town, would certainly not fail to put-up at the " Hotel of the Three Perfections."

CHAPTER VI

WE quitted the Blue Town on the fourth day of the ninth moon. We had already been travelling more than a month. It was with the utmoſt difficulty that our little caravan could get out of the town. The ſtreets were encumbered with men, cars, animals, ſtalls in which the traders displayed their goods; we could only advance ſtep by ſtep, and at times we were obliged to come to a halt, and wait for some minutes until the way became a little cleared. It was near noon before we reached the laſt houses of the town, outside the weſtern gate. There, upon a level road, our camels were at length able to proceed at their ease in all the fulness of their long ſtep. A chain of rugged rocks rising on our right sheltered us so completely from the north wind, that we did not at all feel the rigour of the weather. The country through which we were now travelling was ſtill a portion of Weſtern Toumet. We observed in all directions the same indications of prosperity and comfort which had so much gratified us eaſt of the town. Everywhere around substantial villages presented proofs of successful agriculture and trade. Although we could not set up our tent in the cultivated fields by which we were now surrounded, yet, as far as circumſtances permitted, we adhered to our Tartar habits. Inſtead of entering an inn to take our morning meal, we seated ourselves under a rock or tree, and there breakfaſted upon some rolls fried in oil, of which we had bought a supply at the Blue Town. The passers-by laughed at this ruſtic proceeding, but they were not surprised at it. Tartars, unused to the manners of civilized nations, are entitled to take their repaſt by the roadside even in places where inns abound.

During the day this mode of travelling was pleasant and convenient enough; but, as it would not have been prudent to remain out all night, at sunset we sought an inn: the preservation of our animals of itself sufficed to render this proceeding necessary. There was nothing for them to eat on the way-side, and had we not resorted in the evening to places where we could purchase forage for them, they would, of course, have speedily died.

On the second evening after our departure from Blue Town, we encountered at an inn a very singular personage. We had juſt tied our animals to a manger under a shed in the great court, when a traveller made his appearance, leading by a halter a lean, raw-boned horse. The traveller was short, but then his rotundity was prodigious. He wore on his head a great ſtraw hat, the flapping brim of which reſted on his shoulders; a long sabre suspended from his girdle presented an amusing contraſt with the peaceful joyousness of his physiognomy. "Superintendent of the soup-kettle," cried he, as he entered, "is there room for me in your tavern?" "I have but one travellers' room," answered the inn-keeper, "and three Mongols who have juſt come occupy it; you can ask them if they will make room for you." The traveller walked towards us. "Peace and happiness unto you, Sirs Lamas; do you need the whole of your room, or can you accommodate me?" "Why not? We are all travellers, and should serve one another." "Words of excellence! You are Tartars; I am Chinese, yet comprehending the claims of hospitality, you aƈt upon the truth, that all men are brothers." Hereupon, faſtening his horse to a manger, he joined us, and, having deposited his travelling bag upon the *kang*, ſtretched himself at full length, with the air of a man greatly fatigued. "Whither are you bound?" asked we; "are you going to buy up salt or catsup for some Chinese company?" "No; I represent a great commercial house at Peking, and I am collecting some debts from the Tartars. Where are you going?" "We shall to-day pass the Yellow River to Tchagan-Kouren [Chagan-küren], and then journey westward through the country of the Ortous [Ordos]." "You are not Mongols, apparently?" "No; we are from the West." "Well, it seems as if we are both of one trade; you, like myself, are Tartar-eaters." "Tartar-eaters! What do you mean?" "Why, we eat the Tartars. You eat them by prayers; I by commerce. And why not? The Mongols are poor simpletons, and we may as well get their money as anybody else." "You are mistaken. Since we entered Tartary we have spent a great deal, but we have never taken a single sapek from the Tartars." "Oh, nonsense!" "What! do you suppose our camels and our baggage came to us from the Mongols?" "Why, I thought you came here to recite your prayers." We entered into some explanation of the difference between our principles and those of the Lamas, for whom the traveller had mistaken us, and he was altogether amazed at our disinterestedness. "Things are quite the other way here," said he. "You won't get a Lama to say prayers for nothing; and certainly, as for me, I should never set foot in Tartary but for the sake of money." "But how is it you manage to make such good meals of the Tartars?" "Oh, we devour them; we pick them clean. You've observed the silly race, no doubt; whatever they see when they come into our towns they want, and when we know who they are, and where we can find them, we let them have goods upon credit, of course at a considerable advance upon the price, and upon interest at thirty or forty per cent, which is quite right and necessary.

In China the Emperor's laws do not allow this; it is only done with the Tartars. Well, they don't pay the money, and the intereſt goes on until there is a good sum owing worth the coming for. When we come for it, they've no money, so we merely take all the cattle and sheep and horses we can get hold of for the intereſt, and leave the capital debt and future intereſt to be paid next time, and so it goes on from one generation to another. Oh! a Tartar debt is a complete gold mine."

Day had not broken when the *Yao-Tchang-Ti* [*yao-chang-ti*] "exaċtor of debts" was on foot. "Sirs Lamas," said he, " I am going to saddle my horse, and proceed on my way,—I propose to travel to-day with you." " 'Tis a singular mode of travelling with people, to ſtart before they're up," said we. "Oh, your camels go faſter than my horse; you'll soon overtake me, and we shall enter Tchagan-Kouren 'White Enclosure' together." He rode off, and at daybreak we followed him. This was a black day with us, for in it we had to mourn a loss. After travelling several hours, we perceived that Arsalan was not with the caravan. We halted, and Samdadchiemba, mounted on his little mule, turned back in search of the dog. He went through several villages which we had passed in the course of the morning, but his search was fruitless; he returned without having either seen or heard of Arsalan. "The dog was Chinese," said Samdadchiemba; "he was not used to a nomadic life, and getting tired of wandering about over the desert, he has taken service in the cultivated diſtriċt. What is to be done? Shall we wait for him?" " No, it is late, and we are far from White Enclosure." " Well, if there is no dog, there is no dog; and we muſt do without him." This sentimental effusion of Samdadchiemba gravely delivered, we proceeded on our way.

THIBET, AND CHINA

At first, the loss of Arsalan grieved us somewhat. We were accustomed to see him running to and fro in the prairie, rolling in the long grass, chasing the grey squirrels, and scaring the eagles from their seat on the plain. His incessant evolutions served to break the monotony of the country through which we were passing, and to abridge, in some degree, the tedious length of the way. His office of porter gave him especial title to our regret. Yet, after the first impulses of sorrow, reflection told us that the loss was not altogether so serious as it had at first appeared. Each day's experience of the nomadic life had served more and more to dispel our original apprehension of robbers. Moreover, Arsalan, under any circumstances would have been a very ineffective guard; for his incessant galloping about during the day sent him at night into a sleep which nothing could disturb. This was so much the case, that every morning, making what noise we might in taking down our tent, loading the camels, and so on, there would Arsalan remain, stretched on the grass, sleeping a leaden sleep; and when the caravan was about to start, we had to arouse him with a sound kick or two. Upon one occasion, a strange dog made his way into our tent, without the smallest opposition on the part of Arsalan, and had full time to devour our mess of oatmeal and a candle, the wick of which he left contumeliously on the outside of the tent. A consideration of economy completed our restoration to tranquillity of mind: each day we had had to provide Arsalan with a ration of meal, at least quite equal in quantity to that which each of us consumed; and we were not rich enough to have constantly seated at our table a guest with such excellent appetite, and whose services were wholly inadequate to compensate for the expense he occasioned.

We had been informed that we should reach White

Enclosure the same day, but the sun had set, and as yet we saw no signs of the town before us. By-and-by what seemed clouds of dust made their appearance in the distance, approaching us. By degrees they developed themselves in the form of camels, laden with western merchandise for sale in Peking. When we met the first camel-driver, we asked him how far it was from White Enclosure. "You see here," he said with a grin, "one end of our caravan; the other extremity is still within the town." "Thanks," cried we; "in that case we shall soon be there." "Well, you've not more than fifteen lis to go." "Fifteen lis! why, you've just told us that the other end of your caravan is still in the town." "So it is, but our caravan consists of at least ten thousand camels." "If that be the case," said we, "there is no time to be lost: a good journey to you, and peace," and on we went.

The cameleers had stamped upon their features, almost blackened with the sun, a character of uncouth misanthropy. Enveloped from head to foot in goat-skins, they were placed between the humps of their camels, just like bales of merchandise; they scarcely condescended to turn even their heads round to look at us. Five months journeying across the desert seemed almost to have brutified them. All the camels of this immense caravan wore suspended from their necks Thibetian bells, the silvery sound of which produced a musical harmony which contrasted very agreeably with the sullen taciturn aspect of the drivers. In our progress, however, we contrived to make them break silence from time to time; the roguish Dchiahour attracted their attention to us in a very marked manner. Some of the camels, more timid than others, took fright at the little mule, which they doubtless imagined to be a wild beast. In their endeavour to escape in an opposite direction they drew after them the camels next following them in the procession, so that, by this operation, the caravan assumed the form of an immense bow. This abrupt evolution aroused the cameleers from their sullen torpidity; they grumbled bitterly, and directed fierce glances against us, as they exerted themselves to restore the procession to its proper line. Samdadchiemba, on the contrary, shouted with laughter; it was in vain that we told him to ride somewhat apart in order not to alarm the camels; he turned a deaf ear to all we said. The discomfiture of the procession was quite a delightful entertainment to him, and he made his little mule caracole about in the hope of an encore.

The first cameleer had not deceived us. We journeyed on between the apparently interminable file of the caravan, and a chain of rugged rocks, until night had absolutely set in, and even then we did not see the town. The last camel had passed on, and we seemed alone in the desert, when a man came riding by on a donkey. "Elder brother," said we, "is White Enclosure still distant?" "No, brothers," he replied, "it is just before you, there, where you see the lights. You have not more than five lis to go." Five lis! It was a long way in the night, and upon a strange road, but we were fain to resign ourselves. The night grew darker and darker. There was no moon, no stars even, to guide us on our way. We seemed advancing amid chaos and abysses. We resolved to alight, in the hope of seeing our way somewhat more clearly; the result was precisely the reverse; we would advance a few steps gropingly and slowly; then, all of a sudden, we threw back our heads in fear of dashing them against rocks or walls that seemed to rise from an abyss. We speedily got covered with perspiration, and were only happy to mount our camels once more, and rely on their clearer sight and surer feet. Fortunately the baggage was well secured: what misery would it have been had that fallen off amid all this darkness, as it had frequently done before! We arrived at laſt in Tchagan-Kouren, but the difficulty now was to find an inn. Every house was shut up, and there was not a living creature in the ſtreets, except a number of great dogs that ran barking after us.

At length, after wandering haphazard through several ſtreets, we heard the ſtrokes of a hammer upon an anvil. We proceeded towards the sound, and before long, a great light, a thick smoke, and sparks glittering in the air, announced that we had come upon a blacksmith's shop. We presented ourselves at the door, and humbly entreated our brothers, the smiths, to tell us where we should find an inn. After a few jeſts upon Tartars and camels, the company assented to our requeſt, and a boy, lighting a torch, came out to act as our guide to an inn.

After knocking and calling for a long time at the door of the firſt inn we came to, the landlord opened it, and was inquiring who we were, when, unluckily for us, one of our camels, worried by a dog, took it into his head to send forth a succession of those horrible cries for which the animal is remarkable. The innkeeper at once shut his door in our faces. At all the inns where we successively applied, we were received in much the same manner. No sooner were the camels noticed than the answer was, No room; in point of fact, no innkeeper, if he can avoid it, will receive camels into his ſtables at all: their size occupies great space, and their appearance almost invariably creates alarm among the other animals; so that Chinese travellers generally make it a condition with the landlord before they enter an inn, that no Tartar caravan shall be admitted. Our guide finding all our efforts futile, got tired of accompanying us, wished us good-night, and returned to his forge.

We were exhausted with weariness, hunger, and thirst, yet there seemed no remedy for the evil, when all at once we heard the bleating of sheep. Following the sound, we came to a mud enclosure, the door of which was at once opened upon our knocking. "Brother," said we, "is this an inn?" "No, it is a sheep-house. Who are you?" "We are travellers, who have arrived here, weary and hungry; but no one will receive us." As we were speaking, an old man came to the door, holding in his hand a lighted torch. As soon as he saw our camels and our costume, "*Mendou! Mendou!*" he exclaimed, "Sirs Lamas, enter; there is room for your camels in the court, and my house is large enough for you; you shall stay and rest here for several days." We entered joyfully, fastened our camels to the manger, and seated ourselves round the hearth, where already tea was prepared for us. "Brother," said we to the old man, "we need not ask whether it is to Mongols that we owe this hospitality." "Yes, Sirs Lamas," said he, "we are all Mongols here. We have for some time past quitted the tent, to reside here; so that we may better carry on our trade in sheep. Alas! we are insensibly becoming Chinese!" "Your manner of life," returned we, "may have changed, but it is certain that your hearts have remained Tartar. Nowhere else in all Tchagan-Kouren has the door of kindness been opened to us."

Observing our fatigue, the head of the family unrolled some skins in a corner of the room, and we gladly laid ourselves down to repose. We should have slept on till the morning, but Samdadchiemba aroused us to partake of the supper which our hosts had hospitably prepared—two large cups of tea, cakes baked in the ashes, and some chops of boiled mutton, arranged on a stool by way of a table. The meal seemed, after our long fasting, perfectly magnificent; we partook of it heartily, and then having exchanged pinches of snuff with the family, resumed our slumber.

Next morning we communicated the plan of our journey to our Mongol hosts. No sooner had we mentioned that we intended to pass the Yellow River, and thence traverse the country of the Ortous, than the whole family burst out with exclamations. "It is quite impossible," said the old man, "to cross the Yellow River. Eight days ago the river overflowed its banks, and the plains on both sides are completely inundated." This intelligence filled us with the utmost consternation. We had been quite prepared to pass the Yellow River under circumstances of danger arising from the wretchedness of the ferry boats and the difficulty of managing our camels in them, and we knew, of course, that the Hoang-Ho was subject to periodical overflows; but these occur ordinarily in the rainy season, towards the sixth or seventh month, whereas we were now in the dry season, and, moreover, in a peculiarly dry season.

We proceeded forthwith towards the river to investigate the matter for ourselves, and found that the Tartar had only told us the exact truth. The Yellow River had become, as it were, a vast sea, the limits of which were scarcely visible. Here and there you could see the higher grounds rising above the water, like islands, while the houses and villages looked as though they were floating upon the waves. We consulted several persons as to the course we should adopt. Some said that further progress was impracticable, for that, even where the inundations had subsided, it had left the earth so soft and slippery that the camels could not walk upon it, while elsewhere we should have to dread at every step some deep pool, in which we should inevitably be drowned. Other opinions were more favourable, suggefting that the boats which were ftationed at intervals for the purpose would easily and cheaply convey us and our baggage in three days to the river, while the camels could follow us through the water, and that once at the river side, the great ferry-boat would carry us all over the bed of the ftream without any difficulty.

What were we to do ? To turn back was out of the queftion. We had vowed that, God aiding, we would go to Lha-Ssa whatever obftacles impeded. To turn the river by coafting it northwards would materially augment the length of our journey, and, moreover, compel us to traverse the great desert of Gobi. To remain at Tchagan-Kouren, and patiently await for a month the complete retirement of the waters and the reftoration of solidity in the roads, was, in one point of view, the moft prudent course, but there was a grave inconvenience about it. We and our five animals could not live for a month in an inn without occasioning a moft alarming atrophy in our already meagre purse. The only course remaining was to place ourselves exclusively under the protection of Providence and to go on, regardless of mud or marsh. This resolution was adopted, and we returned home to make the necessary preparations.

Tchagan-Kouren is a large, fine town of recent conftruction. It is not marked on the map of China compiled by M. Andriveau-Goujon, doubtless because it did not exift at the time when the Fathers Jesuits residing at Peking were directed by the Emperor Khang-Hi to draw maps of the empire. Nowhere in China, Mantchouria, or in Thibet, have we seen a town like White Enclosure. The ftreets are wide, clean, and clear ; the houses regular in their arrangements, and of very fair architecture. There are several squares, decorated with trees, a feature which ftruck us all the more that we had not observed it anywhere else in this part of the world. There are plenty of shops, commodiously arranged, and well supplied with Chinese, and even with European goods. The trade of Tchagan-Kouren, however, is greatly checked by the proximity of the Blue Town, to which, as a place of commerce, the Mongols have been much longer accustomed.

Our worthy Tartar host, in his hospitality, sought to divert us from our project, but unsuccessfully; and he even got rallied by Samdadchiemba for his kindness. "It is quite clear," said our guide, "that you've become a mere Kitat, and think that a man must not set out upon a journey unless the earth is perfectly dry and the sky perfectly cloudless. I have no doubt you go out to lead your sheep with an umbrella in one hand and a fan in the other." It was ultimately arranged that we should take our departure at daybreak next morning.

Meantime we went out into the town to make the necessary supply of provisions. To guard against the possibility of being inundation-bound for several days, we bought a quantity of small loaves fried in mutton fat, and for our animals we procured a quantity of the most portable forage we could find.

Next morning we departed full of confidence in the goodness of God. Our Tartar host, who insisted upon escorting us out of the town, led us to an elevation whence we could see in the distance a long line of thick vapour which seemed journeying from west to east; it marked the course of the Yellow River. "Where you see that vapour," said the old man, "you will find a great dike, which serves to keep the river in bounds, except upon any extraordinary rise of the waters. That dike is now dry; when you come to it, proceed along it until you reach the little pagoda you see yonder, on your right; there you will find a boat that will convey you across the river. Keep that pagoda in sight and you can't lose your way." We cordially thanked the old man for the kindness he had shown us and proceeded on our journey.

We were soon up to the knees of the camels in a thick slimy compoſt of mud and water, covering other somewhat firmer mud, over which the poor animals slowly slid on their painful way; their heads turning alternately right and left, their limbs trembling, and the sweat exuding from each pore. Every moment we expected them to fall beneath us. It was near noon ere we arrived at a little village, not more than a couple of miles from where we had left the old man. Here a few wretched people, whose rags scarce covered their gaunt frames, came round us, and accompanied us to the edge of a broad piece of water, portion of a lake which, they told us, and which it was quite clear, we muſt pass before we could reach the dike indicated by the Tartar. Some boatmen proposed to carry us over this lake to the dike. We asked them how many sapeks they would charge for the service :—" Oh, very little; next to nothing. You see we will take in our boats you, and the baggage, and the mule, and the horse; one of our people will lead the camels through the lake; they are too big to come into the boat. When one comes to reckon on all this load, and all the trouble and fatigue, the price seems absolutely less than nothing."
" True, there will be some trouble in the affair, no one denies it; but let us have a diſtinct underſtanding. How many sapeks do you ask?" "Oh, scarcely any. We are all brothers; and you, brothers, need all our assiſtance in travelling. We know that; we feel it in our hearts. If we could only afford it, we should have pleasure in carrying you over for nothing; but look at our clothes. We poor fellows are very poor. Our boat is all we have to depend upon. It is necessary that we should gain a livelihood by that; five lis sail, three men, a horse, a mule, and luggage; but come,

as you are spiritual persons, we will only charge you 2,000 sapeks." The price was preposterous; we made no answer. We took our animals by the bridle and turned back, pretending that we would not continue our journey. Scarcely had we advanced twenty paces before the ferryman ran after us. "Sirs Lamas, are you not going to cross the water in my boat?" "Why," said we drily, "doubtless you are too rich to take any trouble in the matter. If you really wanted to let your boat, would you ask 2,000 sapeks?" "2,000 sapeks is the price I asked; but what will you give?" "If you like to take 500 sapeks let us set out at once; it is already late." "Return, Sirs Lamas; get into the boat;" and he caught hold, as he spoke, of the halters of our beasts. We considered that the price was at last fixed; but we had scarcely arrived on the border of the lake, when the ferryman exclaimed to one of his comrades,— "Come, our fortune deserts us to-day; we must bear much fatigue for little remuneration. We shall have to row five lis, and after all we shall only have 1,500 sapeks to divide between eight of us." "1,500 sapeks!" exclaimed we; "you are mocking us; we will leave you;" and we turned back for the second time. Some mediators, inevitable persons in all Chinese matters, presented themselves, and undertook to settle the fare. It was at length decided that we should pay 800 sapeks; the sum was enormous, but we had no other means of pursuing our way. The boatmen knew this, and took accordingly the utmost advantage of our position.

The embarkation was effected with extraordinary celerity, and we soon quitted the shore. Whilst we advanced by means of the oars, on the surface of the lake, a man mounted on a camel and leading two others after him, followed a path traced out by a small boat rowed by a waterman. The latter was obliged

THIBET, AND CHINA

every now and then to sound the depth of the water, and the camel-driver needed to be very attentive in directing his course in the strait trail left by the boat, lest he should be swallowed up in the holes beneath the water. The camels advanced slowly, stretching out their long necks, and at times leaving only their heads and the extremity of their humps visible above the lake. We were in continual alarm; for these animals not being able to swim, there only needed a false step to precipitate them to the bottom. Thanks to the protection of God, all arrived safe at the dike which had been pointed out to us. The boatmen, after assisting us to replace, in a hasty manner, our baggage on the camels, indicated the point whither we must direct our steps. "Do you see, to the right, that small *Miao* (pagoda) ? A little from the *Miao*, do you observe those wooden huts and those black nets hanging from long poles ? There you will find a ferry-boat to cross the river. Follow this dike, and go in peace."

After having proceeded with difficulty for half an hour, we reached the ferry-boat. The boatmen immediately came to us. "Sirs Lamas," said they, "you intend, doubtless, to cross the Hoang-Ho, but you see this evening the thing is impracticable—the sun is just setting." "You are right; we will cross to-morrow at daybreak: meanwhile, let us settle the price, so that to-morrow we may lose no time in deliberation." The waterman would have preferred waiting till the morrow to discuss this important point, expecting we should offer a much larger sum, when just about to embark. At first their demands were preposterous: happily, there were two boats which competed together, otherwise we should have been ruined. The price was ultimately fixed at 1,000 sapeks. The passage was not long, it is true, for the river had nearly resumed its bed; but the waters were very rapid, and, moreover, the camels had to ride. The amount, enormous in itself, appeared, upon the whole moderate, considering the difficulty and trouble of the passage. This business arranged, we considered how we should pass the night. We could not think of seeking an asylum in the fishermen's cabins; even if they had been sufficiently large, we should have had considerable objection to place our effects in the hands of these folks. We were sufficiently acquainted with the Chinese not to trust to their honesty. We looked out for a place whereon to set up our tent; but we could find nowhere a spot sufficiently dry: mud or stagnant water covered the ground in all directions. About a hundred yards from the shore was a small *Miao*, or temple of idols; a narrow, high path led to it. We proceeded thither to see if we could find there a place of repose. It turned out as we wished. A portico, supported by three stone pillars, stood before the entrance door, which was secured by a large padlock. This portico, made of granite, was raised a few feet from the ground, and you ascended it by five steps. We determined to pass the night here.

Samdadchiemba asked if it would not be a monstrous superstition to sleep on the steps of a *Miao*. When we had relieved his scruples, he made sundry philosophical reflections. "Behold," said he, "a *Miao* which has been built by the people of the country, in honour of the god of the river. Yet, when it rained in Thibet, the Pou-ssa had no power to preserve itself from inundation. Nevertheless, this *Miao* serves at present to shelter two missionaries of Jehovah— the only real use it has ever served." Our Dchiahour, who at first had scrupled to lodge under the portico of this idolatrous temple, soon thought the idea magnificent, and laughed hugely.

After having arranged our luggage in this singular encampment, we proceeded to tell our beads on the shores of the Hoang-Ho. The moon was brilliant, and lit up this immense river, which rolled over an even and smooth bed its yellow and tumultuous waters. The Hoang-Ho is beyond a doubt one of the finest rivers in the world; it rises in the mountains of Thibet, and crosses the Koukou-Noor, entering China by the province of Kan-Sou [Kan-su]. Thence it follows the sandy regions at the feet of the Alechan [Alashan] mountains, encircles the country of the Ortous; and after having watered China first from north to south, and then from west to east, it falls into the Yellow Sea. The waters of the Hoang-Ho, pure and clear at their source, only take the yellow hue after having passed the sands of the Alechan and the Ortous. They are almost, throughout, level with the lands through which they flow, and it is this circumstance which occasions those inundations so disastrous to the Chinese. As for the Tartar nomads, when the waters rise, all they have to do is to strike their tents, and drive their herds elsewhere.[1]

Though the Yellow River had cost us so much trouble, we derived much satisfaction from taking a walk at night upon its solitary banks, and listening to the solemn murmur of its majestic waters. We were contemplating this grand work of nature, when

[1] The bed of the Yellow River has undergone numerous and notable variations. In ancient times, its mouth was situated in the Gulf of Pe-Tche-Li, in latitude 39. At present it is on the 34th parallel, twenty-five leagues from the primitive point. The Chinese government is compelled annually to expend enormous sums in keeping the river within its bed and preventing inundations. In 1779, the embankment for this purpose cost no less a sum than £1,600,000. Yet, despite these precautions, inundations are of frequent occurrence; for the bed of the Yellow River, in the provinces of Ho-Nan and Kiang-Sou [Kiangsu], is higher for 200 leagues than the plain through which it passes. This bed continuing to rise with the quantity of mud deposited, there is inevitably impending, at no remote period, an awful catastrophe, involving in death and desolation all the adjacent district.

Samdadchiemba recalled us to the prose of life, by announcing that the oatmeal was ready. Our repast was as brief as it was plain. We then stretched ourselves on our goat-skins, in the portico, so that the three described the three sides of a triangle, in the centre of which we piled our baggage; for we had no faith at all that the sanctity of the place would deter robbers, if robbers there were in the vicinity.

As we have mentioned, the little *Miao* was dedicated to the divinity of the Yellow River. The idol, seated on a pedestal of grey brick, was hideous, as all those idols are that you ordinarily see in Chinese pagodas. From a broad, flat, red face, rose two great staring eyes, like eggs stuck into orbits, the smaller end projecting. Thick eyebrows, instead of describing a horizontal line, began at the bottom of each ear, and met in the middle of the forehead, so as to form an obtuse angle. The idol had on its head a marine shell, and brandished, with a menacing air, a sword like a scythe. This *Pou-ssa* had, right and left, two attendants, each putting out its tongue, and apparently making faces at it.

Just as we were lying down, a man approached us, holding in one hand a small paper lantern. He opened the grating which led to the interior of the *Miao*, prostrated himself thrice, burned incense in the censers, and lighted a small lamp at the feet of the idol. This personage was not a bonze. His hair, hanging in a tress, and his blue garments, showed him to be a layman. When he had finished his idolatrous ceremonies, he came to us. "I will leave the door open," said he; "you'll sleep more comfortably inside than in the portico." "Thanks," replied we; "shut the door, however; for we shall do very well where we are. Why have you been burning incense? Who is the idol of this place?" "It is the spirit of the Hoang-Ho, who inhabits this *Miao*. I have burned incense before him, in order that our fishing may be productive, and that our boats may float without danger." "The words you utter," cried Samdadchiemba, insolently, " are mere *hou-choue* [*hu-shuo*] (stuff and nonsense). How did it happen that the other day, when the inundation took place, the *Miao* was flooded, and your *Pou-ssa* was covered with mud ? " To this sudden apostrophe the pagan churchwarden made no answer, but took to his heels. We were much surprised at this proceeding; but the explanation came next morning.

We stretched ourselves on our goat-skins once more, and endeavoured to sleep, but sleep came slowly and but for a brief period. Placed between marshes and the river, we felt throughout the night a piercing cold, which seemed to transfix us to the very marrow. The sky was pure and serene, and in the morning we saw that the marshes around were covered with a thick sheet of ice. We made our preparations for departure, but upon collecting the various articles, a handkerchief was missing. We remembered that we had imprudently hung it upon the grating at the entrance of the *Miao*, so that it was half in and half out of the building. No person had been near the place except the man who had come to pay his devotions to the idol. We could, therefore, without much rashness, attribute the robbery to him, and this explained why he had made his exit so rapidly, without replying to Samdadchiemba. We could easily have found the man, for he was one of the fishermen engaged upon the station, but it would have been a fruitless labour. Our only effectual course would have been to seize the thief in the fact.

Next morning, we placed our baggage upon the camels, and proceeded to the river-side, fully persuaded that we had a miserable day before us. The camels having a horror of the water, it is sometimes impossible to make them get into a boat. You may pull their noses, or nearly kill them with blows, yet not make them advance a step: they would die sooner. The boat before us seemed especially to present almost insurmountable obstacles. It was not flat and large, like those which generally serve as ferry-boats. Its sides were very high, so that the animals were obliged to leap over them at the risk and peril of breaking their legs. If you wanted to move a carriage into it, you had first of all to pull the vehicle to pieces.

The boatmen had already taken hold of our baggage, for the purpose of conveying it into their abominable vehicle, but we stopped them. "Wait a moment; we must first try and get the camels in. If they won't enter the boat, there is no use in placing the baggage in it." "Whence came your camels, that they can't get into people's boats?" "It matters little whence they came; what we tell you is that the tall white camel has never hitherto consented to cross any river, even in a flat boat." "Tall camel or short, flat boat or high boat, into the boat the camel shall go," and so saying, the ferryman ran and fetched an immense cudgel. "Catch hold of the string in the animal's nose," cried he to a companion. "We'll see if we can't make the brute get into the boat." The man in the boat hauled at the string; the man behind beat the animal vehemently on the legs with his cudgel, but all to no purpose; the poor camel sent forth piercing cries, and stretched out its long neck. The blood flowed from its nostrils, the sweat from every pore; but not an inch forward would the creature move; yet one step would have placed it in the boat, the sides of which were touched by its fore legs.

We could not endure the painful spectacle. "No more of this," we cried to the ferryman; "it is useless to beat the animal. You might break its legs or kill it before it would consent to enter your boat." The two men at once left off, for they were tired, the one of pulling, the other of beating. What were we to do? We had almoſt made up our minds to ascend the banks of the river until we found some flat boat, when the ferryman all at once jumped up, radiant with an idea. "We will make another attempt," cried he, "and if that fails I give the matter up. Take the ſtring gently," he added, to a companion, "and keep the camel's feet as close as ever you can to the side of the boat." Then, going back for some paces, he dashed forward with a spring and threw himself with all his weight upon the animal's rear. The shock, so violent and unexpeƈted, occasioned the camel somewhat to bend its fore legs. A second shock immediately succeeded the firſt, and the animal, in order to prevent itself from falling into the water, had no remedy but to raise its feet and place them within the boat. This effeƈted, the reſt was easy. A few pinches of the nose and a few blows sufficed to impel the hind legs after the fore, and the white camel was at laſt in the boat, to the extreme satisfaƈtion of all present. The other animals were embarked after the same fashion, and we proceeded on our watery way.

Firſt, however, the ferryman deemed it necessary that the animals should kneel, so that no movement of theirs on the river might occasion an overturn. His proceeding to this effeƈt was exceedingly comic. He firſt went to one camel and then to the other, pulling now this down, then that. When he approached the larger animal, the creature, remembering the man's treatment, discharged in his face a good quantity of the grass ruminating within its jaws, a compliment which the boatman returned by spitting in the animal's face. And the absurdity was, that the work made no progress. One camel was no sooner induced to kneel down than the other got up, and so the men went backwards and forwards, gradually covered by the angry creatures with the green substance, half masticated and particularly inodorus, which each animal in turns spat against him. At length, when Samdadchiemba had sufficiently entertained himself with the scene, he went to the camels, and, exercising his recognized authority over them, made them kneel in the manner desired.

We at length floated upon the waters of the Yellow River; but though there were four boatmen, their united strength could scarcely make head against the force of the current. We had effected about half our voyage, when a camel suddenly rose and shook the boat so violently that it was nearly upset. The boatmen, after ejaculating a tremendous oath, told us to look after our camels and prevent them from getting up, unless we wanted the whole party to be engulphed. The danger was indeed formidable. The camel, infirm upon its legs, and yielding to every movement of the boat, menaced us with a catastrophe. Samdadchiemba, however, managed to get quickly beside the animal and at once induced it to kneel, so that we were let off with our fright, and in due course reached the other side of the river.

At the moment of disembarkation, the horse, impatient to be once more on land, leaped out of the boat, but striking, on its way, against the anchor, fell on its side in the mud. The ground not being yet dry, we were fain to take off our shoes, and to carry the baggage on our shoulders to an adjacent eminence; there we asked the boatmen if we should be any great length of time in traversing the marsh and mud that lay stretched before us. The chief boatman raised his head, and after looking for a while towards the sun, said : " It will soon be noon ; by the evening you will reach the banks of the Little River; to-morrow you will find the ground dry." It was under these melancholy auspices that we proceeded upon our journey, through one of the most detestable districts to be found in the whole world.

We had been told in what direction we were to proceed; but the inundation had obliterated every trace of path and even of road, and we could only regulate our course by the nature of the ground, keeping as clear as we could of the deeper quagmires, sometimes making a long circuit in order to reach what seemed firmer ground, and then, finding the supposed solid turf to be nothing more than a piece of water, green with stagnant matter and aquatic plants, having to turn back, and, as it were, grope one's way in another direction, fearful, at every step, of being plunged into some gulf of liquid mud.

By-and-by, our animals, alarmed and wearied, could hardly proceed, and we were compelled to beat them severely and to exhaust our voices with bawling at them before they would move at all. The tall grass and plants of the marshes twisted about their legs, and it was only by leaps, and at the risk of throwing off both baggage and riders that they could extricate themselves. Thrice did the youngest camel lose its balance and fall; but on each occasion, the spot on which it fell was providentially dry; had it stumbled in the mud, it would inevitably have been stifled.

On our way, we met three Chinese travellers, who, by the aid of long staves, were making their laborious way through the marshes, carrying their shoes and clothes over their shoulders. We asked them in what direction we were likely to find a better road: " You would have been wiser," said they, " had you remained at Tchagan-Kouren; foot passengers can scarcely make their way through these marshes; how do you suppose you can get on with your camels?" and with this consolatory assurance, they quitted us, giving us a look of compassion, certain as they were that we should never get through the mud.

The sun was just setting, when we perceived a Mongol habitation; we made our way direct to it without heeding the difficulties of the road. In fact experience had already taught us that selection was quite out of the question, and that one way was as good as another in this universal slough. Making circuits merely lengthened the journey. The Tartars were frightened at our appearance, covered as we were with mud and perspiration; they immediately gave us some tea, and generously offered us the hospitality of their dwelling. The small mud house in which they lived, though built upon an eminence, had been half carried away by the inundation. We could not conceive what had induced them to fix their abode in this horrible district, but they told us that they were employed to tend the herds belonging to some Chinese of Tchagan-Kouren. After resting for a while, we requested information as to the best route to pursue, and we were told that the river was only five lis off, that its banks were dry, and that we should find there boats to carry us to the other side. "When you have crossed the Paga-Gol [Baga-gol] (Little River)," said our hosts, "you may proceed in peace; you will meet with no more water to interrupt you." We thanked these good Tartars for their kindness, and resumed our journey.

After half an hour's march, we discovered before us a large extent of water, studded with fishing-vessels. The title "Little River" may, for anything we know, be appropriate enough under ordinary circumstances, but at the time of our visit, the Paga-Gol was a broad sea. We pitched our tent on the bank which, by reason of its elevation, was perfectly dry, and the remarkable excellence of the pasturage determined us upon remaining in this place several days, in order to give rest to our animals, which, since their departure from Tchagan-Kouren had undergone enormous fatigue : we ourselves, too, felt the necessity of some relaxation, after the sufferings which these horrible marshes had inflicted upon us.

CHAPTER VII

Upon taking possession of our post our first business was to excavate a ditch round the tent, in order that, should rain occur, the water might be carried into a pond below. The excavated earth served to make a mound round the tent; and, within, the pack-saddles and furniture of the animals formed very comfortable bedsteads for us. Having made our new habitation as neat as possible, the next business was to make our persons neat also.

We had now been travelling for nearly six weeks, and still wore the same clothing we had assumed on our departure. The incessant pricklings with which we were harassed sufficiently indicated that our attire was peopled with the filthy vermin to which the Chinese and Tartars are familiarly accustomed, but which with Europeans are objects of horror and disgust,—lice, which of all our miseries on our long journeys have been the greatest. Hunger and thirst, fierce winds and piercing cold, wild beasts, robbers, avalanches, menaced death and actual discomfort, all had been as nothing compared with the incessant misery occasioned by these dreadful vermin.

Before quitting Tchagan-Kouren we had bought in a chemist's shop a few sapeks' worth of mercury. We now made with it a prompt and specific remedy against the lice. We had formerly got this recipe from some Chinese, and as it may be useful to others, we think it right to describe it here. You take half-an-ounce of mercury, which you mix with old tea-leaves, previously reduced to paste by mastication

THIBET, AND CHINA

To render this softer you generally add saliva, water would not have the same effect. You must afterwards bruise and stir it awhile, so that the mercury may be divided into little balls as fine as dust. You infuse this composition into a string of cotton, loosely twisted, which you hang round your neck; the lice are sure to bite at the bait, and they thereupon as surely swell, become red, and die forthwith. In China and in Tartary you have to renew this sanitary necklace once a month, for, otherwise, in these dirty countries you could not possibly keep clear from vermin, which swarm in every Chinese house and in every Mongol tent.

The Tartars are acquainted with the cheap and efficacious anti-louse mixture I have described, but they make no use of it. Accustomed from their infancy to live amid vermin, they at last take no heed whatever of them, except, indeed, when the number becomes so excessive as to involve the danger of their being absolutely eaten up. Upon such a juncture, they strip off their clothes, and have a grand battue, all the members of the family, and any friends who may have dropped in, taking part in the sport. Even Lamas, who may be present, share in the hunt, with this distinction that they do not kill the game, but merely catch it and throw it away; the reason being, that, according to the doctrine of metampsychosis, to kill any living being whatever is to incur the danger of homicide, since the smallest insect before you may be the transmigration of a man. Such is the general opinion; but we have met with Lamas whose views on this subject were more enlightened. They admitted that persons belonging to the sacerdotal class should abstain from killing animals; but not, said they, in fear of committing a murder by killing a man transmigrated into an animal, but because to kill is essentially antagonistic with the gentleness which should characterize a man of prayer, who is ever in communication with the Deity.

There are some Lamas who carry this scruple to a point approaching the puerile, so that, as they ride along, they are constantly manœuvring their horses in and out, here and there, in order to avoid trampling upon some insect or other that presents itself in their path. Yet say they, the holiest among them occasion, inadvertently, the death, every day, of a great many living creatures. It is to expiate these involuntary murders that they undergo fasting and penitence, that they recite certain prayers, and that they make prostrations.

We who had no such scruples, and whose conscience stood upon a solid basis as to the transmigration of souls, concocted, as effectively as possible, our anti-louse preparation, doubling the dose of mercury in our anxiety to kill the greatest practicable number of the vermin that had been so long tormenting us by day and by night.

It would have been to little purpose merely to kill the present vermin; it was necessary to withhold any sort of shelter or encouragement from their too probable successors, and the first point, with this view, was to wash all our under-clothing, which, for some time past, had not been subjected to any such operation. For nearly two months since our departure, we had been wholly dependent, in all respects, upon ourselves, and this necessity had compelled us to learn a little of the various professions with which we had been previously unacquainted; becoming our own tailors and shoe menders, for example, when clothes or shoes required repairs. The course of nomadic life now practically introduced us also to the occupation of washermen. After boiling some ashes and soaking our linen in the lye, we next proceeded to wash it in an adjacent pond. One great stone on which to place the linen when washed, and another wherewith to beat it while washing were our only implements of trade; but we got on very well, for the softness of the pond water gave every facility for cleansing the articles. Before long, we had the delight of seeing our linen once more clean; and when, having dried it on the grass, we folded and took it home to our tent, we were quite radiant with satisfaction.

The quiet and ease which we enjoyed in this encampment, rapidly remedied the fatigue we had undergone in the marshes. The weather was magnificent; all that we could have possibly desired. By day, a gentle, soothing heat; by night, a sky pure and serene; plenty of fuel; excellent and abundant pasturage; nitrous water, which our camels delighted in; in a word, everything to renovate the health and revive the spirits. Our rule of daily life may appear odd enough to some, and perhaps not altogether in harmony with the regulations of monastic houses, but it was in exact adaptation to the circumstances and wants of our little community.

Every morning, with the first dawn, before the earliest rays of the sun struck upon our tent, we rose spontaneously, requiring neither call-bell nor valet to rouse us. Our brief toilet made, we rolled up our goat-skins and placed them in a corner; then we swept out the tent, and put the cooking utensils in order, for we were desirous of having everything about us as clean and comfortable as possible. All things go by comparison in this world. The interior of our tent, which would have made a European laugh, filled with admiration the Tartars who from time to time paid us a visit. The cleanliness of our wooden cups, our kettle always well polished, our clothes not altogether as yet incrusted with grease; all this contrasted favourably with the dirt and disorder of Tartar habitations.

TRAVELS IN TARTARY,

Having arranged our apartment, we said prayers together, and then dispersed each apart in the desert to engage in meditation upon some pious thought. Oh! little did we need, amid the profound silence of those vast solitudes, a printed book to suggest a subject for prayer! The void and vanity of all things here below, the majesty of God, the inexhaustible measure of His Providence, the shortness of life, the essentiality of labouring with a view to the world to come, and a thousand other salutary reflections, came of themselves, without any effort on our parts, to occupy the mind with gentle musings. In the desert the heart of man is free; he is subject to no species of tyranny. Far away from us were all those hollow theories and systems, those utopias of imaginary happiness which men are constantly aiming at, and which as constantly evade their grasp; those inexhaustible combinations of selfishness and self-sufficiency, those burning passions which in Europe are ever contending, ever fermenting in men's minds and hardening their hearts. Amid these silent prairies there was nothing to disturb our tranquil thoughts, or to prevent us from reducing to their true value the futilities of this world, from appreciating at their lofty worth the things of God and of eternity.

The exercise which followed these meditations was, it must be admitted, far from mystic in its character; but it was necessary, and not wholly without entertainment in its course. Each of us hung a bag from his shoulders and went in different directions to seek *argols* for fuel. Those who have never led a nomadic life will, of course, find it difficult to understand how this occupation could possibly develop any enjoyment. Yet, when one is lucky enough to find, half concealed among the grass, an *argol*, recommendable for its size and dryness, there comes over the heart a gentle joy, one of those sudden emotions which create a transient happiness. The pleasure at finding a fine *argol* is cognate with that which the hunter feels when he discovers the track of game, with which the boy regards, his eyes sparkling, the linnet's neſt he has long sought; with which the fisherman sees quivering at the end of his line a large fish; nay, if we may compare small things with great, one might even compare this pleasure with the enthusiasm of a Leverrier when he has discovered a new planet.

Our sack, once filled with *argols*, we returned, and piled the contents with pride at the entrance of the tent; then we ſtruck a light and set the fire in movement; and while the tea was boiling in the pot, pounded the meal and put some cakes to bake in the ashes. The repaſt, it is observable, was simple and modeſt, but it was always extremely delicious, firſt, because we had prepared it ourselves, and secondly, because our appetites provided moſt efficient seasoning.

After breakfaſt, while Samdadchiemba was collecting round the tent the animals which had dispersed in search of paſturage, we recited a portion of our breviary. Towards noon we indulged in a brief repose, a few minutes of gentle but sound sleep, never interrupted by nightmare or by unpleasant dreams. This repose was all the more necessary that the evenings were prolonged far into the night. It was always with difficulty that we tore ourselves from our walks by moonlight on the banks of the river. During the day all was silent and tranquil around us; but as soon as the shades of night began to overspread the desert, the scene became animated and noisy. Aquatic birds, arriving in immense flocks, diffused themselves over the various pools, and soon thousands of shrill cries filled the air with wild harmony. The cries of anger, the accents of passion, proceeding from those myriads of migratory birds, as they disputed among themselves possession of the tufts of marsh grass in which they desired to pass the night, gave one quite the idea of a numerous people in all the fury of civil war, fighting and clamouring, in agitation and violence, for some supposed advantage, brief as this eastern night.

Tartary is populated with nomadic birds. Look up when you may, you will see them floating high in air, the vast battalions forming, in their systematically capricious flight, a thousand fantastic outlines, dissipating as soon as formed, forming again as soon as dissipated, like the creations of a kaleidoscope. Oh! how exactly are those migrant birds in their place, amid the deserts of Tartary, where man himself is never fixed in one spot, but is constantly on the move. It was very pleasant to listen to the distant hum of these winged bands, wandering about like ourselves. As we reflected upon their long peregrinations, and glanced in thought over the countries which their rapid flight must have comprehended, the recollection of our native land came vividly before us. "Who knows," we would say to each other, "who knows but that among these birds there are some who have traversed—who have, perhaps, alighted for awhile in our dear France: who have sought transient repose and refreshment in the plains of Languedoc, or on the heights of the Jura. After visiting our own country, they have doubtless pursued their route towards the north of Europe, and have come hither through the snows of Siberia, and of Upper Tartary. Oh! if these birds could understand our words, or if we could speak their tongue, how many questions should we not put to them!" Alas! we did not then know that for two years more we should be deprived of all communication with our native land. The migratory birds which visit Tartary are for the most

THIBET, AND CHINA

part known in Europe; such as wild geese, wild ducks, teal, storks, bustards, and so on. There is one bird which may deserve particular mention: the *Youen-Yang* [*yuan-yang*], an aquatic bird frequenting ponds and marshes; it is of the size and form of the wild duck, but its beak, instead of being flat, is round, its red head is sprinkled with white, its tail is black, and the rest of its plumage a fine purple; its cry is exceedingly loud and mournful, not the song of a bird, but a sort of clear, prolonged sigh, resembling the plaintive notes of a man under suffering. These birds always go in pairs; they frequent, in an especial manner, desert and marshy places. You see them incessantly skimming over the surface of the waters without the couple ever separating from each other; if one flies away the other immediately follows; and that which dies first does not leave its companion long in widowhood, for it is soon consumed by sorrow and lonesomeness. *Youen* is the name of the male, *Yang* that of the female: *Youen-Yang* their common denomination.

We remarked in Tartary another species of migratory bird, which offers various peculiarities singular in themselves, and perhaps unknown to naturalists. It is about the size of a quail; its eyes, of a brilliant black, are encircled by a magnificent ring of azure; its body is of ash colour, speckled with black; its legs, instead of feathers, are covered with a sort of long, rough hair, like that of the musk-deer; its feet are totally different from those of any other bird; they exactly resemble the paws of the green lizard, and are covered with scales so hard as to resist the edge of the sharpest knife. This singular creature, therefore, partakes at once of the bird, of the quadruped, and of the reptile. The Chinese call it *Loung-Kio* [*lung-chio*] " Dragon's Foot." These birds make their periodical appearance in vast numbers from the north, especially after a great fall of snow. They fly with astonishing swiftness, and the movements of their wings makes a loud, rattling noise, like that of heavy hail.

While we had the charge, in Northern Mongolia, of the little Christendom of the Valley of Black Waters, one of our Christians, a skilful huntsman, brought us two of these birds which he had caught alive. They were excessively ferocious; no sooner was your hand extended to touch them, than the hair on their legs bristled; and if you had the temerity to stroke them, you instantly were assailed with vehement strokes of the bill. The nature of these Dragon's Feet was evidently so wild as to preclude the possibility of preserving them alive: they would touch nothing we offered them. Perceiving, therefore, that they must soon die of starvation, we determined to kill and eat them; their flesh was of agreeable, pheasant-like savour, but terribly tough.

The Tartars might easily take any number of these migratory birds, especially of the wild geese and ducks, the crowds of which are perfectly prodigious; and take them, moreover, without the expenditure of a single ounce of powder, by merely laying traps for them on the banks of the pools, or by surprising them in the night, amongst the aquatic plants; but as we have before observed, the flesh of wild creatures is not at all to the taste of the Tartars; there is nothing to their palates at all comparable with a joint of mutton, very fat and half boiled.

The Mongols are equally disinclined to fishing; and accordingly, the highly productive lakes and ponds which one meets with so frequently in Tartary have become the property of Chinese speculators, who, with the characteristic knavery of their nation, having first obtained from the Tartar kings permission to fish in their states, have gradually converted this toleration into a monopoly most rigorously enforced. The

THIBET, AND CHINA

Paga-Gol "Little River," near which we were now encamped, has several Chinese fishing stations upon its banks. This Paga-Gol is formed by the junction of two rivers, which, taking their source from the two sides of a hill, flow in opposite directions; the one, running towards the north, falls into the Yellow River; the other, proceeding southwards, swells the current of another stream, which itself also falls into the Hoang-Ho; but at the time of the great inundations, the two rivers, in common with the hill which separates their course, all alike disappear. The overflowing of the Hoang-Ho reunites the two currents, and that which then presents itself is a large expanse of water, the breadth of which extends to nearly two miles. At this period, the fish which abound in the Yellow River repair in shoals to this new basin, wherein the water remains collected until the commencement of the winter; and during the autumn, this little sea is covered in all directions with the boats of Chinese fishermen, whose habitations for the fishing season are miserable cabins constructed on either bank.

During the first night of our encampment in this locality, we were kept awake by a strange noise, constantly recurring in the distance, as it seemed to us, the muffled and irregular roll of drums; with daybreak the noise continued, but more intermittent and less loud; it apparently came from the water. We went out and proceeded towards the bank of the lake, where a fisherman, who was boiling his tea in a little kettle supported by three stones, explained the mystery; he told us that during the night, all the fishermen seated in their barks keep moving over the water, in all directions, beating wooden drums for the purpose of alarming the fish, and driving them towards the places where the nets are spread. The poor man whom we interrogated had himself passed the whole night in this painful toil. His red, swollen eyes and his drawn face clearly indicated that it was long since he had enjoyed adequate rest. "Just now," he said, "we have a great deal of work upon our hands; there is no time to be lost if we wish to make any money of the business. The fishing season is very short; at the outside not more than three months; and a few days hence we shall be obliged to withdraw. The Paga-Gol will be frozen, and not a fish will be obtainable. You see, Sirs Lamas, we have no time to lose. I have passed all the night hunting the fish about; when I have drunk some tea and eaten a few spoonfuls of oatmeal, I shall get into my boat, and visit the nets I have laid out there westward; then I shall deposit the fish I have taken in the osier reservoirs you see yonder; then I shall examine my nets, and mend them if they need mending; then I shall take a brief repose, and after that, when the old grandfather (the sun) goes down, I shall once more cast my nets; then I shall row over the water, now here, now there, beating my drum, and so it goes on." These details interested us, and as our occupations at the moment were not very urgent, we asked the fisherman if he would allow us to accompany him when he went to raise his nets. "Since personages like you," answered he, "do not disdain to get into my poor boat and to view my unskilful and disagreeable fishing, I accept the benefit you propose." Hereupon we sat down in a corner of his rustic hearth to wait until he had taken his repast. The meal of the fisherman was as short as the preparations for it had been hasty. When the tea was sufficiently boiled, he poured out a basin full of it; threw into this a handful of oatmeal, which he partially kneaded with his fore-finger; and then, after having pressed it a little, and rolled it into a sort of cake, he swallowed it without any other preparation. After having three or four times repeated the same operation the dinner was at an end. This manner of living had nothing in it to excite our curiosity; having adopted the nomad way of living, a sufficiently long experience had made it familiar to us.

We entered his small boat and proceeded to enjoy the pleasure of fishing. After having relished for some moments the delight of a quiet sail on the tranquil water, smooth and unbroken as glass, through troops of cormorants and wild geese, which were disporting on the surface of the expanse, and which, half running, half flying, made a free passage for us as we advanced, we reached the place where the nets lay. At intervals we saw pieces of wood floating on the water, to which the nets were attached which rested at the bottom. When we drew them up we saw the fish glitter as they struggled in the meshes. The fish were generally large, but the fisherman only kept the largest; those that were under half a pound he threw back into the water.

After having examined a few of the nets, he stopped to see if the haul had been productive. Already the two wells, constructed at the extremities of the boat, were nearly full. "Sirs Lamas," said the fisherman, "do you eat fish? I will sell you some if you please." At this proposition the two poor French missionaries looked at each other without saying a word. In that look you might see that they were by no means averse from trying the flavour of the fish of the Yellow River, but that they dared not, a sufficient reason keeping them in suspense. "How do you sell your fish?" "Not dear; eighty sapeks a pound." "Eighty sapeks! why that is dearer than mutton." "You speak the words of truth; but what is mutton compared with the fish of the Hoang-Ho?" "No matter; it is too dear for us. We have still far to go; our purse is low, we must economize." The fisherman did not insist; he took his oar and directed the boat towards those nets which had not yet been drawn up from the water. "For what reason," asked we, "do you throw back so much fish? Is it because the quality is inferior?" "Oh, no; all the fish in the Yellow River are excellent, these are too small, that is all." "Ah, juſt so; next year they will be bigger. It is a matter of calculation; you refrain now, so that in the end you may get more by them." The fisherman laughed. "It is not that," he said; "we do not hope to re-capture these fish. Every year the basin is filled with fresh fish, brought hither by the overflowings of the Hoang-Ho; there come great and small; we take the firſt; and the others we throw back, because they do not sell well. The fish here are very abundant. We are able to seleƈt the beſt . . . Sirs Lamas, if you like to have these little fish, I will not throw them back." The offer was accepted, and the small fry, as they came, were placed in a little basket. When the fishing was over, we found ourselves possessors of a very respeƈtable supply of fish. Before leaving the boat, we washed an old basket, and having deposited our fish in it, we marched in triumph to the tent. "Where have you been?" exclaimed Samdadchiemba, as soon as he saw us; "the tea is now boiled and it soon gets cold: I have boiled it up again; it has again got cold." "Pour out some of your tea," answered we. "We will not have oatmeal to-day, but some fresh fish. Place some loaves under the ashes to bake." Our prolonged absence had put Samdadchiemba in an ill humour. His forehead was more contraƈted than usual, and his small black eyes flashed with displeasure. But when he beheld in the basket the fish which were ſtill in motion, his face relaxed into a smile, and his countenance insensibly grew more cheerful. He opened smilingly the bag of flour, the ſtrings of which were never untied except on rare occasions. Whilſt he was busily occupied with the paſtry, we took some of the fish, and proceeded to the shores of a lake at a short diſtance from the tent. We had scarcely got there, when Samdadchiemba ran to us with all his might. He drew aside the four corners of the cloth which contained the fish. "What are you going to do?" said he with an anxious air. "We are going to cut open and scale this fish." "Oh, that is not well; my spiritual fathers, wait a little; you muſt not transgress thus." "What are you talking about? Who is committing a sin?" "Why, look at these fish; they are ſtill moving. You muſt let them die in peace, before you open them: is it not a sin to kill a living creature?" "Go make your bread and let us alone. Are we always to be peſtered with your notions of metempsychosis? Do you ſtill think that men are transformed into beaſts, and beaſts into men?" The lips of our Dchiahour opened for a long laugh. "Bah!" said he, striking his forehead, "what a thick head I have; I did not think of that; I had forgotten the doctrine," and he returned not a little ashamed at having come to give us such ridiculous advice.

The fish were fried in mutton fat, and we found them exquisite.

In Tartary and in the north of China, the fishing continues to the commencement of winter, when the ponds and rivers are frozen. At that time they expose to the air, in the night, the fish they have kept alive in the reservoirs; these immediately freeze, and may be laid up without any trouble. It is in this ſtate that they are sold to the fishmongers. During the long winters of the northern part of the empire, the wealthy Chinese can always, by this means, procure fresh fish; but great care muſt be taken not to make too large a provision of them to be consumed during the time of the great froſts, for on the firſt thaw the fish become putrid.

During our few days' rest, we considered the means of crossing the Paga-Gol. A Chinese family having obtained from the King of the Ortous the privilege of conveying travellers across, we were obliged to address ourselves to the master of the boat. He had undertaken to conduct us to the other side, but we had not yet agreed about the fare; he required upwards of 1,000 sapeks. The sum appeared to us exorbitant, and we waited.

On the third day of our halt, we perceived a fisherman coming towards our tent, dragging himself along with great difficulty by the aid of a long staff. His pale and extremely meagre face showed that he was a man in suffering. As soon as he had seated himself beside our hearth, "Brother," said we, "it seems that your days are not happy." "Ah," said he, "my misfortune is great, but what am I to do? I must submit to the irrevocable laws of heaven. It is now a fortnight since, as I was going to visit a Mongol tent, I was bitten in the leg by a mad dog; there has been formed a wound which grows larger and mortifies day by day. They told me that you were from the Western Heaven, and I am come to you. The men of the Western Heaven, say the Tartar Lamas, have an unlimited power. With a single word they are able to cure the most grievous disorders." "They have deceived you, when they said we had such great powers:" and hereupon we took occasion to elucidate to this man the great truths of the faith. But he was a Chinese, and, like all his nation, but little heedful of religious matters. Our words only glanced over his heart; his hurt absorbed all his thoughts. We resolved to treat his case with the *Kou-Kouo* [*k'u-kuo*], or bean of St. Ignatius. This vegetable, of a brown or ashy colour, and of a substance which resembles horn, extremely hard, and of an intolerable bitterness, is a native of the Philippine

Isles. The manner of using the *Kou-Kouo* is to bruise it in cold water, to which it communicates its bitterness. This water, taken inwardly, modifies the heat of the blood, and extinguishes internal inflammation. It is an excellent specific for all sorts of wounds and contusions, and, enjoying a high character in the Chinese *Materia Medica*, is sold in all chemists' shops. The veterinary doctors also apply it with great success to the internal diseases of cattle and sheep. In the north of China we have often witnessed the salutary effects of the *Kou-Kouo*.

We infused the powder of one of these beans in some cold water, with which we washed the poor man's wound, and we supplied some clean linen, in place of the disgustingly dirty rags which previously served for a bandage. When we had done all we could for the sufferer, we observed that he still seemed very embarrassed in his manner. His face was red with blushes, he held down his eyes, and he began several sentences which he could not complete. " Brother," said we, " you have something on your mind." " Holy personages, you see how poor I am ! you have tended my wound ; and you have given me a great mug of healing water to take ; I know not what I can offer in exchange for all this." " If this be the subject of your uneasiness," said we, " be at once reassured. In doing what we could for your leg, we only fulfilled a duty commanded by our religion. The remedies we have prepared, we freely give you." Our words evidently relieved the poor fisherman from a very grave embarrassment. He immediately prostrated himself before us, and touched the ground thrice with his forehead, in token of his gratitude. Before withdrawing, he asked us whether we intended to remain where we were for any length of time. We told him that we should gladly depart the next day, but that we had not as yet agreed with the ferryman as to the fare. "I have a boat," said the fisherman, "and since you have tended my wound, I will endeavour to-morrow to convey you over the water. If my boat belonged entirely to myself I would at once undertake the matter; but as I have two partners, I muſt firſt get their consent. Moreover, we muſt procure some particulars as to our course; we fishermen are not acquainted with the depth of water at all the points of the passage. There are dangerous places here and there, which we muſt ascertain the exaƈt nature and locality of beforehand, so that we may not incur some misfortune. Don't say anything more about the matter to the ferry people. I will come back in the course of the evening, and we will talk over the subjeƈt."

These words gave us hopes of being able to continue our journey, without too heavy an outlay for the river passage. As he had promised, the fisherman returned in the evening. "My partners," said he, "were not at firſt willing to undertake this job, because it would lose them a day's fishing. I promised that you would give them 400 sapeks, and so the affair was arranged. To-morrow we will make inquiries as to the beſt course to follow on the river. Next morning, before sunrise, fold your tent, load your camels, and come down to the river side. If you see any of the ferry people, don't tell them you are going to give us 400 sapeks. As they have the sole right of carrying passengers for hire, they might prosecute us for carrying you, if they knew you had paid us anything."

At the appointed hour, we proceeded to the fisherman's hut. In a minute the baggage was packed in the boat, and the two missionaries seated themselves beside it, attended by the boatman whose wound they had cured. It was agreed that a young companion of his should ride the horse across the shallows, leading the mule, while Samdadchiemba, in like manner, was to conduct the camels over. When all was ready we started, the boat following one course, the horses and camels another, for the latter were obliged to make long circuits in order to avoid the deeper parts of the river.

The navigation was at first very pleasant. We floated tranquilly over the broad surface of the waters, in a small skiff, propelled by a single man with two light sculls. The pleasure of this water party, amid the deserts of Mongolia, was not, however of long duration. The poetry of the thing, soon at an end, was succeeded by some very doleful prose. We were advancing gently over the smooth water, vaguely listening to the measured dips of the sculls, when, all of a sudden, we were aroused by a clamour behind, of which the shrieks of the camels constituted a prominent share. We stopped, and looking around, perceived that horse, mule and camels were struggling in the water, without making any onward progress. In the general confusion we distinguished Samdadchiemba flourishing his arms, as if to recall us. Our boatman was not at all disposed to accept the invitation, reluctant as he was to quit the easy current he had found; but as we insisted, he turned back, and rowed towards the other party.

Samdadchiemba was purple with rage. A soon as we came up to him, he furiously assailed the boatman with invectives: "Did you want to drown us," bawled he, "that you gave us for a guide a fellow that doesn't know a yard of the way. Here are we amid gulfs, of which none of us know the depth or extent." The animals, in fact, would neither advance nor recede; beat them as you might, there they remained immovable. The boatman hurled maledictions at his partner: "If you did not know the way, what did you come for ? The only thing to be done now is to get back to the hut, and tell your cousin to get on the horse; he'll be a better guide than you."

To return for a better guide was clearly the safest course, but this was no easy matter; the animals had got so frightened at finding themselves surrounded with such a body of water, that they would not stir. The young guide was at his wits' end; it was in vain that he beat the horse, and pulled the bridle this way and that; the horse struggled and splashed up the water, and that was all; not an inch would it move, one way or the other. The young man, no better horseman than guide, at last lost his balance and fell into the water; he disappeared for a moment, to our increased consternation, and then rose at a little distance, just where he could stand and have his head above water. Samdadchiemba grew furious, but at last, seeing no other alternative, he quietly took off all his clothes as he sat on the camel, threw them into the boat, and slipped down the camel's side into the stream. "Take that man into your boat," cried he to our boatman; "I'll have nothing more to do with him. I'll go back and find someone who can guide us properly." He then made his way back through the water, which sometimes rose up to his neck, leading the animals, whose confidence returned when they saw themselves preceded by the Dchiahour.

Our hearts were filled with gratitude at observing the devotion and courage of this young neophyte, who, for our sakes, had not hesitated to plunge into the water, which, at that season, was bitterly cold. We anxiously followed him with our eyes until we saw him close upon the shore. "You may now," said the boatman, "be quite at your ease; he will find in my hut a man who will guide him, so as to avoid the least danger."

We proceeded on our way, but the navigation was

by no means so agreeable as before; the boatman could not find again the clear path on the waters which he was pursuing when we returned to aid Samdadchiemba; and hampered with aquatic plants, the vessel made but very slow progress. We tried to mend matters, by turning to the right and then to the left, but the difficulty only grew greater; the water was so shallow that the boat, in its laboured advance, turned up the mud. We were compelled ourselves to take the sculls, while the boatman, getting into the water and passing across his shoulders a rope, the other end of which was tied to the boat, tried to pull us along. We applied our united efforts to the task of moving the vessel, but all in vain; it scarcely advanced a foot. The boatman at laſt resumed his seat and folded his arms in utter despair: "Since we cannot get on by ourselves," said he, "we muſt wait here until the passage-boat comes up, and then follow in its course." We waited.

The boatman was evidently altogether disconcerted; he loudly reproached himself for having undertaken this laborious business; while we, on our parts, were angry with ourselves for having permitted a consideration of economy to deter us from proceeding with the ferry-boat. We should have got into the water and waded to the shore, but, besides the difficulty connected with the baggage, the undertaking was dangerous in itself. The ground was so irregular that, while at one moment you passed through water so shallow that it would scarcely float the boat, in the next moment you came to a hole, deep enough to drown you three times over.

It was near noon when we saw three passage-boats passing us, which belonged to the family who enjoyed the monopoly of the ferry. After having, with infinite labour, extricated ourselves from the mud and attained the channel indicated by these boats, we were quietly following their course when they stopped, evidently awaiting us. We recognized the person with whom we had tried to bargain for our passage over, and he recognized us, as we could easily perceive by the angry glances which he directed against us. "You tortoise-egg," cried he to our boatman, "what have these western men given you for the passage? They must have handed over a good bagful of sapeks to have induced you to trespass upon my rights! You and I will have a little talk about the matter, by-and-by: be sure of that." "Don't answer him," whispered the boatman to us: then raising his voice and assuming an air of virtuous indignation, he cried to the ferryman: "What do you mean? You don't know what you're talking about. Consult the dictates of reason, instead of getting into a fury about nothing. These Lamas have not given me a sapek; they have cured my leg with one of their western specifics, and do you mean to say that in gratitude for such a benefit I am not to carry them over the Paga-Gol? My conduct is perfectly right, and in conformity with religion." The ferryman grumbling, between his teeth, pretended to accept the statement thus made.

This little altercation was succeeded by profound silence on both sides. While the flotilla was peaceably advancing, pursuing the thread of a narrow current, just wide enough to admit the passage of a boat, we saw galloping towards us, along the shallows, a horseman whose rapid progress dashed aside the water in all directions. As soon as he came within call he stopped short: "Make haste," cried he, "make haste; lose no time, row with all your might! The Prime Minister of the King of the Ortous is yonder on the prairie with his suite, waiting the arrival of your boat. Row quickly." He who spoke was a Tartar Mandarin, his rank being indicated by the blue button which surmounted his hair cap. After issuing his orders he turned round, whipped his horse, and galloped back the same way he had come. When he was out of sight, the murmurs which his presence had restrained burst out. "Here's a day's labour marked out ! A fine thing, truly, to be employed by a Mongol *Toudzelaktsi* [*tusalakchi*] "Minister of State," who'll make us row all day, and then not give us a single sapek for our pains." "As to that, it need not so much matter ; but the chances are that this *Tcheou-ta-dze* [*Sao-ta-tzŭ*] will break every bone in our bodies into the bargain." "Well, row away, it can't be helped ; after all, we shall have the honour of ferrying over a *Toudzelaktsi*." This little piece of insolence excited a laugh, but the prevalent expression was that of furious invective against the Mongol authorities.

Our boatman remained silent ; at last he said to us : "This is a most unfortunate day for me. I shall be obliged to carry some of this *Toudzelaktsi's* suite perhaps to Tchagan-Kouren itself. I am by myself, I am ill, and my boat ought this evening to be engaged in fishing." We were truly afflicted at this unlucky turn of affairs, feeling as we did that we were the involuntary occasion of the poor fisherman's misfortune. We knew very well that it was no trifling matter to be called into the service, in this way, of a Chinese or Tartar Mandarin, for whom everything must be done at once, unhesitatingly and cheerfully. No matter what may be the difficulties in the way, that which the Mandarin desires must be done. Knowing the consequences of the meeting to our poor boatman, we determined to see what we could do to relieve him from the dilemma. "Brother," said we, "do not be uneasy; the Mandarin who awaits the passage-boats is a Tartar, the minister of the king of this country. We will endeavour to manage matters for you. Go very slowly, stop now and then; while we are in your boat no one, attendants, Mandarins, not even the *Toudzelaktsi* himself will venture to say a word to you." We stopped short in our course, and meanwhile the three passage-boats reached the landing-place where the Mongol authorities were waiting for them. Soon two Mandarins, with the blue button, galloped towards us: "What are you stopping there for?" cried they. "Why do you not come on?" We interposed: "Brother Mongols," said we, "request your master to content himself with the three boats already at the shore. This man is ill, and has been rowing a long time; it would be cruel to prevent him from resting himself awhile." "Be it as you desire, Sirs Lamas," replied the horsemen, and they galloped back to the *Toudzelaktsi*.

We then resumed our course, but very slowly, in order to give time for every person to embark before we reached the shore. By-and-by, we saw the three ferry-boats returning, filled with Mandarins and their attendants: the horses were fording the river in another direction, under the guidance of one of the boatmen. As the party approached, our boatman grew more and more afraid; he did not venture to raise his eyes, and he scarcely breathed. At last the boats were level with each other; "Sirs Lamas," cried a voice, "is peace with you?" The red button in the cap of the speaker, and the richness of his enbroidered dress, indicated that it was the prime minister who addressed to us this Tartar compliment. "*Toudzelaktsi* of the Ortous," replied we, "our progress is slow, but it is favourable; may peace also attend you." After a few other civilities, required by Tartar forms, we proceeded on our way. When we had attained a safe distance from the Mandarins, our boatman was perfectly relieved; we had extricated him from a most serious difficulty. The ferry-boats, it was probable, would be engaged at least three days in their gratuitous labour, for the *Toudzelaktsi* not choosing to travel across the marshes, the boats would have to convey him down the Yellow River all the way to Tchagan-Kouren.

After a long, laborious, and dangerous passage, we reached the other side of the waters. Samdadchiemba had arrived long before us, and was awaiting us on the margin of the stream. He was still naked, as to clothes, but then he was covered well nigh up to his shoulders with a thick layer of mud, which gave him a negro aspect. In consequence of the extreme shallowness of the water, the boat could not get within thirty feet of the shore. The boatmen who preceded us has been obliged to carry the Mandarins and their attendants on their shoulders to the boats. We did not choose to adopt the same process, but rather to make use of the animals for our disembarkation. Samdadchiemba accordingly brought them close to the boat; M. Gabet got on the horse, M. Huc on the mule, and so we reached the shore, without having occasion to employ any person's shoulders.

The sun was just about to set. We would willingly have encamped at once, for we were exhausted with hunger and fatigue, but we could not possibly do so, for we had, they told us, fully two lis to journey before we could get out of the mud. We loaded, our camels, therefore, and proceeded onward, completing the miserable day in pain and suffering. Night had closed in before we came to a place where we could set up our tent; we had no strength left for preparing the usual meal, so drinking some cold water, and eating a few handfuls of millet, we lay down, after a brief prayer, and fell into a deep slumber.

CHAPTER VIII

THE sun was already high when we rose. On leaving the tent we looked round us, in order to get acquainted with this new country, which the darkness of the preceding evening had not allowed us to examine. It appeared to be dismal and arid; but we were happy, on any terms, to lose sight of bogs and swamps. We had left behind us the Yellow River, with its overflowing waters, and entered the sandy steppes of Ortous.

The land of Ortous is divided into seven banners; it extends a hundred leagues from east to west, and seventy from south to north. It is surrounded by the Yellow River on the west, east and north, and by the Great Wall on the south. This country has been subjected, at all periods, to the influence of the political revolutions by which the Chinese empire has been agitated. The Chinese and Tartar conquerors have taken possession of it in turns, and made it the theatre of sanguinary wars. During the tenth, eleventh, and twelfth centuries, it remained under the sceptre of the kings of Hia [Hsia], who derived their origin from the Thou-Pa [T'o-pa] Tartars of the land of Si-Fan. The capital of their kingdom, called Hia-Tcheou [Hsia-chou], was situated at the foot of the Alechan mountains between the Hoang-Ho and the Great Wall. At present, this town is called Ning-Hia [Ning-hsia], and belongs to the province of Kan-Sou. In 1227 the kingdom of Hia, and afterwards Ortous, were involved in the common desolation by the victories of Tchinggiskhan, founder of the Tartar dynasty of the Youen [*Yüan*].

After the expulsion of the Tartar Mongols by the Ming, the Ortous fell under the power of the Khan of the Tchakar. When the latter submitted to the Mantchou conquerors in 1635, the Ortous followed his example, and were reunited to the empire as a tributary people.

The Emperor Khang-Hi resided for some time among the Ortous in 1696, when he was on his expedition against the Eleuts [Ölet]; and this is what he wrote of this people in a letter to the prince, his son, who had remained at Peking:—" Till now, I never had at all an accurate idea respecting the Ortous: they are a very civilized nation, and have lost nothing of the old manners of the true Mongols. All their princes live in perfect union among themselves, and do not know the difference between *mine* and *thine*. No one ever heard of a thief amongst them, although they take not the slightest precaution for guarding the camels and horses. If by chance one of these animals goes astray, it is taken care of by him who finds it, till he has discovered its owner, to whom he restores it, without the least payment. The Ortous are extremely skilful in breeding cattle; most of their horses are tame and tractable. The Tchakars, north of the Ortous, enjoy the reputation of training them with more care and success; nevertheless, I believe that the Ortous excel them in this point. Notwithstanding these advantages, they are not at all so rich as the other Mongols."

This quotation, which we take from the Abbé Grosier, is in every point conformable with what we ourselves were able to observe among the Ortous; so that, since the time of the Emperor Khang-Hi, this people has not at all changed in its manners.

The aspect of the country through which we

travelled on the first day of our journey seemed affected by the vicinity of the Chinese fishermen, who reside on the banks of the Yellow River. We saw here and there cultivated grounds, but there can be nothing more wretched and bare looking than this cultivation, except, perhaps, the cultivator himself. These miserable agriculturists are a mixed people, half Chinese, half Tartars, but possessing neither the industry of the former, nor the frank and simple manners of the latter. They live in houses, or rather in dirty sheds built of branches intertwined, rudely covered with mud and cow's excrement. Thirst obliging us to enter one of these habitations to ask for some water, we were able to convince ourselves that the interior did not in any way contradict the misery which appeared outside. Men and animals live together higgledy-piggledy in these abodes, which are far inferior to those of the Mongols, where, at least, the air is not infected by the presence of cattle and sheep.

The sandy soil, which is cultivated by these poor people, beyond a little buck-wheat and millet, produces only hemp, but this is very large and abundant. Though, when we were there, the crop was already gathered in, we could nevertheless judge of the beauty of its stem from what remained in the fields. The farmers of Ortous do not pull up the hemp when it is ripe, as is done in China; they cut it off above the ground, so high as to leave a stump about an inch in diameter. It was accordingly great toil for our camels to traverse those vast fields of hemp; the stumps, occurring at every step beneath their large feet, compelled them to execute all sorts of fantastic movements, which would have excited our mirth, had we not been fearful of seeing them wounded. However, that which so impeded our camels proved of great use to ourselves. When we had set up our tent, these stumps furnished us with a ready and abundant fuel.

We soon entered once more the Land of Grass, if, indeed, one can give this name to such a barren, arid country as that of the Ortous. Wherever you turn you find only a soil, bare, and without verdure; rocky ravines, marly hills, and plains covered with a fine, moving sand, blown by the impetuous winds in every direction; for pasture, you will only find a few thorny bushes and poor fern, dusty and fetid. At intervals only, this horrible soil produces some thin, sharp grass, so firm in the earth that the animals can only get it up by digging the sand with their muzzles. The numerous swamps, which had been so heavy a desolation to us on the borders of the Yellow River, became matter of regret in the country of the Ortous, so very rare here is water; not a single rivulet is there, not a spring, where the traveller can quench his thirst; at distances only are there ponds and cisterns, filled with a fetid, muddy water.

The Lamas, with whom we had been in communication at Blue Town, had warned us of all the miseries we should have to endure in the country of the Ortous, especially on account of the scarcity of water. By their advice we had bought two wooden pails, which proved indeed of the greatest service to us. Whenever we were lucky enough to find on our way pools or wells dug by the Tartars, we filled our pails, without considering too nicely the quality of the water, which we used with the greatest economy, as if it had been some rare and precious beverage. In spite of all these precautions, it happened more than once that we were obliged to pass whole days without getting a single drop of water wherewith to moisten our lips. But our personal privations were trifling compared with the pain we felt at seeing our animals wanting water almost every day in a country where they had nothing to eat beyond a few plants nearly dried up, and, as it were, calcined by nitre, and where they accordingly fell away visibly. After some days' travelling, the horse assumed a truly wretched appearance; it bent down its head, and seemed, at every step, as though it would sink down with weakness; the camels painfully balanced themselves on their long legs, and their emaciated humps hung over their backs like empty bags.

The steppes of the Ortous, though so destitute of water and good pasture, have not been quite abandoned by wild animals. You often find there grey squirrels, agile yellow goats, and beautifully plumed pheasants. Hares are in abundance, and are so far from shy, that they did not even take the trouble to move at our approach; they merely rose on their hind legs, pricked up their ears, and looked at us as we passed with the utmost indifference. The fact is, these animals feel perfectly secure, for, with the exception of a few Mongols who follow the chase, nobody ever molests them.

The herds of the Tartars of the Ortous are not very numerous, and are quite different from those which feed on the rich pastures of the Tchakar, or of Gechekten. The cattle and horses appeared very miserable; the goats, sheep and camels, however, looked very well, which is undoubtedly the consequence of their predilection for plants impregnated with saltpetre, whereas cattle and horses prefer fresh pastures, and pure and abundant water.

The Mongols of Ortous are very much affected by the wretchedness of the soil upon which they live. In the course of our journey we saw no indication that they had become much richer than they were in the time of the Emperor Khang-Hi. Most of them live in tents made of some rags of felt, or of goat-skins framed on a wretched woodwork. Everything about these tents is so old and dirty, so tattered with time and storms, that you would with difficulty suppose they could serve as abodes for human beings. Whenever we happened to pitch our tent near these poor habitations, we were sure to be visited by a crowd of wretches who proftrated themselves at our feet, rolled on the earth, and gave us the moft magnificent titles, in order to extract something from our charity. We were not rich, but we could not refrain from beftowing upon them a part of the modicum which the goodness of Providence had beftowed upon us. We gave them some leaves of tea, a handful of oatmeal, some broiled millet, sometimes some mutton fat. Alas! we would fain have given more, but we were obliged to give according to our means. The missionaries are themselves poor men, who only live upon the alms diftributed among them every year by their brothers in Europe.

Anyone not acquainted with the laws by which the Tartars are ruled, would not readily underftand why men condemn themselves to spend their lives in the wretched country of the Ortous, whilft Mongolia presents, in every direction, immense uninhabited plains, where water and pafture are to be found in abundance. Although the Tartars are nomads, and incessantly wandering about from one place to another, they are, nevertheless, not at liberty to live in any other country than their own. They are bound to remain in their own kingdom, under the dominion of their own sovereign, for slavery is ftill maintained among the Mongol tribes with the utmoft rigour. In order to obtain an accurate idea of the degree of liberty these people enjoy in their desert regions, it is expedient to enter into some details as to the form of their government.

Mongolia is divided into several sovereignties, whose chiefs are subject to the Emperor of China, himself a Tartar, but of the Mantchou race; these chiefs bear titles corresponding to those of kings, dukes, earls, barons, etc. They govern their states according to their own pleasure, none having any right to meddle with their affairs. They acknowledge as sovereign only the Emperor of China. Whenever there arise differences among them, they appeal to Peking. Instead of levelling lances at each other, as used to be done in the middle ages of Europe, among its little sovereigns, so warlike and so turbulent, they always submit with respect to the decision of the Court of Peking, whatever it may be. Though the Mongol sovereigns think it their duty to prostrate themselves, once a year, before the Son of Heaven, Lord of the Earth, they nevertheless do not concede to the Grand-Khan the right of dethroning the reigning families in the Tartar principalities. He may, they say, cashier a king for grave misconduct, but he is bound to fill up the vacant place with one of the superseded prince's sons. The sovereignty belongs, they contend, to such and such a family, by a right which is inalienable, and of which it were a crime to dispossess the owner.

A few years ago, the King of Barains [Barin][1] was accused at Peking of having conspired a rebellion against the Emperor; he was tried by the Supreme Tribunal without being heard, and condemned to be "shortened at both ends," the meaning of the decree being, that his head and feet should be cut off. The king made enormous presents to the officials who were sent to superintend the execution of the imperial edict, and they contented themselves with cutting off his braid of hair, and the soles of his boots. They reported at Peking that the order had been executed, and no more was said about the matter. The king,

---

[1] Barains is a principality situated north of Peking. It is one of the most celebrated in Mongol Tartary.

THIBET, AND CHINA

however, descended from his throne, and was succeeded by his son.

Although it is a sort of customary right that power shall always remain in the same family, it cannot be said that there is anything precisely fixed in this respect. There can be nothing more vague and indefinite than the relations between the Tartar sovereigns and the Grand-Khan or Emperor of China, whose omnipotent will is above all laws and all customs. In practice, the Emperor has the right to do whatever he chooses to do, and the right is never disputed by any person. If doubtful or disputed cases arise, they are decided by force.

In Tartary, all the families that are in any way related to the sovereign, form a nobility, or a patrician caste, who are proprietors of the whole soil. These nobles, called *Taitsi* [*taiji*], are distinguished by a blue button surmounting the cap. It is from among them that the sovereigns of the different states select their ministers, who are generally three in number, and called *Toudzelaktsi*—that is to say, a man who assists or lends his aid. This rank gives them the right of wearing the red button. Below the *Toudzelaktsi* are the *Touchimel* [*tushimel*], subaltern officers, who are charged with the details of government. Lastly, a certain number of secretaries or interpreters, who must be versed in the Mongol, Mantchou, and Chinese languages, complete the hierarchy.

In the country of the Khalkhas, to the north of the desert of Gobi, there is a district entirely occupied by *Taitsi*, who are supposed to be descendants of the Mongol dynasty that was founded by Tchinggiskhan, and which occupied the imperial throne from 1260 to 1341. After the revolution, which restored the national independence of the Chinese, these people sought refuge among the Khalkhas, obtained, without difficulty, a portion of their immense territory, and adopted the nomad life, which their ancestors had led prior to the conquest of China. These *Taitsi* live in the greatest independence, liable to no duty, paying no tribute to any one, and recognizing no sovereign. Their wealth consists in tents and cattle. The country of the *Taitsi* is, of all the Mongol regions, that wherein the patriarchial manners are found to be most accurately preserved, such as the Bible describes them in the lives of Abraham, Jacob and the other pastors of Mesopotamia.

The Tartars who do not belong to the royal family are all slaves, living in absolute subjection to their masters. Besides the rents they pay, they are bound to keep their master's flocks and herds, but they are not forbidden to breed also cattle on their own account. It would be a fallacy to imagine that slavery in Tartary is oppressive and cruel, as amongst some nations; the noble families scarcely differ from the slave families. In examining the relations between them, it would be difficult to distinguish the master from the slave: they live both alike in tents, and both alike occupy their lives in pasturing their flocks. You will never find among them luxury and opulence insolently staring in the face of poverty. When the slave enters his master's tent the latter never fails to offer him tea and milk; they smoke together, and exchange their pipes. Around the tents the young slaves and the young noblemen romp and wrestle together without distinction; the stronger throws the weaker; that is all. You often find families of slaves becoming proprietors of numerous flocks, and spending their days in abundance. We met many who were richer than their masters, a circumstance giving no umbrage to the latter. What a difference between this slavery and that of Rome, for instance, where the Roman citizen, when he made up the inventory of his house, classed his slaves as furniture.

With these haughty and cruel masters the slave did not merit even the name of man; he was called, without ceremony, a domestic thing, *res domestica*. Slavery, with the Mongol Tartars, is even less oppressive, less insulting to humanity, than the bondage of the middle ages. The Mongol masters never give to their slaves those humiliating nicknames which were formerly used to designate serfs; they call them *brothers*; never villeins, never scum, never *gent taillable et corvéable à merci*.

The Tartar nobles have the right of life and death over their slaves. They may administer justice themselves upon their bondsmen, even to sentence of death; but this privilege is never exercised in an arbitrary way. In case a slave has been put to death, a superior tribunal investigates the action of the master, and if it be found that he has abused his right, the innocent blood is revenged. The Lamas who belong to slave families become free, in some degree, as soon as they enter the sacerdotal tribe; they are liable neither to rents nor enforced labour; they are at liberty to quit their country, and ramble through the world at their pleasure, without anybody having the right to stay them.

Although the relations between master and slave are generally full of humanity and good-will, there are, nevertheless, Tartar sovereigns who abuse their right, and oppress their people, and exact exorbitant tributes. We know one who makes use of a system of oppression that is truly revolting. He selects from among his flocks the oldest and sickliest cattle, camels, sheep and goats, and gives them in charge to the rich slaves in his states, who cannot, of course, object to pasture the cattle of their sovereign master, but are fain to consider it rather an honour. After a few years, the king applies for his cattle, by this time all dead or dying of illness or old age, and selects from the flocks of his slaves the youngeſt and ſtrongeſt; often even, not content with this, he demands double or treble the number. " Nothing," says he, " is more juſt; for in two or three years my beaſts have been multiplied, and therefore a great number of lambs, colts calves and young camels belong to me."

Slavery, however mitigated and softened, can never be in harmony with the dignity of man. It has been abolished in Europe, and we hope will be abolished one day among the Mongol people. But this great revolution will, as everywhere else, be operated by the influence of Chriſtianity. It will not be theory-mongers who will liberate these nomad people. The work will be the work of the prieſts of Jesus Chriſt, of the preachers of the Holy Gospel, that Divine Charter, wherein are set forth the true rights of man. So soon as the missionaries shall have taught the Mongols to say, " Our Father who art in Heaven," slavery will fall in Tartary, and the tree of liberty will grow beside the Cross.

After some days' march across the sands of the Ortous, we noticed on our way a small Lamasery, richly built in a picturesque and wild situation. We passed on without ſtopping. We had advanced a gun-shot from the place, when we heard behind us the galloping of a horse. On looking round we saw a Lama following us at full speed. " Brothers," he said, " you have passed our *Soume* [*sümé*] ' Lamasery ' without ſtopping. Are you in such haſte that you cannot repose for a day, and offer your adorations to our saint ? " " Yes, we are rather in a hurry; our journey is not of a few days; we are going to the Weſt." " I knew very well by your physiognomies that you were not Mongols, and that you came from the Weſt; but as you are going so far, you had better proſtrate yourselves before our saint; that will bring you good luck." " We never proſtrate ourselves

THIBET, AND CHINA

before men ; the true creed of the West forbids that." "Our saint is not a mere man; you do not imagine, perhaps, that in our little Lamasery we have the happiness to possess a *Chaberon*, a living Buddha. It is two years since he deigned to descend from the holy mountains of Thibet ; he is now seven years old. In one of his former lives he was Grand Lama of a splendid Lamasery in this vale, which was destroyed, according to the prayer-books, in the time of the wars of Tchinggis. The saint having re-appeared a few years since, we have constructed in haste a small Lamasery. Come, brothers, our saint will hold his right hand over your heads, and luck will accompany your steps ! " " The men who know the Holy Doctrine of the West do not believe in all these transmigrations of the *Chaberons*. We adore only the Creator of Heaven and earth ; his name is Jehovah. We believe that the child you have made superior of your Lamasery is destitute of all power. Men have nothing to hope or to fear from him." When the Lama heard these words, which he certainly never expected, he was quite stupified. By degrees his face became animated, and at last exhibited indignation and anger. He looked at us several times, then, pulling the bridle of his horse, he turned short round and left us hastily, muttering between his teeth some words which we could not exactly hear, but which we were aware did not constitute a benediction.

The Tartars believe with firm and absolute faith in all these various transmigrations. They would never allow themselves to entertain the slightest doubt as to the authenticity of their *Chaberons*. These living Buddhas are in large numbers, and are always placed at the head of the most important Lamaseries. Sometimes they modestly begin their career in a small temple, and have only a few disciples ; but very soon their reputation increases around, and the small

Lamasery becomes a place of pilgrimage and devotion. The neighbouring Lamas, speculating upon the rising fashion, surround it with their cells; the Lamasery acquires development from year to year, and becomes at last famous in the land.

The election and enthronization of the living Buddhas are conducted in so singular a manner as to be well worth relating. When a Grand Lama has gone, that is to say is dead, the circumstance is no occasion of mourning in the Lamasery. There are no tears, no lamentations, for everybody knows the *Chaberon* will very soon reappear. This apparent death is but the beginning of a new existence, as it were, one ring more added to the unlimited, uninterrupted chain of successive lives—a regular palingenesis. While the saint is in a state of chrysalis, his disciples are in the greatest anxiety; for it is their most important affair to discover the place where their master will resume life. A rainbow appearing in the air is considered a signal sent to them by their old Great Lama to aid them in their research. Everyone thereupon says his prayers, and while the Lamasery which has lost its Buddha redoubles its fastings and prayers, a troop of elect proceeds to consult the *Tchurtchun* [*churchun*] or augur, famous for the knowledge of things hidden from the common herd. He is informed that on such a day of such a moon the rainbow of the Chaberon has manifested itself on the sky; it made its appearance in such a place; it was more or less luminous, and it was visible so long; then it disappeared amid such and such circumstances. When the *Tchurtchun* has received all the necessary indications, he recites some prayers, opens his books of divination, and pronounces at last his oracle, while the Tartars who have come to consult him listen, kneeling and full of unction. "Your Great Lama," says he, " has reappeared in Thibet, at such a distance from your Lamasery. You will find him in such a family." When these poor Mongols have heard this oracle, they return full of joy to announce the glad tidings to their Lamasery.

It often happens that the disciples of the defunct have no occasion to trouble themselves at all in order to discover the new birth-place of their Great Lama. He himself takes the trouble to initiate them into the secrets of his transformation. As soon as he has effected his metamorphosis in Thibet, he reveals himself at an age when common children cannot yet articulate a single word. " It is I," he says with the accent of authority ; " it is I who am the Great Lama the living Buddha of such a temple; conduct me to my ancient Lamasery. I am its immortal superior." The wonderful baby having thus spoken, it is speedily communicated to the Lamas of the *soumé* indicated that their *Chaberon* is born in such a place and they are summoned to attend and invite him home.

In whatever manner the Tartars discover the residence of their Great Lama, whether by the appearance of the rainbow, or by the spontaneous revelation of the *Chaberon* himself, they are always full of intense joy on the occasion. Soon all is movement in the tents, and the thousand preparations for a long journey are made with enthusiasm, for it is almost always in Thibet that they have to seek their living Buddha, who seldom fails to play them the trick of transmigrating in some remote and almost inaccessible country. Everyone contributes his share to the organization of the holy journey. If the king of the country does not place himself at the head of the caravan, he sends either his own son or one of the most illustrious members of the royal family. The great Mandarins, or ministers of the King, consider it their duty and an honour to join the party. When everything is at last prepared, an auspicious day is chosen, and the caravan starts.

Sometimes these poor Mongols, after having endured incredible fatigues in horrible deserts, fall into the hands of the brigands of the Blue Sea, who strip them from head to foot. If they do not die of hunger and cold in those dreadful solitudes—if they succeed in returning to the place whence they came—they commence the preparations for a new journey. There is nothing capable of discouraging them. At last, when by dint of energy and perseverance, they have contrived to reach the eternal sanctuary, they prostrate themselves before the child who has been indicated to them. The young *Chaberon*, however, is not saluted and proclaimed Great Lama without a previous examination. There is held a solemn sitting, at which the new living Buddha is examined publicly, with a scrupulous attention. He is asked the name of the Lamasery of which he assumes to be the Great Lama; at what distance it is; what is the number of the Lamas residing in it. He is interrogated respecting the habits and customs of the defunct Great Lama, and the principal circumstances attending his death. After all these questions, there are placed before him different prayer-books, articles of furniture, teapots, cups, etc., and amongst all these things he has to point out those which belonged to his former life.

Generally, this child, at most but five or six years old, comes forth victorious out of all these trials. He answers accurately all the questions that are put to him, and makes without any embarrassment the inventory of his goods. "Here," he says, "are the prayer-books I used; there is the japanned porringer out of which I drank my tea." And so on.

No doubt the Mongols are often dupes of the fraud of those who have an interest in making a Great Lama

THIBET, AND CHINA

out of this puppet. Yet we believe that often all this proceeds on both sides with honesty and good faith. From the information we obtained from persons worthy of the greatest credit, it appears certain that all that is said of the *Chaberons* must not be ranged amongst illusion and deception. A purely human philosophy will, undoubtedly, reject such things, or put them, without hesitating, down to the account of Lama imposture. We Catholic missionaries believe that the great liar who once deceived our first parents in the earthly Paradise still pursues his system of falsehood in the world. He who had the power to hold up in the air Simon Magus may well at this day speak to mankind by the mouth of an infant, in order to maintain the faith of his adorers.

When the titles of the living Buddha have been confirmed, he is conducted in triumph to the Lamasery, of which he is to be the Grand Lama. Upon the road he takes, all is excitement, all is movement. The Tartars assemble in large crowds to prostrate themselves on his way, and to present to him their offerings. As soon as he is arrived at his Lamasery, he is placed upon the altar; and then kings, princes, mandarins, Lamas, Tartars, from the richest to the poorest, come and bend the head before this child, which has been brought from the depths of Thibet, at enormous expense, and whose demoniac possessions excite everybody's respect, admiration, and enthusiasm.

There is no Tartar kingdom which does not possess in one of its Lamaseries, of the first class, a living Buddha. Besides this superior, there is always another Grand Lama, who is selected from members of the royal family. The Thibetian Lama resides in the Lamasery, like a living idol, receiving every day the adorations of the devout, upon whom in return he bestows his blessing. Everything which relates to prayers and liturgical ceremonies is placed under his immediate superintendence. The Mongol Grand Lama is charged with the administration, good order, and executive of the Lamasery; he governs while his colleague is content to reign. The famous maxim, *Le roi règne et ne gouverne pas*, is not, therefore, the grand discovery in politics that some people imagine. People pretend to invent a new system, and merely plunder, without saying a word about it, the old constitution of the Tartar Lamaseries.

Below these two sovereigns are several subaltern officers, who direct the details of the administration, the revenues, the sales, the purchases, and the discipline. The scribes keep the registers, and draw up the regulations and orders which the governor Lama promulgates for the good keeping and order of the Lamasery. These scribes are generally well versed in the Mongol, Thibetian, and sometimes in the Chinese and Mantchou languages. Before they are admitted to this employment they are obliged to undergo a very rigorous examination, in presence of all the Lamas and of the principle civil authorities of the country.

After this staff of superiors and officers, the inhabitants of the Lamasery are divided in Lama-masters and Lama-disciples or *Chabis*; each Lama has under his direction one or more *Chabis*, who live in his small house, and execute all the details of the household. If the master possesses cattle, they take charge of them, milk the cows, and prepare the butter and cream. In return for these services, the master directs his disciples in the study of the prayers, and initiates them into the liturgy. Every morning the *Chabi* must be up before his master; his first task is to sweep the chamber, to light a fire and to make the tea; after that he takes his prayer-book, presents it respectfully to his master, and prostrates himself thrice before him, without saying a single word. This sign of respect is equivalent to a request that the lesson he has to learn in the course of the day may be marked. The master opens the book, and reads some passages, according to the capacity of the scholar, who then makes three more prostrations in sign of thanks, and returns to his affairs.

The *Chabi* studies his prayer-book, when he is disposed to do so, there being no fixed period for that; he may spend his time sleeping or romping with the other young pupils, without the slightest interference on the part of his master. When the hour for retiring to bed has arrived, he recites the lesson assigned him in the morning, in a monotonous manner; if the recitation is good, he is looked upon as having done his duty, the silence of his master being the only praise he is entitled to obtain; if, on the contrary, he is not able to give a good account of his lesson, the severest punishment makes him sensible of his fault. It often happens that under such circumstances the master, laying aside his usual gravity, rushes upon his scholar, and overwhelms him at once with blows and terrible maledictions. Some of the pupils, who are over maltreated, run away and seek adventures far from their Lamasery; but in general they patiently submit to the punishment inflicted on them, even that of passing the night in the open air, without any clothes and in full winter. We often had opportunities of talking with *Chabis*, and when we asked them whether there was no means of learning the prayers without being beaten, they ingenuously and with an accent manifesting entire conviction, replied, that it was impossible. "The prayers one knows best," they said, "are always those for which one has got most blows. The Lamas who cannot recite prayers, or cure maladies, or tell fortunes, or predict the future, are those who have not been beaten well by their masters."

TRAVELS IN TARTARY,

Besides these studies, which are conducted at home, and under the immediate superintendence of the master, the *Chabis* may attend, in the Lamasery, public lectures, wherein the books which relate to religion and to medicine are expounded. But these commentaries are mostly vague, unsatisfactory, and quite inadequate to form learned Lamas; there are few of them who can give an exact account of the books they study; to justify their omission in this respect, they never fail to allege the profundity of the doctrine. As to the great majority of the Lamas, they think it more convenient and expeditious to recite the prayers in a merely mechanical way, without giving themselves any trouble about the ideas they contain. When we come to speak of the Lamaseries of Thibet, where the instruction is more complete than in those of Tartary, we shall enter into some details upon Lama studies.

The Thibetian books alone being reputed canonical, and admitted as such by the Buddhist Reformation, the Mongol Lamas pass their lives in studying a foreign idiom, without troubling themselves at all about their own language. There are many of them well versed in the Thibetian literature, who do not even know their own Mongol alphabet. There are indeed a few Lamaseries where the study of the Tartarian idiom receives some slight attention, and where they sometimes recite Mongol prayers, but these are always a translation of Thibetian books. A Lama who can read Thibetian and Mongol is reputed quite a *savant;* is thought a being raised above mankind, if he has some knowledge of Chinese and Mantchou literature.

As we advanced in the Ortous, the country seemed more and more desert and dismal. To make matters still worse, a terrible storm, solemnly closing in the autumn season, brought upon us the cold of winter.

One day, we were proceeding with difficulty through

the arid sandy desert; the perspiration ran down our foreheads, for the heat was stifling; we felt overpowered by the closeness of the atmosphere, and our camels, with outstretched necks and mouths half open, vainly sought in the air a breath of cooling freshness. Towards noon, dark clouds began to gather in the horizon; fearful of being surprised by the storm, we determined to pitch our tent. But where? We looked round on all sides; we ascended to the tops of the hillocks and anxiously sought with our eyes for some Tartar habitation which might provide us with fuel, but in vain; we had before us on all sides nothing but a mournful solitude. From time to time we saw the foxes retiring to their holes, and herds of yellow goats running to take repose in the defiles of the mountains. Meantime, the clouds continued to rise and the wind began to blow violently. In the irregularity of its gusts it seemed now to bring us the tempest, now to drive it from us. While we were thus suspended between hope and fear, loud claps of thunder and repeated flashes of lightning, that seemed to enkindle the sky, gave us notice that we had no other resource than to place ourselves entirely in the hands of Providence. The icy north wind blowing fiercely, we directed our steps to a defile, which opened near us; but before we had time to reach it the storm exploded. At first, rain fell in torrents, then hail, and at last snow half melted. In an instant we were wet through to the skin, and felt the cold seizing upon our limbs. We immediately alighted, hoping that walking would warm us a little, but we had hardly advanced ten steps amidst the deluge of sand, when our legs sank as in mortar. When we found it impossible to go any further we sought shelter by the side of our camels, and crouched down, pressing our arms closely against our sides, in order to attain, if possible, a little warmth.

TRAVELS IN TARTARY,

While the storm continued to hurl against us its fury, we awaited with resignation the fate which Providence destined for us. It was impossible to pitch the tent; it was beyond human power to spread cloth saturated with rain, and half frozen by the north wind. Besides it would have been difficult to find a site for it, since the water streamed in every direction. Amid circumstances so dreadful, we looked at each other in sadness and in silence; we felt the natural warmth of our body diminishing every minute, and our blood beginning to freeze. We offered, therefore, the sacrifice of our lives to God, for we were convinced that we should die of cold during the night.

One of us, however, collecting all his strength and all his energy, climbed up an eminence, which commanded a view of the contiguous defile, and discovered a footpath, leading by a thousand sinuosities into the depths of the immense ravine; he pursued its direction and after a few steps in the hollow, perceived in the sides of the mountain large openings, like doors. At this sight, recovering at once his courage and his strength, he ascended once more the eminence in order to communicate the good news to his companions. "We are saved," he cried; "there are caves in this defile; let us hasten to take refuge in them." These words immediately aroused the little caravan; we left our animals upon the hill, and speedily descended into the ravine. A footpath led to the opening; we advanced our heads, and discovered in the interior of the mountain, not simple caves formed by nature, but fine, spacious apartments excavated by the hand of man. Our first exclamation was an expression of thankfulness for the goodness of Providence. We selected the cleanest and largest of these caverns, and in an instant passed from the utmost misery to the height of felicity. It was like a sudden and unhoped for transition from death to life.

THIBET, AND CHINA

On viewing these subterranean dwellings, constructed with so much elegance and solidity, we were of opinion that some Chinese families had repaired to this country to cultivate the soil; but that, repelled by its barrenness, they had given up their enterprise. Traces of cultivation, which we perceived here and there, confirmed our conjecture. When the Chinese establish themselves anywhere in Tartary, if they find mountains, the earth of which is hard and solid, they excavate caverns in their sides. These habitations are cheaper than houses, and less exposed to the irregularity of the seasons. They are generally well laid out; on each side of the door there are windows, giving sufficient light to the interior; the walls, the ceiling, the furnaces, the *kang*, everything inside is so coated with plaster, so firm and shining, that it has the appearance of stucco. These caves have the advantage of being very warm in winter and very cool in summer; the want of sufficient air, however, sometimes makes a sojourn in them dangerous to the health. Those dwellings were no novelty to us, for they abound in our mission of Si-Wan. However, we had never seen any so well constructed as these of the Ortous.

We took possession of one of these subterranean abodes, and commenced proceedings by making a large fire in the furnaces, with plentiful bundles of hemp-stems, which we found in one of the caves. Never, on our journey, had we at our disposal such excellent fuel. Our clothes dried very soon, and we were so happy at being in this fine hotel of Providence, that we spent the greater part of the night enjoying the delightful sensation of warmth, while Samdadchiemba was never tired of broiling little cakes in mutton fat. It was altogether quite a festival with us, and our flour felt somewhat the effects of it.

The animals were not less happy than we. We

found for them stables out in the mountains, and, which was better still, excellent forage. One cave was filled with millet stems and oat-straw. But for this horrible storm, which had nearly killed us, our animals would never have got so grand a treat. After having for a long time enjoyed the poetry of our miraculous position, we yielded to the necessity of taking repose, and laid down upon a well-warmed *kang*, which made us forget the terrible cold we had endured during the tempest.

Next morning, while Samdadchiemba was using the rest of the hemp stems, and drying our baggage, we went for a nearer inspection of these numerous subterrenes. We had scarcely gone ten steps, when we beheld, to our great astonishment, whirls of smoke issuing from the door and windows of a cave adjoining our own. As we fancied we were alone in the desert, the sight of this smoke excited a surprise, mingled with fear. We directed our steps to the opening of the cavern, and, on reaching the threshold of the door, perceived within a large fire of hemp stems, whose undulating flame reached the ceiling, so that the place looked like an oven. On further investigation we observed a human form moving amidst the thick smoke; we soon heard the Tartar salute, "*Mendou!*" uttered by a sonorous voice; "Come and sit beside this fire." We did not like to advance. This cave of Cacus, that loud voice, presented to our minds something fantastic. Finding that we remained silent and motionless, the inhabitant of this sort of vent-hole of Erebus, rose and came to the threshold. He was neither a devil nor a ghost, but simply a Mongol Tartar, who, the night before, having been surprised by the storm, had fled to this cave, where he had passed the night. After a few words about the rain, wind and hail, we invited him to breakfast with us, and brought him to our dwelling. While Samdadchiemba, aided by our gueſt, made the tea, we went out again to pursue our researches.

We walked amid these deserted and silent abodes with a curiosity not free from terror. All were conſtruċted upon much the same model, and ſtill preserved their priſtine integrity. Chinese charaċters engraved on the walls, and pieces of porcelain vases, confirmed our impression that these caves had been inhabited not long since by Chinese. Some old women's shoes, which we discovered in a corner, removed any remaining doubt. We could not shake off a feeling of sadness and melancholy, when we thought of those numerous families, who, after having lived a long time in the entrails of this large mountain, had gone elsewhere to seek a more hospitable soil. As we entered the caves, we alarmed flocks of sparrows, which had not yet left these former dwellings of man, but had, on the contrary, boldly taken possession of these grand neſts. The millet and oats ſtrewn around profusely, induced them to remain. "Undoubtedly," said we, "they too will fly away when they no longer find here any more grains, when they find that the old inhabitants of these caves return no more, and they will seek hospitality under the roofs of houses."

The sparrow is a regular cosmopolite; we have found it wherever we have found man; ever with the same vivid, petulant, quarrelsome charaċter; ever with the same sharp, angry cry. It is, however, to be remarked that in Tartary, China, and Thibet it is, perhaps, more insolent than in Europe; because there, nobody makes war upon it, and its neſt and brood are piously respeċted. You see it boldly enter the house, live there on familiar terms, and peck up at its leisure the remnants of man's food. The Chinese call it *Kio-nio-eul* [*Chia-niao-êrh*], " bird of the family ".

After having inspected about thirty of these caves, which did not present anything remarkable, we returned to our own. At breakfast, the conversation naturally turned upon the Chinese who had excavated these dwellings. We asked the Tartar if he had seen them. "What!" said he, "have I seen the Kitats who inhabited this defile ? Why, I knew all of them; it is not more than two years since they left the country. For that matter," he added, "they had no right to remain here; as they were rascals, it was quite proper to turn them out." "Rascals, say you ? Why, what mischief could they do in this wretched ravine ? " "Oh, the Kitats are sly, cheating fellows. At first they seemed very good; but that did not last long. It is more than twenty years ago that a few of their families sought our hospitality; as they were poor, they got permission to cultivate some land in the vicinity, on condition that every year after harvest they should furnish some oatmeal to the *Taitsi* of the country. By degrees, other families arrived, who also excavated caverns wherein to dwell; and soon this defile was full of them. In the beginning, these Kitats showed a gentle, quiet character; we lived together like brothers. Tell me, Sirs Lamas, is it not well to live together like brothers ? Are not all men brothers ? " "Yes, that is true; you speak the words of justice; but why did these Kitats go hence ?" "Peace did not last long; they soon showed themselves wicked and false. Instead of being content with what had been given them, they extended their cultivation at their pleasure, and took possession of a large territory without asking anyone's leave. When they were rich they would not pay the oatmeal they had agreed to pay as tribute. Every year, when we claimed the rent, we were received with insults and maledictions. But the worst thing was that these rascally Kitats turned thieves, and took possession of all the goats and sheep that loſt their way in the sinuosities of the ravine. At laſt, a *Taitsi* of great courage and capacity called together the Mongols of the neighbourhood, and said,— ' The Kitats take away our land, they ſteal our beaſts, and curse us ; as they do not aɛt or speak as brothers, we muſt expel them.' Everybody was pleased with these words of the old *Taitsi*. After a deliberation, it was decided that the principal men of the country should go to the king, and supplicate an order condemning the Kitats to be expelled. I was one of the deputation. The king reproached us for having permitted foreigners to cultivate our lands ; we proſtrated ourselves before him, observing profound silence. However, the king, who always aɛts with juſtice, had the order written, and sealed with his red seal. The ordonnance said, that the king would not permit the Kitats to live any longer in the country ; and that they muſt leave it before the firſt day of the eighth moon. Three *Taitsi* rode off to present the ordonnance to the Kitats. They made no answer to the three deputies, but said amongſt themselves, ' The king desires us to go ; very well.'

" Afterwards we learned that they had assembled and had resolved to disobey the orders of the king and to remain in the country, in spite of him. The firſt day of the eighth moon arrived, and they ſtill occupied calmly their habitations, without making any preparations for departure. In the morning, before daybreak, all the Tartars mounted their horses, armed themselves with their lances, and drove their flocks and herds upon the cultivated lands of the Kitats, on which the crop was ſtill ſtanding: when the sun rose, nothing of that crop was left. All had been devoured by the animals, or trodden down. The Kitats yelled and cursed us, but the thing was done. Seeing that their position was desperate they colleɛted, the same day, their furniture and agricultural implements, and went off to settle in the eastern parts of the Ortous, at some distance from the Yellow River, near the Paga-Gol. As you came through Tchagan-Kouren, you must have met on your route, west of the Paga-Gol, Kitats cultivating some pieces of land; well, it was they who inhabited this defile, and excavated all these caves."

Having finished this narrative, the Tartar went out for a moment and brought back a small packet, which he had left in the cavern where he had passed the night. "Sirs Lamas," he said on his return, "I must depart; but will you not come and repose for a few days in my dwelling? My tent is not far hence; it is behind that sandy mountain which you perceive there towards the north. It is at the utmost not more than thirty lis off." "We are much obliged to you," answered we. "The hospitality of the Mongols of Ortous is known everywhere, but we have a long journey before us; we cannot stop on our way." "What are a few days, sooner or later, in a long journey? Your beasts cannot always be on their feet; they need a little rest. You yourselves have had much to endure from the weather of yesterday. Come with me; all will then be well. In four days we shall have a festival. My eldest son is going to establish a family. Come to the nuptials of my son; your presence will bring him good fortune." The Tartar, seeing us inflexible, mounted his horse, and after having ascended the pathway which led to the defile, disappeared across the heath and sand of the desert.

Under other circumstances, we should have accepted with pleasure the offer thus made; but we desired to make the shortest possible stay amongst the Ortous. We were anxious to leave behind us that miserable country, where our animals were wasting away daily, and where we had ourselves met with such fatigue and misery. Besides, a Mongol wedding was no new thing to us. Since we had entered Tartary we had witnessed, more than once, ceremonies of that kind.

The Mongols marry very young, and always under the influence of the absolute authority of the parents. This affair, so grave and important, is initiated, discussed and concluded, without the two persons most interested in it taking the least part in it. Whatever promises of marriage may take place in youth, or at more advanced age, it is the parents who always settle the contract, without even speaking to their children about it. The two future consorts do not know, perhaps never saw each other. It is only when they are married that they have the opportunity to inquire whether there is any sympathy between their characters or not.

The daughter never brings any marriage portion. On the contrary, the young man has to make presents to the family of his bride: and the value of these presents is seldom left to the generosity of the husband's parents. Everything is arranged beforehand and set forth in a public document, with the minutest details. In fact, the matter is less a marriage present than the price of an object, sold by one party and bought by the other. The thing is indeed very clearly expressed in their language; they say, "I have bought for my son the daughter of so and so." "We have sold our daughter to such and such a family." The marriage contract is thus simply a contract of sale. There are mediators who bargain and haggle, up and down, till at last they come to an agreement. When it is settled how many horses, oxen, sheep, pieces of linen, pounds of butter, what quantity of brandy and wheat-flour shall be given to the family of the bride, the contract is at length drawn up before witnesses, and the daughter becomes the property of the purchaser. She remains, however, with her family till the time of the nuptial ceremonies.

When the marriage has been concluded between the mediators, the father of the bridegroom, accompanied by his nearest relations, carries the news to the family of the bride. On entering, they prostrate themselves before the little domestic altar, and offer to the idol of Buddha a boiled sheep's head, milk, and a sash of white silk. Then they partake of a repast provided by the parents of the bridegroom. During the repast all the relations of the bride receive a piece of money, which they deposit in a vase filled with wine made of fermented milk. The father of the bride drinks the wine, and keeps the money. This ceremony is called *Tahil-Tébihou* [takil-talbikhu] "Striking the bargain."

The day indicated by the Lamas as auspicious for the marriage having arrived, the bridegroom sends early in the morning a deputation to fetch the girl who has been betrothed to him, or rather whom he has bought. When the envoys draw near, the relations and friends of the bride place themselves in a circle before the door, as if to oppose the departure of the bride, and then begins a feigned fight, which of course terminates with the bride being carried off. She is placed on a horse, and having been thrice led round her paternal house, she is then taken at full gallop to the tent which has been prepared for the purpose, near the dwelling of her father-in-law. Meantime all the Tartars of the neighbourhood, the relations and friends of both families, repair to the wedding-feast, and offer their presents to the new married pair. The extent of these presents, which consists of beasts and eatables, is left to the generosity of the guests. They are destined for the father of the bridegroom and often fully indemnify him for his expenses in the purchase of the bride. As the offered animals come up they are taken into folds ready conſtructed for them. At the weddings of rich Tartars, these large folds receive great herds of oxen, horses and sheep. Generally the gueſts are generous enough, for they know that they will be paid in return, upon a similar occasion.

When the bride has finished dressing, she is introduced to her father-in-law; and while the assembled Lamas recite the prayers prescribed by the ritual, she first proſtrates herself before the image of Buddha, then before the hearth, and laſtly before the father, mother, and other near relatives of the bridegroom, who, on his part, performs the same ceremonies towards the family of his bride, assembled in an adjacent tent. Then comes the wedding-feaſt, which sometimes continues for seven or eight days. An excessive profusion of fat meat, infinite tobacco, and large jars of brandy, conſtitute the splendour and magnificence of these repaſts. Sometimes music is added to the entertainment, and they invite *Toolholos*, or Tartar singers, to give more solemnity to the feſtival.

The plurality of wives is admitted in Tartary, being opposed neither to the laws, nor to the religion, nor to the manners of the country. The firſt wife is always the miſtress of the household, and the moſt respected in the family. The other wives bear the name of little spouses (*pagá éme*) [*baga eme*], and owe obedience and respect to the firſt.

Polygamy, abolished by the Gospel, and contrary in itself to the happiness and concord of families, may, perhaps, be regarded as a blessing to the Tartars. Considering the present ſtate of society with them, it is, as it were, a barrier opposed to libertinism and corruption of morals. Celibacy being imposed on the Lamas, and the class of those who shave the head and live in lamaseries being so numerous, it is easy to conceive what disorders would arise from this multiplication of young women without support and abandoned to themselves, if girls could not be placed in families in the quality of second wives.

Divorce is very frequent among the Tartars. It takes place without any participation of the civil or ecclesiastical authorities. The husband, who repudiates his wife, has not even occasion for a pretext to justify his conduct. He sends her back, without any formality, to her parents, and contents himself with a message that he does not require her any longer. This proceeding is in accordance with Tartar manners, and does not offend anyone. The husband thinks himself entitled to the privilege, in consideration of the oxen, sheep and horses he was obliged to give as nuptial presents. The parents of the repudiated wife do not complain at having their daughter back; she resumes her place in the family till another husband presents himself, in which case, they even rejoice over the profit they make by thus selling the same merchandise twice over.

In Tartary, the women lead an independent life enough. They are far from being oppressed and kept in servitude, as with other Asiatic nations. They may come and go at their pleasure, ride out on horseback, and pay each other visits from tent to tent. Instead of the soft, languishing physiognomy of the Chinese women, the Tartar woman presents in her bearing and manners a power and force well in accordance with her active life and nomad habits and her attire augments the effect of her masculine, haughty mien.

Large leather boots, and a long green or violet robe fastened round the waist by a black or blue girdle, constitutes her dress, except that sometimes she wears over the great robe a small coat, resembling in form our waistcoats, but very large and coming down to the hips. The hair of the Tartar woman is divided in two tresses, tied up in taffetas, and hanging down upon the bosom; their luxury consists in ornamenting the girdle and hair with spangles of gold and silver, pearls, coral and a thousand other toys, the form and quality of which it would be difficult for us to define, as we had neither opportunity, nor taste, nor patience to pay serious attention to these futilities.

CHAPTER IX

The Tartar who had just taken his leave had informed us that a short distance from the caverns we should find in a vale the finest pasturages in the whole country of the Ortous. We resolved to depart. It was near noon already when we started. The sky was clear, the sun brilliant; but the temperature, still affected by the storm of the preceding day, was cold and sharp. After having travelled for nearly two hours over a sandy soil, deeply furrowed by the streams of rain, we entered, on a sudden, a valley whose smiling, fertile aspect singularly contrasted with all that we had hitherto seen among the Ortous. In the centre flowed an abundant rivulet, whose sources were lost in the sand; and on both sides, the hills, which rose like an amphitheatre, were covered with pasturage and clumps of shrubs.

Though it was still early, we gave up all idea of continuing our journey that day. The place was too beautiful to be passed by; besides, the north wind had arisen, and the air became intolerably cold. We pitched our tent, therefore, in a corner, sheltered by the hills. From the interior of the tent, our view extentended, without obstruction, down the valley, and we were thus enabled to watch our animals without moving.

After sunset, the violence of the wind increased, and the cold became more and more intense. We thought it advisable to take some measures of security. Whilst Samdadchiemba piled up large stones to consolidate the borders of the tent, we went about the adjacent hills, and made, by aid of a hatchet, an abundant provision of fuel. As soon as we had taken our tea and our daily broth, we went to sleep. But sleep did not laſt long; the cold became so severe that it soon roused us. "We can't remain so," said the Dchiahour; "if we don't want to die of cold on our goatskins, we muſt get up and make a large fire." Samdadchiemba's words were full of sense; it was not advisable to sleep at such a time, and accordingly we rose, and added to our usual dress the great sheep-skin robes that we had bought at Blue Town.

Our fire of roots and green branches was hardly lighted, when we felt our eyes as it were calcined by the biting, acid influence of a thick smoke, which filled the tent. We opened the door; but as this gave admission to the wind, without getting rid of the smoke, we were soon obliged to shut it again. Samdadchiemba was not in any way moleſted by the thick smoke, which ſtifled us and drew burning tears from our eyes. He laughed without pity at seeing us crouched by the fire, our heads bending over our knees, and our faces buried in both hands. "My spiritual fathers," he said, "your eyes are large and bright, but they cannot endure a little smoke; mine are small and ugly, but, never mind, they perform their service very well." The jeſts of our camel driver were not much adapted to cheer us up; we suffered dreadfully. Yet, amid our tribulations, we saw occasion to feel our happiness to be very great. We could not reflect without gratitude upon the goodness of Providence, which had led us to caves, whose great value we now fully appreciated. If we had not been able to dry our clothes, if we had been surprised by the cold in the piteous ſtate in which the ſtorm had left us, we certainly could not have lived long; we should have been frozen with our clothes in one immovable block.

We did not think it prudent to proceed amid such

severe cold, and to leave an encampment, where at least our animals got sufficient herbage to browse upon, and where fuel was abundant. Towards noon, the weather having grown milder, we went out to cut wood on the hills. On our way we observed that our animals had left the pasturage, and collected on the banks of the rivulet. We at once conceived that they were tormented by thirst, and that the stream being frozen, they could not quench it. We bent our steps to them, and found, in fact, the camels eagerly licking the surface of the ice, while the horse and the mule were kicking upon it with their hard hoofs. The hatchet we had brought with us to cut wood, served to break the ice, and to dig a small pond, where our animals could quench their thirst.

Towards evening, the cold having resumed its intensity, we adopted a plan for enabling us to obtain a better sleep than we had in the preceding night. Until morning, the time was divided into three watches, and each of us was charged, in turn, with keeping up a large fire in the tent while the others slept. Thus we did not feel much of the cold, and slept in peace, without fear of setting our linen house on fire.

After two days of horrible cold the wind abated, and we resolved to proceed on our way. It was only with great difficulty that we got down our tent. The first nail that we tried to draw out, broke like glass under the hammer. The sandy, humid soil on which we had made our encampment, was so frozen that the nails stuck in it as if they had been encrusted in stone. To uproot them, we were obliged to wet them several times with boiling water.

At the time of our departure, the temperature was so mild that we were fain to take off our skin coats, and to pack them up until further occasion. Nothing is more frequent in Tartary than these sudden changes of temperature. Sometimes the mildest weather is abruptly followed by the most horrible frost. All that is needed for this is the falling of snow, and the subsequent rise of the north wind. Anyone not inured to these sudden changes of the atmosphere, and not provided, in travelling, with well-furred robes, is often exposed to dreadful accidents. In the north of Mongolia especially, it is not unusual to find travellers frozen to death amidst the desert.

On the fifteenth day of the new moon we came upon numerous caravans, following, like ourselves the direction from east to west. The road was filled with men, women and children, riding on camels, or oxen. They were all repairing, they said, to the Lamasery of Rache-Tchurin [Rash'e-churin (bkra-shis . . .?)]. When they had asked whether our journey had the same object, they were surprised at receiving an answer in the negative. These numerous pilgrims, the astonishment they showed upon hearing that we were not going to the Lamasery of Rache-Tchurin excited our curiosity. At the turn of a defile, we overtook an old Lama, who, laden with a heavy pack, seemed to make his way with great labour and pain. "Brother," said we, " you are old ; your black hairs are not so numerous as the grey. Doubtless your fatigue must be extreme. Place your burden upon one of our camels ; that will relieve you a little." Upon hearing these words the old man prostrated himself before us, in order to express his gratitude. We made a camel kneel, and Samdadchiemba added to our baggage that of the Lama. As soon as the pilgrim was relieved from the weight which had oppressed him, his walk became more elastic, and an expression of satisfaction was diffused over his countenance. "Brother," said we, " we are from the West, and the affairs of your country not being well known to us, we are astonished at finding so many pilgrims here in the desert." "We are all going to Rache-Tchurin," replied he, in accents full of emotion. "Doubtless," said we, "some grand solemnity calls you together." "Yes, to-morrow will be a great day: a Lama *Boktè* [*bogda*] will manifest his power: kill himself, yet not die." We at once understood what solemnity it was that thus attracted the Ortous-Tartars. A Lama was to cut himself open, take out his entrails and place them before him, and then resume his previous condition. This spectacle, so cruel and disgusting, is very common in the Lama-series of Tartary. The *Boktè* who is to manifest his power, as the Mongols phrase it, prepares himself for the formidable operation by many days fasting and prayer, pending which, he must abstain from all communication whatever with mankind, and observe the most absolute silence. When the appointed day is come, the multitude of pilgrims assemble in the great court of the Lamasery, where an altar is raised in front of the temple gate. At length the *Boktè* appears. He advances gravely, amid the acclamations of the crowd, seats himself upon the altar, and takes from his girdle a large knife which he places upon his knees. At his feet, numerous Lamas, ranged in a circle, commence the terrible invocations of this frightful ceremony. As the recitation of the prayers proceeds, you see the *Boktè* trembling in every limb, and gradually working himself up into phrenetic convulsions. The Lamas themselves become excited: their voices are raised; their song observes no order, and at last becomes a mere confusion of yelling and outcry. Then the *Boktè* suddenly throws aside the scarf which envelops him, unfastens his girdle, and siezing the sacred knife, slits open his stomach, in one long cut. While the blood flows in every direction, the multitude prostrate themselves before the terrible spectacle, and the enthusiast is interrogated about all

sorts of hidden things, as to future events, as to the
destiny of certain personages. The replies of the *Boktè*
to all these questions are regarded, by everybody, as
oracles.

When the devout curiosity of the numerous pilgrims is satisfied, the Lamas resume, but now calmly and gravely, the recitation of their prayers. The *Boktè* takes, in his right hand, blood from his wound, raises it to his mouth, breathes thrice upon it, and then throws it into the air, with loud cries. He next passes his hand rapidly over his wound, closes it, and everything after a while resumes its pristine condition, no trace remaining of the diabolical operation, except extreme prostration. The *Boktè* once more rolls his scarf round him, recites in a low voice, a short prayer; then all is over, and the multitude disperse, with the exception of a few of the especially devout, who remain to contemplate and to adore the blood-stained altar which the Saint has quitted.

These horrible ceremonies are of frequent occurrence in the great Lamaseries of Tartary and Thibet, and we do not believe that there is any trick or deception about them; for from all we have seen and heard, among idolatrous nations, we are persuaded that the devil has a great deal to do with the matter; and moreover, our impression that there is no trick in the operation is fortified by the opinion of the most intelligent and most upright Buddhists whom we have met in the numerous Lamaseries we visited.

It is not every Lama that can perform miraculous operations. Those who have the fearful power to cut themselves open, for example, are never found in the higher ranks of the Lama hierarchy. They are generally lay Lamas of indifferent character, and little esteemed by their comrades. The regular Lamas generally make no scruple to avow their horror of the spectacle. In their eyes all these operations are wicked and diabolical. Good Lamas, they say, are incapable of performing such acts, and should not even desire to attain the impious talent.

Though these demoniac operations are, in general, decried in well-regulated Lamaseries, yet the superiors do not prohibit them. On the contrary, there are certain days in the year set apart for the disgusting spectacle. Interest is, doubtless, the only motive which could induce the Grand Lamas to favour actions which in their conscience they reprove. The fact is, that these diabolical displays are an infallible means of collecting together a swarm of stupid and ignorant devotees, who communicate renown to the Lamasery, and enrich it with the numerous offerings which the Tartars never fail to bring with them on such occasions.

Cutting open the abdomen is one of the most famous *sié-fa* [*hsieh-fa*], "supernaturalisms" possessed by the Lamas. There are others of the same class, less imposing, but more common; these are practised in people's houses, privately, and not at the great solemnities of the Lamaseries. For example, they heat irons red-hot, and then lick them with impunity; they make incisions in various parts of the body, which an instant afterwards leave no trace behind, etc. All these operations have to be preceded by the recitation of some prayer.

We knew a Lama who, according to everyone's belief, could fill a vase with water, by the mere agency of a prayer; but we could never induce him to try the experiment in our presence. He told us that as we held not the same faith with him, the experiment in our company would not be merely fruitless, but would expose him to serious danger. One day, however, he recited to us the prayer of his *sié-fa*. It was brief, but we readily recognized in it a direct appeal to the assistance of the demon. " I know thee, thou knowest me ; " thus it ran : " Come, old friend, do what I ask of thee. Bring water, and fill the vase I hold out to thee. To fill a vase with water, what is that to thy vast power! I know thou chargest dear for a vase of water ; but never mind : do what I ask of thee, and fill the vase I present to thee. Some time hence we'll come to a reckoning : on the appointed day thou shalt receive thy due." It sometimes happens that the appeal remains without effect : in such cases, praying is discontinued, and the being invoked is assailed with insults and imprecations.

The famous *sié-fa* that was now attracting so large a number of pilgrims to the Lamasery of Rache-Tchurin inspired us with the idea of repairing thither also, and of neutralizing, by our prayers, the satanic invocations of the Lamas. Who knows, said we to each other, who knows but that God even now has designs of mercy towards the Mongols of the Ortous land ; perhaps the sight of their Lama's power, fettered and overcome by the presence of the priests of Jesus Christ, will strike upon the hearts of these people, and make them renounce the lying creed of Buddha, and embrace the faith of Christianity ! To encourage each other in this design, we dwelt upon the history of Simon Magus, arrested in his flight by the prayer of St. Peter, and precipitated from the air to the feet of his admirers. Of course, poor missionaries such as we had not the insane pretension to compare ourselves with the prince of the Apostles ; but we knew that the protection of God, which is sometimes granted in virtue of the merit and sanctity of him who seeks it, is also often accorded to the omnipotent efficacy in prayer itself.

We resolved, therefore, to go to Rache-Tchurin, to mingle with the crowd, and, at the moment when the diabolical invocations should commence, to place ourselves, fearlessly, and with an air of authority before the *Boktè*, and to solemnly forbid him, in the name of Jesus Christ, to make a display of his detestable power. We did not disguise from ourselves the possible results of this proceeding; we knew that it would assuredly excite the fury and hatred of the adorers of Buddha; and that perhaps a violent death would be an instant reward for the endeavour to convert these Tartars; "But what matter!" exclaimed we; "let us do courageously our work as missionaries; let us employ fearlessly the powers that we have received from on high, and leave to Providence the care of a future which does not appertain to us."

Such were our intentions and our hopes; but the views of God are not always in conformity with the designs of man, even when these appear most in harmony with the plan of His Providence. That very day there happened to us an accident which, carrying us away from Rache-Tchurin, involved us in the most distressing perplexities.

In the evening, the old Lama who was travelling with us asked us to make the camel kneel, so that he might take his pack from its back. "Brother," said we, "are we not going to journey together to the Lamasery of Rache-Tchurin?" "No, I must follow the path which you see meandering towards the north, along those hills. Behind that sand-hill is a trading-place, where, upon festival days, a few Chinese merchants set up their tents and sell goods. As I want to make a few purchases, I cannot continue to walk in your shadow." "Can we buy flour at the Chinese encampment?" "Millet, oatmeal, flour, beef, mutton, tea-bricks, everything is sold there." Not having been able to purchase provisions since our departure from Tchagan-Kouren, we considered this a favourable opportunity for supplying our deficiency in this respect. In order not to fatigue our beasts of burden with a long circuit across stony hills, M. Gabet took the flour-sacks upon his camel, separated from the caravan, and went off at a gallop towards the Chinese post. According to the indications furnished by the old Lama, he was to meet us again in a valley at no great distance from the Lamasery.

After travelling for nearly an hour along a rugged road, continually intersected by pits and quagmires, the Missionary Purveyor reached the small heath, on which he found a number of Chinese encamped, some of their tents serving as shops, and the rest as dwellings. The encampment presented the appearance of a small town full of trade and activity, the customers being the Lamas of Rache-Tchurin and the Mongol pilgrims. M. Gabet speedily effected his purchases; and having filled his sacks with flour, and hung two magnificent sheeps' livers over one of the camel's humps, rode off to the place where it had been arranged the caravan should await him. He soon reached the spot, but he found no person there, and no trace of man or beast having recently passed was visible on the sand. Imagining that perhaps some derangement of the camels' loads had delayed our progress, he turned into the road, which it had been agreed we should follow; but it was to no purpose that he hastened along it, that he galloped here and there, that he ascended every hill he came to,—he could see nothing; and the cries he uttered to attract our attention remained unanswered. He visited several points where various roads met, but he found merely another confusion of the steps of horses, camels, oxen, sheep, tending in every direction, and crossing and recrossing each other, so that he was left, at last, without even a conjecture.

By-and-by he recalled to mind that our aim, as last resolved, had been the Lamasery of Rache-Tchurin;

he turned round, and perceiving the Lamasery in the distance, hurried thither as fast as he could go. When he reached the structure, which stood in the form of an amphitheatre upon the slope of a hill, he looked everywhere for us, and asked everybody about us, for here, at least, there was no lack of persons from whom to seek information, and our little caravan was composed in a manner likely to attract the attention of those who saw it at all: two laden camels, a white horse, and, above all, a black mule, that everyone we passed stopped to remark, on account of its extreme diminutiveness, and the splendid tint of its skin. M. Gabet inquired and inquired, but to no purpose; no one had seen our caravan. He ascended to the summit of the hill, whence the eye extended over a large expanse, but he could see nothing at all like us.

The sun set, yet the caravan did not appear. M. Gabet beginning to fear that some serious accident had befallen it, once more set off, and searched in every direction, up hill and down dale, but he could see nothing of us, and learn nothing of us, from the travellers whom he met.

The night advanced, and soon the Lamasery of Rache-Tchurin disappeared in the darkness. M. Gabet found himself alone in the desert, without path and without shelter, fearing alike to advance or to recede, lest he should fall into some abyss. He was fain, therefore, to stop where he was, in a narrow, sandy defile, and to pass the night there. By way of supper, he had to content himself with an *Impression de Voyage*. Not that provisions were wanting, by any means, but fire was, and water. Besides, the feeling of hunger was superseded by the anxieties which afflicted his heart as to the caravan. He knelt on the sand, said his evening prayer, and then lay down his head upon one of the flour sacks beside the camel, keeping its bridle round his arm lest the animal should stray during the night. It is needless to add that his sleep was neither sound nor continuous; the cold, bare ground is not a very eligible bed, especially for a man preyed upon by dark anxieties.

With the earliest dawn, M. Gabet mounted his camel, and though well nigh exhausted with hunger and fatigue, proceeded anew in search of his companions.

The caravan was not lost, though it was terribly astray. After M. Gabet had quitted us, in order to visit the Chinese post, we at first exactly followed the right path; but before long we entered upon a vast steppe, all trace of road insensibly faded away amidst sand so fine that the slightest wind made it undulate like sea-waves; there was no vestige upon it of the travellers who had preceded us. By-and-by the road disappeared altogether, and we found ourselves environed with yellow hills, which presented not the slightest suggestion even of vegetation. M. Huc, fearing to lose himself amid these sands, stopped the cameleer. " Samdadchiemba," said he, " do not let us proceed at random. You see yonder, in the valley, that Tartar horseman driving a herd of oxen; go and ask him the way to Rache-Tchurin." Samdadchiemba raised his head, and looked for a moment, closing one eye, at the sun, which was veiled with some passing clouds. " My spiritual father," said he, " I am accustomed to wander about the desert; my opinion is, that we are quite in the right road: let us continue our course westward, and we cannot go astray." " Well, well, since you think you know the desert, keep on." " Oh, yes; don't be afraid. You see that long white line on the mountain yonder? that's the road, after its issue from the sands."

On Samdadchiemba's assurance, we continued to advance in the same direction. We soon came to a road, as he had promised, but it was a road disused, upon which we could see no person to confirm or contradict the assertion of Samdadchiemba, who persisted that we were on the way to Rache-Tchurin. The sun set, and the twilight gradually gave place to the darkness of night, without our discovering the least indication of the Lamasery, or, which surprised us still more, of M. Gabet, who, according to the information of the old Lama, ought to have rejoined us long ago. Samdadchiemba was silent, for now he saw that we had lost our way.

It was important to encamp before the night had altogether closed in. Perceiving a well at the end of a hollow, we set up our tent beside it. By the time our linen house was in order, and the baggage piled, the night had completely set in; yet M. Gabet had not appeared. "Get on a camel," said M. Huc to Samdadchiemba, "and look about for M. Gabet." The Dchiahour made no reply; he was thoroughly disconcerted and depressed. Driving a stake into the ground, he fastened one of the camels to it, and mounting upon the other, departed mournfully in quest of our friend. He had scarcely got out of sight, when the camel that was left behind, finding himself alone, sent forth the most frightful cries; by-and-by it became furious; it turned round and round the stake, backed to the very limit of the rope and of its long neck, made longer by painful extension, and applied every effort to get rid of the wooden curl that was passed through its nose: the spectacle of its struggle was really frightful. At last it succeeded in breaking the cord, and then dashed off boundingly into the desert. The horse and mule had also disappeared; they were hungry and thirsty; and about the tent there was not a blade of grass, not a drop of water. The well beside which we had encamped was perfectly dry; in fact, it was nothing more than an old cistern which had probably been for years useless.

THIBET, AND CHINA

Thus our little caravan, which for nearly two months had journeyed without once separating, through the desert plains of Tartary, was now utterly dispersed; man and beaſt—all had disappeared. There remained only M. Huc, solitary in his little linen-house, and a prey to the moſt corroding anxieties. For a whole day he had neither eaten nor drunk; but under such circumſtances you do not ordinarily feel either hunger or thirſt; the mind is too full to give any place to the suggeſtions of the body; you seem environed with a thousand fearful phantoms; and great indeed were your desolation, but that you have for your safety and your consolation, prayer, the sole lever that can raise from off your heart the weight of sombre apprehensions that would otherwise crush it.

The hours passed on, and no one returned. As, in the obscurity of night, persons might pass quite close to the tent, and yet not see it, M. Huc, from time to time, ascended the adjacent hills and rocks, and, in his loudeſt tones, called out the names of his loſt companions, but no one replied; all ſtill was silence, and solitude. It was near midnight, when at length the plaintive cries of a camel, apparently remonſtrating againſt being driven so faſt, were heard in the diſtance. Samdadchiemba soon came up. He had met several Tartar horsemen who had no tidings, indeed, of M. Gabet, but from whom he learned that we had gone altogether aſtray; that the road we were pursuing led to a Mongol encampment, in precisely the contrary direction to Rache-Tchurin. "By day-break," said Samdadchiemba, "we muſt raise the tent, and find the right path; we shall there, no doubt, meet the elder spiritual father." "Samdadchiemba, your advice is a bubble; the tent and the baggage muſt remain here, for the excellent reason, that they cannot be moved without animals." "Animals!" exclaimed the Dchiahour, "where, then, is the camel I fastened to the stake?" "It broke the rope and ran away; the horse and the mule have run away too, and I have not the least idea where any of them are to be sought." "This is a pretty business," grumbled the cameleer; "however, when day breaks we must see what can be done. Meanwhile, let us make a little tea." "Make tea, by all means, if you can make tea without water, but water there is none; the well is perfectly dry." This announcement completed the discomfiture of poor Samdadchiemba; he sank back quite exhausted upon the baggage, and his weariness soon threw him into deep slumber.

With the first streaks of dawn, M. Huc ascended an adjacent hill in the hope of discovering something or somebody. He perceived, in a distant valley, two animals, one black, one white; he hastened to them, and found our horse and mule browsing on some thin, dusty grass, beside a cistern of soft water. When he led the animals back to the tent, the sun was about to rise, but Samdadchiemba still slumbered, lying in exactly the same position which he had assumed when he went to sleep. "Samdadchiemba," cried M. Huc, "won't you have some tea this morning?" At the word *tea*, our cameleer jumped up as though he had been electrified; he looked round, his eyes still heavy with sleep, "Did not the spiritual father mention tea? Where is the tea? Did I dream I was going to have some tea?" "I don't know whether you dreamed it, but tea you may have, if you wish, as there is soft water in the valley yonder, where, just now, I found the horse and the mule. Do you go and fetch some water while I light the fire." Samdadchiemba joyfully adopted the proposition, and putting the buckets over his shoulders, hastened to the cistern.

When tea was ready, Samdadchiemba became quite comfortable; he was absorbed with his beloved beverage, and seemed to have altogether forgotten the disruptions of the caravan. It was necessary, however, to recall the circumstance to him, in order that he might go in search of the camel that had run away.

Nearly one half the day elapsed, yet his companion did not rejoin M. Huc. From time to time there passed Tartar horsemen or pilgrims returning from the festival of Rache-Tchurin. Of these M. Huc inquired whether they had not seen, in the vicinity of the Lamasery, a Lama dressed in a yellow robe and a red jacket, and mounted on a red camel. " The Lama," said he, " is very tall, with a great grey beard, a long pointed nose, and a red face." To this description there was a general answer in the negative : " Had we seen such a personage," said the travellers, " we should certainly have remarked him."

At length, M. Gabet appeared on the slope of a hill ; from its summit he had recognized our blue tent pitched in the valley, and he galloped towards his recovered companion as fast as his camel could go. After a brief, animated conversation, wherein both spoke and neither answered, we burst into a hearty laugh at the misadventure thus happily terminated. The reorganization of the caravan was completed before sunset, by Samdadchiemba's return with the missing camel, which, after a long round, he had found fastened to a tent ; the Tartar, who owned the tent, having seen the animal running away, had caught it, and secured it until some one should claim it.

Though the day was far advanced, we determined to remove, for the place where we had encamped was miserable beyond all expression. Not a blade of grass was to be seen, and the water I had discovered was at so great a distance that it involved quite a journey to fetch it. " Besides," said we, " if we can only, before night, manage to get within sight of the right road, it will be a great point gained." Our departure thus determined, we sat down to tea. The conversation naturally turned upon the vexatious mischance which had given so much fatigue and trouble. Already more than once, on our journey, the intractable, obstinate temperament of Samdadchiemba had been the occasion of our losing our way. Mounted on his little mule, as we have described, it was he who led the caravan, preceding the beasts of burden. Upon his assumption that he thoroughly understood the four cardinal points, and that he was perfectly conversant with the deserts of Mongolia, he would never condescend to inquire the route from persons whom he met, and we not unfrequently suffered from his self-opinion. We were resolved, therefore, to convert the accident which had just befallen us into the basis of a warning to our guide. "Samdadchiemba," said we, "listen with attention to the important advice we are about to impart. Though in your youth you may have travelled a good deal in Mongolia, it does not follow that you are master of all the routes; distrust, therefore, your own conjectures, and be more willing to consult the Tartars whom we meet. If yesterday, for example, you had asked the way, if you had not persisted in your practice of being guided wholly by the course of the sun, we should not have endured so much misery." Samdadchiemba made no reply.

We then got up to make the preparations for departure. When we had put in order the different articles that had been confusedly thrown about the tent, we remarked that the Dchiahour was not occupied, as usual, in saddling the camels. We went to see what he was about, and to our great surprise found him tranquilly seated upon a large stone behind the tent. "Well," exclaimed we, "has it not been determined that we are to encamp elsewhere this evening? What are you seated on that stone for?"

Samdadchiemba made no reply; he did not even raise his eyes, but kept them fixedly directed towards the ground. "Samdadchiemba, what is the matter with you? Why don't you saddle the camels?" "If you wish to go," replied he, drily, "you can go; as for me, I remain here. I cannot any longer accompany you. I am, it seems, a wicked man, devoid of conscience; what occasion can you have for such a person?" We were greatly surprised to hear this from a young neophyte who had seemed so attached to us. We, however, thought it best to attempt no persuasion, lest we should aggravate the sullen pride of his character, and render him still more indocile for the future. We accordingly proceeded to do the necessary work ourselves.

We had already folded the tent and packed it on a camel, not a word being spoken by any of the party. Samdadchiemba remained seated on the stone, covering his face with his hands, and probably watching through his fingers how we got on with the labour which he was accustomed to fulfil. When he saw that we were doing very well without him, he rose, without uttering a word, loaded the other camel, saddled his own mule, mounted it, and led the way as usual. M. Gabet and M. Huc exchanged smiles, but they said nothing, for they feared that any observations at that moment might irritate a temperament which evidently required the greatest care in its management.

We halted in a spot beside the road, not very magnificent, certainly, as a station, but at all events, infinitely preferable to the ravine of desolation in which we had experienced such misery. There was this great blessing, that we were once more united; an immense satisfaction in the desert, and which we had never sufficiently appreciated until the occurrence of the mischance that had for a while separated us. We celebrated the occasion by a splendid banquet, of which the flour and sheep's liver, purchased by M. Gabet, formed the basis. This unaccustomed treat relaxed the frowning brow of Samdadchiemba, who applied himself to the culinary arrangements with absolute enthusiasm, and effected, with very limited resources, a supper of several courses.

Next morning, at daybreak, we were in motion. We had not proceeded far when we discovered before us, outlined on the yellow ground of a sandy hill, several large buildings, surrounded with a multitude of white huts. This was the Lamasery of the Rache-Tchurin, which, as we approached it, seemed to us a well-built, well-kept place. The three Buddhist temples which rise from the centre of the establishment are of elegant, of majestic construction. The entrance to the principal temple is through a square tower of colossal proportions, at each angle of which is a monstrous dragon, elaborately carved in stone. We traversed the Lamasery from one end to the other, along the chief streets. There was throughout a religious and solemn silence. The only persons we saw were a few Lamas enveloped in their large red scarfs, who, after giving us the salutation of the day in a tone scarce above a whisper, gravely continued their melancholy walk.

Towards the western extremity of the Lamasery, Samdadchiemba's little mule shied, and then dashed off at a gallop, followed in its irregular flight by the two baggage camels. The animals on which we were mounted were equally alarmed. All this disorder was occasioned by a young Lama, who was stretched at full length in the middle of the street, performing a rite in great vogue among the Buddhists, and which consists in making the circuit of a Lamasery, prostrating yourself, with your forehead to the ground, at every single step you make. Sometimes the number

THIBET, AND CHINA

of devotees performing together this painful pilgrimage is perfectly prodigious; they follow each other in Indian file, along a narrow path which encircles the entire Lamasery and its appendant buildings. Anyone who deviates in the slightest degree from the prescribed line, is considered to have failed in his devotion, and loses all the fruit he would otherwise have derived from his previous toil. Where the Lamasery is of any extent, the devotees have hard work to get through the ceremony in the course of a long day; so that the pilgrims, who have undertaken this exercise, and have started early in the morning, think themselves lucky if they can complete the operation by nightfall. For the pilgrimage must be performed without intermission, so strictly that the pilgrims are not allowed to stop for a moment even to take a little nourishment. If, after commencing the rite, you do not complete it off-hand, it does not count; and you have acquired no merit, and you are not to expect any spiritual profit.

Each prostration must be perfect, so that the body shall be stretched flat along the ground, and your forehead touch the earth, the arms being spread out before you, and the hands joined, as if in prayer. Before rising, the pilgrim describes each time a semi-circle on the ground by means of a goat's horn, which he holds in either hand, the line being completed by drawing the arm down to the side. You cannot but feel infinite compassion when you look upon these wretched creatures, their face and clothes all covered with dust or mud. The most inclement weather will not check their intrepid devotion; they continue their prostrations amid snow and rain and the most piercing cold.

There are various modes of performing the pilgrimage round a Lamasery. Some persons do not prostrate themselves at all, but carry, instead, a load of prayer-books, the exact weight of which is prescribed them by the Great Lama, and the burden of which is so oppressive at times that you see old men, women and children absolutely staggering under it. When, however, they have successfully completed the circuit, they are deemed to have recited all the prayers contained in the books they have carried. Others content themselves with simply walking round the circuit, telling the beads of their long chaplets, or constantly turning a sort of wheel, placed in the right hand, and which whirls about with inconceivable rapidity. This instrument is called *Tchu-Kor* [*ch'u-'khor*] "turning prayer." You see in every brook a number of these *Tchu-Kor*, which are turned by the current, and in their movements are reputed to be praying, night and day, for the benefit of those who erect them. The Tartars suspend them over the fire-place, and these in their movements are supposed to pray for the peace and prosperity of the whole family, emblemed by the hearth. The movement itself is effected by the thorough draught occasioned by the openings at the top of the tent.

The Buddhists have another mode of simplifying pilgrimages and devotional rites. In all the great Lamaseries you find at short intervals figures in the form of barrels, and turning upon an axle. The material of these figures is a thick board, composed of infinite sheets of paper pasted together, and upon which are written in Thibetian characters the prayers most reputed throughout the country. Those who have not the taste nor the zeal, or the strength to carry huge loads of books on their shoulders, or to prostrate themselves, step after step, in the dust and mire, or to walk round the Lamasery in winter's cold or summer's heat, have recourse to the simple and expeditious medium of the prayer barrel. All they have to do is to set it in motion; it then turns of itself for a long time, the devotees drinking, eating, or sleeping, while the complacent mechanism is turning prayers for them.

One day, on approaching a prayer barrel, we found two Lamas quarrelling furiously, and juſt on the point of coming to blows, the occasion being the fervour of each for prayer. One of them having set the prayer automaton in motion, had quietly returned to his cell. As he was entering it he turned his head, doubtless to enjoy the spectacle of the fine prayers he had set to work for himself, but to his infinite disguſt, he saw a colleague ſtopping his prayers, and about to turn on the barrel on his own account. Indignant at this pious fraud, he ran back, and ſtopped his competitor's prayers. Thus it went on for some time, the one turning on, the other ſtopping the barrel, without a word said on either side. At laſt, however, their patience exhauſted, they came to high words ; from words they proceeded to menaces, and it would doubtless have come to a fight, had not an old Lama, attracted by the uproar, interposed words of peace, and himself put the automaton in motion for the joint benefit of both parties.

Besides the pilgrims whose devotion is exercised within or about the Lamaseries, you find many who have undertaken fearfully long journeys, which they execute with a proſtration at every ſtep. Sad and lamentable is it to see these unhappy victims of error enduring, to no purpose, such terrible and painful labours ; one's heart is pierced with grief, and one's soul impressed with yearning for the day when these poor Tartars shall consecrate to the service of the true God that religious energy which they daily waſte upon a vain and lying creed. We had hoped to profit by the solemnities at Rache-Tchurin to announce the true faith to the Ortous ; but such was doubtless not the will of God, since he had permitted us to lose our way on the very day which seemed most favourable for our project. We accordingly passed through the Lamasery of Rache-Tchurin without stopping, eager as we were to arrive at the very source of that immense superstition, of which, as yet, we had only witnessed a few shallow streams.

At a short distance from Rache-Tchurin we reached a road well marked out, and covered with travellers. It was not, however, devotion that had set these people in motion, as it had the pilgrims whom we saw at the Lamasery; mere matter of business was leading them towards the Dabsoun-Noor [Dabsun-nôr], "the Salt Lakes" celebrated throughout Western Mantchou, and which supplies with salt, not only the adjacent Tartars, but also several provinces of the Chinese Empire.

For a day's journey before you reach Dabsoun-Noor the soil changes by degrees its form and aspect; losing its yellow tint, it becomes insensibly white, as though thinly covered with snow. The earth swelling in every direction, forms innumerable hillocks, cone-shaped, and of a regularity so perfect that you might suppose them to have been constructed by the hand of man. Sometimes they are grouped in heaps, one on the other, like pears piled on a plate; they are of all sizes, some but just created, others old, exhausted, and falling to decay. Around these excrescences grow creeping thorns, long-pointed, without flowers or leaves, which, intertwining spirally, surmount them with a sort of net-work cap. These thorns are never found elsewhere than about these hillocks; upon those of more recent growth they are firm, vigorous and full of shoots. Upon the older elevations they are dried up, calcined by the nitre, brittle, and in shreds.

As you look upon these numerous mounds, covered with a thick efflorescence of nitre, it is obvious to

THIBET, AND CHINA

your sense that beneath the surface, and at no great depth, some great chemical operation is in progress. Springs, generally so rare in the Ortous country, are here of frequent occurrence, but the water is for the moſt part excessively salt. Here and there, however, by the very side of a brackish pool, there is a spring of soft, sweet, delicious water; all such are indicated to travellers by a small flag, fluttering from the end of a long pole.

Dabsoun-Noor is not so much a lake as a reservoir of mineral salt, mixed with nitrous effloresence. The latter, in colour pale white, and crumbling between the fingers, is easily distinguishable from the salt, which is of a grey tint, and glitters like cryſtal when broken. Dabsoun-Noor is about twenty lis in circumference. Around it, at intervals, are the tents occupied by the Mongols who work it, and the Chinese who have thruſt themselves in as partners. It were difficult indeed to find any description of induſtry or commerce within a certain range of their own country in which the Chinese do not contrive to have a hand. The manipulation to which the salt is subjected requires neither great labour nor great science. All the workers do is to pick it up as it comes in the reservoir, to pile it, and, when the heap is of a certain size, to cover it with a thin coating of potter's earth. When the salt has sufficiently purified itself, the Tartars convey it to the neareſt Chinese mart and exchange it for tea, tobacco, brandy, and other commodities. In the locality itself salt is of no value: at every ſtep you see lumps of it, sometimes of remarkable purity. We filled a bag with these for our own use and for that of the camels, which are all very fond of salt. We traversed Dabsoun-Noor throughout its breadth from eaſt to weſt, and we had to take the utmoſt precaution as we proceeded over its loose, and at times almoſt moving, soil. The

Tartars recommended us not to deviate in the least from the path we should find marked out, and by all means to avoid any places where we should see the water bubbling up, for there they informed us, were gulfs which they had frequently endeavoured to sound, but without result. This statement induced us to believe that there is a *noor* [*nôr*], or lake, here, but that it is underground, the place called Dabsoun-Noor being merely the covering or roof of the lake, composed of the saline and saltpetrous matter produced by the constant evaporation of the subterranean waters. Foreign matter, brought by the wind, and consolidated by the rain, would in the lapse of time form a crust upon such a roof strong enough to bear the caravans that incessantly traverse Dabsoun-Noor.

This great salt mine seems to pervade with its influence the whole Ortous district, throughout whose extent the water is brackish, the soil arid, and the surface encrusted with saline matter. This absence of rich pasturage and fresh water is very adverse to the growth of cattle; but the camel, whose robust and hardy temperament adapts itself to the most sterile regions, affords compensation to the Tartars of the Ortous. This animal, a perfect treasure to the dwellers in the desert, can remain a fortnight, or even a month, without eating or drinking. However wretched the land may be on which it is put to feed, it can always find wherewith to satisfy its hunger, especially if the soil be impregnated with salt or nitre. Things that no other animal will touch, to it are welcome; briars and thorns, dry wood itself, supply it with efficient food.

Though it costs so little to keep, the camel is of an utility inconceivable to those who are not acquainted with the countries in which Providence has placed it. Its ordinary load is from 700 to 800 lbs., and it can carry this load ten leagues a day. Those, indeed, which are employed to carry dispatches are expected to travel eighty leagues per diem, but then they only carry the dispatch bearer. In several countries of Tartary the carriages of the kings and princes are drawn by camels, and sometimes they are harnessed to palanquins; but this can only be done in the level country. The fleshy nature of their feet does not permit them to climb mountains, when they have a carriage or litter of any sort to draw after them.

The training of the young camel is a business requiring great care and attention. For the first week of its life it can neither stand nor suck without some helping hand. Its long neck is then of such excessive flexibility and fragility that it runs the risk of dislocating it, unless someone is at hand to sustain the head while it sucks the teats of its dam.

The camel, born to servitude, seems impressed from its birth with a sense of the yoke it is destined to bear through life. You never see the young camel playing and frolicking about, as you see kids, colts, and other young animals. It is always grave, melancholy, and slow in its movements, which it never hastens, unless under compulsion. In the night and often in the day also, it sends forth a mournful cry, like that of an infant in pain. It seems to feel that joy or recreation are not within its portion; that its inevitable career is forced labour and long fastings, until death shall relieve it.

The maturation of the camel is a long affair. It cannot carry even a single rider, until its third year; and it is not in full vigour until it is eight years old. Its trainers then begin to try it with loads, gradually heavier and heavier. If it can rise with its burden, this is a proof that it can carry it throughout the journey. When that journey is only of brief duration, they sometimes load the animal in excess, and then they aid it to rise by means of bars and levers. The camel's capacity for labour endures for a long time. Provided that at certain periods of the year it is allowed a short holiday for pasturing at its leisure, it will continue its service for fully fifty years.

Nature has provided the camel with no means of defence against other animals, unless you may so consider its piercing, prolonged cry, and its huge, shapeless ugly frame, which resembles, at a distance, a heap of ruins. It seldom kicks, and when it does, it almost as seldom inflicts any injury. Its soft, fleshy foot cannot wound, or even bruise you; neither can the animal bite an antagonist. In fact, its only practical means of defence against man or beast is a sort of vehement sneeze, wherewith it discharges, from nose and mouth, a mass of filth against the object which it seeks to intimidate or to annoy.

Yet the entire male camels, *bore* [*bogra*] as the Tartars call them (*temen* [*temên*] being the generic appellation of the animal), are very formidable during the twelfth moon, which is their rutting time. At this period, their eyes are inflamed; an oily, fetid humour exhales from their heads; their mouths are constantly foaming; and they eat and drink absolutely nothing whatever. In this state of excitement they rush at whatever presents itself, man or beast, with a fierceness of precipitation which it is impossible to avoid or to resist; and when they have overthrown the object they have pursued, they pound it beneath the weight of their bodies. The epoch passed, the camel resumes its ordinary gentleness, and the routine of its laborious career.

The females do not produce young until their sixth or seventh year; the period of gestation is fourteen months. The Tartars geld most of their male camels, which, by this operation, acquire a greater development of strength, height, and size. Their voices become at the same time thinner and lower, in some instances wholly lost; and the hair is shorter and finer than that of the entire camels.

The awkward aspect of the camel, the excessive stench of its breath, its heavy, ungracious movements, its projecting hare-lips, the callosities which disfigure various parts of its body, all contribute to render its appearance repulsive; yet its extreme gentleness and docility, and the services it renders to man, render it of permanent utility, and make us forget its deformity.

Notwithstanding the apparent softness of its feet, the camel can walk upon the most rugged ground, upon sharp flints, or thorns, or roots of trees, without wounding itself. Yet, if too long a journey is continuously imposed upon it, if after a certain march you do not give it a few days' rest, the outer skin wears off, the flesh is bared, and the blood flows. Under such distressing circumstances, the Tartars make sheep-skin shoes for it, but this assistance is unavailing without rest; for if you attempt to compel the animal to proceed, it lies down, and you are compelled either to remain with or to abandon it.

There is nothing which the camel so dreads as wet, marshy ground. The instant it places its feet upon anything like mud, it slips and slides, and generally, after staggering about like a drunken man, falls heavily on its sides.

When about to repose, it kneels down, folds its fore legs symmetrically under its body, and stretches out its long neck before it on the ground. In this position it looks just like a monstrous snail.

Every year, towards the close of spring, the camel sheds its hair, every individual bristle of which disappears before a single sprout of the new stock comes up. For twenty days the animal remains completely bare, as though it had been closely shaved all over, from the top of the head to the extremity of the tail. At this juncture, it is excessively sensitive to cold or wet; and you see it, at the slightest chillness in the air or the least drop of rain, shivering and shaking in every limb, like a man without clothes exposed in the snow. By degrees the new hair shows itself in the form of fine, soft, curling wool, which gradually becomes a long, thick fur, capable of resisting the extremest inclemency of the weather. The greatest delight of the animal is to walk in the teeth of the north wind, or to stand motionless on the summit of a hill, beaten by the storm and inhaling the icy wind. Some naturalists say that the camel cannot exist in cold countries; these writers must have wholly forgotten the Tartarian camels, which, on the contrary, cannot endure the least heat, and which certainly could not exist in Arabia.

The hair of an ordinary camel weighs about ten pounds. It is sometimes finer than silk, and always longer than sheep's wool. The hair growing below the neck and on the legs of the entire camels is rough, bushy, and in colour black, whereas that of the ordinary camel is red, grey, and white. The Tartars make no sort of use of it. In the places where the animals pasture, you see great sheets of it, looking like dirty rags, driven about by the wind, until they are collected in sheltered corners, in the hill sides. The utmost use the Tartars make of it is to twist some of it into cord, or into a sort of canvas, of which they construct sacks and carpets.

The milk of the camel is excellent, and supplies large quantities of butter and cheese. The flesh is hard, unsavoury, and little esteemed by the Tartars. They use the hump, however, which, cut into slices, and dissolved in tea, serves the purpose of butter.

It is known that Heliogabalus had camel's flesh served up at his banquets, and that he was very fond of camel's feet. We cannot speak as to the latter dish, which the Roman Emperor piqued himself upon having invented, but we can distinctly affirm that camel's flesh is detestable.

CHAPTER X

The environs of the Dabsoun-Noor abound in flocks of goats and sheep. The animals like to browse on the furze and thorny bushes, the sole vegetation of these barren steppes; they especially delight in those nitrous efflorescences which are found here on all sides in the utmost abundance. The soil, miserable as it is in other respects, seems very favourable to the growth of these animals, which enter largely into the consumption of the Tartars, constituting indeed the basis of their food. If bought on the spot, they are of very moderate price. As we calculated that a pound of meat would cost us less than a pound of flour, we resolved, as a matter of economy, to buy a sheep. The thing was not difficult to find; but as it would of course oblige us to stop at least for a day, we waited till we should come to some place not quite barren, and where our animals could find some pasturage to browse upon.

Two days after crossing Dabsoun-Noor, we entered a long narrow valley, where some Mongol families had stationed themselves. The earth was covered with a close herb, which, in form and character, had much resemblance to thyme. Our beasts, as they proceeded, browsed furtively, right and left, on this plant, and seemed to be very fond of it. This new pasturage gave us the idea of encamping on the spot. Not far from a tent, a Lama was sitting on a hillock, making ropes with camel's hair. "Brother," said we as we approached him, "the flock upon that hill doubtless belongs to you. Will you sell us a sheep?" "Certainly," he answered, "I will let you have an excellent sheep; as to the price, we shall not quarrel about that. We men of prayer are not like merchants." He indicated to us a spot near his own tent, and unloaded our beasts. The entire family of the Lama, when they heard the cries of our camels, hastened to assist us to encamp. We, indeed, were not allowed to do anything to it; for our new friends took delight in making themselves useful, in unsaddling the beasts, pitching the tent, and putting our baggage in order within.

The young Lama, who had received us with so much kindness, after having unsaddled the horse and the mule, perceived that both these beasts were hurt a little on the back. "Brothers," he said, "here is a bad business; and as you are upon a long journey, it must be remedied, or you will not be able to go on." So saying, he took the knife which hung from his girdle, sharpened it with rapidity upon his boot-tops, took our saddles to pieces, examined the rough parts of the wood, and pared them away on both sides till he had removed the slightest unevenness. He then put together again, with wonderful skill, all the pieces of the saddles, and returned them to us. "That will do," said he; "now you may travel in peace." This operation was effected rapidly and in the readiest manner possible. The Lama was then about to fetch the sheep; but as it was already late, we said it was unnecessary, for that we should remain a whole day in his valley.

Next morning, before we were awake, the Lama opened the door of our tent, laughing so loud that he aroused us. "Ah," said he, "I see plainly that you do not intend to depart to-day. The sun is already very high, and you sleep still." We rose quickly, and as soon as we were dressed, the Lama spoke of the sheep. "Come to the flock," he said, "you may choose at your pleasure." "No, go by yourself, and select a sheep for us yourself. At present we have an occupation. With us, Lamas of the Western sky, it is a rule to pray as soon as we rise." "Oh, what a fine thing," said the Lama; "oh, the holy rules of the West!" His admiration, however, did not make him forget his little affair of business. He mounted his horse and rode towards a flock of sheep which we saw undulating upon the slope of a hill.

We had not yet finished our prayers when we heard the Tartar returning at full gallop. He had fastened the sheep to the back of his saddle, like a portmanteau. Hardly arrived at the door of our tent, he dismounted; and in the twinkling of an eye he had put upon its four legs the poor sheep, quite astounded at the ride it had been favoured with. "That is the sheep; is it not fine? Does it suit you?" "Admirably. What is the price?" "One ounce; is that too much?" Considering the size of the animal, we thought the price moderate. "You ask an ounce; here is an ingot, which is just the weight you require. Sit down for a moment; we will fetch our scales, and you shall ascertain whether this piece of silver really weighs an ounce." At these words, the Lama drew back, and cried, stretching out both hands towards us: "Above there is a heaven, below there is the earth, and Buddha is the lord of all things. He wills that men behave towards each other like brothers; you are of the West, I am of the East. Is that any reason why the intercourse between us should not be frank and honourable? You have not cheapened my sheep; I take your money without weighing it." "An excellent principle," said we. "As you will not weigh the money, pray sit, nevertheless, for a moment; we will take a cup of tea together and talk over a little matter." "I know what you mean; neither you nor I may cause the transmigration of this living being. We must find a layman who knows how to kill sheep. Is it not so?" and without awaiting an answer, he added, "another thing; from your appearance, one may easily guess that you are no great hands at cutting up sheep and preparing them." "You are not mistaken," we answered, laughing. "Well, keep the sheep tied to your tent; and for the rest rely upon me; I shall be back in a minute." He mounted his horse, went off at full gallop, and disappeared in a bend of the vale.

According to his promise, the Lama soon returned. He went straight to his tent, tied his horse to a post, took off his saddle, bridle and halter, gave it a cut with his whip, and so sent it off to pasture. He went into his tent for a little while, and then appeared with all the members of his family, that is to say, his old mother and two younger brothers. They advanced slowly towards our tent, in truly ridiculous fashion, just as if they were going to remove all their furniture. The Lama carried on his head a large pot, which covered him as with an enormous hat. His mother had on her back a large basket, filled with *argols*. The two young Mongols followed with a trivet, an iron spoon, and several other minor kitchen implements. At this sight, Samdadchiemba was full of joy, for he saw before him a whole day of poetry.

When the entire *batterie de cuisine* was arranged in the open air, the Lama invited us, in his politeness, to go and repose in our tent for awhile. He judged from our air, that we could not, without derogation, be present at the approaching scene of butchering. The suggestion, however, did not meet our views, and we requested that if we could do so without inconveniencing them, we might sit down on the grass at a respectful distance, and with the promise that we would not touch anything. After some objections, perceiving that we were curious to be spectators, they dispensed with the etiquette of the matter.

TRAVELS IN TARTARY,

The Lama seemed anxious; he kept looking towards the north of the valley, as if expecting someone. "All right," he said at last, with an air of satisfaction, "here he comes." "Who comes? Of whom do you speak?" "I forgot to tell you that I had been just now to invite a layman to come, who is very skilful in killing a sheep. There he is." We rose, and perceived something moving among the heath of the valley. At first we could not clearly distinguish what it was, for though it advanced with some rapidity, the object did not seem to enlarge. At last the most singular person we had ever met with in our lives presented himself to our view. We were obliged to make the utmost efforts to repress the strong impulse to laughter that came upon us. This layman seemed to be about fifty years old, but his height did not exceed three feet. On the top of his head, which terminated like a sugar-loaf, rose a small tuft of badly combed hair; a grey, thin beard descended in disorder down his chin. Finally, two prominences, one on his back, the other on his breast, communicated to this little butcher a perfect resemblance with Æsop, as he appears in various editions of the *Fables de la Fontaine*.

The strong sonorous voice of the layman was in singular contrast with the exiguity of his thin, stunted frame. He did not lose much time in saluting the company. After having darted his small black eyes at the sheep, which was tied to one of the nails of our tent, he said: "Is this the beast you wish to have put in order?" And while feeling its tail in order to judge its fat, he gave it a turn, and placed it on its back with remarkable dexterity. He next tied together its legs; then, while uncovering his right arm by throwing back the sleeve of his leathern coat, he asked whether the operation was to be effected in the tent or outside? "Outside," said we. "Outside, very well, outside;" so saying, he drew from a leathern sheath, suspended from his sash, a knife with a large handle, but whose blade by long use had become thin and narrow. After having examined for a moment its point with his thumb, he plunged it to the hilt into the side of the sheep, and drawing it out quite red, the sheep was dead, dead at once, without making any movement; not a single drop of blood had spouted from the wound. We were greatly astonished at this, and asked the little man how he managed to kill a sheep so very easily and quickly. "We Tartars," he said, "do not kill in the same way as the Kitat; they cut the throat, we go straight to the heart. By our method the animal suffers less, and all the blood is, as it should be, retained in the interior."

The transmigration once operated, nobody had any further scruples. Our Dchiahour and the Tartar Lama turned back their sleeves, and advanced to assist the little butcher. The sheep was skinned with admirable celerity. Meantime the mother of the Lama had made the two pots boil. She now took the entrails of the sheep, washed them pretty clean, and then, with the blood which she took from the interior of the sheep by means of a large wooden spoon, prepared some puddings, the basis of which was the never failing oatmeal. "Sirs Lamas," said the little layman, "shall I bone the sheep?" Upon our answering in the affirmative, he had the animal hooked upon the tent, for he was not big enough to perform that operation himself; he then mounted upon a large stone, and passing his knife rapidly along the bones, he detached, in one piece, all the meat, so as to leave dangling from the tent a mere skeleton, clean, cleared, and nicely polished.

While the little layman was, according to his expression, putting in order the flesh of the sheep, the rest of the company had prepared a gala in the

Tartar fashion. The young Lama was director of the feast. "Now," he cried, "let us all sit round; the great pot is going to be emptied." Forthwith everyone sat down upon the turf. The old Mongol woman plunged both hands into the pot, which was boiling over, and drew out all the intestines—the liver, the heart, the kidneys, the spleen, and the bowels, stuffed with blood and oatmeal. In this gastronomical preparation, the most remarkable thing was, that all the intestines had been retained in their integrity, so that they presented themselves much as they are seen in the living beast. The old woman served up, or rather threw this splendid dish upon the lawn, which was at once our chair, table, plate, and in case of need, our napkin. It is unnecessary to add that we used our fingers instead of forks. Everyone seized with his hands a portion of the bowels, twisted it from the mass, and devoured it without seasoning or salt.

The two French missionaries were not able, despite their utmost willingness, to do honour to this Tartar dish. First we burned our fingers when we tried to touch the hot and smoking repast. Although our guests urged that it ought not to be allowed to grow cold, we waited a little, afraid of burning our lips also. At last we tasted these puddings of sheep's blood and oatmeal, but after getting down a few mouthfuls, we were quite satisfied. Never, perhaps, had we eaten anything so utterly tasteless and insipid. Samdadchiemba, having foreseen this, had withdrawn from the common dish, the liver and the kidneys, which he placed before us, with some salt, which he had previously crushed between two stones. We were thus enabled to keep pace with the company, who, with a devouring appetite, were swallowing the vast system of entrails.

When the whole had disappeared, the old woman brought up the second service, by placing in the midst of us the large pot in which the puddings had been cooked. Instantly all the members of the banquet invited each other, and everyone taking from his bosom his wooden porringer, ladled out bumpers of a smoking, salt liquid, which they dignified with the pompous name of sauce. As we did not wish to appear eccentric, or as if we despised the Tartar *cuisine*, we did like the rest. We plunged our porringer into the pot, but it was only by the most laudable efforts that we could get down this green stuff, which gave us the idea of half masticated grass. The Tartars, on the contrary, found it delicious, and readily reached the bottom of the extempore tureen, not stopping for a moment, till nothing was left—not a drop of sauce, not an inch of pudding.

When the feast was finished, the little layman took leave, receiving as his fee the four feet of the sheep. To this fee, fixed by the old custom of the Mongols, we added, as a supplement, a handful of tea leaves, for we decided that he should long remember and talk to his countrymen of the generosity of the Lamas of the Western sky.

Everyone having now thoroughly regaled, our neighbours took their kitchen utensils and returned home, except the young Lama, who said he would not leave us alone. After much talk about the east and the west, he took down the skeleton, which was still hanging at the entrance of the tent, and amused himself with reciting, or rather singing, the nomenclature of all the bones, large and small, that compose the frame of the sheep. He perceived that our knowledge on this subject was very limited, and this extremely astonished him; and we had the greatest trouble to make him understand that in our country ecclesiastical studies had for their object more serious and important matters than the names and numbers of the bones of a sheep.

TRAVELS IN TARTARY,

Every Mongol knows the number, the name, and the position of the bones which compose the frame of animals; and thus they never break the bones when they are cutting up an ox or a sheep. With the point of their large knife they go straight and at once to the juncture of the bones and separate them with astonishing skill and celerity. These frequent dissections, and especially the habit of being every day among their flocks, makes the Tartars well acquainted with the diseases of animals, and skilful in their cure. The remedies, which they employ internally, are always simples gathered in the prairie, and the decoction of which they make the sick animals drink. For this purpose they use a large cow horn. When they have contrived to insert the small end of this into the mouth of the animal, they pour the physic in at the other extremity, as through a funnel. If the beast persists in not opening its mouth, the liquid is administered through the nostrils. Sometimes the Tartars employ a lavement in their treatment of the diseases of animals; but their instruments are still of primitive simplicity. A cow's horn serves for the pipe, and the pump is a great bladder, worked by squeezing it.

Internal remedies, however, are not very often applied; the Tartars make more frequent use of punctures and incisions in different parts of the body. Some of these operations are extremely ludicrous. One day, when we had pitched our tent beside a Mongol dwelling, a Tartar brought to the chief of the family a cow, which, he said, would not eat, and which was pining away day by day. The chief examined the animal, opened its mouth, and rubbed its fore teeth with his nail. " Fool, blockhead," said he to the man who had come to ask his advice, " why did you not come before ? Your cow is on the verge of death; there is scarce a day's life more in her. Yet, there may be tried one means : I will attempt it. If the cow dies, you will say it is your own fault; if it recovers, you will regard it as a great favour from Hormoustha operated by my skill." He called some of his slaves, and ordered them to keep a firm hold of the beast, while he was operating upon it. Then he entered his tent, whence he soon returned, armed with a nail and a great hammer. We waited with impatience this strange chirurgical operation, which was to be performed with a nail and a hammer. While several Mongols held the cow, in order to prevent its running away, the operator placed the nail under its belly, and then drove it up to the head with a violent stroke of the hammer, next he seized with both hands the tail of the cow, and ordered those who were holding it to let it go. Instantly the animal that had been so very singularly operated upon, dashed off, dragging after it the veterinary Tartar, clinging to its tail. In this fashion, they ran nearly a li. The Tartar then quitted his victim, and came quietly back to us, who were quite amazed at this new method of curing cows. He declared that there was no further danger for the beast; for he had ascertained, he said, by the stiffness of its tail, the good effect of the ferruginous medicine he had administered.

The Tartar veterinarians sometimes perform their operations at the belly, as we have just seen; but it is more generally, with the head, ears, temple, upper lip, and about the eyes that they deal. The latter operation is principally had recourse to, in the disease which the Tartars call Hen's dung, to which mules are greatly subject. When this disease breaks out, the animals leave off eating, and fall into extreme weakness, so that they can hardly keep themselves on their legs; fleshy excrescences, similar to the excrements of poultry, grow under the lids, in the corners of the eyes. If these excrescences are removed in time, the mules are saved, and recover by degrees their ordinary vigour; if not, they pine away for a few days, and then die.

Although cupping and bleeding have great place in the veterinary art of the Tartars, you must not suppose that they have at their disposal fine collections of instruments, such as those of European operators. Most of them have nothing but their ordinary knife, or the small iron awl, which they keep in their girdle, and which they use daily to clear their pipes, and mend their saddles and leathern boots.

The young Lama who had sold us the sheep spent a great part of the day in telling us anecdotes, more or less piquant and curious, about the veterinary science in which he seemed to be very skilful. Moreover, he gave us important instructions concerning the road we had to pursue. He settled the stages we ought to make, and indicated the places where we should encamp so as to prevent our dying from thirst. We had still before us in the country of the Ortous a journey of about fourteen days; in all that time we should find neither rivulet, nor spring, nor cistern; but only, at certain distances, wells of an extraordinary depth; some of them distant from each other two days' march, so that we should have to carry with us our provision of water.

Next morning, after having paid our respects to the Tartar family, who had shown us so much kindness, we proceeded on our way. Towards evening, when it was nearly time to pitch our tent, we perceived in the distance a large assemblage of herds. Thinking that one of the indicated wells lay probably there, we bent our steps in the direction, and soon found that we were correct in our anticipation; the water was before us. The beasts were collected from every quarter, waiting to be watered. We halted accordingly, and set up our encampment. As we gazed upon the assembled flocks, and the well, the covering

THIBET, AND CHINA

of which was a large stone, we recalled with pleasure the passage of Genesis, which relates the journey of Jacob in Mesopotamia, to Laban, son of Bathuel, the Syrian.

"Then Jacob went on his journey, and came into the land of the people of the east.

"And he looked, and behold a well in the field, and, lo, there were three flocks of sheep lying by it; for out of that well they watered the flocks: and a great stone was upon the well's mouth.

"And thither were all the flocks gathered: and they rolled the stone from the well's mouth, and watered the sheep, and put the stone again upon the well's mouth in its place."[1]

The wooden troughs placed around the well, reminded us of the other passage, where the meeting of Rebecca with the servant of Abraham is related.

"And when she had done giving him drink, she said, I will draw water for thy camels also, until they have done drinking.

"And she hasted, and emptied her pitcher into the trough, and ran again unto the well to draw water, and drew for all his camels."[2]

One cannot travel in Mongolia, amongst a pastoral and nomad population, without one's mind involuntarily going back to the time of the first patriarch, whose pastoral life has so close a relation with the manners and customs which we still find amongst the Mongol tribes. But how sad and painful do these coincidences become, when we reflect that these unfortunate people are still ignorant of the God of Abraham, Isaac and Jacob.

We had scarcely pitched our tent, and arranged our modest kitchen, when we saw several Tartar horsemen

[1] Gen. xxix., 1-3.
[2] Gen. xxiv., 19, 20.

advancing at full gallop. They were coming to draw water and give it to the numerous flocks that had been long awaiting them. These animals, which had hitherto stood at a distance, seeing the shepherds approach, hastened to the spot, and soon all were grouped round the well, eager to quench their thirst. This large assemblage of animals, so numerous and so various, created an agitation, a tumult to which we were quite unused amid the silent solitude of the desert; and it was perhaps on account of its novelty that this confusion was, to us, full of entertainment. It was amusing to see the half-tamed horses pushing and struggling to arrive first at the well; then, instead of drinking in peace, biting, quarrelling, and even leaving the water in order to pursue each other on the plain. The scene was especially entertaining and picturesque, when an enormous camel came forward, spreading alarm round the well, and driving away the vulgar herd by its despotic presence.

There were four Mongol shepherds; while two of them, armed with a long rod, ran about trying to effect a little order among the flocks, the two others drew the water in a manner which greatly excited our surprise. First, the utensil they used by way of pail appeared to us very remarkable; it was the entire skin of a goat, solidly fastened at the four feet, the only opening being at the neck. A hoop kept this orifice open; a long, strong rope of camel's hair was fastened at one end to the wooden handle that crossed the diameter of the orifice, and at the other end to the saddle of the horse ridden by one of the Tartars, who, when the skin was filled, rode off, and thus hauled up the bucket to the edge of the well, where it was received by another man, who emptied its contents into the trough.

The well was of astonishing depth; the rope used to raise the bucket seemed more than 200 feet long.

Instead of running in a pulley, it went right over a large stone, in which a large groove was already made by the constant friction. Although the drawing up of the water was performed with great activity, it was nearly dark before all the flock had been watered; we then brought our five animals to participate in the general banquet, and the Tartars had the complaisance to draw water also for us; otherwise it is probable we should never have got it, but have been obliged to suffer thirst beside an abundant well.

These Tartars did not seem contented, like those we had met with in the other parts of Mongolia; we saw they were very depressed at being obliged to spend their lives in such a barren country, where pasturage is so very scarce and water still rarer. They talked to us of the Mongol kingdoms through which we had passed, and where it was so easy, so agreeable, indeed, to feed animals. "Oh, how happy are the inhabitants of these countries!" said they. "How fortunate were we, could we spend our days amidst those rich pasturages."

Before they returned to their dwelling, which lay behind a high mountain, these Tartars told us that we ought to depart next morning before daybreak, for that we should not find any water until we came to the Hundred Wells, which was distant a hundred and fifty lis (fifteen leagues).

Dawn had not yet appeared when we left. The country was, as before, sandy, barren, and dismal. About noon we halted, in order to take a little food, and to make tea with the water we had brought with us on one of the camels. Night was setting in before we reached the Hundred Wells; our poor animals could hardly move for hunger and fatigue; yet, at all costs, we were obliged to reach the encampment. To remain where we were would have caused infinite wretchedness. At last we came to the wells, and without troubling ourselves to ascertain whether or no there were a hundred of them, as the Tartar name of the place imported, we haſtened to pitch our tent. Happily the well was not so deep as that we had seen the night before. Our firſt care was to draw some water for the horse and the mule; but when we went to lead them to the trough, we did not find them near the tent, where they usually ſtood to be unsaddled. This misfortune occasioned us an alarm that made us forget the fatigues of the day. We had, it is true, no fear of robbers, for in this respeƈt no country is more safe than the Ortous; but we thought that our animals, thirſty as they were, had run away in search of water. They will go, meditated we, till they have found water; perhaps they will go without ſtopping to the frontiers of the Ortous to the very banks of the Yellow River.

The night was quite dark; nevertheless, we thought it quite proper to go inſtantly in search of our horses, while Samdadchiemba was preparing supper. We wandered about for a long time in all direƈtions without seeing anything; ever and anon we ſtopped to liſten whether we could diſtinguish the sound of the bells suspended from the horse's neck; but our efforts were vain; nothing interrupted the dead silence of the desert. We went on, without losing courage, ſtill hoping to find animals so very necessary to us, and the loss of which would have placed us in such difficulties. Sometimes we fancied we heard in the diſtance the tinkling of the bells. Then we laid flat down, applying our ears to the earth, in order to catch more readily the slighteſt noise that might occur; but it was all in vain; our search was fruitless.

The fear of losing our way in a dark night in a country, the bearings of which we had not been able to examine, made us think of retracing our ſteps.

Judge of our consternation, when, on turning round we perceived, apparently in the place where we had pitched our tent, a large volume of flame and smoke rising. We did not doubt for an instant that Samdadchiemba also had set out in search of the animals, and that in his absence the tent had caught fire. Oh, how sad and discouraging was that moment. In the middle of the desert, at two thousand lis' distance from our christendom, we contemplated without hope those flames consuming our tent, our sole shelter against the inclemency of the weather. "Alas!" we said, "the tent is certainly destroyed, and doubtless all that was in it has also become a prey to the flames."

We mournfully directed our steps to the place of our encampment. Though anxious to ascertain our misfortune, we advanced slowly, for we were, at the same time, afraid to approach the fearful spectacle, destructive of our plans, and plunging us into misery of every description. As we advanced, we heard loud cries, at last we distinguished the voice of Samdadchiemba, apparently calling for assistance. Imagining that we could still save something from the conflagration, we hastened to the spot, calling out at the pitch of our voices, that we were coming. When we at last arrived at the encampment, we stood for an instant quite stupified upon seeing Samdadchiemba quietly seated beside an immense fire and drinking with the greatest satisfaction bumpers of tea. The tent was untouched, and all our animals lying around it: there had been no conflagration at all. The Dchiahour, having found the horse and the mule, had imagined that, having doubtless got to some distance, we should have a difficulty in finding our way back to the encampment, and therefore he had made a large fire to direct our steps, and sent forth vehement cries inviting us to return. We had so fully believed in the reality of our misfortune that, on beholding our tent again, we seemed to pass at once from the extreme of misery to the height of happiness.

As the night had already made considerable progress, we hastened to eat, with excellent appetite, the soup that Samdadchiemba had prepared, and then laid down upon our goat-skins, where we enjoyed a profound sleep till daybreak.

On getting up next morning a glance round the encampment diffused a shudder of terror through all our limbs; for we found ourselves surrounded on every side by deep wells. We had been, indeed, told that we should not find water until we reached the place called Hundred Wells, but we had never imagined that this denomination, Hundred Wells, was to be taken literally. When we had pitched our tent the night before, it was too dark for us to remark the presence of these numerous precipices, and accordingly we had taken no precautions. When we went out in search of our stray animals we had, without knowing it, made a thousand turnings and windings amongst these deep pits; and that we had thus walked in a dark night, without any accident, could only be attributed to a special protection of Providence. Before our departure, therefore, we planted a small wooden cross on the brink of one of these wells, as a sign of our thankfulness for the goodness of God.

After having made our usual breakfast, we proceeded. Towards noon we perceived before us a great multitude issuing from a narrow defile, formed by two precipitous mountains. We were lost in conjecture as to what this numerous and imposing caravan could be. Innumerable camels, laden with baggage, advanced in single file, one after the other, escorted on either side by a number of horsemen, who, in the distance appeared to be richly attired. We slackened our pace, to obtain a nearer view of this caravan, which appeared to us a very strange affair.

THIBET, AND CHINA

It was still a considerable distance off, when four horsemen, who formed a sort of vanguard, galloped on towards us. They were all four Mandarins, as we perceived from the blue button which surmounted their cap of ceremony. " Sirs Lamas," they said, " peace be with you ! Towards what point of the earth do you direct your steps ? " " We are of the West, and it is to the West we are going. And you, brothers of Mongolia, whither do you travel in so large a troop, and in such magnificent apparel ? " " We are from the kingdom of Alechan [Alashan], and our king is making a journey to Peking to prostrate himself at the feet of Him who dwells above the sky." After these few words the four horsemen rose somewhat in their saddles, saluted, and then returned to their position at the head of the caravan.

We had thus encountered on his way the King of Alechan, repairing to Peking with his gorgeous retinue, to be present at the great meeting of the tributary princes, who, on the first day of the first moon, are bound to offer the compliments of the new year to the Emperor. Behind the vanguard came a palanquin carried by two splendid mules, harnessed, the one before, the other behind, to gilt shafts. The palanquin was square, plain, and by no means elegant; its roof was adorned with some silk fringe, and its four panels were decorated with some pictures of dragons, birds and nosegays. The Tartar monarch was sitting, not upon a seat, but with his legs crossed, in the oriental fashion. He seemed to be about fifty years old; and his full round features gave to his physiognomy a remarkable air of good nature. As he passed us we cried : " King of the Alechan, peace and happiness be on your way ! " " Men of prayer," he answered, " may you also be at peace," and he accompanied these words with a friendly salute. An old white-bearded Lama, mounted upon a magnificent horse, led the fore mule of the palanquin; he was considered the guide of the whole caravan. Generally, the great marches of the Tartars are under the guidance of the most venerable of the Lamas of the district; for these people are persuaded that they have nothing to fear on their way, so long as they have at their head a representative of the divinity, or rather the divinity himself incarnate in the person of the Lama.

A great number of horsemen, who surrounded, as a guard of honour, the royal palanquin, made their horses curvet incessantly, and dash up and down, in and out, from one side to the other, without ever stopping in their rapid movements. Immediately behind the carriage of the king came a white camel of extraordinary beauty and size; a young Tartar, on foot, led it by a silken string. This camel was not laden. From the tip of each hump, which looked like two pyramids, floated pieces of yellow taffeta. There was no doubt that this magnificent animal was a present destined for the Chinese Emperor. The remainder of the troop consisted of numerous camels, carrying the baggage, the boxes, tents, pots, the thousand and one utensils, that are always wanted in a country where no tavern is to be found.

The caravan had passed on a long time, when meeting with a well, we resolved to pitch our tent beside it. While we were making our tea, three Tartars, one decorated with the red, the others with the blue button, alighted at the entrance of our dwelling. They asked for news of the caravan of the King of the Alechans. We answered that we had met it a long time since, that it must already be at a considerable distance, and that it would doubtless arrive, before night, at the encampment of the Hundred Wells. "As it is so," they said, "we would rather remain here, than arrive by night at the Hundred Wells, at the risk of falling into some hole. To-morrow, by starting a little before day, we shall reach the caravan."

No sooner said than done: the Tartars forthwith unsaddled their horses, sent them off to seek their fortune in the desert, and without ceremony took their seat beside our fire. They were all *Taitsi* of the kingdom of the Alechan. One of these, he who wore the cap with the red button, was the king's minister; they all three belonged to the great caravan, but the day before, having started to visit a friend, a prince of the Ortous, they had been left behind by the main body.

The minister of the King of Alechan had an open, frank character, and a very acute understanding; he combined Mongol good nature with vivacious and elegant manners, which he had no doubt acquired in his frequent visits to Peking. He asked many questions about the country which the Tartars call the Western Heaven, and informed us that every three years a great number of our countrymen, from the different western kingdoms, rendered their homage to the Emperor at Peking.

It is needless to observe that, for the most part, the Tartars do not carry very far their geographical studies. The west means with them simply Thibet and some adjacent countries, which they hear mentioned by the Lamas, who have made the pilgrimage to Lha-Ssa. They firmly believe that beyond Thibet there is nothing; there, say they, is the end of the world; beyond, there is merely a shoreless ocean.

When we had satisfied all the inquiries of the red button, we addressed some to him about the country of the Alechan, and the journey to Peking. "Every third year all the sovereigns of the world," said he, "repair to Peking for the feast of the new year. Princes who live near, are bound to go thither every year; those who live at the extremities of the earth, go every second or third year, according to the distance they have to travel." "What is your purpose in going every year to Peking?" "We ourselves go as the retinue of our king; the king alone enjoys the happiness of prostrating himself in the presence of the old Buddha (the Emperor)." He entered then into long details about the ceremony of the first day of the year, and the relations between the Chinese Emperor and the tributary kings.

The foreign sovereigns, under the dominating influence of the China empire, repair to Peking; first, as an act of obeisance and submission; secondly, to pay certain rents to the Emperor, whose vassals they consider themselves. These rents, which are decorated with the fine name of offerings, are, in fact, imposts which no Tartar king would venture to refuse the payment of. They consist in camels, in horses remarkable for their beauty, and which the Emperor sends to augment his vast herds in the Tchakar. Every Tartar prince is, besides, obliged to bring some of the rarer productions of his country; deer, bear and goat venison; aromatic plants, pheasants, mushrooms, fish, etc. As they visit Peking in the depth of winter, all these eatables are frozen; so that they bear, without danger of being spoiled, the trial of a long journey, and even remain good long after they have arrived at their destination.

One of the banners of the Tchakar is especially charged with sending to Peking, every year, an immense provision of pheasant's eggs. We asked the minister of the King of the Alechans, whether these pheasant's eggs were of a peculiar flavour, that they were so highly appreciated by the court. "They are not destined to be eaten," he answered; "the old Buddha uses them for another purpose." "As they are not eaten, what are they used for?" The Tartar seemed embarrassed, and blushed somewhat as he replied that these eggs were used to make a sort of varnish, which the women of the imperial harem used for the purpose of smoothing their hair, and which communicates to it, they say, a peculiar lustre and brilliancy. Europeans, perhaps, may consider this pomatum of pheasant's eggs, so highly esteemed at the Chinese court, very nasty and disgusting; but beauty and ugliness, the nice and the nasty, are, as everybody knows, altogether relative and conventional matters, upon which the various nations that inhabit this earth have ideas remotest from the uniform.

These annual visits to the Emperor of China are very expensive and extremely troublesome to the Tartars of the plebeian class, who are overwhelmed with enforced labour, at the pleasure of their masters, and are bound to provide a certain number of camels and horses to carry the baggage of the king and the nobles. As these journeys take place in the depth of winter, the animals find little food, especially when, after leaving the Land of Grass, they enter upon the districts cultivated by the Chinese; and a great number of them, accordingly, die on the road. Hence, when the caravan returns, it is far from being in such good order and condition as when it started; it presents, one might almost say, merely the skeletons of the animals. Those which have still retained a little strength are laden with the baggage necessary on the way; the others are dragged along by the halter, scarcely able to move one leg before the other. It is a very sad, and, at the same time, singular thing, to see the Mongols walking on foot, and leading behind them horses which they dare not mount for fear of breaking them down.

As soon as the tributary kings are arrived at Peking, they repair to the interior of the city, where they inhabit a quarter especially set apart for them. They are generally two hundred in number, each of whom has his palace or inn, which he occupies, with his retinue. A Mandarin, a great dignitary of the realm, superintends this quarter, and has it in charge to maintain peace and concord amongst these illustrious visitors. The tributes are transferred to the care of a special Mandarin, whom we may consider as steward of the household.

During their stay at Peking, these monarchs have no communication with the Emperor, no solemn audience. Some of them may perchance obtain admittance to the throne; but it is only upon affairs of the highest importance, above the jurisdiction of the ordinary ministers.

On the first day of the year, however, there is a solemn ceremony, at which these two hundred monarchs are admitted to a sort of contact with their suzerain and master, with him who, as they phrase it, sitting beneath the sky, rules the four seas and the ten thousand nations of the world by a single act of his will. According to the ritual which regulates the state proceedings of the Emperor of China, he is bound to visit every year, on the first day of the first moon, the temple of his ancestors, and to prostrate himself before the tablet of his fathers. There is before the entrance of this temple a long avenue, wherein the tributary princes, who have come to Peking to render homage to the Emperor, assemble. They range themselves right and left of the peristyle, in three lines, each occupying the place appertaining to his dignity. They stand erect, grave, and silent. It is said to be a fine and imposing spectacle, to witness all these remote monarchs, attired in their silk robes, embroidered with gold and silver, and indicating, by the variety of their costumes, the different countries they inhabit, and the degrees of their dignity.

Meantime the Emperor issues in great pomp from his Yellow Town. He traverses the deserted and silent streets of Peking; for, when the Asiatic tyrant appears, every door must be closed, and every inhabitant of the town must, on pain of death, remain silent within his house. As soon as the Emperor has arrived at the temple of the ancestors, the heralds, who precede the procession, cry out, at the moment he places his foot on the first step of the stairs that lead to the gallery of the tributary kings : "Let all prostrate themselves, for here is the Lord of the earth." To this the two hundred tributary kings respond in unison : "Ten thousand congratulations!" And, having thus wished a happy new year to the Emperor, they all fall down with their faces towards the earth. Then passes through their ranks the son of heaven, who enters the temple of the ancestors, and prostrates himself, in his turn, thrice before the tablet of his fathers. Whilst the Emperor is offering up his adoration to the spirits of his family, the two hundred monarchs remain prostrate on the earth, and they do not rise until the Emperor has again passed through their ranks; after this they re-enter their litters and return to their respective palaces.

And such is the entire and sole fruit of the long patience of these potentates; after leaving their distant countries, and enduring fatigues and dangers of every description, and a long journey through the desert, they have enjoyed the happiness of prostrating themselves in the path of the Emperor! Such a spectacle would with us Europeans be a matter of pity and disgust, for we could not comprehend how there should be so much humility on one side, so much arrogance on the other. Yet it is the simplest thing in the world to Asiatic nations. The Emperor takes his all-mightiness as a grave matter of course; and the Tartar kings think themselves happy and honoured in paying homage to it.

The prime minister of the king of the Alechan told

us that a sight of the Emperor is not easily obtained. One year, when his master was ill, he was obliged to take his place at Peking, in the ceremony of the temple of the ancestors, and he then hoped to see the old Buddha, on his way down the peristyle, but he was altogether mistaken in his expectation. As minister, the mere representative of his monarch, he was placed in the third file, so that, when the Emperor passed, he saw absolutely nothing at all. "Those who are in the first line," he said, " if they are cautiously dexterous may manage to get a glimpse of the yellow robe of the son of heaven; but they must take heed not to lift up their heads, for such an audacity would be considered a great crime, and be punished very severely."

All the Tartar princes are pensioned by the Emperor; the sum allotted to them is a small matter, but it effects a considerable political result. The Tartar princes, in receiving their pay, consider themselves the slaves, or at least, as the servants of him who pays them; and concede, in consequence, to the Emperor the right of requiring their submission and obedience. It is about the first day of the year that the tributary sovereigns receive, at Peking, the allotted pension, which is distributed by some of the great Mandarins, who are said, by slanderous tongues, to speculate in this lucrative employment, and never fail to make enormous profits at the expense of the poor Tartars.

The minister of the king of the Alechan related, for our edification, that in a particular year, all the tributary princes received their pension in ingots of gilt copper. All found it out at once, but were fain to keep silence, afraid to make public an affair that might result in a catastrophe, compromising not only the highest dignitaries of the empire, but the Tartar kings themselves. As, in fact, the latter were supposed to receive their money from the hands of the Emperor himself, a complaint would, in some sort, have been to charge

THIBET, AND CHINA

the old Buddha, the son of heaven, with being a coiner. They received accordingly, their copper ingots with a proſtration, and it was not until they returned into their own countries, that they declared, not indeed that they had been cheated, but that the Mandarins, charged with diſtributing the money, had been the dupes of the Peking bankers. The Tartar Mandarin who related the adventure gave us completely to underſtand that neither the Emperor, nor the courtiers, nor the Mandarins, had anything to do with the affair. We took good care not to undeceive him : as to us who had no great faith in the probity of the government of Peking, we were convinced that the Emperor had regularly swindled the Tartar kings. We were confirmed in this opinion by the faɕt that the period of this adventure coincided with the British war ; when, as we knew, the Emperor was in the laſt extremity, and knew not where to get the money necessary to keep from ſtarving the handful of soldiers who were charged with the preservation of the integrity of the Chinese territory.

The visit of the three Mandarins of the Alechan was not only pleasant on account of the narrative they gave us of the relations of the Tartar kings with the Emperor, but it was of essential utility to us. When they underſtood that we were direɕting our ſteps towards the Weſt, they asked us whether we intended passing through the diſtriɕt of Alechan. On our answering in the affirmative, they dissuaded us from the projeɕt ; they told us that our animals would perish there, for not a single paſturage was to be met with. We already knew that the Alechan is a traɕt ſtill more barren than the Ortous. It consiſts, in faɕt, of chains of lofty mountains of sand, where you may travel sometimes for whole days together, without seeing a single blade of vegetation. Some narrow valleys, here and there, alone offer to the flocks a few thorny and wretched plants. On this account the Alechan is very thinly inhabited, even in comparison with the other parts of Mongolia.

The Mandarins told us that this year the drought which had been general throughout Tartary had rendered the diſtrict of the Alechan almoſt uninhabitable. They assured us that at leaſt one third of the flocks had perished of hunger and thirſt, and that the remainder were in a wretched ſtate. For their journey to Peking, they had, they said, chosen the beſt they could find in the country; and we might have observed that the animals of the caravan were very different indeed from those we had seen in Tchakar. The drought, the want of water, and paſtures, the deſtruction of the flocks—all this had given birth to an utter ſtate of misery, whence, again, numerous bands of robbers who were ravaging the country, and robbing travellers. They assured us that, being so few in number, it would not be wise for us to enter upon the Alechan mountains, particularly in the absence of the principal authorities.

On receiving this information, we resolved not to retrace our ſteps, for we were too far advanced, but to diverge a little from our route. The night was far advanced ere we thought of taking reſt; we had scarcely slept a few minutes, in fact, when the day broke. The Tartars saddled their ſteeds, and after having wished us peace and happiness, dashed off at full gallop, to overtake the great caravan which preceded them.

As for us, before setting out, we unrolled the excellent map of the Chinese empire published by M. Andriveau-Goujon, and sought upon it to what point we ought to direct our ſteps, so as to avoid the wretched diſtrict of the Alechan, without, however, deviating too much from our route. After looking at the map, we saw no other way than to recross the

THIBET, AND CHINA

Yellow River, to pass the Great Wall of China, and to travel across the Chinese province of Kan-Sou, until we arrived among the Tartars of the Koukou-Noor. Formerly this determination would have made us tremble. Accustomed as we had been to live privately in our Chinese christendom, it would have seemed to us impossible to enter the Chinese empire alone, and without the care of a catechist. At that time it would have seemed to us clear as the day that our strangulation, and the persecution of all the Chinese missions, would have been the certain result of our rash undertaking. Such would have been our fears formerly, but the time of our fear was gone. Indurated by our two months' journey, we had come to the persuasion that we might travel in China with as much safety as in Tartary. The stay that we had already made in several large commercial towns, compelled as we had been to manage our own affairs, had rendered the Chinese manners and customs more familiar to us. The language presented to us no difficulties; besides being able to speak the Tartar idiom, we were familiar with the colloquial phrases of the Chinese, a very difficult attainment to those who reside in the missions, because the Christians there seek to flatter them by only employing, in the presence of the missionaries, the short vocabulary of words that they have studied in books. Besides these purely moral and intellectual advantages, our long journey had been useful in a physical point of view; the rain, the wind, and the sun, which had during the two months raged against our European tint, had in the end embrowned and tanned it so that we looked quite like wild men of the wood in this respect. The fear of being recognized by the Chinese now no longer troubled us.

We told Samdadchiemba that we should cease, in a few days, to travel in the Land of Grass, and that we should continue our route through the Chinese empire. "Travel among the Chinese!" said the Dchiahour; "very well. There are good inns there. They boil good tea there. When it rains you can go under shelter. During the night you are not disturbed by the blowing of the north wind. But in China there are ten thousand roads; which shall we take? Do you know which is the best?" We made him look at the map, pointing out all the places which we should have to pass before we reached Koukou-Noor. We even reduced, for his edification, into lis, all the distances from one town to another. Samdadchiemba looked at our small geographic chart with perfect enthusiasm. "Oh," said he, "how sincerely I regret that I did not study while I was in the Lamasery; if I had listened to my master, if I had paid more attention, I might perhaps now understand the description of the world that is here drawn on this piece of paper. With this, one can go everywhere, without asking the way. Is it not so?" "Yes, everywhere," answered we; "even to your own family." "How is that? is my country also written down here?" and as he spoke he bent over the chart, so as entirely to cover it with his huge frame. "Stand aside, and we will show you your country. Look; do you see this little space beside that green line? That is the country of the Dchiahours, which the Chinese call the Three Valleys (San-Tchouan). Your village must be here; we shall pass not more than two days' journey from your house." "Is it possible?" cried he, striking his forehead; "shall we pass two days' journey from my house? Do you say so? How can that be? Not more than two days' journey? In that case, when we are near it, I will ask my spiritual fathers' permission to go and see once more my country." "What can you have to do now in the Three Valleys?" "I will go and see what is doing there. It is eighteen years since my departure from my house. I will go and see if my old mother is ſtill there; if she is alive, I will make her enter into the Holy Church. As for my two brothers, who knows whether they will have enough sense not to believe any longer in the transmigrations of Buddha. Ah, yes," added he, after a short pause, "I will make a little tea, and we will talk this matter over again."

Samdadchiemba was no longer with us; his thoughts had flown to his native land. We were obliged to remind him of his real position,—" Samdadchiemba, you need not make any tea; and juſt now, inſtead of talking, we muſt fold up our tent, load the camels, and proceed on our way. Look; the sun is already high in the heavens: if we do not get on, we shall never reach the Three Valleys." "True," cried he; and springing up he set himself busily about making preparations for our departure.

On resuming our route, we abandoned the direction towards the weſt, which we had ſtrictly followed during our journey, and diverged a little to the south. After having continued our march for half the day, we sat down for a while under a rock to take our repaſt. As usual, we dined on bread and water; and what bread and water! Dough half baked, and brackish water, which we had to draw up with the sweat of our brow, and to carry about with us during the journey.

Towards the conclusion of our repaſt, while we were trying to scrape together a few grains of tobacco in our snuff phials, by way of dessert, we saw coming towards us a Tartar on a camel; he seated himself beside us. After having wished each other peace, we let him smell at our empty snuff phial, and then offered him a little loaf baked in the ashes. In an inſtant he had swallowed the bread, and taken three sniffs of snuff.

We questioned him about the route; he told us that if we followed the same direction we should arrive in two days at the Yellow River, on crossing which, we should enter the Chinese territory. This information gave us great satisfaction, for it perfectly agreed with our map. We asked him if water was far off. "Yes," answered he, "the wells are distant. If you encamp again to-day, you will find a cistern on the way; but there is little water, and that is very bad. Formerly it was an excellent well, but it is now abandoned, for a *tchutgour* (demon) has corrupted its waters."

This information induced us to proceed at once, for we had no time to lose, if we desired to arrive before night. The Mongol mounted his camel, which bounded across the desert, while our little caravan continued slowly its uniform and monotonous march.

Before sunset, we arrived at the indicated cistern, when we pitched our tent, as there was no hope of finding further on better water; besides, we fancied the cistern might perhaps turn out less diabolical than the Tartar had pretended it to be.

While we were lighting the fire, the Dchiahour went to draw water; he returned in a few moments, saying that it was unfit to be drunk; that it was mere poison. He brought a basin full with him, that we might taste it and judge for ourselves.

The stench of this dirty, muddy water was, indeed, intolerable; and on the surface of the nauseous stuff we saw floating a sort of oily drop, which infinitely increased our disgust. We had not the courage to raise it to our lips; we were satisfied with its sight, and, above all, with its smell.

Still we must either drink or die with thirst; we accordingly resolved to make the best we could of this Cistern of the Devil, as it is called by the Tartars. We collected roots, which were growing abundantly around it, half buried in the sand; a few moments labour supplied us with an ample provision of them. Then, first of all, we made some charcoal which we broke into small pieces; next we filled our kettle with the muddy, stinking water, placed it upon the fire, and when the water boiled, threw in a quantity of charcoal.

While we were engaged upon this chemical operation Samdadchiemba, seated beside the little kettle, kept every moment asking what sort of a soup we intended to make with all those detestable ingredients. We gave him, by way of reply, a complete dissertation upon the discolouring and disinfecting properties of charcoal. He listened to our scientific statement with patience, but appeared in no degree convinced by it. His eyes were fixed upon the kettle, and it was easy to see, from the sceptical expression of his features, that he had no sort of expectation or idea that the thick water bubbling in the kettle could at all become clear and limpid fluid.

By-and-by, we poured out the liquid thus prepared, and filtered it through an impromptu linen sieve. The water realized was not, indeed, delicious, but it was drinkable, having deposited all its salt and all its ill odour. We had more than once, on our journey, used water in no degree superior.

Samdadchiemba was perfectly intoxicated with enthusiasm. Had he not been a Christian, he would assuredly have taken us for living Buddhas. "The Lamas," said he, "pretend they have all knowledge and all power in their prayer books; but I am certain they would have died of thirst, or been poisoned, had they only had the water of this cistern to make tea with. They have no more notion than a sheep how to render this bad water good." And then he overwhelmed us with all sorts of odd questions about the natural properties of things. In relation to the purification of water which we had just operated, he asked whether by rubbing his face hard with the charcoal, he could make it as white as ours; but then, when his eyes turned to his hands, still black with the charcoal he had just broken up, he himself laughed immensely at the idea he had propounded.

Night had set in before we had completed the distillation of the water we required. We then made abundance of tea, and the evening was occupied in drinking it. We contented ourselves with infusing a few pinches of oatmeal in the tea, for the ardent thirst which devoured us absorbed all desire to eat. After having deluged our inner man, we sought repose.

We had scarcely, however, stretched ourselves on the turf, when an extraordinary and altogether unexpected noise threw us into a state of stupor. It was a long, lugubrious, deep cry that seemed approaching our tent. We had heard the howl of wolves, the roar of tigers and of bears; but these in no way resembled the sound which now affrighted our ears. It was something like the bellowing of a bull, but crossed with tones so strange and unintelligible, that we were utterly panic-stricken. And we were all the more surprised and confounded because everybody had assured us that there were no wild beasts of any kind in the whole Ortous country.

Our embarrassment was becoming serious. We were in fear not only for our animals, which were tied round the tent, but also on our own account. As the noise did not cease, but, on the contrary, seemed to approach nearer and nearer, we got up, not, indeed, to go forth in search of the villainous beast that was thus disturbing our repose, but in order to frighten it. To this intent all three of us set to work, shouting at the pitch of our lungs: then we stopped, and so did the beast. After a moment's silence, the roaring was heard once more, but at a considerable distance. We conjectured that in our turn we had frightened the animal, and this somewhat reassured us.

The cries once more approaching, we piled up some brushwood at a few paces from the tent, and made a bonfire. The light, instead of deterring the unknown monster, seemed rather to attract it; and, before long, by the flame of the brushwood, we could distinguish the outline of what appeared to be a great quadruped, of reddish hue, the aspect of which, however, as near as we could judge, was by no means so ferocious as its voice. We ventured to advance towards it, but as we advanced, it retreated. Samdadchiemba, whose eyes were very sharp, and accustomed to the desert, assured us that the creature was either a dog or a stray calf.

Our animals were, at the very least, as absorbed with the subject as ourselves. The horse and the mule pointed their ears, and dug up the earth with their hoofs, while the camels, with outstretched necks and glaring eyes, did not for an instant remove their gaze from the spot whence these wild cries issued.

In order to ascertain precisely with what creature we had to do, we diluted a handful of meal in a wooden dish, and placing this at the entrance of the tent, withdrew inside. Soon we saw the animal slowly advance, then stop, then advance again. At last it came to the dish, and with the most remarkable rapidity, lapped up the supper we had prepared for it. We now saw that it was a dog of immense size. After having thoroughly licked and polished the empty dish, it lay down, without ceremony, at the entrance of the tent; and we forthwith followed its example, glad to have found a protector in the apprehended foe.

Next morning, upon awaking, we were able to examine at leisure the dog which, after having so alarmed us, had so unreservedly attached itself to us. Its colour was red, its size immense; its excessive meagreness showed that it had been wandering about homeless for some time past. A dislocated leg, which it dragged along the ground, communicated to it a sort of swinging motion, which added to its formidable effect. But it was especially alarming when it sent forth its loud, fierce voice. When we heard it, we instinctively looked at the animal whence it proceeded, to see whether it really belonged to the canine race.

We resumed our route, and the new Arsalan accompanied us, its general position being a few paces in advance of the caravan, as though to show us the way, with which it appeared to be tolerably familiar.

After two days' journey we reached the foot of a chain of mountains, the summits of which were lost in the clouds. We set about ascending them, however, courageously, for we hoped that beyond them we should find the Yellow River. That day's journey was very painful, especially to the camels, for every step was upon sharp rugged rock; and their feet, accordingly, were very speedily bleeding. We ourselves, however, were too absorbed with the strange, fantastic aspect of the mountains we were traversing to think of the toil they occasioned us.

In the hollows and chasms of the precipices formed by these lofty mountains, you see nothing but great heaps of mica and laminated stones, broken, bruised, and in some cases absolutely pulverised. This wreck of slate and schist must have been brought into these abysses by some deluge, for it in no way belongs to the mountains themselves, which are of granite. As you approach the summits, the mountains assume forms more and more fantastic. You see great heaps of rock piled one upon the other, and apparently cemented together. These rocks are almost entirely encrusted with shells and the remains of a plant resembling seaweed; but that which is most remarkable is that these granite masses are cut and torn and worn in every direction, presenting a ramification of holes and cavities, meandering in a thousand complicated turns and twists, so that you might imagine all the upper portion of each mountain to have been subjected to the slow and destructive action of immense worms. Sometimes in the granite you find deep impressions, that seem the moulds of monsters, whose forms they still closely retain.

As we gazed upon all these phenomena, it seemed to us that we were travelling in the bed of some exhausted ocean. Everything tended to the belief that these mountains had undergone the gradual action of the sea. It is impossible to attribute all you see there to the influence of mere rain, or still less to the inundations of the Yellow River, which, however prodigious they may be, can never have attained so great an elevation. The geologists who affirm that the deluge took place by sinking, and not by a depolarization of the earth, might probably find in these mountains good arguments in favour of their system.

On reaching the crest of these mountains we saw beneath us the Yellow River, rolling its waves majestically from south to north. It was now near noon, and we hoped that same evening to pass the river and sleep in one of the inns of the little town of Ché-Tsui-Dze [Shih-tsui-tzŭ], which we perceived on the slope of a hill beyond the river.

We occupied the whole afternoon in descending the rugged mountain, selecting as we went, the places right and left that seemed more practicable than the rest. At length we arrived, and before nightfall, on the banks of the Yellow River, our passage across which was most successfully effected. In the first place, the Mongol Tartars who rented the ferry oppressed our purse less direfully than the

Chinese ferrymen had done. Next, the animals got into the boat without any difficulty. The only grievance was that we had to leave our lame dog on the bank, for the Mongols would not admit it on any terms, insisting upon the rule that all dogs must swim across the river, the boat being destined solely for men, or for animals that cannot swim. We were fain to submit to the prejudice.

On the other side of the Yellow River we found ourselves in China, and bade adieu for awhile to Tartary, to the desert, and to the nomadic life.

CHAPTER XI

THE Tartars, descended from the ancient Scythians, have preserved to this day the dexterity of their ancestors in archery and horsemanship. The early part of their history is veiled in obscurity, enveloped as they are by the wonders and prodigies of the exploits of their first conqueror Okhous-Han [Oquzkhan] who seems to be the Madyes of Herodotus. This illustrious leader of the Scythian hordes carried his arms into Syria, and reached even the confines of Egypt.

The Chinese annals frequently mention certain nomad tribes, which they call Hioung-Nou [Hsiung-nu], and which are no other than the Huns. These wandering and warlike tribes gradually extended themselves, and finished by covering the immense deserts of Tartary from east to west. Thenceforward they made continual incursions on their neighbours, and on several occasions made attacks on the frontiers of the empire. It was on such an occasion that Tsin-Chi-Hoang-Ti [Ch'in-Shih-huang-ti] had the Great Wall built in the year 213 B.C. About 134 B.C. the Huns, under the conduct of Lao-Chan [Laoshan], their emperor, made an attack on the Tartars Youei-Tchi [Yüeh-chi] (the Getæ), who dwelt on the confines of the province of Chen-Si [Shensi]. After a series of long and terrible conflicts, Lao-Chan defeated them, slew their chief, and made of his head a drinking cup, which he wore suspended from his girdle. The Getæ did not choose to submit to the victors, and preferred going elsewhere in search of another country. They divided into two principal bands. One advanced towards the north-west, and took possession of the plains situated upon the banks of the river Ili, beyond the glaciers of the Moussour [Muzart] mountains; this is that part of Tartary which is now called the Torgot. The other division marched southwards, associated with it in its course several other tribes, and reached the region watered by the Indus. There it laid waste the kingdom founded by the successors of Alexander, strove for some time against the Parthians, and finished by establishing itself in Bactriana. The Greeks call these Tartar tribes Indo-Scythians.

Meanwhile divisions arose among the Huns; and the Chinese, ever politic and cunning, took advantage of this circumstance to enfeeble them. Towards the year 48 of our era, the Tartar empire was divided into northern and southern. Under the dynasty of Han, the Northern Huns were completely defeated by the Chinese armies. They were obliged to abandon the regions wherein they had settled, and proceeded in large numbers towards the west, to the borders of the Caspian Sea; here they spread themselves over the countries watered by the Volga, and round the Palus Mæotis.

They commenced in 376 their formidable irruptions upon the Roman empire. They began by subduing the territory of the Alani, a nomad and pastoral people like themselves; some of these sought refuge in the Circassian mountains, others migrated further west, and finally settled on the shores of the Danube. Later, they drove before them the Suevi, the Goths, the Gepidæ, and the Vandals, and with these advanced to ravage Germany, in the beginning of the fifth century. These large hordes of barbarians, resembling waves, one driven on by the other, thus formed, in their destructive course, a fearful torrent, which finally inundated Europe.

THIBET, AND CHINA

The Southern Huns, who had remained in Tartary, were for a long time weakened by the dispersion of their northern countrymen; but they recovered by insensible degrees, and again became terrible to the Chinese: though they did not acquire a political and historical importance till the time of the famous Tchinggiskhan, towards the close of the twelfth century.

The power of the Tartars, long confined within the desert steppes of Mongolia, broke at length its bounds, and innumerable armies might be seen descending from the lofty table-lands of Central Asia, and precipitating themselves with fury on horrified nations. Tchinggiskhan carried pillage and death even to the most remote regions. China, Tartary, India, Persia, Syria, Muscovy, Poland, Hungary, Austria,—all these countries successively felt the terrible blows of the victorious Tartar. France, Italy, and the other regions further west, escaped with their fear.

In the year 1260 of our era, Khan-Khoubilai [Khubilai-khan], grandson of Tchinggis, who had commenced the conquest of China, succeeded in subduing that vast empire. It was the first time that it had passed under the yoke of foreigners. Khoubilai died at Peking in the year 1294, aged eighty. His empire was, without dispute, the largest that ever existed. Chinese geographers state that, under the Mongol dynasty of the Youen, the empire northwards went beyond the In-Chan [Yin-shan] mountains; westward it extended beyond the Gobi or sandy desert; to the east it was terminated by the countries situated on the left of the river Siao [Liao]; and in the southern direction it reached the shores of the Youé [Yueh] Sea. It is obvious that this description does not include the countries tributary to the empire. Thibet, Turkestan, Muscovy, Siam, Cochin China, Tonking, and Corea, acknowledged the supremacy of the Grand Khan of the Tartars, and faithfully paid him tribute. Even European nations were from time to time insolently summoned to acknowledge the Mongol supremacy. Haughty and threatening letters were sent to the Pope, to the King of France, to the Emperor, commanding them to send as tribute the revenues of their state to the depths of Tartary. The descendants of Tchinggiskhan, who reigned in Muscovy, Persia, Bactriana, and Sogdiana, received investiture from the Emperor of Peking, and undertook nothing of importance without first giving him notice. The diplomatic papers which the King of Persia sent, in the thirteenth century, to Philip the Fair, are a proof of this dependence. On these precious monuments, which are preserved to this day in the archives of France, are seals in Chinese characters, which testify the supremacy of the Grand Khan of Peking over the sovereigns of Persia.

The conquests of Tchinggiskhan and of his successors; and, in later times, those of Tamerlane or Timour, which transferred the seat of the Mongol empire to Samarcand [Samarkand], contributed, in as great, and perhaps a greater degree than the Crusades, to renew the intercourse of Europe with the most distant states of the East, and favoured the discoveries which have been so useful to the progress of the arts, of the sciences, and of navigation.

On this subject, we will quote in this place, an interesting passage from the Memoirs which M. Abel Rémusat published in 1824, on the political relations of the Christian princes, and particularly of the Kings of France, with the Mongol Emperors :—

"The lieutenants of Tchinggiskhan, and of his first successors, on arriving in Western Asia, did not seek at first, to contract any alliance there. The princes, whose domains they entered, silently permitted the impost of a tribute ; the rest were required to submit.

THIBET, AND CHINA

The Georgians and Armenians were among the firſt. The Franks of Syria, the Kings of Hungary, the Emperor himself, had to repel their insolent demands. The Pɔpe was not exempted, by the supremacy he enjoyed in relation to the other Chriſtian princes; nor the King of France, by the high renown he enjoyed throughout the Eaſt. The terror which the Tartars inspired, precluded a fitting answer to their demands. The course resorted to was conciliation, the seeking their alliance, and the endeavouring to rouse them againſt the Moslems. The latter attempt would scarcely have been successful had not the Chriſtians in the Eaſt, who, by adhesion as vassals, had obtained credit at the courts of their generals and their princes, zealously employed themselves in the matter. The Mongols were induced at laſt to undertake war againſt the Sultan of Egypt. Such were the relations with this nation during the firſt period, which laſted from 1224 to 1262.

"In the second period, the Khalifat [caliphate] was deſtroyed; a Mongol principality was founded in Persia: it bordered on the ſtates of the Sultan of Egypt. A sanguinary rivalry arose between the two countries, which the Eaſtern Chriſtians did all in their power to irritate. The Mongol empire was divided. Those of Persia had need of auxiliaries, which the Armenian vassals procured for them: these auxiliaries were the Franks. From this time, their power declined more and more; and ere long it was annihilated. Fresh crusades might reſtore it. The Mongols excited those in the Weſt. They joined their exhortations to those of the Georgians, Armenians, of the wreck of the crusaders, who had taken refuge in Cyprus, and to those of the sovereign pontiffs. The firſt Tartars had commenced by threats; the laſt came to offers, and even descended to supplications. Twenty ambassadors were sent by them to Italy,

France, and England; and it was no fault of theirs that the fire of the holy wars was not rekindled, and extended over Europe and Asia. These diplomatic attempts, the recital of which forms, so to speak, an epilogue to the transmarine expeditions, scarcely noticed by those who have written their history, and, indeed, unknown to most of them, would deserve, perhaps, our fixed attention. We should have to collect facts, resolve difficulties, and place in a clear point of view the political system to which the negociations with the Tartars belong. Specialities of this class could not be appreciated whilst they were considered isolatedly, and without examining them one with another. We might doubt, with Voltaire and De Guignes, that a king of the Tartars had met Saint Louis with offers of service. This fact might not seem tenable, and its recital paradoxical. Yet such scepticism would be unreasonable, after we had seen that the Mongols had acted upon that principle for fifty years; and when we are assured, by reading contemporary writings, and by the inspection of original monuments, that this conduct was natural on their part, that it entered into their views, that it conformed to their interests, and that it is explained by the common rules of reason and policy.

" The series of events which are connected with these negociations serves to complete the history of the Crusades; but the part they may have had in the great moral revolution, which soon followed the relations which they occasioned between people hitherto unknown to each other, are facts of an importance more general and still more worthy of our particular attention. Two systems of civilization had become established at the two extremities of the ancient continent, as the effect of independent causes, without communication, and consequently without mutual influence. All at once the events of war and political

THIBET, AND CHINA

combinations bring into contact these two great bodies, long ſtrangers to each other. The formal interviews of ambassadors are not the only occasions which brought them together. Other occasions more private, but also more efficacious, were eſtablished by imperceptible, but innumerable ramifications, by the travels of a hoſt of individuals, attraćted to the two extremities of the earth, with commercial views, in the train of ambassadors or armies. The irruption of the Mongols, by throwing everything into agitation, neutralized diſtance, filled up intervals, and brought the nations together; the events of war transported millions of individuals to an immense diſtance from the place where they were born. Hiſtory has recorded the voyage of kings, of ambassadors, of missionaries. Sempad, the Orbelian, Hayton, King of Armenia, the two Davids, Kings of Georgia, and several others were led by political motives to the depths of Asia. Yeroslaf, Grand Duke of Sousdal [Yaroslav, grand duke of Susdal] and vassal of the Mongols, like the other Russian princes, came to Kara-Koroum [Karakorum], where he died of poison, it was said, adminiſtered by the Empress herself, the mother of the Emperor Gayouk [Güyük]. Many monks, Italians, French, Flemings, were charged with diplomatic missions to the Grand Khan. Mongols of diſtinćtion came to Rome, Barcelona, Valencia, Lyons, Paris, London, Northampton; and a Franciscan of the kingdom of Naples was Archbishop of Peking. His successor was a professor of theology of the Faculty of Paris. But how many others, less celebrated, were led in the train of those men, either as slaves, or impelled by the desire of gain, or by curiosity, to countries hitherto unexplored. Chance has preserved the names of a few. The firſt envoy who came on the part of the Tartars to the King of Hungary was an Englishman, banished from his country for certain crimes, and who, after having wandered through Asia, had finally taken service among the Mongols. A Flemish Cordelier met in the depth of Tartary a woman of Metz, named Paquette, who had been carried away from Hungary, a Parisian goldsmith whose brother was established in Paris on the Grand Pont, and a young man from the environs of Rouen, who had been present at the capture of Belgrade; he saw there also Russians, Hungarians, and Flemings. A singer, named Robert, after travelling through the whole of Eastern Asia, returned to find a grave in the Cathedral of Chartres. A Tartar was a helmet-maker in the armies of Philip the Fair. Jean de Plan-Carpin met, near [at the Court of] Gayouk, with a Russian gentleman, whom he calls Temer, who served as interpreter. Several merchants of Breslau, Poland, and Austria, accompanied him in his journey to Tartary; others returned with him through Russia; these were Genoese, Pisans, and two merchants of Venice whom chance had brought to Bokhara. They were induced to go in the suite of a Mongol ambassador, whom Houlagou [Hulagu] had sent to Khoubilai. They sojourned several years in China and Tartary, took letters from the Grand Khan to the Pope, and returned to the Grand Khan, bringing with them the son of one of their number, the celebrated Marco-Polo, and quitted once more the Court of Khoubilai to return to Venice. Travels of this kind were not less frequent in the succeeding age. Of this number are those of John de Mandeville, an English physician; of Oderic of Friuli; of Pegoletti; of Guillaume de Bouldeselle, and several others. We may be certain that the journeys which have been recorded are but a small portion of those which were performed, and that there were at that period more people able to make a long journey than to write an account of it. Many of these adventurers must have established themselves and died in the countries they went to visit. Others returned to their country as obscure as when they left it ; but with their imaginations full of what they had seen, relating it all to their families and friends, and doubtless with exaggerations ; but leaving around them, amidst ridiculous fables, a few useful recollections and traditions productive of advantage. Thus were sown in Germany, in Italy, in France, in the monasteries, among the nobility, and even in the lowest grade of society, precious seeds destined to bud at a later period. All these obscure travellers, carrying the arts of their native country to distant lands, brought back other information about these no less precious, and thus effected, unconsciously, exchanges more productive of good than all those of commerce. By this means not merely the traffic in silks, in porcelains, in commodities from Hindostan, was made more extensive and more practicable, opening new routes to industry and commerce; but, that which was far more valuable, foreign manners and customs of before unknown nations, extraordinary productions, were presented to the European mind, confined, since the fall of the Roman empire, within too narrow a circle. Men began to have an idea that, after all, there was something worthy of notice in the finest, the most populous and the most anciently civilized of the four quarters of the world. People began to think of studying the arts, the religions, the languages of the nations who inhabited it, and there was even a proposition to establish a professorship of the Tartar language in the University of Paris. Romantic narratives, reduced by discussion within reasonable proportions, diffused in all directions juster and more varied information : the world seemed opening towards the East. Geography made immense strides, and ardour of discovery became the new form assumed by the adventurous spirit of

Europeans. The idea of another hemisphere ceased, as soon as our own became better known, to present itself to the mind as a paradox destitute of all probability, and it was in going in search of the Zipangri [Zipangu] of Marco-Polo that Christopher Columbus discovered the New World.

"I should make too great a digression, were I to investigate what were in the East the effects of the Mongol irruption, the destruction of the Khalifat, the extermination of the Bulgarians, of the Komans [Comans], and other northern nations. The decline of the population of Upper Asia, so favourable to the reaction by which the Russians, hitherto the vassals of the Tartars, subdued in their turn all the nomads of the North; the submission of China to the foreign yoke; the definitive establishment of the Indian religion in Thibet and Tartary; all these events deserve to be studied in detail. I will not even pause to inquire what might have been the results, to the nations of Eastern Asia, of the intercourse which they had with the West. The introduction of the Indian numerals into China, a knowledge of the astronomical system of the Moslems, the translation of the New Testament and the Psalms into the Mongol language, executed by the Latin Archbishop of Khan-Balik (Peking), the foundation of the lamanical hierarchy, framed in imitation of the pontifical court, and produced by the fusion effected between the remnants of the Nestorianism established in Tartary and the dogmas of the Buddhist; such were all the innovations of which there are any traces in Eastern Asia, and therewith the commerce of the Franks has very little to do. The Asiatics are punished for their contempt of the knowledge of Europeans by the limited results which that very scorn enables them to derive from it. To confine myself to what concerns the people of the West, and to attempt to justify what I said at the commencement of this Memoir, that the effects of the communications with the nations of Upper Asia, in the thirteenth century, had contributed indirectly to the progress of European civilization, I will conclude with a reflection which I shall offer with the more confidence that it is not entirely new, while, at the same time, the facts we have just investigated seem calculated to give it a sanction it had not before.

"Before the establishment of the intercourse which, first the Crusades, and then, later, the irruption of the Mongols, caused to spring up between the nations of the East and those of the West, the greater part of those inventions, which distinguished the close of the middle ages, had been known to the Asiatics for centuries. The polarity of the lodestone had been discovered and put into operation in China from the remotest antiquity. Gunpowder had been as long known to the Hindoos and the Chinese, the latter of whom had, in the tenth century 'thunder carriages,' which seem to have been cannon. It is difficult to account in any other way for the fire-stone throwers, which are so often mentioned in the history of the Mongols. Houlagou, when he set out for Persia, had in his army a body of Chinese artillerymen. Again, the first edition of the classic books engraved on wooden boards is dated in the year 952. The institution of bank notes, and of banking and exchange offices, took place among the Jou-Tchen [Juchen] in 1154. Bank notes were adopted by the Mongols established in China; they were known to the Persians by the same name as the Chinese gave them, and Josaphat Barbaro was informed in 1450 by an intelligent Tartar whom he met at Asof, and who had been on an embassy to China, that this sort of money was printed in China every year *con nuova stampa*; and this expression is remarkable enough, considering the time when Barbaro made this observation. Laſtly, playing-cards—into the origin of which so many learned antiquarians would not have busied themselves to inquire were it not that it marked one of the firſt applications of the art of engraving on wood—were invented in China in 1120.

"There are, besides, in the commencement of each of these inventions, particular features which seem calculated to show their origin. I will not speak of the compass, the ancient use of which, in China, Hager seems to me successfully to have demonſtrated, and which passed into Europe by means of the Crusades, previous to the irruption of the Mongols, as the famous passage in Jacques de Vitry, and some others, prove. But the oldeſt playing cards, those used in the *jeu de tarots*, have a marked analogy in their form, their design, their size, their number, with the cards which the Chinese make use of. Cannons were the firſt fire-arms made use of in Europe; they are also, it would appear, the only fire-arms with which the Chinese were acquainted at this period. The queſtion as to paper money appears to have been viewed in its true light by M. Langles, and after him by Hager. The firſt boards made use of to print upon were made of wood and stereotyped, like those of the Chinese; and nothing is more natural than to suppose that some book from China gave the idea. This would not be more surprising than the fragment of the Bible, in Gothic characters, which Father Martini discovered in the house of a Chinese at Tchang-Tcheou-Fou. [Chang-chou-fu]. We have the inſtance of another usage, which evidently followed the same route—it is that of the *Souan-pan*, or arithmetical machine of the Chinese, which was, doubtless, introduced into Europe by the Tartars of the army of Batou [Batu], and which has so extensively pervaded Russia and Poland that women who cannot read use nothing else in the settlement of their household accounts, and their little commercial dealings. The conjecture which gives a Chinese origin to the primitive idea of European typography is so natural, that it was propounded before there was any opportunity for collecting together all the circumstances which make it so probable. It is the idea of Paulo Jovio, and of Mendoça, who imagine that a Chinese book may have been brought into Europe before the arrival of the Portuguese in the Indies, by the medium of the Scythians and Muscovites. It was developed by an anonymous Englishman; and carefully putting aside from the consideration the impression in moveable types, which is, no doubt, an invention peculiar to the Europeans, one cannot conceive any sound objection to an hypothesis which bears so strongly the stamp of probability. But this supposition acquires a still greater degree of probability when we apply it to the totality of the discoveries in question. All were made in Eastern Asia; all were unheard of in the West. Communication took place: it was continued for a century and a half, and ere another century had elapsed, all these inventions were known in Europe. Their origin is veiled in obscurity. The region where they manifested themselves, the men who produced them, are equally a subject of doubt. Enlightened countries were not their theatre. It was not learned men who were their authors; it was common men, obscure artisans, who lighted up, one after another, those unexpected flames. Nothing can better demonstrate the effects of a communication; nothing can be more in accordance with what we have said above as to those invisible channels, those imperceptible ramifications, whereby the science of the Eastern nations penetrated into Europe. The greater part of these inventions appear at first in the state of infancy in which the Asiatics left them; and this circumstance alone, almost prevents our having any doubt as to their origin. Some are immediately put in practice; others remain for some time enveloped in obscurity, which conceals from us their progress, and they are taken, on their appearance, for new discoveries; all are soon brought to perfection, and, as it were, fecundated by the genius of Europeans, operating in concert, communicate to human intelligence the greatest impulse known to history. Thus, by this shock of nations, the darkness of the middle ages was dispersed. Calamities which at first aspect seemed merely destined to afflict mankind, served to arouse it from the lethargy in which it had remained for ages; and the subversion of twenty empires was the price at which Providence accorded to Europe the light of modern civilization."

The Mongol dynasty of the Youen occupied the empire for a century. After having shone with a brilliancy, the reflection of which spread over the most remote regions, it ended with Chun-Ti [Shun-ti], a feeble prince, more mindful of frivolous amusements than of the great inheritance which had been left him by his ancestors. The Chinese regained their independence; and Tchou-Youen-Tchang [Chu Yüen'-chang], the son of a labourer, and for some time a servant in a convent of bonzes, was the founder of the celebrated dynasty of the Ming. They ascended the imperial throne in 1368, and reigned in the name of Houng-Wou [Hung-wu].

The Tartars were massacred in great numbers in the interior of China, and the rest were driven back to their old country. The Emperor Young-Lo pursued them three several times beyond the desert, more than 200 leagues north of the Great Wall, in order to exterminate them. He could not, however, effect this object, and, dying on his return from his third expedition, his successors left the Tartars in peace

THIBET, AND CHINA

beyond the desert, whence they diffused themselves left and right. The principal chiefs of the blood of Tchinggiskhan occupied, each with his people, a particular diſtrict, and gave birth to various tribes, which all formed so many petty kingdoms. These fallen princes, ever tormented by the recollection of their ancient power, appeared several times on the frontiers of the empire, and did not cease to disquiet the Chinese princes, without, however, succeeding in their attempts at invasion.

Towards the commencement of the seventeenth century, the Mantchou Tartars having made themselves maſters of China, the Mongols gradually submitted to them, and placed themselves under their sovereignty. The Oelets, a Mongol tribe, deriving their name from Oloutai [Olutai (*read* Aruktai)], a celebrated warrior in the fourteenth century, made frequent irruptions into the country of the Khalkhas and a sanguinary war arose between these two people. The Emperor Khang-Hi, under the pretence of conciliating them, intervened in their quarrel, put an end to the war by subjecting both parties, and extended his domination in Tartary to the frontiers of Russia; the three Khans of the Khalkhas came to make their submission to the Mantchou Emperor, who convoked a grand meeting near Tolon-Noor. Each Khan presented to him eight white horses, and one white camel; from which circumſtance this tribute was called, in the Mongol language, *Yousoun-Dchayan* [*yisun-chagan*], "the nine white"; it was agreed that they should bring every year a similar present.

At the present time the Tartar nations, more or less subject to the sway of the Mantchou emperors, are no longer what they were in the time of Tchinggiskhan and Timour. Since that epoch Tartary has been disorganized by so many revolutions; it has

TRAVELS IN TARTARY,

undergone such notable political and geographical changes, that what travellers and writers said about it in former periods no longer applies to it.

During a length of time geographers divided Tartary into three grand parts—1. Russian Tartary, extending from east to west, from the sea of Kamtchatka to the Black Sea, and from north to south, from the regions inhabited by the Tongous [Tungus] and Samoiede [Samoyed] tribes, to the lakes Baikal and Aral. 2. Chinese Tartary, bounded east by the sea of Japan, south by the Great Wall of China, west by the Gobi or great sandy desert, and north by the Baikal Lake. 3. Independent Tartary, extending to the Caspian Sea, and including in its limits the whole of Thibet. Such a division is altogether chimerical, and without any sound basis. All these immense tracts, indeed, once formed part of the great empires of Tchinggiskhan and Timour. The Tartar hordes made encampments there at their will in the course of their warlike wanderings; but now all this is completely changed, and to form an exact idea of modern Tartary, it is necessary to modify in a great degree the notions that have been transmitted to us by the mediæval authors, and which, in default of better information, have been adopted by all geographers, down to Malte-Brun inclusive. To realize a definite idea about Tartary, we think that the clearest, most certain, and consequently the most reasonable rule is to adopt the opinions of the Tartars themselves, and of the Chinese, far more competent judges of this matter than Europeans, who, having no connection with this part of Asia, are obliged to trust to conjectures which have often little to do with truth. In accordance with a universal usage, the soundness of which we were enabled to confirm in the course of our travels, we will divide the Tartar people into Eastern Tartars (Toung-Ta-Dze [Tung-ta-tzŭ]),

THIBET, AND CHINA
or Mantchous, and Weftern Tartars (Si-Ta-Dze [Hsi-ta-tzŭ]), or Mongols. The boundaries of Mantchouria are very diftinct, as we have already ftated. It is bounded on the north by the Khinggan mountains, which separate it from Siberia; on the south by the gulf of Phou-Hai and Corea; on the eaft by the sea of Japan; and on the weft by the Barrier of Stakes and a branch of the Sakhalien-Oula. It would be a difficult matter to define the limits of Mongolia in an equally exact manner; however, without any serious departure from the truth, we may include them between the 75th and 118th degrees longitude of Paris, and 35th and 50th degrees of north latitude. Great and Little Boukaria [Bukharia], Khalmoukia [Kalmuky], Great and Little Thibet—all these denominations seem to us purely imaginary. We shall enter, by-and-by, into some details on this subject, in the second part of our travels when we come to speak of Thibet and of the neighbouring people.

The people who are comprised in the grand division of Mongolia, that we have juft given, are not all to be indiscriminately considered as Mongols. There are some of them to whom this denomination can only be applied in a reftricted sense. Towards the north-weft, for inftance, the Mongols are frequently confounded with the Moslems; and towards the south, with the Si-Fans, or Eaftern Thibetians. The beft way clearly to diftinguish these people is to pay attention to their language, their manners, their religion, their coftume, and particularly to the name by which they designate themselves. The Mongol Khalkhas are the moft numerous, the moft wealthy, and the moft celebrated in hiftory. They occupy the entire north of Mongolia. Their country is of vaft extent, including nearly 200 leagues from north to south, and about 500 from eaft to weft. We will not repeat here what we have already said about the

Khalkha district; we will merely add that it is divided into four great provinces, subject to four separate sovereigns. These provinces are sub-divided into eighty-four banners, in Chinese called *Ky* [*ch'i*], in Mongol *Bochkhon* [*Khoshigun*]. Princes of different ranks are at the head of each banner. Notwithstanding the authority of these secular princes, it may safely be said that the Khalkhas are all dependent on the Guison-Tamba, the Grand Lama, the Living Buddha of all the Mongol Khalkhas, who consider it an honour to call themselves Disciples of the Holy One of Kouren (*Koure bokte ain Chabi* [*Kürê bogda yin shabi*]).

The Southern Mongols have no special designation; they merely bear the name of the principality to which they belong. Thus they say, "Mongol of Souniot Mongol of Gechekten," etc. Southern Mongolia comprises twenty-five principalities, which, like those of the Khalkhas, are sub-divided into several Bochkhon. The principal are the Ortous, the two Toumet, the two Souniot, the Tchakar, Karatsin [Kharachin], Ouniot, Gechekten, Barin, Naiman, and the country of the Eleuts.

The Southern Mongols, near the Great Wall, have little modified their manners by their constant intercourse with the Chinese. You may remark sometimes in their dress a sort of studied elegance, and in their character pretensions to the refined politeness of the Chinese. Laying aside, on the one hand, the frankness, the good-natured openness of the Mongols of the North, they have borrowed from their neighbours somewhat of their cunning and foppery.

Proceeding to the south-east, we encounter the Mongols of the Koukou-Noor or Blue Lake (in Chinese, Tsing-Hai [Ch'ing-hai] or Blue Sea). This country is far from possessing the extent which is generally assigned to it in geographical charts. The

THIBET, AND CHINA

Mongols of the Koukou-Noor only dwell around the lake, from which they derive their name; and, moreover, they are mixed up to a great extent with Si-Fans, who cannot live secure in their own country, because of the hordes of robbers that are constantly ravaging it.

To the west of the Koukou-Noor is the river Tsaidam on whose banks encamp the numerous tribes, called Tsaidam-Mongols, who must not be confounded with the Mongols of the Koukou-Noor. Farther still, in the very heart of Thibet, we encounter other Mongol tribes. We shall say nothing about them here, as we shall have occasion to speak of them in the course of our narrative. We will revert, therefore, in some detail to the Mongols of the Koukou-Noor and the Tsaidam.

The Torgot-Tartars [Turgût Mongols], who formerly dwelt near Kara-Koroum, the capital of the Mongols in the time of Tchinggiskhan, are now situated to the north-west of Mongolia. In 1672, the whole tribe, having raised their tents and assembled all their flocks, abandoned the district which had served them as a resting-place, migrated to the western part of Asia, and established themselves in the steppes between the Don and the Volga.

The Torgot princes recognized the sovereignty of the Muscovite emperors, and declared themselves their vassals. But these wandering hordes, passionately attached to the independence of their nomad life, could not long accommodate themselves to the new masters they had selected. They soon felt an aversion to the laws and regular institutions which were becoming established in the Russian empire. In 1770, the Torgots again made a general migration. Led by their chief, Aboucha [Ubashi], they suddenly disappeared, passed the Russian frontiers, and halted on the banks of the river Ili. This flight had been concerted with the government of Peking. The Emperor of China, who had been informed beforehand of the period of their departure, took them under his protection, and assigned to them settlements on the banks of the Ili.

The principality of Ili is now the Botany-Bay of China: thither are sent the Chinese criminals condemned to exile by the laws of the empire. Before their arrival in these distant regions they are obliged to cross frightful deserts, and to climb the Moussour (glacier) mountains. These gigantic summits are entirely formed of icebergs, piled one on the top of the other, so that travellers cannot advance except by hewing steps out of the eternal ice. On the other side of the Moussour mountains the country, they say, is magnificent; the climate temperate enough and the soil adapted for every kind of cultivation. The exiles have transported thither a great many of the productions of China; but the Mongols continue to follow their nomad life, and merely to pasture herds and flocks.

We had occasion to travel for some time with Lamas of the Torgot; some of them arrived with us at Lha-Ssa. We did not remark, either in their costume, in their manners, or in their language, anything to distinguish them from the Mongols. They spoke a good deal about the *Oros* (Russians), but in a way to make us understand that they were by no means desirous of again becoming subject to their sway. The Torgot camels are remarkably fine, and generally much larger and stronger than those in the other parts of Mongolia.

It would be a very desirable thing to send missionaries to Ili. We believe that there would be found already formed there a numerous and fervent body of Christians. It is well known that for many years past, it is hither that the Christians who have refused to apostatize, have been exiled from all the provinces of China. The missionary who should obtain permission to exercise his zeal in the Torgot would doubtless have to undergo great privations during his journey thither; but he would be amply compensated, by the thought of carrying the succour of religion to all those generous confessors of the faith, whom the tyranny of the Chinese government has sent to die in these distant regions.

To the south-west of Torgot is the province of Khachghar [Kashgar]. At the present day, this district cannot at all be considered a part of Mongolia. Its inhabitants have neither the language, nor the physiognomy, nor the costume, nor the religion, nor the manners of the Mongols; they are Moslems. The Chinese, as well as the Tartars, call them Hoei-Hoei [Hui-hui], a name by which they designate the Mussulmen who dwell in the interior of the Chinese empire. This description of Khachghar is also applicable to the people to the south of the Celestial Mountains, in the Chinese tongue called Tien-Chan [T'ien-shan], and in Mongol, Bokte-oula "holy mountains".

Not long since, the Chinese government, had to sustain a terrible war against Khachghar. We are indebted for the following details to some military Mandarins who accompanied this famous and distant expedition.

The Court of Peking kept in Khachghar two grand Mandarins, with the title of Delegates Extraordinary (*Kin-Tchai* [*Ch'in-ch'ai*]), who were charged to guard the frontiers and to keep an eye on the movements of the neighbouring people. These Chinese officers, instead of merely watching, exercised their power with such horrible and revolting tyranny that they wore out the patience of the people of Khachghar, who, at length, rose in a body, and massacred all the Chinese resident in the country. The news reaching Peking, the Emperor, who knew nothing of the misconduct of his officers, assembled his troops, and marched them against the Moslems. The contest was long and bloody. The Chinese government had several times to send reinforcements. The Hoei-Hoei were commanded by a hero called Tchankoeul [Chang-ko-êrh (Jehangir)]; his stature, they say, was prodigious, and he had no weapon but an enormous club. He frequently defeated the Chinese army, and destroyed several grand military Mandarins. At length the Emperor sent out the famous Yang, who put an end to the war. The conqueror of Khachghar is a military Mandarin of the province of Chan-Toung, remarkable for his lofty stature, and above all for the prodigious length of his beard. According to the account we heard of him, his manner of fighting was singular enough. As soon as the action commenced, he tied up his beard in two great knots, in order that it might not get in his way, and then he placed himself behind his troops. There, armed with a long sabre, he drove his soldiers on to combat, and massacred, without pity, those who were cowards enough to draw back. This method of commanding an army will seem somewhat peculiar; but those who have lived among the Chinese will see that the military genius of Yang was founded on a thorough knowledge of the soldiers he had to deal with.

The Moslems were defeated, and Tchankoeul was, by means of treachery, made a prisoner. He was conveyed to Peking, where he had to undergo the most barbarous and humiliating treatment, even the being exposed to the people, shut up in an iron cage, like a wild beast. The Emperor Tao-Kouang wished to see this warrior, of whom fame spoke so much, and ordered him to be brought to him. The Mandarins immediately took alarm; they were afraid left the prisoner should reveal to the Emperor the causes which had brought about the revolt of Khachghar, and the horrible massacres which had followed it. The great dignitaries saw that these revelations would be dangerous for them, and make them seem guilty of negligence in the eyes of the Emperor for not having duly observed the conduct of the Mandarins who were placed in charge of distant provinces. To obviate this danger, they made the unfortunate Tchankoeul swallow a draught which took away his speech, and threw him into a disgusting state of stupor. When he appeared in the presence of the Emperor, his mouth, they say, foamed, and his visage was horrible; he could not answer any of the questions which were addressed to him. Tchankoeul was condemned to be cut into pieces, and to be served up as food for the dogs.

The Mandarin Yang was loaded with favours by the Emperor, for having so happily terminated the war of Khachghar. He obtained the dignity of *Batourou* [*Baturu*], a Tartar word signifying valorous. This title is the most honourable that a military Mandarin can obtain.

The Batourou Yang was sent against the English, in their last war with the Chinese; but there it would appear that his tactics did not avail. During our travels in China we inquired of several Mandarins how it was that the Batourou Yang had not exterminated the English: the answer everywhere was that he had had compassion on them.

The numerous principalities of which Mongolia is composed are all more or less dependent on the Mantchou Emperor, in proportion as they show more or less weakness in their relations with the Court of Peking. They may be considered as so many feudal kingdoms, giving no obedience to their sovereign beyond the extent of their fear or their interest;

and indeed, what the Mantchou dynasty fears above all things is the vicinity of these Tartar tribes. The Emperors are fully aware that, headed by an enterprising and bold chief, these tribes might successfully renew the terrible wars of other times, and once more obtain possession of the Empire. For this reason, they use every means in their power to preserve the friendship of the Mongol princes, and to enfeeble the strength of these terrible nomads. It is with this view, as we have already remarked, that they patronize Lamanism, by richly endowing the Lamaseries, and by granting numerous privileges to the Lamas. So long as they can maintain their influence over the sacerdotal tribe, they are assured that neither the people nor the princes will stir from their repose.

Alliances are another means by which the reigning dynasty seeks to consolidate its power in Mongolia. The daughters and nearest relations of the Emperor, intermarrying with the royal families of Tartary, contribute to maintain between the two peoples pacific and friendly relations. Yet these princesses continue to have a great predilection for the pomp and grandeur of the imperial court. The mournful, monotonous life of the desert soon fatigues them, and they sigh for the brilliant fêtes of Peking. To obviate the inconvenience that might attend their frequent journeys to the capital, a very severe regulation has been made to moderate the wandering humour of these princesses. First, for the first ten years after their marriage they are forbidden to come to Peking, under penalty of having the annual pension the Emperor allows to their husbands suspended. This period having elapsed, they are allowed to go to Peking, but never at their own mere fancy. A tribunal is appointed to examine their reasons for temporarily quitting their family. If these are considered valid

THIBET, AND CHINA

they allow them a certain number of days, on the expiration of which they are enjoined to return to Tartary. During their stay at Peking they are supported at the expense of the Emperor, suitably to their dignity.

The most elevated personages in the hierarchy of the Mongol princes, are the *Thsin-Wang* [*ch'in-wang*] and the *Kiun-Wang* [*Chün-wang*]. Their title is equivalent to that of king. After them come the *Beïlé* [*beilê*], the *Beïssé* [*pei-tzŭ*] the *Koung* [*Kung*] of the first and second class, and the *Dchassak*. These may be compared to our ancient dukes, barons, etc. We have already mentioned that the Mongol princes are bound to pay certain rents to the Emperor; but the amount of these is so small that the Mantchou dynasty can only levy it on account of the moral effect that may result. As simple matter-of-fact, it would be nearer the truth to say that the Mantchous are the tributaries of the Mongols; for, in return for the few beasts they received from them, they give them annually large sums of money, silken stuffs, clothes, and various articles of luxury and ornament, such as buttons, sables, peacocks' feathers, etc. Each *Wang* of the first degree receives annually 2,500 ounces of silver (about £800), and forty pieces of silk stuff. All the other princes are paid according to the rank they derive from the Emperor. A *Dchassak*, for example, receives yearly one hundred ounces of silver, and four pieces of silk.

There exist certain Lamaseries, termed Imperial, where each Lama, on obtaining the degree of *Kalon*, [*gelong (dge-slong)*] is obliged to offer to the Emperor an ingot of silver of the value of fifty ounces; his name is then inscribed on the register of the imperial clergy at Peking, and he is entitled to the pension given yearly to the Lamas of the Emperor. It is obvious that all these measures, so calculated to flatter the self-love and avarice of the Tartars, do not a little contribute to maintain their feelings of respect and submission towards a government which takes such pains to court their friendship.

The Mongols, however, of the district of the Khalkhas do not seem to be much affected by these demonstrations. They only see in the Mantchous a rival race, in possession of a prey which they themselves have never ceased to desire. We have frequently heard the Mongol Khalkhas use the most unceremonious and seditious language in speaking of the Mantchou Emperor. " They are subject," they say " to the Guison-Tamba alone, to the *Most Holy*, and not to the black-man (layman), who sits on the throne of Peking." These redoubtable children of Tchinggiskhan still seem to be cherishing in their inmost heart schemes of conquest and invasion. They only await, they say, the command of their Grand Lama to march direct upon Peking, and to regain an empire which they believe to be theirs, for the sole reason that it was formerly theirs. The Mongol princes exact from their subjects or slaves certain tributes, which consist in sheep, and here is the absurd and unjust regulation, in accordance with which this tribute must be paid:

The owner of five or more oxen must contribute one sheep; the owner of twenty sheep must contribute one of them; if he owns forty he gives two; but they need give no more, however numerous their flocks. As may be seen, this tribute really weighs upon the poor only; the wealthy may possess a great number of cattle without being obliged to contribute more than two sheep.

Besides these regular tributes, there are others which the princes are accustomed to levy on their slaves, on some extraordinary occasions; for instance, marriages, burials, and distant voyages. On these occasions each collection of ten tents is obliged to furnish a horse and a camel. Every Mongol who owns three cows muſt pay a pail of milk; if he possesses five, a pot of *koumis* [*kumis*] or wine, made of fermented milk. The owner of a flock of one hundred sheep furnishes a felt carpet or a tent covering; he who owns three camels muſt give a bundle of long cords to faſten the baggage. However, in a country where everything is subject to the arbitrary will of the chief, these regulations, as may be supposed, are not ſtrictly observed. Sometimes the subjects are altogether exempted from their operation, and sometimes also there is exacted from them much more than the law decrees.

Robbery and murder are very severely punished among the Mongols; but the injured individuals, or their parents, are themselves obliged to prosecute the prisoner before the tribunals: the worſt outrage remains unpunished if no one appears to prosecute. In the ideas of a semi-barbarous people, the man who attempts to take the property or life of anyone, is deemed to have committed merely a private offence, reparation for which ought to be demanded, not by the public, but by the injured party or his family. These rude notions of juſtice are common to China and to Thibet; and for that matter, we know that Rome herself had no other until the eſtablishment of Chriſtianity, which caused the right of the community to prevail over the right of the individual.

Mongolia, generally speaking, wears a gloomy and savage aspect; the eye is nowhere recreated by the charm and variety of landscape scenery. The monotony of the ſteppes is only interrupted by ravines, by vaſt rents of the earth, or by ſtone and barren hills Towards the north, in the diſtrict of Khalkhas, nature is more animated; tall foreſts decorate the summits of the mountains, and numerous rivers water the rich pastures of the plains; but in the long winter season the earth remains buried under a thick bed of snow. Towards the Great Wall, Chinese industry glides like a serpent into the desert. Towns arise on all sides. The Land of Grass is crowned with harvests, and the Mongol shepherds find themselves driven back northwards, little by little, by the encroachments of agriculture.

Sandy plains occupy, perhaps, the greater part of Mongolia; you do not see a single tree there; some short, brittle grass, which seems to have much difficulty in issuing from this unfruitful soil, creeping briars, a few scanty tufts of heath, such is the sole vegetation and pasturage of Gobi. Water is very rarely seen; at long intervals you may meet with a few deep wells, dug for the convenience of the caravans that are obliged to cross this dismal tract.

In Mongolia there are only two seasons in the year, nine months for winter, and three for summer. Sometimes the heat is stifling, particularly on the sandy steppes, but it only lasts a few days. The nights, however, are almost invariably cold. In the Mongol countries cultivated by the Chinese, outside the Great Wall, all agricultural labour must be comprehended within three months. As soon as the earth is sufficiently thawed, they hastily set to work, or rather, they do nothing but touch the surface of the ground lightly with the plough; they then immediately sow the seed; the corn grows with astonishing rapidity. Whilst they are waiting for it to come to maturity, the men are incessantly occupied in pulling up the weeds that overrun the plain. Scarcely have they gathered in the harvest when the winter comes with its terrible cold; during this season they thresh the corn. As the cold makes vast crevices in the earth, they throw water over the surface of the threshing-floor, which freezes forthwith, and creates

THIBET, AND CHINA

for the labourers a place always smooth and admirably clean.

The excessive cold which prevails in Mongolia may be attributed to three causes :—to the great elevation of the country; to the nitrous substances with which it is strongly impregnated, and to the almost entire absence of cultivation. In the places which the Chinese have cultivated the temperature has risen in a remarkable degree; the heat goes on increasing, so to speak, from year to year, as cultivation advances; so that particular grain crops, which at first would not grow at all because of the cold, now ripen with wonderful success.

Mongolia, on account of its immense solitudes, has become the haunt of a large number of wild animals. You see at every step, hares, pheasants, eagles, yellow goats, grey squirrels, foxes and wolves. It is remarkable that the wolves of Mongolia attack men rather than animals. They may be seen, sometimes, passing at full gallop through a flock of sheep in order to attack the shepherd. About the Great Wall they frequently visit the Tartaro-Chinese villages, enter the farms, and disdaining the domestic animals they find in the yard, proceed to the inside of the house, and there select their human victims, whom they almost invariably seize by the throat and strangle. There is scarcely a village in Tartary, where, every year, misfortunes of this kind do not occur. It would seem as though the wolves of this country were resolved to avenge on men the sanguinary war which the Tartars make upon their brethren.

The stag, the wild goat, the mule, the wild camel, the yak, the brown and black bear, the lynx, the ounce and the tiger, frequent the deserts of Mongolia. The Tartars never proceed on a journey unless armed with bows, fusils and lances.

When we consider the horrible climate of Tartary,

that climate ever so gloomy and frozen, we should be led to think that the inhabitants of these wild countries must be of an extremely fierce and rugged temperament; their physiognomy, their deportment, the costume they wear, all would seem to confirm this opinion. The Mongol has a flat face, with prominent cheek bones, the chin short and retiring, the forehead sunken, the eyes small and oblique, of a yellow tint as though full of bile, the hair black and rugged, the beard scanty, the skin of a deep brown, and extremely coarse. The Mongol is of middle height, but his great leathern boots and large sheep-skin robe, seem to take away from his height, and make him appear diminutive and stumpy. To complete this portrait, we must add a heavy and ponderous gait, and a harsh, shrill, discordant language, full of frightful aspirates. Notwithstanding this rough and unprepossessing exterior, the disposition of the Mongol is full of gentleness and good nature; he passes suddenly from the most rollicking and extravagant gaiety to a state of melancholy, which is by no means disagreeable. Timid to excess in his ordinary habits, when fanaticism or the desire of vengeance arouses him, he displays in his courage an impetuosity which nothing can stay; he is candid and credulous as an infant, and he passionately loves to hear marvellous anecdotes and narratives. The meeting with a travelling Lama is always for him a source of happiness.

Aversion to toil and a sedentary life, the love of pillage and rapine, cruelty, unnatural debaucheries, are the vices which have been generally attributed to the Mongol Tartars. We are apt to believe that the portrait which the old writers have drawn of them was not exaggerated, for we always find these terrible hordes, at the period of their gigantic conquests, bringing in their train, murder, pillage, conflagration and every description of scourge. But are the Mongols the same now that they were formerly ? We believe we can affirm the contrary, at least to a great extent. Wherever we have seen them, we have found them to be generous, frank, and hospitable; inclined, it is true, like ill-educated children, to pilfer little things which excite their curiosity, but by no means in the habit of practising what is called pillage and robbery. As to their aversion for toil and a sedentary life, they are juſt the same as heretofore. It muſt also be admitted that their manners are very free, but their conduct has more in it of recklessness than of absolute corruption. We seldom find among them those unbridled and brutal debaucheries to which the Chinese are so much given.

The Mongols are ſtrangers to every kind of induſtry. Some felt carpets, some rudely tanned hides, a little needlework and embroidery are exceptions not deserving of mention. On the other hand, they possess to perfection the qualities of a paſtoral and nomad people. They have the sense of sight, hearing, and scent prodigiously developed. The Mongol is able to hear at a very long diſtance the trot of a horse, to diſtinguish the form of objects, and to detect the diſtant scent of flocks, and the smoke of an encampment.

Many attempts have already been made to propagate Chriſtianity among the Tartars, and we may say that they have not been altogether fruitless. Towards the end of the eighth century and in the commencement of the ninth, Timothy, patriarch of the Neſtorians, sent some monks to preach the Gospel to the Hioung-Nou Tartars, who had taken refuge on the shores of the Caspian Sea. At a later period they penetrated into Central Asia, and into China. In the time of Tchinggiskhan and his successors, Franciscan and Dominican missionaries were dispatched to Tartary. The conversions were numerous: even princes, it is said, and emperors were baptized. But we must not entirely credit the statements of the Tartar ambassadors, who, the more easily to draw the Christian princes of Europe into a league against the Moslems, never failed to state that their masters had been baptized, and had made profession of Christianity. It is certain, however, that at the commencement of the fourteenth century, Pope Clement V. erected at Peking an archbishopric, in favour of Jean de Montcorvin, a Franciscan missionary, who preached the Gospel to the Tartars for forty-two years; he translated into the Mongol language the New Testament and the Psalms of David, and left at his death a very flourishing Christendom. We find on this subject some curious details in *Le Livre de l'Estat du Grant Caan*[1] (*The book of the State of the Grand Khan*), extracted from a manuscript of the National Library, and published in the *Nouveau Journal Asiatique* (vol. vi.), by M. Jacquet, a learned orientalist. We conceive that it may be acceptable to quote a few passages from this production.

OF THE MINORITES WHO DWELL IN THIS COUNTRY OF
CATHAY (CHINA)

"In the said city of Cambalech [Khan-balik] was an archbishop, who was called Brother John of Mount Curvin [Monte Corvino], of the order of Minorites, and he was legate there for Pope Clement V. This archbishop erected in that city aforesaid three houses of Minorites, and they are two leagues distant from one another. He likewise instituted two others in the city of Racon [Zaitun], which is a long distance from Cambalech, being a journey of three months, and it is on the sea coast; and in these two places were put two Minorites as bishops. The one was named

[1] This compilation was made in the fourteenth century, by order of Pope John XXII.

THIBET, AND CHINA

Brother Andrew of Paris [Perugia], and the other, Brother Peter of Florence. These brothers, and John the Archbishop, converted many people to the faith of Jesus Chrift. He was a man of irreproachable life, agreeable to God and the world, and very much in the Emperor's favour. The Emperor provided him and all his people with all things necessary, and he was much beloved by both Chriftians and pagans; and he certainly would have converted all that country to the Chriftian and Catholic faith, if the false and misbelieving Neftorian Chriftians had not prevented it. The archbishop had great trouble in reftoring these Neftorians to the obedience of our Holy Mother the Roman Church; without which obedience, he said, they could not be saved; and on this account these Neftorian schismatics disliked him greatly. This archbishop has juft departed, as it pleased God, from this life. A great multitude of Christians and pagans attended his funeral; and the pagans tore their funeral robes, as is their cuftom. And these Chriftians and infidels took, with great reverence, the robes of the archbishop, and held them in great respeƈt, and as relics. He was buried there honourably, in the fashion of the faithful. They ftill visit his tomb with great devotion.

OF CERTAIN NESTORIAN CHRISTIAN SCHISMATICS WHO DWELL THERE

" In the said city of Cambalech there is a sort of Chriftian schismatics whom they call Neftorians. They observe the cuftoms and manners of the Greek Church, and are not obedient to the Holy Church of Rome; but they are of another seƈt, and are at great enmity with all the Catholic Chriftians who are loyal to the Holy Church of Rome aforesaid. And when the archbishop, of whom we spoke juft now, built those abbeys of Minorites aforesaid, the Neftorians deftroyed them in the night, and did them all the mischief in their power; for they dared not injure the said archbishop, or his brethren, or the other faithful Chriſtians publicly and openly, because the Emperor loved them and showed them his favour. These Neſtorians dwelling in the said empire of Cathay, number more that 30,000, and are very rich; but many of them fear the Chriſtians. They have very beautiful and very holy churches, with crosses and images in honour of God and of the saints. They receive from the said Emperor several offices, and he grants them many privileges, and it is thought that if they would consent to unite and agree with these Minorites and with other good Chriſtians who reside in this country, they might convert the whole of this country and the Emperor to the true faith.

OF THE EXTRAORDINARY FAVOUR WHICH THE GRAND KHAN SHOWS TO THE SAID CHRISTIANS

"The Grand Khan proteƈts the Chriſtians who in this said kingdom are obedient to the Holy Church of Rome, and makes provision for all their wants, for he shows them very great favour and love; and whenever they require anything for their churches, their crosses, or their sanƈtuaries, in honour of Jesus Christ, he awards it with great willingness. But they muſt pray to God for him and his health particularly in their sermons. And he is very anxious that they should all pray for him; and he really allows the brethren to preach the faith of God in the churches of the infidel which they call *vritanes* [*vritranes (virkharân ?)*], and he also permits the infidels to hear the brethren preach; so that the infidels go there very willingly and often with great devotion, and give the brethren much alms; and, likewise, the Emperor lends and sends his servants to aid and assiſt the Chriſtians when they require their services, and so solicit the Emperor."

While the Tartars remained masters of China, Christianity made great progress in the empire. At the present day (we say it with sorrow), there is not to be found in Mongolia the least vestige of what was done in ages gone by in favour of these nomad people. We trust, however, that the light of the Gospel will ere long shine once more in their eyes. The zeal of Europeans for the propagation of the faith will hasten the accomplishment of Noah's prophecy. Missionaries, the children of Japhet, will display their courage and devotion: they will fly to the aid of the children of Shem, and will esteem themselves happy to pass their days under the Mongol tents: "God shall enlarge Japhet, and he shall dwell in the tents of Shem."—Gen. ix. 27.

CHAPTER XII

Two months had elapsed since our departure from the Valley of Black Waters. During that period we had undergone in the desert continual fatigue and privations of every kind. Our health, it is true, was not as yet materially impaired, but we felt that our strength was leaving us, and we appreciated the necessity of modifying, for a few days, our late rough manner of living. In this point of view a country occupied by Chinese could not be otherwise than agreeable, and, in comparison with Tartary, would place within our reach all sorts of comforts.

As soon as we had passed the Hoang-Ho, we entered the small frontier town called Ché-Tsui-Dze, which is only separated from the river by a sandy beach. We proceeded to take up our lodging at the Hotel of Justice and Mercy (Jen-y-Ting [Jên-i-t'ing]). The house was large and recently built. With the exception of a solid floor of grey tiles, the whole construction was of wood. The host received us with that courtesy and attention which are always displayed when people desire to give a character to a new establishment; and, besides, the man having a most unprepossessing aspect, was anxious, probably, by his amiability of manners, to redeem his ugliness of feature; his eyes, which squinted horribly, were always turned away from the person whom he was addressing. However, if the organ of sight was defective, the organ of speech had marvellous elasticity. In his quality of an old soldier he had seen much, heard much, and, what is more, he remembered much; he was

THIBET, AND CHINA

acquainted with all countries, and had had to do with all sorts of men. His loquacity was far from being troublesome to us : he gave us details of every kind, as to the places great and small, which we had to visit before our arrival at Koukou-Noor. That part of Tartary was well known to him ; for, in the military part of his career, he had served againſt the Si-Fan. The day after our arrival he brought us, early in the morning, a large scroll on which were written, in order, the names of the towns, villages, hamlets, and places that we had to pass in the province of Kan-Sou ; and then he proceeded to give us a description of the localities with so much enthusiasm, so much gesticulation, and in such a loud key, that he made our heads turn.

The time which was not absorbed in long interviews, partly compulsory, partly voluntary, with our hoſt, was occupied in visiting the town. Ché-Tsui-Dze is built on the corner of an angle, formed on one side by the Alechan mountains, and on the other by the Yellow River. On its eaſtern bank the Hoang-Ho is bordered by dark hills, wherein are abundant coal mines, which the inhabitants work with great activity, and whence they derive their chief wealth. The suburbs of the town are occupied by great potteries, where you observe colossal urns, used in families as reservoirs of water, and large ſtoves of admirable conſtruction, and a large collection of vases of all shapes and sizes. There is in the province of Kan-Sou a large trade in this pottery.

At Ché-Tsui-Dze, provisions are abundant, varied, and of aſtonishingly moderate price. Nowhere, perhaps, can a person live so economically. At every hour of the day and night, itinerant reſtaurateurs bring to your house whatever provisions you need ; soups, ragouts of mutton and beef, vegetables, paſtry, rice, vermicelli, etc. There are dinners for every appetite, and for every purse—from the complicated banquet of the rich, to the simple and clear broth of the beggar. These reſtaurateurs are coming and going to and fro almoſt without interval. They are generally Moslems—a blue cap diſtinguishing them from the Chinese.

After two days' repose in the Inn of Juſtice and Mercy, we proceeded on our way. The environs of Ché-Tsui-Dze are uncultivated. On all sides, nothing is to be seen but sand and gravel, drifted by the annual inundation of the Yellow River. However, as you advance, the soil becoming imperceptibly higher, improves. An hour's diſtance from the town we crossed the Great Wall, or rather, passed over some miserable ruins that ſtill mark the ancient site of the celebrated rampart of China. The country soon becomes magnificent, and we could not but admire the agricultural genius of the Chinese people. The part of Kan-Sou which we were traversing is especially remarkable by its ingenious and extensive works for facilitating the irrigation of the fields.

By means of creeks cut in the banks of the Yellow River, the waters are conveyed into broad artificial canals; these again supply others of a larger size, which, in their turn, fill the ditches with which all the fields are surrounded. Sluices, great and small admirable in their simplicity, serve to raise the water and to carry it over all the inequalities of the land. The diſtribution of the water is perfeċtly arranged; each landowner waters his fields in his turn, and no one is allowed to open his flood-gate before his regularly appointed time.

Few villages are met with; but you observe, in all direċtions, farms of various sizes separated from one another by meadows. The eye does not reſt upon either groves or pleasure-gardens. Except a few large trees round the dwellings, all the land is devoted to the cultivation of corn ; they do not even reserve a space for ſtacking the harveſt, but pile it up on the tops of the houses, which are always flat-roofed. On the days of the general irrigation, the country gives you a perfeƈt idea of those famous inundations of the Nile, the descriptions of which have become so classic. The inhabitants traverse their fields in small skiffs, or in light carts with enormous wheels, and generally drawn by buffaloes.

These irrigations, so conducive to the fertility of the land, are a great peſt to travellers. The roads are generally covered with water and mud, so that you cannot use them, but muſt labour along the mounds which form the boundaries of the fields. When you have to guide camels over such roads it is the height of misery. We did not advance a single ſtep without the fear of seeing our baggage fall into the mud ; and more than once such an accident did occur, throwing us into infinite embarrassment. In faƈt, that the misfortune did not oftener befall us was solely attributable to the skill in mud-walking which our camels had acquired in their apprenticeship amongſt the marshes of the Ortous.

In the evening of our firſt day's march we arrived at a small village called Wang-Ho-Po [Wang-ho-p'o]; we had expeƈted to find here the same facility in obtaining provisions as at Ché-Tsui-Dze, but we were soon undeceived. The cuſtoms were not the same ; those amiable reſtaurateurs, with their baskets of ready dressed viands, were no longer visible. Forage-dealers were the only persons who came to offer their goods. We therefore commenced by giving the animals their rations, and afterwards went into the village to see if we could find any provisions for our own supper. On our return to the inn, we were obliged to cook our own supper ; the hoſt merely furnished us with water, coal, and a meal-kettle. Whilſt we were peaceably occupied in appreciating the results of our culinary labours, a great tumult arose in the court-yard of the inn. It was occasioned by a caravan of camels, conducted by Chinese merchants, who were going to the town of Ning-Hia. Destined for the same route as themselves, we soon entered into conversation. They told us that the direct road to Ning-Hia was so bad as to be impracticable, even for the best camels; but they added, they were acquainted with a cross-road, shorter and less dangerous, and they invited us to go with them. As they were to depart in the night, we called the host in order to settle our account. After the Chinese fashion, when sapeks are in question, on one side they ask much, on the other they offer too little; then there is a long squabble, and after mutual concessions you come to an agreement. As they thought us Tartars, it was quite a matter of course with them to ask us nearly triple the just amount; the result was that the dispute was twice as long as it ordinarily is. We had to discuss the matter vigorously; first, for ourselves, then for our beasts, for the room, the stabling, the watering, the kettle, the coal, the lamp, for every single item, until at length we got the innkeeper down to the tariff of civilized people. The unfortunate Tartar exterior, which, for other reasons, we had assumed, had been the occasion of our acquiring a certain degree of dexterity in discussions of this kind; for not a day passed, during our journey through the province of Kan-Sou, in which we had not to quarrel, in this manner, with innkeepers. Such quarrels, however, involve no disagreeable results; you dispute, and dispute, and then you come to an agreement, and the matter is over, and you are as good friends as ever with your antagonist.

It was scarcely past midnight when the Chinese camel-drivers were on foot, making, with great tumult, their preparations for departure. We rose, but it was to no purpose that we expedited the saddling of our animals; our fellow travellers were ready before us, promising to proceed slowly till we came up with them. The instant that our camels were ready, we departed. The night was dark; it was impossible to discover our guides. With the aid of a small lamp we sought traces of them, but we were not successful. Our only course, therefore, was to proceed, at chance, across these marshy plains, which were altogether unknown to us. We soon found ourselves so involved in the inundated soil that we dared advance no further, and halted at a bank, and there awaited daybreak.

As soon as the day dawned, we directed our steps, by a thousand ins and outs, towards a large walled town that we perceived in the distance; it was Ping-Lou-Hien [P'ing-lu-hsien], a town of the third class. Our arrival in this town occasioned lamentable disorder. The country is remarkable for the number and beauty of its mules; and at this juncture there was one of these standing, fastened by a halter, before each of the houses of the long street, which we were traversing from north to south. As we proceeded, all these animals, seized with fright at the sight of our camels, reared on their hind legs and dashed with violence against the shops; some broke the halters which confined them, tore off at a gallop, and overthrew, in their flight, the stalls of the street merchants. The people gathered together, sent forth shouts, anathematized the stinking Tartars, cursed the camels, and increased the disorder instead of lessening it. We were grieved to find that our presence had such unfortunate results; but what could we do? We could not render the mules less timid, nor prevent the camels from having such a frightful appearance. One of us, at last, determined to run on before the caravan and inform the people of the approach of the camels. This precaution diminished the evil, which did not, however, entirely cease until we were outside the gates of the town.

We had intended to breakfaſt at Ping-Lou-Hien; but, not having conciliated the good-will of its inhabitants, we dared not ſtop there. We had only the courage to purchase some provisions, for which we paid an exorbitant price, the occasion not being favourable for bargaining. At some diſtance from the town we came to a guard-house, where we ſtopped to reſt awhile, and to take our morning repaſt. These guard-houses are very numerous in China, the rule being that there shall be one of them at every half-league, on all the great roads. Of a singular and entirely Chinese conſtruction, these barracks consiſt of a little edifice either of wood or earth, but always whitewashed. In the centre is a kind of shed entirely without furniture, and with one large opening in front. This is reserved for unfortunate travellers, who, during the night, being overtaken by bad weather, cannot take refuge in an inn. On each side is a little room with doors and windows, and sometimes with a wooden bench painted red, by way of furniture. The exterior of the barrack is decorated with rude pictures, representing the gods of war, cavalry, and fabulous animals; on the walls of the shed are drawn all the weapons used in China, matchlock, bows, and arrows, lances, bucklers, and sabres of every description. At a little diſtance from the barracks, you see on the right a square tower, and on the left five small poſts ſtanding in a line. These denote the five lis which are the diſtance from one guard-house to another; frequently a large board, on two poles, informs the traveller of the names of the neareſt towns in that quarter. The directions of the board now before us were these:—

THIBET, AND CHINA

From Ping-Lou-Hien to Ning-Hia, fifty lis.
Northwards to Ping-Lou-Hien, five lis.
Southwards to Ning-Hia, forty-five lis.

In time of war, the square tower serves during the night for giving signals by means of fireworks, combined in particular ways. The Chinese relate that the Emperor Yeou-Wang [Yu-wang], the thirteenth emperor of the Tcheou [Chou] dynasty, 780 B.C., yielding to the absurd solicitations of his wife, ordered one night the signals of alarm to be made. The Empress wanted at once to amuse herself at the expense of the soldiers, and to ascertain, at the same time, whether these fireworks would really bring the troops to succour the capital. As the signals passed on to the provinces, the governors dispatched the military Mandarins and their forces to Peking. When the soldiers learned, on their arrival, that they had been called together for the capricious amusement of a woman, they returned home full of indignation. Shortly afterwards, the Tartars made an irruption into the empire, and advanced with rapidity to the very walls of the capital. This time the emperor gave the alarm in grave earnest, but throughout the provinces not a man stirred, thinking the Empress was again amusing herself; the consequence was that the Tartars entered Peking, and the imperial family was massacred.

The profound peace which China has enjoyed so long has much diminished the importance of these guard-houses. When they decay they are seldom repaired; in most cases their doors and windows have been carried off, and no one lives in them at all. On some of the more frequented roads they keep in repair the direction-boards and the posts.

The barrack where we halted was deserted. After having tied our beasts to a thick post, we entered a room, and took in peace a wholesome refreshment.

Travellers looked at us as they passed, and seemed a little surprised to find the place turned into a dining-room. The finer people, especially, smiled at these three uncivilized Mongols, as they deemed us. Our halt was brief. The direction-board officially announced that we had yet forty-five lis' march before we reached Ning-Hia, so that, considering the difficulty of the road, and the slowness of our camels, we had no time to lose. We proceeded along the banks of a magnificent canal, supplied by the waters of the Yellow River, and destined for the irrigation of the fields. Whilst the small caravan was slowly marching over a muddy and slippery ground, we saw advancing towards us a numerous party of horsemen. As the retinue came up, the innumerable labourers who were repairing the banks of the canal prostrated themselves on the earth, and exclaimed, " Peace and happiness to our father and mother ! " We at once understood that the person so addressed was a superior Mandarin. In accordance with the strict rules of Chinese etiquette, we ought to have dismounted, and have prostrated ourselves, as the others did ; but we considered that, in our quality of priests of the Western Heaven, we might dispense with this troublesome and disagreeable ceremony. We remained, therefore, gravely seated on our steeds, and advanced quietly. At sight of our camels, the other horsemen prudently removed to a respectful distance ; but the Mandarin, to show his bravery, spurred his horse, and compelled it to come towards us. He saluted us politely, and made inquiries in Mongol as to our health and journey. As his horse grew more and more afraid of our camels, he was constrained to cut short the conversation, and to rejoin his retinue, but he went away, triumphant at the reflection that he had found an opportunity of speaking Mongol, and of thus giving the horsemen of his suite a high notion of his knowledge. The Mandarin appeared to us to be a Tartar-Mantchou; he was making an official inspection of the irrigating canals.

We proceeded still some way along the banks of the same canal, meeting nothing on our road but some carriages on large wheels, drawn by buffaloes, and a few travellers mounted on asses of lofty stature. At length we discerned the lofty ramparts of Ning-Hia, and the numerous kiosks of the pagodas, which looked in the distance like tall cedars. The brick-walls of Ning-Hia are ancient, but well preserved. The antiquity, which has almost entirely covered them with moss and lichen, gives them a grand and imposing aspect. On every side they are surrounded by marshes, where canes, reeds, and water-lilies grow in abundance. The interior of the town is poor and miserable; the streets are dirty, narrow and tortuous; the houses, smoke-dried and tottering; you see at once that Ning-Hia is a town of great antiquity. Although situated near the frontiers of Tartary, the commerce there is inconsiderable.

After having gone nearly half up the central street, as we found we had still a league to go before we reached the other extremity, we resolved to make a halt. We entered a large inn, where we were soon followed by three individuals who impudently demanded our passports. We saw at once that we had to defend our purses against three swindlers. "Who are you that dare to demand our passports?" "We are employed by the great tribunal: it is not lawful for strangers to pass through the town of Ning-Hia without a passport." Instead of replying, we called the innkeeper and desired him to write upon a small piece of paper his name and that of his inn. Our demand greatly surprised him. "What is the good of this writing? what are you going to do with it?" "We shall soon have need of it. We are going to the great tribunal, to inform the Mandarin that three thieves have sought to rob us in your inn." At these words the three collectors of passports took to their heels; the landlord loaded them with imprecations, and the mob, who were already assembled in great numbers, laughed heartily. This little adventure caused us to be treated with especial respect. Next morning, ere day had dawned, we were awakened by a terrible noise, which arose all at once in the courtyard of the inn. Amid the confusion of numerous voices that seemed in violent dispute, we distinguished the words, "Stinking Tartar—camel—tribunal." We hastily dressed ourselves, and proceeded to investigate the nature of this sudden uproar, with which it struck us we had something to do, and so it turned out; our camels had devoured, in the course of the night, two cart-loads of osiers which were in the yard. The remnants still lay scattered about. The owners, strangers at the inn like ourselves, required to be paid the price of their goods, and their demand we considered perfectly just, only we thought that the landlord alone was bound to repair the damage. Before going to rest, we had warned him of the danger in which the osiers lay. We had told him that he had better place them elsewhere, for that the camels would certainly break their halters in order to get at them. The owners of the carts had joined with us in advising their removal, but the landlord had laughed at our fears, and asserted that camels did not like osiers. When we had sufficiently explained the matter, the mob, the standing jury among the Chinese, decided that the whole loss should be made good by the landlord; however, we had the generosity not to demand the price of the halters of our camels.

Immediately after this impartial judgment had been pronounced, we departed on our way. The southern part of the town seemed to us in even a worse condition than that which we had passed through on the preceding evening. Several portions were altogether pulled down and deserted; the only living things to be seen were a few swine, raking up the rubbish. The inhabitants of this large city were in a ſtate of utter misery. The greater number of them were covered with dirty rags. Their pale visages, haggard and thin, showed that they were often without the necessaries of life. Yet Ning-Hia was once a royal town, and, doubtless, opulent and flourishing.

In the tenth century, a prince of Tartar race, a native of Tou-Pa [T'o-pa], at present under the dominion of the Si-Fan, having induced a few hordes to follow him, came, and formed, despite the Chinese, a small ſtate not far from the banks of the Yellow River. He chose for his capital Hia-Tcheou, which afterwards came to be called Ning-Hia. It was from this town that this new kingdom was called Hia. It was in a very flourishing ſtate for more than two centuries; but in 1227, it was involved in the common ruin by the victories of Tchinggiskhan, the founder of the Mongol dynaſty. At present, Ning-Hia is one of the towns of the first class in the province of Kan-Sou.

On quitting Ning-Hia, you enter upon a magnificent road, almoſt throughout bordered by willows and jujube trees. At intervals, you find small inns, where the traveller can reſt and refresh himself at small expense. He can buy there tea, hard eggs, beans fried in oil, cakes, and fruit preserved in sugar or salt.

This day's journey was one of absolute recreation. Our camels, which had never travelled except in the deserts of Tartary, seemed thoroughly sensible to the charms of civilization; they turned their heads majeſtically right and left, observing, with manifeſt intereſt, all that presented itself on the way, men and things. They were not, however, so wholly absorbed in the investigations of the industry and manners of China as to withdraw their attention altogether from its natural productions. The willows, especially, attracted their interest; and when at all within their reach, they did not fail to pluck the tender branches, which they masticated with entire satisfaction. Sometimes, also, expanding their long necks, they would smell the various delicacies displayed over the inn doors, a circumstance which, of course elicited vehement protests from the innkeepers and other persons concerned. The Chinese were not less struck with our camels, than our camels were with China. The people collected from all directions to see the caravan pass, and ranged themselves on each side of the road; taking care, however, not to approach too near the animals which excited their surprise, and whose strength they instinctively dreaded.

Towards the close of this day's march we arrived at Hia-Ho-Po [Hsia-ho-p'o], a large village without ramparts. We proceeded to dismount at the Hotel of the Five Felicities (Ou-Fou-Tien [Wu-fu-tien]). We were occupied in giving forage to our beasts, when a horseman bearing a white button on his cap appeared in the court of the inn. Without dismounting, or making the accustomed salutation, he proceeded to bawl for the landlord. "The great Mandarin is on his way here," cried he, in curt and haughty tones; "let everything be clean and well swept. Let these Tartars go and lodge elsewhere; the great Mandarin will not have camels in the inn." Coming from the courier of a Mandarin, these insolent words did not surprise, but they irritated us. We pretended not to hear them, and quietly pursued our occupation. The innkeeper, seeing that we paid no attention to the order that had been made, advanced towards us, and laid before us, with politeness mingled with embarrassment, the state of the case. " Go," we said to him firmly; "go tell this white button that you have received us into your inn, that we will remain there, and that Mandarins have no right to come and take the places of travellers who are already lawfully established anywhere." The innkeeper was spared the trouble of reporting our words to white button, for they had been pronounced in such a manner that he could hear them himself. He dismounted forthwith; and addressing us directly, said, " The grand Mandarin will soon arrive; he has a large retinue, and the inn is small; besides, how would the horses venture to remain in this yard in presence of your camels?" " A man in the suite of a Mandarin, and, moreover, adorned like you with a white button, should know how to express himself—first, politely, and next, justly. We have a right to remain here, and no one shall expel us; and our camels shall remain tied to the door of our room." " The grand Mandarin has ordered me to come and prepare apartments for him, at the Hotel of the Five Felicities." " Very well; prepare them, but don't meddle with our things. If you cannot accommodate yourselves here, reason suggests that you go and seek a lodging elsewhere." " And the great Mandarin?" " Tell your Mandarin that there are three Lamas of the Western Heaven in this place, who are ready to return to Ning-Hia to discuss the matter with him: or before the tribunal, if it be necessary, at Peking; they know their way thither." White button mounted and disappeared. The host came to us immediately, and begged us to be resolute. " If you remain here," said he to us, " I am sure to profit a little by you; but if the Mandarin takes your place, his people will turn my inn upside down, will make us work all night, and then go away in the morning without paying a farthing. And besides that, if I were forced to send you away would not the Hotel of the Five Felicities lose its reputation? Who would afterwards enter an inn where they receive travellers only for the purpose of turning them out again?" Whilst the host was exhorting us to courage, the courier of the Mandarin reappeared; he dismounted and made us a profound bow, which we returned with the best grace possible. "Sirs Lamas," said he, "I have ridden through Hia-Ho-Po; there is no other convenient inn. Who says you are bound to cede to us your place? To speak so were to talk inconsistently with reason! Now, observe, Sirs Lamas; we are all travellers: we are all men far distant from our families; cannot we consult together in a friendly manner and arrange the matter like brothers?" "No doubt," said we, "men ought always to deal together like brothers; that is the true principle. When we travel, we should live like travellers. When each gives way a little, all are, in the end, accommodated." "Excellent saying! excellent saying!" cried the courier; and thereupon the most profound bows recommenced on both sides.

After this brief introduction, which had perfectly reconciled both parties, we deliberated amicably how we should best arrange our common residence in the Hotel of the Five Felicities. It was agreed that we should keep the room in which we were already installed, and that we should tie up our camels in a corner of the court, so that they might not terrify the horses of the Mandarin. The courier was to dispose of the rest of the place as he pleased. We hastened to remove our camels from the door of our room and to place them as had been settled. Just after sunset we heard the Mandarin's party approaching. The two folding doors of the great gate were solemnly opened, and a carriage drawn by three mules advanced into the middle of the court of the inn, escorted by a numerous body of horsemen. In the carriage was seated a man about sixty years old, with grey muſtachios and beard, and having his head covered with a red hood. This was the great Mandarin. On entering, he scanned, with a quick and searching glance, the interior of the inn. Perceiving us, and remarking, above all, three camels at the end of the court, the muscles of his lean face were suddenly contraćted. When all the horsemen had dismounted they invited him to descend from his vehicle. "What!" cried he, in a dry, angry voice; "who are those Tartars? what are those camels? let the landlord be brought to me." On this unexpećted summons the hoſt took to his heels, and white button remained for an inſtant like one petrified; his face turned pale, then red, then olive-colour. However, he made an effort, advanced to the carriage, put one knee to the ground, then rose, and approaching the ear of his maſter, spoke to him for some time, in an undertone. The dialogue ended, the great Mandarin condescended to dismount, and after having saluted us with his hand in a protećting manner, he retired like a simple mortal to the small room which had been prepared for him.

The triumph we had thus obtained in a country, admission even to which was prohibited to us under pain of death,[1] gave us prodigious courage. These terrible Mandarins, who had formerly occasioned us such alarm, ceased to be terrible to us the inſtant that we dared to approach them, and to look at them closely. We saw men puffed up with pride and insolence, pitiless tyrants towards the weak, but dastardly in the extreme before men of energy. From this moment we found ourselves as much at our ease

[1] At this period there was no French embassy in China, and no treaty in favour of Europeans. All missionaries, therefore, who penetrated into the interior were, *ipso facto*, liable to be put to death.

in China as anywhere else, and able to travel without fear, and with our heads erect in the open face of day.

After two days' journey we arrived at Tchong-Wei [Chung-wei], on the banks of the Yellow River, a walled town of moderate size. Its cleanliness, its good condition, its air of comfort, contrasted singularly with the wretchedness and ugliness of Ning-Hia; and judging merely from its innumerable shops, all well stocked, and from the large population crowding its streets, we should pronounce Tchong-Wei to be a place of much commercial importance; yet the Chinese of this district have no notion of navigation, and not a boat is to be seen on the Yellow River in this quarter—a circumstance remarkable in itself, and confirmatory of the opinion that the inhabitants of this part of Kan-Sou are of Thibetian and Tartar origin; for it is well known that the Chinese are everywhere passionately addicted to navigating streams and rivers.

On quitting Tchong-Wei we passed the Great Wall, which is wholly composed of uncemented stones, placed one on top of the other; and we re-entered Tartary for a few days, in the kingdom of the Alechan. More than once the Mongol Lamas had depicted in frightful colours the horrors of the Alechan mountains. We were now in a position to see with our own eyes that the reality exceeds all description of this frightful district. The Alechans are a long chain of mountains, wholly composed of moving sand, so fine that when you touch it, it seems to flow through your finger like a liquid. It were superfluous to add that, amid these gigantic accumulations of sand, you do not find anywhere the least trace of vegetation. The monotonous aspect of these immense sands is only relieved by the vestiges of a small insect, that, in its capricious and fantastical sports, describes a thousand arabesques on the moving mass, which is so smooth and fine that you

THIBET, AND CHINA

can trace upon it the meanderings of an ant. In crossing these mountains, we experienced inexpressible labour and difficulty. At each step our camels sank up to the knees; and it was only by leaps that they could advance. The horses underwent still greater difficulties, their hoofs having less purchase on the sand than the large feet of the camels. As for ourselves, forced to walk, we had to keep constant watch that we did not fall from the top of these mountains, which seemed to disappear under our feet into the Yellow River, whose waters flowed beneath us. Fortunately, the weather was calm. If the wind had blown, we should certainly have been swallowed up and buried alive in avalanches of sand. The Alechan mountains themselves appear to have been formed by the sand which the north wind incessantly sweeps before it from the Chamo [Shamo], or Great Desert of Gobi. The Yellow River arrests these sandy inundations, and thus preserves the province of Kan-Sou from their destructive assaults. It is to the great quantity of sand that falls into it from the Alechan mountains that this river owes the yellow colour which has given to it its name Hoang-Ho (Yellow River). Above the Alechan mountains its waters are clear and limpid.

By degrees, hills succeeded to mountains, the sand heaps imperceptibly diminished, and towards the close of the day we arrived at the village of Ever-Flowing Waters (Tchang-Lieou-Chouy [Ch'ang-liu-shui]). Here we found, amidst those sand hills, an oasis of surpassing beauty. A hundred rills disporting through the streets, trees, little houses built of stone, and painted white or red, communicated to the spot an aspect highly picturesque. Weary as we were, we halted at Ever-Flowing Waters with inexpressible delight; but the poetry of the thing vanished when we came to settle with our host. Not only provisions but forage came from Tchong-Wei, and the transport being very difficult, they were dear to a degree that altogether disconcerted our economical arrangements. For ourselves and our animals, we were obliged to disburse 1,600 sapeks, a matter of nearly seven shillings. Only for this circumstance we should perhaps have quitted with regret the charming village of Tchang-Lieou-Chouy; but there is always something which intervenes to aid man in detaching himself from the things of this world.

On quitting Tchang-Lieou-Chouy, we took the road followed by the Chinese exiles on their way to Ili. The country is somewhat less dreadful than that which we had travelled through on the preceding day, but it is still very dismal. Gravel had taken the place of sand, and with the exception that it produced a few tufts of grass, hard and prickly, the soil was arid and barren. We reached, in due course, Kao-Tan-Dze [Kao-tan-tzŭ], a village repulsive and hideous beyond all expression. It consists of a few miserable habitations, rudely constructed of black earth, and all of them inns. Provisions are even more scarce there than at Ever-Flowing Waters, and correspondingly dearer. Everything has to be brought from Tchong-Wei, for the district produces nothing, not even water. Wells have been sunk to a very great depth, but nothing has been found except hard, rocky, moistureless earth. The inhabitants of Kao-Tan-Dze have to fetch their water a distance of more then twelve miles, and they accordingly charge travellers a monstrous price for every drop. A single bucket costs sixty sapeks. Had we attempted to water our camels we should have had to lay out fifty fifties of sapeks; we were therefore forced to be content with drinking ourselves, and giving a draught to our horses. As to the camels, they had to await better days and a less inhospitable soil.

THIBET, AND CHINA

Kao-Tan-Dze, miserable and hideous as it is, has not even the advantage of that tranquility and security which its poverty and its solitude might reasonably be supposed to give it. It is constantly ravaged by brigands, so that there is not a house in it which does not bear the marks of fire and devastation. At the first inn where we presented ourselves, we were asked whether we desired to have our animals defended against robbers. This question threw us into utter amazement, and we requested further explanation of a point which struck us as so very singular. We were informed that at Kao-Tan-Dze there are two sorts of inns : inns where they fight and inns where they do not fight : and that the prices at the former sort are four times greater than those at the latter. This explanation gave us a general notion of the matter ; but still we requested some details. " How ! " said the people. " Don't you know that Kao-Tan-Dze is constantly attacked by brigands ? " " Yes, we know that." " If you lodge in an inn where they don't fight, any brigands that come will drive off your animals, for no one has undertaken to protect them. If, on the contrary, you lodge in an inn where they fight, you have a good chance of preserving your property, unless the brigands are the more numerous party, which sometimes happens." All this seemed to us to very singular, and very disagreeable. However, it was necessary to make up our minds on the subject. After grave reflection we decided upon lodging in an inn where they fought. It occurred to us that the worthy innkeepers of Kao-Tan-Dze had an understanding with the brigands, having for its result the spoliation of travellers, one way or the other, and that therefore it was better, upon the whole, to pay the larger sum, by way of blackmail, than to lose our animals, whose loss would involve our own destruction.

Upon entering the fighting inn to which we had been directed, we found everything about it on a war footing. The walls were regularly covered with lances, arrows, bows and matchlocks. The presence of these weapons, however, by no means rendered us perfectly satisfied as to our safety, and we resolved not to lie down at all, but to keep watch throughout the night.

Kao-Tan-Dze, with its robber assailants and its pauper population, was to us an inexplicable place. We could not conceive how men should make up their minds to inhabit a detestably ugly country like this, sterile, waterless, remote from any other inhabited place, and desolated by the constant inroad of brigands. What could be their object ? What possible advantage could be their inducement ? We turned the matter over in all ways; we framed all sorts of suppositions ; but we could achieve no likely solution of the problem. During the first watch of the night, we conversed with the innkeeper, who seemed a frank, open sort of man enough. He related to us infinite anecdotes of brigands, full of battle, murder, and fire. "But," said we, "why don't you leave this detestable country ? " "Oh," replied he, "we are not free men ; the inhabitants of Kao-Tan-Dze are all exiles, who are only excused from going to Ili on the condition that we remain here for the purpose of supplying with water the Mandarins and soldiers who pass through the place, escorting exiles. We are bound to furnish water gratuitously to all the government officers who come to the village." When we found that we were among exiles, we were somewhat reassured, and began to think that, after all, these people were not in collusion with the brigands ; for we learned that a petty Mandarin lived in the village to superintend the population. We conceived a hope that we might find some Christians at Kao-Tan-Dze, but the innkeeper informed us that there were none, for that all exiles on account of the religion of the Lord of Heaven went on to Ili.

After what the innkeeper had told us, we conceived that we might, without risk, take a brief repose; we accordingly threw ourselves on our goat-skins, and slept soundly till daybreak, the favour of God preserving us from any visit on the part of the brigands.

During the greater part of the day, we proceeded along the road to Ili, traversing with respect, with a degree of religious veneration, that path of exile so often sanctified by the footsteps of the confessors of the faith, and conversing, as we went, about those courageous Christians, those strong souls, who, rather than renounce their religion, had abandoned their families and their country, and gone to end their days in unknown lands. Let us fervently pray that Providence may send missionaries, full of devotion, to bear the consolations of the faith amongst these our exiled brethren.

The road to Ili brought us to the Great Wall, which we passed over without dismounting. This work of the Chinese nation, of which so much is said and so little known, merits brief mention here. It is known that the idea of raising walls as a fortification against the incursions of enemies was not peculiar in old times to China: antiquity presents us with several examples of these labours elsewhere. Besides the works of this kind executed in Syria, Egypt, Media, and on the continent of Europe, there was, by order of the Emperor Septimus Severus, a great wall constructed in the northern part of Britain. No other nation, however, ever effected anything of the sort on so grand a scale as the Great Wall, commenced by Tsin-Chi-Hoang-Ti [Ch'in Shih-Huang-ti], A.D. 214. The Chinese call it Wan-li-Tchang-Tching [Wan-li-ch'ang-ch'eng] "the Great Wall of ten thousand lis". A prodigious number of labourers was employed upon it, and the works of this gigantic enterprise continued for ten years. The Great Wall extends from the westernmost point of Kan-Sou to the Eastern Sea. The importance of this enormous construction has been variously estimated by those who have written upon China, some of whom preposterously exaggerate its importance, while others laboriously seek to ridicule it; the probability being that this diversity of opinion arises from each writer having judged the whole work by the particular specimen to which he had access. Mr. Barrow, who, in 1793, accompanied Lord Macartney to China as historiographer to the British embassy, made this calculation: he supposed that there were in England and Scotland 1,800,000 houses, and estimating the masonry work of each to be 2,000 cubic feet, he propounded that the aggregate did not contain as much material as the Great Wall of China, which, in his opinion, was enough for the construction of a wall to go twice round the world. It is evident that Mr. Barrow adopted, as the basis of his calculations, the Great Wall such as he saw it north of Peking, where the construction is really grand and imposing; but it is not to be supposed that this barrier, raised against the irruptions of the barbarians, is, throughout its extent, equally high, wide, and solid. We have crossed it at fifteen different points and on several occasions have travelled for whole days parallel with it, and never once losing sight of it, and often, instead of the great double turreted rampart that exists towards Peking, we have found a mere low wall of brickwork, or even earth work. In some places, indeed, we have found this famous barrier reduced to its simplest expression, and composed merely of flint-stones roughly piled up. As to the foundation wall, described by Mr. Barrow, as consisting of large masses of free-stone cemented with

THIBET, AND CHINA

mortar, we can only say that we have never discovered the slightest traces of any such work. It is indeed obvious that Tsin-Chi-Hoang-Ti, in the execution of this great undertaking, would fortify with special care the vicinity of the capital, as being the point to which the Tartar hordes would first direct their aggressive steps. It is natural, farther, to conceive, that the Mandarins charged with the execution of the Emperor's plan, would, with especial conscientiousness, perfect the works which were more immediately under the Emperor's eye, and content themselves with erecting a more or less nominal wall at remote points of the empire, particularly those where the Tartars were little to be feared, as, for example, the position of the Ortous and the Alechan mountains.

The barrier of San-Yen-Tsin [San-yen-tsing], which stands a few paces beyond the wall, is noted for its great strictness towards the Tartars who seek to enter within the intramural empire. The village possesses only one inn, which is kept by the chief of the frontier guards. Upon entering the court-yard we found several groups of camels assembled there belonging to a great Tartar caravan that had arrived on the preceding evening. There was, however, plenty of room for us, the establishment being on a large scale. We had scarcely taken possession of our chamber than the passport question was started. The chief of the guards himself made an official demand for them. " We have none," replied we. At this answer his features beamed with satisfaction, and he declared that we could not proceed unless we paid a considerable sum. " How! a passport or money ? Know that we have travelled China from one end to the other, that we have been to Peking, and that we have journeyed through Tartary, without anything in the shape of a passport, and without having paid a single sapek in lieu of a passport. You, who are a chief of guards, must know that Lamas are privileged to travel wherever they please without passports." "What words are these ? Here is a caravan at this very moment in the house, and the two Lamas who are with it have both given me their passports like the rest of the party." "If what you say be true, the only conclusion is, that there are some Lamas who take passports with them and others who do not. We are in the number of those who do not." Finding at last that the dispute was becoming tedious, we employed a decisive course. "Well, come," said we, "we will give you the money you ask, but you shall give us in return a paper signed by yourself, in which you shall acknowledge that, before you would permit us to pass, you exacted from us a sum of money instead of passports. We shall then address ourselves to the first Mandarin we meet, and ask him whether what you have done is consistent with the laws of the empire." The man at once gave up the point. "Oh," said he, "since you have been to Peking, no doubt the Emperor has given you special privileges," and then he added in a whisper, and smilingly, "Don't tell the Tartars here that I have let you pass *gratis*."

It is really pitiable to observe these poor Mongols travelling in China; everybody thinks himself entitled to fleece them, and everybody succeeds in doing so to a marvellous extent. In all directions they are encountered by impromptu custom-house officers, by persons who exact money from them on all sorts of pretences, for repairing roads, building bridges, constructing pagodas, etc. etc. First, the despoilers proffer to render them great services, call them brothers and friends, and give them wholesale warnings against ill-designing persons who want to rob them. Should this method not effect an unloosening of the purse-strings, the rascals have recourse to intimidation, frighten them horribly with visions of

THIBET, AND CHINA

Mandarins, laws, tribunals, prisons, punishments, threaten to take them up, and treat them, in short, juſt like mere children. The Mongols themselves materially aid the imposition by their total ignorance of the manners and cuſtoms of China. At an inn, inſtead of using the room offered to them, and putting their animals in the ſtable, they pitch their tent in the middle of the court-yard, plant ſtakes about it, and faſten their camels to these. Very frequently they are not permitted to indulge this fancy, and in this case they certainly enter the room allotted to them, and which they regard in the light of a prison; but they proceed there in a manner truly ridiculous. They set up their trivet with their kettle upon it, in the middle of the room, and make a fire beneath with *argols*, of which they take care to have a ſtore with them. It is to no purpose they are told that there is in the inn a large kitchen where they can cook their meals far more comfortably to themselves; nothing will dissuade them from their own kettle and their own aboriginal fire in the middle of the room. When night comes they unrol their hide-carpets round the fire, and there lie down. They would not liſten for a moment to the proposition of sleeping upon the beds or upon the *kang* they find in the room ready for their use. The Tartars of the caravan we found in the inn at San-Yen-Tsin were allowed to carry on their domeſtic matters in the open air. The simplicity of these poor children of the desert was so great that they seriously asked us whether the innkeeper would make them pay anything for the accommodation he afforded them.

We continued on our way through the province of Kan-Sou, proceeding to the south-weſt. The country, interſected with ſtreams and hills, is generally fine, and the people apparently well off. The great variety of its productions is owing partly to a temperate climate and a soil naturally fertile, but, above all, to the activity and skill of the agriculturists. The chief product of the district is wheat, of which the people make excellent loaves, like those of Europe. They sow scarcely any rice, procuring almost all the little they consume from the adjacent provinces. Their goats and sheep are of fine breed, and constitute, with bread, the principal food of the population. Numerous and inexhaustible mines of coal place fuel within everyone's reach. It appeared to us that in Kan-Sou anyone might live very comfortably at extremely small cost.

At two days' distance from the barrier of San-Yen-Tsin we were assailed by a hurricane which exposed us to very serious danger. It was about ten o'clock in the morning. We had just crossed a hill, and were entering upon a plain of vast extent, when, all of a sudden, a profound calm pervaded the atmosphere. There was not the slightest motion in the air, and yet the cold was intense. Insensibly, the sky assumed a dead-white colour; but there was not a cloud to be seen. Soon, the wind began to blow from the west; in a very short time it became so violent that our animals could scarcely proceed. All nature seemed to be in a state of dissolution. The sky, still cloudless, was covered with a red tint. The fury of the wind increased; it raised in the air enormous columns of dust, sand, and decayed vegetable matter, which it then dashed right and left, here, there, and everywhere. At length the wind blew so tremendously and the atmosphere became so utterly disorganized that, at midday, we could not distinguish the very animals upon which we were riding. We dismounted, for it was impossible to advance a single step, and after enveloping our faces in handkerchiefs in order that we might not be blinded with the dust, we sat down beside our animals. We had no notion where we were;

our only idea was that the frame of the world was unloosening, and that the end of all things was close at hand. This lasted for more than an hour. When the wind had somewhat mitigated, and we could see around us, we found that we were all separated from one another, and at considerable distances, for amid that frightful tempest, bawl as loud as we might, we could not hear each other's voices. So soon as we could at all walk we proceeded towards a farm at no great distance, but which we had not before perceived. The hurricane having thrown down the great gate of the court we found no difficulty in entering, and the house itself was opened to us with almost equal facility; for Providence had guided us in our distress to a family truly remarkable for its hospitality.

Immediately upon our arrival our hosts heated some water for us to wash with. We were in a frightful state; from head to foot we were covered with dust which had saturated, so to speak, our clothes and almost our skins. Had such a storm encountered us on the Alechan mountains we should have been buried alive in the sand, and all trace of us lost for ever.

When we found that the worst of the storm was over, and that the wind had subsided to occasional gusts, we proposed to proceed, but our kind hosts would not hear of this; they said they would lodge us for the night, and that our animals should have plenty of food and water. Their invitation was so sincere and so cordial, and we so greatly needed rest, that we readily availed ourselves of their offer.

A very slight observation of the inhabitants of Kan-Sou will satisfy one that they are not of purely Chinese origin. The Tartaro-Thibetian element is manifestly predominant amongst them; and it displays itself with special emphasis in the character, manners, and language of the country people. You do not find amongſt them the exaggerated politeness which diſtinguishes the Chinese; but, on the other hand, they are remarkable for their open-heartedness and hospitality. In their particular form of Chinese you hear an infinitude of expressions which belong to the Tartar and Thibetian tongues. The conſtruction of their phrases, inſtead of following the Chinese arrangement, always exhibits the inversions in use among the Mongols. Thus, for example, they don't say, with the Chinese, open the door, shut the window; but, the door open, the window shut. Another peculiarity is that milk, butter, curds, all insupportably odious to a Chinese, are especially favourite foods with the inhabitants of Kan-Sou. But it is, above all, their religious turn of mind which diſtinguishes them from the Chinese, a people almoſt universally sceptical and indifferent as to religious matters. In Kan-Sou there are numerous and flourishing Lamaseries in which reformed Buddhism is followed. The Chinese, indeed, have plenty of pagodas and idols of all sorts and sizes in their houses; but with them religion is limited to this external representation, whereas in Kan-Sou everyone prays often and long and fervently. Now prayer, as everyone knows, is that which distinguishes the religious from the irreligious man.

Besides differing materially from the other peoples of China, the inhabitants of Kan-Sou differ materially amongſt themselves, the Dchiahours marking that subdivision, perhaps, more diſtinctly than any of the other tribes. They occupy the country commonly called San-Tchouan "Three Valleys," the birthplace of our cameleer Samdadchiemba. The Dchiahours possess all the knavery and cunning of the Chinese, without any of their courtesy, and without their polished form of language, and they are accordingly feared and disliked by all their neighbours. When they consider

THIBET, AND CHINA

themselves in any way injured or insulted, they have immediate recourse to the dagger, by way of remedy. With them the man moft to be honoured is he who has committed the greatest number of murders. They have a language of their own, a medley of Mongol, Chinese, and Eaftern Thibetian. According to their own account, they are of Tartar origin. If it be so, they may fairly claim to have preserved, in all its integrity, the ferocious and independent charaƈter of their anceftors, whereas the present occupiers of Mongolia have greatly modified and softened their manners.

Though subjeƈt to the Emperor of China, the Dchiahours are immediately governed by a sort of hereditary sovereign belonging to their tribe, and who bears the title of *Tou-Sse* [*t'u-ssŭ*]. There are in Kan-Sou, and on the frontiers of the province of Sse-Tchouan [Ssŭ-ch'uan] several other tribes, having their own special rulers and their own especial laws. All these tribes are called Tou-Sse, to which each adds, by way of diftinƈtion, the family name of its chief or sovereign. Samdadchiemba, for example, belonged to the Ki-Tou-Sse [Chi-t'u ssu] tribe of Dchiahours. Yang-Tou-Sse [Yang-t'u-ssu] is the moft celebrated and the moft redoubtable of all these tribes, and for a long time exercised great influence at Lha-Ssa, the capital of Thibet, but this influence was deftroyed in 1845, in consequence of an event which we shall relate by-and-by.

After thoroughly refting from our fatigue, we departed early next morning. Everywhere, on our way, we saw traces of the tempeft, in trees uprooted and torn, houses unroofed, fields devaftated and almoft entirely deprived of their surface soil. Before the end of the day, we arrived at Tchoang-Long [Chuang-lang], more commonly called Ping-Fang [P'ing-fan], an ordinary town, with a tolerable amount of trade, but in no way noticeable, whether for its beauty or for its deformity. We went to lodge at the Hotel of the Three Social Relations (San-Kan-Tien [San-kan-tien]), whose landlord was one of the best humoured and most amusing persons we had hitherto met with. He was a thorough Chinese : to give us a proof of his sagacity he asked us, point blank, whether we were not English ; and that we might thoroughly understand his question, he added that he understood by Ing-Kie-Li [Ying-chi-li], the sea-devils (Yang-Kouei-Dze [Yang-kuei-tzŭ]) who were making war at Canton. "No, we are not English ; nor are we devils of any sort, whether of sea or land." An idler who was standing by, interposed to prevent the ill effect of this awkward question. "You," said he to the innkeeper, "you know nothing of physiognomy. How could you suppose that these people are Yang-Kouei-Dze ? Don't you know that they have all blue eyes and red hair ? " "You're right," returned the host, "I had not thought of that." "No," said we "clearly you had not thought at all. Do you suppose that sea-monsters could live as we do, on land, and ride on horses ? " "You're right, quite so ; the Ing-Kie-Li, they say, never venture to quit the sea, for when they're on land they tremble and die like fish out of water." We were favoured with a good deal more information of the same class, respecting the manners and character of the sea-devils, the up-shot of which, so far as we were concerned, was the full admission that we did not belong to the same race.

A little before night, an immense bustle pervaded the inn. A Living Buddha had arrived, with a numerous train, on his return from a journey into Thibet, his native country, to the grand Lamasery, of which for many years he had been the superior, and which was situated in the country of the Khalkhas, towards the Russian frontier. As he entered the inn,

THIBET, AND CHINA

a multitude of zealous Buddhists, who had been awaiting him in the great court-yard, prostrated themselves before him, their faces to the ground. The Grand Lama proceeded to the apartment which had been prepared for him, and night coming, the crowd withdrew. When the inn had become tolerably clear, this strange personage gave full play to his curiosity; he poked about all over the inn, going into every room, and asking everybody all sorts of questions, without sitting down or staying anywhere. As we expected, he favoured us also with a visit. When he entered our chamber, we were gravely seated on the *kang*; we studiously abstained from rising at his entrance, and contented ourselves with welcoming him by a motion of our hands. He seemed rather surprised at this unceremonious reception, but not at all disconcerted. Standing in the middle of the room, he stared at each of us intently, one after the other. We, like himself, preserving entire silence all the while, exercised the privilege of which he had set us the example, and examined him closely. He seemed about fifty years old; he was enveloped in a great robe of yellow taffeta, and he wore red velvet Thibetian boots, with remarkably thick soles. He was of the middle height, and comfortably stout; his dark brown face denoted extreme good nature, but there was in his eyes, when you attentively examined them, a strange, wild, haggard expression, that was very alarming. At length he addressed us in the Mongol tongue, which he spoke with great facility. In the first instance, the conversation was nothing more than the ordinary phrases exchanged between travellers, about one another's health, destination, horses, the weather, and so on. When we found him prolonging his visit we invited him to sit down beside us on the *kang*; he hesitated for a moment, conceiving, no doubt, that in his quality as Living Buddha it did not become him to place himself on a level with mere mortals like ourselves. However, as he had a great desire for a chat, he at laſt made up his mind to sit down, and in fact he could not, without compromising his dignity, remain any longer ſtanding while we sat.

A Breviary that lay on a small table beside us immediately attraƈted his attention, and he asked permission to examine it. Upon our assenting, he took it up with both hands, admired the binding and the gilt edges, opened it and turned over the leaves, and then closing it again, raised it reverently to his forehead, saying, "It is your Book of Prayer: we should always honour and respeƈt prayer." By-and-by he added, "Your religion and ours are like this," and so saying he put the knuckles of his two fore-fingers together. "Yes," said we, "you are right; your creed and ours are in a state of hoſtility, and we do not conceal from you that the objeƈt of our journey and our labours is to substitute our prayers for those which are used in your Lamaseries." "I know that," he replied, smilingly; "I knew that long ago." He then took up the Breviary again, and asked us explanations of the engravings. He evinced no surprise at what we told him, only, when we had related to him the subjeƈt of the plate representing the crucifixion, he shook his head compassionately, and raised his joined hands to his head. After he had examined all the prints, he took the Breviary once more in both hands, and raised it respeƈtfully to his forehead. He then rose, and having saluted us with great affability, withdrew, we escorting him to the door.

Upon being left alone, we felt for a moment stupified as it were at this singular visit. We tried to conceive what thoughts could have filled the mind of the Living Buddha as he sat there beside us, and what impression he had derived from the sketch we gave him of our holy religion. Now, it seemed to us that ſtrange feelings muſt have arisen in his heart; and then again, we imagined that after all he had felt nothing whatever, but that, a mere ordinary person, he had mechanically availed himself of his position, without refleƈtion, and without himself attaching any real importance to his pretended divinity. We became so intereſted in the point, that we determined to see this personage once more before we departed. As that departure was fixed for an early hour next morning we went, accordingly, to return his visit before we slept. We found him in his apartment, seated on thick large cushions, covered with magnificent tiger-skins; before him ſtood, on a small lacquer table, a silver tea-pot, and a ſteatite cup in a richly worked gold saucer. He was evidently in the laſt ſtage of ennui, and was correspondingly delighted to see us. For fear he should take it into his head to let us remain ſtanding, we proceeded, upon entering the room, to seat ourselves beside him. His suite, who were assembled in a contiguous room, which opened into their principal's, were extremely shocked at this familiarity, and gave utterance to a murmur of disapprobation. The Buddha himself, however, who passed over the circumſtance with a half-angry smile, rang a silver bell, and desired a young Lama, who obeyed the summons, to bring us some tea with milk. "I have often seen your countrymen," said he; "my Lamasery ſtands at no great diſtance from your native land; the Oros (Russians) often pass the frontier, but I have never known any of them before to advance so far as you." "We are not Russians" said we, "our country is a long way from Russia." This answer seemed to surprise the Buddha; he looked at us closely for some time, and then said, "From what country come you, then?" "We are from the Weſtern Heaven." "Oh! you are Peling [Phyiling

TRAVELS IN TARTARY,

(Phyi-gling)],[1] of Dchou-Ganga [Jün-Ganga (Jä'ün-Ganga)] (Eastern Ganges), and your city is Galgata (Calcutta)." The notions of the Living Buddha, it is observable, though not exactly correct, were not altogether destitute of meaning; he could of course only class us among the peoples who were known to him, and in supposing us first Russians and then English, he manifested an acquaintance with geographical terms by no means contemptible under the circumstances. He would not be persuaded, however, that we were not either Oros or Peling of Galgata. "But after all," said he, "what matters it from what country we come, since we are all brothers? Only let me advise you, while you are in China, to be cautious not to tell everybody who you are. The Chinese are a suspicious and ill-conditioned race, and they might do you a mischief." He then talked to us about Thibet, and the dreadful road thither that we should have to traverse. Judging from our appearance, he said he doubted very much whether we were strong enough for the undertaking. The words and the manner of the Grand Lama were perfectly affable and kind, but there was a look in his eye to which we could not reconcile ourselves. We seemed to read there something infernal, fiend-like. But for this circumstance, which perhaps after all was mere fancy on our part, we should have esteemed our Grand Lama friend a most amiable personage.

From Tchoang-Long, or Ping-Fang we proceeded to Ho-Kiao-Y [Ho-chiao-i], or, as it is named on the maps, Tai-Toung-Fou [Ta-t'ung]. The latter is the ancient denomination of the place, and is no longer in popular use. The road was,

[1] The Thibetians call the English in Hindostan, Peling, a word signifying stranger, and equivalent to the Chinese *y-jin* [*I-jen*], which the Europeans translate, barbarian, probably with the notion of flattering their self-love by the implied contrast.

THIBET, AND CHINA

throughout, covered with oxen, asses, and small carts, all with loads of coals. We resolved to sojourn for a few days at Ho-Kiao-Y, for the purpose of giving rest to our animals, whose strength had become almost exhausted; the horses and the mule, in particular, had tumours on their sides, occasioned by the constant rubbing of the saddle, and it was essential to have these cured before we proceeded further. Having formed this project, our next business was to inspect all the inns in the place, for the purpose of selecting as our abode that which presented the most favourable indications, and the Hotel of the Temperate Climates was ultimately honoured with our choice.

Ever since our entry into the province of Kan-Sou, not a day had passed in which Samdadchiemba had not enlarged upon the subject of the Three Valleys and the Dchiahours. Though there was no very immense amount of sentiment about him, he had a great desire to revisit his native place, and to see once more any members of his family who might happen to be surviving there. We could not do otherwise than aid so laudable a purpose. Accordingly, when we were established in the Hotel of the Temperate Climates, we granted to our cameleer eight days' leave of absence, wherein to revisit his so long abandoned home. Eight days appeared to him fully sufficient for the purpose: two to go in, two to come back in, and four to be spent in the bosom of his family, relating to them all the marvels he had witnessed abroad. We allowed him the use of a camel, that he might appear among his friends with the greater distinction; and five ounces of silver which we placed in his purse completed his recommendations to a favourable reception.

While awaiting the return of our Dchiahour, we were exclusively occupied in taking care of our animals, and of ourselves. Every day we had to go into the town to buy our provisions, then to cook them, and, morning and evening, to water our cattle at some distance from the inn. The master of the house was one of those good-natured persons who, in their very eagernesss to oblige, become troublesome; and whose amiability of intention scarcely induces one to pardon their importunity of attention. The worthy man was incessantly thrusting himself into our room, to give us advice how we ought to do this, that and the other. After altering the position of everything in the chamber according to his fancy for the moment, he would go up to the furnace, take off the lid of the saucepan, dip his finger into the ragout, and licking it to see how the mess was going on, add salt or ginger, or other condiment, to the infinite annoyance of M. Huc, who was officially charged with the cooking department. At other times he would loudly protest that we knew nothing about making up a fire, that the coals ought to be laid so, and the wood so, and that a draught of air ought to be kept up in this or that direction; and thereupon he would take up the tongs and overturn our fire, to the immense discomfiture of M. Gabet, who presided over that department. At night he appeared to consider himself especially indispensable, and would skip in every quarter of an hour to see that the lamp was burning properly, and that the wick was long enough, or short enough, and what not. At times he had really the air of asking us how it was possible that we had contrived to live without him, the one of us up to thirty-two years of age, the other up to thirty-seven. However, among the exuberances of attentions with which he bored us, there was one which we readily accepted; it was in the matter of warming our beds, the process of which was so singular, so peculiar, that we had never had the opportunity elsewhere of observing it.

THIBET, AND CHINA

The *kang*, a species of furnace on which you lie, is not in Kan-Sou constructed altogether of brickwork, as is the case in Northern China, but the upper flooring consists of moveable planks, placed closely beside one another. When they want to heat the *kang* for sleeping purposes, they remove the planks, and strew the interior of the *kang* with horse-dung, quite dry and pulverized. Over this combustible they throw some lighted cinders, and then replace the planks; the fire immediately communicates itself to the dung, which, once lighted, continues to smoulder; the heat and the smoke, having no exit, soon warm the planks, and this produces a tepid temperature which, in consequence of the slow combustion of the material, prevails throughout the night. The talent of the *kang*-heater consists in putting neither too much nor too little dung, in strewing it properly, and in so arranging the cinders that combustion shall commence at different points in the same moment of time, in order that all the planks may equally benefit by the warmth. Ashamed to have our bed warmed for us like children, we one night essayed to perform this service for ourselves, but the result was by no means happy, for while one of us was nearly broiled to death, the other trembled with cold all night long; the fact being, that owing to our want of skill, the fire had actually caught the planks on one side of the *kang*, while on the other the fuel had not lighted at all. The host of the Hotel of the Temperate Climates was naturally disgusted at the mischance, and in order to prevent its recurrence, he locked the closing plank of the furnace, and himself came every night to light it.

Our various domestic occupations, and the recitation of our Breviary, passed away the time very smoothly at Ho-Kiao-Y. On the eighth day, as we had agreed, Samdadchiemba returned, but not alone; he was accompanied by a lad, whose features bespoke him the brother of our cameleer, and as such Samdadchiemba presented him to us. Our first interview was very brief, for the two Dchiahours had scarcely presented themselves before they disappeared. We imagined, at first, that they were gone to pay their respects to the host, but it was not so, for they almost immediately re-appeared with somewhat more solemnity of manner than before. Samdadchiemba marched in first: " Babdcho [Babjo]," said he to his brother, " prostrate thyself before our masters, and present to them the offerings of our poor family." The young Dchiahour made us three salutations in the Oriental fashion, and then laid before us two great dishes, one of them full of fine nuts, the other laden with three large loaves, in form resembling those made in France. To afford Samdadchiemba the most practical proof in our power that we were sensible to his attention, we forthwith applied ourselves to one of the loaves, which, with some of the nuts, constituted quite a delicious repast, for never since our departure from France had we tasted such excellent bread.

While engaged upon our banquet, we observed that the costume of Samdadchiemba was reduced to its simplest expression; that whereas he had gone decently attired, he had come back half-covered with a few rags. We asked for an explanation of this change, whereupon he gave us an account of the miserable condition in which he had found his family. The father had been dead for some time; his aged mother had become blind, so that she had not enjoyed the happiness of seeing him. He had two brothers, the one a mere child, the other the young man whom he had brought with him, and who, the sole support of his family, devoted his time to the cultivation of a small field which still belonged to them, and to the tending of the flocks of other people for hire. This narrative at once explained what Samdadchiemba had done with his clothes; he had given them all to his poor old mother, without even excepting his travelling cloak. We thought it our duty to propose that he should remain, and devote himself to the assistance of his wretched family; but he did not at all adopt the suggestion. "What," said he, "could I have the cruelty to do such a thing as that! Could I ever think of going to devour the little subſtance that remains to them ? They can scarcely subsiſt themselves: how could they possibly support me; for I myself have no means of making a livelihood there—I cannot labour at the soil, and there is no other way in which I could help them." We considered this resolution neither good nor great : but knowing, as we did, the character of Samdadchiemba, it in no degree surprised us. We did not insiſt upon his remaining, for we were even better convinced than he himself was, that he could be of no sort of service to his family. We did all we could ourselves to aid these poor people, by giving Samdadchiemba's brother as large an alms as we could spare ; and we then proceeded to the preparations for our departure.

During these eight days of repose, the condition of our animals had so improved as to enable us to venture upon the difficult road we had to traverse. The next day after quitting Ho-Kiao-Y, we began the ascent of the high mountain called Ping-Keou [Ping-kou], the terribly rugged paths of which interposed almost insurmountable difficulties in the way of our camels. On the ascent, we were obliged to be conſtantly calling out, at the pitch of our voices, in order to warn any muleteers who might be coming down the road, which was so narrow and dangerous that two animals could not pass each other abreaſt. Our cries were to enable any persons coming the other way to lead their mules aside, so that they might not take alarm at the sight of our camels, and dash over the precipice. We began the ascent of this mountain before daybreak, and yet it was noon before we reached its summit. There we found a little inn, where, under the denomination of tea they sold a decoction of burned beans. We stopped at this place for a brief period to take a repast, which hunger rendered very succulent and savoury, of some nuts and a slice of the famous bread which the Dchiahour had brought us, and which we expended with the utmost parsimony. A draught of cold water should have been, according to our previous plan, the complement of our feast; but the only water attainable on this mountain was affected with an insupportable stench. We were fain, therefore, to have recourse to the decoction of baked beans, a dreadfully insipid fluid, but for which, notwithstanding, we were charged extortionately.

The cold was by no means so severe as we had expected from the season of the year and the great elevation of the mountain. In the afternoon, indeed, the weather was quite mild; by-and-by, the sky was overcast, and snow fell. As we were obliged to descend the mountain on foot, we soon got absolutely hot in the perpetual struggle, of a very laborious kind, to keep from rolling down the slippery path. One of our camels fell twice, but happily in each instance he was stayed by a rock from tumbling over the mountain's side.

Having placed behind us the formidable Ping-Keou, we took up our lodging in the village of the Old Duck (Lao Ya Pou [Lao-ya-p'u]). Here we found a system of heating in operation different from that of Ho-Kiao-Y. The *kangs* here are warmed, not with dried horse-dung, but with coal-dust, reduced to paste, and then formed into bricks; turf is also used for the purpose. We had hitherto imagined that knitting was unknown in China; the village of the Old Duck removed this misconception from our minds, and enabled us, indeed, to remove it from the minds of the Chinese themselves in other parts of the empire. We found here in every ſtreet men, not women, occupied in this species of induſtry. Their produćtions are wholly without taſte or delicacy of execution ; they merely knit coarse cotton into shapeless ſtockings, like sacks, or sometimes gloves, without any separation for the fingers, and merely a place for the thumb, the knitting needles being small canes of bamboo. It was for us a singular spećtacle to see parties of muſtachioed men sitting before the door of their houses in the sun, knitting, sewing, and chattering like so many female gossips ; it looked quite like a burlesque upon the manners of Europe.

From Lao-Ya-Pou to Si-Ning-Fou [Hsi-ning-fu] was five days' march ; on the second day we passed through Ning-Pey-Hien [Nien-po-hsien], a town of the third order. Outside the weſtern gate, we ſtopped at an inn to take our morning meal ; a great many travellers were already assembled in the large kitchen, occupying the tables which were ranged along the walls ; in the centre of the room were several furnaces, where the innkeeper, his wife, several children, and some servants were actively preparing the dishes required by the gueſts. While everybody seemed occupied, either in the preparation or in the consumption of vićtuals, a loud cry was heard. It was the hoſtess, thus expressing the pain occasioned by a knock on her head, which her husband had adminiſtered with a shovel. At the cry, all the travellers looked in the direćtion whence it proceeded ; the woman retreated, with vehement vociferations, to a corner of the kitchen ; the innkeeper explained to the company that he had been compelled to correćt his wife for insolence, insubordination, and an indifference to the intereſts of the eſtablishment, which eminently compromised its prosperity. Before he had finished his version of the story, the wife, from her retreat in the corner, commenced hers; she informed the company that her husband was an idle vagabond, who passed his time in drinking and smoking, expending the result of her labours for a whole month in a few days on brandy and tobacco. During this extempore performance, the audience remained imperturbably calm, giving not the smallest indication of approbation or disapprobation. At length the wife issued from her retreat, and advanced with a sort of challenging air to her husband: "Since I am a wicked woman," cried she, "you must kill me. Come, kill me!" and so saying, she drew herself up with a gesture of vast dramatic dignity immediately in front of her husband. The latter did not adopt the suggestion to kill her, but he gave her a formidable box on the ears, which sent her back, screaming at the pitch of her voice, into her previous corner. Hereupon, the audience burst into loud laughter; but the affair which seemed to them so diverting, soon took a very serious turn. After the most terrible abuse on the one hand, and the most awful threats on the other, the innkeeper at length drew his girdle tight about his waist, and twisted his tress of hair about his head, in token of some decided proceeding. "Since you will have me kill you," cried he, "I will kill you!" and so saying, he took from his furnace a pair of long iron tongs, and rushed furiously upon his wife. Everybody at once rose and shouted; the neighbours ran in, and all present endeavoured to separate the combatants, but they did not effect the object until the woman's face was covered with blood, and her hair was all down about her shoulders. Then a man of ripe years, who seemed to exercise some authority in the house, gravely pronounced these words by way of epilogue: "How! what!" said he, "husband and wife fighting thus! and in presence of their children, in presence of a crowd of travellers!" These words, repeated three or four times, in a tone which expressed at once indignation and authority, had a marvellous effect. Almoſt immediately afterwards the gueſts resumed their dinner, the hoſtess fried cakes in nut-oil, and the hoſt silently smoked his pipe.

When we were about to depart, the innkeeper, in summing up our account, coolly inserted fifty sapeks for the animals which we had tied up in the courtyard during our meal. He had evidently an idea of making us pay *en Tartare*. Samdadchiemba was indignant. "Do you think," asked he, "that we Dchiahours don't know the rules of inns? Where did you ever hear of making people pay for faſtening their animals to a peg in the wall? Tell me, maſter publican, how many sapeks are you going to charge us for the comedy we've juſt witnessed of the innkeeper and his wife?" The burſt of laughter on the part of the byſtanders which hailed this sarcasm carried the day triumphantly for Samdadchiemba, and we departed without paying anything beyond our personal expenses.

The road thence to Si-Ning-Fou, generally well made and well kept, meanders through a fertile and well cultivated country, picturesquely diversified by trees, hills and numerous ſtreams. Tobacco is the ſtaple of the diſtrict. We saw on our way several water-mills, remarkable for their simplicity, as is the case with all Chinese works. In these mills, the upper ſtorey is ſtationary, while the lower is turned by means of a single wheel, kept in motion by the current. To work these mills, though they are frequently of large proportions, a very small ſtream suffices, as the ſtream plays upon the wheel in the form of a cascade, at leaſt twenty feet high.

On the day before arriving at Si-Ning-Fou, we passed over a road extremely laborious, and so dangerously rugged that it suggested frequent recommendations of ourselves to the protection of the Divine Providence. Our course was amid enormous rocks, beside a deep, fierce current, the tumultuous waves of which roared beneath us. There was the gulf perpetually yawning to swallow us up, should we make but one false step; we trembled, above all, for our camels, awkward and lumbering as they were, whenever they had to pass over an uneven road. At length, thanks to the goodness of God, we arrived without accident at Si-Ning [Hsi-ning]. The town is of very large extent, but its population is limited and itself, in several parts, is falling into absolute decay. The history of the matter is, that its commerce has been in great measure intercepted by Tang-Keou-Eul [Dangar], a small town on the banks of the Keou-Ho [Kou-ho], on the frontier which separates Kan-Sou from Koukou-Noor.

It is the custom, we may say the rule, at Si-Ning-Fou, not to receive strangers, such as the Tartars, Thibetians, and others, into the inns, but to relegate them to establishments called Houses of Repose (*Sie-Kia* [*hsieh-chia*]), into which no other travellers are admitted. We proceeded accordingly to one of these Houses of Repose, where we were exceedingly well entertained. The *Sie-Kia* differ from other inns in this important particular, that the guests are boarded, lodged, and served there gratuitously. Commerce being the leading object of travellers hither, the chiefs of the *Sie-Kia* indemnify themselves for their outlay by a recognized percentage upon all the goods which their guests buy or sell. The persons who keep these Houses of Repose have first to procure a license from the authorities of the town, for which they pay a certain sum, greater or less, according to the character of the commercial men who are expected to frequent the house. In outward show, the guests are well treated, but still they are quite at the mercy of the landlords, who, having an understanding with the traders of the town, manage to make money of both parties.

When we, indeed, departed from Si-Ning-Fou, the *Sie-Kia* with whom we had lodged had made nothing by us in the ordinary way, for we had neither bought nor sold anything. However, as it would have been preposterous and unjust on our part to have lived thus at the expense of our neighbours, we paid the host of the House of Repose for what we had had at the ordinary tavern rate.

After crossing several torrents, ascending many rocky hills, and twice passing the Great Wall, we arrived at Tang-Keou-Eul. It was now January, and nearly four months had elapsed since our departure from the Valley of Dark Waters. Tang-Keou-Eul is a small town, but very populous, very animated, and very full of business. It was a regular tower of Babel, wherein you find collected Eastern Thibetians, Houng-Mao-Eul [Hung-mao-êrh] " Long-haired Folk," Eleuts, Kolos [Kolo], Chinese, Tartars from the Blue Sea, and Mussulmans descended from the ancient migrations from Turkestan. Everything in the town bears the impress of violence. Nobody walks the streets without a great sabre at his side, and without affecting, at least, a fierce determination to use it on the shortest notice. Not an hour passes without some street combat.

The International Library of Sociology

HISTORICAL SOCIOLOGY
In 9 Volumes

I	America: Ideal and Reality	*Stark*
II	British Social Work in the 19th Century	*Young et al*
III	Farewell to European History	*Weber*
IV	A History of Autobiography in Antiquity Part One	*Misch*
V	A History of Autobiography in Antiquity Part Two	*Misch*
VI	Men of Letters and the English Public in the 18th Century	*Beljame*
VII	New Trends in Education in the 18th Century	*Hans*
VIII	Peasant Renaissance in Yugoslavia 1900 - 1950	*Trouton*
IX	Sociology of the Renaissance	*Von Martin*

The International Library of Sociology

MEN OF LETTERS AND THE ENGLISH PUBLIC IN THE EIGHTEENTH CENTURY

Founded by KARL MANNHEIM

For Product Safety Concerns and Information please contact our EU
representative GPSR@taylorandfrancis.com
Taylor & Francis Verlag GmbH, Kaufingerstraße 24, 80331 München, Germany

www.ingramcontent.com/pod-product-compliance
Lightning Source LLC
Chambersburg PA
CBHW070616230426
43670CB00010B/1547

MEN OF LETTERS AND THE ENGLISH PUBLIC IN THE EIGHTEENTH CENTURY
1660 - 1744, DRYDEN, ADDISON, POPE

by
ALEXANDRE BELJAME

Edited, with and Introduction and Notes by
BONAMY DOBRÉE

Translated by
E. O. LORIMER

LONDON AND NEW YORK

English edition first published in 1948 by
Routledge, Trench, Trubner and Co., Ltd

Published 2001 by
Routledge
2 Park Square, Milton Park, Abingdon, Oxfordshire OX14 4RN
711 Third Avenue, New York, NY 10017

First issued in paperback 2014

*Routledge is an imprint of the Taylor and Francis Group,
an informa business*

© 1948 Alexandre Beljame

All rights reserved. No part of this book may be reprinted or reproduced or utilized in any form or by any electronic, mechanical, or other means, now known or hereafter invented, including photocopying and recording, or in any information storage or retrieval system, without permission in writing from the publishers.

The publishers have made every effort to contact authors/copyright holders of the works reprinted in *The International Library of Sociology*. This has not been possible in every case, however, and we would welcome correspondence from those individuals/companies we have been unable to trace.

British Library Cataloguing in Publication Data
A CIP catalogue record for this book
is available from the British Library

Men of Letters and the English Public in the 18th Century
ISBN 0-415-17610-7
Historical Sociology: 9 Volumes
ISBN 0-415-17825-8
The International Library of Sociology: 274 Volumes
ISBN 0-415-17838-X

ISBN 978-1-138-88201-0 (pbk)
ISBN 978-0-415-17610-1 (hbk)

Publisher's Note
The publisher has gone to great lengths to ensure the quality of this reprint but points out that some imperfections in the original may be apparent

CONTENTS

	PAGE
FOREWORD	ix
PREFACE	xi
INTRODUCTION	xiii
BIOGRAPHICAL NOTE	xxiv

CHAPTER I : JOHN DRYDEN AND THE THEATRE (1660–1680) :

I The Restoration of 1660 : King Charles II, the Court.—Anti-Puritan reaction.—Gaming, wine, gallantry, profligacy.—Religion, morals 1

II Art, literature : songs, etc., satires, novels 8

III Writers' hopes after the Restoration.—Disappointment.—Authors friendly to the Court : Cowley, Butler.—Authors hostile to the Court : Bunyan, Milton.—Authors who succeed in living by their pen take to drama : Dryden, Otway, Shadwell, Lee, Crowne, Mrs. Behn, Settle, D'Urfey, Ravenscroft 19

IV What the drama was : actresses, production ; dramatic opera.—Tragedy : heroic plays.—Comedy 30

V Dramatists' difficulty in satisfying the audience.—Audience limited in numbers ; perpetual demand for something new ; collaboration and adaptation.—Frivolity of the audience : Prologues and Epilogues 58

VI Courtiers' literary pretensions.—Authors compelled to seek courtiers' favour : Dedications.—Incidents : Dryden and Sir Robert Howard, the Duke of Newcastle, the Duke of Buckingham, the Earl of Rochester 67

VII Writers' profits : from the theatre, from sale of their books, from gifts 107

VIII Conclusion : As yet, neither public, nor men of letters . 125

CHAPTER II : JOHN DRYDEN AND POLITICS (1680–1688) :

I Re-awakening of political and religious passions : Whigs and Tories.—Political Drama : Dryden, Otway, Lee, Southerne, Crowne, D'Urfey, Shadwell, Settle, Tate, Mrs. Behn, Ravenscroft, Bankes.—Political Prologues and Epilogues . . 136

II Decadence of Drama.—Newspapers.—The Coffee House ; The Newsletter ; The Pulpit 151

III Political Literature under Charles II : Dryden's " Absalom and Achitophel " ; replies of Settle, Buckingham, Pordage, etc.—Dryden's poem " The Medal " ; replies of Hickeringhill, Pordage, Shadwell, etc.—Dryden's Mac Flecknoe.—" Absalom and Achitophel, Part II ", by Nahum Tate and Dryden.—Dryden's " Religio Laici ".—Shadwell and Hunt's replies to Dryden and Lee's " Duke of Guise " ; Dryden's Vindication of " The Duke of Guise " ; Dryden's Translation of Maimbourg's " History of the League " 168

		PAGE
IV	Political Literature under James II : Sprat's Account of the "Horrid Conspiracy against the Late King" (Rye-House Plot).—Dryden and Stillingfleet discuss religion.—The Anglican Clergy join in polemics against the King.—" The Hind and the Panther " by Dryden.—Montague and Prior's "The Country-Mouse and the City-Mouse".—Overthrow of James II	178
V	Conclusion : Authors' services are better appreciated.—The City as counterweight to the Court.—Reciprocal influence of City and Court.—Political competes successfully with frivolous literature.—Jacob Tonson, the first English publisher, tries his strength.—Profits from the theatre increase. This gives promise for the future ; meantime the spiritual and material lot of authors does not improve.—They are " courtiers " in politics as in literature.—Their political changes of front.—Wycherley, Haines and Dryden converted to Roman Catholicism.—Violence of their political passion . .	186

CHAPTER III : JOSEPH ADDISON (1688–1721) :

I	Modifications in monarchical practice introduced by the Revolution.—The King's need of public support.—Rôle of literature in the Government ; Halifax, Somers, Dorset, Montague, etc.—Whigs and Tories enlist writers on their side.—Favour and lucrative posts showered on authors.—Shadwell, Tate, Eusden, Rowe, Smith, Hughes, Ambrose Philips, Parnell, Arbuthnot, Garth, Blackmore, Granville, Stepney, Maynwaring, Walsh, Martyn, Tickell, Locke, Newton, Steele, Swift, Defoe, Congreve, Vanbrugh, Gay, Addison, Prior, Montague .	212
II	Happy results of the writers' new status.—They acquire and deserve respect.—They take a share in the reform of manners	219
III	Current Manners.—Manners reflected in the drama : Dryden, Shadwell, D'Urfey, Southerne, Congreve, Vanbrugh, Mrs. Manley, Granville, Dennis	222
IV	Jeremy Collier's " Short View of the Immorality and Profaneness of the English Stage ".—What Collier was.—Analysis of his book : its faults, merits, effect.—Replies by Congreve, Vanbrugh, D'Urfey, Wycherley, Dennis, Settle, Filmer, Drake, Farquhar, etc.—Collier's triumph ; reform of the theatre	230
V	The Danger of Collier's Attack.—The Danger averted by Addison's " Spectator ".—The Difficulties of Addison's Task	243
VI	The periodical press after the Revolution.—Abolition of the Censorship.—Its consequences.—Birth of the literary journal : John Dunton's " Athenian Mercury " ; Defoe's " Weekly Review of the Affairs of France " ; Steele's " Tatler "	248
VII	The " Spectator ".—A Non-political Daily.—Appeal to new Readers.—Readers' Response.—Moral Rôle of the " Spectator ".—Its Attitude to Cavaliers and Puritans.—Addison's special Qualifications for his Task.—Moral Value of his Paper.—Its Literary and Educational Value.—Its Success.—Contemporary Testimony to the Influence of the " Tatler " and " Spectator "	263

CONTENTS

VIII Increase in the number and quality of readers.—The influence of politics.—The influence of Addison and his imitators.—An English reading-public is well established . . . 307

CHAPTER IV: ALEXANDER POPE (1721–1744):

I Despite Appearances, Writers are not yet wholly independent.—Patronage now based on Politics.—Writers' Services to Politics: Addison, Steele, Swift, Shadwell, Congreve, Vanbrugh, Rowe, Prior, Gay, Defoe, Locke, Newton, Tate, Eusden, Smith, Hughes, Ambrose Philips, Parnell, Arbuthnot, Garth, Blackmore, Granville, Stepney, Maynwaring, Walsh, Martyn, Tickell.—Why the Political Parties cannot dispense with authors.—Effects of Political Patronage.—Dedications to Statesmen, etc.—The Author's uneasy position . . 317

II Walpole at the Head of Affairs (1721–42).—Cessation of political patronage just at the moment when the private patronage of the Great has ceased.—The writer's trials: Steele, Ambrose Philips, Savage, Dennis, Boyse, Johnson, etc. 341

III Dryden and the first English publisher, Jacob Tonson.—The publisher's rôle in literature.—Dryden's translation of Virgil. —His Fables.—Literature increasingly remunerative . . 354

IV Pope and his publishers Tonson and Lintot.—Pope's Translation of Homer.—It made Pope's fortune.—Pope breaks the tradition of interested Dedications.—Preserves a detached attitude to political parties.—Refuses offered pensions.—Sought by the highest society in England.—The first English man of letters 366

V Conclusion 381

BIBLIOGRAPHY:

I General Works (a) Historical 387

(b) Critical 392

II Authors 399

INDEX 476

FOREWORD

Before embarking on my subject, it will be advisable briefly to define the words of my title.

By "Man of Letters" I mean a writer who lives by his pen and who is able by his works alone to achieve independence and, if he deserves it, distinction.

By "Public" I do not mean the public of theatre-goers so much as the body of intelligent people who are interested in the various forms of literature, the people who read and buy books.

So long as a nation lacks such a public, so long as education is the privilege of a chosen few, so long as the taste and habit of reading are not common to a considerable proportion of society, it is obvious that the sale of their works will provide writers with an income so uncertain and so inadequate that they cannot be "men of letters" in any sense of the term.

The starting-point of this study of mine is therefore the gradual growth of an enlightened and interested public.

How does such a public come into being? By what degrees and by what means has it been formed? What part have men played, and what influence have events had, in forming it?

What influence has its development exercised on writers? What effect has its existence had on their position in society?

These are the questions I have tried to answer. It seemed to me that in a country like England, and in a literature like English literature, these questions were not unworthy of some attention.

The data for such a study as this really begin with a people's first literary efforts, and I might well have gone back to the origins of English literature. I preferred to confine myself within more modest limits, and to begin my study with the accession of Charles the Second in 1660. Many reasons moreover combined to make the choice of this date appear a wise one. What may be considered the modern period of English literature begins in fact with Charles II: documents become more numerous and more accurate, facts clearer and more precise. Above all, it is with the Restoration that the picture of literary life begins to assume peculiar interest: the public enters on the scene; during the succeeding reigns we see it little by little developing and taking shape. We see at the same time the writers, after various trials and vicissitudes, begin to rise and take their place.

I have stopped at the death of Pope in 1744, because with Pope we reach the climax : with him a public has been established ; the writer's trade has become a liberal profession ; the man of letters has won for himself the place in society which he occupies to-day.

Moreover, even with these limitations, the field of study was sufficiently vast, comprising, as it does, from different points of view almost a whole century of English social history and of English letters. My bibliography offers sufficient proof of the distance to which my researches have led me.

I should like to record how greatly I have been aided in these researches by the staff of the British Museum. During the frequent and lengthy visits I paid to the admirable library in their charge, I was invariably received by them with goodwill and eagerness to help. It is a most pleasant duty here to express to them my thanks.

In England and the United States, in France and Germany, the press has given my book a cordial welcome, for which on the threshold of its second edition I should like to offer my cordial thanks.

To the present edition, purged of some inaccuracies, I have added an Index which will, I trust, prove useful to students.

PREFACE

The translation of this book has been no easy task, for it has had to be a work of interpretation as well as of idiomatic rendering, and has itself involved scholarship. It has, for instance, been no simple matter to know exactly what, in each instance, Beljame meant by the word *puritan*. Did he mean a Church of England man, a Dissenter, or simply " puritan " ? Again, the tracing of quotations in books which are no longer common reading has been no mean labour, one which has been indefatigably pursued. Often a phrase for which no reference was given had to be hunted up, here and there without result, because most of the work was done during the war when access to books and old periodicals was not easy, and sometimes impossible.[1] An editor can do no less than to give grateful thanks for the scholarly work that Mrs. Lorimer has carried out, as well as for a translation which is as spirited as it is exact. He would also like to thank Mr. Noel F. Sharp of the British Museum for most valuable help in looking up quotations and references not otherwise obtainable during the period when the Reading Room was closed. Thanks are also due to the Curator of the Hampton Court pictures for providing the new number of a portrait referred to by Beljame.

All Beljame's notes have been included in this edition, except such as gave the English of certain passages translated in his text: these have, of course, been transferred to the English text. Any extra notes added—and these have been kept down to a minimum—have been enclosed in square brackets and initialled, so that they are easily distinguishable from Beljame's.

Beljame's Bibliography has also been printed in full (with the excision of shelf numbers which are no longer all of them the same as they were seventy years ago). The bibliography has, however, been reorganized so as to make it more easily used, and to bring it into some conformity with modern practice. A certain number of additions have been made, not in any attempt to give a complete bibliography of the period—which would occupy an inordinate amount of room—but to enable

[1] Very few errors have been found, and these have been silently corrected, as have a few misprints and obviously wrong dates.

the reader who wishes to familiarize himself with more recent scholarship, either on the period or on individuals, to pick up the main strains. I have to thank Mrs. Dorothy Broughton for a great deal of help in this compilation; indeed this part of the work is mainly hers, though it is I who must be responsible for any errors or omissions. Here again the additions are put in square brackets, but without initials, to enable the reader to know which are the books that Beljame used.

B. D.

INTRODUCTION

How did the people who lived by the pen between 1660 and 1740 earn their livelihood? That is the question, with its implications as to the kind of writing produced, which Beljame set himself to answer in this classic work of scholarship. The word classic is used advisedly, since no one interested either in the literature of the period, or in its social history, can afford to neglect it, if only to save himself a deterrent amount of initial spade-work. It is classic also by its form and its method : it is a model of how such things should be done. Moreover, the period chosen by Beljame is one of crucial interest, since it was during those years that a fundamental change in the status of the writer took place, a change which corresponded with the final emergence of society from its mediæval phase into the modern one.

The Revolution of 1688 was the political event which defined, gave legal status to, a profound social development bound to affect the position of the great writer, the man of letters (whom alone Beljame considers), as it also did that of the popular or Grub-Street writer ; the position of the author of sermons, or of polemical theology, however, remained largely unaltered. Beljame's work was thoroughly done ; and however much subsequent studies may have led to revision here and there, however much the attitude, both critical and general, may have varied since 1881—such processes go on continually—*le Public et les Hommes de Lettres en Angleterre au Dix-huitième Siècle* must always remain the groundwork of a similar study, should it ever be undertaken, and the constant recourse of the scholar or the curious.

But before plunging into this work, the reader, especially if he be a student, should perhaps ask himself what it is he is really reading about. A book such as this is commonly regarded as a part of literary studies, and the danger is that it may come to be accepted as a study of literature. It cannot be too plainly stated that a knowledge of the appurtenances of literature, of its social surroundings, of the soil in which it flourished, will not make a fig of difference to its value for us here and now— and it is that which matters. To have a notion of how a thing came about, to undergo the most minute explanation of its appearance, will not make you "understand" it any better, in the sense that a work of art is "understood" as opposed, say, to a piece of machinery. One may begin to wonder whether what is in some places studied as literature is indeed literature or something else; for what the student of literature should aim at is to eat the bread, not analyse the chemical nature of the soil from which the wheat sprang. What the literary addict should do is to taste the bread, analyse how it is made, whether or not it is properly cooked, and how much it nourishes him. Anything else is another study, perhaps a paradise for the specialist, but not half so rewarding for the whole man.

Nevertheless, a study of this kind has enormous value, if properly used : it may remove certain barriers which prevent us from getting into intimate contact with the work of literature. Of course it has its value as a sociological study, but with such, as students of literature, we are not primarily concerned. Yet if we can discount the mental and moral trappings of an age, separate them from what is essential so that they need not distract us from our proper study of the work of art as such, a great deal has been gained. A generation or so ago such a statement would have been regarded as "mere æstheticism", as perhaps a good many now may regard it, with a good deal of stress on the "mere" : but it is time to reconsider the position in view of the danger of the study of literature becoming a sub-department of sociology. This is not the place in which to argue the question—to anyone abreast of recent studies in psychology, education, or scientific philosophy it will need no arguing—but rather to see in what way a book such as Beljame's can be of use to us as students of literature itself.

How the writers earned their livelihood, that is, who paid them, must evidently have some effect upon what they wrote, and how they wrote it; as Dryden, forestalling Dr. Johnson, put it :

> They who have best succeeded on the stage,
> Have still conformed their genius to their age;

and what this book enables us to do is to see how far certain attitudes, methods, materials used, developments of attack, are common form, and have only an accidental connection with the essentials of that unique thing, a work of art. All art is an exploration of reality : and anything which helps us to discard the adventitious paraphernalia of that reality brings us closer to the work of art. To many who have read, say, Restoration drama, all the comedies, or all the tragedies, seem much the same because the reader has never penetrated beneath the paraphernalia, and so has been unable to see what each individual dramatist was presenting or probing. All the comedy writers of that time dealt with cuckoldry; they had to, as Beljame shows: but just because they had to, that is what matters least in their plays. In the same way they all dealt with foppery, because they could hardly avoid it: what matters is the relation of these characteristics to a broader sense of life that each writer may exhibit. Read them carelessly, and they will all seem to say much the same thing: but take the symbols for granted and look to see what they symbolize, and something much more important will come through. It is much the same with the tragedy of the time: the impossible plots, the ravings of heroic love, the bombastic ranting, these again are common form. Once we have discounted these things, we find that Dryden does not say the same thing as Lee, nor Etherege the same thing as Wycherley.

Beljame shows us how these things became counters, so that we can take them for what they are. Yet it must be confessed that in the first part of this book Beljame often leaves the discussion at the point of common form: he seems to us, with another sixty years of scholarship behind us, too much to take the symbols for the reality, and is inclined to handle the counters as though they were all of equal value. If the writers in question treated of certain matters, they did actually treat of them, and did not merely present crude "fact". Nor is it quite certain that their material and their attitude was altogether imposed upon them from without, as Beljame suggests; they may to some extent have shared the likes and prejudices of their audiences. Moreover, we shall probably think that Beljame sees the period a little too black; and a little too naïvely, perhaps, accepts the statements of satirists as police-court evidence. The royal circle was hardly ideal; no one will suggest that it was even decent according to our standards; all would agree with Macaulay that Plato was no doubt a far better man than Sir George Etherege. But the Restoration Court did not invent literary licentiousness; poetry knew it before in such things as *The Loves of Hero and Leander*, published in 1651 at the very height of the puritanical Commonwealth; and editors of school editions of our classics have sometimes experienced certain difficulties with Shakespeare himself. Men cannot live in the sort of world presented by the satirists, and cuckoldry would not have been comic had it not also been painful. There is a real moral basis to Restoration comedy, which laughs at, rather than with.

Nor was the drama of this period a sudden invention of the time. Just as you can trace back much of Restoration comedy, the themes and the manner alike, to earlier work, through Davenant, Wilson and Brome back to Shirley, Massinger and Marston, so you can trace Restoration tragedy not only back to late Jacobean romantic comedy, but to early Jacobean tragedy. Where would one suppose the following to come from? One might easily say, at first reading, Dryden or Lee, or possibly Orrery:

> *Tullia.* I am no wife of Tarquin's, if not King;
> Oh! had Jove made me man, I would have mounted
> Above the base tribunals of the earth,
> Up to the clouds for pompous sovreignty.
> Thou art a man: oh! bear my royal mind,
> Mount heaven, and see if Tullia lag behind.
> There is no earth in me, I am all fire;
> Were Tarquin so, then should we both aspire.

It is actually from Thomas Heywood's *Rape of Lucrece*, and was written in about 1604.

Nor was the licentiousness of the stage a fashion which appeared suddenly. Listen to what Ben Jonson, writing in 1607, had to say about the stage of his time. Does it not seem exactly like what Collier was to say about a hundred years later of the then popular drama? Jonson tells us in the dedication of *Volpone* " that now, especially in dramatic, or, as they term it, stage poetry, nothing but ribaldry, profanation, blasphemy, all license of offence to God and man is practised ". And he adds a little later: " For my particular, I can, and from a most clear conscience, affirm, that I . . . have loathed the use of such foul and unwashed bawdry, as is now made the food of the scene." Jonson, whether he wished to be so or not, was here a satirist; and the danger is that if you argue from literature to life, and then back again from life to literature, you are performing a very pretty circle, but you are not getting very much further. It is a danger which, we feel, Beljame does not always escape. The courtiers whom he dismisses so easily were not, we will be inclined to judge, quite such contemptible literary figures as he makes them out to be. Sir Robert Howard, for example, could argue well on dramatic form, and the debt English prosody owed to Waller is not to be ignored. Beljame, indeed, is a little inclined to be certain that a good writer could not have been well born, and that conversely a well-born writer could not have been a good one : thus Etherege must be made out to spring from a social stratum higher than that of Dryden, a matter which is, to say the least of it, not proven. The reader, then, must be a little on his guard ; we know more about the period now than was possible for Beljame.

But however much—thanks, we may repeat, to the researches of the last sixty years—we may be able here and there to pick out a detail on which we can disagree with Beljame, this does not affect the validity of Beljame's main conclusion as to the way a man of letters made his living until the Revolution of 1688, and a little after : it was entirely by Court patronage ; and the public for the poet, the dramatist, the critic, was the Court. There was, of course, another public, that which devoured religious tracts, sermons, *The Pilgrim's Progress*, commercial treatises, political pamphlets and so on—and even poetry. But those who wrote for this public had another means of subsistence ; they were not primarily " men of letters ", and they wrote mainly for propaganda purposes.

But, little by little, the " general public " as opposed to the Court began to be catered for ; and at the same time this public became larger in its views, so began to appreciate what men of letters would write. It would seem to us that Beljame's version of the change, as exhibited in, say, 1710, presents too sudden a swing. It was not all due to Addison. Beljame, of course, was far too good a scholar to say that it was ; but it must be confessed that his emphasis is such that the careless or hasty reader will suppose that all the credit must go to Mr. Spectator. Beljame, in his admiration for Addison, out-Macaulay's Macaulay ; to-day our admiration is tempered. Addison was indeed a very good writer, a man of taste and discernment, of wide reading, and much worldly wisdom in the best sense. He was a good popular moralist, no doubt, but not the genius in moral thinking that Beljame would have us think ; he was, rather, as Matthew Arnold pointed out, provincial and trite. What made him, we are inclined to think, so notable a figure in the history of our literature, was his journalistic genius in seeing what was wanted, what would take, at exactly the right moment. He had a flair, and it made him almost great : but the question arises, was not the flair really Steele's?

If one cannot ascribe to one man the change brought about in the relation between the man of letters and the public, it is impossible to say exactly what did bring it about. Such social changes are very complex, and we have not enough knowledge at our disposal. The patronage of the politicians who replaced the Court at the Revolution of 1688 was a lucky chance ; but it is possible that this only hastened a process which would in any event have taken place, namely, the writer as such achieving a social status. The more important process, that of the writer gaining a large middle-class audience ready to buy his work in sufficient bulk to support him, was already begun before the turn of the century, though only begun. This was largely owing to the rise of a new middle class. The middle class, as any student of history knows, is always rising—or has been hitherto—and this time it was the mercantilist-manufacturing middle class that was rising, the class represented by Defoe, between, say, 1690 and 1720, and sung by Dyer in *The Fleece* in 1757. There were two other causes, aptly commented on by Beljame ; the lapse of the Licensing Act, and the growth of the coffee-houses. Beyond this, there was the need which the large dissenting class in the middle stratum of society began to feel for some reading other than the long-winded and copiously documented effusions of sectarian protagonists. This public, incidentally, was being enlarged by the growth of dissenting elementary schools, which did not come under the Schism Act, and of the charity schools against which Mandeville was soon to inveigh precisely because they taught people to read when they should be hewing wood and drawing water. And when we consider that the City was largely dissenting, and that the main bulk of readers were townsmen, it is clear that there would be a considerable market for easy reading quite different in tone from what had diverted the Restoration Court. Nor should we ignore the influx of educated Huguenots who certainly helped to form and to influence the reading public.

Moreover, the women of this new group were beginning to join the ranks of readers ; they were becoming leisured, and were not averse from frivolities. The journalistic sense of Steele and especially Addison picked up this fact readily enough, and this will explain why so much of *The Spectator* is addressed to " the fair sex ". Addison certainly wrote for the boudoir as much as for the coffee-house : a paper has to be bought to be read in the home, and this may partly account for Addison's enormous sales.

The ground for a new kind of reading matter was well prepared before the appearance of *The Tatler* by, as Beljame tells us, the various *Mercuries*,[1] and other publications of Dunton, who, as a good if limited journalist, knew his job. These periodicals were not, we may think, so vapid as Beljame suggests. There were, besides, such writers as Tom Brown, whom Beljame too lightly dismisses as " flat ", and Ned Ward, not mentioned at all in this volume. Their works ran into many editions in the reign of Queen Anne (Ward, indeed, wrote on up till 1729), and they had much the same idea as Addison had of civilizing the public, in fact, in Ward's own words, " to expose vice and encourage virtue ". Defoe, with his *Review*, also helped enormously in preparing the way. Without Steele it is doubtful if Addison would have achieved his resounding fame. Had there been no *Tatler*, there would have been no *Spectator* ; and it was Steele who launched *The Tatler* and created Sir Roger, just as it was Defoe who had hit upon the idea of the Scandal Club. Addison was in no way an innovator, nor had he a creative mind : but he did what other people were doing, very much better than they did. And that, at any time whatever, is no mean achievement.

It is to be noted that such things as we have been discussing were not aimed primarily at the more educated reading public, the public that read Locke and Clarendon, D'Avenant's *Essay on the Balance of Power*, Dampier's *Voyages*, the earlier works of Berkeley, Shaftesbury and Mandeville, the critical works of Dennis or Bysshe, or, possibly, *The Tale of a Tub*. Readers of such works did not need the kind of civilizing influence that the great journalists were so active in providing, though they too bought *The Tatler* and its numerous progeny. And besides the above-mentioned works, there were, as there had been in the Restoration period, innumerable works of theological controversy, now more heretical than ever (Asgill, Toland, etc.), which together with the usual routine flood of sermons, *The Practice of Piety* in a diversity of forms, and so on, made up the bulk of published matter, at least as revealed by the Term Catalogues. And no

[1] *Mercuries* appeared as early as 1644 ; but were not of much importance until after the Revolution.

doubt readers of these latter works, anxious for relaxation, would patronize *The Spectator* which could hardly ever be accused of raising a blush in the cheek of any young person. Amongst all this reading there was also an intolerable deal of intolerable verse, and a little that was tolerable, but only a very thin trickle of poetry until Pope came to maturity.

Reading lists might be studied indefinitely without our gaining any real certainty as to what happened. What it is wished to do here is a little to gloss the too simplified picture that Beljame draws of an immoral Court calling forth corrupt or absurd literature, as opposed to a morally regenerated England demanding wholesome moralistic fare. The matter is by no means so simple as that. We may think, perhaps, that Beljame confines himself too much to a special class of writing, a special class of readers, and it is doubtful if one could to-day maintain his statement that Addison "increased the number and the quality of readers". Nevertheless, the facts he adduces as causes are at least symptomatic; they cannot be ignored; and he points out the important fact that by the time of Addison's death in 1719 authors could to some extent rely on a general reading public to help keep body and soul together in some dignity, and were not entirely at the mercy of noble patrons. Yet it is well to insist that very few, if any, actually, did make their livelihood out of the reading public; they were still, in varying degrees, dependent on political, and sometimes noble, patronage. In the age of the new Whig lords these were not always distinguishable: the lords often supported the men of letters out of the public pocket rather than their own. Certainly writers no longer had to grovel to peers who thought they knew something about poetry (some of them did know): but it is difficult to point to a single writer above the scandalous or Grub Street level who made his living by his pen alone. Authors still had to make their terms with peers who had political power. Beljame makes this quite clear, but he a little discounts the purity of motive of some of the peers. Men such as Somers, "the all-accomplished", Dorset, " the grace of courts, the muses' pride ", and Halifax who loved to be thought the Mæcenas of his age, really were concerned for literature; and so long as writers did not make nuisances of themselves politically, did not mind to what party they belonged.

There is one matter which again Beljame seems to us to stress too strongly, namely, the purifying influence of Collier's diatribe,

A Short View, etc. Collier certainly voiced, if he exaggerated, the feelings of the new middle class, the members of which wanted to go to the theatre *en famille*. As a matter of sober fact the actual repertory of the theatre did not alter much as a result of his attack. Dryden, Wycherley, Mrs. Behn, and so on, continued to be acted ; we find Addison as late as the end of the first decade of the century reviewing Etherege's *Man of Mode*, and in a very solemn tone making a social criticism already implicit in what Etherege had written (see p. 282). Taste, of course, brought about a change. It was already beginning with Burnaby (fl. 1702) and made itself manifest in the sentimental comedy of Steele ; it was part of the social process which took the bite out of English comedy, and destroyed it for nearly two hundred years. Yet if, as far as one can judge, Collier had very little effect, he was a flamboyant symptom. He was himself a part of the reading public to whom *The Tatler* would later appeal : the translator of Marcus Aurelius would welcome something better written than the stuff Ned Ward could provide, based on a broader culture, and more representative of the newly-risen middle class which desired nothing better than to attain to the culture of the old aristocracy so long as it could retain something of its fierce and uncomfortable morality.

That we should on many points disagree with Beljame's critical opinions is only right and proper : the value of a work of literature (except perhaps for the very greatest), is relative to the experience any generation passes through. A state of society something analogous with that of the Restoration at one time made us see the point of dramatic work which Beljame believed for ever sunk below the horizon of appreciation : some writers to-day dislike Addison perhaps as much as Beljame adored him. It is not to cross critical swords, to oppose opinions, that objections against the author of this work are raised here and in the notes. What we are concerned to discover is how far, and in what way, a state of society influences writing. Beljame, in his admiration for Addison, ascribed too much to his influence : we are inclined to see Addison more as a product of his time than as its architect. Beljame's view of the personal relation between author and patron will seem to us a little vitiated by his not feeling the relations between the classes quite as we do. For instance, he finds it hard to understand why the political leaders should have been socially friendly with authors unless they had been afraid of them, or, alternatively, enlisting the support of their pens. It does not seem probable to him that, for instance, Congreve and Vanbrugh, or Gay, might have been drawn into close social relations with their patrons because they were good fellows, spoke the same language, had had much the same education. In the main the authors belonged to the same class as the patrons with whom they were friendly; they were "the quality"; though there were exceptions, such as Prior, which reflect the fluidity of the class system as it has always existed in England.

Scholar as Beljame was, we cannot but feel that here and there he was a little too much guided by his thesis; his work seems to us slightly distorted by that unscholarly thing, a point of view. It is this, of course, which gives his book life. You cannot be completely disinterested about human affairs and be a whole human being in the workaday or the moral world. Thus Beljame occasionally lets himself be carried away by his argument, and if we are not on our guard we may obtain a slightly false impression. But only if we are not careful, and fail to read his footnotes, or the paragraphs he himself inserts, as a good scholar must, to redress the balance, though these, perhaps, he presents a little too shyly. For instance, he gives to Addison all the credit for what the *Tatlers* and *Spectators* accomplished; only the careful reader will note that he tells us that for simplicity's sake he has used the name Addison throughout to cover the work of Steele as well; only a reader who checks references will observe that certain essays quoted in glorification of Addison are actually by Steele.

In the same way he paints in too gloomy colours the fate that befell authors when Walpole came into power. It is true that the golden age of authorship was over, and many sad stories are truly told of starving poets. But when we see who these poets were we cannot wonder at their fate—Savage and Boyse, for instance. Many are simply unreadable. But after all, a good many poets and writers managed to live, at least partly if not all of them wholly, by their pens, without patronage, or by the aid of subscription lists : Defoe in his last years, Thomson, Dyer, Shenstone, Akenside, Mrs. Haywood. A certain reading public had indeed come into being, and was prepared to support the authors who gave it what it wanted. After all, it is not in conformity with experience to suggest, as Beljame does, that every young, untried author should be able to make a living out of writing. How many young authors in any country have ever been able to do so? Take this country; take France. How many authors in France since the Revolution have been able to live without either some modicum of private means or a civil service job? How many of our own distinguished poets or men of letters—as opposed to best-selling novelists—live, or have lived in this century without private means, a civil service post, or employment in a publisher's firm? Beljame, we feel, asked for too much. So we must not too readily accept this part of his analysis, especially as here again he is apt to rely a little too much on evidence afforded by the satirists, such as Fielding in his farces. Once more we feel that the picture is a little too simplified. The whole question is, in fact, infinitely complicated.

Beljame's was a great pioneer attempt, the first thoroughly documented attempt of its kind : and because it was so well documented it can never be altogether superseded. Nobody can write with authority about the period covered in this book without having read it, sifted it, found out not only where he disagrees with the conclusions, but why he does so. The main picture is clear, and just enough : it needs amending in detail, and here and there some fresh considerations may have to be introduced. One question, suggested in the previous paragraph, is whether Beljame has not made too rigid a demarcation between the professional writer and the amateur. In this country we have never had that respect for letters that they have so long had in France : we have, indeed, been a little over-proud of our amateur status, an attitude of mind not without its benefits to literature, though they are too easily overrated. That is the kind of point that must be kept in mind when reading this work. It is masterly, it stands the test of time, but it is, naturally, not beyond criticism : nevertheless, it is so well done that it demands the most fundamental criticism. It is with the certainty that this is so that this work is offered in English to the English-reading public, and in the hope that it may find imitators. It has, indeed, been the forerunner of similar works, but it still stands head and shoulders above most of them, and it is doubtful if any has yet equalled it for erudition and thoroughness.

BONAMY DOBRÉE.

BIOGRAPHICAL NOTE

In 1864, when Alexandre Beljame was twenty-two years old, he undertook an English course at the Lycée Louis-le-Grand. He found that English studies were very little considered, in no way regarded as being an important part of humane scholarship. He set himself to remedy this state of affairs, and in 1881 produced *Le Public et les Hommes de Lettres en Angleterre* to establish the dignity of English studies in France on a level with those in the classics. He proved by this masterly book that they involved as much real hard work, as much scrupulous thinking, and as fine a critical acumen as were needed in the time-honoured schools of Greek and Latin.

His efforts were rewarded with the success due to them. He was the first lecturer in English to be appointed at the Sorbonne, and in 1902 the Sorbonne Chair was founded that he might occupy it, which he did until his death some five years later.

The school grew rapidly under him, both in numbers and in prestige, thanks to his single-hearted devotion, his high culture, his deep knowledge, and his loving and fastidious scholarship. He soon attracted brilliant pupils and disciples, to whom he gave a large proportion of his time and energy. It can be said that he was virtually the founder of the English studies which now flourish in French Universities, and it is to him that we are indebted for such noted scholars as Émile Legouis, Louis Cazamian, to name only two, and so many monographs by distinguished scholars which are standard books for English studies in England.

An admirable brief account of his life, work and influence may be found in *Dernière Gerbe*, by Émile Legouis (Paris, Henri Didier, 1940).

CHAPTER I

JOHN DRYDEN AND THE THEATRE
(1660–1680)

I

The Restoration of 1660: King Charles II, the Court.—Anti-Puritan reaction.—Gaming, wine, gallantry, profligacy.—Religion, morals

The story goes, that during his short and unhappy reign amongst the Scots in 1650, Charles II had been subjected by the strict Presbyterians to a severe discipline. Forced to sign their Covenant and to adopt their worship, he was first placed under the surveillance of a committee of stern and vigilant ministers. These fierce Argus-eyed guardians compelled him perpetually to attend interminable prayers, appointed fast-days for him and sometimes doomed him to listen to as many as six sermons running. He was lucky when these sermons were not exclusively pointed at the crimes of his family and his personal impiety. All pleasures were forbidden, including dancing and card-playing. On Sunday he might not take a walk, or smile; the slightest ill-judged gesture, the slightest facial expression of boredom brought down on him terrible reproof. One day he had allowed himself to chat innocently with a woman. One of these austere fanatics came and delivered him a long and solemn reproof on the enormity of his sin, and closed by advising him always to keep the windows shut.[1]

The whole of England had been subjected by the Puritans to the same superhuman discipline. After more than eleven years of it, the country felt stifled for lack of air. When Charles II came back, she flung all windows open—wide. She opened them too wide. The Restoration reacted against exaggerated rigour by exaggerated licence.

In this the King took the lead. After a long exile, a wandering and miserable life, he suddenly ascended one of the leading thrones in Europe amid the acclamation of the whole nation. He was 30, with a graceful figure, seductive manners, a love of pleasure and an admirable constitution. Up to this point he

[1] Clarendon, book XIII; Burnet, *History of my Own Times*, vol. I, pp. 91, 92; Malcolm, p. 154.

had always been short of money; now he was going to have as much as ever he liked, and with it all, companions well able to gratify his wishes and themselves eager for enjoyment.

London in those days was everything. Lacking easy communication with the Capital [2], the provinces did not count, and lived an obscure life of their own. London being the whole of England, the Court was the whole of London. Convicted of Puritanism, the middle classes of the city were rudely brushed aside, or ceased to count; the Court took the only place in the sun and everyone fell into line and adopted its tastes and amusements.

It is easy to formulate the programme followed by the Court: it did everything which the Puritans had forbidden. They had worn short hair and banned every refinement of dress; the Court adopted long wigs in the Louis XIV style, and dress became one of the main preoccupations of people of fashion.[3] They had forbidden gaming: people gambled wildly and cheated into the bargain.[4] As for wine: they drank, they caroused, they got drunk [5]; as for oaths: no one opened his

---

[2] See what Macaulay says about the difficulty of communications at this time (*History*, chap. III).

[3] "A *Town-Gallant* is a Bundle of *Vanity*, composed of *Ignorance and Pride*, *Folly* and *Debauchery*; a silly *Huffing* thing, three parts *Fop* and the rest *Hector* (see note 10): A kind of *Walking Mercers shop*, that shows one Stuff to-day and another to-morrow, and is valuable just according to the price of his *Suit*, and the merits of his *Taylor* . . . His first care is his *Dress*, and next his *Body*, and in the fitting these two together consists his Soul and all its Faculties" (*The Character of a Town-Gallant*, anonymous). Once for all, let me here state that in all my quotations I scrupulously preserve the original orthography which is in my opinion of historic interest. See also *The Man of Mode*; or, *Sir Fopling Flutter*, a comedy by Etherege; and *Tyrannus, or the Mode* by Evelyn, in *Memoirs Illustrative of the Life and Writings of John Evelyn, Esq.*, vol. II.

[Beljame is a little too inclined to accept a satirical picture as a sober statement. Since *A Town Gallant* is frequently referred to as authority for the social background, the reader must be on his guard. B. D.]

[4] Pepys: Feb. 14, 1667-8; Evelyn: *Diary*, Jan. 25, 1685; Butler: *Satire upon Gaming* (in *Genuine Poetical Remains*).—Loaded dice were known as *fulhams*.

[5] See, for example, Pepys, Sept. 23, 1667: "The King and the Duke of York get drunk at a hunting-party; the King kneels down to drink the Duke's health, and all the spectators kiss each other with tears." See also ibid., Oct. 23, 1668. The poet Waller is quoted as an exceptional person because he had the art of being a good companion without drinking (Johnson, *Lives of the English Poets*, Waller).

[Since one of the objects of comedy is to ridicule divergence from the normal, or departure from what ought to be (as Vanbrugh put it: " the business of comedy is to show people what they should do, by representing

mouth without calling in one mood or another on God and the Devil.⁶

The reaction went further. The Puritans had vetoed all pleasures, even the most innocent : the Court plunged into every form of indulgence, even the most unmentionable. The Puritans had preached severity of manners : gallantry was enthroned at Court. Fashionable men called themselves " gallants " and thought of nothing but women and how to charm them.⁷ They had set foot on a steep and dangerous slope ; they soon slid to the bottom. Their gallantry was at first pleasing and in good taste. Polished conversation and courtesy in social intercourse superseded biblical jargon and icy Puritanism ; but this stage was short-lived, and soon no restraint was observed. The King, the " Merry Monarch ", set the pace by openly keeping mistresses and exhibiting himself everywhere in their company. The Palace of Whitehall became a place blatantly consecrated to amorous intrigues ; prostitution flaunted itself without a blush, at Court, at the theatre, everywhere. Woman became accustomed to hearing everything, and those who preserved their own virtue consented to mix freely with those who had never pretended to any.⁸

---

them on the stage doing what they should not "), it is hardly fair to expect comedy at any period to paint a good parson. B. D.]

⁶ " He admires the Eloquence of *Son of a Whore*, when 'tis pronounced with a good Grace, and therefore applyes it to *every* thing : So that if his *Pipe* be faulty, or his *Purge* gripe too much, 'Tis a *Son of a Whores Pipe*, or a *Spawn of a Bitches Purge* . . . he . . . may have a Patent for the sole use (as the first Inventer) of that Noble Complement, *Let me be Damn'd, my Body made a Gridiron to Broil my Soul on, to Eternity, If I do not Madam, love you confoundedly* " (*The Character of a Town-Gallant*).—One of the favourite oaths of Sir Samuel Hearty in Shadwell's *Virtuoso* is : " *your Nose in my Breech* ". Here is a declaration of the Gallant, Wittmore : " Madam,—as Gad shall save me, I'me the Son of a Whore if you are not the most Bell Person I ever saw, and if I be not damnably in love with you, but a pox take all tedious Courtship, I have a free-born and generous Spirit, and as I hate being confin'd to dull cringing, whining, flattering, and the Devil and all of Foppery, so when I give my heart I'me an Infidel, Madam, if I do not love to do't frankly and quickly." (*Sir Patient Fancy*, by Mrs. Behn, II, 1.)

⁷ " His trade is making of *Love*, yet he knows no difference between that and *Lust* ; and tell him of a *Virgin* at Sixteen, he shall swear then Miracles are not ceas'd. He is so bitter an Enemy to *Marriage*, that one would suspect him born out of *Lawful Wedlock* . . . But for the most delicious Recreation of *Whoring*, he protests a Gentleman cannot live without it . . ." (*The Character of a Town-Gallant*).

⁸ See Dryden's *The Kind Keeper* and Walter Scott's note prefixed to this comedy ; and the relations of Theodosia with Mrs. Friske (in Shadwell's *The Humorists*) : " A vain Wench of the Town, debauched and kept by Briske."

Men abandoned themselves to the most outrageous licence.[9] One of their favourite pastimes was to scour the streets at night after their orgies, thrashing the guard, threatening with death belated passers-by, sometimes slitting their noses, detaining women, on occasion hanging them upside down, overturning sedan-chairs, breaking windows and filling the town with cries and oaths. Milton at this very moment was writing:

> In Courts and Palaces he also Reigns
> And in luxurious Cities, where the noyse
> Of riot ascends above thir loftiest Towrs,
> And injury and outrage: And when Night
> Darkens the Streets, then wander forth the Sons
> Of *Belial*, flown with insolence and wine. [10]

Some, and amongst them some of the most highly placed, sank to the lowest depths of debauchery. The Earl of Rochester, one of the merry-makers of this gay Court and an intimate favourite of Charles II, used to disguise himself as a porter or a beggar to run wild through the suburbs (it is said that the King often accompanied him). One day when he and the Duke of Buckingham had fallen into disgrace, Rochester hired an inn on the Newmarket road, and they both settled in there, serving drinks to the carters and debauching their wives and daughters. The King, happening to pass that way, laughed and restored him to favour. Another time Rochester set up trestle tables in the middle of London, played the astrologer and mountebank and peddled medicines: " to relieve poor girls of all the ills and all the accidents into which they may have fallen ". On his own confession he was continuously drunk for five con-

---

[9] Women no less. See the exploits of the Court ladies in Hamilton: *Mémoires de Grammont*, passim.—There was a society of " Ballers " which met to dance naked (Pepys, May 30, 1668).

[10] *Paradise Lost*, I, 496 ff.—See Oldham, *Works*, vol. III, *A Satyr, in Imitation of the Third of Juvenal*; Shadwell: *The Scowrers*; Etherege: *The Comical Revenge*, I, 2; *The Character of a Town-Gallant*; in *Poems on Affairs of State*, 1703, vol. I, p. 147: *On the Three Dukes killing the Beadle on Sunday Morning*, Feb. the 26th, 1671.—There were, to use Macaulay's expression, several dynasties of these terrible jokers: the *Muns*, the *Tityre Tus*, the *Hectors*, the *Scourers* or *Skimmers*; then the *Nickers*, the *Hawkubites*, the *Mohawks*, etc. These last three were still flourishing in the days of Addison and Swift.—Tope in Shadwell's *Scowrers* (I, 1) says: " Why I knew the Hectors, and before them the *Muns* and the *Titire Tu's*: they were brave fellows indeed; in those days a man could not go from the *Rose Tavern* to the *Piazza* once, but he must venture his life twice."—In *The Maid's Last Prayer* by Southerne (II, 2) Drybubb speaks of " your Dammee-Boys, your Swashes, your Tuquoques, and your Titire-Tues ".

secutive years. He ended by dying of old age at thirty-three.[11]

Sir Charles Sedley, whom Charles II used to call the Viceroy of Apollo, was supping one evening in a London tavern with Lord Buckhurst (later the celebrated Earl of Dorset) and Sir Thomas Ogle. Flown with good food and wine, all three went out on to the balcony, hailed and abused the passers-by and exhibited themselves in the most indecent attitudes. Finally, Sedley, in order to outdo his friends, presented himself stark naked and cut such grossly coarse Rabelaisian capers that the crowd rioted, threw stones, and tried to force an entrance in order to knock him down.[12] Fashionable though licence might be, there had been a public scandal and Sedley was consequently cited before Sir Robert Hyde, senior Judge of the Court of Common Pleas, and sentenced to a heavy fine. " I am the first," Sedley commented, " that has had to pay for doing what I did." [13]

Sedley disliked being fined, however, so he begged a friend, Henry Killigrew, to intercede with the King and get the fine remitted. This devoted friend begged the money for himself, obtained it, and pocketed it to the last penny.

That is how friendship was conceived of in those days. Every lofty, or merely delicate, sentiment was similarly debased. Needless to say, there was no longer any question of religion. After the reign of the " saints " it was good taste to be ungodly. It is true that people went to church, but to Anglican churches so as to score off the Presbyterians. The church-goers in any case attended the service without reverence,[14] and lost no oppor-

---

[11] Burnet, *Some Passages in the Life and Death of John, Earl of Rochester*; Johnson, *Lives of the English Poets*, Rochester ; Hamilton, *Mémoires de Grammont*, pp. 245 ff. ; Forgues, *John Wilmot* ; letter of Saint-Evremond (?) prefacing the works of Rochester.

[12] à Wood, *Athenæ Oxonienses*, art. Sedley (Charles) states in unvarnished words : " Putting down their breeches they excrementiz'd in the street."

[13] à Wood quotes his reply more crudely : " He thought he was the first man that paid for shiting." Pepys, July 1, 1663, also records this fact. But his first editor, Lord Braybrooke, suppresses the most characteristic part of it. Mr. Mynors Bright and Mr. Wheatley who promised a more complete text, show the same lacuna at the same spot. It is regrettable that Pepys's *Diary* is not yet in its entirety accessible to the historian, who has no means of consulting the original shorthand manuscript.

[14] " *Wildish :* The Beaux are the most constant Church-men : you shall see Troops of 'em perk'd up in Galleries, setting their Cravats " (Shadwell, *Bury-Fair*, III, 1).—See also Pepys, Oct. 14, 1660.

tunity of showing the poor opinion they held of the officiating clergymen,[15] while the clergy for their part were in no mood to irritate their congregations by ill-directed zeal.[16] Preserved by the memory of the Puritans from any excessive enthusiasm or outbursts of piety, well satisfied to have dispossessed their enemies,[17] they were concerned to display courtesy and good manners,[18] and not to shock their flocks who might have amply supplied them with texts and unwelcome lessons for their sermons. " In short," said one of them, preaching in the King's presence " if you don't live up to the Precepts of the Gospel ; but abandon yourselves to your irregular Appetites, you must expect to receive your Reward in a certain Place which 'tis not good Manners to mention here." [19]

If religion was thus handled within a sacred building, it is not difficult to imagine what was made of it outside. People were atheists,[20] or rather called themselves atheists, for this also

[15] I doubt if there appears in all the dramas of this period, a single priest, Protestant or other, ancient or modern, who is not either odious or ridiculous.—See a characteristic scene in Pepys, Dec. 25, 1662 : the Bishop of Winchester is preaching in the Chapel of Whitehall against the pleasures of the Court ; his audience laughs while he is speaking.

[16] " I took a turn with Mr. Evelyn . . . talking of the badness of the Government, where nothing but wickedness, and wicked men and women command the King . . . that much of it arises . . . from the negligence of the Clergy, that a Bishop shall never be seen about him." (Pepys, April 26, 1667. See also ibid., Nov. 9, 1663, and Feb. 16, 1667–8.)

[17] In 1661 two thousand Presbyterian ministers were driven from their churches.

[18] John Stoughton, *The Church of the Restoration*, vol. I, especially pp. 470–3 and 507–12. When the Plague broke out the entire body of clergy fled from London (ibid., vol. I, p. 337).

[19] " What a fine thing it is to be well-manner'd upon Occasion ! In the Reign of King *Charles* the Second, a certain worthy Divine at *Whitehall*, thus address'd himself to the Auditory at the Conclusion of his Sermon : In short . . ." (Tom Brown, *Works*, vol. IV, p. 124 : Laconicks, *or New Maxims of* State *and* Conversation).—See also Pope, *Moral Essays*, Epistle iv, l. 150 and note.

[20] " . . . They professed themselves atheists, both in word and deed— smiling at the name of the devil, . . . and maintaining with oaths that there were no other angels than those in petticoats, denying any essential difference between good and evil, and deeming conscience a check suited merely to frighten children." (*Proteus Redivivus*, quoted by Malcolm, p. 167.)—" His religion (for now and then he will be pratling of that too) is pretendedly *Hobbian* : And he Swears the *Leviathan* may supply all the lost Leaves of *Solomon*, yet he never saw it in his life, and for ought he knows, it may be a *Treatise* about catching of *Sprats*, or new Regulating the *Green-land* Fishing Trade. However, the Rattle of it at *Coffee-houses*, has taught him to . . . maintain that there are no *Angels* but those in *Petticoats* : And therefore he defies *Heaven* worse than *Maximin* (one of Dryden's characters, see p. 41) ; imagines *Hell*, only a *Hot house* to Flux in for a *Clap*, and calls the *Devil*, the

was a matter of fashion : you professed atheism for the same reason as M. Jourdain wore his embroidered flowers, upside down.[20a] These people were not even sceptics : they denied, so as not to be taken for Roundheads, and to save themselves the trouble of thinking ;—just as ready to believe a thing one minute as they had been to deny it the moment before. Rochester suddenly became edifying when he felt his end approaching ; after having paid court to the Muse of gallantry up to the age of eighty, Waller took to writing pious verses [21]; Charles II on his deathbed surreptitiously received the Eucharist at the hands of a Roman Catholic priest ; a large number verted to Roman Catholicism on the accession of James II.

In short, the sole aim of this Court was pleasure. In Rochester's words :

> Our Sphere of Action is Life's Happiness
> And he who thinks beyond, thinks like an Ass.[22]

The Puritans saw human life as a vale of tears, a road strewn with trials and struggles by which man purchased life eternal. Their successors contented themselves with the present life. But to enjoy it properly—and to make up for the fasting under the Republic a man had to take two mouthfuls at a time—and merrily to perform life's pilgrimage, nothing embarrassing could be tolerated, all impedimenta had to be scrapped. Whence do we come ? Whither are we going ? What matter ! Here we are ; that's enough. Virtue, modesty—lies ! Pity, honour, courage [23]—prejudices of petty men ! You tell me some women are virtuous ? Those are the ones who sell their favours dear. You say some men are honest ? They are either liars or fools.[24]

Parsons *Bugbear*, and sometimes the *Civil Old Gentleman in Black* " (*The Character of a Town-Gallant*).
  [20a] Molière, *Le Bourgeois Gentilhomme*, II, 5.
  [21] Johnson, *Lives of the English Poets*, Waller.
  [22] Rochester, *Satire against Man*, Works, vol. I, p. 5. " She was a Woman of Sense, and by consequence a Lover of Pleasure " (The History of the *Life* and *Memoirs* of Mrs. Behn, By one of the Fair Sex. Prefacing the edition of her novels).
  [23] " . . . all men would be Cowards, if they durst " (Rochester, *Satire against Man*, Works, vol. I, p. 7). We shall see that he dared.—The Duke of Buckingham had a duel with Lord Ossory ; he gave him Chelsea Fields as the rendezvous and went off to await him elsewhere (Cobbett, *Parliamentary History*, I, 342).
  [24] " He denies there is any Essential Difference betwixt *Good* and *Evil*, deems *Conscience* a thing only fit for *Children*, and ascribes all *Honesty* to *simplicity* and an unpractisness in the *Ways* and *Methods* of the *Town* " (*The Character of a Town-Gallant*).

Men of wit were not taken in by such nonsense. So when he wanted money, the King of England thought it quite natural to sell himself to France.[24a] Those around him were no less unscrupulous. Aubrey de Vere, Earl of Oxford, was in love with an actress who rejected his advances; to get his way he agreed to marry her but brought a soldier disguised as a priest to perform the ceremony. When she discovered the base trickery of which she had been the victim, she flung herself at the King's feet demanding justice. To the King, however, her betrayer's conduct seemed perfectly natural and he decreed that an annual pension was quite adequate compensation.[25] Villiers, Duke of Buckingham, lover of the Countess of Shrewsbury, killed her husband in a duel, while she, in the dress of a page-boy, held his horse's bridle. Buckingham boasted that she granted him her caresses before he had removed his blood-stained clothes.[26] Incidents of this type were common. The morals of the day are summed up in the following maxim, borrowed from one of the heroes of a contemporary novel:

A man of Wit cou'd not be a Knave or Villain.[27]

When pleasure called him nothing halted him.

II

Art, literature : songs etc. satires, novels

Literature and the arts naturally took their place among the pleasures, since the Puritans had banned them. Their Parliament had decreed that all pictures in the royal collection which represented the second person of the Trinity or the Virgin Mary, should be burnt, and the rest sold.[28] They were no less

---

[24a] [The politics of this transaction are not so simple as would appear from this statement. In so far as Louis and Charles both wished to re-establish absolute monarchy in England, Charles might well regard Louis as his ally, and honourably accept funds from him. Louis might possibly guess that Charles was double-crossing him, but that is another story, not rare in politics. B. D.]

[25] Hamilton, *Mémoires de Grammont*, pp. 220-1.

[26] *Biographia Britannica*, Villiers.—" 'Tis said the duke slept with her in his bloody shirt " (Spence, p. 164).

[27] *Oroonoko, or the Royal Slave*, by Mrs. Behn; in the volume of her novels.

[28] Cromwell succeeded nevertheless in preserving for England the Raphael cartoons which are now in the South Kensington Museum (Lecky, vol. I, p. 528).

insensitive to music.²⁹ As for literature, they had neither the taste nor the time to read any but polemical writings, and the drama had been rigorously put on their index of forbidden works.³⁰ So the new Court restored the arts to favour. Painters were encouraged (Lely,³¹ Kneller, Cooper the miniaturist) and musicians also (Grabut, Purcell), while everyone took to writing literature. You could not be a gallant without being a man of wit: the two epithets became synonymous. The most fashionable men, the most brilliant courtiers were critics, authors, connoisseurs of literature : the Earl of Rochester, Sir Charles Sedley, Villiers Duke of Buckingham, the Earl of Mulgrave, Sir Car Scroop, Edmund Waller, Lord Buckhurst, the Duke and Duchess of Newcastle and innumerable others.³¹ᵃ

Since women were the main preoccupation of the day, they naturally set the tone, and gallant little verses composed for them were from the first the rage. All the poets of the Court set to work to sing of them.

It must be admitted that the singers' muse showed no overmastering inspiration. It was exhausted after a few strophes, or to be accurate after a few couplets, for it ran more to songs than to anything else, though it occasionally ventured on an elegy.³² The Restoration Muse did not, it is true, aim very high, it sought neither lofty ideas nor style : its ideal was a slight, delicate thought in simple and harmonious form. Its poetry

---

²⁹ See an interesting chapter on Puritanism in relation to music in Chappell, vol. II, p. 401.
³⁰ Prynne's celebrated book, *Histrio-Mastix*, gives a good indication of the Puritans' views on questions of amusement. The book is rare and as there is no copy in the Bibliothèque Nationale I quote its full title in my bibliography. The title is instructive.
³¹ Sir Peter Lely was knighted by Charles II.
³¹ᵃ [Waller and the Duke of Newcastle, and the Duchess had "taken to literature" well before the Restoration. See note 59a. B. D.]
³² In his *Essay on Poetry*, Sheffield, Earl of Mulgrave (later Duke of Buckinghamshire), began with songs :

> " First then, of *SONGS*, which now so much abound
> Without his *Song* no Fop is to be found . . .
> Tho' nothing seems more easie, yet no part
> Of *Poetry* requires a *nicer* Art."

Then comes the elegy :

> " Next *ELEGY* . . .
> The Praise of *Beauty*, *Valor*, *Wit* contains
> And there too oft despairing *Love* complains . . ."

Then the ode ; but he can quote no lyric belonging to the reign of Charles II.

was called " witty "[33]; the most flattering term that could be applied to it was to say that it was " ingenious ". The subjects sung varied little. Poetry devoted itself wholly to " beauty " and " beauties ". Lord Buckhurst on the eve of a great naval battle against the Dutch covered himself with glory by writing verses :

> To all you *Ladies* now at Land
> We *Men* at Sea indite ; etc.[34]

Confessions of love, disdain, desire, contempt, absence, sighs, inconstancy—such are the usual themes which the poets embroider with their monotonous variations. They offer sweet nothings to Chloris (Dorset) ; to Amoret, to Sacharissa (Waller) ; to Celimene, to Phillis, to Celia, to Thireis, to Aurelia, to Amaranta (Sedley). They shrink neither from sentimentality nor subtleties :

> While in this park I sing, the list'ning deer
> Attend my passion, and forget to fear :
> When to the beeches I report my flame,
> They bow their heads, as if they felt the same :
> To Gods appealing, when I reach their Bow'rs
> With loud complaints, they answer me in show'rs.
> To Thee a wild and cruel soul is giv'n,
> More deaf than trees, and prouder than the heav'n ![35]

That is the sort of thing, when it does not descend into sheer silliness. Waller inscribes verses to a " Lady who can do any thing but sleep when she pleaseth " and others to a " Lady who can sleep when she pleases ". He sings " Of a Tree cut in Paper ", of a " Card that her Majesty tore at Omber ".[36] The Earl of Roscommon, famed for the seriousness of his inspirations in this frivolous century,[37] wrote stanzas " On a young Lady

[33] It is from this period that English dates the noun *witticism* : " *A mighty Wittycism (if you will pardon a new word!)* "—Dryden, Preface to *The State of Innocence*.
[34] Song, *Written at Sea, in the first* Dutch-War, 1665, *the Night before an Engagement*. (Printed in the Works of Rochester, vol. II, p. 53.)
[35] Waller, *Works*, p. 42. *At* Pens-hurst.
[36] Waller, *The* Apology *of* Sleep, *Works*, pp. 17, 35 ; also pp. 144, 204.
[The title of a poem is not necessarily a good guide as to its merit. " On a girdle " is not promising, but Waller's poem is one of the most famous in the language. The poems on the tree and on the card are blameless trivialities of " occasional " verse : but the ones on sleeping or sleepless ladies have a certain poetic value. B. D.]

[37] " Unhappy Dryden ! in all Charles's days.
Roscommon only boasts unspotted lays." (Pope.)

who sung finely, and was afraid of a cold " or an elegy " On the Death of a Lady's Dog ".[38]

All these graces, however, all these poetic delicacies, were nothing but false coin. Scratch the elegant nobleman of those days and you find at once the ungoverned and shameless debauchee. The poet of the day is no better : his playful flirtation is wholly superficial ; if he is at pains laboriously to concoct little verses apparently tender and languorous, his main desire is to appeal to the physical senses, to excite desire, and to this end he does not hesitate to use the vivid, at need the coarsest phrase.[39]

But it was particularly in their satires that the " gentlemen-poets " gave a free rein to their pen in such matters. The satires, or as they were then called, the " lampoons ",[40] became in fact the refuge of those at Court who could boast neither wit nor poetic talent. To speak evil of your neighbour is within the powers of the meanest intelligence, and the satirists of those days aimed at nothing else. An old French poet wrote, " I bear no malice against fools, but against Folly."[41] The Restor-

[38] *Works*, pp. 53, 54.
[Beljame might have remembered that Apollo does not always keep his bow at full stretch. Roscommon was a good poet in his own line, the *Essay on Translated Verse* being justly well known. One wonders whether, if Beljame had been studying a later period, he would have commented adversely upon Gray for writing on a cat drowned in a bowl of goldfish. B. D.]

[39] " For *Songs* and *Verses* mannerly obscene,
That can stir *Nature* up by Springs unseen,
And, without forcing Blushes, warm the Queen :
Sedley has that prevailing, gentle Art,
That can with a *Resistless Pow'r* impart
The *Loosest* Wishes to the *Chastest* Heart,
Raise such a Conflict, kindle such a Fire
Betwixt declining Virtue and Desire ;
Till the poor vanquish'd Maid dissolves away
In Dreams all Night, in Sighs and Tears all Day."
(Rochester, Horace's *Tenth Satire of the First Book imitated*. *Works*, vol. I, p. 10.)

Such was the poetic art of this type. To see it in practice the reader has only to choose amongst the verses of the fine gentlemen of that day.
[This again is something of an overstatement : the proposition is true only in the main. B. D.]

[40] " *Lord Lampoon* and *Monsieur Song*
Who sought her [the Muse's] love, and promis'd for't
To make her famous at the Court."
(Otway, *The Poets Complaint of his Muse*.)

[41] Du Lorens, 7th Satire : Je ne'en veux point aux sots, j'en veux à la sottise.

ation satirists laid no claim to such detachment; they never rose to a general point of view; they dreamt of nothing but personal attacks. They hurl abuse at people, and since poetry is all the fashion they hurl it in verse. From the King downwards, who often appears under the nickname of " Old Rowley ", no one is spared. With him everyone runs the gauntlet of a vocabulary drawn from the pigsty and the gutter. No one who has not read these lampoons could conceive the flood of mud and filth with which they unashamedly overflow; having read them, you are driven to marvel how people could be found to write such stuff in such quantities, and readers to understand it when written, especially in a period so near our own time and in a country which has so great a reputation for reserve if not for prudery. But there is no use labouring this point. Apart from the fact that quotations from these satires would, to say the least, be difficult, the drama bears more revealing though weaker witness to the prevailing social conditions. At their worst, a few obscene writings, which may circulate privately and be read in a whisper, need not damn the moral reputation of a period. What a more numerous, more sensitive, more impressionable public openly listens to in a theatre, has far greater significance. Without saying more on the subject, it will suffice to cite as specimens of the coarseness of this satiric verse, Rochester's two satires on the King [42], Etherege's *The Lady of Pleasure* [43] and an imitation of Boileau's *Festin Ridicule* from the uninhibited pen of Villiers, Duke of Buckingham.[44]

Having said so much, it is only fair to recognize that these verses, never lofty and often insipid and coarse, have at moments a touch of elegance, and display a genuine feeling for harmony.[45] It should in justice be added that their noble authors have a real taste and feeling for literature, not very deep perhaps, not very

---

[42] *A Satire which the King took out of his Pocket—The Satire on the King, for which he was banished the Court*; and *turned* Mountebank (*Works*, vol. I, pp. 20 ff. and pp. 24–5).

[43] *The Lady of Pleasure. A Satyr. By Sir George Etheridge, Knight.* Printed in the *Miscellaneous Works* of Buckingham (Villiers).

[44] Timon, a Satyr, *In Imitation of Monsieur* Boleau [sic] (in *Miscellaneous Works*). This satire is included also in the works of Rochester (vol. I, p. 126) under the title of *The Rehearsal. A* Satire. It is possible that the two friends collaborated to produce this charming work.—See also " A Faithful Catalogue of our most Eminent *Ninnies*, Written by the Earl of *Dorset* in the year 1683 " in the works of Rochester (vol. II, p. 23).

[45] For instance, Waller's " Go, lovely rose ! " and Sedley's " *Love* still has something of the Sea " both justly included in the anthologies.

acute, but on the whole worthy of note. The writers have an up-to-date acquaintance with French literature. They know the classic poets, the Latin poets at any rate, especially Horace. When they want something a shade better than usual they translate from the classics. The Earl of Roscommon makes an English verse translation of Horace's *Ars Poetica* [46]; Rochester imitates the tenth satire of the first book of Horace and the first satire of Juvenal [47]; Sedley translates in verse the fourth book of the *Georgics*.[48] It is of course a sign of weakness that they cannot escape from their own rut without other men's aid; but it also demonstrates a degree of culture which must in justice be placed to the credit of their account.

After poetry came romantic fiction. It ran on the same lines; it was gallant too. For years England had rejoiced in Mademoiselle de Scudéry. Her *Clélie* was translated in 1656 (the very year that it appeared in France). The first part of La Calprenède's *Cleopatra* had been translated as early as 1652.[49] Preoccupied as it was with women, the Restoration could not fail to take pleasure in these affected pretentious writings, and people continued to wander in the Land of Tender Sentiment. Ladies found their favourite reading in the most mawkish of these novels [50]; and in writing the dedication of his tragedy *Aureng-Zebe*, Dryden takes pains to defend his play to the ladies by quoting the example of *Le Grand Cyrus*. The theatre borrowed from this romantic literature a whole species of play, and everyday conversation was steeped in its style and vocabulary. A simple bookseller, John Dunton, married Miss Elizabeth Annesley in 1682. She was his " Beautiful Iris " and signed herself " Iris ", while he signed his letters " Philaret ". He called his wife " my beautiful conqueror " and " my dear captive " and published a portrait of " Iris " written by " Arsinda ", with a portrait of " Philaret " by the ingenious " Cleonta, sister of the Beautiful Iris ".[51] Mrs. Katherine Philips, " the matchless Orinda ", bestowed on her husband the name of Antenor, and

[46] *Works*, 1753.
[47] Horace's *Tenth Satire of the First Book imitated* (*Works*, vol. I, p. 10), *Imitation of the First Satire of* Juvenal (ibid., p. 15).
[48] The Fourth Book of Virgil (*Poetical Works*).
[49] See the Bibliography s.vv. Scudéry and La Calprenède.
[50] Pepys, Dec. 7, 1660: " My wife in Great Cyrus till 12 at night."
[51] See The *Life and Errors of John Dunton*, pp. 75 ff.—Swift was still under this spell when he called Miss Waring " Varina ", Miss Esther Johnson " Stella " and Miss Vanhomrigh " Vanessa ".

on his friends the names Silvander, Cratander, Poliarchus, Lucasia, etc.[52]

The Restoration novel, then, drew its inspiration from Mademoiselle de Scudéry and her like. But the gallants of the day needed some livelier and less severe reading. They got exactly what they wanted from " the ingenious Madame Aphara Behn ", or as they called her " the admirable " or even " the divine Astræa ".

Her story of *Oroonoko, or the Royal Slave* written, amongst others, " at the command of King Charles II ", was so popular that more than thirty years afterwards the poet Southerne took it as the subject of one of his most successful tragedies.[53] Yet this famous story has not survived, and the same abyss of forgetfulness has swallowed all the romantic literature of the period. It is all the more necessary to dwell on it for a moment, since it reflects one whole facet of the Restoration spirit.[54]

---

[52] See her *Poems*, passim.

[The fashion recurs at intervals, and is not peculiar to this period, nor originated by it. It is not, perhaps, surprising that the Sidney circle, with Spenser, should have adopted it, as they seem to have done. It is more surprising that in 1730 John and Charles Wesley should, in a special circle, have been called respectively Cyrus and Araspes, while Mrs. Pendarves was known as Aspasia, and Ann Granville as Selina, etc. There is no special significance to be attached to this recurring social-literary game. B. D.]

[53] *Oroonoko* (1696).—Southerne borrowed the tragic part of *The Fatal Marriage* from another of Mrs. Behn's novels, *The Fair Vow-breaker*; see his dedication.—Here is a trifling fact which shows the long-enduring popularity of the novel *Oroonoko*. The heroine of the story is called Imoinda. Now, in 1756 John Buncle met a young woman with whom he had been in love : " What (I said) *Miss Wolf of Balineskay?* *O my Imoinda!* And snatching her to my arms, I almost stifled her with kisses." (*The Life of John Buncle, Esq*re, by Thomas Amory, vol. II, p. 183.)

[54] The oldest edition of Mrs. Behn's novels quoted by Lowndes is 1698 ; but *Oroonoko* must date from the beginning of the reign of Charles II, for it contains an allusion to the production of Dryden's *Indian Queen* in 1665 as to something recent. The 1705 edition is the earliest I have been able to find in the British Museum.

[*Oroonoko* is perhaps the earliest example of " the noble savage ", and the work had a great influence in France, being translated into French in 1745 and in 1788, possibly oftener. The book has been described as " the first English philosophical novel containing dissertations upon abstract subjects, such as the religion of humanity " (Sir Paul Harvey in *The Oxford Companion to English Literature*). Mrs. Behn's novels were edited by E. A. Baker in 1905, and her plays by Montague Summers in 1915. She was later the subject of a monograph by Miss V. Sackville-West. The revival in the interest in her works took place since this book was written, and Beljame could not now say that either she or her works are " forgotten ". The *D.N.B.* article suggests that she was to the writers of her day what George Sand was to the writers of France in the last century. B. D.]

Oroonoko is the grandson and sole heir of the King of Cormantin (Kormantine) on the Gold Coast, where the English go to fetch slaves for their colonies. The inhabitants of this country are children of Nature, whom the author compares to our first parents " before the Fall ". Oroonoko, however, is a model of courtesy, honour and generosity ; he knows French, English and Spanish and even a little history (he admires the Romans and grieves for the death of Charles I of England). It is unnecessary to say that he is handsome and capable of the loftiest sentiments, above all made to love and to be loved.

He meets Imoinda, as perfect in her way as he in his :

Having made his first Complements, and presented her an hundred and fifty Slaves in Fetters, he told her with his Eyes, that he was not insensible of her Charms ; while *Imoinda*, who wish'd for nothing more than so glorious a Conquest, was pleas'd to believe, she understood that silent Language of new-born Love ; and, from that moment put on all her additions to Beauty.

The Prince return'd to Court with quite another Humour than before ; and though he did not speak much of the fair *Imoinda*, he had the pleasure to hear all his Followers speak of nothing but the Charms of that Maid, insomuch that, even in the presence of the old King, they were extolling her, and heightening, if possible, the Beauties they had found in her : so that nothing else was talk'd of, no other sound was heard in every Corner where there were Whisperers, but *Imoinda ! Imoinda !*

So beautiful a love was bound to run unsmoothly. The old King (he was over a hundred years old) is fired by these descriptions and sends Imoinda the royal veil, which compels her on pain of death to attend at his harem. She can but obey, and the amiable monarch receives her at the bath.

Despair ensues for Oroonoko, and a painful conflict between respect for his sovereign-grandsire and his love. At last he calms himself and decides to hide his passion and his troubles, reassured by reflecting that in view of his age the King will be his rival rather in desire than deed.

The King who has not failed to get wind of his grandson's love has kept him somewhat at arm's length, but seeing him so calm and peaceful, supposes him cured, and invites him to a feast at which his lady-love is present. During the meal he leaves his guests to lead Imoinda into an adjacent room where his luckless rival sees : " a Bed of State made ready, with Sweets and Flowers for the Dalliance of the King ".

Oroonoko has meantime succeeded in getting into touch

with inmates of the harem; he contrives to see Imoinda, to tell her of his love and " ravished in a moment, what his old Grandfather had been endeavouring for so many Months ". Unfortunately he is surprised; the King sends him back to the army and has Imoinda sold as a slave, telling her lover that she has been killed.

The youth is disconsolate, he heaves many sighs, weeps copious tears, but comforts himself just enough to continue living and overcome his country's enemy, Jamoan, " a Man very gallant, and of excellent graces, and fine parts ", who, after having been defeated, becomes his best friend.

After this victory Oroonoko, deceived by an English captain, is treacherously seized and sold as a slave to Surinam. There he commands the admiration of all by his merits, entrances the English ladies by his grace, and finds among the slaves in the colony the beautiful Imoinda, a slave like himself, hiding herself under the name of Clemene. He is allowed to marry her and the tale of their love so greatly touches the authorities that they promise to set the couple free and send them both back to their own country. There is delay in fulfilling this promise, and Oroonoko who has once already been deceived by a European, suspects new treachery, enlists the negroes' interest in his case and organizes a general rising of the slaves in the colony. The Deputy-Governor, alarmed, suggests discussion, and by fair words induces Oroonoko to lay down his arms. No sooner is the over-trustful youth disarmed than he is seized and flogged. The " royal slave " trembling with wrath at such an outrage swears to be avenged. He flees to the woods with his pregnant wife. That she may not fall into the white men's power he kills her, and she is happy to die by his hand. Imoinda dead, her lover lingers for two days weeping beside her body. There he is found by the Deputy Governor's people who have the greatest difficulty in approaching him. Finally, however, they capture him and put him to death with refined torture : cutting off his limbs one after the other. Calm and heroic, he smokes his pipe till his last arm is amputated. " Thus died," writes the author in conclusion :

this Great Man ; worthy of a better Fate, and a more sublime wit than mine to write his Praise : Yet, I hope, the Reputation of my Pen is considerable enough to make his Glorious Name to survive to all Ages, with that of the Brave, the Beautiful and the Constant *Imoinda.*

It is obvious that in the matter of fine sentiment and highfalutin language Mrs. Behn is a worthy rival of Molière's *Précieuses Ridicules*. She differs from them in two points, however: she does not impose such severe tasks on her readers (the volume of her novels contains eight other narratives besides the *Royal Slave*) and, secondly, she spices her gallantry with a dash of sensuality. Her heroes imitate the style of the Hotel de Rambouillet, but the style only; none of them is inclined like Montausier to languish for fourteen years.

At other times, however, they wallow in the most utter bathos, for instance, as in *The Lover's Watch, or The Art of Courtship*.[55] Here is the " Argument ":

'*Tis* in the most Happy and August Court of the Best and Greatest Monarch of the World, that *Damon*, a young Nobleman, whom we will render under that Name, languishes for a Maid of Quality,[56] who will give us leave to call her *Iris*:

Their births are equally Illustrious; they are both Young; their Beauty such, as I do not too nicely particularize, lest I should discover (which I am not permitted to do) who these charming Lovers are. Let it suffice that *Iris* is the most fair and accomplisht Person that ever adorn'd a Court: and that *Damon* is only worthy of the Glory of her Favour; for he has all that can render him lovely in the fair Eyes of the Amiable *Iris*. Nor is he Master of those Superficial Beauties alone, that please at first Sight; he can charm the Soul with a thousand Arts of Wit and Gallantry. And in a word, may say, without flattering either, that there is no one Beauty, no one Grace, no perfection of Mind and Body, that wants to compleat a Victory on both sides.

The Agreement of Age, Fortunes, Quality and Humours in these two fair Lovers, made the impatient *Damon* hope, that nothing would oppose his Passion; and if he saw himself every Hour languishing for the Adorable Maid, he did not however despair: And if *Iris* sigh'd, it was not for fear of being one day more happy.

Here we have the refinement of refinement. Iris has to go into the country. It is impossible for Damon to follow her. He consoles himself by writing her the sweetest letters in the world; and she, in payment of a wager she had lost to Damon sends him " the watch ".

[55] This is an imitation of two gallant works of Balthazar de Bonnecorse, the author whom Boileau has linked with Pradon in the following epigram:

" Venez, Pradon et Bonnecorse,
    Grands écrivains de même force . . ."

For the complete titles, see my Bibliography.

[56] Madame la comtesse d'Escarbagnas would have enjoyed reading these novels: all the characters are " persons of quality ".

The face of the watch shows no vulgar numerals, but instead indicates how a tender lover should employ each hour of his day, while a Cupid points the tip of his arrow to each successive hour :

> Eight a Clock. *Agreeable Reverie.*—Nine a Clock. *Design to please no Body.*—Ten a Clock. *Reading of Letters.*—Eleven a Clock. *The Hour to Write in.*—Twelve a Clock. *Indispensible Duty.*—One a Clock. *Forc'd Entertainment.*—Two a Clock. *Dinner Time.*—Three a Clock. *Visits to Friends.*—Four a Clock. *General Conversation.*—Five a Clock. *Dangerous Visits.*—Six a Clock. *Walk without Design.*—Seven a Clock. *Voluntary Retreat.*—Eight a Clock. *Impatient Demands.*—Nine a Clock. *Melancholy Reflections.*—Ten a Clock. *Reflections.*—Eleven a Clock. *Supper.*—Twelve a Clock. *Complaisance.*—One a Clock. *Impossibility to Sleep.*—Two a Clock. *Conversation in Dreams.*—Three a Clock. *Capricious Suffering in Dreams.*—Four a Clock. *Jealousie in Dreams.*—Five a Clock. *Quarrels in Dreams.*—Six a Clock. *Accommodation in Dreams.*—Seven a Clock. *Divers Dreams.*[57]

He then gets up, to begin all over again.

In sending Damon the watch, Iris adjures him to guard it tenderly. Damon replies by pointing out that the watch had no case. He suggests the following scheme : the case for the watch should be in the form of a heart and be decorated with their initials and in addition the initials of the words : *Love Extream . . . Reciprocal Love . . . Constant Love . . . Secret Love.* The fastening of the case should be formed by two hands and inscribed with the motto : *Inviolable Faith.*[58]

Gallant reflections and rhymes are throughout intermingled with the tale. Such embroideries as : " These are little paths all strewn with roses."

Nor is this the end. Our author's imagination is not so quickly exhausted. To balance the watch Damon sends his lady love a mirror : " The Lady's Looking-Glass to dress Herself by : or, the Art of Charming. This speaks to her of *The Shape of* Iris . . . Iris's *Complexion* . . . Iris's *Hair* . . . Iris's *Eyes* . . . *The Mouth of* Iris . . . *The Neck of* Iris . . . *The Arms and Hands of* Iris . . . *The Grace and Air of* Iris . . . *The Discretion of* Iris . . . *The Goodness and Complaisance of* Iris . . . *The Wit of* Iris . . . *The Modesty of* Iris . . . Once started on this line there was

---

[57] Here the *ingenious* Mrs. Behn's imagination would seem to have given out : the adjective *divers* is not very gallant.

[58] Note that during the whole narrative it is not clear whether Damon and Iris are betrothed or are vulgar paramours. It is more delicate not to allude to marriage.

no reason why he should ever stop. Let us leave him to continue by himself.

III

Writers' hopes after the Restoration.—Disappointment.—Authors friendly to the Court : Cowley, Butler.—Authors hostile to the Court : Bunyan, Milton. —Authors who succeed in living by their pen take to drama : Dryden, Otway, Shadwell, Lee, Crowne, Mrs. Behn, Settle, D'Urfey, Ravenscroft

So, what the fashionable society of the Restoration asked first and foremost of literature, was gallant and sensual verse, or free and romantic narrative. But the writers of these things were all wealthy people of high rank, for whom writing was merely a recreation and a means of shining in society. They were amateurs, not authors.[59]

Side by side with them, however, there were others who were forced to seek a livelihood by plying the author's trade on which they depended for their living. It is with these latter that this book intends to deal.

The years of the Civil War and the Republic had been an iron age for literature. For eighteen years there had been an interregnum in public taste. No theatre, no books (except polemics).[59a]

---

[59] All the writers so far quoted belonged to the aristocracy except Waller, Etherege and Mrs. Behn. But Waller and Etherege were rich and in favour at Court. As for Mrs. Behn, she was a political spy in the pay of Charles II, and as a gallant lady she had other sources of income than her pen. Her writing, moreover, was not confined to novels.—See *Biographia Britannica*, under Waller (Edmund), Etherege and Behn.

[59a] [Little theatre, true, till Davenant's *Siege of Rhodes* in 1656 ; yet some surreptitious playing (See L. Hotson : *The Commonwealth and Restoration Stage*). But reference to any compilation, such as the Oxford *Annals of English Literature*, or the Tables in the relevant volume of the Oxford History of English Literature, will show that the output in books was as great in these eighteen years as in the previous eighteen. I name a selection, omitting all polemics. 1642. Denham, *Cooper's Hill* ; Fuller, *Holy State*. 1643. Baker, *Chronicles of the Kings of England* ; Browne, *Religio Medici* (authorized). 1644. Donne, *Biathanatos* ; Quarles, *Barnabas and Boanerges*. 1645. Milton, *Poems* ; Waller, *Poems* ; Howell, *Epistolae Ho-elianae*. 1646. Browne, *Vulgar Errors* ; Crashaw, Quarles, Shirley, Suckling and Vaughan, various volumes of poems. 1647. Corbet, Cleveland, Stanley, and More all published volumes of poetry. 1648. J. Beaumont, *Psyche* ; Herrick, *Hesperides* ; Hooker, *Ecclesiastical Polity*, vi and viii. 1649. D. of Newcastle, *The Country Captain* ; Lovelace, *Lucasta* ; Donne, *Fifty Sermons* ; Taylor, *Great Exemplar* ; Lord Herbert, *Life of Henry VIII* ; R. B., *Lachrymae Musarum* (poems by Dryden, Marvell, Herrick and Denham). 1650. Davenant, *Gondibert* ; Vaughan, *Silex Scintillans* ; Raleigh, *Essays and Observations* ; Taylor, *Holy Living*. 1651. Stanley, *Poems* ; Vaughan, *Olor Iscanus* ;] Donne, *Essays in Divinity* and *Letters* ; Taylor, *Holy Dying* ; Wotton,

Cowley and Denham were exiled with their sovereign; Waller was awed into silence by the rigour of the puritanic spirit; and even the muse of Milton was scared from him by the clamour of religious and political controversy, and returned, like a sincere friend, only to cheer the adversity of one who had neglected her during his career of worldly importance.[60]

When Charles II ascended his father's throne, writers could not contain themselves for joy. It seemed that after long wandering in the wilderness, they had reached at last the Promised Land. They dreamt of marvellous grapes, of rivers flowing with milk and honey, and they immediately vied with each other in trying to attract the attention and favours of the King. Panegyrics and dithyrambs poured in from all directions. Each one reckoned that the King would rain down on him gifts and sinecures.

Disillusionment was swift.

Even those who had quite special claims on the royal favour reaped nothing but indifference. Cowley, who had gone into exile to follow the Queen-Mother to Paris, who had devoted himself heart and soul to the Royalist cause and had endured prison in consequence: even he was brushed aside when the hour of recompense arrived. Yet he had not let himself be overlooked. He had celebrated the Restoration in a pindaric *Ode upon His Majesties Restauration and Return* [61] and requested to be made

---

Reliquiae Wottonianae; Walton, *Life of Wotton*. 1652. Herbert, *Remains*; Crashaw, *Carmen Deo Nostro*; Greville, *Life of Sidney*; Vaughan, *Mount of Olives*. 1653. Cleveland, *Poems*; Basse, *Pastorals*; Taylor, *Sermons*; Urquhart, *Rabelais*; Walton, *Compleat Angler*. 1654. Johnson, *History of New England*; Orrery, *Parthenissa*. 1655. Poems by Marvell, Waller, and Philips; Dugdale, *Monasticon Anglicanum*; Fuller, three *Histories*; Taylor, *Golden Grove*; Vaughan, *Hermetical Physics*. 1656. Cowley, *Poems*; Denham, *Destruction of Troy*; Osborne, *Advice to a Son*; Duchess of Newcastle, *Nature's Pictures*. 1657. Cleveland, *Poems*; King, *Poems*; Raleigh, *Remains*; Taylor, *Discourses and Friendship*. 1658. Waller and Godolphin, *Passion of Dido*; Browne, *Urn Burial*; Ussher, *Annals of the World*. 1659. Further poems (posthumous) by Lovelace and Suckling; Chamberlayne, *Pharonnida*; Baxter, *Holy Commonwealth*; Evelyn, *Character of England*; More, *Immortality of the Soul*.

This is only a selection from the usual lists. Besides such works, a number of the plays of the previous period were printed for the first time in these years. There was obviously plenty to read. Far from there being literary starvation, there was not even literary scarcity. B. D.]

[60] Walter Scott, *The Life of John Dryden* prefixed to his works.

[Scott is not quite right here. Milton's early poems were published in 1645. He deliberately put poetry aside so as to serve, as a good citizen, the cause he believed in. Nevertheless, his sonnets were nearly all written in this period, and he probably began *Paradise Lost* in 1656. B. D.]

[61] *Works*.

Director of *The Savoy*,[62] a post which had been promised him both by Charles I and Charles II. Turned away, rejected, criticised,[63] he bitterly complained ; finally, weary of his devotion, " Melancholy Cowley ", as he called himself, withdrew from the World and the Court, and died in retreat seven years after the Restoration. When he was dead the King remembered him : " Mr. Cowley," he said, " has not left a better man behind him in England."[64]

Butler, whose poem *Hudibras* did good service to the Royalists by enlisting laughter on their side, was treated no better than Cowley. When the first three cantos of his burlesque epic appeared in 1663, Lord Buckhurst introduced the poem to the Court. It at once evoked general enthusiasm. The Presbyterian Don Quixote, setting out for war with his stable-boy Ralph, was hailed with shouts of triumphant laughter. People felt revenged on the *Saints* by this merciless satire on their ridiculous ways. The King was for ever quoting lines of *Hudibras* and the courtiers set about learning it by heart, so as to be able to quote it like their master. All eyes expectantly waited to see " the rain of gold " which was bound to be showered on the author. He himself, living at the time an obscure and precarious life, expected it no less eagerly than his admirers. The royal sky remained without a cloud.

The second part appeared in 1664. The nation's interest was kindled once again, and the author once more vaunted to the skies. Praise was his sole reward.[65] There is, it is true, a story that Clarendon who was then Lord Chancellor promised him posts, but the truth of this is questionable, and it is certain that Butler got nothing. There is another story that the King

[62] *The Savoy* was originally a hospital (now no longer existing) which had gradually become a refuge for professional beggars, a sort of *Cour des Miracles*. The post of Director which Cowley coveted was of course a sinecure. —See W. Thornbury, *Haunted London*, chap. VI.

[63] Amongst other things his *Cutter of Coleman-Street* was made a matter of reproach. It was supposed to be an attack on the Royalists. Cowley himself vigorously protested in his preface how unlikely it was that a man who had suffered for a lost cause would choose the day of its triumph to attack it.—See also his ode, *The Complaint*, in his *Works*.

[64] Johnson, *Lives of the English Poets* : Cowley.

[65] " Did not the celebrated Author of Hudibras bring the king's enemies into a lower contempt with the sharpnesse of his wit, than all the terrors of his administration could reduce them to ? Was not his book always in the pocket of his Prince ? And what did the mighty prowess of his Knight-Errant amount to ? Why—he died, with the highest esteem of the Court—in a garret ! " Cibber, Dedication to Steele of his tragedy *Ximena, or the Heroic Daughter*, 1719. Printed in Steele's *Correspondence*, vol. II, p. 535.

one day gave him three hundred guineas, but there is no proof of this outbreak of generosity.[66]

Wycherley, the writer of comedies, who was in great favour at Court, was astonished at the neglect of his unfortunate fellow-author. He was in the good graces of Buckingham, who at that time was all powerful, and he made representations to the Duke, pointing out how much the royal family owed Butler for having written *Hudibras* and what a disgrace it was to the Court that a man of his "loyalty" and "wit" should be left in penury and obscurity. Buckingham, who fancied himself as a patron of literature, promised to speak of the matter to the King. To strengthen him in these good intentions, Wycherley suggested introducing Butler to him. Buckingham agreed, and on the appointed day Butler and his friend arrived first at the rendezvous. The powerful patron turned up in due course, but as bad luck would have it, the door of the room where the meeting took place was not shut. Two beautiful ladies happened to pass, and catching sight of them the great man left the two friends sitting there, while he dashed out to play the gallant. He did not return, and that was the last Butler heard of His Grace the Duke of Buckingham.[67]

Nevertheless, though discouraged, and more and more forgotten, Butler published a third part of his poem in 1678. But he went no further: *Hudibras* remained unfinished.

Butler died without leaving enough to pay for his own funeral. One of his friends tried to raise a subscription to secure a tomb for him in Westminster Abbey, but without success. The friend had to bury him at his own expense.[68]

---

[66] Johnson, *Lives of the English Poets*: Butler.—*Biographia Britannica*, s.v. Butler.

[It is possible that Butler's extreme poverty has been exaggerated. According to the *D.N.B.* it seems that Butler may have had a pension of £100 a year (no mean sum when compared with the currency values of our day) during the last few years of his life. B. D.]

[67] Pack (Richardson), *Miscellanies in Verse and Prose*, p. 181; *Some Memoirs of William Wycherley, Esq.*

[This sort of gossip is hardly evidence; and in any case the whole of these *Memoirs* is extremely suspect. B. D.]

[68] à Wood, *Athenæ Oxonienses*, s.v. Prynne (William).—*The Genuine Poetical Remains of Samuel Butler*, Preface.

> ". . . you have ev'ry Day before your Face
> Plenty of fresh resembling Instances:
> Great *Cowley's* Muse the same ill Treatment had, ⎫
> Whose verse shall live for ever to upbraid ⎬
> Th'ungrateful World, that left such Worth unpaid. ⎭

If loyal writers were thus treated it is not difficult to imagine how the others fared.

Bunyan, who was of course an apostle rather than a writer, lay twelve and a half years in prison for the crime of having preached in public. His works were too serious to be understood by the frivolous readers of those days. They were not collected till 1736 and such was the vacuum of scorn around him that as late as 1782 Cowper hesitated to name him in his verse.[69]

Great Milton, " on evil dayes though fall'n, and evil tongues ; in darkness, and with dangers compast round, and solitude ",[70] wrote his masterpiece for a scanty audience.[71]

Scant the audience, indeed, and scant their sympathy.

> *Waller* himself may thank Inheritance
> For what he else had never got by Sense.
> On *Butler* who can think without just Rage,
> The Glory and the Scandal of the Age?
> Fair stood his Hopes, when first he came to Town,
> Met ev'ry where with Welcomes of Renown,
> Courted, caressed by all, with Wonder read,
> And Promises of Princely favour fed :
> But what Reward for all had he at last,
> After a Life in dull Expectance pass'd?
> The Wretch, at summing up his misspent Days,
> Found nothing left but Poverty and Praise.
> Of all his Gains by Verse, he could not save
> Enough to purchase Flannel and a Grave :
> Reduc'd to Want, he in due Time fell sick,
> Was fain to die, and be interr'd on Tick :
> And well might bless the Fever that was sent
> To rid him hence, and his worse Fate prevent."
> (Oldham, *A Satire, Dissuading from Poetry, Works*, vol. III.)

Oldham was a contemporary ; he died in 1683 at the age of thirty-two.

[69] *Biographia Britannica*, s.v. Bunyan ; Watt, *Bibliotheca Britannica*, s.v. Bunyan.—The first edition of *The Pilgrim's Progress* is dated 1678 ; Bunyan died in 1688. Here are Cowper's lines :

" I name thee not, lest so despised a name
  Should move a sneer at thy deserved fame."
  (*Tirocinium : or, a Review of Schools.*)

We shall later see, however, that not every reader greeted his writings with indifference.

[70] *Paradise Lost*, VII, 28 ff.—His Book *Defensio Populi* had been burned by the hangman in 1660, and proceedings had been instituted against him. (Neal, *History of the Puritans*, vol. IV, p. 308).—See also Geffroy, pp. 204–9.

[71] ". . . still govern thou my song,
  Urania, and fit audience find, though few.
  But drive farr off the barbarous dissonance
  Of *Bacchus* and his Revellers . . ."
  (*Paradise Lost*, VII, 32 ff.)

On April 27, 1667, the bookseller Samuel Symons bought the manuscript of *Paradise Lost* on conditions which deserve to be remembered.[72] He paid the poet five pounds sterling down ; if he sold 1,300 copies of the first edition he was to pay him another £5 ; a third £5 after the sale of the same number of copies of the second edition and a fourth payment of £5 after an equal sale of the third edition. None of the three editions was to exceed 1,500 copies.

At the end of two years Milton's right to the second payment of £5 matured, and he signed a receipt for this sum on April 26, 1669. So England bought 1,300 copies of *Paradise Lost* in two years.[72a] Neither the author nor his subject was of a type to win popular favour, nor his style either ; the Court compared his verse to the clatter of a wheelbarrow.[73] His brother poets themselves treated his biblical epic no better : Dryden turned it into an opera, *The State of Innocence and Fall of Man*. The publisher, in order to quicken attention, had eight times (perhaps more) renewed the title of the first edition.[74] He did not publish the second edition until 1674 and again made modifications ; the format of the volume was changed and the ten books of the poem were converted into twelve. Readers remained unmoved. The third edition did not appear till 1678, after the poet's death. The widow lost no time in selling her rights in it for £8. As for the bookseller Symons, who, despite the very modest price he had paid the poet, had probably made little enough profit from the bargain, he surrendered his rights to his colleague Brabazon Aylmer for the sum of £25.

It was not Symons who four years after *Paradise Lost* published *Paradise Regained* and *Samson Agonistes*. Milton was obliged to turn to another publisher, on what conditions we do not know. Perhaps he had himself to bear the cost of this double publication.[75]

---

[72] This contract which brought in so little to Milton was bought for 100 guineas by the banker-poet Rogers who presented it to the British Museum. Together with the receipts and contracts quoted below, it is reproduced in Professor Masson's excellent edition of Milton's poetical works.

[72a] [One wonders whether many more would be sold to-day, with a population many times larger, and far more literate. Seventh ed. : 1700 ! B. D.]

[73] Smith, quoted by Johnson, *Lives of the English Poets*: Philips (Appendix).

[74] It is interesting to see in Lowndes the detail of these various modifications.

[75] *The Poetical Works of John Milton*, edited by Professor Masson ; Introduction to *Paradise Regained*.

The great man in his poverty and obscurity continued to the end to write books which were not, and could not hope to be, read : a treatise on Logic in Latin, treatises on True Religion, on Heresy, on Schism, on Tolerance and the best methods of preventing the spread of Popery ; a volume of intimate letters in Latin with oratorical essays of his youth ; a history of Muscovy, etc.[76]

All these subjects accorded ill with " the barbarous dissonance of *Bacchus* and his Revellers ". Yet his funeral was attended by a great concourse of mourners, but his modest grave was left without an inscription.[77]

It is clear that the position of authors was not an easy one and no easier for the friends of the Court than for others.[78]

How did those writers manage, who contrived to live by their pen ?

When Charles II returned to England, John Dryden,[79] the most famous of them, had just published *A Poem upon the Death of his late Highness, Oliver, Lord Protector of England, Scotland and Ireland*. This did not prevent his joining in the poetic chorus which greeted the King's return.[80] He wrote a poem *Astræa*

---

[76] Geffroy, *les Pamphlets de Milton*, pp. 239 ff.

[77] Johnson, *Lives of the English Poets* : Milton and the notes of Cunningham.

[78] I am far from wishing to forget Andrew Marvell amongst the authors hostile to the Court. He was a friend of Milton's, a poet of great merit and one of the rare admirable characters of the period. But Marvell did not live by his pen. He represented the town of Kingston upon Hull in the House of Commons, and what his constituents paid him sufficed for his needs (he was the last Member of Parliament to be thus paid). Let us not mention his name without recording an episode which does him honour. Wanting to buy him over, Charles II sent him a thousand guineas by the hand of Lord Danby. Marvell's reply was to ask his servant : " Pray, what had I to dinner yesterday ? A shoulder of mutton, sir. And what do you allow me today ? The remainder hashed. And tomorrow, my Lord Danby, I shall have the sweet blade-bone broiled ; and when your lordship makes honourable mention of my cook and my diet, I am sure his majesty will be too tender in future, to attempt to bribe a man with golden apples, who lives so well on the viands of his native country." Lord Danby carried back the thousand guineas (Life of Marvell, *Works*, vol. III).

[79] On the subject of Dryden see his *Works* and the authors quoted under his name in my Bibliography. See in addition his life by Johnson in *Lives of the English Poets* and by George Saintsbury ; Macaulay's *History* ; *Biographia Britannica*, s.v. Dryden ; and an article in the *Quarterly Review* for Oct. 1878.

[80] Waller was equally untroubled by scruples. He had sung of Cromwell, he sang of Charles II. When he presented his verses to the King, Charles remarked that the verses in honour of the Protector were better than those the poet was offering him. Waller saved the situation by saying " Poets, Sir, succeed better in fiction than in truth." (Johnson, *Lives of the English Poets*: Waller.)

Redux, A Poem on the happy Restoration and Return of His Sacred Majesty, Charles the Second.

The next year he returned to the charge with a new offering: *To His Sacred Majesty, a Panegyric on his Coronation.* Then, not content with addressing the god, he also offered homage to his saints, and wrote verses to Hyde: *To my Lord Chancellor. Presented on New Year's Day 1662.*

The poet's position at the time was none too brilliant. If we are to believe his enemies, he took up his quarters with Herringman, the bookseller, paying for his board and lodging by writing prefaces, advertisements, etc.[81] There is probably some exaggeration in this, for Dryden had a private income. But this income was very small (about £40 sterling a year), and though it prevented his starving it did not relieve him of the need to work. It is certain that in his early days he led a very modest existence: " I remember plain John Dryden before he paid his court with success to the great," writes a disinterested observer of his fortunes, " in one uniform cloathing of *Norwich* drugget." [82]

Obviously he expected presents or at least promises of protection from the King and the Lord Chancellor. Did he get anything? It is probable: for in those days it was customary to thank poets for their homage by a gift of money. But he certainly did not receive anything which seemed likely to make his future secure, for he set himself at once to try another line.

---

[81] " At first I struggled with a great deal of persecution, took up with a lodging which had a Window no bigger than a Pocket-looking-glass, Dined at a Threepenny Ordinary enough to starve a Vocation (vacation) Taylor, kept little Company, went clad in homely Drugget, and drunk Wine as seldom as a *Rechabite*, or the *Grand Seignior's* Confessor." (Tom Brown, *The Reasons of Mr. Bays Changing his Religion*.) It is Bays (that is to say Dryden) speaking.

> " He turned a Journey-man t'a *Bookseller;
> Writ Prefaces to Books for Meat and Drink,
> And as he paid, he would both write and think.
> Then by th' assistance of a †Noble *Knight*,
> Th' hadst plenty, ease and liberty to write
> First like a *Gentleman* he made thee live
> And on his Bounty thou did'st amply thrive.

* Mr. Herringman, *who kept him in his House for that purpose.*
† Sir R. H. (Robert Howard), *who kept him generously at his own house.*"

(Shadwell (?), *The Medal of John Bayes*, pp. 8–9.)

[82] *The Gentleman's Magazine*; letter of an old correspondent in the issue of Feb. 1745, p. 99.

He turned his attention where the attention of the Court was turned : to the theatre.

He was far from taking this step of his own choice.[83] His genius urged him towards epic and lyric poetry, and all his life his heart was there. But the times had little use for major works and a man had to live. He noted which way the wind was blowing and trimmed his sails accordingly. He decided to write for the stage and everyone else did the same : Otway, Shadwell, Lee, Crowne, Mrs. Behn, Settle, D'Urfey, Ravenscroft ; all writers, without exception, who lived by their pen, tried writing plays.[84]

Cromwell's Puritans had completely suppressed the theatre : the playhouse was a pleasure, and an impious, Royalist pleasure to boot. On February 11, 1647, Parliament had passed an Act by which

All Stage-Players are declared to be Rogues punishable by the Act of the 39th of Queen *Elizabeth* and 7th of King James . . . All Stages, Galleries, Seats and Boxes are ordered to be pulled down by Warrant of two Justice of Peace ; All Actors in Plays for time to come being convicted shall be publickly whipp'd, and find Sureties for their not offending in like manner for the Future ; and all Spectators of Plays for every offence are to pay Five Shillings.[84a]

The Puritan hatred of spectacles went so far as to make them prohibit bear-baiting, not from humanity or pity for the bear, but from horror at the pleasure of the spectators.[85]

---

[83] " For I confess my chief endeavours are to delight the Age in which I live. If the humour of this, be for low Comedy, small Accidents and Raillery, I will force my Genius to obey it, though with more reputation I could write in Verse. I know I am not so fitted by Nature to write Comedy . . ." (*A Defence of an Essay of Dramatique Poesie* . . . prefixed to *The Indian Emperour*. 1668.)

" I have never thought myself very fit for an employment, where many of my predecessors have excelled me in all kinds ; and some of my contemporaries, even in my own partial judgment, have outdone me in Comedy." (Dedication to *Aureng-Zebe*.)—See also his Preface to *An Evening's Love*.

[84] Sheffield's *Essay on Poetry*, already quoted, speaks of the theatre as the supreme goal of the writer's art. This is how he introduces it :

" Here rest, my *Muse*, suspend thy Cares a while,
A greater Enterprise attends thy Toil.
As some young Eagle . . .
The Muse inspires a sharper Note to sing . . .
On then, my Muse, adventrously engage
To give Instructions that concern the Stage."

[84a] Neal, vol. III, p. 478. Theatrical performances were first forbidden in 1642.

[85] On this subject see the curious information quoted by Macaulay : *History of England*, vol. I, chap. 2, p. 161.

Yet so lively was the taste for the drama, implanted in England by the Renaissance, that even under the Republic, despite the penalties incurred—and paid—theatrical performances continued surreptitiously from time to time.[86]

But these rare godsends had been like a few mouthfuls of food to a starving man; they had kept the appetite alive without satisfying it. So when it became possible after weary years of deprivation again to indulge the taste without restraint, the playhouses reopened of themselves, as it were, and found at once actors and audience.

The King for his part, who was used to seeing the continental theatre held in honour, and forming the favourite recreation of princes and society, was bound to be as keenly interested in the matter as his subjects. The organization of the theatres was therefore one of the first affairs of state to which Charles II devoted his attention.

The King returned on May 29, 1660. In August he granted a warrant to establish a theatre to Thomas Killigrew, a former royal page of his father's whom he had appointed his own valet, and another to Sir William D'Avenant, a zealous Royalist whom Charles I had knighted after the battle of Worcester.[87] The company of the former called itself "The King's Servants", the second took the name "The Duke's Company" (after the Duke of York, brother of Charles II, later King James II). A certain number of actors of the royal company were considered part of the Royal Household and were entitled "Gentlemen of the Great Chamber".[88]

---

[86] See Disraeli, *Curiosities of Literature*, the chapter *The History of the Theatre during its Suppression.*—See also Malone: *Historical Account of the Rise and Progress of the English Stage*, pp. 97, 98, notes; and Ebsworth, *Westminster Drolleries*, Introduction.

[87] See the Royal Warrant to the two Directors in Malone, *Historical Account*, pp. 311-14.—Political foresight had no doubt a word to say in the matter. These two privileged companies were easy to supervise. [The political explanation is curious. But see addition to next note. B. D.]

[88] Cibber, *An Apology*, etc., pp. 53 ff.—Under Elizabeth, James I and Charles I some actors had already received the title of Servants of the Queen or King (Malone, *Historical Account*, pp. 49, 55 (note 3), 61 and 62).

[From Elizabethan times, all actors, to save themselves from being treated as rogues and vagabonds, had to be somebody's "servants". In Elizabeth's day there were Lord Strange's Men (or Servants), the Lord Chamberlain's Men (Strange became Lord Chamberlain), the Lord Admiral's Men, and also the Queen's Men. (See E. K. Chambers, *William Shakespeare*, vol. I.) In Jacobean times there were The King's Men, Queen Anne's Company, and so on. Prince Charles I had a company, as had Queen Henrietta, and Charles II himself had a company as Prince Charles. (See G. E. Bentley,

The King and his brother were not content merely to lend the two companies the protection of their name; they took a personal interest in the theatre. Not only did they diligently attend performances,[89] thereby ensuring their success, but they considered no detail beneath their dignity. They condescended to smooth out the squabbles which arose, whether between the actors or between the two theatres. Even the costumes were an object of their royal solicitude. When D'Avenant's *Love and Honour* was being played, the King gave the actor Betterton the robe he had himself worn at his coronation. The Duke of York and Lord Oxford gave two other actors the costumes in which they had appeared at the same ceremony. Another time the Duchess of York gave her wedding dress to Mrs. Barry, and the Duke of Monmouth, one of the King's natural sons, offered his sword to the actor Nokes and himself buckled it on.[90]

Charles II took a personal interest in the actors (not to mention the actresses). The comic actor, Leigh, he called *his* actor,[91] and he took such a fancy to another comedian, John Lacey, that he had his portrait painted in three different rôles.[92]

It was on the King's recommendation that Mrs. Butler, whom he called by her Christian name of Charlotte, made her first appearance on the stage. Cibber, who records the fact, remarks that this was " a provident restitution giving to the stage in kind what he had sometimes taken from it ".[93]

There was also a private theatre at Court and members of the Royal Family were not too proud themselves to act and

---

The Jacobean and Caroline Stage.) So this was no scandalous innovation, but a resumption of what had long been the tradition, and a proper regularization. Under Charles II, besides the King's and the Duke of York's players, there were the Duke of Monmouth's Servants, and the Duchess of Portsmouth's Servants. See Montague Summers : *The Playhouse of Pepys*, Allardyce Nicoll : *Restoration Drama*, and for later history, *Their Majesties' Servants* by J. Doran. B. D.]

[89] This was an innovation. Charles II's predecessors did not go to the theatre. When the sovereign wished to see a play, he summoned the actors to him. Only Charles I's Queen, Henrietta Maria, once attended a public performance. (Malone, *Historical Account*, pp. 183–4 ; P. Cunningham, *The Story of Nell Gwyn*, p. 10.)

[90] Betterton, *The History of the Stage*, p. 17 ; Downes, *Roscius Anglicanus*, pp. 21 and 29.

[91] Cibber, *Apology*, pp. 91 and 92.

[92] à Wood, *Athenæ Oxonienses*, s.v. William Lacey.—This triple portrait, painted by Michael Wright, is now in the Hampton Court Museum where it bears the registered No. 847.

[93] *Apology*, p. 97.

to take lessons in the art of declamation from professional actors.[94]

The theatre being thus under royal patronage it became an act of " loyalty " to attend. (What a dream for the courtier !— to enjoy himself and pay his court at the same time.) This factor combining with the passion for pleasure which had taken possession of society, made dramatic performances *the* fashionable recreation.

IV

What the drama was : actresses, production ; dramatic opera.—Tragedy : heroic plays.—Comedy

On its side, the theatre spared no trouble or expense to delight its audiences.

Hitherto women's parts had always been played by young boys.[95] A few tentative efforts had been made to introduce actresses to the stage, but these had always failed.[96]

Under Charles II the experiment could be renewed without fear of failure. As Cibber says : " We may imagine too that these actresses were not ill chosen, when it is well known that more than one of them had charms sufficient at their leisure hours to calm and mollify the cares of empire." [97]

Following the King's example, the gallants much appreciated this innovation and the new-comers were rapidly well established.

---

[94] Mrs. Betterton " had the honour to teach Queen Anne, when Princess, the part of Semandra in *Mithridates*, which she acted at Court in King Charles's time." (Cibber, *Apology*, p. 96.)
[It was nothing new for royalty to take part in theatricals at Court. Queen Ann of Denmark appeared in masques, though James I held aloof, while Charles I and Queen Henrietta Maria performed frequently. Such a custom was not unknown in France. See Enid Welsford, *The Court Masque*. B. D.]

[95] It will be remembered how in *Midsummer Night's Dream*, Flute protests : " Nay, faith let me not play a woman : I have a beard coming." (Act I, sc. 2.)
[Perhaps such a reminder is unnecessary for English readers, all of whom will know that women did not normally act in plays until after the Restoration, the female parts being taken by boys, of whom the most famous, perhaps, thanks to his being celebrated by Ben Jonson, is " Salathiel " Pavy, who died at the age of thirteen. B. D.]

[96] Prynne, *Histrio-Mastix*, p. 215, speaks of French actresses who have made their appearance " not long since " at the *Blacke-friers* theatre. But he has no word for an actress : he uses only the expression " woman-actor ". In the same way Pepys always says " actor ", not " actress " ; see especially Dec. 27, 1666. Southerne (*The Wives' Excuse*, 1692, p. 48) still says " woman-actor."—On the subject of actresses, see Malone, *Historical Account*, pp. 128-42.

[97] *Apology*, p. 55.

There was not, however, a sufficient supply of actresses all at once, and in default the actor Kynaston, amongst others, still played a woman's part. One day when Charles II was in the theatre he was surprised at a delay in beginning the performance. "Sire," was the reply, "the queen is not yet shaved." The queen, that day, was Kynaston.[98]

The male actors, however, lost no time in giving up feminine rôles (except a few comic parts. Nokes was famous as the Nurse in *Romeo and Juliet* and was known by the nickname of "Nurse Nokes")[99] and actresses took a larger and larger share. Soon they were indispensable. When D'Avenant re-wrote *Macbeth*, he lengthened the rôles of Lady Macbeth and Lady Macduff for no apparent reason except to have women longer on the stage.[100] Ere long the actresses even began to encroach. Men in the past had played women's parts, women now took men's. This was perhaps sometimes due to necessity or to some dramatic advantage. In the *Tempest*, for instance, arranged as a lyric comedy by Dryden and D'Avenant, a woman was entrusted with a young boy's part.[101] For the most part dramatic art had nothing to gain from these disguises. On October 28, 1661, Pepys went to the theatre. He saw an actress who, after having played a woman's part, reappeared on the stage in men's clothes.

[98] This Kynaston was a great favourite with the ladies of quality. They would often take him driving in their carriages in Hyde Park after the performance (which was then held in the afternoon) still wearing his actor's dress. (Cibber, *Apology*, p. 72.)

[99] Otway, *Epilogue* to *The History and Fall of Caius Marius*.

[100] See particularly Act I, p. 10, a whole scene added between Lady Macbeth and Lady Macduff: Lady Macbeth has to find an excuse for expediting Lady Macduff's departure, so as to be free to read Macbeth's letter.—Lady Macduff, who appears in only one scene of Shakespeare's play, is given in D'Avenant's arrangement one scene in the first, second and fourth acts and two scenes in the third.

[101] But then the Prologue took pains to point out to the audience the full piquancy of the situation:

> "But, if for *Shakespeare* we your grace implore,
> We for our Theatre shall want it more:
> Who, by our dearth of youths, are forc'd t'employ
> One of our Women to present a Boy.
> And that's a transformation, you will say,
> Exceeding all the Magick in the Play.
> Let none expect in the last Act to find
> Her Sex transformed from Man to Woman-kind
> What e're she was before the Play began,
> All you shall see of her is perfect Man.
> Or if your fancy will be further led
> To find her Woman, it must be a-bed."

He remarks that "she had the best legs that ever I saw", and adds that he was very well pleased with it all. All the males of the audience were of one mind with Pepys in such matters, and the theatre lost no opportunity of catering for their taste.[102] A large number of prologues and epilogues were recited by women dressed as men, with the evident intention of giving pleasure to spectators who shared Pepys' taste.[103] Sometimes, even, the women took complete possession of the theatre and carried a whole performance through, unsupported by a single male actor. In such cases they chose the most outspoken plays, such as Thomas Killigrew's *Parson's Wedding*.[104] On their lips, ambiguous words evidently had a more piquant flavour, and their acting threw indelicate situations into peculiar relief. They were almost all dancers [105] as well as actresses, and they were given licentious songs to sing with which all plays, even the most tragic, were freely interspersed.[106] In short, no opportunity of thus titillating the spectators' senses was missed.

[102] See Pepys, March 7, 1666-7.

[103] For instance, on the revival of Dryden's *Maiden-Queen*, the Prologue and Epilogue were spoken, the one by Mrs. Boutell, the other by Mrs. Reeves, both dressed as men.—In these and the following quotations " Mrs." is used of an unmarried, not a married woman. The first unmarried actress who was called " Miss " was Miss Crow, who created the part of Miss Hoyden in Vanbrugh's *Relapse* (1697). (Cunningham, *The Story of Nell Gwyn*, p. 14, note.)

[" Miss instead of Mrs. meant that she was a very young girl. Six years was by no means an uncommon age for actresses to make their first appearance in a Prologue or Epilogue, or even as a page, as Mrs. Bracegirdle did in *The Orphan* when she was no older, according to Curll. Seeing what these children had to say, this custom roused very natural moral opposition. See the Epilogue to Farquhar's *Love and a Bottle*, 1699.

O Collier ! Collier ! thou'st frighted away Miss Cross.

But she returned on Jan, 2, 1705, to dance and sing in *The Careless Husband* at Drury Lane." B. Dobrée. Notes on *The Relapse*. Nonesuch Ed. B. D.]

[104] *The Parson's Wedding* (1664).—See Pepys, Oct. 11, 1664.

[105] " Mrs. *Johnson* in this Comedy (Shadwell's *Epsom Wells*) Dancing a Jigg so Charming well, Loves power in a little time after Coerc'd her to Dance more Charming else-where." (Downes, *Roscius Anglicanus*, p. 33.)

[106] Here, for instance, is a song recited by *Betty* in the presence of *Lady Ancient*, Penelope, and Tim, Penelope's betrothed (D'Urfey, *The Fool turn'd Critick*, IV, 2) :

" I

I found my *Caelia* one night undrest,
a precious Banquet for languishing Love,
the charming object a flame increast,
Which never, ah never, till then I prov'd ;

Simultaneously with the advent of the actresses came the arrival of scenery. Previously, the sole decoration consisted of

> her delicate skin, and starry eye,
> made me a secret bliss pursue,
> but with her soft hand she still put it by,
> and cry'd. Fie, *Amintor* what would you do?
>
> 2
>
> Her words and blushes so fir'd my heart,
> I pulled her to me and clasp'd her around,
> And though with Cunning she play'd her part :
> Yet fainter, and fainter, her threats I found.
> But when I least thought on her, least I desir'd,
> My love a forebearance should allow,
> A touch of her hand, my heart so inspir'd :
> My Passion melted I know not how.
>
> 3
>
> Which when fair *Caelia's* quick eye perceiv'd,
> And found by my calmness my passion's decay,
> Her Fate she inwardly seem'd to grieve :
> That Fool'd her and Cool'd her, so base away.
> She sigh'd and look'd pale to see me dull,
> And in her heart, this oath she swore,
> She never again would slight an address ;
> Nor the critical minute refuse no more."

When the song was finished, Tim, the fiancé, found it not " bawdy " enough.

See another song recited by Francisca in Mrs. Behn's *Dutch Lover* (II, 4) and another specimen in Dryden's *Marriage à-la-Mode* (IV, 3).

I have said that the most tragic subjects did not exclude such spicy seasonings. Here is a song recited at the banquet of Atreus in Crowne's tragedy of *Thyestes* :

> " 1
>
> A Lovely pair endowed by Fate
> With Loves and Beauties whole Estate ;
> At the sweetest game have been,
> You know, you know what I mean,
> You know, you know what I mean.
>
> 2
>
> For Kisses first the Lovers play'd
> The pleasant sport provok'd the Maid . . .
>
> 4
>
> To deeper Play, they now begin,
> The happy young man's hand is in,
> Both have stak'd down all their joys,
> But she loses, for she cryes :
> See ! she cryes ! Oh ! see she cryes !
>
> 5
>
> But now the Bride, oh ! tempting sight !
> Has won her lapful of delight,

curtains stretched across the background of the stage (when the walls were not left bare).[107] Sir William D'Avenant was the first to introduce the English public to movable scenery painted in perspective. Before the Restoration he had already shown his skill as a decorative artist [108] in a play which as an exceptional case Cromwell had authorized for political reasons. But it was not until restrictions were removed that he was able to give free rein to his talent. Through him the whole theatre fell under the spell of scenic effects. Battles and sacrifices were shown on the stage, aerial spirits who rose winging into the air, genii,[109] phantoms, sorcerers.[110] The Temple was seen on fire in the *Destruction of Jerusalem* [111]; in the *Empress of Morocco* [112] there was a river covered with a fleet, a tempest of hail and a rainbow; in Lee's *Sophonisba* [113] a sky of blood was suddenly displayed with two suns shining in it; in the same author's *Rival Queens* [114] a battle of crows and ravens took place in the air; in the middle of this

---

      To deeper Play, she urges on;
      But, alas, his stakes are gone,
      But, alas, his stakes are gone.

              6

      And now she locks her Cabinet,
      But he'll play another set,
      When his hand again is in.
      You know, you know what I mean,
      You know, you know what I mean."

[107] Malone, *Historical Account*, pp. 85–115 and p. 348.
[108] "*The Cruelty of the Spaniards in Peru.* Exprest by Instrumentall and Vocall Musick, and by Art of Perspective in Scenes . . . 1658."—He had previously given: "*The Siege of Rhodes.* Made a Representation by the Art of Prospective in Scenes . . . 1656."—See *Biographia Dramatica*; s.vv. Sir William Davenant, and The Cruelty of the Spaniards in Peru.
[It was really the tradition of the masque, especially from the time of Inigo Jones, which gave the impetus to elaborate scenery, and new knowledge of the Italian theatre: but even during the Jacobean period there was sometimes no lack of stage effects in the ordinary theatre. In about 1610–12 some plays of Heywood's required much stage contraption. (See Montague Summers, *The Restoration Theatre*, p. 191.) The scenery of *The Siege of Rhodes* was much restricted by the size of the stage at Rutland House. Davenant certainly did much to bring in scenery and "machinery". (See Montague Summers, *The Playhouse of Pepys*, chap. I.) B. D.]
[109] *The Indian Queen* by Dryden and Sir Robert Howard.—See Evelyn, Feb. 5, 1664.
[110] Tate's *Brutus of Alba*; *Œdipus* by Dryden and Lee.
[111] By Crowne, last act.
[112] By Settle.
[113] Last scene of Act II.
[114] Act II, 1.

battle an eagle and a dragon fought a strange fight in which the eagle was defeated.

Horror played no less a part in these performances : in Dryden's *Amboyna* the English were tortured on the stage by the Dutch. In the same author's *Indian Emperour* Montezuma was handed over to the executioner, and during his torments a Catholic priest conducted a religious discussion with him. In Ravenscroft's *Titus Andronicus* a curtain is drawn aside to show the head and hands of Demetrius and Chiron hung on the wall, while their corpses in chairs are covered with bloodstained cloths.[115]

Songs and dances were introduced wherever possible [116] ; the songs were such as we have seen ; the dances were sometimes strange. In Crowne's *Juliana* two queens, two nuns, two phantoms and two crowned angels danced together. They made an odd company ; but the aim was to strike the eye.

The taste for the spectacular preponderated to the point of giving rise to a peculiar type of play in which decoration, machines, costumes, dance, song and music combined to please both eye and ear. They were called " Dramatic Operas " [117] and corresponded approximately to our pantomimes, except for the difference of subject matter.

These new plays which enjoyed extraordinary success,[118] carried the elaboration of scenery to marvellous heights of magnificence. When Shadwell's *Psyche* was played, the decorations alone cost " more than £800 sterling ".[119] The description of the first production of *The Tempest, or the Enchanted Isle* by Dryden and D'Avenant [120] will give an idea of the degree of costly elaboration attained :

---

[115] Acted in 1678 (Genest, I, 233) but not published till 1686 or 1687. The dates of the performance and the publication of these plays do not always tally. In such cases I quote here the date of performance according to Genest, and in my bibliography the date of the first edition, or if this is not ascertainable, the date of the oldest edition I have been able to consult.—
" A Curtain drawn discovers the heads and hands of *Dem.* and *Chir.* hanging up against the wall. Their bodys in chairs in bloody Linnen:" (Act V.)
[Professor Allardyce Nicoll gives date of first performance *c.* Dec., 1686. B. D.]
[116] In Mrs. Katherine Philips's translation of Corneille's *Pompée*, songs are inserted and at the end " A Grand Masque is Danc'd before Caesar and Cleopatra ".
[117] Cibber, *Apology*, p. 57.
[118] Pepys, July 4, 1661.
[119] Downes, *Roscius Anglicanus*, pp. 35 and 36.
[120] Played in 1667.

Act I.
First Tableau.

The front of the stage is opened, and the band of twenty-four violins, with the harpsicals and theorbos which accompany the voices, are placed between the pit and the stage. While the overture is playing, the curtain rises, and discovers a new frontispiece, joined to the great pilasters, on each side of the stage. This frontispiece is a noble arch, supported by large wreathed columns of the Corinthian order; the wreathings of the columns are beautified with roses wound round them, and several Cupids flying about them. On the cornice, just over the capitals, sits on either side a figure, with a trumpet in one hand, and a palm in the other, representing Fame. A little farther, on the same cornice, on each side of a compass-pediment, lie a lion and a unicorn, the supporters of the royal arms of England. In the middle of the arch are several angels, holding the king's arms, as if they were placing them in the midst of that compass-pediment. Behind this is the scene, which represents a thick cloudy sky, a very rocky coast, and a tempestuous sea in perpetual agitation. This tempest (supposed to be raised by magick) has many dreadful objects in it, as several spirits in horrid shapes flying down amongst the sailors, then rising and crossing in the air. And when the ship is sinking, the whole house is darkened, and a shower of fire falls upon them. This is accompanied with lightning, and several claps of thunder, to the end of the storm.

Second Tableau.

In the midst of the shower of fire, the scene changes. The cloudy sky, rocks, and sea vanish; and, when the lights return, discover that beautiful part of the island, which was the habitation of PROSPERO: 'Tis composed of three walks of cypress-trees; each side-walk leads to a cave, in one of which PROSPERO keeps his daughter, in the other HIPPOLITO: The middle-walk is of great depth, and leads to an open part of the island.

And this is only the beginning of the play with five more acts to come ! The whole performance was on this level of magnificence, varied by surprises from time to time. There were choirs of demons. In the Fourth Act a table rose out of the ground and four spirits entered who danced as they set the table with wine and viands. When the dance was over, bottles and dishes vanished and the table sank again into the ground. But all these marvels culminated in the *apotheosis* of the Fifth Act. Here appeared an arcade of rocks and calm sea. Music being played on the rocks. Neptune, Amphitrite, Oceanus and Tethys drove in a chariot drawn by sea-horses; on each side of the chariot were sea gods and goddesses, Tritons and Nereids. There followed songs and dances the list of which filled four quarto pages.

Authors protested against this invasion of the intellectual sphere by merely decorative effects. Prologues and Epilogues are filled with their wailing.[121] But they complained in vain. Aristocratic taste was against them and in this, as in everything else, it prevailed. Authors were not in a position to put up a fight; they did not even try. They confined themselves to protests, and even while protesting continued to supply plays of a type to gratify both in form and matter the tiresome preferences of their audiences.

As regards matter, the influence to which authors were subjected was not propitious either.

When the theatres first reopened, they were caught unprepared and they began by simply reverting to the rich repertoire of old : Shakespeare, Ben Jonson, above all Beaumont and Fletcher and some plays of D'Avenant that had already been acted.[122] But

---

[121] The Prologue to Dryden's *Limberham, or the Kind Keeper* says, for instance :
"True wit has seen its best days long ago ;
It ne'er looked up, since we were dipt in show."

Shadwell's Prologue to *The Squire of Alsatia* complains :
"Then came Machines, brought from a Neighbour Nation ;
Oh how we suffered under Decoration !"

Here is another protest against the importance assumed by music (the *Timon* alluded to is Shadwell's, 1678) :
"How was the Scene forlorn and how despis'd,
When *Tymon*, without Musick moraliz'd ?
Shakespeare's sublime in vain entic'd the Throng,
Without the charm of *Purcel's* Syren Song."
(Epilogue to *The Jew of Venice* : a Comedy by George Granville, Lord Lansdowne ; produced 1701.)

[122] See Genest, vol. I, *passim*.—"Dryden in his *Essay on Dramatick Poesie* records that they used to play two of Beaumont and Fletcher's plays for one of Shakespeare's (or Jonson's). This proportion is the most conclusive proof of the decadence of the theatre and the change in public taste. To prefer Beaumont and Fletcher to Shakespeare, is to prefer the amusement arising from complicated intrigues and novel subjects to the noblest emotions of dramatic art. Their plays are full of beautiful lines ; like the Spanish poets, they dazzle the eye by a series of brilliant scenes ; but they have neither created a character nor composed a complete drama. Everything they write bears the mark of improvisation. They linger over the portrayal of no feeling ; they skate over the surface touching no moral or psychological problems which the drama raises. Theirs is just the kind of superficial play which suited the courtiers of the Restoration ; avid of enjoyment, eager to vary their pleasures and incapable of any sort of serious concentration.

they soon felt that they could not rest content with these revivals, and frankly set out to replough the old furrows. A plot well worked out, characters vigorously drawn, daring and logical endings, made the theatre a weariness and not a recreation. Downes [123] tells us that people could not long put up with seeing Romeo and Juliet dying; James Howard altered the play to give it a happy ending and it was acted one day as a tragedy and on the morrow as a tragi-comedy. Waller changed the last act of Beaumont and Fletcher's *Maids Tragedie* to let it end as a comedy.[124] The whole repertoire of the old theatre was out of tune with the new taste. A break was therefore made with the glorious tradition of Elizabeth's day, and people devoted themselves to writing tragic and comic plays in the new fashion.[125]

In the tragic plays two influences are observable, equally

Beaumont and Fletcher also offered them voluptuous situations to titillate their senses. On all these grounds they were bound to please, and please they did." (A. Mézières, *Shakespeare, ses œuvres et ses critiques*, pp. 165–6.)

[Shakespeare's comedies were on the whole neglected; the tragedies were often, but not always altered, as much in the interests of new critical theories as to form as of those of sentiment; the histories were popular, and not much tampered with. (See Allardyce Nicoll, *Restoration Comedy*.) The Duke of Marlborough said he got his knowledge of English history chiefly from the plays of Shakespeare, which he probably saw rather than read. The preference for Fletcher (Beaumont should not be included in these strictures; while he lived there was bone in the plays) dates from the days of Charles I, when the theatre became more courtly, puritanism keeping the good bourgeois away. B. D.]

[123] Downes, *Roscius Anglicanus*, p. 22. The play has not been published.

[124] *Biographia Dramatica*, s.v. The Maid's Tragedy. By Edm. Waller, 1690.—The play had been acted in its remodelled form from 1682 onwards.

[125] "I saw *Hamlet, Prince of Denmark* played," writes Evelyn (*Diary*, Nov. 26, 1661); "but now the old plays began to disgust this refined age, since his Majestie's being so long abroad."—For Pepys " *Romeo and Juliet* . . . is a play of itself the worst that I ever heard in my life" (Mar. 1, 1661-2); "*Midsummer Night's Dream* . . . is the most insipid ridiculous play that I ever saw in my life" (Sept. 29, 1662); "the so much cried-up play of *Henry the Eighth* . . . is so simple a thing made up of a great many patches . . ." (Jan. 1, 1663-4); "reading *Othello, Moore of Venice* . . . but having so lately read *The Adventures of Five Houres* (by Sir Samuel Tuke) it seems a mean thing" (Aug. 20, 1666); " *The Tempest* . . . has no great wit . . ." (Nov. 7, 1667).—The Bibliothèque Nationale in Paris possesses a copy of the 1623 edition of Shakespeare which bears this manuscript note beside the title of *The Tempest* : " Much better in Dryden."—To see into what discredit Shakespeare had fallen, see Malone, *Historical Account*, pp. 338–42 and 354–8, and Ingleby, pp. 242 ff.

[Pepys is not a reliable witness as to general taste. The critics and playwrights of the period had an extremely high opinion of, even veneration for, Shakespeare, but they were not " bardolators ", and criticized him according to the standards of criticism of their day—as we do. B. D.]

strong, equally deplorable: the influence of women and the influence of the King. The King who had seen French tragedy in all its glory with Corneille, had brought back to England a passion for French ideas and great difficulty in understanding a theatre different from what he had grown accustomed to during his exile. The Earl of Orrery wrote to a friend : " I have now finished a Play in the *French* Manner ; because I heard the King declare himself more in favour of their Way of Writing than ours : My poor attempt cannot please his Majesty, but my Example may incite others who can."[126]

The things which had particularly impressed him in French tragedy were the externals such as the unity of place, the consistent dignity of the characters and the rhymed verse. As was natural, the King made converts and his taste was unopposed, with grave injury to English drama. No more than formal homage could be paid to unity of place, for it could ill be reconciled with the new methods of production. But dramatists adopted rhyme, which, while it seems necessary to the rhythm of French verse, turns English verse into a lyric chant, quite intolerable in a work of any length, and obviously at variance with the genius of English drama. Rhyme had been dethroned by Marlowe in the sixteenth century, and the Restoration poets succeeded only in giving it an artificial life of a few years, after which it disappeared for ever from the English theatre.[127] They also adopted the convention of showing on the stage only kings and queens, heroes and princesses, and tolerating no discussion of lesser problems than the possession of a crown or the overthrow of an empire.

This tendency to sustained majesty—which is perhaps to be regretted in the classical drama of France—was encouraged and accentuated in England by the influence of women and their preference for gallant and romantic literature.[128] The joint

---

[126] Quoted in the Preface to *The Dramatic Works of Roger Boyle, Earl of Orrery*.

[127] When Waller rewrote the conclusion of *The Maids Tragedie* he wrote the Fifth Act in rhymed verse though the preceding four acts were in blank verse. No. 39 of the *Spectator* discusses the use of rhyme in drama. Addison finds that a rhymed play produces on him the same effect as a Greek or Latin tragedy in hexameters.

[But he ended the Acts of *Cato* with passages in rhyme. B. D.]

[128] " This faulty Manner (Luxury of splendid Words) took its rise from the numerous Romances that were the great delight of Gentlemen and Ladies, after the return of king Charles." (Blackmore, *Essays*, vol. II, p. 266.)—Dryden, in his Essay on *Heroic Plays* (prefixed to the *Conquest of Granada*), claims

effect of these two influences gave birth to a new type of play which was known as the Heroic Play.

The mere titles are sufficient indication of their source of inspiration : *Secret-Love, or the Maiden-Queen* [129] ; *Tyrannick-Love, or the Royal Martyr* [130] ; *Love and Revenge* [131] ; *The Rival Queens, or the Death of Alexander the Great* [132] ; *Theodosius, or the Force of Love* [133] ; *Abdelazer, or the Moor's Revenge* [134] ; *The Rival Kings, or the Loves of Orondates and Statira* [135] ; *Ibrahim, the Illustrious Bassa.* [136] No subject is worthy of treatment, if it is of less importance than the Conquest of Mexico or Granada,[137] the siege of Memphis,[138] the destruction of Jerusalem,[139] or similarly august events which allow the chief actors to display themselves in circumstances worthy of their distinguished birth and noble soul. The women, almost all crowned on the steps of the throne,[140] have characteristic names ; they are called Roxolana,[141], Zempoalla, Orazia,[142], Almeria, Cydaria,[143] Melissa,[144] Almahide, Lyndaraza,[145] Almavanga, Alcinda.[146] Rosalinda,[147] Indamora.[148] The men-folk, lofty in rank,[149] and lofty in sentiment,

---

to have borrowed many features of one of the characters, Almanzor, from the Artaban of " Monsieur Calprenède ". The serious part of his *Marriage à-la-Mode* was furnished by *le Grand Cyrus*.

[129] By Dryden ; borrowed from *le Grand Cyrus*.
[130] By Dryden ; *l'Amour tyrannique* is the title of one of Mademoiselle de Scudéry's tragedies.
[131] By Settle.
[132] By Lee ; inspired by La Calprenède's *Cassandre*.
[133] By Lee ; borrowed from Gomberville's *Pharamond*.
[134] By Mrs. Behn.
[135] By Bankes ; borrowed from La Calprenède's *Cassandre*.
[136] *Ibrahim, ou l'Illustre Bassa* is the name of one of Mademoiselle de Scudéry's novels.
[137] *The Indian Emperour, or the Conquest of Mexico by the Spaniards ; Almanzor and Almahide, or the Conquest of Granada ;* by Dryden.
[138] *The Siege of Memphis, or the Ambitious Queen*, by D'Urfey.
[139] *The Destruction of Jerusalem by Titus Vespasian*, by Crowne.
[140] *The Indian Queen* (by Sir Robert Howard and Dryden) ; *The Empress of Morocco* (by Settle) ; *Juliana, or the Princess of Poland* (by Crowne), etc.
[141] In *Mustapha*, by the Earl of Orrery (1668).
[142] In *The Indian Queen*, by Sir Robert Howard and Dryden.
[143] In *The Indian Emperour*, by Dryden.
[144] In *The Maiden-Queen*, by Dryden.
[145] In *Almanzor and Almahide, or the Conquest of Granada*, Part II, by Dryden ; Mademoiselle de Scudéry wrote a novel called *Almahide*.
[146] In *The Conquest of China, By the Tartars*, by Settle.
[147] In *Sophonisba, or Hannibal's Overthrow*, by Lee.
[148] In *Aureng-Zebe*, by Dryden.
[149] Now, it is Suleiman the Magnificent (in Lord Orrery's *Mustapha* and Settle's *Ibrahim*) ; now, the Great Mogul (in Dryden's *Aureng-Zebe*) ; now, some hero of antiquity dressed up for the occasion.

are genuine heroes of romance, full of love, full of honour, full of courage. Or can we justly speak of love, honour or courage? Are there any words to express such amazing passions, such exalted and extraordinary virtues? Their love is the distilled essence of sentimentality, insipid to the last degree and at the same time to the utmost limit impetuous and violent—a little stream flowing with a gentle murmur or a raging torrent unleashed. Their honour is a blend of delicacy and impulse, both equally incomprehensible; their courage is heroic lunacy. They outdo even the models which gave them birth. Aided by the theatre and by rhyme, they push their chivalrous sentiments to the limit of intensity and clothe them in sonorous tirades that hurl defiance at Gods and men and common sense.

When Maximin is informed that "the gods have claimed" Valeria, he exclaims:

> What had the Gods to do with me or mine?
> Did I molest your heaven?
> Why should you then make Maximin your foe
> Who paid you tribute, which he need not do?
> Your altars I with smoke of gums did crown,
> For which you leaned your hungry nostrils down,
> All daily gaping for my incense there,
> More than your sun could draw you in a year.
> And you for this these plagues on me have sent!
> But by the Gods, (by Maximin, I meant,)
> Henceforth I, and my world,
> Hostility with you and yours declare.
> Look to it, Gods; for you the aggressors are.

This master ranter is mortally wounded; his self-confidence remains unshaken:

> And shoving back this earth on which I sit,
> I'll mount, and scatter all the Gods I hit. (*Dies.*) [150]

If they feel themselves so mighty in face of the gods, it is clear that nothing in Nature is going to halt them:

> ... Where is Clarona gone? (*Grows mad.*)
> Aloft!—I see her mounting to the Sun!—
> The flaming Satyr towards her does roul,
> His scorching Lust makes Summer at the Pole.
> Let the hot Planet touch her if he dares!—
> Touch her, and I will cut him into Stars,
> And the bright chips into the Ocean throw.[151]

---

[150] Dryden's *Tyrannick Love*, V, 1.
[151] Phraartes, in *The Destruction of Jerusalem*, by Crowne, Part II, Act V.

Another declares:

> If she were dead, I would restore her breath,
> And she should live,
> Spight of her self, spight of the gods, and Death.
> My Pow'r's unlimited, as is their own:
> My smile brings Life, and death attends my frown.[152]

After that, who among men could resist them? What dangers or threats could move them? Wounds and death have no terror for them. Every blow struck at them must give them new strength, each limb smitten from their body must become yet another hero.[153] Demetrius is threatened with death:

> Come Villains, level me right against the Clouds,
> And then give fire, discharge my flaming soul
> Against such saucy Destinies as those
> As dare thus basely of my life dispose;
> Then from the Clouds rebounding I will fall,
> And like a clap of thunder tear you all.[154]

They carry off Porphyrius to cut off his head. What cares he? Dead, he will still pursue the enemy who strikes him. To Maximin he cries:

> Where'er thou stand'st, I'll level at that place
> My gushing blood, and spout it at thy face.
> Thus, not by marriage, we our blood will join;
> Nay more, my arms shall throw my head at thine.[155]

Bombast can hardly go further. Almanzor and Maximin,

---

[152] Nero speaking in Lee: *The Tragedy of Nero* (V, 1). The character is conceived in this style throughout.
In *The Destruction of Troy* by Bankes, Achilles beside the corpse of Troilus similarly says:
> "Here by thy Side for ever I'le remain
> Close, till I've hatched thee into Life again."
> (*Actus Quartus*, Scena Prima.)

[153]
> "*Almanzor*: Cut piecemeal in this cause,
> From every wound I shou'd new vigor take:
> And every Limb should new Almanzors make."
> (*The Conquest of Granada*, by Dryden, Part II, v.)

[154] *Juliana, or the Princess of Poland*, by Crowne, Act IV.

[155] Dryden's *Tyrannick Love* (IV, 2). Let us quote yet another sample from Dryden's *Conquest of Granada* (Part I, iii). Almanzor speaking:
> "If I would kill thee now, thy fate's so low
> That I must stoop, e're I can give the blow.
> But mine is fix'd so far above thy Crown,
> That all thy Men,
> Pil'd on thy back can never pull it down."

See also a passage from Lee's *Alexander* quoted in No. 438 of the *Spectator*.

the two model heroes of this type, strike us to-day as two lunatics escaped from their asylum. Yet the Court of Charles II, so subtle, so fastidious, with so many claims to wit—some of them not unjustified [156]—accepted it all, applauded it all, revelled in it all. These bombastic declamations, for which English has the special name of " ranting ", were the delight of the audience,[157] and no dramatic works were more popular than those in which this roaring rhetoric had free play.

It is easy to imagine the kind of intrigues amidst which these superhuman heroes thread their way. Every sort of vicissitude, every imaginable complication multiplies around them ; battles dog their footsteps ; ambuscades await them at every turn ; hurricanes hurl themselves with fury at the ship that carries them ; everywhere there lurks the enemy, the traitor, the assassin.

[156] No one could criticize these Heroic Plays with more wit and judgment than the Duke of Buckingham in his *Rehearsal*, a work too often forgotten. Rochester also expressed himself admirably on the subject to Nathaniel Lee, one of the masters of this balderdash (Horace's *Tenth satire of the First Book*, imitated, *Works*, I, p. 11).—Amongst professional authors there was scarcely one, save Butler and Shadwell, who lodged a protest against this bombast. See Butler's amusing parody " Reparties between Cat and Puss at a caterwauling, in the modern Heroic Way ", in the *Genuine Poetical Remains of Samuel Butler*. Shadwell's protest is less well known and deserves to be quoted here :

" How have we in the space of one poor Age,
Beheld the Rise and Downfal of the Stage !
When, with our King restor'd, it first arose,
They did each Day some good old Play expose ;
And then it flourish'd : Till, with Manna tir'd,
For wholesome Food ye nauseous Trash desir'd.
Then rose the whiffling Scribblers of those days,
Who since have liv'd to bury all their Plays :
And had their Issue full as num'rous been
As *Priam's*, they the Fate of all had seen.
 With what prodigious scarcity of Wit
Did the new Authors starve the hungry Pit ?
Infected by the *French*, you must have Rhime,
Which long, to please the Ladies Ears, did chime.
Soon after this came ranting Fustian in,
And none but Plays upon the fret were seen :
Such Roaring Bombast stuff, which Fops would praise,
Tore our best Actors Lungs, cut short their days.
Some in small time did this distemper kill ;
And had the savage Authors gone on still,
Fustian had been a new Disease i' th' Bill . . ."
 (Prologue to *The Squire of Alsatia*.)

[157] See Cibber, *Apology*, pp. 63 and 64.—In the Dedication to his *Indian Emperour* Dryden writes : " The favour which heroic plays have lately found upon our theatres, has been wholly derived to them from the countenance and approbation they have received at court."

Dame Fortune is proverbially fickle ; the adjective is here inadequate ; in their case she displays a ubiquitous caprice that defeats all foresight, overturns all plans. But nothing disconcerts these champions ; their mere presence routs an enemy [158] ; their enemies bite the dust ; those whom their sword does not lay low are conquered by the greatness of their soul [159] ; if they are surprised by ambushed foes, singlehanded they annihilate them in the twinkling of an eye [160] ; if they are thrown into prison you know that some unexpected miracle [161] will set them free to perform new exploits and recover their mistress.

For these valiant men are tender-hearted, true knights errant that they are. Dryden's Montezuma confesses : " My lion's heart is captive in the toils of love." [162] They are captive and they take captive. When Cortez arrives in Mexico, Cydaria falls in love with him at first sight, Mexican and Spaniard, forthwith consumed by the same fire, exchange their declarations *secundum artem*.[163] All the rules of the game are observed, here, as in the romance. It involves neither love nor affection, it is pure gallantry in the approved form :

> In tedious Courtship we declare our pain
> And ere we kindness find, first meet disdain.[164]

In Dryden, Adam and Eve whom we normally picture to ourselves as less sophisticated, conduct their courtship on the same lines. Eve says to Adam :

> But some restraining thought, I know not why,
> Tells me, you long should beg, I long deny.[165]

The whole is interspersed with the inevitable coquetries and jealousies. So inevitable, that—odd as it may seem—Eve is jealous :

> Or like my self, some other may be made ;
> And her new Beauty may thy heart invade.[166]

---

[158] " But I would give a Crown in open day,
And when the Spaniards their Assault begin
At once beat those without and these within."
(Dryden, *The Conquest of Granada*, Part I, iii.)

[159] Dryden : *The Indian Emperour* (I, 2).—We have seen pretty much the same sort of thing occurring in the romance of *Oroonoko*.
[160] Settle : *The Empress of Morocco* (IV, 2).
[161] Dryden : *The Indian Emperour* (IV, 4, and V, 2).
[162] Ibid. (I, 2).   [163] Ibid. (I, 2).   [164] Ibid. (II, 2).
[165] *The State of Innocence* (II, 2).—This play was never acted.
[166] Ibid. (II, 1).

Sometimes too, in due deference to the convention, love indulges in savage ravings. To the lovely Almahide who is betrothed to another, Almanzor says :

> . . . then a ghost I'll be ;
> And from a ghost, you know, no place is free.
> Asleep, awake, I'll haunt you everywhere ;
> From my white shroud groan love into your ear :
> When in your lover's arms you sleep at night
> I'll glide in cold betwixt, and seize my right.[167]

It was this gallant strain in the Heroic Plays which was evidently counted on to be particularly attractive to audiences of the time. Women, so much exalted, so much sought after, could not but find pleasure in the sight of these proud conquerors humbly prostrate at the shrine of Beauty.[168] Men who prided themselves on their gallantry and eloquence could not but listen with pleasure to these amorous scenes, where action was suspended that the poet might at leisure display his talent for making pretty speeches. Devoted to literature, sensitive to wit, they were carried away by plays written for wit alone and in the rhymed verse they loved.[169] A high-sounding couplet excuses many things, and those which to-day sound the most extravagant to us, must have had for their first hearers the supreme merit of expressing in reverberating language ideas then by no means

---

[167] *The Conquest of Granada*, Part I, iv, 2.—See similar threats of Roxana to Statira in Lee's *Rival Queens* (III, 1).

[168] " As our heroes are generally lovers, their swelling and blustering upon the stage very much recommends them to the fair part of their audience. The ladies are wonderfully pleased to see a man insulting kings, or affronting the gods, in one scene, and throwing himself at the feet of his mistress in another. Let him behave himself insolently towards the men, and abjectly towards the fair one, and it is ten to one but he proves a favourite of the boxes. Dryden and Lee, in several of their tragedies, have practised this secret with good success." (*Spectator*, No. 40.)

In the Dedication of his *Mithridates*, Lee himself claims to have represented Ziphares " for the ladies " as ardent, tender, and passionately in love.

[169] The author pauses every moment to bring in a purely poetic simile or metaphor. In Lee's *Sophonisba*, for instance (V, 1), in a scene of less than twenty lines between Lælius and Scipio, eleven lines are taken up by two similes. In Otway's *Orphan* (V, 1), Monimia and Castalio find occasion for three similes in four small pages. Buckingham wittily makes mock of this practice in his *Rehearsal*.

" *Bayes.* . . . Now, here, she must make a *simile*.
Smith. Where's the necessity of that, Mr. *Bayes* ?
Bayes. Because she's surpris'd. That's a general Rule : you must ever make a *simile* when you are surpris'd ; 'tis the new way of writing." (II, 3.)
See the notes on this passage quoted in the Arber edition, p. 56.

commonplace. It must also be noted that the Heroic Plays were adopted by a poet, a real poet, Dryden himself, who lavished on them the treasures of a luxuriant style and brilliant versification.[170] We must remember too that these plays lent themselves to pompous declamation, and to the elaborate scenery which played so important a part in the dramatic art of the time.

However that may be, the Heroic Plays satisfied only some of the tastes of the day : they reflected the elegance of high society, its external graces, its good manners. Now, we have seen what lay below the surface of this society. This deceptive veneer concealed licentious souls whom tragedy, even rouged and be-jewelled, could not wholly satisfy.

At this point my task as a historian becomes delicate. So far I have revealed only the more respectable aspects of the period I am attempting to portray, those where a relative reticence is observed. Now I must show it as it was, and from the glimpses already permitted, the reader can foresee that no edifying sights await him. Ought the historian in such a case to refrain ? If he does, is he not playing false to that truth to which he owes his duty ? If he does not, must he endeavour by subtleties of phrase and style to convey things difficult to speak of openly ? But if he does not quote his evidence, has not the reader a right to question his interpretations ? And in trying merely to hint at his full meaning, does he not incur the danger of allowing too little to be understood, or, perchance, too much ? It seems to me that the most honourable and the safest course is neither to conceal, nor to take refuge in euphemisms, but to state the facts simply and frankly, without over-emphasizing them, without evading them, with moderation no doubt, with such reserve as respect for a modern reader imposes, but at the same time with the sincerity due to the overriding claims of historic truth.

Tragedy suffered from the grave defect of not being amusing. Comedy was. Good-bye to the sonorous phrase, the grandiloquent language, the fine sentiment, the poetry. In Comedy : reality and prose. Love is no longer gallantry but

---

[170] Even in his normal dramas, the least admirable of his works (except *All for Love*, and *Don Sebastian*), passages occur of rare and lasting beauty. From Voltaire down to Macaulay, people have often quoted Nourmahal's lines about life (*Aureng-Zebe*, IV, 1). But was Dryden's public appreciative of what we of to-day admire in his plays ? We may fairly doubt it.

[Why should we doubt it ? The great Duchess of Marlborough, for instance, frequently quoted those lines, which she had probably heard at an early performance, and read later. And she was no great reader. B. D.]

lust.[171] It goes straight to the point: "To make sure of one good night is as much in reason, as a man should expect from this ill world." [172] So the men run after the women, and the women after the men, by no roundabout route. " Give me leave to lie with you," says one to a woman in front of her husband.[173] There was no more to it than that. Or else: " Come, there is a bed adjacent." [174] The women do not refuse these gentle invitations.[175] The sequel is within an ace of taking place on the stage.[176] For that matter, it might nearly as well. The author wishes us to lose as little as possible. If he consents to screen his heroes from us for a moment, he is at pains to let us know at once what takes place behind the scenes. For fear of any mistake, the actors remaining on the stage are ready at need to supply ample details.[177]

If the women are not attacked, they attack first. Lady Love-All in *The Parson's Wedding* [178] is " An old Stallion-hunting Widow ". Lady Vain in Shadwell's *Sullen Lovers* is a " whore " ; Lady Gimcrack in the same author's *Virtuoso* hires Hazard, and makes explicit suggestions to boot to both Bruce and Longvil, who ask nothing better than to take her at her word.[179] In Dryden's *Kind Keeper* three women at once are a-hunting Woodall, a man whom they have scarcely had time even to see.[180] It

[171] "*Lodwick.* How, love another? in what quality and manner?
Wittmore. As a Man ought to love, with a good substantial Passion without any design but that of right-down honest Injoyment." (Mrs. Behn, *Sir Patient Fancy*, IV.)
"*Stanmore.* My Mistress is not here neither ; her Folly has a little cool'd my Love ; but I have a most abominable lust to her, the wiser Passion of the two ; and no despair : Though that Rogue *Selfish* has her Mind, I do not doubt but to get her Body ; which is worth two of it for my use." (Shadwell, *A True Widow*, IV, 1.)
[172] Dryden : *The Maiden-Queen*, II, 1 (comic part).
[173] Thomas Killigrew : *The Parson's Wedding*, 1664, (IV, 2) in *Comedies and Tragedies*.
[174] Wycherley : *The Plain-Dealer* (IV).
[175] See Dryden : *The Kind Keeper* (II, 2).
[176] See Mrs. Behn : *Sir Patient Fancy* (III and IV) ; Wycherley : *The Plain Dealer* (IV).
[177] "*Pandarus.* There was a creake ! there was a creake : they are both alive and alive like ; there was a creake : a ha boyes ! " (Dryden : *Troilus and Cressida*, III, 2.)—See also Dryden's *Kind Keeper* (III, 1).
[But the curious reader might like also to see Shakespeare's *Troilus and Cressida*, III, ii. B. D.]
[178] By Thomas Killigrew.
[179] "*Lady Gimcrack.* . . . I know not why we Ladies should not keep, as well as Men, sometimes " (III).
"*Hazard.* . . . I am kept by her, as I know you are by him " (IV).
[180] Mrs. Saintly, Mrs. Tricksy, Mrs. Brainsick.

might certainly be argued that these are nothing but vulgar intrigues of no significance. Note, however, that Lady Love-All, Lady Gimcrack and Lady Vain are all members of the aristocracy. Even when intentions are " strictly honourable " the tone is no more delicate.

The naval lieutenant Freeman is seeking the widow Blackacre in marriage : " What mean you, sir ? " she asks. " Why, faith, (to be short) to marry you, widow." . . . " You are an impertinent person ; and go about your business." " I have none, but to marry thee, widow." " But I have other business." . . . " But you have no business a-nights, widow ; and I'll make you pleasanter business than any you have. For a-nights, I assure you, I am a great man of business ; for the business. . . ." " Go, I'm sure you're an idle fellow." [181] Marcella and Cornelia, desiring to win the hearts of two attractive striplings, escape from their uncle's house and pass themselves off as prostitutes. They thus succeed in marrying the husbands of their choice.[182]

Handsome Celadon marries Florimel :

Celadon. None of my privileges to be infringed by thee, Florimel, under the penalty of a month of fasting nights.
Florimel. None of my privileges to be infringed by thee, Celadon, under the penalty of cuckoldom.
Cel. Well, if it be my fortune to be made a cuckold, I had rather thou should'st make me one, than any one in Sicily ; and for my comfort, I shall have thee oftener than any of thy servants.
Flo. Look ye now, is not such a marriage as good as wenching, Celadon ?
Cel. This is very good ; but not so good, Florimel.[183]

And they marry.
It is not easy to see why.

---

[181] Wycherley, *The Plain Dealer* (imitated from *le Misanthrope*), Act II. —A moment later the widow says to Freeman :

" Thou art a foul-mouthed Boaster of thy Lust, a meer Bragadochio of thy strength for Wine and Women . . . I say you are a worn-out Whoremaster, at five and twenty, both in Body and Fortune : And cannot be trusted by the common Wenches of the Town, lest you shou'd not pay 'em, nor by the wives of the Town, lest you shou'd pay 'em," etc.

[182] *The Feign'd Curtizans* by Mrs. Behn.
[183] Dryden, *The Maiden-Queen* (V, last scene).—In Etherege's *Man of Mode* (V, 2) Bellair says to the Chaplain who has come to officiate at his son's marriage : " Please You, Sir, to Commission a young Couple to go to Bed together a God's name ? "—In Mrs. Behn's *Sir Patient Fancy* (IV), Sir Credulous Easy says to Lodwick : " Dost thou know I am to unty the Virgin Zone. tomorrow, that is barter Maiden-heads with thy Sister, that is to be married to her . . . ? "

Such is the consistent picture of "love" in these dramas. There is nothing between the fatuously sentimental and pompously extravagant gallantry of the Heroic Plays, and the barefaced sensuality of the comedies. You cannot find in all the comedies a single husband who is not a figure of fun, not a single married woman who has not a lover (or several) or, at best, is trying to secure at least one. You may search them for a maiden : in vain. The young girls who should be such, command a strange vocabulary.[184] They chatter continually of their maidenhead, but not as virgins.[185] Gertrude in Shadwell's *A True Widow* is described as a fool and "whorish".[186] Timorous, in speaking of Isabella, says : " and therefore I have reason to love her the longest day I have to live ". Isabella, who is present, interjects : " Ay, and the longest night too, or you are to blame. And you have one argument I love you, if the proverb be true, for I took you almost in your bare shirt." [187]

Parents talk of their daughters with the same looseness. One mother, Melissa, frankly says : " Well, I'll be bold to say it, 'tis as easy to bring up a young lion without mischief, as a maidenhead of fifteen, to make it tame for an husband's bed." [188] Another mother tries to wean her daughter from a preference for regular marriage, and persuade her to let herself be kept.[189] Children are no less outspoken with their parents : When Mrs. Blackacre gives her son the good advice : " Do not go to ordinaries and bagnios, good Jerry," the young man retorts : " Why, have you had any dealings there ? you never had any ill by

[184] " I will cuckold thee, look to 't ; I will most damnably," says Isabella to a suitor whom she dislikes (*Sir Patient Fancy*, by Mrs. Behn, V).—Here is a scrap of conversation between young Pleasance and Mrs. Tricksy, a kept woman :

" *Pleasance :* Let but little *Minx* go proud, and the dogs in *Covent-Garden* have her in the wind immediately ; all pursue the Scent.
Mrs. *Tricksy :* Not to a Boarding-house, I hope !
Pleasance : If they were wise, they wou'd rather go to a Brothel house," etc. (*The Kind Keeper*, by Dryden, III, 1).

In Shadwell's *Virtuoso*, Miranda says to Old Snarl : " Such as you should be destroyed, like Drones that have lost their Stings, and afford no Honey." He replies : " Marry come up, you young Slut ! Are you so liquorish after the Honey of Man ? " (I).

[185] In Mrs. Behn's *Sir Patient Fancy* Isabella says to Lucretia : " Thou may'st lay thy Maiden-head upon't . . ."—See also Dryden's *Maiden-Queen*, III, 1, and IV, 1.

[186] In the list of *Dramatis Personæ*. [187] V, 3.

[188] Dryden, *The Maiden-Queen*, IV, 1.

[189] Lady Cheatly, backed up by Lady Busie, in *A True Widow*, by Shadwell (II).

them, had you?"[190] Another youth lives incognito for five acts with his father, a loquacious old debauchee, in order to take advantage of his sorry revelations.[191]

No one would believe that human imagination could thus run riot if he had not the documents under his very eyes. For all this is solely the product of imagination. We are not dealing with the spontaneous exuberance of youth, unconsciously overflowing all bounds, nor with a rude expansive gaiety frankly finding laughter and merriment in highly-spiced jesting. We have to do with a perverted and deliberate search for the smutty and the bawdy; with a cold-blooded, intentional study of the lewd and licentious, with a refinement of unwholesome thinking on the part of debauchees who have drunk of life too deeply.[192]

Are we at least compensated by interesting situations, by humorous observation, by skilful character-studies? Not at all. Obscenity is the least of the failings, which mark the comedies of this period. It would obviously be too much to say that none of them have either wit or zest. But the zest (which is rare) is used to serve worthless intrigues which scarcely deserve to be called farces,[193] in which the same gallants and the same coquettes [194] court each other in the same way. The wit is

[190] Wycherley, *The Plain Dealer*, IV. Later on, she informs him—untruthfully—that he was born out of wedlock. To which he replies: "What, what? Am I then the Son of a Whore, Mother?"
[191] Woodall, in Dryden's *Kind Keeper*.
[192] No one will accuse Voltaire of prudery, yet though he admired and even imitated Wycherley's *Plain Dealer*, he says of it: "The manners portrayed are so shameless that you might suppose the scene set in a house of ill fame adjacent to a guard room." (Foreword to *la Prude*.)—See also his note on Act III, 7, and the beginning of his Letter 19 on the English; the picture he paints is not overdrawn. *La Prude* is an imitation of *The Plain Dealer*, which title Voltaire translates as "l'Homme au franc procédé".
[193] In Dryden's *Wild Gallant* Constance puts a pillow under her dress to make her father believe that she is pregnant and she succeeds in persuading him that he himself is on the point of having a child.
[This may have been a topical allusion. Genest quotes a story of a certain "Dr. Pelling, Chaplain to Charles II, who having studied himself into the disorder of mind called the hyp . . . between the age of forty and fifty imagined himself to be pregnant." The illusion is not unique: Marshal Blucher, of Waterloo fame, was also its victim. B. D.]
[194] "*Character* they supply with a smutty *Song, Humor,* with a Dance, and Argument with *Lightning* and Thunder, which has oft repriev'd many a scurvy Play from *Damning*. A huge great Muff, and a gaudy Ribbon hanging at a Bully's backside, is an excellent Jest: and new-invented curses, as, *Stap my Vitals, Damn my Diaphragm, Slit my Windpipe, Sink me Ten thousand fathom deep,* rig up a new Beau, tho' in the main 'tis but the same everlasting Coxcomb . . ." (Tom Brown, *Amusements Serious and Comical, The Play-House. Works,* vol. III.)

the author's purely verbal wit, never provoked by the situation. It is always the author who is speaking, never his characters [195]; he constantly interrupts the play to let the characters assail each other with repartee and to display to the admiring gallery the skill with which he can parry the thrusts he makes himself.[196] Nothing could be more fatal to dramatic effect, nothing so monotonous, nothing so wearisome as these " compositions where everything is blue, everything is pink, everything is the author ".[197] So we do not find a single living part, a single real character : all these concoctions are artificial, cast in the same conventional mould, the fashionable mould of the day.[198] The most you can hope for is occasionally to see a figure or a type which makes you laugh.[199] You are lucky if the wit does not consist wholly of lewd jests " to make the Ladies look they know not how ".[200]

[195] See Macaulay, *Essays* : The Comic Dramatists of the Restoration.
[196] See, for instance, the dialogue between Courtine and Sylvia in the 5th Act of Otway, *The Souldiers Fortune*. This type of thing was called " slap-dash ". (Lee, *The Princess of Cleve*, II, 2.)—" This, Sirs, might properly enough be call'd a prize of Wit ; for you shall see 'em come in upon one another snip snap, hit for hit, as fast as can be. First one speaks, then presently t'other's upon him slap, with a Repartee ; then he at him again, dash with a new conceipt : and so eternally, eternally, I gad, till they go quite off the Stage." (Buckingham, *The Rehearsal*, III, 1.)—Dryden himself says : " As for Comedy, repartee is one of its chiefest graces ; the greatest pleasure of an audience is a chase of wit, kept up on both sides, and swiftly managed." (*An Essay of Dramatick Poesie*.)
[197] Preface to *le Mariage de Figaro*.
[198] Yet they had models and were acquainted with them. But see what Wycherley makes of Alcestis and of Agnes (*The Plain Dealer* and *The Country Wife*).
[199] The widow *Blackacre*, in *The Plain Dealer* ; Sir Samuel Hearty in Shadwell's *Virtuoso*.
[200]
" Here's nothing you will like ; no fustian Scenes,
And nothing too of—you know what he means ;
No double *Entendrés*, which your Sparks allow ;
To make the Ladies look they know not how."
(Prologue to Dryden's *Love Triumphant*.)

" Alas ! 'tis a meer out-of-fashion Play ;
No Bawdy in 't to make the Ladies glow . . ."
(Prologue to Dogget's *Country-Wake*.)

I suppose the ladies must have looked " they know not how " at passages like this :

" *Young Jorden* : Sure there is no woman so necessitated to venture on him.
Cureal : O, many.
Young Jorden : Not she that wears a stiff Busk to keep down a great belly, and is to pass for a Maid still ; or she that is forc'd to come to a Play in a Vizard-Mask to pick up a gallant to give her a Supper.
Cureal : Ha, ha, ha.

As a consequence this whole comic drama has been expunged

Young Jorden: Nay, not she that has lived to be a stale Maid, and is convinc'd by her own imperfections that she shall never know any pleasure, but what her own art and industry can create, but would think her self cast away on him."

(Ravenscroft, *The Citizen turn'd Gentleman*, II, 1.)

I should not venture to assert that there were any ladies who did not understand.

As further samples of this kind, see the character of Sir Jolly Jumble in *The Souldiers Fortune* by Otway; Mrs. Behn's play *The Town-Fopp*, where one scene is laid in a brothel, and the mistress of the establishment initiates us into the details of her management; the scene in Dryden's *Kind Keeper* where Aldo receives the town prostitutes; or rather, see the whole play: note that it had been *softened down* before being printed.

All the comedies of the time should be quoted. Let it suffice to call attention to some conversations in Etherege's *Comical Revenge*, IV, 5, and still more to others in Shadwell's *Humorists* and *Virtuoso*. In the former of these two plays note particularly the first act and the character of Crazy; in the latter the scenes between old Snarl and Mrs. Figgup. Here is a specimen:

"*Snarl:* . . . Where are the instruments of our Pleasure? Nay, prethee do not frown, by the Mass thou shalt do 't now.

Figgup: I wonder that should please you so much, that pleases me so little?

Snarl: I was us'd to 't at *Westminster*-School, I cou'd never leave it off since.

Figgup: Well, look under the Carpet then if I must.

Snarl: Very well, my dear Rogue. But dost hear, thou art too gentle. Do not spare thy pains. I love Castigation mightily.—So, here's good provision. (Pulls the Carpet, three or four Rods fall down.)" (Act III.)

Contemporary tragedy is not free from similar touches, witness the following taken from the works of Lee:

"*Titus:* Sir, I am marry'd.
Brutus: What, without my knowledge?
Titus: My Lord, I ask your Pardon; but that *Hymen*—
Brutus: Thou ly'st; that honorable God would scorn it.
Some bawdy Flamen shuffled you together;
Priapus lock'd you, while the *Bacchanals*
Sung your detested *Epithalamium*.
Which of thy blood were the curs'd Witnesses?
Who would be there at such polluted Rites
But *Goats*, *Baboons*, some chatt'ring old *Silenus*
Or *Satyrs* grinning at your slimy Joys?"

(*Lucius Junius Brutus*, I, 1.)

"*Ascanio Sforza:* . . . Would he were *Pope*,
Head of the Christian World, and I his Engine,
His particular member, to bring, to cast,
To throw, disperse, convey the warmest
Sprinklings of his benediction."

(*Caesar Borgia*, I.)

See also the same author's *Theodosius* (II, 1) where two women, Pulcheria and Julia, are present.

from English literature.[201] If Dryden's name is still held in high honour, it is because he wrote other things beside comedies. As for Shadwell, Ravenscroft, Mrs. Behn, Etherege and even Wycherley, their names have become mere memories; their works are read only by the curious and by those who seek in them information about the characters they depict, and the people for whose pleasure the writers wrote.

These people had reason to be well satisfied, for everything was made according to their favourite recipe. Reflecting the manners of society, offering its members everything that could allure them, sparing no pains to devise new inventions, patronized by the King, the theatre was the great relaxation of people of fashion. They could not do without it. It was with extreme reluctance that they resigned themselves to its closing during the terrible Plague of 1665. While people were still dying of the scourge, they importuned the Bishops to hasten a Day of Thanksgiving for the Cessation of the Plague, that the playhouses might be re-opened.[202]

V

Dramatists' difficulty in satisfying the audience.—Audience limited in numbers; perpetual demand for something new; collaboration and adaptation.—Frivolity of the audience: Prologues and Epilogues

It might seem that in such circumstances the profession of drama-writer would have been one of the most brilliant and well recompensed. Nothing of the sort.

In the first place the number of enthusiastic theatre addicts was very limited. The City remained Puritan, horrified at the manners of the day and the audacity of the plays; the citizens

---

[201] As early as 1749, Otway's comedy *Friendship in Fashion* was hissed because of its "obscenity" and driven from the stage (Johnson, *Lives of the English Poets*, Otway).—In 1818 Wycherley's *Country Wife* was still being played; but the character of Horner no longer appeared "as Wycherley made him" (Hazlitt, *Lectures*, part II, p. 101).

[It is, of course, no longer true to say that this whole comic drama has been expunged from English literature. Much of it is reprinted in the Mermaid Series and the World's Classics. The Phœnix Society, a private society which employed professionals, revived many of the plays as such in the twenties of this century, and some have become part of the public repertoire. They are, one need hardly say, studied in the universities. B. D.]

[202] Pepys, Nov. 20, 1666.—"Nay, she (Lady Cartaret) told me they have heretofore had plays at Court, the very nights before the fast for the death of the late king." (Ibid., Oct. 15, 1666.)

did not attend the performances at all, or very rarely.[203] "The playhouse was abhorred by the Puritans, and avoided by those who desired the character of seriousness or decency. A grave lawyer would have debased his dignity, and a young trader would have impaired his credit, by appearing in those mansions of dissolute licentiousness."[204] Even works composed to flatter the political views of the citizenry could not break down this aloofness.[205] This meant that a large part of the normal theatre audience was excluded, and perhaps the better part, people sufficiently cultured to appreciate, and at the same time sufficiently unsophisticated and naïve, to recognize honest laughter and genuine emotion, and be carried away by them.[206]

Theatre-goers were thus reduced to the Court and the tribe of officials and idlers who revolved round the King. The fact that the audience was thus limited, and always the same, made it impossible to repeat the same plays with any frequency. A play which had a run of ten consecutive performances was counted a huge success.[207] More often it was played only three to six times.[208] For the same reasons, revivals could not be counted on. *Sir Martin Mar-all* by the Duke of Newcastle and Dryden, and Etherege's *Comical Revenge*, two great successes of the

---

[203] See the Epilogue to Wycherley's *Gentleman Dancing Master*.

[204] Johnson, *Lives of the English Poets*: Dryden—"Of late the playhouses are so extremely pestered with vizard-masks and their trade (occasioning continual quarrels and abuses) that many of the more civilised part of the town are uneasy in the company, and shun the theatre as they would a house of scandal." (Wright, *Historia Histrionica*, 1699, p. 6; quoted by Malone, *Historical Account* . . . p. 127.) Despite the date 1699 Malone says that this applies to "after the Restoration".—"Men of *Figure* and Consideration are known by seldom being there (in the theatre) and Men of *Wisdom* and Business by always being absent." (Tom Brown, *The Play-House*, in Amusements *Serious and Comical, Works*, vol. III.)

[205]   "Our Popes and Fryars on one Side offend,
    And yet alass the City's not our Friend:
    The City neither likes us nor our wit,
    They say their Wives learn *ogling in the Pit;
    They'r from the Boxes taught to make Advances,
    To answer stolen Sighs and naughty Glances . . ."
            (Shadwell, Epilogue to *The Lancashire Witches*.)

* A foolish word among the Canters for glancing.

[206] Even at the time people were well aware of this. "And he (T. Killigrew) tells me plainly that the City audience was as good as the Court; but now they are most gone." (Pepys, Feb. 12, 1666–7.)

[207] Downes (p. 37), speaking of the *Œdipus* by Dryden and Lee, says: "it took prodigiously, being *Acted* 10 Days together".

[208] See Genest, vol. I, *passim*.

day (they were played for a month), were revived after several years, the former being then played three times, the latter twice.[209]

Authors were therefore compelled to write without ceasing; since the audience could not be, the repertoire had to be, constantly renewed, and the paucity of spectators compensated by the abundance of plays.[210] Between 1662 and 1680 Dryden produced eighteen plays, one of which was in two parts, making in all ten acts; the others were of five acts and most of them in verse. In some years his output ran to three: in 1678, for instance, *All for Love*, *The Kind Keeper* and *Œdipus*: ten acts in verse and five in prose. As a natural consequence, an author had to work fast: Dryden wrote *Tyrannick Love* in seven weeks [211] and *Amboyna* in a month.[212] Shadwell wrote *The Miser* in less than a month.[213] In his preface to *The Libertine* the same author tells us: " I must applaud my good Fortune, to have pleased with so little pains: there being no Act in it, which cost me above five days writing; and that the last two (the Play-House having great occasion for a Play) were both written in four days, as several can testifie." [214] Ravenscroft wrote a five-act play in seven days.[215]

These demands of the theatre compelled authors to have recourse to two expedients: collaboration (of the bad kind which springs, not from community of literary interests, but from consideration of self-interest) and *adaptation*, which later became the ruin of English drama.[216] Dryden collaborated with D'Avenant to rewrite *The Tempest*; with Lee in *Œdipus* and

---

[209] Genest, vol. I, pp. 75, 76, 123, 124.

[210] " He still must write; and Banquier-like, each day
Accept new Bills, and he must break, or pay."
(Dryden, Epilogue to *An Evening's Love*.)

[211] See the Preface.

[212] See the Dedication.

[213] " 'Tis not barrenness of wit or invention, that, makes us borrow from the *French*, but laziness; and this was the occasion of my making use of *l'Avare*. This play . . . was wrote in less than a month." (Notice of *The Miser*.)

[214] Preface to *The Libertine*.

[215] " In three dayes time, the Three first Acts were Made, Transcrib'd, and given them (the actors) to write out in Parts.—The Two last Acts took me up just so much time: one Week compleated it." (*The Careless Lovers*: The Epistle to the Reader.)

[216] *Adaptation* consists in taking a foreign play, transferring the scene to England and giving the characters English names. Allusions are modified, touches of wit in the original are replaced by local jests, and the play is finished. An older English play is *adapted* by modernizing it.

The Duke of Guise. Crowne and an unknown collaborator brought out a spiritless reproduction of *Andromache*, partly in verse, partly in prose. The plays of Shakespeare and his contemporaries were rewritten; the French and Spanish drama were plundered. In addition to *The Tempest* Dryden pirated *Troilus and Cressida* and staged *l'Étourdi* as *Sir Martin Mar-All*. D'Avenant combined *Measure for Measure* and *Much Ado about Nothing* into *The Law against Lovers* and concocted an opera out of *Macbeth*. Wycherley borrowed his *Gentleman Dancing Master* from Calderon, his *Plain Dealer* from Molière's *Misanthrope*, and blended *l'École des Maris* with *l'École des Femmes* into *The Country Wife*. Otway's *History and Fall of Caius Marius* is nothing but *Romeo and Juliet*.[216a] Molière supplied Otway with *The Cheats of Scapin*; Racine provided him with *Titus and Berenice*. Tate remodelled *King Lear*. Shadwell rewrote Shakespeare's *Timon* and Molière's *l'Avare*. Lacey converted *The Taming of the Shrew* nto *Sauny the Scott*, manufactured *The Dumb Lady* out of *le Médecin malgré lui* and *l'Amour Médecin*, and *Sir Hercules Buffoon* out of Massinger's *City Madam*.[217] Mrs. Philips translated Corneille's *Pompée*[218] and an anonymous author *le Menteur*.[219] This list might be considerably extended. Almost the whole of Molière was lifted.

All authors of the time borrowed more or less. There was

[216a] [It is not true to say that Otway's *Caius Marius* "is nothing but *Romeo and Juliet*". The play is about Marius, Otway's sources being the usual ones, such as Plutarch, Shakespeare's play providing the sub-plot. The whole paragraph needs some comment. The way the Restoration dramatists treated other people's plays, and turned them to their own use was not an invention of their own, and the practice has luckily not been discontinued. All playwrights, when they need to, borrow and "improve", or at least adapt to their own country and society. If *Sir Martin Mar-All* came from *L'Étourdi*, *L'Étourdi* itself was an adaptation of drama foreign to France. These playwrights, like Molière himself, took their good things where they could find them. B. D.]

[217] In *Sir Hercules Buffoon*, Lacey makes one of his characters rightly remark: "Now Poets are turned cobblers; they vamp and mend old plays." (II, 4.)

[That was in the good old tradition, for it was also the practice of the Elizabethan-Jacobean playwrights, including Shakespeare, to the despair of editors and the delight of writers of Ph.D. theses. With the earlier playwrights also, collaboration often sprang from considerations of self-interest rather than from a community of literary interests, so this harmless practice was no monstrous innovation of the amoral Restoration dramatists. B. D.]

[218] *Pompey*, 1663. The translation was made at the request of the Earl of Orrery. See *Biographia Dramatica*, s.v. Pompey.

[219] *The Lyar*, 1661. See *Biographia Dramatica*, s.v. Mistaken Beauty, or *The Lyar*.

even one who did almost nothing else, a certain Edward Ravenscroft. He is nowadays almost completely forgotten, but for a long time he and his dozen plays held a certain position in the theatre world. He rehashed Shakespeare's *Titus Andronicus*, and pieced together his comedy *The Citizen turn'd Gentleman* from *le Bourgeois gentilhomme*, *Monsieur de Pourceaugnac* and *l'Avare*. *The Careless Lovers* was constructed from such fragments of *Monsieur de Pourceaugnac* as he had not been able to work into his *Citizen*, and a third fine-combing of the same play provided him with his *Canterbury Guests*. *Le Mariage Forcé* combined with the *Fourberies de Scapin* and the unused passages of *le Bourgeois gentilhomme*,[220] yielded yet another play, and so on.

It will be realized that the audiences of those days had an unholy appetite for plays and gave little respite to their suppliers. But this was not their only annoying characteristic. The author's sorrows were not over when his play was ready. We must never forget that people's sole idea was to have a good time, in whatever way and by whatever means they could contrive it.[221] So theatre-goers did not come in the best mood to pay serious attention. They came not so much to enjoy the play as to make merry at the play's expense. They came to look and to listen, but also to be seen.[222] They were more taken up with

---

[220] "Scaramouch a Philosopher, Harlequin a Schoolboy, Bravo, Merchant and Magician."—See *Biographia Dramatica*, s.v. Ravenscroft (Edward) and my bibliography.

[221] They even made merry over affairs of state : "At the daily meeting of the Council, when the great Lord Chancellor, Clarendon, wearing one of the magnificent periwigs of the period, was gravely expounding to Charles II his lengthy and carefully thought out opinions, Buckingham would post himself behind the Chancellor's armchair, mimicking the speaker's attitude and gestures, stretching out his arm and tapping with his foot in time with his model." (Geffroy, p. 199.)

[222] "He fears not Sparks who with brisk Dress and Mien,
Come not to hear or see, but to be seen.
Each prunes himself, and with a languishing Eye,
Designs to kill a Lady, by the by."
(Shadwell, Epilogue to *The Squire of Alsatia*.)

". . . you, the fine, loud gentlemen o' th' Pit,
Who damn all Plays ;
Now, you shrewd Judges, who the Boxes sway,
Leading the Ladies hearts and sense astray,
And for their sakes, see all, and hear no Play :
Correct your Cravats, Foretops, Lock behind ;
The Dress and Breeding of the Play ne'er mind.
(Wycherley, Prologue to *The Plain Dealer*.)

themselves and with the theatre itself than with what was happening on the stage. For women, theatre-going has always been an opportunity for dressing up: *spectatum veniunt, veniunt spectentur ut ipsae*.[223] They naturally continued the custom: they came in order to be admired by the men, as the men came in order to be admired by them. "Really," says Selfish in Shadwell's *True Widow*, "I never come to a Play, but upon account of seeing the Ladies."[224] They had more than enough to choose from. It was customary for women to come masked to the performances, which made it impossible to distinguish honourable women from the others.[225] The masks were a subject of much interest for the gallants:

> ... when vizard-mask appears in pit,
> Straight every man who thinks himself a wit
> Perks up, and, managing his comb with grace,
> With his white wig sets off his nut-brown face;[226]
> That done, bears up to the prize, and views each limb,
> To know her by her rigging and her trim;
> Then, the whole noise of fops to wagers go,—
> "Pox on her, 't must be she"; and—"Damme, no!"[227]

It was evidently the masked women who particularly attracted these gentlemen to comedy at the theatre. People dined at about 1 or 2 o'clock p.m. and went on to the theatre where the performances began about half-past three.[228]

---

[223] Ovid, *Artis Amatoriæ*, I, l. 99.—"Here the Ladies come to shew their Cloaths." (Tom Brown, *Amusements Serious and Comical, The Play-House, Works*, vol. III.)

[224] Act IV, 1.

[225] "... By that Mask of modesty which Women wear promiscuously in publick; they are all alike, and you can no more know a kept Wench from a Woman of Honour by her looks than by her Dress ..." (Wycherley, Dedication to *The Plain-Dealer*.)

> "Audacious Vizards too, so fast do grow,
> You hardly can the Virtuous from 'em know."
> (Crowne, Epilogue to *Sir Courtly Nice*.)

> "The proper Use of Visors once was made,
> When only worn by such as own'd the Trade:
> Tho' now all mingle with 'em so together,
> That you can hardly know the one from t' other."
> (Otway, Epilogue to *Titus and Berenice*.)

[226] A brown complexion was all the fashion, for Charles II's was brown.

[227] Dryden, Prologue to the Second Part of *The Conquest of Granada*.

[228] Dryden, Original Prologue to *The Wild Gallant*. See also Malone, *Historical Account* ..., p. 158.

... A Town Gallant ...
... repairs to th' Play to meet a sinner :
And here with Burgundy and brisk sableé
Inspir'd, with vizard-Masque holds reparteé.²²⁹

Here is a picture of the gallant's arrival :

He advances into the middle of the *Pit*, struts about a while, to render his good parts Conspicuous, pulls out his *Comb*, Carreens his *Wigg*, *Hums* the *Orange-Wench* to give her her own rates for her China-fruit, and immediately *Sacrifices* the fairest of them, to the shrine of the next *Vizor Mask*. Then gravely sits down, and falls half *asleep*, unless some *petulant Wench* hard by, keep him awake by treading on his *Toe*, or a wanton Complement ; Yet all on a sudden to shew his *Judgment*, and prove himself at once a *Wit* and a *Critick*, he starts up and with a Tragical Face, *Damns the Play* though he have not *heard* (at least understood) two Lines of it. However when 'tis done, he picks up a Miss, and pinching her fingers in a soft Tone, and looks abominably *Languishing*, he Whispers, " *Damn me, Madam ! If you were but sensible, and all that of the Passion I have for you ; and the Flames which your irresistable Charms, and all that have kindled in my Breast, you would be merciful, and Honour me with your Angelical Company, to take a Draught of Loves Posset at next Tavern.*" But if he finds her honest and cannot prevail, then he cries aloud, *Damn ye for a Puritanical Whore, what make you in the Pit here : The Twelve penny Gallery with Camlet-Cloaks and Foot-boys is good enough for you.* And so raises his Seige, and leaves her.²³⁰

If the masks were few or uninteresting the gentlemen amused themselves by playing practical jokes on their neighbours. They dug them in the back with their fists or threw their hats into the air. Squabbles and fisticuffs ensued. They shouted ; they criticized the play at the top of their voice ; they teased the orange-women ; they moved from the pit to the gallery and from the gallery to the pit. They thought nothing of turning their back to the stage ; they played cards in the boxes ; they munched fruit while the performance was going on. Everyone had songs, epigrams or satires in his hand.²³¹

²²⁹ Ravenscroft, Epilogue to *The Citizen turn'd Gentleman* :
" Leave coming here, when you do not intend
To see the Play, but pick up a she-friend.
Leave sharping for your selves, and pay your Guinny
For Procuration there to honest Jenny."
(Prologue, Spoken in *Lent*. Preceding Ravenscroft's *Titus Andronicus*. Jenny Cromwell was a well-known procuress.)

²³⁰ *The Character of a Town-Gallant.*—In one of Hogarth's engravings we see two of the " orange-women " here mentioned.

²³¹ " They (the young men of this age) are vitious illiterate foolish Fellows, good for nothing but to roar and make a noise in a Play-house. To

This picture reveals an audience anything but attentive. But these were only the minor incidents common to every performance ; matters sometimes went further. One day some young men, over-stimulated by a heavy meal, burst into the theatre with lighted torches and flung them at the actors, loudly

---

be very brisk with pert Whores in Vizards . . . And when Whores are not there, they play Monkey-tricks with one another . . ." (Shadwell, *The Virtuoso*, II, 2.)

> " Our Gallerys too, were finely us'd of late,
> Where roosting Masques sat cackling for a Mate :
> They came not to see Plays but to act their own,
> And had throng'd Audiences when we had none.
> Our Plays it was impossible to hear,
> The honest Country Men were forc't to swear :
> Confound you, give your bawdy prating o'er
> Or Zounds, I'le fling you i' th' Pitt, you bawling Whore."
> (Crowne, Epilogue to *Sir Courtly Nice*.)

> " The empty Head, that never thought before,
> But on New Fashions, or a fresh new Whore :
> Who without us no Afternoon could spend,
> Nor shew Himself, nor meet a secret Friend ;
> Whom mounting from the Pit we use to see
> (For dangerous Intrigues) to th' Gallery ;
> Where stead of Maidenheads 'tis oft his hap
> By bold advent'ring to atchieve a Clap
> Or down he comes, and lolls i' th' Orange-wenches lap.
> For News he now walks gravely up and down," etc.
> (Shadwell, Prologue to *The Woman-Captain*.)

> " He who comes hither with design to hiss
> And with a bum revers'd to whisper Miss,
> To comb a Perriwig, or to shew gay cloathes,
> Or to vent Antique non-sence with new oaths,
> Our poet welcomes . . . "
> (D'Urfey, Prologue to *The Fool turn'd Critick*.)

" Thou shalt . . . after Noon at the Theatre exalted in a Box, give Audience to ev'ry trim amorous twiring Fop of the Corner, that comes thither to make a Noise, hear no Play, and show himself ; thou Shalt, my *Bona Roba*."
(Otway, *Friendship in Fashion*, V.)

> " . . . Flutt'ring Hectores on the Vizard fall
> One half o' th' Play they spend in noise and braul."
> (Lee, Epilogue to *Sophonisba*.)

In the Prologue to St. Serfe's comedy, *Tarugo's Wiles, or The Coffee House* an actor says : " it may scare the Ladies from eating their fruit."

The fourth Act of Shadwell's *True Widow* is laid in a theatre. Here are a few phrases culled from it : " Several young Coxcombs fool with the Orange-women." A *Bully* says : " What Play do they play ? some confounded Play or other." Another exclaims : " A Pox on't, Madam ! What should we do at this damn'd Play-house ? Let's send for some Cards, and Play at Lang-trilloo in the Box." There are literary discussions, there are intrigues, and a gentleman who refuses to pay the Door-Keeper for his seat, hurling abuse against the Duchess of Portsmouth.[232] On another occasion one of the spectators insulted another of the King's mistresses, Nell Gwyn, who was present; a young gallant [233] took up her defence, and one half of the public drew swords against the other. It even happened that concurrently with the tragedy being enacted on the stage, a real tragedy was taking place in the pit as when Sir Thomas Armstrong one day stabbed and killed Mr. Scroop.[234]

An audience of this kind, irresponsible, temperamental and riotous, was easy neither to attract nor to retain. Strive as they might to cater for its taste, authors were not always successful in combating its wayward caprices. A troup of marionettes was enough completely to empty two theatres and an appeal had to be made to the King to protect them against such dangerous rivalry.[235]

At all costs some means must be devised to satisfy tastes so little interested in drama proper, to fix the wandering attention

---

but will not leave. One of the audience complains of his neighbours: "These Fellows will be witty and trouble us." Another: "See how kind the Ladies are to me: Pretty Rogue! Let me repose my Head in thy soft Bosom." Another uses insulting words (Whore, etc.) to a mask who does not answer. Another "Raps People on the Backs, and twirls their *hats, and then looks demurely, as if he did not do it*." Thereupon there is a fight; swords are drawn, the actors vanish and the women scatter screaming.

Tom Brown represents *Country Gentlemen* in the theatre loudly discussing the hunt. "A *Bully Beau* comes drunk into the Pit, screaming out: *Damn me*, Jack, *'tis a Confounded Play, let's to a* Whore *and spend our time better*." (*The Play-House*; *Works*, vol. III. Amusements Serious and Comical.)

See also *The Tatler*, No. 1; Epilogue to Otway's *Titus and Berenice*; Prologue to Lee's *Rival Queens*; Prologue to Southerne's *Disappointment* (attributed to Dryden); Pepys, Nov. 2, 1667; Prologue, *Spoken in Lent* prefixed to Ravenscroft's *Titus Andronicus*; *Prologue Against the Disturbers of the Pit* by Rochester (*Works*, I, p. 56); Prologue to Dryden's *Cleomenes*.

[232] Malcolm, p. 177.

[233] William Herbert, later Earl of Pembroke and first plenipotentiary at Ryswick. This incident is recorded by M. W. Thornbury, *Haunted London*, p. 461, and by Dr. Doran, *Their Majesties' Servants*, p. 21. Neither quotes his authority.

[234] *Makbeth*, a Tragedy; which was reviv'd by the Dukes Company, and re-printed with Alterations and New Songs, 4°, *Lond.*, 1674 (this is D'Avenant's arrangement).... "At the Acting of this Tragedy, on the Stage, I saw a real one acted in the Pit; I mean the Death of Mr. *Scroop*, who received his death's wound from the late Sir *Thomas Armstrong*, and died presently after he was remov'd to a House opposite to the Theatre, in *Dorset-Garden* (Langbaine, I, p. 460). See also Dryden's Epilogue for the Union of the Two Troops in 1682 (Christie, pp. 457-8).—Reresby tells (Jan. 8, 1679) how one of his friends was nearly wounded in the theatre by a drunken neighbour who had drawn his sword.

[235] Cibber, *Apology*, p. 57.

of gallants and rowdies, to counter the attractions of prostitutes, interrupters and marionettes. To meet the case, recourse was had to prologues and epilogues.

The function of the prologue was, not so much to introduce the author or the play, as to summon the audience as bells call the faithful to church and to compensate them in advance if the play was " dull ". In proportion as the play was " dull " [236] —that is to say serious—the prologue had to be lively and highly spiced.

". . . you think yourselves ill used," says Dryden to his audience,

> When in smart prologues you are not abused.
> A civil prologue is approved by no man ;
> You hate it as you do a civil woman.
> Your fancy's palled, and liberally you pay
> To have it quickened ere you see a play.
> Just as old sinners, worn from their delight
> Give money to be whipped to appetite.[237]

Such was the task assigned to the prologue.

The epilogue's business was to amuse the public and more especially, while feigning to crave indulgence, to offer some broad jokes to make good any tediousness or difficulty of the play. The prologue was the appetizer before the meal, the epilogue a liqueur to aid digestion.

Prologue and epilogue both discharged their duty conscientiously. The author racked his brains to provide the attraction of novelty and originality. The prologue to *The Indian Queen* [238]

---

[236] " Prologues, *like Bells to Churches*, toul you in
With Chimeing Verse ; till the dull Playes begin . . . "
(Dryden, Prologue to *The Assignation*.)

[237] Prologue to *Secret-Love*, or *The Maiden-Queen* ; Lee's Epilogue to *Gloriana* expresses the same idea more vividly :

> " We'l deal with you, Gallants, in your own way,
> And treat you like those Punks that love for pay ;
> *Cartwright* and I, dress'd like two thund'ring Whores,
> With rods will stand behind the Play-house doors,
> And firk you up each day to pleasure duly,
> As *Jenny Cromwell* does, or *Betty Buly*."

It was the actor Haines who spoke this epilogue ; Cartwright was one of his fellow-actors. Jenny Cromwell, already mentioned, and Betty Buly were two procuresses.—There had been prologues before, but how different were those of Shakespeare and Ben Jonson. The epilogue was unusual before the time of Charles II. (Malone, *Historical Account* . . . pp. 123, 124.)

[238] By Sir Robert Howard and Dryden.

was spoken by "two Indian children", the epilogue to *The Indian Emperour* by "a Mercury". The original prologue to *The Wild Gallant* brought "two astrologers" on to the stage, that of *Troilus and Cressida* the "ghost" of Shakespeare.[239] Popular actresses were entrusted with the speaking. The prologue of Sir Robert Howard's *Duke of Lerma* was spoken by Mrs. Ellen (Gwyn) and Mrs. Nepp.[240] We have already seen that on such occasions they were often dressed as men. Sometimes prologues and epilogues were sung.[241] Surprises were introduced: now, two prologues at a time on the stage[242]; now, after about twenty lines the speaker went off to return a moment later crying:

> I had forgot one half, I do protest,
> And now am sent again to speak the rest . . .[243]

But the triumph of this type of thing was the prologue spoken by Nell Gwyn in a large hat. The credit for this invention belongs to the actor Nokes, of the Duke's Company. He was the first to have the bright idea of appearing surmounted by a hat with an enormous brim. It seems that this novelty—the salt of which has perhaps somewhat lost its savour nowadays—was considered extremely witty and made a palpable hit. But it was reserved for Dryden to exploit Nokes's idea to the full. He got a hat made with a brim "as large as a cart-wheel" and presented it to Nell Gwyn who masqueraded in it to speak the prologue to the first part of the *Conquest of Granada*. It was a stroke of genius: "the entire theatre fell into convulsions; the King nearly choked with laughter". Tradition adds that it was in this headgear that Nell Gwyn first attracted the attention of her royal lover: Charles II, swept off his feet with admiration, sought her out behind the scenes and carried her off that very day.[244]

Note that this preposterous kit was used not for the prologue to a comedy but to a tragic drama. Imagine a musician who

---

[239] These three plays are Dryden's.
[240] Obviously Pepys's friend Mrs. Knipp.
[241] *The Man is the Master*, a comedy of D'Avenant's: "The prologue but poor, and the epilogue little in it but the extraordinariness of it, it being sung by Harris and another in the form of a ballad." (ballet? —E. O. L.). (Pepys, March 26, 1667-8.)
[242] Dryden's *Rival Ladies*.
[243] Dryden's *Secret-Love, or the Maiden-Queen*.
[244] Downes, *Roscius Anglicanus*, edited by Thomas Davies, Appendix, pp. 14 and 18.

would allow a medley or a pom-pom-pom to be played as the overture to a tragic opera. Nothing less was customary in those days. Everyone—audience and authors alike—unanimously refused to take anything seriously. The author not only took care to warn his audience in advance against any genuine emotion which his work might evoke, but when the play was over was the first to laugh at it. Like Penelope he hastened to unravel in his epilogue the fabric laboriously woven in his five acts.[245] In Sir Robert Howard's *Vestal Virgin* all the chief characters perished at the close. After this murderous climax, the comic actor Lacey entered *ex abrupto* and chattered nonsense to the audience whom the dramatist had just plunged into grief. Later the climax was altered : only one character was sacrificed. Lacey arrived and finding everybody alive but one, complained that he was no longer wanted and that they had completely ruined his epilogue.[246]

Better still. At the close of Dryden's *Tyrannick Love,* Princess Valeria kills herself rather than marry an unloved husband. Her lifeless body remains stretched out upon the stage and people come to carry it away. But as one of the bearers draws near to raise the corpse, the dead woman cries out :

> Hold ! Are you mad ? You damn'd confounded Dog !
> I am to rise and speak the epilogue.

It was Nell Gwyn who, flinging aside her character of princess, became herself again and took the public into her confidence :

> I come, kind gentlemen, strange news to tell ye,
> I am the ghost of poor departed Nelly.
> Sweet ladies, be not frighted ; I'll be civil ;
> I'm what I was, a little harmless devil . . .
> O poet, damned dull poet, who could prove
> So senseless, to make Nelly die for love !
> Nay, what's yet worse, to kill me in the prime
> Of Easter-term, in tart and cheese-cake time !
> I'll fit the fop ; for I'll not one word say,
> To excuse his godly, out-of-fashion play ;
> A play, which, if you dare but twice sit out,
> You'll all be slandered, and be thought devout . . .[247]

---

[245] See what No. 338 of the *Spectator* has to say about the effect of these comic epilogues to tragedies.

[246] Sir Robert Howard's volume : *Five New Plays* contains both versions and both epilogues.

[247] Dryden tells us that he wrote *Tyrannick Love* in praise of piety.

> As for my epitaph when I am gone,
> I'll trust no poet, but will write my own :—
> Here Nelly lies, who, though she lived a slattern,
> Yet died a princess, acting in St. Catherine.[248]

Highly uplifting and highly favourable to tragic emotion ! But to be given information about the more interesting personalities of the stage ; to hear the back stage gossip was almost as amusing as unveiling masked faces, and so the audience listened. The authors, who knew the type of mind they were catering for, were careful, by prologue and epilogue, to keep the gentlemen informed of the ways and doings of the actress ladies. One poet pleads with his audience that they shall :

> Think him not duller for this year's delay ;
> He was prepared, the women were away ;
> And men, without their parts, can hardly play.
> If they, through sickness, seldom did appear,
> Pity the virgins of each theatre :
> For, at both houses, 'twas a sickly year !
> And pity us, your servants, to whose cost
> In one such sickness nine whole months are lost.[249]

Or it might be an actress [250] who would come to complain of her lovers :

> Who wou'd have thought such hellish times to 've seen
> When I shou'd be neglected at eighteen ?

We are justified in considering these prologues and epilogues not exactly models of reserve. Yet those so far quoted are anything but the most outspoken. Their usual tone is similar to that we have already noted in the songs and satires. Indecent allusions, phrases with a double meaning, often, too, words of incredible coarseness so abound that it is difficult to give the reader an idea of them in any language suited to his ears. Here, however, is a prologue of Dryden's which it is just possible to quote, as a sample of the type. It introduces *An Evening's Love* :

---

[248] St. Catherine is one of the characters in the play.—The epilogue to Otway's *History and Fall of Caius Marius* was similarly spoken by Mrs. Barry who had just been playing Lavinia :

> " A Mischief on't ! though I'm agen alive
> May I believe this Play of ours shall thrive ? " etc.

[249] Dryden, Epilogue to the first part of *The Conquest of Granada*.
[250] Mrs. Currer in Mrs. Behn's Prologue to *The Feign'd Curtizans*.

> When first our poet set himself to write,
> Like a young bridegroom on his wedding-night,
> He laid about him, and did so bestir him,
> His Muse could never lie in quiet for him :
> But now his honey-moon is gone and past,
> Yet the ungrateful drudgery must last,
> And he is bound, as civil husbands do,
> To strain himself in complaisance to you :
> To write in pain, and counterfeit a bliss,
> Like the faint smacking of an after-kiss.
> But you, like wives ill pleased, supply his want ;
> Each writing Monsieur is a fresh gallant :
> And though, perhaps, 'twas done as well before,
> Yet still there's something in a new amour.
> Your several poets work with several tools,
> One gets you wits, another gets you fools :
> This pleases you with some by-stroke of wit,
> This finds some cranny that was never hit.
> But should these jaunty lovers daily come
> To do your work, like your good man at home,
> Their fine small-timbered wits would soon decay ;
> These are gallants but for a holiday.
> Others you had, who oftener have appeared,
> Whom for mere impotence you have cashiered :
> Such as at first came on with pomp and glory,
> But, overstraining, soon fell flat before ye.
> Their useless weight with patience long was borne,
> But at the last you threw them off with scorn.
> As for the poet of this present night,
> Though now he claims in you an husband's right,
> He will not hinder you of fresh delight.
> He, like a seaman, seldom will appear,
> And means to trouble home but thrice a-year ;
> That only time from your gallants he'll borrow ;
> Be kind to-day, and cuckold him tomorrow.

It is not hard to see why ladies took the precaution of wearing a mask when coming to hear such pretty verses. But the limit had not yet been reached : the final triumph was to put the grossest indecencies into women's mouths, ignoring the possibilities of euphemism. But further quotation is impossible.[251]

[251] [Beljame's last sentence reads in the original " But further translation is impossible ". He makes the following note. B. D.] Yet quote I must, for these are historical documents. First, some fragments from the epilogue to Duffett's *Spanish Rogue* spoken by Mrs. Kneppe :

> " . . . Kind Women, new *French* Words, and Fashions got :
> And finding all *French* Tricks so much did please,
> 'T oblige you more, They got—ev'n their Disease . . .

VI

Courtiers' literary pretensions.—Authors compelled to seek courtiers' favour : Dedications.—Incidents : Dryden and Sir Robert Howard, the Duke of Newcastle, the Duke of Buckingham, the Earl of Rochester

When an author had succeeded in satisfying the clamorous impatience of the theatres, and had overcome the frivolity of his audience, he had still not surmounted all his difficulties. One of the most serious remained. The courtiers naturally did not surrender in favour of the theatre their pretensions to being men of wit. On the contrary, it was in the theatre that they most enjoyed displaying their wit. Those who were able to rise above songs and satires could not resist the craving to hear their names bandied about by a larger, though more dangerous, public than that of the drawing-room. Villiers, Duke of Buckingham, Sir Charles Sedley, the Honourable Sir Robert

> O 'tis so gente ! So modish ! and so fine !
> To shrug and cry, Faith *Jack* ! I drink no wine :
> For I've a swinging Clap this very time," etc.

Read the epilogue to Wycherley's *Country Wife* in the same taste, also spoken by a woman ; read also Dryden's prologue written for the revival of *The Wild Gallant* and his Epilogue to *The Assignation*. The works of Dryden and Wycherley are easily come by ; the plays from which I take the following quotations are less accessible.

Epilogue to Settle : *The Empress of Morocco* :

> " This play like Country Girls come up to Town
> Long'd t'appear fine, in Jewels and rich Gown ;
> And so,
>   Hoping it's Pride your Courtiers would support,
> To please You, lost its Maiden-head at Court . . .
> A generous Gallant though tired and Cloy'd,
> Should still speak well of what he has enjoy'd.
> Should you damn this you would your selves reproach,
> 'Tis barb'rous to defame what you debauch.
> Nay, now you've Cast it off, yet do not Frown : ⎫
> Though like the Refuge of a *Miss* o'th' Town   ⎬
> It is turn'd Common, Yours for half a crown . . .⎭
> Thus your applause resembles your Amours,
> Have we not seen (*Oh loves almighty Powers*) !
> A *Wench* with tallow-looks and winter-Face,
> Continue one Man's Favourite seven Years space :
> Some Ravishing knack i'th' sport and some brisk motion,
> Keeps the gilt *Coach* and the gallants Devotion . . ." etc.

Epilogue to Ravenscroft's *Citizen turn'd Gentleman* :

> " . . . Tow'rds morning, when they think of going home,
> Each Gallant on a Couch in the next room,
> In's turn, takes gentle solace with his Punk ;
> Drops her a Guinney, and sends her home half-drunk.

Howard, the Earl of Orrery, the Duke of Newcastle, Sir Robert Stapylton, Gentleman Usher of His Majesty's Most Honourable Privy Chamber, Sir Francis Fane, Knight of the Bath, Sir William Killigrew, the Queen's Vice-Chamberlain, Sir Samuel Tuke, the Earl of Bristol, etc., wrote plays and had them produced.[252] Rochester re-wrote Beaumont and Fletcher's *Valentinian*[253]; Waller and Lord Buckhurst tried their hand at a translation of Corneille's *Pompée*[254]; Sir John Denham helped Mrs. Philips, " the matchless Orinda ", to handle the same author's *Horace*[255]; the Earl of Mulgrave re-modelled Shakespeare's *Julius Cæsar*.[256] Those who, like the Earl of Roscommon[257] and Sir Car Scroop[258] were aware that they possessed no spark of dramatic genius, sought at least to provide the theatre with songs or prologues. The ordinary man of fashion contented himself with theorizing and posing as *arbiter elegantiarum*. The most insignificant little coxcomb assumed, with his fine clothes and his Chedreux wig, the right of passing

---

> . . . Ladies, our Author trusts in you.
> He is a man as modest for his age,
> As most you've seen, who know him dare engage }
> That he has kept 'till now his pusillage."

Epilogue to Lee's *Nero* :

> " . . . May each Gallant that has an assignation,
> Be jilted after four hours expectation ;
> Or if the masked Gentlewoman come
> Spight of long Scarff, may she be dogg'd from home :
> May ye—
> In height of Titilation hear a rapping
> And then the jealous Cuckold take ye napping."

I give it up. But that is not to say that the mine is exhausted.

A point to note in this shameless writing is that all reverence for childhood is lacking. Read for instance this passage from Mrs. Behn's *Abdelazer*, " Spoken by little Mis. *Ariell* " :

> " Your kindness, Gallants, I shall soon repay . . .
> Your last Applauses, like refreshing showrs,
> Made me spring up and bud like early Flow'rs ;
> Since then I'm grown at least an Inch in height,
> And shall e're long be full blown for delight."

[252] See my Bibliography.
[253] See my Bibliography, s.v. Wilmot (John).
[254] *Biographia Dramatica*, s.v. Pompey the Great.
[255] Ibid., s.v. *Horace*.
[256] His version is printed in his *Works*.
[257] Prologue to *Pompey* : *A Tragedy* . . . *Translated from the* French *of Monsr.* Corneille, *by Mrs.* Katherine Philips (in her *Miscellaneous Works*, p. 3).
[258] Prologue for Lee's *Rival Queens* ; song for Lee's *Mithridates* ; prologue for Etherege's *Man of Mode*.

authoritative judgment on literary questions [259]; and it was to comedy that he devoted his severest and noisiest condemnations. At the theatre, writes a contemporary, the gallant " resigns himself to sleep, but roused suddenly proclaims his pretensions to wit and criticism, by loudly damning the play, with a most tragical face ".[260] The spectators whom Shadwell introduces in *A True Widow* noisily express their opinions on what is being acted.[261]

These individual sharpshooters were merely annoying folk who might be tiresome but were not greatly to be feared. There were others more dangerous ; those who were known as *Flag-wits*,[262] comparing them with the admiral's flagship whose signals govern the movements of the whole fleet. As one epilogue puts it :

> . . . And where a lot of smilers lent an ear
> To one that talked, I knew the foe was there.
> The club of jests went round ; he who had none,
> Borrowed of the next, and told it for his own.[263]

These " leading Voters of the Pit " [264] with their following of friends and flatterers always ready to take their lightest expression of opinion as an order to fight, were a serious menace, and in a period when literature was the correct and fashionable thing, there were many of them. The most insignificant scribbler who borrowed a gleam of importance from his rank, his profession or his position near the King, became a literary sun round whom revolved a whole system of inferior planets. All writers of standing had their little courts, their flatterers, their coteries, and became the dispensers of success. Woe to the author who displeased them ! The hounds were unleashed against him,[265]

[259] " How often have I heard true wit call'd stuff,
By Men with nothing in their Brains but Snuff?
Each Shante Spark, that can the Fashion hit.
Place his Hat thus, role full (,) forsooth(')s a Wit ;
And thinks his Cloaths allow him judge of it."
(Crowne, Epilogue to *Sir Courtly Nice*.)

[260] *Proteus Redivivus, the Art of Wheedling*, a little work written in the reign of Charles II, quoted by Malcolm, p. 167. See p. 59, my quotation from *The Character of a Town Gallant* couched in almost identical terms.
[261] See also Pepys, Oct. 4, 1664, and Feb. 18, 1666-7.
[262] St. Serfe, Prologue to *Tarugo's Wiles*.
[263] Dryden, Epilogue to *An Evening's Love*.
[264] Lee : Prologue to *Lucius Junius Brutus*.
[265] " . . . It Met with the clamorous opposition of a numerous party, bandied against it, and resolved, as much as they could, to damn it, right

cat-calls [266] and hisses were the order of the day. When Colonel Henry Howard's *United Kingdoms* was being performed, the Duke of Buckingham, who was the declared enemy of the heroic style, organized a regular attack upon the play. Like a commander-in-chief he disposed his forces throughout the theatre, urged them on and gave the signal for whistles. But the author knew his world and had forces of his own at his disposal and the two parties nearly came to blows. An ambush was laid at the exit of the theatre to manhandle the Duke.[267]

Authors of commoner stock had no such resources at their command. They could neither arm others in their defence nor themselves draw sword against their enemies, as their aristocratic colleagues so readily did.[268] They were driven therefore to diplomacy in order to propitiate the capricious deities of success with whom it was impossible to contend. This required tact and resourcefulness. The great lords considered wit and taste as the prerogative of birth; every author who bore an honoured name had a claim to their admiration or at worst to their tolerance [269] (I know of none save Buckingham who drew the

---

or wrong, before they had heard or seen a word on't." (Shadwell, Preface to *The Humorists*.) See Langbaine, s.v. *Shadwell*.
  "I'm told that some are present here today,
  Who e're they see, resolve to Dam this Play."
                                          (Lee, Prologue to *Nero*.)

[266] One way of expressing disapproval in the theatre was to imitate the mewing of a cat (Malone, *Historical Account* . . . p. 186, note 7).—" *Banditti* or *A Ladies Distress*, a Comedy acted at the Theatre-Royal, printed in quarto, Lond., 1686. This Play was affronted in the Acting by some who thought themselves Criticks, and others with Cat-calls, endeavour'd at once to stifle the Author's Profit, and Fame: which was the occasion, that through Revenge he dedicated it to a certain Knight under this Ironical Title, " To the extream Witty and Judicious Gentleman, Sir *Critick-Cat-call*." (Langbaine, s.v. Thomas Durfey.)

[267] He contrived to elude the author's partisans.—See Arber's reprint of *The Rehearsal*, pp. 46 and 90.

[268] " . . . Some . . . of our Modern Fops, that declare they are resolv'd to justifie their Plays with their Swords . . . such as peep through their loopholes in the Theatre, to see who looks grum upon their Playes: and if they spy a Gentle Squire making Faces, he poor soul, must be *Hector'd* till he likes 'em . . . " (Shadwell, Preface to *The Sullen Lovers*.)—" *Tutor*. When you come to a new Play and know the Author is no fighter, and you may venture to abuse him; first sit grave and unconcern'd, and be sure to cast an eye upon some fam'd wit of the town and take him for your pattern." (Arrowsmith, *The Reformation* II, 2.)

[269]   " From the Court party we hope no success,
       Our Author is not one of the Nobless,
       That bravely does maintain his Miss in Town,
       Whilst my great Lady is with speed sent down,

sword against his friends). A commoner who dared to meddle in the writing business was looked on with another eye; there was no need to spare his feelings. You must note in the many verses Rochester devotes to ordering literature about, the very different tone in which he speaks of writers who are well-born and of those who are not. The plebs had to sue for permission to be witty.

A few succeeded almost without taking thought. Etherege, man of the world, elegant, supplied by an advantageous marriage with ample funds, was, like Waller, speedily accepted by fashionable young men as a social equal.[270] Wycherley, a simple law student, owed the favour of the Court to his distinguished appearance. Pope assures us that he had a "nobleman look".[271] The Duchess of Cleveland, " mistress of the King and of everybody else ",[272] took a fancy to him. Seeing him one day in the Ring, she put her head out of the carriage window and was clearly heard to say in a loud voice : " Sir, you are a rascal ;

   And forc'd in Country Mansion house to fix,
   That Miss may rattle here in Coach and six.
   If one of these the Author was, perchance
   You'd join your int'rest, and the Play advance ;
   For tho' you great ones and you Courtiers be
   Not o'er good natur'd, you've civilitie. '
    (Ravenscroft, Epilogue to *The Citizen turn'd Gentleman.*)

[270] *Biographia Britannica*, s.v. Etherege (George).—

  " E'en gentle *George* (flux'd both in tongue and purse)
  Shunning one Snare, yet fell into a worse.
  A man may be reliev'd once in his Life,
  But who can be reliev'd that has a Wife ? "
   (Villiers, Duke of Buckingham, *A consolatory Epistle to Captain Julian the Muses News-Monger in his Confinement*, in his *Miscellaneous Works.*)

Rochester, in his *Scession of the Poets* (*Works*, I, 133) also calls him " Gentle George ".

[Etherege's marriage, if anything, closed his social career. His last play, *The Man of Mode*, appeared in 1676, and he was regarded as newly married in 1680. (See the Preface of his *Works* edited by F. Brett Smith.) Whether he married wealth to obtain a knighthood, or obtained a knighthood to marry wealth is not clear. As the quotation shows, he only just escaped bankruptcy, so it was not his wealth that made him a playwright acceptable to society. Waller had always been rich, and accepted in society, and, from his teens had been an M.P., in those days an acknowledgment of rank. He was first cousin to John Hampden, and it was not considered at all odd that he should court a daughter of the Earl of Leicester. There is no reason to suppose that she refused him on account of his unequal birth. He published long before the Restoration. B. D.]

[271] Spence, p. 284.
[272] Taine, II, p. 486.

Sir, you are a villain : Sir you are a . . . " and she used a word which, according to Macaulay, " might most justly have been applied to her own children ".[273] He became her lover and dedicated to her his first play, *Love in a Wood*. In it he carefully introduced an allusion to the gallant way in which their acquaintance opened.[274] Without ado she presented him at Court. Charles II, resigned to defeat, developed an affection for him, visited him in person when he was ill, and wanted to entrust him with the education of the Duke of Richmond, one of his natural sons. Buckingham, at that time the King's Minister and Master of his Horse, had been one of the lovers of the indefatigable Duchess. He showed himself at first less complaisant than his master and looked askance at this new rival. But he in turn fell under the spell of Wycherley's good looks and conversation, made friends with him, and gave him not only a regimental commission but a post as equerry in the King's household. Thus introduced and welcomed, the fortunate young man had to do nothing but carry on. His plays were successful. Lord Buckhurst, now Earl of Dorset, made the success of *The Plain Dealer* his personal concern,[275] and forced it on a public at first unappreciative. Thereafter his progress was as easy as Etherege's.[276]

Both men happened to share a qualification which commended them to their noble friends : neither pursued literature for a livelihood.[277] Etherege's private means and Wycherley's emolu-

---

[273] Essays, *The Comic Dramatists of the Restoration*.

[274] In the first Act, Lady Flippant recites a song against marriage, which closes with these lines :

" Great Wits, and great Braves,
Have always a Punk to their Mother."

[275] " Butler owed it to Him (Dorset), that the Court tasted his *Hudibras* : Wicherley [sic], that the town liked his *Plain Dealer*." (Prior, Dedication of *Poems on Several Occasions* to the Earl of Dorset's son.)

[276] Pack, *A New Collection*, etc., p. 113 : Some Remarkable Passages in the Life of Mr. *Wycherley* by *Mr. Dennis*.—Spence, pp. 16–17.

[277] " Brawny *Wycherley* was the next Man shew'd his Face ;
But *Apollo* e'en thought him too good for the Place
[amongst the royalty of Parnassus]
No Gentleman-Writer that Office should bear,
'Twas a Trader in Wit the Laurel should wear."
(Rochester, *A Scession of the Poets, Works*, I, 133.)

[Wycherley was a gentleman of means too narrow to permit of Court life. But he was a law student, not because he wanted to become a barrister or a solicitor, but because in those days a study of the law was still the natural

ments placed them beyond the reach of want. They wrote, like aristocratic amateurs, pleasantly to occupy their leisure, the former composing three plays, the latter four.

The ordinary run of authors, as we have seen, had of necessity to be more active. They had, moreover, to learn how to steer clear of dangers which never threatened the favourites of Fortune. The method was somehow to continue to enlist the interest of some great man possessing influence both at Court and in the world of letters. When Dryden accepted his fate and took to writing drama he approached the theatre only after enlisting as an ally Sir Robert Howard, good courtier and writer of plays, whose favour he won by praising in verse his "excellent poems".[278] Every person of importance who stood well at Court and fancied himself in literature, became a target for the poetry-writing tribe. Authors swarmed round them to beg for their good offices.

Some of the poets, like D'Urfey, were none too fastidious in their approach. He wrote gallant songs which he recited to the applause of society circles. Having thus introduced himself, he soon proceeded to become the professional jester and recognized buffoon of all the young scatter-brains of Charles's Court. He took part in all their pranks, even the King's. Thanks to

---

conclusion of a gentleman's education; it enabled him to look after his estates. After the death of his wife, the Countess of Drogheda, he relapsed for some years into a debtor's prison, from which he was finally rescued by the king. We have already glanced at Etherege's position. As for the remark quoted below by Beljame, you cannot argue to a man's opinions from something that he puts into the mouth of one of his characters. B. D.]
"Writing Madam's a Mechanick part of Witt! A Gentleman should never go beyond a Song or a Billèt." (Etherege, *The Man of Mode*, IV, 1.)

"Sir Courtly : I write like Gentleman, soft and easie.
Servant : Does your Honour write any Plays?
Sir Courtly : No, that's Mechanick; I bestow some Garniture on Plays, as a Song or a prologue."
(Crowne, *Sir Courtly Nice*, III.)

[278] "*To my Honored Friend*, SIR ROBERT HOWARD, On his Excellent Poems." (Signed : John Driden.) Dryden's verses are prefixed to Sir Robert's poems.
[Beljame's remarks again give the wrong emphasis. Dryden and Howard were friends for a long time, Dryden marrying Howard's sister. Howard was an interesting writer, and thinker on literary matters, and in the controversy he had with Dryden over *The Duke of Lerma*, Dryden did not carry off all the laurels. (See the edition of *The Duke of Lerma* by D. Arundell.) As regards birth, Dryden was well qualified to move in Court circles. He was the grandson of a baronet (his uncle succeeded to the title), and was equally well connected on his mother's side. B. D.]

his versatility and accommodating gifts, his adaptable and unscrupulous gaiety, Tom D'Urfey, as his friends called him, was in high favour, if low esteem, with the fashionable world. The question of esteem did not worry him overmuch.[279]

Not all his fellow-poets were inclined to such excess of good nature, and a writer seeking patrons usually had need of more tact and better manners. The height of his art was to infiltrate quietly into high society, posing as a weak and timorous soul who needed the company of superior beings in order to improve himself. He had to worm his way in by the charm of his conversation, to know when to speak and when to hold his tongue, to make himself unobtrusively agreeable until he became the indispensable guest at every gathering and at every banquet.[280] It was particularly important for him not to embarrass those who honoured him with their intimacy by too profuse a display of his own gifts. Without appearing to do so, he must render

---

[279] *Biographia Dramatica*, s.v. D'Urfey (Thomas).
> "And Sing-Song D'Urfey, placed beneath abuses,
>   Lives by his impudence, and not by the Muses."

(Buckingham, *Epistle to Captain Julian*, etc., already quoted, note 270.)

"I myself remember King *Charles* the Second leaning on *Tom D'Urfey's* Shoulder more than once, and humming over a Song with him." (*The Guardian*, No. 67. This number was by Addison.)—Jeremy Collier speaks of D'Urfey with marked contempt. In *A Short View*, etc., p. 208, he says: "His way is rather to cultivate his Lungs, and Sing to other Peoples Sense: For to finish him in a word, he is *Vox et praeterea nihil*." Dunton also writes: "Mr. *Durfey* has but a low *Genius* and yet some of his *Farces* wou'd make a Body laugh." (*Life*, p. 238.)—See also Langbaine, s.v. Thomas Durfey.

> "And all Retreats except *New-Hall* refuse
>   To shelter *Durfey* and his Jocky Muse;
>   There to the Butler and his Grace's Maid,
>   He turns, like *Homer*, Sonnetteer for Bread;
>   Knows his just bounds, nor ever durst aspire
>   Beyond the swearing Groom and kitchin fire."

(A Satyr upon the Poets, being a Translation out of the 7th Satyr of Juvenal. In *Poems on Affairs of State*, vol. II, 1703, pp. 138 ff.)

[280] "We have . . . our Genial Nights, where our discourse is neither too serious nor too light; but always pleasant, and, for the most part, instructive: the raillery neither too sharp upon the present nor too censorious on the absent; and the Cups only such as will raise the Conversation of the Night, without disturbing the Business of the Morrow." (Dryden, Dedication of *The Assignation* "to my most honour'd Friend, Sir Charles Sedley, Baronet.)

". . . My greatest Satisfaction is, that I have the Honour of his Friendship, and my Comedies have had his Approbation, whom I have heard speak more wit at a Supper than all my Adversaries, with their Heads join'd together, can write in a Year." (Shadwell, Dedication of *A True Widow* to the Same.)

discreet assistance with their productions,[281] while welcoming their most trifling suggestions with exuberant expressions of admiration and gratitude. He must give them the credit for any merit in his works and finally succeed in imperceptibly identifying the interests of protégé and patron. Dryden's fortune was secure once he was so high in favour of Sedley and Mulgrave, that he could venture publicly to proclaim himself their friend.[282] Titled critics would have made but one mouthful of plain John Dryden, but when they could attack him only across the body of one of their own kind, they thought twice, and did not dare.

" The Criticks ", says Shadwell frankly to the Duke of Newcastle of his new play, ". . . will not dare to use it roughly, when they see Your Grace's Name in the beginning . . ." [283] Dryden proudly replies to those " cavillers " who failed to appreciate his *Don Sebastian* : " I will give them and their fellows to understand that the Earl of Dorset was pleased to read the tragedy twice over before it was acted, and did me the favour to send me word, that I had written beyond any of my former plays, and that he was displeased anything should be cut away." [284] It would have needed a brave critic to continue the attack after that.

For the ordinary courtier to differ from the literary judgment of a Court favourite, was to forgo his patronage and the hope of a good job. But the overriding consideration which restrained them all, was that the whole body of courtiers saw their interest in preserving intact the reputation for good taste which each had severally acquired. Every nobleman was by birth infallible in such matters. To question the views of one, was to cast a doubt on the infallibility of the rest. If even one was mistaken the others might be too.

The author therefore takes care to efface himself and shelter behind his patron. He never introduces himself to his readers

[281] " *Bayes. Mr. Johnson*, How d'e like that Box ? Pray take notice of it, 't was given me by a *Person of Honour* for looking over a Paper of Verses . . ." (Prior and Charles Montague, *The Hind and the Panther Transvers'd* p. 22.)—D'Alembert called this, being " décrotteur bel esprit ". (Letter to Voltaire, Dec. 26, 1772.)
[282] Dedications to *The Assignation* and to *Aureng-Zebe*.
[283] " And I doubt not, but that Generosity wherewith Your Grace has always succour'd the Afflicted, will make You willing (by suffering me to use the Honour of Your Name) to rescue this from the bloody Hands of the Criticks, who etc." (Dedication of *The Sullen Lovers*.)
[284] Preface. The play appeared in 1690 ; but Dorset retained his literary influence unimpaired under William III.

without the protection of a dedication addressed to some great man.[285] Like a naughty child he seems to cry: "Please, it isn't me." He gets his play read before its appearance on the stage. He gets it approved at the cost, if need be, of a few alterations, and he loudly proclaims how little credit he, the author, deserves for its excellence. Settle owes the subject of his *Empress of Morocco* to the Earl of Norwich.[286] In the Dedication of *A True Widow* Shadwell thanks Sedley for having revised his play.[287] Dryden's *Aureng-Zebe* was corrected by the Earl of Mulgrave; his comedy, *The Assignation*, before being played, had been read "by the best judges".[288] To Sir Robert Howard Dryden writes of his *Annus Mirabilis*:

It is not long since I gave you the trouble of perusing a play for me; and now, instead of an acknowledgement I have given you a greater in the correction of a poem ... I must leave my poem to you with all its faults, which I hope to find fewer in the printing by your emendations ... 'Tis but reason I should do you that justice to the readers to let them know, that, if there be anything tolerable in this poem, they owe the argument to your choice, the writing to your encouragement, the correction to your judgment, and the care of it to your friendship.[289]

The share remaining to the author is small indeed.

To humble himself still further, the author raises his protector to the seventh heaven. Shadwell writes to Sedley: "You have

---

[285] Otway's *Souldiers Fortune* is probably the only play of the period which is not dedicated to a person of quality. He dedicated it to his bookseller, Mr. Bentley.

[286] "... The *Story* ... I owe to your Hands, and your honourable Embassy into *Africa*." (Dedication.)

[287] "... This Comedy, which had the benefit of your Correction and Alteration, and the Honour of your Approbation."

[288] Dedications.

[289] "An Account of the ensuing Poem, in a Letter to the Honourable Sir Robert Howard" prefixed to *Annus Mirabilis*. Dryden is careful to date his letter "From Charlton in Wiltshire", the country house of Lord Berkshire, Sir Robert's father.

[Dedication to noble patrons was no new thing; some of the Jacobean playwrights indulged in the practice, e.g. Webster's dedication of *The Duchess of Malfy* to Lord Berkeley. The language used in this period was courtly to the stage of being, to our minds, ridiculous; but the statements were not altogether devoid of justification, and the noblemen were not addressed merely because they were "by birth infallible in literary matters". It is possible that Settle did get his material from Lord Norwich, who knew Africa. Mulgrave (John Sheffield, afterwards Duke of Buckinghamshire) had set himself to study literature, and if his shorter poems are merely agreeable if skilful trifles, his verse essay on criticism still repays reading. Howard was a fellow-author of distinction, as was Sedley. B. D.]

in the *Mulberry Garden* shown the true Wit, Humour and Satyr of a Comedy ; and in *Anthony and Cleopatra* the true Spirit of a Tragedy ; the only one (except two of *Johnson's* and one of *Shakespear's*) wherein Romans are made to speak and do like Romans." (Dedication to *A True Widow*.)

Crowne's patron, the Earl of Orrery, was also honoured by Dryden's praise. Amongst other things His Lordship had written eight plays, a novel and some poems as well as *A Treatise of the Art of War* [290] which went with him to the grave. When dedicating his rhymed tragedy, *The Rival Ladies*, to this champion of rhyming drama, Dryden says to him :

> Who could so severely judge of faults as he, who has given testimony he commits none ? Your excellent poems have afforded that knowledge of it to the world, that your enemies are ready to upbraid you with it, as a crime for a man of business to write so well. Neither durst I have justified your lordship in it, if examples had not been in the world before you ; if Xenophon had not written a romance,[291] and a certain Roman, called Augustus Caesar, a tragedy and epigrams.

William, Duke, Marquis and Earl of Newcastle, one of the faithful adherents of Charles II who had followed him into exile, was a poet by conviction. Versifying was not his only passion : horses and poetry divided his heart between them. He wrote several plays and devoted two magnificent folio volumes to the art of riding. His *System of Horsemanship* is adorned with engravings depicting His Grace on horseback in every possible attitude and in every conceivable costume, and finally prancing triumphantly on Pegasus and rising towards Olympus from the midst of a circle of horses who gaze on him with admiration and respect.[292] By great good fortune this high-born enthusiast had found a wife after his own heart. The Duchess is the author of philosophic essays, of letters, of discourses, and of nineteen plays, eight of which are in two parts. At night she kept a servant ready to come at her first summons to record in writing

---

[290] See my Bibliography.

[Orrery was a serious writer ; his rhymed tragedies are by no means despicable, and are not disagreeable reading. *Mustapha* might even be recommended. It was not absurd to dedicate works to him, or even to praise him. B. D.]

[291] This romance is no doubt the *Cyropædia*.

[292] See my Bibliography.—" Newcastle and's Horse for entrance next strives . . ." (*The Scession of the Poets, to the Tune of Cook Lawrel*, in *Poems on Affairs of State*, vol. I, p. 209.)

her lightest inspiration.²⁹³ This noble pair formed a natural target for dedications. Flecknoe dedicated *The Damoiselles à la Mode* to them both, and his *Love's Kingdom* to the Duke. Settle inscribed to the Duke his tragedy, *Love and Revenge*. Shadwell dedicated to him his *Virtuoso*, his *Libertine*, *The Sullen Lovers* and *Epsom-Wells* while commending *The Humorists* to the Duchess's protection. Dryden presented *An Evening's Love* to the poet-horseman in a dedication in which no virtue of either spouse is overlooked :

Methinks I behold in you another Caius Marius, who, in the extremity of his age, exercised himself almost every morning in the Campus Martius, amongst the youthful nobility of Rome. And afterwards in your retirements, when you do honour to poetry, by employing part of your leisure in it, I regard you as another Silius Italicus, who, having passed over his consulship with applause, dismissed himself from business and the gown, and employed his age, amongst the shades, in the reading and imitation of Virgil.

In which, lest any thing should be wanting to your happiness, you have, by a rare effect of fortune, found, in the person of your excellent lady, not only a lover, but a partner of your studies ; a lady whom our age may justly equal with the Sappho of the Greeks, or the Sulpicia of the Romans ; who, by being taken into your bosom, seems to be inspired with your genius.

Lee wrote to Dorset : " Your writing dazzles with Clearness and Majesty . . . Whate'er you stamp as Royal, other Pretenders to Satire but file and wash : they live by the Clippings of your Wit, and dip their Silver in your Bath, to make it pass for Gold." ²⁹⁴ He appealed to Rochester in these terms : " From the Criticks . . . I appeal to your Lordship as the Saint did to *Cæser*. To you whose Judgment vies remark with your Grandeiur, who are as absolutely Lord of Wit as those prevaricators are its slaves. To you . . . whose sayings astonish the Censorious, and

---

²⁹³ To summon him, she would call : " John, I conceive . . . ".—She was more or less mad ; the ragamuffins of London used to run after her carriage when she drove out. (Pepys, April 11, 1667 ; April 26, 1667 ; May 10, 1667.)—See H. Walpole : *A Catalogue*, etc., vol. III, s.v.v. Margaret, Duchess of Newcastle and William Cavendish, Duke of Newcastle.

[It is true that the Newcastles appear slightly ridiculous to us, but that is only because they took literature too seriously in view of their own accomplishment. Nobody seems to read their works now, but they were considered capable judges then. In a sense the Duke was Dryden's collaborator ; at least he gave him the translation of Molière's *l'Étourdi*, from which Dryden made *Sir Martin Mar-All*. Why it should be considered a crime in a man who had been a cavalry leader in the Civil War to write two works on horsemanship and horsemastership is not quite clear. B. D.]

²⁹⁴ Dedication of *Mithridates*.

whose Writings are so exactly ingenious ; Princes treasure them in their Memory, as things Divine." [295] In his *Discourse concerning Satire* Dryden simply says to Dorset : " In tragedy and satire . . . this age and the last, particularly in England, have excelled the ancients in both these kinds ; and I would instance in Shakespeare of the former, of your Lordship in the latter sort." [295a]

This was flattery laid on with a trowel. It was sometimes applied with greater restraint and subtlety. In his *Essay of Dramatick Poesie*, for instance, Dryden introduces Sir Charles Sedley, Sir Robert Howard and Lord Buckhurst, in a long and interesting discussion, under the transparent pseudonyms of Lisideius, Crites and Eugenius.[296]

Though the poets aimed their flatteries by preference at literary aristocrats they by no means omitted to cultivate the influential men of the time who were not writers. Literature was in fact so much the fashion in the higher strata of society that it was always possible, whatever the occasion, to find some pretext for a flattering dedication designed effectively to impress the public by the use of a great name. Dryden dedicated *Troilus and Cressida* to the Earl of Sunderland, chief Secretary of State, and his *All for Love* to the Lord Treasurer, the Earl of Danby. He was even mindful of the City, greatly though its influence had waned, and dedicated his poem *Annus Mirabilis* " to The Metropolis of Great Britain, the Most Renowned and Late Flourishing City of London, in its Representatives the Lord Mayor and Court of Aldermen, the Sheriffs and Common Council of it ".

But the *ne plus ultra* of an author's ambition was to enlist the benevolent attention of the supreme judge and patron [297] : an arduous and delicate undertaking. Etiquette forbade a

[295] Dedication of *Nero*.
[295a] The *Discourse* is prefixed to Dryden's translation of Juvenal, dedicated to the Right Honourable Charles Earl of Dorset and of Middlesex, etc.
[296] [Dryden was guilty of no special flattery in his choice of persons for the *Essay of Dramatick Poesie*. They were all people keenly interested in the drama, Sedley and Howard being themselves playwrights. Buckhurst, later Lord Dorset, had certain literary qualifications. It seems likely that these four men had often had similar discussions, which Dryden now put into form. We know, for instance, that Howard did hold the views imputed to him in the *Essay*. When Mr. T. S. Eliot wrote a conversation on dramatic matters as an introduction to a new edition of the *Essay*, he stated that much of the matter came out of conversations with his friends. This would seem to be the way in which Dryden worked. B. D.]
[297] " The Lord of Hearts, and President of Wit " (Otway, Prologue to *The History and Fall of Caius Marius*).

work being dedicated to the King without permission. It was impossible boldly to march to the attack and sue for the royal approval; a repulse would have spelt disaster. So the wise author trod warily, digging trenches at a respectful distance and advancing slowly, patiently and discreetly. The minor out-works leading to the citadel were first captured. Dedications were addressed to the Duchess of Monmouth, wife of the King's natural son, then to the Duke himself, finally to the King's brother or to his Duchess.[298]

Since you could not speak to the King, you lost no opportunity of speaking about him in the hope that something of what you said would reach his ear. Settle writes to the Duke of Newcastle: "Providence has justly lengthened out your happy life to see the prosperous Raign of a Great, a Pious, and Gracious *Monarch.*"[299] Dryden, in addressing the Duke of York, says: "I have always observed in your royal highness an extreme concernment for the honour of your country; it is a passion common to you with a brother, the most excellent of kings; and in your two persons are eminent the character which Homer has given us of heroic virtue; the commanding part in Agamemnon, and the executive in Achilles".[300]

You thus swing the censer round the King's circle praying Heaven that some odour of incense will reach the royal nostrils. Then suppose that the King should learn the name of the burner of incense, that he should remember it, and that one day his august lips should let fall an opinion flattering for his worshipper, in what an ecstasy of happiness the favoured being will trumpet his triumph abroad!

Dryden was frequently reproached for having stolen his plays, a reproach which (we may note in passing) all authors

---

[298] In 1665 Dryden dedicated *The Indian Emperour* to the Duchess f Monmouth; in 1668 *Tyrannick-Love* to the Duke; in 1669 *Almanzor and Almahide* to the Duke of York, the King's brother. The gradation of dates is significant.—This is how he writes to the Duke of York: "Heroic poesy has always been sacred to princes, and to heroes . . . It is from this consideration, that I have presumed to dedicate to your royal highness these faint representations of your own worth and valour in heroic poetry: Or, to speak more properly, not to dedicate, but to restore to you those ideas, which in the more perfect part of my characters I have taken from you . . . You shone to us from afar . . . " In 1674 he dedicated *The State of Innocence* to the Duchess of York. To her he writes: " We think not the day is long enough when we behold you . . . Your person is a paradise, and your soul a cherubim within, to guard it."

[299] Dedication of *Love and Revenge.*

[300] Dedication of *Almanzor and Almahide, or the Conquest of Granada.*

of his day deserve at least as much as he. Hearing someone voice this accusation the King very sensibly retorted, so Dryden tells us : " that he only desired that they who accused me of theft, would always steal him Playes like mine ". It is worth seeing how great was Dryden's delight at this and how, while feigning modesty, he enjoyed quoting the royal saying and therewith firmly stopping the critics' mouths.[301] Crowne's *Calisto* pleased Charles II and the King condescended to mention this to the author. The playwright lost no time in ostentatiously parading the approval of the King " to whose Pleasure all our endeavours ought to be devoted ". Joyously he exclaimed : " the devouring Critick must cease his pursuit, for the poor Sinner is out of his Fangs, and safe in Glory ".[302]

On another occasion the King's intervention was more direct. He liked giving advice to authors. It was on a suggestion of his that Sir Samuel Tuke borrowed from Calderon his *Adventures of Five Hours*.[303] It was also the King who supplied Crowne with the plot of *Sir Courtly Nice* [304] (the rumour even ran that he had actually helped in its composition).[305] One day he suggested a correction to Dryden who hastened to give his play the benefit of the alteration. The poet naturally did not fail to boast of Charles's collaboration and in his enthusiasm applied to him *Si fractus illabitur orbis* . . . [306] But the great day, the day of glory was the day when the royal patron claimed *The Maiden-Queen* as *his* play. Then the entire preface was devoted to singing the praises of a monarch who displayed such good

[301] Preface to *An Evening's Love*.
[302] " It (*Calisto*) attained the felicity for which it was made, to afford some delight to His Royal Mind, to whose Pleasure all our endeavors ought to be, and this more particularly was devoted. And of this I have full assurance by the best and to me most pleasing testimony of it, that of His most Princely Bounty. Having said this, the devouring Critick, etc." (Crowne, Preface to *Calisto*.)
[303] The " Prologue at Court " has the following note : " This refers to the Authors purpose of Retirement, at that time when his Majesty recommended this Plot to him."
[304] " This Comedy was Written by the Sacred Command of our late most Excellent King, of ever blessed and beloved Memory . . . The greatest pleasure he had from the Stage was in Comedy, and he often Commanded me to Write it, and lately gave me a *Spanish* Play called *No Puedeser* (*Non pued esser*) : *Or, It Cannot Be* out of which I took part o' the Name) and design o' this (dedication)."—See also Dennis, *Original Letters*, etc., vol. I, pp. 51 ff.
[305] Crowne showed the King each scene as he wrote it. (Langbaine, manuscript note of Oldys, p. 96.)
[306] *Aureng-Zebe*, Dedication.

taste. The happy author recalls that plays have been dedicated to the Kings of France, and that he has good reason to follow this precedent,

> it having been own'd in so particular a manner by His Majesty that he has graced it with the Title of " His Play " . . . But though a character so high and undeserv'd, has not raised in me the presumption to offer such a trifle to his most serious view, yet I will own it my vanity to say, that after this glory which it has receiv'd from a Soveraign Prince, I could not send it to seek protection from any subject. Be this poem then sacred to him without the tedious form of a Dedication, and without presuming to interrupt those hours which he is daily giving to the peace and settlement of his people.

Nevertheless, the King while adopting his play took exception to one episode in it: the poet humbly bowed to the royal judgement:

" But though the artifice succeeded, I am willing to acknowledge it as a fault, since it pleas'd His Majesty, the best Judg, to think so."

Boileau felt no shame in flattering his royal master either, but on a literary issue he would not so readily have waived his own opinion in favour of the Great King's.[306a]

To gain access to the " Merry Monarch ", there was a surer road than that leading via his family and his favourite courtiers: the road via his mistresses. Men in those days scorned no path that led to success, and writers were no more scrupulous than others. Dryden addressed verses to the Duchess of Portsmouth (Mademoiselle de Kéroualle)[307] and to Lady Castlemaine.[308] He at least confined himself to ephemeral verses of limited circulation. His fellow-authors were less fastidious: Crowne openly dedicated his *Destruction of Jerusalem* to the Duchess of Portsmouth with the words: " I fix then Your Grace's Image at this *Jewish* Temple Gate, to render the Building sacred." Lee offered the same lady his tragedy of *Sophonisba* and praised not only her beauty but " the immortal splendours of an elevated soul ". Duffett went even further. He dedicated his *Spanish*

[306a] [The phrase " although the artifice succeeded " should be enough to indicate how much Dryden (or any other poet) was talking with his tongue in his cheek. Charles II would probably be amused enough to condone the *lèse-majesté*. B. D.]

[307] *The Fair Stranger, A Song* (*Works*, edited by Walter Scott and George Saintsbury, vol. XI, p. 167).

[308] She had been a patron of his early days when he was producing *The Wild Gallant* (*Works*, Scott and Saintsbury, vol. XI, p. 20). He compared her to Cato: to Cato's disadvantage.

Rogue to Nell Gwyn, the least reputable of the royal mistresses, who, as all London well knew, had begun life as barmaid in a brothel and had later been the mistress of Hart, the actor (amongst others),[309] before winning the King's heart in the circumstances already related. This was the person to whom Duffett wrote: " . . . Next to your Beauty, these Virtues are the greatest Miracle of the Age. If I am the first that has taken the boldness to tell you this, in Print, 'tis because *I* am more ambitious than all others, to be known by the Title of, *Madam, Your Admirer and humblest Servant*, T.D." [310]—" Boldness " was certainly the right word.

Authors, as we see, omitted no precaution, neglected no skill, to remedy the weakness of their position *vis-à-vis* an omnipotent Court consumed with vanity. Once embarked on this course, they availed themselves of every facility offered by the period in which they lived.

Their utmost care, however, did not always suffice to steer their fragile bark safely past the rocks. However zealously they practised humbug and self-humiliation, they could not always make themselves sufficiently insignificant and obscure to be invisible amidst the clash of conflicting vanities; they received in consequence their share of bruises.

Let us first consider some minor misadventures.

After having insinuated himself into the good graces of Sir Robert Howard, Dryden collaborated with him in *The Indian Queen*, which was notably successful. But his noble friend, having done him the honour of borrowing his ideas and his style, studiously omitted all mention of him, and the play appeared under Sir Robert's name alone. *Sic vos non vobis* . . .[311]

[309] She used to tell anyone who would listen that Charles II was *her* Charles III (Burnet, *History of my Own Times*, vol. I, p. 457). On the subject of Nell Gwyn, see Pepys, Oct. 26, 1667; Etherege, *The Lady of Pleasure*, already mentioned, p. 12; Betterton, *History of The English Stage*, pp. 55 and 111; Downes, with the Appendix by Davies, pp. 11–20; Cunningham, *The Story of Nell Gwyn*.

[310] Mrs. Behn dedicated her comedy *The Feign'd Curtizans* to Nell Gwyn too, saying: " When you speak, men crowd to listen with that awfull reverence as to Holy Oracles or Divine Prophesies, and bears [*sic*] away the precious words to tell at home to all the attentive family the Gracefull things you utter'd . . . etc." But the two were colleagues.

[311] The first edition which was printed in Sir Robert's *Four New Plays*, is there entitled: " *The Indian-Queen*, a Tragedy. London, Printed for H. Herringman . . . 1665."—The title of the second edition in Sir Robert's *Five new Plays* is: " *The Indian-Queen, a Tragedy*. Written by the Honourable Sir Robert Howard. London . . . DDCXCII." No mention of Dryden. The play is now printed among Dryden's works.

Similar experience with the Duke of Newcastle. The illustrious scribbler handed Dryden a word-for-word translation of Molière's *l'Étourdi*. Dryden took the trouble of working over and modifying the play to suit current taste and created from it *Sir Martin Mar-all*. Only the Duke's name was mentioned.[312] The titled jays refused to flock with the vulgar peacock whose plumage they borrowed. "If together they create a new work," writes Count Almaviva, "it is understood that the nobleman will contribute his name, the poet his talent."[313]

In the case of Sir Robert Howard, Dryden was able to some degree to retrieve the situation. He had the happy idea of writing, without a collaborator, a sequel to *The Indian Queen*, and his *Indian Emperour* benefited from its predecessor's success and drew serious attention to the young playwright.[314] About the same time he married his patron's sister, Lady Elizabeth Howard. This marriage of a young noblewoman with a poet —one of the despicable crew who lived by their pen and had no means of livelihood save an uncertain income from the theatre and presents, scrounged here and there in return for sycophantic dedication—may well cause surprise. Various indications suggest that its background was not entirely honourable.[315] Dryden hoped perhaps to gain a surer footing in good society

---

[312] "To the Duke's playhouse, where we saw the new play acted yesterday, 'The Feign Innocence, or Sir Martin Marall'; a play made by my Lord Duke of Newcastle, but, as everybody says, corrected by Dryden" (Pepys, Aug. 16, 1667).—"Sir *Martin Marral*, The Duke of *Newcastle*, giving Mr. *Dryden* a bare Translation of it, out of a Comedy of the Famous *French* Poet, *Monseur Moleiro* [sic]" (Downes, p. 28).—The first edition bears no author's name (see my Bibliography). The play was registered at Stationers' Hall, June 24, 1668, as the Duke's work without allusion to Dryden (Malone, *Life of Dryden*, p. 93). *Sir Martin Mar-all*, like *The Indian Queen*, is now printed amongst Dryden's works. Thus the collaborator so disdainfully treated by these grand gentlemen has preserved their names for posterity.

[313] *Mariage de Figaro*.

[314] When *The Indian Emperour* was being acted, Dryden was shrewd enough to furnish the spectators of the first performance with a printed slip: "Connexion of *The Indian Emperour* to *The Indian Queen*." There is an allusion to this in *The Rehearsal*.

[315] The marriage took place on Dec. 1, 1663. It would seem that before marrying Dryden, the Lady Elizabeth had had dubious relations with the Earl of Chesterfield. On this point consult Mr. Christie, one of Dryden's biographers. Dryden's enemies phrased the matter more crudely. Here are some verses attributed to Somers:

"Hear me, dull Prostitute, worse than my Wife,
Like her the Shame and Clog of my dull Life . . .
Against my Will, I marry'd a Rank Whore:

and so to better his position as a writer. If so, he had gravely miscalculated, a fact of which he was promptly made aware. The poet soon discovered that, though he had married the daughter of the house, he had by no means become one of the family.

In dedicating his *Rival Ladies* to the Earl of Orrery, Dryden had boasted of the superiority of rhymed plays. Sir Robert suddenly proclaimed himself the champion of blank verse, and in a preface [316] attacked rhyme, making an exception of the Earl of Orrery's works but pointedly abstaining from any praise of his brother-in-law's. The latter, in his *Essay of Dramatick Poesie* introduced Sir Robert Howard—under the pseudonym of Crites —amongst the distinguished persons taking part in the discussion, reserving to himself—as Neander—the pleasure of refuting his arguments. Sir Robert was shocked at Dryden's not leaving him the last word. In his notice of the *Duke of Lerma*, he set out to demonstrate the gulf which had always lain between them and combated the views of his sister's husband in the bored and disdainful tone of a great nobleman who condescends.[317]

Dryden replied with a *Defence of an Essay of Dramatick Poesie*,[318]

> After two Children, and a third Miscarriage
> By Brawny Brothers Hector'd into Marriage," etc,
> (*Satyr to his Muse;* by the author of *Absalom and Achitophel.*)

This satire is attributed to Somers.

Dryden came of good family : Sir John Driden was his uncle ; his mother was a granddaughter of Sir Gilbert Pickering. Nevertheless he was a commoner and worked for his living. One of his brothers was a London tobacconist and two of his sisters had married small tradesmen.

[316] Notice of *Four New Plays*. Two of these are in rhyme.

[317] " I suppose I need not trouble the Reader with so impertinent a delay to attempt a farther Confutation of such ill-grounded reasons, then thus by opening the true state of the Case . . . I will not . . . pretend to say, why I writ this Play, some Scenes in blank Verse, others in Rhime, since I have no better a reason to give then Chance, which waited upon my present Fancy ; and I expect no better a reason from any ingenious person..." He does not even name Dryden ; he calls him " the Author of an Essay of Dramatick Poesie " and " that Author ". The reply is very short.

[318] Prefixed to the second edition of *The Indian Emperour*. There he says : " To begin with me, he gives me the Compellation of *The Author of a Dramatique Essay* . . . therefore, that I may not be wanting to him in civility, I return his Complement by calling him *The Author of the Duke of Lerma.*" The Dyce Collection in the South Kensington Museum contains a copy of this second edition with a note by Dyce to say that when Dryden was reconciled to Sir Robert Howard, *The Defence* was suppressed, and was now rarely to be met with.

[The *Defence*, both a spirited piece of writing and admirable criticism,

contenting himself with quietly aiming a few barbed phrases at Sir Robert without departure from good taste. Nevertheless, his brother-in-law did not forgive him for having dared to defend his own opinion and an estrangement resulted which for some time furnished lively entertainment to the satirists.

Throughout the whole affair Dryden preserved his right to retort, despite the aristocratic scorn with which he was treated. He countered when attacked. It was a duel of equals. The other side might have the advantage of birth; he had the advantage of talent. Worse might be in store for him. He might be taken at a disadvantage and still more vigorously attacked when unable to defend himself, as in fact befell him with the Duke of Buckingham.

In 1671 Buckingham presented *The Rehearsal* which he had written, so it is believed, with the very effective assistance of Butler, and of his chaplain Sprat,[319] and of Matthew Clifford, Master of Charterhouse. Three other unfortunates to whom fell the toil but not the credit; their names were not mentioned. *The Rehearsal* is an extremely clever and witty parody of the Heroic Plays and it appeared most opportunely at the very moment when these extravagant plays were at the zenith of their popularity. However small Buckingham's own share in *The Rehearsal*, it does honour to his wit and to his literary courage, for he was the only man to dare openly to speak his mind about the prevailing fashion and swim against the stream when the current was at its swiftest. His boldness was all the more praiseworthy in that he was challenging a style in which many fellow members of the aristocracy, the Howards, the Orrerys, and so forth, had won distinction. The play itself was an all-round parody and in so far we can applaud it without reserve. But, by the Duke's express intention, the character of Bayes

---

is now to be found in every edition of Dryden's plays or prose works. It is not easy to agree with Beljame that Howard's tone is condescending, but one can certainly agree that Dryden treats him as an equal. B. D.]

[319] His duty as chaplain must have been, as M. Forgues wittily points out, "a curious sinecure".

[But of course the duties of a chaplain in a ducal household were not confined to ministering to the spiritual needs of the duke. Thomas Sprat, afterwards Bishop of Rochester, the historian of the Royal Society, and an acknowledged poet, at that time probably had to conduct the services in the Duke's private chapel, and carry out all the duties with respect to births, deaths and marriages, and consolation in sickness, to a fairly large establishment. It may be doubted whether the post was, after all, such a sinecure. B. D.]

became a personal caricature of Dryden. Buckingham himself took endless pains to coach the actor Lacey, and taught him to reproduce the voice, the gestures and the very mannerisms of the poet. He even went so far as to dress him like Dryden so that there could be no possible mistake.[320] The mockers had scored their point. For the rest of his life Dryden was saddled with the nickname of Bayes.

Some hundred years later the actor-author Foote was planning to impersonate Dr. Johnson on the stage. Johnson happened to be dining with Thomas Davies, the bookseller, when he first heard of Foote's intention : " What ", he promptly asked his host, " is the common price of an oak stick ? "—" Sixpence," was the reply. " Why then, Sir, give me leave to send your servant to purchase me a shilling one. I'll have a double quantity ; for I am told Foote means *to take me off*, as he calls it, and I am determined the fellow shall not do it with impunity." When Foote learned of Johnson's preparations he decided not to risk incurring the Doctor's wrath. He was wise. " Sir," said Johnson to Boswell, " fear restrained him. He knew I would have broken his bones. I would have saved him the trouble of cutting off a leg ; I would not have left him a leg to cut off." [321]

Dryden for his part said not a word.[322] Not only did he fail to wield an oaken stick, he did not even allow his pen to take up the defence of his reputation as a writer. Yet his pen did first-class service whenever it was allowed to turn on his enemies, and many of the wounds his satire inflicted still retain their sting. Nor was the Duke of Buckingham's hide invulnerable to epigrams. This was later proved and more than proved. But what would you ! The Duke was at that time the cherished favourite of Charles II, and Dryden durst not risk annoying the King and bringing at one blow the whole edifice of his literary success tumbling about his ears merely for the pleasure of

---

[320] Spence, p. 63.—Arber's Edition of *The Rehearsal*.
[321] Boswell, vol. V, p. 233, and vol. III, p. 96.
[322] In his *Discourse Concerning Satire*, written in 1693, Dryden gave very inadequate reasons for his silence : " I answered not *The Rehearsal*, because I knew the author sat to himself when he drew the picture, and was the very Bayes of his own farce : because I knew that my betters were more concerned than I was in that satire : and, lastly, because Mr. Smith and Mr. Johnson (two characters in the play), the main pillars of it, were two such languishing gentlemen in their conversation, that I could liken them to nothing but to their own relations, those noble characters of men of wit and pleasure about the town."

avenging himself. So *Bayes* held his tongue and waited ten long years till his tormentor had fallen from grace and lost his unassailable position. Then it was possible to exact a tooth for a tooth. When Dryden drew Zimri's portrait in *Absalom and Achitophel*, it was clear that he had forgotten nothing, and if he had hitherto held his peace this indicated neither indifference nor disdain, nor yet lack of ample material for a reply.

But Dryden's long-suffering was to be put to still more painful tests.

John Wilmot, Earl of Rochester, was one of those noblemen whom it was most difficult, and yet most important, to conciliate. Young, elegant, witty, keen and capricious, without shame or scruple, he lived on a footing of complete equality with the King. He was thus all-powerful. Prolific author of satires which respected no one, not even his royal master, he was a man to fear.[323] A leader of pleasure and fashion, he sought to be also a leader of taste, and as he did nothing by halves, he would fain have ruled as dictator over wit in every form.[324]

One day a new actress, Mrs. Barry, made her appearance on the stage. After three unfortunate attempts of hers all the connoisseurs maintained that she was no good and was utterly unqualified to play a part in tolerable style. Thereupon Rochester, merely "to shew them he had a Judgment superior",[325] fired up on her behalf and loudly asserted that she would be ere long the best actress on the English stage. Not to see this prophecy belied, he devoted six months to teaching her himself. The task is said to have been no easy one, but he persisted in it, and when he thought his pupil sufficiently prepared,

---

[323] "In satire, no pen so ruthless as was his . . . the most dangerous enemy in the world." (Hamilton, p. 206.)

[324] In dedicating his first play, *Nero*, to Rochester, Lee tells him that he is "absolutely Lord of Wit".—Sir Francis Fane calls him "the most accomplish'd of all Mankind that I ever Knew, read, or heard of, by Humane Testimony . . . " and he adds this amazing eulogy : " I never return from your Lordships most Charming and Instructive Conversation, but I am inspir'd with a new Genius, and improv'd in all those Sciences I ever coveted the Knowledge of : I find my self, not only a better Poet, a better Philosopher ; but, much more than these, a better Christian : your Lordship's miraculous Wit, and intellectual pow'rs being the greatest Argument that ever I could meet with for the immateriality of the Soul ; they being the highest exaltation of humane Nature ; and under Divine Authority much more convincing to suspicious Reason, than all the Pedantick proofs of the most Learnedly peevish Disputants ; so that, I hope, I shall be oblig'd to your Lordship, not only for my Reputation of this World, but my future Happiness in the next . . . " (Dedication of *Love in the Dark*).

[325] Betterton, p. 14.

he invited the King with the Duke and Duchess of York to come and applaud her. Such august judges could not be wrong : she proved a great success and Rochester shared her triumph.[326]

Dryden took great care not to ignore a man of so much influence, whose self-conceit was backed by so much passion and perseverance. In 1673 he dedicated his comedy *Marriage à-la-Mode* to " The Right Honourable, the Earl of Rochester " with this significant quotation :

> Quidquid sum ego, quamvis
> Infra Lucilli censum ingeniumque, tamen me
> Cum magnis vixisse invita fatebitur usque
> Invidia, et fragili quaerens illidere dentem
> Offendet solido.[327]

His dedication is a laborious piece of work in which he painstakingly endeavours to flatter from every angle the vain person whose smiles he covets. The long-winded elaborate eulogies make it weary and heavy reading. But the very long-windedness, the insistent flatteries, the pains the poet takes to humble himself, the literary importance of the patron he addresses, make the document interesting and worth quoting almost in full, as one of the most remarkable specimens of its type.

My Lord,
 I humbly dedicate to your Lordship that poem, of which you were pleased to appear an early patron, before it was acted on the stage. I may yet go farther, with your permission, and say, that it received amendment from your noble hands ere it was fit to be presented. You may please likewise to remember, with how much favour to the author, and indulgence to the play, you commended it to the view of his Majesty, then at Windsor, and by his approbation of it in writing, made way for its kind reception on the theatre . . . I am sure, if there be anything in this play, wherein I have raised myself beyond the ordinary lowness of my comedies, I ought wholly to acknowledge it to the favour of being admitted to your Lordship's conversation. And not only I, who pretend not to this way, but the best comic writers of our age, will join with me to acknowledge that they have copied the gallantries of court, the delicacy of expression, and the decencies of behaviour, from your Lordship, with more success than if they had taken their models from the court of France. But this, my Lord, will be no wonder to the world, which knows the excellency

---

[326] " . . . He made her Rehearse near thirty times on the Stage, and about twelve in the Dress she was to Act it in . . . The Dutchess of *York* . . . made her a Present of her Wedding-Suit . . . " (Betterton, pp. 15-17).
[327] Horace, *Satires*, II, 1.

of your natural parts and those you have acquired in a noble education. That which, with more reason, I admire, is, that being so absolute a courtier, you have not forgot either the ties of friendship or the practice of generosity. In my little experience of a court (which, I confess, I desire not to improve), I have found in it much of interest, and more of detraction : Few men there have that assurance of a friend, as not to be made ridiculous by him when they are absent. There are a middling sort of courtiers, who become happy by their want of wit ; but they supply that want by an excess of malice to those who have it. And there is no such persecution as that of fools : They can never be considerable enough to be talked of themselves ; so that they are safe only in their obscurity, and grow mischievous to witty men, by the great diligence of their envy, and by being always present to represent and aggravate their faults . . . These are the men who make it their business to chase wit from the knowledge of princes, lest it should disgrace their ignorance. And this kind of malice your Lordship has not so much avoided, as surmounted. But if by the excellent temper of a royal master, always more ready to hear good than ill ; if by his inclination to love you ; if by your own merit and address ; if by the charms of your conversation, the grace of your behaviour, your knowledge of greatness, and habitude in courts, you have been able to preserve yourself with honour in the midst of so dangerous a course ; yet at least the remembrance of those hazards has inspired you with pity for other men, who, being of an inferior wit and quality to you, are yet persecuted, for being that in little which your Lordship is in great. For the quarrel of those people extends itself to anything of sense ; and if I may be so vain to own it, amongst the rest of the poets, has sometimes reached to the very borders of it, even to me. So that if our general good fortune had not raised up your Lordship to defend us, I know not whether anything had been more ridiculous in court than writers. It is to your Lordship's favour we generally owe our protection and patronage, and to the nobleness of your nature, which will not suffer the least shadow of your wit to be contemned in other men. You have been often pleased, not only to excuse my imperfections, but to vindicate what was tolerable in my writings from their censures ; and, what I never forget, you have not only been careful of my reputation, but of my fortune.[328] You have been solicitous to supply my neglect of myself ; and to overcome the fatal modesty of poets, which submits them to perpetual wants, rather than to become importunate with those people who have the liberality of kings in their disposing, and who, dishonouring the bounty of their master, suffer such to be in necessity who endeavour at least to please him, and for whose entertainment he has generously provided, if the fruits of his royal favour

---

[328] Is this not a delicate invitation to Rochester to show his generosity in the present case ?

[Dedications were not mere idle flattery, but were written chiefly for the purpose of receiving a handsome acknowledgment in cash in return for the compliment. But see Beljame later, and the article on Dryden in the *D.N.B.* B. D.]

were not often stopped in other hands.³²⁹ But your Lordship has given me occasion, not to complain of courts whilst you are there. I have found the effects of your mediation in all my concernments; and they were so much more noble in you, because they were wholly voluntary. I became your Lordship's (if I may venture on the similitude) as the world was made, without knowing him who made it, and brought only a passive obedience to be your creature. This nobleness of yours I think myself the rather obliged to own, because otherwise it must have been lost to all remembrance ! For you are endued with that excellent quality of a frank nature, to forget the good which you have done.

But, my Lord, I ought to have considered, that you are as great a judge as you are a patron ; and that in praising you ill, I should incur a higher note of ingratitude, than that I thought to have avoided. I stand in need of all your accustomed goodness for the dedication of this play ; which, though perhaps it be the best of my comedies, is yet so faulty, that I should have feared you for my critic, if I had not, with some policy, given you the trouble of being my protector. Wit seems to have lodged itself more nobly ³³⁰ in this age than in any of the former ; and people of my mean condition are only writers, because some of the nobility, and your Lordship in the first place, are above the narrow praises which poesy could give you. But, let those who love to see themselves exceeded, encourage your Lordship in so dangerous a quality ; for my own part, I must confess, that I have so much of self-interest, as to be content with reading some papers of your verses, without desiring you should proceed to a scene, or play ; with the common prudence of those who are worsted in a duel, and declare they are satisfied, when they are first wounded. Your Lordship has but another step to make, and from the patron of wit, you may become its tyrant ³³¹ ; and oppress our little regulations with more ease than you now protect them. But these, my Lord, are designs, which I am sure you harbour not, any more than the French king is contriving the conquest of the Swissers. It is a barren triumph, which is not worth your pains ; and would only rank him amongst your slaves who is already,
   My Lord,
    Your Lordship's most obedient,
     And most faithful servant,
      JOHN DRYDEN.

Rochester would have been hard indeed to please if he had not been gratified. He would seem to have expressed his pleasure in a letter of some literary pretensions, to which Dryden replied by yet further abasing himself before the genius of the noble Lord. Rochester's reply dazzled him ; he professes himself conquered with his own weapons.

[329] An obvious allusion to the Poet-Laureate's salary which Dryden should be receiving, but which, as we shall see, was very irregularly paid.
[330] How elegantly the noble habitation is indicated !
[331] O my prophetic soul ! (*Hamlet*, I, 5.)

I find [he adds] it is not for me to contend any way with your Lordship, who can write better on the meanest subject than I on the best. ... My only relief is, that what I have written is publique, and I am so much my own friend as to conceal your Lordship's letter; for that which would have given vanity to any other poet has only given me confusion. ... You are that *rerum natura* of your own Lucretius:
Ipsa suis pollens opibus, nihil indiga nostri.[332]

It looked as if everything were turning out for the best. Unfortunately Rochester was not content with offerings of frankincense unless they burned for him alone and were denied to others. Dryden, busy winning many patrons for himself, had not foreseen this dilemma. He thought himself fortunate in having gained the friendship of Sheffield, Earl of Mulgrave: a friendship which cost him innumerable vexations.

After having been on the best of terms with Mulgrave,[333] Rochester had had a duel with him from which he emerged with scant honour by feigning sudden illness and declaring himself in no condition to fight.[334] His opponent was at little pains to keep the matter secret, and it can well be imagined that Rochester was not over-grateful for his indiscretion. Mulgrave's friendly relations with Dryden further embittered him. To see the man who had snatched from him the palm of courage now stretching out his hand to grasp the palm of wit, was wounding to his vanity. Moreover, Dryden's talent and reputation threatened to cross his own literary ambition; this was salt in the wound. Rochester determined to avenge himself and began hostilities at once: against the poet only. He recommended Elkanah Settle to the King, that Settle might play towards Dryden the part of Pradon against Racine.

Poor Settle, whose works are long since studiously un-read, whose name survives only as the synonym of ridiculous presumption and ludicrous anticlimax [335], had produced his first tragedy in 1666. *Cambyses, King of Persia*, is a miserably bad play, but

---

[332] *Works*, edited by Scott and Saintsbury, vol. XVIII, pp. 91 ff.—Rochester had translated fragments of Lucretius. See his *Poems on Several Occasions*, p. 45.

[333] Witness some verses entitled *An Epistolary Essay from Lord Rochester to Lord Mulgrave upon their mutual poems*. See *The Works of the English Poets*, edited by Chalmers, vol. VIII, p. 244.

[334] See *Memoirs of His Grace* John *Duke of* Buckingham. *Written by himself*, pp. 8, 9, 10 in vol. II of *The Works of John Sheffield*.

[335] For Settle, see Nichols, *Literary Anecdotes*, vol. I, p. 41, note, and Dryden's biographers.

thanks to good acting it had succeeded in achieving six performances.³³⁶ This modest success drew Rochester's attention to him as the suitable instrument for the plan he had in mind. At the instance of the outraged aristocrat, Settle's new tragedy, *The Empress of Morocco*, made its first appearance in the Palace of Whitehall : an honour which had never been accorded to Dryden, Poet Laureate though he was. To make Dryden's humiliation the more complete, the cast was drawn from ladies and gentlemen of the Court. Caring not a whit for the rebuff to his protégé, Mulgrave wrote the prologue for the first performance, and Rochester, to underline his interest in the matter, the prologue for the second.³³⁷

The play had sore need of every adventitious aid. It would not be easy to conceive a more extravagant and complicated plot nor a cruder, more fatuous style.

The Empress of Morocco is a criminal hussy who has skilfully poisoned her husband and is plotting to get rid of the young king, her son, to plant her lover Crimalhaz on the throne. While her people picture her plunged in grief mourning her husband's death, she is carrying on with the said Crimalhaz and the two are discovered by Muly Hamet, Commander in Chief of the royal forces, sleeping side by side. The young king hears the tale and immediately believes it ; but his mother, without turning a hair, accuses Muly Hamet of having attempted to seduce her and persuades her credulous son to throw him into prison on the spot and later send him into exile.

Virtuous Crimalhaz meanwhile is appointed Royal Treasurer and loses no time in making off to the mountains with the army and the treasure. There, with his mistress's co-operation, he tries to lure the king into an ambuscade. Not succeeding in this, he feigns a reconciliation with the king, returns to court and to celebrate his return to favour, he offers his royal master a ballet whose subject—somewhat surprising in Morocco—is Orpheus descending to Hell to seek Eurydice. Now thanks to the machinations of the queen-mother the part of Eurydice is played by the young queen, her daughter-in-law, without the king's knowledge. He, for his part, has disguised himself as Orpheus

---

³³⁶ " The first new Play that was Acted in 1666 was : *The Tragedy of Cambyses, King of Persia*, wrote by Mr. *Settle* : Cambyses, was perform'd by Mr. Betterton : . . . All the other Parts, being perfectly well Acted, it succeeded six Days with a full Audience." (Downes, p. 27.)

³³⁷ These prologues are prefixed to the printed text of *The Empress of Morocco*.

to escape from Crimalhaz who—so he has been told—seeks his life. The young queen has been persuaded that Orpheus is no other than Crimalhaz and at the moment when Orpheus is preparing to carry off Eurydice, she slays with a dagger the husband to whom, after a thousand misadventures, she has just been united.

Crimalhaz becomes king. But without revealing it, he has been secretly in love with the young queen. He offers her his hand to avenge her husband's death. After some hesitation she accepts it and is confronted by the queen mother. Suspecting nothing, the latter urges her lover to put the young widow to death. But it is she herself who is seized by his bodyguard. Seeing herself thus a prisoner, she begs mercy of her young rival, throws herself on her knees before her and then suddenly leaping up, pierces her with a dagger and tries to fling herself on her treacherous lover. Baulked of this, she kills herself.

While the two queens are breathing their last, Crimalhaz learns that his army has been defeated by General Muly Hamet who returns from exile in the nick of time to round off the play. He seizes the usurper and has him put to death. The last scene shows the villain and his accomplices dangling hanged against a wall ornamented with hooks.

The foregoing is only the main plot of the tragedy, but as if it were insufficiently complicated there are subsidiary intrigues: amongst others the love of Muly Hamet for the lovely Mariamne, a princess of the royal family. She is also beloved by her gaoler, Hametalhaz. He is a tool in the hand of Crimalhaz, but when bidden to bring her head to his master he announces *ex abrupto*: " . . . I have . . . the pride to be her Jaylor . . . and her Slave." [338]

The whole play is a tissue of similar surprises. It would seem that the only chord in us which the author seeks to strike is stupefaction. Thus, in the first Act, while the royal prince —who will in the second Act be king—is groaning in his chains, his love, Morena, comes to tell him that his father consents to their union. He is transported with joy. " Yes," she continues, " we are to be united in death." [339]

[338] Act V.
[339]   " I come to tell you that your Father's kind,
        And has our mutual Happiness design'd, etc.
Muly Labas: This does disperse my Fears, checks my Despair:
        And has my Father . . . Shall we then . . . and are
        Our Loves and Hopes . . . Oh my unruly Joy, etc.

When General Muly Hamet in his turn is disgraced and sent to prison (everyone in the play is sooner or later flung into gaol for a bit), Mariamne comes to bring him his sword.

Mariamne: . . . You are free ; fly !
Muly H: And must I from my Princess presence fly ?
Mariamne: No, stay.
Muly H: Kind Stars !
Mariamne: Yes, in my Memory.[340]

There is one scene in particular in the last Act where the surprises are oddly piled up. Muly Hamet enters the capital as conqueror ; fair Mariamne greets her lover from a balcony. Suddenly Crimalhaz appears beside her, and vows to slay her *hic et nunc* if life and crown are not secured to him. She is about to die when in his turn the tender-hearted gaoler, Hametalhaz, pops up on the balcony, disarms Crimalhaz, proclaims his love for Mariamne and forthwith generously resigns her to his rival Muly Hamet. The latter is struck—as well he may be—by so much magnanimity and in testimony of his esteem offers Muly Hamet a crown : duly accepted.

Language and style are on the same lofty level as the plot.

I shed my Tears, as Rain in Egypt falls,
Sent for no common cause, but to foretell
Destructions, Ruins, Plagues and Funerals.
I ne'er draw Tears but when those Tears draw Blood.[341]

As he sets forth to banishment, Muly Hamet is overtaken by a hail shower, an unprecedented phenomenon in Morocco. In his amazement he questions a priest (a bogus priest of course) :

Muly H: Though show'rs of Hail Morocco never see,
Dull Priest, What does all this Portend to me ?
Hametalhaz: It does Portend . . .
Muly H: What ?
Hametalhaz: That the Fates . . . designe . . .
Muly H: To tire me with Impertinence like thine.[342]

Such was the rival set up to outclass Dryden. It is difficult to believe that in this Rochester was inspired by a pure passion for literature. So intelligent a man and especially one so sensitive to the ridiculous in others, could have been under no

Morena: Know then, to grant our Souls a stricter Tye,
He has decreed . . . we shall together Dye."
(I, 1).

[340] III, 2.   [341] III, 2.   [342] IV, 2.

misapprehension. It is obvious that he used the first rhymester he could lay hands on, to make clear in the right quarter that if there were other patrons than Rochester, there were also other poets than Dryden. And no doubt he was glad to find a man unlikely to endanger his own literary fame.

Such as it is, *The Empress of Morocco* was a great success. Apart from the quite exceptional welcome accorded it by the Court, it is fair to admit that the play had extrinsic merits which carried weight in its day. The settings and scenery were varied and magnificent. The hail shower just mentioned fell from a stormy sky with a brilliant rainbow. There was a great river covered with a "magnificent" fleet, there were cannon shots and fanfares, an ambush, choruses, Moors dancing round a palm tree and hell itself opening on the stage.

After having been performed at Court the play was acted continuously for a month by the Duke's Company. The unfortunate Settle's head was turned. He published his tragedy with "sculptures" (it was the first to be illustrated by engravings). On the title-page his name was followed by the words "Servant to His Majesty" [343] clearly proclaiming his rivalry with Dryden whom he attempts to ridicule in his dedication.[344]

Dryden committed the supreme folly of getting angry. With two of his colleagues, Shadwell and Crowne, he wrote *ab irato* some *Notes and Observations on The Empress of Morocco* [345] into which he poured more passion than good taste. Having called Settle "this upstart illiterate scribbler" and "so contemptible a wretch" he goes on : "His king, his two empresses, his villain, and his sub-villain, nay his hero, have all a certain natural cast of the father ; one turn of the countenance goes through all his children. Their folly was born and bred in them ; and something of the Elkanah will be visible." At some length he discusses two of his lines, fastidiously analysing his words and concludes : "Sure the poet writ these two lines aboard some smack in a storm, and, being sea-sick, spewed up a good lump

---

[343] See my Bibliography.—When he published his tragedy, *Ibrahim The Illustrious Bassa* in 1677, Settle resumed the title "Servant to His Majesty" in apparent rivalry to Dryden's title of Laureate.

[344] "But my Lord, whilst I trouble you with this kind of discourse, I beg you would not think I design to give rules to the *Press*, as some of our Tribe have done to the *Stage* ; No, that's a trick I do not pretend to." (An unmistakable allusion to Dryden's *Essay of Dramatick Poesie*.) See below, note 417, another passage of this dedication, evidently aimed at Dryden.

[345] Reprinted in part in the *Works* of Dryden.

of clotted nonsense at once." Dryden sums up his opinion thus : " In short he is an animal of a most deplored understanding, without reading and conversation : his being is in a twilight of sense, and some glimmering of thought, which he can never fashion either into wit or English."

In a Billingsgate battle the better man is always the loser. The fool is more skilled in bandying abuse than argument. Settle replied to the *Remarks* in ninety-five quarto pages in the style in which he had been challenged, and easily proved himself superior in its use. He called Dryden a thief and had the last word.[346] Dryden had succeeded only in prolonging his rival's success.

Settle, however, did not long enjoy his fame. Jealous of his success, Rochester took pleasure in humbling him and transferred his favour to John Crowne. At his suggestion [347] the King commanded Crowne to write the *Masque of Calisto* which was acted at Court in 1675.[348] This was a new and direct blow at Dryden, more cruel than the first. For one of his duties as Poet Laureate was to supply this type of court poetry. He tried to regain a footing by humbly offering an epilogue, but Rochester was on the alert and the epilogue was rejected.[349]

After having tried his hand at the novel,[350] Crowne had so far written only three plays for the theatre : *Juliana, or The Princess of Poland*, a tangled jungle of complications ; *Charles VIII of France, or the Invasion of Naples*, a poor tragedy which he was

[346] " . . . With very little Conjuration, by those three remarkable Qualities of *Railing, Boasting* and *Thieving*, I found a *Dryden* in the frontispiece." (*Notes and Observations*, etc.)

[347] " His (Crowne's) Writings soon made him known to the Court and Town. Yet it was neither to the Favour of the Court, nor of *Wilmot* Lord *Rochester*, one of the shining Ornaments of it, that he was indebted for the Nomination which the King made of him for the writing the Mask of *Calypso* [sic] but to the Malice of that noble Lord, who design'd by that preference to mortify Mr. *Dryden* (Dennis : *Original Letters*, etc., vol. I, p. 49).—See also Saint-Evremond (?), *Lettre à la duchesse de Mazarin*, prefixed to the works of Rochester.

[348] See my Bibliography.—In the Preface he says : " I was invaded, on the sudden, by a Powerful Command, to prepare an Entertainment for the Court . . . it was done by Command." And in his Dedication to " The Lady Mary, Eldest Daughter of His Royal Highness the Duke," he writes : " This Poem, made like the first Man, by the Command, and for the Service of a Divinity . . ."

[349] This epilogue, which was to have been spoken by Lady Henrietta Maria Wentworth who was acting Jupiter, is to be found in Scott and Saintsbury's edition of Dryden's *Works*, vol. X, p. 332.

[350] *Pandion and Amphigenia*. See my Bibliography. It is a romance of 307 pages in Scudéry style.

careful to dedicate to Rochester, and a comedy called *The Countrey Wit*. He had also collaborated in a miserable imitation of Racine's *Andromaque*, half-verse, half-prose. *Calisto* has added nothing to his posthumous fame. The seduction of the nymph Calisto by Jupiter in the guise of Diana, as Ovid tells the story, was a risky subject for the stage. Not that this would in those days have been an objection. But Crowne, diluting his meagre material to spread it over five long acts, yet stopped short of the seduction. In his play Jupiter is converted to virtue by Calisto's resistance and to guard himself against future temptation he gallantly addresses her:

> I then entreat you will (to end this War!)
> Accept the small dominion of a Star.[351]

The most noteworthy thing about the play was the rank of the actors taking part in it: amongst others, the two daughters of the Duke of York, Mary and Anne, both of them later to be Queens of England (Mary played Calisto), the Countess of Sussex, natural daughter of the King, and Mrs. Sarah Jennings, destined to become Duchess of Marlborough. The Duke of Monmouth and other nobles danced with ladies of the Court.[352]

A work thus staged, with scenery and costumes in keeping with the actors, was bound to succeed and did in fact prove a success: it was played more than twenty times at Court, and won for Crowne the King's signal favour.[353]

Dryden swallowed this fresh affront without a word; but in the same year when dedicating his tragedy of *Aureng-Zebe* to Mulgrave he could not conceal his vexation and discouragement. He speaks of " those unhappy people, whom, in our own wrong, we call the great ". " Neither am I formed," he adds, " to praise a court, who admire and covet nothing, but the easiness and quiet of retirement . . . I desire to be no longer the Sisyphus of the stage; to roll up a stone with endless labour . . . which is perpetually falling down again." And he dreams anew of epic poetry.

Rochester, meanwhile, growing more and more capricious, was growing weary of Crowne also (on account of the success

---

[351] Act V.

[352] When the play was printed, Crowne gave the names of noble actors and dancers in great detail.

[353] The *Dramatic Works of John Crown*, 1873–76. See the Preface and the note prefixed to *Calisto*.

of his new play, *The Destruction of Jerusalem*) [354] and was commending Thomas Otway to Charles II and his royal brother. Otway at this time was twenty-five. He had failed to make a success of an actor's career,[355] but his ready wit and pleasant manners won him the society of some gay young nobles,[356] amongst whom were Lord Falkland and the Earl of Plymouth—a natural son of Charles II—who had been fellow-students of his at Oxford. When the need to earn a livelihood became pressing, Plymouth's influence secured him a cornetship in the army. But he was no more successful as a soldier than an actor. Before a year was up, he sold his commission and returned penniless to London. He made his début as an author in 1675 with his tragedy, *Alcibiades*, which, combined no doubt with his value as a boon companion—for the play is a masterpiece of insipidity—drew the attention of Rochester. Thanks to Rochester's patronage, his *Don Carlos*, an incomparably better play than *Alcibiades*, was a great success. In his Preface, the young poet, hitherto little accustomed to good fortune, effusively thanks his patron for his good offices with the King and the Duke of York, and to please him permits himself a sneer at Dryden.[357] He also dedicated his next tragedy, *Titus and Berenice*,[358] to Rochester.

[354] " When *Crown's Hierusalem* had met with as wild, and unaccountable Success, as the *Almanzors*, his Lordship withdrew his Favours, as if he would still be in Contradiction to the Town." (Saint-Evremond (?), Letter prefixed to the works of Rochester.)

[355] Downes, p. 34.

[356] " Gay Coxcombs, Cowards, Knaves and prating Fools,
Bullies of o're-grown Bulks, and little Souls,
Gamesters, Half-wits, and Spendthrifts (such as think
Mischievous midnight Frollicks bred by Drink
   Are Gallantry and Wit,
Because to their lewd Understandings fit)
Were those wherewith two Years at least I spent . . ."
      (Otway, *The Poets Complaint of his Muse*.)

[357] " Though a certain Writer, that shall be nameless (but you may guess at him by what follows) being ask'd his Opinion of this Play, very gravely cock'd, and cry'd, *I gad* (a favourite exclamation of Dryden's, also reproduced in *The Rehearsal*) *he knew not a Line in it he would be Author of.* But he is a fine facetious witty Person, as my Friend Sir Formal has it; and to be even with him, I know a Comedy of his, that has not so much as a Quibble in it that I would be Author of. And so, Reader, I bid him and thee Farewel." (*Works*, 1712. The edition of 1695, the earliest possessed by the British Museum, does not contain the Preface.)

[358] See Johnson, *Lives of the English Poets*, Otway; Otway's *Life* prefixed to his *Works*, 1712; E. W. Gosse: Otway, in *Seventeenth Century Studies*,

But Rochester was born to put everyone out of countenance. He wrote *A Session of the Poets,* and amidst the more or less vulgar shafts aimed at all poets—except aristocrats—he speaks thus of his latest pet :

> *Tom Otway* came next, Tom Shadwell's dear Zany,
> And swears, for Heroicks, he writes best of any :
> *Don Carlos* his Pockets so amply had fill'd,
> That his Mange was quite cur'd, and his Lice were all kill'd.
> But *Apollo* had seen his Face on the Stage,
> And prudently did not think fit to engage
> The Scum of a Play-House for the Prop of an Age.³⁵⁹

As if this were not enough, the noble Earl circulated anonymously—but everyone perfectly well knew the author—Horace's *Tenth Satire of the First Book imitated* in which he sneers at everybody : Dryden whom he is the first to call " Poet Squab " ³⁶⁰ ; " blund'ring Settle " . . . ; " Crown's tedious Scenes " ; " puzzling Otway ".³⁶¹

We can guess what Dryden must have suffered from all these blows and from feeling himself the plaything of the fantastic whims of a conceited ass in face of whom his tongue was tied as surely as in face of Buckingham. How often he must have reread his dedication to " The Right Honourable, the Earl of Rochester " and smiled wryly at his futile flattery of the man whom he had prophetically warned : " Your Lordship has but another step to make, and from the patron of wit, you may become its tyrant " !

But these trials did Dryden good service. From this period, so mortifying to the man, the poet emerged stronger and with greater respect for his own talent. Up to this point he had written to please others : he would now, to use his own ex-

---

pp. 269-305.—*Don Carlos* is dedicated to the Duke of York. The success of this play was so great that Settle, already infuriated at having been supplanted by Crowne, could bear no more and is said to have challenged Otway to a duel.

³⁵⁹ *Works,* vol. I, p. 135.
[Beljame refers to the poem usually printed in Rochester's *Works* (e.g. in Chalmers or Hayward) as " A Trial of the Poets for the Bays ". In the edition Beljame used, it appears to have been called " A Scession of the Poets ". B. D.]

³⁶⁰ " He was as plump as Mr. Pitt," said Pope (Spence, p. 261).

³⁶¹ *Works,* vol. I, pp. 10–11.—Otway in disgust gave vent to his resentment against Rochester in some bitter lines of *The Poets Complaint of his Muse.*

pression, write something to please himself,³⁶² and *All for Love* was the result. This play, Dryden's first real drama (and written under Charles II) is perhaps the only claim Rochester can make on the gratitude of posterity. But for his insolence and disdain, the poet might perhaps never have found himself again and given this tragedy to the world. Defying fashion, he returns to genuine drama and to genuine style ; he forsakes rhyme,³⁶³ he brings real people to life and breathes into them something of Shakespeare's spirit.³⁶⁴

The play itself is a reply to the pretensions of the puppet-rivals who had been set up against him, and a happier reply than that recently to Settle, for not one of them felt strong enough to retort. The Preface disposed not less happily of their patron's pretensions. It is easy to recognise the portrait veiled behind words like these :

Men of pleasant conversation (at least esteemed so), and endued with a trifling kind of fancy, perhaps helped out with some smattering of Latin, are ambitious to distinguish themselves from the herd of gentlemen, by their poetry—

Rarus enim fermè sensus communis in illâ Fortunâ.

And is not this a wretched affectation, not to be contented with what fortune has done for them, and sit down quietly with their estates, but they must call their wits in question, and needlessly expose their nakedness to public view ? Not considering that they are not to expect the same approbation from sober men, which they have found from their flatterers after the third bottle. If a little glittering in discourse has passed them on us for witty men, where was the necessity of undeceiving the world ? Would a man who has an ill title to an estate, but yet is in possession of it, would he bring it of his own accord to be tried at Westminster ? We who write, if we

---

³⁶² " But it (*The Spanish Fryar*) was given to the people ; and I never writ any thing for my self but *Anthony* and *Cleopatra*." (Preface to *The Art of Painting*.) Anthony and Cleopatra are hero and heroine of *All for Love*.

³⁶³ Lee followed his example and gave up rhyme in the same year with *Mithridates* ; Otway followed suit with *The Orphan* in 1680.

³⁶⁴ The title with its " Written in Imitation of *Shakespeare's* Stile ", and the Prologue, betray the poet's joy in reverting to wholesome inspiration :

" He fights this day unarmed,—without his rhyme— . . .
His hero, whom you wits his bully call,
Bates of his mettle, and scarce rants at all . . .
I could name more : a wife, and mistress too ;
Both (to be plain) too good for most of you :
The wife well-natured, and the mistress true."

want the talent, yet have the excuse that we do it for a poor subsistence; but what can be urged in their defence, who, not having the vocation of poverty to scribble, out of mere wantonness take pains to make themselves ridiculous? Horace was certainly in the right, where he said, " That no man is satisfied with his own condition." A poet is not pleased, because he is not rich; and the rich are discontented, because the poets will not admit them of their number. Thus the case is hard with writers: If they succeed not, they must starve; and if they do, some malicious satire is prepared to level them, for daring to please without their leave. But while they are so eager to destroy the fame of others, their ambition is manifest in their concernment; some poem of their own is to be produced, and the slaves are to be laid flat with their faces on the ground, that the monarch may appear in the greater triumph.

Dionysius and Nero had the same longings, but with all their power they could never bring their business well about. 'Tis true, they proclaimed themselves poets by sound of trumpet; and poets they were upon pain of death to any man who durst call them otherwise. The audience had a fine time on 't, you may imagine; they sat in a bodily fear, and looked as demurely as they could: for it was a hanging matter to laugh unseasonably ... but when the show was over, and an honest man was suffered to depart quietly, he took out his laughter which he had stifled, with a firm resolution never more to see an emperor's play though he had been ten years a-making it. In the meantime the true poets were they who ... had wit enough to yield the prize with a good grace, and not contend with him who had thirty legions. They were sure to be rewarded, if they confessed themselves bad writers, and that was somewhat better than to be martyrs for their reputation. Lucan's example was enough to teach them manners; and after he was put to death, for overcoming Nero, the Emperor carried it without dispute for the best poet in his dominions.

These arrows were barbed and struck home. Indignation inspired Dryden better than flattery.

Rochester, however, had not yet said his last word.

In Molière's *Médecin malgré lui*, when Lucas is recalling Jacqueline to the respect due to her master, it is Géronte, unhappily placed between the two, who receives every blow with which the outraged husband reinforces his exhortations to his wife: Mulgrave and Rochester were at war, and it was Dryden who was hit. Things were about to take a tragic turn.

Round about November, 1679, Mulgrave began to circulate in manuscript an *Essay upon Satyr* he had written. It was a fairly crude attack on everybody; on the King, his mistresses, Dorset, Sedley and more particularly on Rochester, to whom a long tirade was devoted, the celebrated duel with Mulgrave forming the main theme.[365]

In view of his relation to the author, it is possible that Dryden may have somewhat touched up Mulgrave's inspired satiric lines. This is one of the accusations that was habitually levelled at poets who cultivated the friendship of lettered amateurs. But it seems probable that the verses owed nothing to him, for Mulgrave expressly asserts that Dryden had nothing to do with

[365] " Nor shall the Royal Mistresses be nam'd,
Too ugly, or too easy to be blam'd ;
With whom each rhyming Fool keeps such a Pother,
They are as common that way, as the other.
Yet sauntering *Charles* between his beastly Brace,
Meets with Dissembling still in either place,
Affected Humour, or a painted Face.
In Loyal Libels we have often told him,
How one has jilted him, the other sold him :
How that affects to laugh, how this to weep ;
But who can rail, so long as he can keep ? . . .
Thus *D—et*, purring like a thoughtful Cat,
Married ; but wiser Puss ne'er thought of that ;
And first he worried her with railing Rhyme . . .
Then for one night sold all his Slavish Life,
A teeming *Widow*, but a barren *Wife* ;
Swell'd by contact of such a fulsome Toad,
He lugg'd about the Matrimonial Load ;
Till Fortune blindly kind as well as he,
Has ill restor'd him to his Liberty.
Which he would use in all his sneaking way,
Drinking all Night, and dozing all the Day . . .
    And little *Sid—y* for *Simile* renown'd
Pleasure has always sought, but never found :
Tho' all his Thoughts on Wine and Women fall,
His are so bad, sure he ne'er thinks at all,
The Flesh he lives upon is rank and strong ;
His Meat and Mistresses are kept too long . . .
No Nastiness offends his skilful Nose ;
Which from all Stink can with peculiar Art
Extract Perfume and Essence, from a *F—t* :
Expecting Supper is his great Delight ;
He toils all Day, but to be drunk at Night :
Then o're his Cups this Night-bird chirping sits,
Till he takes *Hewet* and *Jack Hall* for Wits.
    Rochester I despise for want of Wit . . .
For while he Mischief means to all Mankind,
Himself alone the ill Effects does find . . .
False are his Words, affected is his Wit,
So often he does aim, so seldom hit ;
To ev'ry Face he cringes while he speaks,
But when the Back is turn'd, the Head he breaks.
Mean in each Action, lewd in every Limb,
Manners themselves are mischievous in him . . .

them [366] and the widowed Countess later printed them in the complete edition of her husband's works.[367]

Be this as it may, Rochester well knew who was responsible, for he called Mulgrave to account not long afterwards, chaffing him at length in a set of verses entitled "Rochester's Farewell" about an expedition he had led to Tangier. In them he takes the opportunity of accusing Mulgrave of lack of courage.[368] But he thought it more convenient to pose in public as believing that Dryden alone was the author of the satire. Far from belying the accusation of cowardice that had been flung at him, Rochester further justified it by a vile, cold-blooded ambuscade.

> For (there's the Folly that's still mixt with Fear);
> Cowards more blows than any Hero bear.
> Of fighting-Spraks (Sparks), some (Fame?) may her Pleasures say,
> But 'tis a bolder thing to run away.
> The World may well forgive him all his Ill,
> For ev'ry Fault does prove his Penance still:
> Falsly he falls into some dangerous Noose,
> And then as meanly labours to get loose.
> A Life so infamous is better quitting,
> Spent in base Injury, and low submitting," etc.
>   (*An Essay upon Satyr, By the Earl of* Mulgrave.
>   In *A New Collection of* Poems relating to
>   State Affairs . . . MDCCV, pp. 133 ff.)

[366] See below, note No. 375.

[367] Malone (pp. 129–34) and Walter Scott (pp. 167–72) in their biographies of Dryden have no hesitation in affirming that these verses are not his. Their argument—though it has since been disputed—seems to me irrefutable. Walter Scott's opinion (reinforcing Johnson's) has great weight on the literary side; and the other considerations which he advances are, like Malone's, extremely cogent, especially this: that the Poet Laureate would not have taken the risk of attacking the King and his mistresses. Mulgrave, on the other hand, was at the time in the Opposition and such attacks were part of his rôle, besides being less dangerous for him than they would have been for Dryden. Mr. Bell, who believed in Dryden's authorship, stresses the fact that they contain a eulogy of Mulgrave which he could hardly have written himself. But isn't this obviously a device to throw the hounds off the scent? Mulgrave moreover blows his own trumpet in the *Essay on Poetry* which is unquestionably his.

[368] " First, then, the *Tangier Bullies* must appear,
> With open Brav'ry, and dissembled Fear.
> *Mulgrave*, their Head . . .
> Had it not better been, than thus to roam,
> To stay and tie the Cravat-string at Home?
> To strut, look big, shake Pantaloon, and swear
> With *Hewet, Dam me,* There's no action there.
> Had'st thou no Friend, that would to *Rowley* write,
> To hinder this thy eagerness to fight?
> That without Danger thou a Brave might'st be . . ." etc.
>   (Rochester's *Farewell, Works,* I, pp. 161–2.)

You write me word [he wrote to a friend] that I'm out of Favour with a certain Poet, whom I have ever admir'd for the disproportion of him and his Attributes : He is a Rarity which I cannot but be fond of, as one would be of a Hog that could fiddle, or a singing Owl. If he falls on me at the Blunt, which is his very good Weapon in Wit, I will forgive him, if you please, and leave the Repartee to *Black Will*, with a cudgel.[369]

And thus it was done. One evening on his way home, Dryden was waylaid in Rose Street near Covent Garden by three men posted there, who first overwhelmed him with vulgar abuse, then flung him to the ground and belaboured him with blows.

Dryden, and for that matter everybody else, knew perfectly well who was behind this dastardly attack, but witnesses were lacking. The poet offered £50 reward for anyone who would help to trace the culprits [370]; but in vain. Apart from the fact that episodes of this kind were not infrequent and roused little indignation,[371] Rochester was too highly placed for a mere author to reach him.

Dryden had to abandon hope of obtaining justice and once again decided to keep silence. The whole town, not least his fellow-authors, took sides against him. It seemed that it was

[369] Rochester, *Familiar Letters*, etc., p. 5.

[370] " Whereas *John Dreyden*, Esq. ; was on Thursday, the 18th instant at night barbarously assaulted and wounded in *Rose-street* in *Covent Garden*, by divers men unknown. If any Person shall make Discovery of the said Offenders to the said Mr. *Dreyden*, or to any Justice of the Peace—he shall not onely receive Fifty pounds, which is deposited in the hands of Mr. *Blanchard Goldsmith*, next door to *Temple Bar*, for the said Purpose ; but if he be a Principal or an accessory in the said Fact himself, His Majesty is graciously pleased to promise him his pardon for the same." (*London Gazette*, from Wednesday, Dec. 24, to Monday, Dec. 29, 1679.)

[371] In 1669 the House of Commons proposed to put a tax on theatres. The Court party opposed the motion saying that the actors were the King's Servants and part of his pleasures. Thereupon Sir John Coventry, M.P., asked whether the King's pleasure was in the actors or the actresses. That evening he was assailed in the street by men who cleft his nose to the bone and left him there. No one doubted that this attack was arranged by the King or one of his entourage (probably the Duke of Monmouth) and the House of Commons passed an Act condemning the criminals to banishment, adding that the King should have no power to pardon them. Needless to say they were not found. (Burnet, *History of my Own Times*, I, pp. 468–70.) —See also Pepys, July 29, 1667, and Feb. 1, 1669.—The *Athenæum* of April 17, 1875, quotes a curious document in which Charles II proclaims pardon to his " faithful and well-beloved cousin and counsellor " the Duke of Buckingham for several " murders, treasons and other crimes ". The same monarch held in high favour the celebrated Colonel Blood, who had daringly tried to steal the Crown Jewels and to kidnap the Duke of Ormond.

he who had been guilty of a disgraceful act and who had lost his honour. From this time onwards the cowardly assault of which he had been the victim was constantly cast in his teeth. The satire of Rose-Alley, the ambush of Rose-street, Dryden's good health, became ever-recurring jests at the luckless author's expense and were considered in the best of taste. It is unnecessary to mention that Rochester, far from feeling regret—still less, remorse—joined in the chorus. At the close of some verses in which he reviews the disgraces of his time he can find nothing better for a final line than : " Who'd be a Wit, in Dryden's cudgell'd skin ? " [372]

Otway, whom Rochester had preferred to Dryden, Otway, who had accused Dryden of having said of *Don Carlos* that " I gad, he knew not a line in it he would be Author of ",[373] Otway was alone in defending his hapless colleague, and in the Epilogue to *Venice Preserv'd* he nobly expressed his opinion about ambuscades and those who laid them.[374]

[372] " Who'd be a *Monarch*, to endure the Prating
Of NELL and sawcy OGLETHORPE in Waiting ?
Who would SOUTHAMPTON's driv'ling Cuckold be ?
Who would be YORK, and bear his *Infamy* ? . . .
Who'd be a Wit in DRYDEN's cudgell'd skin ? "
(*An Imitation of the First Satire of Juvenal*, Works, I, 15–16.)

[373] Preface to *Don Carlos* quoted above, note No. 357.

[374] " Poets in honour of the Truth shou'd write,
With the same Spirit brave men for it fight ;
And though against him causeless hatreds rise, ⎫
And dayly where he goes of late, he spies ⎬
The scowles of sullen and revengeful eyes ; ⎭
'Tis what he knows with much contempt to bear
And serves a cause too good * to let him fear :
He fears no poison from an incens'd Drabb—
No Ruffian's five foot-sword, nor Rascal's stab ;
Nor any other snares of mischief laid,
Not a Rose-alley Cudgel-Ambuscade,
From any private cause where malice reigns,
Or general Pique all Block-heads have to brains."

* The defence of the King and the Duke of York.

But *Venice Preserv'd* was acted in 1682 and Rochester had died in 1680.— In the Prologue to Maidwell's comedy, *The Loving Enemies* played in 1680, there is a defence of Dryden :

" Who dares be witty now, and with just rage
Disturb the vice and follies of the Age ?
With knaves and Fools, Satyr's a dang'rous fault,
They will not let you rub their sores with salt.
Else *Rose-Streets* Ambuscade shall break your head,
And life in Verse, shall lay the Poet dead.

Mulgrave, who at the start of this long-drawn-out and disastrous quarrel of which he was the cause, had written a prologue to the play of the rival who was supplanting his protégé, preserved to the end the same haughty detachment. When he wrote his *Essay on Poetry* he found nothing more appreciative to say of Dryden than :

> Tho prais'd and punish'd for another's Rhimes
> His own deserve as great Applause sometimes . . .

and he calmly adds a footnote : " A Libel, for which he was both applauded and wounded, tho entirely innocent of the whole matter." [375] Pope, who revised the poem later,[376] did Mulgrave the service of suppressing both the couplet and the note.[377]

This was the last of Rochester's exploits. He died the following year, worn out with wine and debauchery and—it was said—reconciled with Heaven. Having to mention his name some years later, Dryden's sole revenge was to call him " an author of . . . quality whose ashes I will not disturb ".[378]

VII

Writers' profits : from the theatre, from sale of their books, from gifts

All this makes a sorry tale, and it shows the humiliating moral dependence of the writer on those who called themselves, and whom he called, his patrons. If he had even enjoyed financial independence in return ! But he did not. The income which he drew from his writings was small and precarious, and

---

> Since therefore such unequal Judges sit,
> Who for suspicion punish men of Wit,
> 'Twill be self-preservation to be dull,
> It cracks the credit but preserves the skull."

[375] " The * Laureat here may justly claim our Praise,
Crown'd by † Mac-Fleckno with immortal Bays
Tho *prais'd* " etc.

* Mr. *D—n*. † A famous Satirical Poem of his.

[376] Spence, p. 292.
[377] They are omitted in the edition of his books published by his Widow in 1723. See vol. I, p. 137.
[378] *Discourse concerning the Original and Progress of Satire* prefixed to his translation of Juvenal (1693).

[For Rochester's reconciliation with Heaven, see Burnet's *Some Passages in the Life and Death of the right honourable John Earl of Rochester*, 1680. Rochester was a more interesting character than Beljame would have us think. See the *Cambridge History of English Literature*, or the Preface to his *Works* edited by John Hayward, and Professor V. de S. Pinto's biography. B. D.]

it was this problem of a livelihood which placed him so completely at the mercy of a frivolous society and its capricious leaders.

The rewards which a professional writer might hope for were of three kinds :
1. profits from the theatre,
2. sale of his works to booksellers,
3. gifts.

All three were, as we shall see, very modest and most uncertain.

The rights of an author, as the theatre understands them to-day, were then unknown. All the payment that a playwright could claim for a play's being acted was the profit on the third performance. This profit was his—if there was a third performance; but plays did not always survive so far. For the occasion, the author himself went round selling tickets and was obliged actively to solicit the presence of his patrons and their friends at his benefit performance.[379]

If after all these efforts the third performance yielded him £70 he thought himself incredibly lucky.[380] If his play had a long run, its success benefited the theatre alone; the author had no further share in it.

In view of the popularity the theatres enjoyed, and their brilliant well-attended performances, it seems amazing that they should not have paid their authors more adequately. But closer inquiry explains the phenomenon. First, the brilliant performances were not achieved without immense expenditure

---

[379] ". . . you brought in Her Royal Highness just at the exigent time, whose single Presence on the Poet's Day, is a Subsistence for him all the Year after." (Dedication of Lee's *Theodosius* to the Duchess of Richmond.)

[380] Malone, *Historical Account*, etc., p. 178 note 5.—This was evidently a maximum rarely reached ; for Spence (p. 262) records Pope as saying that it was very good if the third performance brought in £50 to the author. This estimate is confirmed by a passage of Otway's :

> "But which among you is there to be found,
> Will take his Third Day's Pawn for Fifty pound?"
> (Epilogue to *The History and Fall of Caius Marius*.)

Those were fortunate who made even £50. D'Urfey speaks of £20 :

> "He who now, in hopes of equal gain,
> Will needs be Pris'ner . . .
> He melts in durance half his Grease away,
> To get, like us, poor twenty Pounds a day."
> (Prologue to *The Injured Princess*.)

The same lines recur in the Epilogue to *The Fool turn'd Critick* by the same author, with £13 instead of £20.

on scenery and costumes [381] ; to cover this, the management would have needed the guarantee of full houses over a long period. But we have seen how small in number was the regular clientèle of the theatre and how little they could in fact be relied on, for all their enthusiasm. New plays had therefore to be continually provided and fresh expense incurred. Wrestling with these problems, the directors of the theatre did not grow rich : D'Avenant died bankrupt.[382] This was the first reason for offering writers derisory fees. A second factor lessened the commercial value of a play : the nobleman's very passion for drama. It is obvious that when men like Sedley, Buckingham, Orrery, or Howard, gave their plays to the theatre, they were aiming at honour and glory and were little concerned about a financial return.[383] The directors had thus a double induce-

[381] ". . . Scenes, which had been a little before introduced upon the publick stage by Sir William Davenant, at the Duke's old Theatre in Lincolns-inn-fields, but afterwards very much improved, with the addition of curious machines by Mr. Betterton in Dorset Garden, to the great expense and continual charge of the players. This much impaired their profit o'er what it was before . . ." (*Historia Histrionica*, 1699, quoted by Ebsworth, *Westminster Drolleries*, p. xxvi.)

[382] Chalmers, *Biographical Dictionary* : Sir William Davenant.—See also *Sir William D'Avenant's voyage to the other World*, etc., by Richard Flecknoe, quoted by Malone, *Historical Account*, etc., p. 250 ff.

[383] "The *Poet* and the *Whore* alike complains
Of trading Quality, that spoils their Gains ;
The Lords will Write, and Ladies will have Swains."
 (Lee, Prologue to *Constantine the Great*. This Prologue is printed also in Otway's works.)

"You've seen what Fortune other Poets share :
View next the Factors of the theatre :
That constant Mart which all the year does hold,
Where staple Wit is barter'd, bought and sold ;
Here trading Scriblers for their Maintenance
And Livelihood, trust to a Lott'ry chance :
But who his Parts would in the Service spend,
Where all his Hopes on vulgar Breath depend ?
Where ev'ry sot, for paying half a Crown,
Has the Prerogative to cry him down.
Sedley, indeed may be content with Fame,
Nor care, should an ill-judging Audience damn.
But *Settle* and the rest that write for Pence,
Whose whole Estate's an Ounce or two of Brains,
Should a thin House on the third Day appear,
Must starve, or live in Tatters all the Year.
And what can we expect that's brave and great,
From a poor needy Wretch, that writes to eat ?
Who the Success of the next Play must wait

ment to accept their plays : the rank of the author, which ensured the interest of an audience that was almost exclusively aristocratic, and his indifference to money. The professional writer could not compete on either line, and the market, as economists would say, being flooded with goods easily disposed of and offered for nothing, the inevitable result was a fall in prices.

It should be said that authors enjoying the favour of the public were not content with the fluctuating fee of the third performance and dictated other conditions. Thus, after the success of *The Indian Emperour* and *The Maiden-Queen*, Dryden concluded a special agreement with the King's Company, by which he was entitled to one and a quarter shares in the profits of the theatre. But in return he pledged himself to furnish the playhouse with three plays a year. Since all comedies were in five acts and often in verse this meant immense labour, and labour ill-rewarded. The players reckoned the poet's share at £300 to £400 a year, *communibus annis*. The meanest Dryden of modern times would turn up his nose at such a sum—even allowing for the greater value of money in those days.[384] Yet even these figures are certainly an over-estimate. We possess in fact a document [385]

For Lodging, Food and Cloaths, and whose chief Care,
Is how to spunge for the next Meal and where?"
(Oldham, *A Satire, Dissuading from Poetry. Works*, vol. III.)

Sedley handed over the third performance of *Bellamira* to a friend, probably Shadwell (see his Preface).

[384] Money was then worth approximately three times what it is to-day (i.e. 1897. What of 1947? E. O. L.).

[385] " Whereas upon Mr. Dryden's binding himself to write three playes a-yeere, hee the said Mr. Dryden was admitted and continued as a sharer in the king's play-house for diverse years, and received for his *share and a quarter* three or four hundred pounds, *communibus annis* ; but though he received the moneys, we received not the playes, not one in a yeare. After which the house being burnt, the company in building another, contracted great debts, so that shares fell much short of what they were formerly. Thereupon Mr. Dryden complaining to the company of his want of proffit, the company was so kind to him that they not only did not presse him for the playes which he so engaged to write for them, and for which he was paid beforehand, but they did also at his earnest request give him a third day for his last new play called *All for Love* ; and at the receipt of the móney of the said third day, he acknowledged it as a guift, and a particular kindnesse of the company. Yet notwithstanding this kind proceeding Mr. Dryden has now, jointly with Mr. Lee (who was in pension with us to the last day of our playing, and shall continue), written a play called *Œdipus*, and given it to the Duke's company, contrary to his said agreement, his promise, and all gratitude, to the great

in which the actors complain how little the author has done in return for all the advantages they have secured for him. So it is probable that their calculation is considerably exaggerated and that, as Malone believed, we must reduce his maximum receipts to £200.[386] We must also deduct the proceeds of the third performance which seem to have been cancelled by the new agreement,[387] and take account of the continual fluctuation of profits in any undertaking which is so much of a gamble as a theatre exposed to the whims of fashion as well as to the risks of every commercial venture. In 1671, for instance, the building in which the King's Company acted was destroyed by fire, and the shares, to Dryden's great vexation, fell considerably in value.[388] This agreement was in any case only temporary and according to Malone [389] Dryden benefited under it only from 1667 to 1680.

Other authors were employed on similar terms by the players who thus ensured themselves a supply of acting plays. Crowne would seem to have received an annual salary of £112 from the Duke's Company, and Lee to have had some like agree-

---

prejudice and almost undoing of the company, they being the only poets remaining to us. Mr. Crowne, being under the like agreement with the duke's house, writt a play called *The Destruction of Jerusalem*, and being forced by their refusall of it, to bring it to us, the said company compelled us, after the studying of it, and a vast expence in scenes and cloathes, to buy off their clayme, by paying all the pension he had received from them, amounting to one hundred and twelve pounds paid by the king's company, besides near forty pounds he the said Mr. Crowne paid out of his owne pocket.

These things considered, if notwithstanding Mr. Dryden's said agreement, promise, and moneys freely given him for his said last new play, and the many titles we have to his writings, this play be judged away from us, we must submit.

(*Signed*) Charles Killigrew ;
Charles Hart ;
Rich. Burt ;
Cardell Goodman ;
Mic. Mohun."

(Malone, *Historical Account*, etc., pp. 192, 193.) Malone attributes this document—probably addressed to the Lord Chamberlain or to the King—to the year 1678 or thereabouts.

[386] *Life of Dryden*, pp. 444–8. He calculates that each share would have brought in not more than £160 a year.—According to Malone, Dryden's receipts from the theatre between 1665 and 1670 and from 1676 to 1685 did not exceed £100 a year.
[387] See the document quoted above, note No. 385.
[388] See the same.
[389] Life of Dryden, pp. 70–6.

ment with the King's.[390] Others no doubt enjoyed similar advantages.

But, when all is said and done, authors were most reasonably dissatisfied with their income from the theatre. Dryden never made more than £100 with any one of his most successful plays, and this includes not only the profits of the third performance but also the Dedication and the sale of his manuscript to the bookseller.[391] The conclusion authors had arrived at by the end of Charles II's reign, was that the actors had been buying their goods too cheap,[392] and that they were being doomed like Sisyphus " to roll up a stone with endless labour, which, to follow the proverb, gathers no moss ".[393]

That Otway shared this opinion is shown by the quotation which he prefixed to *The Orphan*.[394] Shadwell was of the same mind and expresses himself thus in the Dedication of his *Virtuoso* : " That there are a great many faults in the conduct of this Play, I am not ignorant. But I (having no pension [395] but from the Theatre, which is either unwilling, or unable, to reward a Man sufficiently for so much pains as correct Comedies require) cannot allot my whole time to the writing of Plays, but am forced to mind some other business of Advantage." [396] Lee

---

[390] Document quoted note No. 385.—". . . After the Restoration, when the two houses struggled for the favour of the town, the taking poets were secured to either house by a sort of retaining fee, which seldom amounted to more than 40s. a week, nor was that of any long continuance." (Gildon, *Laws of Poetry*, 1721, quoted by Malone, *Historical Account*, etc., p. 191.) Malone adds that he seems to have underestimated their profits. These cannot in any case have been large for according to the document above quoted (note No. 385) Crowne appears to have had only £112 a year.

[391] Life of Southerne, prefixed to his Works : Johnson, *Lives of the English Poets* : Dryden.—Mr. Gosse also says that Otway made only £100 by *The Orphan*.

[392] Life of Southerne.

[393] Dedication of *Aureng-Zebe*.

[394]   " Qui Pelago credit, magno se fœnore tollit;
    Qui pugnas et Castra petit, præcingitur Auro ;
    Vilis adulator picto jacet Ebrius Ostro ;
    Et qui sollicitat Nuptas, ad præmia peccat :
    Sola pruinosis horret Facundia pannis
    Atque inopi lingua desertas invocat Artes."
                           (Petronius Arbiter, *Sat.*)

[395] An allusion to the pension which Dryden drew, or was supposed to draw, as Poet Laureate.

[396] The same author in his Preface to *The Sullen Lovers*, says : " Look upon it, as it really was, wrote in haste, by a Young Writer, and you will easily pardon it ; . . . Nor can you expect a very correct *Play*, under a Years pains at the least, from the Wittiest Man of the Nation ; It is so difficult to

indulges in similar bemoaning of the unfortunates condemned to count on the uncertain profit of a third-day performance, and to die of hunger.[397] Though Crowne was patronized by the King to the point of being honoured by his advice he calls poetry " a pleasant but barren country ".[398]

It is true that the theatre offered one other source of income to poets : prologues and epilogues were the indispensable garniture of every play and distinguished authors like Dryden [399] were often asked for them. On all-important occasions, for the production of a new play or the revival of an old one, or when the theatre wished to pay tribute to the presence of some highly-placed personage, Dryden was called in. Though he was without a rival in this line, he never got more than five guineas for a set of verses of this sort.[400] This was obviously a source of revenue that could not be counted on. It must further be noted that this represented a real hardship for authors whose own

---

write well in this kind. Men of Quality, that write for their Pleasure, will not trouble themselves with exactness in their *Playes* ; and those, that write for profit, would find too little encouragement for so much *paines*, as a correct *Play* would require."

[397] " What think ye meant wise Providence, when first
Poets were made ? I'd tell you, if I durst,
That 'twas in Contradiction to Heaven's Word,
That when its spirit o're the Waters stir'd,
When it saw All, and said that All was good,
The Creature *Poet* was not understood.
For, were it worth the Pains of six long Days ⎫
To mould Retailers of dull Third-Day-Plays, ⎬
That starve out threescore Years in hopes of Bays ? ⎭
'Tis plain they ne're were of the first Creation,
But came by meer Equiv'cal Generation.
Like Rats in Ships, without Coition bred ;
As hated too as they are, and unfed . . .
Therefore, all you that have Male-Issue born
Under the starving sign of *Capricorn* ;
Prevent the Malice of their Stars in time,
And warn them early from the Sin of Rhyme :
Tell 'em how *Spenser* starv'd, how *Cowley* mourn'd,
How *Butler's* Faith and Service was return'd . . ."
(Prologue to *Constantine the Great*.)

We hear the same wailings by Lee in his Dedication of *The Rival Queens* and in the Prologue to his *Theodosius*.

[398] " Your Grace has been a Princely patron and encourager of Poetry ; a Pleasant but Barren Country where my Genius and inclination has cast me." (Dedication of *Sir Courtly Nice* to the Duke of Ormond.) [Cf. Heine : " Brotloseste der Künste, Poesie." E. O. L.]

[399] It was the custom to have them printed and sold for a penny at the theatre door before the first performance (see Genest, I, p. 236).

[400] *Life of Southerne*, prefixed to his works.

obscurity compelled them to ask a prologue or epilogue from a more famous colleague, for they had to pay him out of their own pocket.

A writer had little more to hope for from the publication of his works. Publishing firms as we know them did not exist: "publishers" were both printers and booksellers and often paper-makers and binders into the bargain.[401] There were, moreover, very few of them. An act passed after the Restoration limited the number to twenty for the whole of England.[402] Of this scanty number not all were at the service of pure literature; we must deduct the printers who specialized in books on medicine, law, theology and the like. A petition presented to Parliament in 1666 reveals that there were in that year only 140 "working printers".[403] It is true that the law limiting the number of printers would seem not to have been very strictly enforced, for the aim of the petitioners was to exclude intruders. But if their number increased, the increase must have been slight, if we may judge by the number of publications. We possess a catalogue (one of the first ever printed in Britain) of "Books, Printed in England Since the Dreadful Fire of London MDCLXVI. To the End of *Trinity Term* MDCLXXX" (that is to say from 1666 to June 12, 1680),[404] and this is how an excellent judge[405] analyses the information yielded by a careful study of this interesting document:

> A great many—we may fairly say one-half of these books, are single sermons and tracts. The whole number of books printed during the fourteen years from 1666 to 1680, we ascertain, by counting, was

---

[401] They were still called "stationers".

[402] Hallam, *Constitutional History of England*, vol. III, p. 4, and Keble, I, pp. 1306 and 1322.—The Act fixing the number of printers at twenty is known as 14 Car. 2, c. 33. It was valid for a limited time but was renewed by Parliament until 1679. The same Act imposed on books a censorship exercised by the Licenser, and limited the number of type-founders to *four* with *two* apprentices. No printer was allowed more than two presses at a time; at the very most three. The text of the Act will be found in Keble, vol. II, pp. 1250 ff. In 1637 a decree of the Star Chamber had already limited the number of printers to twenty and of type-founders to four. See my Bibliography, s.v. Star-Chamber.

[403] Knight, *Shadows of the Old Booksellers*, p. 307.—Timperley, p. 543. According to Timperley there were in London in 1831, 3,628 printers, that is twenty-five times as many as in 1666.—I have myself seen the above-mentioned petition: see my Bibliography, s.v. Printers.

[404] See my Bibliography, s.v. Clavell.

[405] Knight, *Shadows*, etc., p. 308. Knight speaks with peculiar authority since he was himself a publisher.

3,550, of which 947 were divinity, 420 law, and 153 physic,—so that two-fifths of the whole were professional books ; 397 were school books, and 2,653 on subjects of geography and navigation, including maps. Taking the average of these fourteen years, the total number of works produced yearly was 253 ; but deducting the reprints, pamphlets, single sermons and maps, we may fairly assume that the yearly average of new books was much under 100.

It is a remarkable fact—which strengthens the impression produced by these figures of the very limited book trade at the beginning of Charles II's reign—that almost no information beyond the name has come down to us about any one of the booksellers of the time. We know that Henry Herringman " at the Blew-*Anchor* in the Lower Walk of the New-Exchange " was Dryden's first publisher. We know that William Cademan published Settle's plays, and so on. But that is all. Not one of them occupies more space in the history of literature than is taken up by his name on the front page of the books he sold. Jacob Tonson was the first bookseller to acquire personal, independent importance. He made his first timid entry on the scene when, in 1678 he published a tragedy of Tate's, *Brutus of Alba*. In 1679 he took unto himself a partner, Abel Swall, in order to print Dryden's *Troilus and Cressida*, not feeling his financial position sound enough to let him shoulder single handed a commitment of £20, the fee due to the author for his play.[406]

We must admit that the booksellers had every reason to be cautious, for the sale of books was anything but a safe venture.

> To read was not then [says Samuel Johnson] a general amusement ; neither traders, nor often gentlemen, thought themselves disgraced by ignorance. The women had not then aspired to literature, nor was every house supplied with a closet of knowledge. Those, indeed, who professed learning, were not less learned than at any other time ; but of the middle race of students who read for pleasure or accomplishment, and who buy the numerous products of modern typography, the number was then comparatively small.[407]

Many facts bear out Johnson's words and prove that education was not sufficiently widespread in any class to make a taste for reading anything but an exception. We have letters from people in high society which show that they possessed a curiously

---
[406] Disraeli, *The Case of Authors Stated*, in *Calamities of Authors* ; Knight, *Shadows*, etc., p. 52.
[407] *Lives of the English Poets* : Milton.

imperfect knowledge of their own tongue.[408] Milton's eldest daughter could not write,[409] and Dryden's wife, though belonging by birth to a great and noble family and married to the most famous writer of the day, displays an ignorance of English grammar and spelling which to-day would make her maidservant blush.[410] So unenlightened a society was ill calculated to make booksellers enterprising. This explains why their publications were so infrequent and, I might add, why so few copies of an edition were printed. From Milton's contract with Symons we have seen that no printing of *Paradise Lost* was to exceed 1,500 copies. There is every reason to believe that most books did not reach even this figure. We have no precise statistics; it is a subject on which publishers have at all times been very reticent. Failing fuller information, a trustworthy clue is supplied us by the price at which books were sold.

Roger North informs us that a small octavo volume which could be read in an hour and a half was currently sold at six shillings,[411] which, allowing for the difference in money values,

[408] Towards the close of Pepys's Diary, see the letter addressed to him by the Duchess of Norfolk, *née* Lady Mary Mordaunt, daughter of the Earl of Peterborough.—When the fashionable Will Honeycomb was anxious to play the author, the *Spectator* was obliged " to rectify some little orthographical mistakes " (*Spectator*, No. 499).

[409] Masson, *The Poetical Works of John Milton*, I, pp. 64, 65, 74.—She puts her cross as signature to a document. Her two sisters learned to write, but in very imperfect fashion. Deborah signs her name " Deboroh ".

[410] " He (your father) is much at woon as to his health, and his defnesse is not wosce . . . you doe but Gust make shift to live wheare you are, and soe I hope you may doe heare; for I will Leaf noe Ston unturn'd to help my belov'd Sonns . . . I hope I may have some better thinges against you come, than what is sent you in that box; there being nothing Considurabell but my deare Jackes play, who I desire in his next to me to give me a true account how my deare Sonne Charlles is head dus; for I cane be at noe rest till I heare he is better, or rather thourely well, which I dally pray for." (Malone, *Prose Works of John Dryden*, vol. I, part II, pp. 58, 59.)

[411] " It may not be amiss to step a little aside to reflect on the vast Change in the trade of books, between that Time and ours (i.e. between 1666 and 1683). Then little Britain was a plentiful and perpetual Emporium of learned Authors; and men went thither as to a Market. This drew to the Place a mighty Trade, the rather because the shops were spacious, and the learned gladly resorted to them, where they seldom failed to meet with agreeable Conversation. And the booksellers themselves were knowing and conversible men, with whom, for the sake of bookish knowledge, the greatest Wits were pleased to converse . . . But now this Emporium is vanished and the Trade contracted into the Hands of two or three Persons, who, to make good their Monopoly, ransack, not only their Neighbours of the Trade that are scattered about Town, but all over England, aye and beyond Sea too, and send abroad their Circulators, and in that Manner get into their hands all that is valuable. The rest of the Trade are content

would represent 17 or 18 shillings nowadays. Twenty years later the normal price of a similar volume was five shillings.[412] The texts of plays fetched a shilling or eighteenpence, but with their dirty common paper, their coarse type and faulty printing, they would to-day be counted dear at half that price. Now, it is an axiom of economics that supply accommodates itself to probable demand and that the price of goods rises or falls according to their scarcity or abundance on the market. Books are no exception to the rule. We note to-day that books addressed to a necessarily limited number of specialists are issued in smaller editions and cost more than those which appeal to what we call " the general public ". From the price of books at this period we can deduce two things : first, that few copies were printed and, secondly, that buyers were few. We can draw a third conclusion, which follows naturally from the first two : that the booksellers could offer very inadequate payment for the books they printed, when they consented to print them at all.

We have already seen what a meagre sum was paid for the manuscript of *Paradise Lost* and what trouble Symons had to take to sell out the first edition, wooing readers by frequent changes of the title. No doubt the nature of the poem accounted for part of the difficulty, but literary works of the type that was then fashionable were scarcely more eagerly sought after by booksellers or readers.[413] The price at which a bookseller

---

to take their Refuse, with which, and the fresh Scum of the Press, they furnish one Side of a Shop, which serves for the sign of a Bookseller, rather than a real one ; but instead of selling, deal as Factors and procure what the Country Divines and Gentry send for ; . . . And it is wretched to consider what pickpocket work, with Help of the Press, these Demi-booksellers make. They crack their brains to find out selling subjects, and keep hirelings in garrets, on hard meat, to write and correct by the grate ; so puff up an octavo to a sufficient thickness, and there is six shillings current for an hour and a half's reading, and perhaps never to be read or looked upon after. One, that would go higher, must take his Fortune at blank Walls and Corners of Streets, or repair to the sign of *Bateman, Innys* and one or two more, where are best Choice and better pennyworths. I might touch other abuses, as bad Paper, incorrect printing, and false advertising ; all of which and worse is to be expected if a careful Author is not at the heels of them." (*The Life of the Honourable and Reverend Dr. John North*, pp. 241 ff. In the same volume as *The Life of the Honourable Sir Dudley North*.)

[Beljame's figures refer to 1881, when this book was first published. Prices have risen considerably since then. B. D.]

[412] Knight, *Shadows*, etc., p. 309.
[413] Many dramatic works of this period have not come down to us, which suggests that they were perhaps not even printed. (Genest, I, pp. 64, 108, etc.)

bought a successful author's play did not exceed £20 or £25 [414] and he did not always find it easy to sell his copies. The people who read plays were naturally the same, with few exceptions, as those who went to see them and these, as we know, were not a large number. From their frivolous temperament we may assume that they were little inclined to go and seek in the printed play the beauties which might have escaped them in the actual performance.[415] Of those who had seen a play on the stage, it was, in fact, only a small proportion who bought it when published. " I have often heard the stationer sighing in his shop," writes Dryden, " and wishing for those hands to take off his melancholy bargain which clapped its performance on the stage." [416]

An attempt was made to allure readers by adding some new attraction when the play was published. In addition to the obligatory Dedication, it might be reinforced by a Preface handling some literary theme, or perhaps a literary discussion would be introduced with the Dedication. These additions had for the author the merit of swelling the size and consequently raising the price of his manuscript [417]; but the main advantage

---

[414] Malone, *Historical Account*, etc., p. 178, note 5. This is the fee Dryden received at the height of his popularity, and what Otway and Lee got for their best plays.—Pope quotes a smaller figure still. He speaks of " ten broad pieces " (Spence, p. 262).—The *broad piece* was worth 24s., say, therefore, £12.—Gentlemen of quality paid to have their plays printed (*The Tatler*, No. 224).

[415] " His whole Library consists of the *Academy of Complements, Westminster Drollery*, half a dozen *Plays*, and a Bundle of *Bawdy* Songs *in Manuscript* . . ." (*The Character of a Town-Gallant*).

[416] Dedication of *The Spanish Fryar*.—A play was rarely published until its success in the theatre was exhausted. Dryden's *Tyrannick Love*, acted at Easter, 1669, was not " entered in the Stationers' books " until July, 1670.

". . . Few Plays gain Audience by being
In Print, a fewer women get Husbands by
Being too much known."
(Sedley, *The Mulberry-Garden*, III, 2.)

[417] " Read all the prefaces of Dryden,
For these our critics much confide in;
Though merely writ at first for filling,
To raise the volume's price a shilling."
(Swift, *On Poetry. A Rhapsody. Works*, XIV, p. 336.)

In his Dedication of *The Empress of Morocco*, Settle introduces a bookseller saying to a poet : " Sir, Your Play has had misfortune, and all that . . . but if you'd but write a Dedication, or Preface . . . the Poet takes the hint, picks out a person of Honour, tells him he has a great deal of Wit, gives us an account who writ Sence in the last Age, supposing we cannot be Ignorant

was that they persuaded many people to buy the printed play who would otherwise have let it lie at the bookseller's.

D'Avenant was the first to have the idea of prefixing a literary preface to a poem, his *Gondibert* (1651).[417a] Next Flecknoe in 1664 accompanied his play *Love's Kingdom* [418] with " A short Treatise of the *English Stage* ". While following Dame Fashion, Dryden had the genius to carry to perfection her every vagary. He saw all the opportunities, literary and pecuniary, that this innovation offered, and took advantage of it to produce some of the first critical studies which the English language can boast.[419] To *The Conquest of Granada* he added an " Essay on Heroic Plays " ; to *The State of Innocence*, " The Author's Apology for Heroic Poetry and Poetic Licence " ; to *Troilus and Cressida*, a discourse on " The Grounds of Criticism in Tragedy ", etc. And in 1667 he even published by itself (for the theatres were closed on account of the Plague and the Fire of London) his *Essay of Dramatick Poesie*. Their intrinsic value apart, these essays were amazingly well adapted to the readers of the day. The fashionable world talked literature, or aspired to talk it. To embark, however amateurishly, on literary conversation you must have opinions and arguments, and to press an argument home you must have authorities. It was necessarily only a small minority amongst society people who were qualified or inclined to seek enlightenment about the drama at first hand from Aristotle or even Horace. Dryden saved them the trouble of going so far afield, and in his literary prefaces he made them a gift of neat

---

who writes it in This ; Disputes the nature of *Verse*, Answers a Cavil or two, Quibles upon the *Court*, Huffs the *Critiques*, and the work's don. 'Tis not to be imagin'd how far a sheet of this goes to make a *Bookseller* rich, and a *Poet* famous."

[417a] [This preface is interesting also for the further reason that it gave occasion for a reply from Hobbes. See *Critical Essays of the Seventeenth Century*, ed. Spingarn. B. D.]

[418] *Love's Kingdom*. See my Bibliography.

[419] The following paragraph which I borrow from an article on Dryden in the *Quarterly Review* of October, 1878, perfectly sums up the state of literary criticism in England before Dryden : " The treatises of Wilson, Gascoign, Sidney, Webbe, Puttenham, Campion and Daniel ; the occasional discursions of Ascham in his ' Schoolmaster ', and of Ben Jonson in his ' Discoveries ' ; and the incidental remarks of Cowley, Denham, and Davenant—may be said to sum up all that had hitherto appeared in England on this important province of literature." See also Drake, *Essays . . . Illustrative of the Tatler*, II, pp. 121–142.

[Cowley and Davenant wrote more than " incidental remarks ", and Hobbes might be added, both for his answer to Davenant and his Preface to Homer. But in the main the statement is fair enough. B. D.]

little treatises, not too difficult to read, on special aspects of dramatic and poetic art, complete with the opinions of the chief authorities, with quotations and arguments all to hand, everything in short which a gentleman could need to cut a creditable figure in drawing-room conversation.[420] So these prefaces were warmly welcomed ; but though they swelled the author's profits, the total of his gains from theatre and bookseller combined was slight enough.

We now come to the writer's third source of income : gifts. The aim of the dedications was not solely—as the reader will no doubt have divined—to secure patronage and success for the poet. The incense so liberally expended had other functions : to loosen the strings of a well-lined purse as well as to pay homage to an aristocratic name. D'Urfey, making no bones about it, dedicated his tragedy, *The Siege of Memphis*, " to the truly generous Henry Chevers, Esquire ". Such tactful hints were superfluous : there was a tacit understanding between the flattered and the flatterer. The recognized reply to a dedication was a purse sent to the author : the reflex action was automatic. The custom was an old one, going back to Shakespeare's day and surviving under Charles II. In his Dedication of *Aureng-Zebe* Dryden thanks Mulgrave for " the care you have taken of my fortune ". He tenders similar recognition to Sir Robert Howard for having been " careful of my fortune ", in the Introduction to his poem *Annus Mirabilis*. This theme perpetually recurs.

Poets like Dryden confined themselves to adding a dedication to each of their works ; others added books to their dedications : their books were written solely to provide a pretext for a dedication. The poet, Payne Fisher, or as he learnedly subscribed himself Paganus Piscator—incidentally he was a graduate of Oxford and a prolific writer of Latin verse—used to go round knocking at everyone's door, whenever he was planning a new book, showing a specimen of the eulogies he was prepared to address to the highest bidders. When the book appeared he added the coats of arms on the copies supplied to the most generous. If the day of publication was delayed (and we can well believe that this sometimes happened) he would repeat his visits and try to *borrow* small sums from those who had swallowed

---

[420] His *Grounds of Criticism in Tragedy* quotes Aristotle, Euripides, Lebossu, Rymer (who had published critical comments on the English theatre the year before), Rapin, Homer, Racine, Sophocles, Æschylus, Terence, Plautus, Plato, Longinus and discusses the works of Shakespeare, Fletcher and Ben Jonson.

the bait of his praise.[421] Others who specialized in occasional verse kept poems in stock ready for every possible contingency. Was the Duke of York setting sail at the head of some expedition? their accommodating and fertile pen composed simultaneously a victory song to greet his glorious return and a mournful elegy to lament his death. They were thus sure not to be caught napping, and were equally prepared to welcome reward for their poetic inspiration from the triumphant prince himself or from his inconsolable widow.[422]

What sum in cash did these gifts amount to that formed the patron's response to the offerings of flattery?

We have seen that at best the average which Dryden made from a play was £100 sterling. Now, from the information quoted above, we may fairly reckon that the proceeds of the Third-Day performance brought him in £70 and the sale of his manuscript some £20 or £25: this would leave between £5 and £10 as the probable yield from the dedication. This estimate can naturally be approximate only: we can at most take it as a rough average. Obviously the size of these gifts will have varied with the wealth and generosity of the patron [423] and also according to the importance of the author and of his work.

When the Earl of Ossory died, his death gave the poet Flatman inspiration for a Pindaric ode for which the bereaved father, the Duke of Ormond, gave him a diamond ring worth 100 guineas.[424] On the other hand, when Paganus Piscator challenged Pepys's generosity by asking an advance of twenty shillings, Pepys—official of the Admiralty though he was—made no scruple of sending him only ten.[425] Since, by its very nature, this

[421] Pepys, July 14 and 28, 1660: à Wood, *Athenæ Oxonienses*, s.v. Payne Fisher.
[422] Dryden, *Essay Of Dramatick Poesie*.
[423] ". . . To a person of higher Rank and Order, it (the dedication) looks like an Obligation for Praises, which he knows he does not deserve and therefore is very unwilling to part with ready Money for." (Otway, Dedication of *The Souldiers Fortune*.)—" Epistles Dedicatory, and long Prefaces are of late much in Request; no Person of Quality, how remote soever, can escape the Impertinences of *Poets*; . . . But this is excusable in them that Write for *Bread*, and Live by *Dedications*, and *Third-Dayes*. If once in a Year they meet not with a good Audience, or a Bountiful *Mæcenas*, we are to expect no Play from them the next; because they want Money to keep the great Wits company; from whose Conversation, once in Twelve Months, they pick up a Comedy." (Ravenscroft, *The Careless Lovers*, Epistle to the Reader.)
[424] à Wood, *Athenæ Oxonienses*, s.v. Thomas Flatman.
[425] Pepys, July 28, 1660.—See below, note No. 440.

source of revenue was even more variable and uncertain than the others, I mention it only that it may not be overlooked. The point to remember is that the author's custom of begging and accepting alms in return for obligatory flattery—though it certainly did not seem so shocking in those days as it now does to us—was bound to lessen still further the scanty respect in which he was held.[426]

Compared with his fellow-authors, Dryden was particularly fortunate from the financial point of view. First, his talent assured him an absolutely supreme position; then he had wealthy and influential patrons; but in addition he had the good fortune to succeed D'Avenant in 1670 as Poet Laureate, and James Howell as Historiographer Royal. Each of these posts was worth £100 a year, payable quarterly, and the Laureate's also brought a tierce of Canary wine from the King's cellars. It would therefore seem that these salaries, added to his income from theatre and bookseller, ought to have set him at least at ease, and Dr. Johnson[427] appears to have felt little sympathy with the wails of which he is so lavish about the state of his finances.[428] Perhaps there was in truth some exaggeration in his plaints. Poets have at all times been inclined to rate themselves very highly, and as a natural consequence to believe themselves insufficiently appreciated. But Johnson is reviewing his whole life which extended over several reigns, while we are here considering only the early days of his career under Charles II, and it is clear that we must not judge his financial circumstances from outward appearances. His

---

[426] The writers themselves were well aware of this:

"A Poet would be dear, and out o'th'way,
Should he expect above a Coachman's Pay:
For this, will any dedicate and lie,
And daub the gaudy Ass with flattery?
For this, will any prostitute his Sense
To Coxcombs, void of Bounty as of Brains?
Yet such is the hard Fate of Writers now,
They're forc'd, for Alms, to each great Name to bow:
Fawn, like her Lap-dog, on her tawdry Grace . . .
Sneak to his Honour, call him witty, brave,
And just; tho' a known Coward, Fool or knave . . . "

(Oldham, *A Satire. Dissuading from Poetry*, Works, vol. III.)

[427] *Lives of the English Poets:* Dryden.
[428] See, for example, the Dedication of *Aureng-Zebe*, where he speaks of "the lowness of my fortune".

Laureate's salary, of which Shadwell was so jealous,[429] was like all other debts of the Merry Monarch, most irregularly paid [430]; any trifling accident at Court would even completely stop it. Mulgrave fell into disgrace in 1680 and by a sort of ricochet Dryden ceased to receive his pay.[431] We shall see that in 1684, at a moment when he was rendering the King most signal service, it was already four years in arrears. He wrote on the subject to the First Lord of the Treasury a letter, the feeling in which seems anything but feigned. If we further consider that neither he nor his family indulged expensive vices, and that he worked and produced without respite, we must conclude that his distress was genuine.

As for the other writers of the time, there cannot be the slightest doubt about their financial position. The greater number led a hand to mouth existence. We have already seen their complaints. Some like Otway [432] and Lee [433] lived in

---

[429] See note No. 395 above.

[430] Pepys, Dec. 19, 1666, April 4, 1667, and *passim*; Reresby, May 15, 1679; Bell, *Life of Dryden*, prefixed to his *Works*, p. 38, note.—Dryden frequently complains of his salary's being irregularly paid, in his Dedication, for instance, of *Marriage-à-la-Mode* and in his *Discourse concerning the Original and Progress of Satire*. He might have applied to himself with even greater emphasis Corneille's lines:

> Grand roi, dont nous voyons la générosité
> Montrer pour le Parnasse un excès de bonté
> Que n'ont jamais eu tous les autres,
> Puissiez-vous dans cent ans donner encor des lois
> Et puissent tous vos ans être de quinze mois
> Comme vos commis font les nôtres.

> Great King, whose liberality doth flow
> And on Parnassus bounties great bestow
> For which no other king e'er found the treasure,
> May you a hundred years our laws dictate,
> Your every year set in full three months late
> As ours does, at your clerks' good pleasure.

[431] *Biographia Britannica*: Sheffield, note M.

> "Thy pension lost . . .
> That lost, the Visor chang'd, you turn about,
> And strait a True Blue Protestant crept out;
> The Fryar now was writ: and some will say
> They smell a Male-Content through all the Play."
>   (*The Laureat*, anonymous.)

[432] "There was a time when *Otway* charm'd the Stage,
 Otway the Hope, the Sorrow of our Age;
 When the full Pit with pleas'd attention hung,
 Wrapt with each accent from *Castalio's* Tongue,
 With what a Laughter was his *Souldier* read!
 How mourn'd they when his *Jaffier* struck, and bled!

abject poverty. Oldham took the trouble to write a long poem to dissuade any from poetry who might have felt tempted to become his fellow-poets. Besides, contemporary opinion on the professional author's earnings was unambiguous. Here is what a great Lord, the Duke of Buckingham, has to say on the subject in a letter addressed to an odd character of the time, Captain Julian [434]:

> . . . Poetry has been so much your friend:
> On that thou'st liv'd and flourish'd all thy Time;
> Nay more, maintain'd a family by Rhime;
> And that's a Mark that Dryden ne'er could hit.
> He lives upon his Pension, not his Wit:
> E'en gentle George (flux'd both in tongue and purse)
> Shunning one Snare, yet fell into a worse.
> A Man may be reliev'd once in his Life,
> But who can be reliev'd that has a Wife?

> Yet this best Poet, tho with so much ease,
> He never drew his Pen but sure to please;
> Tho Lightning were less lively than his Wit,
> And Thunder-Claps less loud than those o' th' Pit,
> He had of 's many Wants much earlier dy'd,
> Had not kind Banker *Betterton* supply'd,
> And took for Pawn the Embryo of a Play,
> Till he could pay himself the next third Day."
> (A Satyr upon the Poets, being a Translation out of the 7th Satyr of Juvenal.—In *Poems on Affairs of State*, vol. II, 1703, pp. 138 ff.)
> Cf. the quotation from Otway, note No. 380 above.

[433] See *Biographia Britannica*, s.v. Lee.

[434] This Captain Julian, who called himself "Secretary of the Muses" used to haunt Will's Coffee House, and distribute on the quiet manuscript copies of each new "lampoon". (See Dryden's *Works*, edited by Scott and Saintsbury, XV, p. 217.) In a period so prolific of satires, this occupation lent him a certain importance and his name frequently recurs in contemporary literature, notably in the *Poems on Affairs of State*.

> "Now Fop may dine with Half-wit ev'ry Noon,
> And read his Satyr, or his worse Lampoon.
> *Julian's* so furnished by these scribbling Sparks
> That he pays off old Scores and keeps two Clarks."
> (Ravenscroft, Prologue to *The London Cuckolds*.)

"The conscious Tub. Tavern can witness, and my *Berry-Street* Apartment testifie the solicitations I have had, for the first Copy of a new Lampoon, from the greatest Lords of the Court: though their own folly and their Wives Vices were the subject . . . And the Love of Scandal and native Malice that Men and Women have to one another, made me in such request when alive, that I was admitted to the Lord's Closet, when a Man of Letters and Merit wou'd be thrust out of doors." (Tom Brown, *Letters from the Dead to the Living*: From Julian, Late Secretary to the Muses, to Will. Pierre of Lincolns-Inn Fields *Play-House*.)

Otway can hardly Guts from Gaol preserve,
And, tho he's very fat, he's like to starve :
And Sing-song Durfey (plac'd beneath abuses)
Lives by his impudence, and not the Muses :
Poor Crown too has his third days mix'd with Gall,
He lives so ill, he hardly lives at all.
Shadwell and Settle both with Rhimes are fraught,
But can't between them muster up a groat :
Nay, Lee in *Beth'lem* [435] now sees better days,
Than when applauded for his bombast Plays ;
He knows no Care, nor feels sharp want no more,
And that is what he ne'er could say before :
Thus while our Bards are famish'd by their Wit
Thou who hast none at all, yet thriv'st by it.[436]

Now hear what the commoner, John Dunton, bookseller, has to say : " Mr. Settle . . . But alas ! after all, when I see an Ingenious Man set up for a *meer Poet* . . . I give him up as one *prick'd down by Fate*, for misery *and misfortune*." [437]

VIII
Conclusion : As yet, neither public, nor men of letters

Neither money, nor honour—such in a couple of words was the plight of authors after the Restoration.

Need we be surprised ? What else could they expect from the sorry society they had to do with ? Their fate was all the sadder because this society had inspired them with eager and apparently well-founded hopes, and they had trusted it. How natural that they should be taken in ! The King, young and all-powerful, took a pride in being a connoisseur of the beautiful, the great Lords were so much in love with literature that they felt bound to write themselves and thus become in some sort fellow-authors. Surely all this was full of promise ? But the promise was not kept : authors were given nothing but hope.

The fact is that truly to encourage literature you must love her for herself. Now society folk in those days loved her solely for their own sakes. Essentially frivolous, thinking only of having a good time, their one merit is that they counted literature among their pastimes ; but she was for them a pastime only,

---

[435] He was for many years insane.
[436] A Consolatory Epistle to Captain *Julian* The Muses News-Monger, in his Confinement. (In the *Miscellaneous Works* of George Villiers, Duke of Buckingham.)
[437] *The Life and Errors of John Dunton*, Written by Himself, etc., p. 241.

and that in the most literal sense of the word. So they cared only for verses and the theatre; the verses had to be of the lightest kind, and what they asked of the theatre was luxurious scenery, brilliant versification and licentious characters. When fashionable people dabbled in writing or posed as judges of literature, it was merely for personal satisfaction: to gratify their vanity, to please the ladies, to parade a veneer of culture, or to add a few flattering epithets to their name.

What conception could they have of literature who were so preoccupied with themselves? What feeling would they be capable of? Obviously they would disdain its loftier aspects, having disqualified themselves for attaining to them. They might be stirred by the superficial quality of a couplet, by harmony, by a neat turn of phrase. At a pinch they might be able to criticize the choice of words, the conduct of a plot; in a word they would concentrate on outward form. But the soul and spirit would be beyond their ken, and they would carefully guard themselves against too lively an emotion and shrink from being stirred to genuine admiration. They would ban every serious inspiration, every careful delineation of character or passion, everything which might touch the heart or quicken the mind. Even love they would tolerate only on the condition that it should be treated as a sentiment of no depth and of no importance. On the other hand, they would welcome the lightest and most frivolous works, however far they went in frivolity, provided that they were amusing. That is the sole condition they would impose, but that is a *conditio sine quâ non*.

So it comes that this period, in appearance so deeply devoted to letters, proved one of the least favourable to literature. It cast off Shakespeare; it ignored the two great epics of Milton and Bunyan. It must be accused of other literary crimes: the word is not too strong. The age condemned Dryden, one of the most powerful and prolific geniuses which England has ever produced, to squander the best years of his intellectual vigour in the hurried concoction of works for which he knew himself to be unfitted [438]; it drove Otway, with his strong dramatic gifts,

---

[438] "And Dryden, in immortal strain,
Had raised the Table Round again,
But that a ribald king and Court
Bade him toil on, to make them sport,
Demanded for their niggard pay,
Fit for their souls, a looser lay,
Licentious satire, song and play;

to wear out on unworthy compositions the pen which was capable of writing *The Orphan* and *Venice Preserv'd*; and it turned Shadwell, endowed from birth with notable powers of observation and lively comedy, into the reluctant author of contemptible farces.

A society with so base and so narrow a conception of literature could hold its writers in no high esteem. It thought of them only as entertainers and mountebanks, people in whom you took but little interest except so far as they amused you. Such interest as Charles II's Court showed for them, was wholly selfish, superficial and devoid of sympathy. They were praised, it is true, but the patron praised out of vanity to prove his good taste and gain kudos thereby. The society of some was sought, but the host invited them for his own sake, not for theirs, because their friendship was a diploma of wit,[439] because he wanted from them some literary service, because he coveted their praise or simply because he found them merry company. When the patron had praised (or criticized) their work, had invited them to his table, had laughed at their jests or had, in accordance with society custom, flung them a few guineas [440] in payment

---

The world, defrauded of the high design,
Profaned the God-given strength, and marr'd the lofty line."
(Walter Scott, *Marmion*, Introduction to Canto I.)

[439] "There marched the bard and blockhead, side by side,
Who rhym'd for hire, and patroniz'd for pride."
(Pope, *Dunciad*, IV, ll. 99–100.)

[440] Sometimes they got no guineas :
" Sir, I've a Patron, you reply. 'Tis true . . .
Why faith e'en try. Write, Flatter, Dedicate,
My Lord's and his Forefathers Deeds relate :
Yet know he'll wisely strive ten thousand ways,
To shun a needy Poet's fulsom Praise ;
Nay, to avoid thy Importunity,
Neglect his State, and condescend to be
A Poet, tho perhaps a worse than thee.
Thus from a Patron he becomes a Friend ;
Forgetting to reward, learns to commend ;
Receives your twelve long Months successless Toil,
And talks of Authors, Energy and Stile ;
Damns the dull Poems of the scribling Town,
Applauds your Writings, and repeats his own ;
Whilst thou in Complaisance oblig'd must sit
T'extol his Judgment, and admire his Wit ;
And wrapt with his *Essay on Poetry*,
Swear *Horace* writ not half so strong as He,
But that we're partial to Antiquity . . . "
(A Satyr upon the Poets . . . in *Poems on Affairs of State*, vol. II, pp. 138 ff.)

of some panegyric, he had done all that was due to himself and his position; he owed them nothing, neither sympathy nor consideration: and he thought no more about them.

When the King admired *Hudibras* it never occurred to him to wonder how Butler contrived to live. When he took unto himself a Poet Laureate—he had to follow his predecessor's example and have a Poet Laureate—little cared he whether the salary was paid or no. He had shown his good taste; that was enough. On the same principle, Buckingham who fancied himself as a connoisseur, urged Lee to come to London and once he had come, felt no further responsibility for him.[441] Similarly Otway's aristocratic boon-companions let him die in poverty, if not of poverty.[442] Dryden was mercilessly thrashed without one of his patrons turning a hair and Mulgrave looked unconcernedly on while his protégé endured suffering of which he was the cause. Wycherley himself, the special favourite who had mixed on equal terms with the nobility, lay for seven years in prison without any of his dear Court friends appearing to observe his absence, still less dreaming of paying the debts which kept him there.[443] They went on

---

[441] Spence, p. 62.—Lee went out of his mind and the Duke wrote verses on his madness. See above, note No. 435.

[442] "Otway was more beholden to Captain Symonds the Vintner in whose Debt he died four hundred Pounds, than to all his Patrons of Quality." (Manuscript note by Oldys on Langbaine's article: Otway, p. 398.)—In debt, and dying of hunger he asked alms of a passer-by, crying: "I am Otway, the poet." Moved to pity, the stranger gave him a guinea with which Otway dashed to a baker's. He began to eat so greedily that the first mouthful of bread choked him (April 14, 1685). He was thirty-four. This version of his death has been questioned, but Mr. Gosse, his latest biographer, accepts it as true. However that may be, there is no doubt that he died in the extreme of misery.

[443] Oldham was under no illusions about these fine gentlemen:
"*Bless me! how great his Genius! how each Line*
Is big with Sense!
Cries a gay, wealthy Sot, who would not hail
For bare five Pounds, the Author out of Jail."
(*A Satire, Dissuading from Poetry.*)
" Chymists and Whores by *Buckingham* were fed,
Those by their honest Labours gain'd their Bread;
But he was never so expensive yet,
To keep a Creature merely for his Wit; . . .
Pemb—[roke] lov'd Tragedy, and did provide
For Butcher's Dogs, and for the whole Bankside;
The Bear was fed, but Dedicating *Lee*,
Was thought to have a larger Paunch than he."
(A Satyr upon the Poets, being a Translation out of the 7th Satyr of *Juvenal*; in *Poems on Affairs of State*, vol. II, 1703, pp. 138 ff.)

applauding his plays without wondering what had become of the author.[444]

Flattered and made much of to-day while he was amusing, scorned and forgotten to-morrow—such was the writer's fate. Authors were fed on fine words, and that was all. At heart the great looked down on them, as wealthy folk may look down on poor devils whose trade is to amuse them, as the rich landowner of those days, swollen with self-importance, could look down on the serfs who toiled for a living on his land. In short, a poet in the eyes of this gay world was just a variety of buffoon, exercising a skill slightly superior to that of the Court Jester of the good old days, but having no more claim than he to respect or to considerate treatment. Woe betide him when his tricks cease to seem funny! Throw him out, drive him off with contumely, cover him with abuse—without allowing him the right to protest—at need, have him beaten to death! Treat him like a woman of the gutter: enjoy him, then kick him out of doors. The simile is Rochester's.[445]

This is what the fine sentiment of the Court amounted to, and its parade of zeal for literature. Complete neglect would have been of greater value to the poets, for it would have compelled them to rely wholly on themselves and to use their gifts to the best of their power.[446] Instead, they exhausted the bulk of their energy in pursuing a mirage which could lead only to fresh disillusionment. The very fashion for writing affected by elegant society made the poets' position even worse, while evoking more false hopes. It had the result of creating two factions in literature: the patricians and the plebs. The greater the pretensions of the aristocracy, the worse treated was the

---

[444] Pack, *Miscellanies in Verse and Prose*, Some Memoirs of William Wycherley, Esq.,—Spence, pp. 44, 45.

[445]   " For *Wits* are treated just like common *Whores* ;
       First they're *enjoyed*, and then *kick'd out of Doors*."
                               (*Satire against* Man, *Works*, vol. I, p. 2.)

" It is the business of poor Poets to be the diversion of mankind ; pleasure is their being. I think I may call 'em the Mistresses of the World ; which, if granted, I am sure 'tis easie to prove their Gallants very brutish, for they generally loath them as soon as they're enjoy'd."
                               (Lee, Dedication of *Cæsar Borgia*.)

He expresses the same idea with the same comparison in the Epilogue to his *Theodosius*.

[446] We have seen that it was when Dryden felt himself forsaken and alone that he wrote *All for Love*. It is probable that we owe Otway's *Orphan* to the same feeling.

commonalty. Willy-nilly, the author found himself embroiled in the quarrels of his conceited patrons and, as was but natural, suffered the fate of the earthen jar.

It might well seem that so many bitter disappointments would have opened his eyes to the vanity of his hopes. But the King and the Court offered so many allurements that even repeated disappointments could not entirely disillusion him. The English nation had recovered from the Puritan fever only to fall victim to the Royalist, and in enthusiastically recalling Charles II had surrendered itself to him wholeheartedly. Welcomed, flattered, cherished like an idol, the King had become the focus and the symbol of England. Only the Court counted for anything in comparison with him, and the Court was merely the mirror of the King. The citizenry was looked upon askance and kept at arm's length; the citizens maintained their reserve and acquiesced in being nothing. Even if the Court had not seduced him by so many promises, the author had nowhere else to turn, and no hope from any other quarter.

That was the crux. There was as yet no " public ". Neither the word nor the thing existed.[447] The author saw before him only a coterie, too exclusive not to be all-powerful, too powerful not to command obedience. Whatever way he turned, he could find no one to whom he could appeal against the verdict of Court society. There was nothing to be done but to submit with what grace he could muster. From the moment that a man adopted the career of a writer he was obliged to swear allegiance to fashionable society and make himself a courtier— or die of hunger.[448]

The author of the day became the complete and perfect sycophant. He modelled himself meticulously on his masters

---

[447] Dryden always uses the word " people " where we should now say " public ". See in particular his Preface to *The Mock Astrologer* and note No. 362 above. [The " public " meant " public affairs ". B. D.]

[448] " The *Poets* who must live by Courts or starve,
Were proud, so good a Government to serve;
And mixing with Buffoons and Pimps profain
Tainted the Stage, for some small Snip of Gain.
For they, like *Harlots*, under *Bawds* profest,
Took all th'ungodly pains, and got the least.
Thus did the thriving Malady prevail,
The Court, its Head, the *Poets* but the Tail," etc.
   (Dryden, Epilogue written for Fletcher's *Pilgrim*.)

and painstakingly sought to acquire an aristocratic polish.[449] In his plays he introduced on the stage none but persons of social standing,[450] and he adopted their ways of speech. The court indulged the affectation of talking French ; he talked French too, and to such purpose that his fellow-countrymen of to-day often require a translation of his jargon,[451] which must assuredly have been unintelligible to the ordinary citizen of his own time. Once caught up in the machinery, he was helpless. Before sitting down to write, he carefully inquired how the wind was blowing among those on high, and dutifully trimmed his sails accordingly, even when he saw clearly where the chosen course was leading him. Dryden wrote what is perhaps the finest appreciation of Shakespeare which English literature possesses,[452] and yet laid sacrilegious hands on Shakespeare ; he worthily praised the epic genius of Milton [453] and yet dressed his heroes in the costumes of Mademoiselle de Scudéry. Shadwell and Otway passed vigorous and just criticism on contemporary comedy, which no plays deserved more thoroughly than their own.[454] All decried current taste [455] and all pandered to it ;

[449] " I have always acknowledged the wit of our predecessors with all the veneration which becomes me ; but, I am sure, their wit was not that of gentlemen," etc. (Dryden, *Defence of the Epilogue to the Second Part of the Conquest of Granada.*)
[450] When they borrow a play of Molière's, they usually suppress the free natural speech of servant to master ; this would evidently have grated on noble ears. Thus in Ravenscroft's imitation of *le Bourgeois Gentilhomme* all Nicole's remonstrances are put into the mouth of M. Jourdain's daughter. It is difficult to see what propriety gained by this device.
[451] See, for instance, Dryden's *Marriage-à-la-Mode*, the scene between Palamede and Melantha (II, i). In his edition of Dryden, Walter Scott frequently explains the French expressions used and Swift used to say that in his day a large number of the words and phrases introduced by Court influence under Charles II were already barely intelligible. (*A Proposal for improving the English Tongue.*)
[This was probably an affectation confined to a few, and Dryden was sure of support in making fun of it. Palamede sizes up Melantha rapidly enough in II, i, and laughs at her, but she is more especially made fun of in III, i, in her scene with Philotis, where, the reader will remember, the new French words she learns " began at *sottises* and ended *en ridicule* ". B. D.]
[452] *Essay Of Dramatick Poesie.*
[453] In his Preface to *The State of Innocence*, he calls *Paradise Lost* " one of the greatest, most noble and most sublime poems which either this age or nation has produced ".
[As *The State of Innocence* was never acted, Dryden can hardly have clothed the characters in any costume. As for laying sacrilegious hands on Shakespeare, see the addition to note 122. Bardolatry had not begun. B. D.]
[454] " Though I have known some of late so Insolent to say, that *Ben Johnson* wrote his best *Playes* without Wit ; imagining that all the Wit in *Playes* consisted in bringing two Persons upon the Stage to break Jests, and

they inveighed against the over-emphasis on scenery and setting, yet wrote tragedies appealing to the eye; they deplored the debasement of comedy into coarse farce, yet against their better judgment indulged in clowning, garnished with calculated smuttiness.[456] They saw and cursed the current that swept them on, but not one of them attempted to swim against it. Many possessed the necessary strength; but to risk such a

to bob one another, which they call Repartie, not considering that there is more wit and invention requir'd in the finding out good Humor, and Matter proper for it, than in all their smart reparties. For in the writing of a Humor, a Man is confin'd not to swerve from the Character, and oblig'd to say nothing but what is proper to it: but in the *Playes*, which have been wrote of late, there is no such thing as perfect Character, but the two chief Persons are most commonly a Swearing, Drinking, Whoring Ruffian for a Lover, and an impudent ill-bred *tomrig* for a Mistress, and these are the fine People of the *Play*; and there is that Latitude in this, that almost anything is proper for them to say; but their chief Subject is bawdy, and profaness which they call *brisk writing*, when the most dissolute of Men, that relish those things well enough in private, are *chok'd* at 'em in publick: and, methinks, if there were nothing but the ill Manners of it, it should make Poets avoid that Indecent way of Writing." (Preface to Shadwell's *Sullen Lovers*).—" And then their Comedies now a days are the filthiest things, full of Bawdy and nauseous doings, which they mistake for raillery and Intrigue; besides, they have no wit in 'em neither; for all their Gentlemen and men of wit, as they style 'em, are either silly conceited impudent Coxcombs, or else rude ill-mannerly drunken Fellows—fogh——" (Lady Squeamish in Otway's *Friendship in Fashion*, Act I.)

[455] See, amongst others, Dryden in his Dedication of the *Spanish Fryar* and his *Defence of an Essay of Dramatique Poesie*. See also almost all his Prologues and Epilogues.

> "*Dryden* himself, to please a frantick Age,
> Was forc'd to let his Judgment stoop to Rage:
> To a wild Audience he conform'd his Voice,
> Comply'd to Custom, but not err'd by Choice.
> Deem then the Peoples, not the Writer's Sin,
> *Almanzor's* Rage, and Rants of *Maximin*."
> (Granville, *Essay. Upon unnatural Flights in Poetry, Works*, I, p. 93 and note.)

[456] "Then Courts of Kings were held in high Renown,
E'er made the common Brothels of the Town: ...
The King himself to Nuptial Ties a Slave,
No bad Example to his Poets gave:
And they not bad, but in a vicious Age
Had not to please the Prince debauch'd the Stage."
(Dryden, *The Wife of Bath, her Tale,* in *Fables Ancient and Modern*, p. 481.)

"Posterity is absolutely mistaken as to that great man; tho' his comedies are horribly full of double entendres, yet 'twas owing to a false complaisance for a dissolute age. He was in company the modestest man that ever convers'd."

(*Gentleman's Magazine*, Feb. 1745.)

venture, to defy fashion before an audience accustomed to lay down the law and closely united as a body, would have been to play for high stakes. Put your audience òut of humour, and you had no alternative but—to give up writing. Authors did not think the game worth the candle, they recognized the better path, and chose the worse. Dryden's Prologue to *The Kind Keeper* frankly says :

> Let them, who the rebellion first began
> To wit, restore the monarch if they can,
> Our author dares not be the first bold man.
> He, like the prudent citizen, takes care
> To keep for better marts his staple ware.[457]

Weary of struggle and despairing of victory, authors resigned themselves to murmuring a humble little literary credo :

> You now have habits, Dances, Scenes and Rhymes,
> High Language often : I, and Sense sometimes . . .
> But blame your Selves, not him who Writ the Play ; . . .
> He's bound to please, not to Write well ; and knows
> There is a mode in playes, as well as. Cloathes.[458]

If he wins no applause, it is because he has not known how " to lower himself to please his auditors ".[459] Thus driven to make a virtue of necessity, he gave up trying to be himself. In twenty years, only two works are noteworthy as having an intrinsic value : Dryden's *All for Love* and Otway's *Orphan*. And these two plays belong to the close of the period that has been the subject of this first chapter.

Compelled thus to abase themselves in their work, we need not be surprised to see them abasing themselves also in their lives. Powerless to shake off their dependence on those whose

[457] " He who made this, observ'd what Farces hit,
And durst not disoblige you now with wit."
(Dryden, Prologue to *The Assignation*.)

[458] Dryden, Prologue to *The Rival Ladies*
[459] Dryden, Preface to *An Evening's Love*.
" Th' unhappy Man, who once has trail'd a Pen,
Lives not to please himself but other Men."
(Prologue to Lee's *Cæsar Borgia*, written by Dryden.)
" So should wise Poets sooth an awkward Age,
For they are Prostitutes upon the Stage :
Tꝺ stand on Points were foolish and ill-bred,
As for a Lady to be nice in Bed ;
Your wills alone must their Performance measure,
And you may turn 'em ev'ry way for pleasure."
(Lee, Epilogue to *Theodosius*.)

taste governed their writings, they eagerly set about currying their favour and rivalled each other in sycophancy, exceeding all bounds and violating all dignity. Readily donning the livery of Messrs. So and So, they assailed their patrons with flatteries which no one imagined to be sincere.[460] Willingly they made obeisance to folly and to shame provided these were covered by a title. The flattery-competitions which went on among them did nothing to raise them in the eyes of an arrogant society. They grew accustomed to be despised and became despicable.

Their private life suffered. Most of them adopted a devil-may-care philosophy which left little room for self-respect. We have seen the kind of man D'Urfey was ; Lee lived a riotous life in which wine played no small part [461] ; Shadwell was " a brute " in conversation [462] and also drank ; after a week of fashionable orgies with Lord Plymouth, Otway spent whole months with low-caste companies in disreputable taverns [463]; Oldham was of Rochester's gang [464] ; enough said.

Their self-respect being so small, they respected their profession little. They sacrificed their literary pride so cheaply as

---

[460] Dryden wrote to Rochester : " I have sent your Lordship a prologue and epilogue, which I made for our players, when they went down to Oxford. I hear they have succeeded ; and by the event your Lordship will judge how easy 'tis to pass anything upon an university, and how gross flattery the learned will endure."

(*Works*, edited Scott and Saintsbury, vol. XVIII, p. 95.)

[461] " Poor *Nat. Lee* (I cannot think of him without tears) had great merit. In the poetic sense he had, at intervals, inspiration itself : but liv'd an outrageous, boisterous life, like his brethren . . ."

(*Gentleman's Magazine*, Feb. 1745.)

" *Nat. Lee* slept in next, in hopes of a Prize,
Apollo remember'd he had hit once in thrice ;
By the Rubies in's Face, he could not deny,
But he had as much Wit as wine could supply."
(Rochester, *A Scession of the Poets*, *Works*, I, p. 134.)

[462] " Shadwell in conversation was a brute." (*Gentleman's Magazine*, Feb. 1745) ; *Quarterly Review*, Oct. 1878, p. 314, article on Dryden. Like De Quincey later, Shadwell also used opium. On his drunken habits see Dryden : *The Vindication*, etc., where he is introduced under the name of Og.—The coarseness of his conversation is confirmed by a manuscript note of Oldys on the Shadwell article in Langbaine.

[463] " You'll be glad to know any trifling circumstance concerning *Otway* . . . He gave himself up early to drinking, and like the unhappy wits of that age passed his days between rioting and fasting, ranting jollity and abject penitence, carousing one week with Lord *Pl———th*, and then starving a month in low company at an ale-house on *Tower-Hill*." (*Gentleman's Magazine*, Feb. 1745.)—See also Johnson, *Lives of the English Poets* : Otway.

[464] à Wood, *Athenæ Oxonienses*, s.v. John Oldham.

to subordinate their own judgment to the opinion of any titled or moneyed fool, and not even to resent insults offered them. When the most distinguished of their company was outrageously maltreated not more than one or two had the courage to protest. The others laughed and congratulated themselves that a storm which might have broken over them had burst on a fellow-writer's shoulders. Dryden himself swallowed his indignation for fear of damaging his position. Not only did the writers of the day lack, as a body, all *esprit de corps*, they did not even form small literary groups of friends bound together by sympathy, such as gathered later round Addison, Pope and Samuel Johnson. Each played his own hand careless of his dignity, careless of the dignity of his fellows, without, in short, any of the feelings we associate with the man of letters. From this we draw the conclusion that, just as there was no public, there were at this period no men of letters either.

CHAPTER II

JOHN DRYDEN AND POLITICS
(1680–1688)

I

Re-awakening of political and religious passions : Whigs and Tories.—Political Drama : Dryden, Otway, Lee, Southerne, Crowne, D'Urfey, Shadwell, Settle, Tate, Mrs. Behn, Ravenscroft, Bankes.—Political Prologues and Epilogues

The years immediately following the Restoration had been light-hearted and carefree. The King thought only of leading a gay life and in this the Court wholeheartedly co-operated. His subjects, full-fed with strait-laced Puritanism, drifted gently with the stream or at least, beguiled by the good humour and infectious geniality of a Prince, " young, charming, and a winner of all hearts ", had not the courage to swim against the current. Everything smiled on the new régime ; monarchy and the King were immensely popular, and no dissentient voice sounded a discordant note in the general chorus of gaiety and content.

Good order had been established. Pursued and hunted down, liberty and even life endangered,[1] Puritans and Republicans were forced to take refuge in obscurity, and public opinion kept them there. The fallen government now seemed actually an impious usurpation and Charles I a martyr, Cromwell a parricide, and his supporters hateful hypocrites or detestable fanatics. The terrible reprisals taken against everything connected with the Republic, the horrid treatment meted out to all who had in any measure shared the Protector's political or religious views, seemed only the just reward of unprecedented crimes committed without excuse.[1a] So the Puritans lay low, and because they gave no sign of life they were thought to be well and truly dead.

[1] See Neal, vol. IV, chaps. 5 and 6 ; Geffroy, pp. 202–3.
[1a] [This is to exaggerate the very mild retribution visited on the Parliamentarians : there were hardly any executions. The worst sufferers were the many dissenting ministers who were ejected from livings which belonged to the Anglican Church. When one thinks of what happened during the French Revolution, or in many countries in our own generation, one cannot but admire the moderation shown by the victorious royalists. B. D.]

Free from any unwelcome anxieties at home, and firmly determined, whatever happened, not to create trouble for himself either at home or abroad,[2] living in an atmosphere of general approval and unmixed amusement, Charles II had quickly grown accustomed to thinking that life and the exercise of power provided a merry party which would never end.

But the Puritan fires, apparently extinct, were smouldering under their ashes. It was the King himself who blew the embers into flame. First and foremost the excesses of the Court soon re-awakened respect for the stern uprightness of " the Saints ". People had hated exaggerated virtue, they were soon nauseated by exaggerated vice.[3] They were glad to let the King enjoy himself, but when they saw him treat everything as a jest, even the interests of his people, they felt he was carrying merriment too far, and they remembered that if his predecessors had tended to magnify trifles into affairs of State, they had, at least, taken affairs of State seriously, and had not squandered their tax-revenues on enriching mistresses and favourites.[4]

Once people began to make comparisons, they did not stop. Whatever views you might hold about Cromwell, you could not deny that under him England had cut a good figure in Europe.[5] The English had perhaps tended somewhat to forget, but little by little Charles II quickened their memories. The town of Dunkirk had been won from Spain by the Protector's arms, Charles sold it to Louis XIV—for money. Nay, he sold himself to France.[5a] And—unheard-of disgrace—he let the Dutch

---

[2] " It is said the King being one day importuned by the Duke to undertake things which he thought very dangerous, told him, *Brother, I am resolved never to travel again, you may do so if you please.*" (Rapin de Thoyras, vol. II, book 23, p. 725.)

[3] In 1668, the apprentices of London set about " pulling down the bawdy-houses ", saying " that they did ill in contenting themselves in pulling down the little bawdy-houses, and did not go and pull down the great bawdy-house at White Hall." (Pepys, March 24, 25, 1668.)

[4] Macaulay, *History*, chap. II.—" The King hath lately paid about £30,000 to clear debts of my Lady Castlemayn's." (Pepys, Dec. 12, 1666.)

[5] See Geffroy, p. 164.

[5a] [The affair was a little more subtle than that. Charles's ambition, which he pursued stubbornly under the screen of flippancy, was to make himself absolute monarch over a strong England. For this he needed money, and the only way he could get it was by making concessions to Louis. He was playing a dangerous game, but had he lived a few years longer he would probably have succeeded completely, and been in a position to defy France. If his brother had had a tithe of his ability, English history would have been very different. B. D.]

fleet sail up the Thames, and for the first time in history the citizens of London heard the sound of enemy guns. Cromwell had inspired the foe with more respect.[6]

What stirred England more profoundly yet, was the King's religious behaviour. In their horror of Puritanism, the English had forgotten their old hatred of Popery. Having calmed their feelings toward the one, Charles succeeded in reviving their feelings against the other. They soon saw, in fact, that while the King treated the Puritans with extreme severity, he and his brother showed much more tolerance to Roman Catholics. The King married a Portuguese princess [7] and allowed his French mistress, the Duchess of Portsmouth, complete dominion over him.[8] The Duke of York was even less discreet and did not hesitate to make public profession of Roman Catholicism (1671), thus arousing acute Protestant anxiety. Similarly, when the King proclaimed a Declaration of Indulgence in 1672—which under cover of giving relief to all Dissenters was in fact designed to give a free field to the Roman Catholics—the Protestants were not deceived. The Nonconformists themselves were the first to protest against the specious liberty offered them. As an understanding was known to exist between Charles II and Louis XIV, the people—still vividly remembering "Bloody Mary"—

---

[6] See Reresby, p. 74.

[7] The Infanta, Dona Catarina, sister of King Alphonso VI of Portugal (1662).

[8] See Reresby, pp. 234 and 276.—The Duchess of Portsmouth was passionately disliked ; there are innumerable satires on the subject. In vol. II alone of the Luttrell Collection in the British Museum, I find three : "A Pleasant Dialogue betwixt Two Wanton Ladies of Pleasure ; Or, *The Dutchess of* Portsmouths *woful Farwell to her former Felicity*" (1684–5), No. 167 ; "The Dutchess of Portsmouths Farwel" (1684–5), No. 168 ; "Portsmouth Observed and Described," 1684, No. 254.—In *Poems on Affairs of State*, 1703, vol. I, p. 216, I note a piece of verse called *On his Royal Highness's Voyage beyond Sea*, March 3d., 1678, which thus begins :

> "R. H. they say is gone to Sea,
> Design'd for the *Hague*
> But *Portsmouth's* left behind to be
> The Nation's Whorish Plague."

The story goes that Nell Gwyn was driving through the streets of Oxford in her carriage, pursued by the hooting of the crowd, who mistook her for the Duchess of Portsmouth. "She looked out of the window and said, with her usual good humour, 'Pray, good people, be civil ; I am the Protestant whore.' This laconic speech drew upon her the favour of the populace, and she was suffered to proceed without further molestation." (Cunningham, *The Story of Nell Gwynn*, chap. VI, p. 121.)

foresaw a fiery persecution [9] by the Romanists under the direction of the King of France. So, day by day, causes of complaint piled up; the King's popularity was wearing thin; the number of malcontents increased and they dared to make their voices heard. Above all, the national conscience took fright—soon one cry alone was heard throughout the land : the Church in danger ! Since Heaven—endorsing the country's views—had denied children to Charles's marriage to a Roman Catholic, his brother, James, Duke of York, was next in the succession, and with him Romanism in its most fanatic form would mount the throne. This threat to the future was a spark to tinder. From words the nation passed to deeds. The House of Commons began hostilities, by compelling the King to withdraw his Declaration of Indulgence, and by passing the Test Act (1673) against the Roman Catholics, to which—so deep was the people's feeling—Charles did not dare to refuse the royal assent. The Duke of York was obliged to resign his office of Grand Admiral of the Fleet, but in the same year, as if to defy Parliament and nation, he took as his second wife a devout Roman Catholic princess, Maria of Modena, whom the people promptly nicknamed " The Pope's eldest daughter ".[10]

Such was the mood in England when Titus Oates appeared with his sensational revelations of an alleged Popish Plot (1678). The country was in a state of excitement so acute that people believed the whole story; they saw themselves encircled by snares and dangers, prepared themselves for self-defence, and became literally mad with fear and anger. Political and religious passion had seemed dead. They were now rekindled, to burn more fiercely than ever before. It was soon clear that if people had so long kept silence it was not because they had nothing to say.[10a]

[9]
> " What need I to apologize?
> 'Tis said, nothing more true is,
> The chiefest part of 's Errand lies
> To fetch in Cousin *Lewis*.
>
> That both together, as they say,
> If one may dare to speak on 't :
> Thro' Hereticks Throats may cut their way,
> To bring in *James* the Second . . ."
> (*On his Royal Highness's Voyage beyond Sea*, see last note.)

[10] On the state of public opinion at this critical time, see Christie, *Letters Addressed from London to Sir Joseph Williamson, in the Years 1673 and 1674*.

[10a] [The most complete study of the whole affair is Mr. John Pollock's *The Popish Plot*. B. D.]

England was once again divided into two hostile camps : on the one hand were those who looked on the Duke of York as a menace to the English constitution and religion and wished at all costs to exclude him from the succession ; on the other, those who held that his right to the throne came from God and could not be questioned on any grounds whatsoever. Here, the champions of the nation's rights—there, the upholders of the royal prerogative. The one party set about sending petitions to the King, demanding that Parliament be immediately summoned to bring in a Bill of Exclusion directed against the Duke of York. The other showered addresses on him expressing their abhorrence of petitions and of parliaments. In a moment politics dominated everything. Everyone was a prey to quite exceptional mental excitement. Normal social relations were at an end. " I know but four men, in their whole [Whig] party," said Dryden, " to whom I have spoken for above this year last past ; and with them, neither, but casually and cursorily. We have been acquaintance of long standing, many years before this accursed Plot divided men into several parties." [11] " Things have got to such a pass," wrote Reresby,[12] " that there are not only divergencies of interest, but there are almost no business or social relations except between people of the same opinions." Henceforth there were in England neither neighbours, nor friends, nor colleagues, nor families ; there were only Petitioners (also known as Exclusionists or Birminghams [13]) and Abhorrers (also called Anti-Birminghams, Yorkists, Irish, Bogtrotters or Tantivies).[14] All these terms speedily gave way to " Whigs " and " Tories " respectively.

Whig-a-more, abbreviated to Whig, was a term applied to the peasants of the Scottish Lowlands, fanatical Presbyterians who had recently risen and assassinated the Primate. Tory was the Romanist outlaw, half vagabond, half bandit, who had sought refuge in the Irish bogs.[15] This unflattering title was given to the adherents of the Duke of York, while his opponents were branded by the equally unflattering name of Whigs.

[11] *The Vindication*, etc.   [12] Reresby, p. 265.
[13] That is to say, " False Protestants " (North, *Examen*, p. 321). The people of Birmingham were reputed to manufacture false coin.
[14] Stephens, *Catalogue* . . . vol. I *passim* ; North, *Examen*, p. 321 ; Reresby, pp. 187 and 190. " To ride tantivy " means " at headlong pace ". The Tantivies were the extremists who were said to be heading full speed for Rome.
[15] Macaulay, *History*, chap. II, vol. I, pp. 256–7 ; Swift, *Works*, edited Walter Scott, vol. III, p. 508, note.

The Court was naturally on the Tory side; the City, which now re-entered the picture, rallied to the side of the Whigs.[15a] The light-hearted days of irresponsibility and jollity were over. It was impossible for anyone to steer clear of politics, and the writers who had hitherto concentrated only on amusing the Court were compelled, like everybody else, to take sides.

The theatre was still the rage, so it was through the theatre that they first took part in the struggle. Up to now they had ventured no excursions into the political field save by complimentary allusions to the King: [16]

> You, Sir, such blessings to the World dispense,
> We scarce perceive the use of Providence,

or by rhetorical affirmations of the sanctity of royalty: a scarcely veiled protest against republican theories:

> Kings, tho' they err, should never be arraign'd [17];

> But make him know it is a safer thing,
> To blaspheme Heav'n, then to depose a king [18];

> We ought, when Heav'n's Vicegerent does a Crime,
> To leave to Heav'n the right to punish him.
> Those who for wrongs their Monarchs murther act,
> Worse sins than they can punish they contract.[19]

Politics in the theatre were confined to flattering generalities of this type.

It is true that when England was at war with Holland in 1673 Dryden had written his *Amboyna, or The Cruelties of the Dutch to the English Merchants*, with the evident intention of stirring up public opinion to support the policy of the government. The tragedy was dedicated to Lord Clifford who up to that moment had been a Minister. But in 1673 no one took politics seriously. Mrs. Behn—who was, as the reader will recall, a political spy as

---

[15a] [It is true that the City, the dissenting and trading element, was against the King: but the Court was divided. Many great nobles, e.g. Shaftesbury, fought hard against the royal measures. The battle in the House of Lords over the Exclusion Bill was bitter and long-drawn-out. B. D.]

[16] Crowne, Epilogue to *Calisto*, addressed to the King.

[17] Lee, *Sophonisba* (III).

[18] Crowne, *The History of Charles the Eighth of France* (I, 1).

[19] Earl of Orrery, *Tryphon* (I, 1). In the volume entitled *Two New Tragedies*.

[Such statements are not merely flattery. They are, in a sense, Hobbism, and reflect an attitude of mind understandable in a people who did not want another civil war. B. D.]

well as an author—was simply laughed at when she sent from Holland the all-too-accurate news of Ruyter's raid up the Thames.[20] The drama did not follow up this experiment of Dryden's but speedily reverted to its normal fatuity.

Now, however, there was no more laughter. The struggle raged with fury and it was no longer so easy to side-track political issues. Sick as a man might be of them, they were there, they were full of menace, they thrust themselves on his attention. The theatre could not escape them. From 1680 onwards it echoed every passion and reflected every tiny incident of a stormy period that was destined to end in a Revolution.[21]

The titles of plays changed suddenly and significantly. One after another the stage presented :

> Sir Barnaby Whigg.[22]
> The City Heiress.[23]
> The Royalist.[24]
> The Roundheads, or The Good Old Cause.[25]
> The Loyal Brother, or The Persian Prince.[26]
> Venice Preserv'd, or A Plot Discover'd.[27]
> City Politiques.[28]
> A Common-Wealth of Women.[29]

They even dragged Shakespeare—whose plays they continued to remodel—into the politics of the day. In the early days of the Restoration, when Dryden borrowed his *Troilus and Cressida*, he encumbered it with a subsidiary and romantic title *Or, Truth Found too Late* ; when the actor Lacey rewrote *The Taming of the Shrew* he rechristened it *Sauny the Scott*. Crowne now adapted *Henry VI* and called it *The Misery of Civil-War* ; Tate reintroduced

---

[20] Granger, *A Biographical History of England*, s.v. Mrs. Behn.
[21] " All run now into Politicks." (Shadwell, Notice of *The Lancashire Witches*.)—

> " 'Tis Faction buys the Votes of half the Pit."
> (Dryden, Epilogue for Southerne's *Loyal Brother*.)

> " The Stage, like old Rump-Pulpits, is become
> The Scene of News, a furious Party's Drum.
> Here Poets beat their brains for Volunteers
> And take fast hold of Asses by their Ears . . ."
> (Shadwell (?) *A Lenten Prologue*.)

[22] By D'Urfey.	[23] By Mrs. Behn.
[24] By D'Urfey.	[25] By Mrs. Behn.
[26] By Southerne.	[27] By Otway.
[28] By Crowne.	[29] By D'Urfey.

Coriolanus as *The Ingratitude of a Common-Wealth*.[30] The gulf between the two periods is revealed by the contrast between the titles current in each.

The titles just quoted all obviously belong to plays directed against the City and the Whigs. There are two reasons for this: first, the playwrights, long vassals of the Court, were naturally for the most part more inclined to sing its praises than to oppose it; secondly, the Tories, making common cause with the King, had the advantage of being able openly to attack their opponents, while the Whigs enjoyed no such privilege.[31] Such authors as were tempted to take the popular side dare not indulge in provocative titles, but instead of advertising their principles had to content themselves with jests at the expense of the Romanists.[32] Shadwell, for instance, in his *Lancashire Witches* introduces the ridiculous Irish priest Teague O' Divelly; Settle in the *Female Prelate, the Life and Death of Pope Joan* brings his heroine to bed in the streets of Rome. Whig sympathizers had to confine themselves to general allusions of this kind, and even then the allusions must be neither too obvious nor too cutting. Otherwise the play was suppressed. In a transitory fit of Protestant zeal Crowne had spiced his First Part of Henry VI with "a little Vineger against the Pope"[33] only to see his tragedy "e're it liv'd long . . . stifled by command".[34] During the whole of

[30] In his Dedication he says: "Upon a close view of this Story, there appear'd in some Passages no small Resemblance with the busie *Faction* of our own time. And I confess, I chose rather to set the *Parallel* nearer to Sight, than to throw it off at further Distance."

[31] "I am no Politician," says Settle in dedicating his *Pope Joan* to Shaftesbury, "for that Scribler must have no prospect to his Interest, who dares affront so numerous a Party, that are so powerful a Support of the Stage."

[32] As early as 1679, on the occasion of the Popish Plot, Oldham had published his *Satyrs upon the Jesuits*. They were extremely successful: First Edition 1679; Second Edition 1685; Eighth Edition 1782 (Stephens, *Catalogue* . . ., I, p. 649).

[33]
"To-day we bring old gather'd Herbs, 'tis true,
But such as in sweet *Shakespears* Garden grew.
And all his Plants immortal you esteem,
Your mouthes are never out of taste with him.
Howe're to make your Appetites more keen,
Not only oyly Words are sprinkled in;
But what to please you gives us better hope,
A little Vineger against the *Pope*." (Prologue.)

[34] ". . . My aversion to some things I saw acted there (viz. at Court) by great men, carried me against my Interest, to expose Popery and Popish

James II's reign the performance of Dryden's *Spanish Fryar* was forbidden because of the character of Dominick, the Spanish monk.[35] As for direct political allusions, the moment they implied the slightest reflection on the Tories, they were excised. In his *Lancashire Witches* Shadwell had introduced the character of Chaplain Smerk, to poke fun at the Anglican clergy, and in particular at their hatred of Dissenters. This whole part was cut to pieces by the Master of the Revels.[36] Lee's tragedy *Lucius Junius Brutus* was stopped after its third performance, because it talked too much of liberty.[37] In remodelling Shakespeare's *Richard II* Tate had to change the English king into *The Sicilian Usurper*, yet even so the play was banned after the second performance, evidently for political reasons, since he protests in his Dedication that every page of it " breathes loyalty ".[38]

In short, almost the only way by which the Whigs could give vent to their feelings in the theatre, was to hiss whatever the Tories applauded.[39]

The Tories, on the other hand, had more than the privilege of hissing what the Whigs applauded ; the authors who upheld their point of view were on the stronger side, and had therefore complete freedom to air their opinions and attack their opponent's with no beating about the bush. They made full use of their

---

Courts in a Tragedy of mine, call'd *The Murder of Humphry Duke of Gloucester*, which pleas'd the best Men of *England*, but displeas'd the worst ; for e're it liv'd long, it was stifled by command." (Crowne, Dedication of *The English Frier*.)

[35] *Biographia Dramatica*, s.v. Spanish Fryar.

[36] See Shadwell's Preface. In the 1720 edition of his *Works* the excised passages are printed in italics. In one of them Sir Edward Hartford says to Smerk :
"You . . .
Foam at the mouth when a Dissenter's nam'd."

[37] Cibber, *Apology*, p. 200.

[38] See my Bibliography. " I fell upon the new-modelling of this Tragedy (as I had just before done on *The History of King Lear*) charmed with the many Beauties I discover'd in it . . . After this Account it will be askt why this Play shou'd be supprest, first in its own Name, and after in Disguise ? All that I can answer to this is, That it was *Silenc'd on the Third Day* . . . Every scene is full of Respect to Majesty, and the dignity of Courts, not one alter'd Page but what breathes Loyalty ; yet had this Play the hard fortune to receive its Prohibition from Court."

[39] . " That he shall know both Parties, now he Glories ;
By Hisses th' Whiggs, and by their Claps the Tories."
(D'Urfey, Prologue to *Sir Barnaby Whigg*.)

" They themselves (the Whigs) owned openly, by their hissings that they were incensed at it (the play)." (Dryden, *The Vindication*, etc.)

opportunities. Their first move was more than ever to enliven their plays with floods of Royalist fervour. They had frequently in the past put warm professions of faith into the mouths of their characters; but now their passionate loyalty burst all bounds. In any and every context they dragged in such lines as

> . . . Learn here the greatest Tyrant
> Is to be chose before the least Rebellion.[40]

> . . . This Maxim still
> Shall be my Guide (*A Prince can do no ill !*)
> In spight of Slaves, his Genius let him trust;
> For Heav'n ne'er made a King, but made him just.[41]

D'Urfey's Sir Charles Kinglove is about to make a gift of £20,000 to Charles I. In ecstasy he adds: " Oh, did he want as many drops of blood from the dear Centre of my life, my heart, as he does pounds from my now happy Store, should I not freely bleed? Strong in my zeal beyond Mortality, with my own hands I'd crush the trembling Lump, until the Noble Loyal Debt was paid." [42]

Down even to the gallants of the comedies, hitherto accustomed to speeches of a very different sort, there was no character who did not feel an urge to utter similar sentiments. Mrs. Behn's comedy *The Roundheads* shows Loveless and Lady Lambert engaged in an amorous *tête-à-tête*. Lady Lambert chooses this moment—it is difficult to see why—to reveal a crown and sceptre lying on an adjacent table, whereupon Loveless cries:

> Have I been all this while
> So near the Sacred Reliques of my King! . . .
> —Hail Sacred Emblem of Great Majesty, . . .
> —'tis Sacrilege to dally where it is;
> A rude, a Sawcy Treason to approach it
> With an unbended knee; for Heav's [*sic*] sake, Madam,
> Let us not be profane in our Delights
> Either withdraw, or hide that Glorious Object.[43]

Frequent and vehement as such passages were, they were not sufficient to satisfy the public's raging appetite for politics.

---

[40] Crowne, *The Misery of Civil-War*, IV. [See also note 19 above. B. D.]
[41] Bankes, *Vertue Betray'd*. These are the last lines of the play, spoken by the king.
[42] *The Royalist*, V, 1.
[43] IV, 2. Lady Lambert is General Lambert's wife. Lady Cromwell and Lady Fleetwood are also among the Dramatis Personæ.

They were too vague, too general. More outspoken, more direct allusions to current events and people of the day, were needed. Tory authors spared no pains to supply them. Southerne devoted a whole play, *The Loyal Brother or the Persian Prince* to championing the Duke of York. In *The Duke of Guise* Dryden and Lee represented Charles II as Henri III of France, the Duke of York as King of Navarre and the Duke of Monmouth as Guise, and that there might be no mistake began their Prologue with the words " Our play's a parallel." Crowne's *City Politiques* brings on to stage Titus Oates and the venerable Whig lawyer, Maynard.[44] Dryden's opera *Albion and Albanius* is nothing but a long-winded glorification of Charles II and his successor with a violent satire on their enemies. For, as we can well believe, not the slightest chivalry was shown in any quarter towards the Whigs. They were lavishly treated to abuse and the grossest personal insults. It was the fashion to call them "fanatical rogues" and "seditious rascals",[45] and Puritan convictions were freely assumed to be synonymous with the most disreputable practices.[46] "I never knew a religious Fool", says Craffy in Crowne's *City Politiques*, "that was not a Rogue in my life."[47] "Damn the City," says another. "Damn all the Whigs, Charles, All the Whigs," is the reply.[48] The citizenry and their

[44] Maynard was more than eighty years old. When the Prince of Orange met him for the first time he said to him : " You must have survived all the lawyers of your standing."—" Yes, Sir," replied Maynard, " and, but for Your Highness, I should have survived the laws too." (Macaulay, *History*, chap. 10, vol. II, p. 576.) Under the name of *Bartoline* Crowne naturally made him into a corrupt old attorney and his wife—under the name of *Lucinda*—into a coquette. In the printed version of his play he even went so far as to reproduce Maynard's peculiarities of speech, for old age had not spared him all his teeth.—Titus Oates figured as *Dr. Paunchy*.

[45] D'Urfey's list of Dramatis Personæ in *Sir Barnaby Whigg* contains :

"*Wilding*—A Loyal and Witty Gentleman, only addicted to rail against Women."
"*Sir Barnaby Whigg*—a Phanatical Rascal."

In *The Royalist* D'Urfey describes Captain Jonas as " A Seditious Rascal that disturbs the People with News and Lyes to promote his own Interest ".

[46] Mrs. Behn's *City-Heiress* contains, amongst other characters, one, Mrs. Clacket, " A City-Bawd and Puritan ".

[47] I, 1.

[48] "*Closet*. The City, you know, Sir, is so censorious . . .
Sir Charles Meriwell. Damn the City.
Sir Anthony Meriwell. All the Whigs, *Charles*, all the Whigs."
(Mrs. Behn, *The City-Heiress*, IV.)

officials were grossly ridiculed. The rôles of betrayed husbands and self-important fools were reserved exclusively for them. Tate named one of his plays *Cuckolds-Haven or, an Alderman No Conjuror*. In *The London Cuckolds* Ravenscroft introduces two aldermen under the names of Doodle and Wiseacre. Accusing Anne Boleyn of adultery, Henry VIII—in one of Bankes's tragedies—exclaims :

> I have more Horns than any Forrest yields,
> Than *Finsbury*, or all the City musters
> Upon a Training, or a Lord Mayor's day.[49]

The fiercest of the attacks was directed against Shaftesbury, the leader of the Whig party. He was the chief target for jest and abuse. Playing on his name, the Tories called him " Shiftsbury " because of his changes of front.[50] Preachers alluded to him as Mephistopheles or The Demon,[51] Southerne represented him as a sort of political Iago under the name of Ishmael in his *Loyal Brother*; Otway pilloried him in *Venice Preserv'd* as an imbecile old senator bearing the suggestive name of Antonio (Shaftesbury's Christian name was Anthony),[52] and since, despite his sixty years, he was reputed somewhat over-fond of women,[53] the poet devoted a long scene to showing him playing the lapdog to amuse his mistress, barking, biting, yelping, only to be rewarded for his pains by kicks and whippings.[54] Vulgarity went further, publicly alluding to his physical disabilities. He had had a serious fall from a carriage which resulted in an accumulation of fluid that the doctors sought to remedy by

[49] *Vertue Betray'd*, IV.
[50] North, *Examen*, p. 42.
[51] B. Martyn and Dr. Kippis, *The Life of the First Earl of Shaftesbury*, vol. II, p. 285.
[52] The Dramatis Personæ include " Antonio, a fine speaker in the Senate ".

[53]
> " Next is a Senatour that keeps a Whore,
> In *Venice* none a higher office bore :
> To lewdness every night the Letcher ran,
> Shew me, all *London*, such another man,
> Match him at Mother *Creswold* if you can.
> Oh *Poland, Poland*! had it been thy lot
> T'have heard in time of this Venetian Plot,
> Thou surely chosen hadst one king from thence
> And honour'd them as thou hast *England* since."
> (Prologue to *Venice Preserv'd*.) See also note 57 below.

[54] III, 1.

adjusting to his side a silver tap.[55] Party venom eagerly seized on this subject for jesting. A newly-invented wine-jar with a turn-cock was baptized a *Shaftesbury* and installed in the royal taverns.[56] A rumour ran that before the election of John Sobieski Poland had offered the crown to Shaftesbury, who was hence nicknamed *Tapski* or *Potapski*.[57] The theatre did not scorn to exploit these unsavoury jests. In the Prologue to *Cuckolds-Haven* Tate speaks of " Treason's Tap ".[58] Dryden introduces into his opera *Albion and Albanius*, " a Man with a long, lean, pale face, with fiend's wings, and snakes twisted round his body ; he is encompassed by several fanatical rebellious heads, who suck poison from him, which runs out of a tap in his side ".[59]

While tragedies, comedies and operas fought the enemies of the Court with any weapon they could lay hands on, prologues and epilogues carried on a guerrilla warfare in detail. The most trifling incidents and day-to-day happenings of current politics were brought down on the wing. In 1681 Shaftesbury was accused of treason before the Grand Jury ; but this Jury, appointed by the City Magistrates, was composed of Whigs. They refused to find him guilty and brought in a verdict of *Ignoramus*. Prologues and epilogues were forthwith filled with

---

[55] *Biographia Britannica*, s.v. Cooper (Anthony Ashley).—Walter Scott, *A Collection of Scarce and Valuable Tracts* . . . vol. VIII, p. 315, note.

[56] Dryden, *Works*, edited by Scott and Saintsbury, VII, p. 282, note.

[57] " A modest Vindication of the Earl of Shaftesbury : In a Letter to a Friend concerning his being elected king of Poland." (Walter Scott, *A Collection of Scarce and Valuable Tracts* . . . VIII, p. 313.)—The British Museum possesses a Broadside called : *The Last Will and Testament of Anthony King of Poland*. From it I quote the following lines :

> " My Tap is run ; then *Baxter* tell me why
> Should not the *good*, the great *Potapskie* die ? . .
> Ye Mortal Whigs for Death prepare,
> For mighty *Tapski's Guts* lie here.
> Will his great Name keep Sweet, d'y'think !
> For certainly his Entrals stink . . ."
> See my Bibliography, s.v. *Anthony*.

[58] And at the end of Act III :

> " The very dregs of Treason's Tap are out."

[59] " In the Piss and the Spew the poor Cooper did paddle,
To stop up his Tap, but the Knave was not able . . ."
(*The Wine-Cooper's Delight*. See my Bibliography, s.v. *Wine-Cooper*.)

thrusts at the *Ignoramus* verdicts of juries.[60] To avenge himself for this acquittal, the King declared the City's privileges forfeit and set over it new Sheriffs and a new Lord Mayor. Having thus, so to speak, tasted blood, he started a campaign against the Municipal Charters of every town suspected of Whig sympathies [61]; then it was the Sheriffs' turn to submit to cross-examination.[62] During the excitement caused by the Exclusion Bill, Charles II had thought it wise to despatch his brother to Scotland in a sort of diplomatic exile. The Duke returned to London for a momentary stay in 1680 while Parliament was prorogued. Otway's Prologue to *The Orphan* greeted him as he passed through. He was gone again before the end of the year and the Epilogue to *The Royalist* reminded the audience of " the Gentleman in Scotland ".[63] In 1682 he came back to London

[60] " What in my face cou'd this strange Scribler see,
(Uds Heart) to make an *Evidence* of me?
That never cou'd agree with *Ignoramus*,
But for a *Tender Conscience* have been famous."
(D'Urfey, *The Royalist*, Epilogue.)

" Pay Juries that no formal Laws may harm us
Let Treason be secur'd by *Ignoramus*."
(Mrs. Behn, *The Roundheads*, Prologue.)

" But what provok'd the Poet to this Fury,
Perhaps he's piqu'd at by the *Ignoramus* Jury . . ."
(Ravenscroft, *The London Cuckolds*, Epilogue.)

" But, Friends, don't think that you shall longer Sham us,
Or that we'll Bugbear'd be by your *Mandamus*;
You see Dame *Dobsons* Devil long was famous,
But fail'd at last; so will your *Ignoramus*."
(Ravenscroft, *Dame Dobson*, Epilogue.)

" And then in *Ignoramus Holes* they think,
Like other Vermin, to lie close, and stink."
(Anon., *Romulus and Hersilia*, Prologue.)

[61] Cooke, *History of Party*, I, p. 223 ff.

[62] " Now I dare swear, some of you *Whigsters* say
Come on, now for a swinging Tory Play.
But, Noble *Whigs*, pray let not those *Fears* start ye,
Nor fright hence any of the *Sham Sheriffs Party*;
For, if you'l take my censure of the story,
It is as harmless as e're came before ye,
And writ before the times of Whig and Tory."
(Anon., *Romulus and Hersilia*, Prologue.)

The Prologue Dryden wrote for the King and Queen on the union of the two theatres expresses the wish that " Whig poets and Whig sheriffs may hang together ".

[63] " For who are these among you here that have
Not in your Rambles heard of *Tory Cave*;
That rores in Coffee-house, and wasts his Wealth,
Toping the Gentleman in *Scotland's* Health."
(D'Urfey, *The Royalist*, Epilogue.)

for good. Dryden forthwith composed a prologue [64] and Otway an epilogue [65] to celebrate his return; and Otway added to his epilogue an epistle to the Duchess.[66] About the same time the Duke of York's portrait at Guildhall was slashed by an unknown hand; Otway castigated as a " rascal " the " vermin " who had dared to deface this sacred countenance. In 1684 the Court had temporarily triumphed over its enemies, and prologues and epilogues shared in the rejoicing.[67] In 1685 the Duke of York became King James II; the poets lost no time in chanting the long years of prosperity he promised to his people.[68] The same year saw Monmouth's ill-advised insurrection and D'Urfey armed with a scythe the actor who spoke the prologue to his *Common-Wealth of Women*, for scythes were the weapons carried by many partisans of the Protestant Duke.[69]

[64]
[65] } See my Bibliography.

[66] *Works*, III, p. 368.

[67]   " Now would you have me rail, swell and look big,
Like rampant Tory over couchant *Whig*,
As spit-fire Bullies swagger, swear and roar,
And brandish Bilbo, when the Fray is o're,
Must we huff on when we're oppos'd by none? "
            (Prologue intended for (Rochester's) *Valentinian*
              to be spoken by *Mrs*. Barrey.)

" Since the *Whig-Tyde* runs out, the *Loyal* flows.
All you who lately here presum'd to bawl,
Take warning from your Brethren at *Guild-Hall*;
The *Spirit of Rebellion* there is quell'd ...
Impartial *Justice* has resum'd agen
Her awful Seat, nor bears the Sword in vain."
            (Epilogue to Otway's *Atheist*, by Mr. Duke of
              Cambridge.)

[68]   " How greatly Heaven has our great Loss supplyed?
'Tis no small Vertue heales a Wound so wide ...
Verse is too narrow for so Great a name,
Far sounding Seas hourly repeat His Fame.
Our Neighbours vanquished Fleets oft wafted o're
His Name to theirs, and many a trembling Shore;
And we may go, by His great Conduct led
As far in Fame as our Forefathers did ...
These are not all the blessings of this Isle,
Heaven on our Nation in a Queen does smile,
Whose Vertue's Grace by Beauty shines so bright ..."
            (Crowne, *Sir Courtly Nice*, Prologue.)

See also the Epilogue to Dryden's *Albion and Albanius*.

[69] Prologue, Spoken by Mr. *Hains* with a Western Scyth in his Hand:
  " From the *West* as Champion in defence of Wit,
   I come to mow you Critticks of the Pit ...

It would be easy to multiply these quotations, for such allusions abound. It is safe to say that if all other historic documents relating to this stormy period were to be lost, it would almost be possible to reconstruct it in minute detail by consulting the prologues and epilogues to which it gave birth.

II

Decadence of Drama.—Newspapers.—The Coffee House ; The Newsletter ; The Pulpit

Despite the fervour it displayed, and the zeal with which it sought to increase its influence, the theatre could not meet the new demands of the time. First, it was going out of fashion. The public had lost their keenness and become less diligent in their attendance, so much so that the King's and the Duke's Companies had been compelled for lack of spectators to unite their threatened interests in one single royal company in 1682.[70] This decline of the theatre was in the natural course of things. It had been exploited and misused to such a degree that it could not possibly maintain its first brilliance. For twenty years the theatre had been everything. It had exhausted all its resources in order to allure its audiences ; theatre-goers had become blasé, and pampered to saturation-point ; and there were no novel attractions left to offer them.

Secondly, political crises supervened, fatally competing with the theatre in interest. Political sympathies diverged too often for authors to be tempted to write, or directors at vast expense to produce, plays in several acts, which the public were not always in the mood to enjoy or which they listened to with divided attention.[71] Thus, just as Dryden's *Albion and Albanius*—an

>   This Godly Weapon first invented was
>   By Whigs to cut down Monarchy like Grass ;
>   But I know better how to use these Tools,
>   And have reserv'd my Scythe to mow down Fools."

[70] Downes, *Roscius Anglicanus*, p. 39.—Cibber, *Apology*, pp. 57, 58. Cibber is mistaken in dating the union of the two companies 1684.
   [Recent histories, giving accurate detail, may be found in Allardyce Nicoll's *Restoration Drama*, which prints many of the relevant documents, and Montague Summers's *The Playhouse of Pepys*. See also Doran, *His Majesty's Servants*. B. D.]
[71]   " And what can Players hope for, in these Days,
   When e'r the Idle Youth forsake our Plays ?
   The empty Head that never thought before
   But on New fashions, or a fresh new Whore : . . .

opera in verse produced with an amazing and reckless use of music, scenery and costumes—appeared on the stage the news reached London that the Duke of Monmouth had landed at Lyme Regis, laying claim to the throne. It can easily be imagined that the public was more deeply stirred by this invasion than by the adventures of Dryden's heroes, and this new work, on which both the poet and the theatre had built great hopes, was given only six performances in all.[72] But the radical reason for the theatre's receding into the background was that it was a poor instrument for polemics, and polemics now absorbed every man's attention. The original Puritans who formed the backbone of the Whig party, eschewed the theatre and not even plays upholding their point of view could lure them into it. As Shadwell put it :

> Our Popes and Fryars on one Side offend,
> And yet alass the City's not our Friend :
> The City neither likes us nor our Wit,
> They say their wives learn ogling in the Pit ;
> They'r from the Boxes taught to make Advances,
> To answer stolen sighs and naughty glances . . .[73]

The theatre therefore could exercise no influence on the Whigs of the City, and the only thing political plays could hope to do, was to strengthen the Tories in opinions of which they were long since the champions : too slight a reward for too much toil. It was useless to continue the struggle on these lines. It was absolutely necessary to discover another weapon to seek out the elusive foe, to attack him in his lair, above all to reason with him. Each new occurrence, each principle enunciated, each

---

> For News he now walks gravely up and down,
> And every Fop's a Politician grown."
>   (Shadwell, Prologue to *The Woman-Captain*.)

"I cannot easily excuse the printing of a play at so unseasonable a time, when the great plot of the nation, like one of Pharaoh's lean kine, has devoured its younger brethren of the stage."
                    (Dryden, Dedication of the *Kind Keeper*.)

[72] "This being perform'd on a very Unlucky Day, being the Day the *Duke of Monmouth*, Landed in the *West* : The Nation being in a great Consternation, it was perform'd but Six times, which not answering half the Charge they were at, Involv'd the Company very much in debt." (Downes, *Roscius Anglicanus*, p. 40.) Malone says (*Life of Dryden*, p. 186) that if tradition is to be believed the audience withdrew in disorder at the sixth performance and the play was never acted again.

[73] See chap. I, note No. 205, above.

emergent personality, must be discussed with the opponent and with the drifting crowd of waverers—always so important a factor in politics. These are tasks which the theatre can rarely at any time satisfactorily perform, and in which it is bound utterly to fail when auditors are absent, especially those very auditors on whose conversion an author's heart is set.

Nowadays this business of discussion and polemics is handled by the Press. But in the England of those days the Press was embryonic. The first known publications with any resemblance to newspapers were scarcely more than fifty years old.[74] From 1619 onwards [75] modest little pamphlets, not too well printed, had begun to appear, which undertook to supply the curious with news of foreign countries.[76] These news reports were like the famous newspaper of Jérôme Paturot [76a]: they appeared "sometimes". Most of them probably consisted of the one issue only. Where they had a longer life, their name seems to have varied with each new appearance.

The first English journal which aimed at being a regular periodical would seem to have appeared on the 23rd of May 1622 : *Weekely Newes from Italy, Germanie, Hvngaria, Bohemia, the Palatinate, France and the Low Countries*, printed, as the title indicates, once a week. With constant changes of name and publisher it

---

[74] For a long time *The English Mercurie* dated 1588 was quoted as the first English newspaper, but in 1839 a remarkable letter from Thomas Watts of the British Museum to Antonio Panizzi, the then Keeper of the Printed Books, conclusively proved that this ancient newspaper was a fake.—See my Bibliography, s.v. Watts.

[75] The British Museum Catalogue of English newspapers begins with 1604. But prior to 1619 I can find nothing save papers relating to affairs of State, royal proclamations officially published with the superscriptions : " Set forth by Authoritie " or " Commanded by his Maiestie to be published in Print ", and usually printed by the King's Printer. These are political documents, not newspapers.

[76] Such are : *Newes out of* Holland : Concerning Barnevelt . . . London : Printed by T. S. for Nathanael Newbery . . . 1619 (British Museum). It consists of 28 small quarto pages including the title. Twelve of these are devoted to France and the Duke of Épernon.—Newes from Poland . . . Published by Authority . . . *At London* 1621. (British Museum)—*Newes from France* . . . Translated according to the French Copie, *printed at Paris. London* . . . 1621 (British Museum).

[76a] [Jérôme Paturot was a character invented by Louis Reybaud in the forties of the last century as a vehicle for political satire in very amusing novels. Paturot became a sort of legendary hero, after the manner of Tartarin, but at the beginning of this century died out as a familiar reference. Paturot was very up to date, and offered his regular subscribers, on their first subscription, the choice of a pair of boots, an overcoat, or a leg of mutton. B. D.]

struggled on haltingly to 1640.[77] Whether intermittent or recurrent, all these newspapers—if we can already use the word—had one characteristic in common : they invariably confined themselves to foreign news, and were content to print their information dryly, without comment or discussion.

With the Long Parliament and the Civil War, political leaflets quickly increased in number and vigour. From 1640 to the execution of Charles I in 1649, more than a hundred seem to have appeared with different titles, and more than another eighty between 1649 and the Restoration.[78]

Every event, in a period when events followed each other thick and fast, found everywhere and immediately its chronicler. One gave news of Great Britain, another of Ireland, Scotland or Wales. There were " Certain Informations from Severall Places ".[79] This, told people what was happening in Oxford;

[77] " *Translated out of the Low Dutch Copie London*, Printed by I. D. for *Nisholas Bourne* and *Thomas Archer* . . ." 1622 (British Museum). On September 25, 1622, Nathaniel Butter and William Sheffard offered for sale : "Newes from most parts of Christendome " ; then we find Butter joining Bourne to publish " A True Relation of the Affaires of *Europe* (Oct. 4, 1622)." Butter and Bartholomew Downes published on October 15, 1622, " A Continuation of the Affaires of the Low-Countries, and the Palatinate ". Endorsements like the following are frequent : " The Continuation of our Former Newes ", " The Continuation of our Forraine Avisoes ", " The Continuation of the Forraine Occurrents, for 5 weekes last past ", or sometimes the title " The Weekely Newes Continued ". From the format and the names of the publishers—Bourne, Archer, Butter, Downes and Sheffard —it is clear that we are dealing with one and the same journal throughout.

[78] George Chalmers, *The Life of Thomas Ruddiman*, 114, note *m*. This work (pp. 404-42) contains a chronological list of newspapers that had appeared after the Civil War.—See also Andrews, chaps. III to VI.

[79] " *Mercurius Britannicus* : Communicating the affairs of Great Britaine . . 1643 " (British Museum).

" The Victorious proceedings of the Protestants in Ireland ; from the beginning of *March* to this present, being the 22. of the same month . . . Printed at London for *John Wright*, in the Old-baily. 1642 " (British Museum).

" *Aprill the first*, 1642. A Continuation of the Tryumphant and Couragious proceedings of the Protestant Army in *Ireland* . . . London Printed for John Wright, 1642 " (British Museum).

" The late Proceedings of the Scotish Army . . . 1644 " (British Museum).

" The Scotish Dove Sent out and Returning . . . April 1646 Num. 129." (British Museum).

" The Welch Mercury . . . 1643 " (British Museum).

" Speciall Passages And certain Informations from severall places, Collected for the use of all that desire to bee truely Informed . . . 1642 " (British Museum).—I give the dates of the earliest issues I have been able to find.

that, what was being done at Westminster; a third reported what was going on at Court.[80] Similarly each point of view, each tendency, found its champion. On every side there was an outburst of Mercurys of every colour : Mercurius-Civicus, Philo-Monarchicus, Morbicus, Medicus, Bellicus, Pacificus, Problematicus, Veridicus, Candidus, Elencticus, etc.[81] There was even a Mercury giving news of Hell.[82] *The Laughing Mercury* gave " genuine news " of the moon and the antipodes.[83] The Newsbooks, as they were then called, were born—and died, for most were fairly short-lived—with astounding rapidity.

Each new publication immediately provoked one or more hostile retorts : *Mercurius Impartialis* attacked *Mercurius Militaris* [84] ; *Mercurius Aquaticus* replied " to all that hath or shall

---

[80] " Numb. 1. *Mercurius Academicus* : Communicating the Intelligence and Affairs of Oxford ... April 1648 " (British Museum).
" The Spie : Communicating Intelligence from Oxford " (1643 ?) (British Museum).
" *Mercurius Melancholicus* ; or, Newes from Westminster and other parts ... 1647 " (British Museum).
" *Mercurius Aulicus*, A Diurnall, Communicating the Intelligence and Affaires of the Court to the rest of the *Kingdome*. Oxford ... (date added by hand) 1642/43 " (British Museum). The *Mercurius Aulicus* was edited by Sir John Birkenhead.
[81] " *Mercurius Civicus* ... 1643 " ; " *Mercurius Philo-Monarchicus* May 1649 ; " " *Mercurius Morbicus* ... 1647 " ; " *Mercurius Medicus* ... 1647 " ; *Mercurius Bellicus* ... 1647 " ; " *Mercurius Pacificus* ... 1648 " ; " A new Mercury. Called *Mercurius Problematicus* ... 1644 " ; " *Mercurius Veridicus* ... 1646 ; " " *Mercurius Candidus* 1646 " ; " *Mercurius Elencticus* ... 1647." All these are in the British Museum.—Amidst this flood of Mercurys, some had difficulty in finding a name. Witness the following title :

> " 17 Jan, 1643. Mercurius, etc. [*sic*]
> Upon my life new borne, and wants a Name,
> Troth let the Reader then impose the same
> Veridicus—I wish thee ; if not so
> bee—Mutus—for wee Lyes enough doe know."
> (British Museum.)

[82] " *Mercurius Diabolicus, Or Hells Intelligencer* ... 1647 " (British Museum).
[83] " The Laughing Mercury, *or a True and Perfect Nocturnall, Communicating many strange Wonders,* Out of the World in the Moon, *The Antipodes, Maggy-land, Tenebris, Fary-land, Green-land,* and other adjacent Countries. Published for the right understanding of all the Mad-merry-People of *Great-Bedlam. From* Wednes day *Octob.* 27 to *Wednes.* Novem. 3. 1652 Numb. 30 " (British Museum).
[84] " *Mercurius Impartialis* : or, An Answer to that Treasonable Pamphlet *Mercurius Militaris*, ... from Tuesday *December* 5 till Tuesday December 12, 1648 " (British Museum).—" Numb. 1. Mercurius Militaris : ... Beginning on *Tuesday, October* 10, 1648 " (British Museum).

be writ" by *Mercurius Britannicus*[85]; *Mercurius Pragmaticus* was countered by *Mercurius Anti-Pragmaticus*,[86] *Mercurius Melancholicus* by *Mercurius Anti-Melancholicus*.[87] If a *Weekly Discoverer* came out, another paper forthwith undertook to "strip it naked" for its readers.[88] There was even a Mercury which threw down the gauntlet to all its brethren at once, under the name of *Mercurius Anti-Mercurius*.[89] Without even troubling to seek a different designation, one publicist would often simply lift his opponent's title, thus catching the eye of the other's habitual readers. And we not infrequently come across two copies of the same paper in the same format, bearing the same date and the same printer's name, in short, identical in every way except that the two sets of news they bring are entirely contradictory and that the persons lauded by the one are violently attacked by the other.[90]

In addition to these papers, a host of pamphlets and leaflets which seem to have been read no less widely and with equal gusto debated political and religious questions. The Library of the British Museum possesses a collection [91] of these pamphlets published between 1640 and 1660 containing no less than 30,000 specimens, which works out to an average of four or five per day. And collections of this kind are always and inevitably incomplete.

But all this publishing did not yet amount to a "Press". Though passions ran high, though people thirsted after news,

[85] "*Mercurius Aquaticus*, or, the Water-Poets Answer to all that hath or shallbe Writ by *Mercurius Britannicus*. Ex omni ligno non fit Mercurius. Printed in the Waine of the Moone *Pag.* 121, *and Number* 16 *of* Mercurius Britannicus, 1643" (British Museum).

[86] "Num 1 *Mercurius* Pragmaticus.—Communicating Intelligence from all Parts, touching all Affaires, Designes, Humours, and Conditions throughout the Kingdome. Especially from *Westminster* and the *Head-Quarters*. From Tuesday *Septem.* 14, to Tuesday *Septem.* 21, 1647" (British Museum). "Num. 1. *Mercurius* Anti-Pragmaticus. Communicating some remarkable Intelligence. From Tuesday *Oct.* 12 to Tuesday *Oct.* 19, 1647" (British Museum).

[87] "*Mercurius Melancholicus* . . . 1647", First No. Sept. 14 (British Museum). "Mercurius Anti-Melancholicus . . . 1647", First No. Sept. 18 (British Museum). Note that the reply was prompt.

[88] *The Weeckly Discoverer* and *The Discoverer stript Naked*. These titles are quoted by Disraeli, *Curiosities of Literature*, Origin of Newspapers.

[89] "Numb. 1 *Mercurius Anti-Mercurius*. Impartially Communicating Truth, correcting falshood . . . Sept. 1648" (British Museum).

[90] Johnson, *Lives of the English Poets*, Addison.—See also *The Athenæum*, 1858, No. 1594, p. 620.

[91] This Collection goes by the name of *The King's Pamphlets* because it was offered to the Museum by George III. It would more justly be described as the *Thomason Collection* after the indefatigable London bookseller to whose zeal we owe it. See *The English Cyclopaedia*. London, 1859, s.v. British Museum. This article was written by Mr. Thomas Watts.

news still reached them in wholly irregular fashion and never daily. At first the News-books appeared at most once a week. Even when the war grew more lively, and impatient readers would not be kept so long waiting, none was published oftener than twice or thrice a week. Notice also that they continued to be very modest, badly-printed pamphlets, that the news was always dry and scanty and that even when comment began to find a place—as yet a very small place—it was, in accordance with the mood of the day, of the most violent character, usually taking the form of invective.[92]

The Restoration sharply put a full stop to such discussion as there had been. The Press, already subjected to a censorship by the Long Parliament,[93] was ridden on a very tight rein by Charles II's government.[94] Nothing was printed without a permit from the Licenser who allowed none but carefully sifted news to reach the public. To ensure the quality of this news, government set up newspapers of its own. Thus in December 1661 there appeared *The Kingdom's Intelligencer* " to prevent false news "[95]; then in January 1662, *Mercurius Publicus*, also " to prevent false news "[96]; in 1663 *The Intelligencer* and *The Newes*[97] both " published for the satisfaction and information of the people " ; and in 1665 the mouthpiece of the Court, the *Oxford Gazette*, later known as the *London Gazette*.[98]

No publications were tolerated alongside these privileged

[92] In his *Calamities and Quarrels of Authors*, Disraeli quotes some samples under the title *The Paper-Wars of the Civil Wars*.
[93] Decree of Sept. 30, 1647. See Cobbett, III, p. 780.
[94] See chap. I, note No. 402 above.
[95] " Numb. 2. The Kingdom's Intelligencer of the Affairs now in agitation in *England, Scotland* and *Ireland* ; Together with forrain Intelligence ; *To prevent false Newes*. Published by Authority. From Monday, *January* 5 to Monday *January* 12, 1662 " (British Museum).
[96] " Number 1. *Mercurius Publicus, Comprising* The Sum of all Affairs now in agitation in *England, Scotland* and *Ireland*, Together with Foreign Intelligence ; for Information of the People, and to prevent false News. *Published by Authority. From* Thursday *February* 28 to Thursday *March* 7, 1661 " (British Museum).
[97] " Numb. 1. The Intelligencer ; Published *For the Satisfaction and Information of the People. With Privilege. Monday* August 3, 1663 " (British Museum) ;—" Numb. 1. The Newes, Published *For Satisfaction and Information* of the People. *With* Privilege. Thursday September 3, 1663 " (British Museum).
[98] It was first called the *Oxford Gazette* because the Court had fled to Oxford during the London Plague (*Biog. Brit.*, s.v. L'Estrange).—" Numb. 1. The Oxford Gazette. Published by Authority Nov. 7. 1665 " (British Museum).—" Numb. 24. The London Gazette. *Published by Authority.* From Thursday, *February* 1, to Monday February 5, 1665 " [o.s.] (British Museum).

newspapers, except sensational gossip-mongerings or fantastic nonsense. A few sample titles will sufficiently indicate the contents and the value of these latter : " Bloody News from Chelmsford : or, A Proper New Ballad, containing A true and perfect Relation of a most barbarous Murther committed upon the Body of a Country Parson who died of a great Wound given him in the Bottom of the Belly, by a most Cruel Country-Butcher for being too familiar with his Wife "[99] : For which Fact he is to be tried for his Life at this next Assizes. Oxford. Printed in the Year MDCLXIII " ; or in another vein : " Magnifico Smokentissimo Custardissimo Astrologissimo Cunningmanissimo Rabinissimo Viro Iacko Adams de Clarkenwell Greeno Lanc lovelissimam sui Picturam Hobbedeboody pinxit et scratchabat "[100] ; or again : " The Man in the Moon, Discovering a World of Knavery under the Sun, with a perfect *Nocturnal*, containing several strange Wonders out of the *Antipodes, Magyland, Faryland, Greenland, Tenebris*, and other parts adjacent. *Published for the right-understanding of all the mad-merry-people in* Great Bedlam. 1663 "[101] ; or again : " The Infallible Mountebank or Quack Doctor, 1670 " ; " The Extravagant Prentices with their Lasses at a Taverne Frollick, 1672 "[102] ; " The London Prodigal "[103] ; " A Strange Wonder in Wiltshire, Affirmed by Three Ministers that were Eye-Witnesses of this following Relation "[104] ; " Flos Ingenii vel Evacuatio Descriptionis, Being an Exact Description of Epsam and Epsam Wells "[105] ; " Clod-pate's Ghost : or a Dialogue Between *Justice Clod-Pate*, and his (*quondam*) Clerk Honest *Tom Ticklefoot* ; Wherein *is faithfully related all the News* from Purgatory *about* Ireland, Langhorn, etc.".[106] " New News of a Strange Monster found in Stow Woods near Buckingham, of *Human Shape*, with a Double Heart, and no Hands ; a Head with two Tongues, and no Brains "[107]—and so forth.

[99] British Museum, Luttrell Collection, vol. II, No. 144.
[100] Stephens, *Catalogue*, I, No. 1018. [101] British Museum.
[102] Stephens, *Catalogue*, I, Nos. 1032 and 1043.
[103] ". . . Or the Unfortunate Spendthrift " . . . London . . . 1673 (British Museum, Luttrell Collection, vol. II, No. 131).
[104] 1674 (ibid., No. 245). For other similar titles see Andrews, I, pp. 79, 80.
[105] "*London* Printed in the year 1674. folio." British Museum : 816, m. 19/40).—See my Bibliography, s.v. Flos.
[106] "August 25, 1679. folio." (ibid., 816, m. 19/43).—See my Bibliography, s.v. Clod-pate.
[107] 1699 (Luttrell Collection, vol. III, No. 7).
[These are ballads and broadsides rather than newspapers in any accepted sense of the word. B. D.]

It is true that the censorship no longer existed at the date which we have now reached. The Licensing Act, passed shortly after the Restoration, had expired in 1679, and had not been renewed. Every Englishman henceforward had the right to print whatever he wished—at his own risk and peril. But this new freedom was in a general way of little benefit to political discussion—because the carefully packed juries pitilessly condemned every piece of writing to which the government took exception [108]—and it was of no advantage at all to the newspapers. The judges declared unanimously that this freedom did not in fact extend to the " gazettes " [109] and that no one had the right to print political news without the King's permission, which permission the King granted only to the *London Gazette*. Nevertheless, amid the seething political passions aroused by the fights over the Exclusion Bill, and the acute tensions that were caused by the Popish Plot, some political leaflets contrived to appear—whether because the Crown judged it prudent to turn a blind eye, or because the zeal of the parties succeeded in eluding its vigilance. Among these were, for instance : *Domestick Intelligence* ; *The English Intelligencer* ; *The Friendly Intelligence* ; *The English Currant* ; *Poor Robins Intelligence* ; *The True News* ; *The Protestant (Domestick) Intelligence* ; *The True Domestick Intelligence*.[110]

[108] " Mr. Benjamin Harris . . . He sold a *Protestant Petition* in King *Charles's* Reign, for which they fin'd him, Five Hundred Pound, and set him once in the Pillory " (Dunton, *Life* . . . p. 293).—See also Andrews, chap. VI, and my Bibliography, s.v. Smith (Francis).—After the discovery of the Rye-House Plot (1683) censorship was *de facto* re-established and nothing unfavourable to the Court appeared except clandestinely. In July 1685 James II re-established the censorship *de jure*. The best proof of how little weight the Press carried at that date, is the fact that the censorship was reintroduced without the Tories dreaming of rejoicing or the Whigs of complaining (Macaulay, *History*, chap. V).
[109] Hallam, *Constitutional History* III, pp. 4–5.
[110] " Numb. 1. Domestick Intelligence, Or News both from City and Country. Published to prevent false reports. Monday July the 7th 1679 " ;— " The English Intelligencer. Thursday July 24. 1679. Num. 2 " ;—" The Friendly Intelligence. Published for the Accommodations of all sober persons. Munday, September 7th 1679. Numb. 1."—" The English Currant. Or, Advice Domestick and Forreign. Published for general Satisfaction. Monday, September 8, 1679 " ;—" Poor Robins Intelligence, Revived ; Published for the Accommodations of all Ingenious persons. Wednesday *November* the 26th 1679 " ;—" The True News : or, Mercurius Anglicus, Being the Weekly Occurrences Faithfully Transmitted. January 1679. Numb. 15 " ;— " The Protestant (Domestick) Intelligence ; or, News both from City and Country. Published to prevent false Reports. Fryday, *January* 16, 1679 Numb. 56 " ;—" The True Domestick Intelligence, *Or* News both from City and Country. Published to prevent false Reports. Feb. 1680 Numb. 69."
—All these papers are in the British Museum.

Some of these papers even introduced themselves with titles like echoes of the Civil War : *A Pacquet of Advice from Rome* ; *Mercurius Anglicus* ; *The True Protestant Mercury* ; *The Impartial Protestant Mercury* ; *Mercurius Civicus* ; *The London Mercury* ; *Mercurius Infernus* ; *Jesuita Vapulans* ; or, *A Whip for the Fool's Back and a Gag for his Foul Mouth*. There was even a revival of the *Weekly Discoverer* to which retorted, just as under the Republic, *The Weekly Discoverer, stript Naked*.[111]

At this critical moment Government thought it necessary to take an active part in the discussion and to find another medium than the *London Gazette* to convey sound, twenty-four-carat opinions to the public. The *Gazette* was certainly a poor instrument of propaganda. It appeared on Mondays and Thursdays only, on a single sheet like all its predecessors, and gave the scanty news which the Court thought fit, in the most laconic terms without comment of any kind. It is as if the French Government should hope to guide public opinion through *le Journal officiel* or *le Bulletin des lois*. A newspaper was therefore required to provide an orthodox commentary on the news published by the *Gazette*. The Court called its new paper *The Observator* [112] and summoned one, Roger L'Estrange,[113] a prolific and most devoted Royalist scribbler, to edit it.

During the Civil War, L'Estrange had fought in the ranks of the Royal Army. He was captured and condemned to death

[111] " Numb. 1. A Pacquet of Advice from Rome : or, The History of Popery. Begun to be Published on *Tuesday* the 3. of *December*, 1678. and thence to be continued " ; Edited by Henry Care ;—" Mercurius Anglicus : or, The Weekly Occurrences Faithfully Transmitted. Nov. 1679. Numb. 3 " ;—" Numb. 1. The True Protestant Mercury, or Occurrences *Forein* and *Domestick*. Beginning Tuesday the 28 Decemb. 1680 " ;—" Numb. 11. The Impartial Protestant Mercury, or Occurrences Foreign and Domestick. *May* 31. 1681 " ;—" Mercurius Civicus : or, a True Account of Affairs both Foreign and Domestick *Monday* 29 March, 1680, Numb. 3 " ;—" Num. 1, The London Mercury. London Thursday April 6. 1682." These papers are all in the British Museum except the four last, which are quoted by Andrews. I, pp. 73 and 80.

[112] " Numb. 1. The Observator. In *Question and Answer*. Wednesday April 13 1681." (British Museum and Bibliothèque Nationale : Nd. 85.) This paper appeared twice a week, on Wednesdays and Saturdays, occasionally three times, as in the week April 10–17, 1682. It consisted of a single sheet only. The opening of the first issue is a good indication of its aims :

" Q. Well ! They are so. But do you think to bring 'um to their Wits again with a *Pamphlet* ?
A. Come, come ; 'Tis the *Press* that has made 'um Mad, and the *Press* must set 'um Right again."

[113] On L'Estrange, see *Biographia Britannica*, and Stephens, *Catalogue*, I, No. 1083.

by the Parliamentarians, but escaped after four months' imprisonment. Later, people said, Cromwell had pardoned him and set him at liberty, thanks to his skill in playing the violin.[114] This did not prevent his noisily demanding at the Restoration, reward for his devotion to the good cause. Charles II was quick to notice him and gave him a confidential post : making him Licenser of the Press.[115] From this moment L'Estrange became the Court's literary maid-of-all-work—supervising and directing the Press, editing newspapers [116] and pro-Government pamphlets as required.[117] As an ever-ready writer he could not refuse to assume responsibility for the *Observator*. It must be admitted that he was not without a certain gift for brutal argument, and though his style is vulgar and pretentious it does not lack life and vigour. He placed at the service of the Tories all his pamphleteering skill and all the resources of a not over-scrupulous [118]

[114] The pamphlets of the day call him " Cromwell's Fiddler ". In a drawing of 1680 he is represented holding a violin and bow and wearing round his neck this inscription : " Touzer old Nol's Fidler " (Stephens, *Catalogue*, I, No. 1085. See also No. 1110). In volume III of the Luttrell Collection, No. 138, he figures as a dog called Towzer with a violin attached to his tail.

[115] L'Estrange had, so to speak, brought these duties on his own head by publishing in 1663 " Considerations and Proposals in Order to the Regulation of the Press : *Together* with Diverse *Instances of Treasonous*, and *Seditious Pamphlets*, Proving the *Necessity* thereof". See my Bibliography.

[116] Amongst others, *The Intelligencer* and *The Newes* already mentioned and *Heraclitus Ridens*.—" Numb. 1. Heraclitus Ridens : *Or*, A discourse between Jest and Earnest, where many a True Word is spoken in opposition to all Libellers against the Government . . . *Ridentem dicere verum Quis vetat* . . . Horat. *London*, Printed for the Use of the People, *Tuesday*, Feb. 1. 1681 " (Bibliothèque Nationale, No. 61, complete collection).

[117] See a long list of his writings in Watt and in *Biographia Britannica*.— L'Estrange is the *Sheva* of the second part of Dryden and Tate's *Absalom and Achitophel*:

> " Than Sheva, none more loyal Zeal have shown,
> Wakeful as *Judah*'s lion for the Crown,
> Who for that Cause still combats in his Age,
> For which his Youth with danger did engage,
> In vain our factious priests the Cant revive,
> In vain seditious Scribes with Libels strive
> T' enflame the Crowd, while He with watchful eye
> Observes, and shoots the Treasons as They fly :
> Their weekly frauds his keen replies detect ;
> He undeceives more fast than they infect.
> So *Moses*, when the pest on *Legions* prey'd,
> Advanc'd his Signal, and the Plague was stay'd."

[118] He wrote a pamphlet against Milton entitled *No blind Guides* (Johnson, *Lives of the English Poets*, Milton). Dunton held no very favourable opinion of L'Estrange. This is what he says of him (*Life* . . . p. 349) :

enthusiasm, and from 1681 to 1687 his paper passionately upheld all the views dear to the Tory heart.

All his zeal achieved little. In spite of every effort, the Press was not yet in a position to yield the results hoped of it. It did its best : to little purpose. There is no use running a political journal—unless someone reads it. Now the newspaper was still in its infancy and had few readers, for the newspaper habit was as yet no part of English daily life.[119] Its sphere of influence was therefore very limited, and it was not through newspapers that the general public could be reached.

Besides, public opinion flowed through other more important channels.

There were, first, in London the Coffee Houses. They were new to the city—the first dated from 1652—but they had quickly taken root and grown and multiplied with amazing rapidity. By the end of Charles II's reign, there was no class of society, and no profession, which had not its own Coffee House. In the City proper there was one for merchants ; society gentlemen had one near St. James's Park ; men of letters went to The Rose near Covent Garden—later known as Will's Coffee House, where Dryden had an armchair always reserved for him, in winter by the chimney-corner, in summer on the balcony.[120] The Coffee House had gradually come to play an important part in the Londoner's life. It was there that he met his friends, that he made business appointments, that he had his letters addressed, and that he often spent his evenings.[121]

When politics again came to the fore, the Coffee House was there, a ready-made focus for news. People dropped in as a

---

" A Man that betrays his Religion, and Country, in pretending to defend it . . . That was made Surveyor *of the Press*, and wou'd wink at unlicens'd Books, if the Printer's Wife would but———" [*sic*].

[119] Pepys, who talked of everything, mentions the words News-book or Gazette only two or three times in the whole course of his diary.

[120] In 1709 *The Tatler* is dating its articles from the various Coffee Houses according to the subject dealt with. Its first issue says : " *All Accounts of* Gallantry, Pleasure *and* Entertainment, *shall be under the Article of* White's Chocolate-House ; Poetry *under that of* Will's Coffee-house ; Learning *under the Title of* Graecian ; Foreign and Domestick News, *you will have* from St. James's Coffee-house." (Numb. 1.)

[121] " And we may judge the time as well spent there (at the Booksellers') as (in later days) either in Tavern or Coffee-House ; though the latter has carried off (after 1683) the spare hours of most people." (Roger North, *The Life of the Honourable and Reverend Dr. John North* a sequel to *The Life of the Honourable Sir Dudley North*.)—See how large a place the Coffee House takes in the life of Pepys.—Swift had his letters addressed to St. James's Coffee House (Journal to Stella, Oct. 14, 1710).

matter of course to read the News-books,[122] to gather the rumours that were going round, to hear the latest events of the day, to argue, to hammer out their own opinions. Politics ere long enjoyed pride of place. The Coffee House became a sort of small-scale Club [123] where people read newspapers and pamphlets aloud, or where impromptu orators held forth for or against Whigs or Tories. In all these places, views and opinions were poured forth with a freedom which the Press, supervised and spied upon as it was, could not know.[124]

So the Coffee House exercised a most important influence. Hitherto, people holding the same opinion were scattered here

[122] " Syrrop of Soot, or Essence of old Shooes,
Dasht with Diurnals, and the Books of News."
(A Cup of Coffee : or Coffee in its Colours, 1663.)
See my Bibliography, s.v. Coffee.

[123] " I' the Coffee house here one with a grave face
When after salute, he hath taken his place,
His Pipe being lighted begins for to prate
And wisely discourses the affairs of the state."
(A New Satyricall Ballad of the Licentiousness
of the Times . . . *London*, Printed in the
Year 1679. British Museum, Luttrell
Collection, vol. II, No. 116.)

"There's nothing done in all the World,
From *Monarch* to the *Mouse*
But Every Day or Night 'tis hurld
Into the *Coffe*-house . . .
You shall know there, what Fashions are ;
How Perrywigs are Curl'd
And for a Penny you shall heare,
All Novells in the World . . . "
(News from the Coffe-House ; . . . London
. . . 1667. With Alowance. British
Museum, Luttrell Collection, vol. II,
No. 145.)

" Each Coffee-house is fill'd with subtile Folk,
Who wisely talk, and politickly smoke."
(Shadwell, Prologue to *The Woman-Captain*.)

" *Bak'd* in a pan, *Brew'd* in a pot,
The third device of him who first begot
The Printing Libels, and the Powder-plot."
(A Satyr against Coffee. British Museum,
Roxburghe Collection, vol. III, No. 831.)

[124] On Coffee Houses, see Macaulay, *History*, chap. III.— The *Spectator*, No. 305, calls them " our *British* Schools of Politics ".

[For a good account, see Leslie Stephen's *English Literature and Society in the Eighteenth Century*. 1904. He puts the first appearance of the coffee house in 1657. B. D.]

and there. There existed, so to speak, only a multitude of individual opinions, isolated units who but rarely, and only in exceptional circumstances, could find an opportunity of meeting and forming a group. Nowadays, the newspapers link together in groups people sharing the same outlook and give these groups cohesion. But as we have just seen, the newspapers of the late seventeenth century were wholly unqualified to do this. What the newspaper could not compass, was achieved, at least in London, by the Coffee Houses. These eating-places provided rallying-points. People met, exchanged opinions, formed groups, gathered number.[125] It was through them, in short, that a public opinion began to evolve, which thereafter had to be reckoned with. The Government were so fully conscious of this that they began to feel uneasy and the Danby Government would fain have suppressed these hot-beds of political opinion. But the Coffee Houses had already become so indispensable to Londoners that the outcry was violent and general, and Government had to abandon the project.[126]

If London opinion was formed by coffee-house discussion, the provinces found a partial equivalent in a peculiar type of literature known as *Newsletters*, of which we must here take notice.

Outside the capital there were at this time no newspapers in England.[127] The post, as yet barely organized, brought London papers only after much delay,[128] and we already know that they were in any case miserly even of expurgated news.[129] Opposition papers led a precarious existence; of Government papers the *London Gazette* offered no comment, and the *Observator* ventured on discussion only with approval from above. Such a press was lenten fare to people hungry for news, far from the centre of affairs and happenings, and lacking the frank interchanges of

---

[125] Aubrey, quoted by Disraeli, *Curiosities of Literature*, vol. II, *Introduction of Tea, Coffee and Chocolate*, boasts " the modern advantage of coffee-houses in this great city, before which men knew not how to be acquainted except with their own relations and societies ".

[126] North, *Examen*, pp. 138–41.

[127] The first provincial paper was the *Mercurius Caledonicus* which was published in Edinburgh in 1660 and ran to ten issues. The second Edinburgh paper was *The Edinburgh Gazette* of 1699 (George Chalmers, *The Life of Thomas Ruddiman*, pp. 118, 119) :—See chap. I, note No. 402 above. Outside London no printing-press was authorized except at York and at the two universities. James II had this law re-enacted.

[128] On the post of those days, see Macaulay, *History*, chap. III.

[129] " Gazetts no News can tell." (*Clod-pate's Ghost*, already quoted, p. 158 above.)

the Coffee House. Provincial readers found compensation in the Newsletters. These were hand-written letters which important county people, the nobility, the upper middle classes, the clergy, the magistrates, the universities had despatched to them from London at least once a week.[130] There were people—ancestors of our " reporters "—who made a profession of writing Newsletters.[131] They went from Coffee House to Coffee House and to the Law Courts, they prowled about the Court and the City, their ears cocked to gather news and rumours. Fearless of the Censor's watchful eye—in this having the advantage of the newspapers,—they hastened to record everything in detail with their own personal comments in the letter which their provincial correspondent impatiently awaited, for during many long years people in the country had no other news from London.

Another important factor in the formation of public opinion remains to be mentioned : the pulpit. Though the clergy at the beginning of Charles II's reign had to so large an extent resigned themselves to playing a worldly and complaisant part, there were nevertheless among them men of high character who had kept alive the tradition of virtue and hard work : men like Jeremy Taylor, a survival from a preceding age, like Tillotson, Barrow, Stillingfleet, whose sermons and books bear witness to activity and zeal, and who had been able to maintain real and well-deserved influence over an important section of Church-people.[132] When religious and political questions came again to the fore, when the nation realized that despite the reaction against Puritanism it was still stoutly Protestant, the zeal and influence of such men increased, and when the clergy intervened

---

[130] I have handled a collection of these Newsletters, addressed between March 26, 1723 and December 31, 1730, to the Right Honourable Viscount Percivall. In the British Museum Catalogue of Manuscripts they bear the numbers " Additional 27,980 and 27,981 ". The first begins with this sentence which proves that we are dealing with a real manuscript newspaper : " In order to Inform our Readers with y*e* great Application, and Diligence of y*e* Ministry in y*e* Discovery of y*e* Plot, we shall insert . . . " These missives were written every second day on three large unsigned sheets and were conscientiously filled with political and general news including the winning numbers in the lottery.

[131] See in the *Spectator*, No. 625, a letter from one of these newsletter writers.—See also Aubrey, *Letters of Eminent Men*, I, p. 15, and North, *Examen*, p. 133.

[132] Barrow's works run to four folio volumes. Stillingfleet, whom we shall presently see at work, produced six folio volumes (Watt, *Bibliotheca Britannica*). Tillotson's sermons (the earliest dating from 1664) were bought in 1694 for 2,500 guineas (Macaulay, *History*, chap. XX).

in the struggle they proved themselves neither the least ardent nor the least effective of fighters. It goes without saying that the whole body of the clergy rallied to the side of the Tories.[133] First, the clergy formed an integral part of the royal establishment; secondly, their old enemies, the Dissenters, were in the popular camp; a double reason for their lending their support without chaffering to the Court party. Thus, when once battle was joined, Church preachers vied with each other in protestations of loyalty and in invectives against the Whigs.[134] Everywhere they preached passionately in favour of *passive obedience* and *non-resistance* to the King,[135] and expressed their horror of Dissenters and Republicans. We can imagine how great an effect such propaganda was bound to exercise on public opinion when repeated every Sunday in thousands of churches by a unanimous clergy. This effect was particularly strong in the provinces, in the little towns and villages where no newspaper or newsletter ever penetrated, where the clergyman was consequently the first to break the news of events to minds unprepared, telling them at the same time what they ought to think, with all the authority of words pronounced *ex cathedra*. The country clergyman thus wielded great influence over public opinion, and Macaulay has no hesitation in attributing to him a large share in the lively reaction against the Whigs which set in towards the end of Charles II's reign.[136]

This refers of course only to the clergy of the Church of England.[137] The Dissenters had no pulpits, and could preach only surreptitiously in their "conventicles", as their secret meetings were called. If they were caught, as Bunyan and Baxter allowed themselves to be, they were banished or thrown into prison.[138] But if oral preaching was for them attended

[133] There were, naturally some exceptions, like Burnet.
[134] We have already seen that they dubbed Shaftesbury "the Demon" and "Mephistopheles".—They drank to the health of the Duke of York with cheers and cries of "to the confusion of all his enemies!" (Burnet, *History of my Own Times*, I, p. 509, suppressed passage restored.)
[135] Rapin de Thoyras, vol. II, chap. XXIII.
[136] *History*, chap. II.
[137] We must except, however, the brief respites granted by Charles II's *Act of Indulgence* and the two *Declarations of Indulgence* of James II, April 4, 1687, and April 27, 1688.
[138] *Biographia Britannica*, s.vv. Bunyan and Baxter;—Macaulay, *History*, chap. II.—"I saw several poor creatures carried by, by constables, for being at a conventicle. They go like lambs, without any resistance. I would to God they would either conform, or be more wise, or not be catched" (Pepys, August 7, 1664).

with peril, the Dissenters still had the written word at their disposal, books and more especially little religious tracts : which are still amongst their favourite weapons. Bunyan continued his work even in prison, writing *The Pilgrim's Progress* in his cell. It will not be forgotten that the catalogue earlier quoted shows that half the writings published between 1666 and 1680 were separate sermons or tracts, the majority of which may safely be ascribed to the Dissenters, who were always distinguished by the tenacity with which they clung to their own views and the burning zeal with which they defended them. Howe, " the Puritan Plato ", wrote twenty-five books, three of them in two volumes ; Calamy and Owen, two other famous Nonconformists of the day, were the authors of thirty-five and over eighty works respectively, Baxter of more than a hundred and twenty.[139] A religious group possessing apostles like Bunyan and workers like Howe, Calamy, Owen and Baxter, could not—as long as they had the means of fighting—allow their opponents to be the only people to spread ideas. Compelled though they were to lie low, the Puritans had in fact never ceased to teach or to enlist recruits. The bookseller, John Dunton, who set up in London about 1680, counted over fifty Nonconformist ministers (Baxter amongst them) with whom he was in touch, and all of them were writers.[140] During the whole of the early part of Charles II's reign, while on the surface the Court indulged its merry gambollings, and the theatre and frivolous literature appeared to monopolize attention, there was evidently here an underground literature, so to speak, of which we get imperfect glimpses only,[141] but which must have been considerable and which, without noise and without rest, performed its slow and silent task. Not in vain. For there is no doubt that Puritan publications found readers in no negligible number. One fact alone would suffice

[139] See Watt and *Biographia Britannica*, s.vv. Howe & Calamy ; Allibone s.vv. Owen and Baxter.
[140] Dunton says of his patron : " Mr. Tho. Parkhurst (My Honoured Master) the most eminent Presbyterian Bookseller in the Three Kingdoms . . . He has printed more *Practical* books, than any other that can be named in *London* . . . I have known him sell off a whole Impression before the Book had been almost heard of in London " (*The Life and Errors*, etc., p. 281).
[141] Here are two titles which sufficiently indicate the Puritan view of the Restoration carnival ! " A just and seasonable reprehension of naked breasts and shoulders " (with a preface by Baxter).—" New instructions unto youth for their behaviour, and also a discourse upon some innovations of habits and dressing ; against powdering of hair, naked breasts, black spots (or patches) and other unseemly customs. 1672." (Quoted by Disraeli, *Anecdotes of Fashion* in *Curiosities of Literature*.)

to prove this : the Court ignored the very name of Bunyan, yet his *Pilgrim's Progress* which appeared in 1678, read by Puritans alone, ran through eight editions in four years, a success unheard of for any fashionable publication of the time.[142]

III

Political Literature under Charles II : Dryden's " Absalom and Achitophel " ; replies of Settle, Buckingham, Pordage, etc.—Dryden's poem " The Medal " ; replies of Hickeringhill, Pordage, Shadwell, etc.—Dryden's Mac Flecknoe.— " Absalom and Achitophel, Part II", by Nahum Tate and Dryden.— Dryden's " Religio Laici ".—Shadwell and Hunt's replies to Dryden and Lee's " Duke of Guise " ; Dryden's Vindication of " The Duke of Guise " ; Dryden's Translation of Maimbourg's " History of the League "

We now see how the land lay : writers devoted to the Court could not avoid joining in the battle of polemics, but the weapons in their ordinary arsenal were inadequate. Less than ever was the theatre equal to the task ; the newspaper had no appreciable influence. The factors that went to forming public opinion were too many and too complex for the budding Press, still working under restraint, to deal effectively with them all. The newspaper was no less impotent than the theatre to produce those great waves of opinion, those burning expressions of feeling which make a party conscious of its power, which compel opponents to waver, and waverers to think.

Yet something had to be done. The crisis caused by the Popish Plot and by the resurgence of anti-Romanism, was big with menace. Shaftesbury was a doughty champion ; the Duke of Monmouth, whom he had skilfully thrust into the foreground, was winning a disturbing popularity ; the Duke of Buckingham had lent the Whigs the prestige of his powerful name. Unless some means were found to turn the tide, who could foresee how many like deserters [142a] might swell the ranks of the City party,

---

[142] See my Bibliography.

[William Penn might be added to the list of prolific writers who were not members of the Church of England, and whose peculiar position at Court did not save him from imprisonment. In the seventies of the century he produced a spate of pamphlets, some very fat, such as *New Witnesses Prov'd Old Hereticks*, and was copiously answered by dissidents of opposed sects, such as Thomas Hicks, John Faldo, and John Perrot. B. D.]

[142a] [There had always been a group of powerful nobles determined not to be the King's pawns. They were not deserting the Court ; they, and not the King, were to be the Court as far as politics went, and very soon they were. Just as the King made use of French subsidies, so they used the financial power of the City. The Civil War had been fought to counter

how greatly its self-confidence might grow? Who could prophesy the result of the struggle now begun?

The King happily recalled that he possessed a Poet Laureate and begged him to come to the rescue.[143] For some time past the King had given Dryden little cause for gratitude. Charles, who now so opportunely bethought him of his poet, had ignored him during the most painful episodes of his struggle with Rochester. Temporarily sickened of the theatre by the Rochester affair, Dryden's thoughts were turning to epic poetry. He had confided this intention to the King and his brother, and had received fair words from them, but no largesse.[144] Perhaps it was at that very moment—whether because of Mulgrave's disgrace or because of an empty treasury—that the payment of his Laureate's salary had ceased.[145] Weary of struggle, he had detached himself from the Court and had written *The Spanish Fryar* against the Roman Catholics: a play highly distasteful to the Duke of York. But however great and well-founded his grievances, Dryden—like all his fellow-authors—was too much the courtier to resist a royal smile, and the King did not need to woo him over-long in order to obtain what he wanted.[146]

Since 1667, when he had addressed his *Annus Mirabilis* to the City of London, Dryden had given up writing poems or verses. The theatre was financially more profitable, and he had devoted himself entirely to the theatre. Now that the theatre was in eclipse and politics took the first place, he gladly took up verse again and with his political poem *Absalom and Achitophel*, he forthwith showed that the Court was well advised to remember him. For while Dryden unhappily pandered too slavishly and too completely to the taste of his time, he had the redeeming merit of carrying to perfection every literary style he attempted. We have seen him take the first place among the authors of

the arbitrary power of the King in finance, as much as in religious matters. Charles tried to neutralize the results of the Civil War, which were real enough, though seemingly cancelled by the Restoration. This struggle signalized the emergence of the Whig oligarchy which was to rule England for over a century. B. D.]

[143] See Tonson's Notice for the second part of *Absalom and Achitophel* in *Miscellany Poems*, 1716; and Spence, p. 172.
[144] *Discourse concerning... Satire*, dedicated to the Earl of Dorset.
[145] See chap. I, note No. 431.
[146] He very quickly recaptured the Duke's favour by amending *The Spanish Fryar* and writing a political Prologue " to His Royal Highness upon his first Appearance at the Duke's Theatre since his Return from Scotland, April 21, 1682 ".

heroic plays, of prologues, and of literary criticism. Once again he showed that he possessed the rare gift—by no means to be despised—of doing exactly what was wanted exactly when it was wanted, of planting, in fact, " the right thing in the right place at the right time ". Without models, without precursors, he created the political poem, and at the first attempt produced a masterpiece.

It would have been difficult to strike a note more perfectly in tune with the prevailing mood. The choice of an allegory was in itself a happy inspiration. Allegory challenges curiosity by its veil of mystery ; the puzzled reader tries to lift the veil, every discovery he makes flatters and delights him. Admiring the author's wit, he is able to admire also his own shrewdness, and the good opinion of himself thus engendered is reflected back on to the work to which he owes it.[147] But to choose a biblical allegory from the store of allegories available, was a master-stroke. The very title *Absalom and Achitophel* was a find. To French readers it seems strange. The name of Absalom awakes in us, it is true, the memory of an unusual form of death, but Achitophel suggests just nothing at all, and we are tempted to exclaim with Boileau :

> Oh, an ignorant poet's ridiculous plan ! [147a]

It is far worse when we begin to read, and come across Barzillai, Ishbosheth, Zimri, Issachar and the Jebusites : these names defeat and frighten us. But Dryden had good reasons for his choice. To conduct a political discussion under cover of Old Testament characters, was to fight the Puritans with their own weapons, to command their attention, to compel them to read and to recognize in Absalom their Duke of Monmouth,[148] in his counsellor Achitophel their Shaftesbury, and to wonder what modern persons were concealed behind so many names so familiar to their ears.[148a]

---

[147] See *The Spectator*, No. 512.—" Poems of this *Nature have seldom fail'd of Reception ; A Veil drawn over the Design in Poetry creates a Curiosity if not a Reverence.*" (Preface to *Uzziah and Jotham. A Poem 1690.*) See my Bibliography, s.v. Uzziah.

[147a] [*O le plaisant projet d'un poète ignorant !*]

[148] The Duke of Monmouth had already been compared to Absalom in *Absalom's Conspiracy* ; *or, The Tragedy of Treason*. London, 1680. See my Bibliography, s.v. Absalom.

[148a] [It was not, of course, the Puritans alone who would be familiar with the Bible. Even now, anybody born before 1900 would be familiar enough with the names to find no difficulty in following the allegory. This

The work was equally well calculated to succeed in the other camp. For one thing, it was acutely pleasing to see the enemy's own arrows fired back at him; for another, the Court rejoiced in the literary quality of a satire which on so admirable a plane continued the lampoon tradition dear to the courtier's heart. Furthermore, the brevity of the poem allowed it to circulate easily in the Coffee Houses and to scour the provinces in the wake of the Newsletters. The rhymed couplets, well-turned and sonorous, were bound to produce an impression and to linger in the memory, and the biblical subject, while attracting the Puritans, was well calculated to breathe new life and warmth into the sermons of the loyal clergy.[149]

Public opinion, thus catered for, secured for *Absalom and Achitophel* such a welcome as was before unheard of. Johnson's father, who was a bookseller at Lichfield in Staffordshire, told his son that in all his experience he had never known such sales " equalled but by Sacheverell's trial ".[150] This testimony has peculiar importance as showing the provinces entering on the scene and taking part with the Press in a movement of opinion.[151] The poem appeared on November 17, 1681; before the end

---

was not, one need hardly say, the first political poem in the language; even *The Faery Queen* is in some measure a political allegory. Yet the application of Dryden's work was so immediate, the allegory so readily understood, that *Absalom and Achitophel* deserves to be regarded as a literary invention. B. D.]

[149] " Surely a *Politician and a Divine* are scarce Commodities, when we *fly for Refuge to Hakney Poets* and *Hireling Pamphleteers*, with their Juniper-Lectures of *Politicks and Divinity*, to instruct the *Tantivy Clergy*, every Week, against the time that Sunday comes and to Tutor the *Corporations* and *Country Justices*, and Country *Commission-Officers*!" (Hickeringhill, Post-Script to *The Mushroom*).—Malone (*The Prose Works of John Dryden*, II, p. 293) quotes two sermons inspired by Dryden's poem. The allegory set a general fashion; see Walter Scott's Preface to *Absalom and Achitophel*. In the Roxburghe Collection (vol. III, p. 916) I have found " Good News in Bad Times : or *Absaloms* Return to *David's Bosome*, 1683".

[150] Johnson, *Lives of the English Poets*, Dryden.

[151] The success of the poem in the provinces is confirmed by the following quotation : " What sport it is to see an *old Country Justice* (with his *eager* Chaplain at his Elbow) putting his *Barnacles on his nose* (Bless us !) *How he gapes* and admires when he reads *Nat. Thompson*, the Addresses in the *Gazette, Abhorrences, Heraclitus* or the *Observator*? But, shew him but—*Absalom and Achitophel*—oh—then the *man's horn mad*, there's no holding him, then he *Hunts up* (and though in his *Dining-Room*) how he spends *with double mouth*, and whoops and hallows (just *as he hunts his Doggs* when at *full Cry*) That— That—That—That *Rattle—Towzer—Bull-Dog—Thunder*—That—That—whilst the little Trencher-Chaplain *Ecchoes* to him and crys—*Amen*—" (Hickeringhill, Post-Script to *The Mushroom*.)

of December a second edition was called for.[152] Two further editions appeared in 1682.

The reason was, not only that the author had had the skill to take up a favourable theme, but that the poem itself was amazingly well executed. In satire Dryden was on his own home ground. No one can argue better in verse than he, and this time he had a double source of inspiration : the first, the wish to please his King ; the second, the personal pleasure of being on active service against his old enemy Buckingham, on whom he had so far been unable to take vengeance. So he had the satisfaction of serving his own private ends at the same time as the King's, and he made the author of *The Rehearsal* pay dearly for ten years of enforced resentful silence, by painting Buckingham in the immortal character of Zimri :

> In the first rank of these did Zimri stand,
> A man so various that he seemed to be
> Not one, but all Mankind's epitome :
> Stiff in opinions, always in the wrong,
> Was everything by starts and nothing long ;
> But in the course of one revolving moon
> Was chymist, fiddler, statesman and buffoon ;
> Then all for women, painting, rhyming, drinking,
> Beside ten thousand freaks that died in thinking.
> Blest madman, who could every hour employ
> With something new to wish or to enjoy !
> Railing and praising were his usual themes,
> And both, to show his judgment, in extremes :
> So over violent or over civil
> That every man with him was God or Devil.
> In squandering wealth was his peculiar art ;
> Nothing went unrewarded but desert.
> Beggared by fools whom he still found too late,
> He had his jest, and they had his estate.
> He laughed himself from Court ; then sought relief
> By forming parties, but could ne'er be chief :
> For spite of him, the weight of business fell
> On Absalom and wise Achitophel ;
> Thus wicked but in will, of means bereft,
> He left not faction, but of that was left.[153]

---

[152] This second edition appeared with four sets of verses, one of them by Nahum Tate in praise of Dryden.

[153] Dryden probably borrowed the name Zimri (or Zambri) from the 25th chapter of Numbers where Zimri " a Prince of the chief house among the Simeonites ", was slain in adultery with the " daughter of a Prince of Midian ". He wished no doubt to recall Buckingham's liaison with the Countess of Shrewsbury.

[It is much more likely that Dryden took the name Zimri from I Kings 16, where Zimri " conspired against (Tirzah, his king) . . . and

The whole poem has remained one of the most valued show-pieces of English literature. The portraits are remarkable both for sureness of line and richness of colouring. The argument is lively and skilful, and produced on contemporary polemics an effect such as no piece of political writing had produced before. The wrath of the Whigs was proof that Dryden had scored a bull's eye. Replies spurted out from every quarter. Settle, who had recently become a vassal of the City, took up again the pen that had written *The Empress of Morocco* to pit himself once more against Dryden by writing a poem too. He called it *Absalom Senior: Or Achitophel Transpros'd*.[154] Buckingham published some poor *Poetical Reflections* [154a] on the work which had treated him so unkindly. At the same time a wretched dramatist called Samuel Pordage [155] brought out *Azaria and Hushai* (i.e. Monmouth and Shaftesbury); Henry Care, editor of an anti-Catholic paper, *A Packet of Advice from Rome*, produced *Towser the Second* and a Nonconformist minister two replies: *A Whip for the Fools Back*, who styles *Honorable Marriage a Curs'd Confinement in his profane Poem of Absalom and Achitophel* and *A Key (With the Whip) To open the Mystery and Iniquity of the Poem call'd Absalom and Achitophel*.[156]

---

smote him and killed him ". Everyone would be familiar with the still well-known query " Had Zimri peace who slew his master ? " in II Kings ix, 31. The main story, of course, comes from II Samuel xv seq. B. D.]

[154] Spence, p. 67, says that Settle was assisted by Matthew Clifford, Sprat and several of the best writers of the day. No one would think it. This is how Settle repaints Zimri's portrait as a likeness of Dryden:

> " Besides, lewd Fame had told his plighted Vow
> To *Laura's* cooing Love percht on a dropping Bough ;
> *Laura* in faithful Constancy confin'd
> To *Ethiops* Envoy, and to all Mankind.
> Laura, though Rotten, yet of Mold Divine,
> He had all her Cl—ps, and She had all his Coine.
> Her Wit so far his Purse and Sense could drain,
> Till every P—x was sweetn'd to a Strain.
> And if at last his Nature can reform,
> A weary grown of Loves tumultuous storm,
> 'Tis Age's Fault, not His ; of pow'r bereft,
> He left not Whoring, but of that was left."

[154a] [Wood says he is sure that Buckingham either " wrote, or caus'd to be wrote " the *Poetical Reflections*. These are, as Beljame says, very poor stuff, and are almost certainly not by Buckingham. Thorn-Drury ascribed them to Ned Howard. See *Review of English Studies*, Jan. 1925. B. D.]
[155] See Genest, I, 171 and 213.
[156] See my Bibliography, s.vv. Whip and Key.

The extraordinary success of *Absalom and Achitophel* proved beyond a shadow of doubt that Dryden had hit the nail on the head and that no one could do better than follow his example. It also brought home to Court and King the great advantage of alliance with an author. When, before long, a second occasion arose for appealing to Dryden, Charles II's eagerness betrayed that he now attached quite a new value to his Laureate's goodwill.

It will be remembered that Shaftesbury, who had been accused of treason and committed to the Tower, was acquitted by the Grand Jury. Intoxicated by this victory, his adherents kept up for an hour their shouts of triumph, lit bonfires of rejoicing, and finally to commemorate the happy event struck a medal with the inscription *Lætamur* which they ostentatiously displayed.[157] It was an ugly shock to the Court. They must deal an immediate counterstroke to minimize the ill effects. Who could do this better than Dryden? So the King's affection for his Poet Laureate was suddenly redoubled, and seeing him in the Mall one day, he drew him aside and said to him in friendly wise: "Mr. Dryden, if I were a poet, and I believe I am poor enough to be one, I should write a poem on such a subject in the following manner."[158] Dryden was not slow to take the hint. *The Medal, a Satire against Sedition*, appeared anonymously in March 1682 with this motto:

> Per Graium populos, mediæque per Elidis urbem
> Ibat ovans ; Divumque sibi poscebat honores.

This satire produced immense effect, and the anger of the Whigs again vented itself in numerous replies. Hickeringhill, the enlightened pamphleteering preacher who had sent the verses of his *Mushroom*[159] to the printer the very day that Dryden's

---

[157] See Christie's *Life of Anthony Ashley Cooper*, II, pp. 427 ff. Mr. Christie has reproduced this medal on the cover of his book.—See also Cooke, I, pp. 208 ff.

[158] Spence, p. 171.

[159] "God grant that this *Mushroom* be not like Jonas (his) Goard, *that sprung up in a night* and perished *in a night*. *Mushrooms* though they spring up in a night, yet (*well drest and Cook'd*) are served up, for *Daintyes*, and last *long*, not withstanding their *hasty Birth*, like this, far from the Authors Library, his *Notes*, and his *Books*. And if any man *think or say* that it is a Wonder, if this Book and Verses were compos'd and writ in *One Day*, and sent to the Press, since it would employ the *Pen of a ready Writer*, or nimble Scrivener, *to Coppy* this Book *in a Day* (it may be so). But *it is a Truth as certain* and stable as *the Sun* in the Firmament, and which (*if need be*) the Bookseller, Printer and other *Worthy Citizens*, that are privy to it, can *Avouch*, for an *Infallible* Truth.—*Deo soli Gloria*." (Post-Script to *The Mushroom*.)—See also the full title in my Bibliography.

Medal appeared, attributed this important poetic coincidence to divine inspiration. Samuel Pordage launched *The Medal Revers'd a Satyre against Persecution* : while Shadwell contributed *The Medal of John Bayes : a Satyr against Folly and Knavery* and *The Tory Poets a Satyr*. There were further two poems whose authors have remained unknown : *The Loyal Medal Vindicated* [160] and *Dryden's Satyr to his Muse*.[161] Finally, to all these retorts we must add one which was assuredly the wittiest and happiest of all : a reprint of the verses which Dryden had written in other days in praise of Cromwell.[162]

In writing *The Medal* the poet had worked for the King only. He now felt moved to work a little for himself, while continuing to serve the royal cause. He had squared his long-standing account with Buckingham, but there were still two fellow-authors in the Whig camp whose attacks had been peculiarly galling : his old rival Settle—and Shadwell.

In earlier days Shadwell had been one of Dryden's old friends ; the reader will remember that the two had collaborated (with Crowne also) to write *Notes and Observations* on the *Empress of Morocco* ; again in 1679 Dryden wrote the Prologue for Shadwell's comedy, *A True Widow*. But politics had come between them and, as is so often the case, the old friend had become the most violent of enemies. In *The Medal of John Bayes* Shadwell made the most odious accusations against Dryden in the most outrageous language.[163] Dryden could not leave all these attacks unanswered ; and since, amongst all his enemies, Shadwell was not merely the ablest but the only one of any ability at all, he concentrated on him—reserving Settle for a later occasion—and published *Mac Flecknoe*,[164] *or a Satyr upon the true-blew-protestant poet T. S.* (namely Thomas Shadwell). It is a delightful specimen of literary banter which Pope had still in mind when he wrote *The Dunciad*, and it proved a blow to Shadwell from which his reputation has never recovered.[165]

[160] See my Bibliography, s.v. Medal.
[161] Attributed to Somers.
[162] " Three Poems upon the Death of the Late Usurper Oliver Cromwell : " and also " A Panegyrick On the Author of Absolom [*sic*] and Achitophel." See my Bibliography, s.vv. Dryden and *Panegyrick*.
[163] I have not the nerve to quote them, even in a foreign tongue.
[164] That is to say, the son of Flecknoe, the poet already mentioned on pp. 78 and 119. Flecknoe appears to have been the butt of his fellows, for Marvell, III, p. 280, like Dryden, makes him a laughing-stock.
[165] Let me hasten to say that it was most unjust, for Shadwell's work was very much better than Dryden allows.

This successful elimination of a dangerous opponent gave the Court a taste for blood, and Dryden—who up to now had practically confined his attacks to the chiefs of the popular party, Shaftesbury, Monmouth and Buckingham—was urged to administer a little castigation to the mongrel curs who barked to order at their leaders' heels, by writing a further series of Absalom and Achitophel portraits.[166]

But so many repeated efforts had wearied the Laureate; he called in his friend Nahum Tate who had just demonstrated his Tory zeal by writing verses in praise of Dryden's political poems. As soon as they had together laid down the general lines to be followed, Tate got to work to maltreat as best he could the infinitely minor lights of the Whig party; most of them to-day forgotten. He wound up with a pretentious eulogy of the friends of the Court, more especially Dryden and L'Estrange.[167] Dryden reserved for himself only the opposition writers like Pordage, whom he pictured under the name of Mephibosheth, and above all his dear enemies Settle and Shadwell—Doeg and Og—at whom he lashed out vigorously. Shadwell, the only one to attempt a retort, prefixed a bitter Preface against Dryden to a translation of the tenth Satire of Juvenal.

In the same year Dryden, the versatile, brought out a poem of less combative and calmer tone, *Religio Laici, or a Layman's Faith*, in which he upholds the Church of England and seeks to gather both Romanist and Dissenter once more into her arms.

Poems and literary polemics soon superseded theatre and newspaper. This is not to imply that newspapers or theatre held their peace and ceased to function; the dates quoted above sufficiently prove that they did not, and passions ran too high for any means to be neglected. But the theatre dropped back into the second place in public regard, and the newspaper, try as it might, shared at best this second place. The type of writing of which Dryden was the pioneer exercised the sole serious influence. So much was this the case that the play which at this time made the most lively impression on the public mind, *The Duke of Guise* by Dryden and Lee, was impressive not by reason of its own merit, but because of the controversy it evoked. Shadwell brought out *Some Reflections upon the Pretended Parallel in the Play Called The Duke of Guise* and probably also a Prologue

---

[166] The Second Part of *Absalom and Achitophel*.
[167] See above, chap. II, note No. 117. Dryden appears in the poem as Asaph.

claiming to have been "refused by the actors". A lawyer called Thomas Hunt produced *A Defence of the Charter and Municipal Rights of the City of London*. Dryden replied to both by a long *Vindication* (of sixty pages) of his play, and the excitement roused by this battle of words was so great that Hunt, threatened with prosecution, was compelled to take refuge in Holland,[168] and Shadwell in the Dedication of his play *Bury-Fair* maintains that his life was in danger and that for several years he was obliged to give up writing.[169]

Such an expenditure of effort did not fail to bear fruit. Dryden was the first to flutter and halt the Whigs in their triumph, and to revive the flagging courage of the Tories. Hearing his voice, all friends of the Court, foremost among them the clergy, felt their zeal redoubled and gained renewed strength from confidence. Little by little the Whigs lost ground and showed themselves less daring and less self-assured. The discovery of the Rye-House Plot (1683) dealt them a final blow. This Whig conspiracy inspired a horror—skilfully exploited by the Royal party—which immediately hurled back into the Tory camp the numerous proselytes who had flung themselves into the opposition ranks in terror of the Popish Plot. The popular party ceased to be popular. Shaftesbury had already fled and died in Holland (1682).[170] The Rye-House Plot provided a convenient opportunity, which was not missed, for eliminating two other leaders of the Whigs: Lord Russell and Algernon Sidney were executed. The King became once more undisputed master of the situation.

Nevertheless Charles felt that there was more to do and the

---

[168] *Biographia Britannica*, s.v. Shadwell and à Wood, *Athenæ Oxonienses*, IV, columns 81 ff.

[169] "I could never recant in the Worst of Times, when my Ruine was design'd, and my Life was sought, and for near Ten Years I was kept from the exercise of that Profession which had afforded me a competent Subsistence." (Dedication of *Bury-Fair* to the Earl of Dorset.)

" Our *Author*, then opprest, would have you know it
Was Silenc'd for a *Non-conformist* Poet . . . "
(Prologue to the same.)

Shadwell did not begin to write again for the theatre till 1688, the year in which he produced *The Squire of Alsatia*. His last preceding play had been *The Lancashire Witches* in 1681.

[170] " . . . The king's influence increasing every day both in London and the country. A loyal lord mayor was this day chosen for the city of London, and two very good sheriffs. My Lord Shaftesbury stole oversea into Holland, and the charter of London was likely to stoop to the *quo warranto* brought against it." (Reresby, p. 263, Nov. 20, 1682.)

writers' work was not yet done. He bade Dryden translate *The History of the League* by the Jesuit Maimbourg. Obviously the aim of bringing out this translation at this particular moment was to increase the unpopularity of the Whigs by comparing them to the French Leaguers who, clothing themselves in a garment of noble religious zeal, attacked the royal power and plunged their country into a long and bloody civil war. It was, in short, a repetition of the tragedy of the *Duke of Guise*, and the Dedication was designed to make its purpose clear even to purblind eyes. This new work of Dryden's was published with particular care, and this time the title-page bore his name and openly proclaimed that it was written at the King's command.[171]

IV

Political Literature under James II: Sprat's Account of the " Horrid Conspiracy against the Late King " (Rye-House Plot).—Dryden and Stillingfleet discuss religion.—The Anglican Clergy join in polemics against the King.—" The Hind and the Panther " by Dryden.—Montague and Prior's " The Country Mouse and the City Mouse ".—Overthrow of James II

This was destined to be literature's last service to Charles II. In the following year, while Dryden under the royal supervision was working on his opera *Albion and Albanius* to celebrate the King's victory over the Whigs, the Merry Monarch died, leaving his throne to the man who had been the cause of all the heated political feeling of his last years.

The period of hope and calm which normally follows the accession of a new king was this time of short duration. With the accession of James II political passions speedily rekindled. The poets had scarcely time to pay the customary mourning tributes to the deceased monarch, and hail the elevation of his successor,[172] before polemics were again raging more fiercely than ever.

---

[171] Preceding the text was an engraving representing the King on his throne; the heaven opened slightly to reveal a hand holding a crown. A ray of light from the crown illumined the King's head and in it was written: *Per me reges regnant*. Round the throne stood Justice and nobles with a magistrate in the foreground at whose feet were inscribed the words: *Sibi et successoribus suis legitimis*.

[172] Dryden, *Threnodia Augustalis*; apotheosis of James II at the end of *Albion and Albanius*; D'Urfey, *Joy to Great Cæsar*; *An Elegy upon . . . King Charles II*, and two panegyricks upon . . . *King James and Queen Mary . . .*; Charles Montague, *On the Death of His Most Sacred Majesty Charles II*. Montague's verses figure in a collection of poems on the death of Charles II

Blinded by zeal, James II seemed in haste to fan the flames of political passion, by ordering Sprat, the newly appointed Bishop of Rochester, and one of the authors of *The Rehearsal*, to compose a narrative of the Rye-House Plot; the fire of religious passion, by asserting that his brother had died a Roman Catholic, and by publishing two documents—said to have been found in Charles II's safe—which maintained the superiority of the Roman to the Protestant Church.[173]

Stillingfleet, Dean of St. Paul's, promptly replied to this letter.[174] Though his name did not appear on the title-page of his *Answer*, the fact that a distinguished member of the English Church should intervene in opposition to the King deserves attention, for it indicated that under James II discussion was from the start to assume a wholly different complexion from discussion under Charles, and in particular that the clergy were to play a different part.

Up to this point the clergy, passionately devoted to the doctrine of passive obedience, had unanimously supported the King. Whatever doubts might privately be entertained about his personal religious convictions, Charles II throughout his reign remained a Protestant, and the head of the Protestant

---

published by the University of Cambridge (*Biographia Britannica*, s.v. Montague) —Here is a specimen of D'Urfey's enthusiasm:

The Kings Health, *set to* Farinel's *Grounds.*
       First Strain.

  Joy to Great *Caesar,*
  Long Life, Love and Pleasure;
  'Tis a Health that Divine is,
  Fill the Bowl high as mine is . . .
    Second Strain.
  Try all the Loyal
   Defy all
   Give Denial;
  Sure none thinks Glass too big here,
  Nor any *Prig* here,
  Or sneaking *Whig* here
  Of Cripple *Tony's* Crew
  That now looks blew.
  His Heart akes too
  The *Tap* won't do . . .
  (*A Collection of One Hundred and Eighty Loyal Songs.*)

See my Bibliography, s.v. Thompson, N.)

[173] See my Bibliography, s.v. James II.
[174] See my Bibliography, s.v. Stillingfleet.

religion in England. The clergy's interest and the royal interest were therefore one. The situation was now radically altered. James II had not only divorced himself from the Church of England but had clearly shown his determination to smash it. The Anglican clergy correspondingly changed their point of view.

So long as persecution and oppression had hit none but Roman Catholics and Dissenters, they had with one voice maintained that God's law forbade resistance. But as soon as the blast of persecution veered in their direction, as soon as their own interests were threatened, they changed their attitude, if not their manner of speech, and made a duty of vigorously challenging the King's pretensions.[175]

This change of clerical allegiance was serious, for it robbed the King of a very loyal and very influential ally; it was all the more serious because the point at issue had become almost entirely a religious question, and here the clergy were manifestly in strength on their own ground. The consequences were soon seen in the sequel to this first controversy.

It was no light matter to reply to so authoritative a writer as the Dean of St. Paul's. Fortunately, in throwing in his lot with James II, Dryden had become a convert to Roman Catholicism. At the King's request he undertook to answer Stillingfleet. He set to work with heat—with too much heat, for he went so far as to accuse the Dean of disloyalty and "foul dealing"[176]—and devoted all the resources of his skill to the cause of his new religion. But a theologian is not made in a moment. It was not enough to be the best writer of his age, Dryden was no match in battle for a consummate controversialist who had made a life-study of religious questions. Stillingfleet vigorously retorted and easily won the day.

For the writers of the Court, the day of brilliant reply and easy victory was over. They no longer had to contend only with fellow writers, that is to say with their equals, or with political fanatics turned author, whose prose and verse were

---

[175] Amongst the Church of England clergy who at one point had unanimously preached passive obedience, there were not more than 400 who refused allegiance to the revolutionary government of William III. (Macaulay, *Essay on Hallam*.)

[176] " . . . I hope I shall discover the foul Dealing of this Author, who has obscur'd, as much as he is able, the Native Lustre of those Papers, and recommended by a false Light his own sophisticated Ware; part of which may certainly deserve the clearest Light which can be given it by the Hands of the Under-Sheriff, or of somebody, whom I will not name." (*A Defence of the Papers Written by the Late King of Blessed Memory: Preface.*)

little to be feared. Though but a few years had passed, the blissful days were far distant when Dryden, almost single-handed, had kept at bay the Shadwells and Settles, not to mention the Pordages, Hunts and Hickeringhills. The Court writers of old went into battle on familiar ground, wielding well-tried weapons against a foe with whom they were wont to fight. Now, the terrain was new, and not only were they the novices in this type of warfare, but they were face to face with adversaries weighty by the authority alike of their speech and of their position.

In the wake of Stillingfleet we find the most distinguished ecclesiastics joining the fray, some of whom have left their mark in literature apart from their religious learning, men like Tillotson, Prideaux, Burnet, Atterbury.[177] It was in fact the clergy who now seized the initiative and became masters of the argument. While from one end of England to the other every Church of England clergyman passionately preached in protest against James II's religious leanings, the eminent men whose names I have just quoted, took the cue from Dryden and with unwearied vigour—adopting in their varied writings [178] every tone and style in turn, to appeal now to the people, now to society, now to the learned—they expounded, argued, and studied from every angle, the comparative merits of the Roman Catholic and Protestant religions.[179] Here was a formidable army arrayed against the King, attacking every day, every moment, and from every point of the compass at the same time.

Much as he might have wished, it was impossible for him to silence such a multitude of redoubtable opponents. He could do nothing through the Courts, for he would have had to prosecute every clergyman of the National Church; he was equally powerless to do anything against their publications, for though in the very first year of his reign, he had re-established a Press Censorship,[180] the Act contained a clause exempting the two Universities of Oxford and Cambridge, and authorizing the printing of theological works approved by either the Bishop

---

[177] Dryden himself said he had learned to write prose by reading Tillotson. (Congreve, Dedication to Dryden's *Dramatick Works*, 1717.)
[178] Macaulay, *History*, chap. VI, says: "Those which may still be found in our great libraries make up a mass of near 20,000 pages. This I can attest from my own researches. There is an excellent collection in the British Museum."
[179] Neal, IV, chap. XI; Stoughton, vol. II, pp. 117 ff.
[180] Keble, I, p. 1511.

of London or the Archbishop of Canterbury.[181] Now the two Universities were playing a very active part in the fight against Roman Catholicism, and both Compton, Bishop of London, and Sancroft, Archbishop of Canterbury, were far from approving of the King's beliefs.

There was one course only open to James II: to meet argument with argument. To this end he set his machinery in motion. He had his own printing presses in London and Oxford and even at Holyrood in Scotland, and from them he bombarded the whole country with printed matter.

But the writers at his disposal were not of the right calibre to stand up against the Protestant clergy; they were second-rate Roman Catholic priests, not one of whom won distinction in this war of words. Even if they had had more ability, they could not have turned it to full account owing to their imperfect knowledge of English.

For many years the English climate had been inhospitable to Roman Catholics, and the more devout Romanists in England had sent their children to be educated abroad, either at Rome or Douai. When large numbers of these expatriates returned to England on the accession of James II, they came home knowing Italian or French much better than their mother tongue. One of them, Andrew Pulton, was even driven to request Dr. Tenison to write in Greek or Latin, so that the controversial battle between them might be waged on equal terms.[182] Yet another, one William Clenche, writing an English tract on *St. Peter's Supremacy*, reverted in haste to Italian to write his Dedication to the Queen, thus from the first deterring his readers by many pages in a language they could not understand.[183]

Such allies were willing and eager enough no doubt, but of little value. The only serious reading-matter which the King

---

[181] See paragraph III of the Act, already alluded to, chap. I, note 402, in Keble II, 1250 ff.

> "But *Imprimatur*, with a Chaplain's name,
> Is here sufficient licence to defame."
> (Dryden, *The Hind and the Panther*, part III, 11, 256/7.)

[182] "A. P. having been eighteen years out of his Country, pretends not yet to any Perfection of the *English* expression or Orthography, Wherefore for the future he will crave the favour of treating with the Dr. in *Latine* or *Greek*, since the Dr. finds fault with his *English*. (Notice printed on the reverse of the title page of *A True and Full Account of a Conference*, etc.)

[183] See Macaulay, *History*, chap. VI, where samples of their English style are given.—William Clenche's Dedication: "Alla Serenissima Principessa Maria d'Este Reina d'Inghilterra" is twelve pages long.

could offer to confound the Protestants, was some translations of Bossuet [184]—which would have been more effective if they had not been so miserably translated—and Dryden.

Dryden had not emerged too happily from his recent controversy with Stillingfleet. He hoped to recapture his usual success with a return to verse. He fled the noise of London to find a country retreat favourable to study, and there—slowly, painstakingly, with mature thought—he composed his allegoric poem, *The Hind and the Panther*. The unspotted, milk-white Hind is the Church of Rome, contrasted with the mottled Panther, the Church of England. Around these two animals in the same forest, Dryden groups the Independent Bear, the Anabaptist Boar, the Presbyterian Wolf, the Quaking Hare and the Socinian Fox. All the Protestant sects are thus metaphorically reviewed while the Freethinkers are represented by the Ape. Though this poem suffers from a grave fault which Dryden's opponents were not slow to detect, it nevertheless contains some of the most eloquent and powerful passages he ever wrote. The King himself had it printed at his own Holyrood Press and took pains to circulate it through the whole of England. Thanks to such fostering, *The Hind and the Panther* quickly ran into three, if not four editions. Despite all this, however, Dryden failed to recapture the success of earlier days.

No degree of talent, not even of genius itself—for *Absalom and Achitophel* had earned its author the right to this word—can win a struggle against the convictions of a nation. The further things went, the less was England inclined to accept the views of which Dryden had made himself the champion.

How far he had forfeited his early dominion over public opinion is well shown by the fact that a simple reply by two amateurs sufficed to destroy the whole effect of the famous veteran's poem.[185] The two authors of *The Country Mouse and the City Mouse*, Charles Montague and Matthew Prior, collaborated to produce this retort, and though both possessed wit and

[184] See my Bibliography, s.v. Bossuet. It is believed that Dryden undertook to translate Bossuet's *Exposition de la Doctrine de l'Église catholique*. He had also been commanded by the King to translate Varillas's *Histoire des révolutions en matière de religion*; this translation was never published. (Malone, *Life of Dryden*, p. 194.)
[185] There were other replies too : *Reflections upon the Hind and the Panther* by Tom Brown ; *The Laureat* ; *A Poem in Defence of the Church of England* ; *The Revolter. A Trage-Comedy Acted between the Hind and the Panther and Religio Laici*. See my Bibliography, s.vv. Brown (Thomas), *Laureat, Poem* and *Revolter*.

talent, their work looks paltry enough in comparison with the fine verse of Dryden. Their sole merit lies in having detected and revealed the error of design which mars *The Hind and the Panther*. Dryden makes the two animals converse together; now, since each represents a Church, what can they talk about save religion? Here we see to what strange incongruities the allegory leads. The Hind is afraid to go to the common stream to drink, for fear of being attacked by the beasts of the forest. A moment after, she speaks of Jesus Christ as her Saviour, and attempts to convert the Panther by arguments about the Real Presence, the authority of the Popes, the Test Act, the Popish Plot, Stillingfleet's writings and Burnet's conjugal prowess. The Panther who in friendly wise ranges the forest with the Hind, carries a crozier and wears a mitre on her head. Montague and Prior had no difficulty in showing how incongruous and laughable it all was, and having made merry over the form of the poem, they stayed their hand and refrained from discussing the basic problems raised. What good would it have done anyhow? Public opinion had crystallized; no one needed to be convinced. Those who enjoyed a laugh needed no further inducement to join their side.[186] The applause which hailed their literary banter was so great that Dryden, cut to the quick, bitterly complained: "for two young fellows that I have always been very civil to, to use an old man in so cruel a manner!"[187] and *The Country Mouse and the City Mouse* laid the foundations of Montague and Prior's political fortunes.

From this point onwards it was clear that James II was

---

[186] "But to conclude, blush with a lasting Red,
(If thou'rt not mov'd with what's already said)
To see thy Boars, Bears, Buzards, Wolves and Owls,
And all thy other Beasts, and other Fowl's,
Routed by two poor Mice: (Unequal fight)
But easie 'tis to Conquer in the Right."

(*The Laureat.*)

"If you have not yet Mr. Dreydens celebrated poem of the Hinde and Panther wth the no less admired answer to it call'd the Poem of the Panther and Hind transprosed done by a young gentleman Mr. Montagu I will send them both to you."

(Manuscript letter of July 19, 1687; British Museum, Additional: 28,569, p. 65 reverse.)

[187] "Dryden was most touched with 'The Hind and the Panther Transversed'. I have heard him say: 'for two young fellows, that I have always been very civil to; to use an old man in so cruel a manner!'— And he wept as he said it." (Spence, p. 61.)

striding towards his fall with seven-league boots, and that nothing could prevent the collapse of his tottering throne.[188] The war of words continued with the same result to the end : whatever was written in the King's favour missed its mark, whatever was written against him was read throughout England with delight. When James II endeavoured to win over the Puritans by his first Declaration of Indulgence in 1687, a broadside called *Letter to a Dissenter*, which was attributed to Sir William Temple or alternatively to the Marquis of Halifax,[189] warned the country of the King's true intentions and deeply stirred public opinion. Twenty-four replies appeared in the King's interest, one of them by L'Estrange,[190] but did not succeed in weakening the *Letter's* effect.

The King had no grip on the minds of his subjects ; he was powerless to stay the current that was sweeping him away. Clandestine publications followed hard on each other without his being able to stop them. He could not discover the author of the *Letter to a Dissenter*. Similarly in 1688 when he issued his second Declaration of Indulgence and seven bishops presented a famous petition against its being read in the churches, this petition was printed—no one has discovered how—that very evening, cried in the streets, and bought up with extraordinary avidity,[191] despite anything that could be done to suppress it.

Yet so infatuated was the King, that he was unaware how close he was to the abyss. The authors supporting his cause shared his blind confidence. When a son [192] was born to him

[188] See Reresby, from Feb. 10, 1685, to Dec. 28, 1688.
[189] Macaulay (*History*, chap. VII) has no hesitation in deciding on Halifax.—George Savile, Marquis of Halifax, must not be confused with Charles Montague, just mentioned, whom we shall soon see appearing as Baron Halifax and later Earl of Halifax.—*The Letter to a Dissenter* is printed in Walter Scott's *Collection of Scarce and Valuable Tracts*, vol. IX.
[This brilliant work, which Temple could not have accomplished, is now universally conceded to be by Halifax, and is to be found in any edition of his works, e.g. Miss Foxwell's or Sir W. Raleigh's. B. D.]
[190] See my Bibliography, s.v. L'Estrange.
[191] " It was said that the printer cleared a thousand pounds in a few hours by this penny broadside. This is probably an exaggeration but an exaggeration which proves that the sale was enormous." (Macaulay, *History*, chap. VIII.)
[192] The Queen's pregnancy, in which England refused to believe, was the subject of innumerable pamphlets. See in *Poems on Affairs of State*, II, p. 184 : " The Miracle ; how the *Dutchess of Modena* (*being in Heaven*) prayed the *B. Virgin* that the Queen might have a Son, and how our Lady sent the Angel *Gabriel* with her Smock ; upon which the Queen was with *Child* " ; idem, III, p. 267 : " An excellent new Song, call'd, *The Prince of Darkness* ;

on June 10, 1688—the son and heir so long desired—Dryden triumphantly exclaimed: "Britannia Rediviva!"[193] Five months later, the man who was soon to be William III landed on the English coast and James II took flight while his subjects sang their heads off with Lillibulero.[194]

V

Conclusion: Authors' services are better appreciated.—The City as counterweight to the Court.—Reciprocal influence of City and Court.—Political competes successfully with frivolous literature.—Jacob Tonson, the first English publisher, tries his strength.—Profits from the theatre increase. This gives promise for the future; meantime the spiritual and material lot of authors does not improve.—They are " courtiers " in politics as in literature.—Their political changes of front.—Wycherley, Haines and Dryden converted to Roman Catholicism.—Violence of their political passion

The eight years whose stormy history we have been considering and which were so important from the political point of view, were not without some happy turns of fortune for literary men. Let us first note that a shade more importance was being accorded to them, and a shade more consideration shown. When people realized that the author was capable of being something more

---

Showing how three Kingdoms may be set on fire by a *Warming-Pan*";—Stephens, Catalogue I, Nos. 1156/7: "The Warming-Pan, Portraits of the Pretenders, etc."—The story was that another woman's new-born infant was smuggled into the Queen in a warming-pan.

[193] *Britannia Rediviva.* Mrs. Behn congratulated "Her Most Sacred Majesty on the Universal Hopes of all Loyal Persons for a Prince of Wales." See my Bibliography.

[194] "A foolish ballad was made at that time, treating the Papists, and chiefly the *Irish*, in a very ridiculous manner, which had a burden said to be *Irish* words, *lero lero lilibulero*, that made an impression on the Army, that cannot well be imagined by those that saw it not. The whole Army, and at last all the people both in city and country, were singing it perpetually. And perhaps never had so slight a thing so great an effect." (Burnet, *History* . . . , III, p. 319.) See also Macaulay, *History*, chap. IX. This song can be found on p. 9 of *A collection of the Newest and Most Ingenious Songs . . . against Popery.* See my Bibliography, s.v. *Collection.*—In a rhymed broadside of 1688 called *An Epistle to Mr. Dryden* (see my Bibliography, s.v. *Epistle*) I note this couplet:—

"Dryden, thy wit has caterwauld too long,
Now *Lero, Lero,* is the only Song . . . "

[Lord Wharton was said to have been the author of this famous song, set to music by Purcell as A New Irish Tune, which is now well known, and has found favour as a regimental march. Wharton boasted that he had "sung a king out of three kingdoms", but at least as much credit must be given to Purcell's catching lilt, to whistle which was always Uncle Toby's retort to any statements he felt smacked of Toryism or Popery. B. D.]

than an amusement-monger, and that his work might on occasion serve a more useful purpose than pleasantly killing time, they no longer always waited for him to make advances, but began to approach him on their own behalf. The Court laid claim to the services of L'Estrange and Sprat. Charles II personally intervened with Dryden and tried on him the effect of that seductive voice hitherto chiefly used for wooing his mistresses. James II commissioned writings from several writers and printed them himself. Authors were little accustomed to such attentions. They were beginning to be valued. This is the first sign of the changing times.

Another fact carries weight and in part explains the former: The Court was no longer everything. The City had come again into its own, it had its politics, its coffee houses and its newspapers, and for it Whig authors wrote poems and plays. The citizens were not content with this, they coveted authors of their very own. They were wont every year to burn the Pope in effigy; in 1680 they engaged Settle to preside over this ceremony which they wished to make a particularly brilliant one.[195] They aimed even higher; they made Dryden offers of money to come over to their side.[196]

The number of readers increased with the resurgence of the City: the closed and narrow circle of the Court opened, to make way for the middle classes who had too long remained aloof but were at last bent on making their existence felt. Up to now there had been, in fact, two groups of readers of radically different tastes, separated from each other and without mutual intercourse, one of which seemed almost non-existent. While the Court, like a noisy and frothy torrent, filled eye and ear with the boisterous fret of its tumultuous waters, the Puritan river, unseen, unheard, pursued unobserved its clear and tranquil course. The two were now united into a single stream and flowed together between wider shores.

Henceforward we can say that the Court no longer has a monopoly of reading; we may even add that after *Absalom and Achitophel* reading was no longer confined to London.[197]

It was not only the number but also the calibre of readers

[195] Nichols, *Literary Anecdotes*, I, 41; note; Disraeli, *Quarrels of Authors*, Pope's Earliest Satire.
[196] See his letter to the First Lord of the Treasury quoted below, p. 196.
[197] The impetus once given, it did not die down. The *Letter to a Dissenter* was circulated through the post to the tune of 20,000 copies. (Macaulay, *History*, chap. VII.)

which rose. Each of the two components of the enlightened public contributed its qualities and made them felt. Amidst all its frivolity and corruption, we must recognize that the Court had the merit of taste and a desire for refinement, thanks to which English polemics, by care for literary form, acquired a polish and seemliness which had hitherto been almost completely lacking.

Consider the famous wranglings of Milton and Salmasius [198]; without even going back so far, recall the quarrels—wholly literary though they were—between Dryden and Settle. Each of the champions was bent simply on defeating the other, without overmuch concern for the methods by which victory was won. They overwhelmed each other with violent insults and thundering words; they fought with bludgeons. The infuriated assailant launched savage blows that made his victim's body quiver; his antagonist without flinching repaid them with equal weight and vigour. The onlookers applauded the cracked skulls and fractured limbs, and even the most fortunate fighters emerged from the combat a mass of wounds and bruises. The presence of ladies and the atmosphere of the drawing-room now put such brutal struggles out of court, and the foil replaced the bludgeon. The duel now demanded sprightliness and elegance; the attack must be quick, the defence smart and neat. The audience delighted to see skilful passes skilfully parried, and even if the wounds drew blood, at least they did not disfigure the fencers. Rhymed satire became the vehicle of argument and all readers found so much pleasure in a well-turned phrase that versified polemics had the best chance of success. I would not imply that all violence was henceforward banished from discussion. There were plenty of excesses and plenty of vulgarities [199] in the replies which Dryden's political writings brought upon his head, and plenty even in Dryden's work. But however furiously anger might rage—and we shall presently see the extremes of which it was capable—literary considerations moderated the form if not the content. We have seen Dryden's portrait of Zimri which confirms this view. Here is another sample of Dryden's art directed against Shadwell :

Og may write against the king, if he pleases, so long as he drinks for him, and his writings will never do the government so much harm,

---

[198] Taine, II, pp. 357–8; Geffroy, pp. 152–4.
[199] See above, chap. I, note No. 315, and chap. II, note No. 154.

as his drinking does it good ; for true subjects will not be perverted by his libels ; but the wine duties rise considerably by his claret. He has often called me an atheist in print ; I would believe more charitably of him, and that he only goes the broad way, because the other is too narrow for him. He may see, by this, I do not delight to meddle with his course of life, and his immoralities, though I have a long bead-roll of them. I have hitherto contented myself with the ridiculous part of him, which is enough, in all conscience, to employ one man ; even without the story of his late fall at the Old Devil, where he broke no ribs, because the hardness of the stairs could reach no bones ; and for my part, I do not wonder how he came to fall, for I have always known him heavy : the miracle is, how he got up again. I have heard of a sea-captain as fat as he, who, to escape arrests, would lay himself flat upon the ground, and let the bailiffs carry him to prison, if they could. If a messenger or two, nay, we may put in three or four, should come, he has friendly advertisement how to escape them. But to leave him, who is not worth any further consideration, now I have done laughing at him,—would every man knew his own talent, and that they who are only born for drinking, would let both poetry and prose alone ! [200]

It would be possible to cite other similar passages ; *Mac Flecknoe* might almost be quoted *in extenso*. We have, however, quoted enough to show how much milder were the forms polemics now favoured, thanks to a Court which had made literature the fashion.

If the Court had taught the ruder Puritan middle classes to appreciate polish and elegance, they for their part had introduced a wholesome and sustaining element into the courtier's dissolute and superficial life.

We have seen that despite appearances, other matter than plays and songs had been finding readers. This subterranean stream of readers now found its way into the open, happily overwhelming the superficial and degraded, and was soon swelled by the serious-minded Royalists. For there were serious-minded men also in the Royalist camp—though the empty-headed had so long prevented serious voices being heard—if it were only the group of thinkers who, feeling the need of quiet study after the disturbances of the Civil War, founded the Royal Society in 1662.[201]

From this point of view the revival of politics had a fortunate effect. Compelling people to give up the sole pursuit of enjoy-

---

[200] *The Vindication*, etc.
[201] Amongst them were Dryden, Cowley, Denham, Evelyn, Barrow, Waller and Sprat.

ment it turned their minds to wholesomer, more vigorous thought. As regards the reign of James II in particular, we must add that the King's more frigid temperament and the fact that he had passed the age of sensual passion and was wholly preoccupied in seeking the triumph of his religious views, gave far less encouragement to licence than Charles II had done, and thus imposed a measure of restraint.

It would obviously be untrue to imply that the general tone had suddenly improved all at once. A society which for twenty years has devoted itself wholly to pleasure and cast aside all modesty and self-respect, cannot purify itself in a day. Plays in particular—even political plays—were not less licentious or less disgusting than in the first years of Charles II. Ravenscroft's *London Cuckolds*, Rochester's *Valentinian*, Otway's *Souldiers Fortune* and his *Atheist*, Crowne's *City Politiques*, Lee's *Princess of Cleve*, Sedley's *Bellamira* and Mrs. Behn's new comedies, were in no way behind the most audacious of the early Restoration plays in daring and indecency.[202] Prologues and Epilogues likewise were no less shameless than in the past.[203]

---

[202] I shall confine myself to a few quotations: [Rochester d. 1680, B. D.]

"The Love of Women moves even with their Lust.
Who therefore still are fond, but seldom just:
Their Love is Usury, while they pretend,
To gain the Pleasure double which they lend.
But a dear Boy's disinterested Flame
Gives Pleasure, and for meer Loves gathers pain;
In him alone Fondness sincere does prove,
And the kind tender Naked Boy is Love."

(Rochester, *Valentinian*, II, 1.)

"*Beauregard*: Would the Lady of my Motion make haste, and be punctual; the Wheels of my Nature move so fast else, that the weight will be down before she comes." (Otway, *The Atheist*, II, 1.) His father speaks to him of "brawny-bum'd Whores" (III, 1).

"*Nemours*: Let's try how our lips fit.
Marguerite: Is that your fitting?
Nemours: 'Fore Heaven she's wond'rous quick; Nay, my Dear, and you go to that, I can fit you every way——
Marguerite: You are a notorious talker.
Nemours: And a better doer; prithee try."

(Lee, *Princess of Cleve*, II, 3.) And she tries.

"*Poltrot*: ... When you were little Girls of Seven, you were so wanton, your Mothers ty'd your hands behind you——
Elianora: All this we confess to be true," etc.

(Id., IV, 1.)

The whole play is in this tone, especially Nemours' part.

[203] See, amongst others, the Epilogue to Crowne's *Sir Courtly Nice*; the Epilogue by Dryden for Lee's *Constantine the Great*; the Prologue (spoken

Nevertheless we seem to detect some promises of improvement even in the theatre. We begin to hear protests raised against the immoralities displayed on the stage and we see authors compelled to give heed to these protests.[204] From Ravenscroft himself we learn the *The London Cuckolds* did not fail to rouse complaints.[205] Comedy showed a slight, a very

---

by a woman) and the Epilogue to Southerne's *Loyal Brother*, both of them written by Dryden; the Prologue (also by Dryden) and the Epilogue to Southerne's *Disappointment*.

[204] " Of all the things which at this *Guilty time*,
Have felt the honest *Satyr's* Wholsome *Rhime*,
The *Play-house* has scap't best, being most forborn,
Though it, of all things, most deserves our scorn . . .
First to the *Middle-Gallery* we'll go . . .
Where reeking *Punks* like Summer Insects swarm,
And stink like *Pole-cats* when they are hunted warm : . . .
In the *Side-box Moll H . . . n* you may see,
Or *Coquet Moll*, who is as lewd as she :
That is their Throne ; for there they best survey
All the salt Sots that flutter to the *Play* . . .
As the *New-River* does from *Islington*,
Through several pipes supply ev'n half the Town ;
So the Luxurious lewdness of the *Stage*,
Drain'd off, feeds half the *Brothels* of the Age.
Unless these ills, then, we could regulate,
It ought not to be suffer'd in the State."
(*The Play-House, a Satyr* . . . by Robt. Gould.)

" Baudy the nicest Ladies need not fear,
The quickest fancy shall extract none here.
We will not make 'em blush, by which is shown
How much their bought Red differs from their own."
(Shadwell, *The Squire of Alsatia*, Prologue.)

[205] " Gallants, I vow I am quite out of heart,
I've not one smutty Jest in all my part.
Here's not one Scene of tickling Rallery ;
There we quite lose the Pit and Gallery.
His *London Cuckolds* did afford you sport.
That pleas'd the Town, and did divert the Court.
But 'cause some squeamish Females of renown
Made visits with design to cry it down,
He swore in 's Rage he would their humours fit,
And write the next without one word of Wit.
No line in this will tempt your minds to Evil,
It's true, 'tis dull, but then 'tis very civil.
No double sense shall now your thoughts beguile,
Make Lady Blush nor Ogling Gallant smile.
But mark the Fate of this mis-judging Fool !
A Bawdy Play was never counted Dull,
Nor modest Comedy e're pleas'd you much
'Tis relish'd like good Manners 'mongst the *Dutch*.

slight tendency to cease to serve as a market-place for debauchery. Politics had drawn off no small number of its male and female addicts.[206] Southerne, who began his dramatic career in 1682, actually has the courage to introduce virtuous women into his plays, even into his comedies.[207] All these things are of course but straws in the wind, but when you have long been floundering in a cess-pool, stirring up septic filth at every step, the tiniest trickle of pure water rejoices your eye and uplifts your heart.

We find, besides, another indication of mental progress—in the appearance of less frivolous reading matter. Political writing had begun seriously to compete with light literature. Religious discussions in which the most eminent people in the country bore a part and which found readers all over England, had prepared people's minds to accept and demand better fare than stale plays, prologues and songs. The "publisher", just on the point of emerging from the chrysalis of printer-bookseller, would be on the watch for the more substantial work. Jacob Tonson, taking the first steps in publishing, was busy as early as 1683 preparing with Dryden a volume of a new type: a collection of translations from Virgil, Ovid, Horace, etc., and of "original poems by the most eminent hands", a collection

---

"In you, Chast Ladies, then we hope to day,
This is the Poets *Recantation* Play.
Come oft to't that he at length may see
'Tis more than a pretended Modesty:
Stick by him now, for if he finds you falter,
He quickly will his way of writing alter;
And every Play shall send you blushing home.
For, tho you rail, yet then we're sure you'll come..."
(Ravenscroft, Prologue to *Dame Dobson*, spoken by Mrs. *Currer*.)

[206] "Here's such a Rout with Whigging and with Torying,
That you neglect your dear-lov'd sin of Whoring:
The Visor-Mask, that ventur'd her Half-Crown,
Finding no hopes but here to be undone;...
Turns Godly streight and goes to Church in spight;
And does not doubt, since you are grown so fickle
To find more Cullies in a Conventicle."
(Bankes, Epilogue to *Vertue Betray'd*.)

"Our Prologue-Wit grows flat: the Nap's worn off;
And howsoe'ere we turn and trim the Stuff,
The Gloss is gone that look'd at first so gaudy;
'Tis now no Jest to hear young Girls talk Baudy.
But Plots and Parties, give new matter birth;
And State Distractions serve you here for mirth!"
(Shadwell(?), *A Lenten Prologue*.)

[207] Notably in *The Disappointment*.

still known as Dryden's or Tonson's Miscellany. It appeared in 1684.[208] The experiment justified itself, for in 1685 the two partners launched a second, similar volume which was soon followed by a third.[209] Already in 1683 Tonson had foreseen a probable revulsion in the taste of readers and had been courageous enough to buy from his fellow-bookseller, Brabazon Aylmer, half the rights in Milton's *Paradise Lost*. Without haste—obviously not yet feeling quite sure of his ground—he got ready a new edition which he published in 1688. This was the first worthy recognition of the great, under-appreciated poet. This edition was published by subscription with the encouragement of Atterbury, later Bishop of Rochester, and of Somers, a young literature-loving lawyer, destined to fill ere long the highest offices of state.[210] Henceforward the bookseller was no longer content to be merely a seller of books; assured of a reading public on whom he could count, he developed ambition and a spirit of enterprise; he set about seeking out authors and potential books; he was on the alert for new ideas—in short, he became a publisher.

Such were, in brief, the changes we can note in matters which were of concern to writers : the Court was devoting more attention to them and making approaches to them ; the City was offering them a new market ; the number of readers was growing ; literary taste was spreading ; finally, the publishing firm was born. At the same time certain profits from the theatre were proving more remunerative : the author's fee for a prologue

[208] In the same year of 1684 Dryden (see his Letters) advised Tonson to reprint Roscommon's *Essay on Translated Verse* and to run off 1,000 copies. He also revised and reprinted his own *Essay of Dramatick Poesie* in 1684, dedicating it to Dorset.
[209] The first volume is called *Miscellany Poems*, the second *Silvæ*, and the third *Examen Poeticum*. See my Bibliography, s.v. Dryden.
[210] Professor Masson's Edition of the Poetic Works of Milton, *Introduction to Paradise Lost*.—The list of over 500 subscribers, printed at the end of the volume includes, in addition to Somers and Atterbury already mentioned, the names of Dryden, Waller, Lord Dorset, Sir Robert Howard and L'Estrange. It was for this edition that Dryden wrote his verses on Milton :

> " Three *Poets*, in three distant Ages born,
> *Greece, Italy* and *England* did adorn.
> The *First* in loftiness of thought Surpass'd,
> The *Next* in Majesty ; in both the *Last*.
> The force of *Nature* cou'd no further goe ;
> To make a *Third* she joynd the former two."

Tonson later had his portrait painted by Kneller holding his Milton in his hand.

went up, from 5 to 10 guineas [211]; the third performance of *The Squire of Alsatia* brought Shadwell the remarkable sum of £130, a fact which was duly remarked on.[212]

All this is far from being without significance, but it would be a mistake to suppose that these fortunate improvements immediately altered the author's position for the better. These improvements were rather promises for the future than realities of the present. The theatre was going down, and while in detail paying more, was earning less; publishing was still tentative and timid, and only preparing for future expansion. As for the City, it offered a dangerous lure to writers, as many who entered its service discovered to their cost. The reader will remember that after the controversy provoked by Dryden's *Duke of Guise*, Hunt was obliged to quit the country and Shadwell to renounce the theatre which had been his source of livelihood. Another Whig pamphleteer, Robert Ferguson, was likewise compelled to seek refuge in Holland.[213] Henry Care, who had edited *A Packet of Advice from Rome* and was the author of *Towser the Second*, ill satisfied with the support given him by the City, turned his back on the Whigs and rallied in 1687 to the banner of James II.[214] Even Settle, whom the City had more particularly enlisted, having quitted the Court for the City, found his illusions shattered and was driven into quitting the City and returning again to the Court.[215]

---

[211] "Dryden's price for a prologue had usually been five guineas, with which sum Southerne presented him when he received from him a prologue for one of his new plays; Dryden returned the money and said to him, 'Young man, this is too little; I must have ten guineas.' Southerne observing his usual price had been five guineas, 'Yes,' answered Dryden, 'it has been so; but the players have hitherto had my labours too cheap: for the future I will have ten guineas.'" (Life of Southerne, prefixed to his *Works*, p. 5.)

The biographer does not mention the date; but the first prologue Dryden wrote for Southerne was of 1682 (*The Loyal Brother*); the last was 1684 (*The Disappointment*). Pope's lines, *To Mr. Thomas Southern on his Birth-day*, 1742, prove that Dryden's example was applauded by his fellows. Pope calls Southerne

". . . Tom sent to raise
The price of prologues and of plays."

[212] "Note. The Poet receiv'd for his third Day in the House in *Drury Lane* at single Prizes 130l. which was the greatest Receipt they ever had at that House at single Prizes." (Downes, p. 41.)

[213] à Wood, *Athenæ Oxonienses*, s.v. Cooper (Anthony Ashley).

[214] Ibid., s.v. James (Thomas).

[215] See below, p. 201. Settle himself says: "Alas, I was grown weary of my little Talent in Innocent *Dramaticks*, and forsooth must be rambling

All things considered, there was in fact—just as in the past —no harbour of refuge for the author save the Court. Yet the Court, while showing more respect for him than heretofore, still failed to provide practical assistance. Amid all the political difficulties which surrounded the close of his reign, Charles II remained as feather-headed and carefree as at the beginning. Now and again he was seized by an attack of generosity and when Dryden had, at his command, written his poem, *The Medal*, the King suddenly flung him a gift of a hundred " broad pieces " say between £115 and £125.[216] But these noble impulses were exceptional, not recurrent. Whatever hopes the resurgence of politics may have aroused in them, authors were soon compelled to realize that the reign of indifference—at least to all that personally concerned them—was not over. After having collaborated with Dryden in writing *The Duke of Guise*, Lee was driven out of his mind by hope deferred, and was consigned to Bedlam in 1684.[217] Otway, the author of *Venice Preserv'd*, the ardent Tory who turned Shaftesbury to ridicule and wrote such impassioned prologues for the royal cause, died of hunger [218]; Crowne on such good terms with Charles, Crowne, author of *City Politiques*, voiced in 1685 his view of poetry as " a pleasant but barren country " [219]; weary and disheartened by the precariousness of success in the theatre, he begged a post of the King: in vain.[220] The Merry Monarch remained the same to the end. In 1683, when Dryden had just shown himself the gallant champion of the Court, and stunned the triumphant

into *Politicks*; And much I have got by 't, for, I thank 'em, they have undone me." (Dedication of *Distress'd Innocence*.)

" Recanting Settle . . .
Protests his Tragedies and Libels fail
To yield him Paper, Penny-Loaves and Ale,
And bids our Youth by his Example fly
The Love of Politicks and Poetry."
(Poems on Affairs of State, *A Satyr upon the Poets*, II, pp. 138 ff.)

[216] Spence, p. 172. " Broad piece, a golden Coin some worth 23 shillings and others 25." (Bailey, *English Dictionary*, 1736.)
[217] Spence, p. 62.
[218] See above chap. I, note No. 442.
[219] See above chap. I, note No. 398. He was still of the same opinion in 1694: " How many Kings and Queens have I had the honour to divertise? And how fruitless has been all my Labours? . . . a maker of Fires at Court has made himself a better Fortune, than Men much my Superiors in Poetry could do, by all the noble Fire in their Writings." (Dedication of *The Married Beau*.)
[220] Dennis, *Original Letters*, I, pp. 49 ff.

Whigs by writing in breathless succession *Absalom and Achitophel, The Medal*, and *The Duke of Guise*, not to mention *Mac Flecknoe* and *Religio Laici*, his salary as Poet Laureate and Historiographer Royal was four years in arrears, and he was driven to writing the following melancholy letter to the First Lord of the Treasury [221]:

> My Lord ;—I know not whether my Lord Sunderland has interceded with your lordship for half a year of my salary : but I have two other advocates, my extreme wants, even almost to arresting, and my ill health, which cannot be repaired without immediate retiring into the country. A quarter's allowance is but the Jesuit's powder to my disease : the fit will return a fortnight hence. If I durst, I would plead a little merit, and some hazards of my life from the common enemies ; my refusing advantages offered by them, and neglecting my beneficial studies for the King's service ; but I only think I merit not to starve. I never applied myself to any interest contrary to your lordship's, and on some occasions, perhaps not known to you, have not been unserviceable to the memory and reputation of my lord your father.[222] After this, my lord, my conscience assures me, I may write boldly though I cannot speak to you. I have three sons growing to man's estate ; I bred them all up to learning, beyond my fortune ; but they are too hopeful to be neglected, though I want. Be pleased to look on me with an eye of compassion. Some small employment would render my condition easy. The King is not unsatisfied of me ; the Duke has often promised me his assistance ; and your lordship is the conduit through which they pass ; either in the Customs, or the Appeals of the Excise, or some other way, means cannot be wanting, if you please to have the will. 'Tis enough for one age to have neglected Mr. Cowley and starved Mr. Butler ; but neither of them had the happiness to live till your lordship's ministry. In the meantime, be pleased to give me a gracious and speedy answer to my present request of half a year's pension for my necessities. I am going to write somewhat by his Majesty's command,[223] and cannot stir into the country for my studies, till I secure my family from want. You have many petitions of this nature, and cannot satisfy all ; but I hope from your goodness to be made an exception to your general rules, because I am with all sincerity
>   Your lordship's most obedient humble servant
>   JOHN DRYDEN.

In reply to this petition the poet was given a post in the Customs from which the income was fluctuating and uncertain.

---

[221] This letter has neither address nor date. Malone has supplied both. He believes the date to be August 1683. Both his hypotheses seem fully justified.

[222] That is to say Clarendon. The First Lord of the Treasury, Lawrence Hyde, Earl of Rochester, was his second son. Dryden is no doubt referring to the verses he had in earlier days addressed to the Lord Chancellor. See above, p. 26.

[223] Probably his translation of Maimbourg's *History of the League*.

As for his salary they remitted to him in 1684—as a favour—
—not half a year's but a quarter's arrears. Fifteen quarters
remained unpaid. It is true that some years before, the King
had graciously accorded him a supplementary pension of £100,
but this was paid like his salary, and at the end of 1683 four years
of it also were still owing. It was on the same lines that Dorante
discharged his debt to M. Jourdain.

Dorante: How much does that come to?
M. Jourdain: That makes a total of 15,800 francs. Add to that
another 200 louis which you are going to give me and that will make
it exactly 18,000 francs which I shall pay you at the first opportunity.

So much for Charles II.[224] As for his brother, he had neither
time nor taste for literature. Even if his fight for Roman
Catholicism had left him the necessary leisure, he was of too
stern and gloomy a temperament to be moved by art. By
nature he was insensitive to the charms of literature, and saw
nothing in it but its political value. His interest in writers was
measured only by the service they could render towards the
triumph of his views. We have seen that he employed many,
and we may safely assume that he paid them punctually for
the work he commissioned. Being, however, neither cultured
nor generous, he confined himself to paying his debt at the just
price, as a man pays his tailor or his shoemaker, feeling the
transaction ended once the cash had changed hands.[225] Charles,
the slave of pleasure and always penniless, loved literature
without paying for it; James, frigid, miserly, and fanatically
taken up with his religious task, purchased literature without

[224] In his poem *Threnodia Augustalis*, written to mourn the death of
Charles II, Dryden could not refrain from including lines like these:
"Tho little was their [the poets'] Hire, and light their Gain,
Yet somewhat to their share he threw;
Fed from his Hand, they sung and flew,
Like Birds of Paradise, that liv'd on Morning Dew.
Oh never let their Lays his Name forget!
The Pension of a Prince's Praise is great."

[225] How niggardly he was with money, we see from the fact that Dryden,
while rendering him services such as no other man could render, was driven
to interlard his political writing with more remunerative work, to grind out
prologues and epilogues and partner Tonson in his first publishing ventures.
It is true that James II knighted L'Estrange and Etherege and gave Southerne
a commission in the army (*Biographia Britannica*, s.vv. L'Estrange, Etherege;
Life of Southerne prefixed to his works); but these marks of favour cost him
nothing. Talking of Etherege, let me relate his end. He went as English
Plenipotentiary to Ratisbon, got drunk, fell down the well of the staircase
and killed himself. A splendid finale, and a fine text for a sermon!

caring for it. So great was his contempt of it that it amounted to ingratitude. If any man in England had a claim on his gratitude, assuredly Dryden was that man. Dryden, who during the furious controversies over the Bill of Exclusion had struck a staggering blow at the Whigs, rallied the terrified Tories and perhaps—it is not too much to say—secured the Duke of York's accession to the throne.[225a] Yet one of the first acts of this same Duke of York when he became James II was to practise his economies on the author of *Absalom and Achitophel* by cancelling the supplementary pension of £100 granted him by Charles II, and—miracle of meanness—the tierce of Canary wine from the royal cellars which since the days of Ben Jonson the King of England had annually sent his Poet Laureate.

In short nothing, or very little, had radically altered. Writers had to fend for themselves as best they might amid the same old difficulties as in the past, with the result that they continued to be courtiers as they had been before. They remained vassals of the Court and having previously obliged by producing fashionable drama, they now equally obligingly produced fashionable politics. Some of them no doubt overdid the sycophancy a trifle, but it would be unfair to blame them overmuch. It is obvious that they could not yet aspire to independence, as was proved by the unhappy fate of those who tried to emancipate themselves in premature reliance on the City; they dare not yet attempt to walk alone, for the ground under their inexperienced feet was too unstable. *Nolens volens*, they could but accept their fate, cling to the skirts only of the Court, and adapt themselves to its opinions as they had earlier adapted themselves to its tastes. It is easy to imagine that this compulsion always to follow some one, did not help to raise their moral qualities. This subordination, this necessity of winning approval from on high—under pain of getting sacked—compelled them to stifle their own individuality and aim solely at pleasing. Their only ambition was to be a faithful echo; far from seeking to develop their own personal views they tailored their opinions according to those of the people in power and painstakingly strove to avoid running counter to them.

As a sort of compensation, they were wholly unembarrassed

[225a] [This is an exaggeration, if a pardonable one. The issue was fought out in the House of Lords, while Charles lounged by the fireplace pretending amusement. The Exclusion Bill was defeated largely by the efforts of Halifax, and *Absalom and Achitophel* can have had little effect on this crucial point. B. D.]

by their own inconsistency. We have already seen Dryden producing his comedy, *The Spanish Fryar*, calculated to please the Whigs rather than the Court,[226] and then to please the Court fling off his coat to give the Whigs a drubbing. Other authors acted likewise. After having in 1681 produced his tragedy of *Lucius Junius Brutus*, which was promptly suppressed because the over-frequent recurrence of the word "liberty" grated on courtly ears, Lee hastened the next year to make amends by joining Dryden in writing *The Duke of Guise*. In 1679 Crowne was a Tory passionately preaching passive obedience [227]; in 1681 he was a Whig attacking the Roman Catholics [228]; by 1683 he was a Tory again savaging the Whigs and Protestants [229]; after the Revolution he was a Whig once more.[230] Nahum

[226] About this time his reputation as a Whig was so well established that in the anti-Shaftesbury pamphlet above quoted (chap. II, note No. 57) he is named with Shadwell as designated to accompany Shaftesbury to Poland to be an official of his government. His name is followed by this description : "Our poet laureat, for writing panegyrics upon Oliver Cromwel, and libels against his present master, King Charles II of England."

[227]   "Duke—Princes are sacred, ,
What e're Religious Rebels may pretend,
Murderers of Kings are Worshippers of Devils
For none but Devils are worship by such Sacrifices . . .
      . . . No Sacrilege
Greater, than when a Rebel with his Sword
Dare's cut the hand of Heaven from King's Commissions
To hide the Devils' mark upon his own.
I lifted up my Arm against the Dauphin,
It ought to have dy'd and rotted in the Air."
            (*The Ambitious Statesman*, V, last scene.)

[228]   *Henry the Sixth*, see above, p. 143.
"Pagan and Popish priests
Are but two names for the same bloody beasts . . .
Then halter priests and tye 'em to the racks,
If you will keep the Devil off their backs."
            (*Thyestes*, Epilogue.)

[229]   "There is in every true *Protestant* Breast }
A *Heraclitus Ridens*, his Contest,   }
A Knave in Earnest, and a Saint in Jest   }
The Saint looks up to Heaven, the Knave that while
Your Pocket picks and at the Cheat does smile . . ."
            (*City-Politiques* I, i.)

See also above, p. 146.
[230] In his *English Frier* he attacks James II's Court and the Roman Catholics ; in the Prologue he reproaches those who
"... are so Mad, they'd give up *Englands* Glory,
Only to keep the wretched Name of *Tory*."
In the Dedication of his *Caligula*, he celebrates the Revolution, and acidly criticizes Charles II and James II : ". . . this Revolution, which has been

Tate, whose *Sicilian Usurper* was banned by the Court, produced indubitably Tory work in *The Ingratitude of a Common-Wealth* and *Cuckolds-Haven*, and in collaborating in the Second Part of *Absalom and Achitophel*. This did not prevent his accepting from William III the post of Poet Laureate. D'Urfey, who under Charles II and James II had put his dramatic and lyric gifts at the service of the Tories, employed the same gifts against them after the Revolution.[231] Sprat, who had begun his literary career with lines in praise of Cromwell, having obeyed James II's command to write a narrative of the Rye-House Plot, found it simple and natural to disclaim and excuse this work when William III became King.[232] L'Estrange was the complaisant tool of royal politics, whoever might happen to be King. He attacked all Nonconformists under James II. So far did he go in this direction that people thought he had turned Roman Catholic and he had publicly to deny the report. Hunt undertook to defend the City's rights only after having written first in favour of the Court in the hopes of securing an important post and finding it awarded to another aspirant.[233] Henry Care, after violently abusing the Roman Catholics in his news-

---

so happy to England, and the greatest part of Europe. Had not this change been, almost all Europe had been overrun by France; England, for certain, had lost its Rights, Liberties and Religion, and perhaps, been no more a Kingdom, but a Province to France, a Vassal to Vassals, and for all its Wealth had nothing but a Wafer ... And what a glorious Figure does England now make in Comparison of what it did some years ago? It lay one Reign becalm'd in Luxury: In another Fetter'd: In this Reign it has not only freed it self, but humbled France, and protected Germany, Spain and Holland, and appears one of the greatest Powers in Christendom."

[231] "Let's leave this Scene of Death, and to the People,
With kind Oration, settle our new Royalty;
Pull down the Fabrick of ill Government,
And found one upon Justice, Truth and Honour
Whilst all good Subjects, glorying in their Change,
Reflect on Ills from Tyranny did grow,
And bless the happy Revolution now."
(*The Grecian Heroine*. These are the closing lines of the tragedy.)

See also the characters of Lady Addleplot and Lady Stroddle in *Love for Money*. They are thus described: "*Lady Addleplot*, A lusty flaunting imperious Lady, a highflown Stickler against the Government, and always railing at it and talking of Politicks.—*Lady Stroddle*, Her Companion, a Papist and Grumbler."

See also Addison, *The Guardian*, No. 67.

[232] Johnson, *Lives of the English Poets*, Sprat; *Biographia Britannica*, s.v. Sprat.

[233] à Wood, *Athenæ Oxonienses*, s.v. Hunt (Thomas).

paper, did a right-about-turn under James II and abused the Protestants.[234] Settle—having renounced the plaudits of the Court to link his fortunes to the Whigs', having presided over the burning of the Pope's effigy in the City, having written a reply to Dryden's loyal poems and, at Shaftesbury's dictation, *The Character of a Popish Successor*,[235]—became convinced that the City was not going to prove the stronger party, and forthwith unblushingly forswore his Whig convictions in a recantation published in 1683,[236] brutally attacked his former friends, fired off a pamphlet against Russell after his execution, concocted a heroic poem on the coronation of James II, composed a panegyric on the odious Jeffreys, and wound up by enlisting in the army of the "Popish Successor" mobilized on Hounslow Heath. After the Revolution he refurbished his friendship for the City and became its Poet Laureate.[237]

On the accession of James II, when the sole way of currying favour with the King was to adopt his religion, there were many who had no hesitation in staging a conversion.

It seems probable that Wycherley was one of these. The information about him that has come down to us is scanty; but we know for certain that his creditors had detained him in prison for seven years, that James II procured his release by paying his debts, and that he died a Roman Catholic.[238] Are we wronging the Duchess of Cleveland's protégé if we assume that these two facts are related, and that other considerations than his soul's salvation won him for the Roman Church? Are we misjudging James II if we assume that it was not the pure love of literature which loosed his purse-strings—normally so firmly tied—for the sake of a man whose heart seemed promising soil for the good seed? No one can be in much doubt about the answer.

A companion of Wycherley's in opportune conversion was

[234] Ibid., s.v. James (Thomas).
[235] North, *Examen*, p. 96.
[236] A Narrative.—See also *The Present State of England In relation to Popery*.
[237] à Wood, *Athenæ Oxonienses*, s.v. Settle; Scott and Saintsbury, *Works of John Dryden*, IX, p. 355 ff.; Nichols, *Literary Anecdotes*, I, p. 41, note; Disraeli, *Calamities and Quarrels of Authors*: Pope's Earliest Satire; Pope, *Dunciad*, III, ll. 277 ff.; *Biographia Dramatica*, s.v. *Pageants*; see also my Bibliography.
[238] Spence, p. 2; Pack, *Miscellanies*, p. 181 ff.; Allibone, article Wycherley.—Wycherley had first, in France, been a Roman Catholic; when he came back to England he turned Protestant, finally to die as a Roman Catholic.

the author-actor Joseph Haines—known to his intimates as Joe Haines—who was famous for the prologues and epilogues he wrote and himself delivered with great success. When James came to the throne, Haines made a great to-do about a vision he had had of the Virgin Mary, proclaimed himself a convert, was promptly distinguished by the new King and selected as one of the suite to accompany the noble consort of Lady Castlemaine as Ambassador to Rome.[239]

But the most famous and the saddest of these conversions was John Dryden's.

In his case we should prefer to doubt; it is painful to accuse this great genius of a bogus conversion for material advantage. But we seek in vain for sound and convincing reasons to acquit him, and can only exclaim with André de Chénier:

> I'd have liked to believe him, I vow to the skies
> I'd rather have doubted the facts and my eyes.
> But alas, it's not true that outstanding parts
> Cannot flourish in other than high-minded hearts.
> A mortal may strike most sublimely the lyre,
> Yet be weak-kneed, and narrow, and lacking in fire;
> Unskilled in the virtues his songs so well praise,
> In words he extols them, in practice betrays.[240]

It looks sorely as if Dryden went over to Rome out of faint-heartedness.

Johnson and Walter Scott [241]—swayed by their admiration for the poet and perhaps not uninfluenced by their own political sympathies,—believed, and have tried to prove, that his conversion was the result of genuine conviction and untainted by worldly considerations. Unfortunately it is difficult to accept their special pleading. The damning fact remains that Dryden's

---

[239] *Biographia Dramatica*, s.v. Haines; Tom Brown, *The Reasons of Mr. Joseph Hains the Player's Conversion and Re-Conversion*.

[240] "Ah! j'atteste les cieux que j'ai voulu le croire;
J'ai voulu démentir et mes yeux et l'histoire.
Mais non! il n'est pas vrai que des cœurs excellents
Soient les seuls, en effet, où germent les talents.
Un mortel peut toucher une lyre sublime,
Et n'avoir qu'un cœur faible, étroit, pusillanime;
Inhabile aux vertus qu'il sait si bien chanter,
Ne les imiter point et les faire imiter."
(André de Chénier, edited by Gabriel de Chénier, Paris, 1874, II, p. 150.)

[241] Hallam, Professor Masson, Robert Bell, John Skelton and George Saintsbury follow suit. Saintsbury is the author of an admirable Life of Dryden and an excellent edition of his works, both of which have appeared

conversion was extremely opportune. Even while defending him, Johnson is compelled to admit that people will always suspect the worst, where a person derives personal advantage from a change of faith. Now, the moment of Dryden's conversion coincided on the one hand with the King's reinstatement of Roman rites in Westminster after an interval of 127 years, and on the other with the retrenchment of his pension at James's command. The immediate result of his conversion was the restoration of his income in full.[242] If his change of faith was bona fide, how could he bear even to appear to accept a cash reward for it? One wonders.

Dryden had hitherto shown no marked interest of any kind in religious matters. He shared the comprehensive scepticism of the Restoration and its cynical contempt for priests of every church and of every country. A casual glance at any of his plays, tragic or comic, confirms this view of his mental attitude.

If we trace his expressed views on Roman Catholicism and Protestantism, from the moment when the two came into conflict, we shall find him alternately backing the one or the other according as his personal interest or the success of his work seemed to dictate. The Duke of York had chosen a moment when a wave of Protestant feeling was at its height to make public profession of his Roman faith; Dryden promptly exploited

---

since the first edition of this book. He defends Dryden without reserve and yet his view is not fundamentally very different from my own when he says: "It is fully believable that a sense that he was about to be on the winning side may have assisted his rapid determination from Hobbism or Halifaxism to Roman orthodoxy." (G. Saintsbury, *Dryden*, p. 103.)—See the next note. Macaulay (*History*, chap. VII) and W. D. Christie take the other line.

[242] According to Bell's calculations Dryden's conversion took place at the close of 1686 while his pension was restored in full in 1685-6. But Bell himself admits that the conversion probably soon followed, shrewdly adding that if Dryden changed his religion for a pension, the transaction does not become more edifying by proving that he wanted to make sure of the pension before admitting his conversion. I would myself add that it is clear that Dryden did not crudely sell his soul for £100 of pension but that he was certainly influenced by the hope of winning the royal favour.

[Dryden's conversion to Roman Catholicism exposed him to many attacks during his lifetime, as did many of the events of his life (see *Essays and Studies*, xxi, 1936, the article by Hugh Macdonald). In the matter of his religion posterity until lately has not treated him generously. Recent researches, especially by Professor L. Bredvold, have shown that the conversion took place some time before the death of Charles; but his change of faith need cause no surprise. Like many others of his day, permeated by the scepticism made agreeable by Montaigne, he in the end turned to the old faith: his conversion is really implicit in *Religio Laici*, from which it is only a short step to *The Hind and the Panther*. B. D.]

the prevalent emotion by giving the subsidiary title of *Love in a Nunnery* to his new comedy *The Assignation*.

That was as early as 1672. This second title indicated a definite anti-Papist bias which the epilogue reinforced by very outspoken comments on convents in general.[243] The obvious aim was to attract public attention to the new play. When all England was at fever-heat over the Popish Plot in 1681, Dryden sought to curry favour with the mob by a new attack on the Romanists and wrote his *Spanish Fryar* [244] with evident enjoyment. This was ill calculated to please James II—sensitive as he was in such matters—who banned its performance during his reign. That no one might this time mistake his intention Dryden dedicated this play to Lord Haughton, " recommending a Protestant play to a Protestant patron "—the phrase is worth noting. Then, observing that in playing to the gallery he had somewhat compromised his position with the King's brother, he reversed his engine and softened down the anti-Papist tone of his comedy. But he was not yet aware that the King had secret leanings towards the Roman Church, and he continued to make anti-Romanist allusions as occasion offered, and amongst other delicacies he slipped into *Absalom and Achitophel* a fairly vulgar view of transubstantiation.[245] In *Religio Laici* he is still

[243] " Some have expected from our bills today,
To find a *Satire* in our *Poet's Play*.
The *zealous Rout* from *Coleman-Street* did run
To see the Story of the *Fryer* and *Nun*
Or Tales, yet more ridiculous to hear,
Vouch'd by their Vicar of ten pounds a year ;
Of Nuns, who did against Temptation Pray,
And Discipline laid on the Pleasant Way :
Or that to please the Malice of the Town,
Our *Poet* should in some close Cell have shown
Some Sister, Playing at Content alone : " . . .

[244] See above, chap. I, note No. 431. In the first Act he ridicules processions ; in the second, the invocation of saints ; in the third, auricular confession. The Epilogue is supposed to be written by a friend of the Author's, but is in fact too good to be from any other hand than Dryden's own. It contains the line :

" Well may they give the God they can devour."

[245] " Such savory Deities must needs be good,
And serv'd at once for Worship and for Food."

It is amusing to compare this passage with *The Hind and the Panther* (part I, ll. 134 ff.) :

" Could He his Godhead veil with flesh and Bloud,
And not veil these again to be our food ?
His Grace in both is equal in extent,
The first affords us life, the second nourishment."

a Protestant and an orthodox one and is anxious only to lead back into the Anglican fold Roman Catholics [246] and Nonconformists alike. Yet in the very same year his *Vindication of the Duke of Guise* warmly championed the right of a Roman Catholic heir to succeed to the throne in defiance of Protestant prejudice. These two mutually contradictory pieces of special pleading date from 1682. Charles II died in 1685 and the champion of the English Church bade farewell to Protestantism and adopted the religion of his new King. In 1687 he wrote *The Hind and the Panther*, the very negation of *Religio Laici*.

It might well seem that his waverings now were ended, and that in future his path would be undeviatingly straight.[247] Yet even while he was writing *The Hind and the Panther* his point of view shifted on a question of religious sympathy if not of doctrine. When the poem opens, the English Church is flattered and courted; she should make common cause with Rome to silence the dissenting sects. At the close and in the Preface— written last—the suggestion of an alliance is made instead to the Protestant Dissenters, who are now invited to form a common front with the Roman Catholics against the Anglicans. The

[246] Neither Preface nor poem shows much tenderness towards Roman Catholics. Witness the following lines (ll. 370-93) :
"In times o'ergrown with Rust and Ignorance,
A gainfull Trade their Clergy did advance ;
When want of Learning kept the *Laymen* low,
And none but *Priests* were *Authoriz'd* to *know* :
When what small Knowledge was, in them did dwell ;
And he a *God* who cou'd but *Reade* or *Spell* ;
Then *Mother Church* did mightily prevail :
She parcel'd out the Bible by *retail* :
But still *expounded* what She *sold* or *gave* ;
To keep it in *her Power* to *Damn* and *Save* :
Scripture was *scarce*, and as the Market went,
Poor *Laymen* took *Salvation* on *Content* ;
As needy men take Money, good or bad :
God's word they had not, but the *Priests* they had.
Yet, whate'er *false Conveyances* they made,
The *Lawyer* still was *certain* to be paid.
In those dark times they learn'd their knack so well,
That by long use they grew *Infallible* :
At last, a knowing Age began t'enquire
If *they* the Book, or *That* did *them* inspire :
And, making narrower search they found, tho late,
That what they thought the *Priest's* was *Their* Estate :
Taught by the *Will produc'd*, (the written Word)
How long they had been *cheated on Record*."

[247] He himself declared : "My doubts are done." (*The Hind and the Panther*, I, line 78.)

dramatist offers them the rôle of victors instead of vanquished.[248] Why? Because, while the poem was still a-making, the King had without warning switched his religious policy, and since he despaired of winning over the Anglican clergy, was ogling the very fanatics whom he had so recently abhorred. The poet, faithful echo of his master, finished his song on a different note from that he had struck at the beginning.

Such was the man whose admirers would persuade us that genuine conviction prompted his conversion to Rome. But it is impossible to blink the fact that Dryden was perpetually changing, not for those intimate and conscientious reasons which command from everyone a tribute of respect, but for purely worldly motives. It is impossible not to observe that the wind which veered his weathercock, was always his direct and immediate personal advantage.

It is true that his admirers lay weight on the fact that on the accession of William III he remained faithful to his new religion. But surely it was in his own interest not to change again. There is a limit to everything—even to inconstancy. In turning Roman Catholic he had alienated the Whigs but secured the favour of the Tories. If he had turned Protestant again, he would have alienated the Tories without recapturing the confidence of the Whigs. Instead of being despised by one party only, he would have been despised and rejected by both.[249] After the Revolution, the Tories had of course lost the innings, but for many years to come they were by no means without influence, still less without hope. It has been stressed that Dryden " brought up " his sons in the Roman faith,[250] but there are games which you must play to the end or not at all, and in playing a given rôle you may eventually arrive at deceiving even yourself. Besides, at the time of their father's conversion the boys had nearly arrived at manhood, and were of an age to shoulder the responsibility and claim the merit of their own acts.

[248] This has been remarked by Walter Scott in his *Life of Dryden* and by Macaulay in his *History* (chap. VII). Robert Bell, who is violently against Macaulay, has made no comment on this important point.

[249] Joe Haines de-converted himself all right. He publicly displayed his penitence in the theatre, robed in white and bearing a candle in his hand. But Dryden was not Haines. Haines had long since had no character of any kind to lose.

[250] " Brought up " is no apt phrase for children, the youngest of whom was at least sixteen and the eldest nineteen years old. Charles was born in 1666, John in 1667 or 1668, and Erasmus-Henry in 1669. I borrow these dates from Robert Bell, one of the most eager defenders of Dryden.

Lastly, there is something in the last years of Dryden's life which shows that even if he succeeded in taking himself in on the subject,[251] his conversion was not one of those reformations in the presence of which all questioning is silenced. When a man who has long been indifferent or sceptical is suddenly—if belatedly—illumined by the light of faith, his daily life henceforth reflects the new radiance of his soul. Be it Protestant or Roman Catholic, true religion honourably practised imposes respect for certain things, things which Dryden had hitherto treated with scant reverence. To minister to the taste of his contemporaries he had pandered to vice and brought a blush to the cheeks of modesty. He was himself sufficiently aware of the duties which his conversion laid upon him to exclaim: " Good life be now my task." [252] We should therefore expect to see him repenting of his evil ways and turning his back on them for ever. When Racine after the success of *Phèdre*—his genius being then at the height of its power—fèlt called to the serious practice of his religion, he put aside once and for all the work that had been his glory, and did so with an inflexible determination under which his letters groan. Dryden, who had far graver faults to reproach himself with than Racine, remained precisely the sinner he had been before. He staged Molière's *Amphitryon* but packed it full of lasciviousness [253] and in his translation of Roman classics contrived to out-Juvenal Juvenal in daring, to change the outspokenness of Lucretius into disgusting coarseness, and to insinuate indecency even into the *Georgics*.

However reluctantly, and sorely though it be against our will, we are driven to the conclusion that Dryden was no disinterested, single-minded convert. I have dwelt at so much length on this question of Dryden's conversion only because his motives have been so hotly debated. They have been the subject of controversy only because—or so it seems to me—the

---

[251] Professor Masson, a scholar sympathetic to Dryden, justly says: ". . . In consequence of the very obloquy which his change of religion drew upon him from all quarters, he hugged his new creed more closely, so as to coil round him, for the first time in his life, a few threads of private theological conviction." (*Essays*, p. 127.) I am willing to believe that Dryden deceived himself more quickly and more completely than he deceived others, and with a poet's gift of adaptation came to believe himself, and even to be, sincere.

[252] *The Hind and the Panther*, I, l. 78.

[253] It is true that in 1700 he honourably admitted that in many things Collier's indictment of the immorality of the stage had " taxed him justly ". I should reckon his true conversion from this date.

disputants have failed to take due account of the general position of writers at this time.

Thinking of Dryden alone, our minds are dazzled by his genius and chivalrously refuse to believe that his character was unworthy of our homage. Every suspicion of him seems a detraction from his literary glory and we indignantly reject it. Admiration is a jealous mistress; when she falls in love with a man she would fain possess him wholly.

But if we refuse to be hypnotized by a famous name, and extend our researches beyond Dryden himself to the period in which his lot was cast, if we cross-examine his contemporaries, we find that the question solves itself. What was it that Dryden did? Exactly what all his fellow writers of the period did—neither less nor more.[254] Like them, he was unable to make a living by his pen; like them, he was inevitably condemned to seek the patronage of the great; like them, his allegiance changed according to the fortune of the day; like them, he was a writer of his time. The worst we can reproach him with, is that he was not an exception.

But why should he have been an exception? He made no claim to be of other stuff than they. Had he made himself conspicuous by strength of character? Far from it. In politics as in religion his convictions were fluid. He started life as a Republican singing the praises of Cromwell; within two years he was a Royalist enthusiastically hailing the advent of Charles II. In 1673 he wrote *Amboyna* to stir up patriotic feeling in the Dutch War; then in *Absalom and Achitophel* and in *The Medal* he violently attacked Shaftesbury for having been accessory to this war. Even in literary matters we have seen him abase himself—albeit with reluctance—before the gods of fashion and the day.

It is true that he was the greatest of all the living writers of his time. But his temptations were the greater in proportion as his place was the more exalted, and the urgencies of the time pressed on him the more severely. Poet Laureate he might be, but none the less a poet: that is to say a fragile, vulnerable

---

[254] Amongst professional writers I can find none but Shadwell who remained faithful to his political convictions. But Shadwell himself tells us (see above, p. 112 and note No. 396) that he could not give all his time to writing but was "forced to mind some other business of Advantage". I do not know what form this business of advantage took, but whatever it was it probably was his refuge and salvation during the stormy years with which this second chapter deals.

member of society, unable to be self-sufficing, a prey to circumstance.

It is not for us then to be surprised that he gave way as others did : Lee, Crowne, Tate, D'Urfey, Sprat, Hunt, Care, L'Estrange, Settle, Wycherley and Haines. His humiliation, the more striking for the rank he held, should simply throw into relief for us the sorry fate of the writers of his day.

One last touch to the picture will show into what depths they were plunged by the wretched state of dependence to which they were helplessly condemned. Merely to live, they had perforce to adopt the opinions welcome in higher quarters, to ensure attention they had also to prove outstanding zeal. As they had earlier gone to the extreme of indecency to gratify degenerate theatre-goers, so now they exploited political passion—with how little conviction—to the very limit. They had trimmed their sails to one wind, they now trimmed them to another. They championed every violent suggestion ; they showed themselves harsh and cruel ; they trampled under foot all conceptions of friendship, compassion and humanity. The Duke and Duchess of Monmouth had been Dryden's protectors at a time when friends were few and very precious ; yet Dryden boldly attacked the Duke in *Absalom and Achitophel.* He went further. He brought his old patron on the stage in the character of the Duke of Guise rebelling against his father Henry III (that is Charles II), nor did he shrink from following the historic parallel to its end, he showed Henry III murdering the Duke of Guise, thus seeming to advise the royal father to assassinate his son.

After this it is superfluous to go back and re-emphasize the odious forms of his polemic against Shaftesbury. We must dwell, however, on one detail of it. In the Prologue to *Don Sebastian* Dryden had proudly told his fellow-countrymen :

> The British nation is too brave to show
> Ignoble vengeance on a vanquished foe.

When he gave voice to this noble sentiment Dryden was himself on the losing side. As victor, he changed his tune, as did his fellows. They had no chivalry even towards the dead. The coarse allusions to Shaftesbury quoted above from Dryden's *Albion and Albanius* and from Tate's *Cuckolds-Haven* date from 1685, that is to say they appeared after the death of the Whig leader. In the Prologue to the same play Tate thinks it witty to make merry over the Duke of Monmouth, lying under sentence of death if he had not already been executed.[255] Settle attacked Russell after his execution.[256]

The same harshness permeates all they write : they call for the hangman, they cry out for blood. In dedicating to the King his translation of the *History of the League*, Dryden volunteers some political advice. Hark to his counsels :

> Pardons are grown dangerous to your safety, and consequently to the welfare of your loyal subjects . . . you are still forgiving [your enemies] and they still conspiring against your sacred life ; your principle is mercy, theirs inveterate malice ; when one only wards, and the other strikes, the prospect is sad on the defensive side. Hercules, as the poets tell us, had no advantage on Antæus, by his often throwing him on the ground ; for he laid him only in his mother's lap, which, in effect, was but doubling his strength to renew the combat. These sons of earth are never to be trusted in their mother-element ; they must be hoisted into the air and strangled.

There is here nothing ultra-humane, yet this is weak compared with the sinister jesting of the Epilogue to the *Duke of Guise* which, to crown all, was recited by a woman. Just as the dramatists heightened the effect of their indecencies by putting them into the mouths of young actresses, they seem to have sought to emphasize the cynicism of political hatreds by allowing women to give them brutal expression. In this Epilogue the actress Mrs. Cook records a dialogue with a representative of the new party of Trimmers (approximately the type which in French is known as the *Juste-Milieu*). She has just indicated how little love she bears the Whigs, when the Trimmer interjects :

> " Fie, Mistress Cook ! faith, you're too rank a Tory !
> Wish not Whigs hanged, but pity their hard cases ;
> You women love to see men make wry faces."—
> " Pray Sir," said I, " don't think me such a Jew ;
> I say no more, but ' give the devil his due.' "—
> " Lenitives," says he, " best suit with our condition."—
> " Jack Ketch," [257] says I, " 's an excellent physician."—
> " I love no blood."—" Nor I, Sir, as I breathe ;
> But hanging is a fine dry kind of death."—

---

[255] " Our Trinculo and Trapp'lin were undone
When Lime's more Farcy Monarchy begun "
Trinculo is the buffoon in Shakespeare's *Tempest* ; Trappolin is one of the characters in a play of Tate's : *A Duke and No Duke*.
[256] See above, p. 201.
[257] The executioner of the day. He had been with Judge Jeffreys during the Bloody Assizes and had executed Lords Russell and the Duke of Monmouth. His name proverbially denotes a hangman.

" We Trimmers are for holding all things even."—
" Yes ; just like him that hung 'twixt Hell and Heaven."—
" Have we not had men's lives enow already ? "—
" Yes, sure : but you're for holding all things steady.
Now since the weight hangs all on one side, brother,
You Trimmers should, to poise it, hang on the other."

The need to gratify political passion thus led authors to forswear all tolerance, to renounce all humane feeling.

The tragedy is that this could not be otherwise. Appearances notwithstanding, the hapless author had no one he could turn to but the Court. Hence followed two almost fatal results : on the one hand, he must at all costs please the King and Court and in so doing set his feet upon a slippery slope ; on the other hand, though the Court his mistress may value his services a trifle more than of old she makes little effort to reward him, for there he is, for ever thrusting himself on her, and when she wants him she is sure to find him waiting, as submissive as ever, as eager as ever to do her bidding. She may fling him now and then a careless smile, but so little fear has she of losing his devotion that she has no mind to make any sacrifices for his benefit. It is a vicious circle : the more he needs the Court, the more he humbles himself to woo her ; the more he abases himself, the less his graceless mistress does for him.

It is this preponderating influence of the Court which explains why the improvements in the author's lot which we have noted, have as yet borne so little fruit. None the less, these improvements were real, and after the Revolution we shall find them developing in a new atmosphere and beginning to prove effective.

CHAPTER III

JOSEPH ADDISON
(1688–1721)

I

Modifications in monarchical practice introduced by the Revolution.—The King's need of public support.—Rôle of literature in the Government : Halifax, Somers, Dorset, Montague, etc.—Whigs and Tories enlist writers on their side.—Favour and lucrative posts showered on authors.—Shadwell, Tate, Eusden, Rowe, Smith, Hughes, Ambrose Philips, Parnell, Arbuthnot, Garth, Blackmore, Granville, Stepney, Maynwaring, Walsh, Martyn, Tickell, Locke, Newton, Steele, Swift, Defoe, Congreve, Vanbrugh, Gay, Addison, Prior, Montague

The revolution changed many things in England. The sovereign no longer wielded absolute and unquestioned authority by right of birth ; his authority rested on the nation's confidence. The royal power, begotten of public opinion, was obliged to heed the parent's will. Having set up the throne, the public could also overturn it ; and the Jacobite party was there, ever on the alert, awaiting the moment when friction should arise between the King and his subjects.

Those at the head of affairs were therefore continually concerned to preserve harmony and to avert friction. Their task was not merely by their own effort to conciliate public opinion, but to enlist the co-operation of everyone who was in a position to sway people's minds. The King chose ministers who had the ear of Parliament, the ministers sought everywhere to find support for their views and their administration. This being so, they were compelled to enlist the service of authors, who had in recent days so effectively demonstrated the weight their pen could throw into the political scales, and whose importance daily increased with the growth of the Press.

True, the new King whom the Revolution placed on the English throne was no literary connoisseur. William III had but a moderate knowledge of English, and even if he had known enough to appreciate the literature of his new home, we may fairly doubt his having been likely to show much sympathy for writers or to have valued highly the services they could render him. He believed in two things : war and diplomacy.[1] Charles II loved literature without paying for it ; James II paid for it without loving it ; William III neither loved nor paid.[2]

The authors were thereby the gainers. William's ministers appreciated them instead, and with much fuller understanding than the King could have shown.

For amongst the first men whom William III summoned to aid him in the tasks of government, there were many warm friends of literature. Some of them had by their pen helped to ensure the success of the Revolution, and owed no small share of their reputation and influence to their writings. There was Halifax, for instance, head of the Trimmers and probably the author of *Letter to a Dissenter* [3] ; there was Somers, the learned lawyer who encouraged Tonson to re-publish *Paradise Lost*, who had collaborated in a translation of Plutarch for which Dryden wrote a life of the Greek historian, and to whom were attributed many pro-Whig political pamphlets that appeared under James II.[4] Finally there was Dorset, who had put aside the follies of his Buckhurst days, but had retained the courteous manners and fine literary taste of his youth,[4a] and become the discriminating and

---

[1] When he met Swift at Sir William Temple's he offered to make him a Captain in his cavalry. (Forster, *Life of Jonathan Swift*, p. 66.)
[But at that time Swift had hardly begun to write, and nothing noteworthy had come from his pen. It is unlikely that William III would have made him such an offer in 1712, had he been alive, or even in 1704. B. D.]
[2] Yet the story goes that when Dorset presented Montague (one of the authors of *The Country Mouse and City Mouse*) to the King, saying : " Sir, I have brought a *Mouse* to wait on your Majesty ", William replied : " You do well to put me in the way of making a *Man* of Him ", and ordered him a pension of £500. The anecdote is certainly apocryphal, and in any case it is Dorset who is cast in it for the principal part. Dr. Johnson's comment is : " The king's answer implies a greater acquaintance with our proverbial and familiar diction than King William could possibly have attained." (*Lives of the English Poets*, Halifax.)
[3] Another political publication, *The Character of a Trimmer*, is attributed sometimes to Halifax and sometimes to Sir William Coventry. (Stephens, *Catalogue*, I, p. 751.)
[*The Character of a Trimmer*, admirable reading even to-day, and which contains many famous passages, is undoubtedly by Halifax. See any edition of his *Works*. B. D.]
[4] Malone, *Life of Dryden*, p. 180 ; *Biographia Britannica*, s.v. Somers.—" In defense of these *ignoramus* juries, it was said that . . . a book was wrote . . . it passed as writ by Lord Essex, though I understood afterwards it was writ by Somers, who . . . writ the best papers that came out in that time." (Burnet, *History of my Own Times*, II, p. 290.)—See also above chap. II, note No. 161.
[4a] [" Dorset, the grace of Courts, the Muses' pride." B. D.]

open-handed Mæcenas of two reigns.⁵ Later, Charles Montague, one of the lucky authors of *The Country Mouse and the City Mouse*, became a Minister, and since he owed his advancement entirely to literature he could not be indifferent to its fortunes.⁶

These men had seen with their own eyes how powerfully public opinion might be influenced by a happily conceived, well-timed poem or pamphlet. They remembered how Dryden had called a halt to the triumph of the Whigs, and himself had in turn been rendered impotent by their replies. They themselves had personally contributed by their writings to his defeat. They were bound to feel, and did in fact evince, a peculiar sympathy for authors. They succeeded in setting up in ministerial circles a tradition of patronage towards literature which their successors maintained for thirty years to come.

This Whig tradition was promptly adopted by the Tories. The Opposition could ill afford to allow the Revolution to monopolize the credit and the advantage of patronizing writers. If Dorset and Montague were the great Whig patrons of literature, the Tories Harley and Bolingbroke, both in Parliament and in office, rivalled them in munificence and zeal.

The happenings that attended the first appearance of Addison's *Cato* are a good indication of the party attitudes to literature. The author, who was one of the glories of the Whig camp, produced his play at a time when the Tories were temporarily victorious and in power. The Whigs applauded it with an enthusiasm compounded of vexation at their defeat and pleasure in a friend's success. They saw in it a means of scoring off the enemy. But the Tories had no mind to let them do so. They countered the Whig applause by applauding even more loudly,

---

⁵ Halifax, who was already Leader of the House of Lords, was made Lord Privy Seal; Somers became Solicitor-General; Dorset was Lord Chamberlain.—The Queen's Vice-Chamberlain was also an author, though one of dubious repute. He was John Howe, popularly known as Jack Howe, the putative author of many recent lampoons. (Macaulay, *History*, Chap. XI.) —Ferguson (see above chap. II, note No. 213) also held a fat sinecure in the Excise (Macaulay, *History*, chap. XI; Stephens, *Catalogue*, I, p. 703).

⁶ " Wit and Learning have from your Example fallen into a new Æra . . . it is to you we owe, that the Man of Wit has turned himself to be a Man of Business." (Steele, Dedication to Charles, Lord Halifax of the fourth volume of the *Tatler*.)

[It is, to say the least of it, an exaggeration to say that Montague owed his advancement entirely to literature. The Montagues were a powerful family, and he himself had a brilliant financial brain. The first, and so far the only, person in this country to be ennobled purely for literary merit, is Tennyson. B. D.]

and spared no effort to convert the play into a Tory gain. On the evening of the first performance Bolingbroke, Secretary of State and leader of the Tory party, summoned to his box the actor who had played Cato and ostentatiously handed him a purse of fifty guineas, publicly thanking him " for defending the cause of liberty so well against a perpetual dictator ". And Queen Anne, whose sympathies were naturally Tory, sent a message to Addison the Whig, to say that she would be happy to permit the play to be dedicated to her.[7] Each side was eager to claim the author for itself.

It sometimes happened that each party chose a different champion. Addison had sung the glories of the great victory of Blenheim, so that Tories entrusted John Philips with the task of celebrating it on their behalf and the rival poem was written under Bolingbroke's roof.[8]

The author was thus being sought after by Ministers—who, thanks to the daily-increasing importance of the House of Commons, were gradually becoming the real rulers of the country —and at the same time sought after by a powerful and sometimes victorious Opposition, which was in a position to offer him more solid benefits than the City had provided for Settle and his friends. He had henceforward no need to beg for favours, they rained down on him unsolicited. He was being courted and could afford to lie back and enjoy the wooing.

As soon as politics began to come to the fore and his potential power was understood, advances had been made towards him, but the eager warmth he was now meeting with was something entirely new. Godolphin, Lord High Treasurer, personally begged Addison to celebrate the victory of Blenheim, and the Chancellor of the Exchequer himself went to the young poet's modest lodging to present the Minister's request.[9] The Whig, Thomas Parnell,

[7] The " perpetual Dictator " was Marlborough.—See Johnson, *Lives of the English Poets*, Addison ; Spence, pp. 46, 47 ; Pope's Letter to Sir William Trumbull, Elwin's Edition of the *Works*, VI, p. 7.

[8] Bolingbroke was at this date plain Henry St. John. See Johnson, op. cit., s.v. J. Philips.
[The skies at that time snowed poems on Blenheim, anonymous and signed. Addison's is the best of a thoroughly mediocre display. B. D.]

[9] See Johnson, *Lives of the English Poets*, Addison ; Budgell, *Life of Lord Orrery*, quoted in *Addisoniana*, p. 683 ; Addison's *Works* edited by Hurd, vol. VI ; Aikin, I, 168-9.
[Godolphin consulted Halifax, who suggested Addison, insisting that the poet should be personally approached. Godolphin did not go himself, but sent Boyle, who, as Chancellor of the Exchequer, would convey honour enough. See Eustace Budgell, *Memoirs of the Life and Character of the Earl of Orrery and*

transferred his political allegiance to the then triumphant Tories. When Harley, Earl of Oxford, was informed that Dr. Parnell was among the crowd waiting in his antechamber, he allowed Swift to persuade him to bid welcome to the new recruit. With his Treasurer's staff in his hand he went out in person to find and bring him in.[10] On the accession of George I, Parker, the new Lord Chancellor, as soon as he received the seals of office, appointed the poet Nicholas Rowe to be Secretary of the Presentations without Rowe's even having applied for the post.[11]

This last example shows that the authorities now not only smiled on authors and anticipated their desires, but offered them solid advantages. Pensions (now punctually paid) and remunerative posts fell to their lot, and they were not precluded from aspiring to even higher honours.

Shadwell was Poet Laureate and Historiographer Royal,[12] Tate,[13] Rowe and Eusden [14] were all in their turn Poets Laureate, and Rowe was in addition one of the Land Surveyors of the Port of London, Clerk of the Prince of Wales's Council and, as we have seen, Secretary of Presentations.[15] Edmund Smith, whose sole literary glory was his tragedy of *Phaedra and Hippolitus* [sic] which was a miserable failure, had no one but himself to thank for missing the chance of a post worth £300 a year.[16] A brother writer Hughes—brother also in obscurity—was more careful of his own interests and secured himself a place in the Ordnance Office, besides being secretary to various commissions for purchasing lands required for the Royal Docks, and finally secretary to the Commission of the Peace.[17] Ambrose Philips was Lottery Commissioner.[18] Parnell, who was in orders, was given a

---

the family of the Boyles. 1732. Budgell, as a protégé of the Boyles, and one of Addison's " little Senate " would be in a position to know. B. D.]

[10] Johnson, ibid., Parnell; Swift, *Journal to Stella*, Jan. 31, 1712–13.
[11] Johnson, ibid., Rowe.
[12] The title-page of his comedy *The Scowrers* bears both these titles.
[13] Chalmers, *Biographical Dictionary*, s.v. Tate (Nahum).
[14] Drake (Nathan), *Essays . . . Illustrative of the Tatler, Spectator and Guardian*, III, pp. 280–5.
[15] Johnson, *Lives of the English Poets*, Rowe.
[16] Ibid., Smith. Halifax was awaiting Smith with the book the dedication of which he had accepted and was prepared to reward the poet with a post at £300 a year. Smith kept procrastinating about the dedication and had to be vigorously egged on by his publisher before he brought himself to write it. Having at last got it written, he was too lazy or proud or bashful to take it in person to the expectant patron. He was a fantastic type of Bohemian. His friends called him " Captain Rag ".
[17] Ibid., Hughes.   [18] Drake, *Essays . . . Illustrative, etc.*, III, p. 268.

prebend and later presented to a vicarage worth £400 a year.[19] Arbuthnot was appointed Physician in Ordinary to Queen Anne.[20] Garth and Blackmore were knighted.[21] Budgell was First Secretary to the Lords Justices in Ireland, Deputy Clerk to the Council, Member of Parliament and Controller of Revenue. This last post alone brought him in £400 a year.[22] Granville was an M.P., Knight of the Shire for Cornwall, Secretary at War, raised to the peerage as Lord Lansdowne, and became Controller, and later Treasurer, of Queen Anne's Household, and a Privy Counsellor.[23]

Stepney was entrusted with several important diplomatic posts.[24] Arthur Maynwaring was Commissioner of Customs, Auditor of the Imprests and Member of the House of Commons.[25] Walsh was also an M.P. and Gentleman of the Horse to Queen Anne.[26] Henry Martyn was Inspector-General of Imports and Exports.[27] Tickell was Under-Secretary of State.[28] After so many obscure and semi-obscure names, we are not surprised to find John Locke figuring as Commissioner of Appeals and of the Board of Trade, and Sir Isaac Newton with a knighthood as Director of the Mint.[29] Steele was Chief Editor of the *London Gazette*, Gentleman Waiter to Prince George of Denmark, Commissioner of Stamps, M.P., Governor of the Royal Comedians, Judge and Deputy Lieutenant of the County of Middlesex, Surveyor of the Royal Stables at Hampton Court, Commissioner of Forfeited Estates and a knight.[30] If Swift had not written *A Tale of a Tub* and called the Duchess of Somerset " Carrots ", he would have been a bishop ; and even as it was, he was made Dean of St. Patrick's in spite of these misdemeanours.[31] Defoe

---

[19] Johnson, *Lives of the English Poets*, Parnell.
[20] Chalmers, *Biographical Dictionary*, s.v. Arbuthnot (Dr. John).
[21] Johnson, *Lives of the English Poets*, Garth, Blackmore.
[22] Drake, *Essays . . . Illustrative*, etc., III, pp. 1–25.
[23] Johnson, *Lives of the English Poets*, Granville.
[24] The long list of these diplomatic posts will be found in Johnson, ibid., Stepney.
[25] *Biographia Britannica*, s.v. Maynwaring (Arthur).
[26] Johnson, ibid., Walsh.
[27] Drake, *Essays . . . Illustrative*, etc., III, p. 287.
[28] Johnson, ibid., Tickell.
[29] *Biographia Britannica*, s.vv. Locke, Newton.
[30] For Steele I have consulted (in addition to his own works) : *The Epistolary Correspondence of Sir Richard Steele* ; Drake, *Essays . . . Illustrative*, etc., and Forster, *Biographical Essays*, Steele.
[31] See *The Windsor Prophecy* (Scott's Edition of Swift, XII, p. 297 ff. ; *The Author upon Himself*, 1713 (ibid., XII, pp. 315–18). In addition, I have

held a post as Accountant to the Commissioners of Glass Duty and was entrusted with various diplomatic missions.[32] After publishing his first comedy—shortly after his 24th birthday—Congreve was appointed Commissioner of Hackney Coach and Wine Licences, and held also posts in the Treasury and Customs. On the accession of the House of Hanover he was made Secretary for Jamaica.[33] Vanbrugh discharged the duties of " Clarenceux King at Arms ", was despatched by Queen Anne to Hanover to convey to the future George I the insignia of the Garter, appointed Controller of the Council of Public Works and Inspector of the Royal Gardens. He was also given a knighthood.[34] Gay, *who began life as a silk-merchant's apprentice, became Secretary* to an Embassy at the age of 25.[35] After having filled several political posts Addison was made Secretary of State and ultimately retired from public life with a pension of £1,600 a year.[36] The less famous author of *Country Mouse and City Mouse*, Matthew Prior, was appointed successively Secretary to the Earl of Berkeley, Ambassador at the Hague, Gentleman of the Bed Chamber to King William III, Secretary to the Embassy at the Treaty of Ryswick, Ambassador to Versailles, Commissioner of Customs and M.P.[37] His more fortunate collaborator, Montague, who became—as we have seen—a Minister, was made Baron, then Viscount and finally an Earl, and received the Order of the Garter.[38]

Never had writers found life so easy or so brilliant. Almost

---

consulted Lives of Swift by Johnson (*English Poets*), by Scott (prefixed to the edition of his Works), by Forster and by Craik, also Professor Masson's Essay on Swift in *Essays Biographical and Critical*.

[32] On Defoe (in addition to his own works listed in my Bibliography), I have consulted the lives by Wilson, William Lee and Minto and Forster's study in his volume of *Biographical Essays*.

[33] On Congreve, see Drake, *Essays . . . Illustrative*, etc., III, pp. 307 ff. ; Johnson, *Lives of the English Poets* ; and Gosse, *Life of William Congreve*.

[34] *An Account of the Life and Writings of the Author* prefixed to Vanbrugh's Works, 1776, and *Biographia Dramatica*, s.v. Vanbrugh.

[35] Drake, *Essays . . . Illustrative*, etc., III, pp. 23–4 ; Johnson, *Lives of the English Poets*, Gay.

[36] On Addison I have consulted (in addition to his own works) Miss Aikin's *Life of Addison* ; Johnson, *Lives of the English Poets* ; Drake's *Essays . . . Illustrative*, etc. ; *Biographia Britannica* ; Tickell's Preface to his edition of Addison 1721 ; Steele's letter to Congreve prefixed to Addison's Comedy, *The Drummer* ; Macaulay's Essay on Addison.

[37] Johnson, *Lives of the English Poets*, Prior.

[38] Ibid., Halifax.—Voltaire comments : " In France Addison might have been Member of some Academy and might have obtained, through some woman's good offices, a pension of 1200 *livres* . . . in England he became Secretary of State. Newton was Comptroller of the Mint ; Congreve held

without transition, they leapt from a precarious and despised position to secure and honourable posts, and found themselves courted on every side. They gained a footing in society which they had never before enjoyed, and which a few short years before they would not have dared to dream of attaining even in the distant future.[38a]

II

*Happy results of the writers' new status.—They acquire and deserve respect.—
They take a share in the reform of manners*

This marked change in their position brought the happiest results.

First, their profession rose in public estimation. As soon as it was clear that literature might be the road to wealth and dignity, it was no longer scorned and looked down upon.

Hitherto literature had seemed—not unjustifiably—a career which led only to endless disillusionment, if not to irretrievable misery. The luckless wight who was trying to live by his pen met only with contempt—tempered, in exceptional cases only, by the respect which talent commands—such contempt as the world

---

an important post; Prior has become a Plenipotentiary; Dr. Swift is a Dean in Ireland and is there accounted a much more important person than the Primate . . ." (*Lettres Philosophiques*, Letter XXIII, Garnier's Edition, XXII, pp. 179-80.)

[38a] [While this picture is in the main true, a few cautions may be suggested. Many of the authors named received their posts for reasons other than literary. Montague was a brilliant financier; Granville, later Lord Lansdowne, owed his advancement to the fact that he was an able man and member of a rich and powerful family which had many Cornish boroughs in its pocket; Vanbrugh became Controller of Public Works not because of his plays, but because he was a brilliant architect; Lord Carlisle obtained for him the post of Clarenceux King at Arms because he was building Castle Howard for him. He was the first knight made by George I mainly as a reward for being a stout Whig, and a protégé of the Duke of Marlborough, for whom he had built Blenheim. He, as herald, had presented the King with the Garter in 1706. Defoe got his post in the glass office because he was a man of business and a manufacturer; at that time he had no fame as a writer, his chief work at that date being his *Essay on Projects*, a business hand-book. Many, such as Walsh and Maynwaring, were simply amateur writers who would have held the posts they did even if they had never written a line. But it is true that men such as Addison, Congreve, Steele, Prior, etc., obtained their posts, many of them sinecures, solely because they were writers. It was certainly a golden age for authors, but even they had to be efficient in their posts, under pain of losing them, as Gay did his. Ability in literature alone was not enough, social charm counted for a good deal, and there were plenty of writers who got nothing. B. D.]

is wont to bestow on those whose livelihood is painfully and precariously earned, if not actually won by subterfuge and dishonour.

The moment that the author became eligible for high employment and fat salaries, he was looked on with another eye and granted what he had never enjoyed before : respect and esteem.[39] Writing was no longer a trade but a career—a career leading to riches and honour ; and this new respect for literature inspired a new attitude to authors. They no longer formed a class apart, they were received in high society not as protégés but on terms of full equality with the greatest.

Prior invited Harley to his house.[40] Swift was on terms of intimacy with the most important figures of his day ; Harley and Bolingbroke habitually addressed him by his Christian name.[41] Congreve's friendship with the Duke of Marlborough's daughter is well known. Addison married the Dowager Countess of Warwick. Commoners such as Vanbrugh, Congreve, Addison, Garth, Steele, Maynwaring, Stepney, Walsh [42] took their seats in the Kit-Cat Club alongside politically-minded peers like the Earls of Dorset and Sunderland, the Dukes of Somerset, Newcastle and Marlborough. In the Scriblerus Club, Swift, Pope, Arbuthnot and Gay rubbed shoulders with Harley and Bolingbroke.[43] Without having to abase themselves as of old, authors

---

[39] " What most encourages men of letters in England is the esteem in which they are held . . . " (ibid., p. 180).

[40] See " An Extempore Invitation to the Earl of Oxford, Lord High Treasurer ", 1712, in his *Poems on Several Occasions*, p. 286.

[41] See his Correspondence, *Works*, XVI, pp. 108, 143, 150, 367, 454, and his *Journal to Stella*, Feb. 17, 1710–11.

Swift sometimes treated Harley pretty cavalierly, sending him into the House of Commons one day to inform the Secretary of State " to let him know I would not dine with him if he dined late " (*Journal to Stella*, Feb. 12, 1710–11). On July 29, 1711, he wrote to Stella : " I was at Court . . . today . . . I generally am acquainted with about 30 in the drawing-room, and am so proud I make all the lords come up to me : one passes half an hour pleasant enough." Again he writes (Oct. 7, 1711) : " The Duchess of Shrewsbury came up and reproached me for not dining with her. I said that was not so soon done ; I expected more advances from ladies, especially duchesses : she promised to comply with any demands I please ; and I agreed to dine with her tomorrow, if I did not go to London too soon, as I believe I shall before dinner. Lady Oglethorpe brought me and the Duchess of Hamilton together today in the drawing-room and I have given her some encouragement, but not much . . . Lord Keeper . . . said : ' Dr. Swift is not only all our favourite, but our governor.' "

[42] *Addisoniana* in vol. VI of Hurd's edition of Addison, p. 676 ; Spence, pp. 46 and 338.

[43] *Life of Swift* prefixed to Scott's edition of his *Works*, p. 200. [For Scriblerus read Brothers'? B. D.]

were introduced and received into every grade of society and all hastened to bid them welcome.

The natural consequence was that literature attracted more recruits than ever before. It was no longer the pastime of the idle rich, the refuge of the outcast, or the dream of the young enthusiast. As soon as he realized that it offered its votaries not the chance of dubious fame but of assured fortune, a hope of rising not falling in the social scale, everyone who felt he could handle a pen, aimed at a literary career. There was now no reason why any man of talent should hesitate to enter the lists.[44] If other periods of English literature can boast of greater names than this, none can show a larger galaxy of authors famous in so many varied styles. Thinking only of Addison, Swift, Defoe, Steele, Congreve, Farquhar, Vanbrugh, Locke and Newton, we have here famous names enough to make the glory of any literature, and yet we have only skimmed the cream of the brilliant period which has long been known as the Augustan Age of English literature.

We see literature held in greater honour and writers more highly esteemed, but this is by no means the whole story. Exalted in others' eyes by the position accorded them in society, authors themselves rose higher in their own estimation. They acquired a loftier conception of their profession and a better opinion of themselves, and as a natural consequence they became more worthy of popular esteem. Well-paid posts released them from the daily struggle for mere subsistence. They were no longer reduced to the degradation of scheming and self-abasement. Life was not only regular but honourable.[45] They played a dignified part in society and in the posts they held, and one

[44] Vanbrugh held the rank of ensign when he began writing (*An Account of the Life and Writings of the Author* prefixed to his *Works*, p. 4); Farquhar was a captain (*Some Memoirs of Mr. George Farquhar* prefixed to his *Works*); Steele was a captain; Addison was about to take Orders; Swift was in Orders; Parnell was Archdeacon of Clogher in Ireland (Johnson, *Lives of the English Poets*, Parnell); Rowe had an income of £300 a year (Spence, p. 257).

[45] A correspondent addressed the following question to the *Spectator*:

" Sir,—Pray be so kind as to let me know what you esteem to be the chief qualification of a good poet, especially of one who writes plays; and you will very much oblige, Sir,
                         Your very humble Servant,
                                  N. B."

The *Spectator* answered: " To be a very well-bred man." (No. 314.)

amongst them, Joseph Addison, still remains the model of an English gentleman in the noblest sense of the term.

The new position of the political parties contributed not a little to this happier state of affairs, for it permitted a writer to hold his personal opinions and remain faithful to them, without fear of being plunged into penury. He was no longer face to face with an omnipotent Court to whose whims he must submit or starve, but with two great parties equally balanced which offered him approximately equal advantages. He was not compelled by material considerations to let his views be swayed by his interest, but was at liberty to choose his own road. In short, he was free to be himself and not the mouthpiece of another. Henceforward such weaknesses as he might betray were such as are at all times inherent in human nature.

The only influence an author had previously wielded—and that rarely—was the influence due to talent. He now enjoyed the influence of position and of character.

He was thus able to take a share, an authoritative share, in the great revolution of manners and morals which was coming.

III

Current Manners.—Manners reflected in the drama : Dryden, Shadwell, D'Urfey, Southerne, Congreve, Vanbrugh, Mrs. Manley, Granville, Dennis

The reader will remember the type of manners and morals that had prevailed under Charles II, and will remember too that during the Merry Monarch's last years, and under James II, people were beginning to weary of so much licence and of so much shame, and that many circumstances combined to heighten this weariness : political preoccupation, the dour temperament of James II and even the King's age.

The Revolution of 1688 and the accession of William III encouraged the nation's return to decency and morality. Politics continued to exercise a wholesomely counter-active effect on impulses of unbridled enjoyment, while the King's personal character and Queen Mary's influence combined to calm and steady people's minds.[46] William was cold and by nature

---

[46] In dedicating *The Mourning Bride* to Princess Anne, the Queen's sister, Congreve writes : " It is from the example of princes that virtue becomes a fashion in the people ; for even they who are averse to instruction will yet be fond of imitation." (*Works*, 1752. The oldest edition in the British Museum—noted in my Bibliography—lacks this Dedication.)

taciturn, and more taciturn than ever in England owing to his very imperfect knowledge of the language. The Queen's life was so entirely beyond reproach that it inspired respect even amid the passion of politics. With two such people on the Stuart throne the Court inevitably ceased to be the haunt of pleasure which Charles II had made it : no more gay festivities, no more gaming, no more theatrical performances, no more " gallantry ". William was not the man to be his courtiers' comrade in revelry, and the Queen's example imposed on the ladies of Whitehall at least the semblance of virtue, and of respect for seemly behaviour.[47] So the Court changed completely in character, and its attractions were further diminished by the fact that the King's health compelled him to leave the capital and emigrate to Kensington. It was in very truth an " emigration ", for Kensington, which is nowadays a part of London, was then in open country [48] and thus less easily accessible than Whitehall, a circumstance which in itself made Court entertainments less frequent and less brilliant.

William and Mary were succeeded by Queen Anne and she by George I. It was not a woman—particularly not a thrifty and puritanical woman like Anne [49]—nor yet a foreign prince of fifty-five like George I, who knew not a word of his new subjects' tongue and who was bourgeois even in his royal amours,[50] who could revive the Restoration days. Thus the English court tradition of irresponsible gaiety was broken : for ever.

[47] We shall presently see that almost all the protests against the excesses of the theatre come from women. In this I divine the influence of Queen Mary. Hampton Court possesses a collection of portraits of Charles II's Court, most of them painted by Lely, and another collection of William and Mary's Court almost all by Kneller. It is interesting to compare the two sets of women's portraits. The " beauties " of Charles II's time are voluptuous courtesans clad—as scantily as possible—in lustrous materials of bright colour. Under William III the ladies' dress has become most markedly more modest and more discreet.

[48]   " Where *Kensington* high o'er the neighb'ring lands
        'Midst greens and sweets, a Regal fabrick, stands,
        And sees each spring, luxuriant in her bowers,
        A snow of blossoms, and a wilde of flowers,
        The Dames of *Britain* oft in crowds repair
        To gravel walks, and unpolluted air.
        Here, while the Town in damps and darkness lies
        They breathe in sun-shine, and see azure skies . . . "
                (Tickell, *Kensington Garden*, 1772. See my Bibliography.)

[49] See Swift, *Journal to Stella*, Aug. 8 and Sept. 2, 1711.
[50] See Lecky, I, p. 221.

The reform was, however, superficial only. Debauchery was no longer acceptable in high places; that was an important point. But it is obvious that the basis of manners and morals could not be transformed in a night. A whole society cannot switch over from unbounded licence to the worship of moral purity, or—since this is scarcely to be found on earth—let me rather say to respect for virtue and honourable conduct.

After the Revolution, everything, or almost everything, still remained to be done. It is true that some reassuring signs had indicated that people were tired of irregularity and licence, some genuine protests had made themselves heard, but momentum in the wonted direction was too powerful to be immediately brought to a standstill. Objectors were not yet numerous enough, or sufficiently confident of their strength, at once to silence the din of libertines and scatter-brains. Morality was still looked on as bad form and the same set of people still held the centre of the stage.[51] Fashionable diversions remained unaltered and such as we have seen: young sparks scoured the streets at night to the terror of passers by,[52] they cheated at cards,[53] they drank, they

[51] ". . . 'Tis to be hop'd this once wise and sober Nation will awaken from its Lethargy. That notwithstanding the present Popularity of Vice, Levity and Impiety, it may one Day recover its Relish of solid Knowledge and real Merit. That Buffoons themselves may one Day be expos'd, the Laughers in their turn become ridiculous, and an Atheistical Scoffer be as much out of Credit as a sober and religious Man is at present . . . 'Tis great Pity that in so noble a Cause any should shew such Poorness of Spirit as to be asham'd of asserting their Religion, and stemming the Tide of Impiety, for fear of becoming the Entertainment of scoffing Libertines." (Blackmore, *Creation*, Preface.)

[52] "Now is the Time that Rakes their Revels keep;
Kindlers of Riot, Enemies of Sleep.
His scatter'd Pence the flying *Nicker* flings,
And with Copper the Show'r the Casement rings.
Who has not heard the *Scowrer's* Midnight Fame?
Who has not trembled at the *Mohock's* name?
Was there a Watchman took his hourly Rounds,
Safe from their Blows, or new-invented Wounds?
I pass their desp'rate Deeds, and Mischiefs done
Where, from *Snow-Hill* black sleepy Torrents run;
How Matrons hoop'd within the Hogshead's Womb,
Were tumbled furious thence; the rolling Tomb
O'er the Stones thunders; bounds from side to side:
So Regulus to save his Country dy'd."
(Gay, *Trivia*.)
[Book III, l. 321.]

See also the *Spectator*, Nos. 324, 332, 335, 347; Swift, *Journal to Stella*, March 8, 9, 12, 15, 16, 18, 22, 26, 1711-12; and my Bibliography, s.v. Mohocks.

got drunk,[54] women were as brazen as ever.[55] If we search the drama for indications of morality, we find that licentiousness and the extravagances of debauched imaginations still hold the stage. The old comic authors remained faithful to the old tradition : Dryden's *Amphitryon*,[56] D'Urfey's *Don Quixote*, Shadwell's *Scowrers* and his *Volunteers* are no less outrageous than earlier comedies by the same authors.[57] Newcomers followed faithfully in their footsteps. To be fully convinced on this score, it is enough to cast a glance on Southerne's *Sir Anthony Love* or the

[53] " Mrs. *Foresight* : . . . do you think any Woman honest ?
Scandal : Yes, several, very honest ; —they'll cheat a little at Cards, sometimes, but that's nothing."
(Congreve, *Love for Love*, III.)

" *Sir Ruff Rancounter* : Madam, I have some Doctors in my Pocket, if you please to use 'em.
Lady *Malepart* : What Doctors, Sir ?
Sir *Ruff* : Why, don't you know the Doctors ? The Dice that only run the high Chances. I'll put 'em into your Box, and no body the wiser.
Lady *Mal* : You shou'd ha' don 't without telling me.
Sir *Ruff* : So I can still, Madam——"
(Southerne, *The Maids Last Prayer*, III, 1.)

See also Southerne's *Wives Excuse*, IV, 1.
[54] The first Mutiny Bill, passed in 1689, contained a clause forbidding any Court Martial to pass sentence of death after dinner. It was foreseen that " a gentleman who had dined could not safely be trusted with the lives of his fellow creatures ". (Macaulay, *History*, chap. XI, vol. III, p. 45.)—See also Rémusat, vol. L, p. 285 ; Swift, *Journal to Stella*, April 9 and 21, 1711 ; Oct. 29, 1711 ; Feb. 17, 1711–12.
[55] See their dialogues in the Comedies.
[56] See especially I, 2.
[57] In *The Scowrers* Lady Maggot ranges the streets alone looking for gallants to oblige her. Tope, a Scowrer, accosts her saying : " Pray Heaven she be sound—she's of Quality—hah ! may be ne'ere the sounder for that neither." In *The Volunteers* Nickum is described in the list of Dramatis Personæ as " Mrs. *Hackwell's* Stallion ; a Sharper, which is a new name for a Rogue and a Cheat."

" *Teres*.—Here *Mary*, prithee thread my Needle, good girl, whilst I turn down this Selvidge here.
Mar.— Ay, come, let's see 't. (*rises from the Stool*), And so, Mother, you say you had a main deal of Prate about me with Vather and my Man that is to be—hoh, hah, hoh, hah—What a dickins, I think I Can't do't here—I'm blind, I think, with living so long a Maid, hoh, hoh. D'ye think I shall thread it better tomorrow, Mother ? Hoh, hoh, hoh.—
Teres.—Ay, ye Jade," etc.
(D'Urfey, *The Comical History of Don Quixote*, part III, II, 1. See also I, 1.)

comic parts of his *Oroonoko*,[58] or to skim the early plays of Congreve and Vanbrugh. Comedy paints the same manners with the same lack of restraint.[59] Tragedy took a slight pull on the

[58] As a specimen, let us take a fragment of *Oroonoko*, the first scene of Act IV between the Widow Lackitt, her son Daniel and his wife Lucy (whom he had married in Act II):

"*Dan:* I am alter'd for the worse mightily since you saw me; and she has been the cause of it there.
Wid: How so, Child?
Dan: I told you before what wou'd come on't, of putting me to bed to a strange Woman: but you would not be said nay.
Wid: She is your Wife, now, Child, you must love her.
Dan: Why, so I did, at first.
Wid: But you must love her always.
Dan: Always! I lov'd her as long as I cou'd, Mother, and as long as loving was good, I believe, for I find now I don't care a fig for her ... She may call me Hermophrodite, if she will, for I hardly know whether I'm a Boy or a Girl ... I have no more Manhood left in me already, than there is, saving the mark, in one of my Mother's old under Petticoats here."

See also I, 1, and II, 1.
See the character of the Abbé in *Sir Anthony Love* and the comments on him in II, 1.—This character in conjunction with Coupler in Vanbrugh's *Relapse* (especially I, 3) would seem to indicate that English society had sunk to the very depths of despicable vice. Among the arguments in favour of the theatre which Dennis brings forward in his *Usefulness of the Stage* is the following (p. 26): "And now lastly, for the Love of Women, fomented by the ... Stage ... it may be in some measure excus'd ... Because it has a check upon the other Vices, and peculiarly upon that unnatural sin, in the restraining of which the happiness of mankind is in so evident a manner concern'd." Tom Brown, too, says: "... *Sue Frousie* that came hither the other day, assures me ... that the practical Vices of the Town boaded an eternal breach betwixt the Sexes, while Each confin'd itself to the same Sex, and so threatened a cessation of Commerce in Propagation betwixt 'em." (*Letters from the Dead to the Living*, p. 64: From Julian, Late Secretary to the Muses, to Will. Pierre of Lincolns-Inn Fields *Play-House*.)

[59] "*Belinda*. ... my Glass and I could never yet agree what Face I should make when they come blurt out with a nasty thing in a Play: For all the Men presently look upon the Women, that's certain; so laugh we must not, tho' our Stays burst for 't, because that's telling Truth, and owning we understand the Jest: and to look serious is so dull when the whole House is a laughing ... For my part, I always take that occasion to blow my Nose.
Lady Brute: You must blow your Nose half off, then, at some Plays."
(Vanbrugh, *The Provok'd Wife*, III, 3.)

"While our Authors took the extraordinary Liberties with their Wit, I remember the Ladies were then observ'd, to be decently afraid of venturing bare-fac'd to a new Comedy, 'till they had been assur'd they might do it, without the Risque of an Insult, to their Modesty; or, if their Curiosity were too strong, for their Patience, they took care, at least, to save Appearances and rarely came upon the first Days of Acting, but in Masks (then daily worn, and admitted, in the Pit, the Side-Boxes, and Gallery) which Custom,

reins, the worship of Mademoiselle de Scudéry began to make way for an imitation of the great writers of tragedy, but there was still an eager welcome for sensuous scenes and daring descriptions. Congreve did not stint such things in his *Mourning Bride*.[60] Mrs. de la Rivière Manley, who inherited the mantle of Mrs. Behn, introduced into *The Royal Mischief* a love scene which her model would not have disclaimed.[61] Granville's *Heroick Love* has passages which are amongst the most risky that anyone had so far ventured to offer to the English stage.[62] The songs,[63]

---

however, had so many ill Consequences attending it, that it has been abolish'd these many Years."
(Cibber, Apology, p. 154.)

See also *Spectator*, No. 51.

[60] Act III, Scene 6. Enter Osmyn and Almeria :
" *Osmyn :* Then *Garcia* shall lie panting on thy Bosom,
    Luxurious, revelling amidst thy Charms
    And thou perforce must yield, and aid his Transport."

[61] At the close of a love scene between Homais and Prince Levan, Acmat, one of the characters, says :
    " We'll not intrude into a Monarch's Secrets,
    The God of Love himself is painted Blind ;
    To teach all other Eyes they shou'd be vail'd
    Upon his Sacred Misteries."   (*Shuts the Scene.*)
(The Royal Mischief, III, 1.)

[62] Briseis has been stolen from Achilles during his absence. When he sees her again he says to her :
    " The stain of violation is upon thee . . .
    Didst thou resist ? or didst thou early yield ? . . .
    Met'st thou with willing warmth his brutal lust ?
    Had'st thou thy share of Bliss ? With amorous rage
    Improving Joy with Art ? . . . "
(V, 1.)

[63]
I

" As *Amoret* and *Thyrsis* lay
Melting the Hours in gentle Play ;
Joining Faces, mingling kisses
And exchanging harmless Blisses
He trembling cry'd, with eager haste
O let me feed as well as taste,
I die, if I'm not wholly blest.

II

The fearful Nymph reply'd—*Forbear* ;
I cannot, dare not, must not hear :
Dearest Thyrsis, *do not move me,*
Do not—do not—if you Love me.
O let me—still the Shepherd said ;
But while she fond Resistance made,
The hasty Joy, in strugling fled.

epilogues and prologues remain as indelicate as ever [64] and one of D'Urfey's epilogues surpasses in audacity anything heard before.[65]

Nevertheless, there really was something in the air. Free and reckless as his plays are, the greatest writer of comedies at this time, William Congreve, betrays by his diction a change of taste. Whatever you may reproach his characters with, they have the new virtue of being a trifle more restrained in their expression; bullying scoundrels and frequenters of brothels they remain, but they do not use the language of the brothel. They set no good example, but at least they are good company. Voltaire's phrase hits them off exactly: they act like rascals but talk like honest men.[66] The same may be said of the characters in Southerne's comedies.

III

Vex'd at the Pleasure she had miss'd
She frown'd and blush'd, then sigh'd and kiss'd
And seem'd to moan in sullen Cooing
The sad miscarriage of their Wooing:
But vain alas! were all her Charms;
For *Thyrsis* deaf to Loves allarms
Baffled and senseless, tir'd her Arms.

(Congreve, *The Old Batchelour*, III, 2.)

See also Congreve's *Love for Love* (III, 1), and the song which closes Vanbrugh's *Provok'd Wife*.

[64] Notably the Epilogue of *A Plot and no Plot* by Dennis. It was spoken by a woman:

"... The Poet was inclin'd to chuse
Your humble Servant to sustain his Muse:
He knew, if I would beg, I should not want
A favour, who you know have one to grant.
I've kept it long; There's an old Dame—Pox on her,
An old, morose, damn'd grinning Jade, call'd Honour;
Who with her coldness checks my forward Nature,
Else should I quickly prove—The happiest creature!
I'll throw her off, if possibly I can,
Throw the grim Goddess off, and put on Man ...
Now who shall first be my man? He, I swear,
Who for this Play most warmly shall declare ... "

[65] *The Comical History of Don Quixote*, part I. The Epilogue is spoken by Sancho, mounted on a donkey called Dapple:

"But for some other Gifts—mind what I say,
Never compare, each *Dapple* has his Day,
Nor anger him, but kindly use this Play
For should you, with him, conceal'd Parts disclose,
Lord, How like Ninneys, would look all the *Beaus*."

[66] "In them [viz. Congreve's comedies] you find everywhere the speech of honest men and the actions of rascals." (*Lettres philosophiques*, Letter XIX. On Comedy. *Works*, XXII, p. 160.)

The public too were no longer willing to tolerate the smuttinesses for which they had earlier shown so much appetite. Protests were frequent. Downes tells us that Granville's *She-Gallants* had but a short run, though " extraordinary witty and well Acted " for " offending the Ears of some Ladies who set up for Chastity, it made its Exit ".[67] D'Urfey's *Don Quixote* [68] and Congreve's *Double-Dealer* [69] also shocked some of the audience. A play of Fletcher's, which a certain Thomas Scott in 1697 worked over in Restoration style, also gave offence.[70] Mrs. Manley's tragedy of which I spoke just now and Vanbrugh's *Relapse* were not—if we can trust their Prefaces—immune from reproach. An Epilogue, also of 1697, sadly complains :

> Once only smutty Jests would please the Town,
> But now (Heav'n help our Trade) they'll not go down.[71]

It seems as if authors no longer felt themselves on firm ground. There was a scene in *Sir Anthony Love*—fairly scandalous, it must be admitted—between his priest and his heroine [72] which Southerne did not dare to put on the stage. In dedicating *The Mourning Bride* to Princess Anne, Congreve eloquently pleads extenuating circumstances for drama, hoping, as he says, " to convince your Royal Highness that a play may . . .

---

[67] Downes, *Roscius Anglicanus*, p. 45, on " *The She-Gallants*, a Comedy, wrote by *Mr. George Greenvil*, when he was very Young ".
[68] J. Collier, *A Short View*, etc., p. 204.
[69] " His Double Dealer is much censur'd by the greater of the Town : . . . The women think he has expos'd their Bitchery too much ; and the gentlemen are offended with him for the discovery of their follyes : and the way of their Intrigues, under the notion of Friendship to their Ladyes Husbands." (Letter from Dryden to Walsh, probable date 1693 ; first published in R. Bell's *Life of Dryden*, p. 76.) Congreve himself says in his Dedication, " Some of the Ladies are offended."
[70] " The last Scene in the Third Act had the Misfortune to offend some . . . " (Preface to *The Unhappy Kindness*.)
[71] Hopkins, *Boadicea, Queen of Britain*. The Epilogue was spoken by Mrs. Bowman.—In the Prologue to *Sir Anthony Love*, spoken by Mrs. Bracegirdle, Southerne says :

> " O ! would our peaceful days were come agen ; . . .
> When once the Child was turn'd into her Teens,
> You cou'd not find a Maid behind the Scenes.
> But now your Keeping humor's out a door,
> We must dye Maids : or marry to be poor."

[72] V, 1. See the Preface. It was in order not to offend the ladies that he suppressed it, so he tells us. It is printed in the 1774 Edition of his *Works*.

become sometimes an innocent, and not unprofitable entertainment ".[73]

All these signs evidently foreshadow a coming revolution in taste. At last, thirty years after the Restoration, people had the courage to mention the words modesty and restraint. This was much : but still too little. Protests were still too vague and too weak to be effective. The Anti-Puritan reaction had been too acute and too vigorous to yield to such hesitant attacks.

IV

Jeremy Collier's " Short View of the Immorality and Profaneness of the English Stage ".—What Collier was.—Analysis of his book : its faults, merits, effect.—Replies by Congreve, Vanbrugh, D'Urfey, Wycherley, Dennis, Settle, Filmer, Drake, Farquhar, etc.—Collier's triumph : reform of the theatre

In 1698 a little book of less than 300 pages opportunely came to speak for, and to rally, the opposition : Jeremy Collier's *Short View of the* Immorality *and* Profaneness *of the English Stage*.[74] A zealous clergyman of the Church of England and an ardent Tory, Collier refused to swear allegiance to King William. He

[73] *Works*, 1752 Ed. See also above chap. III, note No. 46.
[74] On Collier, see *Biographia Britannica* ; Allibone, and Macaulay's Essay on the *Comic Dramatists of the Restoration*.—Before Collier, an estimable but intolerable writer, Richard Blackmore, had begun the attack on the stage. As early as 1695 in the Preface to a heroic poem called *Prince Arthur* he wrote : " Our poets seem engaged in a general *Confederacy* to ruin the End of their own Art, to expose *Religion* and *Virtue*, and bring *Vice* and *Corruption of Manners*, into Esteem and Reputation. The Poets that write for the Stage (at least a great part of 'em) seem deeply concern'd in this *Conspiracy*." Here he added five folio pages of well-aimed criticism.—In 1697 he returned to the attack in the Preface to his *King Arthur* : " The Reasons which induc'd me to make the former, did likewise engage me in this second Attempt in *Epick* Poetry ; and among the rest, particularly this, that the young Gentlemen and Ladys who are delighted with Poetry might have a useful, at least a harmless Entertainment, which in our Modern Plays and Poems cannot ordinarily be found . . . that leud and abominable way of writing which was encourag'd in the late Reigns . . . And tho' these mischievous ways of Writing are still endur'd to the great prejudice of Religion and good Manners, yet if ever the *English* Nation recovers it's ancient Vertue and a just Tast of these Matters, I do not doubt but most of those Writers who have been esteem'd and applauded in the late loose and vicious Times, will be rejected with Indignation and Contempt, as the Dishonour of the Muses, and the Underminers of the Publick Good." This is all sensibly and justly said ; but Blackmore had not lung-power enough to sound a trumpet round the walls of Jericho.

resigned his offices in the Church, and being a born controversialist girded his loins for battle. He prepared himself for his task by wide reading—more extensive perhaps than well digested —and then flung himself heart and soul into the political and religious fray with a Loyalist passion which earned him several months' imprisonment in Newgate.[75]

Restored to liberty and not a whit repentant, he set himself with increased vigour to maintain the rights of James II and to attack the usurper. Suspected of being a party to Jacobite plots, he was imprisoned again in 1692. He was not long in bringing graver trouble on himself. Sir John Friend and Sir William Parkyns were condemned to death in 1696 for a plot against King William's life. Collier stood by them to the last and at the foot of the scaffold publicly and solemnly gave them absolution. This created no small scandal. He was accused from every side of having absolved unrepentant assassins and of thus having appeared to cloak a crime with the mantle of the Church. The Bishops rebuked him in due form.[76] He was summoned before the Court of King's Bench, but refused to give obedience to an illegal tribunal, and was thereupon outlawed. He was under this ban, that is to say threatened and hunted, when he published his book against the contemporary theatre. This fact alone is enough to show the mettle of the man, and the spirit he was bringing to his attack on the English stage. He was of the breed of the apostles. Neither his personal danger, nor the fame of the authors whom he was attacking, nor the brilliance of recent dramatic triumphs could halt him in his course, or for an instant delay him. He believed that he had a mission to fulfil, and he set out to war against the theatre as the Crusaders of old took the Cross against the Infidel.

Plunging head foremost into battle, he launched a vigorous frontal attack. Striking ahead of him, striking to right of him, striking to left of him, he let fly uncounted blows of his brawny arm, returning perpetually on his tracks as if he feared to have let his foes escape too lightly. He called to his aid Aristotle,

[75] Allibone gives a list of his political writings. The work for which he was imprisoned was *The Desertion Discuss'd*. See my Bibliography.

[76] " Mr. *Collier* the absconding, absolving Parson, has been so bold as to print a second Vindication of the practice of himself and his Comerades at Tyburn, wherein he pretends to prove the Lawfulness [sic] of his and their practice, by Councils and Fathers, in answer to the Declaration of our Bishops." (The London News-Letter Numb. 13. From Monday, May 25th, to Wednesday, May 27th, 1696 : *British Museum*.)—See also my Bibliography, s.v. Letter.

Plato, Horace, Tacitus, Boileau, Rapin, the Ancients and the Moderns, philosophers, orators and historians, poets, Greek tragedians and Latin comedians, Athenians, Lacedæmonians and Romans, the Law, the Councils, the Fathers of the Church down even to Minutius Felix. With these allies he pushed his charge home, strewing his path with the mangled remains of authors and their plays. Pretty well every English dramatist was more or less battered in the fray, but his severest blows were aimed at his contemporaries, at Dryden, Wycherley, Congreve, D'Urfey and Vanbrugh, especially in their latest works. To prove that they were no models of virtue and chastity was an easy task. He piles up quotations from their plays, he singles out each passage which outrages religion, morality, and seemliness, and even (while he's on the job) each which offends orthodox literary convention.[77] One by one in full detail he picks out every fault —even the minutest peccadillo. Every page lengthens the indictment against them. Pressing in turn into his service indignation, sarcasm, contempt, anathema, he thunders out his fiery speech for the prosecution, leaving his victim no chance to plead extenuating circumstances.

Criticisms in plenty may be made against this passionate and uncompromising attack. Its form is anything but attractive. Its style is heavy and verges on the brutal, though it does not lack energy or a certain felicity of phrase. As a whole the book is nothing but a monotonous sermon, a long homily, scrupulously divided into sections, many of which are again minutely subdivided. The effect on the reader is markedly wearisome, and fatigue is increased by a laborious erudition which obscures rather than clarifies the argument. Collier never allows you to forget that he was in his day a student of Cambridge University, and at every turn of his discourse he pedantically and coquettishly displays his knowledge of Greek and Latin authors if he does not hark back to still older authority. So dear is his hobbyhorse to him, that he often lets her take the bit between her teeth and completely forgets—and the reader forgets of course even more completely—the destination he was heading for. While he devotes, for instance, thirteen pages to proving that the English drama treats the clergy badly,[78] he spends twenty-eight pages in

---

[77] The passages in Section III, for instance, that are particularly devoted to Vanbrugh's *Relapse* reproach the dramatist with failure to observe the unities of time, place and action.

[78] In Chapter III.

discussing the part which priests play in the works of Homer and Virgil, in Greek tragedy, in Aristophanes, Plautus, Terence, Corneille and Molière,[79] in Racine, Shakespeare, Ben Jonson, Beaumont and Fletcher, etc. Then, like M. Jourdain's teacher, he gives three reasons why it is a duty to respect the clergy: namely, the first, the second and the third. Next, he fine-combs history for proof that they have always and everywhere commanded respect from the days of Jews, Egyptians and Persians down to French and Muscovite times. It must be admitted that in a discussion devoted to the clergy of the Church of England, arguments from foreign civilizations and pagan—or at any rate non-Protestant—religions, are unexpected and not exactly cogent. This notwithstanding, every step in his logic is supported anew by a review of the ancients, equally uninteresting, equally out of place.

Apart from this craze for erudition, Collier is the victim of another obsession, no less damaging to his book. If he can never forget that he is a Cambridge man, still less can he forget that he is in Holy Orders. We have just seen how elaborately he insists that the drama should respect the cloth, but his sensitivity on this point rises to almost unimaginable heights. If he were content to plead merely for respect, he would win his case too easily; but he is not content to protest against the coarse and vulgar jokes perpetually levelled at the clergy and at religion by the Restoration drama, he must, if you please, deny that any dramatist in tragedy or comedy has the right to stage any scene implying that any parson could be subject to any human passion, fault or eccentricity.[80] He lays claim to absolute immunity, not limited, as we might expect, to clergymen of the English Church but extended—a most remarkable fact when we remember the religious hatreds of his day—to Roman Catholic priests[81] and Nonconformist ministers.[82] Nor is this enough. He grows indignant to think of a mufti or a priest of Jupiter[83] being represented in an ugly light, and he cannot forgive Dryden for having spoken lightly of Muhammad or taken the names of Phœbus and Mercury in vain, and for having applied disrespectful adjectives

---

[79] All that he can say about clerics in the plays of Corneille and Molière is that there are none.
[80] Vanbrugh retorts—justly if somewhat brutally—" A Clergyman is not in any Country exempted from the Gallows: . . . A Hangman then may jerk him; Why not a Poet?" (*A Short Vindication* . . . p. 54.)
[81] Pp. 98 and 99. [82] Pp. 101 and 102.
[83] Pp. 103, 105, and 120.

to the bull Apis.[84] He goes even further in retrospective zeal and picks a quarrel with Aristophanes for showing lack of reverence towards Neptune, Bacchus and Hercules.[85]

Worst of all, Collier's book suffers from two grave defects: want of perception and injustice.

He is completely lacking in artistic feeling.[86] His pages contain not one word of admiration for any of the authors ancient or modern that he names. It is clear that he has no spark of sympathy for dramatic literature of any kind—which frequently prevents his judging it fairly. Because Shakespeare has at times used phrases which he—like everyone else—considers too vigorous, he puts Shakespeare on the same level as the comic dramatists of the Restoration.[87] He does not understand that the flavour of words alters with time,[88] that it is not the word but the underlying meaning which is dangerous and that no sane moralist could hesitate to prefer the outspoken crudities of Shakespeare to the ingeniously veiled vileness of some of his successors. Collier never judges things from the dramatic point of view but focuses his mind on the words alone, and thus makes the dramatist personally responsible for every syllable uttered by his characters. If a rascal or a libertine enters and speaks as suits his character, the author is accused of himself deliberately attacking honesty and virtue.[89]

The root of Collier's injustice is that he considers the theatre, and the theatre alone, guilty of the vices of his time and makes it the scapegoat of his contemporaries' sins. If licence is the fashion, that is the theatre's fault; if irreverence reigns, the theatre only is the cause; if high principle is at a discount, the

---

[84] Pp. 61, 184 and 105.

[85] Pp. 38 and 45.

[86] On p. 123 he praises "the famous Corneille" for not having introduced Tiresias into his *Oedipus*, tho' he himself admits that this omission is injurious to the tragedy.

[87] Pp. 10, 50 and 125.

[88] Collier himself uses words of which an English writer would to-day be chary. (See particularly, pp. 70 and 73.)

[89] Vanbrugh admirably countered this point: ". . . his Lordship's Words [i.e. Lord Foppington's in *The Relapse*] which he [Collier] quotes about St. *James's* Church, are beyond all dispute on the Minister's side, though not on his Congregation's . . . For though my Lord *Foppington* is not supposed to speak what he does to a Religious End, yet 'tis so ordered, that his manner of speaking it, together with the Character he represents, plainly and obviously instructs the Audience (even to the meanest Capacity) that what he says of his Church Behaviour, is design'd for their Contempt, and not for their Imitation . . ."

(*A Short Vindication* . . . pp. 16 and 17.)

theatre is the villain of the piece. It would seem that Collier had never met undesirable people off the stage, that the theatre had deliberately invented vice in order to set an evil example. He would imply that all England was peopled with innocent and simple souls who would have been to the world a model of all the virtues, if dramatists had not, out of pure wickedness, turned them from the straight and narrow way and hunted them along the road to perdition. This was to shut his eyes to the broader issues and oddly to misplace responsibility.[90]

But having made these reservations—as we are bound to do—we must concede that Collier's book is the sincere testimony of a brave and honest man. How brave he was, he had already proved. He proved it yet again—obscure writer as he was—by boldly attacking the greatest authors of his day, then at the zenith of their powers and popularity. Honest he was, for though a partisan in every fibre of his being, he banished every trace of party spirit from his work. This fervent Tory, who chose to embrace the cause of James II at the very moment when loyalty to it could spell for him nothing but risk and danger, this passionate politician, lays aside all political sympathies when his task is to defend outraged morals. He does not hesitate to lash out at such Tories as he encounters in his course and even those works of theirs which had performed the greatest service to the cause so near his heart.[91] This burning sincerity gives his *Short View of the Immorality and Profaneness of the English Stage* a value of which no criticism can rob it. Each page is steeped in sincere conviction and impresses even the most recalcitrant reader. One-sided and violent as was the attack, it had the merit of being radically just and singularly opportune. It would be unreasonable to ask of a controversialist the stern and impartial

[90] " Perhaps the Parson stretch'd a point too far,
When with our *Theatres* he wag'd a War.
He tells you, That this very Moral Age
Receiv'd the first Infection from the Stage.
But sure, a banisht Court, with Lewdness fraught,
The Seeds of open Vice returning brought.
Thus Lodg'd (as Vice by great Example thrives)
It first debauch'd the Daughters and the Wives . . .
(Dryden's Epilogue to Fletcher's *Pilgrim*; see the lines that follow, quoted above chap. I, note No. 448.)

Dennis in *The Usefulness of the Stage* (chap. III), like Dryden, replaces responsibility on the right shoulders.

[91] P. 183 violently attacks Dryden's *Absalom and Achitophel.*

detachment of a historian. Collier sounded the call to action stations, and sounded it at the right moment. No doubt he lacked a sense of proportion in attacking the theatre only ; but it is only fair to recognize that the theatre was one of the last fortresses in which fashionable vice was entrenched and also the most glaring symbol of the country's demoralization.[92]

With these various merits, the author of the *Short View* combined another which contributed not a little to the success of his book : the advantage of being incontestably Anglican and Tory. For more than forty years—we have seen why and how— virtue had in England been considered Puritan, and we know what reactions the term " Puritan " evoked. These anti-Puritan prejudices, firmly held and violently expressed during the first post-Restoration years, had been somewhat modified by time which had assuaged the ancient hatreds.

Those who had witnessed and those who had taken part in the Civil War had almost all passed on. The Puritans had mellowed both in politics and religion, and had gradually become assimilated in the Whig party and the various dissenting bodies. But a match to the tinder of slumbering prejudice and the old passions would have blazed up as furiously as ever.[93] If Collier had been even slightly suspect of being a Whig or a Dissenter— let alone a Puritan—people on hearing him play the moralist would have begun by shouting " fanatic " and ended by dubbing him " regicide ". He would have been accused of concealing beneath a hypocritical display of virtue the wish to restore the reign of " The Saints " and violently to overthrow the monarchy.[94]

---

[92] " The Seat of Wit, when one speaks as a Man of the Town and the World, is the Play-House ", so says No. 65 of *The Spectator*.

[93] Note how comedy still represents the Puritans and their friends : Fondlewife in Congreve's *Old Batchelour* and Saygrace in his *Double-Dealer*.

[94] D'Urfey made the attempt. See the lines of a song called *The New Reformation*, which he introduced into his comedy, *The Campaigners* (IV, 1) :

" Cuckolds and Canters,
    With Scruples and Banters,
Th' Old Forty One peal against Poetry ring.
    But let State revolvers,
    And *Treason-Absolvers*,
Excuse if I sing,
    The Scoundrel that chooses
    To cry down the Muses,
Would cry down the King."

Congreve's *Way of the World* also ranks Collier among the Puritans : " There are Books over the Chimney—*Quarles* and *Pryn*, and the *Short View of the Stage*, with *Bunyan's* Works to entertain you." (III, 1.)

It is easy to guess how the moral question would have been sidetracked amid such recriminations. It would have been swamped under an avalanche of accusation and insult of every kind.

Fortunately for the cause he was championing, Collier was a Tory and a Church of England clergyman of such quality that every misinterpretation of this kind fell to the ground in advance. So people kept to the point at issue and the book produced its full effect.

The effect was great. The theatre world and the literary world were immediately shaken to their foundations. On every side authors and playwrights girded on their armour to give battle to the foe. Congreve, Vanbrugh and D'Urfey, directly indicted, hastened to reply: Congreve and Vanbrugh in specially-written vindications, D'Urfey in a " Familiar Preface " and a Prologue to *The Campaigners*.[95] Wycherley no doubt also replied.[96] Others who had not been pilloried by name, or were not personally interested in the controversy—Dennis, Settle, Drake, Filmer, Motteux, Tom Brown [97]—took up the defensive: not to mention those who wrote anonymously.[98] Two newcomers to drama hastened to enrol themselves under the war-banner of their fellow-playwrights: Farquhar with the Epilogue to his first play *Love and a Bottle* and Cibber with the Prologue to his tragedy of *Xerxes*.[99] A hail of missiles—pamphlets, dissertations, prologues, epilogues, prefaces—rained down on Collier from every side,

[95] See my Bibliography, s.vv. Congreve, Vanbrugh and D'Urfey.
[96] See Macaulay's Essay, *Comic Dramatists of the Restoration*, and Allibone, s.v. Collier (Jeremy). Neither gives a clue that would have enabled me to trace Wycherley's reply.
[Wycherley's answer may be the anonymous *A Vindication of the Stage*, a light, amusing, ineffective piece of writing. Others ascribe it to Gildon. The only really good answer was Dennis's *The Usefulness of the Stage*; he could meet Collier on his own ground as far as erudition went, but his argument is rather above the head of the general reading public. B. D.]
[97] See my Bibliography, s.vv. Dennis, Drake (J.), Filmer, Motteux, Tom Brown. Macaulay and Allibone quote Settle as amongst those who replied, but give no more clue than in the case of Wycherley. The British Museum Catalogue is silent on all three.
[98] *The Immorality of the English Pulpit* ; *A Vindication of the Stage* ; *Some Remarks upon Mr. Collier's Defence* . . . ; *The Stage Acquitted*, edited by A. D. See my Bibliography, s.vv. Pulpit, Stage, Remarks, A. D.
[99] The Epilogue to *Love and a Bottle* was by the actor Haines who got himself up in mourning to recite it:

"Royal Theatre, I come to *Mourn* for thee . . .
Oh Collier, Collier! thou'st frighted away *Miss C—s* . . ."
(Farquhar's *Works* 1760 ; the British Museum has no separate edition of this play.)

and coming from men who were nearly all fighting *pro aris et focis*, we can well understand that the defence was not less lively than the attack. They attacked the enemy at close quarters. He was spared neither heavy blows nor coarse abuse.[100] Another man might have been dazed by so much noise and so many assaults, might have been bewildered, might have hesitated ; but not Collier. Trifles of this kind could not move him. Controversy was the breath of his life. He had the temperament of the political orator who far from being flustered by interruptions is stimulated thereby to greater eloquence. All these replies merely spurred him to exertion. He parried every blow and let fly his return blows in every direction at once. For ten consecutive years, with inexhaustible energy, he held his own against all comers.[101]

It was he who remained master of the field. This result of the battle might from the outset have been easily foreseen by any attentive observer. It had indeed immediately been evident that public opinion was behind Collier, and would ensure his final victory.[102] We may go so far as to say that his ultimate

---

For the Prologue to *Xerxes* (1699), see Genest, II, p. 169. The British Museum has no separate edition of this play and it is not included in Cibber's *Works*.

[100] " I have no intention to examine all the Absurdities and Falshoods in Mr. *Collier's* Book ; . . . I will remove 'em (the passages quoted by Collier from his plays) from his Dunghil, and replant 'em in the Field of Nature ; and when I have wash'd 'em of that Filth which they have contracted in passing thro' his very dirty hands, let their own Innocence protect them." (Congreve, *Amendments*, etc., pp. 2 and 4.)—" In reading this Gentleman's Book I have been often at a loss to know when he's playing the Knave, and when he's playing the Fool . . . But this I'm sure, *Young Fashion* is no more the Principal Person of the Play, than He's the best Character in the Church." (Vanbrugh, *A Short Vindication*, p. 58.)—In his " Familiar Preface " D'Urfey's wit consists solely in calling Collier " the *Absolver* ", " Doctor Absolution ", " Doctor *Crambo* ", " Hypocrite " and " canting Fool ". The anonymous author of *The Immorality of the English Pulpit* is vulgar and stupid from end to end ; here is one of the phrases he hurls at Collier : " A wicked Parson is the most potent Villain upon Earth " (p. 7).

[101] *A Defence of the Short View* . . . 1699, reply to Congreve and Vanbrugh ; *A Second Defence* . . . 1700, reply to Drake ; *Dissuasive from the Play-House* . . . 1703 (Dennis replied to this last by " The Person of Quality's Answer to Mr. Collier's Letter : *Containing a Defence of a Regulated Stage* " ; (see his *Original Letters*, II, p. 228) ; *A Farther Vindication* . . . 1708, reply to Filmer. See my Bibliography, s.v. Collier. This controversy did not prevent his writing on other subjects ; see *Biographia Britannica*.

[102] He was himself confident of this from the start. In the preliminary notice of *A Defence of the Short View* he already said : " Notwithstanding the singular Management of the *Poets* and *Play-House*, I have had the satisfaction to perceive, the Interest of Virtue is not altogether Sunk, but that Conscience and Modesty have still some Footing among us."

success was manifest from the very manner of his opponents' replies to his attack. The man who might have proved his sturdiest antagonist, Dryden, was weary of the theatre and had already reached the age at which a man looks back on his life to survey the road he has travelled. Convinced that his road had been the wrong one; and that he had squandered his genius, Dryden at first kept silence and then in 1700 in the Preface to his *Fables* he passed judgment on himself with a candour which did honour to him at the end of his career. (He died the same year.) He frankly admitted that in many things Collier had " taxed him justly " : " I have pleaded guilty ", he writes, " to all thoughts or expressions of mine that can be truly accused of obscenity, immorality, or profaneness, and retract them. If he be my enemy, let him triumph ; if he be my friend, as I have given him no personal occasion to be otherwise, he will be glad of my repentance." Vanbrugh cleared his conscience in some sixty pages where a few telling retorts are drowned in colourless and tedious argument. We might have expected a brilliant reply from a man of Congreve's wit, but he writes like an incompetent attorney defending a bad case. He raises minor points only, counters Collier's learning with Greek and Latin quotations of his own, argues about Collier's style [103] and indulges in irrelevant personalities unworthy of his own talent.[104] In a word, he was neither able to establish his innocence nor honest enough, like Dryden, to confess his faults. Even where Collier laid himself open to easy refutation, Congreve contrived to put himself in the wrong by concocting ridiculous evasions. Collier had for instance reproached him for giving the name of Mr. Prig to a chaplain. We might think that on such a point Congreve might have thrown himself on the mercy of the court ; it was not a hanging matter. He preferred to deny having had any ulterior motive whatever in the choice of this name rather than another : " Well, but supposing his name really had been Mr. Prig ? " [105] says he. This is typical of the whole style of his defence:

It is clear that the accused conducted their defence without conviction. They felt at heart that they were in the wrong, and the ground gave way under their feet. Public opinion

[103] Pp. 15, 28–9 and 94 (wrongly numbered 84).
[104] Pp. 21 and 106 (wrongly numbered 96).
[105] P. 58.

which had immediately taken sides for the prosecution [106] exerted a pressure to which everybody gradually yielded. Approval was so strong and so unanimous that William III was willing to forget that Collier was politically his enemy, and issued a *nolo prosequi* quashing all legal proceedings against him.[107] Eager recruits flung themselves passionately into the Crusade whose Peter the Hermit was Jeremy Collier.[108] Morality was the watchword of the day. Societies for the Reformation of Manners, which during the reign of James II had been born in obscurity in London, now came to the fore with ardour and with zest. They lay in wait for every word uttered on the stage that might be at variance with morals or religion, they sent their spies to the performances and brought actors and theatres into court.[109] William III insistently renewed the orders he had already issued in 1697

[106] By 1699 his book had already reached its fourth edition. See my Bibliography.
[107] Cibber, *Apology*, p. 159.
[108] Defoe, *The Poor Man's Plea*, 1698; *The Stage Condemn'd*, 1698; *Some Considerations about the Danger of going to Plays*, 1698 and 1704; *Animadversions on Mr. Congreve's Late Answer to Mr. Collier*, 1698; *A Representation of the Impiety and Immorality of the English Stage*, 1704; *Some Thoughts Concerning the Stage*, 1704; *Plain English, A Sermon . . . for Reformation of Manners*, 1704, by William Bisset; Four Pamphlets by Arthur Bedford; *Serious Reflections on the Scandalous Abuse and Effects of the Stage*, 1705; *A Second Advertisement concerning the Profaneness of the Play-House*, 1705; *The Evil and Danger of Stage Plays*, 1706; *A Serious Remonstrance in Behalf of the Christian Religion, against the Horrid Blasphemies and Impieties which are still used in the English Play-Houses*, 1719. See my Bibliography, s.vv. Defoe, Stage, Considerations, Animadversions, Plays, Bisset and Bedford (Arthur).—Collier's book was even translated into French. See my Bibliography, s.v. Collier.
[109] Lecky, II, pp. 546-7. According to their 40th Annual Report these societies had by 1735 instituted 99,380 proceedings in London and Westminster alone. At a certain point Queen Anne was obliged to temper their passion for prosecutions (Genest, II, p. 124). These Societies for the Reformation of Manners are frequently mentioned in the literature of the time, notably in John Dunton's *Life and Errors* (passim); in *A Representation of the Impiety and Immorality of the English Stage*, pp. 6-7; in Collier's *Dissuasive from the Play-House*, p. 9; in Swift's *Advice to a Young Poet*; and in Tom Brown. Amongst other passages here is what Tom Brown has to say: "There has a terrible enemy arose to the Stage; an abdicated Divine, who when he had escaped the Pillory for Sedition and reforming the State, set up for the Reformation of the Stage; the Event was admirable . . . one grave Citizen . . . laid out Threescore Pound in the Impression to distribute among the Saints . . . There is yet a greater mischief befall'n the *Stage*; here are Societies that set up for *Reformation of Manners*: Troops of *Informers* . . . serve God for Gain, and ferret out Whores for Subsistence" (*Letters from the Dead to the Living*: Will. Pierre's Answer (to Julian), Lincoln's Inn Fields, Novem. 5, 1701. Behind the Scenes).—These societies published numerous pamphlets, etc. Some are mentioned in my Bibliography, s.v. Reformation.

suppressing immoral or irreligious passages in any play,[110] and the Master of the Revels, whose duty it was to authorize a play, could pass it only after rigorous scrutiny.[111] At the beginning of her reign Queen Anne impressed on actors the need for the greatest self-restraint, forbade the admission behind the scenes of anyone, of whatever rank, unconnected with the theatre, and forbade women to come masked to performances.[112]

There was, however, little need of threats and law-givings. The seed Collier had sown germinated of itself, and the change spontaneously brought about by the exercise of men's free will, produced more far-reaching and speedier results than could have been achieved by the wisest of laws or the fear of serious punishment.

The theatre voluntarily reformed its erring ways. Authors flung into the melting-pot plays that had already been acted, to recast them in finer mould : Congreve deleted several phrases

---

[110] " His Majesty has been pleased to Command that the following Order should be sent to both Playhouses.

"*His Majesty*, being informed, That, notwithstanding an Order made the 4th of *June*, 1697, by the Earl of *Sunderland*, then Lord Chamberlain of his Majesty's Household, to prevent the Prophaneness and Immorality of the Stage [Note that these are the very words of Collier's title] ; several Plays have lately been Acted, containing Expressions contrary to Religion and good Manners : And whereas the Master of the Revels has represented, That, in Contempt of the said Order, the Actors do often neglect to leave out such Prophane and Indecent Expressions, as he has thought proper to be omitted. These are therefore to signify His Majesty's Pleasure, That you do not hereafter presume to Act anything in any Play contrary to Religion and good Manners, as you shall answer it at your utmost peril. *Given under my Hand this 18th of* February 1698. In the Eleventh year of His Majesty's reign. *Pere. Bertie.* [Peregrine Bertie was Vice Chamberlain. B. D.]

" An Order has likewise been sent by His Majesty's Command to the Master of the Revels, not to License any plays containing Expressions contrary to Religion and good Manners, and to give Notice to the Lord Chamberlain of His Majesty's Household, or in his absence to the Vice-Chamberlain if the Players presume to Act anything which he has struck out." (*The London Gazette*, No. 3,474, Monday, Feb. 27, 1698-9.)

On Dec. 11, 1699, he returns to the charge : " Whitehall, Dec. 11. This day was Published, His Majesty's Proclamation for Preventing and Punishing Immorality and Prophaneness." (*The London Gazette*, No. 3,557 of 11-14th Dec. 1699.)

[111] Cibber, *Apology*, pp. 159, 160.

[112] See Genest, II, pp. 296-7. In order to court Queen Anne's favour, Swift published in 1707 *A Project for the Advancement of Religion, and the Reformation of Manners. By a Person of Quality.* One important passage in it is devoted to the theatre. See Scott's Edition of his *Works*, VIII, pp. 79 ff. and Forster, *The Life of Jonathan Swift*, p. 213.—Similarly Tate published in 1712 *The Monitors. Intended for the Promoting of Religion and Virtue, and Suppressing of Vice and Immorality.* See my Bibliography.

in his *Double-Dealer*,[113] and in *The Mourning Bride*,[114] and *Love for Love*[115] amended passages which had shocked Collier. In *The Provoked Wife* Vanbrugh rewrote a scene in which Sir John Brute, dressed as a parson, was found by the Watch drunk and brawling in the streets, and was taken before a Justice of the Peace whom he scandalized by his language. In the new version the parson's frock is exchanged for a woman's.[116] At the same time new plays were written to a new recipe. Congreve in *The Way of the World* and Vanbrugh in *The Provok'd Husband*[117] were

[113] " This day was played a revived comedy of Mr. Congreve's called ' The Double Dealer ' . . . In the play-bill was printed.—" Written by Mr. Congreve ; with several expressions omitted." (Dryden, *Correspondence*, letter to Mrs. Steward, 1698.)

[114] Genest, II, p. 121.

[115] Genest, II, p. 125.—Congreve had no luck with Collier : for a second time he unnecessarily put himself in the wrong. Valentine is pretending to be mad and Congreve makes him say : " 'Tis strange ! but I am Truth . . ." (IV, 6). Collier scented blasphemy as if Valentine were claiming to be God. Quite evidently he was not, but Congreve substituted the words : " I am honest." [This alteration is not noted in Leigh Hunt's Edn.]

[116] IV, 6. See Genest, II, p. 347, and III, pp. 171-2.

[117] The Prologue to *The Provok'd Husband* was written by Cibber and begins :

" This Play took Birth from Principles of Truth,
To make Amends for Errors past, of Youth.
A Bard, that's now no more, in riper Days,
Conscious review'd the Licence of his Plays :
And though Applause his wanton Muse had fir'd,
Himself condemn'd what sensual Minds admir'd.
At length, he own'd, that Plays should let you see
Not Only, What you Are, but Ought to be :
Though Vice was natural, 'twas never meant,
The Stage should shew it ; but for Punishment !
Warm with that Thought, his Muse once more took Flame,
Resolv'd to bring licentious Life to Shame.
Such was the Piece his latest Pen design'd . . ."

As early as 1702 Vanbrugh wrote in the Prologue to *The False Friend* :

" You dread Reformers of an Impious Age
You awful Catta-nine-Tailes, to the Stage,
This once be Just, and in our Cause engage.
To gain your Favour, we your Rules Obey,
And Treat you with a Moral Piece to Day ;
So Moral, we're afraid 't will Damn the Play . . ."

Farquhar also paid honourable tribute to Collier : " I have not displeas'd the Ladies, nor offended the Clergy, both which are now pleased to say, that a Comedy may be diverting without Smut or Profaneness." (Preface to *The Constant Couple* ; see also the Prologue.)—" The Success and Countenance that Debauchery has met with in Plays ; was the most Severe and Reasonable Charge against their Authors in Mr. *Collier's Short View* : and indeed this Gentleman had done the *Drama* considerable Service, had he

both more guarded than they had been before. The later comedies of Farquhar and Vanbrugh mark a gradual transition. These plays were still daring enough, but their natural high spirits and frank merriment carried off anything that was at times a trifle too audacious.[117a] Little by little the English drama sobered down, mended its ways and grew calmer, till we ultimately sail into the quiet waters of Addison's *Cato*, of Rowe's monotonous and sentimental tragedies and of Steele's moral comedies.[118]

V

The Danger of Collier's Attack.—The Danger averted by Addison's " Spectator ".—The Difficulties of Addison's Task

There are some who think that the theatre overdid its reformation.[119] According to them, the English drama after Collier's day partakes too much of Florian's pastoral fables, and they

---

Arraign'd the Stage only to Punish it's Misdemeanours, and not to take away it's Life ; but there is an Advantage to be made sometimes of the Advice of an Enemy, and the only way to disappoint his Designs, is to improve upon his invective, and to make the Stage flourish by vertue of that Satyr, by which he thought to suppress it." (Preface to Farquhar's *Twin-Rivals*.)

Lastly, Cibber wrote in 1708 : " A Play, without a just Moral, is a poor mercenary Undertaking ; and 'tis from the Success of such Pieces that Mr. Collier was furnish'd with an Advantageous Pretence of laying his unmerciful Axe to the Root of the Stage." (Dedication of *The Lady's Last Stake*.)

[117a] [The best account of the Collier controversy may be found in *Comedy and Conscience after the Restoration*, by J. W. Krutch. 1924. See also the chapter on Vanbrugh in *Essays in Biography* by B. Dobrée.

However much Collier, together with the sentiment of the time, may have influenced the way in which plays were written, and hastened the decline of the drama by depriving it of its satirical bite, the theatres did not change much, nor the taste of the audiences. In about 1706 the author of *Hell upon Earth, or the Language of the Playhouse* bewailed the fact that the public was still enticed by " horrid comedies ". " The more they have been exposed by Mr. Collier and others," he groaned, " the more they seem to be admir'd." The controversy rumbled on through half the century, the stage being attacked by numerous Societies for the Prevention of Other People's Enjoyment. But the plays continued to be acted. For instance, I have before me a *Daily Post* of 1743, advertising *The Plain Dealer*, *The Country Wife*, and *The Constant Couple*, while offering the playgoer little else, except farce and pantomime. For the stage history of Restoration and early eighteenth-century plays, see the Notes in the Nonesuch Editions of the principal playwrights. B. D.]

[118] See in particular Steele's *Lying Lover* and *The Conscious Lovers*.—In Fielding's *Joseph Andrews* (book III, chap. XI) Parson Adams says : " I never heard of any plays fit for a Christian to read, but *Cato* and *The Conscious Lovers* ; and I must own that in the latter there are some things almost solemn enough for a sermon."

[119] Hazlitt amongst others. He expresses this opinion in a few pages

would fain cry with Lebrun : " Oh, how welcome a little wolf would be ! "

There is some justification for these regrets, though they are unnecessarily acute. They are, besides, actuated by an admiration for Restoration drama which we cannot easily share, and by a contempt for Collier which we cannot justly endorse. It is, however, fair to say that if Collier—or, worse, his friends—had had their way, that would have been the end of English drama and of many other things besides.[120] Their way led straight back to Puritanism. Collier was not himself a Dissenter, but he had a Dissenter's puritanical ideas about many things, and above all he had re-kindled puritanic fires slumbering in many a fanatic heart. Some were already talking of suppressing the theatre altogether.[121] That would have meant a return to the views of Prynne. If these plans had been carried out, England would have been put back for nearly a century, and her whole moral progress would have had to start again from scratch.

I have neither the wish nor the intention here to say anything against the Puritans. Whatever objections I might raise, I cannot but recognize in them the firm, honest and energetic core of the English nation. It is nevertheless certain that in pushing their principles to the furthest extreme, in seeking to deny to

---

of delicate wit and of sound judgment to boot. (*Lectures on the English Poets, and the English Comic Writers,* part II, pp. 117 ff.)

[120] Filmer in a *Defence of Plays* rightly contends : ". . . Many great and Unexpected Events do frequently flow from very slight and trivial Beginnings. We, or our Fathers, have seen Three flourishing Kingdoms brought to the very Brink of Ruin, a great, good and pious King murder'd on a Scaffold . . . and all by the Unnatural Violence of some hot-headed Zealots, who ran their first Heat indeed against Lawful Sports after Evening Service on *Sundays,* against Wakes, Feasts, Garlands and Maypoles on Holy-Days, and other such like innocent Diversions of the Vulgar ; but never stopp'd in their Career, 'till in Contempt of the Laws, both Divine and Human, they had utterly, and as they thought, irrecoverably, overthrown both Church and State . . . had those strait-lac'd Gentlemen (Collier's over-zealous partisans), with Mr. *Collier's* charitable Assistance once gain'd their Point against Plays, we should find them quickly nibbling at most our other Diversions, and giving our Ladies as frightful an Idea, perhaps of *Hidepark* or the *Mall* as Mr. *Collier* has already done of the Play-house . . ." By 1711 Bedford was tilting at Music. See my Bibliography, s.v. Bedford (Arthur), *The Great Abuse of Musick.*

[121] The anonymous author of *A Representation of the Impiety and Immorality of the English Stage* proposed " a total suppression of the Play-house " (p. 4).— Bedford wrote : " It is high Time to suppress such Places of *Iniquity.*" (*The Evil and Danger of Stage-Plays,* p. 218.)—In 1726 William Law published a book called : *The Absolute Unlawfulness of the Stage Entertainment Fully Demonstrated,* to which Dennis replied by : *The Stage defended from Scripture, Reason,* etc.

human nature the most innocent relaxation, and especially in trying to impose by force their own asceticism on everyone, they had exercised a tyranny over the consciences of their fellow-countrymen, and had seriously compromised the very cause of virtue and morality. You cannot establish the empire of Virtue on a sure foundation by making of her a scowling and repellent monster ; Virtue can be a kindly, humane, responsive goddess. The only logical ascetics are the folk who withdraw from the world. If you live in society, you must be genial, and not demand of other men inflexible and unrelaxing self-discipline. Those who fail to understand this truth, and seek to banish from life that beneficent and wholesome element which we call joy, defeat themselves—as do those English sabbatarians of to-day who deny the people Sunday recreation, and thereby encourage drunkenness.[121a] People who are cut off from innocent pleasures take refuge in vicious ones, and the more they are restrained in one direction the more they let themselves go in another. Outraged human liberty reacts against constraint: by licence. That is what happened at the Restoration. That is what would have happened again. If England had had to undergo another spell of exaggerated rigour, she would inevitably have reacted with a new outburst of exaggerated libertinism. The pendulum having been insanely forced to the right, would have swung with equal violence to the left, and Englishmen would have squandered their strength in perpetual oscillations from one excess to the other.

Happily, a man stepped forward at this very juncture to save English society from the threatening danger, to teach men moderation, and introduce them to a safe and level road, to link together in unique and lasting union the two admirable elements in the nation which had so long been striving against each other for supremacy, to fuse the best qualities of Puritan and Cavalier. This man was Addison. The work which confirmed and established England's moral reformation was the periodical which he modestly christened *The Spectator*.

The task which Addison undertook was one of supreme difficulty and delicacy. The urgent need was, not to oppose Collier's campaign, but to carry it on, while moderating its ruthlessness and guiding it into less narrow paths. The immorality

---

[121a] [It must be remembered that Beljame was writing some fifty years ago ; Sundays are less grim now than they were then, but the battle still goes on. B. D.]

and corruption which had been poisoning the whole social fabric must be attacked and driven out—and here Collier was an ally—but many things must be protected from the iconoclastic zeal of Collier and his disciples : all the genuine manifestations of literature and art, all the subtle pleasures which lend courtesy and charm to social intercourse, and in so doing ennoble and refine man's soul. The virtue of the Puritan must be reconciled with the elegance of the Cavalier. The one must be won over to a moral life by finding there good fellowship and pleasant company, the other must be won over to good manners by being shown that these were not incompatible with good morals.

That is to say—and herein lay the major difficulty of Addison's task—he had to distribute praise and blame to each of the two parties ; he had to be with the Puritans, but not in their excess of rigour ; he had to part company with the Cavaliers when their fine manners turned to licence. In other words, he had to try to find the golden mean. Now, at all times the golden mean is a thing most difficult to find. The man who has a foot in both camps can satisfy neither. Both are against him. Neither party can tolerate his criticism, neither can bear that he should praise the other. A mediator in such a case has been wittily compared to the French National Guard during the civil wars, where the first rank was exposed both to the fire of the insurgents and the fire of their comrades behind.[122]

To escape this fate, to succeed merely in making himself heard ; still more, to succeed in convincing his readers, a man needs gifts of persuasiveness, of tact and of impartiality such as are rarely united in one person, and he needs also to enjoy—a thing equally unusual—an authority which is recognized and respected, alike by friend and foe.

Every one of these conditions was fulfilled by Addison. No writer has ever had to the same degree so many attractive and delightful qualities, and none has more admirably devoted all his gifts to the service of the cause he had at heart. His own personal character and his position in the government invested him with an authority such as no English author had ever exercised before.

Joseph Addison was the son of an eminent clergyman of the

---

[122] A. Mézières, *le Spectateur d'Addison*, in the *Revue des cours littéraires*, Paris, March 19, 1870. This essay contains another very pertinent observation : " The part to be played in such a case is far from brilliant. If your sole aim is to mediate, and to temper excessive zeal, you cannot let yourself indulge in sounding phrases and telling effects."

Church of England, and distinguished himself at Oxford. His intention was to take Orders. His early literary efforts, however, won him admittance to the circle of which Dryden was the presiding genius. He was introduced to Montague and Somers, who shrewdly perceived his unusual talent and sought to enlist him for the service of their party. They persuaded the young Oxonian to give up the idea of the Church and embark on a political career. Through their good offices he was given a pension of £300 a year to enable him to travel in Europe. Poems addressed to his two benefactors proclaimed his allegiance to the Whig party.[123] William III's death, entailing the fall from power of his political friends, seemed for a moment likely to impair the young writer's prospects. But Queen Anne's ministers were semi-Tories, constrained to preserve the outward semblance of a Whig policy, and they turned to him (as we have seen above) to sing the victory of Blenheim. His poem, *The Campaign*, written for this occasion, immediately proved that the apprentice had become the master. Godolphin was so greatly delighted by *The Campaign* that he made its author Commissioner of Appeals in the Excise. He was next given the duty of accompanying Montague (now Lord Halifax) to Hanover, to convey to the Prince Elector the insignia of the Garter; then appointed Under Secretary of State, and finally Secretary to the Marquis of Wharton,[123a] Lord-Lieutenant of Ireland. This last post brought him in close on £2,000 a year. The Queen made him in addition Keeper of the Irish Records, with an annual salary of £400 a year, and the Irish electors voted him into the Irish Parliament.

Such was Addison's standing when he undertook the work which has deserved the undying gratitude of his fellow-countrymen. After *The Campaign*, he had published an account of his travels in Italy,[124] accompanied by some graceful verses, all of which had won him the attention of the cultured public. His public posts gave him a status which was enhanced by his personal reputation. His attachment to the Whig party, with which his career had begun, never flagged through fair weather or foul, and this earned him general respect. He had addressed verses to Montaguê the minister, he was no less the friend of Montague

---

[123] *A Poem to his Majesty*, presented to the Lord-Keeper (Somers), 1695; *Pax Guglielmi Auspiciis Europae reddita*, dedicated to Montague, 1697.

[123a] [At this time, Dec. 1708, Wharton was an Earl, having been made such in 1706. He was not created Marquis until 1715. B. D.]

[124] *Remarks on Several Parts of Italy*, dedicated to Lord Somers, 1705.

out of office.[125] He was made a member of the Kit-Cat Club even after his party had fallen from power.[126] He inspired so much respect by his principles—moderate without weakness, and firm without ostentation—that when the Tories were inclining towards a Whig policy he was one of the first to whom they turned. He was therefore well qualified to speak to the English public as a whole, and to exercise serious and lasting influence on his compatriots.

Before we proceed further, we must show what tools lay ready to his hand, and pay a just tribute to those who, by preparing the way for his journal, made his path straight and enabled him successfully to carry out his task.

VI

The periodical press after the Revolution.—Abolition of the Censorship.—Its consequences.—Birth of the literary journal : John Dunton's " Athenian Mercury " ; Defoe's " Weekly Review of the Affairs of France " ; Steele's " Tatler "

One of the great reforms consequent on the Revolution of 1688, and one of the most fruitful, was the emancipation of the Press. Except for rare intervals of liberty, Censorship had existed in one form or another under every English Government, royal or republican. On May 3, 1695, it passed away, never to be reinstituted. Parliament refused—almost certainly without suspecting the future consequences of its decision—to renew a law which subjected the Press to any man's good pleasure.[127]

William III's accession had already brought a measure of release to the Press. The new political situation encouraged writers to resume a certain freedom of expression, and some thirty

---

[125] *A Letter from Italy*, 1701, dedicated to Charles (Montague), Lord Halifax.

[126] In 1704.

[It is not quite correct to say that in 1704 the Whigs had fallen from power. Queen Anne's first House of Commons was Tory, and her ministers were such ; but by 1704 the Tories had suffered a decline, while the House of Lords continued strongly Whig. In 1705 the Whigs were returned to power, and did not fall until 1710. But in any event the Kit-Cat was a Whig social club with no political aims, and whether the Whigs were in or out made no difference to membership. Addison was introduced to the club by his friend and patron Halifax. Whig though he was, Addison did not mind taking a place under so firm a Tory as Sir Charles Hedges. B. D.]

[127] Macaulay, *History*, chap. XXI ; Hallam, *Constitutional History of England*, III, chap. XV.

new journals had appeared between 1688 and 1694.[128] But their existence had always been uneasy and precarious, and their anxiety was to escape, rather than to attract, attention. During the early years of William's reign, the only paper which provided serious political information was still the *London Gazette*, published as before under the eye of Government and supplying only favourable news, and none too much even of that. The *Gazette* was so dull that though it had no rivalry to fear, it circulated 8,000 copies only, not even one apiece for every parish in England. Other papers were shy of handling news, and when they did, it was usually copied from the *Gazette*.[129] The Coffee-Houses, which were growing in number and importance and beginning to develop into clubs,[130] remained, with the Newsletters,[131] the chief sources of information and the foci of political debate.

The abolition of the Censorship changed all that. A trusty old Whig, Harris by name, had been publishing a paper called *Intelligence Domestick and Foreign* during the last years of Charles II's reign, and had been obliged to discontinue it and go into voluntary exile. Within a fortnight of the abrogation of the Censorship he announced that his paper, sometime suppressed by " the violators of both the Laws and Liberties of England ", was about to reappear.[132] Ten days after Harris's *Intelligencer*,

[128] See a chronological list of these papers in George Chalmers, *Life of Thomas Ruddiman*, pp. 404-42.
[See also *Government and the Press, 1695-1763*, by L. Hanson. 1936. B. D.]
[129] Macaulay, *History*, chap. XXI.—Some years later Steele was made editor of the *Gazette*. He vowed that in this capacity he had never transgressed the rules observed by every administration : to keep the *Gazette* very harmless and very tame.
[130] On Coffee-Houses, see the *Spectator*, Nos. 1, 49 and 403 ; on Clubs, id., No. 9.
[See also Leslie Stephen, *English Literature and Society in the 18th Century*: 1904. Ashton, *Social Life in the Reign of Queen Anne*. T. H. S. Escott, *Club Makers and Club Members*. E. Ward, *A Compleat and Humorous Account of all the Remarkable Clubs and Societies in the Cities of London and Westminster*. Printed anon.: 1756. B. D.]
[131] Especially noteworthy are the Newsletters of a certain Dyer, which were much to the taste of Tories and High Churchmen. See Macaulay, *History*, chap. XX : *The Lancashire Prosecutions* ; Steele's *Tatler*, No. 86 ; the *Spectator*, No. 45.
[132] Benjamin Harris in the first number of the new *Intelligence Domestick and Foreign* dated Tuesday, May 14, 1695 (in the British Museum) writes : " Some time since I Published an *Intelligence*, with the like Title, wherein upon all Occasions, I Vigorously Asserted, the Laws and Liberties of *England*, against the Bold and Open Violators of both, which Procur'd me so many Inveterate Enemies, that to Save my Life, and my Family from Ruin, I was Compel'd to be an *Exile* from my Native Countrey, for above *Eight Years* : But being now Return'd, I know no reason, why, I may not endeavour, in some Measure,

appeared the first issue of *The English Courant*.[133] Then there poured out in rapid succession *The Post Man*, *The Post Boy*, *The Harlem's Courant*, *The Weekly News-Letter*, *Foreign and Domestick News*, *The London News-Letter*, *With Foreign and Domestick Occurrences*, *Pegasus*, *The Old Post-Master*, *Lloyd's News*, etc.[134]

So far, these newspapers were nothing much to boast of. They invariably consisted of a single sheet only, and that often printed only on one side.[135] Even *The Post Boy* and *The Post Man*, which were amongst the best produced and the most prosperous (*The Post Man* brought its editor in £600 a year),[136] were miserably printed on dirty paper, sometimes adorned with primitive engravings like those of the French *Liège Almanach*.

---

to Retrieve my Losses, and Misfortunes, by the same Methods, under the Happy Government of His Present Majesty, who hath so Gloriously Restored and Confirmed, our Rights and Privileges to us . . . I shall Write nothing but Truth, and certainty, and if I thereby Disoblige my Old Implacable Adversarys, the Care is taken ; since I doubt not but to Please my Old *Protestant Friends*, whose Zeal for their Freedoms of the Land of their Nativity, in the Worst of Times, I shall have a Just Value for ; While I am, Benjamin Harris."—On Harris, see above, chap. II, note No. 108.

[133] " The English Courant. Numb. 1. *To be published every* Wednesday *and* Saturday . . . Saturday, May 25, 1695." (British Museum.)

[134] " Numb. 72. The Post Man, and the Historical Account, etc. From Tuesday, October 22d. to Thursday, Oct. 24th 1695."—" Numb. 9. The Post Boy. With Foreign and Domestick News. From Saturday, June 1. to Tuesday, June 4. *London*, Printed for *A. Roper*, *E. Wilkinson* and *R. Clavel* in *Fleetstreet*, 1695."—" Numb. 1. The Harlem's Courant, *Publish'd at* Harlem Saturday, May 28. 1695. *N.S.*" " Numb. 4. The Weekly News-Letter : or, An Exact and Impartial Account of the most Remarkable Occurences. Foreign and Domestic . . . From *Saturday*, June 29. to *Saturday*, *July* 6. Printed for *J. Whitlock* near *Stationers-Hall*. 1695."—" (Numb. 1). Foreign and Domestic News : with the Pacquet-Boat from Holland and Flanders . . . Tuesday, July the 2. 1695."—" Numb. 1. The London News-Letter. With *Foreign* and *Domestick* Occurrences, Wednesday, April 29 1696."—" Numb. 1. Pegasus, With *News*, an *Observator*, and a *Jacobite Courant*. Monday June the 15th 1696." (printed by John Dunton).—" (Numb. 1.) The Old Post-Master. With the Occurrences of Great Britain and Ireland, and from Foreign Parts ; Collected and Published. From Saturday *June* the 20th. to Tuesday *June* the 23rd. 1696."—" Numb. 43. Lloyd's News. London, Tuesday. December 8, 1696. *Printed for Edward Lloyd* (*Coffee-Man*) *in Lombard Street*."—All these papers are in the British Museum.

[135] No. 12, for instance, of *The Post Boy*.—It should be said, however, that sometimes even both sides of one printed sheet did not suffice, and supplements were issued like : " A postscript to the Post Boy, in n°. 23 Wednesday July 3^d, 1695."

[136] Dunton, quoted by Andrews, I, p. 103.—". . . my most ingenious and renowned Fellow-Labourer, the *Post-Man*." (*Tatler*, No. 178) [but surely this is said ironically ?]. " The Post-Man, who is one of the most celebrated of our Fraternity." (*Tatler*, 204.)

They never appeared oftener than three times a week, and each issue contained about as much matter as would fill one column of a modern newspaper. They were anything but venturesome, and their excursions on to political ground were cautious in the extreme.

They were in fact still mindful of the unanimous pronouncement of Charles II's legal advisers, that the liberty of the Press did not imply liberty to print political news, for which royal permission was always necessary. What would be the judges' ruling on this point now? No one knew, and no one was anxious to challenge them on the question, lest their decision should be unfavourable. It is amusing to see how careful every editor was not to commit himself; though the papers continued to publish none but foreign political news, he always contrived to keep open a way of retreat by prefacing his statements with some precautionary formula like " it is said that . . ." or " people say . . ." or " it is thought that . . ." [137]

The proof that readers were not entirely satisfied by this procedure, is that the years 1695 and 1696 saw the birth of a hybrid type of paper intended to give the newspaper something of the attractive quality of the news-letter. The first specimens of this were *The Flying Post* and *Dawks's News-Letter*. Like other papers, these provided the current news, but they left a good proportion of their paper blank, so that anyone posting a copy to a friend could add by hand the latest information available, and more especially those items which the editor thought it more expedient not to print.[138]

[137] See Andrews, I, p. 101.—" The *Daily Courant*, says he, has these Words, *We have Advices from very good Hands, That a Certain Prince has some Matters of great Importance under Consideration.* This is very mysterious ; but the *Post-Boy* leaves us more in the Dark, for he tells us, *That there are private Intimations of Measures taken by a certain Prince which Time will bring to Light.* Now the *Post-Man*, says he, who used to be very clear, refers to the same News in these Words ; *The late Conduct of a certain Prince affords great Matter of Speculation.*" (*Tatler*, No. 155.)

[138] Andrews, I, p. 86 : " The *Flying Post* thus announces its design : ' If any gentleman has a mind to oblige his country friend or correspondent with this account of public affairs, he may have it for twopence . . . on a sheet of fine paper, half of which being blank, he may thereon write his own private business, or the material news of the day.' "

The earliest issue I have been able to find in the British Museum is " Numb. 281. The Flying Post : or, The Post Master. From Saturday February 27 to Tuesday March 2 1697. Printed for John Salusbury at the *Rising Sun* in *Cornhill*." By this date the *Flying Post* had become just an ordinary newspaper of the time.—The earliest issue of *Dawks's News-Letter* I have been able to get hold of has no title. It begins " London S^r 7 January 1698." Like the other

Nevertheless, despite uncertainty and hesitation, the free Press speedily took root in England, and when a bill to subject it anew to regulation was introduced in the House of Commons in 1697, it was defeated by 200 votes to 16.[139]

The painful and trying years of childhood and adolescence were past, the newspaper had attained its majority and achieved emancipation. The first daily newspaper was published in London on March 11, 1702. It was called *The Daily Courant*. At first it found some difficulty in filling both sides of the single sheet on which it was printed, and left one side blank [140]; but after a dozen numbers or so, it regularly appeared fully printed on both sides, and it succeeded in surviving till 1735.[141]

The number of newspaper readers in England must have multiplied mightily in a few years to ensure from the very start the successful survival of a daily paper, and we may fairly attribute a large share of this progress to the emancipation of the Press. This was not the only happy consequence that followed the change of policy. The freedom and development of the Press regularized and moderated its ways.

During the first years of William III's reign, political controversy, and more especially the ventilation of Jacobite sympathies, could not be carried on save by clandestine methods. The only means were secret printing presses, anonymous pamphlets surreptitiously smuggled from the printer's and circulated on the sly. Such a state of affairs produced the inevitable consequences. Reputable people of the opposition party, finding that they could not express their views without transgressing the law, and having recourse to endless subterfuge, held their peace and left their cause at the mercy of fanatics. These folk, who staked liberty and even life on every illegal publication, naturally wanted value for the risks they ran, and no scruple deterred them from any violence which lent weight to their blows. A baser

---

numbers which I have seen in the Newspaper Collection of the British Museum (1698, vol. II), it is printed in italics and consists of two and a half pages of print; half of the third and the whole of the fourth page are left blank. This part is filled with hand-written news. This copy bears the post-mark and is addressed: "To Mᵉ Dorothy Day in Oxon." The earliest numbered copy (No. 358) in the British Museum Collection bears the title: "Dawks's News-Letter" and is dated October 1, 1698. On Dawks and his paper, see the *Tatler*, No. 178.

[139] Macaulay, *History*, chap. XXII.
[140] "Numb. 1. *The Daily Courant*. Wednesday, March 11, 1702." (British Museum.)
[141] Andrews, I, p. 101.

type still, was the low-caste scribbler dealing in witless platitude, who was prepared to sell his pen to anyone for a consideration, and use it to spread stupid and filthy slanders. These things gave rise to a virulent and cynical literature exploiting lies and abuse, and circulating in shameless language the most odious accusations and the coarsest invective.[142] In a few years there had assembled in the attics and outhouses of Grub Street—a street whose name was henceforth a literary symbol—a sort of beggars' nest of all the starveling quill-drivers of London, outlaws and social outcasts, ready to write anything for the most trifling payment [143] and pouring forth a host of minor pamphlets nicknamed " Grub-streets ", so despicable that the adjective has passed into English as a synonym for mean and vile.[144]

The emancipation of the Press happily altered this state of affairs. As soon as everyone was at liberty freely to print what he thought, clandestine publishing lost its attraction and all reason for its continued existence. The Grub-street gradually died out, supplanted by the newspaper. With their future secure, the newspapers grew and developed and soon won a recognized place of their own. Hitherto political controversy

[142] See Macaulay, *History*, chap. XVI : The Jacobite Press ; chap. XX : Jacobite Libels : William Anderton, Writings and Artifices of the Jacobites ; chap. XXI : Effect of the Emancipation of the English Press.

[143] They were commonly known as " Grub-street hacks ".—Grub Street is frequently mentioned in writings of the time ; see Addison, *The Freeholder*, No. 35. Also, Swift's *Journal to Stella*, Aug. 21, Dec. 5 and 18, 1711, Nov. 15 and Dec. 12, 1712 ; likewise Swift's *Answer to Bickerstaff . . . By a Person of Quality* ; *A Letter of Advice to a Young Poet* ; to Dr. Delany, *On the Libels written against him* ; *A Scheme to make an hospital for incurables*. The earliest allusions I have met to Grub Street are of 1685 and 1689 : the Prologue to Rochester's *Valentinian*, written for Mrs. Barrey, speaks of " Grub-street *Pens* " and the Prologue to Shadwell's *Bury-Fair* of " *Silly* Grub-street *Songs* ".—The following sketch applies no doubt to one of the denizens of this street : " Mr. Ames, originally a *Coat-seller* . . . You might engage him upon what Project you pleas'd, if you'd but conceal him, for his *Principles* did never resist in such Cases . . . Wine and Women were the great Bane of his Life and Happiness." (John Dunton, *Life and Errors* . . . p. 247).—See also Dunton's portrait of Mr. Bradshaw (ibid., p. 241).

[144] *The Imperial Dictionary* (London, 1882) defines the adjective Grub-street as " mean, low, vile ".

[" Originally the name of a street near Moorfields in London (now Milton-Street), ' much inhabited by writers of small histories, dictionaries, and temporary poems ' (Johnson) ; hence used allusively for the tribe of mean and needy authors, or literary hacks." *N.E.D.* This is the sense in which it is now, and has always been, used. The name was first used by Taylor, the Water Poet, in 1630, the term by Shadwell in 1689. Beljame is a little harsh here, and has slightly misunderstood the term, which does not necessarily convey a moral stigma. B. D.]

had not been confined to one branch of literature ; it was liable to break out anywhere : in the theatre, in prologues and epilogues, in verses, in leaflets or in pamphlets. It now made a home for itself in the newspaper, and tended more and more to stay at home. It formed a new branch of literature and ceased, so to speak, to trespass on its neighbours. Every type of literature was thereby the gainer : drama, poetry and above all, controversy. In becoming centralized, controversy attained self-mastery, coherence and discipline ; it recruited its own specialists, and organized regular discussion. "Journalism" came into being, where previously there had been only individual newspapers ; and journalism lived in the public eye, open to the criticism of the nation : a fact which moderated and humanized debate. The change was, naturally, neither immediate nor complete. It was long before the English press wholly purged itself of baseness and violence ; Grub Street did not give up the ghost without a prolonged death rattle. But from the moment the Press was free, disreputable pamphleteers no longer called the tune of political discussion ; their sober rivals daily won a larger and larger circle of readers. Now that journalism had become a recognized and responsible branch of literature, it ceased to draw recruits from the dregs of society, but attracted able men who had something of value to say. After a few years, journalists numbered in their ranks writers, divines and statesmen of the calibre of Addison, Swift, Steele, Defoe, Garth, Kennet, Berkeley, Atterbury (the last three later to become bishops), Bolingbroke, Prior, and so on.[145]

Thus launched, the English newspaper grew in strength and made its power felt. It had a large and reliable reading public ; the most distinguished men in the country used it to address their fellow countrymen. But it was still one-sided ; it dealt exclusively with politics and was at the service of the parties. It is Addison's glory that he had vision to perceive that the time was come when the reading public, whom the controversialists had enlisted, might be invited to consider other

---

[145] Addison in *The Tatler, The Whig Examiner, The Medley, The Guardian, The Freeholder, The Old Whig* ; Swift in *The Examiner* ; Steele in *The Tatler, The Medley, The Guardian, The Englishman, The Plebeian* ; Defoe in *The Review*, etc. (See the Bibliography prefixed to William Lee's *Life and Writings of Defoe*) ; Garth and Kennet in *The Medley* (Andrews, I, p. 111) ; Berkeley in *The Guardian* (N. Drake, *Essays Illustrative*, etc., III, pp. 50 ff.) ; Atterbury, Bolingbroke and Prior in *The Examiner* (Swift, *Memoirs relating to that Change which happened in the Queen's Ministry in the Year 1710*).)

subjects than day-to-day politics, and when a paper might handle wider and more fertile themes.

It is a bookseller of those days—a fantastically-minded but inventive fellow—who can claim credit for having been the first to divine that a paper might serve to purvey other things than news. On Tuesday, March 17, 1690, John Dunton of the Black Crow in Gracechurch Street brought out a penny paper first called *The Athenian Gazette*. The second issue, however, was— " to oblige Authority "—rechristened *The Athenian Mercury*.[146] It was an odd production, proceeding by question and answer, and aiming at " Resolving Weekly all the most Nice and Curious Questions Propos'd by the Ingenious ". It would be impossible to conceive a more extraordinary collection of infantile queries and quibblings. Most of the questions relate to the casuistries of light love-making [147] or to microscopic and obscure points of religion and natural history, which are generally further obscured by the replies. " Whether the Torments of the damn'd are visible to the Saints in Heaven ? And vice versa ? "—" Whether 'tis lawful for a Man to beat his wife " ;—" Where was the soul of Lazarus for the four days he lay in the grave ? " ;—" Suppose Lazarus had an estate, and bequeathed it to his Friends, whether ought he or his Legatees to enjoy it after he was rais'd from the Dead ? " ;—" Where extinguish'd Fire goes ? " ;—" What became of the Waters after Noah's Flood ? " ;—" Why a Horse with a round Fundament emits a square Excrement ? " [148]

The editorial board or, as Dunton calls it, " The Athenian Society ",[149] replied to all these questions, and to others odder

[146] My information about *The Athenian Mercury* is drawn from the paper itself, and from Dunton's own *Life and Errors*, pp. 256 ff.
[147] No. 13, amongst others, is devoted entirely to questions of love and marriage. [A good deal of the correspondence in *The Tatler* and *The Spectator* is given to such matters. B. D.]
[148] The first three of these questions occur in the first issue ; Lazarus's estate in the fourth ; Fire in the sixth ; the Flood waters in the sixteenth and the Horse in the twenty-third. On the subject of wife-beating the paper dare not frankly say " yes " for fear of alienating its woman readers. But it argues thus : man and wife are one ; now, a man often inflicts suffering on himself : he lets the surgeon bleed him or amputate a limb, therefore, etc. Congratulations on such skilful tight-rope-walking !—The Horse question is a quaint specimen.
[*The Athenian Mercury* was not really quite so silly as Beljame suggests. It interested Temple, and Swift was all cock-a-whoop at having his early verses published in it. But see Beljame later. B. D.]
[149] It was composed of Dunton himself, Richard Sault, a Cambridge theologian, the Reverend Dr. John Norris and Dunton's brother-in-law Samuel Wesley, father of the future founder of Methodism.

still, with imperturbable gravity and a conscientious industry that never flagged.[150]

This eccentric paper demonstrates better than anything else how willing to learn were the readers of those days, and how much remained to be done towards their education. And nothing shows more clearly how the Press had already penetrated into daily life and how ready and willing people were to read other subjects than politics. For *The Athenian Mercury*, whose origin we have just seen, was a great success. It had begun as a modest weekly, but its third number already announced that so many questions had poured in that it would appear twice a week—and so in fact it did. After two years of life, it tried the experiment of four issues a week [151]; but this was too much, and the attempt had promptly to be given up.[152] Its success soon raised up rivals and imitators : *The Lacedemonian Mercury* edited by the prolific and commonplace Tom Brown,[153] *The Ladies Mercury*,[154] *The British Apollo*.[155] Dunton proudly quotes testimonies of approval

---

[150] They received this request one day : " Since in your Advertisement you make it known that a *Chyrurgeon* is taken into your Society, I have thought fit to propound the following Question, withal assuring you that the matter of the Fact is true. A Sailor on board the Fleet by an unlucky Accident broke his Leg, being in Drink, and refusing the assistance of the Surgeon of the Ship, called for a piece of new *Tarpauling* that lay on the Deck, which he rolled some turns round his Leg, tying up all close with a few Hoop-sticks, and was able immediately after to walk round the ship, never keeping his Bed one Day. I would know whether the Cure is to be attributed to the Emplastick Nature of the tarr'd and pitch'd Cloth bound on strait with the Hoop-sticks etc. or rather whether it may not be solved according to the *Cartesian Philosophy* ? " The Athenian Society solemnly replied with a discourse on fractures of the focile and of bones in general, on the catagmatic properties of tarred cloth and on Copernicus, without perceiving that they were dealing with a practical joker and a wooden leg. (No. 16.)—Some replies are of more value, this, for instance : " What is Platonick Love ? "— " Nothing at all, unless it be Friendship " (No. 16).—Let us note to the credit of Dunton's paper that it contains notices of new books, both English and foreign.

[151] No. of March 1, 1692.

[152] No. of March 14, 1692.

[153] A. Wood, *Athenæ Oxonienses*, s.v. Browne (Thomas). See also my Bibliography.—Dunton records how he compelled Tom Brown to resign from this paper by threatening to publish his life.

[Tom Brown may be commonplace, but he is by no means flat (*plat* is Beljame's phrase for him). The *Amusements Serious and Comical*, reprinted in 1927, are full of vigorous idiom and lively description. B. D.]

[154] " Vol. I. Numb. 1. *The Ladies Mercury*, Munday, *February* 17, 1693." (British Museum.)

[155] " Numb. 1. The British Apollo or *Curious Amusements for the Ingenious*. To which are added the most material Occurrences Foreign and Domestic *Perform'd by a society of Gentlemen.*" (British Museum.)—The collected numbers

which reached him from various quarters: the Marquis of Halifax, " The great and learned nobleman ", read *The Athenian Mercury* regularly and said he " had received great satisfaction from many of the answers " ; Sir William Temple, " a man of clear judgment and wonderful penetration ", sent frequent letters and questions ; Dunton received verses from Tate, Defoe and Motteux, and " Mr. Swift, a Country Gentleman " sent the Athenian Society an Ode which " being an ingenious poem was prefixed to the Fifth Supplement of the Athenian Mercury ".[156] Thus encouraged, the paper continued its bi-weekly appearance until 1696. At that point the competition of politics became too acute, and Dunton decided that it would pay better to issue quarterly numbers. He continued until the collection ran to twenty folio volumes. This did not satisfy readers' demands, and he had to publish a three-volume selection, under the title of *The Athenian Oracle*.

Dunton's idea had been a happy one, and odd as his *Mercury* may seem to us, we cannot deny him the honour of having successfully founded the first literary journal in England.

Dunton's example was not lost on Defoe. We tend too much to think of Daniel Defoe as the author of *Robinson Crusoe* only, and to forget that among many other titles to fame, he has the honour of being the founder of the English literary press. Born of dissenting parents, young Defoe early and passionately flung himself into politics and religious controversy. At twenty-four he was fighting under the banner of Monmouth, " the Protestant Duke ", and it was only by a happy chance that he escaped the fierce reprisals of the Bloody Assizes. In 1688 he was one of the strongest supporters of William III and in 1700 he wrote a poem, *The True-Born Englishman*, to defend the King against those who reproached him with his foreign birth and his Dutch friendships. Eighty thousand copies of the poem were sold.[157] Under Queen

---

of this paper form three volumes, beginning Feb. 13, 1708 and ending March 23, 1711. Note that it includes political news.

[156] This Ode is reprinted in Swift's *Works*. It was when he saw these verses that Dryden said to their author : " Cousin Swift, you will never be a poet."

[It is true that on the whole the Ode deserved Dryden's comment ; but it contains a great deal of characteristic Swiftian philosophy, and, in a wrong form (he should not have followed the fashion of the Pindaric), many of the poetic virtues he was later to use so effectively. B. D.]

[157] See my Bibliography.

[It is impossible to do more than guess at the circulation of *The True-Born Englishman* because of the many pirated editions. At any rate it was huge. B. D.]

Anne, Defoe was again on the war-path. To satirize the intolerant pretensions of the Church of England, he wrote in 1702 a pamphlet, *The Shortest Way with the Dissenters*, which created as great a stir as his poem, but for which he was sentenced to a fine, to the pillory, and to imprisonment during the Queen's pleasure.[158] On the very day that he was subjected to public disgrace he brought out *A Hymn to the Pillory* [159] and in his Newgate cell [160] he began the publication of a weekly paper, the first number of which appeared on Saturday, February 19, 1704, under the title: "A Weekly Review of the Affairs of *France* : Purged from the Errors and Partiality of *News-Writers* and *Petty-Statesmen*, of all Sides ".[161]

Possessed as he was by the spirit of controversy, Defoe was incapable of producing a non-political paper. This makes it the more noteworthy that he did not feel it possible to confine it to purely political topics. Following in Dunton's footsteps, he introduced a literary section which he called " Mercure Scandale : or, Advice from the Scandalous Club : Being A Weekly History of Nonsense, Impertinence, Vice and Debauchery ".[162] This programme clearly points to more ambitious aims than Dunton's. While imitating Dunton, he did more, and did it better, than his predecessor. For one thing, a new spirit was abroad. Since *The Athenian Mercury* was launched, Jeremy Collier had called public attention to more serious matters than those dealt with by the Athenian Society. Defoe, who had already crossed swords with Collier, did not neglect to handle moral questions in his

---

[158] In this anonymous pamphlet Defoe posed as a die-hard High-Churchman and suggested the complete suppression of the Dissenters, by force and violence if need be. Churchmen loudly applauded, but they soon learned the author's name, and the trap into which they had fallen. *Inde iræ*.

[159] I am here mentioning only the most important of Defoe's early works. He was one of the most prolific of English writers. The *Review of the Affairs of France* was his 67th publication [at least. B. D.]. According to William Lee he was the author of 254 works.

[160] He spent more than a year in prison.

[Investigations undertaken since Beljame wrote show that Defoe was in prison for only five and a half months (20th May–4th Nov. 1703), so the *Review* was not begun while he was in gaol. See additions to Defoe bibliography. B. D.]

[161] As its title indicates, the *Review* was at first a weekly, but from the eighth issue onwards it came out twice a week, on Tuesdays and Saturdays, and by 1705 it was appearing three times, on Tuesdays, Thursdays and Saturdays, the days on which the post went out from London to the provinces. It was sold at a penny. Defoe reverted to the size and lay-out of the Newsbooks ; his *Review* consisted of eight small quarto pages instead of a folio sheet.

[162] I take this title from No. 3 of the *Review*.

literary section. He discusses several aspects of contemporary manners, attacks drunkenness, swearing, marital unfaithfulness, the licence of the theatre, and duelling. His Scandalous Club accepts questions and letters [163] and offers varied and often ingenious advice on the reforms of which social life appeared to stand in need.[164] Here was already in outline the sketch of what the literary and moral Press was to be. But the detail had still to be filled in. Many and great as his qualities were, Defoe lacked those which would have enabled him successfully to address the majority of his fellow-countrymen. He was not a man of the world. His robust, straightforward style was without grace or art, and was not calculated gently to inculcate lessons of virtue and the good life in his contemporaries. What most seriously restricted Defoe's influence, was the fact that he was a Dissenter, and therefore suspect to that considerable section of English society to whom every form of Puritanism was hateful and intolerable. The influence of the *Review*, which was one of the most important and widely-read papers of its day,[165] was therefore chiefly political, and practically limited to Whig circles.

Nevertheless, Defoe was on the right tack, and it is thanks

[163] The issue dated Tuesday, September 19, 1704, contains, for instance, a letter from a correspondent signed " Arabella " to the Scandalous Club.— In the same year Defoe started " A Supplementary Journal, to the Advice from the Scandal Club ; *for the Month of* September 1704. To be Continued Monthly." This part of the *Review* consists of questions and answers like Dunton's paper, of verses, etc.
[164] Forster's *Biographical Essays* (Defoe) and Walter Wilson's *Memoirs of Daniel De Foe* (chap. XVI) contain interesting extracts from this section of the *Review*.
[The Review is now easily consulted in the facsimile reprint edited by Arthur W. Secord. Columbia University Press. 1938. B. D.]
[165] Bolingbroke's *Examiner* was founded largely to counter the *Review* (Andrews, I, p. 104). In *A Letter from a Member of the House of Commons in Ireland to a Member of the House of Commons in England Concerning the Sacramental Test*, 1708, Swift says that the *Review* was an indispensable item of Coffee-House furniture. But all the same, Swift had no love for Defoe ; in the same letter he alludes to him as " that fellow who was put in the pillory—I forget his name ". The influence of the *Review* spread quickly in the provinces. *Notes and Queries* (April 3, 1875) quotes some correspondence between Defoe and one John Fransham of Norwich. In it I find this passage dated Nov. 10, 1704 : " It was with no small Satisfaction that I read your Justification in your Review . . . I had read it to several Gentlemen . . . in the chief Coffee-house here where we have it as oft as it comes out and is approv'd as the politest paper we have to entertain us with. I had some difficulty to prevail with the Master of the house to take it in but now he finds I advis'd him well there being no paper more desir'd . . ."—Defoe edited his *Review*, single-handed, for over nine years.

to him that his imitators were able to do better. Imitators were not long in making their appearance. As early as 1708, while the *Review* was still going strong, Richard Steele—writing under the pseudonym of Isaac Bickerstaff [166]—published the *Tatler*, which like the *Review* appeared tri-weekly and on the same days. Steele possessed many of the qualities in which Defoe was deficient. He had been to Oxford, he was a soldier, a playwright, a Government office-holder and a man of the world. Having tasted of life pretty freely, he had studied men and things from many angles, and was able with his well-tried, smoothly-running pen to tackle the most varied subjects in such a way as to interest the great majority of the reading public. He belonged to the same political party as Defoe, but his attitude was less tainted with proselytizing intolerance. Defoe (I speak here only of his early days) was one person only and that a controversialist, while Steele was a many-sided character. In him politics had not swallowed up the man of the world nor the lover of literature. His views were strong and decided, but they were genial. He belonged to the new Whig generation to which no odour of Puritanism clung.

Steele embarked at once on a comprehensive programme, taking for the motto of his paper :

Quicquid agunt homines nostri farrago libelli.

In his first issue he announced that articles on questions of gallantry, pleasure and entertainment, poetry and learning would come from different Coffee-Houses ; while he would write on various other subjects " from my own apartment " ; and he

---

[166] The year before, Swift had been campaigning against the Almanack makers, especially a certain Partridge, an ex-cobbler who successfully retailed his prophecies in London. Taking the name of Isaac Bickerstaff, Swift gave himself out to be a genuinely learned astrologer who maintained the wholesome ancient traditions of his art. As such he blushed at the productions of his would-be co-astrologers and wished to recapture for Astrology its old-time brilliance and prestige. He began by predicting that Partridge would die on the 29th of March of a raging fever, and on the 30th he announced with the most circumstantial detail the precise manner of Partridge's death on the predicted day. Partridge vigorously protested that he was still alive. Bickerstaff replied with cogent proof that he was on the contrary well and truly dead, and to the great delight of London, Rowe, Steele, Addison, Prior, Congreve and Yalden amused themselves by prolonging the jest. The Stationers' Company gravely walked into the trap, and officially forbade the publication of further Almanacks bearing Partridge's name, because no one had a right to misuse the name of a dead writer. It is easy to picture the wrath of the unfortunate cobbler-prophet. London's laughter had not died away when Steele bethought him of publishing his *Tatler* under the popular name of Isaac Bickerstaff.

would deal also with home and foreign news. In common with Defoe, Steele did not banish politics,[167] but whereas the *Review* gives them the major space and the post of honour, the *Tatler* treats them as accessory and thrusts them into the background. Little by little even news became less important and scantier, and from the eighty-third issue onwards it disappeared entirely. Thus it came about that in the course of his progress Steele recruited an unexpected and invaluable collaborator. Addison was at the time in Ireland, and presently discovered that the name of Bickerstaff cloaked his old school and college friend Richard Steele. His co-operation, warmly and eagerly accepted, rapidly made his influence on the paper felt.[168] The *Tatler* brought Addison the revelation of his true vocation, and newcomer though he was, he was soon taking the lead. " I fared," says Steele, " like a distressed Prince, who calls in a powerful Neighbour to his Aid ; I was undone by my Auxiliary ; when I had called him in, I could not subsist without Dependance on him." [169] And, true enough, Addison's inspiration soon preponderated in the *Tatler* and little by little changed its character in the happiest way. Steele had wit, observation and imagination, and he wrote with ease and elegance. The pages of his paper for which he alone is responsible, provide many most pleasing passages, and the reader will there find in embryo the whole programme which the two friends developed in the later numbers of the *Tatler* and in the *Spectator*.[170] But everything with Steele is tentative and vague. We get flashes of light rather than illumination. His invention is happy and fertile, but he

---

[167] He was at the moment editor of the *London Gazette* and thus had all the political news at first hand.
[168] Addison's collaboration begins with No. 18. He detected Steele's hand in a comment on Virgil which he himself had once made to his friend. This remark in *Tatler* No. 6 relates to Virgil's good sense in substituting the epithet *Dux Trojanus* for the usual *Pius Æneas* and *Pater Æneas*, either of which would have been out of place when Æneas and Dido sought the shelter of the cave for their love-making.
[169] Preface to fourth vol. of the *Tatler*.
[170] See, for instance, No. 3, where he condemns the dubious morality of Wycherley's *Country-Wife* and at the same time confesses that he cannot endorse the severity towards the theatre shown by his friends and " collaborators ", the reformers of manners. The same number contains this passage : ". . . if a fine Lady thinks fit to giggle at Church, or a Great Beau come in drunk to a Play, either shall be sure to hear of it in my ensuing Paper : for meerly as a well-bred Man, I cannot bear these Enormities." Here Steele anticipates the programme and the tone of Addison.—See also No. 8 with Steele's criticism of Ravenscroft's *London Cuckolds*.

does not in practice turn it to full account; his genius deserts him halfway. He gropes and taps in every direction like a man uncertain where he wants to go, or rather, like one who wants to go to several different places at once. This uncertainty of aim is very marked in the first issues of the *Tatler*. The paper, seeking to be at once literary and political, ends by being neither. Steele touches on everything and handles nothing exhaustively. He had promised his readers too much, and each number is a medley of odds and ends in which nothing stands out and nothing is emphasized. The final impression is confused and blurred.

Addison made a clearance of the undergrowth and brought air and light to the saplings. He clearly saw that the *Tatler* must decide whether it was to be a political or a literary paper, and he saw that politics were amply catered for in a period wholly given over to party strife. He saw too—what his predecessors had but dimly suspected—that a literary paper had a special part to play and a new influence to exert on surrounding society.[171] So, little by little, politics disappeared from the *Tatler* and left the field free for other developments. The delineation of character and social eccentricities, the discussion of literary works, discreet and witty dissertations on morals, claimed every day more and more space. In proportion as the two friends' collaboration grew more intimate and Addison's gifts developed, gaining confidence and strength,[172] the *Tatler*

---

[171] " I must confess I am amazed that the press should only be made use of in this way (i.e. in periodic sheets) by news-writers, and the zealots of parties : as if it were not more advantageous to mankind to be instructed in wisdom and virtue than in politics ; and to be made good fathers, husbands, and sons, than counsellors and statesmen. Had the philosophers and great men of antiquity, who took so much pains to instruct mankind, and leave the world wiser and better than they found it ; had they, I say, been possessed of the art of printing, there is no question but they would have made such an advantage of it, in dealing out their lectures to the public. Our common prints would be of great use were they thus calculated to diffuse good sense through the bulk of a people, to clear up their understandings, animate their minds with virtue, dissipate the sorrows of a heavy heart, or unbend the mind from its more severe employments with innocent amusements. When knowledge, instead of being bound up in books, and kept in libraries and retirements, is thus obtruded upon the public ; when it is canvassed in every assembly, and exposed upon every table, I cannot forbear reflecting upon that passage in the *Proverbs* : ' Wisdom crieth without ; she uttereth her voice in the streets : she crieth in the chief place of concourse, in the openings of the gates : in the city she uttereth her words, saying, How long, ye simple ones, will ye love simplicity ? and the scorners delight in their scorning, and fools hate knowledge ? ' " (*Spectator*, No. 124, and Proverbs i, 20–22.)

[172] Addison's best essays occur fairly late in the *Tatler*. Afterwards he grew surer of himself and did even better, but some are charming and deserve

became what has been justly called a "journal of manners",[173] a gallery of delightful subject-pictures, a faithful but kindly mirror of society, ever mindful quietly to drive home some delicate and useful lesson in pleasing and attractive guise. With glad surprise, Steele confessed that he scarcely recognized his own child.[174]

VII

The "Spectator".—A Non-political Daily.—Appeal to new Readers.—Readers' Response.—Moral Rôle of the "Spectator".—Its Attitude to Cavaliers and Puritans.—Addison's special Qualifications for his Task.—Moral Value of his Paper.—Its Literary and Educational Value.—Its Success.—Contemporary Testimony to the Influence of the "Tatler" and "Spectator"

Let us, however, not linger over the rough sketch, when the finished masterpiece is calling us. The two friends soon became conscious that however skilfully they retouched and elaborated their first draft it would remain an imperfect patchwork and could never be turned into a first-class picture. There was nothing to be done but leave this first experiment as it stood, for what it in itself was worth and start work on something new. On January 2, 1710-11, Isaac Bickerstaff made his exit from the literary stage, where for nearly two years he had played no undistinguished part, and in the following March Addison and Steele—no longer Steele and Addison [175]—the richer by

---

to be quoted : The politically-minded Upholsterer, Nos. 155, 160, 178, 232 ; Tom Folio, Nos. 158, 160 ; Ned Softly, No. 163 ; The Political Barometer, No. 214 ; The Adventures of a Shilling, No. 249 ; The Court of Honour, Nos. 250, 252, 253, 256, 259, 261, 262, 265. It will be noticed that most of these subjects take up several numbers. Addison taught Steele the art of keeping the reader's interest from one day to the next.

[173] Rémusat, I, p. 195.

[174] "He (Tickell) very justly says, the occasional Assistance Mr. *Addison* gave me in the Course of that Paper [the *Tatler*] did not a little contribute to advance its Reputation especially when, upon the Change of the Ministry, he found leisure to engage more constantly in it. It was advanced, indeed, for it was rais'd to a greater thing than I intended it." (A letter of Steele's prefixed to *The Drummer*, addressed "To Mr. *Congreve* Occasion'd by Mr. *Tickell's* Preface to the Four volumes of Mr. *Addison's* Works ".)

[This Preface of 1721 is, however, an angry reply to Tickell for claiming too much for Addison. Steele, bountifully generous, gave Addison more than his due. See *Essays in Biography*, B. Dobrée, pp. 339 seq. B. D.]

[175] While Steele had written 188 and Addison 42 (and the two friends jointly 36) of the 271 *Tatlers*, Addison wrote 250 and Steele only 240 out of the 555 *Spectators*.—In reckoning 555 *Spectators* I am not counting in the eighth volume of the *Spectator*, which was in fact an entirely new venture.

experience gained, made their bow to the public in the *Spectator*.

Encouraged by the success of the *Tatler* they ventured on two daring innovations : from the beginning the new paper was to be solely literary and it was to appear daily, except on Sundays, instead of only three times a week. The experiment was plucky and arduous. While editing the *Tatler* Steele had already groaned over the difficulty of supplying the public regularly with the promised reading matter :

> When a Man has engaged to keep a Stage-Coach, he is obliged, whether he has Passengers or not, to set out : Thus it fares with us weekly Historians.[176]

How much greater would be the difficulty of running a daily paper which denied itself the advantage of utilizing political news ! In renouncing politics, the editors were forgoing not only a sure and easy means of daily filling up blank spaces in the paper, but at the same time the faithful circle of partisan readers on whom a party journal can always safely count.

There were other potential subscribers to whom the *Spectator* deliberately scorned to appeal : those who had been wont to devour the lampoons and comedies of the Restoration, and were now greedily fattening on pamphlets and Grub-streets. These readers could easily have been wooed and won, if the new paper had been willing to bespatter its pages with slanders, scandals and uncharitable personalities. But Addison would not purchase success at the price

> of those seasonings that recommend so many of the writings which are in vogue among us.[177] As, on the one side, my paper has not in it a single word of news, a reflection in politics, nor a stroke of party ; so, on the other, there are no fashionable touches of infidelity, no obscene ideas, no satires upon priesthood, marriage, and the like popular topics of ridicule ; no private scandals, nor anything that may tend to the defamation of particular persons, families, or societies.

This dual ordinance of self-denial was highly creditable,[178]

---

[176] *Tatler*, No. 12.
[177] *Spectator*, No. 262. See also Nos. 33 and 355.
[178] The merit was all the greater that from every side pressure was brought to bear on the *Spectator* to take up politics and personalities. This is Addison's simple and dignified reply : " There is another set of correspondents to whom I must address myself . . . I mean such as fill their letters with private scandal, and black accounts of particular persons and families. The world is so full of ill-nature, that I have lampoons sent me by people who cannot spell, and satires composed by those who scarce know how to

for, as Addison says, " there is not one of the above-mentioned subjects that would not sell a very indifferent paper ". Nor was this self-denial without its dangers, for, more than any other literary product, a paper which does not immediately command readers, is doomed to speedy and inevitable death.

The truth is that Addison had the courage to disregard the normal supporters of his brother-editors because he divined that there existed, ready and waiting, the makings of another reading public, to whom no one had hitherto given thought. Poets and playwrights had written for the Court and for Society (with a capital S) ; Church of England clergymen and dissenting ministers had written tracts and sermons for their

---

write. By the last post in particular I received a packet of scandal which is not legible ; and have a whole bundle of letters in women's hands that are full of blots and calumnies, insomuch that when I see the name Caelia, Phillis, Pastora, or the like, at the bottom of a scrawl, I conclude of course that it brings me some account of a fallen virgin, a faithless wife, or an amorous widow. I must therefore inform these my correspondents, that it is not my design to be a publisher of intrigues and cuckoldoms, or to bring little infamous stories out of their present lurking-holes into broad daylight. If I attack the vicious, I shall only set upon them in a body ; and will not be provoked by the worst usage I can receive from others, to make an example of any particular criminal. In short I have so much of a Drawcansir * in me, that I shall pass over a single foe to charge whole armies. It is not Lais or Silenus, but the harlot and the drunkard whom I shall endeavour to expose ; and shall consider the crime as it appears in a species, not as it is circumstanced in an individual. I think it was Caligula who wished the whole city of Rome had but one neck, that he might behead them at a blow. I shall do out of humanity, what that Emperor would have done in the cruelty of his temper, and aim every stroke at a collective body of offenders. At the same time, I am very sensible that nothing spreads a paper like private calumny and defamation ; but as my speculations are not under this necessity, they are not exposed to this temptation.

" In the next place, I must apply myself to my party correspondents, who are continually teasing me to take notice of one another's proceedings. How often am I asked by both sides, if it is possible for me to be an unconcerned spectator of the rogueries that are committed by the party which is opposite to him that writes the letter. About two days since, I was reproached with an old Grecian law that forbids any man to stand as a neuter or looker-on in the divisions of his country. However, as I am very sensible that my paper would lose its whole effect, should it run into the outrages of a party, I shall take care to keep clear of everything which looks that way. If I can any way assuage private inflammations, or allay public ferments, I shall apply myself to it with my utmost endeavours ; but will never let my heart reproach me with having done anything towards increasing those feuds and animosities that extinguish religion, deface government, and make a nation miserable." (*Spectator*, No. 16.)

* A character in Buckingham's *Rehearsal* :
 "Others may boast a single man to kill,
 But I the blood of thousands daily spill."

respective followings; scholars had written for the universities, and newspapers had written to gratify the passions of one party or another. But outside the radius of the Court, the Churches and the Universities, outside political cliques, were there not somewhere other readers, possibly even women readers? [179] Might there not be, perchance, in the professions, in commerce, amongst provincial folk, some persons ready to welcome intelligent mental fare? [180] In a society where the Court had first

[179] "But there are none to whom this paper will be more useful than to the female world. I have often thought there is not sufficient pains taken in finding out proper employments and diversions for the fair ones. Their amusements seem contrived for them rather as they are women than as they are reasonable creatures, and are more adapted to the sex than to the species. The toilet is their great scene of business, and the right adjusting of their hair the principal employment of their lives. The sorting of a suit of ribbons is reckoned a very good morning's work; and if they make an excursion to the mercer's or a toy-shop, so great a fatigue makes them unfit for anything else all the day after. Their more serious occupations are sewing and embroidery, and their greatest drudgery the preparation of jellies and sweetmeats. This, I say, is the state of ordinary women; though I know there are multitudes of those of a more elevated life and conversation, that move in an exalted sphere of knowledge and virtue, that join all the beauties of the mind to the ornaments of dress, and inspire a kind of awe and respect, as well as love, into their male beholders. I hope to increase the number of these by publishing this daily paper, which I shall always endeavour to make an innocent if not an improving establishment, and by that means at least divert the minds of my female readers from greater trifles. At the same time, as I would fain give some finishing touches to those who are already the most beautiful pieces in human nature, I shall endeavour to point out all those imperfections that are the blemishes, as well as those virtues which are the embellishment of the sex. In the meanwhile I hope these my gentle readers, who have so much time on their hands, will not grudge throwing away a quarter of an hour in a day on this paper, since they may do it without any hindrance to business." [No. 10—not 50 as in the text. E. O. L.]—Addison kept the promise here made to give attention to his woman-readers. See No. 205 for a list of 24 numbers devoted to women's affairs. Swift was of the opinion that he overdid it: "I will not meddle with *The Spectator*," he writes to Stella, Feb. 8, 1711-12, "let him fair-sex it to the world's end."

[180] "I would recommend this paper to the daily perusal of those gentlemen . . . who live in the world without having anything to do in it, and either by the affluence of their fortunes or laziness of their dispositions, have no other business with the rest of mankind but to look upon them. Under this class of men are comprehended all contemplative tradesmen, titular physicians, Fellows of the Royal Society, Templars that are not given to be contentious, and statesmen that are out of business; in short every one that considers the world as a theatre, and desires to form a right judgment of those who are the actors in it.

"There is another set of men that I must likewise lay a claim to, whom I have lately called the blanks of society, as being altogether unfurnished with ideas till the business and conversation of the day has supplied them. I have often considered these poor souls with an eye of great commiseration, when I have heard them asking the first man they have met with whether

made literature fashionable, where, next, the development of the Press had spread the habit of reading, ought there not to exist—if it could be discovered—a whole army of intelligent, open-minded people who might be attracted without too great difficulty? Who could tell? Perhaps among newly-won readers, in drawing-rooms, amongst scholars, amid the congregations of church or even of dissenting chapel, perchance even amongst those whose interest had hitherto been wholly monopolized by politics,[181] there might be found some whose minds had been

there was any news stirring? and by that means gathering together materials for thinking. These needy persons do not know what to talk of till about twelve o'clock in the morning, for by that time they are pretty good judges of the weather, know which way the wind sits, and whether the Dutch mail be come in. As they lie at the mercy of the first man they meet, and are grave or impertinent all the day long, according to the notions they have imbibed in the morning, I would earnestly entreat them not to stir out of their chambers till they have read this paper, and do promise that I will daily instil into them such sound and wholesome sentiments as shall have a good effect on their conversation for the ensuing twelve hours." (No. 10.)

[181] " There is no humour in my countrymen which I am more inclined to wonder at, than their general thirst after news. There are about half a dozen ingenious men, who live very plentifully upon this curiosity of their fellow-subjects. They all of them receive the same advices from abroad, and very often in the same words; but their way of cooking it is so different, that there is no citizen, who has an eye to the public good, that can leave the coffee-house with peace of mind, before he has given every one of them a reading. These several dishes of news are so very agreeable to the palate of my countrymen, that they are not only pleased with them when they are served up hot, but when they are again set cold before them, by those penetrating politicians who oblige the public with their reflections and observations upon every piece of intelligence that is sent us from abroad. The text is given us by one set of writers and the comment by another.

" But notwithstanding we have the same tale told us in so many different papers, and if occasion requires in so many articles of the same paper; notwithstanding in a scarcity of foreign posts we hear the same story repeated, by different advices from Paris, Brussels, the Hague, and from every great town in Europe; notwithstanding the multitude of annotations, explanations, reflections, and various readings which it passes through, our time lies heavy on our hands till the arrival of a fresh mail. We long to receive further particulars, to hear what will be the next step, or what will be the consequences of that which has been already taken. A westerly wind keeps the whole town in suspense, and puts a stop to conversation.

" This general curiosity has been raised and influenced by our late wars, and, if rightly directed, might be of good use to a person who has such a thirst awakened in him. Why should not a man, who takes delight in reading everything that is new, apply himself to history, travels, and other writings of the same kind, where he will find perpetual fuel for his curiosity, and meet with much more pleasure and improvement, than in these papers of the week? An honest tradesman, who languishes a whole summer in expectation of a battle, and perhaps is balked at last, may here meet with half a dozen in a day. He may read the news of a whole campaign, in less time than he now bestows upon the products of any single post. Fights, conquests, and revolu-

influenced by the course of events, and who would no longer be content with the only reading up to now supplied them : books, tracts, pamphlets, broadsides, Grub-streets, which, when not blazing with political passion, had been either wholly frivolous or wholly ascetic.

Addison was the first to formulate these questions clearly to himself. He divined the existence of such a public and marched forth to conquer it with clear-cut ideas and a well-defined plan of campaign.

The first problem to be faced was how to catch the ear of this multiple and scattered audience ; how to capture the interest of so many diverse listeners distributed through every stratum of society. From his first entry on the scene Addison succeeded by an ingenious stage-device.[182]

His paper was supposed to be edited by a Club in which people of the most varied characters and professions were represented.[183] Chief amongst them towers the Spectator, a calm and meditative person who goes through life as a silent observer. The gravity of his behaviour was remarked even in babyhood ; before he was two months old he threw away his rattle and would not use it till they had removed the bells from it. At the University, apart from College exercises, he did not during

---

tions lie thick together. The reader's curiosity is raised and satisfied every moment, and his passions disappointed or gratified, without being detained in a state of uncertainty from day to day, or lying at the mercy of sea and wind. In short, the mind is not here kept in a perpetual gape after knowledge, nor punished with that eternal thirst, which is the portion of all our modern news-mongers and coffee-house politicians.

"All matters of fact, which a man did not know before, are news to him ; and I do not see how any haberdasher in Cheapside is more concerned in the present quarrel of the Cantons, than he was in that of the League. At least, I believe every one will allow me, it is of more importance to an Englishman to know the history of his ancestors, than that of his contemporaries, who live upon the banks of the Danube or the Borysthenes." (No. 452.)

"Is it not much better to be let into the knowledge of one's self than to hear what passes in Muscovy or Poland, and to amuse ourselves with such writings as tend to the wearing out of ignorance, passion, and prejudice, than such as naturally conduce to inflame hatreds, and make enmities irreconcilable ? " (No. 10.)

[182] I shall henceforward speak of Addison as if he were the sole author of the *Spectator*, partly for brevity but more because he is obviously its life and soul and it is he who gives it all its value. But I am not forgetting Steele who has been unduly eclipsed by his friend's lustre. He deserves an ample share in the applause showered on Addison and it is pertinent and only fair here to recall that he had his part in staging the *Spectator*.

[183] See Nos. 1 and 2. The idea of Addison's Club existed already in embryo in Dunton's Athenian Society and Defoe's Scandalous Club. No. 132 of the *Tatler* contains a foreshadowing of the *Spectator* Club.

the space of eight years utter more than a hundred words. But if he kept his mouth shut, his eyes and mind were open, and there were few celebrated books, either in the learned or modern tongues, which he did not read and ponder during his student years. Having arrived at man's estate, he travelled over all the countries of Europe to satisfy his thirst for knowledge, and even made a special journey to Cairo to take the measure of a pyramid. Returning to London to settle down, he continued to observe men and things with curiosity. There was no place of general resort where his face was not known : the coffee-houses, the theatres, the Exchange, were in turn recipients of his long and silent visits. Having slowly and perseveringly accumulated such a mass of observations he made himself, as he says, " a speculative statesman, soldier, merchant, and artisan, without ever meddling with any practical part in life ". He goes on to say :

I am very well versed in the theory of a husband, or a father, and can discern the errors in the economy, business, and diversion of others, better than those who are engaged in them, as standers-by discover blots which are apt to escape those who are in the game. I never espoused any party with violence, and am resolved to observe an exact neutrality between the Whigs and Tories [184] . . . In short,

---

[184] He scrupulously keeps his word. Not more than once or twice are the Whig sympathies of the author allowed an airing, and then a slight one : in No. 3 for instance the vision of the Bank of England presided over by the beautiful maiden Public Credit on her throne of gold, and No. 139 (by Steele) in eloquent praise of the Duke of Marlborough. But this latter may fairly be considered patriotic rather than political. The only excursions the *Spectator* makes into politics are counsels of tolerance and moderation. How evenly he holds the balance in offering good advice alike to Whigs and Tories, may be judged from the following quotations :

" My worthy friend, Sir Roger, when we are talking of the malice of parties, very frequently tells us of an accident that happened to him when he was a school-boy, which was at the time when the feuds ran high between the Roundheads and Cavaliers. This worthy knight being then but a stripling, had occasion to inquire which was the way to St. Anne's Lane, upon which the person whom he spoke to, instead of answering his question, called him a young popish cur, and asked him who had made Anne a saint ? The boy being in some confusion, inquired of the next he met, which was the way to Anne's Lane ; but was called a prick-eared cur for his pains, and instead of being shown the way, was told, that she had been a saint before he was born, and would be one after he was hanged. ' Upon this,' says Sir Roger, ' I did not think fit to repeat the former question, but going into every lane in the neighbourhood, asked what they called the name of that lane.' By which ingenious artifice he found out the place he inquired after, without giving offence to any party." (No. 125.)

History repeats itself ; the following anecdote sounds like an echo from the French Revolution. Four Indian kings had come on a visit to England

I have acted in all the parts of my life as a looker-on, which is the character I intend to preserve in this paper.[185]

This unusual being was known only to "not above half a dozen select friends" and it was only in their company tha his tongue was loosed, and he consented to allow others a glimpse of the treasure he had accumulated from day to day by observation and reflection.[186] His friends frequently urged him to permit his fellow citizens to benefit by the fruits of his experience. As it was a question not of speaking but of writing, he yielded to their importunity and resolved to "publish a sheetful of thoughts every morning" with the assistance and collaboration of his friends, whom he then introduces to us one by one.[187]

The first is "a gentleman of Worcestershire of ancient descent, a baronet, his name Sir Roger de Coverly", who divides his time between London and the country. In his early days Sir Roger was "what you call a fine gentleman" who moved in the society of the Rochesters and the Etheregcoes. But being "crossed in love by a perverse beautiful widow" he has long since grown careless of his dress, and "continues to wear a coat and doublet of the same cut that were in fashion at the time of his repulse, which, in his merry humours, he tells us has been

---

and one of them is giving his impressions of their stay : " The queen of the country appointed two men to attend us that had enough of our language to make themselves understood in some few particulars. But we soon perceived these two were great enemies to one another, and did not always agree in the same story. We could make a shift to gather out of one of them that this island was very much infested with a monstrous kind of animals, in the shape of men, called Whigs ; and he often told us that he hoped we should meet with none of them in our way, for that if we did, they would be apt to knock us down for being kings. Our other interpreter used to talk very much of a kind of animal called a Tory, that was as great a monster as the Whig, and would treat us as ill for being foreigners. These two creatures, it seems, are born with a secret antipathy to one another, and engage when they meet as naturally as the elephant and the rhinoceros. But as we saw none of either of these species, we are apt to think that our guides deceived us with misrepresentations and fictions and amused us with an account of such monsters as are not really in their country." (No. 50.)

I should like to go on and quote his advice to political women (No. 57), his witty No. 81 on the use of "patches" in politics, and a host of others. As it is, I refer the reader to A. Mézières, *le Spectateur d'Addison* in the *Revue des cours littéraires*, March 19, 1870.

[185] No. 1.

[186] Nos. 1 and 4.—This peculiarity was certainly characteristic of Addison himself. He was shy and unwilling to talk except in a circle of intimate friends. He used himself to say that he could write a cheque for £1,000 but never had a guinea in his pocket.

[187] In No. 2.

in and out (of fashion) twelve times since he first wore it ". He is now in his fifty-sixth year and devotes himself entirely to his friends and the care of his estates which he administers with paternal kindness, looking on all around him, tenants, servants and guests, as his family, happy to be beloved by his own circle. He is both a good man and a genial companion, " cheerful, gay, and hearty ", with certain eccentricities of character which are no less lovable than his virtues and good qualities.

The gentleman next in esteem and authority to whom the Club introduces us is " another bachelor, who is a member of the Inner Temple ", who has, however, taken up Law only to satisfy his father's whim. If filial duty compels his residence in the Temple, his tastes carry him elsewhere. He prefers to study the passions themselves rather than the lawsuits to which they give rise, and is more diligent in attendance at the theatre than in the Courts. He is besides a man of wide reading and fastidious taste. The next member is " a merchant of great eminence in the City ", Sir Andrew Freeport, a convinced believer in trade and commerce, and an equally convinced enemy of war. Next to him sits a retired Army officer, Captain Sentry, a man " of great courage, good understanding but invincible modesty " ; then " a clergyman . . . of general learning, great sanctity of life and the most exact good breeding " ; and lastly, " that our society may not appear a set of humorists unacquainted with the gallantries and pleasantries of the age we have among us the gallant Will Honeycomb ", who has always kept himself up to date in matters of elegance and fashion [and who " where women are not concerned is an honest worthy man ". B. D.].

How skilful this preamble is ! Every class of society is represented in this Club [188] over which the Spectator presides as detached and impartial arbiter : landed interests, commerce, the Army, the Church, the Law. Literature and art are represented in some degree by all the members, who are all men of taste and culture. Amorous dalliance—note that Addison never

[188] " The club of which I am a member is very luckily composed of such persons as are engaged in different ways of life, and deputed, as it were, out of the most conspicuous classes of mankind. By this means I am furnished with the greatest variety of hints and materials, and know everything that passes in the different quarters and divisions, not only of this great city, but of the whole kingdom. My readers, too, have the satisfaction to find that there is no rank or degree among them who have not their representative in this club, and that there is always somebody present who will take care of their respective interests, that nothing may be written or published to the prejudice or infringement of their just rights and privileges." (No. 34.)

forgets the ladies—has its advocate in Will Honeycomb. Every type of reader will therefore find some one in whom to take an interest; each will feel curiosity about one member or another whose character and outlook, developed from one number to another, [189] will challenge his attention and keep it constantly on the alert. In the wake of one or another we visit in turn the theatre, the coffee-houses, society, the streets of London, the courts, the church, the Exchange, the army, and when Sir Roger visits his estates he will take us with him into the country.

This variety of personalities supplies another element of interest. The same problem is approached from different angles, and opposing points of view give rise to discussion, made more attractive and more stimulating by the clash of opinions. [190]

The whole paper in its variety fulfils—and that right royally —the promise of its opening numbers. Every day, with amazing fertility and elasticity, the subject changes, and in each subject Addison is at home. Following him from page to page, the reader is astounded at the ease with which he handles one after another the most varied material, and leads perpetually and smoothly "from grave to gay, from lively to severe". A character sketch is followed by an episode of history; a witty fantasy by a moral discussion or a literary criticism; a tale of country life by a story of the town; a picture of social whimsicalities by a discourse on the most profound matters of religion. After a disquisition on anger comes a chat about dancing [191]; after a discourse on modesty, a discussion about dreams [192]; from the consideration of envy and effrontery we are led straight on to an appreciation of trade and commerce [193]; from luxury and avarice to the immortality of the soul [194]; from matters of dress to gardens. [195] I must pull myself up; I should have to quote everything. For the truth is that no one who has not

---

[189] These portraits built up by successive strokes contain the germ of the English character novel. The Sir Roger de Coverly articles have been reprinted in one volume; they make the most delightful reading. See my Bibliography, s.v. Addison.

[190] See, for instance, No. 34.—Addison enjoys giving play to opposing views. See in particular Nos. 88, 96, 107 and 137, where the servant question is treated in its different aspects. [All these four papers are Steele's.]

[191] Nos. 438 and 466.

[192] Nos. 484 and 487.

[193] Nos. 19, 20 and 21.—The praise of commerce is again taken up in No. 69—one of the best of the essays—and in No. 174.

[194] Nos. 55, 56 and 111.

[195] Nos. 129, 360, 477 and 478.

read the 555 numbers of the *Spectator*, and read them consecutively, can possibly imagine the infinity of resource they display, the wealth of invention and exposition which varies and sustains the reader's interest, leading him irresistibly on from one essay to the next. It is not only the choice of varied subjects that is so happy, but also the changes of form and modulations of tone. Now a portrait,[196] now a letter or an anecdote, or perhaps a parable,[197] now a conversation ; prose to-day, to-morrow poetry.[198] Addison is master of the art of quickening and holding the attention. Once you have started for a stroll with him as your companion, you follow his lead to the end, enchanted by the beauty and variety of the scenes through which he takes you, delighted and led on by the chat which enlivens the walk, and you never dream of looking back to survey the road you have travelled till you and he have reached your journey's end.

If we, people of to-day, and of another type of society, thus fall under the spell of this versatile mind, how much more magically must that spell have worked on his contemporaries, to whom almost every essay brought a fresh and acutely pertinent line of thought, and who—more fortunate in this than we— were alive to every one of his allusions. They would have been perverse indeed, and hard to please, if they had found nothing to appeal to them in this rich collection. Addison however had another trump card up his sleeve to win them to him. He puts himself into intimate touch with his readers ; he invites their comments,[199] prints and replies to their letters [200] in such a way as to establish and constantly renew mutual intercourse.

This plan of campaign, so skilfully conceived and so brilliantly

[196] Nos. 15, 58, 59, etc. These portraits were evidently inspired by La Bruyère, and here Addison owes a share of his glory to France. In No. 77 he translates the greater part of La Bruyère's *le Distrait*.
[197] It is scarcely necessary here to recall the celebrated *Vision of Mirzah* (No. 159) which Burns called " that glorious paper in the *Spectator* ".
[198] It was in the *Spectator* (No. 378) that Pope's *Messiah* appeared for the first time. See also Nos. 461, 465, 489 and 551.—The *Spectator* even includes passages in French and Italian, Nos. 229, 513, 545.
[199] In the very first number he says : " Those who have a mind to correspond with me may direct their letters to the Spectator, at Mr. Buckley's in Little Britain." See also Nos. 16, 37 and 428. In No. 442 he even suggests to his readers a subject for them to write on : Money. No. 450 is an essay on it by one of them.
[200] Not a week passes without some letter from a correspondent appearing in the *Spectator*. We might suppose that Addison wrote these himself—as was no doubt sometimes the case. But he rebuts the general accusation in No. 271 and we know from Johnson (*Lives* . . .) that Steele often relied on letters received to provide matter for the essays which it fell to his lot to supply.

executed, was successful. He soon found his readers grouping themselves together and thronging round him. As early as his tenth number he was able to say—with an elation he made no attempt to conceal : " It is with much satisfaction that I hear this great city inquiring day by day after these my papers . . . My publisher tells me that there are already 3,000 of them distributed every day, so that if I allow twenty readers to every paper, which I look upon as a modest computation, I may reckon about three-score thousand disciples in London and Westminster." [201]

A woman-reader writes to him :

" Your *Spectator* is a part of my tea equipage ; and my servant knows my humour so well, that calling for my breakfast this morning (it being past my usual hour) she answered, The Spectator was not yet come in ; but that the tea-kettle boiled, and she expected it every moment." [202]

Another reader thus testifies to his approval : " I love and thank you for your daily refreshments. I constantly peruse your paper as I smoke my morning's pipe (tho' I can't forbear reading the motto before I fill and light), and really it gives a grateful relish to every whiff." [203]

---

[201] The sales of the *Spectator* progressively increased from the beginning, as the following statements show :
No. 1 on sale only at one bookseller's ; No. 16 onward on sale at two booksellers' ; No. 29 at six ; No. 39 at seven ; No. 49 at eight ; No. 133 at nine ; No. 135 at ten ; No. 147 at eleven ; No. 221 at twelve.
The first number states " *London* : Printed for *Sam.* Buckley, at the *Dolphin* in *Little Britain* : and Sold by *A. Baldwin* in Warwick-Lane." The 16th adds : " as also by *Charles Lillie*, Perfumer, at the Corner of *Beauford-Buildings* in the *Strand*."—We shall later see how considerable the sales became.

[202] No. 92. The *Spectator* was daily taken in to Queen Anne with her breakfast.

[203] No. 134.—These were not the only encouraging signs which he received : see No. 124 : people write him approving letters ; his bookseller tells him that the demand for his paper increases daily ; many readers make separate collections of sets of numbers in which the same subject is dealt with. When the members of the Club begin to disappear, readers fear that it portends the winding up of the paper and " some of the most out-lying parts of the kingdom are alarmed " (Nos. 542 and 553). The *Spectator* found its way even as far as Scotland. " Rare as was the intercourse between the capital and the highlands of Scotland, the Spectator soon found its way regularly to that part of the kingdom. Mr. Stewart, of Dalguise, a gentleman of Perthshire, of very great respectability, who died near ninety, about twelve or fourteen years ago [this was written in 1803] informed us, that, when as usual in that country, the gentlemen met after church on Sunday to discuss the news of the week, the Spectators were read as regularly as the Journal. He informs us also that he knew the perusal of them to be general through the country." (Hurd's Addison, VI, p. 688.)

Thus the first English literary daily at once recruited readers and, it must be noted, faithful readers. When the Ministry of Oxford and Bolingbroke, hoping thus to rid themselves of the bitter and persistent opposition of the Whig Press, imposed a halfpenny tax on each half-sheet of print, the *Spectator* cheerfully shouldered this extra expense, doubled its price and kept afloat in defiance of wind and wave, while numbers of other papers foundered with all hands.[204]

" Do you know," Swift writes to Stella on August 7, 1712, " that Grub Street is dead and gone last week ? No more ghosts or murders now for love or money . . . Now every single half-sheet pays a half-penny to the Queen *The Observator* is fallen ; the *Medleys* are jumbled together with *The Flying Post* ; *The Examiner* is deadly sick ; *The Spectator* keeps up and doubles its price ; I know not how long it will hold."

The *Spectator* " held " for another hundred issues, and when it ultimately disappeared, its place was immediately filled by another paper, the *Guardian*.[205] Addison's prophetic insight had not been at fault : he had, and held, his audience.

This first victory gained, there remained another, and one in our eyes neither less difficult nor less interesting. If the *Spectator* were nothing more than a paper which succeeeded in finding readers (though the material success of the first literary daily was in itself a fact of major importance), it would not command so large a share of our attention. We must not forget that Addison had a moral and intellectual task to perform.

We cannot better formulate his own conception of this task than by borrowing his very words :

Since I have raised to myself so great an audience, I shall spare no pains to make their instruction agreeable, and their diversion useful, for which reasons I shall endeavour to enliven morality with wit, and to temper wit with morality, that my readers may, if possible, both ways find their account in the speculation of the day. And to the end that their virtue and discretion may not be short, transient, intermitting starts of thought, I have resolved to refresh their memories

---

[204] See No. 445 dated July 31, 1712 (the Stamp tax came into force on August 1st) and also No. 488. The tax on newspapers was introduced indirectly in an Act which also taxed soap, paper, vellum, cloth, silk, calicos, etc. (Andrews, I, pp. 106–9 ; see also *Spectator*, No. 488, and the complaints of the Soap-merchant.)

[205] The last number of the *Spectator* is dated Dec. 6, 1712. The first number of the *Guardian* is March 12, 1713.—On June 18, 1714, Addison tried to revive the *Spectator*. It then came out tri-weekly till the end of the year.

from day to day, till I have recovered them out of that desperate state of vice and folly into which the age is fallen. The mind that lies fallow but a single day sprouts up in follies that are only to be killed by a constant and assiduous culture. It was said of Socrates that he brought philosophy down from heaven to inhabit among men; and I shall be ambitious to have it said of me that I have brought philosophy out of closets and libraries, schools and colleges, to dwell in clubs and assemblies, at tea-tables and in coffee-houses.[206]

This quotation alone suffices to show the spirit in which Addison approached his work. and his whole programme is comprehended in the two equally important phrases: "to enliven morality with wit—to temper wit with morality". On fundamental questions he is wholly at one with Collier and with the Puritans. He is as deeply alarmed as they at the relaxation of all moral standards that prevails among his fellow-citizens; like them, he believes that this state of affairs cannot continue without danger and dishonour. But while his predecessors saw this side of the question only, and consequently only one factor of the problem to be solved, Addison faced it in its entirety. Like them, he stands for religion and morality (which, like them, he considers essentially one), but he avoids their error of making these things cheerless and harsh, and of denying a rightful place to wit and merriment. Wiser and more reasonable than they, he is content to aim at the possible, and he asks only that—after a period of so much folly and licence—merriment and wit should settle down, happily wedded to decency and virtue. Others before Addison had diagnosed the evil, but no one before him had so clearly perceived its causes. Therein lies his originality and undeniable claim to credit. No one else understood as he did, that it was the long divorce of wit from virtue [206a] which had produced in England that profound moral disturbance from which people were now just trying to escape, that if the patient's disease were to be cured without fear of a relapse, if his shaken organism were to recover its equilibrium, it was essential to re-establish harmony between these two necessary elements in life, which according to the decrees of natural law must live together, but which of late had been at variance to the equal injury of both.

[206] No. 10.
[206a] [This is an exaggeration; wit had not always been opposed to virtue between 1660 and Addison's appearance. To name a few there were Halifax, Garth, Defoe; and even the most virtuous were sometimes witty, e.g. William Penn. B. D.]

But how was this harmony to be established? What methods of persuasion or diplomacy could avail to reconcile the two sections of the nation, embittered by the political and religious differences of nearly a century? Each looked with horror on the other, and when unable to oppress, was ever ready with insult and contempt.

Addison succeeded by reason of neither insulting nor despising anyone whether of Right or Left. He excluded not only party politics from his paper but also partisan and sectarian morality. He never names either the Court or the City, the Puritans or the Cavaliers; he never contrasts them. If he points out the errors of one side, it is never to the advantage of the other.[207] In short, he introduces moderation, calm and impartiality.

Above all, he takes the greatest care not to pose as a reformer. Before him, the champions of morality, lay or clerical, had been little but cantankerous and monotonous preachers fulminating against sinners, drawing a gloomy picture of their vices and impurity and threatening them—unless they should repent— with the wrath of heaven. Addison does not belong to this surly, bitter school. He does not mount the pulpit. He does not preach. No one was ever less of a pedagogue or sermonizer than he. He does not essay to teach people a lesson. He is content to show them what is desirable and seemly, and lead them to prefer it.

Picture to yourself a man of the world unselfconsciously cultured, serious but not starched, learned without pedantry, loving and savouring intellectual pleasures, a Christian withal, a believing Christian, but not bigoted, not puritanical, not intolerant, practising charity as the foremost element in his religion.[208] Picture such a man chatting informally in a company

---

[207] It is extremely rare for him to make direct allusion to the Puritans. Towards the end of No. 161 he mentions them in connection with certain popular amusements they sought to suppress, and he alludes to them again at the close of No. 458. No. 494 which I quote later on (p. 284 f.) is entirely devoted to their conception of religion; but he does not mention them by name.

[208] In the dream-allegory of No. 3 Religion makes her appearance among the " very amiable phantoms ", but she is led in by Moderation. In another context the *Spectator* (No. 459), quoting " an excellent author ", says : " We have just enough religion to make us hate, but not enough to make us love one another."—And again : " Without a good grace valour would degenerate into brutality, learning into pedantry, and the genteelest demeanour into affection. Even religion itself, unless decency be the handmaid which waits upon her, is apt to make people appear guilty of sourness and ill-humour " (No. 292).—See also No. 516 devoted to the virtue of tolerance. In No. 432

of distinguished and cultivated people, and sharing with them his views on all the subjects which may be debated in such a gathering—as the chances of conversation may suggest—on literature, on the amusements and manners of the day, on more serious topics concerning this life and the next. In all these talks, varied as they are in subject and in tone, he is genial, witty, always interesting, often high-minded, but never dogmatic or sententious.[209] He unobtrusively avoids hammering away at the same theme, for he would think it both bad taste and bad policy to bore his hearers. He is averse from all exaggeration; he uses neither high-sounding phrase nor dramatic gesture; he is readier to praise than to find fault. If he is compelled to blame, he avoids the wounding word which would be as inconsistent with his natural courtesy as with his religion. He implies his censure by a quiet word, more often by an ironic tone of voice, by the twitch of an eyelid or a curl of the lip. His conversation never has the formal well-prepared character of a lecture, yet it conveys instruction, and no one could live long in communion with his mind without drawing from such intercourse both the most subtle enjoyment and the greatest intellectual and moral advantage. Such are Addison's essays: delightful talks of a man of the world, whose mind is ennobled by reason and knowledge, and mellowed by kindliness.

What makes Addison's essays so peculiarly gracious, is that it cost him no effort to strike the friendly note of good will which makes them so effective. In reading them you do not feel that you are dealing with a self-conscious man, ordering his thoughts and keeping guard over his tongue. The man and the author in him are one. He is the same in public among his fellow men as in the privacy of his diary. With him mental integrity was allied by nature to kindness and courtesy. I have already mentioned the high respect he had won in political circles by the charm and the firmness of his character. This respect was so solidly and securely based, that when the feeling stirred up by the Sacheverell Trial brought about the downfall of the Whigs,[210] Addison, without any concession to his opponents,

---

he displays tolerance even towards Roman Catholics: "Though I am a firm Protestant I hope to see the Pope and Cardinals without violent emotions."— In 1689 John Locke had published his first *Letter on Toleration*, first in Latin, then in English.

[209] "A man may appear learned without talking sentences, as in his ordinary gesture he discovers he can dance, though he does not cut capers." (No. 4.)   [210] See Lecky, I, pp. 51–9.

escaped the unpopularity which suddenly overwhelmed his friends. In the 1710 elections, which left so many of his party in the wilderness, he was once more returned to Parliament. Swift, whose feelings towards the Whigs were tainted by that bitterness which a political renegade always feels towards the friends he is deserting, [210a] wrote to Stella : "... new elections, where the Tories carry it among the new members six to one. Mr. Addison's election has passed easy and undisputed ; and I believe if he had a mind to be chosen king he would hardly be refused ".[211] These remarkable words admirably reveal the nature of Addison's peculiar influence on his contemporaries. It was an influence springing from contagious sympathy. He lived in an aura of seductive charm ; whoever came near him fell under the spell.

In his immediate circle this influence showed itself in the unusually deep affection and respect which he enjoyed. Pope tells us that Steele's friendship for him bordered on veneration.[212] When Garth lay on his death-bed he sent to ask Addison whether he ought to believe in the Christian religion.[213] Mediocre poet though Tickell was, he was inspired to write on his dead friend one of the finest elegies in the English language.[214] One particular case will show the kind of tie which bound Addison's friends to him. Amongst the authors who grouped themselves

[210a] [This scarcely does Swift justice. Though he was Whig enough to support the Revolution, the dogmatic beliefs which he sincerely held made it impossible for him to be wholly Whig or to support occasional conformity ; and he really believed that a Whig triumph would mean ruin to the country and the Church. He was no renegade, and it was Addison, not Swift, who turned personally bitter over politics. After all, he tried to keep Steele in his place of Commissioner of Stamps—hardly the rôle of a party-embittered man. See the *Journal to Stella*, 22nd and 23rd Oct., 1710, and *passim* till 14th Dec. B. D.]

[211] *Journal to Stella*, Oct. 12, 1710.
[212] Spence, p. 197.
[Steele's schoolboy veneration survived a good many shocks, but not, ultimately *The Plebeian—The Old Whig* quarrel. Pope, when he reported this to Spence, was thinking of the Button's days, of the Little Senate, where he himself was a somewhat strange intruder. B. D.]
[213] Spence, p. 2, note.
[This is an agreeable anecdote of Edward Young's, with little real authority, being *via* Addison himself, or Tickell, " which is much the same ". Garth who, being the fattest man in London, died with the comment that life was hardly worth the bother of bending down to tie one's shoe laces, was far too confirmed a sceptic to believe in a religion because an Addison told him that he ought. B. D.]
[214] This Elegy is prefixed to Tickell's Edition of Addison, printed in 1721.

round him was a certain Eustace Budgell, who was distantly related to him, and in whom he had always taken an active interest, bringing him to live in London with him and securing for him various public posts under his wing, allowing him to collaborate in the *Spectator* and the *Guardian*, and even exercising ingenuity in helping him to gain a literary success which he would certainly never have attained without his kinsman's kindly aid.[215] While Addison lived, Budgell's conduct was blameless; but no sooner was his protector taken from him, than the younger man began speculating in public funds, got himself into debt, and quickly slipping down the fatal incline, attempted to pay his debts by forgery. Finally, detected, despised, consumed with remorse, he decided to end his wretched life by committing suicide in the Thames. It was eighteen years after Addison's death that the unhappy man, reviewing in his last hours the course of his life, still thought of Addison, who if he had lived would undoubtedly have saved him from evil courses. His last thought was for his lost friend, and for the marks of kindness and consideration Addison of old had shown him.[216]

In social relationships Addison's moral and mental qualities combined to cast a spell on his fellows. The charm of his companionship was felt to an extraordinary degree by all, even by the most exacting critics and the most reluctant admirers. He was a "favourite" of Mrs. Steele, a woman by no means easy to please, and inclined to view with jealous eye the place Addison

---

[215] Addison completely overhauled, or perhaps even himself wrote the whole Epilogue to Ambrose Philips' tragedy *The Distrest Mother*. The Epilogue was much admired and praised and Addison allowed it to pass as Budgell's unaided work.

[216] They found on his desk a sheet of paper with the words:

"What Cato did, and Addison approv'd
Cannot be wrong."

See Spence, p. 145; Drake, *Essays . . . Illustrative of the Tatler, Spectator and Guardian*, III, pp. 1–25.

[Addison seems to have had a great affection for this most adoring of his "little Senate", and appears to have had a most disastrous influence on him. He obtained him a post in Ireland, and Budgell did well so long as Addison was there to mother him—but only so long. Later he lost heavily when the South Sea Bubble burst, and tried to retrieve himself by gambling, thinking, as Addison had taught him to think, that fortune would always shower favours on him. It is hardly fair to accuse him of forgery. The affair over Dr. Tindal's will, and *Christianity as Old as the Creation* is ugly enough, but it was not forgery. And by that time he was notoriously lunatic, and was so adjudged by the Coroner's jury. See the *D.N.B.* B. D.]

took in her husband's life.[217] Pope, who was filled with bitter malice towards him, Pope who drew the portrait of *Atticus*,[218] vowed that he had never met anyone whose conversation was so delightful.[219] At the very moment that Swift was openly at war with the Whigs and cold-shouldering Addison, he wrote to Stella : " I yet know no man half so agreeable to me as he is." [220] Lady Mary Wortley Montagu used to say that she had known all the famous wits of her time, but never one who was better company than Addison.[221] A private conversation with Addison was for Steele a pleasure beyond all others : it was Terence and Catullus in one, with an added something, indefinable, exquisite and delightful, of which Addison alone held the secret.[222] Edward Young of the *Night Thoughts* often said that when Addison felt at ease his talk had a splendid flow of thought and expression which captured the attention of all.[223]

These eloquent testimonies show how admirably Nature had equipped the author of the *Spectator* successfully to carry out a task of pure conciliation and persuasion. With his readers, as with his friends, he had only to be himself to win their ears and their affections. In writing his paper he simply enlarged the circle of his friends. Delicate as was the reform he aimed at, formidable as were the passions which lay in his way, he overcame all difficulties with the same ease as enabled him in his more immediate circle to triumph over prejudice and ill will. We shall see how impossible it was for the persons involved not to be won over by advice so tactfully tendered, phrased

---

[217] See Steele's Correspondence, *passim*, especially vol. I, pp. 158 and 171.

[218] This unfair portrait of Addison occurs in Pope's *Epistle to Dr. Arbuthnot* [usually known as *The Prologue to the Satires*. The worst of the portrait was that it was true—if one-sided. B. D.]. (Warburton's Edition of Pope, vol. IV.)

[219] Spence, p. 50.

[220] *Journal to Stella*, Sept. 14, 1711. Sheridan reports that Swift was wont to say that a *tête-à-tête* conversation with Addison was the pleasantest he had ever known, and that in all the many hours they had thus spent alone together neither had ever wished for the arrival of a third party. (*Life of Swift* quoted by Drake, *Essays . . . Illustrative*, etc., III, p. 144.)

[221] Spence, p. 232.

[222] " I have often reflected, after a Night spent with him apart from all the World, that I had the Pleasure of conversing with an intimate Acquaintance of *Terence* and *Catullus*, who had all their Wit and Nature heighten'd with Humour, more exquisite and delightful than any other Man ever possessed." (Letter from Steele to Congreve, prefixed to *The Drummer*.)

[223] Spence, p. 355.

with so much wit and good will, and so strongly backed by reason and good sense.

Here, for instance, are some remarks aimed at those who were carrying on the traditions of Charles II's reign; they occur at the close of a critical analysis of a play of Etherege's, *Sir Fopling Flutter*, which was still a popular favourite in the *Spectator's* day :

> According to the notion of merit in this comedy, I take the Shoemaker to be, in reality, the fine gentleman of the play : for it seems he is an atheist, if we may depend upon his character as given by the Orange-woman, who is herself far from being the lowest in the play.[224] She says of a fine man who is Dorimant's companion, " There is not such another heathen in the town, except the shoemaker." His pretension to be the hero of the drama appears still more in his own description of his way of living with his lady. " There is," he says, " never a man in town lives more like a gentleman with his wife than I do ; I never mind her motions ; she never inquires into mine. We speak to one another civilly, hate one another heartily ; and because it is vulgar to lie and soak together, we have each of us our several settle-bed." That of " soaking together " is as good as if Dorimant had spoken it himself ; and I think, since he puts human nature in as ugly a form as the circumstance will bear, and is a staunch unbeliever, he is very much wronged in having no part of the good fortune bestowed in the last act.[225]

This is no flattering likeness, and no gentleman with aspirations after social elegance could easily feel flattered at being thus compared to—a shoemaker. But how kindly and ingenious the satire is![225a] How skilfully this irony says all that needs be said without fine phrases or wounding words! How could anyone whom the cap fitted take umbrage and having once begun to read, fail to read to the end ? And when the *Spectator* returns in another passage to the same subject—one which lies very near his heart—in graver mood, how could the most recalcitrant reader fail to be unwittingly carried away by such calm and temperate language which unpretentiously and easily rises to that natural eloquence which impresses and persuades ?

> I know no one character that gives reason a greater shock, at the same time that it presents a good ridiculous image to the imagination,

---

[224] The Shoemaker, the Orange-Woman and Dorimant are characters in the play.
[225] No. 65.
[225a] [The kindly and ingenious satire is, of course, Etherege's rather than Addison's. That the play was still a favourite at this time is no tribute to Collier's success, and scarcely bears out Beljame's earlier contention. B. D.]

than that of a man of wit and pleasure about the town. This description of a man of fashion, spoken by some with a mixture of scorn and ridicule, by others with great gravity as a laudable distinction, is in everybody's mouth that spends any time in conversation. My friend Will Honeycomb has this expression very frequently ; and I never could understand by the story which follows upon his mention of such a one, but that his man of wit and pleasure was either a drunkard too old for wenching, or a young lewd fellow with some liveliness, who would converse with you, receive kind offices of you, and at the same time debauch your sister or lie with your wife. According to his description, a man of wit, when he could have wenches for crowns apiece whom he liked quite as well, would be so extravagant as to bribe servants, make false friendships, fight relations ; I say, according to him, plain and simple vice was too little for a man of wit and pleasure ; but he would leave an easy and accessible wickedness, to come at the same thing with only the addition of certain falsehood, and possible murder. Will thinks the town grown very dull, in that we do not hear so much as we used to do of these coxcombs, whom (without observing it) he describes as the most infamous rogues in nature, with relation to friendship, love, or conversation.

When pleasure is made the chief pursuit of life, it will necessarily follow that such monsters as these will arise from a constant application to such blandishments as naturally root out the force of reason and reflection, and substitute in their place a general impatience of thought, and a constant pruriency of inordinate desire.

Pleasure, when it is a man's chief purpose, disappoints itself ; and the constant application to it palls the faculty of enjoying it, though it leaves the sense of our inability for that we wish, with a disrelish of everything else. Thus the intermediate seasons of the man of pleasure are more heavy than one would impose upon the vilest criminal. Take him when he is awaked too soon after a debauch, or disappointed in following a worthless woman without truth, and there is no man living whose being is such a weight or vexation as his is. He is an utter stranger to the pleasing reflections in the evening of a well-spent day, or the gladness of heart or quickness of spirit in the morning after profound sleep or indolent slumbers . . .

You may indeed observe in people of pleasure a certain complacency and absence of all severity, which the habit of a loose unconcerned life gives them ; but tell the man of pleasure your secret wants, cares, or sorrows, and you will find he has given up the delicacy of his passions to the cravings of his appetites. He little knows the perfect joy he loses, for the disappointing gratifications which he pursues. He looks at pleasure as she approaches, and comes to you with the recommendation of warm wishes, gay looks and graceful motion ; but he does not observe how she leaves his presence with disorder, impotence, downcast shame and conscious imperfection. She makes our youth inglorious and our age shameful . . .

No, there is not in the world an occasion wherein vice makes so fantastical a figure, as at the meeting of two old people who have been partners in unwarrantable pleasure. To tell a toothless old lady that she once had a good set, or a defunct wencher that he once was the admired thing of the town, are satires instead of applauses : but on the other side, consider the old age of those who have passed their days in labour, industry and virtue ; their decays make them but appear the more venerable, and the imperfections of their bodies are beheld as a misfortune to human society that their make is so little durable.[226]

Addison, as I have said, holds the balance even, between the two extremes. Having shown how he speaks to the libertine I must now show his approach to the puritanical. This time I shall quote not passages merely but an entire number of his paper, so that the student may form an idea of how a *Spectator* was composed. The reader will gladly forgive me these lengthy quotations and be grateful only that I allow Addison to speak instead of holding the floor myself.

Friday, Sept. 26, 1712.
Ægritudinem laudare, unam rem maxime detestabilem, quorum est tandem philosophorum ? Cic.

About an age ago it was the fashion in England, for every one that would be thought religious, to throw as much sanctity as possible into his face, and in particular to abstain from all appearances of mirth and pleasantry, which were looked upon as the marks of a carnal mind. The saint was of a sorrowful countenance, and generally eaten up with spleen and melancholy. A gentleman, who was lately a great ornament to the learned world, has diverted me more than once with an account of the reception which he met with from a very famous Independent minister, who was head of a college in those times. This gentleman was then a young adventurer in the republic of letters, and just fitted out for the university with a good cargo of Latin and Greek. His friends were resolved that he should try his fortune at an election which was drawing near in the college of which the Independent minister, who I have before mentioned, was governor. The youth, according to custom, waited on him in order to be examined. He was received at the door by a servant, who was one of that gloomy generation that were then in fashion. He conducted him, with great silence and seriousness, to a long gallery which was darkened at noonday, and had only a single candle burning in it. After a short stay in this melancholy apartment, he was led into a chamber hung with black, where he entertained himself for some time by the glimmering of a taper, until at length the head of the college came out to him from an inner room, with half-a-dozen nightcaps upon his head, and a religious horror in his countenance. The young man trembled ; but his fears increased when, instead of being asked what progress he had made in learning, he was examined how he

---

[226] No. 151.—See also No. 358.

abounded in grace. His Latin and Greek stood him in little stead. He was to give an account only of the state of his soul, whether he was of the number of the elect ; what was the occasion of his conversion ; upon what day of the month and hour of the day it happened ; how it was carried on, and when completed ? The whole examination was summed up with one short question, namely, whether he was prepared for death ? The boy, who had been bred up by honest parents, was frighted out of his wits at the solemnity of the proceeding, and by the last dreadful interrogatory ; so that upon making his escape out of this house of mourning, he could never be brought a second time to the examination as not being able to go through the terrors of it.[227]

Notwithstanding this general form and outside of religion is pretty well worn out among us, there are many persons who, by a natural uncheerfulness of heart, mistaken notions of piety, or weakness of understanding, love to indulge this uncomfortable way of life, and give up themselves a prey to grief and melancholy. Superstitious fears and groundless scruples cut them off from the pleasures of conversation, and all those social entertainments, which are not only innocent but laudable ; as if mirth was made for reprobates, and cheerfulness of heart denied those who are the only persons that have a proper title to it.

Sombrius is one of these sons of sorrow. He thinks himself obliged in duty to be sad and disconsolate. He looks on a sudden fit of laughter as a breach of his baptismal vow. An innocent jest startles him like blasphemy. Tell him of one who is advanced to a title of honour, he lifts up his hands and eyes ; describe a public ceremony, he shakes his head ; show him a gay equipage, he blesses himself. All the little ornaments of life are pomps and vanities. Mirth is wanton and wit profane. He is scandalized at youth for being lively, and at childhood for being playful. He sits at a christening or a marriage feast as at a funeral ; sighs at the conclusion of a merry story ; and grows devout when the rest of the company grow pleasant. After all, Sombrius is a religious man, and would have behaved himself very properly had he lived when Christianity was under a general persecution.

I would by no means presume to tax such characters with hypocrisy, as is done too frequently, that being a vice which I think none but He who knows the secrets of men's hearts should pretend to discover in another, where the proofs of it do not amount to a demonstration. On the contrary, as there are many excellent persons who are weighed down by this habitual sorrow of heart, they rather deserve our compassion than our reproaches. I think, however, they would do well to consider, whether such a behaviour, does not deter men from a religious life, by representing it as an unsociable state, that extinguishes

---

[227] This anecdote is not of Addison's invention. The interview really took place, just as he describes it, between Dr. Goodwin, President of Magdalen College, Oxford, and young Anthony Henley, one of the collaborators of the *Tatler*. See N. Drake, *Essays . . . Illustrative*, etc., III, pp. 340-7.

all joy and gladness, darkens the face of nature, and destroys the relish of being itself.

I have, in former papers,[228] shown how great a tendency there is to cheerfulness in religion, and how such a frame of mind is not only the most lovely, but the most commendable in a virtuous person. In short, those who represent religion in so unamiable a light, are like the spies sent by Moses to make a discovery of the Land of Promise, when by their reports they discouraged the people from entering upon it. Those who show us the joy, the cheerfulness, the good humour, that naturally spring up in this happy state, are like the spies bringing along with them the clusters of grapes, and delicious fruits, that might invite their companions into the pleasant country which produced them.

An eminent Pagan writer [229] has made a discourse, to show that the atheist, who denies a God, does Him less dishonour than the man who owns His being, but at the same time believes Him to be cruel, hard to please, and terrible to human nature. "For my own part," says he, "I would rather it should be said of me, that there was never any such man as Plutarch, than that Plutarch was ill-natured, capricious, or inhuman."

If we may believe our logicians, man is distinguished from all other creatures by the faculty of laughter. He has an heart capable of mirth, and naturally disposed to it. It is not the business of virtue to extirpate the affections of the mind, but to regulate them. It may moderate and restrain, but was not designed to banish, gladness from the heart of man. Religion contracts the circle of our pleasures, but leaves it wide enough for her votaries to expatiate in. The contemplation of the Divine Being, and the exercise of virtue, are in their own nature so far from excluding all gladness of heart, that they are perpetual sources of it. In a word, the true spirit of religion cheers, as well as composes the soul : it banishes indeed all levity of behaviour, all vicious and dissolute mirth, but in exchange fills the mind with a perpetual serenity, uninterrupted cheerfulness, and an habitual inclination to please others, as well as to be pleased in itself.[230]

Addison felicitously groups round these serious subjects of religion and morals an analysis of the main duties of life and expounds them with the same high-principled common sense. It would be easy to extract from his paper a code of practical morality.[231] He writes repeatedly and at length on the question

---

[228] Amongst others, Nos. 302 and 381.

[229] Plutarch.

[230] No. 494.—Another aspect of the same subject is dealt with in No. 354 ; this time it is the portrait of a she-bigot.—See also the first letter quoted in No. 46 and No. 201, from which I cull this sentence : "The two great errors into which a mistaken devotion may betray us are enthusiasm and superstition."

[231] Professor M. L. Mézières collected from Addison's works, the *Spectator* in particular, an anthology which he justly called *Encyclopédie morale*. See my Bibliography.

of marriage,[232] which it had been the fashion to ridicule and scoff at, on education and instruction [233] which were still gravely neglected.[234] In dealing with important subjects such as these, he does not forget that a host of minor questions arise in daily life which from their constant recurrence in all sorts of circumstances acquire real importance. He does not omit to treat of customary conventions, courtesy, good breeding, and the everyday forms of politeness which contribute so greatly to the pleasure and dignity of life.[235] In short, wherever he detects an error

---

[232] Nos. 149, 170, 171, 203, 261, 299, 364, 437, 479, 482, 486, 490, 500, 520, 522, 525. " Nothing is a greater mark of a degenerate and vicious age ", he says, " than the common ridicule which passes on this state of life." (No. 261.)

[233] Nos. 66, 215, 307, 353, 426, etc. No. 215 opens with a beautiful paragraph on education : " I consider an human soul without education like marble in the quarry, which shows none of its inherent beauties, till the skill of the polisher fetches out the colours, makes the surface shine, and discovers every ornamental cloud, spot, and vein that runs through the body of it. Education, after the same manner, when it works upon a noble mind, draws out to view every latent virtue and perfection, which without such helps are never able to make their appearance.

" If my reader will give me leave to change the allusion so soon upon him, I shall make use of the same instance to illustrate the force of education which Aristotle has brought to explain his doctrine of substantial forms, when he tells us that a statue lies hid in a block of marble ; and that the art of the statuary only clears away the superfluous matter and removes the rubbish. The figure is in the stone, the sculptor only finds it. What sculpture is to a block of marble, education is to an human soul. The philosopher, the saint, or the hero, the wise, the good, or the great man, very often lie hid and concealed in a plebeian, which a proper education might have disinterred, and have brought to light." (This passage was translated by Professor M. L. Mézières, in his *Leçons anglaises de Littérature et de morale*. Paris, 1826, I, p. 300.)—In 1693 Locke had published his *Thoughts Concerning Education*. Following in Locke's footsteps Addison anticipates Rousseau in advising women to suckle their infants themselves (No. 246). In Nos. 157 and 168 he writes pages against corporal punishment in schools, pages which his fellow countrymen of today might still ponder with advantage.

[234] Steele recommended to his readers a certain English Grammar in these terms : " I therefore enjoin all my female correspondents to buy and study that grammar, that their letters may be somewhat less enigmatic ; and on all my male correspondents likewise, who make no conscience of false spelling and false English, I lay the same injunction, on pain of having their epistles exposed in their own proper dress in my lucubrations." (Drake, *Essays . . . Illustrative*, etc., III, pp. 348-9.)

[235] No. 100, on good humour in society ; No. 104, on decorum ; No. 148, on breaches of good taste ; No. 155, on undue licence in conversation ; No. 302, on women's carelessness in indoor dress ; No. 371, against swearing ; No. 430, on the strange freedoms some married people take in company ; No. 503, on the misbehaviour of people at church ; No. 508 (2nd letter), on the way some men behave towards women ; Nos. 242 and 533, against lewd conversation in public conveyances, etc. etc.

to be corrected, a bad habit to be cured, a step forward to be made—however trifling these may be—he mounts guard like a sentinel at his post, fighting against accepted follies, from duelling to vulgar superstitions,[236] on the alert, as he himself says, to serve the public " by reprehending those vices which are too trivial for the chastisement of the law, and too fanatical for the cognizance of the pulpit ".[237]

It would, however, be a grave mistake to picture the *Spectator* as nothing but a monotonous collection of lessons in morals and good manners. Anything but that. And therein lies Addison's originality. Other moralists usually point out the evils of contemporary ways, laying bare their causes, effects and dangers with more or less justification and vigour, and consider their task then ended. Addison goes further : he is not content to diagnose and locate the malady, he points out and supplies the remedy.

This remedy, as the intelligent reader will already have perceived, is—pleasure. Pleasure, which the Puritans had indiscreetly banned, which the Restoration libertines had dishonoured, must be restored to her due place in social life. Despite her enemies, above all, despite her friends, she must be reinstated. Widely and wisely interpreted, refined intelligent pleasure could supply Puritanism with a most necessary safety valve [238]; and so-called high society with a wholesome and lasting corrective to its base and vulgar amusements.[239] When once innocent pleasure had taught the " unco guid " to relax, and had extricated the licentious from their mire, the most difficult part of her task would be accomplished. So having attacked with just as much warmth as his predecessors—but in another tone and

---

[236] Nos. 84 and 97, against duelling ; No. 7, on the folly of superstitions ; No. 505, against belief in portents, prodigies and the interpretation of dreams. —There are, however, some superstitions which he shares : he is prepared to admit the possibility of apparitions and witchcraft (Nos. 110 and 117).

[237] No. 34.

[238] " Pleasure and reaction of one kind or other are absolutely necessary to relieve our minds and bodies from too constant attention and labour." (No. 258.)

" A man that is temperate, generous, valiant, chaste, faithful and honest, may at the same time have wit, humour, mirth, good breeding and gallantry." (No. 51.)

[239] " Delicacy in pleasure is the first step people of condition take in reformation from vice " (No. 370). For this reason Addison attacks the brutalities of the Mohocks in their nocturnal expeditions (Nos. 324, 332, 335, etc.) ; excessive drinking (No. 474) ; barbarous spectacles (No. 436) ; and so on.

with more moderation—the excesses of the fashionable play,[240] the *Spectator* by no means demands the suppression of the theatre.[241] He asks only that it be chastened and purified that he may commend it to his fellow citizens as a " noble entertainment ".[242] In the same way he continually recommends to his readers everything which can offer pleasurable recreation to mind or body : reading,[243] music,[244] dancing,[245] conversation [246] or painting.[247] Setting an example in his own practice, he hopes to provide recreation for his readers at the same time as he offers useful information. Not only does he enliven his lessons—so pleasant in themselves—by amusing anecdote and witty comment,[248] he often devotes a whole issue to pure mental entertainment, and such numbers are by no means the least happily inspired. Let us consider a sample specimen :

Thursday, April 3, 1712.

'*Errat, et illinc
Huc venit, hinc illuc, et quoslibet occupat artus
Spiritus : eque feris humana in corpora transit,
Inque feras noster.*

Ovid., Met. XV, 165.

Will Honeycomb, who loves to show upon occasion all the little learning he has picked up, told us yesterday at the club, that he thought there might be a great deal said for the transmigration of souls and that the eastern parts of the world believed in that doctrine to this day. " Sir Paul Rycaut ", says he, " gives us an account of several well-disposed Mahomedans that purchase the freedom of any little bird they see confined to a cage, and think they merit as much by it, as we should do here by ransoming any of our countrymen from their captivity at Algiers. You must know ", says Will, " the reason is, because they consider every animal as a brother, or a sister in disguise, and therefore think themselves obliged to extend their charity to them, though under such mean circumstances. They'll tell you ",

---

[240] I have quoted above his criticism of Etherege's comedy, *Sir Fopling Flutter*.—See also Nos. 51, 446, etc.
[241] Steele firmly said to Cibber : " To talk of suppressing the Stage, because the Licentiousness, Ignorance, or Poverty, of its former Professors may have abus'd the proper Ends of its Institution, were, in Morality as absurd a violence, as it would be in Religion to silence the Pulpit, because Sedition or Treason had been preach'd there." (Cibber, Dedication to *Ximena*.)
[242] No. 141.—See also No. 370.   [243] Nos. 37, 80, 92, etc.
[244] No. 405. He recommends, contrary to Puritan ideas, the use of music, even in churches.
[245] No. 67.   [246] Nos. 68, 138, 409.
[247] Nos. 83, 226, 244.
[248] See, amongst others, Nos. 491, 509, 535.

says Will, " that the soul of a man, when he dies, immediately passes into the body of another man, or of some brute, which he resembled in his humour or his fortune when he was one of us."

As I was wondering what this profusion of learning would end in, Will told us that Jack Freelove, who was a fellow of whim, made love to one of those ladies who throw away all their fondness on parrots, monkeys, and lap-dogs. Upon going to pay her a visit one morning, he writ a very pretty epistle upon this hint. " Jack ", says he, " was conducted into the parlour, where he diverted himself for some time with her favourite monkey, which was chained in one of the windows ; till at length, observing a pen and ink lie by him, he writ the following letter to his mistress, in the person of the monkey ; and upon her not coming down so soon as he expected, left it in the window, and went about his business.

" The lady soon after coming into the parlour, and seeing her monkey look upon a paper with great earnestness, took it up, and to this day is in some doubt," says Will, " whether it was written by Jack or the monkey."

Madam,—

Not having the gift of speech, I have a long time waited in vain for an opportunity of making myself known to you ; and having at present the conveniences of pen, ink, and paper by me, I gladly take the occasion of giving you my history in writing, which I could not do by word of mouth. You must know, madam, that about a thousand years ago I was an Indian Brahmin and versed in all those mysterious secrets which your European philosopher, called Pythagoras, is said to have learned from our fraternity. I had so ingratiated myself by my great skill in the occult sciences with a demon whom I used to converse with, that he promised to grant me whatever I should ask of him. I desired that my soul might never pass into the body of a brute creature ; but this he told me was not in his power to grant me. I then begged that into whatever creature I should chance to transmigrate, I might still retain my memory, and be conscious that I was the same person who lived in different animals. This he told me was within his power, and accordingly promised me on the word of a demon that he would grant me what I desired. From that time forth I lived so very unblamably, that I was made president of a college of Brahmins, an office which I discharged with great integrity till the day of my death.

I was then shuffled into another human body, and acted my part so very well in it, that I became first minister to a prince who reigned upon the banks of the Ganges. I here lived in great honour for several years, but by degrees lost all the innocence of the Brahmin, being obliged to rifle and oppress the people to enrich my sovereign ; till at length I became so odious, that my master, to recover his credit with his subjects, shot me through the heart with an arrow, as I was one day addressing myself to him at the head of his army.

Upon my next remove I found myself in the woods under the shape of a jackal, and soon enlisted myself in the service of a lion. I used to yelp near his den about midnight, which was his time of rousing and seeking after his prey. He always followed me in the rear, and when I had run down a fat buck, a wild goat, or an hare, after he had feasted very plentifully upon it himself, would now and then throw me a bone that was but half-picked for my encouragement; but upon my being unsuccessful in two or three chases, he gave me such a confounded gripe in his anger that I died of it.

In my next transmigration I was again set upon two legs, and became an Indian tax-gatherer; but having been guilty of great extravagances, and being married to an expensive jade of a wife, I ran so cursedly in debt that I durst not show my head. I could no sooner step out of my house, but I was arrested by somebody or other that lay in wait for me. As I ventured abroad one night in the dusk of the evening, I was taken up and hurried into a dungeon, where I died a few months after.

My soul then entered into a flying-fish, and in that state led a most melancholy life for the space of six years. Several fishes of prey pursued me when I was in the water, and if I betook myself to my wings, it was ten to one but I had a flock of birds aiming at me. As I was one day flying amidst a fleet of English ships, I observed an huge seagull whetting his bill and hovering just over my head. Upon my dipping into the water to avoid him, I fell into the mouth of a monstrous shark that swallowed me down in an instant.

I was some years afterwards, to my great surprise, an eminent banker in Lombard Street; and remembering how I had formerly suffered for want of money, became so very sordid and avaricious that the whole town cried shame of me. I was a miserable little old fellow to look upon, for I had in a manner starved myself, and was nothing but skin and bone when I died.

I was afterwards very much troubled and amazed to find myself dwindled into an emmet. I was heartily concerned to make so insignificant a figure, and did not know but, some time or other, I might be reduced to a mite if I did not mend my manners. I therefore applied myself with great diligence to the offices that were allotted me, and was generally looked upon as the notablest ant in the whole molehill. I was at last picked up, as I was groaning under a burden, by an unlucky cock-sparrow that lived in the neighbourhood, and had before made great depredations upon our commonwealth.

I then bettered my condition a little, and lived a whole summer in the shape of a bee; but being tired with the painful and penurious life I had undergone in my two last transmigrations, I fell into the other extreme, and turned drone. As I one day headed a party to plunder an hive, we were received so warmly by the swarm which defended it, that we were most of us left dead upon the spot.

I might tell you of many other transmigrations which I went through; how I was a town rake, and afterwards did penance in a bay gelding for ten years; as also how I was a tailor, a shrimp, and a tom-tit. In the last of these my shapes I was shot in the Christmas holidays by a young jackanapes, who would needs try his new gun upon me.

But I shall pass over these and several other stages of life to remind

you of the young beau who made love to you about six years since. You may remember, madam, how he masked, and danced, and sung, and played a thousand tricks to gain you; and how he was at last carried off by a cold that he got under your window one night in a serenade. I was that unfortunate young fellow, whom you were then so cruel to. Not long after my shifting that unlucky body, I found myself upon a hill in Ethiopia, where I lived in my present grotesque shape till I was caught by a servant of the English factory, and sent over into Great Britain: I need not inform you how I came into your hands. You see, madam, this is not the first time that you have had me in a chain; I am, however, very happy in this my captivity, as you often bestow on me those kisses and caresses which I would have given the world for when I was a man. I hope this discovery of my person will not tend to my disadvantage, but that you will still continue your accustomed favours to
     Your most devoted humble Servant,
               PUGG.

P.S. I would advise your little shock-dog to keep out of my way; for as I look upon him to be the most formidable of my rivals, I may chance one time or other to give him such a snap as he won't like.[249]

The Spectator often offers his readers similar titbits, in the belief that he is contributing to their moral education when he provides their mind with subtle amusement of good quality. Nor is this all. Fully and permanently to restore to cultured pleasure its rightful place in life, Addison sets himself to explain and demonstrate its charm and value; he undertakes in short—and a most interesting element in his work it is—the intellectual education of his fellow-countrymen.

We might even say that he laid the foundation of literary criticism in England. I have already pointed out that the first tentative but significant steps in this direction were taken by Dryden. But Dryden never passed beyond slight essays on particular points, chosen according to the mood and interest of the moment, with no defined aim, no sequence, and no attempt to consider any work as a whole.[249a] He was writing, moreover, for the frivolous Court society, for readers almost incapable of

---

[249] No. 343. See also the amusing petition of *Who and Which* in the second letter of No. 78 and the reply of *That* in the second letter of No. 80.
[249a] [To readers of Dryden this must seem an incredible statement. Think of the *Essay of Dramatick Poesie*, of the *Preface to the Fables*, or half a dozen other critical passages! It is true that Dryden did not describe what he was criticizing; he was writing for a more cultivated public, and assumed that they knew what he was talking about. There had been a good deal of good critical writing in the seventeenth century—not to mention the sixteenth —Hobbes and Rymer, for instance, coming within the period here studied. See Spingarn's edition of *Critical Essays of the Seventeenth Century*. O.U.P. B. D.]

sustained thought and attention, and his aim was to please rather than to instruct. Graceful and ingenious as his discourses are, they neither had, nor were intended to have, any deep or extensive influence. The author's highest purpose was fulfilled if he had succeeded in providing some new material for the friendly conversations of the Sedleys, the Dorsets, the Mulgraves and their like.[250] Addison's circle had a much wider radius, and his readers were more serious-minded. His conception of a writer's role was entirely different from Dryden's. So it happened that when he came in his turn to cultivate the field where his predecessor had traced the first furrow, he brought to his task more serious intention and a wider vision. He fixed his eyes not on the Court alone, but on society as a whole, and he sought to open Everyman's eyes to literature ; better still, to open his mind, form his judgment, teach him to think and provide him with general ideas on life and art. He made it his business to conduct a course on literature and æsthetics. Not indeed speaking from pulpit or professorial chair, nor taking his readers back to distant origins, nor dogmatically propounding elaborate theories ; such procedure was ruled out by the limited size of each number of his paper and by the novelty of the subjects he handled, new at least to most of his readers.[251] He had, besides, no wish to play the pedagogue. His literary lessons, scattered through the *Spectator*, are much more modest. Like his moral lessons, they are practical and simple. His aim is not to supply accurate and detailed knowledge, but to awaken taste and the power of worthily enjoying the delicate pleasure of which he invites his readers to partake.[252] Nevertheless, by

[250] There had since appeared, of course, Thomas Rymer's letter, *The Tragedies of The last Age consider'd* (1678) and his *Short View of Tragedy* . . . (1693) (see my Bibliography), and above all the Essays of Sir William Temple : I. *Upon* Antient *and* Modern Learning : II. *Upon* the Gardens of Epicurus (in the body of the volume this essay is dated 1685) : III. *Upon* Heroick Virtue : IV. *Upon* Poetry (*Works*, I, pp. 147 ff.).
But these things were still addressed to a limited circle of the learned and fashionable world.
[251] The *Spectator's* method in these matters was so new that he was reproached with " prostituting learning to the Embraces of the vulgar " and making her " a common strumpet " (No. 379).
[252] " As the great and only end of these my speculations is to banish vice and ignorance out of the territories of Great Britain, I shall endeavour as much as possible to establish among us a taste of polite writing " (No. 58).
—In the Dedication of his first volume he speaks of his paper as a work which " Endeavours to cultivate and polish human life, by promoting virtue, knowledge, and by recommending whatsoever may be either useful or ornamental to society."

recurring several times to the same question, from one number to another, he covers the ground little by little, and soon succeeds in providing his readers with quite a respectable outfit of literary ideas. Briefly and without pedantry, he sets forth the principal rules which in his opinion should govern various types of composition,[253] warns them when he thinks their enthusiasm or admiration is wrongly directed,[254] puts them on their guard against specious work, advises them [255] what to read [256] and above all—with catholic taste and infectious sympathy which knows no national boundaries, no limitation of period—he calls their attention to the masterpieces of every country and of every age,[257] introduces these works and puts the reader into a position adequately to appreciate their beauties.[258] From end to end of his paper, he never loses sight of this side of his task. In varying forms, directly or indirectly, he perpetually returns to it, and there is scarcely any subject which does not give him opportunity to introduce a relevant parallel, or a literary fact, or a happily appropriate quotation. The product of a classical education which he had constantly refreshed and increased by reading and conversation, his memory was never at a loss. At the required moment it supplied without fail the author and the passage that he needed. I need no proof beyond the Latin and Greek mottos which he habitually prefixed to each number. These offered his readers a rich and instructive collection of

---

[253] See his remarks on Tragedy Nos. 39, 40, 42. His Essays on Milton which I deal with later formulate the rules for epic poetry.

[254] See in particular his articles against "false wit", Nos. 58, 59, 60, 61, 62 and 63.

[255] Especially his women readers.

[256] "We know the highest pleasure our minds are capable of enjoying with composure, when we read sublime thoughts communicated to us by men of great genius and eloquence" (No. 146). See also his articles on the pleasures of imagination, Nos. 411-21.

[257] A glance at an Index to the *Spectator* is enough to show how wide and varied is the range of his literary studies. I shall mention only some numbers devoted to then—recent works—the first essays in literary criticism ever published in England : No. 253 on Pope's *Essay on Criticism* which had just appeared (1711) ; No. 290 written after the performance of Ambrose Philips's *Distrest Mother* ; No. 400 on the same author's *Pastoral Verses* ; No. 523 on the *Miscellany* of Pope and Philips (1709).

[258] "The criticisms which I have hitherto published have been made with an intention rather to discover beauties and excellences in the writers of my own time, than to publish any of their faults and imperfections." (No. 262.) "It is a very honest action to be studious to produce other men's merit ; and I make no scruple of saying I have as much of this temper as any man in the world." (No. 532.)

interesting quotations that were never commonplace or hackneyed.[259]

In his literary passages Addison naturally never forgot the theatre which he so greatly valued. To make it the "noble entertainment" of which he dreamed, he demanded many reforms and improvements. The vigorous indictments I have quoted of the licence in which comedy indulged, were far from being the only ones he drew up. From the artistic point of view he made many strictures on contemporary drama, and stated his case with remarkable accuracy and judgment. When you have just been studying Restoration drama, it is a joy to hear him protesting with his usual wit against the use of rhyme in tragedy,[260] and the ridiculous rantings worn so threadbare by the Lees and Drydens,[261] against facetious epilogues gaily terminating a tragedy,[262] and especially against the abuse of stage costumes and decorations.[263] With all these cheap and tawdry devices he contrasts the graver beauties of Greek and French drama, which he himself was to imitate in his *Cato* when he turned his own hand to tragedy.

[259] "When I have finished any of my speculations, it is my method to consider which of the ancient authors have touched upon the subject that I treat of. By this means I meet with some celebrated thought upon it, or a thought of my own expressed in better words, or some similitude for the illustration of my subject. This gives birth to the motto of a speculation, which I rather choose to take out of the poets than the prose writers, as the former generally give a finer turn to a thought than the latter, and by couching it in few words and in harmonious numbers, make it more portable to the memory. My reader is therefore sure to meet with at least one good line in every paper." (No. 221.)
[260] No. 39.   [261] No. 40.
[262] Nos. 338 and 341.
[263] I should like to show by at least one example the tone in which he handles these subjects: "Aristotle has observed, that ordinary writers in tragedy endeavour to raise terror and pity in their audience, not by proper sentiments and expressions, but by the dresses and decorations of the stage. There is something of this kind very ridiculous in the English theatre. When the author has a mind to terrify us, it thunders; when he would make us melancholy, the stage is darkened. But among all our tragic artifices, I am the most offended at those which are made use of to inspire us with magnificent ideas of the persons that speak. The ordinary method of making a hero is to clap a huge plume of feathers upon his head, which rises so very high that there is often a greater length from his chin to the top of his head than to the sole of his foot. One would believe that we thought a great man and a tall man the same thing. This very much embarrasses the actor, who is forced to hold his neck extremely stiff and steady all the while he speaks; and notwithstanding any anxieties which he pretends for his mistress, his country or his friends, one may see by his action that his greatest care and concern is to keep the plume of feathers from falling off his head." (No. 42.)
—No. 44 on the same subject is also extremely witty.

He formulates another contrast too. However great were the services which Addison rendered to his contemporaries by initiating them into opinions which had up to that time been the privilege of a chosen few, however timely and wise were his literary teachings, he has yet other merits as a critic, and we must recognize to his honour that he helped to rediscover the literary title-deeds of his country and became one of the promoters of a kind of English Renaissance. I must explain myself. At the Restoration the works which are still the greatest achievements of the English genius, fell into neglect, indeed, it may be said into temporary oblivion. Political and religious preoccupations, French culture—which Charles II made fashionable—and frivolous taste, all combined to spread a thick mist of forgetfulness over the fairest flowers which the strength and richness of this genius had brought forth. We have seen how Shakespeare had been brushed aside or, worse, disrespectfully remodelled. The most famous of his predecessors and contemporaries had been equally ill-treated. The only new poet who deserved a place of honour at their side, Milton, author of *Paradise Lost*, had reaped little but silence and indifference. The sound core of truly English literature had been swamped by the futile babblings of the Restoration. So much so, that Saint-Evremond, who lived in England from 1661 to 1703 and moved in the most cultured circles, appears scarcely to have heard Shakespeare mentioned.[264] Sir William Temple, unquestionably one of the most distinguished Englishmen of his day, in his essay *Upon Ancient and Modern Learning* [265] omits all mention of Chaucer, Spenser, Shakespeare and Milton. Swift, in all his writings, only once alludes to Shakespeare [266] and is so ill acquainted with his works that he attributes to him one of Chaucer's.[267] Even Addison, in his versified *Account of the Greatest English Poets*,[268] also forgot to

---

[264] He mentions him once only and then quite casually. Writing to the Duchess of Mazarin : " Hear every evening the comedy of Henry VIII or of Queen Elizabeth " . . . and notes to this passage add :

" *by the famous *Shakspear* who died in 1616 ;

†by *Thomas Heywood* who flourished under *Elizabeth* and *James I.*

All the plays of this period are very long and extremely boring." (*Œuvres meslees*, 1705, II, p. 306.)—This is the first allusion to Shakespeare by any French author.

[265] *Works*, I, pp. 151 ff.   [266] Journal to Stella, Jan. 8, 1711-12.

[267] Letter to Gay dated Nov. 20, 1729 (Elwin's Edition of Pope, VII, p. 167).—In his *Life of Swift* (p. 466) Walter Scott says that Swift does not appear to have possessed a copy of Shakespeare.

[268] *Addressed to Mr. H. S.*, 1694.—We should remember that Dryden, whose magnificent tribute to Shakespeare in his Essay on Dramatick Poesie

include Shakespeare. But when he wrote the *Account* he was young, and was reflecting merely the current valuations of his day. When he came to write the *Spectator*, age and meditation had matured him. Steeped though he was in French literature and criticism [269]; dearly though he loved continually quoting Boileau, Racine, Corneille, even Bouhours and Lebossu [270]; faithfully—too faithfully—though he fashioned his own tragedy of *Cato* on the French pattern, he yet had come to understand that a people cannot safely betray its national genius by imitating a foreign literature however splendid. He saw that the spirit of England was in danger of losing its bearings and, if writers did not beware, of drifting into long stretches of sterile production like that of the Restoration period. His artistic instinct rose above his literary theories and his own poetic predilections, and revealed to him that true English poetry must be English—not foreign-born. Its wealth of glory, too long obscured, must be brought again to light and English genius referred back to its native, undervalued origins. To his readers he spoke with admiration of Shakespeare,[271] of Spenser,[272] of Bacon,[273] of Ben Jonson,[274] and especially of Milton, to whose masterpiece he devoted no less than eighteen articles.[275] Apart from Tonson's edition of *Paradise Lost*, to which I have already referred, this

---

I have spoken of above (p. 81), introduces this tribute with caution and diffidence.—Pope thought " it was mighty simple in Rowe to have written a play (*Jane Shore*) professedly in Shakespeare's style, that is professedly in the style of a bad age ". (Spence, p. 174.)

[269] His admiration for French literature was, however, neither uncritical nor unreserved. See especially No. 44, where he criticizes Corneille's *Horace*.

[270] Nos. 62, 369, 409.

[271] Nos. 22, 39, 40, 42, 44, 45, 48, 116, 141, 160, 206, 208, 210, 218, 230, 235, 279, 285, 346, 360, 370, 396, 397, 400, 419, 468, 474, 484, 485, 541. In some of these numbers (eleven of which are Addison's own) Shakespeare is mentioned several times, and the Spectator's admiration is unstinted: he calls him " the admirable Shakespeare " (No. 210), classes him amongst the " great geniuses " (No. 160) and suggests young men's being set to act scenes from his plays, as well as from Terence and Sophocles (No. 230). He contrasts Shakespeare's plays with the popular plays of the day (No. 208), and finally—this fact is specially noteworthy—vigorously condemns the current practice of " reforming " a play of Shakespeare's at the cost of " half its beauty " (No. 40). A fine passage about Shakespeare also occurs in No. 402.

[272] Nos. 62, 297, 390, 419, 510.

[273] Nos. 10, 19, 160, 411, 447, 554.

[274] Nos. 28, 510, 527.

[275] Nos. 267, 273, 279, 285, 291, 297, 303, 309, 315, 321, 327, 333, 339, 345, 351, 357, 363, 369.—These are not the only articles in which Milton is mentioned; see also Nos. 12, 33, 62, 89, 160, 173, 304, 425, 472, etc.

L

was the first reparation England made to the great poet who had died forgotten.[276] Addison went further; he recalled to mind the old popular ballads,[277] thus anticipating the movement by which Percy later so profoundly and so happily requickened English poetry.[278]

Thus, approaching at once from every point of the compass, Addison entered into, and took possession of, the minds of his fellow-countrymen. By addressing himself to their reason, their conscience and their good taste in turn; by interesting and instructing them; by reasoning with them and teaching them to reason; by awakening or re-awakening them to lofty and sensitive feeling, he gradually won their affection and their confidence. The net of his gracious and irrefutable argument was so well and closely woven, that none of those on whom his heart was set was able to slip through its meshes. Before his time the Cavaliers had one answer ready made for anyone who cast their dissolute manners in their teeth: "He's a fanatic." The Puritans similarly dismissed everyone who challenged their gloomy code with: "He's an infidel", and with averted face passed by on the other side. In the case of Addison, neither party could file its favourite plea. There was no denying it—here was a man who was both a gentleman and a Christian: as true a gentleman as the most polished of Charles II's courtiers, as sincere a Christian as the most devout Presbyterian apostle.

[276] The *Tatler* had already begun to redirect attention to the authors of the great century. He speaks of Bacon (Nos. 108, 247), of Spenser (No. 194), of Ben Jonson (No. 267), of Milton (Nos. 6, 40, 79, 98, 114, 137, 149, 237, etc.), of Shakespeare (Nos. 8, 41, 47, 53, 68, 90, 106, 111, 117, 167, 251, 271, etc.). When he wished, however, to quote passages from *Macbeth* in Nos. 68 and 167, he used Davenant's pitiably "modified" version.

[277] Nos. 70 and 74: Chevy Chase; No. 85: The Babes in the Wood. He is of the same opinion as Alceste:

"Et je prise bien moins tout ce que l'on admire,
Qu'une vieille chanson que je m'en vais vous dire"

(Good what the world admires. To me more dear
The fine old song that I shall let you hear.)

[278] Percy's *Reliques of Ancient English Poetry* was published in 1765.
[The Ballads were never wholly neglected. When John Prideaux was made Bishop of Oxford in 1641, a friend wrote to him: "Send me what ballads you have, and I will let *you* see what I have." Various collections were made, e.g. at Shirburn Castle c. 1610. Selden (1584–1654) made a collection, as did Anthony à Wood (1632–95), Pepys (1633–1703), not to mention Harley. The manuscript on which Percy founded his edition appears to have dated from about 1650. What Addison did was to make respected by a snobbish middle class, work which might otherwise have remained the delight of the few. B. D.]

So much was this the case, that the reader who was tempted to vote him too pious, was won over by his easy and genial humour, and another who was inclined to think him too worldly, could not resist the genuine moral and religious temper which breathes from every page of his paper. The one forgave his piety because of his wit, the other forgave his wit because of his piety, neither perceiving that he himself was being gradually converted : in the one case to virtue, in the other case to innocent enjoyment. Addison's readers were like an encircled army, whose retreat is cut off, whose resistance is vain ; no course was open to them save surrender.

And surrender they did—with the utmost good will. The moral success of the *Spectator* equalled, or exceeded, its material success. Not only was it read, as no other periodical had ever been read before, but it was not read in vain. The good seed, widely scattered in the soil prepared by Collier, by Defoe and by Steele, was quick to germinate and strike root. Vice, though already shaken and weakened, did not of course immediately disappear for ever and leave a clear field for a Golden Age of purity and innocence. But Vice was thrust aside, and could no longer count on the general admiration of her charms ; immorality was no longer considered fashionable or in good taste. A cheap reputation for wit could no longer be acquired by sneers at everything worthy of respect ; threadbare jests at the expense of religion were no longer considered funny ; well-worn epigrams about marriage and wedded misadventures no longer raised a laugh (the Englishman of to-day doesn't even get the point). New subject-matter for jesting had to be found. True, there were sceptics and free-thinkers still ; but scepticism had gone out of fashion, and serious discussion had taken the place of the sneer that had served as a cheap substitute for thought.[279] True also, there were libertines still, but they no longer openly gloried in their debauchery, and they no longer commanded admiration. In short, no one was compelled to choose between a parade of

---

[279] Toland, *Christianity not Mysterious* (1696), *Nazarenus* (1718), *Pantheisticon* (1720), etc. etc. ; Collins, *Priestcraft in Perfection* (1710), *A Discourse of Free-Thinking* (1713), etc. Tindal, *Christianity as old as the Creation* (1730), etc. ; Bolingbroke, *Letters on the Study and Use of History* (1752) ; etc. etc. See my Bibliography.—The doctrines of scepticism, moreover, proved unable to exert a lasting influence. In 1790 Burke was able to ask : " Who, born within the last 40 years, has read one word of Collins, and Toland, and Tindal . . . and that whole race who called themselves Freethinkers ? " (*Reflections on the French Revolution.*) [But Mandeville ? B.D.]

vice and irreligion or the stigma of being an unmannerly rustic. Society had changed its tone. It was thought neither ridiculous nor strange to hear men talk seriously of serious things. Virtue could show herself openly without a blush, and raise her head —never to lower it again. As Macaulay says, in his Essay on Addison :

" So effectively did he retort on vice the mockery which had recently been directed against virtue, that, since his time, the open violation of decency has always been considered among us as the sure mark of a fool."

It may seem a matter of surprise that I should attribute so much influence to a modest leaflet which London booksellers sold for a penny, and we must not fail to remember that others had prepared Addison's path and that influences of many kinds had inclined men's minds to a moral rebirth.[280] But no one who reads contemporary tributes can for an instant doubt that the *Spectator* and its predecessor the *Tatler* played a major part in this happy reformation, nor that Addison's peculiar merit was, that he brought high principles home to all and made them common currency, at once cultivating men's minds and mending their manners.

As early as 1711, just when the *Spectator* had succeeded the *Tatler*, a writer—believed to be the poet Gay—bore this testimony :

> His disappearing (i.e. the Tatler's) seem'd to be bewailed as some general Calamity,[281] everyone wanted so agreeable an Amusement, and the Coffee-houses began to be sensible, that the Esquires Lucubra-

---

[280] There is no doubt that there was in England at this moment an upsurging of virtue, which manifested itself in a general hunger for religious propaganda. Within a few years of each other the learned botanist Ray brought out *The Wisdom of God, manifested in the Works of Creation* (1691), the philosopher, Locke, his *Reasonableness of Christianity, As delivered in the Scriptures* (1695) ; the cleric, Clark, *A Discourse concerning the Unchangeable Obligations of Natural Religion, and the Truth and Certainty of the Christian Revelation* (1706) ; and the journalist, Addison, *The Evidence of the Christian Religion*, a work which appeared after his death. See my Bibliography. It is appropriate to remember also the influence which sermons were to exert, and the writings of clergymen like Tillotson, Stillingfleet, Sherlock and South and of Nonconformists like Matthew Henry whose Bible Commentaries are still popular.

[281] This is corroborated by the following verses :

> " When first the *Tatler* to a *Mute* was turn'd,
> Great Britain for her *Censor's* Silence mourn'd ;
> Robb'd of his sprightly Beams, she wept the Night,
> 'Till the SPECTATOR rose, and blaz'd as Bright.

tions alone, had brought them more Customers, than all their other News Papers put together.

It must indeed be confess'd that never Man threw up his Pen under Stronger Temptations to have employed it longer; His Reputation was at a greater height than, I believe, ever any living Author's was before him ... Everyone read him with Pleasure and Good-Will; and the *Tories*, in respect to his other Good Qualities, had almost forgiven his unaccountable Imprudence in declaring against them. Lastly it was highly improbable, that if he threw off a Character, the Ideas of which were so strongly impress'd on everyone's mind, however finely he might write in any new form, that he should meet with the same reception.

To give you my own thoughts of this Gentleman's Writings, I shall, in the first place, observe, that there is this noble difference between him and all the rest of our Polite and Gallant Authors: the latter have endeavoured to please the Age by falling in with them, and incouraging them in their fashionable Vices, and false notions of things. It would have been a jest, sometime since, for a Man to have asserted, that anything Witty could be said in praise of the Marry'd State; or that Devotion and Virtue were in any way necessary to the Character of a fine Gentleman. *Bickerstaff* ventur'd to tell the Town, that they were a parcel of Fops, Fools and Vain Cocquets; but in such a manner, as even pleased them, and made them more than half inclin'd to believe that he spoke Truth.

Instead of complying with the false Sentiments, or Vicious tasts of the Age, either in Morality, Criticism, or Good Breeding, he has boldly assur'd them, that they were altogether in the wrong, and commanded them, with an Authority, which perfectly well became him, to surrender themselves to his Arguments for Vertue and Good Sense.

'Tis incredible to conceive the effect his Writings have had on the Town; How many Thousand follies they have either quite banish'd, or given a very great check to; how much Countenance they have added to Vertue and Religion; how many People they have render'd happy, by shewing them it was their own fault if they were not so; and lastly, how intirely they have convinc'd our Fops and Young Fellows of the value and advantages of Learning.

He has indeed rescued it out of the hands of Pedants and Fools; and discover'd the true method of making it amiable and lovely to all

---

So the first Man, the SUN's first Setting view'd,
And sigh'd, till circling Day his Joys renew'd;
Yet doubtful how that second SUN to name,
Whether a bright *Successor* or the *Same*.

So we—but Now from this Suspence are freed
Since all must own, who Both with Judgment read
'Tis the Same SUN, and does *Himself* succeed."

(An Epigram on the *Spectator*, in the *Tunbridge-Miscellany*, 1712. See my Bibliography, s.v. Tunbridge.)

mankind : In the dress he gives it, 'tis a most welcome guest at Tea-Tables and Assemblies and is relish'd and caressed by the Merchants on the Change ; . . .[282]

Lastly, His Writings have set all our Wits and Men of Letters upon a new way of Thinking, of which they had little or no Notion before ; and tho' we cannot yet say that any of them have come up to the Beauties of the Original, I think we may venture to affirm, that every one of them Writes and Thinks much more justly than they did some time since . . .[283]

You may remember I told you before that one Cause assign'd for the laying down the *Tatler* was want of Matter ; and indeed this was the prevailing Opinion in Town, when we were surpris'd all at once by a Paper called the *Spectator*, which was promised to be continued every day, and was writ in so excellent a Stile, with so nice a Judgment, and such a noble profusion of Wit and Humour, that it was not difficult to determine it could come from no other hands but those which had penn'd the *Lucubrations* . . .

Mean while, the *Spectator* . . . is in every one's Hand, and a constant Topic for our Morning Conversation at Tea-Tables and Coffee-Houses. We had at first, indeed, no manner of Notion how a *Diurnal Paper* could be continu'd in the Spirit and Stile of our present Spectators ; but to our no small Surprise, we find them still rising upon us, and can only wonder from whence so Prodigious a Run of Wit and Learning can proceed ; since some of our best Judges seem to think that they have hitherto, in general, out-shone even the

---

[282] "How long and happily did *Old Isaac* triumph in the universal Love and Favour of his Readers ? The Grave, the Chearful, the Wise, the Witty, Old, Young, Rich, and Poor, all Sorts, though never so opposite in Character, whether Beaux or Bishops, Rakes or Men of Business, Coquets or Statesmen, Whigs or Tories, All were equally his Friends, and thought their Tea in a Morning had not its Taste without him." (Dedication to Steele of Cibber's *Ximena*.)

[283] "While the World was under the daily Correction and Authority of your *Lucubrations* ; their Influence on the Publick was not more visible in any one Instance than the sudden Improvement (I might say Reformation) of the Stage that immediately follow'd them : From whence it is now apparent, that many Papers (which the Grave and Severe then thought were thrown away upon that Subject) were, in your speaking to the *Theatre*, still advancing the same Work, . . . ; to the end that whenever you thought fit to be silent, the Stage, as you had amended it, might by a kind of substituted Power, continue to Posterity your peculiar manner of making the Improvement of their Minds their public Diversion."

"Nothing but a Genius so universally rever'd could, with such Candour and Penetration, have pointed out its Faults and Misconduct, and so effectually have redeem'd its Uses and Excellence from Prejudice and Dis-favour. How often have we known the most excellent Audiences drawn together at a Day's Warning, by the Influence or Warrant of a single *Tatler*, in a Season when our best Endeavours without it could not defray the Charge of the Performance ? This powerful and innocent Artifice soon recover'd us into Fashion, and spirited us up, to think such new Favour of our Auditors worthy of our utmost Industry, and 'tis to that Industry, so instructed, the Stage now owes its Reputation and Prosperity " (ibid.).

Esquires first *Tatlers*. Most People Fancy, from their frequency, that they must be compos'd by a Society ; I, with all, Assign the first Places to Mr. *Steele* and *His Friend* . . .

Mean time, all our unbyassed well-wishers to Learning are in hopes, that the known Temper and Prudence of one of these Gentlemen, will hinder the other from ever lashing out into Party, and rend'ring that Wit, which is at present a Common Good, Odious and Ungrateful to the better part of the Nation." [284]

A continuation of the *Tatler* that appeared in January 1711 speaks of Steele as ". . . A Gentleman who has so eminently obliged the Publick, and whose Lucubrations have done more Good than all the Moral Discourses that were ever written in our tongue ".[285] An anonymous poet writing in 1712 paid this tribute :

> Improving youth, and hoary age,
> Are better'd by thy matchless page ;
> And, what no mortal could devise,
> Women, by reading thee grow wise . . .
> . . . wedlock by thy art is got
> To be a soft and easy knot . . .
> The ladies, pleas'd with thee to dwell,
> Aspire to write correct, and spell : . . .
>   Maintain, great Sage, thy deathless name,
> Thou can'st no wider stretch thy fame,
> Till, gliding from her native skies,
> Virtue once more delighted flies,
> By each adoring Patriot own'd,
> And boasts herself by thee enthron'd.[286]

While the *Spectator* was still appearing, Tickell warmly congratulated its author on having reformed the fops of both sexes, and restored English society to health :

> . . . Nor harsh thy Precepts, but infus'd by Stealth,
> Please while they cure, and cheat us into Health.
> Thy Works in *Chloe's* Toilet gain a part;
> And with his Tailor share the Fopling's heart : . . .
> His Miss the frolick Viscount dreads to toast,
> Or his third Cure the shallow Templar boast ;
> And the rash Fool, who scorn'd the beaten Road,
> Dares quake at Thunder, and confess his God . . .[287]

---

[284] *The Present State of Wit* by J. G. (Gay ?). [Now usually assigned to Gay. B. D.]

[285] " The Tatler, with the Character of Mr. Steele, alias *Isaac Bickerstaff*, Esq., No. 272. From *Tuesday, January* 2 to *Thursday, January* 4, 1711." This number is bound in at the close of the *Tatler* in the British Museum copy.

[286] *Bibliotheca* : *a Poem occasioned by the Sight of a Modern Library*, quoted by Drake, *Essays* . . . *Illustrative*, etc., III, pp. 394 ff.

[Drake ascribes it to Newcomb : Nichols had given it to Dr. King. B. D.]

[287] *Spectator*, No. 532 : " To the supposed Author of the Spectator." In the Preface to his edition of Addison Tickell says : " The world became

While greatly admiring the *Tatler* and the *Spectator*, Blackmore was at first inclined to question their influence in curing fools of their folly,[288] but was ultimately forced to recognize that their moral value was as evident as their beauty, and that they had taught men to despise irreligious and indecent writing.[289]

Somerville wrote to Addison :

> When panting Virtue her last efforts made,
> You brought your Clio to the virgin's aid :
> Presumptuous Folly blush'd, and Vice withdrew,
> To vengeance yielding her abandon'd crew . . .
> Hard was the task, and worthy your great mind,
> To please at once, and to reform mankind :
> Yet, when you write, Truth charms with such address,
> Pleads Virtue's cause with such becoming grace,
> His own fond heart the guilty wretch betrays,
> He yields delighted, and convinc'd, obeys.[290]

---

insensibly reconciled to wisdom and goodness, when they saw them recommended by him (Addison) with at least as much spirit and elegance, as they had been ridiculed for half a century."

[288] " Let the famous Author of the *Tatlers* and *Spectators* declare his Experience, who, if Wit could have made Men wiser, must certainly have succeeded ; that Gentleman says, in one of his Discourses, *I have many Readers but few Converts* ; I believe he might have said none : For it is my opinion, that all his fine Raillery and Satire, though admirable in their kind, never reclaim'd one vicious Man, or made one Fool depart from his Folly." (*Essays*, vol. I, 1716, Preface.)—". . . The Productions of this Nature, which have of late appeared in this Nation, whether we regard the just and generous sentiments, the fertile Invention, the Variety of Subjects, the surprizing Turns of Wit and facetious Imagination, the genteel Satire, the Purity and Propriety of the Words, and the Beauty and Dignity of the Diction, have surpass'd all the Productions of this Kind, that have been publish'd in any Age or Country. The Reader is no doubt before-hand with me, and concludes, that I mean the *Tatler* and *Spectator*, which for the greatest Part, have all the Perfection of Writing, and all the Advantages of Wit and Humour, that are requir'd to Entertain and instruct the People : And it must chiefly be owing to the great Depravity of Manners of these loose and degenerate Times, that such worthy Performances have produc'd no better Effects." (*Essays*, 1716, I, p. 203.)—Blackmore had been somewhat cruelly handled in the third number of the *Tatler*. This may perhaps account for his scepticism.

[289] " It was with great Pleasure and Satisfaction that Men, who wish'd well to their Country and Religion, saw the People delighted with Papers which lately came Abroad as daily Entertainments ; in which rich Genius and polite Talents were employ'd in their proper Province, that is, to recommend Vertue and regular Life, and discourage and discountenance the Follies, Faults and Vices of the Age ; . . . Nor was it without good Effect, for the People in some measure recover'd their true Relish, and discern'd the Benefit and moral Advantages as well as the Beauties of these daily Pieces, and began to have profane and immodest Writings in Contempt." (*Essays*, II, 1717, p. 268.)

[290] A. Chalmers, *The Works of the English Poets*, XI, p. 190.—Addison's own articles in the *Spectator* are signed by one of the letters of the name Clio.

Another witness, a clergyman, destined later to become a bishop, said: "'To him we owe, that swearing is unfashionable, and that a regard to religion is become a part of good breeding . . . He had an art to make people hate their follies, without hating themselves for having them; he shewed gentlemen a way of becoming virtuous with a good grace." [291]

Yet another testified:

None ever attempted with more Success to form the Mind to Virtue, or polish the Manners of common Life; none ever touched the Passions in that pleasing, prevailing Method, or so well inculcated the most useful and instructive Lessons. I say, none did ever thus happily perform so important a Work as these illustrious Colleagues, who, by adapting themselves to the Pleasures, promoted the best Virtues of human Nature; insinuated themselves by all the Arts of fine Persuasion; employ'd the most delicate Wit and Humour in the Cause of Truth and good Sense; nor gave Offence to the most rigid *Devotees* or the loosest *Debauchees*, but soon grew popular, tho' advocates of Virtue . . . All the *Pulpit Discourses* of a Year scarce procur'd half the Good as flow'd from the SPECTATOR of a Day. They who were tir'd and lulled to Sleep by a long and labour'd Harrangue, or terrify'd at the Appearance of large and weighty Volumes, could chearfully attend to a single Half-sheet, where they found the Images of Virtue so lively and amiable, where Vice was so agreeably ridicul'd that it grew painful to no Man to part with his beloved Follies; nor was he easy till he had practis'd those Qualities which charm'd so much in Speculation. Thus good Nature and good Sense became habitual to their Readers. Every morning they were instructed in some new Principle of Duty, which was endear'd to them by the Beauties of Description; and thereby impress'd on their Minds in the most indelible Characters.[292]

---

[291] "Anticipation of the Posthumous Character of Sir Richard Steele." By the Rev. Dr. Thomas Rundle. Written about 1720. Quoted in Nichols' Edition of Steele's *Correspondence*, II, pp. 685 ff. Dr. Rundle later became Bishop of Derry.

[292] "*An Essay, sacred to the Memory of Sir Richard Steele*, in The British Journal, or the Censor. By Roger Manley, of Lincoln's Inn, Esq., No. 89. Saturday, September 13, 1729." (British Museum.)

There are other curious testimonies to the *Spectator's* influence. It is said that a few lines of No. 173 put a stop to a "grinning match" which was to have taken place in a remote county (*Addisoniana*, Hurd's Addison, VI, p. 690). Again, it was considered a matter of pride to have collaborated, even once, in the paper (Boswell, VI, p. 151). But nothing seems to me to redound more to the *Spectator's* honour than the following letter in No. 208:

"Mr. Spectator,—I have been out of town, so did not meet with your paper dated September the 28th, wherein you to my heart's desire expose that cursed vice of ensnaring poor young girls, and drawing them from their friends. I assure you without flattery it has saved a prentice of mine from ruin, and in token of gratitude, as well as for the benefit of my family, I have put it in a frame and glass, and hang it behind my counter. I shall take care

The salutary effect thus produced, was so obvious that Addison, modest and reserved though he was, when referring in later years to his work, did not hesitate to congratulate himself on the good he had accomplished.[293]

If, therefore, others share with Addison the credit of having laboured for the renewal of England, the greatest of the glory is his alone; his is the honour of having extended the scope, secured and strengthened the foundations, of this renewal, by robbing vice of its deceptive veneer of elegance; of having—if the phrase be allowed—brought virtue into fashion. It has been wittily said that he won the laughers over to virtue's side. But this happy phrase does not cover everything. Not only did he bring laughter to the reinforcement of virtue, he brought virtue over to the side of moderation and good sense.[294] While sobering the Cavalier, he humanized the Puritan.[295] He was so successful that ere long his fellow-countrymen marvelled that fashionable society could ever have been so corrupt, and that religious folk could ever have seemed so surly and morose. Since his day, England has had relapses into libertinism and puritanism;

---

to make my young ones read it every morning, to fortify them against such pernicious rascals. I know not whether what you write was matter of fact, or your own invention, but this I will take my oath on, the first part is so exactly like what happened to my prentice, that had I read your paper then, I should have taken your method to have secured a villain. Go on and prosper."

[293] "There are very good Effects which visibly arose from the above-mentioned Performances [the *Tatlers* and *Spectators*] and others of the like Nature; as, in the first Place, they diverted Raillery from improper Objects, and gave a new Turn to Ridicule, which for many Years had been exerted on Persons and things of a secret and serious Nature." (*The Free-Holder*, No. 45, May 25, 1716.) See also the remainder of this article. Addison is replying to Blackmore's cynicism quoted just above in note No. 288. The *Spectator's* reputation was not confined to England.—Translations into other languages followed immediately. See L. Mézières (Preface to the *Encyclopédie morale*).

[294] "The last Advantage I shall mention from compositions of this Nature, ... is, that they show Wisdom and Virtue are far from being inconsistent with Politeness and good Humour. They make Morality appear amiable to People of gay Dispositions, and refute the common Objection against Religion, which represents it as only fit for gloomy and melancholy Tempers. It was the Motto of a Bishop very eminent for his Piety and good Works, in King *Charles* the Second's reign, *Inservi Deo et Laetare, Serve God and be cheerful*." (The *Free-Holder*, No. 45, May 25, 1716.)

[295] "Lash'd in thy Satyr, the penurious Cit
Laughs at himself and finds no Harm in Wit."
(Tickell, the *Spectator*, No. 532: "To the supposed Author of the *Spectator*".)

but since his day two extremes have become alike impossible : the moral tyranny of Cromwell's partisans, and the cynical immorality of Charles II's court.

VIII
Increase in the number and quality of readers.—The influence of politics.— The influence of Addison and his imitators.—An English reading-public is well established

Addison's influence was real and salutary : in yet another way he increased the number and quality of readers.

The emancipation of the Press had already greatly stimulated the habit of reading, and had taught people to feel the need of it. The political circumstances of the day contributed not a little to the same result. Round William III, round Queen Anne, and round George I, a great battle was raging between Whigs and Tories. The battle was feverish and fiery, the issue uncertain. During this period of continuous emotional tension, when England daily wondered anew whether the Revolution of 1688 was final, or whether it was to be erased from English history by a return to the Stuart succession, men's minds were in an extraordinary state of commotion and hyper-excitement. No Englishman was indifferent. No deed could be done, no question be raised, without provoking passionate pro-and-con argument. So violent was discussion that, despite their recent expansion, the newspapers alone could not cope with it. Political pamphlets fought side by side with the papers, and so torrential was the flow of them, that Swift said a man would have to spend the entire day in this kind of reading if he were to keep pace with them.[296]

From time to time Ministers and Parliament, galled and irritated by the unceasing din in their ears, attempted to silence these publications. Bolingbroke sent twelve printers or journalists to prison in one day.[297] William Hart, printer of the

---

[296] " Meantime the pamphlets and half-sheets grow so upon our hands, it will very well employ a man every day from morning till night to read them, and so out of despair I never read any at all." (Letter from London, dated Sept. 26, 1710 (Scott's Edition of his *Works*, XV, p. 380.) See also Lord Mahon, *History of England*, I, pp. 119, 120 ; Swift, *Journal to Stella*, passim ; Lecky, I, p. 61 ; and Doran, *London in the Jacobite Times*, especially vol. I, chaps. III and V.)

[297] Swift, *Journal to Stella*, Oct. 24, 1711 : and Stanhope, *History of* . . . *the Reign of Queen Anne*, II, p. 237.

paper called *The Flying Post*, was sentenced by the Court of Queen's Bench to stand twice in the pillory and be imprisoned for two years, besides being fined £50.[298] Not satisfied with individual repressions of this kind, the Tory Government imposed, as we have seen, a heavy general tax on periodicals and pamphlets. For its part, the House of Commons expelled Steele on account of a pamphlet called *The Crisis* and two numbers of his paper *The Englishman*. The House of Lords offered a reward of £300 for anyone who would betray the author of an anonymous pamphlet—actually Swift's—*The Public Spirit of the Whigs*, and not being able to track down the offender himself, they prosecuted the printer.[299] Defoe's book, *The Shortest Way with the Dissenters*, was publicly burnt by order of the House of Commons; the author was sentenced to a heavy fine and condemned to stand thrice in the pillory and to be imprisoned during the Queen's pleasure. Parliament also ordered Tutchin, of the *Observator*, to be flogged by the hangman. Fleetwood, Bishop of St. Asaph, wrote a Preface expressing in calm and dignified language his respect for the memory of William III, his sermons were consequently burnt. A clergyman named Steevens was fined, and but narrowly escaped the pillory, for having written over-sympathetically of his clerical brethren, the Non-Jurors, who refused to swear allegiance to the Government of the Revolution. Wellwood, editor of *Mercurius Rusticus*, Mist, editor of *Mist's Journal*,[299a] and Dyer, editor of the *Newsletter* that bore his name, were all compelled to attend a session of the House of Commons and do penance on their knees.[300]

All this severity was vain.[301] Papers and pamphlets swarmed

---

[298] Walter Scott's Edition of Swift, II, p. 136, note.
[299] Lord Mahon, *History of England*, I, pp. 67 ff.
[299a] [There may be a certain confusion here in the mind of the forgetful reader: it may be as well to give a few dates. *The Shortest Way with the Dissenters*, 1702. Tutchin's *Observator*, 1702. Leslie's *Observator*, 1702. Bolingbroke's coup, 1711. *The Public Spirit of the Whigs*, 1714. *The Crisis*, 1714. *Mist's Journal*, 1725–8 (it then became *Fog's Journal*). B. D.]
[300] Townsend, *History of the House of Commons*, chap. VII.
[301] "These devils of Grub Street rogues, that write *The Flying Post and Medley* in one paper, will not be quiet. They are always mauling Lord Treasurer, Lord Bolingbroke and me. We have the dog under prosecution, but Bolingbroke is not active enough; but I hope to swinge him. He is a Scotch rogue, one Ridpath. They get out upon bail and write on. We take them again, and get fresh bail; so it goes round." (Swift, *Journal to Stella*, Oct. 28, 1712.)

The Stamp Act proved no more efficacious than prosecutions and sentences. Here also, Tory hopes were foiled: Whig papers gained in influence as before, and the pamphlets in particular were bought up with unprecedented avidity.

Within four years Defoe's *True-born Englishman* [1701] went through nine editions on good paper, and twelve cheap pirated editions of which 80,000 copies were sold in the London streets. The famous sermon of Dr. Sacheverell which, at the close of her reign, caused the downfall of Queen Anne's Whig Ministry, and the temporary triumph of the Tories, sold 40,000 copies in a few days.³⁰² The trial of the too-famous preacher provoked a Whig pamphlet, *A Letter to Sir J(acob) B(anks)*, by one Benson, which enjoyed a sale of 60,000 copies in London alone, and in addition appeared in one Edinburgh and in two Dublin editions.³⁰³ An anti-Sacheverell pamphlet of William Bisset's, *The Modern Fanatick*, ran to at least twelve editions.³⁰⁴ A small twopenny pamphlet by Swift about Prior's secret diplomatic trip to Paris, sold 2,000 copies in a fortnight, " though the Town is empty ".³⁰⁵ A more important work of the Dean's, *The Conduct of the Allies*, sold 2,000 copies in two days, and by the end of two months, sales had reached the 11,000 mark, not to mention three Irish editions.³⁰⁶ One political poem of Tickell's quickly ran into six editions, another into five.³⁰⁷ The first sermon Sacheverell preached after the three years' compulsory silence that followed his impeachment, sold over 40,000 copies.³⁰⁸

These returns are significant. Never before had so many purchasers so faithfully responded to the writer's appeal.

Still, if none but political writings had been in question, we should have been no further on than in James II's day; we should merely have had to record a marked increase in the

---

what they lost in numbers, and kept the field in triumph. Swift later confessed that the effect of the tax had been " to open the mouths of our enemies and shut our own ". (*History of the Four Last Years of Queen Anne, Works*, IV, p. 301.) The net result of the tax was to deal an effective blow at the feeble and detestable publications of Grub Street; it cleansed the Press.

³⁰² Burnet, *History of my Own Times*, V, p. 422.
³⁰³ Wilson, III, p. 129. See my Bibliography.
³⁰⁴ See my Bibliography, s.v. Bisset.
³⁰⁵ *A New Journey to Paris*; *Works*, IV, p. 59.—See Swift's *Journal to Stella*, Sept. 11 and 24, 1711.
³⁰⁶ See my Bibliography and *Journal to Stella*, Nov. 30, Dec. 2 and 5, 1711; Jan. 28 and Feb. 8, 1711–12.
³⁰⁷ *A Poem ... on the Prospect of Peace*; *Epistle ... to a Gentleman at Avignon*. See Johnson, *Lives of the English Poets*, Tickell.
³⁰⁸ *Journal to Stella*, April 2, 1713.—N. Drake, *Essays ... Illustrative of the Tatler*, etc., I, p. 91, note.

number of readers. To Addison we owe it that there was at the same time a rise in their quality.

This was primarily his personal achievement. We have seen the zeal with which he devoted himself to the intellectual education of his fellow-countrymen, and the eagerness with which they flocked to his banner. Reading his paper consecutively, it is easy to observe that, as he proceeds, he comes to count more and more on the intelligence of his public, and increases the scope and seriousness of his writing.[309]

It was secondarily the work of Addison's imitators. He had so whetted the public's appetite that demand immediately called forth a swarm of what were known in England as " Essay-papers ", modelled on Addison's happily-inspired articles. For the most part these papers eschewed politics, and supplied short articles of varying tone, on moral and literary subjects, addressed to different classes of society. Apart from many papers which followed the *Tatler* and *Spectator* and simply annexed the names which Steele and Addison had made so popular, there appeared *The Growler*, *The Whisperer*, *The Tell-Tale*,[310] *The Female Tatler*,

[309] " I have endeavoured to set my readers right in several points relating to operas and tragedies ; and shall from time to time impart my notions of comedy, as I think they may tend to its refinement and perfection. I find by my bookseller that these papers of criticism, with that upon humour, have met with a more kind reception than indeed I could have hoped for from such subjects ; for which reason I shall enter upon my present undertaking with greater cheerfulness." (*Spectator*, No. 58.)

Addison's eighteen articles on Milton began with No. 267 and were continued every Saturday. His eleven numbers on the Pleasures of the Imagination ran from No. 411 to 421 without a break.

[310] " *The Expiration of Bickerstaff's Lucubrations* was attended with much the same Consequences as the Death of *Melibœus's* Ox in Virgil ; as the latter engendred Swarms of Bees, the former immediately produc'd Swarms of little Satirical Scribblers."

One of these authors called himself The Growler ; " and assur'd us, that to make amends for Mr. *Steel's* Silence, he was resolv'd to *Growl* at us Weekly, as long as we should think fit to give him any Encouragement. Another Gentleman, with more modesty, call'd his paper *The Whisperer* ; and a Third, to Please the Ladies, Christen'd his *The Tell-Tale*. At the same time came out several Tatlers, each of which, with equal Truth and Wit, assur'd us, That he was the Genuine Isaac Bickerstaff . . . some of our Wits were for forming themselves into a Club, headed by one Mr. *Harrison*, and trying how they could shoot in this Bow of *Ulysses* " (*The Present State of Wit*).—Harrison's *Tatler* ran to 52 numbers. (Drake, *Essays . . . Illustrative of the Tatler*, etc.) Swift frequently alludes to Harrison and his *Tatler* in his *Journal to Stella*, especially on Jan. 11 and 13, 1710-11. On the latter date he writes : " You must understand that upon Steele's leaving off, there were two or three scrub *Tatlers* came out, and one of them holds on still, and today it advertized against Harrison's ; and so there must be disputes which are genuine like the straps for razors."—In Walter Scott's Edition of Swift, vol. IX, there are

The Rambler, The Lay Monk, The Historian, The Censor, The Hermit, The Silent Monitor, The Inquisitor, The Pilgrim, The Instructor, The Wanderer, The Freethinker, The Observator, etc.³¹¹ Dr. Drake has counted 106 of these essay-papers between Steele's *Tatler* and the publication of Dr. Johnson's *Rambler* in 1750 and yet his list is probably incomplete.³¹² There speedily sprang up, in fact, a whole literature *sui generis,* so prolific and so vigorous, that it has left its characteristic imprint on this period of English letters, which may justly be called The Age of Essayists.

The pattern set by Steele and Addison was so appropriate and so impressively successful, that none of their successors dreamt of adopting any other form than that of their invention. Not only did they steal their very titles, as we have seen, but like them they introduced to their readers characters who were —or would fain have been—near relatives of Isaac Bickerstaff and of the silent gentleman of the *Spectator. The Whisperer* was edited by Miss Jenny Bickerstaff,³¹³ a half-sister of Isaac ; *The Female Tatler* by " Mrs. Crackenthorpe " ³¹⁴ ; *The Lay Monk,* by a group of the same type as the Spectator Club ³¹⁵ ; *The Observator,* by " Humphrey Medlecott " ³¹⁶ ; others, by John Partridge, Walter Wagstaff, Sir Heister Ryley,³¹⁷ " Jeremy Quick ", and " Sir John Falstaff ".³¹⁸

I should be reluctant to maintain that all these newcomers

---

some issues of Harrison's *Tatler* which Swift must have retouched.—There was at least one " scrub " *Spectator* (Drake, *Essays . . . Illustrative of the Tatler,* etc., I, p. 348, and *Essays . . . Illustrative of the Rambler,* etc., I, p. 29).

³¹¹ *The Female Tatler,* 1709 ; *The Rambler,* 1712 ; *The Lay Monk,* 1713, edited by Blackmore and Hughes ; *The Historian,* 1713 ; *The Censor,* 1715, edited by Theobald ; *The Hermit,* 1715 ; *The Silent Monitor,* 1715 ; *The Inquisitor,* 1715 ; *The Pilgrim,* 1715 ; *The Instructor,* 1715 ; *The Wanderer,* 1717 ; *The Freethinker,* 1718, edited by Ambrose Philips. (Drake, *Essays . . . Illustrative of the Rambler,* etc., I, pp. 4 ff. ; II, pp. 490 ff.) ; *The Observator,* 1718 (Andrews, I, p. 114).

³¹² This number (106 papers) includes those published by Addison and Steele after the *Tatler* : a few deductions should perhaps be made of papers too exclusively political. Dr. Drake continues his list to 1809 and reckons 221 papers which still betray the influence of the *Tatler* and *Spectator*. The list might well be extended beyond 1809.

³¹³ Drake, *Essays . . . Illustrative of the Rambler,* etc., II, pp. 6 and 7.
³¹⁴ Andrews, I, p. 114.
³¹⁵ Johnson, *Lives of the English Poets,* Blackmore.
³¹⁶ Andrews, I, p. 114.
³¹⁷ *Tit for Tat,* 1709–10 ; *Annotations on the Tatler,* 1710 ; *The Visions of Sir Heister Ryley,* 1710 ; —See Drake, *Essays . . . Illustrative of the Rambler,* etc., I, pp. 4–10.
³¹⁸ *The Medley, or Daily Tatler,* 1715 ; *The Anti-Theatre,* 1720.—See Andrews, I, p. 114.

were creditable disciples of their masters, or that Bickerstaff, Sir Roger de Coverley and Will Honeycomb would have recognized as of the family, and welcomed with open arms, all the would-be relatives who mustered on every side.[319] The likeness was assuredly remote and superficial.

These over-faithful copies,[320] made for the most part by men lacking both talent and originality, were little more than watered-down imitations of their models. Even the best of them, and those a very few, succeeded in preserving only a faint suggestion of their perfume and savour.[321]

Such as they were, however, they found readers, and performed the useful office of maintaining and extending the taste for intellectual reading, especially amongst the middle-classes, who had hitherto taken little heed of literature. Nor did Addison and Steele quit the field. After the *Spectator* had closed down, they still continued their work in various papers, of which at least one, the *Guardian*, can still claim a place of honour alongside their masterpiece.[322]

---

[319] Without incurring the accusation that he lacked modesty, Addison was justified in saying :

" I cannot but observe with some secret pride, that this way of writing diurnal papers has not succeeded for any space of time in the hands of any persons who are not of our line. I believe I speak within compass when I affirm that above a hundred different authors have endeavoured after our family-way of writing : some of which have been writers in other kinds of the greatest eminence in the kingdom ; but I do not know how it has happened, they have none of them hit upon the art. Their projects have always been dropt after a few unsuccessful essays. It puts me in mind of a story lately told me by a pleasant friend of mine who has a very fine hand on the violin. His maid-servant seeing his instrument lying upon the table, and being sensible there was music in it, if she knew how to fetch it out, drew the bow over every part of the strings, and at last told her master she had tried the fiddle all over, but could not for her heart find where-about the tune lay." (*Guardian*, No. 98.)

[320] " They seem'd, indeed, at first to think, that what was only the *Garnish* of the former *Tatlers*, was that which recommended them, and not those *Substantial Entertainments* which they every were [sic] abound in. Accordingly they were continually talking of their *Maid*, *Night-Cap*, *Spectacles* and *Charles Lillie*. However there were now some faint endeavours at Humour and *Sparks* of Wit ; which the Town, for want of better Entertainment, was content to hunt after, through a heap of Impertinencies." (*The Present State of Wit*.)

[321] In the four volumes of his *Gleaner*, Drake has collected from these inferior works everything which could possibly survive.

[322] Addison and Steele, singly or together, published successively *The Guardian*, March 12, 1713 ; *The Englishman*, Oct. 6, 1713 ; *The Lover*, Feb. 14, 1714 ; *The Reader*, April 22, 1714 ; the eighth volume of the *Spectator*, Jan. 3, 1715 ; *Town Talk*, Dec. 17, 1715 ; *The Free-Holder*, Dec. 23, 1715 ; *The Tea-Table*, Feb. 6, 1716 ; *Chit-Chat*, March 6, 1716 ; *The Plebeian*, March 14,

I fear that to-day justice is hardly done to these Essayists, even to those who deserve the name of Classics.[323] They are certainly not as much read as they deserve to be.[324] The difficulty of now grasping the allusions of which they are full, no doubt accounts in part for this neglect, but I suspect that people are nowadays inclined to think them too short-winded, and to accuse them of being too sketchy and commonplace.[325] Without lingering to discuss how much exaggeration there is in this complaint, I must confess that it seems to me in certain points not without some justification. I admit that in publishing their opinions fragmentarily and in instalments, they often narrowed their horizon and shut out a comprehensive view. I also admit that in writing with a practical aim, they forewent loftier inspiration on many subjects.

But everything which we of to-day count as a flaw, was a definite asset at the time when they were writing. Their dishes were dressed for delicate or diseased stomachs, accustomed to inadequate or over-sophisticated fare, lacking wholesome appetite or digesting with difficulty. What can the best physician prescribe in such a case? What, but a diet of light and varied meals to tempt the appetite, to sustain and strengthen, without relaxing, an undernourished system, and gradually restore it to normal vigour? What better method could be devised than to serve each item in thin, easily-digested slices and offer every day a new menu to give each meal the charm of novelty?

1719; *The Old Whig*, March 19, 1719; *The Spinster*, Dec. 19, 1719; *The Theatre*, Jan. 2, 1720.

[323] By the term " Classic Essayists ", I personally denote solely Addison and Steele; but the epithet is generally used to include several authors whose publications are not without interest, since they were born of the success of the *Tatler* and the *Spectator* : Samuel Johnson's *Rambler* (1750-2) ; Hawkesworth and Johnson's *Adventurer* (1752-4) ; *The World* (1753-6) by Dr. Moore with the collaboration of Lord Chesterfield and Horace Walpole ; *The Connoisseur* (1754-6) by George Colman and Bonnel Thornton, with the collaboration of Cowper; Johnson's *Idler* (1758-60) ; Henry Mackenzie's *Mirror* (1779-80) and *Lounger* (1785-7) ; Cumberland's *Observer* (1785-90) and William Roberts' *Looker-on* (1792-4).

[324] *The Cornhill Magazine* for October, 1876, in an article on Sir Richard Steele laments, that " whereas there was a time when everyone who reads at all was perfectly familiar with the *Spectator*, and when an allusion to a paper would have sufficed without quotation. But time, though it cannot destroy our finest literature, is apt to rust it. Even Sir Roger is known by name only to many well-informed readers."

[325] Jeffrey raised this complaint, with some skill, not against the Essayists alone, but against the whole eighteenth century. See his Contributions to the *Edinburgh Review*, I, pp. 160 ff.

Stout volumes and lengthy treatises would have rebuffed readers so lacking in self-confidence as those of Addison's day. They would not even have been opened. High-flying speculation and long-drawn-out argument would have uselessly wearied and repelled the reader. The paper that consisted of short essays tempted the timorous by its brevity and variety, and held them by never overtiring them. Its unambitious modesty won their confidence. People who would otherwise never have read at all, unconsciously acquired the habit, and the taste for reading thus became widespread.[326]

After the Restoration, the theatre had become the literature of those who did not read. Later, politics did indeed compel the Englishman to read—but only in the fever of the moment. Addison's triumph was that he proved that the spice of politics was not indispensable, and that he won for his literary paper at least as many readers as all the party writings of the day put together. Having begun with a printing of 3,000 copies, the *Spectator* rapidly rose to 4,000, then to 20,000 and often as high as 30,000.[327] These figures apply to the daily sales; to these we must add the sale of the volumes. After the publication in separate numbers, readers immediately demanded a reprint in volumes in two different sizes. Each of these two issues ran to close on 10,000 copies, and before the daily *Spectator* had ceased to appear, more than 9,000 copies of the first four volumes had been sold.[328]

It is true that the *Spectator* had been obliged to keep each essay brief; and to offer its physic in small doses. But gradually and unawares the reading public found its mental power growing stronger, its taste more formed, and its enlightenment greater, and such precautions ceased to be necessary. The more serious works of English literature were re-edited and read, people

---

[326] "An *Essay* is an instructive writing, either in Prose or Verse, distinguished from compleat Treatises and voluminous Works, by its shorter extent and less accurate Method . . . the disrelish of such diffusive Pieces in these Times is . . . carry'd so far, that great Books are look'd on as oppressive . . . ; while those in which the principal End, as well as the sentiment of the Author, are contracted into a Narrower Compass, if well writ, meet with general Approbation." (Blackmore, *Essays*, vol. I, Preface.)

[327] *Addisoniana*, in Hurd's Edition of Addison, VI, p. 688; Forster, *Biographical Essays*, Steele; Drake, *Essays . . . Illustrative of the Tatler*, etc., I, p. 82 and III, p. 326.

[328] See the announcements in Nos. 227 and 283 [I can't see the relevance of either of these two essays. E. O. L.] and Nos. 488 and 555.—The *Tatler* had also had to be immediately reprinted in volume form.

returned to Milton [329] and to Shakespeare.[330] Soon the magazine followed the literary essay, but without supplanting it.[331] The two survived side by side for many years. Finally the novel—not the fantastic romance, but the novel of manners and real life—was born with *Robinson Crusoe* in 1719, and developed with much distinction in the works of Defoe, Richardson, Fielding and Smollett.[332] The spread of general culture in every direction united all classes of society. Readers were no longer segregated into watertight compartments of Puritan and Cavalier, Court and City, the metropolis and the provinces : all the English were now readers.

[329] Between 1688 and 1730 the Tonsons published twelve editions of *Paradise Lost*, either by itself or in conjunction with other works of Milton (Masson, *The Poetical Works of John Milton*, Introduction to Paradise Lost).
[330] The fourth and last reprint of the 1623 folio edition had appeared in 1685 (the second and third were of 1632 and 1663–4 respectively). In 1709 after the lapse of twenty-four years, Rowe published his edition of Shakespeare (a second edition in 1714) ; then came Pope's edition in 1725 (with a second in 1728) ; Theobald's, 1733 ; Hanmer's, 1744 ; Warburton's, 1747 ; Johnson's, 1765.—In 1741 Garrick made his first appearance on the London stage in *Richard III* and with him there began a brilliant Shakespeare revival.
[All this is slightly exaggerated : Shakespeare never sank very low. Dryden's praise was by no means apologetic ; and if Addison left him out of reckoning that was because it was not in his day the fashion at Oxford to consider him, and Addison always followed the fashion. He did so after Rowe's edition of 1709 was on the stocks. Garrick, and others of his time, " improved ". Shakespeare to their hearts' content, and so did Dr. Bowdler, if for other reasons. The Victorians improved him by careful selection, while latterly Robertson, and other " disintegrators " improved him almost out of existence in another way. Why attribute to the Restoration alone what is a habit common to all ages, and, with respect to the Restoration, call it a degrading folly ? B. D.]
[331] " The *Gentleman's Magazine*, For January, 1731 " ; " The *London Magazine*, April 1732 " ; " The *Scots Magazine*, January, 1739, Published in Edinburgh " ; " The *Universal Magazine of Knowledge and Pleasure* : for June, 1747 " ; The *Grand Magazine* : for January, 1758 " ; " The *Town and Country Magazine or Universal Repository of Knowledge, Instruction and Entertainment* : for January, 1769."—These titles are those of the first numbers preserved in the British Museum. On the Magazines and their contents see an article called *Last Century Magazines* in *Fraser's Magazine* for September, 1876, and Cucheval Clarigny, chap. XIV.—The *Gentleman's Magazine* appeared regularly without intermission from 1731 till 1907.
[332] Defoe : *Memoirs of a Cavalier* (1720), *The Life, Adventures and Piracies of the Famous Captain Singleton* (1720), *A Journal of the Plague Year* (1722), *The History and Remarkable Life of the truly Honourable Colonel Jacque* (1722), etc. ; —Swift : *Gulliver's Travels* (1726) ;—Richardson : *Pamela* (1741), *Clarissa Harlowe* (1751), *Sir Charles Grandison* (1754) ;—Fielding : *Joseph Andrews* (1742), *Tom Jones* (1749), *Amelia* (1751), etc. ;—Smollett : *Roderick Random* (1748), *Peregrine Pickle* (1751), *Ferdinand Count Fathom* (1753), *Humphrey Clinker* (1771), etc.

In a word, authors were henceforth provided with a public, that is to say a sufficiently numerous body of readers on whom they could count, and readers sufficiently cultivated to welcome and to purchase every type of literature.

CHAPTER IV

ALEXANDER POPE

(1721-1744)

I

Despite Appearances, Writers are not yet wholly independent.—Patronage now based on Politics.—Writers' Services to Politics : Addison, Steele, Swift, Shadwell, Congreve, Vanbrugh, Rowe, Prior, Gay, Defoe, Locke, Newton, Tate, Eusden, Smith, Hughes, Ambrose Philips, Parnell, Arbuthnot, Garth, Blackmore, Granville, Stepney, Maynwaring, Walsh, Martyn, Tickell.— Why the Political Parties cannot dispense with authors.—Effects of Political Patronage.—Dedications to Statesmen, etc.—The Author's uneasy position

So now we have a reading-public in England. This was a fact of capital importance to the author : an importance impossible to over-estimate. For this reading-public, created by the Essayists [0a], was destined ultimately to emancipate the writer and secure him his independence.

For the moment, however, high though they had climbed in the social scale, honourable as was the position they enjoyed, great as was the respect accorded them, authors were not yet independent.

Queen Anne's reign, the peak of the period we have just been studying, is remembered by Englishmen as a Golden Age of Literature, a writer's paradise of encouragement and patronage. But my reader will probably have noticed that this patronage was by no means wholly disinterested. No doubt one factor therein was pure love of literature. Charles II's reign had sown in high society the seed of literary enjoyment which was now bearing fruit. In this connection it would be unjust to forget that when Dorset's duty as Lord Chamberlain compelled him after the Revolution to cancel Dryden's pension as Poet Laureate and Historiographer Royal, he compensated the poet by generous gifts from his own private purse.[1] It was

---

[0a] [This is to go too far. The essayists no doubt helped the growth to some extent ; but the public was already growing from different causes. See my Introduction. B. D.]

[1] Dryden, Dedication to Dorset of his *Discourse on Satire*, 1693. I should hate to seem cynical, but perhaps the idea was that Dryden should not be driven to extremes. He might have made a dangerous enemy.

[This does indeed seem to be unduly cynical. Dorset, " the grace of courts, the Muses' pride " had been one of the old group of literary roisterers,

Dorset, too, who came to Tate's rescue when nothing further was to be hoped or feared from that aged and impoverished man.² Somers also, enlightened lover as he was of literature and the arts, was not wont to take heed of the personal opinions of those whom he succoured or encouraged.³ All the statesmen of the day, in fact, had the admirable virtue of being genuinely cultured men and good judges of literature, which qualities they proved by bringing to light so many valuable men of letters, to the honour of their own memory and the glory of their country.

None the less, the patronage they extended to authors had an entirely political basis. No crude bargaining took place between statesman and author, nor was the author in any statesman's pay. But the statesman won the author's attachment, and skilfully contrived to link the latter's interest with his own fortunes. The two formed a sort of mutual-aid society. The one said: "You stand by me, and I shall see that you do not suffer by it", the other answered: "You secure me a livelihood and I shall support you." Thus, no actual demand was made of the author, but he felt himself obliged to give; he was no mercenary, but he was an ally. The most distinguished of them, men like Addison, Newton, Locke, Prior and Steele, were entrusted with public office in which they could be directly of value to the party appointing them. Others were offered posts less in the limelight, in the hope—rarely falsified—that they would render to their patron-friends the type of service which Dryden had performed for Charles II and his royal brother. Others again were supplied with a comfortable sinecure—a sop, as it were, to Cerberus—to secure at least their silence and neutrality.

At this distance of time, it is easy for us to be taken in by the gracious urbanity of the statesman of those days and his friendly attitude towards the author, an attitude in which lay no trace

---

but had himself great taste and was something of a poet. He had little to fear from Dryden, and would be glad to help him. B. D.]

² Chalmers, *Biographical Dictionary*, s.v. Tate. Tate died hopelessly in debt. In earlier days Dorset had financed Prior's education. Prior is said to have been the son of a joiner. He was early left an orphan, and his uncle, who was a vintner, sent him to school at Westminster. Visiting the uncle's tavern, Dorset found the boy reading Horace and from that day undertook the care and cost of Prior's further studies. (Johnson, *Lives* . . . , Prior.)

³ Macaulay, *History*, chap. XX, Somers. He encouraged and protected the antiquary, Hickes " the fiercest and most intolerant of all the Non-Jurors ", and the engraver Vertue, who was a devout Roman Catholic.

[Somers was known as " the all-accomplisht ". B. D.]

of patronizing superiority towards a subordinate. This pleasant relationship of equal to equal, is all the more attractive by contrast with the disdainful patronage of men like Rochester and Mulgrave. No wonder that the author welcomed with delight the new régime which suddenly made life so pleasant for him, and recorded it with so much appreciation that we are tempted to see it with his eyes. We are the more inclined to share this illusion, because, while we remember that some writers were frankly political partisans—Steele and Addison were, for instance, zealous Whigs and Swift an ardent Tory— the greater number of names mentioned in the preceding pages are for us nowadays politically colourless, and their connotation is purely and solely literary. We remember only the comedies of Shadwell, Congreve and Vanbrugh, the tragedies of Rowe, the light poetry of Prior, the verses and fables of Gay. How many people connect Defoe's name with anything but *Robinson Crusoe*? Who dreams of inquiring about the political sympathies of Locke or Newton? As for most of the others, their works and their opinions are equally buried in oblivion. Yet, if we look more closely, we note that the writers of the day were one and all involved in political strife and zealously took a more or less active share in it.

Shadwell, who had, as we saw, entered the lists before the Revolution, wrote a poem to commemorate the arrival in England of the Prince of Orange, and another Congratulatory Poem to greet the arrival of " The Most Illustrious Queen Mary ". He also celebrated various events of the reign of William III : the King's return from Ireland, the King's birthday, etc.[4] Congreve, a member of the Kit-Cat Club, mourned Queen Mary's death in a pastoral elegy and " humbly offered " to Queen Anne a Pindaric Ode on the capture of Namur and the victories of Marlborough.[5] Vanbrugh, who knew French well, undertook to keep William III's Government informed of what was going on in France, and did so to such good purpose that he was arrested and spent nearly two years in the Bastille.[6]

---

[4] See my Bibliography. Queen Mary landed on Feb. 12, 1689; Shadwell's verses are dated Feb. 20. Rymer, who later succeeded Shadwell as Historiographer Royal, was even more expeditious : on Feb. 15 he addressed a poem to the Queen on her safe arrival. (Malone, *Life of Dryden*, pp. 207-8.)
[5] See my Bibliography.
[6] Ravaisson, *Archives de la Bastille*, IV, pp. 338-446. It is not expressly stated that he was arrested as a spy. But other documents quoted by Ravaisson show that William III had an excellently-organized system of espionage

Like Congreve, he was a member of the Kit-Cat club. Rowe, "who was so keen a Whig that he did not willingly converse with men of the opposite party",[7] sang the Union of England and Scotland, the victories of Marlborough, the House of Brunswick [8] and introduced party allusions into his verses—even into his translation of Lucan.[9] Prior collaborated in the Tory *Examiner* and wrote a number of political poems which he carefully reprinted in his *Works*.[10] The sole reason for Gay's being appointed Secretary to the Ambassador in Hanover was that he had dedicated some verses to Bolingbroke; he also wrote an Epistle to the Princess of Wales.[11] Defoe, whom we saw supporting the Revolution of William III with so much

---

in France. Now, in view of the fact that Vanbrugh had a perfect command of French, that he was a supporter of the English Revolution and on good terms with people who stood well at Court (see the *Life* prefixed to his Works) it would seem that his arrival in France without a passport, at a time when the two countries were at war, made him justifiably suspect to the French authorities.—See also *Biographia Dramatica*, s.v. Vanbrugh.

[Vanbrugh was arrested at Calais in 1690. At that time he had no connection with courtly circles; he may have been known to one or two senior officers in the army, but that is all. It is most unlikely that he was directly employed as a spy. He did not go to the Bastille till 1692, and was not, of course, a Kit-Cat till a good deal later, since the club then hardly existed, if at all. See Ravaisson, *loc. cit.*, and my Introduction to the Nonesuch edition of Vanbrugh's *Works*. B. D.]

[7] Johnson, *Lives* . . . etc. Rowe.

[8] *Unio*, a little Latin poem, "English'd *by the* Author" in his *Poems on Several Occasions*, 1714, p. 29; *A Poem upon the Late Successes of Her Majesties Arms*, etc., in his *Works*, II, p. 283; *Ode for the New Year*, addressed to George I. See my Bibliography.

[9] In his *Tamerlane*, Bajazet represented Louis XIV and Tamerlane William III. See my Bibliography for the quotation from Virgil which precedes the play.—His tragedy, *The Royal Convert*, 1707, ends with a prophetic compliment to Queen Anne and the Union of England and Scotland.—Henry Cromwell wrote to Pope on Nov. 5, 1710: "I have just read and compared Mr. Rowe's version of the ninth (book) of Lucan with very great pleasure . . . He is so arrant a Whig, that he strains even beyond his author, in passion for liberty, and aversion to tyranny." (Elwin, VI, p. 108.)

[10] See my Bibliography and p. 66 of his *Poems on Several Occasions*: "Presented to the King, at his Arrival in Holland, after the Discovery of the Conspiracy, 1696";—p. 133, "*Carmen Seculare*, for the year 1700; to the King";—p. 181, "Prologue spoken at Court before the Queen on Her Majesty's Birth-Day, 1704";—p. 183, A Letter to Monsieur Boileau Despreaux, occasioned by the Victory at Blenheim, 1704;—p. 245, "An Ode humbly inscribed to the Queen on the Glorious Success of Her Majesty's Arms, 1706. Written in Imitation of Spenser's Style";—p. 285, "To Mr. Harley wounded by Guiscard, 1711: An Ode."—On this last item see Swift's *Journal to Stella*, March 30, 1710-11.

[11] *The Shepherd's Week*, 1714, with a "*Prologue*. To the Right Honourable the Ld. Viscount of Bolingbroke."—"*Epistle* to a Lady. Occasion'd by the Arrival of Her Royal Highness" in his *Poems on Several Occasions*, II, p. 271.

vigour, left over two hundred political writings. In 1690 Locke, who was Shaftesbury's friend and collaborator, published two *Treatises of Government* in which he warmly defended the principles of the Revolution against the Tories.[12] Newton, M.P. for Cambridge, actively upheld the rights of the University against the illegal encroachments of James II.[13]

Tate's genuine grief at the death of the sovereigns whom he survived, did not prevent his hailing the accession of their successors and the principal events of subsequent reigns.[14] Eusden's first step on the road to literary success was a Latin verse translation of Lord Halifax's poem on the Battle of the Boyne, and he repaid favours received with several pieces whose subjects were calculated to give pleasure in exalted circles.[15] The interest Lord Halifax displayed in Edmund Smith, was not evoked solely by Smith's tragedy of *Phædra*; the poet had previously celebrated the accession of William and Mary and the Battle of the Boyne, mourned the death of William III and sung the victory of Blenheim.[16] Hughes wrote verses on the Duke of Gloucester, the House of Nassau, the Princess of Wales, the Peace of Ryswick and the return of William III in 1699.[17] Ambrose Philips in his *Pastorals* set his shepherds Lobbin, Albino and Lanquet to sing poetic eulogies of Dorset and Queen Anne

[12] See H. R. Fox Bourne, *The Life of John Locke* and Villemain, *Tableau de la littérature au XVIIIe siècle, 5e leçon*.—In his Preface to the *Two Treatises*, Locke says: "These (Papers) I hope are sufficient to establish the Throne of our Great Restorer, Our present King *William*; to make good his Title, in the Consent of the People, which being the only one of all lawful Governments, he has more fully and clearly than any Prince in *Christendom*. And to justify to the World, the People of *England*, whose love of their Just and Natural Rights, with their Resolution to preserve them, saved the Nation when it was on the very brink of Slavery and Ruine."

[13] *Biographia Britannica*, s.v. Newton.

[14] See my Bibliography.—Some verses of his to Queen Anne, "*Britannia's Prayer to the Queen*, 1706. By Mr. *Tate*, Poet Laureat to her Majesty" may be found in *Poems on Affairs of State*, IV, 1707, p. 129.

[15] See N. Drake, *Essays . . . Illustrative of the Tatler*, etc., III, p. 280, and my Bibliography.

[16] On the Inauguration of *King William and Queen Mary*, An. Dom. 1689; On the Return of King William to Ireland, After the battle of the Boyne 1690 (In A. Chalmers, *The Works of the English Poets*, IX, pp. 203-4); *A Pindarique Poem Sacred to the Glorious Memory of King William III*, 1702 (see my Bibliography); Ode for the Year 1705 (A. Chalmers, op. cit., p. 207).

[17] *The Triumph of Peace* (see my Bibliography);—"The Court of Neptune. On King William's Return from Holland, 1699" (in his *Poems on Several Occasions*, p. 19);—"Song. Written for the Late Duke of Gloucester's Birthday, 1699" (A. Chalmers, op. cit., X, p. 24);—*The House of Nassau*; —*An Ode for the Birth-Day of Her Royal Highness The Princess of Wales* (see my Bibliography).

and in his *Life of Archbishop Williams* aired Whig opinions in prose.[18] Parnell, whom Swift introduced to Harley, paid his court with a poem *On Queen Anne's Peace*.[19] At Swift's instigation, Arbuthnot wrote his *History of John Bull* [20] to ridicule Marlborough and turn men's minds to thoughts of peace, and his *Pseudologia Politike* or *The Art of Political Lying* to make merry at the expense of the Whigs.[21] Garth backed the views of his Kit-Cat friends in several poems, in Epistles to Godolphin and to Marlborough, in verses on Queen Anne and on the Jacobin rising of 1715.[22] Blackmore was the author of *A True and Impartial History of the Conspiracy Against the Person and Government of King William III of Glorious Memory*, verses in praise of Marlborough, etc.[23] Before being raised to the peerage by Harley's Government, Granville had committed himself to the Tories by poems in honour of Mary of Modena and of James II.[24] Stepney sang in Latin the virtues of Charles II, the Marriage of Princess Anne, and in English the accession of James II, William III's journey to Holland and the death of

[18] See my Bibliography. In Charles I's day Archbishop Williams had been one of the promoters of the Petition of Right.

[19] *On Queen Anne's Peace (Written in December,* 1712) (A. Chalmers, op. cit., IX, p. 405).—See Swift, *Journal to Stella,* Dec. 22, 26, 31, 1712 ; Jan. 6, Feb. 19, March 27, 1712-13.

[20] Usually quoted under this title, but the original title is *Law is a Bottomless-Pit.* See my Bibliography.

[21] See Swift, *Journal to Stella,* Oct. 9 and Dec. 12, 1712.—This pamphlet of Arbuthnot's, revised by Swift, is reprinted in Scott's Edition of Swift, vol. VI.

[22] *To the Duke of Marlborough,* on his Voluntary Banishment ; *To the Earl of Godolphin* ; *On Her Majesty's Statue,* in St. Paul's Church-Yard ; *On the New Conspiracy,* 1716 (A. Chalmers, op. cit., IX, pp. 449-50).

[23] *A True and Impartial History,* etc., and *Advice to the Poets* (see my Bibliography) ; " Instructions to *Vander Bank.* A Sequel to the Advice to the Poets. A Poem Occasioned by the Glorious Success of Her Majesty's Arms, under the Conduct of the Duke of Marlborough, the last Year in *Flanders.* Printed in the Year 1709 (In *A Collection of Poems on Various Subjects.* By Sir Richard Blackmore).—In the Dedication of his poem *Alfred* he says : ". . . I had the Honour to contribute more to the Succession of the Illustrious House of *Hanover* to the Crown of *Great-Britain,* than I ever boasted of, contenting my Self with this, that what I had done was for the Service of reformed Religion, and the Good of my Country."

[24] See in his *Genuine Works,* III, pp. 1 and 6-8 : " To the Earl *of* Peterborough, *on his Happy Accomplishment of the Marriage between His* Royal Highness *and the Princess* Mary d'Este *of* Modena " ; " *To the* King *in the First Year of His* Majesty's *Reign* " ; " *To the* King " ; " *To the* King ;—At the age of eighteen he had been eager to fight against the Duke of Monmouth ; in 1688 he had volunteered to maintain in arms the rights of James II ; under William III he remained in retirement." (Johnson, *Lives,* etc., Granville.)

Queen Mary, etc.[25] Maynwaring, having first given rein to his high spirits in verses against the Whigs, allowed them a long canter against the Tories and attacked Swift and Bolingbroke's *Examiner* in the paper known as *The Medley*.[26] Walsh pressed Horace and Virgil into his service to glorify William III's courage and the merits of Whig politics.[27] Henry Martyn actively collaborated in *The British Merchant, or Commerce Preserv'd*, a paper founded to oppose the commercial treaty with France which was concluded at Utrecht.[28] Tickell, whom Swift dubbed " Whiggissimus ", wrote several sets of verses in favour of the House of Brunswick.[29]

It is not possible to doubt the motives underlying the favour accorded to authors, when we observe that the Whigs reserve it exclusively for ·Whigs, and the Tories for Tories, and that each triumph of one party or the other is the signal for a distribution of lucrative posts.

On the accession of William III, Dryden, the Tory, was released from his duties and deprived of his salaries, while Shadwell, an over-night Orangeman, was appointed Poet Laureate in his stead. Under William, the Whig Newton was called to be Master of the Mint.[29a] Locke, who by order of Charles II had been driven out of the University of Oxford,

[25] *In Obitum* Caroli *Secundi*. He speaks of " Caroli Mores Cœlestibus æquos " ; *In Nuptias* P. Georgii et D. Annæ ; *To King James II. Upon his Accession to the Throne. The Author then of Trinity-College, Cambridge*; *On the late horrid Conspiracy* (in *The Works of Celebrated Authors, of whose writings there are but small Remains*, II, pp. 58, 56, 3, 11). *An Epistle to Charles Montague, Esq.* ; *on his Majesty's Voyage to Holland* ; *A Poem Dedicated to the Blessed Memory of Her late Gracious Majesty Queen Mary* (see my Bibliography).

[26] See *Biographia Britannica*, s.v. Maynwaring, which quotes the titles of some fifteen writings of his against the Tories.

[27] *Horace. Ode III. Book III* Imitated 1705 ; *The Golden Age restored*, 1703. An Imitation of the Fourth Eclogue of Virgil. Supposed to have been taken from a Sibylline Prophecy (A. Chalmers, op. cit., VIII, pp. 417–18).

[28] N. Drake, *Essays . . . Illustrative of the Tatler*, etc., III, pp. 285 ff. See also my Bibliography, s.v. Martyn (Henry).

[29] *The Prospect of Peace* (see my Bibliography). This poem favouring the policy of Harley and Bolingbroke was little calculated to please the Whigs, but the wrong thereby done them Tickell repaired in his later verses : *The Royal Progress*, on the arrival of George I, first published in No. 620 of the *Spectator*, Nov. 15, 1714 ; *An Imitation of the Prophecy of Nereus*. From Horace, II, Ode XV, on the Jacobite rising of 1715 (A. Chalmers, op. cit., XI, p. 108) ; *Epistle from a Lady in England to a Gentleman at Avignon*, against the Jacobites (see my Bibliography) ; *Kensington Garden* in praise of George I (see my Bibliography).

[29a] [But might it not be that Newton's appointment to the Mint was made on technical grounds ? B. D.]

had followed Shaftesbury to Holland, and had been unable to return home until he came in King William's train, was appointed Commissioner of Appeals. Blackmore, who had all his life been an Anti-Jacobite, was knighted and appointed Physician to the King. It was to his Tory friends that Swift owed the Deanery of St. Patrick's, and it was likewise the Tories who appointed Gay Secretary to the Embassy in Hanover, who entrusted Prior with important diplomatic missions and elevated Granville to the peerage. Those who throughout the days of Tory triumph had remained faithful to the House of Brunswick, came into their own when George I came to the throne. Addison and Steele, who had been ousted by the previous ministry, were rewarded in overflowing measure. Even before the new King's arrival, Addison was appointed Secretary to the Council of Regency, and was later made Secretary to the Lord-Lieutenant of Ireland and Under-Secretary of State. Steele was made Inspector of the Royal Stables, J.P. and Deputy Lieutenant for the County of Middlesex, Director of the Theatre Royal in Drury Lane and received a knighthood. Garth was also knighted. Tickell was rewarded with a public post in Ireland under Addison.[30] Henry Martyn, who had opposed the Tories' commercial policy, was made Inspector-General of Exports and Imports. It was at this time too that Ambrose Philips, a member of the Hanover Club, secured two of his posts, and that Rowe was made Poet Laureate (before the death of his predecessor, Tate) and provided with other highly remunerative sinecures.

We even see a service reap instantaneous reward. Addison's *Blenheim* had got no further than the simile of the angel, when Godolphin testified his appreciation by appointing him Commissioner of Appeals.

Powerful political motives underlay this eager haste to enlist the author's allegiance and secure his loyalty by every possible device. I have already pointed out how urgently necessary it was for the very existence of any Government after the Revolution, to ensure the support of public opinion, to keep in touch

[30] In his *Royal Progress* he prophetically said of George I :

"Now to the Royal Towers securely brought,
He plans *Britannia's* Glories in his Thought,
Resumes the delegated Pow'r he gave,
Rewards the Faithful, and restores the Brave."

[It might also be noted that Vanbrugh was the first man to be knighted by George I. B. D.]

with the nation, and to influence it from day to day. Nowadays, the propaganda indispensable to a constitutional government, is almost entirely supplied by parliamentary debate. An evening speech by a Minister, or by a leader of the Opposition, is read throughout England next morning, and penetrates into even the tiniest village, to challenge the attention and invite the opinion of millions of readers. But at the period of which I am writing, parliamentary eloquence died within the walls of St. Stephen's, unechoed in the outside world. The publication of debates was strictly forbidden,[31] and the words which swayed the votes of Lords and Commons remained a dead letter in the country at large. Bolingbroke has left a reputation of eloquence unequalled in England, rich as that country is in political oratory, yet not a phrase of any of his speeches has been preserved.[32] It was therefore imperative that the work of discussion, already accomplished in Parliament, should be carried on afresh in the world outside, and contact incessantly renewed with the coffee-houses and clubs and with the provincial electorate. This could be done only by the perpetual publication of fresh matter.[33] The influence nowadays exerted by parliamentary speeches then belonged solely to the Press, which means not only newspapers and pamphlets but every literary work, and even verses handling political ideas. It has been justly said that Addison's *Campaign* is merely a rhymed *Gazette*. Every man capable of wielding a pen was a valuable and important ally, and a party chief who neglected to enlist him by flattering attentions, and retain his loyalty by substantial marks

[31] See Lecky, I, pp. 442-6, and Andrews, I, pp. 142-9 and 196-203. It was not until 1771 that parliamentary debates began to be freely reported. —In 1745 the *Gentleman's Magazine* was still giving them—and not without risk—under the headline of "Discussions in the Lilliput Senate". The Lords were the *Hurgoes* : Lord Chesterfield appeared as *Hurgo Castroflet*, Lord Hardwicke as *Hurgo Hickrad* ; the Archbishop of Oxford as Archbishop of *Oxdorf*. The House of Commons became the *Clinabs* and the speakers were *Snadsy, Gamdahm, Feaucs, Pulnub*, that is Sandys, Wyndham, Fox and Pulteney. Europe was *Degulia*, France *Blefuscu*, London *Mildendo*, the Jacobites, *Jacomites*.—The *Scots Magazine* adopted Roman pseudonyms : Sir Robert Walpole was M. Tullius Cicero ; Pulteney, M. Cato ; The Duke of Newcastle, Cn. Domitius Calvinus ; and Lord Chesterfield, L. Piso, etc.
[32] Stanhope, *History of . . . the Reign of Queen Anne*, II, p. 175.
[33] We have already seen Bolingbroke collaborating in the *Examiner* ; he was at that time a member of the Ministry. Harley wrote *A Vindication of the Commons in the last Session of Parliament*, 1701 (Townsend, I, p. 157). Watt quotes some dozen political works written by Walpole. On this point, and on the active part played by Walpole and Pulteney in press polemics, see Macaulay's *Essay on Addison*.

of esteem, would have been failing in his duty towards his party and towards himself. If it was not possible to make the author an active partisan, it was at least expedient to prevent his swelling the ranks of the enemy.

So we find both parties on the alert to detect budding talent, in order to have a nursery of useful collaborators to draw on. When Congreve called Whig attention to young Addison's promise, Halifax personally intervened to prevent the young man's taking orders and to maintain him firmly in his expressed opinions. It is curious to note Swift recording the solicitude shown by Harley and Bolingbroke towards the very modest signs of talent in a Diaper,[34] a Trapp,[35] a Harrison.[36]

For the same reason, turn-coat writers were welcomed with enthusiasm: there was a double advantage in roping in a renegade—gain to your own party, loss to the other. We have already seen the attention lavished on Parnell when Swift brought him to pay his respects to Harley. Prior also who, under the wing of his friend and collaborator Montague, had found both honour and profit in the ranks of the Whigs, went over to the Tories, who received him with open arms, entrusted him with negotiations abroad and rewarded him with lucrative posts. Having won his first literary distinction with a Tory poem, so good that it was attributed to Dryden, Maynwaring was not long in showing his appreciation of the courtship of the Whigs. Halifax hastened to encourage so happy a frame of mind by securing for him a job in the Customs, and Godolphin's kindness went so far as to purchase from its holder a post worth £2,000 a year to present it as an offering to the repentant Tory. Nothing in this mart-and-barter business, however, is more illuminating than the competition of the two parties to capture Swift. He was the incumbent of a small Irish parish when he ventured for the first time into politics with a Whig-flavoured pamphlet published anonymously in 1701. It was *A Discourse*

---

[34] *Journal to Stella*, March 12, 13, 21, 1711–12; Dec. 23, 1712; Feb. 12, 13, 1712–13.

[Diaper does not deserve the neglect into which he has fallen: Trapp and Harrison are not to be mentioned in the same breath with him. It is extremely difficult to see copies of Diaper's three works, which should be reprinted. He is beginning to be quoted in anthologies, being far better than the average ruck of Eusdens, Philips, Hughes, Parnells, *et hoc genus omne*. B. D.]

[35] Ibid., Jan. 7, 1710–11; April 1, 2, 1713.

[36] Ibid., Oct. 13, 1710; March 15, 1710–11; April 19, 1711; March 12, 1711–12; Jan. 30, 31 and Feb. 12, 13, 14, 1712–13.

of the Contents and Dissensions between the Nobles and the Commons at Athens and Rome and it produced so much effect that it was popularly ascribed either to Somers or to Burnet. As soon as the author declared himself, Halifax and Somers both expressed a wish to meet him, received him graciously, promised him their support and proposed him for a bishopric.[37] They were unfortunate in being unable to make good their promises, or perhaps they pressed his case too half-heartedly, and Swift, filled with bitter disappointment and resentment, was left to vegetate in his modest benefice. So when the Whig Ministry fell, and the Tories came to power, the disgruntled author hastened across the water and came to London to study the situation.[38] He had meantime written *The Tale of a Tub* which placed beyond all doubt his remarkable talent as a writer, and showed what service he could render to his friends, and how much damage he could inflict on those of the other side.[39] No sooner had he arrived in the capital than the Whigs, anticipating his resentment, laid hold on him and overwhelmed him with compliments and excuses, blaming themselves for having been able to do so little for a man of his calibre. While the Whigs were profuse in compliments, protestations and attentions, the Tories frankly told him that the moment had come to lay the foundation of his fortunes if he had a mind. Harley made personal approaches to him with a courtesy all the more seductive that it was in pleasing contrast to the cold reserve of Somers, one of the Whig leaders. He frequently invited Swift to dine, introduced him to his family circle, treated him as an intimate, called him his friend, and addressed him without formality by his Christian name, till the guest recorded with delight that his position amongst " the people of to-day " was ten times better than with their predecessors and that he was forty times more sought after. So it was " the people of to-day " who won him over and the acquisition of a writer of the first rank was undoubtedly one of the most valuable achievements of the new Ministry. Swift's writings alone did greater service to the Tory

[37] This proposal, previously a matter of conjecture only, has been documented by papers reproduced in Forster's *Life of Jonathan Swift*, pp. 210 ff.
[38] He carried off a book which Halifax had given him [Jolivet's *Poésies Chrétiennes*. B. D.], and wrote in it : " Given me by my lord Halifax, May 3, 1709. I begged it of him, and desired him to remember, *it was the only favour I ever received from him or his party*."
[39] Bolingbroke later told him : " We were determined to have you ; you were the only one we were afraid of."

cause than all the delicate political manœuvres of Harley and the eloquent speeches of Bolingbroke.[40]

About this same time Harley exerted his diplomacy to retain in neutrality, if he could not win over to an offensive alliance, the two Whig writers, Steele and Congreve. As Editor of the *London Gazette* and Commissioner of Stamps, Steele played an active part in politics. In the hope of securing him, Harley retained him in these two posts, assured him of the high esteem he felt for his character and promised to show practical proof of his wish to be of service to him. Two unpleasing anti-Tory articles which Steele printed in the *Tatler* [41] cost him the editorship of the *Gazette*. But the Tories did not wish to push matters to extremes and Harley sent Swift as his ambassador with general instructions " to clear matters with Steele " and request him to continue " in his office of stamped paper ". Swift's overtures were ill received. Steele, who was always hasty and passionate in politics, resigned his commissionership and launched a merciless campaign against the Tories.[42]

Congreve, who was of milder temper than Steele and appreciative of the easy life which his posts assured him, begged Swift to intercede on his behalf. Delighted to find the dramatist so amenable, Harley sent a gracious reply in Latin :

> Non obtusa adeo gestamus pectora Pæni,
> Nec tam aversus equos Tyriâ sol jungit ab urbe.

This quotation completely won Congreve's heart, and his political muse kept silence through all the remainder of Queen Anne's reign.[43]

---

[40] For details of Swift's first steps in politics see his own works, especially *Memoirs relating to that Change which happened in the Queen's Ministry in the Year 1710* ; *Imitation of part of the Sixth Satire of the Second Book of Horace 1714* and the *Journal to Stella.*

[What Swift always worked for was the security and betterment of the Church of England. Though as a churchman he would welcome the Revolution as removing the Catholic menace, it was soon pretty clear that the Whigs of Queen Anne's day, with their strong support from the Dissenters, would and could do little for it. Swift had no choice but to be a Tory, which he was from the conviction of a practical man quite apart from his personal ambition. B. D.]

[41] The numbers of June 29 and July 4, 1710. The former contained a portrait of Harley under the name of Polypragmon ; the latter a letter purporting to be by Downes, the prompter, criticizing the new Ministry under the pretence of describing a change of theatrical management.

[42] Swift, *Journal to Stella*, Oct. 22 and Dec. 15, 1710. Harley even offered Steele a better post. See Steele's fine letter to Harley in N. Drake, *Essays . . . Illustrative of the Tatler*, etc., I, pp. 95 ff.

[43] *Journal to Stella* : June 28, 1711, and Swift's *Works*, XVI, p. 349, his letter to Pope from Dublin, dated Jan. 10, 1720–1.

It is clear that Congreve had no illusions about the disinterested kindness of statesmen, but was fully alive to the connection between politics and patronage. His brother-authors were no less wide-awake than he, and the eagerness with which they entered the fray shows that they clearly perceived where their own best interests lay. Those I have so far mentioned all succeeded in securing more or less important posts, and we might assume that special talent prompted them to embark on a career in which they believed themselves destined to succeed. But if we look outside the circle of the specially privileged, we notice that all employed the same procedure for drawing attention to themselves. They understood full well that if they were to derive effective benefit, more was expected of them than proof of purely literary talent. Farquhar—who however died too young to attain distinction—wrote Pindaric verses on the death of General Schomberg, who fell in the Battle of the Boyne, and mourned Queen Mary's death.[44] John Philips also paid his tribute to the memory of the dead Queen,[45] and, as already mentioned, celebrated for the Tories the victory of Blenheim. The critic Dennis composed one poem on Queen Mary's death, another on Marlborough's victories and yet a third, mourning the death of Queen Anne and in the same breath hailing the accession of George I.[46] In 1712 Young made his first literary appearance with a political *Epistle* to Granville newly created Lord Lansdowne; in 1713 he offered verses to Queen Anne in a political dedication, and in 1714 he wrote a poem on the Queen's death and the New King.[47] Aaron Hill was another who lamented the death of Queen Anne.[48] The Deist, Toland, wrote a pamphlet on the destruction of Dunkirk, and another

---

[44] *On the Death of General* Schomberg, *Kill'd at the* Boyn; *On the Death of the late* Queen (*Works*, I, pp. 16 and 41).
[45] *In Memory Of Our Late Most Gracious Lady* (see my Bibliography).
[46] *The Court of Death: A Pindarick Poem dedicated to the Memory of her most Sacred Majesty Queen* Mary (*The Select Works of Mr. John Dennis*, I, p. 33); *Britannia Triumphans* (see my Bibliography); *The Battle of Ramillia* (ibid.); *A Poem on the Death of Her late Sacred Majesty Queen Anne, And the Most Happy and Auspicious Accession of his Sacred Majesty King George* (ibid.).—We may note that he obtained a minor post through Marlborough's kind offices. (*Biographia Dramatica*, s.v. Dennis).
[47] *An Epistle.* To the Right Hon. George, Lord Lansdowne, MDCCXII (A. Chalmers, *The Works of the English Poets*, XIII, p. 509); *A Poem On the last Day*, dedicated "To the Queen" (see my Bibliography); *On the Late Queen's Death. And His Majesty's Accession to the Throne* (ibid.).
[48] *The Dream. Occasioned by the Death of* Q. Anne. *By* Aaron Hill, *Esq.* (In the *Works of Rochester*, M.DCC.XXXI, II, p. 159.)

attacking Harley, now Lord Oxford.[40] I could add many other examples, but let these suffice.

In quoting these facts to show that authors had not yet escaped from serfdom, I have no intention of weakening what I have said of their greatly improved position. In proving that they were still dependent on politics, I am far from wishing to imply that they were degrading themselves by taking part in them. No doubt a few trimmed their sails to suit a change of wind and forfeited some self-respect by so doing; but Newton, Locke, Addison, Steele and many others are no less worthy in my eyes for having taken part in party controversy. I should not even contend that they were wrong to do so or that they would have been better to abstain. It would be absurd to suggest that an author—simply because he is an author—should hold himself aloof from the business of his time and country. There are periods in history, moreover, when no citizen has the right to be a passive spectator of the happenings that are taking place before his eyes. The years which followed the English Revolution of 1688 were a period of this kind. Besides, it is obvious that politics offer a writer natural and frequent opportunity to practise his art and to serve his country. It would be regrettable and unjust to forbid him thus to employ his gifts. I feel therefore no regret that English writers of this time occupied themselves with politics; but I do regret that circumstances compelled their so doing, and I am bound to record that they owed their new position in society solely to their political activity and that, whether they were aware of the fact or not, this activity was the *sine quâ non* of their very existence. They had, in fact, simply exchanged Court patronage for the patronage of politicians, and they were as powerless to escape the one as the other.

It is manifest that this new form of patronage was pleasanter and less undignified than the earlier. First, because they were not compelled, as of old, to stake all their hopes on Court favour; they had the choice of allegiance to either of two parties, and this freedom of choice conferred a real liberty of movement. Secondly, the important service they were able to render to their patrons ensured that their value was appreciated. The statesman, wooing the author not for his personal pleasure, nor

---

[40] Scott's Edition of Swift, XII, p. 305, note. I have been unable to find either of these pamphlets in the British Museum. The second was called *The Art of Reasoning*.

for the fleeting need of the moment, but as a permanent ally and for serious purposes, was compelled to give thought to his qualities and qualifications and could not—without danger to himself and to his party—let a mere whim dictate his choice, nor afterwards capriciously discard his protégé. Thirdly, since author and statesman had interests in common, the author became partner and collaborator rather than client. His position was no longer the subordinate one of other days.

It is none the less true that he remained dependent on others. He lived, not by his pen, but by the post he held, and to obtain it he had to incur certain inevitable obligations. He therefore still chafed under the inconvenient consequences of dependence. He still had to pander and pay his court to the influential persons of the day, to be diligent in his attendance at levées and audiences, or risk being overlooked, and to spend long hours in antechambers. " We had much company to-day at dinner at Lord Treasurer's," writes Swift to Stella,[50] " Prior never fails : he is a much better courtier than I ; and we expect every day that he will be a Commissioner of the Customs." So the author was still constrained humbly to issue his work under the aegis of some famous name. He had been wont to write dedications ; he went on writing them, but now to a different address. Instead of offering them to those in high favour at Court, he sent them now to Ministers or high officials, or to men influential in public affairs.

Congreve dedicated one of his comedies to the Right Honourable Charles Montague, one of the Lords of the Treasury ; another to the Right Honourable Charles, Earl of Dorset and Middlesex, Lord Chamberlain of his Majesty's Household ; a collection of his occasional verses again to Charles Montague now become Lord Halifax. The collection contains a poem addressed to Halifax, and another to Godolphin, Lord High Treasurer of Great Britain [51] ; all this without prejudice to the political works already entered to the author's account. Rowe's *Ulysses* was offered to Godolphin ; his *Royal Convert* to Halifax. Southerne presented his *Wives' Excuse* to The Right Honourable Thomas Wharton, Controller of His Majesty's Household, his

---

[50] June 26, 1711.
[51] Poems upon *Several Occasions* (*Works*, III, p. 57) : " The Birth of the Muse. To the Right Honourable *Charles*, Lord *Hallifax* " ; p. 193 : " To the Right Honourable the Earl of *Godolphin*, Lord High Treasurer of *Great Britain*. Pindarique Ode."

Oroonoko to His Grace the Duke of Devonshire, Lord Intendant of His Majesty's Household. Mrs. Manley likewise dedicated *The Royal Mischief* to the Duke of Devonshire. Mrs. Centlivre *The Man's Bewitch'd* to the same, and her *Busie Body* to Somers. Hughes presented his tragedy *The Siege of Damascus* to Cowper, the Lord Chancellor, Ambrose Philips addressed a poetic letter to Dorset [52] and commended his *Pastorals* to his protection. The classical scholar Richard Bentley dedicated an edition of Horace to the Earl of Oxford, and, if we are to believe a footnote of Pope's to the *Dunciad*, he would have dedicated it to Halifax, if the Tories had not meantime come into power. Bentley's nephew, following in his uncle's footsteps, offered yet another edition of the Latin poet to Lord Harley, the new minister's son.[53] John Philips addressed a Latin ode to Bolingbroke,[54] to whom also Gay dedicated *The Shepherd's Week*. Swift laid his *Tale of a Tub* at Somers' feet. Young offered his tragedy of *Busiris* to His Grace the Duke of Newcastle, Lord Chamberlain of His Majesty's household, etc., and his *Paraphrase* of a part of the Book of Job to Parker, the Lord Chancellor.[55] Cibber dedicated *She wou'd and She wou'd not* to the Duke of Ormond who had been commanding the English forces before Cadiz, *The Lady's Last Stake* to the Marquis of Kent, Lord Chamberlain to Her Majesty's household. Addison dedicated his *Remarks on Several Parts of Italy* to Somers, and his opera of *Rosamund* to the Duchess of Marlborough. The third volume of the *Tatler* was inscribed to the Lord Chancellor, Cowper, the fourth to Halifax; the first volume of the *Guardian* to Lieutenant-General Cadogan, Marlborough's friend and second in command, the second to Pulteney, already a man of influence in the House of Commons. The first volume of

---

[52] Published in No. 12 of the *Tatler*.

[53] *The Dunciad*, II, line 205, note. The uncle's edition is inscribed to "Nobilissimo et Præstantissimo Viro Roberto Harleio, Baroni de Wigmore, Comiti Oxonii, et Comiti Mortimero, Magnæ Britanniæ Thesaurario"; the nephew's to "Nobilissimo et Eruditissimo Juveni Edwardo Harleio, Baroni de Wigmore".

[54] Ad Henricum S^t. John, Armig. 1706 (A. Chalmers, op. cit., VIII, p. 384).

[55] *A Paraphrase* On part of the *Book of Job*. To the Right Honourable Lord Parker, Baron of Macclesfield, Lord High Chancellor of Great-Britain, etc. etc. (A. Chalmers, op. cit., XIII, p. 408).—Johnson (*Lives* . . . Young) wittily remarks: "Parker, to whom it is dedicated, had not long, by means of the seals, been qualified for a patron . . . The Dedication, which was only suffered to appear in Tonson's edition . . . is addressed, in no common train of flattery, to a Chancellor, of whom he clearly appears to have had no kind of knowledge."

the *Spectator* was offered to Somers; the second to Halifax; the third to the Right Honourable Henry Boyle, principal Secretary of State; the fourth to Marlborough; the fifth to the Earl of Wharton, ex-Lord-Lieutenant of Ireland; the sixth to the Earl of Sunderland, a former Minister and Marlborough's son-in-law; the seventh to Methuen, English Ambassador at the Court of Savoy.[56]

These Dedications are unquestionably more dignified than those I have quoted earlier. The Author no longer prostrates himself before his patrons as if they were gods, since he has been rubbing shoulders with them, and no longer sees them merely from a distance, and they have lost for him that aura of religious awe which used to surround them amid the radiance of their inaccessible majesty. The patron has in fact resumed human proportions. You cannot, however, habitually indulge in flattery and compliments without forfeiting some fraction of your self-respect and occasionally lapsing into regrettable exaggeration as, for instance, when Addison and Congreve place Halifax on the same plane as Virgil and Homer [57]; when

[56] By a kind of boomerang effect, highly-placed authors became in their turn the target for dedications and petitions. Young dedicated verses to Addison " Secretary to their Excellencies, the Lords Justices " (*On the Late Queen's Death*). See my Bibliography. Swift was courted by a number of his brother-authors (See *Journal to Stella*, especially Jan. 7 and 15, 1712-13).

[57] In *A Letter from Italy* Addison speaks to him of

". . . lines like Virgil's or like yours."

Congreve writes:

"O had Your Genius been to Leisure born,
And not more bound to Aid us than Adorn!
Albion in Verse with antient *Greece* had vy'd,
And gain'd alone a Fame, which, there, seven States divide " . . .
(Dedication to Halifax of his *Miscellaneous Poems*.)

Compare the verses in which Pope caricatures Halifax as Bufo:

"Proud as *Apollo* on his forked hill,
Sate full-blown *Bufo*, puff'd by ev'ry quill;
Fed with soft Dedication all day long,
Horace and he went hand in hand in song,
His library, where busts of Poets dead
And a true *Pindar* stood without a head,
Receiv'd of wits an undistinguish'd race,
Who first his judgment ask'd, and then a place:
Much they extoll'd his pictures, much his seat,
And flatter'd ev'ry day, and some days eat:" etc.
(*Epistle to Dr. Arbuthnot, being the Prologue to the Satires*. Warburton's *Pope*, IV, p. 9.)

Ambrose Philips addresses the Honourable Miss Carteret in her cradle [58]; when Young fills his first verses and dedications with so much extravagant eulogy that he is later ashamed to include them amongst his works.[59]

In addition to this compulsory flattery, the humiliating practice continued of openly offering an author gifts of money. Tickell tells us that Halifax left " no dedicator unrewarded ".[60] When Colley Cibber presented his *Non-Juror* to George I, the King paid him £200.[61] Steele's *Conscious Lovers*, dedicated to the same monarch, earned for its author a purse of £500.

Apart from these drawbacks, the inevitable accompaniment of any form of dependence, and only a repetition of those we have commented on when the author was at the mercy of the Court, the compulsory liaison between literature and politics had its own peculiar inconveniences. In speaking of the *Tatler*, I said that in seeking to be both a political and literary journal it had failed to be either. We may apply the same remark to the writers of this period. They are neither politicians nor authors in the proper sense of either term. Politics and literature were alike the poorer.

Driven to take part in public affairs rather by circumstances than by natural inclination or special talent, the author was not infrequently the victim of the patron's miscalculation. If we are to take Pope's word for it, Prior had little understanding of government or administration.[62] Neither he nor Maynwaring ventured to open his mouth in Parliament.[63] Steele, whose supple and elegant style had tempted his friends to hope that he would prove at least a fluent speaker, made in fact a very poor showing in the House of Commons. Addison failed even

---

[58] See my Bibliography.
[59] For details of these prose and verse flatteries and their suppression, see Johnson's *Lives* . . . Young.
[60] Johnson's *Lives* . . . Halifax.
[61] Genest, II, p. 216.—Note that Cibber was a Whig and had taken up arms for the Revolution of 1688 (Boswell, II, p. 175, note). As its title indicates, the *Non-Juror* was a political work. Cibber was later appointed Poet Laureate and attributed his nomination to this comedy.
[62] Spence, p. 175. [Pope's judgment here is hardly to be relied on. Prior was, as a matter of fact, rather able. B. D.]
[63] " What *Qualities* must we therefore conceive requisite to form a *Publick Speaker*? When we see such Men as the late Earl of *Orrery*, the late Earl of *Shaftesbury*, the late Mr. *Addison*, Mr. *Prior*, and Mr. *Maynwaring*, sit silent; while —— and —— and —— hold forth upon every Subject that falls under Debate ? " (Budgell, *Memoirs of the Life and Character of the late Earl of Orrery*, p. 208).

more lamentably. Filling a higher post than his friend, he himself felt how far his performance fell short of what was expected from a Secretary of State and begged leave to resign.[64]

On the other side, the competing interest of politics was unfortunate and harmful to literature. A distinguished contemporary historian [65] justly wrote:

It is, I think, a recognized truth, almost a harmless commonplace, that Liberty is the very soul of Literature. Let us, however, draw a distinction. In antiquity Liberty was a heroic figure who attuned man's soul to the sublime and whose spirit passed from civil life into his works of art and thought. The passions born of her were eloquent and poetic. Such is not the case with that other Liberty, wiser and more self-controlled, regulated and formalized, such as is recognized in one modern society based on constitutional monarchy, Liberty as we have seen her evolving in England since the Revolution of 1688.

This Liberty gives birth rather to vexatious frictions than to mighty battles, rather to intrigue than to passion. No doubt, in its ultimate repercussions and long-term results, this Liberty raises both the dignity of intelligence and the national well-being. But while she establishes and organizes herself, her machinery is too complex and cumbersome not to overwhelm public attention with a thousand details and rob the soul of that creative impulse and undisturbed independence which foster great gifts in literature and art. The mechanism of a constitutional government, if we may use the phrase, makes too great a demand on the mind to be favourable to genius. It fails to provide either the grandeur or the passion of republican liberty or the leisure offered by a peaceful and glorious monarchy.

---

[64] There is a yarn that in 1706 when the Act of Union was being debated in the House, Addison rose to speak and addressing the Speaker began: "Mr. Speaker, I conceive . . ." and stopped short. A second and a third time he started, but could never get beyond the words: "Mr. Speaker, I conceive . . ." Hereupon another Member is reputed to have said: "Mr. Speaker, I regret to note that the honourable member has thrice conceived and brought forth nothing." There is also a story that when it was his business to announce Queen Anne's death to the Elector of Hanover who was to become George I, Addison was so preoccupied with phrase and style that the drafting of the official letter had to be handed over to a clerk who finished it in a few minutes. Both these anecdotes would appear to have been concocted after the event, but, exaggerated though they may be, they are certainly expressing the essential truth.

[" Mr. Addison could not give out a common order in writing, from his endeavouring always to word it too finely."—so Pope in Spence, ed. cit., p. 175. This remark is corroborated in a footnote, but Pope's hearsay evidence in these matters is not to be trusted: we certainly need not take his word that Prior understood little of government or administration, and facts would seem to contradict this. It might be added here that a good writer is not necessarily a good speaker. Gibbon could not speak in Parliament. B. D.]

[65] Villemain, *Tableau de la littérature au XVIII siecle*, 6e leçon.

From this point of view the parliamentary government of 1688, highly favourable to gifted men of letters whose fortunes it improved, whose influence it created, seems to have been less propitious to the progress of literature.

The demands of parliamentary government, then, absorbed the greater part of a writer's intellectual energy, threw him with no hope of escape into the fever of election contests and political meetings, into pamphlet and newspaper controversy, and thus encumbered literature with a mass of ephemeral work, extravagant political poems, panegyrics, topical and occasional verse, whose futility and banality was patent, most of all to their authors, and whose life was inevitably short. Such political writing or controversial work as allowed its author to put his mark on it might pass muster and survive its maker, if he had been fortunate enough to stumble on some happy stroke of satire or some inspiring subject transcending the petty issues of every day.[66] But are we not entitled to grieve over the time squandered on official duties, the days spent in finding and filing papers, in running offices and appending signatures, and to mourn for the more enduring works of which these occupations have robbed us? People grieved even at the time: " As for *Comedies*, ther's not great Expectation of any thing of that kind, since Mr. *Farquhar's* Death. The two Gentlemen, who would probably always succeed in the *comick* vein, Mr. *Congreve* and Captain *Steele* having Affairs of much greater Importance to take up their Time and Thoughts."[67] Consider what were the " Affairs of much greater Importance " which in 1707 were taking up the time and thought of Steele and Congreve. Steele was editing the *London Gazette*, Congreve was issuing licences for the plying of hackney coaches and the sale of wines. That is to say, both were doing work which an honest civil service clerk could have done at least as well as they. But what civil

---

[66] See Swift's witty attack on Marlborough in the *Examiner*, quoted by Villemain in his 6th lesson.

[Nevertheless, it was politics which brought out Swift's best writing, *The Dissensions in Athens and Rome*, the *Tale of a Tub*, *The Conduct of the Allies*, *The Public Spirit of the Whigs*, *The Last Four Years of Queen Anne's Reign* and the *Drapier Letters*. Moreover, *Gulliver's Travels* is largely political. It is likely that but for politics he would not have written at all, except for admirable light verse. B. D.]

[67] *The Muses Mercury*, Sept. 1707, *Of the new* Opera's *and* Plays *preparing for the* Theatres. See my Bibliography, s.v. Muses Mercury.

[This is probably true of Steele: but Congreve was not busy, other reasons operated there. B. D.]

service clerk could fill their vacant place in literature? How many similar cases awake our regret! Is it not grievous to see Swift harness himself to the party waggon and "toil like a horse" as he phrases it himself,[68] in the daily controversies of Harley and Bolingbroke, leaving a gap of fourteen years [68a] between the *Tale of a Tub* and *Gulliver's Travels*? Is it not grievous to find amongst Addison's collected works almost a whole volume devoted to administrative scribblings which are rightly reprinted out of respect for his memory, but which usurp the place of unwritten work that would have been worthier of posterity? We know, moreover, that if Addison's party had remained in power, it is more than probable that we should have forgone the writings that are his glory. We remember that he was in Ireland as Secretary to the Lord-Lieutenant when Steele in London began the publication of the *Tatler*. Even from Ireland Addison came to his friend's assistance, but it was not until the fall of the Whig Ministry relieved him of his official duties, that he was able actively to collaborate on the paper and make his influence felt in it.[69] So we owe the *Spectator* to the enforced leisure thrust on him by the triumph of the Tories. When Queen Anne died, and the Whigs resumed control of the government, Addison gave up working on the English Dictionary he had begun. His last return to politics similarly cost us the tragedy of *Socrates* which he had been planning and left his *Evidences of the Christian Religion* incomplete.

Writers themselves were well aware how ill literature consorted with administration and public business. Prior jestingly complains that "he hates his Commission of the Customs, because it spoils his wit. He says he dreams of nothing but cockets, and dockets, and drawbacks, and other jargon, words of the Custom House."[70] Addison wrote to Swift that "Multiplicity of Businesse and a long dangerous fit of sicknesse have prevented me from answering the obliging letter you honoured me with some time since, but God be thanked I can not make use of either of these Excuses at present being entirely free both of my office and my Asthma." It was Addison also who wrote to Pope advising him "not to content your self with one half

---

[68] "I toil like a horse, and have hundreds of letters still to read: and squeeze a line out of each, or at least the seeds of a line . . . I have about thirty pages more to write (that is to be extracted) which will be sixty in print." (*Journal to Stella*, Oct. 28, 1712.)   [68a] [Twenty-four. B. D.]
[69] See above, chap. III, note No. 174.
[70] Swift, *Journal to Stella*, March 13, 1711–12.

of the Nation for your Admirers when you might command them all ", and added that " I think you are very happy that you are out of the Fray ".[70a]

But the most serious drawback of the author's position has not yet been mentioned. He was not given his due recognition, he was not appreciated at his true value. " Literature for its own sake had not yet acquired its true place in society." [71] People in those days took no heed of literature as such, but valued only the practical use to which it could be turned. The respect accorded to it was conditioned by circumstance and paid, not to its intrinsic merit, but to its accidental value. It is certain, for instance, that Addison—to quote no other case— owed his success less to his literary gifts than to the first use he made of them,[72] and if he had not been Secretary of State it is unlikely that the Countess of Warwick would have married him.[72a] In short, the writer figured in society not in virtue of being a writer, but as an official and a politician. He was thus himself tempted to consider literature as a means to an end. He devoted himself to his profession, not for its own sake, but for the material advantage it might bring. Swift held his literary reputation cheap, signed none of his works with his name,[73] never thought of publishing a complete edition of them

---

[70a] [Letter to Swift, March 26, 1717–18, and letter to Pope, November 2, 1713. See *Letters of Joseph Addison*, ed. Walter Graham, 1941, pp. 692 and 44. B. D.]

[71] Villemain, 5th Lesson. Villemain is speaking of the reign of Charles II, but his comment is no less applicable to the reign of Queen Anne.

[72] " *Addison* and his Advancement hardly need be mentioned, the Instance is so notorious ; but every body may not so readily recollect that his party-Services contributed more to it than all his laudable Efforts to refine our Manners and perfect our Taste." (Ralph, *The Case of Authors by Profession*, p. 34.)

[72a] [Lady Warwick married Addison before he became Secretary of State. B.D.]

[73] The one exception in his letter to Oxford *A Proposal for Correcting, Improving, and Ascertaining, the English Tongue*. " My letter to Lord Treasurer, about the English tongue, is now printing ; and I suffer my name to be put at the end of it, which I never did before in my life." [*Journal to Stella*, May 10, 1712.)

[This refusal to sign works was hardly indifference. It was possibly because of fear of political pursuit (e.g. *A Tale of a Tub*) and partly to a sort of pride. He knew that everyone that mattered would be aware of his authorship, so why expose his name, especially as he was a parson, to the rabble? Anonymity was by no means singular in those days, even with those who were the most eager for literary fame. Addison loved to write behind a veil, as Gay said (e.g. the *Tatlers* and *Spectators*, and *The Drummer*) and Pope himself often practised it (e.g. *The Dunciad*). B. D.]

and quite obviously used his gift of writing as a springboard to a bishopric : which he never attained. Even those possessed of means enough to need no man's patronage, and free to put all their ambition into writing worthy of being valued by posterity, men like Rowe and Parnell,[74] had not enough pride to stay at home in lonely independence soliciting no favours. Parnell even stooped to a recantation to win the smiles of men in power. Neither they nor their brother-authors had yet achieved that detachment from outward success that makes a man find honour and satisfaction in his work alone, and concentrate his whole ambition on satisfying himself and his readers, becoming, in a word, a man of letters, living by literature and for literature alone. One even went so far as to affect to despise the work that is now his glory. When Voltaire visited England, eager to see everything, people and places, and to mix in English society, he went to call on Congreve. The young and enthusiastic Frenchman naturally spoke of the dramatist's plays ; but Congreve dismissed these as trifles beneath his dignity, and begged his visitor to see in him nothing but a gentleman who lived very contentedly. " Sir," replied Voltaire, who for his part was a man of letters, " if you had the misfortune to be only a gentleman like any other, I should never have come to see you." [75]

The shadows in the picture are finally darkened by uncertainty and disappointment. The man who relies on the favour of a patron, be he who he may, is building on sand ; and no sand is more shifting than the soil of politics. Many discovered this to their sorrow. Addison's friend Budgell, whose

[74] See above, chap. III, note No. 44.—Apart from his ecclesiastical income Parnell had private means.

[75] *Voltaire, Lettres philosophiques*, Letter XIX, Garnier's edition, XXII, p. 161.—A few years later the English author's attitude was different. In recording this interview Johnson sternly says that Congreve had "treated the Muses with ingratitude" and had displayed a "despicable foppery in desiring to be considered not as an author but a gentleman" (*Lives . . . Congreve*).

[It is time this silly story was scotched ; it will, alas ! never be killed. Voltaire, anxious to meet great authors, visited Congreve some twenty years after *The Way of the World* had been written, and wanted to discuss it with Congreve. Heavens, what a boring prospect for Congreve ! What he said in effect was that he would be delighted to talk generally with Voltaire, as an amateur of letters if you will, but not as an expert. One is inclined to agree with Lamb that "the impertinent Frenchman was properly answered ". For a fuller discussion, see my preface to Vol. II of Congreve's *Works* in the World's Classics Edition, reprinted in *Variety of Ways*. B. D.]

tragic end I have already related, lost the posts he had held in Ireland because of an untoward attack on the Lord-Lieutenant, and forfeited all hope of office by asserting his independence in criticism of a Government bill. This was the beginning of his downfall. Opposition to the same bill cost Steele his directorship of Drury Lane theatre. Like Addison, he had lost his other posts when Harley and Bolingbroke came to power. Gay, who had banked on the Tory party, lost his post as secretary and all chance of serious promotion on the death of Queen Anne. On the accession of George I, Prior was accused of treason and imprisoned, forfeiting all his handsome salaries and retaining only his meagre income as a Cambridge fellow. Swift, who had hoped by means of politics to win a bishopric, kept an ever-watchful eye on the health of ailing prelates,[76] addressed himself first to the Whigs and then transferred his allegiance to the Tories, wearily discharging the crushing labour of their controversies,[77] haughtily rejecting their gifts of money, because he hoped for other things at their hand.[78] Swift, flattered, pampered, consulted, influential—a

---

[76] In June, 1710, he writes to Halifax: "Pray, my lord, desire Dr. South" (now on the verge of eighty) "to die about the fall of the leaf, for he has a prebend of Westminster which will make me your neighbour, and a sinecure in the country, both in the Queen's gift, which my friends have often told me would suit me extremely." In November of the same year he again writes to Halifax "that 'if the gentle winter should not carry off Dr. South', perhaps Lord Halifax might so use his credit, that, as Lord Somers thought of him last year for the bishopric of Waterford so my Lord President might now think of him for that of Cork if the incumbent died of the fever he was under". (Forster, *Life of Jonathan Swift*, pp. 259–61.)

So much for the Whigs. Now for the Tories: "We hear your Bishop Hickman is dead; but nobody here will do anything for me in Ireland, so they may die as fast or slow as they please." (*Journal to Stella*, May 29, 1711.) "Did the Bishop of London die in Wexford? poor gentleman!" (Ibid., Aug. 24, 1711.) "The Bishop of Gloucester is not dead, and I am as likely to succeed the Duke of Marlborough as him if he were." (Ibid., Feb. 8, 1711–12.) "The Bishop of Dromore . . . has been very near dying." (Ibid., Jan. 9, 1712–13.)

[77] See *Journal to Stella*, especially Aug. 25, Nov. 15, 1711; July 18, 1712; Jan. 1, 1712–13.

[78] See *Journal to Stella*, Feb. 6, 13 and 16 and March 7, 1710–11.—This refusal of money is often quoted as an example of lofty disinterestedness. But Prévost-Paradol shrewdly divined the underlying motive: "Swift", he says, "indignantly rejected so unworthy a reward for his services. Humbly to accept payment from the Ministry would have been to renounce the hope of a more useful and permanent recognition of his share in its victory. Swift wanted a bishopric." (*Étude sur Jonathan Swift*, p. 40.)

[Towards 1714, perhaps earlier, he hankered after a Deanery rather than a Bishopric—but he wanted it in England. Addison behaved in

small-scale minister in fact—securing posts for his friends but nothing for himself,[79] not even succeeding in getting audience of the Queen,[80] let alone a nomination to his coveted bishopric, ended by becoming only Dean of St. Patrick's in Dublin, and going over to bury in Ireland his thwarted ambition and his savage bitterness against others and against himself.

II

Walpole at the Head of Affairs (1721-42).—Cessation of political patronage just at the moment when the private patronage of the Great has ceased.—The writer's trials: Steele, Ambrose Philips, Savage, Dennis, Boyse, Johnson, etc.

The advent to power of a new Ministry soon showed how unstable were the foundations of an author's good fortune.

In 1721 Walpole became head of the Government.[81] With him the patronage extended by statesmen to anyone who could write, came abruptly to an end.

The motives underlying this new attitude seem to have been varied and complex. Neither George I nor George II was the stuff of which an Augustus is made. George I, a stranger in his own kingdom, was so completely ignorant of English that Walpole, who did not know a word of German, had to converse with him in dog Latin. George II made no effort to conceal his complete contempt for "bainting" and "boetry" as he called them.[82] Walpole felt no more warmly towards

---

exactly the same way as Swift did in rejecting pecuniary reward when he hoped for a Secretaryship of State; see his letter to Halifax of November 30, 1714 (Graham, p. 306). B. D.]

[79] *Journal to Stella*, March 17, 1711-12.
[80] Ibid., Feb. 9, 1710-11.
[81] On Walpole see Coxe, *Memoirs of the Life and Administration of Sir Robert Walpole*; Lecky, I; Lord Mahon, *History of England from the Peace of Utrecht* . . . ; Macaulay, *Essays, Walpole's Letters to Sir Horace Mann*; Walpole (Horace) *Reminiscences*.

[82]   "Alas! few verses touch their nicer ear;
   They scarce can bear their *Laureate* twice a year;
   And justly Caesar scorns the Poet's lays,
   It is to *History* he trusts for Praise."
   (Satire I. To Mr. Fortescue. Warburton's *Pope*, IV, p. 57.)

See also Clerk, *The Works of William Hogarth*, I, p. 181; and Lord Hervey, *Memoirs*, I, chap. XIV and II, chap. XXI.—It is true that Queen Caroline, wife of George II, showed an interest in writers, but whatever her influence and intelligence, she could not fill the place left vacant by the King and his chief Minister.

such matters than did his sovereigns and masters. He was himself indifferently educated and thoroughly unsentimental. Possibly he perceived that political patronage was an artificial system and if continued would give rise to embarrassment. The number of aspiring authors would perpetually increase with the encouragement offered, and the number of jobs available for them would not rise proportionately. Besides, in making a friend of one, you made an enemy of another, and, since spite and malice are emotions more enduring than gratitude, what is precariously gained on one side is lost for certain on the other. Walpole had not failed to notice that no Minister had been more savagely attacked by authors than Halifax, the great patron of men of letters.[83] He decided to ignore the lot, rather than hurt the feelings of one. It is possible that he saw yet another unpleasant result of political patronage: the ambition to achieve distinction, the desire to repay favours received and qualify for greater favour, tempted an author to write and write, and willy nilly to prolong and exacerbate political controversy. This passion for polemics could make little appeal to Walpole, whose maxim of government was *quieta non movere*. Perhaps while constitutional government in England was evolving amid the throes of complex struggle, political controversy had been inevitable and necessary. But once the Hanoverian succession had been accepted, the first difficult phases of its establishment were over; and now the Whig Minister's primary aim was to create an atmosphere of greater calm and stability in public affairs and in the mind of the people. Nor could Walpole overlook the fact that many of the authors who had recently taken a hand in public affairs had been either very ineffective allies—like Addison as Secretary of State, like Prior and Maynwaring in the House of Commons—or even very embarrassing ones, subject to fits of over-independence like Steele and Budgell. He was fond of saying that writers were ill-adapted to practical life, they tended to trust theory rather than experience and were guided by principles invalid in everyday affairs. And in Queen Anne's reign, when he was already a member of the Government but not yet its chief, he was reluctant to endorse Congreve's appointment as Commissioner of Customs, opining that he would prove to have "no head for business". So when he himself became head of the Government he preferred to choose as collaborators men who were administrators pure and

[83] Macaulay, *History*, chap. XXIV.

simple. If he then needed press-support for his measures, he either did his own writing [84] or entrusted it to hack scribblers whom he crudely hired—men like Concanen, Arnall, Welsted or Henley—who had too little brain to possess opinions of their own, or be tempted to differ from the views of the employer from whom they drew their pay.[85] The main reason, however, which dictated his procedure, was undoubtedly his conviction that the House of Commons was daily growing in power, and was becoming more and more the centre of Government. Walpole was a man of positive and practical views, who possessed great parliamentary gifts. He devoted his entire attention and activity to Parliament [86]; and the result proved how sound his judgment was. Never was Minister pursued with more unrelenting violence or by more distinguished and dangerous opponents; never before had a Minister accorded such freedom of speech to his enemies,[87] and yet despite the freedom and fury of their attacks, despite the strength of an opposition in which were ranged men like Bolingbroke, Carteret, Chesterfield, Pulteney, Wyndham, Pitt, Lyttelton, Swift, Gay, Pope, Fielding, Thomson, Glover—Walpole governed England for more than twenty consecutive years.

[84] I have already mentioned his political writings, chap. IV, note No. 33.
[85] Walpole paid more than £50,000 in the course of ten years to writers supporting his administration (Lecky, I, p. 372). Arnall boasted of having made £10,997 6s. 8d. in four years by his political writing (Scott's Edition of *Swift*, vol. XII, pp. 103-4).—
> "A pamphlet in Sir Bob's defence
> Will never fail to bring in pence:
> Nor be concerned about the sale,
> He pays his workmen on the nail."
> (Swift, *On Poetry: A Rhapsody*, 1733. Ibid., XIV, p. 334.)

On Walpole's hireling writers, see also Pope's *Dunciad*, especially II, lines 305-14.
[86] When it was learnt in England that Louis XV had pensioned Crébillon, the following epigram (which I find quoted in Belsham, II, p. 54) became current:
> "At reading this, great Walpole shook his head;
> How! wit and genius help a man to bread;
> With better skill we pension and promote;
> None eat with us who cannot give a vote."

Swift called Walpole: "Bob, the poet's foe." (*An Epistle to Mr. Gay*, 1731.)
[87] In one of his speeches Walpole remarked that no Government had prosecuted so few pamphleteers and no Government had ever had provocation to prosecute so many.

Whatever were the motives which actuated the new Minister's conduct, the patronage hitherto so extravagantly extended to authors ceased completely. Suddenly they found themselves hurled from their heights of prosperity and success. Everything combined to make the fall a cruel one : it was unforeseen and carried no compensation. But yesterday, Whigs and Tories had alike been the author's patrons. To-day, Tories and Whigs alike failed him. The Whigs, represented by Walpole, offered nothing, and Walpole remained omnipotent Minister from 1721 to 1742. The prolongation of his reign rendered the Tories for their part impotent. Having neither pensions nor posts at their command, the most they could offer was a meagre diet of unfulfilled promises. " St. James's would give nothing ; Leicester House had nothing to give." [88] When he lost the patronage of the politicians, the unfortunate author did not regain the patronage of the aristocracy. The nobleman's importance had yielded to that of the politician and his tradition of literary patronage had been broken.

So there was our author, abruptly planted down to face the facts of existence, thrown back wholly on his own strength and his own resources. His only hope was to get down to business and write for the publishers. But the publishing business was still in its infancy, undeveloped, only half awake, and with but little capital behind it. To make matters worse, the number of authors had been much swollen by reason of the alluring prospects opened to professional literature in the two preceding reigns. The whole crowd of needy and disillusioned writers competed for booksellers' contracts, besieged reviews and magazines with offers of service, and thus put themselves at the publishers' mercy. The publisher naturally took advantage of the position to sweat and exploit the whole scribbling pack. The work he demanded of his victim was often peculiarly laborious and sometimes very odd.

In one of his earliest plays [89] Fielding shows us three luckless devils, Dash, Blotpage and Quibble, whom a publisher lodges in his house and compels to write the livelong day on a starvation

---

[88] Macaulay's *Essays*, Samuel Johnson.—After breaking with his father George II in 1737, the Prince of Wales, in a spirit of opposition set himself up in his little court as a patron of literature. But his means were limited and his protégés but few : I can think of no more than three : Lyttelton, Mallet and Thomson.—Thomson enjoyed £100 a year, Mallet £200, and Lyttelton, who was his secretary probably a little more.

[89] *The Author's Farce* (1730).

diet of "good milk porridge, very often twice a day, which is good wholesome food and proper for students". Here are some scraps of their instructive conversation:

Dash: Pox on 't, I'm as dull as an ox, tho' I have not a bit of one within me. I have not dined these two days, and yet my head is as heavy as any alderman's or lord's. I carry about me symbols of all the elements; my head is as heavy as water, my pockets are as light as air, my appetite is as hot as fire, and my coat is as dirty as earth.
Blot: Lend me your Bysshe (i.e. a rhyming dictionary), Mr. Dash, I want a rhime for wind.
Dash: Why there's blind, and kind, and behind, and find, and mind: it is of the easiest termination imaginable; I have had it four times in a page.
Blot: None of those words will do.
Dash: Why then you may use any that end in ond, or and, or end. I am never so exact: if the two last letters are alike, it will do very well. Read the verse.
Blot: "Inconstant as the seas, or as the wind."
Dash: What would you express in the next line?
Blot: Nay, that I don't know, for the sense is out already. I would say something about inconstancy.
Dash: I can lend you a verse and it will do very well too.

"Inconstancy will never have an end"

End rhimes very well with wind.
Blot: It will do well enough for the middle of a poem.
Dash: Ay, Ay, anything will do well enough for the middle of a poem. If you can but get twenty good lines to place at the beginning for a taste, it will sell very well.
Quib: So that, according to you, Mr. Dash, a poet acts pretty much on the same principles with an oister-woman.
Dash: Pox take your simile, it has set my chaps a watering.

At this point the publisher arrives on the scene, scolds them all and complains of their sloth. One ought by now to have finished the answer to a letter which was in fact of his own composition. He points out that it is "harder to write on this side the question, because it is the wrong side". To which his employer retorts: "Not a jot. So far on the contrary that I have known some authors choose it as the properest to show their genius." Another has to finish an account of a murder and is just adding a few moral reflexions as preface to it. Then there is a ghost which must be finished. The last was a pale one, "then let this be a bloody one". Next, a prospectus for *Bailey's English Dictionary*, but this should not be a lengthy job for it will suffice to copy the proposals for printing *Bayle's Dictionary* —"The same words will do for both." Someone's obituary is also on the stocks, but it seems that the fellow is not dead, so that must be held up pending better news. Some allowance must of course be made for dramatic exaggeration; but the accuracy of the main lines of Fielding's picture is established by other contemporary evidence.

Cave, the owner of the *Gentleman's Magazine*, used to buy Boyse's verses at so much a hundred. After some time, gambling on the poet's poverty, he would insist for good measure on having " a long hundred ", that is to say ten or twenty extra lines for nothing.[90] Smollett tells of an author of twenty-four living in an attic who wrote, at a guinea a sheet, historical works which another man published under his own name.[91] In *Joseph Andrews* Mr. Wilson is represented as spending several years in translating for a bookseller, exercising no part of his body but his right arm. The result was illness and disability, and his employer denounced him to his colleagues as a lazy-bones.[92] The hack translators, whom the bookseller Curll kept permanently employed, used to work without remission and to sleep three in a bed.[93] Payment was always precarious. Most writers were reduced to living in misery from day to day, in everlasting anxiety about the morrow, at the mercy of moneylenders to whom they had to pledge their wages, in perpetual dread of the bailiff and the gaol. The chronicle of literature became a collection of strange adventures which far exceed anything to be found in what the French call Bohemia.

Steele, Savage and Ambrose Philips were strolling together in London one evening. A kindly merchant, apologizing for the liberty he was taking, warned them that he had noticed some suspicious characters at the end of the street, who looked uncommonly like bailiffs. If any of them was afraid of bailiffs, he suggested their altering their course. The three asked no questions but made off as fast as they could, without even waiting to thank their benefactor.[94]

[90] Lawrence, *Life of Fielding*, pp. 125-8. See also Boyse's Life in the collection known as *The British Poets* (see my Bibliography, s.v. Boyse); and Boswell, VIII, pp. 410-11; IX, p. 46; X, pp. 63-4.—Boyse was the son of a Nonconformist minister in Dublin. He wrote a poem called *The Deity* which Fielding paid him the compliment of quoting in *Tom Jones* (book VII, chap. I).
[91] *Humphrey Clinker*. This novel came out in 1771, but Smollett began his literary career in 1739.
[92] Fielding: *Joseph Andrews*, book III, chap. III.
[93] Amory, *The Life of John Buncle*, II, pp. 381 ff.
[94] N. Drake, *Essays . . . Illustrative of the Tatler*, etc., I, p. 180.

It was Steele too who once requested Savage to call for him at his house at an early hour. Savage was punctual and found Steele already awaiting him and a carriage at the door. They drove off together and the carriage stopped at a small tavern where the two authors closeted themselves in a private room. Savage was not a little mystified by all this curious procedure, and Steele explained that he wanted to publish a pamphlet and had asked Savage to come and act as his amanuensis. They set to work, Steele dictating and Savage writing until dinner was served. Savage was surprised at the meanness of the entertainment and ventured to ask for wine, which Steele ordered with some reluctance. When dinner was over, they set to work again and completed their task in the course of the afternoon. Savage supposed their work was now done, and expected that his host would call for the bill and set his guest free. But Steele now confessed that he had no money and that he must get his manuscript sold before he could pay for the dinner. So Savage was obliged to scour the booksellers and sell his friend's prose, for which after a good deal of trouble he secured two guineas. Steele had left home solely to evade his creditors and had written his pamphlet to pay for his meal.[95]

Dennis took endless pains to keep clear of the duns and creditors who were a perpetual threat to him, but he imprudently relaxed his precautions one Saturday evening in a wine shop. For two long hours he stayed, not daring to make a movement or to say a word lest he should attract attention to himself, and doing his best to remain concealed. Midnight struck at last and the author rose triumphantly to his feet crying : " Now Sir, bailiff or no, I snap my fingers at you ; you have no hold on me." His distress finally became so acute that his fellow-authors organized a benefit performance for him at the theatre.[96] Of Savage, Johnson writes :

> During a considerable part of the time in which he was employed upon this performance (i.e. writing his tragedy of Sir Thomas Overbury), he was without lodging, and often without meat ; nor had he any other conveniences for study than the fields or the street allowed him ; there he used to walk and form his speeches, and afterwards

---

[95] Johnson, *Lives* . . . Savage.—I know of course that Steele was never at any time a model of prudence or economy. But up to the period we are now discussing, his posts had enabled him to avoid any distressing situations. Unemployed, bankrupt and abandoned by his party, he died in poverty and oblivion in 1729.
[96] *Biographia Dramatica*, s.v. Dennis (John).

step into a shop, beg for a few moments the use of pen and ink, and write down what he had composed, upon paper which he had picked up by accident.[97]

He kept alive in the most miserable fashion on sums of money which his poverty or his importunity extorted from one person or another, from actors or fellow-writers, from Lord Tyrconnel, from Walpole, from Queen Caroline. When such succour failed him, he lived from hand to mouth, eating when his friends invited him to share a meal—which the shabbiness of his clothes often prevented their doing—sleeping where he could, in a basement lodging, in a noisome cellar, amongst the dregs of the population. Often he was too poor to afford the luxury of such quarters, and walked the streets of London till fatigue overcame him, and he slept in summer on a bulk in the open air, in winter with thieves and beggars among the warm ashes of a glass-house. He was ultimately arrested and imprisoned at the instance of his creditors —his sole fortune at the time was threepence-halfpenny. He died in prison and had to be buried at the generous keeper's expense.[98]

Boyse would spend whole days in bed for lack of outdoor clothes, when his coat, his shirt and even his sheets were at the pawnbroker's. He used to wrap himself in his blanket, in which he had made a hole so that he could put his arm out to write on his knee. At other times, when important items of his wardrobe were in pawn, he would replace his vanished shirt with paper collar and cuffs, and disguise his lack of breeches by carefully buttoning down his coat. He was often without food for days at a time, witness the following letter and Latin verses which he addressed to his publisher from a sponging-house:

I am every moment threatened to be turned out here, because I have not money to pay for my bed two nights past, which is usually paid beforehand . . . I hope therefore you will have the humanity to send me half a guinea for support, till I finish your papers in my hands. . . . I humbly entreat your answer, having not tasted anything since Tuesday evening I came here, and my coat will be taken off my back for the charge of the bed, so that I must go into prison naked, which is too shocking for me to think of.

> Hodie, teste cælo summo,
> Sine pane, sine nummo,
> Sorte positus infeste,
> Scribo tibi dolens mæste.

---

[97] Johnson, *Lives* . . . Savage.
[98] Ibid.; and Boswell, I, p. 187; X, p. 122.

Fame, bile, tumet jecur :
Urbane,⁹⁹ mitte opem, precor ;
Tibi enim cor humanum
Non a malis alienum :
Mihi mens nec male grata,
Pro a te favore dato.

Ex gehenna debitoria.
Vulgo, domo spongiatoria.

In the early days of his literary life, Samuel Johnson himself sometimes spent the night wandering through the streets of London for lack of a lodging, and at times went fasting for forty-eight hours on end. At such times he avoided passing near Porridge Lane, for the delicious odours of the cook-shops were intolerably tantalizing to an empty stomach.¹⁰⁰ When he ate, he spent fourpence-halfpenny a day on food. If he was able to allow himself a feast he " dined very well for eightpence with very good company . . . It used to cost the rest a shilling, for they drank wine ; but I had a cut of meat for sixpence, and bread for a penny, and gave the waiter a penny ; so that I was quite well served, nay better than the rest, for they gave the waiter nothing." ¹⁰¹

Of the authors whom Smollett presents in *Humphrey Clinker*, some have no known domicile, the others go to prison. They eat in nauseating cookhouses, sleep under the stars on a bench, or under a church porch with ladies of the gutter. Their publisher brings them together round his table on a Sunday, the only day when the bailiff has no hold over them. The profession of literature, which a few short years before led a man so easily to prosperity and social position, if not to wealth and honour,

⁹⁹ In his Diary Cave called himself " Mr. Urban ".
¹⁰⁰ Mrs. Thrale said to a friend one day, in front of Johnson, that she did not like roast goose, because it smells so when roasting. " But you, Madam," replies the Doctor, " have been at all times a fortunate woman, having always had your hunger so forestalled by indulgence, that you never experienced the delight of smelling your dinner beforehand." " Which pleasure," answered I pertly, " is to be enjoyed in perfection by such as have the happiness to pass through Porridge Island of a morning."——" Come, come," says he gravely, " Let's have no sneering at what is serious to so many : hundreds of your fellow-creatures, dear lady, turn another way, that they may not be tempted by the luxuries of Porridge Island to wish for gratifications they are not able to obtain : you are certainly not better than all of *them* ; give God thanks that you are happier." Mrs. Piozzi, quoted by Boswell, IX, p. 40.—" Porridge Island was a mean street in London, filled with cook-shops for the poorer inhabitants " (Croker's footnote).
¹⁰¹ See Boswell, *passim*, especially I, pp. 112-14, 151, 187 ; V, pp. 8-9 ; IX, pp. 40 and 235.

now offered nothing but a dreary prospect of struggle, privation and disappointed hope. Under Queen Anne, an author was a gentleman, fashionably dressed, living a regular and reputable life, provided with a fixed income, cutting a figure in the drawing-room, playing a rôle in the state. Now he was a wretched outcast, tattered, dirty and starving,[102] living how or where no one knew. There was practically no distinction between author and beggar. As a natural consequence the writer's trade fell cruelly in public estimation. It seemed a compendium of human misery, one of the most cheerless careers on which a man could embark. When Johnson first arrived in London " Mr. Wilcox, the bookseller, on being informed by him that his intention was to get his livelihood as an author, eyed his robust frame attentively, and with a significant look said, ' You had better buy a porter's knot.' "[103] Pope writes :

> One Cell there is, conceal'd from vulgar eye,
> The Cave of Poverty and Poetry.[104]

Another contemporary wrote :

Hath Literature been thy choice and thy occupation and hast thou food and raiment? be contented, be thankful, be amazed at thy good fortune—Art thou dissatisfied and desirous of other things, go and make 12 votes at an Election—It shall do thee more service, than to make a Commentary on the 12 Minor Prophets.[105]

Johnson applied Virgil's lines to the literary profession :

> Vestibulum ante ipsum, primisque in faucibus Orci
> Luctus et ultrices posuere cubilia Curæ ;
> Pallentesque habitant Morbi, tristisque Senectus,
> Et Metus, et malesuada Fames et turpis Egestas,
> Terribiles visu formæ ; Lethumque Laborque.[106]

Finally Hogarth, the painter, in a famous picture [107] showed a poet living in a miserable hovel wrapped in a dressing-gown as he worked, while his wife was mending his only pair of breeches, and interrupted in his work by the demands of a creditor.

The distressing element in such a disorganized life, especially when it overtakes a whole class of people, is, not so much the suffering it inflicts, as the consequences it entails. In the first

---

[102] See Pope's letter to Burlington and his amusing account of how the bookseller Lintot calmed an irate critic by offering to share his modest dinner with him. Warburton's Edition of *Pope*, VII, p. 336.
[103] Boswell, I, p. 112 note.
[104] *Dunciad*, I, lines 33-4. See ibid., II, lines 419-28.
[105] Jortin, quoted by Genest, I, p. 416.
[106] Boswell, V, p. 43.
[107] *The Distressed Poet*, which dates from 1736.

place, once a man has been divorced from the routine of well-regulated living, he is almost incapable of reconciling himself to it again, unless he has unusual energy or unusual luck. Bitter as is the first experience of uneasy and ill-ordered life, he quickly becomes accustomed to it; he grows less fastidious; privation, humiliation even, become less painful; he resigns himself to them and at last ceases to notice them. Carelessness and improvidence become principles of conduct, and happy-go-lucky irregularity a habit and a tradition. Whatever may be the trials and the uncertainties of an existence unfettered by rule, they are often accompanied by a feeling of independence which is not without a certain charm, and which a man may ultimately learn to prize. We have seen the same thing in France where Bohemian life has found affectionate chroniclers, who even sing its praises.

Boyse's friends, scarcely less poor than he, once clubbed together to redeem his clothes from the pawnbroker (Johnson later says that the sum was made up of sixpenny pieces "at a time when sixpence meant a great deal to me") only to find him pawning them again two days later. Another time, when he was almost dying of hunger, they gave him money to buy himself a dinner; but he could not enjoy his meat without kitchen, and he spent half a guinea on mushrooms and truffles which he enjoyed in bed, since he had not at the moment a shirt to his back. Nothing could wean Savage from his irregular life. One day when the Goddess of Wealth smiled on him, he hastened off to buy himself a gold-embroidered cloak in which he proudly masqueraded, though his bare feet were peeping through the holes in his shoes. Lord Tyrconnel took him to live with him and gave him an annual allowance of £200 to boot. Savage turned his host's house into a tavern, acted as if he were the master of his lodging, feasted boisterously with chance acquaintances, wallowing with them in punch and wine, singing and loudly making merry till sunrise, until at last he was naturally shown the door. At another time Queen Caroline granted him a pension of £50 a year, enough in those days to supply him with daily bread. But each time the money was paid, Savage disappeared for two entire months, without telling his friends where he was going, and as soon as the windfall was exhausted he returned penniless to his beloved hand-to-mouth existence. Towards the end of his life, some brother-authors combined to subscribe a considerable sum, sufficient to provide a regular and peaceful existence for him, on condition that he would leave London and settle down quietly by the seaside. Savage set out, but stopped halfway and resumed his usual disorderly way of life in Bristol.

This haphazard way of living has other and graver results. It is rare to find that it does not corrupt the character of those who adopt it. Men of firm principle like Johnson are unaffected ; but others, and inevitably a vastly greater number, yield and become demoralized. Living outside the pale of society, they gradually and unconsciously begin to despise its laws ; irregular life begets easy morals. Living by their wits, they cease little by little to distinguish the line that separates the ingenious expedient from the barefaced fraud. Their self-respect is lowered, their conscience becomes less sensitive, their principles less rigid.

Smollett's *Humphrey Clinker* portrays a group of authors who would appear to have been drawn from life. The philosopher amongst them has been sent down from Oxford as an atheist, and prosecuted for blaspheming the Sabbath in a wine-shop. He undertakes to refute Bolingbroke's metaphysical writings. The Scotsman gives lessons in English pronunciation ; the man from Piedmont writes a satire on the English poets ; a cockney, who is the victim of " agrophobia ", and does not know Indian corn from rice, composes a treatise on agriculture. An Irishman publishes a pamphlet in favour of a Minister in the hope of receiving some token of gratitude ; when disappointed, he passes off his pamphlet as the Minister's own production and writes a reasoned refutation. Another, who has never ventured to show his face outside the privileged quarters where debtors of the day were safe from the bailiff, writes an account of travels in Europe and Asia. In Fielding's portrait gallery [108] there is an author who offers his publisher a pamphlet against the Ministry. This is rejected because two others are already in the press. He then suggests a defence of the Ministry, but this is similarly rejected because it would command no sale. So he falls back on an annotated edition of the *Æneid*. " But I am afraid I am not qualified for a translator, for I understand no language but my own."—" What, and translate Virgil ? "—" Alas, I translated him out of Dryden."—" Lay by your hat, sir—lay by your hat, and take your seat immediately. Not qualified !—thou art as well versed in thy trade as if thou hadst laboured in my garret these ten years ! " In his admiration the publisher becomes familiar and addresses him with " thou ".

" Translators . . ." the publisher Lintot said to Pope, " are

[108] *The Author's Farce.*

the saddest pack of rogues in the world : in a hungry fit, they'll swear they understand all the languages of the universe. I have known one of them take down a Greek book upon my counter, and cry, Ah, this is Hebrew, I must read it from the latter end." One of the translators whom the same publisher had employed and commissioned to make an English translation of Lucretius only wrote the first page himself and then simply copied out an existing translation.[109]

It was not only in literary matters that dishonesty was practised. Authors frequently transgressed the frontiers of professional fraud. They would sometimes publish the prospectus of, and accept subscriptions for, a work which never appeared. Fielding's *Index* sends the publisher *Bookweight* the draft of a prospectus asking him to print five hundred copies with the same number of receipt forms, for a new translation of Cicero's *De Natura Deorum* and the *Tusculan Disputations*. " I am sorry ", says the publisher, " you have undertaken this, for it prevents a design of mine."—" Indeed, sir, it does not ; for you see all of the book that I ever intend to publish. It is only a handsome way of asking one's friends for a guinea." [110]

Savage and Boyse spent part of their lives announcing and discounting new editions of their works. A certain Cooke, who had translated Hesiod, lived for twenty years on a projected translation of Plautus.[111] These swindles became so general that people of standing formed a defensive alliance against importunate petitioners, and entered into a formal agreement with each other not to subscribe in advance to any work.[112] Breach of this agreement entailed a fine. Mallet undertook to write a Life of the Duke of Marlborough and on this understanding accepted for many years a pension from his family. But he never wrote a line.[113] Smollett tells of a certain author who borrowed a horse on the pretext of having to make a journey. He went off at once and sold it and ended by stealing his publisher's riding-boots.[114] Fielding presents a translator who ultimately found his way to prison for " the rogue had a trick of translating out of the shops as well as the languages ".[115] Savage helped himself from the shelves of Lord Tyrconnel's library, and his host

---

[109] Pope's *Letter to the Earl of Burlington*.
[110] *The Author's Farce*. [111] Boswell, IV, p. 26.
[112] Fielding, *Joseph Andrews*, book III, chap. 3.
[113] Johnson, *Lives* . . . Mallet.
[114] *Humphrey Clinker*. [115] *The Author's Farce*.

used to find handsomely bound books of his, stamped with his arms, displayed for sale in second-hand bookshops. This same wastrel committed manslaughter in a low drinking den and was condemned to death. Thanks to powerful influence, he was let off with six months' imprisonment. It is more than likely that this man—over whose hard lot so many tears have been wasted—was an impostor who deceived innocent Johnson and all his contemporaries by posing as the illegitimate son of the Countess of Macclesfield. We are probably justified in interpreting his dramatic and touching story as nothing but an ingenious fiction cleverly devised to blackmail a great lady by importunity, insult and the threat of scandal.[116]

Having already steeply declined in public favour, the literary profession was on the verge of completely forfeiting all respect and esteem.

III

Dryden and the first English publisher, Jacob Tonson.—The publisher's rôle n literature.—Dryden's translation of Virgil.—His Fables.—Literature increasingly remunerative

While the majority of authors were pleasantly drifting downstream with the placid current of political patronage, there was —fortunately for literature—one amongst them whom the Revolution robbed of all hope of post or pension, and who, thus driven to rely solely on himself, prepared a better future for his brother-writers.

We opened our study with Dryden, and to him we now return. Having, as a Roman Catholic, forfeited his position of Historiographer Royal and Poet Laureate, and also his post in the Customs, being deprived of all useful patronage, now that those whom he had so vigorously opposed had come to power, he set himself to work again with renewed energy—in defiance of shattered hopes and the onset of old age. His genius faltered neither under the weight of years nor the bitterness of trial. He turned first to drama, but with dubious success and inadequate reward. Then, adopting another line, he linked his fortunes with those of his publisher, Jacob Tonson.

---

[116] See W. Moy Thomas's researches in *Notes and Queries*, Nov. and Dec. 1858, pp. 361, 385, 425 and 445.

I have already mentioned Tonson, an interesting figure, who deserves our closer attention, for with him a new character enters the literary scene.

The production of every literary work involves two distinct processes : an intellectual act and a commercial transaction. As long as the reading public was confined to a restricted circle, the commercial transaction was of little importance. The author was himself responsible for extracting from his labour the reward he was entitled to claim. He relied little on publisher or purchasers ; he dedicated his book and looked for a gift in return. The printer-publisher played an altogether minor part : it was his modest place to print a limited number of copies, without incurring much risk or aspiring to much profit. But as the number and discernment of readers increased, and people began eagerly to look out for and to purchase books, the author saw a vision of more serious and more legitimate advantage and his thoughts turned to the buyers of his books. The more numerous book-buyers became, the more impossible it grew for him to keep directly in touch with them, without squandering thought and energy, which ought properly to be devoted to his writing. The proprietor of a small piece of land can well work it single-handed ; if his property increases, he needs a steward. The author similarly requires an intermediary between himself and his reader, and the reader equally requires an intermediary between himself and the writer of books. It is at this point that the duties of a publisher become changed and enlarged, and he himself a necessary and most important agent for the intellectual producer. It must be his care to study the literary market ; to keep the author informed of the tastes and inclinations of readers ; to seek out for the reader works of value and writers of talent. If he has rivals in the business, he will try to secure good authors to himself by paying them generously. At the same time, foreseeing a certain sale for his publications, he forges ahead, becomes adventurous and risks his capital.

It is to Tonson's credit that he first scented the breath of a new era opening for literature, and at once foresaw that publishing was destined to play an important rôle therein. Taking intelligent advantage of favourable circumstances as they arose, he skilfully contrived to prepare the way for, and ensure the success of, the new development. With him, and largely thanks to him, the publisher proper evolved out of the printer-bookseller.

Jacob Tonson [117] was the son of a London barber-surgeon who at his death bequeathed £100 to each of his children. Jacob set up as a publisher " at the Judge's Head in Chancery Lane, near Fleet Street " in 1678, at a moment when his fellows were cutting a poor enough figure in the world, and when rigorous legislation, and still more the scarcity of readers, imposed such severe limits on their activities that they were solely—and that very modestly—printers and booksellers, occupying a very subordinate place in literature.[118] Divining that the refined literary taste of the Court, combined with the mental awakening produced by political controversy, might prove the herald of better days, Tonson was the first to display serious, though still very cautious, publishing initiative. I have already spoken [119] of his timid ventures with Dryden's plays, his purchase of *Paradise Lost* and particularly of his partnership with Dryden in the publication, before the Revolution of 1688, of two volumes of *Miscellanies*. After the Revolution, the re-establishment of political calm and the success of his first tentative experiments inspired Tonson with courage. He had gained experience, he felt sure of his readers and sure of himself, and his spirit of enterprise gradually grew stronger. In 1688 he published his reprint of *Paradise Lost* and in 1693 translations by Dryden of Juvenal, of Persius and of other Latin authors. At the same time he suggested to Dryden to bring out a third volume of *Miscellanies*, which was soon followed by a fourth.[120] Meantime public opinion was stirring, which ultimately led to the emancipation of the Press.[121] The abolition of restrictive legislation gave new impetus to the book-trade ; the number of booksellers quickly swelled : a few years later Dunton [122] mentioned more than 130 in London alone, which marks a great advance on the figures for Charles II's reign.[123] More and more elated by propitious fortune, Tonson

---

[117] On Tonson, see Knight, *Shadows of the Old Booksellers*, pp. 48 ff., and Malone's *Life of Dryden*, pp. 523 ff.

[118] See above, pp. 114 ff.

[119] See above, pp. 114 ff. and pp. 192 ff.

[120] *Examen Poeticum* : being The Third Part of Miscellany Poems ; *The Annual Miscellany* : for The Year 1694, Being The Fourth Part of Miscellany Poems. See my Bibliography, s.v. Dryden.

[121] Macaulay, *History*, chap. XXI.

[122] *The Life and Errors* . . . pp. 280 ff.

[123] See above, pp. 114 ff. For all its immense advantages, the abolition of the Censorship had one serious drawback. The preliminary authorization to publish, confirmed the author's property rights in a book. Its abolition left the field open to unauthorized reprints, and there were plenty of people

suggested to Dryden a more ambitious undertaking than they had previously ventured on : a verse translation of the complete works of Virgil.[124] The poet accepted the suggestion, and after three years' work his translation appeared in 1697.

The English Virgil was published by subscription. It was the fourth publication to appear under a new system, which Tonson had successfully adopted in his reprint of *Paradise Lost*.[125] The venture was ingeniously organized to attract subscribers and obviate miscalculations. There were two series of subscribers. The first paid five guineas, the second, two. The five-guinea subscriber was offered a special bait : his copy was enriched with many engravings, under one of which his own coat of arms appeared. The name of the two-guinea subscriber was modestly recorded on a list published with the translation. It is noteworthy that under this subscription system the author was entitled to a proportion of the sums subscribed. It was therefore directly to his interest to recruit as many subscribers as he could, and bring his personal influence to bear on his friends and patrons. The publisher thus enlisted the author as a partner in his enterprise, and made him shoulder a part of the work and of the risk entailed.

In this way, while showing himself more enterprising than his fellows, Tonson continued to display his prudence and commercial acumen. In every venture he proceeded most cautiously, narrowly weighing expenditure and risk, and keeping a watchful eye on his own interest. Dryden, for his part, was no less energetic and alert. We get the feeling that both were exploring uncharted regions, on the look out for surprise and misadventure at every step. This was the beginning of the relations between publisher and author, relations marked at first neither by great mutual confidence, nor by excess of courtesy.

---

eager to take advantage of this loophole in the law. Complaints against the " pirates ", as they were called, were frequent. See in particular Smith, quoted in Johnson's *Lives* . . . John Philips ; No. 101 of the *Tatler* and the Preface to the Second Part of *Robinson Crusoe*. But it's an ill wind that blows nobody good : these pirated editions, by offering readers the opportunity to buy cheap, helped to spread a taste for reading.

[124] In the Dedication of his *Æneid*, Dryden himself states that the idea was Tonson's.

[125] The earlier three were : Walton's *Polyglot Bible*, 1654–7 (Nichols, *Literary Anecdotes*, IV, p. 8) ; the reprint of *Paradise Lost*, 1688, and à Wood's *Athenæ Oxonienses*, 1691 (Malone, *Life of Dryden*, p. 234).

As the following letter shows, the publisher haggled over lines and prices :

Letter from Jacob Tonson to John Dryden, Esq. (probably written in Jan. or Feb. 1692–3 **).*

SIR,

I have here returned ye Ovid, wch I read wth a great deal of pleasure, and think nothing can be more entertaining ; but by this letter you find I am not soe well satisfied as perhaps you might think. I hope at ye same time the matter of fact I lay down in this letter will appear grounds for it, and wch I beg you wou'd consider of ; and then I believe I shall at least bee excused.

You may please, S^r, to remember, that upon my first proposal about ye 3^d Miscellany, I offer'd fifty pounds, and talk'd of several authors, without naming Ovid. You ask'd if it shou'd not be guyneas, and said I shou'd not repent it ; upon wch I imediately comply'd, and left it wholly to you what, and for ye quantity too : and I declare it was the farthest in ye world from my thoughts that by leaving it to you I shou'd have the less. Thus the case stood when you went into Essex. After I came out of Northamptonshire I wrote to you, and reseived a letter dated Monday Oct. 3^d, 92, from wch letter I now write word for word what followes :

" I' am translating about six hundred lines, or somewhat less, of ye first book of the Metamorphoses. If I cannot get my price, wch shall be twenty guynnees, I will translate the whole book ; wch coming out before the whole translation, will spoyl Tate's undertakings. 'Tis one of the best I have ever made, and very pleasant. This, wth Heroe and Leander, and the piece of Homer (or, if it be not enough, I will add more), will make a good part of a Miscellany."

Those, S^r, are ye very words, and ye onely ones in that letter relating to that affair ; and ye Monday following you come to town.—After your arrivall you shew'd Mr. Motteaux what you had done (wch he told me was to ye end of ye story of Daphnis), [Daphne], and demanded, as you mention'd in your letter, twenty guyneas, wch that bookseller refus'd. Now, S^r, I the rather believe there was just soe much done, by reason ye number of lines you mention in yor letter agrees wth ye quantity of lines that soe much of ye first book makes ; wch upon counting ye Ovid, I find to be in ye Lattin 566, in ye English 759 ; and ye bookseller told me there was noe more demanded of him for it.—Now, S^r, what I entreat you wou'd please to consider of is this : that it is reasonable for me to expect at least as much favour from you as a strange bookseller ; and I will never believe y^t it can be in yor nature to use one ye worse for leaveing it to you ; and if the matter of fact as I state it be true (and upon my word what I mention I can shew you in yor letter), then pray, S^r, consider how much dearer I pay then you offered it to ye other bookseller ; for he might have

---

* The Third Miscellany was published in July 1693.

had to ye end of ye story of Daphnis for 20 guynneas, wch is in yor
translation 759 lines ;
And then suppose 20 guyneas more for the
same number . . . . 759 lines ;
that makes for 40 guyneas . . . . . . 1518 lines ;
and all that I have for fifty guyneas are but 1446 ; soe that, if I have noe more, I pay 10 guyneas above 40, and have 72 lines less for fifty, in proportion, than the other bookseller shou'd have had for 40, at ye rate you offered him ye first part. This is, Sir, what I shall take as a great favour if you please to think of. I had intentions of letting you know this before ; but till I had paid ye money, I would not ask to see the book ; nor count the lines, least it shou'd look like a design of not keeping my word. When you have looked over ye rest of what you have already translated, I desire you would send it ; and I own y^t if you don't think fit to add something more, I must submit : 'tis wholly at your choice, for I left it intirely to you ; but I believe you cannot imagine I expected soe little ; for you were pleased to use me much kindlyer in Juvenall, wch is not reckon'd soe easy to translate as Ovid. S^r, I humbly beg yor pardon for this long letter, and upon my word I had rather have yor good will than any man's alive ; and, whatever you are pleased to doe, will alway acknowledge my self, S^r,

Yo^r most obliged humble Servt,
J. Tonson.[126]

Tonson, who was in politics an ardent Whig, pestered Dryden to dedicate his Virgil to William III. The poet, ill-disposed to change his political allegiance, resisted ; and the subject gave rise to long argument between them. The publisher, hoping to carry his point at the last moment, and perhaps to bluff Dryden by confronting him with a *fait accompli*, had the plates touched up, which were to form the engravings destined to illustrate the book, so as to give Æneas the King of England's features. Tonson lost the trick and his expenses, for Dryden stood firm, but the poet had to remain on the defensive and fight to the bitter end.[127]

---

[126] This and the following letters will be found in *Dryden's Correspondence*.

[127] " But, however, he (Tonson) has missed of his design in the dedication, though he had prepared the books for it ; for in every figure of Eneas he has caused him to be drawn like King William, with a hooked nose." (Dryden. Letter to his sons.)—Hence this epigram :

> " Old Jacob by deep judgment sway'd,
> To please the wise beholders,
> Has placed old Nassau's hook-nosed head
> On poor Æneas' shoulders.
>
> To make the parallel hold tack,
> Methinks there's a little lacking ;
> One took his father pick-a-pack,
> And t'other sent his packing."

The state of the silver currency in England was at this time deplorable. The country was flooded with clipped and depreciated coins.[128] When a payment was due to Dryden, Tonson usually tried to unload on to him all the most under-weight coins he had at the moment in his till. The unfortunate author had continually to complain:

You know money is now very scrupulously receiv'd : in the last which you did me the favour to change for my wife, besides the clip'd money, there were at least forty shillings brass.

I shall loose enough by your bill upon Mr. Knight*; for after having taking it all in silver, and not in half-crowns neither, but shillings and sispences, none of the money will go ; for which reason I have sent it all back again, and as the less loss will receive it in guinneys at 29 shillings each.

. . . if you have any silver which will go, my wife will be glad of it. I lost thirty shillings or more by the last payment of fifty pounds, wch you made at Mr. Knights.

When it sometimes happened that Dryden was behind time in delivering his manuscript, the treatment he received was rough and uncivil. One day when St. John (later Bolingbroke) was visiting Dryden, they heard a knock at the front door. "This", said Dryden, "is Tonson. You will take care not to depart before he goes away ; for I have not completed the sheet which I promised him ; and if you leave me unprotected I must suffer all the rudeness to which his resentment can prompt his tongue." [129]

Dryden was not to be outdone. On one occasion, when Tonson no doubt had pressed some petty calculations on his attention, such as those we have seen above, he wrote acidly :

October the 29th, (f. 1695).

MR. TONSON,

Some kind of intercourse must be carryed on betwixt us, while I am translating Virgil. Therefore I give you notice, that I have done the seaventh Eneid in the country † ; and intend some few days hence, to go upon the eight : when that is finished, I expect fifty pounds in good silver ; not such as I have had formerly. I am not obliged to take gold,‡ neither will I ; nor stay for it beyond four-and-twenty houres after it is due. I thank you for the civility of your last letter

---

* A banker or goldsmith, afterwards notorious for his share in the South Sea scheme, to which Company he was cashier.

† At Burleigh, the seat of John, the fifth Earl of Exeter.

‡ Both the gold and silver coin were at this time much depreciated ; and remained in a fluctuating state till a new coinage took place.

---

[128] See Macaulay, History, chap. XXI.
[129] Johnson, *Lives* . . . Dryden.

in the country; but the thirty shillings upon every book remains with me. You always intended I should get nothing by the second subscriptions, as I found from first to last. And your promise to Mr. Congreve, that you had found a way for my benefit, which was an encouragement to my paines, came at last, for me to desire Sir Godfrey Kneller and Mr. Closterman to gather for me. I then told Mr. Congreve, that I knew you too well to believe you meant me any kindness: and he promised me to believe accordingly of you, if you did not. But this is past; and you shall have your bargain, if I live and have my health. You may send me word what you have done in my business with the Earl of Derby: and I must have a place for the Duke of Devonshyre. Some of your friends will be glad to take back their three guinneys. The Countess of Macclesfield gave her money to Will Plowden before Christmas; but he remembered it not, and payd it not in. Mr. Aston tells me, my Lord Chesterfield and my Lord Petre are both left out; but my Lady Macclesfield must have a place, if I can possibly: and Will Plowden shall pay you in three guinneys, if I can obtain so much favour from you.* I desire neither excuses nor reasons from you: for I am but too well satisfyed already. The Notes and Prefaces shall be short; because you shall get the more by saving paper.†

JOHN DRYDEN.

Once again he wrote in the same style:

Friday forenoon, (f. Feb. 1695–6).

SIR,

I receiv'd your letter very kindly,‡ because indeed I expected none; but thought you as very a tradesman as Bentley,§ who has cursed our Virgil so heartily.

. . . Upon triall I find all of your trade are sharpers, and you not more than others; therefore I have not wholly left you. Mr. Aston does not blame you for getting as good a bargain as you cou'd, though I cou'd have gott an hundred pounds more; and you might have spared almost all your trouble if you had thought fit to publish the proposalls for the first subscriptions; for I have guynneas offered me every day, if there had been room; I believe modestly speaking I have refused already 25. I mislike nothing in your letter therefore, but onely your upbraiding me with the publique encouragement, and my own reputation concerned in the notes; when I assure you I

---

* From inspecting the plates of Dryden's Virgil, it appears that the Earl of Derby had one inscribed to him, as had Lord Chesterfield. But this wrathful letter made no further impression on the mercantile obstinacy of Tonson; and neither the Duke of Devonshire, Lord Petre, nor Lady Macclesfield, obtained the place among the first subscribers, which Dryden so peremptorily demands for them.

† This seems to be a bitter gibe at Jacob's parsimony.

‡ Tonson's answer to the foregoing letter seems to have been pacific and apologetical, yet peremptory as to his terms.

§ Richard Bentley, a bookseller and printer, who lived in Russel Street, Covent Garden.

cou'd not make them to my mind in less than half a year's time. Get the first half of Virgil transcribed as soon as possibly you can, that I may put the notes to it ; and you may have the other four books which lye ready for you when you bring the former ; that the press may stay as little as possibly it can. My Lord Chesterfield has been to visite me, but I durst say nothing of Virgil to him, for feare there should be no void place for him ; if there be, let me know ; and tell me whether you have made room for the Duke of Devonshire. Haveing no silver by me, I desire my Lord Derby's money, deducting your own. And let it be good, if you desire to oblige me, who am not your enemy, and may be your friend,

JOHN DRYDEN.

One day when Tonson had refused an advance of money, Dryden sent him the following opening lines of a projected portrait :

> With leering looks, bull-faced, and freckled fair,
> With two left legs, and Judas-colour'd hair,
> And frowzy pores, that taint the ambient air . . .

And in committing the letter to the person entrusted with its delivery, he added : " Tell the dog that he who wrote these lines can write more."

But savage as were these squalls, they passed over : and calm reigned once more. The sky was not continuously fraught with storm.

Dryden wrote :

(*Wednesday the* 13*th of* 7 *ber f.* 1695.)

MY GOOD FRIEND,

. . . I assure you I lay up your last kindnesses to me in my heart ; and the less I say of them, I charge them to account so much the more ; being very sensible that I have not hitherto deserved them.

JOHN DRYDEN.

And again :

August 30, (1693).

MR. TONSON,

I am much asham'd of my self, that I am so much behind-hand with you in kindness. Above all things I am sensible of your good nature, in bearing me company to this place, wherein, besides the cost, you must needs neglect your own business ; but I will endeavour to make you some amends ; . . .

JOHN DRYDEN.

Tonson, for his part, was lavish of minor courtesies. Not content with accompanying the author to the country, he would send him gifts of melons and sherry, both of which were gratefully appreciated.

The truth is that the two men were indispensable to each other. Without Dryden, Tonson would have been nobody, and Dryden had no choice of publishers. However justly founded the complaints to which his behaviour gave rise, Tonson had one virtue—imposed by his own interest—to which Dryden could not be insensible : he was a more solvent debtor than Charles II and a more open-handed giver than Charles's royal brother James. Each volume of the *Miscellanies*, which they jointly produced, brought Dryden £50, and his Virgil some £1,400,[130] that is to say, approximately as much profit as he had reaped in earlier days from fourteen successful plays (counting the sale of the manuscript, the gift evoked by the Dedication and the third-night earnings).[131] Tonson meantime was laying the foundations of his fortune.

Despite their bickerings, author and publisher were in fact so well satisfied with their partnership that after Virgil they undertook yet another joint publication. This was the volume of verse which is known as Dryden's *Fables*. For this volume, the last he was ever to write, Dryden was paid 250 guineas, which for 12,000 lines works out, as Pope calculated,[132] to approximately sixpence a line.

Adversity had opened Dryden's eyes to the fact that henceforth the true patrons of literature would be the publishers. Or, more correctly, that henceforth there would be neither patron nor protégé. The two contracting parties would enter into voluntary collaboration, each making his appropriate contribution : the author his talent, the publisher his commercial experience ; the one risking his labour, the other his capital, and both according to their desert and to their luck, good or ill, would have their share of failure or success. Under these new conditions the author could of course no longer count on pleasant windfalls, on generous gifts, on fortune falling from heaven while he slept. He would have to earn his bread in the sweat of his brow, the

---

[130] Pope (as reported by Spence, pp. 262–3) reckoned it as about £1,200, Malone over £1,300 and Bell about £1,400. A document based on Dryden's personal authority points to the figure of £1,400 (*Notes and Queries*, May 19, 1877, p. 386). Everyone agrees that from a financial point of view the Virgil was a considerable success. The first edition was exhausted in a few weeks. There had been 102 five-guinea and 250 two-guinea subscribers. The second edition appeared early in the following year.

[131] See above, p. 112 f.

[132] Spence, pp. 262–3. Tonson might on this occasion be well content. Dryden had contracted to supply 10,000 lines for 250 guineas and furnished actually another 2,000 over and above the tally.

publisher paying nothing for nothing. But by his work, severe and toilsome though it might be and frequently coupled with rebuffs, the author acquired, if he deserved them, two precious imponderables for which no price is too high—independence and dignity.

Furthermore, in proportion as a reading-public evolved and the publishing trade developed, the opportunity of achieving this independence presented itself more freely to writers, until by slow degrees literature became a remunerative profession.

After the Revolution, dramatists had the benefit not of one performance only, but of two, and sometimes even of three,[133] and the profit of these performances was considerable. With one single play Southerne earned as much as £700, a sum so vastly in excess of those current in the preceding reigns that he was ashamed to confess it to Dryden. True, Southerne had many wealthy and highly-placed friends, and he possessed a quite peculiar gift of arousing their generosity when he hawked his tickets round their great houses.[134] Apart from Southerne, however, we hear of a quite obscure writer who derived £300 from a play that ran only for seven nights.[135] The sale of the manuscript to publishers also became markedly more profitable. The price of a play rose gradually from £20 or £25 to a more serious figure. Dryden sold the text of *Cleomenes* (1691) for thirty guineas,[136] Southerne *The Fatal Marriage* (1695) for £36, Edmund Smith *Phædra and Hippolitus* (1708) for £60.[137] Tonson paid John Philips forty guineas for his little poem on *Cider* (1703).[138] In 1694 Tillotson's *Sermons* were bought for the unheard-of sum of 2,500 guineas, which " in the wretched state in which the silver coin then was ", as Macaulay says,[139] was " the equivalent of at least £3,600 ".[140]

[133] Genest, II, pp. 7, 166 and 316; Malone, *Historical Account*, pp. 174-5. According to Malone, Farquhar—quite exceptionally—was allowed as many as four performances for *The Constant Couple* in 1700.
[134] Life of Southerne prefixed to his *Works*; Malone, *Historical Account*, p. 175.
[135] " We have had a poor comedy of Johnson's (not Ben) which held seven nights and has got him three hundred pounds." (Letter of Cromwell to Pope, Dec. 7, 1711. Elwin's Edition of *Pope*, VI, p. 128.)—The author was one Charles Johnson, and the play was called *The Wife's Relief, or The Husband's Cure*.
[136] Malone's *Dryden*, II, p. 230, note No. 2.
[137] Malone, *Historical Account*, p. 180.
[138] Johnson, *Lives* . . . John Philips.   [139] *History*, chap. XX.
[140] The risking of so large a sum on one publication shows how far the spirit of enterprise had already carried the publishers. It must be admitted,

After the appearance of the *Tatler* and the *Spectator* and the definite formation of an English reading-public, the rewards of literary work rose still higher. His publisher paid Sacheverell £100 for the first sermon he preached after his suspension (1713).[141] Rowe received £75 for the manuscript of *Lady Jane Grey* (1715); Cibber £105 for the *Non-Juror* (1718)[142]; Southerne, of whom Pope said that he was

> ... sent to raise
> The price of prologues and of plays,[143]

got as much as £120 for his *Spartan Dame* (1719).[144] From 1720 onwards the three benefit nights for the author of a play, which had hitherto been an exceptional concession, became the rule.[145] A few years later Gay received more than £1,000 for *The Captives*, and George Jeffreys at least the same sum for his tragedy of *Edwin* (1724). Fenton made more than £1,500 from his tragedy of *Mariamne*.[146] In 1712 Addison and Steele sold half their rights in the first seven volumes of the *Spectator* for £575, which implies a value for the whole copyright of £1,150.[147] In 1716 after his fall from glory, Prior organized the publication of his poems by subscription and made 4,000 guineas[148] by the transaction. In 1720 Gay published his poems in the same way at a profit of £1,000.[149]

If publishers were disposed to be as generous as all this, we may fairly conclude that they had their sound reasons, and that their receipts encouraged them to bold adventure and taught

---

however, that the fact is not of purely literary significance. Tillotson occupied a unique place in England's religious life, and the payment of so high a price for the copyright of his sermons must be attributed more to his fame as an Archbishop than to his gifts as a writer, great though these unquestionably were. His posthumous works run to fourteen octavo volumes.

[141] Swift, *Journal to Stella*, April 2, 1713.
[142] Johnson, *Lives . . . Dryden*, p. 390, Cunningham's note.
[143] See above, chap. II, note No. 211.
[144] Malone, *Historical Account*, p. 181, note. See above chap. II, note No. 211.
[145] Ibid., p. 175.
[146] Young's Letter to Lady Mary Wortley Montagu in her *Works*, II, p. 11.
[147] The record of the sale is in the British Museum: *Additional Manuscripts*, No. 21,110.—The daily sales of the paper had no doubt brought them considerable profits, for we know that Berkeley was paid a guinea for each article he contributed to the *Guardian*, in addition to being given a dinner by Steele. (Nichols' Edition of *Steele's Correspondence*, I, p. 329, note.)
[148] Johnson, *Lives . . . Prior*.
[149] N. Drake, *Essays . . . Illustrative of the Tatler*, etc., III, p. 242.

them not to be too sparing of their guineas. The first volume of *Robinson Crusoe* alone brought in more than £1,000 to its publisher, who died a few years later worth over £40,000.[150] Soon after Dryden's death, Tonson bought property in the country, and was well on the way to a fortune which ultimately rose to £80,000. The hundred pounds with which he started life had bred handsomely under his care.

IV

Pope and his publishers Tonson and Lintot.—Pope's Translation of Homer.—It made Pope's fortune.—Pope breaks the tradition of interested Dedications.—Preserves a detached attitude to political parties.—Refuses offered pensions.—Sought by the highest society in England.—The first English man of letters

What was now needed was a man capable of drawing full advantage from all the recent progress made, and establishing, on the existence of an enlightened public and on the rivalry of competing publishers, an author's complete independence.

The man appeared. He was Alexander Pope.[151]

His parents were Roman Catholics, his father, before retirement, a London linen-draper. He spent his childhood and early boyhood in Windsor Forest, whither his father had prudently withdrawn with a modest competence, after the fall of James II and the triumph of the Protestant party, to devote himself to his son's education.

Delicate and deformed, the boy early showed promise of great poetic talent. When he came to London to mix in literary society his verses at once attracted notice, and one of the first persons whose attention was drawn to them was Dryden's publisher, Jacob Tonson. Pope had so far published nothing, and was not yet eighteen when he received the following letter:

GRAY'S INN GATE.
April 20, 1706.

SIR,—

I have lately seen a Pastoral of yours in Mr. Walsh's and Congreve's hands, which is extremely fine, and is (generally) approved of by the best judges in poetry. I remember I have formerly seen you at my shop, and am sorry I did not improve my acquaintance with you. If you design your poem for the press, no person shall be more careful

---

[150] Spence, p. 340; William Lee, *Daniel Defoe*, p. 293.
[151] In addition to Pope's own works, I have consulted especially Johnson, Carruthers, Dilke, Elwin and Leslie Stephen.

in the printing of it, nor no one can give (a) greater encouragement to it than, sir, your, etc.
(Pray give me a line per post).[151a]

Pope succumbed at once to so courteous and so flattering an overture and his *Pastorals* appeared in 1709 in a new volume of *Miscellanies* published by Tonson.

The first English editor had drawn another ace. Having been the mainstay of Dryden's last years, and helped him to bring out some of his finest work, he rendered literature the further service of encouraging the first steps of a new poet.

So Pope, still a youth, still unknown, entered on the scene, not under the protection of a great lord, nor of a statesman, but under the immediate auspices, and almost at the request, of a publisher.

This fact was bound, or so it seems to me, to have a serious influence on the course of his later life. From the very beginning of his career he saw—what Dryden's latest experiences had no doubt already shown him—that the future of literature lay in the intelligent collaboration of author and publisher, and that he had no need to look further afield for support.

His position was immeasurably more favourable than Dryden's. Dryden had behind him no one but Tonson, which placed him in some sort at the publisher's mercy; and in Dryden's day Tonson was making, with justifiable caution, his first publishing experiments. Since then Tonson had prospered; he had become wealthy; he had become a person of importance, so much so that he had been elected secretary of the Kit-Cat Club. Political and literary authorship had moreover extended its range in every direction, creating a need and a taste for reading, and the publishing trade had consequently expanded. Tonson had not long remained the sole expert in the marketing of books. He was soon confronted by a serious rival, Bernard Lintot.[152] The subsequent competition between the two publishers was a thing wholly new in English literature, and in a host of ways beneficial. There is nothing like competition to make a business man active, clear-sighted and generous. If Tonson brought out an edition of Shakespeare's plays, Lintot capped it with a new edition of his poems. No sooner had Lintot announced the first volume of Pope's verse translation of the *Iliad* than Tonson offered

---

[151a] [Elwin, IX, p. 545. B. D.]
[152] On Lintot, see Knight, *Shadows* . . . pp. 100 ff.

the public Tickell's version of the first book. If Tonson was preparing a translation of Lucretius, Lintot set about finding a translator of the same poet " to publish against Tonson's ".[153] The two of them, hearing that Young had a new work ready for printing, wrote simultaneously to the poet requesting the honour of publishing it.[154] The man whom Pope himself styled " the enterprizing Mr. Lintot, the redoubtable rival of Mr. Tonson ",[155] wasted no time in competing with his brother-publisher for the young poet's work, and in 1712 he secured Pope's collaboration for a collection of *Miscellanies* compiled in imitation of Tonson's.[156] Pope had meantime entrusted his *Essay on Criticism* to another publisher called Lewis. Thereafter his work was divided between Lintot and Tonson. Lintot published *Windsor Forest*, *The Rape of the Lock*, *The Temple of Fame*; Tonson published several poems of Pope's in a volume of his *Miscellanies* which came out under Steele's editorship.[157]

These works, by which the young poet continued to maintain and even increase the promise of his talent, won him an enviable reputation; but they were far from enriching him. The income from his father's legacy was very modest.[158] He was inclined to try whether his literary reputation and an enlightened public might not between them enable him to conquer fortune.

Dryden had toyed with the plan of following up his Virgil with a translation of Homer. Pope took the idea up again and began to think of tackling the *Iliad*. The publishers hailed

---

[153] Pope's *Letter to the Earl of Burlington*.
[154] Spence, p. 355 [2nd edn., p. 269].—This double attack gave rise to an amusing blunder. Young wrote to both publishers the same day and in his haste transposed the two addresses so that Lintot got a letter beginning " That Bernard Lintot is so great a scoundrel that . . . "
[155] *Letter to the Earl of Burlington*.
[156] It was called Pope's *Miscellany*. It was in this volume that appeared the first version of the *Rape of the Lock*.
[157] Pope subsequently gave Tonson his edition of Shakespeare, and Lintot his translation of the *Iliad* and the *Odyssey*. His other works he entrusted mainly to Gilliver and to Dodsley. He had given Dodsley £100 to set him up in business.
[158] ". . . The translation of the Iliad. What led me into that . . . was purely the want of money. I had then none; not even to buy books." Spence, p. 304 [2nd edn., p. 231].—Pope's father had possessed a capital sum of £10,000; and when he died in 1717 he left his son an income of between £280 and £400 a year. But Roman Catholics paid double taxes and the uncertainty of their position compelled them to leave a part of their money unproductive or to invest it disadvantageously. After his father's death, Pope wrote to a co-religionist : " He has left me to the ticklish management of a narrow fortune, where every false step is dangerous." (Elwin, VI, p. 377, also VI, pp. 189, 201 and 214.)

the project with enthusiasm, and Lintot outbid all competitors by offering terms more generous than any English publisher had previously ventured on. Like Dryden's Virgil, Pope's *Iliad* was published by subscription. The edition consisted of six quarto volumes at a guinea apiece. Lintot allowed Pope the entire revenue from subscriptions, undertook to bear the cost of supplying the volumes subscribed for, and in addition paid the translator £200 a volume.[159] There were 575 subscribers who took 654 copies and Pope's receipts finally reached the total of £5,320 4s. This success encouraged him to persevere, and he undertook, still with Lintot, the translation of the *Odyssey*.[160] These two translations, which kept him busy for ten years (from 1715 to 1725) brought him a fortune of about £9,000. If we compare this with the £1,400 which Dryden made by his Virgil we can see what great strides have been made in twenty years.[161]

Pope was now thirty-five; he was rich and, we must hasten to add, independent. His translation of Homer is interesting, not only because of its brilliant financial success, nor because of the intelligence which enabled Pope to acquire by his pen a fortune of that most honourable kind which a man owes to his own labour; it is interesting also because of the means the poet used to introduce it to the world.

From the moment of his first literary successes Pope had been welcomed into the most distinguished London society. He had been able to count among his friends both writers like

---

[159] Lintot reserved for himself only the profit from subsequent editions. The *Iliad* by itself made a rich man of him and provided further a considerable income for his heirs.

[160] Pope translated only a part of the *Odyssey* himself. He called in the assistance of two collaborators, Fenton and Broome.

[161] Gay and Swift both commemorated Pope's success, Gay in the verses *Alexander Pope and his Safe Return from Troy. A Congratulatory Poem on his Completing his Translation of Homer's Iliad* (Carruthers, pp. 198 ff.); Swift in *A Libel on the Reverend Dr. Delany* (Scott's Edition of *Swift*, XIV, pp. 246 ff.).— It is useful to note that other cases than Pope's confirm the steady rise in literary fees. The performance of *The Beggar's Opera* brought Gay in between £700 and £800 (Letter from Gay to Swift, March 30, 1727-8) (Scott's *Swift*, XVII, p. 181). His opera of *Polly* (1729), a sequel to *The Beggar's Opera*, was banned from the stage, but he published it by subscription and benefited to the tune of at least £2,000 (Johnson, *Lives* . . . Gay). In 1727 Voltaire published in London, by subscription, an English edition of his *Henriade*, dedicated to Queen Caroline, which earned him £6,000 (Garnier's Edition of Voltaire's *Œuvres*, VIII, p. 5). Young made £3,000 by a volume of seven satires on *The Love of Fame* (1728) (*Johnson, Lives* . . . Young). In 1738 Henry Brooke, finding his tragedy of *Gustavus Vasa* banned, published it by subscription, making a profit of £800 (Boswell, I, p. 156, note).

Wycherley, Walsh, Congreve, Granville, Garth, Swift, Steele, Addison, Gay, Arbuthnot, Parnell, and statesmen like Harley, Bolingbroke, Halifax, Somers and Craggs. All of these, authors and politicians alike, were ranged on one side or other in politics. To which party did Pope owe allegiance? Was he a Whig? Or a Tory?[162] Since he was a Roman Catholic, the Tories from the start reckoned him as one of themselves, and towards the close of his poem, *Windsor Forest*, there were some lines in praise of Peace, calculated to please them. But he had written a Prologue for Addison's *Cato* which the Whigs enthusiastically applauded,[163] and the *Spectator* and the *Guardian*, edited by two Whigs, had welcomed his verse and his prose. So each party in turn laid claim to the new-comer: his most trivial actions were noted and criticized from two sides; his very friendships were analysed; and each camp showed its longing to annex him, and its still stronger hope that he would not be captured by the other. Some extracts from his correspondence at this time will show the degree to which people were preoccupied with the question of his political opinions:

An honest Jacobite . . . spoke to me the sense, or nonsense, of the weak part of his party very fairly and innocently—that the good people took it very ill of me that I write with Steele, though upon never so indifferent subjects.[164]

The little I have done (for the *Guardian*) and the great respect I bear Mr. Steele as a man of wit, has rendered me a suspected Whig to some of the over-zealous and violent.[165]

I have also encountered much malignity on the score of religion, some calling me a papist and a tory, the latter because the heads of the party have been distinguishingly favourable to me; but why the former I cannot imagine, but that Mr. Caryll and Mr. Blount have laboured to serve me. Others have styled me a whig, because I have been honoured with Mr. Addison's good word, and Mr. Jervas's good deeds, and of late with my Lord Halifax's patronage.[166]

---

[162] Swift writes to Pope, Aug. 30, 1716: "I had the favour of yours by Mr. F(ord), of whom before any other question relating to your health or fortune, or success as a poet, I inquired your principles in the common form, 'Is he a whig or a tory?'" (Elwin's *Pope*, VII, p. 14).

[163] "The prologue-writer . . . was clapped into a stanch whig, sore against his will, at almost every two lines." (Letter from Pope to Caryll, April 30, 1713, Elwin's *Pope*, VI, p. 184.)

[164] To the same, June 12, 1713 (ibid., VI, p. 185).

[165] To the same, Oct. 17, 1713 (ibid., VI, p. 197).

[166] To the same, May 1, 1714 (ibid., VI, p. 208).— Caryll and E. Blount were both, like Pope, Roman Catholics; Jervas was a painter of repute who belonged in politics to the Whig party.

Some modern rumours have been thrown about, which would have represented me as more concerned in party affairs than I ever dreamed on ; in so much that I had the honour to be named in the London Gazette for an enemy to the Grande Société at Button's.[167]

Mr. Phillips did express himself with much indignation against me one evening at Button's Coffee-house, as I was told, saying that I was entered into a cabal with Dean Swift and others to write against the whig interest.[168]

For all that passed betwixt Dr. Swift and me, you know, the whole, without reserve, of our correspondence. The engagements I had to him, were such as the actual services he had done me in relation to the subscription for Homer, obliged me to. I must have leave to be grateful to him, and to any one who serves me, let him be never so obnoxious to any party.[169]

And in the midst of these perpetual commentaries on his conduct inspired by political passion, of these efforts by left and right to capture him, the poet wrote to his co-religionist Caryll :

Yet let me tell you, you can hardly guess what a task you undertake when you profess yourself my friend ; there are some tories who will take you for a whig, some whigs who will take you for a tory, some protestants who will esteem you a rank papist, and some papists who will account you a heretic. I find, by dear experience, we live in an age where it is criminal to be moderate ; and where no one man can be allowed to be just to all men.[170]

Meantime the translation of the *Iliad* appeared.[171] It was an important book, long expected, in which the whole literary world was interested. To which party would it be dedicated ? Dryden, in whose steps Pope was following, had been lavish of his Virgil dedications. He had presented the *Eclogues* to Lord Clifford, the *Georgics* to the Earl of Chesterfield, the *Æneid* to Mulgrave, Marquis of Normanby. What would Pope do ? To whom would he offer his work ? To a Whig or to a Tory ? [172] Neither the one nor the other. He dedicated it to a brother-author, to a famous and honoured man, who, at a time when all men were passionate political partisans, had taken no doubt

---

[167] To the same, Feb. 25, 1714 (ibid., VI, p. 202).—Button's Coffee-House was the Whig rendezvous.
[168] To the same, June 8, 1714 (ibid., VI, p. 209).
[169] To Jervas, August 27, 1714 (ibid., VIII, p. 9).
[170] To Caryll, July 25, 1714 (ibid., VI, p. 215).
[171] The first volume was published in 1715.
[172] It is said that Halifax had expressed the wish that it should be dedicated to him.

a modest part in politics, but with so much calm restraint as to win the favour and goodwill of both parties,[173] and he wrote his dedication in the following simple and straightforward terms :

> I beg to be excused from the ceremonies of taking leave at the end of my work ; and from embarrassing myself, or others, with any defences or apologies about it. But instead of endeavouring to raise a vain monument to myself, of the merits or difficulties of it (which must be left to the world, to truth and to posterity), let me leave behind me a memorial of my friendship, with one of the most valuable men, as well as finest writers, of my age and country : one who has tried, and knows by his own experience, how hard an undertaking it is to do justice to *Homer* : and one, who (I am sure) sincerely rejoices with me at the period of my labours. To him, therefore, having brought this long work to a conclusion, I desire to dedicate it ; and to have the honour and satisfaction of placing together, in this manner, the names of Mr. CONGREVE and of
>
> A. POPE.
>
> *March* 25, 1720.

This dedication is a very important landmark in the history of English literature. It was nothing less than revolutionary. With it Pope shattered at a blow the long tradition of self-seeking dedications, whether political or personal.[174]

To mark still more clearly his wish to remain independent of party, Pope took pains to hold the balance exactly even between Whig and Tory, when expressing in his Preface his gratitude to all who had taken a sympathetic interest in himself or in his great undertaking. Side by side with Addison,

---

[173] Macaulay was the first to point out the motive underlying this dedication from one author to another. In his Essay on *The Comic Dramatists of the Restoration*, he writes : " It was necessary to find someone who was at once eminent and neutral. It was therefore necessary to pass over peers and statesmen. Congreve had a high name in letters. He had a high name in aristocratic circles. He lived on terms of civility with men of all parties."

See also the beginning of Macaulay's Essay on Robert Montgomery.

[174] In the 4th number of the *Guardian*, that is to say, as early as March 16, 1713, Pope had expressed in no uncertain terms his opinion of the fashionable type of dedication :

" To say more to a Man than one thinks, with a Prospect of Interest, is dishonest ; and without it, foolish. And who ever has had Success in such an Undertaking, must of necessity at once, think himself in his Heart a Knave for having done it, and his Patron a Fool for having believed it."

He continued the campaign against dedications : see the *Dunciad*, II, lines 191–206, and IV, lines 101–2.—Before the publication of the *Iliad* Steele had dedicated *The Tender Husband* to Addison (1705) and Gay his *Rural Sports* to Pope (1713) ; but these were both works of slight importance, and the dedications were not designed to catch public attention.

Steele, Garth and Rowe, he named Swift, Parnell and Granville. Finally, amongst the statesmen to whom he offered a tribute of thanks, he particularly singled out Halifax; but with singular audacity—which did not pass unnoticed [175]—he immediately coupled this name with Bolingbroke's. Now Bolingbroke was at the time an exile and under sentence for high treason, yet Pope was not afraid to write: " Such a genius as my Lord Bolingbroke, not more distinguished in the great scenes of business than in all the useful and entertaining parts of learning." And he closed his paragraph of thanks with the significant remark that the patronage he had received " was the more to be acknowledged, as it is shown to one whose pen has never gratified the prejudices of any party nor the vanity of any man ".[176]

It was no small merit, in an age entirely given over to political struggle, to adopt an attitude so independent as Pope's. First, as we have just seen, it was by no means easy to avoid being sucked into the vortex, and it required both imperturbability and active effort to resist persuasive advances, and even more to resist the temptation of establishing truth by replying to attack and misrepresentation, a course which frequently entangles a man in controversy against his will. Secondly, Pope's aloofness did not spring from indifference. Pope was a Roman Catholic, that is member of a conquered, proscribed and persecuted class, victim of Draconian laws.

[175] Swift wrote to Pope, June 28, 1715: "You are pretty bold in mentioning Lord Bolingbroke in that preface." (Elwin, VII, p. 11.) And Jervas also wrote on the same date: " The Whigs say Bolingbroke is the hero of your preface. Pray make room for Walpole in your next, to keep the balance of power even." (Elwin, VIII, p. 14. Walpole had been the president and reporter of the commission which decided on the impeachment of Bolingbroke and of Lord Oxford.) Pope replied : " If the whigs say now that Bolingbroke is the hero of my preface, the tories said, you may remember, three years ago, that Cato was the hero of my poetry. It looks generous enough to be always on the side of the distressed, and my patrons of the other party may expect great panegyrics from me (when) they come to be impeached by the future party rage of their opponents. To compliment those who are dead in law, is as much above the imputation of flattery, as Tickell says it is, to compliment those who are really dead, and perhaps too there is as much vanity in my praising Bolingbroke, as in his praising Halifax. No people in this world are so apt to give themselves airs as we authors." (Elwin, VIII, p. 15.)—Tickell had dedicated his translation of the first book of the *Iliad* to Lord Halifax who died a month before it was published.

[176] The Preface was published with the first volume of the *Iliad* in 1715; the Dedication with the sixth and last volume in 1720.

Every Roman priest convicted of having celebrated mass or exercised his ministry in any manner whatsoever (unless it were in the house of a foreign ambassador) ran the risk of imprisonment for life. Denunciation was encouraged by a reward of £100. To conduct a boarding-school, or in general to play any part in education, was similarly to incur a life sentence. Young Roman Catholics were not eligible for any public school, college or university, and if a father sent his child abroad to be educated in his own faith, he rendered himself liable to a fine of £100, which became the reward of the man who had denounced him. Every Englishman on reaching the age of eighteen was obliged to take an oath of allegiance to the Crown and another acknowledging its religious supremacy. Nonjurors could neither purchase nor inherit land, which passed by right to the Protestant next of kin. A Roman Catholic paid double taxes. Civil and military service, teaching, the bar and legal professions were closed to him. He was even forbidden to own a horse worth more than £5.[177] If a Roman Catholic was suspected of opposition, two Justices of the Peace could at any moment summon him to take the oaths of allegiance and supremacy, and if he refused, he put himself in the position of a released convict. He had not the right to go to law, to approach within five miles of London or, without a special permit, to travel more than five miles from his home. The penalty for infringement of these regulations was confiscation of goods. He might moreover be challenged either to renounce his errors or to quit the country ; if he did not obey, or if he returned without the royal permission, the penalty was death. It is true that these repressive laws were not applied in all their rigour, but they remained a perpetual menace. If a personal enemy, or a delator tempted by the reward, drew attention to a Roman Catholic, if Government was—rightly or wrongly—apprehensive of some disturbance brewing, these laws could be instantly brought into play.[178]

Pope had suffered, and continued to suffer, for his religion.

---

[177] " Horses by Papists are not to be ridden :
But sure the Muse's Horse was ne'er forbidden.
For in no Rate-Book, it was ever found
That *Pegasus* was valued at Five-pound."
(Dryden, Prologue to *Don Sebastian*.)

[178] Lecky, I, pp. 272–6 and 303–10. Lecky attributes the laxity with which these laws were enforced, in part at least to the fact that a Roman Catholic was at the time acknowledged leader of English literature.

As a child, he had seen his parents take refuge in the solitude of Windsor Forest, seeking to be overlooked, hiding themselves to practise their religion, compelled to give their children an imperfect education. He had witnessed their sorrow and anxiety.[179] As a man, he heard the complaints of his co-religionists, he shared their hourly apprehensions and vexations.[180] Sorrowfully he said : " It is not for me to speak of England with tears in my eyes. I cannot consider that country mine where I am not allowed to call a foot of ground my own."

There was therefore good reason, enough and to spare, why Pope's sympathy did not go forth to the Whigs and the Protestant party, but naturally inclined him towards the Tories, if not actually towards the Jacobites. His chief personal friends were in fact Tories, and as he grew older his ideas approximated more and more to theirs. He frequently expressed in verse the views they cherished, and in one of his works, his *Epistle to Augustus*, did so with so much vigour that the poem narrowly escaped being proscribed. But his main concern was to be an author, and not to allow himself in his own despite, to be lured like his fellows into politics on the slightest provocation. While neither disguising nor concealing his opinions, he did not wish

[179] " Bred up at home, full early I begun
To read in Greek the wrath of Peleus' son.
Besides, my Father taught me, from a lad,
The better art, to know the good from bad :
(And little sure imported to remove,
To hunt for Truth in Maudlin's learned grove.)
But knottier points we knew not half so well,
Depriv'd us soon of our paternal Cell ;
And certain Laws, by suff'rers thought unjust,
Deny'd all posts of profit or of trust :
Hopes after hopes of pious Papists fail'd,
While mighty William's thund'ring arm prevail'd.
For Right Hereditary tax'd and fin'd,
He stuck to poverty with peace of mind ;
And we, the Muses help'd to undergo it ;
Convict a Papist he, and I a Poet."
(*Satires and Epistles*, VI, Horace 2 Epist. 2, lines 52–69, Warburton's Edition, p. 209.)

[180] See Pope's letters to Caryll dated Aug. 16, 1714, and March 2, 1715–16, and those to Blount, March 24, 1715–16 and June 23, 1716 (Elwin VI, pp. 217, 238, 372 and 374). In 1730 one of his nephews was prevented, after fourteen years of preparation, from qualifying as an attorney because oaths were unexpectedly required of him which his religion forbade him to take. (Letters to Caryll, Dec. 1730 and Jan. 31, 1732–3. Elwin, VI, pp. 325, 337.) In 1744 when the Pretender's activities were causing alarm, a royal proclamation, which Pope was obliged to obey, forbade Roman Catholics to live in London.

to air them where they had no relevance, but sought to devote himself wholly and freely to his profession, unhampered by any commitment of his own or other people's. This single-minded concentration on his profession, this concern to exercise it in dignity and independence, was the dominating principle of his life. Not only did he bear witness to it in his own conduct but he strove to convert his brethren to it.

One day, for instance, when Gay, cheated of the ambitious hopes he had centred on the Court, haughtily refused as beneath him, a post he was offered in the household of one of the royal children, Pope wrote to him :

> I could find it in my heart to congratulate you on this happy dismission from all court dependency . . . You are happily rid of many cursed ceremonies, as well as of many ill and vicious habits, of which few or no men escape the infection, who are hackneyed and trammelled in the ways of a court. Princes indeed, and peers (the lackeys of princes) and ladies (the fools of peers), will smile on you the less ; but men of worth and real friends will look on you the better. There is a thing, the only thing which kings and queens cannot give you—for they have it not to give—liberty, which is worth all they have, and which, as yet, I hope Englishmen need not ask from their hands. You will enjoy that, and your own integrity . . . While you are nobody's servant, you may be anyone's friend, and as such, I embrace you in all conditions of life.[181]

Similarly when Swift, yearning again to take a hand in politics, seemed for a moment on the brink of yielding to Pulteney's blandishments, Pope offered him this advice :

> Surely, without flattery, you are now above all parties of men, and it is high time to be so, after twenty or thirty years' observation of the great world.
>
> Nullius addictus jurare in verba magistri.
>
> I question not, many men would be of your intimacy, that you might be of their interest : but God forbid an honest or witty man should be of any, but that of his country. They have scoundrels enough to write for the passions and their designs ; let us write for truth, for honour, and for posterity.[182]

---

[181] Letter dated Oct. 16, 1726 (Elwin, VII, p. 427).
[182] Letter dated Nov. 16, 1726 (ibid., p. 87).—On Dec. 1, 1731, he again wrote him :

> "I am glad you resolve to meddle no more with the low concerns and interests of parties . . .
>
> *Quid verum atque decens, ourare, at rogare, nostrum sit.*"
>
> (Elwin, VII, p. 258.)

It would be wrong to picture Pope's religion as having made this independence of his a compulsory virtue, whose restraint he could not have shaken off even if he had wished. It is true that as a Roman Catholic he was debarred from public office; but that did not deter either Whigs or Tories from making him tempting offers which he was free to accept had he so desired.

When Harley was in office, he expressed on several occasions his regret at not being able to give Pope a place in the administration, and made it clear that the poet need only turn Protestant to have what he liked for the asking. Pope, who had never been over-zealous in his faith—if indeed he was not all his life more Deist than Papist—had no other reason for not following Dryden's example than the fear of wounding his aged parents, yet he would not even toy with the suggestion: " I could not ... without giving a great deal of pain to my parents; such pain, indeed, as I would not have given to either of them, for all the places he could have bestowed upon me."[183]

---

[183] Spence, pp. 304–5 [2nd Ed. of Spence, 1858, the page reference is 231].—The following passage from a letter of Pope's to Caryll, dated May 1, 1714, seems to have reference to Harley's proposal:

" Though I find it an unfortunate thing to be bred a papist, when one is obnoxious to four parts in five as being so too much, and to the fifth part for being so too little, I shall yet be easy under both their mistakes ... God is my witness, that I no more envy the protestants their places and possessions than I do our priests their charity or learning. I am ambitious of nothing but the good opinion of all good men of all sides, for I know that one virtue of a free spirit is more worth than all the virtues put together of all the narrow-souled people in the world. If they promise me all the good offices they ever did, or could do, I would not change for them all one kind word of yours." (Elwin, VI, pp. 208–9.)

See also letters from Swift to Pope, July 19 and Sept. 29, 1725 (Elwin, VII, pp. 49 and 53).—After the death of Pope's father in 1717, Bishop Atterbury—with the utmost delicacy, be it said—drew Pope's attention to the advantage which would accrue from his conversion. Pope replied in a long letter which deserves to be read in its entirety; I confine myself to quoting a passage:

" As to the *temporal* side of the question, I can have no dispute with you. It is certain, all the beneficial circumstances of life, and all the shining ones, lie on the part you would invite me to. But if I could bring myself to fancy, what I think you do but fancy, that I have any talents for active life, I want health for it; and besides it is a real truth, I have less inclination (if possible) than ability. Contemplative life is not only my scene, but my habit too. I began my life where most people end theirs, with a disrelish of all that the world calls ambition. I do not know why it is called so; for to me it always seemed to be rather *stooping* than *climbing*." (Carruthers, pp. 162–4.)

Again, in a letter to Swift, Nov. 28, 1729, Pope writes:

" Yet am I of the religion of Erasmus, a catholic. So I live, so I shall die; and hope one day to meet you, Bishop Atterbury, the younger Craggs,

At the beginning of George I's reign, Halifax asked to see the poet. He had, he said, noted with regret that Pope had not received the recognition he deserved. He rejoiced to be now in a position to be of service to him : if Pope felt inclined to accept the offer, he would be granted a pension with no condition attached. Pope thanked him, but, as if he needed leisure for reflection, returned no immediate answer. Later he wrote to Halifax, renewing his thanks, and saying that he had given the offer mature consideration. With the pension, he would no doubt be able " to live more at large in town " and drive his carriage, but that without the pension he could live " happily enough in the country ". His choice was made, and he preferred " liberty without a coach ".[184]

Later, his intimate friend Craggs, happening to have at his disposal a secret fund of public money, pressed him most insistently to accept from this source a pension of £300 a year, which no one would ever know about. This offer also Pope refused. In thanking Craggs for this proof of his friendship he added simply that if he ever needed to borrow money Craggs was the first to whom he would turn.[185]

On another occasion Swift took it upon himself to speak to Carteret of a pension for Pope. No sooner had Pope heard of this, than he wrote with some acrimony to his friend :

I was once displeased before at you, for complaining to Mr. Dodington of my not having a pension, and am so again at your naming it to a certain lord. I have given " some " proofs, in the course of my whole life (from the time when I was in the friendship of Lord Bolingbroke and Mr. Craggs, even to this, when I am civilly treated by Sir R. Walpole), that I never thought myself so warm in any party's cause as to deserve their money ; and, therefore, never would have accepted it ; but give me leave to tell you, that of all mankind the two persons I would least have accepted any favour from are those very two, to whom you have unluckily spoken of it. I desire you to take off any impressions which that dialogue may have left on his lordship's mind, as if I ever had any thought of being beholden to him or any other, in that way. And yet you know I am

---

Dr. Garth, Dean Berkeley, and Mr. Hutchenson, in that place, to which God in his infinite mercy bring us, and everybody ! " (Elwin, VII, p. 175.)

[184] Spence, pp. 305-6 [1858 Ed., pp. 231-2]. See also in Johnson Pope's letter to Halifax, dated Dec. 1, 1714.—Pope was no doubt alluding to Halifax's offer when some years later he wrote to Swift : " Horace might keep his coach in Augustus's time if he pleased. But I will not in the time of our Augustus." (Letter of Oct. 22, 1727, Elwin, VII, p. 104.)

[185] Spence, pp. 307-8 [1858 Ed., p. 232].

no enemy to the present constitution—I believe as sincere a well-wisher to it, nay, even to the church established, as any minister in or out of employment whatever.[186]

Rather than accept as a favour money from other men, Pope preferred to live, with lesser luxury and greater dignity, on what he earned by his own work. He rented on a long lease a house at Twickenham on the Thames in the neighbourhood of London. There he made his home, living in his own house like a landed proprietor, tending his garden, working at his leisure, receiving his friends, caring tenderly for his old mother, and proudly exclaiming:

> But (thanks to Homer) since I live and thrive,
> Indebted to no Prince or Peer alive.[187]

He was thus the first to set a noble example to his fellow-authors. He demonstrated to them that they could at last live as independent men, that literature was now a liberal profession, and that henceforth they need owe their due place in society to nothing but their own talent. This poet, who sought favours from none, was sought after by all, and the house at Twickenham became the trysting-place of a company which would have done honour to a royal palace. There were seen not only distinguished intellectuals like Swift, Atterbury, Gay and Arbuthnot, artists like Jervas and Kneller, politicians like Murray, Pulteney, Lyttelton and Wyndham, but those most eminent by birth, rank and station. Thither came Bolingbroke, the brilliant orator, the statesman who at one moment had held the destiny of England in his hand; Lord Oxford, colleague and rival of Bolingbroke, and his son, later the inheritor of his title (1724); Lord Peterborough, gallant and chivalrous commander of the English army in Spain; the fashionable and witty Chesterfield; Lords Burlington, Bathurst and Cobham; the Earls of Orrery and Marchmont; the Dukes of Shrewsbury and Argyle, in a word, all the most brilliant stars of aristocratic England. Even the King's son and heir, the Prince of Wales,

---

[186] Nov. 28, 1729 (Elwin, VII, pp. 174–5).
[187] *Satires and Epistles*, VI, Horace 2 Epist. 2, lines 68–9; Warburton, IV, p. 209.—Again, in prefacing *The Dunciad* he says: "But it happens that this our poet never had any place, pension, or gratuity, in any shape, from the said glorious Queen, or any of her Ministers. All he owed, in the whole course of his life, to any court, was a subscription, for his Homer, of £200 from King George I, and £100 from the Prince and Princess."

went out of his way to call on the poet and accepted his invitation to dinner.[188]

With all these great folk Pope mixed on the same terms as with his brother authors—on a footing of perfect equality. He took his place among them as of natural right. If they entertained him in their houses, he entertained them in his. All were his friends; none was his patron. If at one time or another he dedicated one of his books to one of them, it was not to flatter him or invite his support—as had so recently been the accepted practice of writers—it was merely to give public expression to genuine esteem.

On their side the haughty arrogance of other days was completely forgotten: the aristocracy of birth at last paid homage without reserve to the aristocracy of genius. Neither as an act of condescension, nor from motives of self-interest did the great ones of the land seek social contact with the poet. They came out of admiration for his gifts, out of liking for his personality, out of the feeling that it was an honour to be admitted to the circle of his friends.[189] Bolingbroke loved to discuss philosophy and literature with Pope; Peterborough amused himself by working in the garden [190]; Bathurst, whose hobby

[188] "Oft in the clear, still Mirrour of Retreat,
I study'd Shrewsbury, the wise and great;
Carleton's calm Sense, and Stanhope's noble Flame,
Compar'd, and knew their gen'rous End the same:
How pleasing Atterbury's softer hour!
How shin'd the Soul, unconquer'd in the Tow'r!
How can I Pult'ney, Chesterfield forget,
While Roman Spirit charms, and Attic Wit:
Argyll, the State's whole Thunder born to wield,
And shake alike the Senate and the Field:
Or Wyndham, just to Freedom and the Throne,
The Master of our Passions, and his own.
Names, which I long have lov'd, nor loved in vain,
Rank'd with their Friends, not number'd with their Train.
And if yet higher the proudest List should end,
Still let me say! No Follower, but a Friend."
(*Epilogue to the Satires*, lines 78–93. Warburton, IV, p. 324.)

[189] On Nov. 6, 1721, the Earl of Oxford writes to Pope: "I should be glad the world knew you admitted me to your friendship." (Elwin, VIII, p. 189.)

[190] "There, my retreat the best Companions grace,
Chiefs out of war, and Statesmen out of place.
There St. John mingles with my friendly bowl
The Feast of Reason and the Flow of Soul:
And He, whose lightning pierc'd th' Iberian Lines,
Now forms my Quincunx, and now ranks my Vines,

was building and plantation, consulted him about his plans. All of them valued his company and his conversation, and if they were cut off from the pleasure of seeing him, they kept up a regular correspondence with him. One and all were eager to do him service; and the Prince of Wales himself sent him busts for his library.

Finally, nothing shows more clearly the profound change which the Restoration had wrought in the author's status, than the fact that members of the aristocracy addressed to Pope poetic compliments on his work. Among these flattering tributes it is quaint to find verses of Mulgrave's—now Duke of Buckinghamshire [191] (currently known as Duke of Buckingham). The Merry Monarch's brilliant courtier, Dryden's haughty patron, the literary Mæcenas who had seen so many poets bend the servile knee before him, had come to this, that in the reign of George I it was he who paid homage to Alexander Pope.

Alexander Pope, the little, deformed and ailing man, the Roman Catholic, the London linen-draper's son, had become the social equal of the greatest; and that by dint of minding his own affairs, of wishing to be, and wishing to remain, simply a man of letters.

V

Conclusion

This is a matter in which less than justice has been done to Pope.

First, his biographers have almost always treated his life in isolation, taking too little heed of preceding history. As a

---

Or tames the Genius of the stubborn plain,
Almost as quickly as he conquer'd Spain."
(*Satire* I. To Mr. Fortescue, lines 124-32.
Warburton, IV, p. 69.)

[191] This was Mulgrave's legal title. He formally avoided the title of "Duke of Buckingham" lest it might be claimed by the Villiers family.—The verses by Mulgrave, the Countess of Winchelsea and the Hon. Simon Harcourt, may be found in Elwin's *Pope*, I, pp. 19 ff.—Swift had already tried the Duke's pride severely. In a letter to Stella (May 19, 1711) he writes: "Mr. Secretary told me the Duke of Buckingham had been talking to him much about me, and desired my acquaintance. I answered it could not be; for he had not made sufficient advances. Then the Duke of Shrewsbury said he thought that duke was not used to make advances. I said I could not help that; for I always expected advances in proportion to men's quality, and more from a duke than other men."

natural consequence, though they have usually noted his independent attitude, they have failed to appreciate how much credit he deserved for adopting, and how great service he rendered by maintaining it. Themselves rejoicing in their independence, they troubled little to inquire whether their predecessors had in the past enjoyed the same boon, and they saw nothing remarkable in the conduct of the man who had won this independence for them.

Pope has suffered in yet another way at his biographers' hands. It has become a commonplace to say that a biographer is usually inclined to conceal or minimize the failings and mistakes of the man whose life he undertakes to write. This disease, to which the biographer is particularly liable, if it be a disease, is that of over-admiration which Macaulay wittily diagnosed—after one of the most distinguished sufferers from it —as *lues Boswelliana*. But in the case of those who have written of Pope we find a strange phenomenon : they have been inspired not by admiration but by the very reverse, a desire to depreciate. Because Pope has been convicted of sharp practice and bad faith at certain moments in his life, they would have us believe that he was capable of nothing but duplicity, perfidy and treachery. In the whole of English literature there is perhaps no figure which has been painted so black as Pope's. Not only are his proven frailties displayed with a ruthlessness that takes no heed of extenuating circumstances, not only is any ambiguous act of his given the most damaging interpretation possible, not only is every ugly deed attributed to him by his enemies, accepted with almost no attempt at verification ; but his biographers appear to take so much pleasure in the unpleasant side of their task that it exercises a sort of hypnotic fascination over them which prevents their perceiving even his most manifest good qualities.

This is not the place to make a detailed study of the accusations with which he has been overwhelmed, or to examine the exaggeration and even errors which many of them may contain. Charles Dilke, one of those who knew Pope best and perhaps the only man who has been just to him, has already disproved some of these accusations, and I refer the reader to his valuable work. As for me, I have not undertaken to write the poet's life and I have no mind to counter relentless criticism with unqualified praise. There are certain stains on Pope's character which will unfortunately not wash off. Yes. In his desire to publish his correspondence during his own lifetime Pope played for a long time a curious comedy. The same desire led him to take unfair advantage of his friend Swift when Swift's mental powers were failing. Yes. When asked to explain certain personal allusions in his verse, he had not the courage to answer honestly, and stooped to contemptible and useless evasions. I know these faults of his, and they grieve me the more in proportion as I admire other sides of his character. But who can claim to be without fault? Is it fair that the blame justly incurred by Pope should blot out the praise that he has rightly earned? In any case, not one of the just accusations which besmirch his memory detracts from his independence as a writer, or the faithfulness with which he devoted himself to his profession.

As an example of the injustice with which he has too frequently been treated, I should like, however, to make mention of one reproach that has been levelled at him, because this bears on the subject of my study.

In his life of Pope Dr. Johnson says: " Next to the pleasure of contemplating his possessions, seems to be that of enumerating the men of high rank with whom he was acquainted . . . His admiration of the Great seems to have increased in the advance of life . . . To his later works he took care to annex names dignified with titles."

And in conversation he commented with more asperity:

" How foolish was it in Pope to give all his friendship to lords, who thought they honoured him by being with him ! . . . And then always saying : ' I do not value you for being a lord ' ; which was a sure proof that he did." [192]

To which Dilke has vigorously retorted : " So far indeed was Pope from seeking Lords for his acquaintance, that those he did know sought him ; and those who sought him were amongst the most distinguished and intellectual men of his age. Was he to refuse such associates?—was he to refuse such testimony to his worth—such worshippers of his genius—because they were men of distinguished rank and high position ? " [193]

I would add that even if we admit that Pope took a certain pleasure in mentioning his noble friends, a spice of vanity was not unnatural. He was the first English writer to be thus

[192] Boswell, VII, p. 208.
[193] *Papers of a Critic*, I, p. 116.—See also his further very just and very eloquent remarks.

honoured. Before his time the great lord and the holder of great office had looked down on the author; it was only recently that they had condescended to show the writer a modicum of respect, and that in return for services rendered. Pope had rendered service to none; he had devoted himself wholly to his profession, which was the sole occupation and passion of his life, and despite this, the most highly placed persons had made advances and rendered homage to him. How could he have avoided feeling proud? We may rather marvel that his head was not turned, as Swift's was in his days of fame.[194] Johnson, himself a great man of letters, ought better than anyone to have understood the justifiable pride of a man who rejoices to note that, thanks to his own merit, and to that alone, he need envy none the advantages conferred by birth or office. When George III sought out Dr. Johnson for a talk, did Johnson not feel himself highly honoured and afterwards remark " he is the finest gentleman I have ever seen "? Is it not true that " he loved to relate the incident with all its circumstances among his friends "? And did he not like to boast, as Boswell records, " that he talked to His Majesty with profound respect, but still in his firm manly manner, with a sonorous voice, and never in that subdued tone which is commonly used at the levee and in the drawing-room "? [195]

Shall we in our turn find fault with Johnson? Shall we accuse him of vanity? By no means. He was moved by precisely the same natural instinct as Pope. He was justly proud of the flattering step the King took to meet him; but he preserved his professional pride, and on principle would not appear to humble himself even before his sovereign.

There is a story that Piron was one day invited to dine at some great seigneur's. As the guests were moving into the

[194] See above, chap. III, note No. 41, and chap. IV, note No. 191.—Nor, for all his grand friends, did he ever forget his fellow-authors. Not to speak of his friendship for Swift, for Gay and for Arbuthnot, he never deserted Savage, who had worn out all his friends in turn. He helped to organize a benefit performance for Dennis who had made savage attacks on him, not sparing even his physical infirmities. He brought strong persuasion to bear on Dodsley, the publisher, to pay a liberal fee to Akenside for a remarkable poem. After reading some verses of Johnson, a man whom he did not know, he wrote spontaneously to Lord Gower commending Johnson to his favour. The *Dunciad* might seem to belie the benevolence of these acts, but above and beyond personal attacks the *Dunciad* shows a predominating desire to rid literature of the type of writer who in Pope's opinion brought it into dishonour.

[195] Boswell, III, pp. 19 ff.

dining-room he made way for one whom he did not know; the other refused to take precedence. The master of the house put a stop to this competition in courtesy by saying: " Come on first, Duke, he is only an author."—" Since our ranks are known," retorted Piron, " I claim my own ", and he led the way.

Pope, similarly, claimed his own rank, and his whole profession claimed it with him. Whether or not they recognized their debt to him, his immediate successors, inheriting the rank he had won for them, adopted his attitude and maintained the tradition he had begun.

At present [writes Goldsmith] the few poets of England no longer depend on the Great for subsistence, they have now no other patrons but the public, and the public, collectively considered, is a good and generous master . . . Every polite member of the community, by buying what a man of letters writes, contributes to reward him. The ridicule therefore of living in a garret, might have been wit in the last age, but continues such no longer, because no longer true. A writer of real merit now may easily be rich if his heart be set only on fortune: and for those who have no merit, it is but fit that such should remain in merited obscurity. He may now refuse an invitation to dinner, without fearing to incur his patron's displeasure, or to starve by remaining at home. He may now venture to appear in company with just such clothes as other men generally wear, and talk even to princes, with all the conscious superiority of wisdom. Though he cannot boast of fortune here, yet he can bravely assert the dignity of independence.[196]

Goldsmith's practice harmonized with his theory. When the Earl of Northumberland was appointed Lord-Lieutenant of Ireland he told Goldsmith that he had read his *Traveller* with much enjoyment, and that it would be a great pleasure to him if, in his new capacity, he could do something for him. In recounting this gracious offer, Goldsmith said: " I could say nothing, but that I had a brother there [in Ireland], a clergyman, that stood in need of help: as for myself, I have no dependence on the promises of great men; I look to the booksellers for support; they are my best friends, and I am not inclined to forsake them for others." [197]

This testimony is doubly interesting. First, because of the important place Goldsmith occupies in English literature, and secondly because his career as a man of letters was by no means all plain sailing, and was punctuated by long and painful periods

---

[196] *The Citizen of the World*, Letter 84. *Works*, II, pp. 369-70. These letters first appeared in the paper called *The Public Ledger* in 1760.
[197] Hawkins, quoted by Boswell, II, p. 200.

of hardship. The same interest attaches to a testimony of Johnson's that occurs in a conversation of his with his friends Boswell and Watson :

"Now learning is itself a trade. A man goes to a bookseller and gets what he can. We have done with patronage. In the infancy of learning, we find some great man praised for it. This diffused it among others. When it becomes general, an author leaves the great, and applies to the multitudes." *Boswell :* "It is a shame that authors are not now better patronized." *Johnson :* "No, Sir. If learning cannot support a man, if he must sit with his hands across till somebody feeds him, it is as to him a bad thing, and it is better as it is. With patronage, what flattery ! What falsehood ! While a man is in equilibrio, he throws truth among the multitude, and lets them take it as they please : in patronage, he must say what pleases his patron, and it is an equal chance whether that be truth or falsehood." *Watson :* "But is it not the case now, that instead of flattering one person, we flatter the age ? " *Johnson :* "No, Sir. The world always lets a man tell what he thinks his own way." [198]

Again, in the *Rambler* Johnson repeated the same view but with greater seriousness :

"The Sciences, after a thousand indignities, retired from the palace of Patronage, and having long wandered over the world in grief and distress, were led at last to the cottage of Independence, the daughter of Fortitude ; where they were taught by Prudence and Parsimony to support themselves in dignity and quiet." [199]

So it is clear that Pope had founded a school of thought. It was he who introduced this attitude of proud independence into English literature, a virtue which it has never lost.

I have tried to do justice to his predecessors, and we should not forget how much they did to open and prepare the road. But if it was thanks to their pioneer work that he was able to be an independent man of letters, the personal honour is his, of having desired to be such, and of having invested the literary profession in England with the rank and dignity it enjoys to-day.

---

[198] Boswell, IV, p. 55.   [199] *The Rambler*, No. 91.

BIBLIOGRAPHY

I. GENERAL WORKS

A. Historical

AUBREY (John).
Letters written By Eminent Persons in the Seventeenth and Eighteenth Centuries : . . . 'And Lives of Eminent Men, by John Aubrey, Esq. In two Volumes. London : Printed for Longman, Hurst, Rees, Orme, and Brown, Paternoster-Row; and Munday and Slatter, Oxford. 1813. 8º.

BELSHAM (W.).
Memoirs Of the Kings of Great Britain of the House of Brunswic-Lunenburg. By W. Belsham. Ac mihi quidem videntur huc omnia esse referenda ab iis qui praesunt aliis, ut ii qui eorum in imperio erunt, sint quam beatissimi. Cicero. London : Printed for C. Dilly, in the Poultry. 1793. 2 vol. 8º.

BURKE (Edmund).
Reflections on the Revolution in France, and on the Proceedings in certain Societies in London relative to that event. In a Letter intended to have been sent to a Gentleman *in Paris*. By the Right Honourable *Edmund Burke*. London : Printed for J. Dodsley, in Pall-Mall. MDCCXC. 8º. [Ed. Sir S. Lee. 1905.]

CHALMERS (George).
The Life of *Thomas Ruddiman*, A.M. The Keeper, for almost Fifty Years, of the Library belonging to the Faculty of Advocates at Edinburgh. To which are subjoined New Anecdotes of *Buchanan*. By George Chalmers, F.R.S.S.A. London : Printed for John Stockdale. Piccadilly : and William Laing, Edinburgh. M.DCC.XCIV. 8º.

CHARLES II.
Copies of two papers Written by the late King Charles the Second. Together with a copy of a Paper written by the late Dutchess of York. Published by his Majestie's special Command. London : Printed by Henry Hills Printer to the Kings most excellent Majesty, for his household and Chappell. 1686. 4º. (This is in manuscript.)

CHRISTIE (W. D.).
Letters addressed from London to Sir Joseph Williamson while Plenipotentiary at the Congress of Cologne in the Years 1673 and 1674. Edited by W. D. Christie, C.B. Author of the Life of the First Earl of Shaftesbury. In Two Volumes. Printed for the Camden Society. M.DCCC.LXXIV. 4º.

CLARENDON (Edward Hyde, Earl of).
The History of the Rebellion and Civil Wars in England, together with an Historical View of the Affairs of Ireland, by Edward Earl of Clarendon now for the first time carefully printed from the original MS. preserved in the Bodleian Library. To which are subjoined the notes of Bishop Warburton. In seven volumes. Oxford, at the University Press. MDCCXLIX. 8º.
[First edition : 3 vols. 1702–4. Ed. W. Dunn Macray. 1888.]

CLARK (G. N.).
[*The Later Stuarts, 1660–1714.* 1934.]

COBBETT (William).
Cobbett's Parliamentary History of England. From the Norman Conquest, in 1066, to the Year 1803. From which last-mentioned Epoch it is continued downwards in the Work entitled, " Cobbett's Parliamentary Debates ". London : Printed by T. Curson Hansard, Peterborough-Court, Fleet street. Published by R. Bagshaw, Brydges-Street, Covent-Garden ; and sold by J. Budd, Pall-Mall ; R. Faulder, New Bond-Street ; H. D. Symonds, Paternoster-Row ; Blacks and Parry, Leadenhall-Street ; and J. Archer, Dublin. October 1806. 36 vols. 8º.

COOKE (Wingrove George).
The History of Party ; From the rise of the Whig and Tory Factions, in the Reign of Charles II., To the passing of the Reform Bill. By George Wingrove Cooke, Esq., Barrister at Law, Author of " Memoirs of Lord Bolingbroke ", etc. 3 volumes. London : John Macrone, St. James's Square. MDCCCXXXVI. 8º.

DORAN (Dr.).
London in the Jacobite Times By Dr Doran, F.S.A. . . . In Two Volumes. London, Richard Bentley and Son, New Burlington Street, Publishers in Ordinary to Her Majesty the Queen. 1877. 8º.

EVELYN (John).
Memoirs, Illustrative of the Life and Writings of John Evelyn, Esq. F.R.S. Author of the " Sylva ", etc. etc. Comprising his Diary from the Year 1641 to 1705–6, and a Selection of his familiar Letters. To which is subjoined, The private Correspondence between King Charles I. and his Secretary of State, Sir Edward Nicholas, whilst His Majesty was in Scotland, 1641, and at other times during the civil war ; also between Sir Edward Hyde, afterwards Earl of Clarendon, and Sir Richard Browne, Ambassador to the Court of France, in the time of King Charles I. and the Usurpation. The Whole now first published, from the Original MSS. In two Volumes. Edited by William Bray, Esq. Fellow and Treasurer of the Society of Antiquaries of London. London : Printed for Henry Colburn, Conduit Street. And Sold by John and Arthur Arch, Cornhill. 1818. 4º.
Diary and Correspondence of John Evelyn, F.R.S., Author of the " Sylva ". To which is subjoined The Private Correspondence between King Charles I. and Sir Edward Nicholas, and between Sir Edward Hyde, afterwards Earl of Clarendon and Sir Richard Browne. Edited from the Original MSS. at Wotton. By William Bray, Esq., F.A.S. A new edition, in four Volumes. Corrected, revised, and enlarged. London : Henry Colburn, Publisher, . . . 1850. 8º.
[4 vols. Bohn's Library. 1859. Reprinted : Routledge. 1906.]

GRANGER (J.).
A Biographical History of England, From Egbert the Great to the Revolution : Consisting of Characters disposed in different Classes, and adapted to a Methodical Catalogue of Engraved British Heads. Intended as an Essay towards reducing our Biography to System, and a Help to the Knowledge of Portraits. Interspersed with Variety of Anecdotes, and Memoirs of a great Number of Persons, not to be found in any other Biographical Work. With a Preface, shewing the Utility of a Collection of Engraved Portraits to supply the Defect, and answer the various Purposes of Medals. By the Rev. J. Granger, Vicar of Shiplake, in Oxfordshire. Animam pictura pascit inani. Virg. Celebrare domestica facta. Hor. London, Printed for T. Davies, in Russel-Street, Covent-Garden. 1769–1774. 2 vols. 4º.
[3 vols. 1806. Cont. M. Noble.]

HALLAM (Henry).
The Constitutional History of England From the Accession of Henry VII. to the Death of George II. By Henry Hallam, LL.D., F.R.A.S. Foreign Associate of the Institute of France. Seventh Edition. In Three volumes. London : John Murray, Albemarle Street. 1854. 8º.

HAMILTON (Antoine).
Mémoires du Chevalier de Grammont. Précédés d'une notice sur la vie et les ouvrages d'Hamilton, par M. Auger, secrétaire perpétuel de l'Académie française. Suivis de la table des noms propres des mémoires de Grammont et d'un choix de ses épîtres en vers et de la correspondance . . . Paris, Librairie de Firmin-Didot, freres, fils et Cie. 1861. 12º.

HERVEY (John, Lord).
Memoirs of the Reign of George the Second, from his Accession to the Death of Queen Caroline. By John, Lord Hervey. Edited from the original manuscript at Ickworth, By The Right Hon. John Wilson Croker, LL.D., F.R.S. In Two Volumes. London : John Murray, Albemarle Street. 1848. 8º.
[Ed. R. Sedgwick. 3 vols. 1931. With a memoir of the life of Hervey.]

KEBLE (Joseph).
The Statutes at Large in Paragraphs and Sections or Numbers, from Magna Charta To the End of The Reign of King Charles II. (Carefully Examined by the Rolls of Parliament ; with the Titles of such Statutes as are Expired, Repealed, Altered, or out of Use.) Together with the Heads of Pulton's or Rastal's Abridgments in the Margin, And the Addition of above a Thousand New References from other Books of Law. By Joseph Keble of *Grays-Inn*, Esquire. In this Impression are added All the Statutes in the Reigns of King *James* II. King *William* and Queen *Mary*, to the End of the last Session of Parliament, May 3. 1695. In the Seventh Year of the Reign of His Majesty King *William* III. All the Statutes of the said Reigns are Alphabetically Tabled with the other Statutes, and the former Table much Improved by Notes on all the Paragraphs or Heads, whereby any Thing that is look'd for may be much sooner found. In Two Volumes. *London,* Printed by *Charles Bill,* and the Executrix of *Thomas Newcomb,* deceas'd, Printers to the Kings most Excellent Majesty, And by the Assigns of *Richard Atkins,* and *Edward Atkins,* Esquires. MDCXCV. folio.

LECKY (William Edward Hartpole).
A History of England in the Eighteenth Century by William Edward Hartpole Lecky. London : Longmans, Green, and Co. 1878–1886. 6 vols. 8º.
[8 vols. 1878–90.]

LODGE (Sir Richard).
[*The History of England from the Restoration to the death of William III. 1660–1702.* Vol. VIII of *The Political History of England.* 1910.]

MACAULAY (Thomas Babington, Lord).
The History of England from the accession of James the Second By Thomas Babington Macaulay. Twelfth Edition. London : Longman, Brown, Green and Longmans, 1856. 5 vols. 8º.
[Ed. T. F. Henderson. 5 vols. 1931. World's Classics.]

MAHON (Lord). See STANHOPE.

MALCOLM (James Peller).
Anecdotes of the Manners and Customs of London from the Roman Invasion

to the Year 1700; including the origin of British Society, Customs and Manners, with a General Sketch of the State of Religion, Superstition, Dresses, and Amusements of the Citizens of London during that period. To which are added, Illustrations of the Changes in our Language, Literary Customs, and gradual Improvement in style and versification, and various particulars concerning public and private libraries. Illustrated by Eighteen Engravings. By James Peller Malcolm, F.A.S. Author of " Londinium Redivivum " ; and of " Anecdotes of the Manners and Customs of London, during the eighteenth century ". London: Printed for Longman, Hurst, Rees, Orme, and Brown, Paternoster Row. 1811. 4º.

NEAL (Daniel).
The History of the Puritans or *Protestant Non-Conformists*, from the Reformation to the Death of Queen Elizabeth : With An Account of their Principles ; their Attempts for a further Reformation in the Church ; their Sufferings ; and the Lives and Characters of their principal Divines, By Daniel Neal, M.A. *Now all these Things happened unto them for Ensamples ; And they are written for our Admonition.* 1 Cor. x. 11. London : Printed for Richard Hett, at the Bible and Crown in the Poultry. M.DCC.XXXII. The 2nd volume, dated M.DCC.XXXIII, " from the Death of Queen Elizabeth to the Beginning of the Civil War in the Year 1642 ", has the motto : *But if ye bite and devour one another, take heed ye be not consumed one of another,* Gal. v. 15. The 3rd volume dated M.DCC.XXXVI, " from the Beginning of the Civil War in the Year 1642. to the Death of King Charles I. 1648 ". has the motto : *Think not that I am come to send Peace on Earth, I came not to send Peace but a Sword,* Matth. x. 34. The 4th volume dated M.DCC.XXXVIII, " from the Death of King Charles I. to the Act of *Toleration* by King William and Queen Mary, in the Year 1689 ", has the two following mottoes : *This know also, that in the last Days perilous Times shall come,* 2 Tim. III. 1. *They shall put you out of the Synagogues ; yea, the Time cometh, that whosoever killeth you will think that he doth God Service.* John xvi. 2. 4 vols. 8º.
[Ed. J. Toulmin. 1822. With a life of Neal.]

PEPYS (Samuel).
Diary and Correspondence of Samuel Pepys, F.R.S. Secretary to the Admiralty in the Reigns of Charles II. and James II. With a Life and Notes by Richard Lord Braybrooke. The Third Edition, Considerably enlarged. Five Volumes. London : Henry Colburn, Publisher, Great Marlborough Street. 1848. 8º.
Diary and Correspondence of Samuel Pepys, Esq. F.R.S., from his MS. cypher in the Pepysian Library, with a Life and Notes by Richard Lord Braybrooke. Deciphered, with additional notes, by Rev. Mynors Bright, M.A. President and Senior Fellow of Magdalene College, Cambridge. With numerous portraits from the Collection in the Pepysian Library, printed in permanent Woodburytype. London : Bickers and Son, 1, Leicester Square. 1875. 5 vols. 8º.
The Diary of Samuel Pepys M.A. F.R.S. Clerk of the Acts and Secretary to the Admiralty transcribed from the Shorthand Manuscript in the Pepysian Library Magdalene College Cambridge by the Rev. Mynors Bright M.A. Late Fellow and President of the College with Lord Braybrooke's Notes Edited with Additions by Henry B. Wheatley, F.S.A. London : George Bell & Sons York St. Covent Garden. . . 1893–1896. 8º.
[Ed. H. B. Wheatley. 1920.]

[Samuel Pepys. By Arthur Bryant.
Vol. I. The Man in the Making. 1933.
Vol. II. The Years of Peril. 1935.
Vol. III. The Saviour of the Navy. 1938.]

PHILIPS (Ambrose).
The Life of John Williams, Ld Keeper of the Great Seal, Bp. of Lincoln, and Abp. of York. In the Reigns of King James, and King Charles the First. Wherein *Are related several Remarkable Occurences of those Times both in Church and State*. With an *Appendix* Giving a just Account of his Benefactions to *St. John's* College in *Cambridge*. By *Ambr. Philips*, Fellow of the same College. Cambridge, Printed at the University Press, for *A. Bosvile*, at the Sign of the *Dial* over against St. *Dunstan's* Church in Fleetstreet. 1700. 8º.

RAPIN de Thoyras.
The History of England. Written in French by Mr Rapin de Thoyras. Translated into English With Additional Notes, by N. Tindal, M.A. Vicar of Great Waltham, in Essex. The Second Edition. London : Printed for James, John and Paul Knapton, at the Crown in Ludgate-street, near the West-End of St. Paul's. MDCCXXXIII. folio.

RAVAISSON (François).
Archives de la Bastille. Documents Inédits recueillis et publiés par François Ravaisson. Règne de Louis XIV (1687 to 1692). Vol. IX. Paris, 1877. 8º.

RÉMUSAT (Charles de).
L'Angleterre au dix-huitième siecle. Études et portraits pour servir à l'histoire du gouvernement anglais depuis la fin du règne de Guillaume III, par M. Charles de Rémusat. Paris, Didier et Cie, libraires-éditeurs, 36, Quai des Augustins. 1856. 2 vols. 8º.

RERESBY (Sir John).
The Memoirs of Sir John Reresby of Thrybergh, Bart. M.P. for York, etc. 1634–1689. *Written by Himself.* Edited from the Original Manuscript By James J. Cartwright, M.A. Cantab. Of H.M. Public Record Office. Author of " Chapters of Yorkshire History ". London : Longmans, Green, And Co. 1875. 8º.

SCOTT (Sir Walter).
A Collection of Scarce and Valuable Tracts, on the most interesting and entertaining subjects : but chiefly such as relate to the History and Constitution of these Kingdoms. Selected from an infinite number in print and manuscript, in the Royal, Cotton, Sion, and other public, as well as private, libraries, particularly that of the late Lord Somers. The Second Edition, revised, augmented, and arranged, by Walter Scott, Esq. The bent and genius of the age is best known in a free country, by the pamphlets and papers that come daily out, as the sense of parties, and sometimes the voice of the nation. Preface to Kennet's Register. *Judex qui aliquid statuit, una parte audita tantum et inaudita altera, licet aequum statuerit, haud aequus fuerit.* Ld. Cook and Just. Inst. London : Printed for T. Cadell and W. Davies, Strand ; W. Miller, Albemarle-street ; R. H. Evans, Pall-Mall ; J. White and J. Murray, Fleet-street ; and J. Harding, St. James's-street. 1809–15. 13 vols. 4º.

SKELTON (John).
The Impeachment of Mary Stuart Sometime Queen of Scots and other Papers Historical and Biographical. (With this epigraph : " In defence ! ") By John Skelton Advocate. London, William Blackwood and Sons, 1876. 8º.

STANHOPE (Philip Henry, 5th Earl of Stanhope).
History of England from the peace of Utrecht to the peace of Versailles, 1713–1783. By Lord Mahon. In seven volumes. Leipzig, Bernhard Tauchnitz. 1853. 12º.
History of England comprising the reign of Queen Anne until the peace of Utrecht, by Earl Stanhope, 1701–1713, In two volumes. Leipzig, Bernard Tauchnitz, 1870. 12º.

STOUGHTON (John).
Ecclesiastical History of England. The Church of the Restoration. By John Stoughton. D.D. In two volumes, London : Hodder and Stoughton. 27, Paternoster Row, etc. MDCCCLXX. 8º.

THORNBURY (Walter).
Haunted London, by W. Thornbury. *Illustrated by F. W. Fairholt, F.S.A.* London : Hurst and Blackett, Publishers, Successors to Henry Colburn, 13, Great Marlborough Street. 1865. 8º.

TOWNSEND (W. Charles).
History of the House of Commons, from the Convention Parliament of 1688–9 to the Passing of the Reform Bill in 1832. By W. Charles Townsend, Esq. ; A.M., *Recorder of Macclesfield*. London : *Henry Colburn, Publisher*, Great Marlborough Street. 1834–4. 2 vols. 8º.

TREVELYAN (G. M.).
[*England under Queen Anne.* 3 vols. 1930–4.]
[*English Social History* : *a survey of six centuries, Chaucer to Queen Victoria.* 1944.]

TURBERVILLE (A. S.).
[*English Men and Manners in the Eighteenth Century.* 1929.]

WALPOLE (Sir Robert).
Memoirs of the Life and Administration of Sir Robert Walpole, *Earl of Orford.* With original correspondence and authentic papers, never before published. In Three Volumes. By William Coxe, M.A. F.R.S. F.A.S. Rector of Bemerton. *London* : Printed for T. Cadell Jun. and W. Davies, in the Strand. 1798. 4º.

WILLEY (Basil).
[*The Seventeenth Century Background.* 1934.]
[*The Eighteenth Century Background.* 1940.]

B. Critical.

ALLIBONE (S. Austin).
Critical Dictionary of English Literature and British and American Authors Living and Deceased From the Earliest Accounts to the Latter End of the Nineteenth Century. Containing over forty-six thousand articles (Authors). With Forty Indexes of Subjects. By S. Austin Allibone . . . Philadelphia. J. B. Lippincott and Co. 1872. 3 vols. 8º.

ANDREWS (Alexander).
The History of British Journalism, from the Foundation of the Newspaper Press in England, to the Repeal of the Stamp Act in 1855, with Sketches of Press Celebrities, by Alexander Andrews. In two Volumes. London : Richard Bentley, New Burlington Street, Publisher in Ordinary to Her Majesty. MDCCCLIX. 8º.

ὰ WOOD (Anthony).
Athenæ Oxonienses, an Exact History of all the Writers and Bishops who have had their education in the University of Oxford. To which are added the Fasti, or Annals of the Said University. By Anthony

à Wood, M.A. of Merton College. A new edition, with additions and a continuation By Philip Bliss, Fellow of St. John's College . . . *Antiquam exquirite matrem.* Virgil. London : . . . 1813-1820. 4 vols. folio.

BATESON (F. W.).
[*English Comic Drama. 1700-1750.* Oxford. 1929.]

BETTERTON (Thomas).
The History of the English Stage, from the Restauration to the Present Time. Including the Lives, Characters and Amours, of the most Eminent Actors and Actresses. With Instructions for Public Speaking ; Wherein The Action and Utterance of the Bar, Stage, and Pulpit are Distinctly Considered. By Mr. Thomas Betterton. Adorned with Cuts. London : Printed for E. Curll, at *Pope's Head* in *Rose-Street, Covent-Garden.* MDCCXLI. Price 5^s. Bound. 8º. (The attribution of this work to the celebrated actor Betterton was no doubt a convenient guess of bookseller Curll.)

Biographia Britannica.
Biographia Britannica : or, the Lives of the Most eminent Persons Who have flourished in Great Britain and Ireland, From the earliest Ages, down to the present Times : Collected from the Best Authorities, both Printed and Manuscript, And digested in the Manner of Mr. Bayle's Historical and Critical Dictionary. London : Printed for W. Innys, W. Meadows, . . . MDCCXLVII. 6 vols. folio.

Biographia Dramatica.
Biographia Dramatica ; or, a Companion to the Playhouse : Containing *Historical and critical Memoirs, and original Anecdotes* of British and Irish Dramatic Writers, from the Commencement of our Theatrical Exhibitions ; among whom are *some of the most celebrated Actors* : Also an Alphabetical Account, and Chronological Lists of their Works. The Dates when Printed, and Observations on their Merits : Together With *An Introductory View of the Rise And Progress* of the British Stage. Originally Compiled, to the Year 1764, by David Erskine Baker. Continued thence to 1782 by Isaac Reed. F.A.S. *And brought down to the End of November 1811, with very considerable Additions and Improvements throughout, by* Stephen Jones. In three Volumes. London : Printed for Longman, Hurst, Rees, Orme, and Brown, T. Payne, G. and W. Nichols and Son, Scatchard and Letterman, J. Barker, W. Miller, R. H. Evans, J. Harding, J. Faulder, and Gale and Surtis. 1812. 3 vols. 8º.

BOSWELL (James).
The Life of Samuel Johnson, LL.D. Including his Tour to the Hebrides, Correspondence with Mrs. Thrale, etc. etc., by James Boswell. With numerous additions, by John Wilson Croker. *Revised and enlarged under his direction by John Wright.* London, Bell and Daldy, York street, Covent Garden. 1868. 10 vols. 8º.
[Ed. G. Birkbeck Hill. 6 vols. 1887. Revised L. T. Powell. 6 vols. 1934-40.]

BOYSE (Samuel).
The British Poets. Including Translations. In one Hundred Volumes, LIX. Grainger—Boyse, Chiswick : Printed by Whittingham, College House, for J. Carpenter, J. Booker, Rodwell and Martin. G. and W. B. Whittaker, R. Triphook, J. Ebers, Taylor and Hessey, R. Jennings, G. Cowie and Co. N. Hailes, J. Porter, B. E. Lloyd and Son, G. Smith, and C. Whittingham. 1822. 12º.

[*Cambridge History of English Literature.*
Ed. A. W. Ward and A. R. Waller. 1907-27. Vols. VII, VIII, IX, X.]

CHALMERS (Alexander).
  The Works of the English Poets, from Chaucer to Cowper; including
  the series Edited with Prefaces, Biographical and Critical, By Samuel
  Johnson: And the most approved Translations. The Additional Lives
  by Alexander Chalmers F.S.A. In Twenty one Volumes, London:
  printed for J. Johnson; J. Nichols and son; R. Baldwin; F. and C.
  Rivington; etc. 1810. 4º.
  The General Biographical Dictionary: ... A New Edition, Revised and
  Enlarged by Alexander Chalmers, F.S.A. 30 volumes. London: ...
  1812. 8º.

CHAPPELL (William).
  Popular Music of the Olden Time; a Collection of Ancient Songs, Ballads,
  and Dance Tunes, Illustrative of the National Music of England. With
  short Introductions to the different Reigns, and Notices of the Airs
  from Writers of the Sixteenth and Seventeenth Centuries. Also A Short
  Account of the Minstrels. By W. Chappell, F.S.A. The Whole of the
  Airs harmonized by G. A. Macfarren. Two Volumes. Prout sunt illi
  Anglicani concentus suavissimi quidem ac elegantes. *Thesaurus Harmonicus* Laurencini, *Romani*. 1603. London: Cramer, Beale and
  Chappell, 201. Regent Street. (1856–59.) 8º.

CIBBER (Colley).
  [*A Short Account of the Rise and Progress of the English Stage*. 1750. (With
  the *Apology*. See Cibber, Section II.)]

CLAVELL (Robert).
  The General Catalogue of Books, Printed in England Since the Dreadful
  Fire of London MDCLXVI. To the End of *Trinity-Term* MDCLXXX.
  Together with the Texts of Single Sermons, With the Authors Names:
  Plays Acted at both the Theaters: And an Abstract of the General
  Bills of Mortality since 1660. With an Account of the Titles of all the
  Books of *Law, Navigation, Musick, etc.* And a Catalogue of School Books.
  To which is now added a Catalogue of Latin Books Printed in Foreign
  Parts and in *England* since the Year MDCLXX. Collected by *R. Clavell,
  London*, Printed by *S. Roycroft* for *Robert Clavell* at the *Peacock* in St. *Paul's
  Church-Yard*. 1680. folio.

CUCHEVAL CLARIGNY.
  Histoire de la Presse en Angleterre et aux États-Unis, par M. Cucheval
  Clarigny, ancien rédacteur en chef du *Constitutionnel*. Paris, Amyot,
  éditeur des oeuvres de Napoléon III et de la *Semaine politique*. 8, rue de
  la Paix. 1857. in-12.

DILKE (Charles Wentworth).
  The Papers of a Critic. Selected from the writings of the late Charles
  Wentworth Dilke. With a biographical sketch by his Grandson, Sir
  Charles Wentworth Dilke, Bart., M.P., author of " Greater Britain "
  and of " The Fall of Prince Florestan of Monaco." In two volumes.
  London: John Murray, Albemarle Street. 1875. 8º.

D'ISRAELI (Isaac).
  Curiosities of Literature. By Isaac D'Israeli. A New Edition, Edited,
  with Memoir and Notes, By his Son The Right Hon. B. Disraeli, Chancellor of Her Majesty's Exchequer. In Three Volumes. London:
  G. Routledge and Co., Farringdon Street. New York: 18, Beekman
  Street. 1858. 8º.
    [A selection from the above ed. E. V. Mitchell. 1932.]
  Amenities of Literature. Consisting of Sketches and Characters of English
  Literature. By Isaac D'Israeli. A New Edition, Edited by his Son,

The Right Hon. B. Disraeli, Chancellor of Her Majesty's Exchequer. In Two Volumes. London : Routledge, Warnes, and Routledge, Farringdon Street, New York : 18, Beekman Street. 1859. 8⁰.
The Calamities and Quarrels of Authors : With some inquiries respecting their moral and literary Characters, and Memoirs for our Literary History. By Isaac D'Israeli. A New Edition, Edited by his Son The Right Hon. B. Disraeli, Chancellor of Her Majesty's Exchequer. London : Routledge, Warnes, and Routledge,. . . . 1859. 8⁰.

DOBRÉE (B.).
[*Essays in Biography 1680–1726.* Oxford. 1925. (Vanbrugh, Addison, Etherege.)]
[*Restoration Comedy.* Oxford. 1924.]
[*Restoration Tragedy.* Oxford. 1930.]
[*Variety of Ways.* 1932. (Dryden, Halifax, Steele, Mandeville.)]

DORAN (Dr.).
" Their Majesties' Servants." Annals of the English Stage, from Thomas Betterton to Edmund Kean. Actors—Authors—Audiences. By Dr. Doran, F.S.A., Author of " Table Traits," " History of Court Fools," " Queens of England of the House of Hanover," etc. Second Edition. (Revised, corrected, and enlarged.) London : Wm. H. Allen and Co., 13. Waterloo Place, S.W. 1866. 8⁰.

DOWNES (John).
Roscius Anglicanus, Or An Historical Review of the Stage : After it had been Suppress'd by means of the late Unhappy Civil War, begun in 1644, till the Time of King *Charles* the II⁸. Restoration *in May* 1660. Giving an Account of its Rise again ; of the Time and Places the Governours of both the Companies first Erected their Theatres. The Names of the Principal Actors and Actresses, who Perform'd in the Chiefest Plays in each House. With the Names of the most taking Plays ; and Modern Poets. For the space of 46 Years, and during the Reign of Three Kings, and part of our present Sovereign Lady Queen *Anne*, from 1660, to 1706. *Non Audita narro, sed Comperta. London.* Printed and sold by *H. Playford,* at his House in *Arundel-street,* near the Water side, 1708 (date cancelled by hand and altered to 1712). 8⁰.
Roscius Anglicanus, or, An Historical Review of the Stage . . . With Additions, By the late Mr. Thomas Davies, Author of *The Life of Garrick,* and *Dramatic Miscellanies.* London, Printed for the Editor, and Sold at No. 62. *Great Wild-Street,* near *Lincoln's*-Inn-Fields, by Mess. Egerton, *Whitehall* ; Mess. Cox and Phillipson, *James-Street, Covent-Garden* ; R. Ryan. No. 351, Oxford-Street ; H. D. Symonds, No. 20, *Pater-Noster-Row* ; and W. Richardson, under the *Royal-Exchange.* 1789. 8⁰. (Edited by F. G. Waldron.)
[Ed. M. Summers. 1928.]

DRAKE (Nathan). See p. 423.

DYSON (H. V. D.) and John Butt.
[*Augustans and Romantics. 1689–1830.* 1940. Vol. III of *Introductions to English Literature.* Ed. B. Dobrée.]

FORSTER (John).
Oliver Cromwell. Daniel De Foe. Sir Richard Steele. Charles Churchill. Samuel Foote. Biographical Essays. By John Forster. Third Edition. London : John Murray, Albemarle Street. 1860. 8⁰.

GENEST (John).
Some Account of the English Stage, from the Restoration In 1660, to 1830. In ten Volumes.

'Ει δε τι παρωπται, ή ούκ ακριβως ανειληπται, μηδεις ήμας γραφετω μεμψεως, εννοων ως πεπλανημενην ιστοριαν συνελεξαμεν.
  Evagrius, p. 473. If any thing be overlooked, or not accurately inserted, let no one find fault, but take into consideration that this history is compiled from all quarters. Bath : Printed by H. E. Carrington. Sold by Thomas Rodd, Great Newport Street, London. 1832. 8º.

GOSSE (E. W.).
  Seventeenth Century Studies A Contribution to the History of English Poetry by Edmund W. Gosse London Kegan Paul, Trench and Cº, Paternoster Square, 1883, 8º. (P. 269–305 : Otway.)

HALLAM (Henry).
  Introduction to the Literature of Europe, in the Fifteenth, Sixteenth and Seventeenth Centuries. By Henry Hallam, LL.D., F.R.A.S., Foreign Associate of the Institute of France. De modo autem hujusmodi historiae conscribendae, illud imprimis monemus, ut materia et copia ejus, non tantum ab historiis et criticis petatur, verum etiam per singulas annorum centurias, aut etiam minora intervalla, seriatim libri praecipui, qui eo temporis spatio conscripti sunt, in consilium adhibeantur ; ut ex eorum non perlectione (id enim infinitum quiddam esset), sed degustatione, et observatione argumenti, styli, methodi, genius illius temporis literarius, veluti incantatione quadam, a mortuis evocetur. Bacon de Augm. Scient. Fifth Edition in Four Volumes. London : John Murray, Albemarle Street. 1855. 8º.

HAZLITT (William).
  Lectures on the English Poets, and the English Comic Writers. By William Hazlitt, Author of " *Table Talk, or Essays on Men and Manners* ; " " *Essays on the Literature of the Age of Elizabeth* ; " " *Characters of Shakspeare's Plays, etc. etc. etc.*" A New Edition, Edited by *William Carew Hazlitt*. London : Bell and Daldy, York Street, Covent Garden. 1870. 8º.

HETTNER (Hermann).
  Geschichte der englischen Literatur von der Wiederherstellung des Königthums bis in die zweite Hälfte des achtzehnten Jahrhunderts. 1660–1779. Von Hermann Hettner. Dritte verbesserte Auflage. Braunschweig, Druck und Verlag von Friedrich Vieweg und Sohn. 1872. 8º.

HUNT (J. H. Leigh).
  [*The Dramatic Works of Wycherley, Congreve, Vanbrugh and Farquhar.* 1840.]

JOHNSON (Samuel).
  Lives of the most eminent English Poets, with critical observations on their works. By Samuel Johnson. With notes corrective and explanatory, by Peter Cunningham, F.S.A. In three volumes. London : John Murray, Albemarle Street. 1854. 8º.
    [Ed. G. Birkbeck Hill. 3 vols. Oxford. 1905.]

KNIGHT (Charles).
  Shadows of the Old Booksellers. By Charles Knight. " Now learning itself is a trade. A man goes to a bookseller, and gets what he can. We have done with patronage. In the infancy of learning, we find some great man praised for it. This diffused it among others. When it becomes general, an author leaves the great, and applies to the multitude."—Johnson, in 1773. London : Bell and Daldy, 186, Fleet-street. 1865. 8º. [Reprinted 1927.]

KRUTCH (J. W.).
  [*Comedy and Conscience after the Restoration.* New York. 1924.]

BIBLIOGRAPHY 397

LAMB (Charles).
[*On the Artificial Comedy of the Last Century.* 1821. In *Essays of Elia.*]
LANGBAINE (Gerard).
An Account of the English Dramatick Poets. Or, Some Observations And *Remarks* On the Lives and Writings, of all those that have Publish'd either Comedies, Tragedies, Tragi-comedies, Pastorals, Masques, Interludes, Farces, or Opera's in the *English Tongue*. By Gerard Langbaine. Oxford, Printed by L. L. for George West, and Henry Clements. *An. Dom.* 1691. 8º.
[The essay on Dryden is reprinted in *Critical Essays of the Seventeenth Century*. Ed. J. E. Spingarn. Vol. III. 1909.]
LOWELL (James Russell).
Among my Books. By James Russell Lowell, A.M., Professor of Belles-Lettres in Harvard College. Boston : James R. Osgood and Company, 1875. 12º.
LOWNDES (William Thomas).
The Bibliographer's Manual of English Literature . . . revised by Henry G. Bohn. London, 1864. 6 vols. 8º.
Luttrell Collection
Vol. I : Eulogies and Elegies. Vol. II : Humorous, Political, and Miscellaneous Ballads. Vol. III : Proclamations and Broadsides. folio.
LYNCH (K. M.).
[*The Social Mode of Restoration Comedy*. University of Michigan. 1926.]
MACAULAY (Thomas Babington, Lord).
Critical and Miscellaneous Essays. By T. Babington Macaulay. New and Revised Edition. In Five volumes. New York : D. Appleton and Company, 346 and 348 Broadway. M. DCCC.LVII. 8º.
[*Critical and Historical Essays.* Ed. F. C. Montague. 3 vols. 1903.]
MALONE (Edmond).
Historical Account of the Rise and Progress of the English Stage, and of the Economy and Usages of the Ancient Theatres in England ; by Edmund Malone, Esqur. Basil : Printed and sold by J. J. Tourneisen. M.DCCC. 8º.
MASSON (David).
Essays Biographical and Critical : chiefly on English Poets. By David Masson. A.M. Professor of English Literature in University College, London. Cambridge : Macmillan and Co. 1856. 8º.
MEREDITH (George).
[*An Essay on Comedy.* 1877.]
NICHOLS (John).
Literary Anecdotes of the Eighteenth Century, Comprizing Biographical Memoirs of William Bowyer, Printer, F.S.A. and many of his learned friends ; an incidental view of the progress and advancement of literature in this kingdom during the last century ; and Biographical Anecdotes of a considerable number of eminent Writers and ingenious Artists : with a very copious index. By John Nichols F.S.A. in six volumes. London, Printed for the author by Nichols, son and Bentley, at Cicero's head Red Lion-passage, Fleet Street, 1812. 8º.
NICOLL (Allardyce).
[*A History of Restoration Drama.* 1923.]
[*A History of Early Eighteenth Century Drama.* 1919.]
PALMER (John).
[*The Comedy of Manners.* 1913.]

PERRY (H. Ten Eyck).
[*The Comic Spirit in Restoration Drama.* New Haven. 1925.]

PINTO (V. de Sola).
[*The English Renaissance. 1510–1688.* 1938. Vol. II. *Introductions to English Literature.* Ed. B. Dobrée.]

REID (G. W.).
Catalogue of Prints and Drawings in the *British Museum.* Div. I. Political and Personal Satires. Vol. II. June 1689 to 1733. By G. W. Reid. 8º.

Roxburghe Collection.
Ancient Songs and Ballads : Written on Various Subjects, and Printed between the Years MDLX and MDCC. Chiefly Collected by Robert Earl of Oxford, and purchased at the Sale of the late Mr. West's Library, in the Year 1773. Encreased by several Additions . . . London, Arranged and Bound in the Year 1774. 2 vols. folio.

SPENCE (Joseph).
Anecdotes, Observations, and Characters of Books and Men. Collected From The Conversation of Mr. Pope, and *Other Eminent Persons of His Time.* By the Rev. Joseph Spence. Now First Published From The Original Papers, With Notes And A Life of The Author. By Samuel Weller Singer.
     Apis matinae
     More modoque
     Grata carpentis thyma.
London : Published By W. H. Carpenter, Lower Brook Street ; And Archibald Constable And Co. Edinburgh. MDCCC.XX. 8º.

SPINGARN (J. E.).
[*Critical Essays of the Seventeenth Century.* Ed. J. E. Spingarn. 3 vols. Oxford. 1908–9.]

STEPHEN (Leslie).
[*English Literature and Society in the Eighteenth Century.* 1904.]

STEPHENS (Frederic George).
Catalogue of Prints and Drawings in the British Museum. Division. Political and Personal Satires (No. 1 to No. 1235). Vol. I. 1320 to April 11, 1689. Printed by order of the Trustees. 1870. 8º.

SUMMERS (M.).
[*The Restoration Theatre.* 1934.]

TAINE (H.).
Histoire de la Littérature Anglaise, par H. Taine. Paris, Hachette et Cⁱᵉ. 1863. 4 vols. 8º.
[Trans. H. Van Laun. 2 vols. 1871.]

THOMPSON (N.).
A Collection of One Hundred and Eighty Loyal Songs, All written since 1678. And Intermixt with several New Love Songs. To which is Added, The Notes Set by Several Masters of Musick. With a Table to find every Song. The Fourth Edition with many Additions. *London,* Printed, and are to be sold by *Richard Butt,* in *Princess-street* in *Covent-Garden.* 1694. Price Bound 2s. 12º.

TIMPERLEY (C. H.).
Encyclopaedia of Literary and Typographical Anecdote : Being a Chronological Digest of the most interesting facts illustrative of the History of Literature and Printing from the earliest Period to the present Time. Interspersed with Biographical Sketches of Eminent Booksellers, Printers, Type-founders, Engravers, Bookbinders and Paper makers, of all ages

and Countries, but especially of Great Britain. With Bibliographical and Descriptive Accounts of their principal Productions and occasional Extracts from them. Including Curious Particulars of the first introduction of Printing into various Countries, and of the Books then printed. Notices of early Bibles and Liturgies of all Countries, especially those printed in England or in English. A History of all the Newspapers, Periodicals, and Almanacks published in this Country. An Account of the Origin and Progress of Language, Writing and Writing Materials, the Invention of Paper, Use of Paper Marks, etc. Compiled and Condensed from Nichols's Literary Anecdotes, and numerous other Authorities, By C. H. Timperley. Second Edition, to which are added, A Continuation to the present Time, Comprising recent Biographies, Chiefly of Booksellers, and A Practical Manual of Printing. London : Henry G. Bohn, York Street, Covent Garden. MDCCCXLII. 8º.

VILLEMAIN.
Cours de Littérature Française, par M. Villemain. Tableau de la Littérature au xviiiᵉ siècle. Paris, Didier et Cᵗᵉ. 1864. 4 volumes 12º.

WALPOLE (Horace).
A Catalogue of the Royal and Noble Authors of England, Scotland, and Ireland ; with *Lists of their Works*. By the late Horatio Walpole, Earl of Orford, Enlarged and Continued to the present Time, *By* Thomas Park, F.S.A. These sheets are calculated for the closest of the idle and inquisitive ; they do not look up to the shelves of what Voltaire happily calls . . . "·La Bibliothèque du Monde." See Vol. II, p. 76. *London :* Printed for John Scott, No 442, Strand. 1806. 5 vols. 8º.
Reminiscences : *Written in* 1788, for the amusement of Miss Mary and Miss Agnes B—— Y ; By Horace Walpole, late Earl of Orford. *No wit is needed by the man concerned with past occurrences.* Voltaire. London, Published by John Sharpe, Piccadilly. 1819. 32º.
[Ed. P. Toynbee. 1924.]

WATT (Robert).
Bibliotheca Britannica ; or A General Index to British and Foreign Literature. By Robert Watt, M.D. In Two Parts :—Authors and Subjects . . . Edinburgh and London. 1824. 4 vols. 4º.

II. AUTHORS

ABSALOM.
Absalom's Conspiracy ; or, the Tragedy of Treason. *London,* Printed in the Year, 1680. folio.

ADDISON (Joseph).
Poems.
A Poem to his Majesty, Presented to the Lord Keeper. By Mr. *Addison*, of *Mag.* Coll. *Oxon.* London : Printed for *Jacob Tonson,* at the *Judge's Head* near the *Inner-Temple-Gate* in *Fleetstreet.* MDCXCV. folio.
The Campaign, A Poem, To his Grace the Duke of *Marlborough.* By Mr. *Addison.*
> *Rheni pacator et Istri*
> *Omnis in hos Uno variis discordia cessit*
> *Ordinibus ; laetatur. Eques plauditque Senator,*
> *Votaque Patricio certant Plebeia favori.*
> Claud. de Laud. Stilic.

London, Printed for *Jacob Tonson,* within *Grays-Inn Gate* next *Grays-Inn Lane.* 1705. folio.

Dramatic Works.
   Rosamond. An Opera. Inscrib'd to Her Grace, The Duchess of Marlborough,
        Hic quos durus amor crudeli tabe peredit
        Secreti celant calles, et myrtea circum
        Sylva tegit.
                            Virg. Æn. VI.
   By the late Right Honourable Joseph Addison Esq.; Glasgow. Printed and Sold by Robert and Andrew Foulis. M. DCC. LI. 8⁰. [First edition : 1707. 4⁰.]
   Cato. A Tragedy. As it is Acted at the Theatre-Royal in *Drury-Lane*, By Her Majesty's Servants. By Mr. *Addison. Ecce Spectantibus dignum, ad quod respiciat, intentus operi suo, Deus! Ecce par Deo dignum vir fortis cum mala fortuna compositus! Non video, inquam, quid habeat in terris Jupiter pulchrius, si convertere animum velit, quam ut spectet Catonem, jam partibus non semel fractis, nihilominus inter ruinas publicas erectum.* Sen. de Divin. Prov. N. B. *This book in a fair large Print is Sold by* M. Gunne, at the *Bible and Crown* at Essex-Street *Gate*, and R. Gunne *in* Capel-Street. 1713. 8⁰.
   [In *Five Restoration Tragedies*. World's Classics. 1927.]
   The Drummer : or, the Haunted-House. A Comedy. As it is Acted at the *Theatre-Royal* in *Drury-Lane*, By His Majesty's Servants.
        Falsis terroribus implet.
        Ut magus.   Hor.*
   The Third Edition. With a Preface by Sir *Richard Steele*, in an Epistle Dedicatory to Mr. *Congreve*, occasioned by Mr. *Tickell's* Preface to the Four Volumes of Mr. *Addison's* Works, *London* : Printed for J. Darby : and Sold by Thomas Combes at the *Bible* and *Dove* in *Pater-Noster-Row*. 1722. 12⁰. [First edition : 1716. 4⁰.]
Periodical Essays.
   Numb. 1. The Spectator.
        Non fumum ex fulgore, sed ex fumo dare lucem
        Cogitat, ut speciosa dehinc miracula promat.
                            Horac.
   To be Continued every Day. *March* 1. 1711. folio.
   The Spectator. *London* : Printed for *S. Buckley*, at the *Dolphin* in *Little-Britain* ; and *J. Tonson*, at *Shakespear's-Head* over-against *Catherine-Street*, in *the Strand*. 1712. 7 vols. 8⁰. (The first edition to be published in volume form.)
   Numb. 1. The Guardian.—*Ille quem requiris.* Mart. To be Continued Every Day. *Thursday*, March 12. 1713. folio.
   The Guardian. *London : Printed for Mess.ʳˢ Longman, Law, Johnson, Nichols, Dilly, Robinson, Richardson, Baldwin, Rivington, Otridge and Son, Hayes, Wilkie ; W. Lowndes, Ogilvie and Son, J. Edwards, Vernor and Hood, Cadell and Davies, H. Lowndes and Lee and Hurst.* 2 vols. 8⁰. 1714.
   The Free-Holder, or Political Essays. London. Printed for D. Midwinter at the *three Crowns* in *St. Paul's Churchyard* ; and J. Tonson at *Shakespear's Head* in the *Strand*. 1716. N⁰. 1. *Friday, December 23, 1715. Rara temporum felicitas, ubi sentire quae velis, et quae sentias dicere licet.* Tacit. 8⁰.
Miscellaneous Prose.
   Remarks on Several Parts of *Italy*, etc. In the Years 1701, 1702, 1703.
        Verum ergo id est, si quis in caelum ascendisset, naturamque mundi et

pulchritudinem siderum perspexisset, insuavem illam admirationem ei fore, quae jucundissima fuisset, si aliquem cui narraret habuisset. Cicer. de Amic. London, Printed for *Jacob Tonson,* within *Grays-Inn* Gate next *Grays-Inn* Lane. 1705. 8º.

The Evidences of the Christian Religion, By the Right Honourable *Joseph Addison,* Esq. To which are added, Several Discourses against Atheism and Infidelity, and in Defence of the Christian Revelation, occasionally published by Him and Others : *And Now collected into one Body and digested under their proper Heads.* With a Preface, containing the Sentiments of Mr. Boyle, Mr. Locke, and Sir Isaac Newton, concerning the *Gospel-Revelation.* London : Printed for J. Tonson in the *Strand.* MDCCXXX. 8º.

Sir Roger de Coverley, by the Spectator. The Notes and Illustrations by W. Henry Wills, London, Longmans, Green and Co. 1 shilling. 12º. 1850.

[*The Letters of Joseph Addison.* Ed. Walter Graham. 1941.]

Collected Works.

The Works of the Right Honourable *Joseph Addison,* Esq. : In Four Volumes. London : Printed for Jacob Tonson, at *Shakespear's-Head,* over against *Katharine-street* in the Strand. MDCCXXI. 4º. (Tickell's edition.)

Bohn's British Classics. The Works of the Right Honourable Joseph Addison. With Notes by Richard Hurd, D.D. Lord Bishop of Worcester. A New Edition with large additions, chiefly unpublished, collected and edited by Henry G. Bohn. London : Henry G. Bohn, York Street, Covent Garden. MDCCCLIV–MDCCCLVI. 6 vols. 8º.

[*Miscellaneous Works.* Ed. A. C. Guthkelch. 2 vols. 1914.]

Biography and Criticism.

Aiken, Lucy.
The life of Joseph Addison. By Lucy Aikin. In two volumes. London : Printed for Longman, Brown, Green and Longmans, Paternoster-Row. 1843. 8º.

Macaulay, T. B.
The Life and Writings of Addison. Edinburgh Review. July, 1843.

Courthope, W. J.
[*Addison.* 1884.]

AMORY (Thomas).
The life of John Buncle, Esq. ; Containing Various Observations and Reflexions, Made in several Parts of the World ; and Many extraordinary Relations.

> *Felix ille animi, Divisque simillimus ipsis,*
> *Quem non mendaci resplendens gloria fuco*
> *Sollicitat, non fastosi mala gaudia luxus.*
> *Sed tacitos sinit ire dies, et paupere cultu*
> *Exigit innocuae tranquilla silentia vitae.*
>   Volusenus.

London : Printed for *J. Noon,* at the *White Hart* in *Cheapside,* near the *Poultry.* MDCCLVI. 2 vols. 8º. [Ed. E. A. Baker. 1904.]

ANTHONY.
The Last Will and Testament of Anthony, King of Poland : Printed for S. Ward, 1682. folio.

ARBUTHNOT (John).
Law is a Bottomless-Pit. Exemplify'd in the Case of The Lord *Strutt,*

John Bull, Nicholas Frog, and *Lewis Baboon*. Who spent all they had in a Law-Suit. *Printed from a Manuscript found in the Cabinet of the famous* Sir Humphry Polesworth. The Second Edition. London : Printed for *John Morphew*, near Stationers' Hall. 1712. Price 3d. 8º. (First edition : 1712.)

[This pamphlet was incorporated into *The History of John Bull*. 1727. In the latter form it is contained in *The Life and Works of John Arbuthnot*. George A. Aitken. 1892.]

Proposals for Printing A very curious Discourse, in two Volumes in *Quarto*, Intitled, ψευδολογα Πολιτικη, or A Treatise of the Art of Political Lying, With An Abstract of the First Volume of the said Treatise. Edinburgh : Reprinted in the Year MDCCXLVI. 8º. (The 1st Edition is dated 1712.) [Ed. George A. Aitken. See above.]

Biography and Criticism.

Beattie, L. M.
[*John Arbuthnot, Mathematician and Satirist.* Cambridge. U.S.A. 1935.]

ARROWSMITH (Joseph).
The Reformation. A Comedy. Acted At the Dukes Theater.

> *Sunt, quibus in Satyra videor nimis acer . . .*
> Horat. lib. 2. Sat. 1.

London, Printed for *William Cademan,* at the Popes-Head, in the Lower walk of the New *Exchange* in the *Strand.* MDCLXXIII. 4º.

BANKES (John).
The Rival Kings Or the Loves of Oroondates and Statira, a Tragedy. Acted at the Theatre-Royal. Written by Mr. Bankes.

> *Divesne Prisco natus ab* Inacho,
> *Nil interest, an Pauper, et infima*
> *De gente sub dio moreris,*
> *Victima nil miserantis Orci.*
> Horat., lib. 2. Ode 3.

London, Printed for *Langley Curtis* in Goat Court on *Ludgate-Hill,* 1677. 4º.

The Destruction of Troy, a Tragedy, Acted at His Royal Highness The Duke's Theatre. Written by *John Bankes.*

> Fortunam Priami cantabo et Nobile Bellum.
> *Quid dignum tanto feret hic Promissor hiatu ?*
> Hor. de Art. Poet.

London, Printed by *A.G.* and *J.P.* and are to be sold by *Charles Blount* at the *Black-Raven* in the *Strand,* near the *Savoy.* 1679. 4º.

Vertue Betray'd : or, Anna Bullen. A Tragedy. Acted at His Royal Highness The Duke's Theatre, Written by *John Banks, Crescit sub Pondere Virtus.* London, Printed for *R. Bentley,* in *Russel-Street* in *Covent-Garden.* MDCXCII. 4º. [First edition : 1682.]

BEDFORD (Arthur).
Serious Reflections on the Scandalous Abuse and Effects of the Stage : in a Sermon preach'd at the Parish-Church of *St. Nicolas* in the City of *Bristol,* on *Sunday* the 7th Day of *January,* 1704/5. By Arthur Bedford, M.A. Vicar of *Temple-Church* in the aforesaid City. *Bristol,* Printed and sold by *W. Bonny* in *Corn-street,* 1705. 8º.

A Second Advertisement concerning the Profaneness of the Play-House. *Bristol.* Printed by *W. Bonny* in *Corn-street.* 1705. 8º.

The *Evil* and *Danger* of Stage-Plays : Shewing their Natural Tendency to Destroy Religion, And introduce a General *Corruption of Manners* ; In almost Two Thousand *Instances*, taken from the *Plays* of the two last Years, against all the *Methods* lately used for their *Reformation.* By *Arthur Bedford*, M.A. Chaplain to his Grace *Wriothesly* Duke of *Bedford* ; and Vicar of *Temple* in the City of *Bristol.*
(Ovid. Metam. lib. 1.)
Cuncta prius tentanda, sed immedicabile vulnus
Ense recidendum est, ne pars sincera trahatur.
Printed and Sold by *W. Bonny*, and the Booksellers of *Bristol* : And by *Henry Mortlock* at the Sign of the *Phoenix* in St. *Paul's Church-Yard, London*, 1706. 8º.
The Great Abuse of Musick. In Two Parts, Containing an Account of the Use and Design of Musick among the Antient *Jews, Greeks, Romans*, and others ; with their Concern for, and Care to prevent the Abuse thereof. And also An Account of the *Immorality* and *Profaneness* which is occasioned by the Corruption of that most Noble Science in the Present Age. By Arthur Bedford, *M.A. Chaplain to His Grace* Wriothesly *Duke of* Bedford, *and Vicar of* Temple *in the City of* Bristol. London : Printed by *J.H.* for John Wyatt at the *Rose* in St. *Paul's* Church-Yard. 1711. 8º.
A serious Remonstrance In Behalf of the Christian Religion, against The Horrid Blasphemies and Impieties which are still used in the *English* Play-Houses, to the great Dishonour of Almighty God, and in Contempt of the Statues of this Realm. Shewing their plain Tendency to overthrow all Piety, and advance the Interest and Honour of the Devil in the World ; from almost Seven Thousand Instances, taken out of the Plays of the present Century, and especially of the five last Years, in defiance of all Methods hitherto used for their Reformation. By *Arthur Bedford*, M.A. Chaplain to the most Noble Wriothesly Duke of *Bedford*, and Rector of *Newton St. Loe* in the County of *Somerset. Jer.* 7, 8, 9, 10. *Behold, ye trust in lying Words, that cannot profit. Will ye steal, murder, and commit Adultery, and swear falsly, and burn Incense unto Baal, and walk after other Gods whom ye know not ; and come and stand before me in this House, which is called by my Name, and say, We are delivered to do all these Abominations ?* Caetera Deus avertat. To treat Honour and Infamy alike, is an Injury to Virtue, and a sort of Levelling in Morality. I confess, I have no Ceremony for Debauchery ; for to compliment Vice, is but one Remove from worshipping the Devil.—*Preface* to Collier's *Book of the Stage.* London : Printed by John Darby, for Henry Hammond, Bookseller in *Bath* ; Richard Gravett, Bookseller on the *Tolzey* in *Bristol* ; and Anth. Piesley, Bookseller in *Oxford.* 1719. 8º.

BEHN (Aphra).
Poems.
A Congratulatory Poem To Her Most Sacred Majesty on the Universal Hopes of all Loyal Persons for a Prince of Wales. By Mrs. *A. Behn. London,* Printed for *Will. Canning,* at his Shop in the *Temple-Cloysters.* 1688. 4º.
Fiction.
All the Histories and Novels Written by the Late Ingenious Mrs. *Behn,* Entire in One volume. Viz. I. *The History of* Oroonoko, *or the Royal Slave. Written by the Command of King* Charles *the Second.* II. *The* Fair Jilt, *or Prince* Tarquin. III. Agnes de Castro, *or the Force of Generous Love.* IV. *The* Lover's Watch, *or the Art of making Love ; being Rules for Courtship for every Hour of the Day and Night.* V. *The* Ladies Looking-glass *to Dress themselves by, or the whole Art of Charming*

all Mankind. VI. *The Lucky Mistake.* VII. *Memoirs of the Court of the King of* Bantam. VIII. *The Nun, or the Perjured Beauty.* IX. *The Adventure of the Black Lady.* Together with The History of the Life and Memoirs of *Mrs. Behn.* By one of the Fair Sex. Intermix'd with Pleasant Love-Letters that pass'd betwixt her and Minheer *Van Bruin,* a *Dutch* Merchant ; with her Character of the Country and Lover : And her Love-Letters to a Gentleman in *England.* The Fifth Edition, Corrected from the many Errors of former Impressions. *London* ; Printed for *R. Wellington,* at the *Dolphin* and *Crown* in St. *Paul's* Church-yard : 1705. 1 vol. 8º.
[*The Novels of Aphra Behn.* Ed. E. A. Baker. 1913. Contains all the above novels.]

Dramatic Works.
    The Amorous Prince, or, the Curious Husband. A Comedy. As it is Acted at his Royal Highness, the Duke of *York's* Theatre. Written by Mrs. *A. Behn. London,* Printed by *J.M.* for *Thomas Dring,* at the *White Lyon,* next *Chancery-Lane-End,* in *Fleet-street.* 1671. 4º.
    The Dutch Lover : A Comedy, acted at the *Dukes Theatre.* Written by Mrs. *A. Bhen* [*sic*]. *London :* Printed for *Thomas Dring* at the Sign of the *Harrow* at *Chancery-lane-end,* over against the Inner Temple Gate in *Fleet-Street,* 1673. 4º.
    The Town-Fopp : Or, Sir Timothy Tawdrey. A Comedy. As it is Acted at his Royal Highness the Duke's Theatre. Written by Mrs. *A. Behn.* Licensed *September* 20. 1676. *Roger L'Estrange. London,* Printed by *T.N.* for *James Magnes,* and *Rich. Bentley,* in *Russel-Street* in *Covent-garden* near the *Piazza's.* M. DC. LXXVII. 4º.
    The Rover or the Banish't Cavaliers. As it is Acted at his Royal-Highness The Duke's Theatre. Licensed *July* 2d 1677. *Roger L'Estrange. London,* Printed for *John Amery,* at the *Peacock,* against St. *Dunstan's* Church in *Fleet-Street.* 1677. 4º.
    Abdelazer, or the Moor's Revenge. A Tragedy. As it is Acted at his Royal Highness the Duke's Theatre. Written by Mrs. *A. Behn, London,* Printed for *J. Magnes* and *R. Bentley,* in *Russel-Street* in *Covent-Garden,* near the *Piazza's,* 1677. 4º.
    Sir Patient Fancy : A Comedy. As it is Acted at the Duke's Theatre. Written by *Mrs. A. Behn,* the Author of the *Rover.* Licensed *Jan.* 28. 1678. *Roger L'Estrange. London,* Printed by *E. Flesher* for *Richard Tonson,* within *Grays-Inn-gate* in *Grays-Inn-lane* and *Jacob Tonson,* at the *Judge's Head in Chancery-lane.* 1678. 4º.
    The Feign'd Curtizans, or, A Nights Intrigue. A Comedy. As it is Acted at the Dukes Theatre. Written by Mrs. *A. Behn.* Licensed *Mar.* 27. 1679. *Roger L'Estrange. London,* Printed for *Jacob Tonson* at the *Judges Head* in *Chancery-Lane* near *Fleet-street.* 1679. 4º.
    The Second Part of the Rover. As it is Acted by the Servants of His Royal Highness. Written by *A. Behn. London :* Printed for *Jacob Tonson* at the *Judges-Head* in *Chancery Lane.* MDCLXXXI. 4º.
    The City-Heiress : or, Sir Timothy Treat-all. A Comedy. As it is Acted At his Royal Highness his Theatre, Written by Mrs. *A. Behn. London :* Printed for *D. Brown,* at the *Black Swan* and *Bible* without *Temple-bar* ; and *T. Benskin* in St. *Brides* Church-yard ; and *H. Rhodes* next door to the *Bear-Tavern* neer *Bride-lane* in *Fleetstreet.* 1682. 4º.
    The False Count, or, a New Way to play an old game. As it is Acted at the Dukes Theatre. Written by Mrs. *A. Behn. London,* Printed by *M. Flesher,* for *Jacob Tonson,* at the *Judge's Head* in *Chancery-lane,* near *Fleetstreet.* 1682. 4º.
    The Roundheads or, The Good Old Cause, A Comedy As it is Acted

at His Royal Highness the Dukes Theatre. *BY* Mrs. A. Behn. *London*, Printed for *D. Brown* at the *Black Swan* and *Bible* without *Temple bar*, and *T. Benskin* in *St. Brides* Church Yard, and *H. Rhodes* next door to the *Bear Tavern* near *Bride Lane* in *Fleetstreet*. MDCLXXXII. 4º.
The Luckey Chance, or an Alderman's Bargain. A Comedy, As it is Acted by their Majesty's Servants. *Written by* Mrs. A. Behn. This may be Printed, *April* 23. 1686. *R. P. London*, Printed by *R.H.* for *W. Canning*, at his Shop in *Vine-Court, Middle-Temple*. 1687. 4º.
Collected Works.
[*The Plays, Histories, and Novels of the Ingenious Mrs. Aphra Behn.* Ed. R. H. Shepherd. 6 vols. 1871.]
[*The Works of Aphra Behn.* Ed. M. Summers. 6 vols. 1915. (Omits the pindarics.)]
Biography and Criticism.
[*Aphra Behn or the Incomparable Astræa.* V. M. Sackville West. 1927.]

BENSON (William).
A Letter to Sir *J.—— B.——* (Jacob Banks). By Birth a *S——* (Swede), but Naturaliz'd and now a *M——r* of the Present p——t : Concerning the late *Minehead* Doctrine which was established by a certain *Free Parliament* of *Sweden*, to the utter *Enslaving* of that Kingdom. Si, mehercle, peccato locus esset, facile paterer vos ipsa re corrigi, sed undique circumventi sumus. Non nunc agitur de Vectigalibus, non de Cociorum Injuriis agitur ; *Libertas et Anima* nostra in dubio est. *Sallust. Bell. Catilinar.* London : Printed for *A. Baldwin* in *Warwick-Lane*. M. DCC. XI. 8º.

BENTLEY (Richard).
Q. Horatius Flaccus, Ex Recensione et cum Notis Atque Emendationibus Richardi Bentleii. Cantabrigiae. MDCCXI. 4º.

BENTLEY (Thomas).
Q. Horatius Flaccus Ad Nuperam *Richardi Bentleii* Editionem accurate expressus. Notas addidit *Thomas Bentleius*, A.B. Collegii S. Trinitatis Cantabrigienses Alumnus. *Cantabrigiae* : Typis Academicis. Impensis Cornelii Crownfield, Celeberrimae Academiae Typographi. MDCCXIII. 8º.

BISSET (William).
Plain English. A Sermon Preached at St. *Mary-le-Bow*, on *Monday*, March 27. 1704. For Reformation of Manners. With Some Enlargements. By William Bisset, *One of the Ministers of St* Catherine's *by the* Tower, London : Printed for the Author ; and Sold by *A. Baldwin* in *Warwick-Lane*. 1704. 8º.
The Modern Fanatick. With a Large and True Account of the Life, Actions, Endowments, *etc.* Of the Famous Dr. *Sa.....l. Veritas magna est, et praevalebit.* By *William Bisset*, Eldest Brother of the Collegiate-Church of St. *Katherine*, and Rector of *Whiston* in *Northamptonshire, London* : Printed : And Sold by *A. Baldwin*, near the *Oxford-Arms* in *Warwick-Lane* : And *T. Harrison* at the *West* Corner of the *Royal Exchange* in *Cornhill*. 1710. Price Six-pence. 8º.

BLACKMORE (Sir Richard).
Poems.
Prince Arthur. An Heroick Poem. In Ten Books. By *Richard Blackmore* M.D. And Fellow of the College of Physicians in *London*. The Second Edition Corrected. To which is added, An Index, Explaining the Names of *Countries, Cities,* and *Rivers,* etc. *London* : Printed for *Awnsham* and *John Churchil* at the *black Swan* in *Pater-Noster-Row*. MDCXCV. folio.

BIBLIOGRAPHY

King Arthur. An Heroick Poem. In Twelve Books. By *Richard Blackmore*, M.D. Fellow of the College of Physicians in *London*, and One of His Majesty's Physicians in Ordinary. To which is Annexed, An Index, Explaining the Names of *Countrys*, *Citys*, and *Rivers*, etc. *London* : Printed for *Awnsham* and *John Churchil* at the *Black Swan* in *Pater-Noster-Row*, and *Jacob Tonson* at the *Judges Head* in Fleet-street, MDCXCVII. folio.

A Satyr Against Wit. *London* : Printed for *Samuel Crouch*, at the Corner of *Pope's-Head-Alley*, over against the *Royal Exchange* in *Cornhill*. 1700. folio.

Advice to the Poets. A Poem. Occasion'd by the Wonderful Success of her Majesty's Arms, under the Conduct of the duke of *Marlborough*, in *Flanders*. *London* : Printed by *H.M.* for *A.* and *J. Churchill*, at the *Black Swan* in *Pater-Noster-Row*. MDCCVI. folio.

Creation. A Philosophical Poem. In Seven Books. By Sir *Richard Blackmore*, Knt. M.D. and Fellow of the College of Physicians in London.

> *Principio Caelum, ac terras camposque liquentes*
> *Lucentemque globum lunae, Titaniaque astra*
> *Spiritus intus alit, totamque infusa per artus*
> *Mens agitat molem, et magno se Corpore miscet.*
> *Inde hominum, pecudumque genus, vitaeque Volantum,*
> *Et quae marmoreo fert monstra sub aequore pontus.*
> Virg.

London : Printed for *S. Buckley* at the *Dolphin* in *Little-Britain* ; and *J. Tonson*, at *Shakespear's Head*, over against *Catherine-street* in the *Strand*. MDCCXII. 8º.

A Collection of Poems on Various Subjects. By *Sir* Richard Blackmore, Kt. *M.D.* Fellow of the Royal-College of Physicians. *London* : Printed by *W. Wilkins*, for Jonas Browne at the *Black-Swan* without *Temple-Bar* ; and J. *Walthoe*, *Jun.* over-against the *Royal-Exchange* in *Cornhill*. MDCCXVIII. 8º.

Alfred. An Epick Poem. In Twelve Books. Dedicated to the Illustrious Prince *Frederick* of *Hanover*. By Sir Richard Blackmore. Kt. *M.D.*

> *Tu regere imperio Populos, Romane, memento*
> *(Hae tibi erunt Artes) Paciq; imponere Morem*
> *Parcere Subjectis et debellare superbos.*
> Virg., Æneid., Lib. VI.

London, Printed by *W. Botham*, for James Knapton, at the *Crown* in St. *Paul's* Church-Yard. MDCCXXIII. 8º.

[*The Works of the English Poets.* Ed. A. Chalmers. 1810. Vol. X.
The Works of the British Poets. Ed. T. Park. 1818. Vol. 33.
Contain poems by Blackmore.]

Prose.

Essays upon Several Subjects. By Sir Richard Blackmore, *Kt. M.D.* and Fellow of the College of Physicians in *London*. *London* : Printed for E. Curll at the *Dial* and *Bible*, and J. Pemberton at the *Buck* and *Sun*, both against St. *Dunstan's* Church in *Fleet-street*. M.DCCXVI. 8º.

Essays upon Several Subjects. By *Sir* Richard Blackmore, *Kt. M.D.* and Fellow of the College of Physicians in *London*. Vol. II. *London* : Printed by W. Wilkins, for A. Bettersworth, at the *Red Lyon* in *Pater-Noster-Row* ; and J. Pemberton, at the *Buck* and *Sun* against St. *Dunstan's* Church in *Fleetstreet*. 1717. 8º.

A True *and* Impartial History of the Conspiracy Against the Person *and* Government of King *William* III. Of Glorious Memory, in the Year 1695. By Sir Richard Blackmore, Kt. M.D. *London,* Printed for James Knapton, at the *Crown* in St. *Paul's* Church-Yard. MDCCXXIII. 8º.

BOLINGBROKE. See ST. JOHN (Henry).

BONNECORSE (Balthazar de).
La Montre. *Par Monsieur* De Bonnecorse. A Cologne Chez Pierre Miceel. M.DC.LXVI. 8º.
La Montre. *Seconde Partie.* Contenant La Boëte, et le Miroir. *Par M. de* Bonnecorse. Dédiée à Monseigneur de Vivonne. A Paris, Chez Claude Barbin, au Palais, sur le second Perron de la Ste Chapelle, M.DC.LXXI. *Avec Privilege du Roy.* 8º.

BOSSUET (Jacques-Bénigne).
An Exposition of the Doctrine of the Catholic Church in Matters of Controversie. By the Right Reverend *James Benigne Bossuet,* Counsellor to the King, Bishop of *Meaux,* formerly of *Condom,* and Preceptor to the Dauphin ; First Almoner to the Dauphiness. Done into *English* from the Fifth Edition in *French. London,* Printed in the Year 1685. 4º.
A Treatise of Communion under Both Species. *By the Lord* James Benigne Bossuet, *Bishop of Meaux, Councellour to the King, heretofore Preceptor to Monseigneur le* Dauphin, *first Almoner to Madame la* Dauphine. Printed at Paris by Sebastian Mabre Cramoisy, Printer to his Majesty. MDCLXXXV. With Priviledge. 12º.
A Pastoral Letter From the Lord Bishop of Meaux, To The New Catholics of His Diocess, Exhorting them to keep their Easter. And giving them Necessary Advertisements against the *False Pastoral Letters* of their *Ministers.* With Reflections upon the Pretended Persecution. Translated out of *French,* and Publish'd with Allowance. *London,* Printed by *Henry Hills,* Printer to the King's most excellent Majesty, for His Household and Chappel. 1686. 4º.
A Discourse on the History of the Whole World, Dedicated to his Royal Highness the Dauphin, and Explicating the Continuance of Religion with the Changes of States and Empires ; from the Creation till the Reign of *Charles* the Great. Written Originally in French by *James Benigne Bossuet,* sometimes Bishop of *Condom,* and now of *Meaux,* Counsellor of State to the Most Christian King, heretofore Tutor to the Dauphin, and now Chief Almoner to the Dauphiness. Faithfully Englished. *London,* Printed for *Matthew Turner* at the *Lamb* in *High-Holborn.* MDCLXXXVI. 8º.
A Conference with Mr. Claude Minister of Charenton, Concerning The Authority of the Church. By *James Benigne Bossuet,* Bishop of Meaux, Councellor to the most Christian King, and formerly Preceptor to the Dauphin : First Almoner to the Dauphiness. *Faithfully done into English out of the French original.* Publish with Allowance. *London,* Printed for *Matthew Turner,* at the *Lamb* in *High Holbourn.* 1687. 4º.

BOYLE (Roger, 1st Earl of Orrery).
Poems.
The following collection contains verse by the Earl of Orrery : A Collection of Poems : Viz. *The Temple of Death* : By the marquis of *Normanby. An Epistle to the Earl of* Dorset : By *Charles Montague,* Lord *Halifax. The Duel of the Stags* : By Sir *Robert Howard.* With Several Original Poems, Never before printed, By the E. of *Roscommon.* The E. of *Rochester.* The E. of *Orrery.* Sir *Charles Sedley.* Sir ़*George Etherege.* Mr. *Granville.* Mr. *Stepney.* Mr. *Dryden,* Etc. *London* :

Printed for *Daniel Brown*, at the *Black Swan* and *Bible* without *Temple-Bar*: And *Benjamin Tooke* at the *Middle-Temple-Gate* in *Fleetstreet.* 1701. 8º.

Dramatic Works.
The Dramatic Works of *Roger Boyle*, Earl *of* Orrery. To which is Added A Comedy, intitled, *As you find it.* By the Honourable Charles Boyle, Esq; Afterwards Earl of *Orrery*. Vol. I. Containing: The Black Prince. Tryphon. Henry the Fifth. Mustapha. London: Printed for R. Dodsley, at *Tully's-Head*, in Pall-Mall. M.DCC.XXXIX. The second volume is entitled: The Dramatick Works of *Roger Boyle*, Earl of Orrery. Volume II. Containing: Herold the Great. Altemira. Guzman, *a Comedy*. Also as you find it, *a Comedy*. By Charles late Earl of *Orrery*. London: Printed for R. Dodsley, in *Pall-Mall*. M.DCC.XXXIX. 8º. (*Henry V*, a historical play, was acted in 1664; *Mustapha*, a tragedy, in 1665; *The Black Prince*, a tragedy, in 1667; *Tryphon*, a tragedy, in 1668; *Guzman*, a comedy, between 1667 and 1672; *Herold the Great*, tragedy, was not acted; *Altemira*, tragedy, was acted in 1702 after the author's death. Orrery also wrote a comedy called *Mr. Anthony* which was acted about 1671.)

Two New Tragedies. The Black Prince, and Tryphon. The first Acted at the Theatre Royal *by His Majesties Servants*; The Other *by his Highness the Duke* of York's *Servants*. Both Written by the Right Honourable the Earl of Orrery. London, Printed for H. *Herringman*, at the Sign of the *Blew Anchor*, in the Lower Walk of the New Exchange. 1672. folio. [First edition: 1669.]

[*The Dramatic Works of Roger Boyle, Earl of Orrery*. Ed. W. S. Clark. 2 vols. Cambridge. U.S.A. 1937. (Includes from MS. *The Tragedy of Zoroastres*.)]

Prose.
Parthenissa That most fam'd Romance: Composed by the Right Honoble The Lord *Broghill*, And Dedicated to the Lady *Northumberland*. London: Printed for *Richard Lownes* at the *White Lyon* in St *Pauls* Church-yard. 1654. 4º.

A Treatise of the Art of War: Dedicated to the Kings Most Excellent Majesty. *And Written by the Right Honourable* Roger Earl of Orrery. *In the Savoy*: Printed by *T.N.* for *Henry Herringman* at the Anchor in the *Lower Walk* of the *New Exchange*. M.DC.LXXVII. folio.

Biography.
Memoirs of the Life and Character Of the Late Earl of *Orrery*, And of the Family of the Boyles. Containing Several Curious *Facts*, and *Pieces of History*, from the Reign of Queen Elisabeth, to the present Times: Extracted from Original Papers and Manuscripts never yet Printed. With A Short Account of the Controversy between the late Earl of Orrery and the Reverend Doctor *Bentley*; and some *Select Letters* of Phalaris, the famous *Sicilian* Tyrant: Translated from the *Greek*. By Eustace Budgell Esq;

  Te, animo repetentem Exempla tuorum
  Et Pater Aeneas, *et* Avunculus *excitet* Hector. Virg.

London: Printed for W. Mears, at the Lamb in the Old Bailey. M.DCCXXXII. 8º.

BRISTOL (Earl of). See DIGBY.

BROWN (Tom). See also DRYDEN and COLLIER.
Numb. 9. The Lacedemonian Mercury. Being A Continuation of the *London Mercury*. Monday March 7. 1692. folio.
Letters from the Dead to the Living. By *Mr*. Tho. Brown, *Capt*. Ayloff,

Mr. Hen. Barker, etc. *Viz. from Jo. Haines* of Merry Memory, to his Friends at *Wills. Perkin Warbeck*, to the pretented Prince of *Wales, Abraham Cowley*, to the *Covent Garden Society. Charon*, to the Illustrious and Highborn *Jack Ketch. James* the 2^d, to *Lewis* the 14th. *Julian* late Secretary to the Muses, to *Will Peirre* of *Lincolns-Inn* Play-house. *Scarron*, to *Lewis Le Grand. Hannibal* to the Victorious Prince *Eugene* of *Savoy.* Pindar of *Thebes*, to *Tom. D.* —— *Catharine* of *Medicis*, to the Dutchess of *Orleans.* Queen *Mary* to the Pope. *Harlequin*, to Father *Le Chaise*. The Duke of *Alva*, to the Clergy of *France. Philip* of *Austria*, to the *Dauphin. Juvenal*, to *Boileau. Diana of Poitiers*, to Madam *Maintenon*. Hugh Spencer, the younger to all the Favourites and Ministers whom it may concern. *Julia*, to the Princess of *Conti. Christina* Queen of *Sweden*, to the Women. *Rabelais*, to the Physicians. The *Mitred Hog* ; a Dialogue between *Furetiere* and *Scarron*. Beau *Norton*, to his Brothers at *Hippolito's*. Sir *Bartolomew* ——, to Serjeant *S.* —— And several others with their Answers.

Infanti Melimela dato, fatuasq; mariscas,
Sed mihi, quae novit pungerem Chia *Sapit.* Mart.

London, Printed in the Year, 1702. 8º.

Collections.

The Works of Mr. *Thomas Brown*, Serious and Comical, In Prose and Verse. In Four volumes. *The* Fifth Edition, *Corrected from the Errors of the former Impressions.* With the Life and Character of Mr. *Brown*, And a Key to all his Writtings. *Adorn'd with Cuts.* London : Printed for Sam Briscoe, at the *Bell-Savage* on *Ludgate Hill* ; and sold by *R. Smith, A. Bell, J. Round, G. Strahan, E. Symons, J. Osborne, J. Brotherton, A. Bettsworth, W. Taylor, J. Batley, R. Robison, C. Rivington, R. King, J. Pemberton, T. Corbet, D. Browne, W. Mears, F. Clay and T. Warner* in Paternoster-Row, 1720. 12º. The fifth volume of this edition is entitled : The Remains of Mr. *Thomas Brown*, Serious and Comical, In Prose and Verse. In one Volume. Collected from scarce Papers and Original Mss. never Printed in his Works. With Mr. Brown's Legacy for the Ladies ; or Characters of the Women of the Age. To which is prefix'd, A Key to all his Prophesies, Dialogues, Satyrs, Fables, and Poems, *London*, Printed for *Sam. Briscoe*, at the *Bell-Savage Inn* on *Ludgate-Hill.* 1720. 12º. [First edition : 3 vols. 1707. 8º.]
[*The Beauties of Tom Brown.* E. C. H. Wilson. 1808.]
[*Amusements Serious and Comical and other works.* By Tom Brown. Ed. with notes by Arthur L. Hayward. 1927. (Contains Letters from the Dead to the Living.)]

BUCKHURST (Lord).
Sackville (Charles), Earl of Dorset. See WILMOT (John).

BUCKINGHAM (Duke of). See VILLIERS (George).

BUCKINGHAM (Duke of). See SHEFFIELD (John).

BUNYAN (John).
The Pilgrim's Progress from this World to That which is to come : delivered under the Similitude of a Dream. Wherein is Discovered, The manner of his setting out, His Dangerous Journey, and Safe Arrival at the Desired Country. By *John Bunyan,* The second Edition, with Additions. *I have used similitudes,* Hosea 12. 10. Licensed and Entered according to Order. *London* : Printed for *Nath. Ponder,* at the Peacock in the *Poultrey,* near *Cornhil.* 1678. 12º. [The first edition also 1678.]
[Ed. J. Wharey. Oxford. 1928.]
[Ed., with *Mr. Badman*, G. B. Harrison. Nonesuch. 1928.]

Biography and Criticism.
    Brown, J.
        [*John Bunyan his Life and Work.* 1885. Revised F. M. Harrison. 1928.]
BURNET (Gilbert). See also WILMOT (John).
    Bishop Burnet's History of his own time ; with the suppressed passages of the first volume, and notes by the Earls of Dartmouth and Hardwicke, and Speaker Onslow. hitherto unpublished. To which are added the cursory remarks of Swift, and other observations. Oxford, at the Clarendon Press. MDCCCXXIII. 6 vols. 8º. [First edition : 2 vols. 1724–34.]
        [Ed. M. J. Routh. 7 vols. Oxford. 1823. Reprinted 6 vols. 1833.]
        [Ed. O. Airy. Oxford. 1897–1900. (Vols. 1 and 2 only.)]
BUTLER (Samuel).
    Hudibras. The First Part. *Written in the time of the late Wars.* London, Printed by G. J. for *Richard Marriot,* under Saint *Dunstan's* Church in Fleetstreet. 1663. 8º.
        [Ed. A. R. Waller. Cambridge. 1905. Forming Vol. 1. of *Collected Works.* Vol. 2 : Characters and passages from notebooks. Ed. A. R. Waller. 1908. Vol. 3 : Satires and miscellaneous poetry and prose. Ed. R. Lamar. 1928.]
    The Genuine Poetical Remains of Samuel Butler. With Notes, By Robert Thyer, Keeper of the Public Library, Manchester. With a Selection from the Author's Characters in Prose. Illustrated with humorous Wood-cuts, and Portraits of Butler and Thyer. London : Printed for Joseph Booker, 61, New Bond Street, 1827. 8º.
Biography and Criticism.
    Veldkamp, J.
        [*Samuel Butler, the author of Hudibras.* 1924.]
    Gibson, D.
        [*Samuel Butler.* 1932.]
CAVENDISH (William, 1st Duke of Newcastle). See also DRYDEN. *Sir Martin Mar-all.*
    A General System of Horsemanship in All it's Branches : Containing a Faithful Translation Of that most noble and useful Work of his Grace, *William Cavendish,* Duke of *Newcastle,* entitled, the Manner of Feeding, Dressing, and Training of Horses, for the Great Saddle, and Fitting them for the Service of the Field in Time of War, or for the Exercise and Improvement of Gentlemen in the Academy at home : A Science peculiarly necessary throughout all *Europe,* and which has hitherto been so much neglected, or discouraged in *England,* that young Gentlemen have been obliged to have recourse to foreign Nations for this Part of their Education. With all the original Copper-Plates, in Number forty-three, which were engrav'd by the best Foreign Masters, under his Grace's immediate Care and inspection, and which are explained in the different Lessons. London : Printed for J. Brindley, Bookseller to His Royal Highness the Prince of Wales, in New Bond-street. MDCCXLIII. 2 vols. folio.
        [First published Antwerp. 1658. *Méthode et invention nouvelle de dresser les chevaux.*]
Dramatic Works.
    The Humorous Lovers. A Comedy, Acted by His Royal Highness's Servants. Written by His Grace the Duke of *Newcastle.* London, Printed by J.M. for *H. Herringman,* at the Sign of the *Blew Anchor* in the Lower-Walk of the *New-Exchange,* 1677. 4º.

The Triumphant Widow, or the Medley of Humours. A Comedy, Acted by His Royal Highnes's Servants. Written by His Grace the Duke of *Newcastle*. London, Printed by *J.M.* for *H. Herringman*, at the Sign of the *Blew Anchor in the Lower-Walk* of the *New-Exchange*, 1677. 4º.

CENTLIVRE (Susanna).
The Busie Body. A Comedy. *Written by Mrs.* Susanna Centlivre. The Fifth Edition.

    Quem tulit ad scenam ventoso Gloria curru,
    Exanimat lentus Spectator, sedulus inflat.
    Sic Leve, sic parvum est, animum quod laudis avarum
    Subruit aut reficit.
                                        Hor. Epist. Lib. II. Ep. 1.

London : Printed for Bernard Lintot ; and sold by Henry Lintot, at the Cross-Keys, against St. Dunstan's Church in Fleet-street. M.DCC.XXXII. 8º. (This play was acted in 1709.)
[Reprinted vol. 4. *Modern British Drama*. 1811.]
The Man's bewitch'd ; or, The Devil to do about Her. A Comedy, As it is Acted at the New-Theatre in the Hay-Market ; By Her *Majesty's Servants*. By Susanna Cent-Livre. *London*, Printed for Bernard Lintott, between the Two *Temple-Gates* in Fleet-street. (1710) 4º.
Collected Works.
[*The Works of the celebrated Mrs. Centlivre.* 3 vols. 1761. 3 vols. 1872. (As *The Dramatic Works.*)]
Character.
The Character of A Town-Gallant ; Exposing the Extravagant Fopperies of some vain Self-conceited Pretenders to Gentility, and good Breeding. *London*, printed for *Rowland Reynolds* in the Strand, 1680. folio.

CIBBER (Colley). See also VANBRUGH, *The Provok'd Husband*.
Dramatic Works.
She wou'd, and She wou'd not, or The Kind Imposter. A Comedy. As it is Acted at the Theatre-Royal in *Drury-Lane*. By Her Majesties Servants. *Written by Mr.* Cibber. London : Printed for *William Turner* at the *Angel* at *Lincolns-Inn* Back-Gate, and *John Nutt* near *Stationers-Hall*. 1703. 4º.
[Reprinted : vol. 3. *Modern British Drama*. 1811.]
The Lady's last Stake, or, The Wife's Resentment, A Comedy. As it is Acted at the Queen's Theatre in the *Hay-Market*, By Her Majesty's Servants. *Written by Mr.* Cibber. *London* : Printed for Bernard Lintott, at the *Cross-Keys* next *Nando's* Coffee-House in Fleet-street. (1708.) 4º.
The Non-Juror. A Comedy. *Written by* Mr. Cibber.

                —*Pulchra Laverna*
    Da mihi fallere ; da justum, sanctumque videri,
    Noctem peccatis, et fraudibus objice nubem. Hor.

London, Printed for T.J. and are sold by the Booksellers of London and Westminster. M.DCC.XVIII. 8º.
[Reprinted : *Plays from Molière by English Dramatists*. H. Morley. 1885.]
Ximena, or, The Heroick Daughter. As it is Acted at the Theatre-Royal By His Majesty's Servants. Written by Mr. *Cibber*.

                Face nuptiali
           Digna, et in omne Virgo
              Nobilis Ævum. Hor.

London : Printed for B. Lintot, between the *Temple-Gates* ; A. Bettersworth, at the *Red Lyon* in *Pater-noster-Row* ; and W. Chetwood, at *Cato's-Head*, in *Russell-street, Covent Garden*. 1719. 8º.

Autobiography.

An Apology for the Life of Mr. Colley Cibber, Comedian, and Late Patentee of the *Theatre-Royal*. With an *Historical View of the* Stage *during his* Own Time. Written by Himself.

> Hoc est
> Vivere bis, vita posse priore frui.   Mart. lib. 2.

> When *Years no more of active Life retain,*
> '*Tis Youth renew'd to laugh 'em o'er again.* Anonym.

London : Printed by John Watts for the Author. MDCCXL. 4º.
[Reprinted : Everyman's Library. 1906.]

Biography and Criticism.

Senior, Dorothy.
[*The Life and Times of Colley Cibber.* 1928.]

CLARK (Samuel).

A Discourse Concerning the Unchangeable Obligations of Natural Religion, and the Truth and Certainty of the *Christian Revelation*. Being Eight Sermons Preach'd at the Cathedral-Church of St *Paul*, in the Year 1705, at the Lecture Founded by the Honourable *Robert Boyle*, Esq. By *Samuel Clark*, M.A. Chaplain to the Right Reverend Father in God *John*, Lord Bishop of *Norwich*. Isa. 5. 20. *wo unto them that call Evil Good, and Good Evil ; that put Darkness for Light and Light for Darkness ; that put Bitter for Sweet and Sweet for Bitter.* Rom. 1. 22. *Professing themselves to be Wise, they became Fools.* 1. Cor. 2. 10. *But God hath revealed them unto us by his Spirit.* London : Printed by *W. Botham*, for *James Knapton*, at the *Crown* in St. *Paul's* Church-Yard. 1706. 8º.

CLENCHE (William).

St *Peter's* Supremacy faithfully discuss'd according to Holy Scripture, and *Greek* and *Latin* Fathers. With a Detection and Confutation of the Errors of Protestant Writers on this Article. Together with A Succinct Handling of several other Considerable Points. *The First Book, Divided into Three Parts.*

> *Romae nutriri mihi contigit atq; doceri,*
> *Scilicet, ut possem Curvo dignoscere Rectum.*
> Chryst. 67. Hom. John.

Permissu Superiorum. London, Printed by *Henry Hills*, Printer to the Kings Most Excellent Majesty, for His Household and Chappel. 1686. And are to be sold by *Matthew Turner*, at the *Lamb*, in *Holborn*. 4º. (The dedication is signed : Guglielmo Clenche.)

Clod-pate.

Clod-pate's Ghost : or a Dialogue Between *Justice Clod-Pate*, and his (*quondam*) Clerk Honest *Tom Ticklefoot* ; Wherein *Is Faithfully Related all the News from* Purgatory, *about* Ireland, Langhorn, etc. Aug. 25. 1679. folio.

Coffee.

A Cup of Coffee : or, Coffee in its Colours. *London*, Printed in the year 1663. folio, broadside.

Collection.

A Collection of The Newest and Most Ingenious Poems, Songs, Catches, etc. Against Popery. Relating to the Times. Several of which never before Printed, *London*, Printed in the Year MDCLXXXIX. 4º.

COLLIER (Jeremy).
The Desertion discuss'd In a Letter to a Country Gentleman. (1688.) 8º.
The Stage Controversy.
[For accounts, see *Comedy and Conscience after the Restoration.* J. W. Krutch. New York. 1924.
Essays in Biography, 1680–1726. (Vanbrugh.) B. Dobrée. 1925.]
Works by Collier.
A Short View of the *Immorality*, and *Profaneness* of the English Stage, Together with the Sense of Antiquity Upon this Argument, By *Jeremy Collier*, M.A. London, Printed for S. Keble at the *Turk's Head* in *Fleet-street*, R. Sare at *Gray's-Inn-Gate*, and H. Hindmarsh against the *Exchange* in *Cornhil*, 1698. 8º. The Third Edition. 1698. The Fourth Edition. 1699.
A Defence of the Short View of the Profaneness and Immorality of the English Stage, *etc.* Being a Reply to Mr. *Congreve's* Amendments, *etc.* And to the Vindication of the Author of the Relapse. By *Jeremy Collier*, M.A. Fortem animum praestant rebus quas turpiter audent. Juv. Sat. 6. London : Printed for S. Keble at the *Turks-head* in *Fleetstreet*, R. Sare at *Gray's-Inn-Gate*, and H. Hindmarsh against the *Exchange* in *Cornhil*. 1699. 8º.
[In reply to Congreve and Vanbrugh.]
A second Defence of the Short View of the Prophaneness and Immorality of the *English Stage*, *etc.* Being *A Reply* to a Book, Entituled, *The Ancient and Modern Stages Surveyed, etc.* By *Jeremy Collier*, M.A. London : Printed for *S. Keble* at the *Turk's Head* in *Fleetstreet*, R. Sare at *Gray's Inn-Gate* in *Holborn*, and *G. Strahan* against the *Exchange* in *Cornhill*. 1700. 8º.
[In reply to Drake.]
Mr. *Collier's* Dissuasive from the *Play-House* ; in a Letter to a Person of Quality, Occasion'd By the late Calamity of the Tempest. London : Printed for Richard Sare, at *Grays-Inn-Gate* in *Holborn*. 1703. 8º.
Mr. *Collier's* Dissuasive from the *Play-House* ; in A Letter to a Person of Quality. Occasion'd By the late Calamity of the Tempest. To which is added, A Letter written by another Hand ; in Answer to some Queries sent by a Person of Quality. Relating to the Irregularities charged upon the *Stage*. London Printed for Richard Sare, at *Grays-Inn-Gate* in *Holborn*. 1704. 8º.
A Farther Vindication of the Short View of the Profaneness and Immorality of the English Stage, In which the Objections of a late Book, Entituled, *A Defence of Plays*, are consider'd. By *Jeremy Collier*, M.A. London : Printed for *R. Sare*, at *Gray's-Inn-Gate* in *Holborn*, and *G. Strahan* at the *Golden Ball* in *Cornhill*. 1708. 8º.
[In reply to Filmer.]
La Critique du Theatre Anglois, Comparé au Theatre d'Athenes, de Rome et de France. *Et* L'Opinion *des Auteurs tant profanes que sacrez, touchant les Spectacles.* De l'Anglois de M. Collier. A Paris, chez Nicolas Simart, Imprimeur et Libraire ordinaire de Monseigneur le Dauphin, ruë S. Jacques, au Dauphin couronné. M.DCC.XV. *Avec Privilege du Roy.* 8º. (The *Biographia Britannica* ascribes this translation to Pere de Courbeville.)
Works by other hands.
Brown, Tom.
The *Stage-Beaux toss'd in a Blanket*, or Hypocrisie Alamode. Expos'd in a True Picture of Jerry . . . , a Pretending Scourge to the

English Stage. A Comedy; with a *Prologue* on *Occasional Conformity*; being a full Explanation of the *Poussin Doctor's* Book; and an *Epilogue* on the *Reformers*. Spoken, at the *Theatre-Royal* in *Drury-Lane*. Simulant Curios, et Bacchanalia vivunt. Juv. London, Printed and Sold by *J. Nutt*, near *Stationers' Hall*. 1704. 4⁰.

Congreve, William.
Amendments of *Mr.* Collier's *False and Imperfect Citations*, etc. From the Old Batchelour, Double Dealer, Love for Love, Mourning Bride. By the Author of those Plays.

> *Quem recitas meus est o Fidentine Libellus,*
> *Sed male dum recitas incipit esse tuus.*
>   Mart.

Graviter, et iniquo animo, maledicta tua pateter, si te scirem Judicio magis, quem [sic] *morbo animi, petulantia ista uti. Sed, quoniam in te neque modum, neque modestiam ullam animadverto, respondebo tibi : uti, si quam maledicendo voluptatem cepisti, eam male-audiendo amittas.* Salust. Decl. London, Printed for *J. Tonson*, at the *Judge's Head* in *Fleet-street*, near the *Inner-Temple-Gate*. 1698. 8⁰.

[In *Complete Works*. World's Classics. 1925–8.]

Dennis, John.
The Usefulness of the Stage, *To the Happiness of Mankind. To Government*, and *To Religion*. Occasioned by a late Book, written by *Jeremy Collier*, M.A. By Mr. *Dennis*. London, Printed for *Rich. Parker* at the *Unicorn* under the Piazza of the *Royal Exchange*. 1698. 8⁰.

[In *Critical Works*. Ed. E. N. Hooker. 1939–43. Vol. 1.]

Drake, J.
The Antient and Modern Stages survey'd. Or, Mr *Collier's* View of the Immorality and Profaness of the *English* Stage Set in a True Light. Wherein some of Mr *Collier's* Mistakes are rectified, and the comparative Morality of the *English* Stage is asserted upon the Parallel.

> *Rode* Caper *vitem, tamen hic cum stabis ad Aram*
> *In tua quod fundi* Cornua *possit, erit.* Ov.

London : Printed for *Abel Roper*, at the *Black Boy* over against St. *Dunstans* Church in *Fleetstreet*. 1699. 8⁰.

D'Urfey, Thomas.
The Preface to *The Campaigners*. See D'URFEY.

Filmer, Edward.
A Defence of Dramatick Poetry : Being a Review of Mr. *Collier's* View of the Immorality and Profaneness of the Stage. London : Printed for *Eliz. Whitlock*, near *Stationer's Hall*. 1698. 8⁰.

A Farther Defence of Dramatick Poetry : Being the Second Part of the Review of Mr. *Collier's* View of the Immorality and Profaneness of the Stage. *Done by the same Hand*. London : Printed for *Eliz. Witlock*, near *Stationer's Hall*. 1698. 8⁰.

A Defence of Plays : or, The Stage vindicated, From several Passages in Mr. *Collier's Short View*, etc. Wherein is offer'd The most Probable Method of Reforming our Plays. With a Consideration How far Vicious Characters may be allow'd on the Stage. By *Edward Filmer*, Doctor of the Civil Laws. London, Printed for *Jacob Tonson* within *Grays-Inn* Gate next to *Grays-Inn* Lane. 1707. 8⁰.

Vanbrugh, John.
A Short Vindication of the *Relapse* and the Provok'd Wife, from

Immorality and Prophaneness. By the Author. *London* : Printed for H. Walwyn, at the *Three Legs* in the *Poultrey*, against the Stocks-Market. MDCXCVIII. 8º.
[In *Complete Works*. Ed. B. Dobrée and G. Webb. 1927.]

Anonymous.
Animadversions on Mr. Congreve's Late Answer to Mr. *Collier*. In a Dialogue between Mr. *Smith* and Mr. *Johnson*. With the Characters of the present *Poets* ; And some Offers towards New-Modeling the *Stage*.

Sr. Jos. *Egad, there are good Morals to be pick'd out of* Æsop's Fables, *let me tell you that, and* Reynard the Fox *too*.
Bluff. *Damn your Morals*.
Sr. Jos. *Prithee don't speak so Loud*.
Bluff. *Damn your Morals, I must revenge the Affront done to my Honor*.
Old Batch. *Page* 47.

London, Printed for *John Nutt*, near Stationers-Hall. 1698. 8º.
Some remarks upon *Mr*. Collier's *Defence of his Short View of the English Stage*, etc. in Vindication of Mr. *Congreve*, etc. In a Letter to a Friend. *London* : Printed for A. Baldwin, near the *Oxford Arms*, in *Warwick-Lane*. 1698. 8º.

The Immorality of the English Pulpit, as Justly Subjected to the Notice of the *English Stage*, as The Immorality of the Stage is, to that of the Pulpit. *In a Letter to Mr*. Collier. Occasion'd by the Third Chapter of his Book, Entit'ld, *A Short View of the Immorality of the* English Stage, etc. *London* : Printed in the Year MDCXCVIII. 4º.

The Stage Condemn'd, and The Encouragement given to the Immoralities and Profaneness of the Theatre, by the English Schools, Universities and Pulpits, *Censur'd*. King *Charles I*. Sundays Mask and Declaration for Sports and Pastimes on the Sabbath, *largely Related and Animadverted upon*. The Arguments of all the Authors that have Writ in Defence of the Stage against Mr, *Collier, Consider'd*. And The Sense of the Fathers, Councils, Antient Philosophers and Poets, and of the Greek and Roman States, and of the First Christian Emperours concerning the Drama, *Faithfully Deliver'd*. Together with The Censure of the English State and of several Antient and Modern Divines of the Church of *England* upon the Stage. And Remarks on diverse late Plays, as also on those presented by the two Universities to King *Charles* I. *London* : Printed for John Salusbury, at the *Angel* in St. *Paul's* Church-Yard, 1698. 8º.

A Vindication of the Stage. With the Usefulness and advantages of Dramatick Representations. In Answer to Mr. Collier's Late Book, Entituled, *A View of the Prophaneness* [sic] *and Immorality*, etc. *In a Letter to a Friend. Aut Prodesse volunt, aut Delectare Poetae. Delectant homines, mihi crede, ludi, non eos solum, qui fatentur ; sed illos etiam qui dissimulant*. Cicero. *London* : Printed for *Joseph Wild*, at the Sign of the *Elephant* at *Charing-Cross*. MDCXCVIII. 4º.

The *Stage Acquitted*. Being A Full Answer to Mr. *Collier*, and the other Enemies of the Drama. With A Vindication of King *Charles* the Martyr, and the Clergy of the Church of *England*, From the Abuses of a Scurrilous Book, called, *The Stage Condemned*. To which is added, The Character of the Animadverter, and the Animadversions on Mr. *Congreve's* Answer to Mr. *Collier*. London :

Printed for John *Barnes* at the *Crown* in the *Pall-mall*, and sold by M. *Gilliflower* in *Westminster-hall*, D. *Brown* near *Temple-bar*, and R. *Parker* at the *Royal Exchange*. MDCXCIX. 8º.

A Representation of the *Impiety* and *Immorality* of the English Stage, with Reason *for putting a stop thereto* : *and some* Questions *addrest to those who frequent the* Play-Houses. London, Printed, and are to be sold by *J. Nutt* near *Stationers-Hall*, 1704. 8º.

COLLINS (Anthony).
Priestcraft in Perfection : Or, a Detection of the Fraud of Inserting and Continuing this Clause (*The Church hath Power to Decree Rites and Ceremonys, and Authority in Controversys of Faith*) In the Twentieth Article of the Church of England. *To forge an Article of Religion, either in Whole or in Part, and then thrust it upon the Church, is a most heinous Crime, far worse than Forging of a Deed.* Archbishop Laud's Speech in the Starchamber. *Remains*, Vol. 2. pag. 82. Maxime habenda sunt pro suspectis, quae quomodocunque dependent a Religione. *Baconis Nov. Org. lib.* 2. *Aph.* 29. London : Printed for B. *Bragg* in *Pater-noster-Row*. 1710. 8º.

A Discourse of Free-Thinking, Occasion'd by The Rise and Growth of a Sect call'd Free-Thinkers. Mundum tradidit *hominum* disputationi *Deus. Eccl.* 3. 11. Vulg. Unusquisque suo sensu abundet. *Rom.* 14. 5. Ib. Nil tam temerarium, tamque indignum sapientis gravitate atque constantia, quam, quod non satis explorate perceptum sit et cognitum sine ulla dubitatione defendere. *Cic. de Nat. Deor.* 1. 1. '*Tis a hard Matter for a* Government *to settle*. Wit. Characteristicks. *vol.* 1. *p.* 19. Fain *would they* confound Licentiousness in Morals *with* Liberty in Thought, *and make* the Libertine *resemble his* direct Opposite. Ib. *vol.* 3. *p.* 306. London, Printed in the Year M.DCC.XIII. 8º.

CONGREVE (William). See also COLLIER and DRYDEN.
Poems.
A Pindarique Ode, Humbly Offer'd to the King On His Taking Namure. By Mr. *Congreve*.

> *Praesenti tibi Maturos largimur Honores :*
> *Nil oriturum alias, nil ortum tale fatentes.*
> Hor. ad Augustum.

London : Printed for *Jacob Tonson* at the *Judge's Head* near the *Inner-Temple-Gate* in *Fleetstreet*. MDCXCV. folio.

The Mourning Muse of Alexis. A Pastoral. Lamenting the Death of our late Gracious Queen Mary Of ever Blessed Memory. By Mr. Congreve. *Infandum Regina Jubes renovare dolorem!* Virg. London : Printed for *Jacob Tonson*, at the *Judge's Head*, near the *Inner-Temple Gate* in Fleet Street. 1695. folio.

A Pindarique Ode, Humbly Offer'd to the Queen, On the Victorious Progress of Her Majesty's Arms, under the Conduct of the Duke of Marlborough. To which is prefix'd, A Discourse on the Pindarique Ode. By Mr. *Congreve*.

> *Operosa parvus*
> *Carmina fingo.*   Hor. Ode 2. L. 4.

> *Tuque dum procedis, Io triumphe*
> *Non semel dicemus, Io triumphe*
> *Civitas omnis; dabimusq; Divis*
> *Thura benignis.*   Ibid.

London : Printed for *Jacob Tonson*, within *Grays-Inn* Gate next *Grays-Inn* Lane. 1706. folio.

Dramatic Works.
The Old Batchelour, A Comedy. As it is Acted at the Theatre Royal, By Their Majesties Servants. Written by Mr. *Congreve.*

Quem tulit ad Scenam ventoso gloria Curru,
Exanimat lentus Spectator ; sedulus inflat.
Sic leve, sic parvum est, animum quod laudis avarum
Subruit, aut reficit. Horat. Epist. I. Lib. II.

The second Edition. *London,* Printed for *Peter Buck* at the Sign of the *Temple* near the *Inner Temple-Gate* in *Fleet-street,* 1693. 4°.
The Double-Dealer. A Comedy. As it is Acted at The Theatre Royal. By Their Majesty's Servants, Written by Mr. *Congreve. Interdum tamen, et vocem Comedia tollit.* Hor. Art. Po. *Huic equidem Consilio palmam do ; hic me magnifice effero, qui vim tantam in me et potestatem habeam tantae astutiae, vera dicendo ut eos ambos fallam.* Syr. in Terent. Heaut. *London :* Printed and sold by *H. Hills,* in *Black-Fryars,* near the *Water-side.* 1694. 8°.
Love for Love. A Comedy. Acted at the Theatre in *Little-Lincoln's-Inn-Fields,* By His Majesty's Servants. Written by Mr. *Congreve.*

Nudus Agris, nudus nummis paternis,
Insanire parat certa ratione modoque.

London : Printed and Sold by *H. Hills,* in *Black-Fryars,* near the *Water-side.* 1695. 8°.
The Mourning Bride. A Tragedy. As it is Acted at the Theatre in *Lincoln's-Inn-Fields.* By His Majesty's Servants. Written by Mr. *Congreve.*

Neque enim lex aequior ulla,
Quam necis artifices arte perire sua.
Ovid. de Arte Am.

London : Printed and Sold by *H. Hills,* in *Black-Fryars* near the *Water-side.* 1697. 8°.
The Way of the World. A Comedy. As it is Acted at the Theatre in *Lincoln's-Inn-Fields,* By His Majesty's Servants. Written by Mr. *Congreve.*

Audire est Operae pretium, procedere recte
Qui Moechis non vultis. Hor. Sat. 2. L. 1.

Metuat doti deprensa. Ibid.

London : Printed for *Jacob Tonson* within *Gray's-Inn-Gate* next *Gray's-Inn-Lane.* 1700. 4°.
Prose.
The Occasional Paper : Number IX. Containing some Considerations about the Danger of going to Plays. In a Letter to a Friend. *London,* Printed for *M. Wotton,* at the Three Daggers in *Fleet-street.* 1698. 8°.
Some Considerations about the Danger of going to Plays. In a Letter to a Friend. *London,* Printed for *M. Wotton,* at the *Three Daggers* in *Fleet-street.* And Sold by *J. Nutt* near *Stationers-Hall.* 1704. Price Three Pence. 8°.
Collected Works.
The Works of Mr. *William Congreve.* In three volumes. Consisting of his Plays and Poems. *The Fifth Edition.* London : Printed for Tonson, in the *Strand.* MDCCLII. 12°. [First edition 1710.]
[*Plays.* Ed. Montague Summers. 4 vols. Nonesuch Press. 1923.]
[*Complete Works.* Ed. B. Dobrée. 2 vols. World's Classics. 1925–8.]
[*Comedies.* Ed. F. W. Bateson. 1930.]

Biography and Criticism.
>   Gosse, E.
>>   "Great Writers." Edited by Professor Eric S. Robertson, M.A. Life of William Congreve, by Edmund Gosse, M.A. Clark Lecturer in English Literature at Trinity College, Cambridge. London, Walter Scott. 1888. 8º.
>>>   [Revised edition. 1924.]
>>   Hodges, J. C.
>>>   [*William Congreve, the man : a biography from new sources.* 1941. Modern Language Association of America. General Series II.]
>>   Protopopesco, Dragosh.
>>>   [*William Congreve.* 1924.]

COOPER (Anthony Ashley, First Earl of Shaftesbury).
>   *Biography.*
>>   Martyn, B., and Kippis, Dr.
>>>   The Life of the First Earl of Shaftesbury, from Original documents in possession of the family. By Mr. B. Martyn and Dr. Kippis. Now First Published. Edited By G. Wingrove Cooke. Esq. Author of "Memoirs of Lord Bolingbroke." In two Volumes. London : Richard Bentley, New Burlington Street. Publisher in Ordinary to His Majesty. 1836. 8º.
>>   Christie, W. D.
>>>   A Life of Anthony Ashley Cooper, First Earl of Shaftesbury. 1621–1683. By W. D. Christie, M.A. Formerly Her Majesty's Minister to the Argentine Confederation and to Brazil. Two Volumes. London and New York : Macmillan & Co. 1874. 8º.
>>   Traill, H. D.
>>>   [Shaftesbury (the first earl). 1886.]

COWLEY (Abraham).
>   The Works of Mr. Abraham Cowley, Consisting of *Those which were formerly Printed* : And *Those which he Design'd for the Press*. Now Published out of the Author's Original Copies. To this Edition are added Cutter of *Coleman-Street* : And Several Commendatory Copies of Verses on the Author, by Persons of Honour. As Also, A Table to the whole Works, never before Printed. The Eighth Edition. *London*, Printed for *Henry Herringman* ; and are to be Sold by *R. Bentley*, *J. Tonson*, F. Saunders, and T. Bennet. MDCXCIII. folio.
>>   [First edition 1668.]
>>   [Ed. A. R. Waller. 2 vols. Cambridge. 1905–6.]
>   *Biography and Criticism.*
>>   Nethercot, Arthur H.
>>>   [*Abraham Cowley. The Muse's Hannibal.* Oxford. 1931.]

CROWNE (John).
>   *Fiction.*
>>   Pandion and Amphigenia : or the History of the Coy Lady of Thessalia Adorned with *Sculptures*. By *J. Crowne*. *London*, Printed by *I.G. for R. Mills*, at the sign of the *Pestel* and *Mortar* without *Temple-Barr, Anno*, 1665. 8º.
>   *Dramatic Works.*
>>   Juliana, or the Princess of Poland. *A Tragicomedy.* As it is *Acted* at His Royal Highness the Duke of York's Theatre. By *J. Crown*, Gent. *Presto, e bene, di rado riesce bene.* Licensed, *sept.* 8. 1671. *Roger L'Estrange. London,* Printed for *Will. Cademan* at the *Popes-Head* in the lower Walk in the *New-Exchange,* and *Will. Birch* at the lower end of *Cheapside,* 1671. 4º.

BIBLIOGRAPHY 419

The History of Charles the Eighth of France, or the Invasion of *Naples* by the *French*. As it is acted at his Highnesses the Duke of *York's* Theater. Written by Mr. *Crowne, Honestum est secundis tertijsve consistere*. Qu. *London*, Printed by *T.R.* and *N.T.* for *Ambrose Isted*, at the Sign of the *Golden Anchor*, over against St. *Dunstan's* in *Fleet-street*. 1672. 4°.

Andromache. A Tragedy. As it is Acted at the Dukes Theatre. *London*, Printed by *T. Ratcliffe*, and *N. Thompson*, for *Richard Bentley*, and Sold by the Book-sellers of *London* and *Westminster*. 1675. 4°.

The Countrey Wit. A Comedy : Acted at the Dukes Theatre, Written by Mr. *Crown, London*, Printed by *T.N.* for *James Magnes*, and *Richard Bentley*, at the *Post-Office*, in *Russel-street* in *Covent-Garden*. 1675. 4°.

Calisto : or, The Chaste Nimph. The late Masque at Court, As it was frequently Presented there, By several Persons of Great Quality. With the Prologue, and the Songs betwixt the Acts. *All Written by J.* Crowne, *London*, Printed by *Tho: Newcomb*, for *James Magnes* and *Richard Bentley*, at the *Post-Office* in *Russel-street* in *Covent-Garden*. 1675. 4°.

The Destruction of Jerusalem by Titus Vespasian. In two Parts. As it was Acted at the Theatre Royal. Written by Mr. *Crowne*. Part the First. *London*, Printed for *R. Bentley*, at the *Posthouse* in *Russel-street* in *Covent-Garden*, 1677. 4°.

The Destruction of Jerusalem by Titus Vespasian. The Second Part. As it is Acted at the Theatre Royal By Their Majesties Servants. Written by Mr. *Crown*. *London*, Printed for *J. Magnes* and *R. Bentley*, in *Russel-street* in *Covent-Garden*, near the *Piazza's*, Anno. Dom. 1677. 4°.

The Ambitious Statesman, or the Loyal Favourite. As it was Acted at the theatre *Royal*, by His Majesties Servants. Written by *Mr. Crowne*. *London*, Printed for *William Abington*, at the *Black-spread-Eagle*, at the West-end of St *Paul's*. 1679. 4°.

The Misery of Civil-War. A Tragedy, As it is Acted at the Duke's Theatre, By His Royal Highnesses Servants. Written by Mr. *Crown*, *London*, Printed for *R. Bentley* and *M. Magnes*, in *Russel-Street* in *Covent-Garden*. 1680. 4°. (Though it was printed in 1680, this play was not acted till 1681 ; see Genest, I, p. 307.)

Henry the Sixth, The First Part. With the Murder of *Humphrey* Duke of Glocester. As it was Acted at the Dukes Theatre. Written by Mr. *Crown*. *London*, Printed for *R. Bentley* and *M. Magnes*, in *Russel-Street*, in *Covent-Garden*. 1681. 4°.

Thyestes, A Tragedy. Acted at the Theatre-Royal, By their Majesties Servants. *Written by Mr.* Crown. *London*, Printed for *R. Bently* and *M. Magnes*, in *Russel-street*, in *Covent-Garden* near the *Piazza's*. Anno Domini MDCLXXXI. 4°.

City Politiques. A Comedy. *As it is Acted* By His Majesties Servants. Written by Mr. *Crown*. *London*, Printed for R. Bently in *Covent-Garden*, and *Joseph Hindmarsh*, Book-Seller to His Royal Highness. M.DC.LXXXIII. 4°.

Sir Courtly Nice : Or it Cannot Be. A Comedy. As it is Acted by His Majesties Servants. *Written by Mr.* Crown. *London*, Printed by *H.H.* Jun. for *R. Bently*, in *Russell-street, Covent-Garden*, and *Jos: Hindmarsh*, at the *Golden-Ball* over against the *Royal Exchange* in Cornhill. MDCLXXXV. 4°.

[In *Restoration Comedies*. Ed. M. Summers. 1921.]

The English Frier : or, The Town Sparks. A Comedy, As it is Acted by Their Majesty's Servants. By Mr. *Crowne*. London : Printed for *James Knapton*, at the Crown in St. *Paul's* Churchyard. 1690. 4°.

The Married Beau : or, the Curious Impertinent, A Comedy : Acted at the Theatre-Royal, By their Majesties Servants. Written by Mr. Crowne. London : Printed for *Richard Bentley*, at the Post-House in *Russell-Street* in *Covent-Garden*. 1694. 4º.

Caligula, a Tragedy, as it is acted at the *Theatre Royal*, By His Majesty's Servants. Written by Mr. *Crowne*. London : Printed by *J. Orme*, for *R. Wellington*, at the *Lute* in St *Paul's* Church-Yard, and sold by *Percivil Gilborne*, at the *Harrow*, at the Corner of *Chancery-Lane*, and *Bernard Lintott*, at the *Cross-Keys* in St *Martins-Lane*, near *Long-Acre*. 1698. 4º.

Collected Works.
The Dramatic Works of John Crowne. With Prefatory Memoir and Notes. Edinburgh : William Paterson, London : H. Sotheran and Co. MDCCCLXXIII. 4 vols. 8º.
[In *Dramatists of the Restoration.* Ed. J. Maidment and W. H. Logan. Omits *Andromache, Misery of Civil War, Henry the Sixth.*]

Biography and Criticism.
White, A. F.
[*John Crowne, His Life and Dramatic Works,* Cleveland. 1922.]

D'AVENANT (Sir William).
Poems.
Gondibert : An Heroick Poem, Written by Sr *William D'Avenant.* London, Printed by *Tho. Newcomb*, for *John Holden*, and are to be sold at his Shop at the sign of the Anchor in the New-Exchange. 1651. 4º.
[Chalmers, Vol. VI. Also Southey's *Select Works of the British Poets.* 1841.]

Dramatic Works.
The Siege of Rhodes Made a Representation by the Art of Prospective in Scenes, And the Story sung in *Recitative* Musick. At the back part of *Rutland*-House in the upper end of *Aldergate*-Street *London.* London, Printed by *J.M.* for *Henry Herringman*, and are to be sold at his Shop, at the Sign of the *Anchor*, on the Lower-Walk in the *New-Exchange*, 1656. 4º.

The Cruelty of the Spaniards in Peru. Exprest by Instrumentall and Vocall Musick, and by Art of Perspective in Scenes, etc. Represented daily at the *Cockpit* in *Drury-Lane*, At Three after noone punctually. *London*, Printed for *Henry Herringman*, and are to be sold at his Shop at the *Anchor* in the Lower walk in the *New-Exchange.* 1658. 4º.

Law against Lovers. (This play, acted in 1662, is not to be found in a separate edition, but is in the following volume :) The Works of Sr William D'Avenant K^t Consisting of *Those which were formerly Printed*, And *Those which he design'd for the Press* : Now Published Out of the Authors Originall Copies. London : Printed by *T.N.* for *Henry Herringman*, at the Sign of the *Blew Anchor* in the Lower Walk of the *New-Exchange*. 1673. folio.

Macbeth, a Tragedy. With all the Alterations, Amendments, Additions, and New Songs. As it's now Acted at the Dukes Theatre. *London*, Printed for P. Chetwin, and are to be sold by most Booksellers, 1674. 4º.

The Tempest. *See* DRYDEN.

Collected Works.
[*The Dramatic Works.* 5 vols. 1872-4. (*Dramatists of the Restoration.* Ed. J. Maidment and W. H. Logan.)]

Biography and Criticism.
Harbage, Alfred.
[*Sir William Davenant. Poet Venturer. 1606–1668.* Philadelphia, 1935.]
Dowlin, C. M.
[*Sir William Davenant's Gondibert, its preface, and Hobbes' answer : a study in English neo-classicism.* 1935.]

DEFOE (Daniel).
Poems.
   The True-Born *Englishman* a Satyr *Statuimus Pacem et Securitatem, et Concordiam, Judicium et Justitiam, inter* Anglos *et* Normannos, Francos *et* Britones, Walliae *et* Cornubiae, Pictos *et* Scotos, Albaniae, *similiter inter Francos et Insulanos Provincias, et Patrias, quae pertinent ad Coronam nostram, et inter omnes nobis Subjectos, firmiter et inviolabiliter observari.* Charta Regis Willielmi Conquisitoris de Pace Publica, Cap. 1. Printed in the Year MDCC. 4°.
   A Hymn to The Pillory. London : Printed in the Year MDCCIII. 4°.
   [Both the above reprinted : E. Arber. *The English Garner.* Vol. VII. 1883.]
Prose.
   The Poor Man's Plea, In Relation to all the *Proclamations, Declarations, Acts of Parliament,* etc. Which Have been, or shall be made, or publish'd, for a Reformation of Manners, and suppressing Immorality in the Nation. London : Printed in the Year MDCXCVIII. 4°.
   The Shortest-Way With the Dissenters : or Proposals for the Establishment of the Church. *London* : Printed in the Year MDCCII. 4°.
   [Reprinted : E. Arber. *The English Garner.* Vol. VII. 1883. Also H. Morley. *Famous Pamphlets.* 1886.]
   The Shortest-Way With the Dissenters : Or Proposals for the Establishment of the Church. With its Author's Brief Explications *Consider'd*; His Name *Expos'd,* His Practices *Detected,* and his Hellish Designs set in a true Light, that the Party which stickles for Him, may rightly know Him, and that Which is against Him continue to Triumph over Him. The Second Edition, Corrected and Amended. To which is Added A *Post-Script,* By Way of Answer to some *Malicious and False Aspersions,* etc.

   Disce Omnes.

   Tempus eget.

   Crimine ab Uno

   Nec Defensoribus istis
   Virg., Æn.

   London : Printed in the Year 1703. 4°.
   A Weekly Review of the Affairs of *France* : Purg'd from the Errors and Partiality of *News-Writers* and *Petty-Statesmen,* of all Sides. Numb. 1. Saturday, Feb. 19 1704. 4°.
   [Facsimile edition : 22 vols. A. W. Secord. New York. 1938.]
Collected Works.
   [*Novels and Miscellaneous Works.* 7 vols. 1854–67. (Bohn's British Classics.)]
   [*Novels and Selected Writings.* 14 vols. Oxford. 1927–8.]
Biography and Criticism.
   Wilson, Walter.
      Memoirs of the Life and Times of Daniel De Foe ; Containing A Review of his Writings, and his opinions upon a Variety of important Matters, Civil and Ecclesiastical. By Walter Wilson, Esq. of the Inner Temple. In Three volumes. London : Hurst, Chance and Co. 1830. 8°.
   Lee, William.
      Daniel Defoe : His Life, and recently discovered writings : extending from 1716 to 1729. By William Lee. London : John Camden Hotten, Piccadilly. 1869. 3 vols. 8°.
   Minto, William.
      English Men of Letters Edited by John Morley. Daniel Defoe By William Minto. London Macmillan and Co. 1879. 1 vol. 12°.

Trent, W. P.
  [*Daniel Defoe. How to know him.* Indianapolis. 1916.]
Dottin, Paul.
  [*Daniel De Foe et ses Romans.* 3 vols. Paris. 1924. Trans. Eng. (vol. 1 only). 1929.]
Sutherland, J. R.
  [*Defoe.* 1937.]

DENNIS (John). See also COLLIER.
Poems.
  Britannia Triumphans : Or the Empire Sav'd, and *Europe* Deliver'd. By the Success of her Majesty's Forces under the Wise and Heroick Conduct of his Grace the Duke of Marlborough. A Poem, By Mr. Dennis. Ab Jove Principium Musae. Virg. London : Printed for *J. Nutt* near *Stationers-Hall.* 1704. 8⁰.
  The Battle of Ramillia : or, the Power of Union. A Poem. In Five Books By Mr. *Dennis. London,* Printed for *Ben Bragg* at the *Raven* in *Pater-Noster-Row,* 1706. 8⁰.
  A Poem Upon the Death of Her late Sacred Majesty Queen *Anne,* And the Most Happy and most Auspicious Accession Of his Sacred Majesty King George. To the Imperial Crowns of *Great Britain, France and Ireland.* With an Exhortation to all True *Britons* to Unity. *Rege incolumi mens omnibus una est.* Virg. Georg. I. 4. London : Printed by H. Meere, and Sold by J. Baker at the Black Boy in Pater-Noster-Row. 1714. (Price Six Pence.) 8⁰.
Prose.
  A Plot, and no Plot. A Comedy, As it is Acted at the Theatre-Royal, in *Drury Lane.* Written by Mr. *Dennis.*

  > Militiae quamvis piger et malus, utilis urbi,
  > Si das hoc, parvis quoque rebus magna Juvari.
  >   Horace Epist.

  London, Printed for *R. Parker,* at the Sign of the *Unicorn* under the *Royal Exchange* in *Cornhil* : *P. Buck,* at the Sign of the *Temple,* near the *Inner Temple Gate, Fleet street* : and *R. Wellington,* at the *Lute* in St. *Paul's* Church Yard. (1697), 4⁰.
  Original Letters, Familiar, Moral, *and* Critical. By Mr. *Dennis.* In Two Volumes. London : Printed for W. Mears, at the Lamb without Temple-Bar. MDCCXXI. 8⁰.
  The Stage defended from Scripture, Reason, Experience and the Common Sense of Mankind, for Two Thousand Years. Occasion'd by Mr. *Law's* late Pamphlet against Stage-Entertainments. In a Letter to . . . By Mr. *Dennis,* London : Printed for N. Blandford, at the *London-Gazette, Charing-Cross* ; and sold by J. Peele, at *Locke's-Head* in *Pater-Noster-Row.* MDCCXXVI. (Price one Shilling.) 4⁰.
Collected Works.
  The Select Works of Mr. *John Dennis.* In Two Volumes.

  > Neque, Te ut miretur Turba, labores ;
  > Contentus paucis Lectoribus.   Hor.

  London, Printed by John Darby in Bartholomew-Close. MDCCXVIII. 8⁰.
  [*The Critical Works of John Dennis.* Ed. E. N. Hooker. 2 vols. Baltimore. 1939–43.]
Biography and Criticism.
  Paul, H. G.
    [*John Dennis, His Life and Criticism.* New York. 1911.]

BIBLIOGRAPHY 423

DIAPER (William).
[*Nereides: or, Sea-Eclogues.* London. 1712.]
[*Dryades.* London. 1713.]
[Verse translation of the first two books of Oppian's *Halieuticks*. Oxford. 1722.] Ed. in preparation by D. Broughton.

DIGBY (George, 2ᵈ Earl of Bristol).
Elvira : or The Worst not always True. A Comedy, Written by a Person of Quality. Licens'd May 15. 1667. Roger L'Estrange. *London*, Printed by E. Cotes for *Henry Brome* in Little-Britain. 1667. 4°.
[Reprinted : R. Dodsley, *A Select Collection of Old Plays*. Vol. XII. 1744. Revised W. C. Hazlitt. Vol. XV. 1876.]

DILLON (Wentworth, Earl of Roscommon.) See also WILMOT (John).
Miscellaneous Works By The Right Honourable. The *Earl of* Roscommon. *London*: Printed in the Year MDCCIX, 8°.
The Works of the right honourable Wentworth Dillon, Earl of Roscommon. Glasgow : Printed by Robert and Andrew Foulis. MDCCLIII. 12°.
[See Chalmers, Vol. VIII. Also T. Park, *Works of the British Poets*. Vol. 32.]

DOGGET (Thomas).
The Country-Wake: A Comedy. As it is Acted at the New Theatre in *Little Lincoln's-Inn-Fields* by His Majesty's Servants. *Written by Mr. Tho. Dogget, Comedian. London*, Printed for *Sam. Briscoe* at the Corner of *Charles-street*, in *Russel-street, Covent Garden* ; Sold by *R. Wellington*, at the *Lute* in St. *Paul's* Church-yard ; *R. Parker* at the *Royal-Exchange*. 1696. *Price*, One Shilling, Six Pence. 4°.

DORSET (Charles Sackville, Earl of). See WILMOT (John).

DRAKE (Nathan).
Essays, Biographical. Critical, and Historical, Illustrative of the Tatler, Spectator, and Guardian. *By Nathan Drake, M.D.* Author of Literary Hours, etc. ['Αγαθούς άγαθοις άντεξεταζειν.] Dionysius Halicarnasseus. In three Volumes.—The second Edition. *London* : Published by Suttaby, Evance, and Fox. Stationers'-Court, Ludgate-Street ; and Sharpe and Hailes, Piccadilly. 1814. In-12.
Essays, Biographical, Critical, and Historical, Illustrative of the Rambler, Adventurer, Idler, and of the Various Periodical Papers which, *In Imitation of the Writings of Steele and Addison*, have been published between the Close of the eighth volume of the Spectator, and the commencement of the year 1809. *By Nathan Drake, M.D.* Author of Literary Hours, and of Essays on the Tatler, Spectator, and Guardian. Evolvendi penitus auctores qui de virtute praecipiunt, ut—vita cum scientia divinarum rerum sit humanarumque conjuncta. Quintilianus. In two Volumes. Printed by J. Seeley, Buckingham, for W. Suttaby, Stationers Court. London. 1809. In-12.
The Gleaner : A series of Periodical Essays ; Selected and arranged From scarce or neglected volumes, with an introduction, and notes, By Nathan Drake, M.D. Author of " Literary Hours," And of " Essays, on Periodical Literature."

Apis Matinae
More modoque,
Grata carpentis thyma per laborem
Plurimum.   Hor.

In four volumes. London : Printed for Suttaby, Evance and Co. Stationers' Court ; And Robert Baldwin, Pater-Noster Row ; Also for William Blackwood, Edinburgh, and Michael Keene. Dublin 1811. 8°.

DRYDEN (John).
  Poems.
    Astraea Redux. A Poem on the happy Restoration and Return of His Sacred Majesty Charles the Second. By *John Driden*. *Jam Redit et Virgo, Redeunt Saturnia Regna.* Virgil. *London* Printed by *J.M.* for *Henry Herringman*, and are to be sold at his shop, at the Blew-*Anchor*, in the Lower Walk of the New-Exchange. 1660. folio.
    Annus Mirabilis: the year of Wonder, 1666: an Historical Poem: Containing The Progress and various Successes of our Naval War with *Holland*, under the Conduct of His Highness Prince Rupert and His Grace the Duke of Albemarl. And describing The Fire of London. By John Dryden, Esq.; *Multum interest res poscat, an homines latius imperare velint.* Trajan. Imperator. ad Plin. *Urbs antiqua ruit, multos dominata per annos.* Virg. *London*, Printed for *Henry Herringman*, at the *Anchor* in the Lower Walk of the *New Exchange*: 1677. 8º.
    [Facsimile reprint: Clarendon Press. 1927.]
    Absalom and Achitophel. A Poem.
      . . . *Si Propius stes*
      Te Capiet Magis . . .
    London, Printed for *J.T.* and are to be Sold by *W. Davies* in *Amen-Corner*. 1681. folio.
    The second part of Absalom and Achitopel. A Poem.
      Si quis tamen Haec quoque, Si Quis
      Captus Amore Leget.
    London: Printed for *Jacob Tonson*, at the *Judges Head* in *Chancery Lane*, near *Fleet-Street*. 1682. folio. (In collaboration with Nahum Tate.)
    [Both parts ed. W. D. Christie. Fifth edition revised C. H. Firth. Clarendon Press. 1911.]
    The Medall. A Satyre against Sedition By the Author of *Absalom* and *Achitophel*.
      Per Graium *populos, mediaeque per* Elidis Urbem
      Ibat ovans: Divumque *sibi poscebat honores.*
    London, Printed for *Jacob Tonson* at the *Judge's Head* in *Chancery-Lane* near *Fleet-street*. 1682. 4º.
    [Facsimile reprint: Oxford. 1924.]
    Mac Flecknoe, or a Satyr upon the true-blew-protestant poet T.S. London. Printed for D. Green. 1682. 4º.
    [Facsimile reprint: Oxford. 1924.]
    Three Poems Upon the Death of the Late Usurper Oliver Cromwel. Written by Mr. *Jo. Drydon* [sic]. Mr. *Sprat*, of Oxford. Mr. *Edm. Waller*. London: Printed by *William Wilson*, in the Year 1659. And Reprinted for *R. Baldwin* 1682. 4º.
    [Originally published as: Three Poems upon the Death of his late Highnesse Oliver Lord Protector of *England, Scotland,* and *Ireland*. By Mr. Edm. Waller. Mr. Jo. Dryden. Mr. Sprat of *Oxford*. 1659. Later reprinted with the above heading by Dryden's enemies, to remind the public of his earlier sympathies. See *Dryden Bibliography*. Hugh Macdonald. 1939. pp. 3-7.]
    Religio Laici or a Laymans Faith. A Poem. Written by Mr. *Dryden*: *Ornari res ipsa negat: contenta doceri.* London, Printed for *Jacob Tonson* at the *Judge's Head* in *Chancery-lane*, near *Fleet-street*. 1682. 4º.
    Prologue To His *Royal Highness*, Upon His first appearance at the *Duke's Theatre*, since his Return from *Scotland*. *Written by Mr. Dryden. Spoken by Mr.* Smith. *London*, Printed for *J. Tonson*. (21st April 1682.) folio.

Miscellany Poems. Containing a New Translation of *Virgil's* Eclogues, *Ovid's* Love Elegies, Odes of *Horace*, And Other Authors; With Several Original Poems. By the most Eminent Hands.

   Et Vos, O Lauri, *carpam, et Te, proxima* Myrte :
   Sic posita quoniam suaveis miscetis odores.
               Virg. *Ecl.* 2.

London, Printed for *Jacob Tonson*, at the *Judges-Head* in *Chancery-Lane* near Fleet-street, 1684. 8º.

Sylvae : Or, The Second Part of Poetical Miscellanies.

       Non deficit alter
  Aureus ; et simili frondescit virga metallo. Virg.

London, Printed for *Jacob Tonson*, at the *Judges-Head* in *Chancery-lane* near *Fleet-street*. 1685. 8º.

The Second Part of Miscellany Poems. Containing Variety of New Translations of the *Ancient Poets* : Together with Several Original Poems. *By the Most Eminent Hands.* Publish'd by Mr. *Dryden.*

       Non deficit alter
  Aureus ; et simili frondescit virga metallo. Virg.

The Fourth Edition. London : Printed for Jacob Tonson at *Shakespear's Head* over-against *Katharine-Street* in the *Strand*. MDCCXVI. 8º.

Examen Poeticum : being The Third Part of Miscellany Poems. Containing Variety of New Translations of the *Ancient Poets*. Together with many Original Copies, by the *Most Eminent Hands.*

   Haec potior soboles : hinc Caeli tempore certo,
   Dulcia mella premes.   Virg. Geor. 4.
   In Medium quaesita reponunt. Ibid.

London, Printed by R.E. for *Jacob Tonson*, at the *Judges Head* in *Chancery-Lane* near *Fleetstreet.* MDCXCIII. 8º.

The *Annual Miscellany* : for The Year 1694, Being The Fourth Part of Miscellany Poems Containing Great Variety of New Translations and Original Copies by the *Most Eminent Hands.* London : Printed by *R.E.* for *Jacob Tonson*, at the *Judges Head* near the *Inner Temple-Gate,* in *Fleetstreet.* M.D.CXCIV. 8º.

[For details of the above miscellanies see *Dryden Bibliography.* Hugh Macdonald. 1939.]

Threnodia Augustalis : a Funeral-Pindarique Poem Sacred to the Happy Memory of King Charles II. By *John Dryden* Servant to His late Majesty and to the Present King.

   Fortunati Ambo, si quid mea Carmina possunt,
   Nulla dies unquam memori vos eximet aevo !

London : Printed for *Jacob Tonson*, at the *Judges Head* in *Chancery-lane*, near *Fleet-street.* 1685. 4º.

The Hind and the Panther. A Poem. In Three Parts.

     Antiquam exquirite matrem } Virg.
   Et vera, incessu, patuit Dea.

Holy-Rood-House. Re-printed by *James Watson*, Printer to His most Excellent Majesties Royal Family and House-hold. MDCLXXXVII. 4º.

Britannia Rediviva : A Poem on the Birth of the Prince. Written by Mr. *Dryden.*

   Dii Patrii Indigetes et Romule, Vestaque Mater,
   Quae Tuscum Tiberim, et Romana Palatia servas

P

> *Hunc saltem everso* Puerum *succurrere saeclo*
> *Ne prohibete : satis jampridem sanguine nostro*
> *Laomedonteae luimus* Perjuria *Trojae.*
> Virg. Georg. I.

London. Printed for *J. Tonson* at the *Judges-Head* in *Chancery-Lane* near *Fleet-Street.* 1688. folio.

The Satires of Decimus Junius Juvenalis. Translated into English Verse. By Mr. *Dryden* And Several other Eminent Hands. Together with the Satires of Aulus Persius Flaccus. Made English by Mr. *Dryden.* With Explanatory Notes at the end of each Satire. To Which is Prefix'd a Discourse concerning the Original and Progress of Satire. Dedicated to the Right Honourable *Charles* Earl of *Dorset,* etc. By Mr. *Dryden.*

> *Quicquid agunt homines, votum, timor, Ira, Voluptas,*
> *Gaudia, discursus, nostri est farrago libelli.*

London, Printed for *Jacob Tonson* at the *Judge's Head* in *Chancery-Lane,* near *Fleetstreet.* MDCXCIII. folio.

[The Juvenal satires 1, 3, 6, 10 and 16, and all those of Persius are translated by Dryden.]

The Works of Virgil : Containing His Pastorals, Georgics, and AEneis. Translated into English Verse ; by Mr. *Dryden.* Adorn'd with a Hundred Sculptures. *Sequiturque Patrem non passibus AEquis.* Virg. AEn. 2. The Second Edition. *London,* Printed for *Jacob Tonson,* at the *Judges-Head* in *Fleetstreet,* near the *Inner-Temple-Gate.* MDCXCVIII. folio.

Fables *Ancient* and *Modern* ; Translated into Verse, From Homer, Ovid, Boccace, and Chaucer : with Original Poems. By Mr *Dryden.*

> *Nunc ultro ad Cineres ipsius et ossa parentis*
> *(Haud equidem sine mente, reor, sine numine divum)*
> *Adsumus.* Virg. Æn. lib. 5.

London : Printed for *Jacob Tonson,* within *Gray's Inn Gate* next *Gray's Inn Lane.* MDCC. folio.

Collected Poems.

The Annotated edition of the English Poets. Edited by Robert Bell. Author of ' The History of Russia,' ' Lives of English Poets,' etc. London : John W. Parker and Son, West Strand. The Poetical Works of J. Dryden. 1854. 3 vols. in-12.

The Globe Edition. The Poetical Works of John Dryden Edited with a Memoir, Revised text, and Notes by W. D. Christie, M.A. of Trinity College, Cambridge. New Edition. London : Macmillan and Co. 1870. 8⁰.

The Works of John Dryden. Illustrated with Notes, Historical, Critical, and Explanatory, and A Life of the Author. By Sir Walter Scott, Bart. Revised and Corrected by George Saintsbury. Edinburgh : Printed for William Paterson, Princes Street, by T. and A. Constable, Printers to Her Majesty. 1882–1893. 18 vols. 8⁰. [Contains all the above poems.]

[*Poetical Works.* Ed. G. R. Noyes. New York. 1909.]

[*Poems.* Ed. John Sargeaunt. 1910.]

Dramatic Works.

The Wild Gallant : A Comedy, As it was acted at the Theater-Royal, By His Majesties Servants. Written *By* John Dryden, *Esq.* ; In the Savoy. Printed by *Tho. Newcomb.* for *H. Herringman,* at the *Blew-Anchor,* in the Lower-Walk of the *New-Exchange.* 1669. 4⁰. (Acted in 1662.)

The Rival Ladies. A Tragi-Comedy. As it was Acted at the *Theatre Royal*. Nos. haec Novimus esse nihil. Written by *John Driden* Esquire. *London*, Printed for *H. Herringman*, and are to be sold at his shop in the Lower walk in the *New Exchange*. 1669. 4°. (Acted in 1664.)
The Indian Queen 1664. See HOWARD (Sir Robert).
The Indian Emperour, or, the Conquest of Mexico By the Spaniards. Being the Sequel of the *Indian Queen*. By John Dryden Esq. ;

> Dum relego scripsisse pudet, quia plurima cerno
> Me quoque, qui feci, judice, digna lini.
>   Ovid.

London, Printed for *H. Herringman*, at the Sign of the *Blew Anchor* in the Lower Walk of the *New Exchange*, 1667. 4°. (Acted in 1665.)
Secret-Love, or the Maiden-Queen. As it is Acted By His Majesties Servants at the *Theater-Royal*. Written by John Dryden, Esq ;

> Vitis nemo sine nascitur ; optimus ille
> Qui minimis urgetur.   Horace.

London, Printed for *Henry Herringman*, at the Sign of the *Anchor* on the lower walk of the *New-Exchange*. 1668. 4°. (Acted in 1667.)
Sʳ Martin Mar-all, or the Feign'd Innocence ; A Comedy. As it was Acted at His Highnesse the Duke of *York's* Theatre. *London*, Printed for *Henry Herringman*, at the Sign of the *Blew Anchor* in the Lower Walk of the *New Exchange*. 1668. 4°. (Acted in 1667.)
[In collaboration with William Cavendish, Duke of Newcastle.]
Sʳ Martin Marr-all : Or, the Feign'd Innocence. A Comedy. As it is Acted By Their Majesties Servants. By Mʳ *Dryden*. *London*, Printed for *Henry Herringman*, and are to be sold by *Francis Saunders* at the *Blue Anchor* in the Lower Walk of the *New-Exchange*, 1691. 4°. (From the year 1691, still in Dryden's lifetime, the play has been printed under Dryden's name alone.)
The Tempest, or the Enchanted Island. A Comedy : As it is now Acted At His Highness the Duke of York's Theatre. *London*, Printed by *J. Macock*, for *Henry Herringman* at the Sign of the *Blew Anchor* in the Lower Walk of the *New Exchange*. M.DC.LXXVI. 4°. (In collaboration with D'Avenant ; acted in 1667.)
An Evening's Love. Or the Mock-Astrologer. Acted at the Theatre-Royal by His Majesties Servants. Written by *John Dryden* Servant to His Majesty. *Mallem Convivis quam placuisse Cocis.* Mart. In the *Savoy*, Printed by *T.N.* for *Henry Herringman*, and are to be sold at the *Anchor* in the Lower Walk of the *New Exchange*. 1671. 4°. (Acted in 1668.)
Tyrannick-Love : or, the Royal Martyr. A Tragedy. As it is Acted by his Majesties Servants, at the *Theatre Royal*. By *John Dryden*, Servant to his *Majesty*.

> Non jam prima peto—neq; vincere certo ;
> Extremum rediisse pudet.   Virg.

London, Printed for *H. Herringman*, at the Sign of the *Blew Anchor* in the Lower Walk of the *New Exchange*. 1670. 4°.
The Conquest of Granada by the Spaniards : In Two Parts. Acted at the *Theater-Royall*. Written by *John Dryden* Servant to His Majesty.

> Major rerum mihi nascitur Ordo ;
> Majus Opus moveo.   Virg. Æneid : 7.

In the *Savoy*. Printed by T.N. for *Henry Herringman*, and are to be sold at the *Anchor*, in the Lower Walk of the *New Exchange*. 1672. 4°. [Acted in 1670.]

Almanzor and *Almahide*. Or the Conquest of Granada. The Second Part. As it is Acted at the *Theater-Royal*. Written by *John Dryden* Servant to his Majesty—*stimulos dedit aemula virtus*. Lucan. In the *Savoy*, Printed by *T.N.* for *Henry Herringman*, and are to be sold at the Anchor in the Lower Walk of the *New Exchange*. 1673. 4°. [Acted in 1671.]

The Assignation : Or, Love in a Nunnery. As it is Acted, at the *Theatre Royal*. Written by *John Dryden* Servant to His Majesty. *Successum dea dira negat*. Virg. London : Printed by *T.N.* for *Henry Herringman*, and are to be sold at the *Anchor* in the Lower Walk of the *New Exchange*. 1673. (Acted in 1672.) 4°.

Marriage-à-la-Mode. A Comedy. As it is Acted at the Theatre-Royal. Written by *John Dryden*, Servant to His Majesty.

> *Quicquid sum ego, quamvis*
> *Infra Lucilli censum ingeniumque, tamen me*
> *Cum magnis vixisse, invita fatebitur usque*
> *Invidia, et fragili quaerens illidere dentem*
> *Offendet solido.* Horat. Serm.

London, Printed by *T.N.* for *Henry Herringman*, and are to be sold at the Anchor in the Lower Walk of the *New-Exchange*. 1673. 4°.

Amboyna : A Tragedy. As it is Acted at the *Theatre-Royal*. Written by *John Dryden* Servant to His Majesty. *Manet alta mente repostum*. London, Printed by *T.N.* for *Henry Herringman*, and are to be sold at the Anchor in the Lower Walk of the *New Exchange*. 1673. 4°.

The State of Innocence, and Fall of Man : an Opera. Written in Heroique Verse, And Dedicated to Her *Royal Highness*, the Dutchess. By *John Dryden*, Servant to His Majesty.

> *Utinam modo dicere possem*
> *Carmina digna Dea : certe est Dea Carmine digna.*
> Ovid. Metam.

London : Printed by *T.N.* for *Henry Herringman*, at the Anchor in the Lower Walk of the *New Exchange*. 1677. 4°.

Aureng-Zebe : A Tragedy. Acted at the Royal Theatre. Written by John Dryden, Servant to his Majesty.

> *Sed, cum fregit subsellia versu,*
> *Esurit, intactam Paridi nisi vendat Agaven.*
> Juv.

Licensed, *Roger L'Estrange*. *London*, Printed by *T.N. for Henry Herringman*, at the *Anchor* in the Lower Walk of the *New Exchange*. 1676. 4°.

All for Love : Or, the World well Lost. A Tragedy, As it is Acted at the *Theatre Royal* ; And Written in Imitation of *Shakespeare's* Stile. By *John Dryden*, Servant to His Majesty. *Facile est verbum aliquod ardens (ut ita dicam) notare : idque restinctis animorum incendiis irridere*. Cicero. *In the Savoy* : Printed by *Tho. Newcomb*, for *Henry Herringman*, at the Blew Anchor in the Lower Walk of the *New-Exchange*. 1678. 4°.

Œdipus : A Tragedy. As it is Acted at his Royal Highness The Duke's Theatre. The Authors Mr. *Dryden*, and Mr. *Lee*.

> *Hi proprium decus et partum indignantur honorem*
> *Ni teneant.* Virgil.
>
> *Vos exemplaria Graeca,*
> *Nocturna versate manu, versate diurna.* Horat.

Licensed, *Jan*. 3. 1678/9. *Roger L'Estrange. London*, Printed for *R. Bentley* and *M. Magnes* in *Russel-street* in *Covent-Garden*. 1679. 4°.
Troilus and Cressida, Or, *Truth Found too Late*. A Tragedy As it is Acted at the Dukes Theatre. To Which is Prefix'd, A Preface Containing the Grounds of Criticism in Tragedy. Written by *John Dryden* Servant to His Majesty.

Rectius, Iliacum carmen deducis in actus,
Quam si proferres ignota indictaque primus. Hor.

London, Printed for *Abel Swall*, at the Unicorn at the West-end of S. Pauls, and *Jacob Tonson* at the *Judges-Head* in *Chancery-lane* near *Fleet-street*, 1679. 4°.
The Kind Keeper ; Or, Mr Limberham : A Comedy : As it was Acted at the Duke's Theatre by His Royal Highnesses Servants. Written by *John Dryden*, Servant to his Majesty. Κἤν μεφάγης ἐπὶ ῥίζαν, ὅμως ἔτι καρποφορήσω. Ἀντολογία Δευτέρα

Hic nuptarum insanit amoribus ; his meretricum :
Omnes hi metuunt versus ; odere Poetas. Horat.

London : Printed for *R. Bentley*, and *M. Magnes*, in *Russel-Street* in *Covent-Garden*, 1680. 4°.
The Spanish Fryar, Or, The Double Discovery. Acted at the Duke's Theatre.

Ut melius possis fallere, sume togam. Ma.
Alterna revisens
Lusit, et in solido rursus fortuna locavit. Vir.

Written by *John Dryden*, Servant to His Majesty. *London*, Printed for *Richard Tonson* and *Jacob Tonson*, at *Grays-inn-gate*, in *Grays-inn-lane*, and at the *Judge's Head*, in *Chancery-lane*, 1681. 4°.
The Duke of Guise. A Tragedy. Acted By Their Majesties Servants. Written by Mr. *Dryden*, and Mr. *Lee* ‛Οὕτως δὲ φιλότιμοι φύσεις ἐν τᾶις πολιτείαις τὸ ἄγαν μὴ φυλαξάμεναι τοῦ ἀγαθοῦ μεῖζον τὸ κακὸν ἔχουσι. Plutarch. in Agesilao. *London*, Printed by *T.N.* for *R. Bentley* in *Russel-street*, near the *Piazza* in *Covent-Garden*, and *J. Tonson* at the *Judge's Head* in *Chancery-lane*. M. DC. LXXXIII. 4°.
Albion and Albanius : an Opera Perform'd at the Queens Theatre in *Dorset* Garden. *Written by Mr*. Dryden. *Discite justitiam moniti, et non temnere Divos*. Virg. *London*, Printed for *Jacob Tonson*, at the *Judge's Head* in *Chancery-lane*, near *Fleet-street*. 1685. folio.
Amphitryon ; or, The Two Sosia's. A Comedy. At it is Acted at the Theatre Royal.

Egregiam vero laudem, et spolia ampla refertis ;
Una, dolo, Divum, si Foemina victa duorum est. Virg.

Written by Mr. *Dryden*. To which added, The Musick of the Songs Compos'd by Mr. *Henry Purcel*. *London*, Printed for *J. Tonson*, at the *Judge's Head* in *Chancery-lane* near *Fleet-street* ; and *M. Tonson* at *Grays-Inn-Gate* in *Gray's-Inn-Lane*. 1691. 4°. (Played in 1690.)
Don Sebastian, King of Portugal : A Tragedy Acted at the Theatre Royal. Written by Mr. *Dryden*.

Nec tarda Senectus
Debilitat vires animi, mutatque vigorem. Virgil.

London : Printed for *Jo. Hindmarsh*, at the *Golden Ball* in *Cornhill*. MDCXC. 4°.
Cleomenes, the Spartan Heroe. A Tragedy, As it is Acted at the Theatre Royal. *Written by* Mr. Dryden. To which is prefixt The Life of

Cleomenes. His Armis, illa quoque tutus in aula, Juv. Sat. IV. *London,* Printed for *Jacob Tonson,* at the *Judge's-Head* in *Chancery-Lane* near *Fleet-Street.* 1692. 4º.

Love Triumphant; Or, Nature will Prevail, A Tragi-Comedy. As it is Acted at the Theatre-Royal, By Their Majesties Servants.

    Quod optanti Divum promittere nemo
    Auderet, volvenda dies, en, attulit ultro. Virg.

Written by Mr. *Dryden. London,* Printed for *Jacob Tonson,* at the *Judges Head* near the *Inner-Temple-Gate* in *Fleet-street.* 1694. 4º.

The Pilgrim, a Comedy: As it is acted at the *Theatre Royal* in Drury-Lane. *Written Originally by Mr.* Fletcher, *and now Very much Alter'd with several Additions.* Likewise A Prologue, Epilogue, Dialogue *and* Masque, *Written by the late Great Poet Mr.* Dryden *just before his Death, being the last of his Works. London :* Printed for *Benjamin Tooke,* near the *Middle-Temple-Gate,* in *Fleet-street.* 1700. 4º.

The Dramatick Works of *John Dryden,* Esq; in Six Volumes. London: Printed for *J. Tonson :* And Sold by *R. Knaplock, W. Taylor, W. Mears, J. Browne, W. Churchill, E. Symon,* and *J. Brotherton.* (With Congreve's Dedication to the Duke of Newcastle.) MDCCXVII. 8º.

[*The Dramatic Works.* Ed. M. Summers. 6 vols. The Nonesuch Press. 1931–2. (Contains all the above plays.)]

Miscellaneous Prose.

Of Dramatick Poesie, An Essay. By *John Dryden* Esq;

    Fungar vice cotis, acutum
    Reddere quae ferrum valet, exsors ipsa secandi.
    Horat. de Arte Poet.

London, Printed for *Henry Herringman,* at the Sign of the *Anchor,* on the Lower-Walk of the New *Exchange.* 1668. 4º.

[Reprinted: 1928. Etchells and Macdonald. Preceded by T. S. Eliot's *Dialogue on Poetic Drama.*]

The Vindication: or the Parallel of the *French* Holy-League, and the English League and Covenant, Turn'd into a Seditious Libell against the King and his Royal Highness, by *Thomas Hunt* and the Authors of the *Reflections* upon the Pretended Parallel in the Play Called The Duke of *Guise.* Written by Mr. *Dryden.*

    Turno tempus erit magno cum optaverit emptum
    Intactum Pallanta ; et cum spolia ista, diemq;
    Oderit.

London, Printed for *Jacob Tonson* at the *Judges Head* in *Chancery-Lane* near *Fleet-street.* MDCLXXXIII. 4º.

Plutarchs Lives Translated *from the Greek* by Several Hands. To which is prefixt the *Life* of *Plutarch. London,* Printed for *Jacob Tonson,* at the Sign of the *Judges-Head* in *Chancery-Lane* near *Fleet-street.* 1683–1686. 5 vols. 8º. (The 1st vol. is headed: The Life of Plutarch, *written by Mr Dryden.*)

[Reprinted: Everyman's Library.]

The History of the League. Written in *French* by Monsieur *Maimbourg.* Translated into *English,* according to His Majesty's Command, By Mr. *Dryden.*

    Neque enim libertas gratior ulla est
    Quam sub Rege Pio.

London, Printed by *M. Flesher,* for *Jacob Tonson,* at the *Judge's-Head* in *Chancery-lane* near *Fleetstreet.* 1684. 8º.

[In the Scott-Saintsbury edition of *The Works.*]

A Defence of the Papers Written by the Late King of Blessed Memory. and Duchess of York, against The Answer made to Them. By Command. London : Printed by *H. Hills*, Printer to the King's Most Excellent Majesty for His Houshold and Chappel. 1686. 4º.
[Dryden wrote the defence of the third paper, that of the Duchess of York. In the Scott-Saintsbury edition of *The Works*.]
De Arte Graphica. The Art of Painting. By *C. A. Du Fresnoy*. With Remarks. Translated into *English*, Together with an *Original Preface* Containing A Parallel betwixt Painting and Poetry. By Mr. *Dryden*. As also a Short Account of the most Eminent Painters, both *Ancient* and *Modern*, continu'd down to the *Present Times*, according to the Order of their Succession. *By Another Hand. Ut Pictura Poesis erit.* Hor. de Arte Poetica. *London*, Printed by *I. Heptinstall* for W. Rogers, at the Sun against St. *Dunstan's* Church in *Fleet-street*. M.DC.XCV. 4º.
[In the Scott-Saintsbury edition of *The Works*.]
[*The Letters of John Dryden*. Ed. Charles E. Ward. Duke University Press. 1942.]
Collected Works (Prose).
  The Critical and Miscellaneous Prose Works of John Dryden, now first collected : With Notes and Illustrations ; An Account of the Life and Writings of the Author, Grounded on Original and Authentick Documents ; And A Collection of his Letters, the greater Part of which has never before been Published. By Edmond Malone, Esq. London : Printed by H. Baldwin and Son, New Bridge-street, for T. Cadell, jun. and W. Davies, in the Strand. M,DCCC. 8º.
  [*The Essays of John Dryden*. Ed. W. P. Ker. 2 vols. Oxford. 1900, 1926.]
Collected Works (Poems, Dramatic Works, Prose).
  The Works of John Dryden. Illustrated with Notes, Historical, Critical, and Explanatory, and a Life of the Author. By Sir Walter Scott, Bart. Revised and Corrected by George Saintsbury. Edinburgh : Printed for William Paterson, Princes Street, by T. and A. Constable, Printers to Her Majesty. 1882–1893. 18 vols. 8º.
Drydeniana.
  Care, Henry.
    Towser the Second, a Bull-dog, or a short Reply to Absalom and Achitophel, 10th December 1681. 8º.
  Hickeringhill, Edmund.
    The Mushroom : or a Satyr against *Libelling Tories* and *Prelatical Tantivies* : In Answer to A Satyr against Sedition called The Meddal, by the Author of *Absalom* and *Achitophel*. And here Answered By the *Author* of the *Black Nonconformist*. The *Next Day* after the Publication of the *Meddal* : To *Help the* sale *thereof. Nitimur in vetitum ? Quousque ?* London, Printed for *Fra* : *Smith* Jun. at the Elephant and Castle, in *Cornhill*. MDCLXXXII. folio. (The end of the work is dated London, March 17, 1681.)
  Villiers, George, Duke of Buckingham.
    Poetical Reflections on a late Poem entituled, Absalom and Achitophel. *By a Person of Honour*. London : Printed for Richard Janeway. 1682. folio.
    [Ascribed to Villiers by Anthony à Wood.]
  Pordage, Samuel.
    Azaria and Hushai, A Poem *quod cuique visum est sentiant.* London : Printed for *Charles Lee*. An. Dom. 1682. 4º.
    The Medal Revers'd a Satyre against Persecution By the Author of Azaria and Hushai. *Laudatur ab his, Culpatur ab illis.* London : Printed for *Charles Lee*, Anno 1682. 4º.

Settle, Elkanah.
  Absalom Senior : Or, Achitophel Transpros'd. a Poem. *Si Populus vult decipi, etc.* London : Printed for *S.E.* and Sold by *Langley Curtis*, at the sign of Sir *Edmondbury Godfrey*, near *Fleetbridge*. 1682. folio.
Shadwell, Thomas.
  The Medal of John Bayes : A Satyr against Folly and Knavery. *Facit indignatio versus*, London : Printed for *Richard Janeway*. 1682. 4°. (Attributed to Shadwell.) [See *Dryden Bibliography*. Hugh Macdonald. 1939. pp. 232–3.]
  The Tory Poets a Satyr. 4°. 1682. "A sad paltry performance against Dryden, Otway, etc.," says Oldys in a Ms. note on Langbaine's Shadwell article. Attributed to Shadwell also by Malone. (See *Life of Dryden*, p. 165), who gives the following extract :

> The laurel makes a wit ; a brave, the sword ;
> And all are wise men at a Council-board :
> Settle's a coward, 'cause fool Otway fought him,
> And Mulgrave is a wit, because I taught him.

  Some Reflections upon the Pretended Parallel in the Play Called The Duke of Guise. In a Letter to a Friend. *London*, Printed for *Francis Smith*, sen. 1683. 4°.
  The Tenth Satyr of Juvenal. English and Latin. The English by *Tho. Shadwell*. With Illustrations upon it. Licensed, *May* 25 1687. London : Printed by *D. Mallet*, for *Gabriel Collins* at the Middle-Temple Gate, in *Fleet-street*. 1687. 4°. (This is a reprint ; the satire must have been 1682.)
Somers, John, Lord.
Satyr to his Muse by the Author of *Absalom* and *Achitophel*.

> *Quo liceat libris non licet ire mihi.*
> *Turpiter huc illuc Ingeniosus eat.*

  London, Printed for D. *Green* 1682. 4°. (Attributed to Somers.)
Prior, Matthew.
  The Hind and the Panther Transvers'd To the Story of the *Country Mouse* and the *City-Mouse*. Much Malice mingled with a little Wit. *Hind. Pan. Nec vult Panthera domari.* Quae Genus. London : Printed for *W. Davis*, MDCLXXXVII. 4°. (In collaboration with Charles Montague.)
Brown, Tom.
  Notes Upon Mr. Dryden's Poems in Four Letters. By *M. Clifford* late Master of the *Charter-House, London*. To which are annexed some Reflections upon the *Hind and Panther*. By another Hand.

> *Et Musarum et Apollinis aede relicta,*
> *Ipse facit versus.*
>   Juv. Sat. 7.

  London, Printed in the Year 1687. 4°.
  The Reasons of Mr. Bays Changing his Religion. Considered in a Dialogue between *Crites, Eugenius*, and Mr. *Bays*.

> *Quo teneam vultus mutantem Protea nodo ? . . .* Hor.
> *Ante bibebatur, nunc quas contingere nolis*
> *Fundit Anigrus aquas. . . .* Ovid. Met.

  London, Printed for *S.T.* and are to be Sold by the Booksellers of London and *Westminster.* 1688. 4°.
  The Late Converts Exposed : Or the Reasons of Mr Bays's Changing his Religion. Considered in a Dialogue. Part the Second. With

Reflections on the Life of St *Xavier*. Don *Sebastian* King of *Portugal*. As Also the Fable of the Bat and the Birds.
> *Parcite* Oves *nimium procedere, non bene ripae*
> *Creditur, ipse* Aries *etiam nunc vellera siccat.*
> Virg. Ecl. 3.
> *Rode* Caper *vitem, tamen hinc sum stabis ad aram,*
> *In tua quod fundi* Cornua *possit, erit.*
> Ovid, Fast.

Licensed, *January*, 8. 1689. *London*, Printed for *Thomas Bennet*, at the Sign of the *Half-Moon* in St. Paul's Church-Yard. 1690. 4°.

The Reasons of Mr Joseph Hains The Player's Conversion and Re-Conversion. Being the Third and Last Part To The Dialogue of Mr. Bays.
> *Ecce iterum* Crispinus, *et est mihi saepe vocandus*
> *Ad partes.* Juv. Sat. 4.
> *Non compositus melius cum* Bitho Bacchius. Hor. Serm.

London, Printed for *Richard Baldwin*, near the *Black-Bull* in the *Old-Baily.* 1690. 4°.

Anonymous.

A Key (With the Whip) To open the Mystery and Iniquity of the Poem call'd *Absalom* and *Achitophel* (1682). 4°.

A Whip for the Fools Back, who styles Honorable Marriage a Curs'd Confinement in his profane of Absalom and Achitophel. Printed by T. Snowden for the author. 1682. folio.

A Poem, in Defence of the Church of England ; In Opposition to the Hind and Panther. Written by Mr. *John Dryden*. *Omnia Subsidunt, meliori pervia Causae.* Claudian. London : Printed in the Year, MDCLXXXVIII. folio.

The Revolter. A Trage-Comedy Acted between the Hind and Panther, and *Religio Laici*, etc. London, Printed in the Year 1687. 4°.

A Panegyrick On the Author of *Absolom* [*sic*] and *Achitophel*, occasioned by his former writing of an *Elegy* in praise of *Oliver Cromwell, lately Reprinted.* Reprinted in the Year MDCLXXXII. folio.

Biography and Criticism.

Saintsbury, George.
English Men of Letters, Edited by John Morley. Dryden by G. Saintsbury. London : Macmillan and Co. 1881. 8°.

Verrall, A. W.
[*Lectures on Dryden.* Cambridge. 1914.]

Nicoll, A.
[*Dryden and his Poetry.* 1923.]

Lubbock, Alan.
[*Character of John Dryden.* 1928.]

Eliot, T. S.
[*Homage to John Dryden.* 1924.]
[*John Dryden.* New York. 1932.]
[*The Use of Poetry and the Use of Criticism.* 1933.]

Van Doren, Mark.
[*The Poetry of John Dryden.* 1931.]

DUFFET (Thomas).
The Spanish Rogue. As it was Acted By His Majesties Servants. Written by *Tho : Duffett*. Hor. Serm.
> *O bone ! ne te*
> *Frustrere : Insanis et tu, Stultique prope omnes.*

London : Printed for *William Cademan* at the *Pope's Head* in the *Lower Walk* in the *New Exchange* in the *Strand*. M.DC.LXXIV. 4º.

DUNTON (John).
Numb. 1. The Athenian Gazette Resolving weekly all the most *Nice and Curious Questions* Propos'd by the Ingenious. Tuesday, March 17th 1690. After the first number the title was changed to :
Numb. 2. The Athenian Mercury. Resolving Weekly all the most *Nice and Curious Questions* Propos'd by the Ingenious. *Licensed and Entered according to Order.* Tuesday, March 24*th*. 1690. folio.
The Athenian Oracle : Being an Entire Collection of the Valuable Questions and Answers in the old *Athenian Mercuries*. Intermix'd with many Cases in *Divinity, History, Philosophy, Mathematicks, Love, Poetry,* never before *Published.* To which is Added, An *Alphabetical* Table for the speedy finding of any Questions. By a *Member* of the Athenian *Society. London,* Printed for Andrew Bell, at the *Cross-Keys* and *Bible,* in *Cornhill,* near *Stocks Market,* 1704. 3 vols. 8º.
The Life and Errors of John Dunton Late Citizen of *London ; Written by Himself in Solitude.* With an Idea of a New Life ; Wherein is Shewn How he'd Think, Speak, and Act, might he Live over his Days again. Intermix'd with the New Discoveries The Author has made in his Travels Abroad, And in his Private Conversation at Home. Together with the Lives and Characters of a Thousand Persons now Living in *London,* etc. Digested into *Seven Stages,* with their Respective Ideas.

> *He that has all his own Mistakes confest,*
> *Stands next to him that never has transgrest,*
> *And will be censur'd for a Fool by none,*
> *But they who see no Errors of their own.*
> Foe's *Satyr upon himself,* P. 6.

London : Printed for S. *Malthus,* 1705. 8º.
[Ed. J. Nichols. With memoir. 1818.]

D'URFEY (Thomas).
Dramatic Works.
The Siege of Memphis, or the Ambitious Queen. *A Tragedy,* Acted at the *Theater-Royal.* Written by *Tho. Durfey,* Gent. *Non fit sine Periculo facinus magnum et memorabile.* Terent. *London,* Printed for *W. Cademan* at the Popes Head at the entrance of the *New Exchange* in the *Strand.* 1676. 4º.
The Fool Turn'd Critick : A Comedy : As it was Acted at the Theatre-Royall. *By His Majesties Servants.* By *T. D.* Gent. *London,* Printed for *James Magnes* and *Richard Bentley,* at the *Post-Office* in *Russel-street* in *Covent Garden,* 1678. 4º.
Sir Barnaby Whigg : or, *No Wit like* a Womans. A Comedy As it is Acted by their Majesties Servants at the Theatre-Royal. *Written by* Thomas Durfey, *Gent.*

> *Quidquid agunt homines, votum, timor, Ira, voluptas,*
> *Gaudia, discursus nostri farrago libelli est.*
> Juvenal.

London, Printed by *A.G.,* and *J.P.* for *Joseph Hindmarsh,* at the *Black Bull* in *Cornhill.* 1681. 4º.
The Royalist. A Comedy ; As it is Acted at the Duke's Theatre. By *Thomas Durfey,* Gent. *London,* Printed for *Jos. Hindmarsh* at the Sign of the Black-Bull near the Royal-Exchange in *Cornhill,* Anno Dom. 1682. 4º.
The Injured Princess, or The Fatal Wager : As it was Acted at the

Theater-Royal, By His Majesties Servants. By *Tho. Durfey*, Gent. London : Printed for *R. Bentley* and *M. Magnes* in *Russel-street* in *Covent-Garden*, near the Piazza, 1682. 4º.

A Common-Wealth of Women. A Play : As it is Acted at the Theatre Royal, By their Majesties Servants. By Mr. D'*Urfey*. *Anguillam Cauda tenes*. Eras. Licensed. Sept. 11. 1685. Roger *L'Estrange*. London, Printed for *R. Bentley* in *Russel-street* in *Covent-Garden* ; and *J.* Hindmarsh at the *Golden Ball* in *Cornwell*, over against the *Royal Exchange*. 1686. 4º.

Love for Money : or, the Boarding School. A Comedy, Written by Mr. D'*Urfey*. London : Printed for *Abel Roper* at the *Mitre* in *Fleet-street*, and are to be sold by *Randal Taylor* near *Stationers-Hall*. 1691. 4º.

The Comical History of Don Quixote. As it was Acted at the *Queen's Theatre* in Dorset-Garden, By Their Majesties Servants. Part I. Written by Mr. D'Urfey. *London*, Printed for *Samuel Briscoe*, at the Corner of *Charles-street*, in *Russel-street*, *Covent-Garden*, 1694, 4º.

The Comical History of Don Quixote, As it was Acted at the Queen's Theatre in *Dorset Garden*. By Their Majesties Servants. Part the Second. Written by Mr. D'*Urfey*. *London*, Printed for *S. Briscoe*, in *Russel-street, Covent-Garden*, and *H. Newman* at the *Grashopper* in the *Poultry*, 1694. 4º.

The Comical History of Don Quixote. The Third Part. With The Marriage of Mary the Buxome. *Written by Mr.* D'Urfey. *Non omnes Arbusta juvant humilesq; myricae.* Virg. London, Printed for *Samuel Briscoe*, at the Corner of *Charles-street*, in *Russel-street, Covent-Garden*. 1696. Where is Also to be had the Songs, set to Musick by the late famous Mr. *Pursel*, Mr. *Courteville*, Mr. *Aykerod*, and other eminent Masters of the Age. 4º.

[Reprinted (three parts) 1889.]

The Campaigners : Or, The *Pleasant Adventures* at Brussels. A Comedy. With a Familiar Preface upon *A Late Reformer of the Stage*. Ending with a Satyrical Fable of *The* Dog *and the* Ottor. Written by Mr. D'*Urfey*. London, Printed for *A. Baldwin*, near the *Oxford Arms* Inn in *Warwick Lane*. MDCXCVIII. 4º.

The Grecian Heroine : or, the Fate of Tyranny. A Tragedy, Written 1718. *London* : Printed for William Chetwood, at *Cato's* Head in *Russel-street, Covent-Garden.* 1721. 8º.

Poems.

An Elegy upon the late Blessed Monarch King Charles II. And Two Panegyricks upon their Present Sacred Majesties, King James and Queen Mary. Written by Mr. *Durfey, London* : Printed for *Jo.* Hindmarsh, at the *Black Bull* in *Cornhill*. MDCLXXXV. folio.

Criticism.

[*A Study of the Plays of Thomas Durfey.* R. Forsythe. 2 vols. Cleveland. 1916–17.]

EBSWORTH (J. Woodfall).

Westminster Drolleries, Both Parts, of 1671, 1672 ; being a Choice Collection of Songs and Poems, Sung at Court and Theaters : *With Additions made by* '*A Person of Quality.*' Now First Reprinted from the Original Editions. Edited, With an Introduction on the Literature of the Drolleries ; a Copious Appendix of Notes, Illustrations, and Emendations of Text ; *A Table of Contents, and Index of First Lines of Songs and Poems* ; By J. Woodfall Ebsworth, M.A. Cantab. R. Roberts, Boston, Lincolnshire. M.DCCCLXXV. 8º.

ETHEREGE (George).
  Dramatic Works.
    The Comical Revenge; or Love in A Tub. Acted at His Highness the Duke of *York's* Theatre in *Lincolns-Inn-Fields.* Licensed, *July* 8, 1664. Roger L'*Estrange. London,* Printed for *Henry Herringman,* and are to be sold at his Shop at the *Blew-Anchor* in the Lower Walk of the *New-Exchange.* 1677. 4º.
    She Wou'd if she Cou'd, A Comedy. Acted at His Highnesse the Duke of York's Theatre. Written by George Etherege Esq. *London,* printed for *H. Herringman,* at the Sign of the *Blew Anchor* in the Lower walk of the New Exchange. 1668. 4º.
    The Man of Mode, or, Sr Fopling Flutter. A Comedy. Acted at the *Duke's Theatre.* By *George Etherege* Esq. Licensed, *June* 3 1676. *Roger L'Estrange. London,* Printed for *J. Macock,* for *Henry Herringman,* at the Sign of the *Blew Anchor* in the Lower Walk of the *New Exchange,* 1676. 4º.
  Collected Works.
    The Works of Sir *George Etherege*: Containing His Plays and Poems. *London,* Printed for *H.H.* And Sold by *J. Tonson,* within *Grays Inn* Gate, next *Grays-Inn* Lane; and *T. Bennet,* at the *Half-Moon* in St. *Paul's* Church-yard. 1704. 8º.
    [*The Works of Sir George Etheredge. Plays and Poems.* Ed. A. W. Verity. 1888.]
    [*The Works of Sir George Etherege.* Ed. H. F. B. Brett-Smith. 3 vols. Oxford, 1927–. (The first two volumes contain the above three plays.)]
    [*The Letter-Book of Sir George Etherege.* Ed. Sybil Rosenfeld. 1928.]
  Biography and Criticism.
    Dennis, John.
      [*A Defense of Sir Fopling Flutter.* 1722. In *The Critical Works.* Ed. E. N. Hooker. 1939–43. Vol. 2.]
    McCamie, F. S.
      [*Sir George Etherege. A Study in Restoration Comedy.* Iowa. 1931.]

EUSDEN (Laurence).
  The Royal Family! A Letter to Mr. *Addison,* On the King's *Accession to the Throne.* By Mr. *Eusden.* London: Printed for *J. Tonson.* And Re-printed and Sold by *E. Waters* in *Essex-street.* 1714. 8º.
  A Poem to Her Royal Highness On the Birth *of the* Prince. By Mr. *Eusden.*

    Ille Deum vitam accipiet, Divisque videbit
    Permixtos Heroas, et ipse videbitur illis. Virg.

  London: Printed for *Jacob Tonson,* at *Shakespear's-Head* over-against *Katharine-street* in the *Strand.* MDCCXVIII. folio.
  An Ode for the Birth-Day, MDCCXXI. As it was Sung before His Majesty.

    Aggrederem O! magnos (aderit jam tempus) honores!
    Hic Vir, Hic est, tibi quem promitti saepius audis!
    Virg.
    Plurima securi fudistis Carmina Bardi. Lucan.

  Written by *L. Eusden,* Esquire, Servant to his Majesty. *London*: Printed for Jacob Tonson, at *Shakespear's-Head,* over-against *Katharine-Street* in the *Strand.* MDCCXXI. folio.
  Three Poems: The First, Sacred to the Immortal Memory of the late King; The Second, On the happy Succession, and Coronation of His

present Majesty; And a Third Humbly Inscrib'd to the Queen. By *Laurence Eusden*, Servant to His Majesty.

*Ille Deum Vitam accipiet, Divisque videbit
Permixtos Heroas, et Ipse videbitur Illis!* Virg.
Strepitus fastidit inanes,
Inque Animis Hominum Pompa meliore triumphat. Claud.
Utinam modo dicere possem
Carmina digna Dea, certe Dea Carmine digna est! Ovid.

London: Printed for J. Roberts in *Warwick-Lane.* MDCCXXVII. folio.

FANE (Sir Francis).
Love in the Dark, or The Man of Bus'ness. A Comedy: Acted at the Theatre Royal By His Majesties Servants. Written By Sir *Francis Fane, Junior*, Knight of the Bath. *Naturam expellas furca licet, usque recurret.* Hor. In the *Savoy.* Printed by T.N. for *Henry Herringman*, and are to be sold at the Anchor in the Lower Walk of the *New Exchange.* 1675. 4°.

FARQUHAR (George).
The Constant Couple or, A Trip to The Jubilee. A Comedy. By Mr. George Farquhar.

*Sive favore tuli, sive hanc ego carmine famam
Jure tibi grates, Candide lector, ago.*
Ovid. Trist. lib. 4. Eleg. 10.

London, Printed in the Year 1710. 8°. (Played in 1699.)
The Twin-Rivals. A Comedy. Acted at the *Theatre Royal* by Her Majesty's Servants. *Written by Mr.* Farquhar. *Sic vos non vobis.* London: Printed for *Bernard Lintott* at the Post-House in the *Middle-Temple-Gate* in *Fleet-street.* MDCCIII.
Collected Works.
The Works Of the late Ingenious Mr. *George Farquhar*: Containing all his Poems, Letters, Essays and Comedies, Publish'd in his Life-time. In Two Volumes. The Ninth Edition. Corrected from the Errors of former Impressions. To which are added some Memoirs of the Author, never before Publish'd. *London*, Printed for J. Clarke, John Rivington, James Rivington and James Fletcher, S. Crowder and Co. T. Caslon, T. Lownds, H. Woodgate and S. Brookes. MDCCLX. 8°.

[Second edition: 1711. Earlier collections were made up from various copies of separate works with a general title-page.]
[*Works.* Ed. W. Archer. 1906. (Mermaid Series.) This edition contains both the above plays.]
[*Complete Works.* Ed. Charles Stonehill. Nonesuch. 1930.]

FIELDING (Henry).
The History of the Adventures of *Joseph Andrews*, And his Friend Mr. *Abraham Adams.* Written in Imitation of the *Manner* of Cervantes, Author of *Don Quixote.* In Two Volumes. London: Printed for A. Millar, over against *St. Clement's-Church*, in the *Strand.* M.DCC.XLII. 12°.
[Ed. G. Saintsbury. 1910. Everyman's Library.]
[Ed. L. Rice-Oxley. 1929. World's Classics.]
Biography and Criticism.
Lawrence, Frederick.
The Life of Henry Fielding; with Notices of his Writings, his Times, and his Contemporaries. By Frederick Lawrence, of the Middle Temple, Barrister-at-Law.—" Mores Hominum multorum vidit."

Horace. *De Arte Poetica*. London : Arthur Hall, Virtue and Co, 25, Paternoster Row. 1855. 8⁰.

Cross, W. L.
[*The History of Henry Fielding*. 3 vols. New Haven. 1918.]

Blanchard, F. T.
[*Fielding the Novelist. A Study in Historical Criticism*. New Haven. 1926.]

Voorde, F. P. van der.
[*Henry Fielding, Critic and Satirist*. The Hague. 1931.]

FLECKNOE (Richard).
Love's Kingdom, A Pastoral Trage-Comedy. Not as it was Acted at the Theatre near *Lincoln's-Inn*, but as it was written, and since corrected By Richard Flecknoe. With a short Treatise of the *English Stage, etc.* by the same Author. *London*, Printed by *R. Wood* for the Author. 1664. 8⁰.
 [The treatise to the above is reprinted in W. C. Hazlitt's *English Drama and Stage*. 1869. Also in *Critical Essays of the Seventeenth Century*. Ed. J. E. Spingarn. Vol. 2. 1908.]
The Damoiselles à la Mode. A Comedy. Compos'd and Written by Richard Flecknoe. *London*, Printed for the Author. 1667. 8⁰.

Flos.
Flos Ingenii vel Evacuatio Descriptionis. Being an Exact Description of Epsam and Epsam Wells. *London* Printed in the year 1674. folio.

GAY (John).
The Present State of Wit, in a Letter to a Friend in the Country. *London*, Printed in the Year, MDCCXI. (Price 3d.) 8⁰. (Signed J. G. and attributed to Gay.)
 [In *Critical Essays*. Ed. J. Churton Collins. 1903.]
The *Shepherd's Week*. In Six Pastorals. *By Mr.* J. Gay.

> Libeat mihi sordida rura,
> Atque humiles habitare Casas.   Virg.

The Second Edition. London, Printed for *J.T.* and Sold by W. Taylor at the *Ship* in *Pater-noster-Row*. MDCCXIV.
 [Ed. H. F. B. Brett-Smith. Oxford. 1924.]
Trivia : or, The Art of Walking The Streets of London. By Mr. *Gay*.

> Quo te Moeri pedes ? An, quo via ducit, in Urbem ?   Virg.

London : Printed for *Bernard Lintott*, at the *Cross-Keys* between the *Temple* Gates in *Fleetstreet*. (1716.) 8⁰.
 [Ed. W. H. Williams. 1922.]
Collected Works.
Poems on several Occasions. By Mr. *John Gay*. *London* : Printed for Jacob Tonson, at *Shakespear's-Head* in the *Strand*, and Bernard Lintot, between the *Temple-Gates* in *Fleetstreet*. MDCCXX. 2 vols. 4⁰.
 [*The Poems of John Gay*. Ed. Francis Bickley. 1923.]
Biography and Criticism.
 [*The Life and Letters of John Gay*. L. Melville. 1921.]

Gentleman's Magazine (The).
1731–1833. New Series : 1834–1851 : 138 volumes 8⁰. [–1907.]

GOULD (Robert).
The Play-House a Satyr written in the Year 1685. By Rob*t*. Gould. To the Right Honourable Charles Earl of Dorset and Middlesex, etc.

GRANVILLE (George, Lord Lansdowne).
The She-Gallants : A Comedy. As it is Acted at the Theatre in Little-Lincoln-Inn-Fields, By His Majesty's Servants. *London* : Printed for

BIBLIOGRAPHY 439

Henry Playford in the *Temple-Change*. And Benj. Tooke at the *Middle-Temple-Gate*, in *Fleetstreet*. 1696. 4º.
Heroick Love : A Tragedy, As it is Acted at The Theatre in *Little-Lincolns-Inn-Fields*. Written by the Honourable George Granville Esq. ;
    Rectius Iliacum Carmen deducis in Actus,
    Quam si proferres ignota indictaque primus.
                                 Hor. de Arte Poetica.
London : Printed for *F. Saunders*, in the New-Exchange in the *Strand* : H. Playford in the *Temple-Change*, and *B. Tooke* at the *Middle-Temple-Gate, Fleet-street*. 1698. 4º.
Three Plays, *Viz.* The She-Gallants, A Comedy. Heroick-Love, A Tragedy. And The Jew of Venice, A Comedy. Written by the Right Hon[ble] George Granville, Lord Landsdowne. *London* : Printed for *Benj. Took* at the *Middle-Temple-Gate*, and *Bern. Lintott*, between the Two *Temple-Gates*, MDCCXIII. 8º.
The Genuine Works in Verse and Prose, Of the Right Honourable George Granville, Lord *Lansdowne*. *London* : Printed for J. and R. Tonson, at *Shakespear's* Head in the *Strand*, and L. Gilliver, J. Clarke, at *Homer's* Head in *Fleetstreet*. MDCCXXXVI. 3 vols. 12º.
[For verse by Granville, see Johnson, vol. 25 ; Chalmers, vol. II ; Park, vol. 34.]
Biography and Criticism.
  Handasyde, Elizabeth.
    [*Granville the Polite.* Cambridge. 1933.]
GWYN (Nell).
The Story of Nell Gwyn : and the Sayings of Charles the Second. Related and collected by Peter Cunningham, F.S.A. London : Bradbury and Evans, 11. Bouverie street, 1852. 8º.
HALIFAX (Marquis of). See SAVILE (George).
HOGARTH (William).
The Works of William Hogarth (*Including " the Analysis of Beauty "*) Elucidated by Descriptions, Critical, Moral, and Historical (Founded on the Most Approved Authorities). To which is prefixed Some Account of his Life. By Thomas Clerk. In Two Volumes. *London* : Printed for R. Scholey, 46, Paternoster Row ; *By T. Davison, Lombard Street, Whitefriars*. 1810. 8º.
HOPKINS (Charles).
Boadicea Queen of Britain. A Tragedy, As it is Acted by His Majesty's Servants at the Theatre in *Lincolns-Inn-fields*. Written by Mr. *Charles Hopkins*. *London*, Printed for *Jacob Tonson*, near the *Inner-Temple-Gate* in *Fleet-street*. 1697. 4º.
HOWARD (The Honourable Edward).
The Usurper, A Tragedy. As it was Acted at the *Theater Royal* by his Majesties Servants. Written by the Honourable Edward Howard, *Esq.* Licens'd *August* 2. 1667. *Roger L'Estrange. London*, Printed for *Henry Herringman* at the *Anchor* in the *Lower Walk* of the *New Exchange*. 1668. 4º.
HOWARD (Sir Robert).
Poems, Viz.—1. A Panegyrick to the King.—2. Songs and Sonnets.—3. The Blind Lady, a Comedy.—4. The Fourth Book of Virgil.—5. Statius his Achilleis, with Annotations.—6. A Panegyrick to Generall Monck. By the Honourable S[r] Robert Howard. London, Printed for *Henry Herringman*, and are to be sold at his shop at the sign of the *Anchor* on the Lower Walk of the New Exchange. 1660. 8º.

Four New Plays, viz : The Surprisal, Committee, Comedies, The Indian Queen, Vestal Virgin. Tragedies. As they were Acted by His Majesties Servants at the *Theatre-Royal.* Written by the Honourable Sir *Robert Howard.* Imprimatur, March 7 1664/5. *Roger L'Estrange. London,* Printed for *Henry Herringman,* and are to be sold at his Shop at the *Blew-*Anchor in the Lower Walk of the New-Exchange. 1665. folio. (Following, the titles of each of the four plays : The Surprisal, A Comedy. Written by the Honourable Sir *Robert Howard.* Imprimatur, *March* 7. 1664/5. *Roger L'Estrange. London,* Printed for *Henry Herringman,* and are to be sold at his Shop at the *Blew-Anchor* in the Lower Walk of the New-Exchange. 1665.—The Committee, A Comedy. Written by the Honourable Sir *Robert Howard.* Imprimatur, March 7 1664/5, *Roger L'Estrange, London,* Printed for *Henry Herringman,* at the *Blew Anchor* in the Lower Walk of the New-Exchange, 1665.—The Indian-Queen, A Tragedy. *London,* Printed for *H. Herringman,* at the *Blew-Anchor* in the Lower Walk of the New-Exchange. 1665.—The Vestal-Virgin, or the Roman Ladies, A Tragedy, *London,* Printed for H. Herringman, at the *Blew-Anchor* in the Lower Walk of the New-Exchange. 1665.)

[*The Indian Queen* was written in collaboration with Dryden. In *The Dramatic Works of John Dryden.* Ed. M. Summers. 1931–2. *The Committee* is contained in *Modern British Drama,* vol. 3.]

The Great Favourite, Or, the Duke of Lerma, As it was Acted at the Theatre-Royal, by His Majesties Servants. *Written by the Honourable Sir* Robert Howard. *In the* Savoy : Printed for *Henry Herringman,* at the Sign of the *Anchor, on the Lower-walk of the New-Exchange.* 1668. 4º.

[See *Critical Essays of the Seventeenth Century.* Ed. J. E. Spingarn. 1908–9. Vol. II includes the prefaces to *Four New Plays* and *The Great Favourite.*]

Five New Plays, Viz. The Surprisal, Committee, Comedies. And The Indian Queen, Vestal Virgin, Duke of Lerma, Tragedies. As they were Acted by His Majesty's Servants at the *Theatre-Royal.* Written by the Honourable Sir *Robert Howard.* The Second Edition Corrected. *London,* Printed for *Henry Herringman,* and are to be Sold by *Francis Saunders,* at the *Blue-Anchor* in the Lower-Walk of the *New-Exchange.* 1692. folio.

Criticism.
Arundell, D. D.
[*Dryden and Howard.* Cambridge. 1929.]

HUGHES (John).
Poems.
The Triumph of Peace. A Poem.

> *Aggredere O magnos (aderit jam tempus) honores*
> *Chara Deum Soboles, magnum Jovis incrementum !*
> *Aspice convexo nutantem Pondere mundum,*
> *Terrasque, tractusque maris, Caelumque profundum*
> *Aspice, venturo laetantur ut omnia Saeclo !*   Virg.

London : Printed for *Jacob Tonson,* at the *Judges-Head* in *Fleet street* near the *Inner-Temple-Gate.* 1698. folio.

The House of Nassau. A Pindarick Ode. By *J. Hughes.*

> *Caelo demittitur alto*
> *Chara Deum Soboles.*   Virg.

London : Printed for *D. Brown* at the Black Swan and Bible without *Temple-bar,* and *A. Bell* at the Cross-Keys and Bible in Cornhill. M.DCC.II. folio.

An Ode for the Birth-Day of Her Royal Highness The Princess of Wales, St. David's Day, the First of March, 1715/16. Set to Musick by Dr. J. C. Pepusch, And Perform'd at the Anniversary Meeting of the Society of Ancient *Britons*, establish'd in Honour of Her Royal Highness's Birth-Day, and of the Principality of *Wales*. Written by Mr. Hugues.

   Salve laeta Dies ! meliorque revertere semper,
    A Populo rerum digna potente coli !   Ovid.

London : Printed for *Jacob Tonson*, at *Shakespear's-Head* over-against *Catherine-Street* in the *Strand*. 1716. 4º.

Poems on Several Occasions, with some Select Essays in Prose. In Two Volumes. By *John Hughes*, Esq ; Adorn'd with Sculptures. London : Printed for J. Tonson *and* J. Watts. MDCCXXXV. 8º.
[The following collections contain poems by Hughes : Chalmers, vol. 10 ; Anderson, vol. 8 ; Johnson, vol. 22.]

Dramatic Works.
The Siege of *Damascus*. A Tragedy. As it is Acted at the Theatre-Royal in *Drury-Lane* By His Majesty's Servants. *By* John Hughes, *Esq* ; London : Printed for John Watts at the Printing Office in Wild Court near Lincolns-Inn-Fields. MDCCXX. 8º.

HUNT (Thomas).
An Argument for the Bishops Right In Judging in Capital Causes in Parliament : For their Right unalterable to that Place in the Góvernment that they now enjoy. With several Observations upon the Change of our English Government since the Conquest. To which is added a Postscript, being a Letter to a Friend, for Vindicating the Clergy, and rectifying some mistakes that are mischievous to Government and Religion. By Tho. Hunt, Esquire. *In Turbas et Discordias pessimo cuique plurima vis Pax et quies bonis artibus indigent.* Tacit. Hist. 1. 4. *London*, Printed for *Thomas Fox*, at the *Angel* and Star in *Westminster-Hall*. 1682. 8º.

A Defence of the Charter, and Municipal Rights of the City of London. And the Rights of other Municipal Cities and Towns of *England*. Directed to the Citizens of *London*. By Thomas Hunt. *Si populus vult decipi decipiatur. London,* Printed and are to be sold by *Richard Baldwin* near the *Black Bull* in the *Old-bailey*. (1682.) 4º.

JEFFREY (Francis).
Contributions to the Edinburgh Review. By Francis Jeffrey. Now one of the Judges of the Court of Session in Scotland. In Four Volumes. London : Printed for Longman, Brown, Green, and Longmans, Paternoster-Row. 1844. 8º.

KILLIGREW (Thomas).
Comedies and Tragedies, Written by Thomas Killigrew, Page of Honour to King *Charles* the First. And Groom of the Bed-Chamber to King *Charles* the Second. *London,* Printed for *Henry Herringman,* at the Sign of the *Anchor* in the Lower Walk of the *New-Exchange.* 1664. folio.

Biography and Criticism.
Harbage, Alfred.
[*Thomas Killigrew.* Philadelphia. 1930.]

KILLIGREW (Sir William).
Three Playes Written by Sir *William Killigrew*, Vice-Chamberlain to Her Majesty the Queen Consort. 1664. Viz. *Selindra. Pandora. Ormasdes.* London, Printed by *T. Mabb* ; for *John Playfere,* at the *White Lion,* in the Upper Walk of the *New Exchange* ; and *Thomas Horsman,* at the three *Kings* in the *Strand,* 1665-64 [*sic*].

Four new Playes, *viz*: The *Seege* of *Urbin. Selindra. Love* and *Friendship.* (The running title is: *Ormasdes*; Or *Love,* and *Friendship.*) Tragy Comedies. *Pandora* (in the volume the piece has for its second title: Or the Converts). A Comedy. Written by Sr William Killigrew. Vice-Chamberlaine to Her *Majesty*. Oxford, Printed by *Hen: Hall,* printer to the University, for *Ric: Davis,* 1666. folio.

KING (Charles). See MARTYN (Henry).

LA CALPRENÈDE (Gautier de Costes, sieur de).
Hymen's Praeludia: or, Love's Master-piece: Being the first Part of that so much admir'd *Romance,* intituled, *Cleopatra. Written Originally in the* French *and now rendred into* English By R. Loveday. Whereunto is annexed, A succinct Abridgement of what is extant in the succeeding Story *By the same Hand.*

> Evand. *Quid magis optaret* Cleopatra *parentibus orta,*
> *Conspicuis, Comiti quam placuisse Thori?*

London, Printed for *George Thompson,* at the White-Horse in *Chauncery*-lane, neere *Lincolnes*-Inn. 1652. 12º.
Criticism.
Hill, H. W.
[*La Calprenède's Romances and the Restoration Drama.* Chicago. 1910.]

LACEY (John).
Sauny the Scott: or, the Taming of the Shrew: A Comedy. As it is now *Acted* at the Theatre-Royal. *Written by* J. Lacey, *Servant to* His Majesty. And Never before Printed.

> Then I'll cry out, Swell'd with Poetick Rage,
> 'Tis I, John Lacy, have Reform'd your Stage. Prol. *to* Rehers.

London, Printed and Sold by *E. Witlock,* near *Stationers-Hall.* 1698. (Acted in 1667.) 4º.
Sr Hercules Buffoon, Or the Poetical Squire. A Comedy, As it was Acted at the Duke's Theatre. *Written* by John Lacy, *Com. London*: Printed for *Jo. Hindmarsh,* Bookseller to His Royal Highness, at the Black Bull in Cornhill, 1684. 4º.
[*Dramatic Works.* Ed. J. Maidment and W. H. Logan. Edinburgh. 1875.]

LANSDOWNE (Lord). See GRANVILLE (George).
Laureat.
The Laureat.

> *Jack Squabbs Hystory in a little drawn,*
> *Down to his Evening, from his early dawn.*

4 pages folio. (1687.)

LAW (William).
The Absolute Unlawfulness of the Stage-Entertainment Fully Demonstrated By *William Law,* A.M. London: Printed for W. and J. Innys, at the *West*-End of St. *Paul's.* MDCCXXVI. 8º.
[*Works.* 9 vols. Ed. G. B. Morgan. Brockenhurst. 1892–3.]

LEE (Nathaniel).
The Tragedy of Nero, Emperour of Rome: As it is Acted at the Theatre-Royal, By his Majesties Servants. By *Nathaniel Lee,* Gent. *London,* Printed by *T. R.* And *N. T. James Magnus* and *Richard Bentley,* at the *Post Office* in *Russel-street* in *Covent-Garden.* 1675. 4º.
Sophonisba, or Hannibal's Overthrow. A Tragedy, Acted at the Theatre-Royal, By their Majesties Servants. *Written by* Nathaniel Lee, *Gent.*

Praecipitandus est liber spiritus, *Petronius*. *London*, Printed for *J. Magnes* and *R. Bentley* in *Russel-street*, in *Covent-Garden* near the *Piazza's*. Anno Domini, MDCLXXVI. 4°.
(This edition does not contain the Epilogue which appears, however, in the following edition :)
Sophonisba : or Hannibal's Overthrow. A Tragedy. Acted at the Theatre Royal, By Their Majesties Servants. Written by Nathaniel Lee, Gent. Praecipitandus est liber Spiritus. *Petronius*. *London*, Printed for *Tho. Chapman*, at the *Golden-Key* over against the Mews, near *Charing-Cross*. MDCXCII. 4°.
Gloriana, or the Court of Augustus Caesar. Acted at the Theatre-Royal By Their Majesties Servants.

Quibus haec, sint qualiacunque
Arridere velim, doliturus si placeant spe
Deterius nostra. Nor. Sat. 10.

By *Nat. Lee*. *London*, Printed for *J. Magnes* and *R. Bentley*, in *Russel-street* in *Covent-Garden*, near the *Piazza's*. Anno Dom. MDCLXXVI. 4°.
The Rival Queens, or the Death of Alexander The Great. Acted at the Theater-Royal. By Their Majesties Servants. By *Nat. Lee*, Gent.

Natura sublimis et acer,
Nam spirat tragicum satis, et feliciter audet.
Horat. Epist. ad Aug.

London, Printed for *James Magnes* and *Richard Bentley*, at the Post-house in *Russel-street* in *Covent-Garden*, near the *Piazza's*, 1677. 4°.
[In *Modern British Drama*. Vol. 1.]
Mithridates King of Pontus. A Tragedy ; Acted at the Theatre Royal, By their Majestie's Servants. Written by *Nat. Lee*.

Hi motus animorum atque haec certamina tanta,
Pulveris exigui jactu compressa quiescent.
Virg. Georg. 1. 4.

Licensed March 28 1678. Roger l'Estrange. *London* : Printed by R. E. for *James Magnes* and *Rich. Bentley*, in *Russel-street* in *Covent-Garden*, near the Piazza's. 1678. 4°.
Theodosius : or The Force of Love, A Tragedy. Acted By their Royal Highnesses Servants, At the Duke's Theatre. Written by *Nat. Lee* With the Musick betwixt the Acts.

Nec minus periculum ex magna
Fama quam ex mala. Tacit.

London, Printed for *R. Bentley* and *M. Magnes*, in *Russell-street* near *Coventgarden*. 1680. 4°.
[In *Modern British Drama*. Vol. 1.]
Caesar Borgia ; Son of Pope Alexander the Sixth : A Tragedy Acted at the Duke's Theatre by Their Royal Highnesses Servants. Written by *Nat. Lee*. *London* : Printed by R. E. for *R. Bentley*, and *M. Magnes*, in *Russel-street* in *Covent-Garden*, near the *Piazza*, 1680. 4°.
The Princess of Cleve, As it was Acted At the Queens Theatre in Dorset-Garden. By *Nat. Lee*, Gent.

Tuque, dum procedis, Io Triumphe,
Non semel dicemus : Io Triumphe,
Civitas omnis, dabimusque divis,
Thura benignis. Horat.

London, Printed in the Year, 1689. 4°. (Acted in 1681.)

Lucius Junius Brutus; Father of his Country. A Tragedy. Acted at the Duke's Theater, by their Royal Highnesses Servants. Written by *Nat. Lee.*
> *Caeloque invectus aperto*
> *Flectit equos, curruque volans dat lora Secunda.*
> Virg. lib. 4.

London, Printed for *Richard Tonson*, and *Jacob Tonson*, at *Grays-Inn* Gate, and at the Judges Head in *Chancery-Lane* near *Fleet-street*; 1681. 4º.
Criticism.
Ham, R. G.
[*Otway and Lee.* New Haven. 1931.]

L'ESTRANGE (Sir Roger).
No Blinde Guides. In Answer To a seditious Pamphlet of *J. Milton's* intituled *Brief Notes upon a late Sermon Titl'd*, the fear of God and the King; *Preached and since Publishd, By* Matthew Griffith, D.D. *And Chaplain to the late King*, etc. Addressed to the Author. *If the Blinde Lead the Blinde Both shall fall into the Ditch.* London, Printed for *Henry Brome April* 20. 1660. 4º. (Attributed to L'Estrange by Samuel Johnson, *Lives of the English Poets*, Milton.)
Considerations and Proposals in Order to the Regulation of the Press: *Together with* Diverse *Instances* of *Treasonous*, and *Seditious Pamphlets*, Proving the *Necessity* thereof. *By* Roger L'Estrange. London, Printed by *A. C. June* 3ᵈ M.DC.LXIII, 4º.
An Answer to a Letter to a Dissenter, Upon Occasion of His Majesties Late Gracious Declaration of Indulgence. By Sir *Roger L'Estrange*, Knight. London, Printed for *R. Sare* at *Grays-Inn-Gate* in *Holborn*. 1687. 4º.
Criticism.
Kitchen, G.
[*Sir Roger L'Estrange: a Contribution to the History of the Press in the Seventeenth Century.* 1913.]
Letter.
A Letter to the Three Absolvers, Mr. *Cook*, Mr. *Collier* and Mr. *Snett*, Being Reflections on the Papers Delivered by Sir *John Friend*, and Sir *William Parkyns*, to the Sheriffs of *London* and *Middlesex*: At *Tyburn*, the Place of Execution, *April* 3. 1696, which said Papers are Printed at Length, and answered Paragraph by Paragraph. London: Printed for *R. Baldwin* near the *Oxford-Arms* in *Warwick*-Lane. 1696. folio.

LOCKE (John).
Two Treatises of Government: In the Former, *The False Principles and Foundation* of Sir *Robert Filmer*, and His Followers, are Detected and, Overthrown. The Latter is an Essay concerning the true Original, Extent, and End of Civil-Government. London: Printed for *Awnsham* and *John Churchill*, at the *Black Swan* in *Pater-Noster-Row*. 1698. 8º. (Published for the first time in 1690.)
[Ed. F. W. Carpenter. 1924. Everyman's Library.]
Some Thoughts concerning Education.
> *Doctrina vires promovet infinitas* [sic]
> *Rectiq; cultus pectora roborant:*
> *Utcunq; defecere mores,*
> *Dedecorant bene nata culpae.* Horat. L. IV. Od. 4.

The Fourth Edition Enlarged. London, Printed for *A.* and *J. Churchill*, at the *Black Swan* in *Pater-noster-row*. 1699. 8º. (The first edition was published in 1693.)
[Ed. R. N. Quick. Cambridge. 1880.]

BIBLIOGRAPHY 445

The Reasonableness of Christianity, As delivered in the Scriptures. *London* : Printed for *Awnsham* and *John Churchil*, at the *Black-Swan* in *Pater Noster Row*. 1695. 8º.
Collected Works.
[*Works*. 10 vols. 1823.]
[*The Philosophical Works*. Ed. J. A. St. John. 1843-54.]
[*The Educational Writings*. Ed. J. W. Adamson. Cambridge. 1912, 1922 (revised edition).]
Biography and Criticism.
Bourne, H. R. Fox.
  The Life of John Locke, By H. R. Fox Bourne. *In Two Volumes*. Henry S. King and Co. London. 1876. 8º.
Aaron, R. I.
  [*John Locke*. 1937.]
MacLean, K.
  [*John Locke and English Literature of the Eighteenth Century*. New Haven. 1936.]
MAIDWELL (John).
  The Loving Enemies : A Comedy, As it was Acted at His Highness the Duke of York's Theatre. Written by *L. Maidwell*.

> *Inventum secuit primus qui nave profundum,*
> *Et rudibus remis sollicitavit aquas*
> *Tranquillis primum trepidus se credidit undis,*
> *Littora securo tramite summa legens :*
> *Mox vagus exultat pelago, caelumque secutus*
> *Aegeas hyemes Ioniasque domat.*   Claudian.

London, Printed for *John Guy* at the Sign of the *Flying Horse* between St. *Dunstan's* Church, and *Chancery* Lane. 1680. 4º.
MANLEY (Mrs. de la Riviere).
  The Royal Mischief. A Tragedy, As it is Acted By His Majesties Servants. By Mrs *Manley*. London, Printed for *R. Bentley, F. Saunders*, and *J. Knapton*. MDCXCVI. 4º.
MARTYN (Henry).
  The British Merchant; or Commerce Preserv'd. In Three Volumes. By Mr. Charles King, *Chamber-Keeper to the Treasury, and late of London Merchant*, London : Printed for John Darby in *Bartholomew-Close*, M.DCC.XXI. 8º. (Although the title of this edition gives Mr. Charles King as the author of *The British Merchant*, the preface says : The Person to whom our Country is chiefly obliged for these Papers, and who had the Greatest Hand in them, is *Henry Martin* Esq. ; lately deceased, who, for his great Merit and Abilities, was made *Inspector-General* of the *Exports* and *Imports*.)
[The British Merchant : or, Commerce Preserv'd in answer to Mercator. By Charles King, etc., twice a week. 7 Aug. 1713-30 July 1714. 3 vols. 1721, 1743, 1748.]
MARVELL (Andrew).
  The Works of Andrew Marvell, Esq. Poetical, Controversial, and Political, containing Many Original Letters, Poems, and Tracts, never before printed, With a new life of the author, By Capt. Edward Thompson . . . In three volumes. London : Printed for the Editor, by Henry Baldwin, And sold by Dodsley, in Pall-Mall ; . . . MDCCLXXVI. 4º.
[*Poems and Satires of Andrew Marvell*. Ed. G. A. Aitken. 2 vols. 1892, 1901.]

[*Poems and Letters of Andrew Marvell.* Ed. H. M. Margoliouth. 2 vols. Oxford. 1927.]
Biography and Criticism.
  Legouis, P.
    [*André Marvell, Poète, Puritain, Patriote.* Paris. 1928.]
  Bradbrook, M. C.
    [*Andrew Marvell.* Cambridge. 1940.]
Medal.
  The Loyal Medal Vindicated. A Poem. *Crescit sub pondere Virtus.* London : Printed for *R. Janeway* in *Queen's Head* Alley. 1682. folio.
MILTON (John).
  Paradise Lost, a Poem Written in Ten Books by *John Milton.* Licensed and Entred according to Order. *London,* Printed, and are to be sold by *Peter Parker* under *Creed* Church neer *Aldgate* ; And by *Robert Boulter* at the *Turks Head* in *Bishopsgate-street* ; And *Mathias Walker,* under St. *Dunstons* Church in *Fleet-street,* 1667. 4º.
  Paradise Lost. A Poem in Twelve Books. The Authour *John Milton.* The Fourth Edition, adorn'd with Sculptures. *London,* Printed by *Miles Flesher,* for *Jacob Tonson,* at the Judge's Head in *Chancery-lane* near *Fleet-street.* MDCLXXXVIII. folio.
  The Poetical Works of John Milton : *Edited, with Introductions, Notes, and an Essay on Milton's English,* By David Masson, M.A., LL.D., Professor of Rhetoric and English Literature in the University of Edinburgh. Three volumes. London : Macmillan and Co. 1874. 8º.
  [*The Works of John Milton.* 18 vols. General editor : Frank Allen Paterson. Columbia. 1931.]
Biography and Criticism.
  Addison, Joseph.
    [*Notes on Paradise Lost.* In the *Spectator,* 5 Jan.—3 May 1712.]
  Geffroy, A.
    Etude sur les Pamphlets politiques et religieux de Milton, par A. Geffroy, professeur d'histoire au Lycée Descartes, à Paris. Paris, Dezobry, F. Magdeleine et C^{le}, libr.—Editeurs, Rue des Macons-Sorbonne, 1. Stassin et Xavier, 9, Rue du Coq, près le Louvre. 1848. 8º.
  Masson, D.
    [*Life of John Milton.* 7 vols. 1849–80.]
  Cook, A. S. (editor).
    Criticism on Paradise Lost. Boston. 1892.]
  Saurat, Denis.
    [*Milton the Man and the Thinker.* 1924.]
  Tillyard, E. M.
    [*Milton.* 1930.]
    [*The Miltonic Setting : past and present.* 1938.]
  Lewis, C. S.
    [*A Preface to Paradise Lost.* 1942.]
  Darbishire, Helen.
    [*Early Lives of Milton.* 1932.]
Mohocks.
  The Town-Rakes or The Frolicks of the *Mohocks or Hawkubites.* With an Account of their Frolicks last Night and at several other Times ; shewing how they slit the Noses of several Men and Women, and wounded others : Several of which were taken up last Night by the Guards, and Committed to several Prisons, the Guards being drawn out to disperse them. 1712. folio.

MONTAGU (Lady Mary Wortley).
The Letters and Works of Lady Mary Wortley Montagu. Edited by her Great-Grandson Lord Wharncliffe. Third edition, with additions and corrections derived from the original manuscripts, illustrative notes, and a new Memoir By W. Moy Thomas. In two volumes. London : Henry G. Bohn, York Street, Covent Garden. MDCCCLXI. 8º.
[3 vols. 1837.]

MONTAGUE (Charles). See DRYDEN. (Collaboration with Matthew Prior in *The Hind and the Panther Transvers'd*. Drydeniana.)

MOTTEUX (Peter Anthony).
Beauty in Distress. A Tragedy. As it is Acted at the Theatre in *Little Lincolns-Inn-Fields*, By His Majesty's Servants. Written by Mr. *Motteux*. With a Discourse of the *Lawfulness and Unlawfulness of Plays*, Lately written in *French* by the Learned Father *Caffaro*, Divinity-Professor at Paris. Sent in a Letter to the Author, *By a Divine of the Church of* England. *London*, Printed for *Daniel Brown*, at the *Black Swan and Bible* without *Temple-bar* ; and *Rich. Parker* at the *Unicorn* under the Piazza of the *Royal Exchange*. 1698. 4º.
Biography and Criticism.
[Peter Anthony Motteux. A Biographical and Critical Study. R. N. Cunningham. Oxford. 1933.]

MULGRAVE (Earl of). See Sheffield (John).

Muses Mercury (The).
The Muses Mercury : or the Monthly Miscellany. Consisting of Poems, Prologues, Songs, Sonnets, Translations, and other Curious Pieces, Never before Printed. By The Earl of *Roscommon*, Mr. *Dryden*, Dr. G——*th*, *N. Tate*, Esquire. Mr. *Dennis*, Dr. *N*——*n*, Capt. *Steel*. Mr. *Manning*, etc. To which is added An account of the Stage, of the New *Opera's* and *Plays* that have been Acted, or are to be Acted this Season ; And of the New Books relating to *Poetry*, *Criticism*, etc. lately Publish'd. For the month of *January*. To be continued Monthly. *Ex Quovis Ligno non fit Mercurius*. *London*, Printed by *J.H.* for Andrew Bell, at the *Cross Keys and Bible* in *Cornhill*, near *Stocks-Market*. 1707. 4º.
[—Jan. 1708. Ed. John Oldmixon.]

NEWCASTLE (Duke of). See CAVENDISH.

NORTH (The Honourable Roger).
Examen : or, an Enquiry into the Credit and Veracity of a *Pretended Complete History* ; shewing The Perverse and Wicked Design of it, and the Many Falsities and Abuses of Truth contained in it. Together with some Memoirs Occasionally inserted. All tending to vindicate the Honour of the late King *Charles* the Second, and his Happy Reign, from the intended *Aspersions* of that *Foul Pen*. By the Honourable *Roger North*, Esq. ; *London*, Printed for Fletcher Gyles against *Gray's-Inn* Gate in *Holborn*. MDCCXL. 4º.
The Life Of the Honourable Sir Dudley North, Kn^t. Commissioner of the *Customs*, and afterwards of the *Treasury* to his Majesty King *Charles* the Second. And of the Honourable and Reverend Dr. John North, Master of *Trinity College* in *Cambridge*, and *Greek Professor*, Prebend of *Westminster*, and sometime Clerk of the Closet to the same King *Charles* the Second. By the Honourable *Roger North*, Esq. ; *Ea complectitur quibus ipse interfuit*. Cic. de Leg. Lib. 1. *London*, Printed for the Editor, And sold by John Whiston, at Mr. Boyle's Head in *Fleet-street*, MDCCXLIV. 4º.
[Both lives edited A. Jessopp. 3 vols. 1890.]

OLDHAM (John).
Satyrs upon the Jesuits; Written in the Year 1679. *upon occasion of the Plot, Together with the Satyr against Vertue, and* Some other Pieces by the same Hand. London: Printed for *Joseph Hindmarsh*, at the *Black Bull* in *Cornhill*. 1681. 8º.
The Compositions in Prose and Verse of Mr. John Oldham. To which are added memoirs of his life, and explanatory notes upon some obscure passages of his writings. By Edward Thompson.

> Farewell, too little and too lately known.
> Whom I began to think and call my own:
> For sure our Souls were near ally'd, and thine
> Cast in the same poetic Mould with mine.

In three volumes. London: Printed for W. Flexney, opposite Gray's-Inn Gate, Holborn. MDCCLXX. 8º.
[*Poetical Works*. Ed. R. Bell. 1854, 1871.]
ORRERY (Earl of). See BOYLE (Roger).
OTWAY (Thomas).
Poems.
The Poets Complaint of his Muse; Or, A Satyr against Libells. A Poem. By *Thomas Otway. Si quid habent veri vatum praesagia, vivam.* London, Printed for *Thomas Norman*, at the *Pope's Head* in *Fleetstreet* near *Salisbury-Court*. 1680. 4º.
Dramatic Works.
Alcibiades. A Tragedy, Acted at the Duke's Theatre. Written by *Tho. Otway. Laudetur ab his Culpetur ab illis. Horat: Serm: Lib.* 1st. Sat. 2. London: Printed for *William Cademan* at the sign of the *Popes Head* in the Lower Walk of the *New-Exchange* in the *Strand*, 1675. 4º.
Don Carlos Prince of Spain A Tragedy. As it was Acted at the Duke's Theatre. Written by *Tho. Otway. Principibus placuisse Viris non ultima Laus est.* Hor. *The Fourth Edition Corrected.* Licensed, *June* 15. 1676. *Roger L'Estrange.* London: Printed for *R. Bentley* at the Post-House in *Russel-Street*, in *Covent-Garden.* 1695. 4º. (The play was acted in 1676.)
Titus and Berenice, A Tragedy, Acted at the Duke's Theatre. With a Farce called the Cheats of Scapin. By *Tho. Otway*.

> Grandis Oratio non est Turgida
> Sed Naturali pulchritudine exsurgit.   Pet. Arb.

Licensed *Febr.* the 19th 1676–7. *Roger L'Estrange.* London: Printed for *Richard Tonson* at his Shop under *Grays-Inn-Gate*, next *Grays-Inn-Lane*. 1677. 4º.
Friendship in Fashion. A Comedy, As it is Acted at his Royal Highness the Dukes Theatre. Written by Thomas Otway. *Archilochum Rabies armavit Iambo.* Licensed *May* 31. 1678. *Roger L'Estrange.* London, Printed by *E.F.* for *Richard Tonson*, at his Shop within *Grays-Inn-Lane*. 1678. 4º.
The Orphan: or, the Unhappy-Marriage: A Tragedy, As it is Acted At his Royal Highness The Duke's Theatre. Written by *Tho. Otway*.

> Qui Pelago credit magno, se foenore tollit;
> Qui Pugnas et Castra petit, praecingitur Auro;
> Vilis Adulator picto jacet Ebrius Ostro;
> Et qui sollicitat Nuptas, ad praemia peccat: ....
> Sola pruinosis horret Facundia pannis,
> Atque inopi lingua desertas invocat Artes.
>   Petron. Arb. Sat.

London, Printed for R. Bentley and M. Magnes, in Russel-Street in Covent-Garden, 1680. 4º.
The History and Fall of Caius Marius. A Tragedy. As it is Acted at the Theatre Royal. By Thomas Otway. Qui color Albus erat nunc est contrarius Albo. London, Printed for R. Bentley in Russel-street, Covent-Garden. 1692. 4º. (Acted in 1680.)
The Souldiers Fortune : A Comedy, Acted by their Royal Highnesses Servants At the Duke's Theatre. Written by Thomas Otway.

>Quem recitas meus est O Fidentine libellus,
>Sed male cum recitas incipit esse tuus.

London, Printed for R. Bentley and M. Magnes, at the Post-House in Russel-Street in Covent-Garden, 1681. 4º.
Venice Preserv'd, or, A Plot Discover'd. A Tragedy. As it is Acted at the *Duke's Theatre*. Written by *Thomas Otway*. London, Printed for *J. Hindmarsh* at the Sign of the Black Bull, over against the Royal Exchange in *Cornhill*. 1682. 4º.
The Epilogue. Written by Mr. Otway *to his Play call'd* Venice Preserv'd, or a Plot Discover'd ; *spoken upon his Royal Highness the Duke of York's Coming to the* Theatre, *Friday*, April 21. 1682. *Printed for* Joseph Hindmarsh *at the* Black Bull in Cornhill. 1682. folio.
The Atheist : or The Second Part of the Souldiers Fortune. Acted at the Duke's Theatre. Written by *Tho. Otway*.

>Hic noster Authores [sic] habet ;
>Quorum aemulari exoptat negligentiam
>Potius, quam istorum obscuram diligentiam,
>Dehinc ut quiescant porro moneo, et desinant
>Maledicere, malefacta ne noscant sua.   Terence.

London, Printed for R. Bentley, and J. Tonson, in Russel-street in Covent-Garden, and at the Judges Head in Chancery-Lane, near Fleet-street. MDCLXXXIV. 4º.
Collected Works.
The Works of Mr. Thomas Otway ; In three volumes. Consisting of his Plays, Poems, and Letters. London : Printed for C. Hitch and L. Hawes, D. Browne, H. Lintot, J. and R. Tonson, J. Hodges, C. Bathurst, J. Brindley, C. Corbet, T. Waller, A. Strahan, and T. Longman. MDCCLVII. 8º.
[2 vols. 1712.]
[*The Works*. Ed. M. Summers. 3 vols. 1926.]
[*The Works*. Ed. J. C. Ghosh. 2 vols. Oxford. 1932.]
Criticism.
Ham, F. G.
[*Otway and Lee*. New Haven. 1931.]
PACK (Richardson).
Miscellanies in Verse and Prose.

>   *Si quis tamen haec quoque, si quis*
>*Captus amore leget*   Virgil.

The Second Edition. London : Printed for E. Curll in *Fleet-street*. M.DCC.XIX. 8º. (The author's name occurs at the foot of the Dedication.)
A New Collection of Miscellanies in *Prose* and *Verse*. *Quod si non hic tantus fructus ostenderetur, et si ex his studiis delectatio sola peteretur ; tamen ut opinor, hanc animi remissionem, humanissimam, ac liberalissimam judicaretis. Nam cetera neque temporum sunt, neque aetatum omnium, neque locorum. Haec studia adolescentiam alunt, senectutem oblectant, secundas res ornant, adversis perfugium,*

ac solatium praebent ; delectant domi, non impediunt foris, pernoctant nobiscum, peregrinantur, rusticantur.

Cicero *Orat. pro* Archia *Poeta.*
Multa satis lusi. Non est Dea nescia nostri
Quae dulcem curis miscet amaritiem. Catull.

London : Printed for E. Curll, in the *Strand*. MDCCXXV. 8°.

PERCY.
Reliques of Ancient English Poetry : Consisting of Old Heroic Ballads, Songs, and other Pieces of our earlier Poets (Chiefly of the Lyric Kind). Together with some few of later Date. Durat Opus Vatum. London : Printed for J. Dodsley in Pall-Mall. MDCCLXV. 8°.
[Ed. H. B. Wheatley. 3 vols. 1876–7.]
[Ed. M. M. A. Schroer. 2 vols. Berlin. 1893. (A reprint of the first edition with later variants.)]

PHILIPS (Ambrose).
Poems.
Pastorals, By Mr. *Phillips*. *Nostra nec erubuit Silvas habitare Thalia.* Virg. Ecl. 6. (In *Poetical Miscellanies : The Sixth Part.* 1709). See POPE.
To the Honourable Miss Carteret. By Mr. *Ambrose Philips. London* : Printed for J. Roberts, near the Oxford-Arms in Warwick-Lane. MDCCXXV. folio.
[*The Poems of Ambrose Philips.* Ed. M. G. Segar. Oxford. 1937. (Contains a biographical introduction.)]
Dramatic Works.
The Distrest Mother. A Tragedy. As it is Acted at the Theatre-Royal in *Drury-Lane*. By Her Majesty's Servants. Written by Mr. *Philips. London* : Printed for *S. Buckley* at the *Dolphin in Little-Britain ;* and *J. Tonson*, at *Shakespear's Head* over-against *Catherine-street* in the Strand. MDCCXII. 4°.
[In *Modern British Drama.* vol. 2. 1811.]

PHILIPS (John).
Blenheim a Poem, Inscrib'd to the Right Honourable *Robert Harley*, Esq ; London, Printed for *Tho. Bennet*, at the *Half-Moon* in *St. Paul's* Churchyard. 1705. folio.
In Memory of Our Most Gracious Lady, Mary Queen of *Great Britain, France,* and *Ireland,* a Poem. By *John Phillips. London*, Printed for John Harris, at the Harrow in the *Poultry.* MDCXCV. folio.
[*The Poems of John Philips.* Ed. M. G. Lloyd Thomas. Oxford. 1927.]
Poems.
Poems on Affairs of State ; From the Time of *Oliver Cromwell,* to the Abdication of K. *James* the Second. *Written by the greatest Wits of the Age.* Viz. Duke of *Buckingham,* Earl of *Rochester,* Lord *B...st,* Sir *John Denham, Andrew Marvell,* Esq ; Mr. *Milton,* Mr. *Dryden,* Mr. *Sprat,* Mr. *Waller,* Mr. *Ayloffe,* etc. With some Miscellany Poems by the same : Most whereof never before Printed. *Now carefully examined with the Originals, and Published without any Castration.* The Fifth Edition, Corrected and much Enlarged. Printed in the Year 1703. 8°. (This volume composed of two parts, the second having a special title :) State-Poems ; Continued From the time of *O. Cromwel,* to the Year 1697. Written by the Greatest Wits of the Age, *viz. The Lord* Rochester, *The Lord* D——t, *The Lord* V——n, *The Hon,* Mr. M——ue, Sir F. S.——d, *Mr.* Milton, *Mr.* Prior, *Mr.* Stepney, *Mr.* Ayloffe, *etc.* With Several Poems in Praise of *Oliver Cromwel,* in *Latin* and *English,* by *Dr.* South,

BIBLIOGRAPHY

Dr. Locke, *Sir* W. G——n, *Dr.* Crew, *Mr.* Busby, *etc.* Also some Miscellany Poems by the same, never before Printed. Now carefully Examined with the Originals, and Published without any Castration. Printed in the Year MDCCIII. 8º. [First edition: 1697.]
Poems on Affairs of State, from the Reign of K. *James* the First, to this Present Year 1703. Written by the Greatest Wits of the Age. *Viz.* The Duke of *Buckingham*, The Earl of *Rochester.* The Earl of *D——t.* Lord *J——s.* Mr. *Milton,* Mr. *Marvel.* Mr. *St. J——n.* Mr. *John Dryden.* Dr. *G——th.* Mr. *Toland.* Mr. *Hugues.* Mr. *F——e.* Mr. *Finch.* Mr. *Harcourt.* Mr. *T——n, etc. Many of which never before Publish'd.* Vol. II. Printed in the Year 1703. 8º.
Poems on Affairs of State, From 1640, to this present Year 1704. *Written by the greatest wits of the Age, Viz.* The late Duke of *Buckingham,* Duke of *D——re,* Late E. of *Rochester,* Earl of *D——t,* Lord *J——rys.* Ld *Hal——x, Andrew Marvel,* Esq ; Col. *M——d——t,* Mr. *St. J——ns,* Mr. *Hambden,* Mr. *Dryden,* Mr. *St——y,* Mr. *Pr——r,* Dr. *G——th, etc.* Most of which were never before published. Vol. III. Printed in the Year 1704. 8º.
A New Collection of Poems Relating to State Affairs, from Oliver Cromwell To this present Time : By the Greatest Wits of the Age : Wherein, not only those that are Contain'd in the Three Volumes already Published are inserted, but also large Additions of chiefest Note, never before Published. The whole from their respective Originals, without Castration. *London,* Printed in the Year, MDCCV. 8º.
[This was a pirated edition, repudiated as spurious in vol. II of the genuine edition, 1707.]
Poems on Affairs of State, From 1620, to this present Year 1707. *Many of them by the most eminent Hands. Viz.* Mr. *Shakespear.* Mr. *Waller.* D. of *D——re.* Mr. *Dryden.* Mr. *W——sh.* Mr. *D——y.* Dr. *Wild.* Mr. *Brady.* Mr. *Tate.* Mr. *Hughes.* Mr. *Manning.* Mr. *Arwaker, etc. Several of which were never before publish'd. To which is added,* A Collection of some Satyrical Prints against the *French* King, Elector of *Bavaria, etc.* Curiously ingraven on Copper-Plates. Vol. IV. *London,* Printed in the Year 1707. 8º.

PHILIPS (Katherine).
Poems By the most deservedly Admired Mrs. *Katherine Philips* The matchless Orinda. To which is added *Monsieur Corneille's* Pompey and Horace Tragedies. With several other Translations out of *French. London,* Printed by *J.M.* for *H. Herringman,* at the Sign of the *Blew Anchor* in the Lower Walk of the New Exchange. 1667. folio.
[In *Minor Poets of the Caroline Period.* Ed. G. Saintsbury. Vol. I. Oxford. 1905.]
Biography.
Souers, P. W.
[*The Matchless Orinda.* 1931.]

POPE (Alexander).
Poetical Miscellanies : The Sixth Part. Containing a Collection of *Original Poems,* With several New Translations. *By the Most Eminent Hands. London,* Printed for *Jacob Tonson,* within *Grays-Inn* Gate, next *Grays-Inn* Lane. 1709. 8º.
The Works of Alexander Pope Esq. In Nine Volumes Complete. With his last Corrections, Additions, and Improvements ; As they were delivered to the Editor a little before his Death : Together with the Commentaries and Notes of Mr. Warburton. London, Printed for J. and P. Knapton, H. Lintot, J. and R. Tonson, and S. Draper. MDCCLI. 8º.

[For earlier collections supervised by Pope see *Alexander Pope, a bibliography*. R. H. Griffith. Vol. I. 2 parts. 1922–7.]
The Works of Alexander Pope. Including several hundred unpublished letters, and other new materials. Collected in part by the late R^t. Hon. John Wilson Croker. With Introduction and Notes. By Rev. Whitewell Elwin and William John Courthope, M.A. With portraits and other illustrations. London : John Murray, Albemarle Street. 1871–1886. 10 vols. 8º.
[*The Poems of Alexander Pope*. The Twickenham Edition. General editor : John Butt.
Imitations of Horace, with an epistle to Dr. Arbuthnot, and the epilogue of the satires. Ed. John Butt. 1939.
The Rape of the Lock and other Poems. Ed. Geoffrey Tillotson. 1940.
The Dunciad. Ed. J. Sutherland. 1943.]
[*The Prose Works of Alexander Pope*. Ed. Norman Ault. vol. 1. (1711–1720.) Oxford. 1936.]
Biography and Criticism.
Carruthers, Robert.
The Life of Alexander Pope. Including Extracts from his Correspondence. By Robert Carruthers. Second Edition, revised and considerably enlarged. With numerous engravings on wood. London : Henry G. Bohn, York-Street, Covent Garden. MDCCCLVII. 8º.
Stephen, Leslie.
English Men of Letters, Edited by John Morley. Alexander Pope. By Leslie Stephen. London : Macmillan and Co. 1880. 8º.
Warren, A.
[*Alexander Pope as Critic and Humanist*. Princeton. 1929.]
Sherburn, George.
[*The Early Career of Alexander Pope*. Oxford. 1934.]
Root, R. K.
[*The Poetical Career of Alexander Pope*. Princeton. 1938.]
Tillotson, G.
[*On the Poetry of Pope*. Oxford. 1938.]

Printers.
The Case and Proposals of the Free-Journeymen Printers, in and about London, humbly submitted to Consideration. Licensed October 23. 1666. Roger L'Estrange. folio.

PRIOR (Matthew). See also DRYDEN (Drydeniana).
To the King, An Ode on His Majesty's Arrival in Holland, 1695. By Mr. Prior.

> *Quis desiderio sit pudor aut Modus*
> *Tam Chari capitis ?* Hor.

London, Printed for *Jacob Tonson* at the *Judge's Head* near the *Inner-Temple-Gate* in *Fleetstreet*, 1695. folio.
An English Ballad : In Answer to Mr. *Despreaux's* Pindarique Ode on the Taking of Namure. *Dulce est desipere in loco*. London, Printed for *Jacob Tonson*, at the *Judge's Head* near the *Inner-Temple Gate* in *Fleetstreet*. MDCXCV. folio.
Poems on *Several Occasions*. London : Printed for Jacob Tonson at *Shakespear's Head*, over against *Katharine-Street* in the *Strand*, and John Barber, upon Lambeth-Hill. MDCCXVIII. folio.
[*The Writings of Matthew Prior*. Ed. A. R. Waller. 2 vols. Cambridge. 1905–7.]

BIBLIOGRAPHY

Biography and Criticism.
Bickley, F.
    [*The Life of Matthew Prior.* 1914.]
Legg, L. G. W.
    [*Matthew Prior.* 1921.]
PRYNNE (William).
    Histrio-Mastix. The Players Scourge, or, Actors Tragaedie, *Divided into Two Parts.* Wherein it is largely evidenced, by divers *Arguments*, by the concurring Authorities and Resolutions of *Sundry texts of Scripture*; of the *whole Primitive Church*, both under the *Law and Gospell*; of 55 *Synodes and Councels*; of 71 *Fathers and Christian Writers*, before the yeare of our Lord 1200; and above 150 *foraigne and domestique Protestant and Popish Authors*, since; of 40 *Heathen Philosophers, Historians*, Poets; of many *Heathen*, many *Christian Nations, Republiques, Emperors, Princes, Magistrates*; of sundry *Apostolicall, Canonicall, Imperiall Constitutions*; and of our owne *English Statutes, Magistrates, Universities, Writers, Preachers, That popular Stage-playes (the very Pompes of the Divell which we renounce in Baptisme,* if we beleeve the Fathers) *are sinfull, heathenish, lewde, ungodly Spectacles, and most pernicious Corruptions; condemned in all ages, as intolerable Mischiefs to Churches, to Republickes, to the manners, mindes, and soules of men. And that the Profession of Play-poets, of Stage-players; together with the penning, acting, and frequenting of Stage-playes, are unlawfull, infamous and misbe-seeming Christians.* All pretences to the contrary are here likewise fully answered; and the unlawfulness of acting, or beholding Academicall Enterludes, briefly discussed; besides sundry other particulars concerning *Dancing, Dicing, Health-drinking, etc.,* of which the *Table* will informe you. *By* William Prynne, *an Utter-Barrester of* Lincolnes Inne. Cyprian. De Spectaculis lib. p. 244. *Fugienda sunt ista Christianis fidelibus, ut iam frequenter diximus, tam vana, tam perniciosa, tam sacrilega Spectacula.: quae, et si non haberent crimen, habent in se et maximum et parum congruente fidelibus vanitate.* Lactantius de Vero Cultu cap. xx. *Vitanda ergo Spectacula omnia, non solum ne quid vitiorum pectoribus insideat, etc. sed ne cuius nos voluptatis consuetudo detineat, atque a Deo et a bonis operibus avertat.* Chrysost. Hom. 38. in Matth. Tom. 2. Col. 299. B. et Hom. 8. De Paenitentia, Tom. 5. Col. 750. *Immo vero, his Theatralibus ludis eversis, non leges, sed iniquitatem evertetis, ac omnem civitatis pestem extinguetis: Etenim Theatrum, communis luxuriae officina, publicum incontinentiae gymnasium, cathedra pestilentiae; pessimus locus; plurimorumque morborum plena Babylonica fornax, etc.* Augustinus De Civit. Dei. 1. 4. c. i. *Si tantummodo boni et honesti homines in civitate essent, nec in rebus humanis Ludi scenici esse debuissent.* London, Printed for *A.E.* and *W.I.* for *Michael Sparke*, and are to be sold at the Blue Bible, in Greene Arbour, in little Old Bayly. 1633. 4°.
Criticism.
Kirby, E. W.
    [*William Prynne: a Study in Puritanism.* Cambridge. U.S.A. 1931.]
PULTON (Andrew).
    A True and Full Account of a Conference Held about Religion Between Dr. Tho. Tenison and A. Pulton one of the Masters in the Savoy. Published by Authority. *London*, Printed by *Nathaniel Thompson* at the Entrance of *Old-Spring-Garden*, near *Charing-Cross.* 1687. 4°.
RALPH.
    The Case of Authors by Profession or Trade, Stated. With Regard to Booksellers, the Stage, and the Public. No Matter by Whom. "The question is not to make people read, but to make them think." L'esprit

des Loix, I. Part. p. 183. *London* : Printed for R. Griffiths, Bookseller, in *Paternoster Row*. MDCCLVIII. 8º.

RAVENSCROFT (Edward).
The Citizen turn'd Gentleman : a Comedy. Acted at the *Duke's Theatre*. By *Edw. Ravenscroft*. Gent. *London*, Printed for *Thomas Dring*, at the *White-Lyon* next *Chancery-Lane* and in *Fleetstreet*. 1672. 4º.
The Careless Lovers : A Comedy Acted at the Duke's *Theatre*. Written by *Edward Ravenscrofts* [sic], Gent. *London* : Printed for *William Cademan*, at the *Popes Head* in the Lower Walk in the *New Exchange*. 1673. 4º.
Scaramouch a Philosopher, Harlequin a School-Boy, Bravo, Merchant, and Magician. A Comedy After the Italian Manner acted at the Theatre-Royal. *Written by Mr*. Edward Ravenscroft. *Spe Incerta certum mihi laborem sustuli.* Terent. in Hecyram. Printed for *Robert Sollers* at the Flying Horse, in St. *Pauls Church-yard*. MDCLXXVII. 4º.
The London Cuckolds. A Comedy ; As it is Acted at the Duke's Theatre. By *Edward Ravenscroft*, Gent. *London*, Printed for *Jos*. Hindmarsh at the Sign of the Black-Bull near the Royal-Exchange in *Cornhill*. Anno Dom. 1682. 4º.
[In *Restoration Comedies*. Ed. M. Summers. 1921.]
Dame Dobson : or, The Cunning Woman. A Comedy As it is Acted at the Dukes Theatre, By *Edward Ravenscroft*, Gent. *London*, Printed for *Joseph Hindmarsh*, Bookseller to His Royal Highness, at the *Black Bull* in *Cornhill*. 1684. 4º.
Titus Andronicus, or the Rape of Lavinia. Acted at the Theatre Royall, A Tragedy, Alter'd from *Mr. Shakespears* Works, by Mr. *Edw. Ravenscroft*. Licensed, *Dec*. 21. 1686. *R.L.S. London*, Printed by *J.B.* for *J. Hindmarsh*, at the *Golden-Ball* in *Cornhill*, over against the *Royal Exchange*. 4º. (Acted in 1687.)
The Canterbury Guests : or A Bargain Broken. A Comedy. Acted at the *Theatre-Royal*. *Written by* Mr. Edward Ravenscroft, *London*, Printed for *Daniel Brown* at the *Bible* without *Temple-Barr* ; and *John Walthoe*, at his Shop in *Vine-Court, Middle Temple*. 1695. 4º. (Acted in 1694.)

RAY (John).
The Wisdom of God, Manifested in the Works of the Creation. Being the Substance of some common Places delivered in the Chappel of *Trinity-College* in *Cambridge*. By *John Ray*, M.A. sometimes Fellow of that, and now of the *Royal Society*. *London* : Printed for *Samuel Smith*, at the *Princes Arms* in S. *Pauls* Church-Yard. 1691. 8º.

Reformation.
An Account of the Societies for *Reformations of Manners*, in England And Ireland. With a Persuasive to Persons of all Ranks, to be Zealous and Diligent in Promoting the Execution of the Laws against *Prophaneness* and *Debauchery*, for the Effecting *A National Reformation*. Published with the Approbation of a Considerable Number of the *Lords Spiritual* and *Temporal*, and Honourable *Judges* of both Kingdoms. The Third Edition. *Who is on the Lord's side, let him come unto me ?* Exod. 32. 20. *Who will rise up with me against the Wicked ? Or who will take my part against the Evil doers ?* Psal. 94. 16. N. Tr. *London*, Printed for *B. Aylmer* and *Bell*, in *Cornhill* ; *D. Brown* without *Temple-Bar* ; *T. Parkhurst*, in *Cheapside* ; *J. Robinson, D. Midwinter* and *T. Leigh*, and *R. Sympson*, in St. *Paul's Church-Yard* ; *T. Godwin* and *W. Rogers*, in *Fleet-street* ; *J. Walthoe*, in the *Temple* ; *Is. Harrison*, at *Lincolns-Inn* ; *S. Heyrick*, at *Grays-Inn-Gate* in *Holbourn*, and *J. Fox*, in *Westminster-Hall*. 1700. For the

more general Benefit of the Publick, this Book is Sold at One Shilling Bound. 8º.
The Fifth Edition. *London*, Printed by *J. Downing*, in *Bartolomew Close* near *West-Smithfield* : And are to be Sold by him and *D. Brown*, Bookseller, without *Temple-Bar*. 1701. 12º.
A Help to a National Reformation. Containing An Abstract of the Penal-Laws against Prophaneness and Vice. A Form of the Warrants issued out upon Offenders against the said Laws. Directions to Inferior Officers in the Execution of their Office. Prudential Rules for the giving of Informations to the Magistrates in these Cases. A specimen of an Agreement for the Forming of a Society for *Reformation of Manners* in any City, Town, or larger Village of the Kingdom. And Her Majesty's Proclamation for Preventing and Punishing Immorality and Prophaneness; and the late Act of Parliament against prophane Swearing and Cursing. To which is added, An Account of the Progress of the Reformation of Manners in *England* and *Ireland*, and other parts of the World. With Reasons and Directions for our Engaging in this Glorious Work. And the Special Obligations of Magistrates To be diligent in the Execution of the Penal-Laws against Prophaneness and Debauchery, for the Effecting of a National Reformation. As also, some Considerations offered to such unhappy Persons as are guilty of prophane Swearing and Cursing, Drunkenness, and Uncleanness, and are not past Counsel. *Printed for the Ease of Magistrates, Ministers, and Inferior Officers, and the Direction and Encouragement of private Persons, who in any part of the Kingdom are engaged in the Glorious Work of Reformation or are Religiously disposed to contribute their Endeavour for the Promoting of it.* The Fifth Edition with great Additions. London, Printed and sold by *Joseph Downing* in *Bartholomew-Close*, near *West-Smithfield*, 1706. 12º.
A Letter to a Minister of the Church of England, Concerning the Societies for Reformation of Manners. London : Printed and Sold by *Joseph Downing* in *Bartholomew-Close*, near *West-Smithfield*. 1710. 4º.

ROCHESTER (Earl of). See WILMOT (John).

Romulus.
Romulus and Hersilia ; Or, The Sabine War. A Tragedy Acted at the Dukes Theatre. *Militat omnis Amans, et habet sua Castra Cupido.* Ovid. *London*, Printed for *D. Brown*, at the *Black-Swan* and *Bible* without *Temple-Bar*, and *T. Benskin* in St. Brides Church-yard, Fleet-street. 1683. 4º.

ROSCOMMON (Earl of). See DILLON (Wentworth).

ROWE (Nicholas).
Poems.
Poems on Several Occasions. By *N. Rowe*, Esq ; Printed for E. Curll at the Dial and Bible against S^t. Dunstan's Church in Fleet-street. 1714. 4º.
Ode for the *New Year* MDCCXVI. By *N. Rowe*, Esq ; Servant to His Majesty.

> *Custode rerum Caesare, non furor*
> *Civilis, aut vis eximet otium :*
>   *Non ira quae procudit enses,*
>   *Et miseras inimicat urbes.*
>   Hor. Lib. 4. Ode 15.

London : Printed for *J. Tonson*, at *Shakespear's-Head*, overagainst *Catherine Street* in the *Strand*. 1716. folio.
[See Chalmers, vol. 9 ; Park, vols. 32, 53, 54.]

Dramatic Works.
  Tamerlane. A Tragedy. As it is Acted at the New Theater in *Little Lincoln's-Inn-Fields.* By His Majesty's Servants. Written by *N. Rowe* Esq ;

> *Magnus ad altum*
> *Fulminat Euphraten bello, Victorque volentes*
> *Per Populos dat jura, viamq; affectat Olympo.*
>   Virg. Georg. 4.

  London, Printed for *Jacob Tonson,* within *Gray's-Inn-Gate,* next *Gray's-Inn-Lane.* 1702. 4º.
  Ulysses : A Tragedy. As it is Acted at the Queen's Theatre in the Hay-Market. By Her Majesty's Sworn Servants. Written by *N. Rowe,* Esq. ;

> *Stultorum Regum et Populorum Continet aestus—*
> *Rursus quid Virtus, et quid Sapientia possit*
> *Utile proposuit Nobis exemplar Ulyssem.*
>   Horat. Epist. Lib. I. Epist. 2.

  London, Printed for *Jacob Tonson,* within *Grays-Inn* Gate next Grays-Inn Lane. 1706. 4º.
  The Royal Convert. A Tragedy. Written by Nicholas Rowe, Esq. ; *Laudatur et Alget.* London : Printed for Jacob Tonson in the *Strand.* MDCCXXXV. 8º. (Acted in 1707.)
  The Tragedy of *Jane Shore.* Written in Imitation of Shakespear's Style. By *N. Rowe,* Esq.

> *Conjux ubi pristinus illi*
> *Respondet Curis.*   Virg.

  The Second Edition. London : Printed for Bernard Lintott, at the *Cross-Keys,* between the *Two Temple-Gates,* Fleet-*street,* 1714. 12º. (Acted in 1714.)
  [*Three Plays : Tamerlane, The Fair Penitent, Jane Shore.* Ed. J. R. Sutherland. 1929. (With a biographical introduction.)]
Collected Works.
  The Works of Nicholas Rowe, *Esq.* ; *London : Printed for* H. Lintot, J. *and* R. Tonson *and* S. Draper. MDCCLXVII. 2 vols. 12º.
    [3 vols. 1728.]

RYMER (Thomas).
  The Tragedies of The last Age Consider'd and Examin'd By the Practice of the Ancients, and by the Common sense of all Ages. In a Letter to *Fleetwood Shepheard,* Esq ; By Thomas Rymer, of *Grays-Inn,* Esquire.

> *Clament periisse pudorem.*
> *Cuncti pene patres ; ea quum reprehendere coner*
> *Quae gravis AEsopus, quae doctus Roscius egit.*   Hor.

  London, Printed for *Richard Tonson* at his Shop under *Grays-Inn* Gate, next *Grays-Inn.* (1678.) 8º.
  A Short View of Tragedy ; It's *Original, Excellency,* and *Corruption.* With some Reflections on *Shakespear,* and other Practitioners for the Stage. By Mr. *Rymer,* Servant to their Majesties. *Hodieque manent vestigia ruris.* Hor. London, Printed and are to be sold by *Richard Baldwin,* near the *Oxford Arms* in *Warwick-Lane,* and at the *Black Lyon* in *Fleetstreet,* between the two Temple-Gates. 1693.

SAINT-EVREMOND.
  Œuvres Meslees de Mʳ. *de Saint-Evremond,* Publiées sur les Manuscrits de

l'Auteur. A Londres, chez *Jacob Tonson*, Marchand Libraire, à *Grays-Inn-Gate*. MDCCV. 2 vols. 4⁰.
[The Letters, in translation, were edited by John Hayward, 1927.]

ST. JOHN (Henry, Viscount Bolingbroke).
Letters on the Study and Use of History. To which are added, Two other Letters, and Reflections upon Exile. By the late Right Honourable Henry St. John, Lord Viscount of Bolingbroke. In Two Volumes. London : Printed for A. Millar, in the Strand. MDCCLII. 8⁰.
[Reprinted : 1870. Ed. G. M. Trevelyan. Cambridge. 1935. (Letters 6–8 only.)]
Biography.
Hassall, A.
[*Life.* 1915.]
Petrie, Sir C.
[*Bolingbroke.* 1937.]

ST. SERFE.
Tarugo's Wiles : or, the Coffee-House. A Comedy. As it was Acted at his Highness's, the Duke of *York's* Theater. Written *By* Tho. St Serfe, *Gent. London*, Printed for *Henry Herringman* at the Sign of the Anchor, on the Lower-walk of the *New-Exchange*. 1668. 4⁰.

SAVILE (George, Marquis of Halifax).
The Character of a Trimmer. His Opinion of I. The Laws and Government. II. Protestant Religion. III. The Papists. IV. Foreign Affairs. By the Honourable Sir *W. Coventry*. The Second Edition, carefully Corrected, and cleared from the Errors of the first Impression. Licensed December 27. 1688. *London*, Printed for Richard Baldwin, next the *Black-Bull* in the *Old-Bailey*, MDCLXXXIX. 4⁰. (For the ascription of this work to the Marquis of Halifax, see text.)
[*Complete Works.* Ed. W. Raleigh. Oxford. 1912.]
Biography.
Foxcroft, N. C.
[*Life and Letters of Sir George Savile, Bart. ; first Marquis of Halifax.* 2 vols. 1898.]

SCOTT (Thomas).
The Unhappy Kindness : or A Fruitless Revenge. A Tragedy, As it is Acted at the Theatre Royal.
  Ad Generum Cereris sine Caede et sanguine pauci
  Descendunt Reges.   Juv. Sat. 10.
Wrirten [*sic*] by Mr. *Scot. London*, Printed for *H. Rhodes* in *Fleet-street, S. Briscoe* in *Covent-garden*, and *R. Parker* at the *Royal Exchange* : 1697. 4⁰.

SCUDÉRY (Magdeleine de).
Clelia. An Excellent *New* Romance : Dedicated to *Mademoiselle de Longueville*. Written in *French* by the Exquisite Pen of *Monsieur de Scudery*, Governour of *Nostredame de la Gard. London* [*sic*], Printed for *Humphrey Mosely* and *Thomas Dring*, and are to be sold at their Shop, at the Princes Arms in St. *Pauls* Church-yard, and at the George in Fleet-street, near *Cliffords*-Inne, 1656–61. 5 vols. folio.

SEDLEY (Sir Charles).
Poems.
- The Poetical Works of the Honourable Sir *Charles Sedley* Baronet, and his Speeches in Parliament. With *Large Additions never before made Publick*. Published from the Original M.S. by Capt. *Ayloffe*, a near Relation of the Authors. With a New Miscelany of Poems by several of the most

Q

Eminent Hands. And a Compleat Collection of all the Remarkable Speeches in both *Houses of Parliament*: Discovering the Principles of all *Parties* and *Factions*; the Conduct of our *Chief Ministers*, the Management of Publick Affairs, and the Maxims of the Government, from the year 1641, to the Happy Union of *Great Britain*: By several Lords and Commoners. Viz. The Duke of *Albemarle*, Earl of *Clarendon*, Earl of *Bristol*, Lord *Wharton*, Earl of *Pembrook*, Lord *Hollis*, Lord *Brook*, Lord *Essex*, Earl of *Argile*, Lord *Melvil*, Lord *Haversham*, Lord *Belhaven*, etc. *Algernon Sidney* Esq.; Mr. *Waller*, Sir *Francis Seymor*, Mr. *Pym*, *Richard Cromwell*, Mr. *Strode*, Sir *William Parkins*, Sir *William Scroggs*, Sir *J—— P——*, And several other Lords and Commoners. *London*, Printed for Sam. Briscoe, and Sold by *B. Bragg* at the *Raven* in *Paternoster-Row*. 1707. 8º.

Dramatic Works.

The Mulberry-Garden, A Comedy, As it is Acted by His Majestie's Servants, At the Theatre-Royal, Written by the Honourable Sir *Charles Sidley*. *London*, Printed for *H. Herringman*, at the Sign of the *Blew Anchor* in the Lower walk of the *New Exchange*. 1668. 4º.

Antony and Cleopatra: A Tragedy. As it is Acted at the Dukes Theatre. Written by the Honourable Sir Charles Sedley, Baronet, Licensed *Apr.* 24. 1677. *Roger L'Estrange. London.* Printed for *Richard Tonson* at his Shop under *Grayes-Inne-Gate* next *Grayes-Inn-lane.* MDCLXXVII. 4º.

Bellamira, or the Mistress, A Comedy: As it is Acted by Their Majesties Servants. Written by the Honourable Sir Charles Sedley Baronet. Licensed, *May* 24. 1687. *Rog. L'Estrange. London*, Printed by *D. Mallet*, for L. C. and *Timothy Goodwin*, at the Maiden-Head over against St *Dunstans* Church, in *Fleet-Street.* 1687. 4º.

Collected Works.

[*The Poetical and Dramatic Works.* Ed. V. de S. Pinto. 2 vols. 1928. (Contains a complete bibliography.)]

Biography and Criticism.

Pinto, V. de S.

[*Sir Charles Sedley.* 1927.]

SETTLE (Elkanah). See also DRYDEN (Drydeniana.)

Poems.

An Heroick Poem on the Coronation of the High and Mighty Monarch, James II. King of England, etc.

Caesar
Imperium Oceano, Famam qui terminet Astris.

By *E. Settle. London*, Printed by *J.L.* for *Benjamin Needham*, in *Duck-Lane*, MDCLXXXV. folio.

Dramatic Works.

Cambyses King of Persia: A Tragedy. Acted by His Highness the Duke of York's Servants. *Written by* Elkanah Settle, *Gent.*

Aut Faman sequere, aut sibi convenientia finge
Scriptor.   Hor. de Arte Poët.

Licensed, *March* 6. 1670. *Roger de l'Estrange. London*, Printed for *William Cademan*, at the *Pope's Head* in the Lower Walk of the New-Exchange. 1671. 4º.

The Empress of Morocco. A Tragedy with Sculptures. As it is Acted at the Duke's Theatre. Written by *Elkanah Settle*, Servant to his Majesty. *Primos da versibus annos.* Petr. Arb. *London,* Printed for

William Cademan at the Popes-head in the Lower Walk of the New-Exchange in the Strand, 1673. 4°.
[Ed. M. Summers. 1935.]
Notes and Observations on the Empress of Morocco Revised. With some few Errata's to be Printed instead of the Postscript, with the next Edition of the Conquest of Granada.
Impune ergo mihi recitaverit ille Togatas?
Hic. Elegos?   Juven.
London, Printed for William Cademan at the Popes-Head in the Lower Walk of the New Exchange in the Strand. 1674. 4°.
Love and Revenge, a Tragedy. Acted at the Duke's Theatre. Written by Elkanah Settle, Servant to his Majesty. London, Printed for William Cademan, and are to be sold at the Sign of the Popes-head in the New-Exchange in the Strand. 1675. 4°.
The Conquest of China, By the Tartars. A Tragedy Acted at the Duke's Theatre. Written by Elkanah Settle, Servant to His Majesty.
Multum sudet frustraque laboret
Ausus idem, tantum series juncturaque pollet. Hor.
London, Printed by T.M. for W. Cademan, at the Popes-Head in the Lower-Walk of the New-Exchange, in the Strand. 1676. 4°.
Ibrahim The Illustrious Bassa. A Tragedy. Acted at the Duke's Theatre. Written by Elkanah Settle, Servant to His Majesty.
Te
Nos facimus Fortuna Deam.   Juven.
Licensed *May* the 4th. 1676. *Roger L'Estrange.* London, Printed by T.M. for W. Cademan, at the Popes-Head in the Lower Walk of New-Exchange in the Strand. 1677. 4°.
The Female Prelate: Being The History of the Life and Death of Pope Joan. A Tragedy. As it is Acted at the Theatre Royal. Written by Elkanah Settle, Servant to His Majestie. *Facit Indignatio Versus.* Juven. London, Printed for W. Cademan, at the Popes head in the New Exchange. 1680. 4°.
[Ed. M. Summers. 1935.]
Distress'd Innocence: Or, The Princess of Persia. A Tragedy. As it is Acted at the Theatre Royal by Their Majesties Servants. Written by E. Settle.
Ut ridentibus arrident, ita flentibus adsunt
Humani vultus: Si vis me flere dolendum est
Primum ipsi Tibi, tunc tua me infortunia laedent
Telephe vel Peleu . . . Horat. de Arte Poetica.
London, Printed by E(?) I. for Abel Roper at the Mitre near Temple-Bar in Fleet street, 1691. 4°.
Miscellaneous Prose.
The Character of a Popish Successour, and What England May expect From Such a One. Humbly offered to the Consideration of both Houses of Parliament, Appointed to meet at Oxford, On the One and Twentieth of *March.* 1680/1. The Third Edition Corrected. London: Printed for R. *Janeway.* 1681. folio.
A Narrative Written by E. Settle.
Humano capiti cervicem pictor equinam
Jungere si velit, et varias inducere plumas
Undique collatis membris, ut turpiter Atrum
Desinat in piscem, Mulier formosa superne,
Spectatum admissi risum teneatis, amici.

Q*

London, Printed, and are sold by *Thomas Graves* for the Author. 1683. folio.

The Present State of England In relation to Popery. Manifesting the Absolute Impossibility of Introducing Popery and Arbitrary Power into this Kingdom. Being a Full *Confutation* of all Fears and Apprehensions of the Imagined Dangers from thence: And particularly of a Certain *Pamphlet* Entituled The Character of a Popish Successor. By E. Settle. London, Printed by *J. Gain*, for *William Cademan*, at the *Popes-Head* in the Lower Walk of the *New Exchange*, in the *Strand*; anno MDCLXXXIV. folio.

Biography and Criticism.
Brown, F. C.
[*Elkanah Settle: his Life and Works.* Chicago. 1910.]

SHADWELL (Thomas). See also DRYDEN (Drydeniana).
Poems.
A Congratulatory Poem On His Highness the Prince of Orange His Coming into England. Written by T.S. A True Lover of his Countrey. *London*, Printed for *James Knapton*, at the *Sign* of the *Crown* in St. *Pauls* Church-yard. MDCLXXXIX. folio.

A Congratulatory Poem To the Most Illustrious Queen Mary Upon Her Arrival in England. By *Tho. Shadwell.* London: Printed for James Knapton, at the Sign of the Crown in St Paul's Church-Yard. MDCLXXXIX. folio.

Ode On the Anniversary of the King's Birth. By *Tho. Shadwell*, Poet Laureat, and Historiographer Royal.

Steriles Transmisimus annos
Haec Ævi prima Dies.

London: Printed for *James Knapton*, at the Sign of the *Crown* in St. *Paul's* Church-Yard. 1690. folio.

Ode to the King. On His Return from Ireland. By *Tho. Shadwell*, Poet Laureat, and Historiographer-Royal to their Majesties. 1690. folio.

Votum Perenne. A Poem to The King On New-Years-Day. By Thomas Shadwell, Esq; Poet Laureat, and Historiographer Royal. *London*, Printed for *Samuel Crouch*, at the Corner of *Pope's-Head-Alley*, over against the *Royal-Exchange*, 1692. folio.

Dramatic Works.
The Sullen Lovers: or, the Impertinents. A Comedy Acted by his Highness the Duke of *Yorkes* Servants. Written by Tho. Shadwell.

Num satis est dixisse, Ego mira Poemata pango,
Occupet extremum scabies, mihi turpe relinqui est
Et quod non didici sane nescire fateri.
Hor. de Art. Poet.

In the *Savoy*, Printed for *Henry Herringman* at the Sign of the *Anchor* in the Lower-Walk of the *New-Exchange*. 1668. 4°.

The Royal Shepherdess. A Tragi-Comedy, Acted By his Highness the Duke of *York's* Servants. *Non Quivis videt immodulata Poemata Judex.* Hor. de Arte Poet. *London*, Printed for *Henry Herringman*, at the Sign of the Blew-Anchor, in the Lower-Walk of the *New-Exchange*. 1669. 4°.

The Humorists; A Comedy. Acted By his Royal Highnesses Servants. Written By Tho. Shadwell, *Poet-Laureat*, and *Historiographer-Royal*.

Quis inique
Tam patiens urbis tam ferreus utteneat [sic] *se.*

London, Printed for *Henry Herringman*, and are to be Sold by *Francis Saunders* at the *Blew Anchor* in the *Lower Walk* of the *New Exchange*, and *James Knapton* at the *Crown* in *St. Pauls Churchyard*. 1691. 4°. (First edition: 1671. Acted in 1670.)

The Miser: A Comedy Acted by His Majesties Servants, At the Theatre Royal. Written by *Thomas Shadwell*. *London*, Printed for *Hobart Kemp*, at the sign of the *Ship*, in the upper Walk of the *New Exchange*. 1672. 4°. (Acted in 1671.)

Epsom-Wells. A Comedy, Acted at the Duke's Theatre. Written by *Tho. Shadwell*. Μεγάλων ἀπολισθαίνειν ἁμάρτημα εὐγενές. Licensed, *Feb.* 17 1672/3. *Roger L'Estrange*. *London*, Printed by *J.M.* for *Henry Herringman* at the Sign of the *Blew Anchor* in the Lower Walk of the *New Exchange*. M.DC.LXXIII. 4°. (Acted in 1672.)

Psyche: A Tragedy, Acted at the Duke's Theatre. Written by *Tho. Shadwell*. *London*, Printed by *T.N.* for *Henry Herringman*, at the *Anchor* in the Lower Walk of the *New Exchange*. 1675. 4°.

The Libertine: A Tragedy, Acted by His Royal Highness's Servants. Written by *Tho. Shadwell*. *London*, Printed by *T.N.* for *Henry Herringman*, at the *Anchor*, in the Lower Walk of the *New Exchange*. 1676. 4°.

The Virtuoso. A Comedy, Acted at the Duke's Theatre, Written by *Thomas Shadwell*. Licensed *May* 31. 1676. *Roger L'Estrange*. *London*. Printed by *T.N.* for *Henry Herringman*, at the *Anchor* in the Lower Walk of the *New Exchange*. 1676. 4°.

The History of Timon of Athens, The Man-Hater. As it is acted at the *Dukes Theatre*. Made into a Play. By *Tho. Shadwell*. Licensed, *Feb.* 18. 1677/8. *Ro. L'Estrange*. London, Printed by *J.M.* for *Henry Herringman*, at the *Blue Anchor*, in the Lower Walk of the *New-Exchange*. 1678. 4°.

A True Widow. A Comedy, Acted by the *Duke's* Servants. Written by *Tho. Shadwell*. *Odi profanum Vulgus et Arceo*. Printed for *Benjamin Tooke*, at the *Ship* in St *Paul's* Church-Yard. 1679. 4°.

The Woman-Captain: A Comedy Acted by His Royal Highnesses Servants. Written by *Tho. Shadwell*. *London*, Printed for *Samuel Carr*, at the *King's-Head* in St *Paul's Church-yard*. 1680. 4°.

The Lancashire Witches, and Tegue O Divelly The Irish Priest. A Comedy. Part the First. The Amorous Bigot, with Second Part of Tegue O Divelly, A Comedy. Both Acted by their Majesties Servants. Written by *Thomas Shadwell* Poet Laureat, and Historiographer Royal to their Majesties. *London*, Printed for *R. Clavell, J. Robinson, A.* and *J. Churchill* and *J. Knapton*, and are to be Sold at the *Crown* in St. *Pauls* Church-yard, 1691. 4°. [First edition: 1682. Acted in 1681.]

A Lenten Prologue, Refus'd by the Players. 1683. folio. (Attributed to Shadwell.)

The Squire of Alsatia. A Comedy, As it is Acted by Their Majestys' Servants. Written by *Tho. Shadwell*.

> *Creditur, ex medio quia res arcessit, habere*
> *Sudoris minimum, sed habet Comaedia tanto*
> *Plus oneris, quanto veniae minus.*
> Hor. Ep. ad Aug. I. lib. 2.

London, Printed for *James Knapton*, at the *Queens-Head* in St. *Paul's* Church-Yard. 1688. 4°.

Bury-Fair. A Comedy, As it is Acted by His Majesty's Servants. Written by *Tho. Shadwell*, Servant to His Majesty. *London*, Printed for *James Knapton*, at the *Crown* in S^t. *Paul's* Church-yard: 1689. 4°.

The Scowrers. A Comedy, Acted by Their Majesties Servants. Written by *Tho. Shadwell*, Poet Laureat, and Historiographer-Royal. *London* : Printed for James *Knapton*, at the *Crown* in St. *Paul's* Church-yard. 1691. 4°.

The Volunteers, or The Stock-Jobbers. A Comedy, As it is Acted by Their Majesties Servants, At The Theatre Royal. Written by *Tho.* Shadwell, Esq. Late Poet-Laureat. and Historiographer Royal. Being his last Play. *London,* Printed for *James Knapton*, at the *Crown* in St. *Paul's* Church-yard. 1693. Where are also to be had all Mr. Shadwells 17 Plays etc. Bound up, or single. 4°. (Played in 1692.)

Collected Works.

The Dramatick Works of *Thomas Shadwell,* Esq ; In Four Volumes. London : Printed for J. Knapton, at the *Crown* in St. *Paul's Church-Yard* ; and J. Tonson, at *Shakespear's Head* over-against *Katharine-Street* in the *Strand.* MDCCXX. 12°.

[*The Complete Works.* Ed. M. Summers. 5 vols. 1927.]

Biography and Criticism.

Borgman, A. S.

[*Thomas Shadwell : His Life and Comedies.* New York. 1928.]

SHAKESPEARE (William).

Mézières, A.

Shakspeare, ses oeuvres et ses critiques. Par A. Mézières, Professeur de littérature étrangère à la faculté des lettres de Paris. Deuxième édition. Ouvrage couronné par l'Académie française. Paris, Charpentier, libraire-éditeur, 28, Quai de l'École. 1865. 12°.

Ingleby, Clement Mansfield.

Shakespeare's Centurie of Praise ; Being Materials for a History of Opinion on Shakespeare and his Works, *Culled from Writers of the first Century after his Rise.*

> *Praestanti tibi maturos largimur honores,*
> *Jurandasque tuum per nomen ponimus aras,*
> *Nil oriturum alias, nil ortum tale fatentes.*
> Horat. Epist., *lib. ii. ep. i. l.* 73.

London : For the Editor : *Printed by* Josiah Allen, of Birmingham, *and published by* Trübner and Co., 57 et 59, *Ludgate Hill.* 1874. 8°.

SHEFFIELD (John), Earl of Mulgrave, Duke of Buckingham and Normanby.

An Essay on Poetry : By the Right Honourable The Earl of Mulgrave. The Second Edition. London, Printed for *Jo. Hindmarsh,* at the *Golden Ball* over against the *Royal Exchange* in *Cornhil.* MDCXCI. folio.

The Works of John Sheffield Earl of Mulgrave, Marquis of *Normanby,* and Duke of *Buckingham.*

> *Nec* Phoebo *gratior ulla est*
> *Quam sibi quae* Vari *praescripsit pagina nomen.* Virg.

London. Printed by John Barber, Alderman of *London.* MDCCXXIII. 2 vols. 4°.

[*Miscellanea from the works of John Sheffield, Duke of Buckingham.* The Haworth Press. 1933.]

SMITH (Edmund).

A Pindarique Poem Sacred to the Glorious Memory of King William III.

> *Ignis utique quo clarius effulsit, citius*
> *Extinguitur, eripit se aufertque ex Oculis*
> *Subito perfecta Virtus.* Cambden de Phil. Syd.

BIBLIOGRAPHY 463

By *M. Smith* Gent. London, Printed for *Andrew Bell* at the Cross-Keys and Bible in Cornhil. MDCCII. folio.
Phaedra and Hippolitus. [*sic*]. A Tragedy. At it is Acted at the Queen's Theatre in the *Hay-Market*, By Her Majesty's Sworn Servants. By Mr. Edmund Smith. London, Printed for Bernard Lintott at the *Cross-Keys* between the two Temple-Gates in *Fleetstreet*. 1709. (Acted in 1707.) 4º.

SMITH (Francis).
An Account of the Injurious Proceedings of Sir George Jeffrey K^{nt}. Late Recorder of London, against Francis Smith, Bookseller. With his Arbitrary Carriage towards the Grand-Jury, at *Guild-Hall*, Sept. 16. 1680. Upon an Indictment then Exhibited against the said *Francis Smith*. For Publishing a Pretended *Libel*, entitled, An act of Common-Council for Retrenching the Expences of the Lord Mayor and Sheriffs of the City of London, etc. Together with an Abstract of very many former Losses, and Publick Sufferings Sustained by Him both in his *Person* and *Estate*. *Humbly submitted to the Consideration of all* True English-Men. London, Printed for Francis Smith at the *Elephant and Castle* in Cornhill near the Royal-Exchange. folio.

SMOLLETT (Tobias).
The Expedition of Humphry Clinker. By the Author of Roderick Random. In Three Volumes.
       Quorsum haec tam putida tendunt,
 Furcifer ? at te, inquam.   Hor.
London, Printed for W. Johnston, in Ludgate-Street ; and B. Collins, in Salisbury. MDCLXXI. 12º.
[Ed. R. Rice-Oxley. World's Classics. 1925.]
Biography and Criticism.
Hannay, David.
 [Tobias Smollett. 1887.]
Lewis Melville.
 [The Life and Letters of Tobias Smollett. 1926.]

Some thoughts.
Some Thoughts Concerning the Stage in a Letter to a Lady. London : Printed, and are to be Sold by *J. Nutt.* near *Stationers-Hall*. 1704. 8º.

SOUTHERNE (Thomas).
The Loyal Brother or the Persian Prince. A Tragedy As it is Acted at the Theatre Royal by their Majesties Servants. By *Thomas Southern*. *I, fuge ; sed poteras tutior esse Domi*. Mart. London, Printed for *William Cademan* at the *Popes Head* in the New *Exchange* in the *Strand*. 1682. 4º.
The Disappointment, or The Mother in Fashion. A Play As it was Acted At the Theatre Royal. Written by *Thomas Southerne*.
    Neque tu divinum Æneada tenta,
  Sed longe sequere, et vestigia semper adora. Stat.
London, Printed for *Jo. Hindmarsh*, Bookseller to his Royal Highness, at the Black Bull in *Cornhil*. 1684. 4º.
Sir Anthony Love : Or, The Rambling Lady. A Comedy. As it is Acted at the Theatre-Royal by Their Majesties Servants. Written by *Tho. Southerne.*
    Artis severae si quis amat effectus,
    Mentemque magnis applicat
      det primos versibus annos,
    Maeoniumque bibat foelici [sic] *pectore fontem.*
        Petro. Arb. Satyr. pag. 3.

London : Printed for *Joseph Fox* at the *Seven Stars* in *Westminster Hall*, and *Abel Roper* at the *Mitre* near *Temple Bar*. 1691. 4º.

The Wives Excuse : Or, Cuckolds make Themselves. A Comedy. As it is Acted at the Theatre-Royal, By Their Majesties Servants. Written by *Tho. Southern*. *Nihil est his, qui placere volunt, tam adversarium, Quam expectatio.* Cicero. *London*, Printed for *Samuel Brisco*, over against *Will's Coffee-house*, in *Russel-Street*, in *Covent-Garden*. 1692. 4º.

The Maids last Prayer : or Any, Rather than Fail. A Comedy. As it is Acted at the Theatre Royal, By Their Majesties Servants. Written by *Tho. Southerne*.

Valeat res ludicra, si me
Palma negata, macrum ; donata reducit opimum.
Hor. Epist. 1. lib. 2.

London, Printed for *R. Bentley*, in *Russell-street* in Covent-Garden, and *J. Tonson*, at the *Judges Head* in *Chancery-Lane*. 1693. 4º.

The Fatal Marriage : or the Innocent Adultery, A Play, Acted at the Theatre Royal, By Their Majesties Servants. *Written by* Tho. Southerne. *Pellex ego facta mariti.* Ovid. *London*, Printed for *Jacob Tonson*, at the *Judges Head* near the Inner-Temple-Gate in Fleetstreet, 1694. 4º.

Oroonoko : A Tragedy As it is Acted at the Theatre-Royal, By His Majesty's Servants. Written by *Tho. Southerne*.

Quo fata trahunt, virtus secura sequetur. Lucan.
Virtus recludens immeritis mori.
Caelum, negata tentat iter Via.
Hor. Od. 2, lib. 3.

London : Printed for *H. Playford*, in the *Temple-Change*. *B. Tooke* at the *Middle-Temple-Gate*. And *S. Buckley* at the *Dolphin* against St Dunstan's Church in Fleet-street. MDCXCXVI. 4º.

[In *Modern British Drama*. vol. 1.]

Collected Works.

Plays Written by Thomas Southerne, Esq. now first Collected. With An Account of the Life and Writings of the Author.

  Your tributary tears we claim,
 For scenes that Southerne drew ; a fav'rite name.
 He touch'd your fathers heart with gen'rous woe,
 And taught your mothers youthful eyes to flow ;
 For this he Claims hereditary praise,
 From wits and beauties of our modern days.
         Hawkesworth.

London, Printed for T. Evans near York-buildings : and T. Becket, corner of the Adelphi, Strand. MDCCLXXIV. 3 vols. 8º.

Biography and Criticism.

Dodds, J. W.
[*Thomas Southerne, Dramatist*. New Haven. 1933.]

SPRAT (Thomas).
A True Account and Declaration of The Horrid Conspiracy against the Late King, His Present Majesty and the Government : *As it was order'd to be Published by His late Majesty*. The second edition. *In the Savoy* : Printed by *Thomas Newcomb*, One of His Majesties Printers ; and are to be sold by *Sam. Lowndes* over against *Exeter-Change* in the *Strand*. 1685. folio. [First edition also 1685.]

STAPLETON or STAPYLTON (Sir Robert).
The Slighted Maid, A Comedy, Acted with great Applause at the Theatre

in Little *Lincolns-Inn*-Fields, *By His Highness the* Duke of York's *Servants. London,* Printed for *Thomas Dring* at the *George* near St. *Dunstan's* Church in *Fleet-street.* 1663. 4º.
The Step-Mother A Tragi-Comedy, Acted with great Applause at the Theatre in Little *Lincolns-Inn* Fields, *By His Highness the Duke of* York's *Servants.* Imprimatur, *Decemb.* 26. 1663. *Roger L'Estrange. London,* Printed by J. *Streater*; And are to be sold by *Timothy Twy* . . . (The rest of the title eroded.)
The Tragedie of Hero and Leander. Written by S^r. Robert Stapylton Kt. One of the Gentlemen Ushers of his Majesty's Most Honorable Privy Chamber, Licensed August 25. 1668. *Roger L'Estrange. London,* Printed for *Thomas Dring,* the Younger, at the *White Lyon* next *Chancery-Lane* in *Fleet-street,* 1669. 4º.

Star-Chamber.
A Decree of Starre-Chamber, concerning Printing, *Made the eleuenth day of July last past.* 1637. Imprinted at London by *Robert Barker,* Printer to the Kings most Excellent Maiestie: And by the Assignes of John Bill. 1637. 4º.

STEELE (Richard).
Dramatic Works.
The Lying Lover: or The Ladies Friendship. A Comedy. As it is Acted at the Theatre Royal by Her Majesty's Servants. Written by Mr. *Steele.* Haec nosse salus est adolescentulis. Tertul. London: Printed for Bernard Lintot at the *Middle-Temple-Gate* in Fleetstreet. 1704. Price. 1s. 6d. 4º.
The Conscious Lovers. A Comedy. As it is Acted at the Theatre Royal in *Drury-Lane.* By His Majesty's Servants. Written by Sir *Richard Steele.*
Illud Genus Narrationis, quod in Personis positum est, debet habere Sermonis Festivitatem, Animorum Dissimilitudinem, Gravitatem, Lenitatem, Spem, Metum, Suspicionem, Desiderium, Dissimulationem, Misericordiam, Rerum Varietates, Fortunae Commultationem, Insperatum Incommodum, Subitam Laetitiam, Jucundum Exitum rerum. Cic. Rhetor. ad Herenn. Lib. 1. London: Printed for J. Tonson at *Shakespear's Head* over against *Katharine-Street* in the *Strand.* 1723. 8º.
[Ed. M. J. Moses. *British Plays.* Vol. 1. Boston. 1929.]
[*The Plays.* Ed. G. A. Aitken. 1894. (Mermaid Series. 1903.)]
Periodicals. See also ADDISON (*The Spectator* and *The Guardian*).
Numb. 1. The Tatler, By *Isaac Bickerstaff* Esq; *Quicquid agunt Homines nostri Farrago Libelli.* Tuesday, April 12. 1709. folio.
[Ed. G. A. Aitken. 4 vols. 1898-9.]
The Lucubrations of *Isaac Bickerstaff* Esq; Οὐ χρὴ παννύχιον εὕδειν βοσληφόρον ἄνδρα. Homer. *London,* Printed: And to be deliver'd to Subscribers, by *Charles Lillie,* Perfumer, at the Corner of *Beauford-Buildings,* in the *Strand*; and *John Morphew* near *Stationers-Hall.* MDCCXIII. 4 vols. 8º.
[Ed. H. R. Montgomery. 1861.]
Encyclopédie Morale, ou Choix des Essais du Spectateur, du Babillard et du Tuteur; traduits en français, par M. L. Mézières, Docteur ès-Lettres, ancien professeur de Rhétorique . . . Paris, F. M. Maurice, libraire-éditeur, rue de Sorbonne, nº 5. MDCCCXXVI. 2 vols. 8º.

Miscellaneous Prose.
The Epistolary Correspondence of Sir Richard Steele; including *his familiar letters* to his wife and daughters; to which are prefixed, *fragments of three plays*; two of them undoubtedly Steele's, the third supposed to be Addison's. Faithfully printed from the originals; and

illustrated with literary and historical. anecdotes, *by John Nichols*, F.S.A.E. and P. In two volumes. London : Printed by and for John Nichols and Son, Red Lion Passage, Fleetstreet ; and sold by Messrs. Longman, Hurst ; Rees, and Orme, Paternoster-Row. 1809. 2 vols. 8⁰.
[*The Correspondence of Richard Steele.* Ed. Rae Blanchard. 1941.]
[*Tracts and Pamphlets.* Ed. Rae Blanchard. Baltimore. 1944.]
Biography and Criticism.
  Dennis, John.
    [*Remarks on a Play called the Conscious Lovers.* 1723. (In *Critical Works.* Ed. E. N. Hooker. 1939. vol. 2.)]
  Dobson, Austin.
    [*Richard Steele.* 1886.]
  Aitken, G. A.
    [*Richard Steele.* 2 vols. 1889.]
  Connely, W.
    [*Sir Richard Steele.* 1934.]

STEPNEY (George). -
An Epistle to Charles Montague Esq. ; on his Majesty's Voyage to Holland, by Mr. *George Stepney.* Licensed *Jan.* 31 1690/1. *J. Fraser.* London : Printed for *Francis Saunders* at the *Blue Anchor* in the *Lower Walk* of the *New Exchange.* 1691. folio.
A Poem Dedicated to the Blessed Memory of Her late Gracious Majesty Queen Mary. By Mr. Stepney. *London* : Printed for *Jacob Tonson*, at the *Judge's Head,* near the *Inner-Temple Gate* in *Fleetstreet.* 1695. folio.
[Poems by Stepney are contained in Johnson vol. XII and Chalmers vol. VIII.]

STILLINGFLEET (Edward).
An Answer to some Papers Lately Printed concerning the Authority of the Catholick Church In Matters of Faith, and the Reformation of the Church of England. *London* : Printed for *Ric. Chiswell* at the *Rose* and *Crown* in St *Paul's* Church-yard. MDCLXXXVI. 4⁰.
A Vindication of the Answer to some Late Papers Concerning The Unity and Authority of the Catholick Church and the Reformation of the *Church of England. London* : Printed for Richard Chiswell, at the *Rose* and *Crown* in St *Paul's* Church-yard. MDCLXXXVII. 4⁰.

SWIFT (Jonathan).
A Tale of A Tub. Written for the Universal Improvement of Mankind. *Diu multumque desideratum.* To which is added, An Account of a Battel Between the Antient and Modern Books in St. *James* Library. Basima cacabasa eanaa irraumista, diarbada caëota bafobos camelanthi. *Iren.* Lib. I. c. 18.

    Juvatque novos decerpere flores,
    Insignemque meo capiti petere inde coronam,
    Unde prius nulli velarunt tempora Musae.   Lucret.

The Second Edition Corrected. *London* : Printed for *John Nutt,* near *Stationers-Hall.* MDCCIV. 8⁰. (First edition also 1704.]
[Ed. A. Guthkelch and D. Nichol Smith. 1920.]
A Letter from a Member of the House of Commons in Ireland to a Member of the House of Commons in England, Concerning the *Sacramental Test. London* : Printed for *John Morphew,* near *Stationers-Hall.* 1709. 4⁰. [First edition : 1708.]
The W—ds—r Prophecy. Printed in the Year, 1711. folio.
The Conduct of the Allies, and of the Late Ministry, In Beginning and Carrying on The Present War.

> *Partem tibi Gallia nostri*
> *Eripuit: partem duris Hispania bellis:*
> *Pars jacet Hesperiae: totoq; exercitus orbe*
> *Te vincente perit. Terris fudisse cruorem*
> *Quid juvat Arctois, Rhodano, Rhenoq; subactis?*
> *Odimus accipitrem quia semper vivit in armis.*
> *Victrix Provincia plorat.*

The Second Edition, Corrected. London, Printed for *John Morphew*, near *Stationers-Hall*. 1711. 8º. (First edition also 1711.)
A Proposal for *Correcting, Improving* and *Ascertaining* the English Tongue; In a Letter To the Most Honourable Robert *Earl of* Oxford *and* Mortimer, *Lord High Treasurer* of Great Britain. The Second Edition. London: Printed for Benj. Tooke, at the *Middle-Temple-Gate, Fleetstreet*. 1712. 8º.
A Letter of Advice to a Young Poet: together with a Proposal for the Encouragement of Poetry in this Kingdom.

> *Sic honor et nomen divinis vatibus atq;*
> *Carminibus venit.*   Hor.

By J. Swift. Printed at *Dublin*, Reprinted at *London*, and Sold by *W. Boreham* at the *Angel* in *Pater-Noster-Row*. 1721. 8º.
Collected Works.
The Works of Jonathan Swift, D.D. Dean of St. Patrick's, Dublin; containing Additional Letters, Tracts and Poems, not hitherto published; with Notes, and a Life of the Author, by Sir Walter Scott, Bart. Second Edition. Edinburgh: Printed for Archibald Constable & Co. and Hurst, Robinson and Co. London. 1824. 19 vols. 8º.
[*The Prose Works*. Ed. Herbert Davis. Oxford. 1939–
  1. *The Tale of a Tub*. 1939.
  2. *Bickerstaff papers and Pamphlets on the Church.* 1939.
  3. *Examiner and other pieces (1710–11).* 1939.
  10. *The Drapier's letters and other works (1724–26).* 1941.
  11. *Gulliver's travels.* 1941.]
[*The Correspondence of Jonathan Swift. D.D.* Ed. F. Elrington Ball. 6 vols. 1910–14.]
[*The Letters of Jonathan Swift to Charles Ford.* Ed. D. Nichol Smith. Oxford. 1935.]
[*The Poems*. Ed. Harold Williams. 3 vols. Oxford. 1937.]
Biography and Criticism.
Prevost-Paradol, M.
  Jonathan Swift, his life and his works, by M. Prevost-Paradol: Paris, A Durand, 7, rue des Grès-Sorbonne, near the Panthéon. 1856. 8º.
Forster, John.
  The Life of Jonathan Swift. By John Forster. Volume the First. 1667–1711. London: John Murray, Albemarle Street. 1875. 1 vol. 8º. (Only this volume ever appeared. The author died after having published it.)
Craik, Henry.
  The Life of Jonathan Swift, Dean of St. Patrick's, Dublin, By Henry Craik, M.A. with Portrait. London, John Murray. 1882. 8º.
Stephen, Leslie.
  [*Jonathan Swift*. 1882.]
Moriarty, G. P.
  [*Dean Swift and his Writings*. 1892.]
Van Doren, C.
  [*Swift*. 1930.]

Quintana, R.
[*The Mind and Art of Jonathan Swift.* 1936.]
Newman, B.
[*Jonathan Swift.* 1937.]
Pons, Émile. [*La Jeunesse de Swift.* 1925.]

TATE (Nahum). See also DRYDEN (*The Second Part of Absalom and Achitophel*).
Poems.
  On the Sacred Memory Of Our Late Sovereign : With a Congratulation To His Present Majesty.
   Non deficit Alter
    Aureus.
  Written by *N. Tate*. London, Printed by *J. Playford*, for *Henry Playford*, near the *Temple*-Church : 1685. folio.
  The Triumph of Union : With the Muse's Address For the Consummation of it in the Parliament of Great Britain. Written by Mr. *Tate* Poet-Laureat to Her Majesty. London : Printed in the Year 1707. 4⁰.
  A Congratulatory Poem To His Royal Highness Prince George of Denmark, Lord High Admiral of Great Britain. Upon the Glorious Successes at Sea. By N. Tate, Esq ; Poet-Laureat to Her Majesty. London : Printed by H. Meere, for J.B. and sold by R. Burrough and J. Baker, at the *Sun* and *Moon* in *Cornhill* ; and J. Morphew, near *Stationers-Hall*. 1708. folio.
  An Entire Set of The Monitors. Intended for the Promoting of Religion and Virtue, and Suppressing of Vice and Immorality. Containing Forty One Poems on Several Subjects, *In Pursuance of Her* Majesty's *Most Gracious Directions.* Perform'd by Mr. Tate, Poet Laureat to Her Majesty, Mr. Smith, and Others. This Undertaking was Encourag'd by the *Subscription* of the following Gentlemen of the Clergy (besides *That* of Many of the Nobility, and great Numbers of the Gentry) His Grace my Lord Arch-Bishop of *York*, my Lord Bishop of *Lincoln*, my Lord Bishop of St. *Davids*, my Lord Bishop of *Gloucester*, Dr. *Moss*, Dean of *Ely*, Dr. *Brailsford*, Dean of *Wells*, Dr. *Williams*, Dr. *Bedfourd*, Dr. *Brown*, Dr. *Fog*, Dr. *Pelling*, Dr. *Bray*, Dr. *Hoadley*, Dr. *Blake*, Dr. *Hunt*. Dr. *King*, Dr. *Waugh*, Dr. *Wells*, Dr. *Only*, Dr. *Heath*, with about Fifty more of that Reverend Order. N.B. When the *Authors* had publish'd these Twenty One Papers, they were oblig'd (by being engag'd in other Affairs) to decline further proceeding in this Undertaking. folio.
  A Poem Sacred to the Glorious Memory of Her Late Majesty *Queen* Anne. By N. Tate, Esq ; Poet Laureat to King William, Queen Mary, Queen Anne, and to His present Majesty, till the Day of his Decease. Printed in the Year MDCCXVI. 8⁰.
  A Poem. Occasioned by the Late Discontents and Disturbances in the State. With Reflections upon the Rise and Progress of Priest-Craft. Written by *N. Tate*.
   Liberius si
   Dixero quid, si forte Jocosius, Hoc mihi juris
   Cum Venia dabis.   Hor.
   Vincit Amor Patriae.   Virg.

  London : Printed for *Richard Baldwin*, near the *Oxford-Arms* in *Warwick-Lane*. MDCXCI. folio.
  Mausolaeum : A Funeral Poem On our late Gracious Sovereign Queen Mary, Of Blessed Memory. By N. Tate, *Servant to His Majesty*. London : Printed for *B. Aylmer*, at the *Three Pigeons* against *St. Dunstan's* Church in *Fleet-street*. And *R. Baldwin*, near the *Oxford-Arms* in *Warwick-Lane*. 1695. folio.

A Congratulatory Poem On the New Parliament Assembled On This Great Conjuncture of Affairs. By *N. Tate*, Esq ; Poet-Laureat to His Majesty. London : Printed for W. Rogers, at the *Sun* against St. *Dunstan's* Church in Fleetstreet, MDCCI. folio.
Dramatic Works.
Brutus of Alba : or, the Enchanted Lovers. A Tragedy. Acted at the Duke's Theatre. Written by N. Tate. *Neque ut te miretur Turba, Labores,* Hor. Licensed *July* 15. 1678. *Roger L'Estrange. London,* Printed for *E.F.* for *Jacob Tonson,* at the Sign of the *Judge's-Head* in *Chancery-Lane,* near *Fleet-Street,* 1678. 4º.
The History of King Lear. Acted at the Duke's Theatre. Reviv'd with Alterations. By *N. Tate. London,* Printed for *E. Flesher,* and are to be sold by *R. Bentley,* and *M. Magnes* in *Russel-street* near *Covent-Garden,* 1681. 4º.
The *History* of King *Richard* the Second Acted at the Theatre Royal, Under the Name of the *Sicilian Usurper.* With a Prefatory *Epistle* in Vindication of the Author. Occasion'd by the Prohibition of this *Play* on the Stage. By *N. Tate. Inultus ut Flebo Puer* ? Hor. *London,* Printed for *Richard Tonson,* and *Jacob Tonson,* at *Grays-Inn* Gate, and at the Judges-Head in *Chancery-Lane* near *Fleet-street.* 1681. 4º.
The Ingratitude of a Common-Wealth ; or, the Fall of Caius Martius Coriolanus. As it is Acted at the Theatre-Royal. By N. Tate.

> *Honoratum si forte reponis Achillem,*
> *Impiger, Iracundus, Inexorabilis, Acer,*
> *Jura neget sibi nata, nihil non arroget Armis.* Hor.

London, Printed by T.W. for *Joseph Hindmarsh,* at the *Black-Bull* in *Cornhill.* 1682. 4º.
Cuckolds-Haven : or, an Alderman No Conjuror, A Farce acted at the Queen's Theatre in *Dorset Garden.* By *N. Tate. London,* Printed for *J.H.* and are to be sold by *Edward Poole,* next door to the *Fleece Tavern* in *Cornhill.* 1685. 4º.
A Duke and no Duke a Farce. As it is Acted by Their Majesties Servants. Written by *N. Tate.* With The several Songs set to Music, With thorow Basses for the *Theorbo,* or *Basse Viol. London,* Printed for *Henry Bonwicke,* at the *Red-Lyon* in St. *Pauls* Church-Yard. 1685. 4º.

TEMPLE (Sir William).
The Works of Sir *William Temple,* Bart. In Two Volumes. To which is Prefix'd Some Account of the Life and Writings of the Author. London : Printed for *A. Churchill, T. Goodwin, J. Knapton, R. Smith, B. Tooke, J. Round, J. Tonson, O. Lloyd, W. Meres, T. Woodward,* and *F. Clay.* MDCCXX. folio.
[4 vols. Edinburgh. 1814.]
[*Essays of Sir William Temple.* Ed. J. A. Nicklin. 1911.]
Biography.
Marburg, Clara.
[*Sir William Temple.* 1932.]

TICKELL (Thomas). See also ADDISON (Preface to Addison's *Works* 1721, and to *The Drummer*).
A Poem To His Excellency The Lord Privy-Seal, on the *Prospect* of *Peace.* By Mr. *Tickell.*
Sacerdos
Fronde super Mitram *faelici insignis Olivae.* Virg.

London : Printed for J. Tonson, at *Shakespear's-Head* over against *Catherine-street* in the Strand. 1713. folio.

Epistle from A Lady in *England*; To A Gentleman at *Avignon*. By Mr. *Tickell*. The Third Edition. London, Printed for *J. Tonson*, at Shakespear's-Head over against *Katharine-street* in the *Strand*. 1717. folio.
Kensington Garden. *Campos, ubi Troja fuit*. Virg. London: Printed for J. Tonson, in the Strand. MDCCXXII. 4º.
[*The Poetical Works*. Boston. 1894.]
Biography and Criticism.
  Tickell, R. E.
  [*Thomas Tickell and the Eighteenth Century Poets*. 1931.]

TINDAL (Matthew).
  Christianity as old as the Creation: Or, the Gospel, A Republication of the Religion of Nature. Est autem jus naturale adeo immutabile, ut ne quidem a Deo mutari potest. *Grot. de Jure Belli et Pacis*, 1. 1. C. 1. 10. n. 5. The Gentiles, *which have not the Law, do by Nature the Things contained in the Law*. Rom. ii. 14.—*God is no Respecter of Persons; but in Every Nation, he that feareth him, and worketh Righteousness, is accepted with him*. Acts. x. 34, 35, Proinde perfectam illam Religionem quae Christi praedicatione nobis tradita est, non Novam aut Peregrinam, sed si verum dicere oportet, primam, solam veramque esse liquido apparet. *Euseb*. Eccl. Hist. 1. 1. C. 4. *Valesius's* Transl. Res ipsa quae nunc Christiana Religio nuncupatur, erat et apud Antiquos, nec defuit ab Initio generis humani, quousq; ipse Christus veniret in Carne; unde vera Religio quae jam erat, caepit appellari Christiana. *Aug*. Oper. To. 1. p. 17. C. *Retract*. 1. 1. C. 13. The Religion of the Gospel, is the true original Religion of Reason and Nature.—And its Precepts declarative of that original Religion, which was as old as the Creation. *Serm. for prop. the Gosp. in for. Parts*, by Dr. *Sherlock*, now Bp. of *Bangor*, p. 10. and 13. God does nothing in the Government of the World by mere Will and Arbitrariness.—The Will of God always determines itself to act according to the eternal Reason of Things.—All rational Creatures are oblig'd to govern themselves in ALL their Actions by the same eternal Rule of Reason. Dr. S. *Clark's* Unchang. Oblig. of Nat. Relig. Edit. 4. p. 47, 48, 49. London, Printed in the Year MDCCXXX. 4º.

TOLAND (John).
  Christianity not Mysterious: or a Treatise Shewing, That there is nothing in the Gospel Contrary to Reason, Nor Above it: And that no Christian Doctrine can be properly call'd A Mystery. *We need not desire a better Evidence that any Man is in the wrong, than to hear him declare against Reason and thereby acknowledge that Reason is against him*. ABp. Tillotson. London, Printed in the Year 1696. 8º.
  Nazarenus: Or *Jewish, Gentile*, and *Mahometan* Christianity. Containing The history of the antient Gospel of Barnabas, and the modern Gospel of the Mahometans, attributed to the same Apostle: this last Gospel being now first made known among Christians. Also, The Original Plan of Christianity occasionally explain'd in the history of the Nazarens, wherby diverse Controversies about this divine (but highly perverted) Institution may be happily terminated. With The relation of an Irish Manuscript of the Four Gospels, as likewise a Summary of the antient Irish Christianity, and the reality of the Keldees (an order of Lay-religious) against the two last Bishops of Worcester. By Mr. *Toland*.

Intacta et Nova? graves Offensae, levis Gratia. }Plin. lib. 10.
}Epistl. 8.

*Ast ego Caelicolis gratum reor ire per omnes
Hoc opus, et Sacras populis notescere Leges.*
Lucan. lib. 10, ver. 197.

London, Printed : And Sold by J. Brown without Temple-Bar, J. Roberts in Warwick-Lane, and J. Brotherton at the Black Bull in Cornhill. 1718. 8º.

Pantheisticon : or the Form Of Celebrating the *Socratic-Society*. Divided into Three Parts. Which Contain, I. The Morals and Axioms of the Pantheists; or the Brotherhood. II. Their Deity and Philosophy. III. Their Liberty, and a Law, neither deceiving, nor to be deceived. To which is prefix'd A Discourse upon the Antient and Modern Societies of the Learned, as also upon the Infinite and Eternal Universe. And subjoined, A short Dissertation upon a Two-fold Philosophy of the Pantheists, that is to be followed ; together with an Idea of the best and most accomplished Man. Written Originally in Latin, by the ingenious Mr. *John Toland*. And now, for the first Time, faithfully rendered into English. *London* : Printed for Sam. Paterson, at *Shakespear's-Head* opposite *Durham-yard*, in the *Strand* ; and Sold by M. Cooper, in *Pater-noster Row*. 1751. 8º. (First edition : 1720.)

TUKE (Sir Samuel).
The Adventures of Five Hours. A Tragi-Comedy. *The Second Edition. Non ego Ventosae Plebis suffragia venor*. Horat. Feb. 12. 1662. Imprimatur. *John Berkenhead*. *London*, Printed for *Henry Herringman*, and are to be sold at his Shop at the Sign of the *Anchor* in the Lower Walk of the *New Exchange*. 1664. 4º.
[Ed. B. Van Thal and M. Summers. 1927.]
[*Sir Samuel Tukes Adventures of the Five Hours in relation to the Spanish Plot and to Dryden*. A. Gaw. Baltimore. 1917.]

Tunbridge.
The Tunbridge-Miscellany : Consisting of Poems, etc. Written at *Tunbridge-Wells* this Summer. By Several Hands.

Carminibus meritas celebrare Puellas
Dos mea. Ovid.

London. Printed for E. Curll at the Dial and Bible, against St. *Dunstan's* Church in Fleetstreet. MDCCXII. 8º.

Uzziah.
Uzziah and Jotham. A Poem. Licensed and Entred according to Order. *Obscuris vera involvens*. Virg. Æneid. 1. 6. *London* : Printed for *B. Motte*, and are to be sold by *Randall Taylor* near *Stationers-Hall*. 1690. folio.

VANBRUGH (John). See also COLLIER (The Stage Controversy).
The Relapse or Virtue in Danger : Being the Sequel of The Fool in Fashion, A Comedy. Acted at the Theatre-Royal in *Drury-Lane*. By the Author of a late Comedy Call'd *The Provok'd Wife*. *London*, Printed for S.B. and Sold by *R. Wellington* at the Lute, in St. *Paul's* Church-Yard. 1698. 4º. (Acted in 1697.)
The Provok'd Wife : A Comedy. Written by *Mr. Vanbrug*. *Author of the Relapse*. London, Printed in the Year 1710. (Acted in 1697.)
[First edition : 1697.]
Æsop. A Comedy. With the Addition of a Second Part. Written by Mr. Vanbrug. Printed for T. Johnson. Bookseller at the Hague. MDCCXI. 8º. (Acted in 1697.) [First edition : 1697.]
The False Friend. A Comedy. As it is Acted at the *Theatre-Royal* in *Drury-Lane*, By His Majesty's Servants. *London* : Printed for *Jacob Tonson*, within *Gray's Inn Gate*, next *Grays Inn Lane*, 1702. 4º.
The Provok'd Husband : or *A Journey to* London, A Comedy, As it is Acted at the Theatre-Royal, By His Majesty's Servants. Written by the Late Sir John Vanbrugh, *and Mr*. Cibber, *Vivit Tanquam Vicina Mariti*.

Juv. Sat. VI. London : Printed for J. Watts, at the Printing-Office in
Wild-Court near *Lincolns-Inn Fields*. MDCCXXVIII. 8º.
Collected Works.
Plays, Written by Sir John Vanbrugh. In two volumes. London :
Printed for J. Rivington, T. Lowndes, S. Caslon, C. Corbett, S. Bladon,
W. Nicoll, T. Evans, and M. Waller. MDCCLXXVI. 12º.
[2 vols. 1719.]
[*The Complete Works*. Ed. B. Dobrée and G. Webb. 4 vols. 1927.]
Biography and Criticism.
Ward, W. C.
[Preface to edition of the *Plays*. 1893.]
Whistler, Laurence.
[*Sir John Vanbrugh. Architect and Dramatist. 1664–1726.* 1938.]

VILLIERS (George, Duke of Buckingham). See also DRYDEN (Drydeniana).
Dramatic Works.
The Rehearsal, As it was Acted at the Theatre-Royal, *London*, Printed
for *Thomas Dring*, at the *White-Lyon*, next *Chancery-Lane* end in *Fleet-
street*. 1672. 4º.
English Reprints. George Villiers, Second Duke of Buckingham. The
Rehearsal. First acted 7 Dec. 1671. Published (? July) 1672. With
Illustrations from Previous Plays, etc. Carefully edited by Edward
Arber, *Associate, King's College, London, F.R.G.S.*, etc., London : Alex.
Murray and Son. 30, Queen Square, W.C. *Ent. Stat. Hall.* 2 Novem-
ber, 1868. (*All Rights reserved.*) 12º.
[Ed. M. Summers. 1914. Ed. A. C. Barnes. 1927.]
The Chances, A Comedy : As it was Acted at the Theatre Royal. Cor-
rected and Altered by a Person of Honour. *London*, Printed for A.B.
and S.M. and Sold by *Langley Curtis* on Ludgate Hill, 1682. 4º.
Miscellaneous.
Miscellaneous Works, Written by His Grace *George* Late Duke of *Buckingham*.
Collected in One Volume from the Original Papers. Containing Poems on
several Subjects. Epistles. Characters. Pindarics. The Militant
Couple, a Dialogue. And the Farce upon *Segmoor*-Fight. With
Letters by and to the Duke of *Buckingham*. By Persons of Quality.
Also *State Poems* on the Late Times, by Mr. *Dryden*, Sir *George Etherage*,
Sir *Fleetwood Sheppard*, Mr. *Butler*, Author of *Hudibras*, Earl of *D———*,
Mr. *Congreve*, Mr. *Otway*, Mr. *Brown*, Capt. *Ayloffe*; etc. Never before
Printed. With the late Duke of *Buckingham's* Speeches in the *House
of Lords*, upon Conference with the *Commons*. To which is added,
*A Collection of Choice remarkable Speeches, that were spoken in both Houses of
Parliament, by several Noblemen, and Commoners, in relation to the Government
and Liberty of the Subject.* In the Reigns of K. *Charles* I. The Usurpation
of the *Rump*, and *Oliver Cromwell*. K. *Charles* II. and K. *William* III,
etc. London : Printed for and Sold by *J. Nutt* near *Stationers-hall*.
1704. 8º.

VOLTAIRE.
Œuvres Complètes. *Nouvelle Édition* . . . par Louis Moland . . . Paris,
Garnier Frères, Libraires-Éditeurs. 1877–1885. 52 vols. 8º.

WALLER (Edmund).
The Maid's Tragedy altered. With some other Pieces. By Edmund
Waller, Esq. ; Not before Printed in the several Editions of his Poems.
London, Printed for *Jacob Tonson*, at the *Judges Head* in *Chancery-Lane*,
near *Fleet-street*. 1690.
The Works of *Edmund Waller*, Esq. ; in Verse *and* Prose. Published By

BIBLIOGRAPHY 473

Mr. *Fenton.* London : Printed for J. Tonson in the *Strand.* MDCCXXX. 12º.
[Ed. G. Thorn Drury. 2 vols. 1905. (Muses Library.)]

WATTS (Thomas).
A Letter to Antonio Panizzi, Esq. Keeper of the Printed Books in the British Museum, on the reputed earliest printed newspaper, "The English Mercurie, 1588." By Thomas Watts of the British Museum. London : . . . 1839. 8º.

WILMOT (John, Earl of Rochester).
Valentinian : A Tragedy, As 'tis Alter'd by the late Earl of Rochester, And Acted at the Theatre-Royal. Together with a Preface, concerning the Author and his Writings. *By one of his Friends.* London : for *Timothy Goodwin* at the *Maiden-head* against St. *Dunstans* Church in *Fleetstreet.* 1685. 4º.
Familiar Letters : Written by the Right Honourable *John,* late Earl of *Rochester,* And several other Persons of Honour and Quality. With letters Written by the most Ingenious Mr. *Thomas Otway* and Mrs. *K. Philips.* Publish'd from their Original Copies. With other Modern Letters, By *Tho. Cheek,* Esq. ; Mr. *Dennis,* and Mr. *Brown,* London : Printed by *W. Onley* for *Sam. Briscoe,* at the Corner of *Charles-street,* in *Russel-street, Covent-Garden.* 1697. 8º.
Poems on Several Occasions : With Valentinian ; a Tragedy. *To Which is added,* Advice to a Painter. Written by the Right Honourable *John,* late Earl of *Rochester.* London : Printed by H. Hills, and Sold by the Booksellers of *London* and *Westminster.* 1710. 8º.
The Works of the Right Honourable The Earls of *Rochester* and *Roscommon.* With some Memoirs of the Earl of *Rochester's* Life, by Monsieur *St. Evremont* : In a Letter to the Dutchess of *Mazarine.* The Third Edition. *To Which is added,* A Collection of Miscellany *Poems,* By the most Eminent Hands. London : Printed for E. Curll, at the *Peacock,* without *Temple-Bar.* 1709. 8º.
The Works of the Earls of Rochester, Roscommon, and Dorset. The Dukes of Devonshire, *Buckinghamshire* etc. With Memoirs of their Lives. In Two volumes. Adorned with Cuts. London : Printed in the Year M.DCC.XXXI. Price 5s.
[*The Collected Works.* Ed. John Hayward. 1926.]
Biography and Criticism.
Burnet, Gilbert.
Some Passages of the Life and Death Of the Right Honourable John Earl of *Rochester,* Who died the 26th of *July,* 1680. Written by his own Direction on his Death-Bed, By *Gilbert Burnet,* D.D. London, Printed for *Richard Chiswell,* at the *Rose* and *Crown* in St. *Pauls Church-Yard.* 1680. 8º.
Forgues, E. D.
John Wilmot, comte de Rochester. Revue des Deux Mondes, August and September 1857.
Prinz, J.
John Wilmot Earl of Rochester his Life and Writings. Leipzig. 1927.]
Whitfield, F.
[*Beast in View. A Study of the Earl of Rochester's Poetry.* Cambridge. U.S.A. 1930.]
Williams, Charles.
[*Rochester.* 1935.]
Pinto, V. de S.
[*Rochester. Portrait of a Restoration Poet.* 1935.]

Wine-Cooper.
  The Wine-Cooper's Delight, To the Tune of, *The Delights of the Bottle* . . .
  London, Printed for the *Protestant Ballad-Singers.* (1681). folio.
Works.
  The Works of Celebrated Authors, Of whose Writings there are but small
  Remains. London : Printed for J. and R. Tonson and S. Draper in the
  Strand. MDCCL. 2 volumes 12º. (1st volume: *The Earl of* Ros-
  common, *The Earl of* Dorset, *The Earl of* Halifax, and *Sir* Samuel Garth ;
  2nd volume : *George* Stepney, Esq. ; William Walsh, *Esq.* ; and Poems
  by *Bishop* Sprat.)

WYCHERLEY (William).
  Love in a Wood, or St. James's Park. A Comedy. As it is Acted By Their
  Majesties Servants. Written by Mr *Wycherley.*

> *Exclùdit sanos Helicone poetas*
> *Democritus ;* Horat.

  London, Printed by *T. Warren* for *Henry Herringman,* and are to be Sold
  by *R. Bentley, J. Tonson, F. Saunders,* and T. Bennet, 1694. 4º.
  [First edition : 1672. Acted in 1671.]
  The Gentleman Dancing Master. A Comedy, Acted at the Duke's Theatre.
  By Mr. *Wycherley.*

> Horat. *Non Satis est risu diducere rictum*
> *Auditoris : et est quaedam tamen hic quoq; virtus.*

  London, Printed by *J.M.* for *Henry Herringman,* and *Thomas Dring* at the
  Sign of the *Blew Anchor* in the Lower Walk of the *New-Exchange,* and at
  the Sign of the *White Lyon* in *Fleetstreet* near *Chancery-Lane* end. 1673.
  (Played in 1672.) 4º.
  The Country-Wife, A Comedy, Acted at the Theatre-Royal. Written by
  Mr. *Wycherley.*

> Indignor quicquam reprehendi, non quia crasse
> Compositum illepideve putetur, sed quia nuper :
> Nec veniam Antiquis, sed honorem et praemia posci. Horat.

  London, Printed for *Thomas Dring,* at the *Harrow,* at the Corner of *Chan-
  cery-Lane* in *Fleet-street.* 1675. (Acted in 1673.) 4º.
  The Plain-Dealer. A Comedy. As it is Acted at the Theatre Royal.
  Written by Mr Wycherley.

> Horat.—*Ridiculum acre*
> *Fortius et melius magnas plerumque secat res.*

  Licensed *Jan.* 9. 1676. Roger L'Estrange. *London,* Printed by *T.N.* for
  James Magnes and *Rich. Bentley* in *Russel-Street* in *Covent-garden* near the
  Piazza's M.D.C.LXXVII. (Acted in 1674.) 4º.
  [*Complete Works.* Ed. M. Summers. 4 vols. 1924.]
  Biography and Criticism.
    Perromat, C.
      [*William Wycherley.* Sa vie—son Oeuvre. Paris. 1921.]
    Barker, H. Granville.
      [*Wycherley and Dryden.* In *On Dramatic Method.* 1931.]

YOUNG (Edward).
  Busiris, King of Egypt. A Tragedy. *By* E. Young, *LL.B.* O triste plane
  acerbumque funus ! O morte ipsa mortis tempus indignius ! Jam
  destinata erat egregio Juveni, Jam electus nuptiarum dies ; quod
  gaudium, quo maerore mutatum est ? Plin. Epist. London, Printed
  for *T. Johnson.* M.DCCXIX. 12º.

A Poem on the *Last Day*. By Edward Young Fellow of *All-Souls* College, *Oxon*. *Venit Summa Dies*, Virg. Oxford. Printed at the Theatre for *Edward Whistler*, MDCCXIII. 8º.
On the Late Queen's Death. And His Majesty's *Accession to the* Throne. Inscribed to *Joseph Addison*, Esq.; Secretary to their Excellencies the Lords Justices. By Edward Young, Fellow of *All-Souls* College, *Oxon*. *Gaudia Curis*. Hor. *London* : Printed for *J. Tonson*, at *Shakespear's Head* over against *Catherine street* in the *Strand*. 1714. folio.
[*The Complete Works*. Ed. E. J. Doran. 2 vols. 1854.]
Biography and Criticism.
  Mackail, J.
    [*Edward Young*. 1926.]

INDEX

NOTE.—Numbers in brackets and italics refer to notes: thus, the entry 343 (*85*) is a reference to note 85 on page 343. But reference to the subject of the entry is often made in the body of the text on the page concerned, as well as in the note so referred to. Thus, " Arnall, Wm., 343 (*85*) " is to be taken to mean that, while a specific reference to Arnall is made in note 85 on page 343, there may be (and in fact is) also a reference to him in the text of that page.

Numbers in heavy type refer to the pages of the bibliography.

Abhorrers, 140
Absalom, **399**
Act of Indulgence, 166 (*137*)
Actors, patronage of, 28 (*88*)
Actresses, 30–2
Adaptation, dramatic, 55–7
Addison, Joseph, xvii–xviii, xix, xx, xxi, xxii, 39 (*127*), 215, 220, 221 (*44*), 222, 245–8, 254 (*145*), 307, 310–11, 312 (*319*), 318, 319, 337, 338, 340 (*78*), 370, **399–401**
  Campaign, The, 247, 325
  Cato, 214–15, 243, 297
  Dictionary, 337
  Evidence of the Christian Religion, 300 (*280*), 337
  Guardian, 275
  Remarks on ... Italy, 247 (*124*)
  Socrates, 337
  Spectator, 245
  official appointments, 218, 247, 324
  and *Tatler*, 261–3
  and *Spectator*, 263 ff.
  as critic, 292 ff.
  and Shakespeare, 296–7 (*271*), 315 (*330*)
  post-*Spectator* periodicals, 312 (*322*)
  Halifax and, 326
  dedications to, 333 (*56*)
  as public servant, 335 (*64*), 337
  Pope on, 335 (*64*)
  anonymity, 338 (*73*)
  See also *Spectator*
Adventurer, The, 313 (*323*)
Akenside, Mark, xxii
  Pope and, 384 (*194*)
Allegory, 170
Allibone, S. A., **392**
Amateur and professional writers, xxiii
Amery, Thomas, **401**
Andrews, Alex, **392**

Ann of Denmark, Queen, 30 (*94*)
Anne, Queen, 30 (*94*), 98, 215, 222 (*46*), 223, 240 (*109*), 241 (*112*)
Annesley, Elizabeth, 13
Anonymity, 338 (*73*)
Anthony, **401**
Arbuthnot, John, 217, 220, 322 (*20–21*), 370, 379, **401**
Argyll, John Campbell, Duke of, 379
Aristophanes, 234
Armstrong, Sir Thomas, 61
Arnall, Wm., 343 (*85*)
Arnold, Matthew, xvii
Arrowsmith, Joseph, 70 (*268*), **402**
Asgill, John, xix
Atheism, 6–7
Athenian Gazette, 255, **434**
Athenian Mercury, 255–6 (*148*), **434**
Atterbury, Francis, 181, 193, 254 (*145*)
  and Pope, 377 (*183*), 379
Aubrey, John, **387**
Audience, theatre
  effect of licentiousness on, 53–4
  attitude of, 58–61
Augustan Age, 221
Author's rights, 108
à Wood, Anthony, 5 (*12, 13*), 22 (*68*), 173 (*154a*), 298 (*278*), **392**
Aylmer, Brabazon, 24, 193

Bacon, Addison and, 297, 298 (*276*)
Ballads, 158, 298 (*277*), **450**
Bankes, John, **402**
  Destruction of Troy, 42 (*152*)
  Rival Kings, 40 (*135*)
  Vertue Betray'd, 145 (*41*), 147 (*49*), 192 (*206*)
Barrow, Isaac, 165, 189 (*201*)
Barry, Mrs., 29, 65 (*248*), 88–9
Bateson, F. W., **393**
Bath, Earl of, see Pulteney

INDEX 477

Bathurst, Allen, Lord, 379, 380–1
Baxter, Richard, 166–7
Bear-baiting, 27
Beaumont and Fletcher, 37
  Maids Tragedie, 38, 39 (*127*)
  Valentinian, 68
Bedford, Arthur, 240 (*108*), 244 (*120–1*), **402–3**
Behn, Mrs. Aphra, xxi, 7 (*22*), 14 ff., 19 (*59*), 27, 141–2, 186 (*193*), 190, **403–5**
  Abdelazer, 40 (*134*), 68 (*251*)
  City Heiress, The, 142, 146 (*46, 48*)
  Dutch Lover, The, 33 (*106*)
  Fair Vow-Breaker, The, 14 (*53*)
  Feign'd Curtizans, The, 48 (*182*), 65 (*250*), 83 (*310*)
  Lover's Watch, The, 17–18
  Oroonoko, 8 (*27*), 14–16
  Roundheads, The, 142, 145 (*43*), 149 (*60*)
  Sir Patient Fancy, 3 (*6*), 47 (*171, 176*), 48 (*183*), 49 (*184–5*)
  Town-Fopp, The, 52 (*200*)
Belsham, W., **387**
Benson, Wm., 309, **405**
Bentley, Richard (bookseller), 361
Bentley, Richard (scholar), 332, **405**
Bentley, Thomas, **405**
Berkeley, George, xix, 254 (*145*)
Bertie, Peregrine, 241 (*110*)
Betterton, Mrs., 30 (*94*)
Betterton, Thomas, 29, **393**
Bibliotheca, 303 (*286*)
Bickerstaff, Isaac, 260 (*166*)
  See also Steele ; Swift
Biographia Britannica, **393**
Biographia Dramatica, **393**
Birminghams, 140
Bisset, William, 240 (*108*), 309, **405**
Blackmore, Sir Richard, 39 (*128*), 217, 304 (*288–9*), 311 (*311*), 314 (*326*), 322 (*23*), 324, **405–7**
  Creation, 224 (*51*)
  King Arthur, 230 (*74*)
  Prince Arthur, 230 (*74*)
Blenheim, Battle of, 215
Blood, Colonel, 105 (*371*)
Blount, E., 370 (*166*)
Blucher, Marshal, 50 (*193*)
Bogtrotters, 140
Bohemianism, 346 ff.
Boileau, 12, 17 (*55*), 82, 97
Bolingbroke, Henry St. John, Viscount, 214, 215 (*8*), 220, 299 (*279*), 307, 326, 343, 379, **457**

Bolingbroke, Viscount (*contd.*)
  Examiner, 254 (*145*), 259 (*165*), 325 (*33*)
  on Swift, 327 (*39*)
  dedications to, 332
  Pope and, 370, 373 (*175*), 379, 380
Bonnecorse, Balthazar de, 17 (*55*), **407**
Books,
  number issued, 114–15
  number printed, 116
  prices, 116–17
Booksellers, 115
Bossuet, Jacques-Bénigne, 183, **407**
Boswell, James, *Life of Johnson*, 349, 350, 384, 386, **393**
Bouhours, 297
Boutell, Mrs., 32 (*103*)
Bowdler, Thomas, 315 (*330*)
Boyle, Henry (Lord Carleton), dedications to, 333
Boyle, *see* Orrery
Boyse, Samuel, xxii, 346 (*90*), 348–9, 351, 353, **393**
Bracegirdle, Mrs., 32 (*103*)
Bredvold, L., 203 (*242*)
Bristol, George Digby, Earl of, 68, **423**
British Apollo, 256 (*155*)
Broadsides, 158
Brome, Richard, xvi
Brooke, Henry, 369 (*161*)
Broome, William, 369 (*160*)
Brothers' Club, 220 (*43*)
Brown, Tom, xix, 6 (*19*), 26 (*81*), 50 (*194*), 54 (*204*), 58 (*223*), 61 (*231*), 124 (*434*), 183 (*185*), 226 (*58*), 237, 240 (*109*), 256 (*153*), **408–9, 413, 432**
Buckhurst, Lord, *see* Dorset
Buckingham, George Villiers, Duke of, 8, 9, 12, 57 (*221*), 67, 70, 71 (*270*), 72, 86–8, 105 (*371*), 124–5, 168, 173, **431, 472**
  Rehearsal, The, 43 (*156*), 45 (*169*), 51 (*196*), 86, 265 (*178*)
  Timon, 12 (*44*)
  and Butler, 22
  Dryden and, 87–8, 172, 175
  and Lee, 128
Buckinghamshire, Duke of, *see* Mulgrave, Earl of
Budgell, Eustace, 215 (*9*), 217, 280, 334 (*63*), 339–40
Buly, Betty, 62 (*237*)
Buncle, John, 14 (*53*), **401**
Bunyan, John, 23, 126, 166–8, **409–10**

Burke, Edmund, 299 (*279*), **387**
Burlington, Richard Boyle, Lord, 379
Burnaby, Charles, xxi
Burnet, Gilbert, 166 (*123*), 181, 186 (*194*), 213 (*4*), 327, **410**
Burns, Robert, 273 (*197*)
Butler, Mrs. Charlotte, 29
Butler, Samuel, 21–2, 43 (*156*), 86, 128, **410**
  Hudibras, 21
Button's Coffee-House, 371 (*167*)

Cademan, Wm., 115
Cadogan, Wm., Lieut.-Gen. the Earl of, 332
Calamy, Edmund, 167
Calderon, 56
Calprenède, *see* La Calprenède
Cambridge History of English Literature, **393**
Care, Henry, 173, 194, 200–1, 209, **431**
Caroline, Queen, 341 (*82*)
  and Savage, 351
Carteret, John, Earl Granville, 343, 378
Carteret, Hon. Miss, 334
Cartwright (actor), 62 (*237*)
Caryll, John, 370 (*166*), 371
Case and Proposals of the Five Journeymen Printers, **452**
Castlemaine, Lady, 82
Catcalls, 70
Catherine of Braganza, 138 (*7*)
Catholics, *see* Roman Catholics
Cave, Edward, 346
Cavendish, William, *see* Newcastle, Duke of
Censor, The, 311
Censorship
  of books, 114 (*402*), 356 (*123*)
  of the press, 157, 159 (*108*), 181, 248–9
Centlivre, Mrs. Susanna, **411**
  dedications, 332
Chalmers, A., **394**
Chalmers, George, **387**
Chappell, Wm., **394**
Character of a Town-Gallant, The, 2 (*3*), 3 (*6*), 3 (*7*), 6 (*20*), 7 (*24*), 59, 118 (*415*), **411**
Charles I, 30 (*94*), 136
Charles II, 1, 7, 8, 20–1, 130, 136–7, 178, 222, **387**
  and Marvell, 25 (*78*)

Charles II and Waller, 25 (*80*)
  and theatre, 28–30, 39
  and Nell Gwyn, 63
  and Wycherley, 72
  as literary patron, 80–3, 195–7, 213
  and religion, 138–9
  and Dryden, 169, 174, 177–8, 187, 195
Chénier, André, 202
Chesterfield, Philip Stanhope, 2nd Earl of, 84 (*315*)
Chesterfield, Philip Dormer Stanhope, 4th Earl of, 313 (*323*), 343, 371, 379
Chevers, Henry, 120
Christie, W. D., **387**
Cibber, Colley, 29, **394, 411–12**
  Apology, 30 (*97*), 226 (*59*)
  Lady's Last Stake, 243 (*117*)
  Non-Juror, 365
  Prologue to *Provok'd Husband*, 242 (*117*)
  Xerxes, 237 (*99*)
  Ximena, 21 (*65*), 302 (*282–3*)
  dedications, 332
  George I and, 334
  Poet Laureate, 334 (*61*)
City,
  and stage plays, 53–4
  and Exclusion controversy, 141
  withdrawal of privileges, 149
  growing importance under James II, 187
Clarendon, Edward Hyde, Earl of, xix, 21, **387**
Clark, G. N., **387**
Clark, Samuel, 300 (*280*), **412**
Class relations, and authors, xxi–xxii
Classics, Restoration poets and, 13
Clavell, Robert, **394**
Clenche, William, 182, **412**
Clergy,
  Restoration, 6
  and public opinion, 165–8
  and James II, 179 ff.
Cleveland, Duchess of, 71–2
Clifford, Matthew, 86, 173
Clifford, Lord, 141, 371
Clod-pate's Ghost, **412**
Cobbett, Wm., 7 (*23*), **388**
Cobham, Richard Temple, Lord, 379
Coffee-houses, 162–5, 249; *see also* Button's, Will's
Collaboration, dramatic, 55–6
Collection of the Newest . . . Poems, **412**
Collier, Jeremy, xvi, 207 (*253*), 230 ff.,

INDEX 479

Collier, Jeremy (*contd.*)
   238 (*101*) 243, (*117a*), 243–4, 258, **413–16**
   Desertion Discuss'd, 231 (*75*)
   Short View, xx–xxi, 74 (*279*), 230 ff.
Collins, Anthony, 299 (*279*), **416**
Colman, George, 313 (*323*)
Comedy, Restoration,
   moral basis of, xvi
   licentiousness of, 46 ff.
Commonwealth, books published under, 19 (*59a*)
Compton, Henry, 180
Concanen, Matthew, 343
Congreve, William, xxii, 218, 220, 221, 226, 228, 237, 319, 329, 336, 370, **414, 416–18**
   Amendments, etc., 238 (*100*)
   Double-Dealer, 229 (*69*), 236 (*93*), 241–2 (*113*)
   Love for Love, 225 (*53*), 228 (*62*), 242 (*115*)
   Mourning Bride, 222 (*46*), 227 (*60*), 229, 242
   Old Batchelour, 227 (*62*), 236 (*93*)
   Way of the World, 236 (*94*), 242
   and Addison, 326
   Harley and, 328
   dedications, 331
   on Halifax, 333 (*57*)
   Voltaire and, 339 (*75*)
   Walpole and, 342
   Pope's dedication to, 372
Connoisseur, The, 313 (*323*)
Conventicles, 166
Conversions, of authors, 201 ff.
Cooke, Thomas, 353
Cooke, W. G., **388**
Cooper, Anthony Ashley, *see* Shaftesbury, Earl of
Cooper, Samuel, 9
Corneille, 56, 68, 123 (*420*), 234 (*86*), 297
Cornhill Magazine, 313 (*324*)
Corporal punishment, Addison on, 287 (*233*)
Court patronage, xvii
   See also Patronage
Court,
   position at Restoration, 2–3
   Restoration, attitude to writers, 127
Courtiers,
   as playwrights, 67–8
   relation to authors, 72 ff.
Coventry, Sir John, 105 (*371*)
Coventry, Sir William, 213 (*3*)

Cowley, Abraham, 20–1 (*62*), 119 (*419*), 189 (201), **418**
Cutter of Coleman-Street, 21 (*63*)
Cowper, William, 23 (*69*), 313 (*323*)
Cowper, William, Lord, dedications to, 332
Craggs, James, 370, 378
Crébillon, 343 (*85*)
Cromwell, Henry, 320 (*9*)
Cromwell, Jenny, 59 (*229*), 62 (*237*)
Cromwell, Oliver, 136, 137, 138
Crow, Miss, 32 (*103*)
Crowne, John, 27, 96, 97–9, 111, 113, 175, 195, 199, 209, **418–20**
   Ambitious Statesman, 199 (*227*)
   Andromache, 56, 98
   Caligula, 199 (*230*)
   Calisto, 81 (*302*), 97, 98, 141 (*16*)
   Charles VIII of France, 97, 141 (*18*)
   City Politiques, 142, 146 (*47*), 190, 199 (*229*)
   Countrey Wit, 98
   Destruction of Jerusalem, 34 (*111*), 40 (*139*), 41, 99, 111 (*385*)
   English Frier, 143 (*34*), 199 (*230*)
   Henry VI, 143 (*33*), 199 (*228*)
   Juliana, 35, 40 (*140*), 42 (*154*), 97
   Married Beau, 195 (*219*)
   Misery of Civil-War, 142, 145 (*40*)
   Murder of Humphry Duke of Gloucester, 143 (*34*)
   Pandion and Amphigenia, 97 (*350*)
   Sir Courtly Nice, 58 (*225*), 60 (*231*), 69 (*259*), 73 (*277*), 81, 113 (*398*), 150 (*68*), 190 (*203*)
   Thyestes, 33 (*106*), 199 (*228*)
Cucheval Clarigny, **394**
Cumberland, Richard, 313 (*323*)
Cup of Coffee, A, **412**
Curll, Edmund, 346
Currer, Mrs., 65 (*250*)

Daily Courant, 252
D'Alembert, 75 (*281*)
Dampier, Wm., xix
Danby, Thomas Osborne, Earl of, 25 (*78*), 79
D'Avenant, Sir William, xvi, xix, 28, 31, 34, 37, 55, 109, 119 (*419*), 122, **420**
   Cruelty of the Spaniards in Peru, 34 (*108*)
   Gondibert, 119
   Law Against Lovers, 56

INDEX

D'Avenant, Sir William (contd.)
  Love and Honour, 29
  Macbeth, 31, 56, 61 (*234*)
  Man is the Master, 63 (*241*)
  Siege of Rhodes, 34 (*108*)
Davies, Thomas, 87
Dawkes's News-Letter, 251 (*138*)
Debauchery, Restoration, 3–5
Declaration of Indulgence, 138–9, 166 (*137*), 185
Dedications, 76 ff. (*289*), 90 (*328*), 120, 331–3
  Pope and, 371–2 (*174*)
Defoe, Daniel, xviii, xix, xxii, 221, 240 (*108*), 254 (*145*), 257–60, 319, 320–1, **421–2**
  Hymn to the Pillory, 258
  Review, 258–9 (*161–5*)
  Robinson Crusoe, 315, 366
  Shortest Way, 258 (*158*), 308 (*299a*)
  True-Born Englishman, 257 (*157*), 309
  official posts, 217–18, 219 (*38a*)
  imprisonment, 258 (*160*)
  and Steele, compared, 620
  novels, 315 (*332*)
Denham, Sir John, 68, 189 (*201*)
Dennis, John, 238 (*101*), 244 (*121*), 329, 347, **414, 422**
  Plot and No Plot, 228 (*64*)
  Usefulness of the Stage, 226 (*58*), 235 (*90*), 237 (*96*)
  Pope and, 384 (*194*)
Devonshire, Wm. Cavendish, Duke of, dedications to, 332
Diaper, Wm., 326 (*34*), **423**
Digby, George, see Bristol, Earl of
Dilke, Charles W., on Pope, 382, 383, **394**
Dillon, Wentworth, see Roscommon, Earl of
D'Israeli, I., 28 (*86*), **394**
Dissenters, xviii, 166–7
Dobrée, B., **395**
Dodsley, Robert, 368 (*157*)
Dogget, Thomas, **423**
  Country-Wake, 51 (*200*)
Domestick Intelligence, 159
Doran, Dr., **388, 395**
Dorset, Charles Sackville, Earl of, xx, 9, 10 (*34*), 21, 68, 72, 75, 78–9, 213 (*2*), 214 (*5*,) 220, 317–18 (*1, 2*), **473**
  dedications to, 331–2
Downes, John, 38, 54 (*207*), 152 (*72*), 229 (*67*), **395**

Drake, James, 237, **414**
Drake, Nathan, **423**
Drama,
  Puritans and, 9
  under Commonwealth, 19
Dramatists, financial returns, 107 ff., 193–4, 364
Dress, Restoration, 2
  women's, under William III, 223 (*47*)
Drunkenness, 2
Dryden, Lady Elizabeth, 73 (*278*), 84 (*315*), 116
Dryden, John, xxi, 25–7, 44–6, 73 (*278*), 75, 80–1, 82 ff., 110–12, 113, 162, 169 ff., 180 (*176*), 183 ff., 187, 188 ff., 195, 213, 214, 233, 239, **424–33**
  Absalom and Achitophel, 88, 161 (*117*), 169 ff., 183, 204 (*245*), 208, 209
  Albion and Albanius, 146, 148, 150 (*68*), 151–2, 178, 209
  All for Love, 55, 79, 101–2, 129 (*446*), 133
  Almanzor and Almahide, see *Conquest of Granada, Part II*
  Amboyna, 35, 55, 141, 208
  Amphitryon, 207, 225
  Annus Mirabilis, 76, 79, 120, 169
  Assignation, 62 (*236*), 67 (*251*), 74 (*280*), 76, 133 (*457*), 204 (*243*)
  Aureng-Zebe, 13, 27 (*83*), 40 (*148–9*), 46 (*170*), 76, 81 (*306*), 98, 120, 122 (*428*)
  Cleomenes, 364
  Conquest of Granada, Part I, 42 (*155*), 44 (*158*), 45 (*167*), 63, 65 (*249*), 119
  Conquest of Granada, Part II, 40 (*145*), 42 (*153*), 58 (*227*), 80 (*298*)
  Defence of an Essay of Dramatique Poesie, 27 (*83*), 85–6 (*318*), 132 (*455*)
  Defence of Epilogue to Conquest of Granada, 131 (*449*)
  Discourse Concerning Satire, 79 (*295a*), 87 (*322*), 123 (*430*), 169 (*144*)
  Don Sebastian, 75, 209
  Duke of Guise, 56, 210, 146, 176, 199, 209
  Epilogue to Fletcher's *Pilgrim*, 130 (*448*), 235 (*90*)
  Epilogue to Lee's *Constantine the Great*, 190 (*203*)
  Epilogue to Southerne's *Loyal Brother*, 142 (*21*), 190 (203)

INDEX

Dryden, John (contd.)
Essay of Dramatick Poesie, 37 (*122*), 51 (*196*), 79 (*296*), 85, 119, 131 (*452*), 193 (*208*)
Essay on Heroic Plays, 39 (*128*), 119
Evening's Love, An, 27 (*83*), 55 (210), 65–6, 69 (*263*), 78, 81 (*301*), 130 (*447*), 133 (*459*)
Fables, 239, 363
Grounds of Criticism in Tragedy, 120 (*420*)
Hind and the Panther, 182 (*181*), 183, 184, 204 (*245*), 205 (*246*), 206
History of the League (Maimbourg), 178, 196 (*223*), 210
Indian Emperour, 35, 40 (*137, 143*), 43 (*157*), 44 (*159*), 63, 80 (*298*), 84, 110
Indian Queen, 34 (109), 40 (*140, 142*), 62 (*238*), 83, 84
Kind Keeper, 3 (*8*), 37 (*121*), 47 (*175, 177, 180*), 49 (*184*), 50 (*191*), 52 (*200*), 55, 133, 152 (*71*)
Love Triumphant, 51 (*200*)
Mac Flecknoe, 175, 189
Maiden Queen, 32 (*103*), 40 (*144*), 47 (*172*), 48 (*183*), 49 (*188*), 81–2, 110
Marriage à la Mode, 33 (*106*), 39 (*128*), 89–91, 123 (*430*), 131 (*451*)
Medal, 174–5, 195, 208
Miscellanies, 193, 356, 363
Mock Astrologer, see Evening's Love
Œdipus, 34 (*110*), 54 (*207*), 55
Prologue to Lee's Cæsar Borgia, 133 (*459*)
Prologue to Shadwell's True Widow, 175
Prologue and Epilogue to Southerne's Disappointment, 190 (*203*)
Religio Laici, 176, 204–5 (*246*)
Rival Ladies, 63 (*242*), 77, 85, 133 (*458*)
Secret Love, 40, 62 (*237*), 63 (*243*); see also Maiden Queen
Sir Martin Mar-All, 54, 56, 78 (*293*), 84
Spanish Fryar, 118 (*416*), 132 (*455*), 144, 204 (*244*), 169 (*146*), 199 (*226*)
State of Innocence, 10 (*33*), 24, 44 (*165–6*), 80 (*298*), 119, 131 (*453*)
Tempest, 31 (*101*), 35–6, 55
Threnodia Augustalis, 178 (*172*), 197 (*224*)

Dryden, John (contd.)
Troilus and Cressida, 47 (*177*), 56, 63, 79, 115, 119, 142
Tyrannick Love, 40, 41, 42 (*155*), 55, 64, 80 (*298*), 118 (*416*)
Vindication of the Duke of Guise, 205
Wife of Bath, 132 (*456*)
Wild Gallant, 50 (*193*), 58 (*228*), 63, 67 (*251*)
financial position, 26, 112, 122–3
and Howard, 73 (*278*), 83, 84
cudgelling, 105–6, 128, 135
agreement with King's company, 110–11
official posts, 122
conversion to Roman Catholicism, 180, 202 ff.
on Milton, 193 (*210*)
appeal to Treasury for salary, 196–7
and James II, 198
sons, 207 (*250*)
on Swift, 257 (*156*)
as critic, 292–3 (*249a*)
on Shakespeare, 296 (*268*)
Dorset and, 317
deprived of Laureateship, 323, 354
and Tonson, 354 ff.
translation of Virgil, 357, 363 (*130*), 369 (*161*)
dedications, 371
Dryden's Satyr to His Muse, 84 (*315*), 175 (*161*), **432**
Duffett, Thomas, 66 (*251*), 82–3, **433-4**
"Duke's Company", 28, 151
Du Lorens, 11 (*41*)
Dunkirk, 137
Dunton, John, xix, 13 (*51*), 74 (*279*), 125, 161 (*118*), 167 (*140*), 253 (*143*), 255, 256–7, **434**
D'Urfey, Thomas, 27, 73–4, 134, 200, 209, 237, 238 (*100*), **414, 434-5**
Campaigners, 236 (*94*), 237 (*95*)
Common-Wealth of Women, 142, 150 (*69*)
Don Quixote, 225 (*57*), 228 (*65*), 229 (*231*), 108 (*380*)
Fool Turn'd Critick, 32 (*106*), 60 (*231*), 108 (*380*)
Grecian Heroine, 200 (*231*)
Injured Princess, 108 (*380*)
Joy to Great Cæsar, 178 (*172*)
Love for Money, 200 (*231*)
Royalist, 142, 145 (*42*), 146 (*45*), 149 (*60, 63*)
Siege of Memphis, 40 (*138*), 120

D'Urfey, Thomas (*contd.*)
  Sir Barnaby Whigg, 142, 144 (*39*), 146 (*45*)
  Vindication, etc., 144 (*39*), 177, 188–9 (*200*)
Dutch wars, 137–8, 141
Dyer, John, xxii, 249 (*131*), 308
  Fleece, The, xviii
Dyson, H. V. D., **395**

Ebsworth, J. Woodfall, 28 (*87*), **435**
Edinburgh Gazette, 164 (*127*)
Education, Addison on, 287 (*283*)
Eliot, T. S., 79 (*296*)
English Courant, 250 (*133*)
English Currant, 159
English Intelligencer, 159
English Mercurie, 153 (*74*)
Epilogues, 62–6, 113–14, 148–50, 190 (*203*), 227–8
Essay-papers, 310
Essex, William Capel, Lord, 213 (*4*)
Etherege, Sir George, xvii, 19 (*59*), 71 (*270*), 72–3 (*277*), 197 (*225*), **436**
  Comical Revenge, 52 (*200*), 54
  Lady of Pleasure, 12
  Man of Mode, xxi, 2 (*3*), 48 (*183*), 71 (*270*), 73 (*277*), 282
  Sir Fopling Flutter, see *Man of Mode*
Eusden, Laurence, 216, 321, **436**
Evelyn, John, 189 (*201*), **388**
  Diary, 38 (*125*)
  Tyrannus, 2 (*3*)
Exclusion Bill, 140, 141 (*15a*), 198 (*225a*)
Exclusionists, 140

Faldo, John, 168 (*142*)
Falkland, Lord, 99
Fane, Sir Francis, 68, 88 (*324*), **437**
Farquhar, George, 221 (*44*), 243, 329, **437**
  Constant Couple, 242 (*117*), 364 (*133*)
  Love and a Battle, 237 (*99*)
  Twin-Rivals, 242 (*117*)
Female Tatler, The, 310, 311
Fenton, Elijah, 365, 369 (*160*)
Ferguson, Robert, 194, 214 (*5*)
Fiction, romantic, 13–19
Fielding, Henry, 243 (*118*), 315 (*332*), 343, 346, **437–8**
  Author's Farce, 344 (*89*), 352 (*108*), 353 (*115*)

Filmer, Edward, 237, 244 (*120*), **414**
Financial position of authors, 107 ff.
Fisher, Payne, 120, 121
Flagwits, 69
Flatman, Thomas, 121
Flecknoe, Richard, 78, 119, **438**
Fleetwood, Wm., 308
Fletcher, John, 229
Florian, 243
Flos Ingenii, **438**
Flying Post, The, 251 (*138*)
Foote, Samuel, 87
Forster, John, **395**
France, Charles II and, *see* Louis XIV
Fransham, John, 259 (*165*)
Frederick Prince of Wales, 344, 379, 381
Free-Holder, The, 306 (*293–4*)
Freethinker, The, 311
French tragedy, Charles II and, 39
Friend, Sir John, 231
Friendly Intelligence, 159

Gallantry, 3
Gambling, 2
Garrick, David, 315 (*330*)
Garth, Sir Samuel, 217, 220, 254 (*145*), 279 (*213*), 322 (*22*), 324, 370
Gay, John, xxii, 218, 219 (*38a*), 220, 224 (*52*), 303 (*284*), 319, 320 (*11*), 324, 340, 343, 365, 369 (*161*), **438**
  Beggar's Opera, 369 (*161*)
  Captives, 365
  Polly, 369 (*161*)
  dedications, 332
  Pope and, 369 (*161*), 370, 376, **379**
Genest, John, **395**
Gentleman's Magazine, 26 (*82*), 132 (*456*), 134 (*461–3*), 315 (*331*), 325 (*31*), **438**
George I, 223
  and Cibber, 334
  Walpole and, 341
George II, 341
George III, Johnson and, 384
Gibbon, Edward, 335 (*64*)
Gifts, to authors, 120 ff.
Gildon, Charles, 237 (*96*)
Gilliver, L., 368 (*157*)
Glover, Richard, 343
Godolphin, Sidney, Earl of,
  and Addison, 215, 247
  and Maynwaring, 326
  dedications to, 331

Goldsmith, Oliver, 385
Goodwin, Dr. Thomas, 285 (*227*)
Gosse, E. W., **396**
Gould, Robert, 191 (*204*), **438**
Grabut, 9
Grand Cyrus, Le, 13
Granger, J., **388**
Granville, George, Lord Lansdowne, 132 (*455*), 217, 219 (*38a*), 322 (*24*), 324, 370
   Heroick Love, 227 (*62*)
   Jew of Venice, 37 (*121*)
   She-Gallants, 229 (*67*)
   Johnson on, 322 (*24*)
Granville, Earl, *see* Carteret, John
Growler, The, 310 (*310*)
Grub Street, 253
Guardian, 74 (*279*), 200 (*231*), 275 (*205*), 332
Gwyn, Nell, 61, 63, 64–5, 83, 138 (*8*), **439**

Hack writers, 346
Haines, Joseph, 62 (*237*), 202, 206 (*249*), 209, 237 (*99*)
Halifax, Charles Montague, Earl of, xx, 178 (*172*), 183, 185 (*189*), 213 (*2*), 214 (*5, 6*), 218, 219 (*38a*), 248 (*126*), 370, **447**
   and Addison, 247, 326
   and E. Smith, 321
   and Maynwaring, 326
   and Prior, 326
   dedications to, 331, 333
   Addison, Congreve and Pope on, 333 (*57*)
   and dedicators, 334
   and Pope's *Iliad*, 371 (*172*)
   and Pope, 378 (*184*)
   See also Prior, *City Mouse*
Halifax, George Savile, Marquis of, 198 (*225a*), 213 (*3*), 214 (*5*), 257, **457**
Hallam, Henry, **389, 396**
Hamilton, Antoine, 4 (*9*), **389**
Hanmer, Sir Thomas, 315 (*330*)
Harley, *see* Oxford
Harris, Benjamin, 159 (*108*), 249 (*132*)
Harrison, Wm., 310 (*310*), 326 (*34*)
Hart, Charles, 83
Hart, William, 307
Hats, worn by prologuists, 63
Haughton, Lord, 204
Hawkesworth, John, 313 (*323*)
Haywood, Mrs., xxii

Hazlitt, William, 243 (*119*), **396**
Hedges, Sir Charles, 248 (*126*)
Hell upon Earth, 243 (*117a*)
Henley, Anthony, 285 (*227*)
Henley, John, 343
Henrietta Maria, Queen, 30 (*94*)
Henry, Matthew, 300 (*280*)
Heraclitus Ridens, 161 (*116*)
Herbert, William, 61 (*233*)
Hermit, The, 311
Heroic Plays, 40 ff.
Herringman, Henry, 26, 115
Hervey, John, Lord, **389**
Hettner, Hermann, **396**
Heywood, Thomas, xvi, 34 (*108*)
Hickeringhill, Edmund, 171 (*149–50*), 174–5 (*159*), **431**
Hickes, George, 318 (*3*)
Hicks, Thomas, 168 (*142*)
Hill, Aaron, 329
Historian, The, 311
Hobbes, Thomas, 119 (*417a, 419*), 292 (*249a*)
Hobbism, 141 (*19*)
Hogarth, William, 59 (*230*), 350, **439**
Hopkins, Charles, 229, **439**
Horror, on stage, 35
Howard, Edward, 173 (*154a*), **439**
Howard, Lady Elizabeth, *see* Dryden, Lady Elizabeth
Howard, Col. Henry, 70
Howard, James, 38
Howard, Sir Robert, xvii, 68, **439–40**
   Duke of Lerma, 63, 73 (*278*), 85
   Vestal Virgin, 64
   and Dryden, 73 (*278*), 76, 79, 83, 84–6, 120
   See also Dryden, *Indian Queen*
Howe, John, 167, 214 (*5*)
Howell, James, 122
Huguenots, xviii
Hughes, John, 216, 311 (*311*), 321 (*17*), 332, **440–1**
Hunt, J. H. Leigh, **396**
Hunt, Thomas, 177, 194, 200, 209, **441**

Idler, The, 313 (*323*)
Ignoramus verdicts, 149, 213 (*4*)
Immorality of the English Pulpit, The, 238 (*100*)
Inconsistency, political, of authors, 199–200
Inquisitor, The, 311
Instructor, The, 311

484 INDEX

Intelligence Domestick and Foreign, 249 *(132)*
Intelligencer, 157 *(97)*, 161 *(116)*

Jacobites, 212
James I, 30 *(94)*
James II, 80 *(298)*, 138, 139, 140, 149–50, 169, 178 ff., 184–5, 187, 213, 222
   and theatre, 28–9
   and Dryden, 169, 180
   and patronage of letters, 187, 197–8
   and Wycherley, 201
Jargon, Court, in drama, 131
Jeffrey, Francis, 313 *(325)*, **441**
Jeffreys, George, Baron, 201
Jeffreys, George (author of *Edwin*), 365
Jervas, Charles, 370 *(166)*, 373 *(175)*, 379
Jesuita Vapulans, 160
Johnson, Charles, 364 *(135)*
Johnson, Michael, 171
Johnson, Samuel, 2, 25 *(80)*, 54 *(204)*, 87, 115, 213 *(2)*, 253 *(144)*, 313 *(323)*, 315 *(330)*, 332 *(55)*, 350, 384, 386, **396**
   and Dryden, 122, 202–3
   on Savage, 347–8
   on Boyse, 351
   on Pope, 383
   Pope and, 384 *(194)*
Jones, Inigo, 34 *(108)*
Johnson, Ben, 37
   Volpone, xvi
   on stage licentiousness, xvi
   Addison and, 297, 298 *(276)*
Jortin, 350
Journalism, birth of, 254
Julian, Capt., 124

Keble, Joseph, **389**
Kennet, White, 254 *(145)*
Kensington, Court at, 223
Kent, Marquis of, dedications to, 332
Ketch, Jack, 210 *(257)*
Key (with the Whip) . . ., A, 173, **433**
Killigrew, Henry, 5
Killigrew, Thomas, 28, **441**
   Parson's Wedding, 32, 47 *(172, 178)*
Killigrew, Sir William, 68, **441**
King, Charles, **445**
King, Dr., 303 *(286)*

Kingdom's Intelligencer, 157 *(95)*
King's Pamphlets, 156
"King's Servants", 28, 151
Kit-Cat Club, 220, 248, 319, 320
Kneller, Sir Godfrey, 9, 223 *(47)*, 379
Kneppe, Mrs., *see* Nepp
Knight (banker), 360
Knight, Charles, **396**
Knipp, Mrs., *see* Nepp
Krutch, J. W., **396**
Kynaston, Edward, 31

La Bruyère, 273 *(196)*
La Calprenède, 13, 40, **442**
Lacey, John, 29, 64, 87, **442**
   Dumb Lady, 56
   Sauny the Scott, 56, 142
   Sir Hercules Buffoon, 56
Ladies Mercury, 256 *(154)*
Lætamur medal, 174
Lamb, Charles, **397**
Lampoons, 11
Langbaine, Gerard, **397**
Lansdowne, Lord, *see* Granville, George
Laughing Mercury, 155
Law, William, 244 *(121)*, **442**
Lawreat, The, **442**
Lay Monk, The, 311
Leaflets, Political, 154 ff.
Lebossu, 297
Lecky, W. E. H., **389**
Lee, Nathaniel, 27, 55, 78, 111, 112, 123, 125, 128, 134, 195, 209, **442–4**
   Alexander, 42 *(155)*
   Cæsar Borgia, 52 *(200)*, 129 *(445)*
   Constantine the Great, 109 *(383)*, 113 *(397)*, 190 *(203)*
   Gloriana, 62 *(237)*
   Lucius Junius Brutus, 52 *(200)*, 144, 199
   Mithridates, 45 *(168)*, 78 *(294)*, 101 *(363)*
   Princess of Cleve, 190 *(202)*
   Rival Queens, 34, 40 *(132)*, 113 *(397)*
   Sophonisba, 34, 40 *(147)*, 45 *(169)*, 60 *(231)*, 82, 141 *(17)*
   Theodosius, 40 *(133)*, 52 *(200)*, 108 *(379)*, 113 *(397)*, 129 *(445)*, 133 *(459)*
   Tragedy of Nero, 42, 68 *(251)*, 70 *(265)*, 79 *(295)*, 88 *(324)*
Leigh, Anthony, 29
Lely, Sir Peter, 9, 223 *(47)*

L'Estrange, Roger, 160-2, 176, 185, 187, 197 (*225*), 200, 209, **444**
Letter to a Dissenter, 185, 187 (*197*), 213
Letter to the Three Absolvers, **444**
Lewis (publisher), 368
Licensing Act, 159
Licentiousness, in Restoration comedy, 46 ff.
after Revolution, 224 ff.
Lillibulero, 186 (*194*)
Lintot, Bernard, 350 (*102*), 367-9
on Translators, 352-3
Locke, John, xix, 217, 221, 278 (*208*), 287 (*233*), 300 (*280*), 318, 319, 321 (*12*), 323-4, 330, **444-5**
Lodge, Sir Richard, **389**
London, position at Restoration, 2
See also City
London Gazette, 157 (*98*), 159, 160, 164, 249 (*129*), 261 (*167*), 328
Looker-On, The, 313 (*323*)
Louis XIV, Charles II and, 8, 137, 138
Lounger, The, 313 (*323*)
Loves of Hero and Leander, The, xv
Lowell, J. R., **397**
Lowndes, W. T., **397**
Loyal Medal Vindicated, 175, **446**
Luttrell Collection, **397**
Lynch, K. M., **397**
Lyttelton, George, Baron, 343, 344 (*88*), 379

Macaulay, T. B., Lord, 2 (*2*), 27 (*85*), 72, 166, 180 (*175*), 181 (*178*), 185 (*191*), 225 (*54*), 382, **389, 397**
on Addison, 300
on Tillotson, 364
on Pope's dedication of *Iliad*, 372 (*173*)
Magazine, the, 315
Mahon, Lord, *see* Stanhope
Maidwell, John, 106 (*374*), **445**
Maimbourg's *History of the League*, 178, 196 (*223*)
Majesty, in dramatic subjects, 39-40
Malcolm, J. P., **389**
Mallet, David, 344 (*88*), 353
Malone, Edmund, 28 (*87-8*), 111, 112 (*390*), **397**
Mandeville, Bernard, xviii, 299 (*279*)
Manley, Mrs. de la Rivière, 229, **445**
Royal Mischief, 227 (*61*)
dedications, 332
Manley, Roger, 305 (*292*)

Marchmont, Hugh Hume, Earl of, 379
Marlborough, John Churchill, Duke of, 38 (*122*), 215 (*7*), 220
Marlborough, Sarah Jennings, Duchess of, 46 (*170*), 98
Marlowe, 39
Marston, John, xvi
Martyn, Henry, 217, 323, 324, **445**
Marvell, Andrew, 25, **445-6**
Mary II, Queen, 98, 222-3 (*47*)
Mary of Modena, 139
Masks, of women playgoers, 58
Massinger, Philip, xvi
Masson, David, 397
on Dryden, 207 (*251*)
Master of the Revels, 241
Maynard, Sir John, 146 (*44*)
Maynwaring, Arthur, 217, 219 (*38a*) 220, 323, 326, 334
Mercuries, xix, 154 (*79*), 155-6, 160, 256
Mercurius Caledonicus, 164 (*127*)
Meredith, George, **397**
Methuen, Sir Paul, dedications to, 333
Mezières, A., 37 (*122*), 246 (*122*), 286 (*231*)
Middle Class, rise of, xviii
Milton, John, 4, 20, 23-5, 126, 188, 296, **446**
Defensio Populi, 23 (*70*)
Paradise Lost, 23-4 (*70-2*), 24, 116, 117, 131 (*453*), 193, 297, 315 (*329*), 356
Addison on, 297-8 (*276*)
Mirror, The, 313 (*323*)
Mist, Nathaniel, 308 (*299a*)
Mistresses, royal, and patronage, 82-3
Molière, 102
adaptations of, 56, 57, 131 (*450*)
Monmouth, Duchess of, 80
Monmouth, James Scott, Duke of, 29, 80, 98, 150, 152, 168, 170 (*148*), 209
Montagu, Lady Mary Wortley, 281, **447**
Montague, Charles, *see* Halifax, Earl of
Moore, Dr. Edward, 313 (*323*)
Morals, Addison and, 287-8, 299
Motteux, Peter A., 237, 257, **447**
Mulgrave, John Sheffield, Earl of, 9, 68, 75, 76, 92-3, 107, 120, 123, 128, 319, 371, 381 (*191*), **462**

Mulgrave, Earl of (*contd.*)
　　Essay on Poetry, 9 (*32*), 27 (*84*), 104 (*367*), 107
　　Essay on Satyr, 102–5
Murray, William, Earl of Mansfield, 379
Muses Mercury, **447**
Music, Puritans and, 9
Mutiny Act (1689), 225

Names, fictitious, 13
Neal, Daniel, **390**
Nepp, Mrs., 63, 66 (*251*)
Newcastle, Duchess of, 9 (*31a*), 77–8
Newcastle, William Cavendish, Duke of, 9 (*31a*), 54, 68, 75, 77–8, 80, 84, 220, 332, **410–11**
　　See also Dryden, Sir Martin Mar-all
Newcomb, Thomas, 303 (*286*)
Newes, The, 157 (*97*), 161 (*116*)
Newes from France, 153 (*76*)
Newes from Poland, 153 (*76*)
Newes out of Holland, 153 (*76*)
News-books, 155 ff.
Newsletters, 164–5, 249–50
Newspapers, 153 ff., 249 ff.
　　provincial, 164
Newton, Sir Isaac, 217, 221, 318, 319, 321, 323, 330
Nichols, John, **397**
Nicoll, Allardyce, **397**
Nobles, anti-Court, 168 (*142*)
Nokes, James, 29, 31, 63
Nonconformists, *see* Dissenters
Non-resistance, 166
Norfolk, Mary Mordaunt, Duchess of, 116 (*408*)
Normanby, Marquis of, *see* Mulgrave, Earl of
Norris, John, 255 (*149*)
North, Roger, 116, 117 (*411*), 147 (*50*), 162 (*121*), **447**
Northumberland, Hugh Smithson, Earl of, 385
Norwich, Earl of, 76
Novel, the, 315

Oates, Titus, 139, 146
Observator, 160 (*112*), 161, 164, 311
Observer, 313 (*323*)
Oldham, John, 134, 143 (*32*), **448**
　　Satire, Dissuading from Poetry, 22–3 (*68*), 109 (*383*), 122 (*426*), 124, 128 (*443*)

Operas, Dramatic, 35
Ormond, James Butler, Duke of, 121, 332
Orrery, Charles Boyle, Earl of, 215 (*9*)
Orrery, Roger Boyle, Earl of, 39, 40 (*141*, *149*), 68, 77, 85, **407–8**
　　Tryphon, 141 (*19*)
Ossory, Thomas Butler, Earl of, 121
Otway, Thomas, 27, 99–100, 106, 123, 126, 128 (*442*), 131, 134 (*463*), 150, 195, **448–9**
　　Alcibiades, 99
　　Atheist, 150 (*67*), 190 (*202*)
　　Caius Marius, 56, 65 (*248*), 79 (*297*), 108 (*380*)
　　Cheats of Scapin, 56
　　Don Carlos, 99, 100 (*358*), 106 (*373*)
　　Friendship in Fashion, 53 (*201*), 60 (*231*), 131 (*454*)
　　Orphan, 45 (*169*), 101 (*363*), 112 (*391*, *394*), 129 (*446*), 133, 149
　　Poets Complaint, 11 (*40*), 99 (*356*), 100 (*361*)
　　Souldiers Fortune, 51 (*196*), 52 (*200*), 76 (*285*), 121 (*423*), 190
　　Titus and Berenice, 56, 58 (*225*), 99
　　Venice Preserv'd, 106 (*374*), 142, 147 (*52–3*)
Owen, John, 167
Oxford, Aubrey de Vere, Earl of, 8, 29
Oxford, Robert Harley, Earl of, 214, 298 (*278*), 325 (*33*), 332
　　and Swift, 220 (*41*), 326, 327
　　and Pope, 370, 379, 380 (*189*)
Oxford Gazette, 157 (*98*)

Pack, Richardson, 22 (*67*), **449–50**
Pacquet of Advice from Rome, 160
Paganus Piscator, *see* Fisher, Payne
Palmer, John, **397**
Pamphlets, sales of, 309
Parker, Sir Thomas, Earl of Macclesfield, 216, 332 (*55*)
Parkhurst, Thomas, 167 (*140*)
Parkyns, Sir Wm., 231
Parliamentary Debates, reporting of, 325 (*31*)
Parnell, Thomas, 216, 217, 221 (*44*) 322 (*19*), 326, 339, 370
Partridge, John, 260 (*166*)
Passive obedience, 166, 179
Patronage, 73 ff., 127
　　under Queen Anne, 317 ff.

INDEX

Patronage (contd).
  cessation under Walpole, 341 ff.
  political, 330 ff.
Paturot, Jérôme, 153
Pavy, Salathiel, 30 (*95*)
Penn, William, 168 (*142*), 276 (*206a*)
Pepys, Samuel, 5 (*13*), 162 (*121*), **390**
  Diary, 2 (*5*), 5 (*13*), 6 (*15*, *16*), 13 (*50*), 31-2, 53 (*202*), 54 (*206*), 63 (*241*), 78 (*293*), 84 (*312*), 121, 137 (*3*, *4*), 162 (*119*), 166 (*138*)
  on Shakespeare, 38 (*125*)
  and ballads, 298 (*278*)
Percy, Bishop, 298 (*278*), **450**
Perrot, John, 168 (*142*)
Perry, H. Ten Eyck, **398**
Peterborough, Charles Mordaunt, Earl of, 379, 380
Petitioners, 140
Philips, Ambrose, 216, 311 (*311*), 321-2, 324, 332, 334, 346, **391**, **450**
  Distrest Mother, 280 (*215*), 294 (*257*)
  Pastoral Verses, 294 (*257*), 321, 332
Philips, John, 215, 329, 332, 364, **450-1**
Philips, Katherine, 13-14, 35 (*116*), 56, 68, **451**
Phœnix Society, 53 (*201*)
Pictures, Puritans and, 8
Pilgrim, The, 311
Pinto, V. de S., **398**
Pirated books, 357 (*123*)
Piron, 384-5
Pitt, William, 343
Plague (1665), 53
Plays,
  booksellers' price for, 118
  additions on printing, 118-19
Pleasure, Addison and, 288-9
Plutarch, 213
Plymouth, Charles Fitzcharles, Earl of, 99, 134
Poetry, Restoration, 9-13
Political news, and liberty of Press, 251
Political favour, and authors, 323 ff.
Poor Robin's Intelligence, 159
Pope, Alexander, 220, 279, 315 (*330*), 343, 366 ff., **451-2**
  Dunciad, 127 (*439*), 175, 350 (*104*), 379 (*187*), 384 (*194*)
  Epilogue to *Satires*, 380 (*188*)
  Epistle to Augustus, 375
  Essay on Criticism, 294 (*257*), 368
  Iliad, 367, 368 (*157-8*), 369, 371-2

Pope, Alexander (contd.)
  Messiah, 273 (*198*)
  Miscellany, 368 (*156*)
  Odyssey, 368 (*157*), 369 (*160*)
  Pastorals, 367
  Rape of the Lock, 368
  Satires and Epistles, 375 (*179*), 379 (*187*), 380 (*190*)
  Temple of Fame, 368
  Windsor Forest, 368, 370
  on Roscommon, 10 (*37*)
  on Dryden, 100 (*360*)
  on Southerne, 194 (*211*), 365
  and Addison, 281 (*218*)
  on Bentley, 332
  on Halifax, 333 (*57*)
  on Prior, 334 (*62*)
  anonymity, 338 (*73*)
  his Shakespeare, 368 (*157*)
  prologue to *Cato*, 370
  and politics, 370-1, 372-3, 375
  and Swift, 371, 376 (*182*), 378, 383
  dedication of *Iliad*, 371-2
  on dedications, 372 (*174*)
  as Roman Catholic, 373-5, 377
  and Gay, 376
  and Halifax, 378
  social position, 379-80
  Johnson on, 383
  and his literary friends, 384 (*194*)
Popish Plot, 139, 168, 204
Pordage, Samuel, 173, 175, 176, **431**
Portsmouth, Duchess of, 61, 82, 138
Post, the, 164
Post Boy, The, 250 (*135*)
Post Man, The, 250 (*136*)
Practice of Piety, The, xix
Prefaces to plays and poems, 118-20
Present State of Wit, The, 310 (*310*), 312 (*320*)
Press, the, beginnings of, 153 ff.
Presses, provincial, 164 (*127*)
Prideaux, Humphrey, 181
Prideaux, John, 298 (*278*)
Printers, limitation of numbers, 114
Prior, Matthew, xxii, 72 (*275*), 218, 220, 254 (*145*), 318, 319, 320 (*10*), 324, 340, 365, **432, 452**
  Country Mouse and the City Mouse, 183-4, 213 (*2*)
  Dorset and, 318 (*2*)
  goes over to Tories, 326
  Swift and, 331
  Pope on, 334 (*62*)
  Swift on, 337
Profits, theatrical, 108

Prologues, 62–6, 113–14, 148–50, 190 (*203*), 227–8
Protestant Intelligence, 159
Prynne, William, 9 (*30*), 30 (*96*), 244, **453**
"Public", the, 130
Public Spirit of the Whigs, 308
Publishers, 192–3, 344 ff., 354 ff.
Publishing, 114
Pulpit, and public opinion, 165–8
Pulteney, Sir William, Earl of Bath, 332, 343, 376, 379
Pulton, Andrew, 182 (*182*), **453**
Purcell, Henry, 9, 186 (*194*)
Puritanism, reaction against, 2–3
Puritans, in Restoration epoch, 136 ff.
  influence on Court, 189
  Congreve and, 236 (*93*)
  attitude to theatre, 244–5
  Spectator and, 277 (*207*), 284–6

Racine, 207, 297
Ralph, **453**
Rambler, The, 311, 313 (*323*)
Rape of Lucrece (Heywood), xvi
Raphael cartoons, 8 (*28*)
Rapin de Thoyras, 137 (*2*), **391**
Ravaisson, F., **391**
Ravenscroft, Edward, 27, 57, **454**
  Careless Lovers, 55 (*215*), 57, 121 (*423*)
  Citizen turn'd Gentleman, 51 (*200*), 57, 59 (*229*), 67 (*251*), 70 (*269*), 131 (*450*)
  Dame Dobson, 149 (*60*), 191 (*205*)
  Titus Andronicus, 35, 57, 59 (*229*)
Ray, John, 300 (*280*), **454**
Readers, number of, 115
Reading public, extension of, 187–8
Reeves, Mrs., 32 (*103*)
Reformation, Help to a National, **455**
Reformation of Manners, Societies for, 240 (*109*)
Reformations of Manners, Account of the Societies for, **454–5**
Reid, G. W., **398**
Rémusat, Charles de, **391**
Renegade writers, 326
Repartee, 51
Reresby, Sir John, 61 (*234*), 140, 177 (*170*), **391**
Revivals, stage, 54
Rewards, writers', 107 ff., 121
Reybaud, Louis, 153 (*76a*)
Rhyme, in plays, 39 (*127*), 101 (*363*)

Richardson, Samuel, 315 (*332*)
Richmond, Charles Lennox, Duke of, 72
Roberts, William, 313 (*323*)
Robertson, J. M., 315 (*330*)
Rochester, John Wilmot, Earl of, 4–5, 7, 9, 13, 71, 78, 88–107, 134, 169, 319, **473–4**
  Farewell, 104
  Horace's Tenth Satire, 11 (*39*), 13 (*47*), 43 (*156*), 100
  Rehearsal, 12 (*44*)
  Satire Against Man, 7 (*22–3*), 129 (*445*)
  Satires, 12 (*42*)
  Scession of the Poets, 72 (*277*), 77 (*292*), 100, 134 (*461*)
  Valentinian, 68, 150 (*67*), 190 (*202*)
Rochester, Lawrence Hyde, Earl of, 196 (*222*)
Rogers, Samuel, 24 (*72*)
Roman Catholicism, conversions of authors to, 201 ff.
Roman Catholics,
  under Charles II, 138–9
  under James II, 182
  penal laws, 374
Romulus and Hersilia, 149 (*60, 62*), **455**
Roscommon, Wentworth Dillon, Earl of, 10 (*37*), 11 (*38, 39*), 13 (*46*), 68, **423, 473**
Rowe, Nicholas, 221 (*44*), 243, 315 (*330*), 320 (*7–9*), 331, 339, **455–6**
  Lady Jane Grey, 365
  Royal Convert, 320 (*9*)
  Tamerlane, 320 (*9*)
  Poet Laureate, 216, 324
Roxburgh Collection, **398**
Royal Society, 189
Rundle, Thomas, 305 (*291*)
Runs, stage, length of, 54
Russell, William, Lord, 177, 201, 210
Rye-House Plot, 159, 177, 179
Rymer, Thomas, 292 (*249a, 250*), 319 (*4*), **456**

Sabbatarianism, 245
Sacheverell, Henry, 309, 365
Sackville, Charles, *see* Dorset, Earl of
Saint-Evremond, 296, **457–8**
St. John, Henry, *see* Bolingbroke, Viscount
Saintsbury, George, 202 (*241*)
St. Serfe, Thomas, 60, **457**

Salmasius, 188
Sancroft, William, 181
Satires, 11–12
Satyr upon the Poets, 74 (*279*), 123 (*452*), 127 (*440*), 128 (*443*), 195 (*215*)
Sault, Richard, 255 (*149*)
Savage, Richard, xxii, 346, 347–8, 351–2, 353, 354
  Johnson on, 347–8
  Pope and, 384 (*194*)
Savile, George, *see* Halifax, Marquis of
Savoy, The, 21
Scandalous Club, Defoe's, 258–9, 268 (*183*)
Scenery, stage, 33–4, 35–6
  expense of, 109
Scotland, *Spectator* in, 274 (*203*)
Scots Magazine, 315 (*331*), 325 (*31*)
Scott, Thomas, 229, **457**
Scott, Sir Walter 20 (*60*), 126 (*438*), 131 (*451*), 148 (*57*), 202, **391**
Scroop, Sir Car, 9, 68
Scroop, Mr., 61
Scudéry, Mlle. de, 13, 40 (*136*), 227, **457**
Sedley, Sir Charles, 5 (*12*), 9, 10, 12 (*45*), 13 (*48*), 67, 74 (*280*), 75, 76–7, 79, **457-8**
  Bellamira, 110 (*383*), 190
  Mulberry-Garden, 77, 118 (*416*)
Selden, John, 298 (*278*)
Settle, Elkanah, 27, 92 ff., 175–7, 187, 188, 194 (*215*), 201, 209, 210, 237, **432**, **458–60**
  Absalom Senior, 173
  Cambyses, 92, 93 (*336*)
  Conquest of China, 40 (*146*)
  Distress'd Innocence, 195 (*215*)
  Empress of Morocco, 34 (*112*), 40 (*140*), 44 (*160*), 67 (*251*), 76, 93–6, 118 (*417*), 173, 175
  Female Prelate, 143 (*31*)
  Ibrahim, 40 (*149*), 96 (*343*)
  Love and Revenge, 40, 78, 80 (*299*)
  Pope Joan, see *Female Prelate*
Shadwell, Thomas, 27, 76–7, 96, 110 (*383*), 123, 127, 131, 134 (*462*), 175–6, 177, 188, 194, 208 (*254*), 216, 253 (*144*), 319, **432**, **460–2**
  Bury-Fair, 5 (*14*), 177 (*169*)
  Epsom-Wells, 78
  Humorists, 3 (*8*), 52 (*200*), 69 (*265*), 78
  Lancashire Witches, 54 (*205*), 142 (*21*), 143, 144 (*36*), 152 (*73*), 177 (*169*)
  Lenten Prologue, 142 (*21*), 192 (*206*)

Shadwell, Thomas (*contd.*)
  Libertine, 55, 78
  Medal of John Bayes, 26 (*81*), 175
  Miser, 55, 56
  Psyche, 35
  Scowrers, 4 (*10*), 216 (*12*), 225 (*57*)
  Squire of Alsatia, 37 (*121*), 43 (*156*), 57 (*222*), 177 (*169*), 191 (*204*), 194 (*212*)
  Sullen Lovers, 70 (*268*), 75 (*283*), 78, 112 (*396*), 131 (*454*)
  Timon, 56
  Tory Poets, 175
  True Widow, A, 47 (*171*), 49, 58, 60 (*231*), 69, 74 (*280*), 76, 77, 175
  Virtuoso, 3 (*6*), 49 (*184*), 51 (*199*), 52 (*200*), 78, 112
  Volunteers, 225 (*57*)
  Woman-Captain, 60 (*231*), 151 (*71*), 163 (*123*)
  made Laureate, 323
Shaftesbury, Anthony Ashley Cooper, Earl of, xix, 147–8, 168, 174, 177, 199 (*226*), 208, 209, **418**
Shakespeare, 37, 38 (*122*, *125*), 47 (*177*), 126, 234, 269–7 (*264*, *268*, 271), 298 (*276*), 315 (*330*), 462
  adaptations of, 38, 56
  Dryden and, 131, 142
Sheffield, John, *see* Mulgrave, Earl of
Shenstone, Wm., xxii
Sheridan, R. B., 281 (*220*)
Sherlock, Thomas, 300 (*280*)
Shirley, James, xvi
Shrewsbury, Charles Talbot, Duke of, 379
Shrewsbury, Countess of, 172 (*153*)
Sidney, Algernon, 177
Silent Monitor, The, 311
Silver, clipped, 360
Similes, 45 (*169*)
Skelton, John, **391**
Smith, Edmund, 216, 321 (*416*), 364, **462-3**
Smith, Francis, **463**
Smollett, Tobias, 315 (*332*), **463**
  Humphrey Clinker, 346 (*91*), 349, 352, 353 (*114*)
Sobieski, John, 148
Some Thoughts Concerning the Stage, **463**
Somers, John, Baron, xx, 193, 213, 214 (*5*), 318 (*3*), 327, 370, **432**
  and Addison, 247
  and Swift, 327
  dedications to, 332, 333
  See also *Dryden's Satyr to His Muse*

Somerset, Duchess of, 217
Somerset, Charles Seymour, Duke of, 220
Somerville, William, 304
South, Robert, 300 (*280*)
Southerne, Thomas, 14, 192, 194 (*211*), 197 (*225*), 228, 364, **463-4**
  Disappointment, 190 (*203*), 192 (*207*)
  Fatal Marriage, 14 (*53*), 364
  Loyal Brother, 142, 146, 147, 190 (*203*)
  Maid's Last Prayer, 4 (*10*), 225 (*53*)
  Oroonoko, 14, 226 (*58*)
  Sir Anthony Love, 225, 226 (*58*), 229 (*71, 72*)
  Spartan Dame, 365
  Wives Excuse, 225 (*53*)
  dedications, 331-2
  Pope on, 365
Spectator, xviii, xix, xx, xxii, 45 (*168*), 64 (*245*), 116 (*408*), 163 (*124*), 165 (*131*), 221 (*45*), 224 (*52*), 236 (*92*), 262 (*171*), 263 ff., 310 (*309*)
  Club, 268 ff.
  and parties, 269 (*184*)
  sales, 274 (*201*), 314
  and Puritans, 277 (*207*)
  Imitations of, 310-12
  dedications, 333
  sums received for, 365
Spence, Joseph, **398**
Spenser, Addison on, 297, 298 (*276*)
Spingarn, J. E., **398**
Sprat, Thomas, 86 (*319*), 173 (*154*), 179, 187, 189 (*201*), 200, 209, **464**
Stanhope, Philip Henry, Earl of, **392**
Stapleton, Sir Robert, 68, **464-5**
Stapylton, Sir Robert, *see* Stapleton
Starre-Chamber, Decree of, **465**
Statesmen and authors, relations, 318
Steele, Richard, xviii, xix, xxi, xxii, 214 (*6*), 220, 221 (*44*), 243, 254 (*145*), 308, 319, 339-40, 346, 347, 370, **465-6**
  Conscious Lovers, 243 (*118*), *334*
  Lying Lover, 243 (*118*)
  Tatler, 260-3
  official appointments, 217, 318, 324
  and *London Gazette*, 249 (*129*), 261 (*167*), 336
  and *Spectator*, 263 ff., 268 (*182*), 303
  veneration for Addison, 279 (*212*)
  on Addison, 281 (*222*)

Steele, Richard (*contd.*)
  Harley and, 328 (*42*)
  Swift and, 328
  and George I, 334
  in Parliament, 334
  see also Tatler, Spectator
Steele, Mrs., 280
Steevens, Wm., 308
Stephen, Sir Leslie, **398**
Stephens, F. G., **398**
Stepney, George, 217, 220, 322-3 (*25*), **466**
Stillingfleet, Edward, 165, 179-80, 183, 300 (*280*), **466**
Stoughton, John, **392**
Subscription publication, 357
Sunderland, Charles Spencer, 3rd Earl of, 220, 333
Sunderland, Robert Spencer, 2nd Earl of, 79
Sussex, Countess of, 98
Swall, Abel, 115
Swearing, 2
Swift, Jonathan, xix, 13 (*51*), 118 (*417*), 131 (*451*), 162 (*121*), 213 (*1*), 217, 220 (*41*), 221 (*44*), 241 (*112*), 254 (*145*), 257 (*156*), 296, 307 (*296*), 308, 309, 340-1, 343, 369 (*161*), 370, **466-8**
  Conduct of the Allies, 309
  Gulliver's Travels, 315 (*332*)
  Journal to Stella, 220 (*41*), 223 (*49*), 224 (*52*), 225 (*54*), 266 (*179*), 275, 279 (*211*), 281 (*220*), 308 (*301*), 310 (*310*), 319, 324, 326 (*34*), 331, 337 (*68, 70*), 338 (*73*), 340 (*76*), 381 (*191*)
  Tale of a Tub, 327, 332
  and Defoe, 259 (*165*)
  "Isaac Bickerstaff", 260 (*166*)
  and the Whigs, 279 (*210a*)
  on Addison, 279, 281 (*220*)
  and Shakespeare, 296
  and Parnell, 326
  party competition for, 326-8
  political writings, 336 (*66*)
  on Prior, 337
  works unsigned, 338 (*73*)
  Pope and, 370 (*162*), 376, 378, 379
Swindles, literary, 353-4
Symons, Samuel, 24, 116, 117

Taine, H., **398**
Tantivies, 140

Taste, change in, after Revolution, 222–30
Tate, Nahum, 172 (*152*), 176, 200, 209, 216, 241 (*112*), 257, 321 (*14*), **468–9**
  Brutus of Alba, 34 (*110*), 115
  Cuckolds-Haven, 147, 148 (*58*), 200, 209
  Duke and No Duke, 210 (*255*)
  Ingratitude of a Common-Wealth, 143 (*30*), 200
  King Lear, 56, 144 (*38*)
  Sicilian Usurper, 144, 200
  Dorset and, 318 (*42*)
  see also Dryden, *Absalom and Achitophel*
Tatler, xix, xxii, 162 (*120*), 251 (*137*), 328 (*41*), 332, 334
Tax, newspaper, 275 (*204*), 308 (*301*)
Taylor, Jeremy, 165
Taylor, John, 253 (*144*)
Tell-Tale, The, 310 (*310*)
Temple, Sir William, 185, 257, 293 (*250*), 296, **469**
Tenison, Thomas, 182
Tennyson, 214 (*6*)
Test Act, 139
Theatre,
  Puritans and, 27–8
  author's profit from, 107 ff., 193–4, 364
  decline of, 151
  Collier's attack on, 231 ff.
  suppression proposed, 244 (*121*)
  Addison and, 289 (*263*)
  Steele and, 289 (*241*)
Theobald, Lewis, 311 (*311*), 315 (*330*)
Theological writing, xix
Thompson, N., **398**
Thomson, James, xxii, 343, 344 (*88*)
Thornbury, Walter, **392**
Thornton, Bonnel, 313 (*323*)
Tickell, Thomas, 217, 223 (*48*), 263 (*174*), 279 (*214*), 303 (*287*), 306 (*295*), 309, 323 (*29*), 324 (*30*), 334, 373 (*175*), **469–70**
Tillotson, John, 165, 181, 300 (*280*), 364 (*140*)
Timperley, C. H., **398**
Tindal, Matthew, 299 (*279*), **470**
Toland, John, xix, 299 (*279*), 329–30 (*49*), **470–1**
Tonson, Jacob, 115, 192–3, 213, 354 ff.
  Miscellany, 193
  Dryden and, 192–3, 354 ff., 367

Tonson, Jacob (*contd.*)
  Pope and, 366–8
Town-Rakes, The, **446**
Townsend, W. C., **392**
Tragedy, Restoration and Jacobean, xvi
Trapp, Joseph, 326 (*34*)
Trevelyan, G. M., **392**
True Domestick Intelligence, 159
True News, 159
Tuke, Sir Samuel, 68, 81, **471**
Tunbridge-Miscellany, 300 (*281*), **471**
Turberville, A. S., **392**
Tutchin, John, 308 (*299a*)
Tyrconnel, Lord, 351, 353–4

Uzziah and Jotham, 471

Vanbrugh, Sir John, xxii, 218, 219 (*38a*), 220, 221 (*44*), 226, 237, 243, 319 (*6*), 324 (*30*), **414, 471–2**
  False Friend, 242 (*117*)
  Provok'd Husband, 242 (*117*)
  Provok'd Wife, 226 (*59*), 228 (*62*), 242
  Relapse, 32 (*103*), 226 (*58*), 229, 230, 232 (*77*)
  Short Vindication . . ., 233 (*80*), 234 (*89*), 238 (*100*)
  on comedy, 2 (*5*)
Varillas, 183 (*184*)
Vertue, George, 318 (*3*)
Villemain, 335, 338 (*71*), 399
Villiers, George, *see* Buckingham, Duke of
Vindication of the Stage, 237 (*96*)
Virgil, 350, 357
Voltaire, 50 (*192*), 218 (*38*), 228 (*66*), 369 (*161*), **472**
  and Congreve, 339 (*75*)

Waller, Edmund, xvii, 2, 7, 9 (*31a*), 10 (*35–6*), 12 (*45*), 19, 25 (*80*), 38, 39 (*127*), 68, 71 (*270*), 189 (*201*), **472–3**
Walpole, Horace, 313 (*323*), 325 (*33*), **399**
Walpole, Sir Robert, 341 ff., **392**
  Swift on, 343 (*86*)
Walsh, William, 217, 219 (*38a*), 220, 323 (*27*), 370
Wanderer, The, 311
Warburton, Wm., 315 (*330*)

Ward, Ned, xix, xxi
Warming-Pan legend, 185 (*192*)
Warwick, Dowager Countess of, 220, 338 (*72a*)
Watt, Robert, **399**
Watts, Thomas, **473**
Webster, John, 76 (*289*)
Weekely Newes from Italy, 153, 154 (*77*)
Weekly Discoverer, 160
Wellwood, James, 308
Welsted, Leonard, 343
Wesley, John and Charles, 14 (*52*)
Wesley, Samuel, 255 (*149*)
Westminster Drolleries, **435**
Wharton, Thomas, Lord, 186 (*194*), 247 (*123a*), 331, 333
Whip for the Fools Back, 173, **433**
Whisperer, The, 310 (*310*), 311
Willey, Basil, **392**
William III, 186, 212 ff., 222–3, 240, 359
Williams, Archbishop, 322 (*18*)
Will's Coffee House, 162
Wilmot, John, *see* Rochester, Earl of
Wilson, John, xvi
Wine-Cooper's Delight, **474**
Wit, and virtue, 276 (*206a*)
Witticism, origin of word, 10 (*33*)

Women,
  as readers, xviii–xix, 39
  and poetry, 9
Women's rôles, acted by men, 30–1
Works of Celebrated Authors, **474**
World, The, 313 (*323*)
Wycherley, William, xxi, 22, 71–2 (*277*), 128, 209, 237 (*96*), 370, 474
  Country Wife, 51 (*198*), 53 (*201*), 56, 67 (*251*)
  Gentleman Dancing Master, 54, 56
  Love in a Wood, 72
  Plain Dealer, 47 (*174*, *176*), 48 (*181*), 49 (*190*), 50 (*192*), 51 (*198–9*), 56, 57 (*222*), 58 (*225*), 72
  conversion, 201
Wyndham, Sir Wm., 343, 379

York, Duchess of, 29
York, Duke of, *see* James II
Yorkists, 140
Young, Edward, 279 (*213*), 281 (*223*), 329, 334, 369 (*11*), **474–5**
  dedications, 332, 333 (*56*), 334
  publishers and, 368 (*154*)

For Product Safety Concerns and Information please contact our EU
representative GPSR@taylorandfrancis.com
Taylor & Francis Verlag GmbH, Kaufingerstraße 24, 80331 München, Germany

www.ingramcontent.com/pod-product-compliance
Lightning Source LLC
Chambersburg PA
CBHW051133230426
43670CB00007B/787